International Business

A MANAGERIAL PERSPECTIVE   SECOND EDITION

International Business

A MANAGERIAL PERSPECTIVE   SECOND EDITION

RICKY W. GRIFFIN
Texas A&M University

MICHAEL W. PUSTAY
Texas A&M University

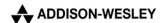 **ADDISON-WESLEY**

An imprint of Addison Wesley Longman, Inc.

Reading, Massachusetts • Menlo Park, California • New York • Harlow, England
Don Mills, Ontario • Sydney • Mexico City • Madrid • Amsterdam

Executive Editor:	Michael Roche
Senior Project Manager:	Mary Clare McEwing
Production Supervisor:	Heather Bingham
Art Editor:	Meredith Nightingale
Assistant Editor:	Ruth Berry
Editorial Assistant:	Adam Hamel
Administrative Assistant:	Dottie Dennis
Design Manager:	Regina Hagen
Text Design:	Linda Manly Wade
Supplements Editor:	Karen Stevenson
Senior Marketing Manager:	Julia Downs
Senior Marketing Coordinator:	Joyce Cosentino
Manufacturing Coordinator:	Sheila Spinney
Electronic Production Administrator:	Michael Strong
Text Illustrations:	GeoSystems
Cover Image:	Bill Frymire/Masterfile
Cover Design:	Cindy Nelson and Kevin Toler for Black & Copper
Photo Research:	Billie Porter
Permissions Editor:	Mary Dyer

International Business: A Managerial Perspective, Second Edition
Copyright © 1999 by Addison-Wesley Publishing Company, Inc.

Photo credits appear on page 791, which constitutes a continuation of this copyright page.

Library of Congress Cataloging-in-Publication Data

Griffin, Ricky W.
    International business : a managerial perspective / Ricky W.
    Griffin, Michael W. Pustay. — 2nd ed.
        p.   cm.
    Includes bibliographical references and indexes.
    ISBN 0-201-85767-7 (hardcover)
    1. International business enterprises—Management.   I. Pustay,
    Michael W.   II. Title.
    HD62.4.G74   1998
    658'.049—dc21   98-16009
                                                      CIP

1 2 3 4 5 6 7 8 9 10–RNV–02 01 00 99 98

To my wife—Glenda
R. W. G.

To my wife—Zandra
M. W. P.

About the Authors

RICKY W. GRIFFIN is the Lawrence E. Fouraker Professor of Business Administration and professor of management at Texas A&M University. He is also head of the Department of Management at Texas A&M. After receiving his Ph.D. from the University of Houston in 1978, he joined the faculty at the University of Missouri–Columbia before moving to Texas A&M University in 1981.

Professor Griffin teaches international management, organizational behavior, human resource management, and general management. He has taught both undergraduate and graduate students, participated in numerous executive training programs, and taught in Europe. A member of the Academy of Management, he has served as division chair of that group's Organizational Behavior division. He also is a member of the Southern Management Association and the board of directors of the Southern Management Association.

Professor Griffin has written several successful textbooks, including *Management, Organizational Behavior* (with Greg Moorhead), and *Business* (with Ron Ebert). He is currently conducting research on workplace violence in Canada and job design differences and similarities among firms in Japan, Europe, and the United States.

MICHAEL W. PUSTAY is professor of management at Texas A&M University. He currently serves as associate director of the Center for International Business Studies and as associate director of the Center for International Business Education and Research at Texas A&M. He is the North American editor of the British journal *Transport Reviews.* Professor Pustay received his B.A. in economics *summa cum laude* from Washington and Lee University in 1969 and his Ph.D. in economics from Yale University in 1973. He taught at Purdue University and Bowling Green State University prior to joining Texas A&M's business school faculty.

Professor Pustay, who has taught international business for 12 years, focuses his teaching and research efforts on international business and business-government relations. His work has appeared in such professional journals as the *Journal of Management, Southern Economic Journal, Land Economics,* and *Transportation Journal.* He is currently researching the role of regional trading blocs on the world economy and the impact of domestic economic policies on international competition.

Professor Pustay is a member of numerous professional organizations, including the Academy of International Business, the American Economic Association, the Association for Canadian Studies in the United States, and the Transportation Research Forum. He has served as a consultant for a variety of public and private organizations, including the U.S. Department of Transportation, the Small Business Administration, the Civil Aeronautics Board, and Houston Power & Light.

Contents

PART 2 — The International Environment **81**

CHAPTER 3

International Trade and Investment Theory **82**

CHAPTER 4

The International Monetary System and the Balance of Payments **120**

PART 3 *The National
Environment* **201**

CHAPTER 5

Foreign Exchange and International Financial Markets 160

CHAPTER 6

Formulation of National Trade Policies 202

**PART 4 *Managing in the
International
Environment* 367**

CHAPTER 11

Strategies for Analyzing and Entering Foreign Markets 402

CHAPTER 12

International Strategic Alliances 448

CHAPTER 17

International Operations Management 620

CHAPTER 18

International Financial Management 652

CHAPTER 19

International Accounting and Taxation 694

CHAPTER 20

International Human Resource Management and Labor Relations 728

Maps

'T'O PRODUCE STUDENTS WHO WILL BE COMFORTABLE AND EFFECTIVE in a worldwide marketplace—this remains our vision in writing this book. As we prepared this revision of our very successful first edition, we were struck by the fact that interest in international business has never been higher. Students are well aware of the importance of international business and its impact on their careers and everyday lives. Yet they often feel overwhelmed by the amount of new knowledge they must assimilate in order to master the subject. Further, many of the existing textbooks are written in needlessly technical terms and seem to be concerned only with students who are specializing in international business. However, *all* students—even those who will never have an overseas assignment—need to be knowledgeable about the global economy.

This is why we feel so strongly about our vision for this book. We want students to attain "cultural literacy" in international business. We want them, for example, to be able to talk knowledgeably with a visiting executive from a French multinational corporation or to understand and analyze the impact on themselves and their firms of trade negotiations with Mexico, an Asian currency crisis, economic growth in China or Brazil, or political uncertainties in the Caspian Sea oil fields. To accomplish this task, we present in the text a comprehensive discussion and analysis of international business and the environment in which international businesses compete. We describe the global economy, the forces that have created this economy, and the businesses—both large and small—that compete in it.

Distinctive Coverage

We approach the study of international business from the standpoint of *managers* who must function in a global competitive environment. Our presentation of international accounting in Chapter 19 is a good example of how we do this. Some books attempt to make students into international accountants; we leave that task to specialized accounting courses. Our coverage, in line with our vision, provides students with information about those aspects of international accounting that are necessary for them to function effectively as managers. Our goal is to equip students with the knowledge, tools, and insights necessary to succeed in a business environment that is becoming increasingly and inevitably global.

Chapter by Chapter. We have organized our coverage of international business to progress from the broad, general context of international business to the more specific managerial and operational elements of managing in an international business environment.

- We begin in Part 1 by devoting two chapters to introducing students to the contemporary international business world. Chapter 1 provides a broad overview of international business—what it is, how it has evolved, the reasons for its growth, and its importance to students. Chapter 2—a unique chapter among international business textbooks—equips students with a basic foundation in economic geography. In addition to detailed maps of the world's major marketplaces, we provide students with relevant historical, political, and economic information about these marketplaces so that they can better understand and appreciate the impacts of these factors on opportunities available to contemporary businesses.

◆ Part 2 describes the international environment of business—the institutional framework that shapes the opportunities available to firms. Our discussion of international trade and investment theories, the international monetary system, the balance of payments, the foreign exchange market, and the global capital market gives students the information they need to succeed in the global marketplace.

◆ Part 3 shifts from the international environment to the domestic environment. This part explores how domestic politics, laws, and culture affect international business activities. It also examines the formulation of national trade policies and cooperative agreements among countries to promote their mutual prosperity.

◆ Part 4 describes the overall set of issues and challenges associated with managing international businesses. The major topics discussed are international strategic management, modes of entry into international markets (with special emphasis on strategic alliances), international forms of organization design, behavioral processes in different cultures, and issues associated with international control. Several elements of Part 4 are unique. This is the only book in the market, for example, to devote full chapters to coverage of strategic alliances, organization design, behavioral processes, and control in international business. Such coverage is clearly warranted because these are all fundamental business functions.

◆ Part 5 focuses on how international businesses manage specific business operations. Separate chapters explore marketing, operations management, finance, accounting, and human resource management—all from an international business perspective.

Changes from the First Edition. The first edition of *International Business* was one of the most successful new books to be published in this market in many years. While we were gratified by the response to our book, we wanted to make it even better. Thus, when we began planning this revision, we obtained extensive feedback and suggestions from a wide array of instructors. Based on their reviews and our own experiences with the text, we made the following major changes in this edition:

◆ Chapters 4 and 5 provide full coverage of the Asian currency crisis, including a new Point/Counterpoint debating the role of the IMF in bailing out countries in crisis.

◆ Chapter 7 has been substantially updated to include the Treaty of Amsterdam and the advent of the euro. This chapter also has expanded coverage of ASEAN and new coverage of the APEC initiative.

- Chapter 8 features an expanded and substantially revised discussion of political risk.

- Chapter 9 now includes coverage of Hofstede's framework of cultural differences. In response to user feedback, we transferred this material, previously covered in Chapter 14, to provide a stronger theoretical framework for the discussion of culture.

- Chapter 10 includes an improved discussion of international strategic management, including Bartlett and Ghoshal's framework for analyzing the internationalization strategies adopted by businesses.

- Chapter 14 highlights stronger and more complete coverage of international organizational behavior, including personality and individual differences across cultures, made possible by the movement of the Hofstede discussion to Chapter 9.

- Chapter 17 presents new material on the growing importance of information technology in operations management.

- Woven throughout the second edition are discussions of the Asian currency crisis, the growing importance of Caspian Sea oil, the emerging role of China in the world economy, and the impact of the euro and the WTO on business behavior.

In addition to these major changes, we have also maintained our overall commitment to currency. Throughout the book, we have made every effort to be as current and up to date as possible in the presentation of theories, concepts, and examples. While some especially useful and still timely examples from the first edition have been retained, most have been replaced or updated. In addition, many of the cases and boxed inserts are new, and those brought forward from the first edition have been updated wherever necessary. Half of the book's opening and closing chapter cases are new to this edition.

Historical Perspective. While we do not wish to overwhelm students with history, we have tried to provide relevant historical and political background information to allow them to better understand the environment in which international businesses compete. For example, Chapter 4 examines the political forces that induced the World Bank to create its various subsidiaries. Chapters 2 and 7 discuss the political infighting among members of the European Union and how businesses can exploit these differences to achieve their goals. As future managers, students need to be aware of how these political and historical issues affect the world today.

Examples. International business is one of the liveliest subjects taken by business majors, yet many existing textbooks manage to make it dry and lifeless. We think good examples are critical to students' mastery of the material, so we include more than 1,000 company examples to illustrate the theory and practice of international business. We have worked hard to find a variety of examples that are both relevant to the subject and memorable to the students. Consider Chapter 1. We have utilized the Olympic Games and *Anne of Green Gables* to depict the internationalization of business. In Chapter 19, we discuss a *Monty Python* sketch about a chartered accountant, Mr. Anchovy, to introduce (with some humor) the treatment of international accounting and taxation. Similarly, in Chapter 6 we discuss the importation of Star

Trek dolls into the European Union to illustrate the complexity of classifying goods for tariff and quota purposes. Students learn that the question of whether Mr. Spock is human or nonhuman is of interest to customs officials and international businesspersons as well as to Trekkies.

Furthermore, many international business textbooks focus on large firms and almost exclusively on Japanese, German, British, and U.S. examples. The authors of these books also fail to realize the types of businesses in which non-industrialized, less developed countries are involved. This limiting of exposure to a handful of manufacturing firms and a select group of countries means that students miss the opportunity to learn about the truly *global* aspects of international business. While our book presents a balanced coverage of material taken from the major industrial powers, it also covers events in less visible countries like Belgium, Kenya, Mexico, Namibia, the Philippines—even the Spratly Islands. Maps, photographs, cases, boxes, and our unique Building Global Skills and Working with the Web exercises supplement and expand the book's coverage of these wide-ranging examples.

Ethics. No international business textbook would be complete without a detailed presentation of ethics. In this book, we integrate throughout the text the ways in which ethical issues affect international business. Ethical insights are also found in many of the Going Global boxes and Point/Counterpoints, as well as in selected Building Global Skills exercises and Closing Cases (see Learning Features below for a description of these features).

Our book looks at three levels of ethical behavior: individual, organizational, and governmental. For example, as future managers, students must consider whether bribery is ever appropriate, whether they should obey foreign laws they believe are unjust, and whether they should comply with local customs and cultures they find inappropriate or abhorrent. They must also confront ethical issues at an organizational level: for example, does a firm have a moral responsibility to monitor the human and workers' rights policies of its foreign subcontractors, or should a firm take into account the impact of its foreign investment policies on the local economy? Finally, students must grapple with the ethical issues facing countries: for example, whether a government's sole responsibility is to its citizens, regardless of the impact its actions have on the world economy, or whether developed countries have obligations to promote the economic prosperity of poorer countries.

Learning Features

In addition to providing thorough and comprehensive coverage of international business, we include a complete, integrated learning system designed to help students master the book's material. Each chapter opens with an outline and a series of learning objectives and closes with a summary, review questions, and discussion questions. The book offers numerous learning features designed to enhance students' understanding, several of which are unique to this book.

Point/Counterpoint. All too often, students are exposed only to a single point of view in international business textbooks. They don't understand the ways in which two countries or firms can perceive the same situation in different ways. Our Point/Counterpoint feature addresses this teaching and learning challenge by taking a series of important but controversial issues relevant to international business today and providing a discussion—in almost a debate format—of opposite points of view. No right answers are provided—instead, the basic pros and cons of each side are highlighted and discussed. Accompanying questions are designed to stimulate classroom discussion and provide food for thought for students. Where appropriate, we have also highlighted ethical implications of these debates.

Cases. Cases are also an important learning feature. Each chapter's opening case is designed to introduce the student to a particular international business or situation that is relevant to the chapter. This case then serves to motivate the material that opens the chapter and is referenced throughout the chapter as a running example. For example, the opening case of Chapter 10, the strategic management chapter, discusses Disneyland Paris. The case introduces the strategic thinking that led to the original idea of a theme park in Europe, the disastrous early days of what was first called Euro Disneyland, and the eventual turnaround that has made the park into a money-making operation. Disney's strategy formulation and implementation processes are then used as a running example throughout the chapter.

Each closing case provides a different perspective on the material covered in the chapter and includes several questions that help students analyze the case itself in light of the chapter content. These cases enable students to delve more deeply into important issues. For example, the closing case for Chapter 8 deals with political risk and the Caspian Sea oil fields. Students are required to conduct their own political risk analyses and make choices about pipeline routes based on the results of these analyses.

Finally, at the end of the book, we include several additional cases for analysis. These cases are longer than the chapter cases and relate to various international business topics and issues that span the contents of several chapters. Thus they serve an integrative function as well as allow instructors and students to examine issues more deeply. For example, "The Ethics of Global Tobacco Marketing" draws on material found in Chapter 3 (international trade), Chapter 6 (national trade policies), Chapter 8 (domestic laws and politics), Chapter 9 (culture), and Chapter 16 (marketing), as well as the discussion of ethics found throughout the text.

Maps. Too few U.S. students today can identify the countries of Western Europe, let alone those that comprise the Four Tigers. Our book includes over forty maps, including nine in Chapter 2 alone, to help students better visualize where various countries and firms are located and how international business transactions occur. The maps also help students better understand political boundaries and national geography, for example:

- Chapter 2 presents a topographic map of South America to demonstrate the physical barriers to trade among South American countries.
- Chapter 3 uses a map to demonstrate the economic interdependence of Indonesia, Malaysia, and the Philippines.

- Chapter 5 presents a map of Africa showing how countries using the CFA franc have maintained close political and economic ties to France.

- Chapter 18 includes a map that helps students visualize a complex, multi-country countertrade deal.

The maps also contain "talk boxes" to highlight aspects important to international businesses. For example, in Chapter 2, the map of the former Soviet Union highlights differences among the Newly Independent States; in Chapter 11, a map focuses on the role of Turkey as an entry point for doing business in the Central Asian Republics.

Photographs. Photographs are integrated throughout the chapters and serve to reinforce and/or expand the material covered. Each has a content-driven caption that explains its importance and relevance to the text. For example, one in Chapter 9 illustrates the cultural adaptation of Barbie dolls that are manufactured in Indonesia and destined for the Asian market. Others, in Chapter 16, depict differences in advertising messages in rich and poor countries.

Going Global Boxes. All chapters contain one or more boxed features called "Going Global." Each feature highlights an especially interesting and important concept, topic, or example that justifies extra attention. Many also address ethical issues, for example:

- The linking of trade with human rights (Chapter 7)
- The ethics of bribery (Chapter 8)
- The uses and abuses of financial derivatives (Chapter 18)
- The ethics of transfer pricing (Chapter 19)

Building Global Skills. Most international business textbooks present theory and concepts but do not provide students with the opportunity to use them in practice. If students are to truly understand international business and master the theories presented, they must take an active role in the learning process. The Building Global Skills exercises found at the end of each chapter require students, alone or in groups, to solve problems, find information in the library, analyze it, and critique it. Some examples of these exercises are as follows:

- Chapter 2 asks students to obtain basic information about the Belgian economy, which requires them to learn about sources of international business data. They will use such knowledge throughout the rest of the course.

- Chapter 12 invites students to evaluate potential joint venture partners, requiring them to apply the concepts introduced in the chapter.

- Chapter 18 asks students to develop a currency netting operation so that they can experience first-hand the complexities of dealing with numerous currencies and also learn implications of transfer pricing in a more vivid way than they would by simply reading about them.

Working with the Web: Building Global Internet Skills.

A new feature for the second edition of *International Business*, these chapter-closing exercises are generally similar to the acclaimed *Building Global Skills* exercises in the first edition, as described above, but add an Internet component to the learning experience. Students are asked to make decisions, provide assessments and evaluations, and obtain data and information, all using the Internet as a resource tool. Representative examples of these exercises include:

◆ Chapter 5 requires students to develop a pricing strategy for goods to be delivered in the future when no forward market exists in a country's currency.

◆ Chapter 7 asks students to use information from the Internet to assess potential new entrants in the EU.

◆ Chapter 18 invites students to assess the export financing needs of new exporters.

Ancillaries

Many busy instructors find themselves teaching several different classes and/or teaching classes with large enrollments. To encourage more effective instruction and to help instructors use their time more efficiently, we have developed a high-quality set of ancillary materials for instructors.

Instructor's Resource Manual.

The Instructor's Resource Manual, prepared by Veronica Horton of the University of Akron, contains valuable materials for all faculty, especially those new to teaching international business. Suggested course outlines with teaching notes will assist instructors in preparing both lectures and class discussions. Detailed chapter outlines, lecture support, discussions of introductory and end-of-chapter cases, answers to case questions, answers to review questions, discussions of Building Global Skills features and answers to followup questions, and discussions of Point/Counterpoint features and of Comprehensive Cases all provide in-depth assistance to the busy instructor.

Test Bank.

The Test Bank, prepared by Sesan Kim Sokoya of Middle Tennessee State University, includes varied true-false, multiple-choice, short-answer, and essay questions. Each chapter includes 50–60 questions, which have been reviewed and edited from a student's perspective. Misleading words and phrases, "all of the above" and "none of the above" answers, and trivia-type questions have been eliminated.

Computerized Test Bank and Network Testing (TestGen Eq with QuizMaster).

This test generation software for Windows is fully net-workable. TestGen EQ's graphical interface allows instructors to view, edit, and add questions, transfer questions to tests, and print tests in various fonts and forms. Search-and-sort features allow the instructor to locate questions quickly and arrange them in a preferred order. Quizmaster will grade tests automatically and provide detailed feedback analysis. Both these programs are components of the CD-ROM, described below.

FastFax Testing. As an additional service to instructors using this text, FastFax testing is available through our Glenview Software Products and Services Group. This group will create tests based on instructions from the professor and send a hard copy of the test within two business days via fax or mail. To receive more information, or forms for requesting tests, please contact your local Addison Wesley Longman sales representative.

PowerPoint Presentations. An extensive set of PowerPoint slides has been prepared to accompany this edition. This selection of slides includes most of the text illustrations. The presentation is included as a component of the Instructor's CD-ROM, described below.

Web Site. A web site has been developed for this book. Here you can find links to other web sites to help you with the "Working with the Web" exercises, as well as other useful information. Visit the site at http://hepg.awl.com. Use the keyword Griffin-IB. The password is IB2.

Videos. A video collection is available, consisting of business news segments from the MacNeil/Lehrer Newshour. Each segment is reported by Paul Solman, MacNeil/Lehrer's special business correspondent. The videos have been selected to correspond to key international business concepts presented in this text.

Instructor's CD-ROM. This Windows-based CD-ROM contains the computerized test bank, PowerPoint presentation, and Instructor's Manual. This innovative technology supplement is now programmed for instant installation with a user-friendly interface.[*]

---

[*] The supplement package is available to qualified adopters, and in some cases all supplements may not be available to adopters because of legal and other restrictions.

Acknowledgments

The cover of this book identifies two authors by name. In reality, *International Business: A Managerial Perspective* represents a true team effort involving literally dozens of skilled professionals. While any and all errors of fact, omission, and emphasis are solely our responsibility, we would be remiss if we did not acknowledge those who helped us create this book.

First of all, a dedicated team of publishing experts from Addison-Wesley played an integral part in shaping this book into its final form. Michael Roche as Sponsoring Editor and Mary Clare McEwing as Senior Project Manager each played a major role in formulating and implementing our plans for this edition. Ruth Berry, Heather Bingham, Joyce Cosentino, Dottie Dennis, Julia Downs, Adam Hamel, Meredith Nightingale, Billie Porter, Karen Stevenson, Gina Hagen, and Michael Strong were also major players at one stage or another as we moved from blank sheets of paper to bound book.

Next, we gratefully acknowledge the contributions of our colleagues at other universities. Veronica Horton of the University of Akron and Sesan Kim Sokoya of Middle Tennessee State University have produced an outstanding instructor's manual and test bank to supplement the main text. A large team of reviewers and focus group participants have also contributed mightily to our work. The reviewers, for example, pored over the manuscript through each draft, providing suggestions and noting weaknesses, all with the same goal: to produce a new generation of international business textbook for today's students. These reviewers continuously displayed conscientious and expert oversight to the development of the manuscript, and we tip our hats to each and every one of them:

Richard A. Ajayi
University of Central Florida

Bill Anthony
Florida State University

Jeffrey Arpan
University of South Carolina

Nicholas Athanassiou
Northeastern University

Robert Aubey
University of Wisconsin–Madison

Jay Barney
Ohio State University

Larry Barton
University of Nevada–Las Vegas

Tom Bates
San Francisco State University

Jean Boddewyn
CUNY Bernard Baruch College

Sharon Browning
Northwestern Missouri State University

Dharma deSilva
Wichita State University

Gary Dicer
University of Tennessee

Susan Douglas
New York University

Johnny Duisend
Stetson University

Brian Engelland
Mississippi State University

Dorothee Feils
University of Regina

Esra Gencturk
University of Texas–Austin

Gary Hannen
Mankato State University

Veronica Horton
University of Akron

Donald Howard
University of Akron

Basil Janavaras
Mankato State University

Bruce Johnson
Gustavus Adolphus College

Thomas Jones
Southern Oregon College

Robert Kemp
Drake University

Dara Khambata
American University

Rose Knotts
University of North Texas

Scott Kramer
University of Wisconsin

Jeffrey Krug
University of Memphis

Jim Kuhlman
University of South Carolina

John Lehman
University of Alaska—Fairbanks

Arvind Mahajan
Texas A&M University

Roderick J. Matthews
University of Wisconsin—Madison

Charles Newman
Florida Atlantic University

David Oh
California State University
Los Angeles

Jerry Ralston
University of Washington

Bill Renforth
Florida International University

Cathy Rich-Duval
Merrimack College

Jeffrey Rosensweig
Emory University

John Scheidhut
North Dakota State University

Nader Shoostari
Radford University

Sesan Kim Sokoya
Middle Tennessee State University

Michael Song
University of Tennessee

John Stanbury
Indiana University–Kokomo

Owais Succari
De Paul University

Rosalie Tung
Simon Fraser University

Arieh Ullmann
SUNY–Binghamton

Philip Van Auken
Baylor University

Heidi Vernon
Northeastern University

Robert Vichas
Florida Atlantic University

George Westacott
SUNY–Binghamton

At Texas A&M University, we have had the good fortune to work with one of the finest groups of professional colleagues anyone could imagine. We also appreciate the support of other colleagues, past and present, whose expertise and insights have been incorporated into this manuscript. These include Barbara Bartkus, Tina Dacin, Lorraine Eden, Benito Flores, Julian Gaspar, Rafael Gely, Javier Gimeno, Mike Hitt, Bob Hoskisson, Gareth Jones, Arvind Mahajan, Ramona Paetzold, Peter Rodriguez, Peter Rose, Glenn Rowe, Steve Salter, Larry Walker, Asghar Zardkoohi, and Jing Zhou.

Our staff assistant, Phyllis Washburn, also played an integral part in the development and preparation of this book. Her professionalism and skill were key ingredients in our ability to write it. Thank you, Phyl, for all that you do.

Finally, we would also like to acknowledge the contributions made by our families—Glenda, Dustin, and Ashley Griffin and Zandy, Scott, and Katie Pustay. They didn't write a single word of the book or draw any of the maps or artwork, but their imprint can be found on everything we do. They support us, encourage us, and inspire us. They give our work—and our lives—meaning. It is with all our love and affection that we thank them.

International Business

A MANAGERIAL PERSPECTIVE   SECOND EDITION

PART 1

Introduction to International Business

An Overview of International Business

After studying this chapter you should be able to:

Discuss the meaning of international business.

Explain the importance of understanding international business.

Identify and describe the basic forms of international business.

Discuss the evolution of international business.

Describe international business during the 1950s, the 1960s, and the 1970s.

Characterize the global environment from the 1980s forward, focusing on global competitiveness and the emerging global marketplace.

Describe the growth of international business over the last half-century.

T HE MODERN OLYMPIC GAMES HAVE OFTEN REFLECTED THE prevailing world order. (The first modern summer games were held in 1896; the winter games were added in 1920.) Adolf Hitler sought to use the 1936 games in Berlin to showcase the superiority of the Nazi political system. Arab terrorists used the 1972 games in Munich as a platform for a highly publicized attack against Israeli athletes, killing sixteen people. The United States led a boycott of the 1980 games in Moscow to protest the Soviet invasion of Afghanistan. And the Soviet Union reciprocated during the 1984 games in Los Angeles with a boycott of its own. ▮▮ Given that international business and the global economy play such a dominant role in the world today, it should come as no surprise that the Olympic games have also come to reflect international business at its most

The Business of the Olympics[1]

intense. The games are governed by the International Olympic Committee (IOC), which is based in Switzerland. The IOC decides where the games will be held and which sports will be represented and oversees the selection of judges and referees. Each country wanting to send athletes to compete in the games establishes a national committee to organize its Olympic effort. These committees are supervised by and report to the IOC. The IOC has an annual budget of hundreds of millions of dollars, yet the cost of running the games far exceeds this budget. Thus the IOC relies heavily on the host cities to help cover much of the cost. And each national committee is responsible for raising the funds to sponsor its own teams. ▮▮ Potential host cities must prepare elaborate presentations for the IOC and make substantial commitments in terms of facilities, a volunteer work force, and related organizational support. For example, as part of its winning bid to host the 1998 Winter Olympics, Japan promised to build a new high-speed rail line between Tokyo and Nagano, the site of the games. Further, the infighting to be selected is vicious. For example, China threatened a trade war with the United States after the U.S. Senate passed a resolution that hurt Beijing's chances to host the Summer Olympics in 2000, a prize eventually seized by Sydney, Australia. ▮▮ Why would a city want to host the Olympic games? Most compete for the privilege because the games would thrust them into the international spotlight and promote economic growth. When Athens was selected as the host city for the 2004 summer games, Greek officials proclaimed that the selection would spur new foreign investments, improve Athens' infrastructure, and boost tourism. And the tourism benefits are long-lived; for example, skiers, skaters, and snowboarders continue to enjoy the facilities at previous

Olympic sites such as Nagano, Lillehammer, Calgary, Albertville, and Lake Placid, pouring money into the local economies long after the Olympic torch has been extinguished. The games also are frequently a catalyst for improvements in a city's infrastructure. For example, the high-speed rail line between Tokyo and Nagano halves the travel time between the two cities—a benefit that continues for local residents and future visitors. ■ ■ Because of the high cost of running the Olympics—the 1996 Summer Olympics in Atlanta cost in the neighborhood of $1.6 billion—both the IOC and national Olympic committees are always on the alert for ways to generate revenue. Television coverage provides one significant source of revenue for both the IOC and national committees. NBC paid $1.27 billion for the rights to broadcast in the United States the 2000 Sydney summer games and the 2002 Salt Lake City winter games. It then shelled out a further $2.3 billion to lock up the U.S. broadcast rights for the 2004, 2006, and 2008 games—even though their sites had not yet been determined. Broadcast rights for Europe, Australia, Asia, and the rest of the Americas will sell for smaller, but still breathtaking, amounts to local broadcasters. NBC and these broadcasters, in turn, will sell advertising time to companies eager to market their goods to Olympic fans throughout the world. For example, in July 1997—three years before its first ad would run—General Motors contracted with NBC to be the exclusive advertiser of automotive products for the 2000, 2002, 2004, 2006, and 2008 Olympics, a package worth over half a billion dollars. ■ ■ Another important source of revenue for the IOC and each national committee is corporate sponsors. Many firms have come to believe that being associated with the games confers a high degree of prestige and status. They can participate in Olympic sponsorship in various ways. The highest-profile—and most expensive, at $40 million—level is that of worldwide sponsor. Firms that market their products to consumers throughout the world, such as Coca-Cola, Eastman Kodak, and Visa, pay these millions of dollars to be official Olympic sponsors. The primary benefit of sponsorship is that sponsors get priority advertising space during Olympic broadcasts, if they choose to buy it. For example, Coca-Cola paid $60 million above and beyond its sponsorship fee for television advertising during the 1996 games. Not only did this provide valuable advertising exposure for the firm, but it also kept rival PepsiCo from buying any advertising time during Olympic broadcasts. ■ ■ Firms also pay for licenses to market their products or services in conjunction with the Olympics. For example, during the 1992 games, Evian was the games' official water, Ray Ban the official sunglasses, Bell the official bicycle helmets, and Reebok provided the suits some athletes wore during medal ceremonies. ■ ■ Sponsorship is even more complex at the level of national teams. National teams typically maintain ongoing and costly training programs and facilities for which there is usually little publicity. Thus opportunities to raise money from the public are limited. Teams consequently depend heavily on corporate sponsorships to cover their costs. But because of the international character of both the games and the businesses, unusual partnerships of teams and firms often are created. For example, Subaru, a Japanese firm, is an official sponsor of the U.S. ski team. Seiko, another Japanese firm, also supports U.S. Olympic teams. Eastman Kodak supports twenty-four national Olympic teams, and Coca-Cola supports eighty-two as part of its efforts to maintain a domestic image within each of those individual countries. ■ ■ ■ ■

The Olympic games are supposed to be about sportsmanship and the joys of athletic competition. But in a world of rapidly expanding international markets, they also have come to be about money and international economic competition. Cities on six continents vie to host the games, television and radio networks bid for the rights to broadcast them, and manufacturers of everything from athletic shoes to sunglasses compete for the opportunity to have world-famous athletes showcase their products on the international stage. Millions of dollars hinge on the success of each city, network, and manufacturer in its efforts to become affiliated with the games. Very clearly, then, the Olympics are international business in every sense of the word.

Moreover, the forces that have made the Olympics a growing international business are the same as those that affect firms worldwide as they compete in domestic and foreign markets. Changes in communications, transportation, and information technology not only facilitate domestic firms' foreign expansion but also aid foreign firms in their invasion of the domestic market. Those millions of dollars spent on the Olympics by television networks and corporate advertisers are symptomatic of the internationalization of business—the result of the desire of firms such as Coca-Cola, Sony Corporation, and Daimler-Benz to market their products to consumers worldwide.

The global economy profoundly affects your daily life—from the products you buy to the prices you pay to the interest you are charged to the job you hold. By writing this book, we hope to help you become more comfortable and effective in this burgeoning international business environment. To operate comfortably in this environment, you need to learn the basic ideas and concepts—the common body of knowledge—of international business. Further, you must understand how these ideas and concepts affect managers as they make decisions, develop strategies, and direct the efforts of others. You also need to be conversant with the fundamental mechanics and ingredients of the global economy and how they affect people, businesses, and industries. You need to understand the evolution of this economy and the complex commercial and political relationships among Asia, Europe, North America, and the rest of the world.

To help ensure your future effectiveness in the international business world, we plan to equip you along the way with the knowledge, insights, and skills that are critical to your functioning in a global economy. To that end, we have included hundreds of examples to help demonstrate how international businesses succeed—and how sometimes they fail. You also will read boxed tips and examples about global companies ("Going Global"), and you will have the chance to practice your growing skills in end-of-chapter "Building Global Skills" and "Working with the Web" exercises and cases.

What Is International Business?

Any business transaction between parties from more than one country is part of international business. Examples of such transactions include buying raw materials or inputs in one country and shipping them to another for processing or assembly, shipping finished products from one country to another for retail sale, building a plant in a foreign country to capitalize on lower labor costs there, or borrowing money from a bank in one country to finance operations in another. The parties involved in such transactions may include private individuals, individual companies, groups of companies, and/or governmental agencies.[2]

How does international business differ from domestic business? Simply put, domestic business involves transactions occurring within the boundaries of a single country, while international business transactions cross national boundaries. More substantively, international business can differ from domestic business for a number of reasons, including the following:

- ◆ The countries involved may use different currencies, forcing at least one party to convert its currency into another.

- ◆ The legal systems of the countries may differ, forcing one or more parties to adjust their behavior to comply with local law. Occasionally, the mandates of the legal systems may be incompatible, creating major headaches for international managers. For example, U.S. law promotes equal employment opportunities for women, while Saudi Arabian law discourages the employment of women when they will have to interact with adult males to whom they are not related.

- ◆ The cultures of the countries may differ, forcing each party to adjust its behavior to meet the expectations of the other. For example, U.S. businesspeople prefer to start meetings on time and to get down to specifics quickly, whereas Latin American businesspeople are less concerned about promptness and more concerned with learning more about the people with whom they are doing business.

- ◆ The availability of resources differs by country. One country may be rich in natural resources but poor in skilled labor, while another may enjoy a productive, well-trained work force but lack natural resources. Thus the way products are produced and the types of products that are produced vary among countries.

In most cases the basic skills and knowledge needed to be successful are conceptually similar whether one is doing business domestically or internationally. For example, the need for marketing managers to analyze the wants and desires of target audiences is the same regardless of whether the managers are engaged in international business or purely domestic business. But although international and domestic business are conceptually similar, there is little doubt that the complexity of skills and knowledge needed for success is far greater for international business. International businesspeople must be knowledgeable about cultural, legal, political, and social differences among countries. They must choose the countries in which to sell their goods and from which to buy inputs. International businesses also must coordinate the activities of their foreign subsidiaries, while dealing with the taxing and regulatory authorities of both their home countries and all the countries in which they do business.

Why Study International Business?

There are many different reasons why students today need to learn more about international business. First, almost any large organization you work for will have international operations or be affected by the global economy. You need to understand this increasingly important area in order to better assess career opportunities and to interact effectively with other managers. For example, as part of your first job assignment, you could be part of a project team that includes members from Mexico, Uruguay, Peru, and the United States. A basic grasp of international business would help you to understand more fully why this team was formed, what the company expects it to accomplish, and how you might most effectively interact with your colleagues.

Small businesses also are becoming more involved in international business. If after graduation you plan to start your own business, you may find yourself using foreign-made materials or equipment, competing with foreign firms, and perhaps even selling in foreign markets. For example, a small U.S. firm may buy raw materials from BASF AG (German), communications equipment from Northern Telecom (Canadian) or Nokia (Finnish), office equipment from Canon (Japanese), business forms from Moore Corporation (Canadian), and manufacturing equipment and machinery from the Daewoo Group (Korean).

You also need to study international business because you may eventually work for a firm that is owned by a corporation headquartered in another country. British Petroleum PLC, Siemens AG, and Toyota, for example, employ thousands of U.S. citizens. Overall, 4.9 million U.S. citizens work for U.S. affiliates of foreign-owned corporations.[3]

Still another reason for you to study international business is to keep pace with your future competitors. Business students in Europe have traditionally learned multiple languages, traveled widely, and had job experiences in different countries. And more European universities are launching business programs, many of which require students to spend one or more semesters in different countries. Japanese students, too, are actively working to learn more about foreign markets and cultures, especially those of the North American and European countries. These students, training to become managers, will soon be in direct competition with you, either in jobs with competing companies or in positions within your own company. You need to ensure that your global skills and knowledge will aid your career, rather than allowing their absence to hinder it.[4]

You also need to study international business in order to stay abreast of the latest business techniques and tools, many of which are developed outside North America. For example, Japanese firms have pioneered inventory management techniques such as **just-in-time (JIT) systems.** Under JIT, suppliers are expected to deliver necessary inputs just as they are needed. Similarly, European firms such as Volvo and Japanese firms such as Honda were among the first to experiment with such labor practices as empowerment, quality circles, autonomous work groups, and cross-functional teams to raise the productivity and satisfaction of their work forces. Managers who remain ignorant of the innovations of their international competitors are doomed to fail in the global marketplace.

Finally, you need to study international business to obtain cultural literacy. As global cultures and political systems become even more intertwined, understanding and appreciating the similarities and differences of the world's peoples will become increasingly important. You will more often encounter colleagues, customers, suppliers, and competitors from different countries and cultural backgrounds. Knowing something about how and where their countries and companies fit into the global economy—or at least knowing where to go to find that information—can help you earn their respect and confidence as well as give you a competitive edge in dealing with them (see "Going Global"). Conversely, if you know little or nothing about the rest of the world, you may very well come off as being provincial, arrogant, or simply inept. And this holds true regardless of whether you are a manager, a consumer, or just an observer of world events.

International Business Activities

Historically, international business activity first took the form of exporting and importing. **Exporting** is the selling of products made in one's own country for use or resale in other countries. **Importing** is the buying of products made in other countries for use or resale in one's own country. Today many firms' first ventures into the international marketplace begin with exporting or importing. In this way they often can limit their investments to little more than the value of what is being traded, thereby controlling their direct financial risk in their initial international endeavors.

Exporting and importing activities often are subdivided into two groups:

1 Trade in goods, that is, tangible products such as clothing, computers, and raw materials. Official U.S. government publications call this type of trade **merchandise exports and imports.** The British call it *visible trade*.

2 Trade in services, that is, intangible products such as banking, travel, and accounting activities. In the United States this type of trade is called **service exports and imports.** The British call it *invisible trade*.

Exports are often critical to a firm's financial health. For example, about 64 percent of Boeing's commercial aircraft sales are to foreign customers, creating 64,000 jobs at the company and thousands more at the factories of its parts suppliers. But international sales often are equally important to smaller firms, particularly those that serve niche markets. For example, exports generate 60 percent of the revenues of Weather Modification, Inc., a small (45 person) North Dakota

GOING GLOBAL

A Rose by Any Other Name …

Most people in the United States are familiar with the abbreviation **Inc.** and are accustomed to seeing business names such as Southwest Airlines, Inc. and Lands' End, Inc. The term, of course, stands for *incorporated* and means that the liability of the company's owners is limited to the extent of their investments if the company fails or encounters financial or legal difficulties. But other countries have different terminology when dealing with this concept of *limited liability*.

For example, Germany uses three different terms to reflect different forms of limited liability. **Aktiengesellschaft (AG)** is used for a large, publicly held firm that must have a management board and a board of directors. Examples include Deutsche Bank AG and Volkswagen AG. **Kommanditgesellschaft auf Aktien (KGaA)** is used for a firm that is owned by limited partners but has at least one shareholder with unlimited liability. Henkel KGaA, a German chemicals manufacturer, is an example. Finally, **Gesellschaft mit beschränkter Haftung (GmbH)** applies to smaller, privately held companies.

In Japan, **kabuskiki kaisha (KK)** is used for all limited-liability companies. In the Netherlands **BV (besloten vennootschap)** refers to a privately held, limited-liability firm and **NV (naamloze vennootschap)** to a publicly held, limited-liability firm, such as Philips NV. The United Kingdom also distinguishes between privately held and publicly held limited-liability companies, using **Ltd.** for the former and **PLC** for the latter. Examples are Swire Pacific Ltd. and Glaxo Wellcome PLC. Italy uses **SpA (la società per azioni)** to denote a limited-liability firm, for example, Benetton Group SpA and Fiat SpA. France uses **SA (société anonyme)** for the same purpose, as in Carrefour SA and Hachette SA.

weather monitoring and cloud seeding company. And trade is important to countries as well, as Fig. 1.1 shows.

Exporting also is important in an economy's service sector. Today services generate over 60 percent of the gross domestic products (GDPs) of the world's industrialized countries and account for an increasing proportion of global imports and exports.[5] Consulting, communications, transportation, tourism, and information services, for example, are all becoming more important in international trade, partly because they help facilitate other forms of international business.[6] For example, in 1976 U.S. service exports equaled $28 billion, or 20 percent of total U.S. exports of goods and services. By 1996 that figure had reached $237 billion, or 28 percent of total exports of goods and services.

The second major form of international business activity is **international investments**—capital supplied by residents of one country to residents of another. Traditionally, such investments are divided into two categories:

I **Foreign direct investments (FDI)** are investments made for the purpose of actively controlling property, assets, or companies located in host countries. (The country in which the parent company's headquarters is located is called the **home country;** any other country in which it operates is known as a **host country.**) An example of FDI is the purchase of all the common stock of Jaguar Motor Company (U.K.) by Ford Motor Company. After the purchase, Ford installed its own executives to oversee

FIGURE 1.1

Merchandise Exports as a Percentage of GDP for Some Key Countries (1995 Data)

Source: World Bank, *World Development Report*, 1997, pp. 236–237, 242–243.

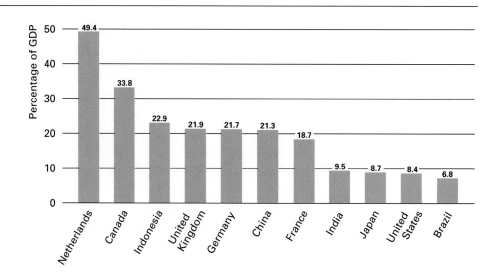

Jaguar's operations and integrate them into Ford's European procurement and marketing programs.

2 Portfolio investments are purchases of foreign financial assets (stocks, bonds, and certificates of deposit) for a purpose other than control. An example of a portfolio investment is the purchase of 1000 shares of Sony's common stock by a Danish pension fund. With this investment, the pension fund was trying to raise the attractiveness of its asset portfolio rather than to control Sony's decision making. For the same reason many investors in recent years have bought shares of mutual funds that specialize in foreign stocks and bonds.

International business activity can take several other forms, among the most important of which are licensing, franchising, and management contracts:

♦ **Licensing.** A firm in one country licenses the use of some or all of its intellectual property (patents, trademarks, brand names, copyrights, or trade secrets) to a firm in a second country in return for a royalty payment. For example, the Walt Disney Company may permit a German clothing manufacturer to market children's pajamas embroidered with Mickey Mouse's smiling face in return for a percentage of the company's sales.

♦ **Franchising.** A firm in one country (the franchisor) authorizes a firm in a second country (the franchisee) to utilize its brand names, logos, and operating techniques in return for a royalty payment. For example, McDonald's Corporation franchises its fast-food restaurants worldwide.

♦ **Management contracts.** A firm in one country agrees to operate facilities or provide other management services to a firm in another country for an agreed-upon fee. Management contracts are common, for example, in the upper end of the international hotel industry. Hoteliers such as Marriott and Hilton often do not own the expensive hotels outside the United States that bear their brand names but rather operate them under management contracts.

International business is extremely important to Boeing. In 1996, for example, the firm's exports exceeded $10 billion. Boeing sells aircraft to virtually every major airline in the world. Its biggest competitor is Airbus Industrie, a European consortium of aerospace firms.

The Extent of Internationalization

To aid in understanding international business activity, experts have categorized firms according to the extent of their international activities. The broadest category is **international business,** an organization that engages in cross-border commercial transactions with individuals, private firms, and/or public-sector organizations. But note that we have also used the term *international business* to mean cross-border commercial transactions. Whenever you see this term, you need to determine from the context in which it is being used whether it is referring to a general process involving transactions across borders or a single organization engaging in specific transactions across borders.

The term **multinational corporation (MNC)** is used to identify firms that have extensive involvement in international business. A more precise definition of a multinational corporation is a firm "that engages in foreign direct investment and owns or controls value-adding activities in more than one country."[7] In addition to owning and controlling foreign assets, MNCs typically buy resources in a variety of countries, create goods and/or services in a variety of countries, and then sell those goods and services in a variety of countries. They generally coordinate their activities from a central headquarters, but may also allow their

TABLE 1.1

The World's Largest Corporations, 1996

RANK	CORPORATION	SALES $ MILLIONS	PROFITS $ MILLIONS	PROFITS RANK	ASSETS $ MILLIONS	ASSETS RANK	EMPLOYEES NUMBER	EMPLOYEES RANK
1	General Motors (U.S.)	168,369.0	4,963.0	8	222,142.0	42	647,000	3
2	Ford Motor (U.S.)	146,991.0	4,446.0	11	262,867.0	33	371,702	7
3	Mitsui (Japan)	144,942.8	321.9	292	61,144.5	135	41,694	276
4	Mitsubishi (Japan)	140,203.7	394.1	271	77,871.5	121	35,000	308
5	Itochu (Japan)	135,542.1	110.9	411	59,179.6	140	6,999	470
6	Royal Dutch/Shell Group (U.K./Neth.)	128,174.5	8,887.1	1	124,373.4	80	101,000	98
7	Marubeni (Japan)	124,026.9	178.6	370	60,865.4	136	65,000	175
8	Exxon (U.S.)	119,434.0	7,510.0	2	95,527.0	102	79,000	141
9	Sumitomo (Japan)	119,281.3	(1,292.8)	491	43,506.3	173	26,200	354
10	Toyota Motor (Japan)	108,702.0	3,426.2	18	102,417.0	95	150,736	51
11	Wal-Mart Stores (U.S.)	106,147.0	3,056.0	22	39,501.0	186	675,000	2
12	General Electric (U.S.)	79,179.0	7,280.0	3	272,402.0	31	239,000	22
13	Nissho Iwai (Japan)	78,921.2	136.9	395	43,647.6	172	17,497	407
14	Nippon Telegraph & Telephone (Japan)	78,320.7	1,330.3	100	115,864.5	84	230,300	25
15	International Business Machines (U.S.)	75,947.0	5,429.0	6	81,132.0	115	268,648	19
16	Hitachi (Japan)	75,669.0	784.2	186	80,328.2	116	330,152	10
17	AT&T (U.S.)	74,525.0	5,908.0	5	55,552.0	148	130,400	65
18	Nippon Life Insurance (Japan)	72,575.0	2,799.1	33	322,759.2	20	86,695	126
19	Mobil (U.S.)	72,267.0	2,964.0	24	46,408.0	166	43,000	272
20	Daimler-Benz (Germany)	71,589.3	1,776.1	73	72,331.5	126	290,029	12

Source: From "Fortune's Global 500," *Fortune*, August 4, 1997, p. F-2. © 1997 Time, Inc. All rights reserved.

affiliates or subsidiaries in foreign markets considerable latitude in adjusting their operations to local circumstances. Table 1.1 lists the world's largest MNCs.

Because some large MNCs—such as accounting partnerships and Lloyd's of London—are not true corporations, some writers distinguish between multinational corporations and *multinational enterprises (MNEs)*. Further, not-for-profit organizations—such as the IOC and the International Red Cross—are not true enterprises, so the term *multinational organization (MNO)* can be used when one wants to refer to both not-for-profit and profit-seeking organizations. Because of the common use of *multinational corporation* in the business press, however, we use it in this book, even though technically its use should be restricted to businesses that are legal corporations.

The term *multinational corporation* generally can be applied to most of the world's larger, well-known businesses. At times, however, this terminology is too broad, and more precise terms are needed to further categorize MNCs. International business experts often find it useful to refer to three different types of MNCs:

1 A **multidomestic corporation** views itself as a collection of relatively independent operating subsidiaries, each of which is focused on a specific domestic market and is free to customize its products, marketing campaigns, and production techniques to best serve the needs of its local customers. The multidomestic approach is particularly useful when distinct differences exist among national markets; economies of scale in production, distribution, and marketing are low; and coordination costs between the parent corporation and its foreign subsidiaries are high. Because each subsidiary needs to be responsive to the local market, the parent typically delegates much power and authority to managers of its subsidiaries in host countries.

2 A **global corporation** views the world as a single marketplace and strives to create standardized goods and services that will meet the needs of customers worldwide. The underlying philosophies of a multidomestic corporation and a global corporation are antithetical. The former believes consumers in each country are basically different; the latter believes consumers are basically similar regardless of their nationalities. A global corporation thus views the world market as a single entity as it develops, produces, and sells products. It seeks to capture economies of scale in production and marketing by concentrating production in a handful of highly productive factories and creating global advertising and marketing campaigns. Because of the global corporation's need to coordinate its worldwide production and marketing strategies, it often concentrates power and responsibility at the parent's headquarters.[8]

3 A **transnational corporation** seeks to combine the benefits of global-scale efficiencies (the hallmark of a global corporation) with the benefits of local responsiveness (the advantage of the multidomestic approach). In transnational corporations,

> key activities and resources are neither centralized in the parent company, nor decentralized so that each subsidiary can carry out its own tasks on a local ... basis. Instead, the resources and activities are dispersed but specialized, so as to achieve efficiency and flexibility at the same time. Further, these dispersed resources are integrated into an interdependent network of worldwide operations.[9]

A high degree of interdependence among operating units is required in order for the transnational corporation to combine global efficiencies with local responsiveness; thus these firms often require complex organizational structures and two-way coordination mechanisms between the parent and its subsidiaries. In practice, they tend to centralize decision making at the parent's headquarters for some functions (such as production and research and development, which require uniform standards and benefit from economies of scale) and decentralize it at the local level for others (such as marketing and human resource management, which may need to be attuned to local cultural differences).

Yet another category of international business exists, although presently only hypothetically. There is no generally accepted term for these organizations, so we will refer to them as world companies. A **world company** is a firm that transcends national boundaries and in so doing loses its national identity. Presently the term represents a theoretical level of internationalization that may or may not ever be achieved in reality. No company has actually reached this level, although some are moving toward it.[10] One firm that is approaching this hypothetical level is Nestlé. While legally a Swiss company, Nestlé has 95 percent of its assets and earns 98 percent of its revenues outside Switzerland. Fewer than 10 percent of Nestlé's employees are Swiss. Moreover, its CEO is German and only five of its top ten executives are Swiss. Another example is Asea Brown Boveri, Ltd. (ABB), an electrical engineering firm that is legally Swedish but is headquartered in Switzerland. About half of ABB's stock is owned by investors outside these two countries. Its top managers are Swiss, Swedish, and German, but its official language, which is used for intracorporate communications and meetings, is English.[11] Service firms such as Reuters (a news agency), Bertelsmann (a publishing company), and Royal Dutch/Shell (an oil company) also are moving toward such a worldwide perspective.

National identity is becoming less important for many multinational corporations. Asea Brown Boveri, Ltd. (ABB), an electrical engineering firm that is legally Swedish but headquartered in Switzerland, is one such company. As shown here, the firm employs a work force that reflects considerable diversity.

The Evolution of International Business

Although the volume of international business has exploded in recent years, its origins developed thousands of years ago. Indeed, many events of the past have played a major role in defining contemporary markets, trade patterns, and financial centers. Moreover, history has played a major role in shaping the faces of many of today's dominant international businesses.[12]

The Early Era of International Business

International business originally consisted of international trade. Trade between nations can be traced back as far as 2000 B.C., when tribes in Northern Africa took dates and clothing to Babylonia and Assyria in the Middle East and traded them for spices and olive oil. This trade continued to expand over the years, encompassing more regions and a growing list of resources and products. Even the Olympic games have their roots in this early era, with the first being held in Greece in 776 B.C. By 500 B.C. Chinese merchants were actively exporting silk and jade to India and Europe, and common trade routes were being established.

Success in international trade often led to political and military power. First Greece and then the Roman Empire prospered in part because of exploitation of international trade. Ancient wars were fought to maintain trade dominance. For example, the Northern African city of Carthage became an international business center that rivaled Rome in the third century B.C., as merchants from Europe brought precious metals and glass to trade for the grains, ivory, and textiles offered by African merchants. Over a period of 100 years, Rome fought three bloody wars with Carthage to maintain its trade supremacy, finally beating the Carthaginians in 146 B.C. The victorious Romans burned the city and plowed salt into the soil (so that crops could not grow) to ensure that Carthage would never again rise as a rival.

During the Middle Ages, Italy became a focal point for international business because of its central location in what was then the world market. The political and military strength of Venice, Genoa, and Florence reflected their roles as major centers of international commerce and banking that linked trade routes between Europe and China.[13] Indeed, some of today's most significant trading relationships were established during this period. Some of the more important international trade routes of the era are illustrated in Map 1.1.

In 1453 these trade routes were severed when the Turks conquered Constantinople (now Istanbul) and gained control of the Middle East. Europe's trade with China had been particularly profitable, so European governments became interested in finding new ocean routes to the Far East. Backed by the Spanish government, Christopher Columbus sailed west from Europe looking for such routes. His landing in the Caribbean islands instead served to identify an important new source of resources and, eventually, led to the colonization of the Americas by European countries. At the same time, new trade routes to India and China were opened by Vasco da Gama's voyage around the Cape of Good Hope to India in 1498 and Ferdinand Magellan's voyage around the world from 1519 to 1522.

As European countries colonized the Americas, new avenues of trade opened. Settlers throughout the Americas sold raw materials, precious metals, and grains to Europe in exchange for tea, manufactured goods, and other commodities. Most of the American territories eventually became independent countries and important contributors to the world economy.

Another phenomenon of great importance to international business developed during the colonial period and the subsequent Age of Imperialism: the growth of FDI and MNCs, both of which involve foreigners supplying and controlling investments in a host country. European capitalists from such imperialist powers as Great Britain, France, the Netherlands, Spain, Belgium, and Portugal nurtured new businesses in their colonial empires in the Americas, Asia, and Africa, establishing networks of banking, transportation, and trade that persist to this day. The earliest of these firms founded during this period include the Dutch East India Company (established 1600), the British East India Company (1602), and the Hudson's Bay Company (1670). These and latter-day trading companies such as Jardine Matheson Holdings, Ltd., owned copper mines, tea and coffee estates, jute and cotton mills, rubber plantations, and the like as part of their global trading empires.[14]

In the nineteenth century the invention and perfection of the steam engine, coupled with the spread of railroads, dramatically lowered the cost of transporting goods over land and thereby made larger factories more economical. This development in turn broadened the extent of FDI. The forerunners of such large contemporary multinational corporations as Unilever, Ericsson, and Royal Dutch/Shell took their first steps on the path to becoming international giants by investing in

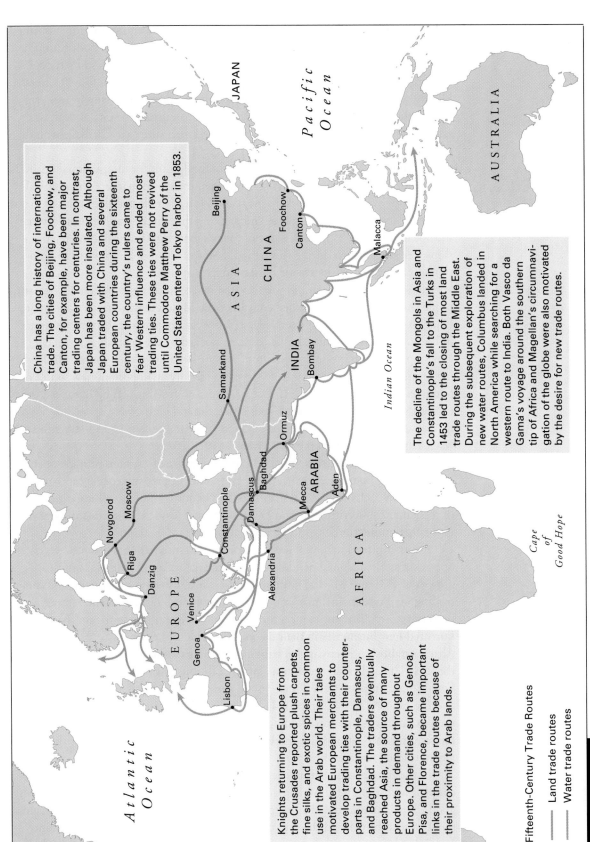

China has a long history of international trade. The cities of Beijing, Foochow, and Canton, for example, have been major trading centers for centuries. In contrast, Japan has been more insulated. Although Japan traded with China and several European countries during the sixteenth century, the country's rulers came to fear Western influence and ended most trading ties. These ties were not revived until Commodore Matthew Perry of the United States entered Tokyo harbor in 1853.

The decline of the Mongols in Asia and Constantinople's fall to the Turks in 1453 led to the closing of most land trade routes through the Middle East. During the subsequent exploration of new water routes, Columbus landed in North America while searching for a western route to India. Both Vasco da Gama's voyage around the southern tip of Africa and Magellan's circumnavigation of the globe were also motivated by the desire for new trade routes.

Knights returning to Europe from the Crusades reported plush carpets, fine silks, and exotic spices in common use in the Arab world. Their tales motivated European merchants to develop trading ties with their counterparts in Constantinople, Damascus, and Baghdad. The traders eventually reached Asia, the source of many products in demand throughout Europe. Other cities, such as Genoa, Pisa, and Florence, became important links in the trade routes because of their proximity to Arab lands.

Fifteenth-Century Trade Routes

—— Land trade routes

—— Water trade routes

MAP 1.1   Ancient Trade Routes

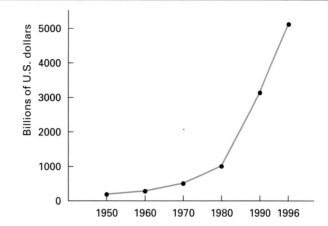

FIGURE 1.2

The Growth of World Merchandise Exports since 1950

Source: *International Monetary Fund Supplement on Trade Statistics* (International Monetary Fund, Washington, D.C.: 1990); *World Development Report, 1997* (World Bank).

facilities throughout Asia, Europe, and the Americas during this period. New inventions promoting technological change further stimulated FDI. For example, in 1852 Samuel Colt built a factory in Great Britain to produce his famous firearms, and later in the century Dunlop built factories in Belgium, France, and Japan to exploit its tire-making expertise.[15]

International Business Growth since World War II

Although international trade has been common for five millennia and international investment for five centuries, these two forms of international business activity have enjoyed unprecedented growth in the past five decades. Figure 1.2 illustrates growth trends in world merchandise exports for each ten-year period since 1950. The trend is both obvious and dramatic—world exports of goods have increased steadily at a significant pace. In 1950 they were around $53 billion.[16] In 1996 they were estimated to be slightly over $5.1 trillion, accounting for 18 percent of the world's $29 trillion economy. Most economists expect this trend to continue for the rest of this century and well into the next.

The statistics for FDI tell much the same story. As Table 1.2(a) indicates, in 1967 the total stock (or cumulative value) of FDI made by countries worldwide was slightly over $112 billion, but this figure more than quadrupled by 1980, then tripled by 1990, and rose an additional sixty percent from 1990 to 1995. Current worldwide FDI is about $2.7 trillion. As you might expect, the source of most FDI is the developed countries, which have consistently accounted for over 92 percent of all direct investments in foreign countries, as the first highlighted line in Table 1.2(a) indicates. If, in the 1990s, the Four Tigers (Hong Kong, Singapore, South Korea, and Taiwan) are included among the developed countries, then the enlarged group of developed countries accounts for over 97 percent of FDI between 1967 and 1995. Now let's look more closely at some significant shifts in the stock of FDI over the past 30 years:

I As shown in the second highlighted line in Table 1.2(a), the United States has become a less important source of FDI. FDI by U.S. firms has continued to increase in absolute terms but has shrunk in relative terms. The United States accounted for over half of the stock of FDI in 1967 but only 25.9 percent in 1995.

TABLE 1.2

Destination and Source of FDI, 1967–1995 (billions of U.S. dollars)
a. Source of FDI by major home countries and regions

COUNTRIES/REGIONS	1967 Value	1967 Percent of total	1980 Value	1980 Percent of total	1990 Value	1990 Percent of total	1995 Value	1995 Percent of total
Developed market economies	109.3	97.3	507.5	98.8	1614.5	95.9	2514.3	92.2
United States	56.6	50.4	220.2	42.9	435.2	25.8	705.6	25.9
United Kingdom	15.8	14.1	80.4	15.7	230.8	13.7	319.0	11.7
Japan	1.5	1.3	18.8	3.7	204.7	12.2	305.5	11.2
Germany	3.0	2.7	43.1	8.4	151.6	9.0	235.0	8.6
Switzerland	2.5	2.2	21.5	4.2	65.7	3.9	108.3	4.0
Netherlands	11.0	9.8	42.1	8.2	109.1	6.5	158.6	5.8
Canada	3.7	3.3	22.6	4.4	78.9	4.7	110.4	4.0
France	6.0	5.3	23.6	4.6	110.1	6.5	200.9	7.4
Italy	2.1	1.9	7.3	1.4	56.1	3.3	86.7	3.2
Sweden	1.7	1.5	5.6	1.1	49.5	2.9	61.6	2.3
Other developed	5.4	4.8	22.3	4.3	122.8	7.3	222.7	8.2
Developing countries	3.0	2.7	6.2	1.2	69.4	4.1	214.5	7.9
Four Tigers*	NA	NA	1.0	0.2	33.0	2.0	134.4	4.9
Total	112.3	100.0	513.7	100.0	1683.9	100.0	2728.8	100.0

b. Destination of FDI by major host countries and regions

COUNTRIES/REGIONS	1967 Value	1967 Percent of total	1980 Value	1980 Percent of total	1990 Value	1990 Percent of total	1995 Value	1995 Percent of total
Developed market economies	73.2	69.4	373.5	77.5	1373.3	80.1	1932.7	73.6
United States	9.9	9.4	83.0	17.2	394.9	23.0	564.6	21.5
Canada	NA	NA	54.2	11.2	113.1	6.6	116.8	4.4
Western Europe	31.4	29.8	200.3	41.6	758.7	44.2	1087.6	41.4
European Union	NA	NA	185.0	38.4	712.2	41.5	1028.1	39.2
United Kingdom	7.9	7.5	63.0	13.1	218.2	12.7	244.1	9.3
France	NA	NA	22.6	4.7	86.5	5.0	162.4	6.2
Germany	3.6	3.4	36.6	7.6	111.2	6.5	134.0	5.1
Spain	NA	NA	5.1	1.1	66.3	3.9	128.9	4.9
Japan	0.6	0.6	3.3	0.7	9.9	0.6	17.8	0.7
Australia	NA	NA	13.2	2.7	75.8	4.4	104.2	4.0
Developing countries	32.3	30.6	108.3	22.5	341.7	19.9	693.3	26.4
Africa	5.6	5.3	20.8	4.3	41.6	2.4	59.6	2.3
Latin America and Caribbean	18.5	17.5	48.0	10.0	121.3	7.1	225.8	8.6
Asia	8.3	7.9	38.0	7.9	175.9	10.3	403.3	15.4
Four Tigers*	NA	NA	11.5	2.4	63.9	3.7	106.9	4.1
China	negl.	negl.	negl.	negl.	14.1	0.8	129.0	4.9
Total	105.5	100.0	481.8	100.0	1715.0	100.0	2626.0	100.0

* Singapore, Taiwan, South Korea, and Hong Kong.
NA = not available

Source: World Bank, *World Investment Report 1996*, pp. 245–246; John H. Dunning, *Multinational Enterprises and the Global Economy*. Wokingham, England: Addison-Wesley Publishers Ltd., 1993. Reprinted with permission.

2 Japan's and Germany's importance as sources of FDI has increased dramatically over the same period, as shown by the third and fourth highlighted lines in Table 1.2(a).

3 Note from the first two highlighted lines in Table 1.2(b) that the share of FDI *received* by the developed countries increased from 1967 to 1990, as did that of the United States. Although the shares of both the developed countries and the United States fell from 1990 to 1995, this occurred primarily because of the large influx of FDI into China seeking access to the world's most populous market. These data reflect a shift toward FDI motivated by penetration of large consumer markets and away from FDI designed to exploit natural resources.[17]

4 Finally, although FDI by Japan has increased (see Table 1.2(a)), Japan's role as a destination country has remained about the same (Table 1.2(b)).

The growth of international trade and investment reflects the economic, political, and technological forces that are leading to the globalization of industries and the marketplace. Let's briefly review the evolution of international business over the past half-century to see how these forces have interacted to create today's economic and political climate.

The Golden Era of U.S. Business: 1945–1960. Consider the situation at the end of World War II in 1945: air, ground, and sea battles had devastated much of Europe; most Japanese business centers had been bombarded into rubble; and of the major industrial powers, only the United States had an infrastructure and industrial base that were unscathed. As a result, U.S. businesses faced relatively little foreign competition at home and also enjoyed considerable success abroad. During the 1950s American Motors (now a part of Chrysler), Chrysler, Ford, and General Motors seemingly sold all the automobiles they could produce. General Electric and RCA were leading electronics suppliers in most world markets. U.S. Steel and Bethlehem Steel faced virtually no foreign competition. Boeing, McDonnell Douglas, and Lockheed dominated the commercial aircraft market internationally. There were, of course, non-U.S. firms that were successful during this era. But giant U.S. corporations were the primary global suppliers for most industries. Indeed, by the decade's end, 70 of the world's 100 largest businesses were based in the United States.

Quite understandably, the energies of the other major combatants were focused on rebuilding their own economies and infrastructures. Japan, Germany, the Soviet Union, and France had to reconstruct or repair their highways, railroads, and communications systems. A fair amount of this reconstruction in Western Europe was financed with direct or indirect aid from the United States through the Marshall Plan. The **Marshall Plan,** named for U.S. Secretary of State George C. Marshall, was a massive aid program to help European countries work together to rebuild themselves. Some of the work was performed by U.S. firms, thus generating profits for the firms and jobs for U.S. workers. But much of the work in each country was done by local businesses. Thus the reconstruction process revitalized both the infrastructures and the economies of those countries.

The U.S. military also directly affected many foreign economies in the 1950s. For example, during the Korean conflict the United States based many of its supply operations in Japan, resulting in a tremendous infusion of capital, jobs, and technology to that country. Massive postwar U.S. troop deployments throughout Europe also created a similar benefit for European countries. Partly because of U.S. support, many industrialized countries, such as France, Italy, and Japan, achieved annual GNP growth rates of 10 percent or more throughout the 1950s. By the end of the 1950s, the process of rebuilding the infrastructures of Europe and Japan was essentially completed.

The Resurgence of Europe and Japan: 1960–1980. As the 1960s began, European and Japanese firms were well prepared to reclaim their traditional shares of the international marketplace.[18] The stage was set for foreign companies to aggressively seek new market opportunities and to expand their operations abroad. For example, Nissan Motor Company started shipping cars to the United States in 1958 under the Datsun name. It established the Nissan Motor Corporation in Los Angeles in 1960 and built its first factory abroad, in Mexico, in 1961. That same year, Alcan Aluminum (Canadian) opened its first foreign plant, in the United States. In 1962 Fuji initiated a joint venture with Xerox to build copiers. In 1967 Mazda introduced its rotary engine in Japan, and the Daewoo Group was created in Korea. And Toyota shipped its first Corona to the United States in 1965, followed by its first Corolla in 1968.[19] The initiatives undertaken by European and Asian firms during this period created the underpinnings of the complex global competitive environment in which firms operate today.

Nor was global expansion limited to industrial firms. For example, in 1961 Japan Air Lines launched the first nonstop flights between Japan and Europe. Deutsche Bank AG expanded from 345 branches in 1957 to 1100 by 1970, many of them in other European countries and in the Far East, Middle East, and North Africa. Other countries' banks and service firms also were expanding rapidly into foreign markets.

Of course, U.S. firms were expanding their global operations as well. For example, in the 1960s Ford built manufacturing facilities in England and Germany. In 1960 Polaroid was selling film in 10 countries; by 1969 it was selling film in 62. Borden, too, expanded aggressively into foreign markets in the 1960s, as did Merck, IBM, Caterpillar, and Goodyear. By 1970, 64 of the world's 100 largest firms were U.S.-based.

In the 1970s, however, several events weakened the position of the United States in the world economy.[20] Some were a backlash from a decade of heated competition. Others resulted from unpredictable turns in the world economy. During the 1950s and the 1960s demand for products and services had been so great that U.S. businesses did not have to be overly concerned with costs, efficiency, or quality. At the same time, however, many companies in other countries had been waging fiercely competitive domestic battles and had grown quite proficient at using cost and quality for gaining competitive advantage. The Japanese in particular had long been dedicated to maximizing product quality and were among the first to realize that efforts to increase quality actually lowered, rather than increased, costs. Thus, during the 1970s Japanese firms were perhaps better prepared for global competition than were most U.S. ones.[21]

Another significant but unforeseen event of the 1970s was the change in world oil prices and supplies. At that time the Middle Eastern countries took center stage in the global economy (see Map 1.2). The key oil-exporting countries in the region (Libya, Iran, Saudi Arabia, Kuwait, and others) forged a

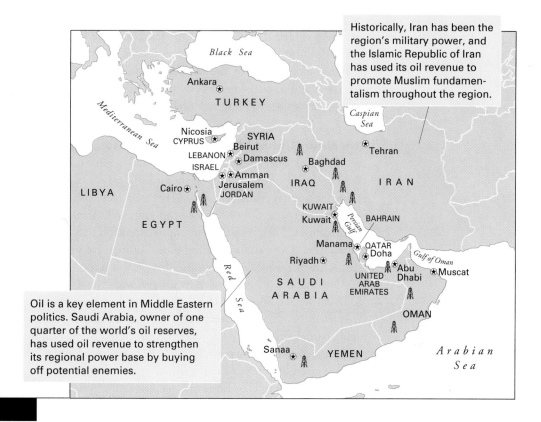

Historically, Iran has been the region's military power, and the Islamic Republic of Iran has used its oil revenue to promote Muslim fundamentalism throughout the region.

Oil is a key element in Middle Eastern politics. Saudi Arabia, owner of one quarter of the world's oil reserves, has used oil revenue to strengthen its regional power base by buying off potential enemies.

MAP 1.2

The Middle East

strong cartel, the Organization of Petroleum Exporting Countries (OPEC), which limited production of crude oil and simultaneously raised prices. OPEC's actions affected countries and companies around the world and triggered a massive wealth redistribution from oil-consuming to oil-producing countries. OPEC's policies had a particularly heavy impact on the United States because much of the competitive strength of the U.S. economy was based on the country's cheap energy policies. U.S. consumers and businesses faced the difficult task of adjusting their behavior and purchasing decisions in light of higher energy prices. For example, petrochemical companies such as DuPont, Monsanto, and Dow Chemical had prospered in international markets by converting low-priced petroleum into petrochemicals, plastics, and synthetic fibers. They had to rethink their operating practices and even their corporate missions in light of dramatically higher input costs. The adjustment problem was worsened by the U.S. government's inconsistent and constantly changing energy policies, which alternately created shortages and surpluses in critical markets for electricity, gasoline, and natural gas. Airlines and industrial consumers dependent on reasonably priced energy from reliable sources were particularly victimized by these shifting governmental policies. Further, the U.S. automobile industry suffered major losses in market share because its products were much less fuel-efficient than those of its Japanese competitors.

These forces enabled firms from Europe, Japan, and elsewhere to significantly increase their shares of the U.S. and world markets. With the enhanced profits generated by the increased demand for their products, these firms were able to expand their manufacturing capacities and increase their research and development expenditures. During the 1970s entire industry structures shifted.[22] For example, the Japanese came to dominate the steel and electronics industries. European automakers ruled the high end of the market, while Japanese automakers displaced General Motors, Ford, and Chrysler as leaders in the market's middle and low end. Japanese banks, fueled by the success of Japan's manufacturing sector, came to reign over the world financial system. By the end of the 1970s, the number of U.S. firms among the world's 100 largest had dropped to 49.

The New Global Marketplace: 1980 to the Present. By the end of the 1970s managers at many U.S. firms had begun to realize their companies could no longer remain complacent and still expect continued growth and prosperity, let alone world leadership. Many managers also realized that the emerging global marketplace not only posed monumental threats but also offered enormous opportunities. They began paying more attention to what their competitors from abroad were doing and emulating those competitive practices that were most effective, while improving on those that were less so.

One manifestation of this new interest was several best-selling books such as William Ouchi's *Theory Z* (1981) that focused on how Japanese organizations differed from their U.S. counterparts. Ouchi noted that Japanese organizations were highly participative and every worker contributed to making the highest-quality products possible. In contrast, many U.S. firms were highly centralized and workers were given little input into how the organizations were run. As these differences became clear, many U.S. firms began copying the competitive management tactics of Japanese firms. For example, they adopted such techniques as quality circles, autonomous work groups, JIT systems, and statistical quality control procedures because they believed those techniques contributed to Japanese success.[23]

However, U.S. firms discovered that simply imitating Japanese practices did not always work in the highly individualistic U.S. culture. This discovery reinforced the importance of carefully assessing the extent to which specific practices are transferable across cultures. U.S. firms, by emulating their foreign competitors in some areas and using new ideas and strengths developed from their own experiences in others, became better able to compete. For example, Ford and Chrysler, following the lead of Honda and Toyota, began emphasizing product quality, and subsequently each was able to regain lost market share and profitability. Companies in the electronics industry, such as Texas Instruments and Motorola, were reminded of the importance of research and development and cost control by Japanese competitors such as Hitachi and Toshiba. And Xerox redoubled its product development and marketing efforts after closely studying Canon. In virtually every international market the increasingly intense competition meant that firms that relied on the old way of doing things fell by the wayside—pushed aside by innovative, quality-conscious competitors better able to satisfy the needs of customers worldwide.[24]

As MNCs in Europe and Japan grew in size and wealth, they also began to escalate their direct investment in the United States. This strategy became popular for several reasons. Some firms wished to quickly establish a major presence in the U.S. market. Canada's Campeau Corporation achieved this goal by buying several prominent U.S. retailers, including Allied Stores and Federated Department Stores. Other MNCs acquired U.S. firms for their unique assets; for example, music libraries and copyrights motivated Bertelsmann AG's purchase of RCA Records and Sony's purchase of CBS Records. Some MNCs acquired U.S. assets

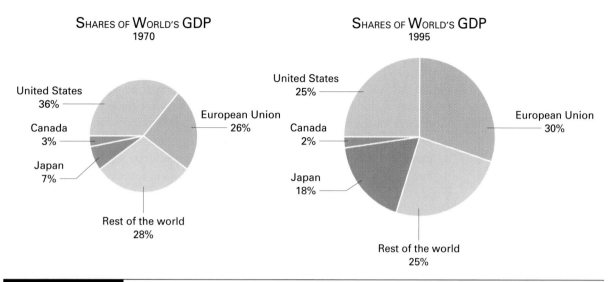

FIGURE 1.3

The World Economy: 1970 and 1995

Source: World Bank, *World Development Report, 1997.*

as part of their globalization strategies, such as Hoechst AG's acquisition of Celanese. Some companies believed that a strong U.S. presence helps them keep abreast of rapidly evolving technologies. As one senior executive of Japan's NEC Corp. noted, a U.S. location allows "you [to] stay in the flow of how the technology is evolving long before the product is available, and you get to see how the market is reacting to the technology so you can see if it's going to play well elsewhere."[25] Other FDI has been motivated by political and/or marketing factors. Mazda, Nissan, and Toyota have built auto assembly plants in the United States to defuse political criticisms and to counteract "Made in America" advertising campaigns by GM, Ford, and Chrysler. Similar patterns are occurring in Europe, as North American and Asian firms increase their investments to tap Europe's large, prosperous consumer markets and its technological prowess, and in Asia, where European and North American firms seek improved access to some of the fastest growing economies in the world.

By the dawn of the 1990s, a competitive global economy was beginning to take shape.[26] There was no single moment in time that marked the beginning of the global era. But today managers in every international business know that the rules of the game have changed dramatically. The old rules, already made brittle by the changes wrought during the 1960s and 1970s, were shattered during the highly competitive 1980s. And the new rules are still being written as the 1990s close out this century.[27]

As Fig. 1.3 shows, three geographic marketplaces now dominate the world economy:

1 United States and Canada

2 The European Union (EU)

3 Japan

While other marketplaces are important, and promise to become even more so in the years ahead, these three regions produce and consume the majority of the world's output of goods and services. Chapter 2 discusses each of these major marketplaces, as well as developing marketplaces, in more detail.

The structures of many industries are changing in response to the globalization of the world economy.[28] While some industries remain essentially domestic in nature (such as commercial printing, residential construction, health services, and regional transportation), an increasing number are truly global in nature (including automobiles, consumer electronics, chemicals, and aviation). In these global industries individual firms find that, to compete effectively, they must serve all the world's major markets. For some industries, these global pressures result from economies of scale in production, marketing, or research and development (R&D). For example, aircraft manufacturers such as Boeing and Airbus Industrie must sell their products to customers worldwide in order to amortize their multibillion-dollar R&D costs. Matsushita Electric Industrial Co., the Japanese giant whose brand names include JVC, Panasonic, and Quasar, has successfully sought market leadership not only in Japan but also in Europe and the United States in order to maximize the value of those brand names. Similarly, airlines such as Delta, American, and United have recognized that their carefully constructed hub-and-spoke systems designed to corral domestic passengers can also capture international ones. Other industries, such as accounting, advertising, banking, express parcel delivery, legal services, and telecommunications, are globalizing because their customers are globalizing. For example, no fewer than three international telecommunications consortia were launched in the 1990s with the explicit strategy of meeting the communications needs of the world's 100 largest companies. Of course, in between these extremes are other industries that have a clear international dimension but still have many firms with limited international operations. These industries include furniture, mining, publishing, and retailing.[29]

Reasons for International Business Growth

Our brief history of international business provides clear and dramatic documentation of the rate of international business growth in recent years. But why has this growth occurred? And why is international business activity likely to continue to escalate during the next several years? Several factors have contributed to this growth: market expansion, resource acquisition, competitive forces, technological changes, social changes, and changes in government trade and investment policies.

Market expansion is perhaps the most significant catalyst for international business growth.[30] As the productive capacities of firms' factories outgrow the size of their home markets, firms often internationalize their operations to seek new marketing opportunities. In many smaller economies, such as those of Singapore, Switzerland, and the Netherlands, firms quickly recognized that they had to look beyond national boundaries if they were to continue to grow. For example, one of the first international businesses was Nestlé. Because its home country, Switzerland, is so small, Nestlé was shipping milk to sixteen different countries as early as 1875. In contrast, the large size of the U.S. market initially caused many U.S. firms to remain content to sell only within that market. This attitude is disappearing as more U.S. companies recognize the rich commercial opportunities available outside the United States.

International business activity also is growing as firms seek to facilitate *resource acquisition*. These resources may be materials, labor, capital, or technology. In some cases, organizations must go to foreign sources because certain products or services are either scarce or unavailable locally. For example, U.S. grocery wholesalers buy coffee and bananas from South America, Japanese firms buy forest products from Canada, and firms worldwide buy oil from the Middle East and Africa. In other cases, firms simply find it easier and/or more economical to buy from other countries. For example, firms in many countries buy their communications equipment from Northern Telecom because they can obtain a complete system relatively inexpensively, which is easier than buying from multiple vendors and then assembling the components. Some firms move their manufacturing facilities abroad because of cheaper labor; for example, Sony and Matsushita Electric have stereo assembly plants in Malaysia. And with the development of the global capital market, many firms are seeking capital from foreign investors and lenders. For example, Disney used European investors for over half of the financing for its European theme park outside Paris.

Competitive forces also spur growth in international business activity. Because of economies of scale and the financial strength that comes with larger organizational size, smaller firms often have difficulty competing with larger ones. Thus, when a firm's competitors begin to grow by expanding into new foreign markets, that firm may have little choice but to follow suit. For example, Mazda struggled for years because it lacked the resources of its larger domestic competitors—Toyota and Nissan. It entered the U.S. market in order to keep pace with these Japanese rivals. In the early 1990s, Mazda aggressively introduced several new models that exploit market niches (such as the Miata convertible) and increased its worldwide automobile production. It adopted these tactics to increase its market share, sales, and profits, with the eventual goal of putting it on an equal footing with its major competitors. Similarly, the H.J. Heinz Company, a U.S. food processing firm, increased its international presence largely because it felt the need to keep pace with its primary competitors—Nestlé, Kellogg, and Philip Morris—each of which has operations in many foreign markets. A vivid demonstration of this need to keep up with one's competitors can be seen in Central and Eastern Europe, especially Russia. As these formerly inaccessible markets opened, literally thousands of businesses raced to capture new customers. Each one realized that if it fell behind its competitors, it might have a difficult time ever catching up.

Technological changes—particularly in communications, transportation, and information processing—are another important cause of the growth in international business activity. Think about the difficulties of conducting business internationally when the primary form of transportation was the sailing ship, the primary form of data processing was pencil and paper, and the primary form of communication was the letter delivered by a postman on horseback. Transportation improvements in the past 150 years—from sailing ship to steamship to seaplane to modern jet airliners—mean that a manager in London no longer needs to spend weeks traveling in order to confer with colleagues in Bombay, Toronto, or New York. The increasing ability of computers to rapidly handle and process vast quantities of information allows firms to manage offices and factories located in every corner of the globe. Exxon, for example, relies on its computers to adjust continuously the output of its refineries and the sailings of its tanker fleet in order to meet changes in worldwide demand for its products. Changes in

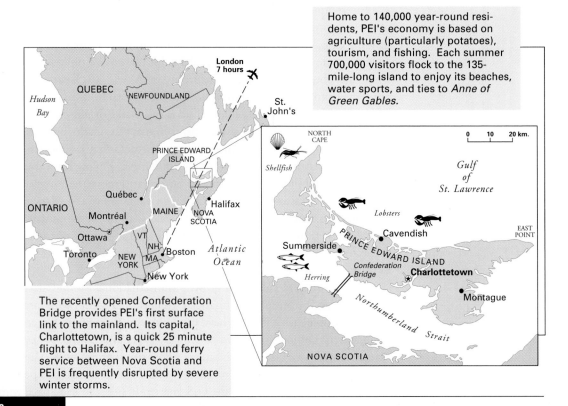

Home to 140,000 year-round residents, PEI's economy is based on agriculture (particularly potatoes), tourism, and fishing. Each summer 700,000 visitors flock to the 135-mile-long island to enjoy its beaches, water sports, and ties to *Anne of Green Gables.*

The recently opened Confederation Bridge provides PEI's first surface link to the mainland. Its capital, Charlottetown, is a quick 25 minute flight to Halifax. Year-round ferry service between Nova Scotia and PEI is frequently disrupted by severe winter storms.

MAP 1.3

Prince Edward Island, Home of *Anne of Green Gables*

communications technology, such as the advent of facsimile transmission and electronic mail, enable a manager in Tokyo to receive reports from colleagues in Amsterdam, Abidjan, and Auckland in minutes rather than days. These technological advances make managing distant businesses far easier today than executives would have dreamed possible just a few decades ago and so have facilitated expansion into international markets.

Social changes also have served to increase international business activity. Products and services too strongly identified with a particular culture were once shunned in certain societies. During the 1950s, for example, U.S. consumers avoided Japanese products, partly because they perceived those products to be of poor quality and partly because of lingering resentment from World War II. Similarly, Kellogg struggled in its attempts to open markets in Europe and Pacific Asia partly because many people in those regions traditionally did not eat processed cereals for breakfast: Europeans ate bread and natural grains, and fish was the choice in much of Asia. But because of long and intensive advertising campaigns, Kellogg is now finding its products becoming more accepted abroad. Today, as consumers worldwide tune into MTV and CNN, they are more likely than in the past to seek out foreign-made products. This global awareness boosts sales of such products as exotic bottled waters from France, television sets from Japan, and expensive cars from Germany. See "Going Global" for another example of this phenomenon.

Finally, changes in *government trade and investment policies* have expanded growth opportunities for international businesses. In the past fifty years, countries have negotiated reductions in import tariffs (taxes placed on imported goods) and eliminated barriers to FDI within their borders. Many of the reductions were nego-

GOING GLOBAL

What was Yoshiko Nishimura's reaction upon arriving at Cavendish on Prince Edward Island? "I cried for happiness upon arrival. Every Japanese girl dreams of one day paying respect to the land of Anne of Red Hair. She is much beloved."

Prince Edward Island (PEI), the smallest of Canada's Maritime Provinces, routinely attracts summer visitors from Central Canada and the Northeastern United States. While they enjoy PEI's rural scenery and charming towns and villages, few North Americans share, let alone understand, Ms. Nishimura's intense reaction to the island. Yet she is not alone. Thousands of her countrywomen annually make the trek—maybe a better word would be pilgrimage—to visit an old farmhouse in Cavendish that supposedly served as the model for the home where Anne Shirley, the fictional heroine of Lucy Maud Montgomery's *Anne of Green Gables*, grew up. One Japanese travel magazine found that among its female readers Cavendish

Anne of Red Hair

was the fourth most popular choice among foreign cities that they wished to visit, being topped only by New York, Paris, and London, even though it's not an easy trip. It takes at least twenty hours to fly from Tokyo to Toronto, catch a connecting flight to Halifax, and then another connecting flight to Charlottetown, PEI's capital, and then travel the last thirty miles or so by road to Cavendish.

Montgomery's book has long been a favorite of preteens in Canada and the United States. It has been translated into numerous languages and sells well in many markets. But in Japan the book has achieved cult-like status subsequent to its publication in 1952 under the title *Anne of Red Hair*. Today, thousands of Japanese girls subscribe to "Anne" magazines that explore in loving detail the lives of L.M. Montgomery, Anne, and her fictional family and friends.

Thousands more journey to Cavendish to visit sites associated with Anne and her creator. Some wear red pigtail wigs and paint freckles on their faces to better honor their idol. They spend millions of dollars purchasing Anne place mats, Anne key chains, and other Anne memorabilia that PEI merchants are only too happy to sell them. Some enroll in classes taught by the L.M. Montgomery Institute at the University of Prince Edward Island. The truly dedicated Anneophiles even drag their fiances to PEI so they can be married in the same front parlor of the farmhouse where Montgomery was wed in 1911.

Why is *Anne of Red Hair* so popular among Japanese women? No one really knows. Perhaps Anne's rebelliousness and frankness appeal to Japanese women who are expected to conform to the restrictive roles laid out for them by their culture. Or maybe Anne's love of nature and her loyalty to her family are the key to her allure. Whatever the reason, it's obvious that Lucy Maud Montgomery's spunky little heroine—whether she's known as Anne of Green Gables or as Anne of Red Hair—has touched the hearts of young readers around the globe. And she's also linked the merchants of PEI into the largest component of the $1.2 trillion trade in international services—tourism.

Many Japanese women journey to Cavendish, Prince Edward Island, to get married or to renew their wedding vows at the *Anne of Green Gables* house. Since its publication in Japan in 1952, *Anne of Red Hair* (as the novel is known there) has been beloved by generations of readers.

Sources: "Green Gables books a crowd," *Boston Globe,* August 10, 1997, p. A1; Calvin Trillin, "Anne of Red Hair," *The New Yorker,* August 5, 1996, pp. 56-61.

tiated through the General Agreement on Tariffs and Trade (GATT) and its successor, the World Trade Organization (WTO), Geneva-based organizations to which most of the world's major trading countries belong. Regional accords, such as the EU and the North American Free Trade Agreement (NAFTA), also have resulted in relaxed trade and investment barriers among their members. Consequently, international business has become more important to the world's economy.

An Overview of the Contents of This Book

As we noted earlier, our mission with this book is to help you become comfortable and effective in the competitive global economy. We use the fundamental perspective of a manager or employee who is or will be competing in the international arena and focus on identifying the major similarities and differences in doing business in domestic versus international settings. That is, we start with the assumption that most users of this book will eventually work for or own a business that is affected by international business activity.

To provide you with the common body of international business knowledge and skills to use in international business, we have structured the contents to move from relatively macro, or general, issues to increasingly micro, or specific, issues that managers deal with regularly. Our rationale is that managers must fully understand the context of international business in order to work effectively within that context. This broad, general context provides the backdrop within which all international business occurs. At each increasingly specific level within that context, the international manager is faced with more specific and operational issues, problems, challenges, and opportunities.

Part I comprises Chapters 1 and 2. Chapter 1 has supplied some background definitions and a history of how the contemporary global business environment evolved to its present form. Chapter 2 provides a wealth of economic and geographical information about the world's major marketplaces and business centers. Together Chapters 1 and 2 lay a foundation of the common body of international business knowledge that provides a useful context for the later chapters. Chapter 2 is especially important because of its coverage of international economics and geography.

Parts II through V follow a logical progression of topics, moving from the broad, general issues confronting international business to increasingly more specific, focused issues that managers face daily (see Fig. 1.4). Part II discusses in more detail the *international* environment itself, addressing the overall context of international business and introducing many of the global forces and conditions that affect organizations and managers. Part III describes the *national* environment of international business—the more specific country-level environmental context of today's organizations.

Part IV adopts the perspective of a specific organization, focusing on general management issues such as international strategies, modes of entry into foreign markets, joint ventures and strategic alliances, organization design, individual behavior, and control in international business. Part V covers the management of specific international business functions: marketing, operations, finance, accounting, and human resource management.

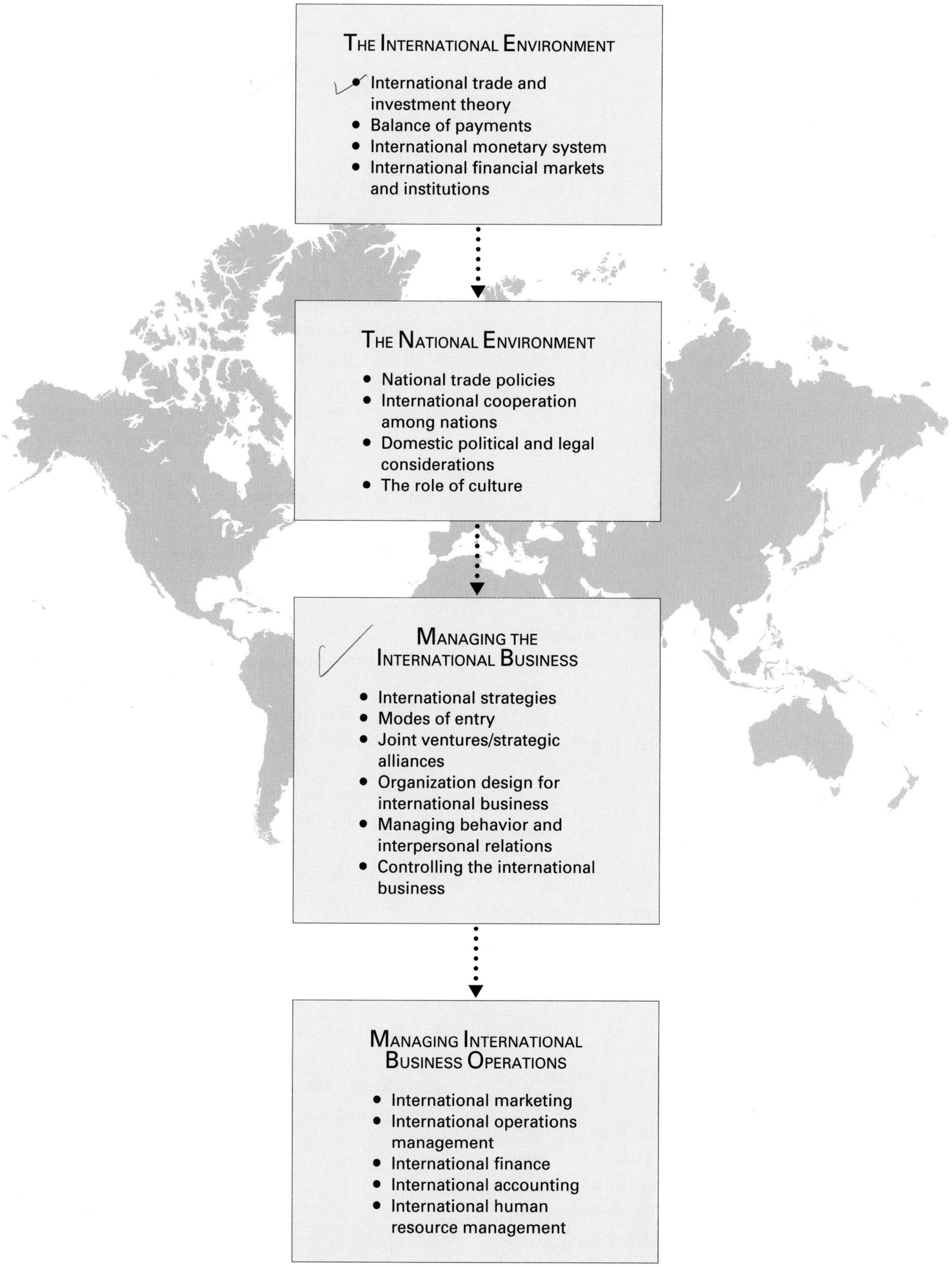

THE INTERNATIONAL ENVIRONMENT

- International trade and investment theory
- Balance of payments
- International monetary system
- International financial markets and institutions

THE NATIONAL ENVIRONMENT

- National trade policies
- International cooperation among nations
- Domestic political and legal considerations
- The role of culture

MANAGING THE INTERNATIONAL BUSINESS

- International strategies
- Modes of entry
- Joint ventures/strategic alliances
- Organization design for international business
- Managing behavior and interpersonal relations
- Controlling the international business

MANAGING INTERNATIONAL BUSINESS OPERATIONS

- International marketing
- International operations management
- International finance
- International accounting
- International human resource management

FIGURE 1.4   **Framework for This Book**

CHAPTER REVIEW

Summary

International business encompasses any business transaction that involves parties from more than one country. These transactions can take various forms and can involve individual companies, groups of companies, and/or government agencies.

International business can differ from domestic business because of differences in currency, legal systems, cultures, and resource availability.

Studying international business is important for several reasons:

♦ Any organization you work for, even if small, is likely to be affected by the global economy.

♦ You some day may work for a foreign-owned firm.

♦ You need to keep pace with other managers who are learning to function in international settings.

♦ You need to be culturally literate in today's world.

International business activity can take various forms. Exporting involves selling products made in one's own country for use or resale in another country. Importing involves buying products made in other countries for use or resale in one's own country. Foreign direct investment is investment made for the purpose of controlling property, assets, or companies located in foreign countries. Other common forms of international business activity include licensing, franchising, and management contracts.

An international business is one that engages in commercial transactions with individuals, private firms, and/or public-sector organizations that cross national boundaries. Firms with extensive international involvement are called multinational corporations, or MNCs. Special forms of multinational corporations include multidomestic corporations, global corporations, and transnational corporations.

Evidence of international business activity can be traced back thousands of years; many of today's major international trading patterns have evolved over several centuries. During the 1950s the United States dominated the global economy because many other industrialized countries were rebuilding after World War II. But international competition began to increase during the 1960s and eventually led to the end of U.S. dominance in the 1970s. In the 1980s many U.S. firms gradually began to regain their competitiveness. As the 1990s dawned, global marketplaces and global industries were becoming fairly well defined.

International business has grown dramatically in recent years because of market expansion, resource acquisition, competitive forces, technological changes, social changes, and changes in government trade and investment policies.

Review Questions

1. What is international business? How does it differ from domestic business?

2. Why is it important for you to study international business?

3. What are the basic forms of international business activity?

4. How do merchandise exports and imports and service exports and imports differ?

5. What is portfolio investment?

6. Identify and describe the various kinds of international businesses that exist today.

7. Briefly summarize the evolution of international business.

8. How did World War II shape international business? How might business have shaped the war?

9. Trace the U.S. role in international business through the 1950s, 1960s, and 1970s.

10. What are the basic reasons for the recent growth of international business activity?

Questions for Discussion

1. Do you think true world companies will ever really exist? Why or why not?

2. If the trade routes through the Middle East had not been closed in 1453, how might the history of international business have been different?

3. What types of firms were likely to prosper during World War II? What types were more likely to have suffered during the war?

4. Why do some industries become global while others remain local or regional?

5. Under what circumstances might a firm want to decrease its level of international activity?

6. Does your college or university have any international programs? Does this make the institution an international business? Why or why not?

7. What are some of the skill differences that may exist between managers in a domestic firm and those in an international firm?

8. Would you want to work in a foreign-owned firm? Why or why not?

9. Are the Olympics and business too intertwined? What are the pros and cons of the increased commercialization of the Olympics?

10. How is managing the IOC similar to and different from managing a business?

BUILDING GLOBAL SKILLS

List ten different products you use on a regular basis, such as your alarm clock, camera, car, coffee maker, computer, razor, sneakers, telephone, television, or VCR—perhaps even your favorite movie, shirt, fruit juice, or type of recording tape.

After you have developed your list, go to the library and research the following for each item:

1. What firm made the item?

2. In which country is that firm based?

3. What percentage of the firm's annual sales comes from the United States? What percentage comes from other countries?

4. Where was the item most likely manufactured?

5. Why do you think it was manufactured there?

Follow up by meeting with a small group of your classmates and completing these activities:

1. Discuss the relative impact of international business on your daily lives.

2. Compile a combined list of the ten most common products the average college student might use.

3. Try to identify the brands of each product that are made by U.S. firms.

4. Try to identify the brands of each product that are made by non-U.S. firms.

5. Does either of your lists of ten products include items that have components that are both U.S.-made and non–U.S.-made?

WORKING WITH THE WEB: Building Global Internet Skills

Marketing Tourism in Prince Edward Island

Let's go back to the "Going Global" on page 29, which discussed the growing market of Japanese tourists—primarily young female adults—visiting Prince Edward Island. The Worldwide Web is becoming an important mechanism for selling goods and services internationally. Visit the web site of the PEI government. Suppose you were thinking about visiting PEI. What information would you like to have to plan your visit? Does this web site provide that information? Now put yourself in the shoes of a young Japanese Anne-loving female. Does the web site meet her needs? What changes would you recommend in the PEI government's web site to cater to this market?

Now examine how the private sector deals with some of these questions. Do a web search on *Anne of Green Gables* and a search on tourist accommodations and attractions on the island. Which web sites are of most value to prospective tourists?

Each chapter of this book contains a "Working with the Web" skill-building exercise. The textbook's web site contains linkages to some web sites that may be of use in doing this assignment and those found in later chapters. Visit the web site at http://hepg.awl.com. Use the keyword "Griffin-IB" (password = IB2).

CLOSING CASE

The Rise and Fall of the British Sportscar [31]

Imagine being the world's largest exporter of a product and controlling the lion's share of the world's biggest market for that product. Now imagine first losing the export title and then being forced to drop completely out of the business—all in relatively few years. Could such a debacle occur? Yes—and it involved the British firms that first created, then dominated, and eventually dropped out of the market for low- to- mid-priced sportscars.

During the first six decades of this century, the MG Car Company became a major player in the British auto industry. Mirroring the strategy used by Alfred Sloan, president of GM from 1923 to 1937, MG developed and sold a variety of cars in every price range. This allowed the firm to sell entry-level cars to young families and later to get them to "trade up" to more expensive models. One part of the MG product line was an inexpensive, two-seat sportscar called—simply enough—the MG; the Morris and the Riley were two of the firm's most successful family cars.

At the conclusion of World War II, two things happened to create a golden opportunity for MG. First, the British government, in dire need of hard currency, pressured domestic automobile manufacturers to export 70 percent of their output to the United States, where hard currency was readily available. To reinforce this pressure, the British government restricted domestic sales of automobiles. Thus MG, along with other British automakers, began shipping large quantities of cars to the U.S. market.

The second factor underlying MG's golden opportunity was unexpected demand in the United States. While most British models were undistinguishable from their U.S. counterparts, the MG sportscar was unique—it essentially had no competitors. Moreover, since many U.S. soldiers had already seen and admired the MG during the war, they eagerly snapped up every unit the firm could ship to dealers in the United States. Thus, the MG emerged as one of the hottest exports from Britain after the war. Indeed, that country was the world's largest exporter of automobiles from 1947 until the early 1960s, fueled in part by the extraordinary success of the MG.

Of course, the MG was not the only sportscar made in Britain, and its success was quickly noticed. Triumph Motor Company made some modifications to its own sportscar line and, in 1950, began shipping units to the United States. And Jaguar, which had been selling its cars in the United States for decades, increased its sales and marketing efforts dramatically. Throughout the 1950s and into the 1960s, MG controlled the low-priced segment of the U.S. sportscar market, Triumph controlled the mid-priced segment, and Jaguar controlled the higher-priced niche.

Blinded by a decade of success, however, the British firms made a classic error of many highly successful businesses—they grew complacent. Each firm saw its position in both the world and the U.S. market as totally secure, refusing to acknowledge that it faced potential competitive threats. For example, the British firms did not continue to invest in new technology, and, as a result, their production methods became relatively inefficient as other automakers built new, more modern plants. Similarly, with demand for their products so strong, the British firms saw little reason to improve the quality and reliability of those products. And when change was necessary, they tended to approach it superficially. For example, when the U.S. government mandated that all cars sold within the United States had to have stronger bumpers, MG simply added larger, bulkier bumpers to its sportscars without altering their design in any other way.

Because the British firms enjoyed what was essentially a monopoly in the U.S. sportscar market, these weaknesses were hidden from managers. In the 1960s, however, two events occurred that led to the eventual downfall of British sportscar makers. The first event took place in 1964, when Ford unveiled the Mustang. Its jaunty styling, low price, and "muscle car" image made it a big success and soon a formidable competitor for the MG and the Triumph. This weakened MG and the other British firms and, more significantly, revealed their vulnerabilities to all their competitors. Unfortunately for Ford, however, its managers also failed to fully understand the sportscar market. They soon began to add features and gimmicks to the Mustang while also increasing its size and price, overlooking the fact that simplicity, small size, and low price were three determinants of the car's appeal. Thus Ford began to lose momentum and the British companies breathed a brief—and unjustified—sigh of relief.

Waiting in the wings were the Japanese, led by

Nissan (which used the name "Datsun" in the United States during this era). The Datsun 240-Z, introduced in the United States in 1969, was in its own way a bigger success than the Mustang. Nissan avoided Ford's mistake of forgetting its target market. The 240-Z had numerous innovative mechanical and design features, was more reliable than other sportscars, and sold for about the same price as the Triumph. Soon the Datsun 240-Z ruled the highways and crippled its British competitors. Two years after the car was introduced it was the best-selling sportscar in the United States, and a year later it was outselling the MG and the Triumph combined in that market.

As a result of financial difficulties caused by loss of market share, MG merged with Triumph to create what was known as British Leyland Motor Corporation. Managers hoped that this combination would have the size and clout to regain the top market position and to compete more effectively with both U.S. and Japanese firms. The new firm quickly tried to develop new products, but these were poorly designed and underengineered, having numerous flaws and weaknesses when they hit the market. Among the more spectacular failures for British Leyland was the Triumph TR7, a wedge-shaped car designed to compete with the Datsun 240-Z. The TR7 sold a respectable 32,743 cars in the United States in 1975 (its first full year of production), but sales dropped to only 22,939 the next year and continued to plummet until the model was eventually discontinued in 1981. The TR7 took with it British Leyland's entire sportscar line; the firm announced it was abandoning the sportscar market altogether. Today, the only British-made sportscar sold in the United States is the Jaguar, now produced by a division of Ford.

The British sportscars did leave an interesting legacy, however. One of the most successful sportscars introduced in recent years is the Mazda Miata. The Miata was intentionally designed and marketed to evoke memories of the 1950s in general and the MG in particular. The Miata is small, with only two seats, has a spartan but functional interior and a jaunty overall look, and carries a modest price tag. Its tremendous success serves to remind the automobile world of a bygone era and to help managers remember the importance of keeping focused on their markets and in tune with their customers.

Case Questions

1. What are the basic lessons international managers can learn from the experiences of the British sportscar manufacturers?

2. Can you identify any firms today that have the same market position as that occupied by the British automobile manufacturers during the 1950s?

3. If you were a British auto executive today, would you consider reentering the sportscar market? Why or why not?

4. Ford recently introduced a new model of the Mustang designed to take the car back to its roots. Comment on the success of this effort.

CHAPTER NOTES

1. "Catalonia Basks in the Olympic Light," *World Press Review,* January 1992, pp. 17–18; "NBC's Olympic Gamble," *Newsweek,* January 13, 1992, p. 44; "The Olympics: Brought to You by ...," *USA Today,* July 21, 1992, pp. 1B, 2B; "Let the Bidding Begin for the TV Rights to '96 Olympics, and Watch It Heat Up," *Wall Street Journal,* August 7, 1992, p. B1; "Going for the Gold, Merchandisers and Retailers Promote the Olympics Two Years in Advance," *Wall Street Journal,* December 7, 1993, pp. B1, B16; "Japan's Nagano, Site of 1998 Games, Faces Problems of Olympic Proportions," *Wall Street Journal,* March 15, 1994, p. A14; "Olympics Strategy Has Its Rewards," *USA Today,* February 21, 1994, pp. 1B, 2B; "Greek Leaders See Winning Olympic Bid as an Endorsement of Market Reforms," *Wall Street Journal,* September 8, 1997; "NBC Wraps Up the Olympics through 2008," *Wall Street Journal,* December 13, 1995, p. B1; "GM to Spend Up to $1 Billion on Olympics through 2008 in Pact with USOC, NBC," *Wall Street Journal,* July 29, 1997, p. B5.

2. See Mira Wilkins, "The Conceptual Domain of International Business" (paper presented at a conference entitled "Perspectives on International Business: Theory, Research, and Institutional Arrangements," University of South Carolina, May 21–23, 1992).

3. *Survey of Current Business* (Washington, D.C.: U.S. Department of Commerce), June 1997, p. 42.

4. Jeremy Main, "B-Schools Get a Global Vision," *Fortune,* July 17, 1989, pp. 78–86.

5. "The *Fortune* Global Service 500," *Fortune,* August 22, 1994, pp. 180–208.

6. Hermann Simon, "Lessons from Germany's Midsize Giants," *Harvard Business Review,* March–April 1992, pp. 115–125.

7. John H. Dunning, *Multinational Enterprises and the Global Economy* (Wokingham, England: Addison-Wesley Publishing Company, 1993), p. 3.

8. See Erdener Kaynak (ed.), *The Global Business* (New York: International Business Press, 1993), for a discussion of global corporations.

9. Christopher Bartlett and Sumantra Ghoshal, *Transnational Management* (Homewood, Ill.: Irwin, 1992), p. 14.

10. Larry Hirschhorn and Thomas Gilmore, "The New Boundaries of the 'Boundaryless' Company," *Harvard Business Review,* May–June 1992, pp. 104–115.

11. "The Stateless Corporation," *Business Week,* May 14, 1990, pp. 98–104.

12. Richard Thurnwald, *Economics in Primitive Communities* (London: Oxford University Press, 1932).

13. Simcha Ronen, *Comparative and Multinational Management* (New York: John Wiley & Sons, 1986).

14. S. D. Chapman, "British-based Investment Groups before 1914," *Economic History Review,* Vol. 38 (1985), pp. 230–235.

15. John H. Dunning, op. cit., pp. 106ff.

16. *International Monetary Fund Supplement on Trade Statistics* (Washington, D.C.: International Monetary Fund, 1990).

17. John H. Dunning, op. cit., p. 21.

18. Richard J. Barnett and Ronald E. Muller, *Global Reach— The Power of the Multinational Corporations* (New York: Simon and Schuster, 1974).

19. Alan Chai, Alta Campbell, and Patrick J. Spain, *Hoover's Handbook of World Business 1993* (Austin, Tex.: The Reference Press, 1992).

20. Michael E. Porter, "The Competitive Advantage of Nations," *Harvard Business Review,* March–April 1990, pp. 73–93.

21. Lloyd Dobyns and Clare Crawford-Mason, *Quality or Else* (Boston: Houghton Mifflin, 1991).

22. Michael Prowse, "Is America in Decline?" *Harvard Business Review,* July–August 1993, pp. 34–45.

23. David A. Ricks, Brian Toyne, and Zaida Martinez, "Recent Developments in International Management Research," *Journal of Management,* June 1990, pp. 219–245.

24. Sylvia Nasar, "America's Competitive Revival," *Fortune,* January 4, 1988, pp. 44–52.

25. "Foreign Executives See U.S. as Prime Market," *Wall Street Journal*, February 3, 1997, p. A1.

26. Michael E. Porter, *The Competitive Advantage of Nations* (New York: Free Press, 1990).

27. Rosabeth Moss Kanter, "Transcending Business Boundaries: 12,000 World Managers View Change," *Harvard Business Review,* May–June 1991, pp. 151–164.

28. Michael A. Hitt, Robert E. Hoskisson, and Jeffrey S. Harrison, "Strategic Competitiveness in the 1990s: Challenges and Opportunities for U.S. Executives," *The Academy of Management Executive,* May 1991, pp. 7–22.

29. Richard I. Kirkland, Jr., "Entering a New Age of Boundless Competition," *Fortune,* March 14, 1988, pp. 40–48.

30. Raj Aggarwal, "The Strategic Challenge of the Evolving Global Economy," *Business Horizons,* July–August 1987, pp. 38–44.

31. Timothy R. Whisler, "Defeating the Triumph," *Audacity,* Fall 1993, pp. 17–25; "Triumph Takes a Holiday," *Automobile Quarterly*, Fall 1993, pp. 23–35; "Triumph Before Tragedy: The Odyssey of the TR Sports Car," *Automobile Quarterly*, Summer 1990, pp. 10–29.

Global Marketplaces and Business Centers

CHAPTER

2

After studying this chapter you should be able to:

Describe the value of economic geography to international businesspeople.

Evaluate the impact on business of the political and economic characteristics of the world's various marketplaces.

Appreciate the uses of national income data in making business decisions.

Discuss North America as a major marketplace and business center in the world economy.

Describe Western Europe as a major marketplace and business center in the world economy.

Discuss the problems facing the economies of the former communist countries of Eastern and Central Europe.

Discuss Asia as a major marketplace and business center in the world economy.

Assess the development challenges facing African, Middle Eastern, and South American countries.

HILE WAL-MART HAS BECOME THE NUMBER ONE RETAILER IN the United States through a combination of aggressive cost cutting, efficient distribution, and careful selection of merchandise, it has stubbed its toe in the Brazilian marketplace. Few Brazilians bought the American footballs prominently displayed in Wal-Mart stores in suburban Sao Paulo, for no one plays that sport there. They also snubbed the cordless tools and leaf blowers that are so popular in the U.S. market. The forklifts Wal-Mart procured in the United States failed to work with the standardized pallets used by Brazilian distributors. And its Sam's Clubs have performed below expectations, in part because most Brazilian consumers don't have enough storage space to take advantage of buying in bulk. ▮▮Advertisements for the Energizer Bunny were spectacular failures when they were run on Hungarian television. Most view-

The First Rule: Know the Territory[1]

ers there assumed that the ads were for toy bunnies. One U.S. baby care company tried to boost sales of its products to Hungarians by featuring a mother warmly embracing her baby. Unfortunately, the model in the ad was wearing a ring on her left hand; Hungarians, however, wear their wedding rings on their right hands. Noted one Hungarian advertising executive, "It was so obvious to viewers that this woman was telling everyone in Hungary that she wasn't married. And then Western marketers wonder why people here won't buy their products." ▮▮Rich farmland has made Ukraine one of the world's premier granaries. In 1993 Monsanto targeted this market, selling $38 million in fertilizers and herbicides to the agricultural ministry. However, it took Monsanto a year to receive payment, and then only after the U.S. State Department interceded on its behalf with the newly elected president, Leonid Kuchma. Burned by this experience, Monsanto decided to bypass the agricultural ministry and sell directly to private distributors and collective farms. This did not prove to be a wise move, for it enraged *apparatchiks* (a Soviet-era term for bureaucrats), who disliked any attempt to reduce their power. Ukrainian prosecutors, acting on behalf of the agricultural ministry, began harassing Monsanto's customers, asking why they were buying foreign products. Ukrainian courts declared Monsanto's chemicals unsafe, even though they had passed strict U.S. regulatory requirements. And farmers using Monsanto products were denied licenses needed to export their crops. ▮▮DHL International sought to trumpet the speediness of its courier services in the fast-growing Asian market by placing a seemingly amusing ad in the *Asian Wall Street Journal* and the *International Herald Tribune*. The ad pictured a DHL courier and five Asian heads of state along with text that questioned, "Who keeps the world's fastest moving economies moving faster?" However, Indonesian President Suharto, one of the five heads of state depicted in the ad and Indonesia's ruler since he seized power in 1968, was not amused at being compared to a mere courier. That country's Information Minister, denouncing the ads as unethical and contrary to the "moral values of Indonesian culture," promptly canceled circulation of both newspapers in the country. While both newspapers and DHL quickly printed apologies for the misunderstanding, none are likely to be invited to the presidential palace any time soon. ▪▪▪▪

Businesses trying to internationalize their operations often blunder because they fail to obtain vital information. Ignorance of basic geography, market characteristics, culture, and politics may lead to lost profits or, in the extreme, doom a venture to failure. Linguistic and cultural ties, past political associations, and military alliances play significant roles in the world pattern of trade and investment and in shaping the opportunities available for businesses today. For example, London's contemporary importance as a world financial center arises from the political and military power of the British Empire in the nineteenth century. Similarly, Austria serves as a bridge between Western and Eastern Europe because of transportation, educational, and cultural linkages that remain from the 600-year reign of the Hapsburg dynasty over the Austro-Hungarian empire.

Take a moment now to assess your own understanding of today's important global marketplaces and business centers by answering the following questions:

1 How far apart geographically are Tokyo and Singapore?

2 What is Ukraine's capital?

3 What is Brazil's official language?

4 What is the largest city in Brazil?

5 What countries border France?

6 Which is farther south: Miami, Florida, or Monterrey, Mexico?

It is perhaps surprising that many people cannot answer these questions. People often think, for example, that Tokyo and Singapore are close neighbors. In fact, they are over 3300 miles apart, about the same distance that separates New York from London and Montreal from Paris. People also may not know that Kiev is Ukraine's capital (many pick St. Petersburg); that Portuguese is Brazil's official language (many pick Spanish, the dominant language throughout the rest of South America); that Sao Paulo, Brazil's commercial capital, is the most populous city in Brazil, although Rio de Janeiro, with its famed beaches like Ipanema, is better known; that France's neighbors are Andorra, Belgium, Luxembourg, Monaco, Germany, Switzerland, Italy, and Spain (many people can name some, but few can name all); and that Miami is farther south than Monterrey (people "know" Mexico is south of the United States). Anyone involved in international business needs to know the basic structure of the world economy and where on a globe or map to find the major countries and cities that are home to the world's major marketplaces and business centers. (See Map 2.1.) This chapter provides a basic understanding of the geographical, economic, and political foundations of the world economy.

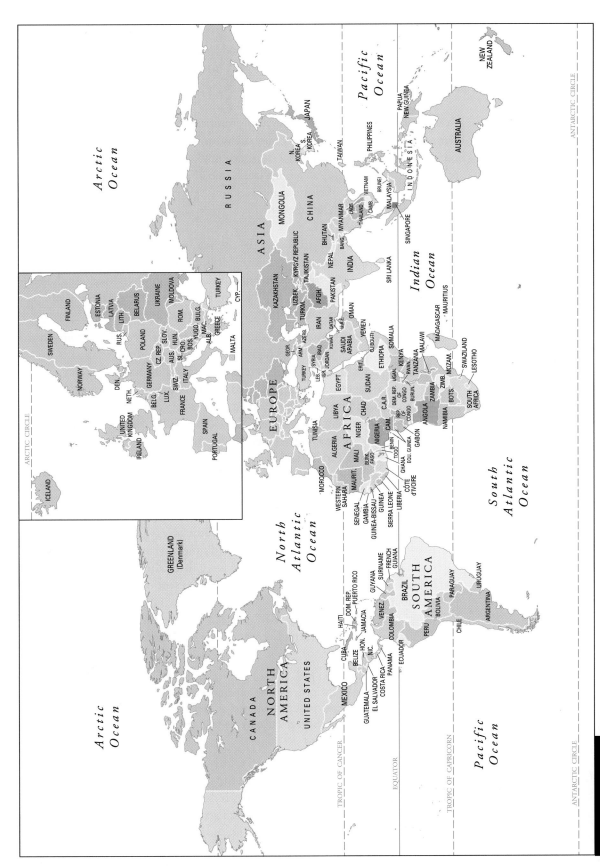

MAP 2.1   **World Map**

The Structure of the World Economy

Because of the vast size of the world economy—an estimated $29 trillion in 1996—providing an overview of it is not simple. To ease this task, international businesspeople often group countries by common features, such as their political systems (democracy, monarchy, or totalitarian state) or their economic systems (communist, socialist, or free market). Geography, however, plays an important, and often underappreciated, role in international business.

Among the factors of cultural and economic geography that affect international trade and investment flows are

1 *Shared borders.* Proximity lowers the costs of transporting and distributing goods. Proximity also makes it easier for firms to stay abreast of foreign markets and to monitor the performance of their foreign investments and operations. For example, Canada and the United States are major trading and investment partners, as are France and Germany.

2 *Common heritage.* Countries that have a common heritage arising from ethnic or political bonds often have extensive international business relations. For example, much of China's initial postwar trade and investment activity with the Western democracies was funneled through Hong Kong because geographical proximity and ethnic and family ties between capitalist Hong Kong and communist China overcame Cold War hostilities. Similarly, trade and investment ties between the United Kingdom and its former colonies of Australia, Canada, India, and New Zealand remain strong because of common political, legal, and educational traditions.

3 *Similar income levels.* Countries with similar per capita incomes (see "Going Global" on page 44) often trade with each other because of similarities in the needs and wants of their consumers. This phenomenon is particularly noticeable among the world's industrialized countries and often colors the strategic thinking of large firms. In the judgment of Kenichi Ohmae, the former managing director of McKinsey & Company's Tokyo office, the world economy is increasingly being dominated by the **Triad:** Japan, the European Union, and the United States. To survive in the increasingly competitive global market any MNC must, according to Ohmae,

> become an insider in each of the Triad regions. Failure in any one would be like losing one leg of a tripod, with a consequent loss of stability. Transforming branches of the enterprise into insiders at overseas locations through one's own effort, or indirectly through effective tie-ups with local firms, is now a matter of corporate life or death.[2]

Many MNCs have operationalized Ohmae's warning and recognized the importance of competing globally in order to expand their customer bases. Such global strategic thinking typifies industries such as airlines, banking, securities, automobiles, computers, and accounting services.

Other experts, recognizing the increasing integration of the large North American market, have broadened the scope of the Triad to include Canada, thus creating a grouping known as the **Quad.** The Quad countries provide international businesses with a pool of 790 million high-income buyers with common needs and account for 75 percent of the world's GDP.

4 *Ownership of natural resources.* Countries with many natural resources sell them to those with fewer. For example, Saudi Arabia, with abundant oil reserves, sells crude oil to the rest of the world. Canada, with its extensive forests, is the world's largest exporter of forest products.

Because most students using this book have already taken college courses in economics and political science, we concentrate here on providing an overview of the economic geography of the world marketplace. We examine the major centers of international business and analyze existing patterns of trade among them. Factors that we will discuss within this geographical framework include population, income, trading and investment patterns, and the public infrastructure (transportation facilities, communications networks, and utilities). We will also explore an individual country's history to the extent that it illuminates that country's contemporary character. We hope you will consider this chapter as an economic travel guide for the international businessperson.

The Marketplaces of North America

North America includes the United States, Canada, Mexico, Greenland, and the countries of Central America and the Caribbean. Home to 454 million people, these countries produce approximately 29 percent of the world's output.

The United States

The United States has only the world's third-largest population and fourth-largest land mass, yet it possesses the largest economy. With a 1996 gross domestic product (GDP) of $7.6 trillion, it accounts for approximately one quarter of the world's GDP. As Map 2.2 shows, the United States enjoys the highest per capita income of the North American countries.[3]

The United States occupies a unique position in the world economy because of its size and political stability. It accounts for about one seventh of world trade in goods and services. It is the prime market for lower-income countries trying to raise their standards of living through export-oriented economic development strategies and for firms from higher-income countries trying to attract business from the country's large, well-educated middle class. The U.S. dollar serves as the **invoicing currency,** that is, the currency in which the sale of goods and services is denominated, for about half of all international transactions and is an important component of foreign-currency reserves worldwide.[4] Because of its political stability and military strength, the United States also attracts **flight capital,** that is, money sent out of a politically or economically unstable country to one perceived as a safe haven. Citizens unsure of the value of their home country's currency often choose to keep their wealth in dollars.[5] The United States also is an important recipient of long-term foreign investment. Foreigners have invested an estimated $630 billion in U.S. factories, equipment, and property.

GOING GLOBAL

Often the single most important piece of information needed by international businesspeople about a country is its income level. Income levels provide clues about the purchasing power of residents, the technological sophistication of local production processes, and the status of the public infrastructure. Such information is useful to international businesses that are contemplating exporting to a new market or investing in a local economy. For example, higher-income countries often offer prime markets for expensive consumer goods, such as luxury automobiles, advanced consumer electronic goods loaded with the latest features, and expensive status goods like Scotch whiskeys and French perfumes. Lower-income countries offer a better market for lower-priced staple goods. Such economies also may interest firms seeking access to large pools of low-wage workers. On the other hand, in these countries electricity distribution often is unreliable and roads often are in disrepair, so a firm needing a reliable public infrastructure might want to look elsewhere.

Classifying Countries by Income Levels

A country's income is normally measured as the total market value of its output of goods and services produced during some time period, such as a year. Until the 1990s most governmental statisticians calculated the **gross national product (GNP)**, a measure of the market value of goods and services produced by property and labor owned by the country's residents. In the 1990s most governmental accounting systems focus on the **gross domestic product (GDP)**, a measure of the market value of all goods and services produced in the country. The difference between GNP and GDP is subtle: GNP focuses on ownership of production, whereas GDP concentrates on the location of production. For example, the dividends returned to Japan by Nissan's U.K. subsidiary, which assembles automobiles in Sunderland, England, would be included in Japan's GNP, but not in its GDP. In most cases, international businesspeople can ignore this difference and use whichever measure is more easily obtainable, for the relative difference between a country's GNP and GDP is usually small. For example, in 1996 the U.S. GNP was $7,637.7 billion, and the U.S. GDP was $7,636.0 billion—a difference of only 0.02 percent. So an international market researcher who has GDP information about one country and GNP information about a second can normally compare the two without worrying that the results will be terribly distorted.

In assessing a foreign country as a potential market, international marketers often ignore total GNP or total GDP and instead look at **per capita income**—the average income per person in a country. Per capita GDP is calculated by dividing the country's total GDP by its population. Which income concept to use—total GDP or per capita GDP—depends on the problem facing the business. Total GDP indicates the economy's overall size, which may be important in a market assessment for durable equipment or bulk goods such as grain, steel, or cement. Per capita income indicates the average income of consumers, which may be important when marketing upscale personal care products or consumer durables. For example, China has a large GDP—$698 billion in 1995—but a very low per capita income —$620. In contrast, Switzerland has a much smaller population and correspondingly smaller GDP—$301 billion—yet Swiss residents enjoy a per capita income of $40,630. Thus China may represent a better market for agricultural products than for 31-inch color TVs.

Although international trade has become increasingly more important in the past decade, it is a relatively small component of the U.S. economy. U.S. exports of goods and services in 1996 totaled $849 billion, but were only 11.1 percent of U.S. GDP. However, this figure is somewhat misleading. Because of the country's large size and large internal market, trade that might be counted as international in smaller countries is considered domestic in the United States. For example, the money spent for a hotel room in neighboring Belgium by a Dutch motorist trapped in a thunderstorm fifty miles from home late at night is counted in the international trade statistics of both Belgium and the Netherlands. A similar

At times international comparisons may be misleading, for they depend on converting one currency to another at existing exchange rates and may fail to adjust for differences in the cost of living in that country. A better comparison of relative incomes may often be obtained by adjusting per capita GDP for differences in purchasing power (the concept of purchasing power parity is discussed in Chapter 5). Japan's per capita GDP in 1996, for example, was $40,726; adjusted for purchasing power, Japan's per capita GDP was only $21,795.

International marketers also are concerned about a country's **income distribution**—the relative numbers of its rich, middle class, and poor. This information is not evident from GNP or GDP alone. Manufacturers of expensive prestige items such as Rolls-Royces are interested in the number of millionaires in the country, while producers of consumer durables such as refrigerators and automobiles may want to know the size of the country's middle class.

One important source of these income statistics is the World Bank, an agency of the United Nations. The World Bank divides the world's countries into high-income, middle-income, and low-income categories. High-income countries are defined as those that enjoy annual per capita incomes of at least $9,386. The high-income group comprises three clusters of countries. The first cluster is drawn from the **Organization for Economic Cooperation and Development (OECD),** a group of twenty-nine market-oriented democracies formed to promote economic growth. The OECD includes twenty-two Western European countries (the EU plus the Czech Republic, Hungary, Iceland, Norway, Poland, Switzerland, and Turkey), four Pacific Rim countries (Australia, Japan, New Zealand, and South Korea), and Canada, Mexico, and the United States. Twenty-three of the OECD's twenty-nine members fall in the high-income category. (The remaining members—the Czech Republic, Greece, Hungary, Mexico, Poland, and Turkey—are classified as middle-income.) The second cluster comprises oil-rich Kuwait and the United Arab Emirates. The third cluster consists of smaller industrialized countries—Hong Kong, Israel, Singapore, and Taiwan.

Middle-income countries have per capita incomes of more than $765 but less than $9,386. This category includes most of the former Soviet bloc, which generally enjoyed high levels of development in the 1930s but stagnated economically since World War II. Other countries in this category, such as Argentina, Slovenia, and Uruguay, have been undergoing successful industrialization and economic growth and may be elevated to the high-income category by the end of this decade.

Lower-income countries, often called *developing countries,* have per capita incomes of $765 or less. This category includes some countries, such as China or Sri Lanka, whose economies are growing substantially because of external aid, sound domestic economic policies, FDI, and/or exploitation of valuable natural resources. Officially labeled "underdeveloped" by the United Nations General Assembly in 1971, these countries have the potential for above-average economic growth. Other countries, designated "undeveloped" and "least developed" by the United Nations, have low literacy rates, per capita incomes, and economic growth. They are less attractive to international businesses because they offer less consumer demand and lack the public infrastructure necessary for reliable production and distribution of goods and services. A prime example of this latter category is Somalia, an East African country wracked by drought, civil war, and starvation.

Sources: *Survey of Current Business* (October 1997); Central Intelligence Agency, *The World Factbook 1996* (Washington, D.C.: U.S. Government Printing Office, 1996), p. 376; World Bank, *World Development Report 1997* (Washington, D.C.: World Bank, 1997).

expenditure by a Connecticut motorist stuck in New Jersey after watching a football game at the Meadowlands is a purely domestic transaction.

As discussed throughout this book, MNCs heavily influence international trade and investment. In 1996, the world's 500 largest corporations had total sales of $11.4 trillion. Given the importance of the United States in the world economy, it should come as no surprise that 162 of these corporations, or about 32 percent, are headquartered in the United States, including 24 of the largest 100 (see Fig. 2.1). General Motors is currently the world's largest company, with 1996 sales of $168.4 billion.[6]

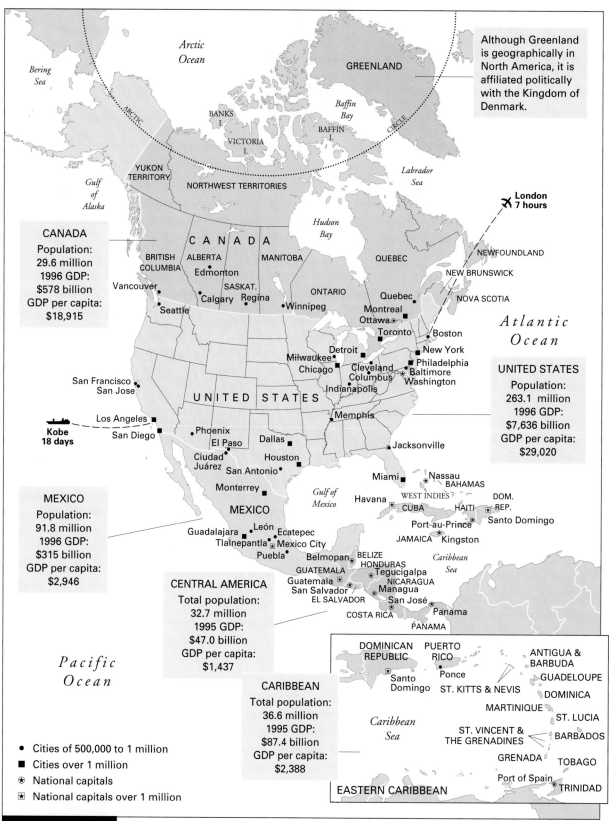

Although Greenland is geographically in North America, it is affiliated politically with the Kingdom of Denmark.

London 7 hours

CANADA
Population:
29.6 million
1996 GDP:
$578 billion
GDP per capita:
$18,915

UNITED STATES
Population:
263.1 million
1996 GDP:
$7,636 billion
GDP per capita:
$29,020

Kobe
18 days

MEXICO
Population:
91.8 million
1996 GDP:
$315 billion
GDP per capita:
$2,946

CENTRAL AMERICA
Total population:
32.7 million
1995 GDP:
$47.0 billion
GDP per capita:
$1,437

CARIBBEAN
Total population:
36.6 million
1995 GDP:
$87.4 billion
GDP per capita:
$2,388

• Cities of 500,000 to 1 million
■ Cities over 1 million
⊛ National capitals
⊞ National capitals over 1 million

EASTERN CARIBBEAN

MAP 2.2   **North America**

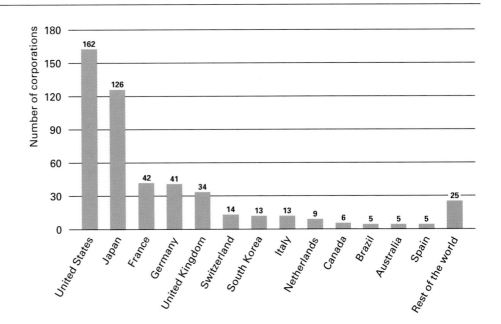

FIGURE 2.1

Headquarters of the World's Largest Corporations in 1996 by Country

Source: *Fortune*, August 4, 1997.

Canada

Canada has the world's second-largest land mass, although its population is only 29.6 million. Eighty percent of the population is concentrated within a 100-mile band along the country's southern border with the United States. Much of Canada's political and economic history reflects its close geographical and economic ties to the United States as well as its attempts to maintain a cultural identity separate from its more populous southern neighbor. The Liberal Party, under the leadership of Prime Minister Pierre Trudeau (1968–1979, 1980–1984), adopted nationalistic and protectionist policies designed to minimize U.S. influence on the Canadian economy. These policies were later reversed by Progressive Conservative Brian Mulroney, elected Prime Minister in 1984. Mulroney opened the Canadian economy, reduced state influence on business by deregulating important industries and selling state-owned enterprises (for example, Air Canada) to the private sector, and forged closer economic ties with the United States. In October 1993, Mulroney's party was voted out of office, and Liberal Jean Chretien was elected Prime Minister. Chretien's government has maintained Canada's economic openness. Shortly after taking office, Chretien endorsed ratification of the North American Free Trade Agreement (NAFTA) in order to increase trade among Canada, Mexico, and the United States and to maintain Canada's access to the U.S. market (see Chapter 7 for more discussion of NAFTA). Under Chretien's leadership, Canada has also signed a free trade agreement with Chile and been an important force in the creation of the World Trade Organization.

Exports are vital to the Canadian economy, accounting for 39 percent of its 1996 GDP. Canada's most important exports reflect its rich natural resources: forest products, petroleum, minerals, and grain. The importance to the Canadian economy of access to the U.S. market cannot be underestimated. The United States is the dominant market for Canadian goods, receiving over three quarters of Canada's exports in a typical year. Two-way trade between the United States and Canada forms the single largest bilateral trading relationship in the world.

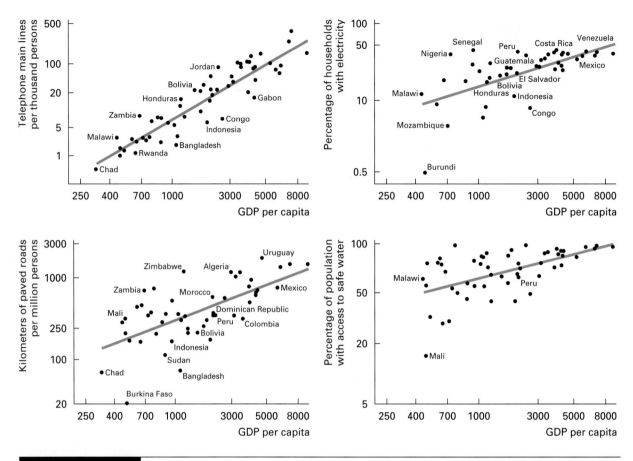

FIGURE 2.2

Per Capita Availability of Major Infrastructure

Source: World Bank, *World Development Report 1994*, p. 16.

International investors have long been attracted to Canada because of its proximity to the huge U.S. market and the stability of its political and legal systems. Canada's excellent infrastructure also contributes to the performance of its economy. The importance of this factor is reflected in Fig. 2.2, which indicates the close linkage between infrastructure and income level. Lack of infrastructure is often an impediment to a country's economic development, for low-wage countries are not necessarily low-cost ones: "If power is expensive and intermittent, … if transport is problematic and … cumbersome, then the fact that [workers] make a few cents less a day is not going to make much of a difference to an investor."[7] Recognizing that its telecommunications, transportation, and utilities networks, which rank among the world's best, lower costs of doing business and raise its appeal as a market and production site for international businesses, Canada has paid close attention to maintaining the quality of its infrastructure.

However, a major threat to Canada's political stability—and to its ability to attract foreign investment—is the long-standing conflict between French-speaking Canadians (most of whom live in the province of Quebec) and English-speaking Canadians. A strong separatist movement has existed in Quebec since the 1960s, and English-speaking Canada has been pressured to adopt policies to diffuse separatism. This conflict has affected domestic and international businesses in many ways. For example, firms exporting products to Canada must be aware of the country's bilingual labeling laws. Also, the riskiness of loans to Quebec firms would increase substantially, at least in the short run, if the province were to become a separate nation.

Mexico

The third major economic power in North America is Mexico. Mexico's political history, like Canada's, is tied to its geography. Now the world's largest Spanish-speaking nation, Mexico declared its independence from its Spanish conquerors in 1810. Its modern boundaries were not established, however, until after its unsuccessful wars with Texan rebels (1836) and the United States (1846–1848). In the 1850s the Mexican economy was wracked by a civil war, which led to a period of political instability until General Porfirio Diaz seized control of the government in 1876. Diaz's 35-year reign encouraged foreign investment in key sectors of the economy, including oil, mining, and railroads. However, his policies became increasingly unpopular as Mexican patriots claimed that the country's resources were being used to benefit foreigners (in other words, U.S. citizens) rather than Mexicans. A peasants' revolt led by Francisco Madero, Venustiano Carranza, Emiliano Zapata, and Pancho Villa ended Diaz's rule in 1911.[8]

Modern Mexican political history begins with the adoption of the 1917 Mexican Constitution, which embodies the nationalistic spirit of the peasants' revolt. Like the United States, Mexico is a federal system whose head of government, a president, is elected by popular vote every six years. Mexican politics have been dominated by the Institutional Revolutionary Party (PRI), which has won every presidential election since its founding in 1929. Historically, the PRI promoted a program of economic nationalism under which Mexico discouraged foreign investment and erected high tariff walls to protect its domestic industries.

President Miguel de la Madrid began to abandon these policies in 1982 after the country's inflation rose as high as 132 percent annually, its trade balance fell into deficit, and it was unable to service its massive external debts. President Carlos Salinas de Gortari, after his election in 1988, completed the reversal of the PRI's traditional economic policies. He reduced the government's role in the economy by selling many publicly owned firms, such as Aeromexico and Telefonos de Mexico. Salinas also opened more sectors of the economy to foreign investors and lobbied vigorously for the passage of NAFTA.

As a result of NAFTA and Salinas's economic reforms, Mexico attracted much attention from international businesses seeking new markets, sources of inputs, and production facilities. Unfortunately, in 1994 foreign investors' confidence in the Mexican economy was shaken by the country's political instability and its expanding deficit. Newly elected President Ernesto Zedillo was forced to allow the peso to devalue in December 1994; within six weeks, the peso's value had fallen 45 percent, and the country plunged into a recession. In 1995, Mexico's real GDP fell 6.2 percent, creating much hardship for Mexico's lower and middle classes. To help restore its economic health, a consortium of international lenders provided Mexico $40 billion in financial assistance. By 1997, Mexico's economy was growing again, helped in part by Zedillo's sound policies and leadership and by its ability to expand its exports as a result of NAFTA and the peso devaluation.

Central America and the Caribbean

The North American continent is also occupied by twenty other countries that are divided geographically into two groups: Central America and the island states of the Caribbean. Collectively their populations equal 69 million—over double Canada's. However, their total GDP of $134 billion is far less than Canada's

$578 billion. With a few exceptions (notably Costa Rica), the economic development of these countries has suffered from a variety of problems, including political instability, chronic U.S. military intervention, inadequate educational systems, a weak middle class, economic policies that have created large pockets of poverty, and import limitations by the United States and other developed countries on Central American and Caribbean goods, such as sugar and clothing.

The Marketplaces of Western Europe

Western European countries are among the world's most prosperous and compose the second component of Kenichi Ohmae's Triad. They can be divided into two groups: (1) members of the European Union (EU), and (2) other countries in the region (see Map 2.3).

The EU, which we discuss in greater detail in Chapter 7, comprises fifteen countries that are seeking to promote European peace and prosperity by reducing mutual barriers to trade and investment. In the past decade, the EU has made tremendous strides in achieving this objective. With a 1996 GDP of $8.4 trillion and a population of 372 million, it is the world's richest market. EU members can be subdivided into three groups:

1 The rich, populous, and politically powerful: Germany, France, the United Kingdom, and Italy

2 The rich, less populous, and less politically powerful: Denmark and the Benelux countries (Belgium, the Netherlands, and Luxembourg), as well as Austria, Finland, and Sweden, which joined the EU in 1995

3 The relatively poor: Greece, Ireland, Portugal, and Spain

The World Bank classifies all EU members except Greece as high-income countries. The EU members are free-market–oriented, parliamentary democracies. However, government intervention and ownership generally play a more important role in these countries' economies than in that of the United States.

From an economic perspective, Germany is the EU's most important member. With a 1996 GDP of $2.4 trillion, it possesses the world's third-largest economy, after those of Japan and the United States. It is a major player in international business; in most years it is the world's second largest exporter, trailing only the United States. Because of the strength of the German economy and the government's strict anti-inflation policies, the mark has been the dominant currency in Europe. In practice the Bundesbank, the German central bank, has controlled the monetary policy of the EU. However, as we will discuss in Chapter 7, the EU is in the process of creating a single currency, the euro, that will be used by most of its members. When the European Central Bank comes into existence, it will supplant the Bundesbank as the master of EU monetary policy.

Politically, France exerts strong leadership within the EU. The French government has been a leading proponent of increased political, economic, and military union within Europe and of strengthening the powers of the EU's government. France also has advocated restricting free trade in commodities important to its economy, such as agricultural goods, automobiles, fish, and semiconductor chips.

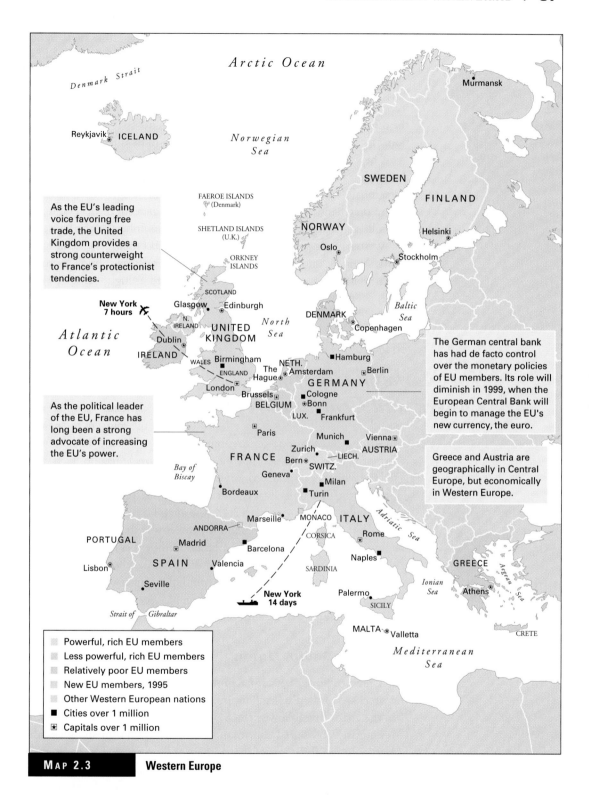

As the EU's leading voice favoring free trade, the United Kingdom provides a strong counterweight to France's protectionist tendencies.

As the political leader of the EU, France has long been a strong advocate of increasing the EU's power.

The German central bank has had de facto control over the monetary policies of EU members. Its role will diminish in 1999, when the European Central Bank will begin to manage the EU's new currency, the euro.

Greece and Austria are geographically in Central Europe, but economically in Western Europe.

New York 7 hours

New York 14 days

- Powerful, rich EU members
- Less powerful, rich EU members
- Relatively poor EU members
- New EU members, 1995
- Other Western European nations
- ■ Cities over 1 million
- ⊞ Capitals over 1 million

MAP 2.3 **Western Europe**

France's positions have not gone unchallenged, however. Under the leadership of Conservative Prime Ministers Margaret Thatcher (1979–1990) and John Major (1990–1997), the United Kingdom in particular has steadfastly resisted French initiatives to expand the EU's powers. Although the Conservatives were routed in the

1997 general election, the new Labor Prime Minister, Tony Blair, has generally maintained the U.K.'s cautious attitude toward strengthening the EU's powers. As a traditionally strong supporter of free trade, the United Kingdom provides an important counterweight to French protectionist tendencies. Because of the U.K.'s free-trade policies, London has been a center of international business activity since the nineteenth century. Along with New York and Tokyo, it is a major international finance center, employing over 300,000 in its financial services sector.

The United Kingdom is a major exporter and importer of goods, an important destination for and source of foreign investment, and the home to the headquarters or regional divisions of numerous MNCs. In 1996, U.K. firms generated $261 billion in merchandise exports, approximately 23 percent of the country's GDP, with the bulk of these goods destined for other EU members or the United States.

Western European countries that are not EU members include Iceland, Malta, Norway, and Switzerland, plus several "postage stamp" countries such as Andorra, Monaco, and Liechtenstein. Classified as high income by the World Bank, collectively these free-market–oriented countries account for 2 percent of the world's GDP.

The Marketplaces of Eastern and Central Europe

No region of the world is undergoing as much economic change as is Eastern and Central Europe, which is in the midst of the painful process of converting from communism to capitalism. Soviet leader Mikhail Gorbachev's 1986 reform initiatives of *glasnost* (openness) and *perestroika* (economic restructuring) triggered the region's political, economic, and social revolutions. Eastern Europe now comprises the fifteen separate countries that resulted from the disintegration of the Soviet Union in 1991 (see Map 2.4). (Geographically, several of these countries are in Asia, but since they share economic problems with their European counterparts, they are discussed in this section.) Central Europe is composed of Albania, Austria, and the former Soviet satellite states of Bulgaria, Czechoslovakia (now divided into the Czech Republic and the Slovak Republic), Hungary, Poland, and Romania. It also includes Bosnia-Herzegovina, Croatia, Macedonia, and Slovenia, which were carved out of Yugoslavia (see Map 2.5 on page 56).

The Former Soviet Union

The Union of Soviet Socialist Republics (Soviet Union or USSR) emerged from the wreckage of the Russian empire, which was caused by its defeat in World War I. In the chaos that followed the March 1917 abdication of Czar Nicholas II, the Communist Party seized control of the Russian government and established the Soviet Union in the name of the workers and peasants. The communists outlawed the market system, abolished private property, and collectivized the country's vast rich farmlands. By so doing, they succeeded in reducing the enormous income inequalities that had existed under czarist rule. Despite this success the population's standard of living increasingly fell behind that of the Western democracies.

Gorbachev's economic and political reforms led to the Soviet Union's collapse in 1991 and the subsequent declarations of independence by the fifteen Soviet republics, which are now often referred to as the **Newly Independent States,** or

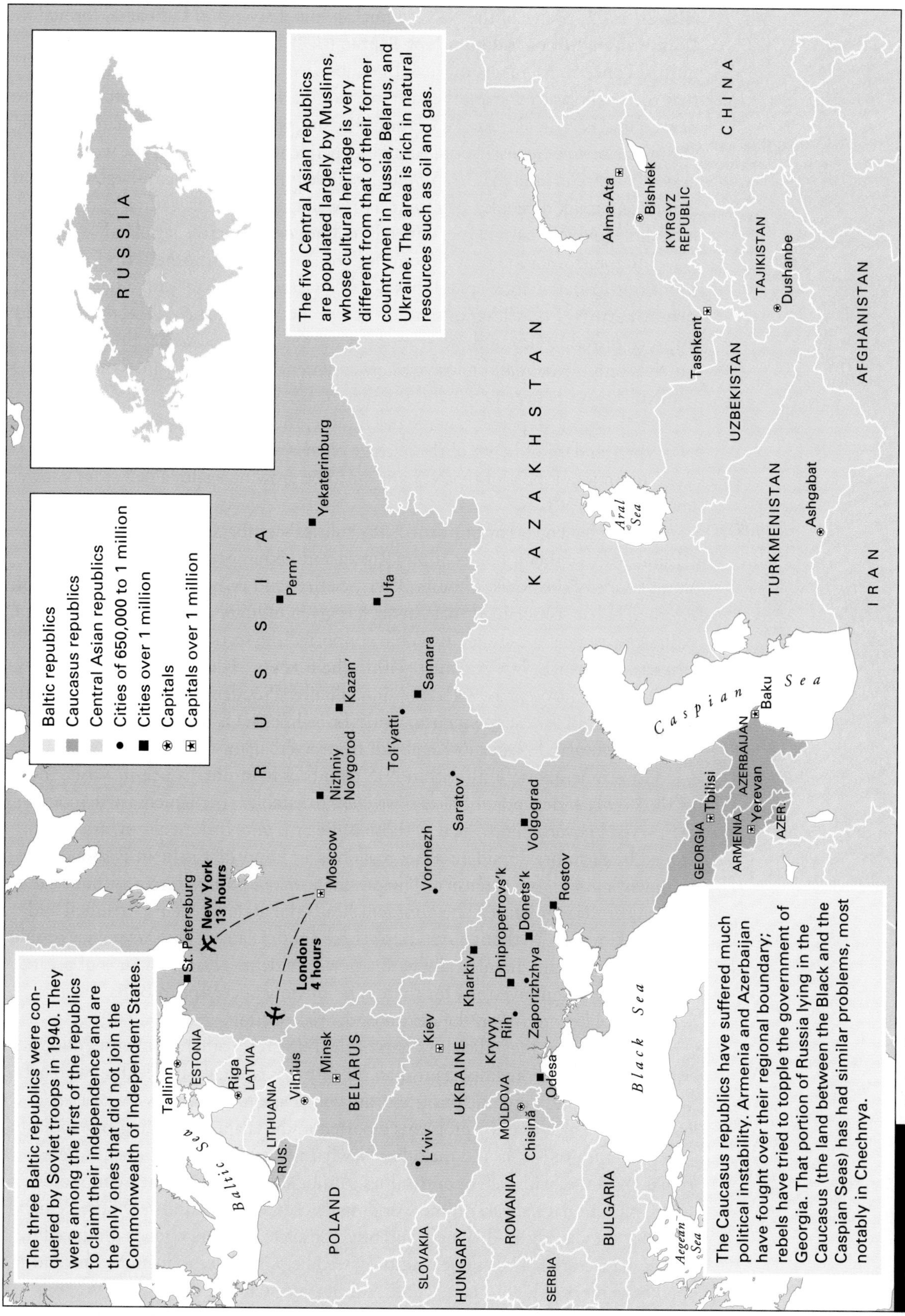

The three Baltic republics were conquered by Soviet troops in 1940. They were among the first of the republics to claim their independence and are the only ones that did not join the Commonwealth of Independent States.

The five Central Asian republics are populated largely by Muslims, whose cultural heritage is very different from that of their former countrymen in Russia, Belarus, and Ukraine. The area is rich in natural resources such as oil and gas.

The Caucasus republics have suffered much political instability. Armenia and Azerbaijan have fought over their regional boundary; rebels have tried to topple the government of Georgia. That portion of Russia lying in the Caucasus (the land between the Black and the Caspian Seas) has had similar problems, most notably in Chechnya.

Legend:
- Baltic republics
- Caucasus republics
- Central Asian republics
- • Cities of 650,000 to 1 million
- ■ Cities over 1 million
- ⊛ Capitals
- ⊠ Capitals over 1 million

RUSSIA

CHINA

KAZAKHSTAN

Alma-Ata
Bishkek
KYRGYZ REPUBLIC
TAJIKISTAN
Dushanbe
Tashkent
UZBEKISTAN
AFGHANISTAN

Yekaterinburg
Perm'
Ufa
Kazan'
Samara
Tol'yatti
Nizhniy Novgorod
Saratov
Voronezh
Volgograd
Rostov
Moscow

Aral Sea

Ashgabat
TURKMENISTAN
IRAN

Caspian Sea
Baku
AZERBAIJAN
Yerevan
AZER.
GEORGIA
Tbilisi
ARMENIA

St. Petersburg
New York 13 hours
London 4 hours

Kharkiv
Dnipropetrovs'k
Donets'k
Zaporizhzhya
Kryvyy Rih
Odesa
Kiev
Minsk
BELARUS
Vilnius
L'viv
UKRAINE
MOLDOVA
Chisinǎu

Tallinn
ESTONIA
Riga
LATVIA
LITHUANIA
RUS.
Baltic Sea

Black Sea

POLAND
SLOVAKIA
HUNGARY
ROMANIA
SERBIA
BULGARIA

Aegean Sea

MAP 2.4   Eastern Europe

NIS. In 1992, twelve of the NIS (all but Estonia, Latvia, and Lithuania) formed the **Commonwealth of Independent States (CIS)** as a forum to discuss issues of mutual concern. Members of the CIS established a free-trade area, which means that their exports to one another are free from tariffs. The most important of these new countries is the Russian Federation (Russia), which was the dominant republic within the former Soviet Union. As an independent state, Russia is the world's largest country in land mass (6.5 million square miles) and the sixth-largest in population (148 million people). The country is well endowed with natural resources, including gold, oil, natural gas, minerals, diamonds, and fertile farmland.

The transformation of the economies of Russia and the other NIS from communism to a free-market system has not been easy, to say the least. The process of **privatization**—the selling of state-owned property to the private sector—should improve the efficiency of these economies in the long run, but has produced much economic pain and massive unemployment in the short run, for most state-owned firms were overstaffed and inefficient. Between 1992 and 1996, Russia's GDP fell almost 40 percent, while in Ukraine, the second-most populous of the NIS, the standard of living of the average citizen was halved. However, by 1997 the economies of most of the NIS appear to be growing again, albeit from a lower level than in 1991.

Other challenges confront the NIS. Political conflicts exist between and within many of them. For example, Russia and Ukraine squabbled over who should control the Soviet Union's Black Sea fleet and its home port of Sebastopol. Azerbaijan has complained that Russia has given military aid to its rival, Armenia, while Georgia believes that Russia has supported the secession attempts of its Abkhazia province. One province within the Russian Federation, Chechnya, fought Russian troops to a bloody standstill after President Boris Yeltsin attempted to quash its bid for independence, while Transdniestria is trying to break away from Moldova and Nagorno-Karabakh from Azerbaijan.

Governmental stability within NIS countries is another concern. While most of the Newly Independent States have tried to establish parliamentary democracies, several governments, such as those of Belarus and Turkmenistan, are controlled by dictators. Presidential succession is an important issue in Russia, for its president's powers are extensive. The president may impose decrees without the consent of the legislature. The president heads the national security council and the armed forces. Without a system of checks and balances, Russia's policies could change quickly and dramatically with a new president. This problem is of great concern to foreign investors, for there is no obvious successor to Boris Yeltsin, who is not likely to run in the next presidential election.

Weaknesses in the judicial systems of the NIS create other problems. Political influence is often more important than the terms of contracts in deciding who gets what. Foreign and domestic businesses are vulnerable to the whims of Soviet-era bureaucrats, as Monsanto's problems reported in the chapter's opening case indicate.

Nonetheless, Russia and the other Newly Independent States present international businesses with rich opportunities. Although they can sell their commodities (gold, oil, and natural gas) on the world market, they have found very little demand there for the shoddy, ill-designed, and often obsolete consumer goods produced by Soviet-era factories. Thus these countries need help. In order to manufacture and market all types of high-quality goods, private and state enterprises seek Western capital and technology by forming joint ventures with Western firms. Virtually every large MNC and thousands of small businesses are flocking to these new nations to access the potentially lucrative market of 290 million consumers that opened with the collapse of the Soviet Union. Because of the political importance of these fifteen new countries, the Western nations have facilitated such private initiatives by providing grants and development assistance to strengthen their economies.

Central Europe

Central European countries that were aligned with the former Soviet Union also face serious challenges (see Map 2.5). Poland, Hungary, the Slovak Republic, Bulgaria, Romania, and the Czech Republic have different abilities to respond to the disintegration of the Soviet bloc. However, they share some common problems. (Because East Germany has been reintegrated into the Federal Republic of Germany, it faces its challenges as part of the much stronger German economy.)

The first common problem is the loss of export markets within the Soviet bloc. The former Soviet Union and its satellite states developed a regional trading bloc called the Council for Mutual Economic Assistance (COMECON) to integrate their economies tightly. The former Soviet Union benefited from COMECON by dictating the goods and services each satellite country should specialize in. The satellites benefited by having guaranteed markets within COMECON for their exports and by receiving subsidized goods from the Soviet Union in order to maintain their political fealty. Of particular value was the crude oil they received at prices well below world market prices.

With the 1989 collapse of Central European communism, COMECON broke down and was finally abandoned in 1991. The former satellite states had to adjust to the loss of guaranteed export markets. For example, many COMECON armaments factories were located in the Slovakian portion of Czechoslovakia. After COMECON disintegrated, Slovakian military goods lost their natural market and unemployment rates in that region skyrocketed. These economic pressures contributed to the 1993 split of Czechoslovakia into two countries (the Slovak Republic and the Czech Republic).

A second common problem is the restructuring of the various Central European economies from centrally organized communist systems to decentralized market systems. The Czech Republic, Hungary, and Poland—all of which are now classified as middle-income countries by the World Bank—are further along in this process than other Central European countries, although they have all followed different paths. The three have attracted more FDI than their neighbors, as Table 2.1 indicates, and have become members of the OECD.

The Czech Republic's transformation to capitalism got off to a fast start. Czech Prime Minister Vaclav Klaus enjoyed strong support for his efforts to build a society based on democracy and a free market. He initiated a privatization scheme that was highly praised at the time. Klaus's privatization program utilized vouchers, which were sold to Czech citizens for a nominal 1000 Czech crowns (about $34) and gave them the right to purchase shares in state-owned industries. By the summer of 1994 these vouchers were worth between 20,000 and 30,000 crowns, thereby benefiting the average Czech participating in the economy's privatization. Most Czechs used their vouchers to buy shares in investment funds controlled by Czech banks, which then bought shares in state-owned companies being privatized. However, this approach brought neither new capital nor new management to these

Communist support of heavy industry and indifference to pollution contributed to environmental havoc throughout much of Central Europe. One particularly devastated region is the industrial triangle between Dresden, Katowice, and Mlada Boleslav.

Following the revolutions of the 1980s, four of Yugoslavia's six republics broke away to become independent nations. The status of the two remaining republics, Serbia and Montenegro, remains uncertain. While some blood was shed when Macedonia, Slovenia, and Croatia separated from Yugoslavia, several hundred thousand lives were lost in Bosnia-Herzegovina's quest for independence. At issue is the extent of Serbia's control over the Balkan peninsula.

Albania is Europe's poorest country, the result of its Stalinist-style economy, which eliminated the private sector. Albania split from the Soviet bloc in 1961, believing the bloc's policies were insufficiently Marxist. Today, about one fifth of its labor force works abroad, sending home funds vital to Albania's survival.

London
3 hours

New York
15½ days

Former Yugoslavia
Cities of 350,000 to 1 million
Capitals
Capitals over 1 million

MAP 2.5 **Central Europe**

TABLE 2.1

Foreign Direct Investment in Central Europe

	POPULATION (IN MILLIONS)	FDI (IN MILLIONS OF DOLLARS)					
		1992	1993	1994	1995	1996	TOTAL 1992–1996
Albania	3.3	20	58	53	70	90	291
Croatia	4.8	n.a.	74	98	81	349	602*
Czech Republic	10.3	n.a.	654	878	2568	1435	5535*
Hungary	10.2	1479	2350	1144	4519	1982	11474
Poland	38.6	678	1715	1875	3659	4498	12425
Romania	22.7	77	94	341	419	263	1194
Slovak Republic	5.4	n.a.	199	203	183	281	866*
Slovenia	2.0	111	113	128	176	186	714

*1993–1996
Source: International Monetary Fund, International Financial Statistics, March 1998.

companies. As a result, many of these firms ignored the painful process of cutting payrolls and improving their efficiency. While the Czechs avoided the massive lay-offs and wage cuts suffered by other Central European countries, their firms were less ready and less able to compete in world markets. The Czech Republic now faces massive trade deficits and the onerous task, initially deferred by its privatization approach, of improving the efficiency of its formerly state-owned firms.[9]

In contrast, Poland's first post-communist government adopted a policy of "shock therapy" to reform its economy. It opened the country to imported goods, provided tax breaks to new companies, and relaxed price controls on basic goods. State employees, farmers, and welfare recipients were hurt by the rapid transformation to a free-market economy and reductions in state subsidies. Another key initiative was the encouragement of entrepreneurship. For example, the Polish government cut red tape, designing its company registration form so that it fit on a single page. Two million new businesses were created as a result, approximately one new business per nineteen Poles. Poland's policies have attracted FDI from a who's who list of MNCs, such as Daewoo, Nestlé, General Motors, and ABB Asea Brown Boveri.[10]

Hungary was the least communist of the communist countries. In 1968 it instituted market-oriented reforms within the context of communism, known as **market socialism** or, more colorfully, "goulash communism." After the Berlin Wall fell, Hungary passed new laws covering bankruptcy, accounting practices, and banking, which forced Hungarian firms to be profitable or go out of business. Over 30,000 bankruptcies resulted. While this sink-or-swim approach caused hardships for the average Hungarian, it swept the deadwood out of the economy and encouraged foreign firms to invest in the country. On a per capita basis, Hungary has received more FDI than any other country in the region, as Table 2.1 shows. Particularly notable is investment by foreign automobile manufacturers. Ford, General Motors, Suzuki, and Volkswagen have all built new factories in the country, employing thousands of the country's skilled workers.[11]

Economic reforms are less advanced in Albania, Bulgaria, and Romania because these countries were slower to develop a political consensus as to the direction they wanted their economies to take. The situation is far worse in parts of what was Yugoslavia. Slovenia avoided almost all of the chaos that surrounded the disintegration of Yugoslavia. This was true to a lesser extent in Croatia and Macedonia. However, the economies of Serbia, Montenegro, and Bosnia were devastated by the brutal war over control of Bosnia, which, needless to say, discouraged most MNCs from investing there.

The Marketplaces of Asia

Asia is home to over half the world's population, yet it produces only 26 percent of the world's GDP. (See Map 2.6.) Asia's importance to international business cannot be minimized. The region is a source of both high-quality and low-quality products and of both skilled and unskilled labor. It is both a major destination for foreign investments by MNCs and a major supplier of capital to non-Asian countries. More important, its aggressive, efficient entrepreneurs have increasingly put competitive pressure on European and North American firms to improve the productivity and quality of their operations.

Japan

Japan, an island country of 126 million people, rose from the ashes of World War II to become the world's second-largest economy (with a GDP of $4.6 trillion in 1996) and an important member of the Triad. Between 1980 and 1990, the Japanese economy grew at an average annual rate of 4.0 percent, compared to only 3 percent for the United States and 2.2 percent for Germany. Japan's per capita GDP in 1996 was $40,726.

Japan's rapid growth in the past fifty years is due in part to the partnership between its Ministry of International Trade and Investment (MITI) and its industrial sector. MITI has used its formal and informal powers to guide the production and investment strategies of the country's corporate elite. Immediately after World War II, MITI encouraged Japanese firms to concentrate their efforts on such basic industries as steel and shipbuilding. As other countries entered these industries, MITI and Japan's MNCs shifted their focus to producing automobiles, consumer electronics, and machinery.

MITI has been aided by Japan's concentrated industrial structure. Japanese industry is controlled by large families of interrelated companies, called *keiretsu,* that are typically centered around a major Japanese bank. The bank takes primary responsibility for meeting the keiretsu's financing needs. The members often act as suppliers to each other, thus making it more difficult for outsiders to penetrate Japanese markets. Members are also protected from hostile takeovers by an elaborate system of cross-ownership of shares by which members of a keiretsu own shares in one another. Toyota Motors, for example, owns 19 percent of the common stock of Koito Manufacturing, and other members of Toyota's keiretsu own 40 percent of Koito's stock. Koito in turn is the primary supplier for Toyota's automotive lighting needs. Keiretsu members often rely on a *sogo sosha,* an export trading company, to market their exports worldwide. Typically the sogo sosha is also a keiretsu member.

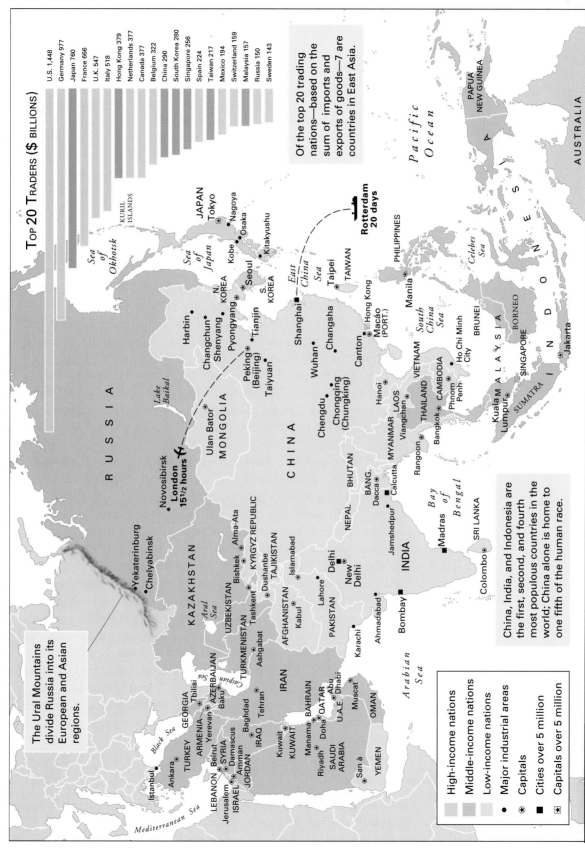

TOP 20 TRADERS ($ BILLIONS)

U.S. 1,448
Germany 977
Japan 760
France 666
U.K. 547
Italy 518
Hong Kong 379
Netherlands 377
Canada 377
Belgium 322
China 290
South Korea 280
Singapore 256
Spain 224
Taiwan 217
Mexico 194
Switzerland 159
Malaysia 157
Russia 150
Sweden 143

Of the top 20 trading nations—based on the sum of imports and exports of goods—7 are countries in East Asia.

The Ural Mountains divide Russia into its European and Asian regions.

China, India, and Indonesia are the first, second, and fourth most populous countries in the world; China alone is home to one fifth of the human race.

London 15½ hours

Rotterdam 20 days

MAP 2.6 | **Asia**

High-income nations
Middle-income nations
Low-income nations
• Major industrial areas
⊛ Capitals
■ Cities over 5 million
✴ Capitals over 5 million

Although most political commentators note that exports have spurred Japan's postwar growth, exports of goods and services are a smaller portion of Japan's GDP—only 9.9 percent—than is the case for many countries, such as Germany (23.3 percent) and France (24.0 percent). Yet Japanese exports have become a lightning rod for international criticism because of the perception that Japan employs unfair trading practices to market its exports while using numerous non-tariff barriers to restrict imports to its domestic market (we'll discuss this further in Chapter 6). The large *balance of trade* (exports greater than imports) that Japan has enjoyed in the past two decades has enabled it to invest heavily overseas and purchase extensive assets in many countries. It is now the world's largest creditor country.

Australia and New Zealand

Australia and New Zealand are the other traditional economic powers in Pacific Asia. Although they share a common cultural heritage, significant differences exist between the two countries, which are separated by 1200 miles of ocean (see Map 2.7). Australia's 18.3 million people live in an area of 2.97 million square miles. Because of the aridity of much of the continent, most of the population is concentrated in the coastal regions, with approximately 40 percent living in either Sydney or Melbourne. With a 1996 GDP of $392 billion, Australia is the world's thirteenth-largest economy. It is rich in natural resources but suffers from a relatively small work force. As a result, its exports, which account for 20 percent of GDP, are concentrated in natural resource industries (such as gold, iron ore, and coal) and in land-intensive agricultural goods (such as wool, beef, and wheat).

New Zealand's 3.6 million people live on two main islands—the more populous North Island and the more scenic but less temperate South Island. With a GDP of $64 billion and a per capita GDP of $16,689 in 1996, New Zealand was one of the slowest-growing of the OECD countries in the early post–World War II period. Much of the blame for this was placed on overregulation of the country's business sector. As a result, beginning in 1984, the Labor Party began systematically deregulating and privatizing the economy, including such key industries as telecommunications, transportation, and financial services. This policy shift proved successful. By the mid-1990s New Zealand had achieved one of the fastest growth rates in the OECD, and has gained an international reputation as being at the forefront of the worldwide shift toward greater reliance on market-based policies. Trade is extremely important to the country; 1996 exports of $14.5 billion constituted 22.5 percent of its GDP. Over half of New Zealand's exports are attributable to its extensive pasture lands—these exports include dairy products, meat, and wool. Australia, Japan, and the United States account for approximately half of New Zealand's exports and imports.

The Four Tigers

Pacific Asia is one of the world's most rapidly industrializing regions. South Korea, Taiwan, Singapore, and Hong Kong in particular have made such rapid strides since 1945 that they are collectively known as the "Four Tigers," a reference to the Chinese heritage that three of the four share. You may also see the four referred to

Cities of 45,000 to 950,000
Capitals
Capitals over 1 million

Although manufacturing is a major contributor to Australia's GDP, its share has been steadily declining. One of the country's biggest challenges is to supplement its small domestic market with new trade links. Currently, Japan and the Pacific Rim have replaced the U.K. as the principal trading partners.

Despite its vast regions of desert and savanna, Australia is highly urbanized, with 80% of its population living in cities along the well-watered coast.

MAP 2.7

Australia and New Zealand

as the newly industrialized countries (NICs) or the newly industrialized economies (NIEs), because Hong Kong is not legally a country and whether Taiwan is an independent country is a sensitive diplomatic issue disputed by China and Taiwan. The Four Tigers are the only countries once categorized as less developed by the World Bank that have subsequently achieved high-income status. However, their growth prospects for the rest of the century have dimmed as a result of a currency crisis that swept the area in 1997–1998. (This crisis is discussed in more detail in Chapters 4 and 5.)

South Korea. The Republic of Korea, more commonly known as South Korea, was born of the Cold War. After the Soviets declared war on Japan in August 1945, the Korean peninsula north of the 38th parallel was occupied by Soviet troops, and the area south of the 38th parallel fell under U.S. influence. North Korean troops invaded South Korea in 1950, triggering the Korean War. Three years of bloody conflict ensued. Peace talks at Panmunjom left the peninsula divided into communist North Korea and capitalist South Korea approximately along the prewar boundaries.

The contrast between the economic performance of communist North Korea (left) and that of capitalist South Korea (right) has been dramatic. After the Korean War ended in 1953, both countries ranked among the world's poorest. Housing, food, and other consumer goods are still scarce in North Korea, and its per capita income has fallen below $1,000. The export-oriented economic policies of South Korea have generated an economic boom. The country's per capita income is $10,155, and it is a major force in the world economy.

Since the 1960s, South Korea has been one of the world's fastest growing economies: its 1995 GDP of $455 billion made it the eleventh largest. A major source of growth is its merchandise exports, which totaled $125 billion in 1995, or 27 percent of its GDP.

This growth has been accomplished through tight cooperation between the government and thirty or so large, privately owned, and family-centered conglomerates that dominate the Korean economy. The most important of these conglomerates, or *chaebol*, are Samsung, Hyundai, Daewoo Group, and LG (formerly Lucky-Goldstar). In many ways, the Korean government has tried to follow the economic path established by the Japanese: discouragement of imports, governmental leadership of the economy, and reliance on large economic combines for industrialization.

Unfortunately, Korea's growth came to a screeching halt as a result of the 1997–1998 Asian currency crisis, and many of the country's chaebol were plunged into financial difficulties. Some observers argued their problems were due to overexpansion and poor lending practices of Korean banks. Many of the chaebol seemed to be more interested in size than profitability, and borrowed money to enter industries already burdened by overcapacity, such as automobiles. To restore its economy to health, Korea is tightening its regulatory controls over the chaebol and its banking sector and reducing barriers to imports and FDI. The International Monetary Fund has also assembled a multi-billion dollar loan package to aid Korea's efforts.

Taiwan. Taiwan, as the Republic of China is commonly known, is a small (13,969 square miles) island country off the coast of mainland China that is home to 21.6 million people. Taiwan was annexed by the victorious Japanese in 1895 at the conclusion of the Sino-Japanese War but was returned to Chinese control at the end of World War II. In the civil war that followed, the Chinese communists under Mao Tse-Tung defeated Chiang Kai-Shek's armies. Chiang's troops and government fled to Taiwan in 1949.

Declaring the island "the Republic of China" and himself the rightful governor of the mainland, Chiang undertook to develop the Taiwanese economy to support a promised invasion of the mainland. Redistribution of land from large estate holders to peasants increased agricultural productivity. Reliance on family-owned private businesses and export-oriented trade policies has made Taiwan one of the world's fastest-growing economies over the past three decades, with a real growth rate averaging over 9 percent annually.[12] Exports were $116 billion in 1996, or 42 percent of the country's GDP of $275 billion. The United States is the destination of 24 percent of Taiwan's exports, followed by China (17 percent) and Japan (12 percent).

Taiwan's economic development has been so fast-paced that it can no longer compete as a low-wage manufacturing center. Consequently Taiwanese businesses more recently have focused on high-value-added industries such as electronics and automotive products. However, they still need low-wage workers. Despite the lack of diplomatic relations between Taiwan and China, these businesses increasingly are investing in factories and assembly plants in China in order to access the low-wage workers they need. Therefore, Taiwanese investments on the mainland are substantial.

Singapore. The Republic of Singapore is a former British colony and a small island country (only 239 square miles) off the southern tip of the Malay peninsula. Since becoming independent in 1965, the country has been governed by a parliamentary democracy. To remedy chronic unemployment, Lee Kuan Yew, the country's first Prime Minister, who served from independence until 1991, emphasized development of labor-intensive industries such as textile production. This economic policy proved so successful that Singapore shifted to higher-value-added activities such as oil refining and chemical processing in the late 1960s and high-tech industries such as computers and biotechnology in the late 1970s. Today Singapore has a population of 3 million and an unemployment rate of less than 2 percent. In fact, it suffers from a labor shortage and can no longer compete with such countries as Honduras and Indonesia in the production of price-sensitive, labor-intensive manufactured goods.

In 1995 Singapore's per capita income was $26,730 and its exports totaled $118.3 billion, or *141 percent* of its GDP of $84 billion. That figure is not a misprint. Singapore thrives on **re-exporting.** Singapore's firms take advantage of the country's excellent port facilities to import foreign goods and then re-export them to other countries (particularly neighboring Malaysia). Besides being an important port and center for oil refining, Singapore provides sophisticated communications and financial services for firms in Pacific Asia and is well on its way to becoming the region's high technology center.

Hong Kong. Hong Kong was born out of the "opium war" fought between the United Kingdom and China (1839–1842). As a consequence of this war, Hong Kong was ceded to the British. Historically, the major attraction of Hong Kong was its deep sheltered harbor and its significance as an entry point to mainland China. In 1860 the British obtained possession of Kowloon on the Chinese mainland, and in 1898 were granted a 99-year lease on an area of the mainland known as the New Territories. The lease expired on July 1, 1997.

In June 1985, the United Kingdom and China agreed on the terms by which China would again assume political control of Hong Kong. On July 1, 1997, Hong Kong became a Special Administrative Region of China. While the agreement reached left Hong Kong fairly autonomous, with its own legislature (in which key appointments would be made by Beijing), its central feature was to ensure economic freedom in terms of the foreign-exchange market, free port status, and a separate taxation system. These features are to prevail for a period of fifty years after 1997. However, China has made it clear that it will impose its own political will on Hong Kong.

Over 6.3 million people are packed into Hong Kong's small (411 square miles) land mass. Hong Kong offers highly educated, highly productive labor for industries such as textiles and electronics and provides banking and financial services for much of East Asia. Hong Kong also has thrived as an entrepôt for China, receiving goods from it and preparing them for shipment to the rest of the world, and vice versa. Moreover, as a result of common culture and geography, Hong Kong entrepreneurs often act as intermediaries for companies around the world that want to conduct business with China.

Export statistics for Hong Kong reflect its role as a re-exporter of goods to and from China. Hong Kong exported $174 billion of goods in 1995, or 121 percent of its $144 billion GDP. Half of its exports are bound for China or the United States. Of Hong Kong's $193 billion in imports, China supplied 35 percent, followed by Japan (15 percent), Taiwan (9 percent), and the United States (8 percent). Hong Kong also serves as a bridge between Taiwan and its political enemy, China. Because Taiwanese goods are somewhat politically tainted in China, and vice versa, Hong Kong provides the valuable service of converting goods produced by one political enemy into Hong Kong goods so that they can be exported to the other political enemy.[13]

India

India is the world's second most populous country, with approximately 936 million people in 1995. It also is one of the poorest countries, with a per capita GDP of only $340. India was part of the British empire until 1947, when British rule ended. The Indian subcontinent subsequently was partitioned along religious lines into India, where Hindus were predominant, and Pakistan, where Muslims were dominant. The eastern part of Pakistan became the independent nation of Bangladesh in 1971. The new country of India adopted many of the formalities of the British governmental system, including the parliamentary system, a strong independent judiciary, and a professional bureaucracy. For most of its postwar history, the country has relied on state ownership of key industries, including power, transportation, and heavy industry, as a critical element of its economic development efforts.

India's bureaucracy can be cumbersome and slow to provide documents necessary to conduct business within the country. Until 1991 India discouraged foreign investment, limiting foreign owners to minority positions in Indian enterprises and imposing other onerous requirements. For example, as a condition for remaining in the country, the Coca-Cola Company was retroactively required by India in the 1970s to divulge its secret soft-drink formula. Coca-Cola refused and chose to leave the market. Coca-Cola subsequently reentered the market as a result of Prime Minister Rao's 1991 market-opening reforms, which reduced trade barriers, opened the doors to increased FDI, and modernized the country's financial sector.

These reforms have begun to pay off. India has attracted much FDI from MNCs based in the Quad countries, and its real GDP growth has averaged 7 percent in the past three years. However, problems remain. A lack of clarity in government policy has created enormous confusion for some foreign investors. The World Bank has warned that failure to trim red tape may threaten the flow of foreign capital into sectors crucial for India's economic growth.

Because of India's past economic policies, international trade has traditionally not been as important to it as it has been to other countries in the region. In 1995 India exported $31 billion of goods, about 9.6 percent of its GDP of $324 billion.

China

With over 1.2 billion people, China is the world's most populous country. It also is one of the world's oldest, ruled by a series of emperors from 2000 B.C. until the early 1900s, when a republic was founded. A chaotic civil war facilitated a Japanese invasion in 1931. After expulsion of the Japanese at the end of World War II, the civil war renewed. Finally, in 1949 the communist forces of Mao Tse-Tung defeated the nationalist army led by General Chiang Kai-Shek.

Communism in China under Mao Tse-Tung went through several stages. The "Great Leap Forward" was a program undertaken from 1958 to 1960 to force industrialization through the growth of small labor-intensive factories. The program's failure led eventually to the "Cultural Revolution" in 1966, during which youthful communist cadres indiscriminately purged any Communist Party member suspected of deviating from Mao's doctrines. Neighbor turned against neighbor. Family members turned on each other. Professors' books were destroyed, and farmers were brought in from the countryside to teach in the universities or to practice medicine. The political chaos that followed set back the country's economic progress, as many of its most productive and educated members were exiled to the countryside to repent their ideological sins.

After Mao's death in 1976, the government adopted limited free-market policies that called for returning agriculture to the private sector and allowing entrepreneurs to start small businesses such as restaurants and light manufacturing. Foreign companies were permitted to establish joint ventures with Chinese firms. As a result, FDI in China and economic growth soared, as did hopes for increased political freedom. However, Communist Party leaders were unwilling to relinquish their powers. The conflict that resulted led to the massacre of pro-democracy demonstrators in Beijing's Tiananmen Square in June 1989. Western countries quickly demonstrated their objections to the massacre by cutting off aid and investment capital to China.

Nonetheless, China is following a unique path. It continues to adopt market-oriented economic policies under the Communist Party's watchful eye. In the 1980s it established numerous special economic development zones to attract foreign capital. It also invested in many Hong Kong companies to better learn the ways of capitalism. In July 1992 the Chinese government granted all enterprises increased independence from the state's central planners, including the right to engage in international trade, the ability to negotiate with foreigners, and the freedom to adjust production, merge, or go bankrupt without permission from governmental planners. As a result, China's economy is becoming increasingly schizophrenic. Half of the country's output is produced by state enterprises noted for their low productivity and shoddy products; the remainder is produced by private firms. For example, in the Wenzhou region, which is home to 6.5 million people, private entrepreneurs have responded to economic liberalization by creating 153,000 small businesses and 42 private banks. Over 88 percent of Wenzhou's output is produced by the private sector. Typical of these firms is the Zhejiang Spark Industrial Automatic Meter Industrial Development Group. A machinist employed by the state-owned meter factory who hadn't been paid for a year started the firm with borrowed money. The privately owned Zhejiang factory now annually sells $2 million in meters and gauges to petroleum and chemical refineries.[14]

FIGURE 2.3

Annual FDI Flows to China, 1982–1996

Source: Data from International Monetary Fund, *International Financial Statistics Yearbook 1997*, p. 299, and *International Financial Statistics*, March 1998.

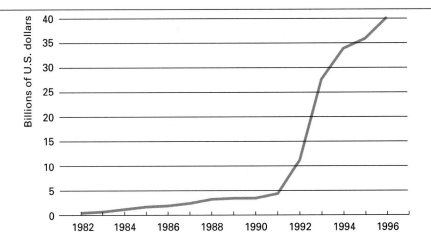

Private-sector development has attracted the attention of firms worldwide. Foreign direct investment in China has exploded since 1992, as Fig. 2.3 indicates. Of particular note are the increased investments in China by overseas Chinese investors living in Taiwan, Hong Kong, and Singapore, who see the country as a source of hard-working, low-cost labor, an increasingly scarce commodity in their own communities.

China's merchandise exports totaled $149 billion in 1995, or 21 percent of its GDP of $698 billion. Hong Kong and Macau (a small Portuguese colony near Hong Kong) accounted for over 40 percent of China's exports and over 20 percent of its imports. Most of Hong Kong and Macau's trade with China represents re-exports to or from third countries.

Southeast Asian Countries

Asia is home to numerous other countries at various stages of economic development. Of particular note are Thailand, Malaysia, and Indonesia, countries with low labor costs that have been recipients of significant FDI in the 1980s and 1990s. As labor costs have risen in their homeland, many Japanese MNCs have sprinkled these three countries with satellite plants designed to supply low-cost parts to parent factories in Japan. U.S. and European MNCs have used these three countries as production platforms as well. The Thai, Malaysian, and Indonesian economies boomed as a result of exports generated by FDI. Their GDPs enjoyed annual growth rates averaging over 7 percent from 1980 to 1995. However, the 1997–1998 currency crisis damaged these three countries badly, with Indonesia bearing the heaviest blows.

Another potentially important economy in this region is Vietnam. At the end of the Vietnam War, the U.S. government imposed a trade embargo on this country; most industrialized countries followed suit. Over the last several years, however, most of those countries have dropped their embargoes and businesses from them have been setting up shop in Vietnam. Many experts believe that Vietnam is poised for a major economic surge similar to that of the Four Tigers.[15] Pressure from major U.S. MNCs that saw how aggressively their foreign competitors were moving into Vietnam resulted in President Clinton's dropping the U.S. trade embargo in early 1994. Consequently, experts believe the Vietnamese economy will increase in importance in the next decade.

The Marketplaces of Africa and the Middle East

The continent of Africa covers approximately 22 percent of the world's total land area and is rich in natural resources. Egypt occupies the northeastern tip of the African continent and represents the western boundary of what is commonly known as the Middle East.

Africa

The African continent, shown in Map 2.8, is home to 701 million people and 55 countries. Most of Africa was colonized in the late nineteenth century by the major European powers (France, Spain, Belgium, Germany, Italy, Portugal, and Great Britain) for strategic military purposes or to meet domestic political demands. The tide of colonialism reversed beginning in the mid-1950s, as one by one these countries surrendered power over their African colonies. Vestiges of colonialism remain in today's Africa, affecting opportunities available to international businesses. For example, Chad, Niger, and the Côte d'Ivoire (Ivory Coast) retain close economic and cultural ties to France. They link their currencies to the French franc and follow French legal, educational, and governmental procedures. Because of these ties, French manufacturers, financial institutions, and service-sector firms often dominate international commerce with these countries. Similarly, the public institutions of Kenya, Zimbabwe, and the Republic of South Africa are modeled along British lines, giving British firms a competitive advantage in these countries.

The history of the newly independent African countries since 1960 has not always been happy. After obtaining their independence, many of these countries attempted to expand their economies along socialist principles. But developmental efforts were hindered by political unrest and civil war, which often occurred along tribal lines, as authoritarian, one-party governments were installed throughout the continent. In the past decade, however, some African countries have shifted away from socialist economics and authoritarian politics and toward market-oriented policies and multi-party democracies, making them more attractive to international businesses.

Much of Africa's economy is tied to its natural resources. Libya enjoys the continent's highest per capita income—$6,500 in 1995—because of its substantial oil reserves. However, the support of terrorist organizations by Libya's Revolutionary Leader Muammar Qadhafi has prompted Western countries to ostracize Libya and cut off economic aid to it. Crude oil production also accounts for one half of the GDPs of Angola, Gabon, and Nigeria and one quarter of that of Algeria.

Agriculture also is important to many African countries. For some, agricultural products are their major exports. For example, coffee, cocoa, and palm oil account for 80 percent of Côte d'Ivoire's exports, and coffee and tea comprised 80 percent of Rwanda's prior to the eruption of tribal conflict there. Unfortunately, the population in many African countries is largely employed in subsistence farming. These countries include Gambia, Mozambique, Sierra Leone, Tanzania, and Zambia.

As its economies grow, Africa will become a more attractive market for MNCs and a source of low-cost labor. The African island of Mauritius, which lies 900 kilometers east of Madagascar in the Indian Ocean, provides a model of suc-

The Sahara Desert divides Africa into two economic areas: the richer northern region and the poorer sub-Saharan region. Over the past 25 years, the desert has advanced southward because of overgrazing, overcultivation, and deforestation. Sub-Saharan economic development has been hindered by political instability, tribal rivalries, and unsuccessful reliance on socialist economic principles.

Legend:
- Desert/shrub
- Grassland
- Woodland/shrub
- Light tropical forest
- Tropical rainforest
- Cities of 500,000 to 1 million
- Cities over 1 million
- Capitals
- Capitals over 1 million

MAP 2.8   **Africa and the Middle East**

cessful economic development for African countries. (See Map 6.2.) Formerly dependent on sugar cane, Mauritius has become an important center for textile and apparel manufacturing by providing a tax-free zone for goods destined for export. Mauritius's economy has been growing at a real rate of 4.9 percent annually. Another likely center of growth is South Africa, which possesses fertile farmland and rich deposits of gold, diamonds, chromium, and platinum. Until the 1970s, many MNCs used South Africa as the base for their African operations. Then the United Nations imposed trade sanctions against the country because of the government's apartheid policies (which called for the separation of blacks, whites, and Asians). As a result of these external pressures, the government extended voting rights to all of its citizens in 1994. Nobel Peace Prize winner Nelson Mandela was elected president in May 1994 in the country's first multiracial elections. In 1995 South Africa's exports—primarily minerals—totalled $25 billion and accounted for 18 percent of the country's GDP of $136 billion.

Middle East

The term Middle East is used to describe the region located between southwestern Asia and northeastern Africa (see Map 2.8 and Map 1.2). The Middle East carries the title "cradle of civilization," as the world's earliest farms, cities, governments, legal codes, and alphabets had their origin there. The region was also the birthplace of several of the world's major religions, including Judaism, Christianity, and Islam. The Middle East has a history of conflict and political unrest and in the latter half of this century has seen the Arab-Israeli wars, the Iran-Iraq war, and the Persian Gulf war.

In 1995 Saudi Arabia, with a GDP of $126 billion, had the largest economy in the Middle East, but Israel enjoyed the highest per capita income, at $15,920 per annum. As explained in Chapter 1, the region is home to many oil-rich economies. In Saudi Arabia, for example, oil accounts for 35 percent of GDP and around 90 percent of total export earnings.[16]

The oil-rich nations of the Middle East are attempting to diversify their economies for "life after oil." Kuwait has used its oil revenues to develop an impressive portfolio of investments; Dubai, which is one of the seven United Arab Emirates, offers foreign investors all of the benefits of a foreign-trade zone (discussed in Chapter 6), an excellent infrastructure, and an entry point for exports to the region. For example, an Australian company, Davey Pumps, has established a considerable market presence in the Middle East because the pumps built for the severe Australian climate work equally well in the Middle East.[17]

The Marketplaces of South America

South America's thirteen countries, shown in Map 2.9, share a common political history as well as many economic and social problems. A 1494 papal decree divided colonization privileges regarding the continent between Portugal (Brazil) and Spain (the rest of the continent). Spanish and Portuguese explorers subjugated the native populations, exploited their gold and silver mines, and converted their fields to sugar cane, tobacco, and cacao plantations. By the

During the late 1980s, many South American governments stimulated economic growth by adopting policies promoting free trade and private enterprise, thereby increasing the continent's appeal to U.S., European, and Asian MNCs. Chile now has one of the most free-market economies in the world.

International business in South America is affected by its physical geography. The Andes Mountains make it difficult to transport goods between Pacific Coast countries and their inland neighbors. Other mountain ranges, as well as the dense forests of the Amazon River Basin, similarly limit transport of goods.

- Cities of 350,000 to 1 million
- Cities over 1 million
- Capitals
- Capitals over 1 million

MAP 2.9　　**South America**

end of the eighteenth century, the hold of the two European empires on their South American colonies had weakened. Led by such patriots as Simon Bolivar, one colony after another won its independence. By 1825 the Spanish flag remained flying over only Cuba and Puerto Rico.

The independent South American countries have not enjoyed a happy economic history. Descendants of the European colonialists have dominated their economies, resulting in huge income disparities. Historically, many of these nations have been characterized by political instability, frequent changes in governments (often headed by military dictators), and inward-looking economic policies that have generated inflation, inefficient production, and widespread poverty.

For much of the post–World War II period most South American countries followed what international economists call **import substitution policies** as a means of promoting economic development. With this approach, a country attempts to stimulate the development of local industry by discouraging imports via high tariffs and nontariff barriers. (The opposite of import substitution is **export promotion,** whereby a country pursues economic growth by expanding its exports. This is the developmental approach successfully adopted by Taiwan, Hong Kong, and Singapore, as discussed earlier in this chapter.) For most South American industries, however, the domestic market is too small to enable domestic producers to gain economies of scale through mass production techniques or to permit much competition among local producers. Thus prices of domestically produced goods tend to rise above prices in other markets. These policies benefit domestic firms that face import competition. But they cripple the ability of a country's exporters to compete in world markets because the companies must pay higher prices for domestically produced inputs than do their foreign competitors. Inevitably, the government must subsidize these firms and often nationalize them in order to preserve urban jobs. The high costs of doing this are passed on to taxpayers and to consumers through higher prices, but over time the government runs a budget deficit. The result is inflation and destruction of middle-class savings.

Many major South American countries—including Argentina, Brazil, and Chile—adopted these well-intentioned but ultimately destructive import substitution policies. In the late 1980s, however, they began to reverse their policies. They lowered tariff barriers, sought free-trade agreements with their neighbors, privatized their industries, and positioned their economies to compete internationally. Chile, for example, now has one of the strongest free-market orientations in the world. These policy shifts are expanding South America's role in world trade, attracting foreign capital to the continent, and increasing productivity and per capita incomes.

CHAPTER REVIEW

Summary

Geography plays an important role in international business. International trade and investment flows are often affected by cultural and economic geography—factors such as shared borders, similar income levels, ownership of natural resources, and common ethnic and political heritages. International businesspeople who understand geographic principles can better select new markets and new countries in which to invest.

A key indicator of a country's desirability to international businesses is its per capita income, which provides information about its consumers and its value as a production site. The World Bank has developed a commonly used scheme for classifying income levels; it divides the world's countries into high-income, middle-income, and low-income categories based on per capita income.

The Quad countries—Japan, members of the EU, the United States, and Canada—are of particular importance to MNCs. Some experts believe that firms cannot succeed in the global economy unless they have a significant presence throughout these areas.

The North American market—Canada, Mexico, the United States, Central America, and the island countries of the Caribbean—is one of the world's largest and richest. The United States and Canada have the largest bilateral trading relationship in the world. Mexico's economic reforms, initiated in 1982, have made it a more important force in the world economy.

Another large, rich market for international businesses is Western Europe, particularly the 15-member EU. The EU members are free-market–oriented, parlimentary democracies.

With the 1989 collapse of European communism, Eastern and Central European countries are undergoing a transition from communism to capitalism. Most have adopted market-oriented policies in order to stimulate economic growth. Their growth prospects and unmet consumer demand are attractive to many Asian, North American, and European MNCs.

Asia is home to several of the fastest-growing economies of the postwar period. Japan and the Four Tigers—South Korea, Hong Kong, Singapore, and Taiwan—have grown dramatically because of economic policies that focus on export promotion. Because of the economic successes of Japan and the Four Tigers, other countries such as India and China have begun to reverse their inward-looking economic policies. Australia and New Zealand are also important economies in this region.

The African countries are among the world's poorest. Their economies primarily rely on natural resources and agriculture. After declaring independence from their European colonizers in the 1950s and 1960s, most of these nations adopted socialist economic principles and subsequently suffered substantial political unrest. In the 1980s, however, several African countries became more market-oriented

and politically stable, thus raising their attractiveness to international businesses. Mideastern countries have played an important role in the world economy thanks to their oil wealth.

The South American countries have been independent since the early nineteenth century. While many are rich in natural resources and farmlands, the continent's economic development since World War II has been hindered by chronic political unrest and import-substitution policies. In the 1980s, however, key South American nations—including Argentina, Brazil, and Chile—shifted toward more market-oriented, export-promotion growth strategies. Privatization and reduced governmental regulation have prompted renewed interest from international businesses in the continent.

Review Questions

1. Discuss the cultural and economic geographical factors that affect international trade and investment activity.

2. What is the Triad? What is the Quad? Why are they important to international businesses?

3. How do differences in income levels and income distribution among countries affect international businesses?

4. Describe the U.S. role in the world economy.

5. How did COMECON's breakup affect its members?

6. What is a sogo sosha?

7. Who are the Four Tigers? Why are they important to international businesses?

8. What is a chaebol?

9. Discuss the reasons for Africa's slow economic development in the past three decades.

10. How did import-substitution policies affect the economies of Brazil and Argentina?

Questions for Discussion

1. Regional trading blocs, such as the EU and NAFTA, are growing in importance. What are the implications of these trading blocs for international businesses? Are they helpful or harmful? How may they affect a firm's investment decisions?

2. Discuss the problems facing Central and Eastern European countries in the 1990s. What opportunities are available to international businesses in these countries?

3. Many American and European businesspeople argue that the keiretsu system in Japan acts as a barrier to foreign companies' entering the Japanese market. Why do you think they believe this?

4. Ethnic ties, old colonial alliances, and shared languages appear to affect international trade. Why might this be so? If true, how does this affect international businesses' strategies regarding which markets to enter?

5. What can African countries do to encourage more foreign investment in their economies?

BUILDING GLOBAL SKILLS

Success in international business often depends on a firm's obtaining information it needs about foreign countries and markets so that it can make exporting, importing, and investment decisions. Fortunately, many published sources of information are available to help firms do this. Among the most useful are the following.

Survey of Current Business The U.S. Department of Commerce publishes the *Survey of Current Business* monthly. The survey is a basic source of statistical data on the U.S. economy. It provides detailed, accurate, and up-to-date analyses of international trade and investment activities affecting the United States.

The World Factbook The U.S. Central Intelligence Agency publishes *The World Factbook* annually. This document provides basic geographic, ethnic, religious, political, and economic information on all countries. It is particularly useful because it compiles data about small, obscure, and politically controversial areas. For example, the Falkland Islands, the object of a short war in 1982 between the United Kingdom and Argentina, both of which claim ownership of the islands, has its own entry. Or, if you were an executive for Crestone Energy Corporation, which was hired by China's government to hunt for oil and gas around the Spratly Islands, *The World Factbook* is one of the few sources available in which you could learn that the islands, many of which

are under water at high tide, have no permanent population yet are claimed and garrisoned by five different countries—China, Malaysia, the Philippines, Taiwan, and Vietnam. Armed with this information, you would realize that Crestone's explorations would be extremely sensitive and possibly the target of political conflict.[18]

Background Notes The U.S. State Department periodically publishes short (10–14 pages) profiles of individual countries called *Background Notes*. Each is intended to provide government employees with a quick overview of a country's geography, culture, living conditions, political orientation, economic policies, and trading patterns. *Background Notes* are particularly useful for briefing employees who are given temporary assignments in a foreign country.

World Development Report Published annually by the staff of the World Bank, the *World Development Report* presents numerous tables detailing information about World Bank members, including population, income and income distribution, infrastructure, government expenditures, trade, production, living standards, health, education, and urbanization.

Commodity Trade Statistics Published by the United Nations, *Commodity Trade Statistics* provides detailed data, compiled annually, on each country's exports and imports, which are classified by commodity and by country of destination or origin. It is an excellent source of minutia, for example, the value of pork exports from Denmark to Portugal in 1998. However, it is rather clumsy to use when time-series information is required, for example, Denmark's total exports from 1983 to 1998.

Balance of Payments Statistics, International Financial Statistics, and Direction of Trade Statistics These reports are published by the International Monetary Fund (IMF). *Balance of Payments Statistics,* issued annually, contains data about balance of payments performances of IMF members. The monthly *International Financial Statistics* offers international and domestic financial data on members' domestic interest rates, money and banking indicators, prices, exports, and exchange rates. *Direction of Trade Statistics* details the exports and imports of each IMF member on a quarterly basis.

National Trade Data Bank (NTDB) One of the newest data sources, the NTDB is distributed monthly by the U.S. Department of Commerce. It is packed with information assembled from other data sources, including some of those listed here. The NTDB differs from the others in its format: it is distributed on a CD-ROM disk. An annual subscription costs $575. Many university libraries and all federal depository libraries receive the NTDB. Because an enormous amount of data can be crammed on a CD-ROM disk, the NTDB contains data bases not readily available elsewhere. Suppose, for example, that your company produces mountain bikes and is looking for a German distributor. The NTDB provides information on whether any existing German sporting equipment distributor is interested in distributing foreign-made mountain bikes. The NTDB also contains *A Basic Guide to Exporting,* a step-

by-step guidebook developed by the U.S. Department of Commerce to assist first-time exporters. This guide contains an extensive list of other standard sources of information often used by international businesses.

Assignment

Go to your library and examine each of these standard references. (If your library subscribes to the NTDB, make an appointment with a reference librarian to play with it so that you can appreciate its capabilities.) Then answer the following questions:

1. What was the total value of U.S. imports from Belgium last year? Of U.S. exports to Belgium?

2. What is the total level of U.S. investments in Belgium? Of Belgian investments in the United States?

3. Profile the economy of Belgium: What is its GDP? What is its per capita income? How fast is its economy growing? What are its major exports and imports? Who are its major trading partners?

4. Profile the people of Belgium: What languages do they speak? What is their average educational level? What is their life expectancy? How fast is the population growing?

Now try to obtain the same information using the Internet. (The textbook's web site provides linkages to some web sites that may be of help, although you should search out other sites as well.) Which questions were easier to answer using printed material? Which were easier to answer using the Internet?

WORKING WITH THE WEB: Building Global Internet Skills

Traveling the Globe

Assume that you are responsible for planning business trips for five of your company's managers. Travel for each manager will originate in St. Louis, Missouri. The destinations are as follows:

- ◆ London, England
- ◆ Ho Chi Minh City, Vietnam
- ◆ Moscow, Russia
- ◆ Cairo, Egypt
- ◆ Warsaw, Poland

Use the Internet to locate answers to the following questions:

1. What is the best way for each manager to get from St. Louis to her/his destination?

2. What are the likely transportation costs for each trip?

3. Assuming a three-day stay for each manager, what additional travel costs are likely to be incurred?

4. Assuming the trip is in January, what weather conditions might be anticipated? What if the trip is in July?

5. What travel documents are required for each trip?

6. Are there any health or safety warnings currently applicable to each destination city?

7. What is the local language and currency?

CLOSING CASE

The Chinese Treasure Chest[19]

China's vast population and untapped business potential make it one of the world's largest potential commercial treasure chests. Businesses that are able to enter and function effectively in the Chinese market face an enviable future. But those that attempt to exploit the Chinese market without fully understanding its complexities are certain to fail.

It is easy to understand the allure of China for international businesses. The country offers over 1.2 billion consumers whose per capita income is rising rapidly. Already over 60 million Chinese residents have annual incomes of $1000 or more, the level at which experts believe consumerism begins to emerge. These consumers, in turn, will want to buy everything from McDonald's hamburgers to fashion apparel to color televisions.

Firms that risk entering the Chinese market are finding one surprise after another—some good, some not so good. For example, in the early 1990s Motorola, the U.S. electronics giant, built a small, makeshift factory in the northern Chinese port city of Tianjin to manufacture electronic paging devices. The firm expected demand for the pagers to be minimal in China and thus planned to ship most of them to other Asian markets. To Motorola's surprise, the factory's entire weekly output of 10,000 pagers has been sold exclusively in China. But Motorola has had to invest more heavily than expected in training local employees to work in a market-oriented business and to emphasize quality in manufacturing. Still, the company has been so enamored of the Chinese market that it built two more new plants in Tianjin, representing a total investment of $400 million, to produce everything from cellular telephones to advanced microprocessors.

China's international business appeal is not restricted to U.S. firms. Siemens and Philips are among the European firms moving aggressively into China. Canada's Seagram has invested $55 million to produce orange juice in the Chongqing area. To boost the supply of oranges for a juice-processing facility it is building in conjunction with a local partner, it is providing local farmers with technical assistance, a seedling nursery, and soil analyses. Even Taiwanese firms see the potential in China. For example, a few years ago, Taiwan's Chung Shing Textile Company opened a plant in Shanghai to make underwear for shipment to Western markets. But local demand was so great that the plant's total output of Three Guns underwear has been snapped up by buyers for local Chinese department stores. Similarly, Ting Hsin International Group, another Taiwanese firm, dominates China's $2 billion instant noodle market.

Among the most competitive areas, however, has been the automobile industry. To encourage domestic production, China slaps a 100 percent tariff on imported autos; even then, imported cars must be distributed by state-owned trading companies, which are not known for their eagerness or skill in mass marketing foreign-made goods. Accordingly, big automakers from the United States, Germany, and Japan have been jockeying for the rights to produce in China, which is likely to become the world's biggest automobile market in the third millennium. Recognizing its position of strength, the government has carefully limited entry and dictated the terms of entry so as to maximize the benefit to China. For example, foreign automakers must team with domestic partners, ensuring that China benefits from technology transfer from the foreign companies. In order to obtain a license to build midsize Buick sedans in Shanghai, for example, General Motors agreed to design much of the car in China and to establish dozens of joint ventures to produce parts for the car. It also promised to set up five research institutes to train Chinese engineers and advance China's technological know-how in such areas as fuel injection systems and power trains.

Meanwhile local Chinese firms are trying to keep a piece of the action for themselves. Local firms producing everything from furniture to processed food are desperately trying to remain competitive. A few Chinese businesses, such as Brilliance China Automotive Holdings and Shanghai Petrochemical, are even listed on the New York Stock Exchange. Unfortunately, many lack modern production equipment, and their managers do not fully understand the nature of free-market competition.

Not everyone agrees that doing business success-fully in China is a sure thing. While the country's economic growth has been nothing short of spectacular for most of the decade, inflation remains a lurking problem. Of the hundreds of thousands of state-owned enterprises, more than half are losing money. Cumulatively, they require enormous subsidies from the government, yet continue to churn out goods in competition with privately owned firms. Political instability also is a major concern of international businesses. China's leadership continues to promote free-market business practices even as it attempts to maintain its tight political control over the country. The risk is that as Chinese consumers grow more accustomed to free-market practices, they will begin to demand more freedom in other areas of their lives. Thus the potential for civil unrest will likely remain a fact of life for some time.

Case Questions

1. Assess the potential advantages and disadvantages of the Chinese market for international businesses.

2. What advice would you give a firm that is considering entry into the Chinese market?

3. What kinds of products are most likely to succeed in China in the short run? Which may need more time to be accepted?

CHAPTER NOTES

1. "The Wal-Mart Way Sometimes Gets Lost in Translation Overseas," *Wall Street Journal*, October 8, 1997, p. A1; "Ad Agencies Are Stumbling in East Europe," *Wall Street Journal*, May 10, 1996, p. B1; "Ukraine's Bureaucrats Stymie U.S. Firms," *Wall Street Journal*, November 4, 1996, p. A14; "Two Papers Are Halted in Indonesia Due to Ad," *Wall Street Journal*, August 10, 1992, p. B8.

2. Kenichi Ohmae, "The Triad World View," *Journal of Business Strategy*, Vol. 7, No. 4 (Spring 1987), p. 18.

3. This chapter reports population, GDP, and per capita GDP data for the world's countries. Data for the United States are

taken from the *Survey of Current Business*, various issues. Data for the OECD nations are taken from "OECD in Figures: 1997 Edition" obtained from the OECD web site. All other data are taken from the World Bank's *World Development Report 1997*.

4. Morris Goldstein et al., "Policy Issues in the Evolving International Monetary System," Occasional Paper #96, International Monetary Fund, Washington, D.C. (June 1992), p. 8.

5. "Counterfeit Bills Confound Detectors at the Fed, Sleuths at the Secret Service," *Wall Street Journal*, July 3, 1992, p. A8.

6. *Fortune,* August 4, 1997, pp. F-1 ff.

7. "Sinecures vs. Sewing Machines," *Wall Street Journal,* August 7, 1992, p. A12.

8. T. R. Fehrenbach, *Fire and Blood* (New York: Bonanza Books, 1985), pp. 440–497.

9. "Czech Republic Is Free, Fun to Visit and Rich, but Only Superficially," *Wall Street Journal,* July 15, 1997, p. A1; "Czech's Economic Success Loses Edge," *Wall Street Journal,* May 28, 1997, p. A12; "Bohemia's fading rhapsody," *The Economist,* May 31, 1997, p. 65.

10. "Booming Economy in Poland Brings Jobs, Wealth and Apathy," *Wall Street Journal,* November 25, 1996, p. A1.

11. "Hungary Begins to Reach Steady Growth," *Wall Street Journal,* July 16, 1997, p. A17; "Bohemia's fading rhapsody," *The Economist,* May 31, 1997, p. 65; "Hungary's Privatization Czar is Unloaded," *Wall Street Journal,* October 21, 1996, p. A19.

12. Family-owned businesses tend to be small by world standards. Only one Taiwanese company is a member of *Fortune's* Global 500, for example.

13. "Taiwan Trade Surplus, at Odds with Policy, Increased 6.4% in 1991," *Wall Street Journal,* January 7, 1992, p. A14.

14. "Free Enterprise Comes Naturally to Residents of Wenzhou, China," *Wall Street Journal,* August 13, 1992, p. A1.

15. Colin Leinster, "Vietnam—Business Rushes to Get In," *Fortune,* April 5, 1993, pp. 98–104.

16. Microsoft Encarta, "Middle East," 1994; Australian Department of Foreign Affairs and Trade, *Country Economic Brief, Saudi Arabia,* March 1995.

17. Michael Wilson, "Dubai Wins Favour as Middle East Trade Oasis," *Overseas Trading,* December 1993, p. 23.

18. "Spratly Islands Dispute in Southeast Asia Spotlights U.S. Role in Regional Security," *Wall Street Journal,* July 27, 1992, p. A6; Central Intelligence Agency, *The World Factbook 1997* (CIA Web Site)

19. John J. Curran, "China's Investment Boom," *Fortune,* March 7, 1994, pp. 116–124; "China—The Emerging Economic Powerhouse of the 21st Century," *Business Week,* May 17, 1993, pp. 54–68; "Taiwanese Firms Are Returning to China with Aim of Investing for Long Term," *Asian Wall Street Journal Weekly,* December 12–13, 1993, pp. 2, 4; "Tea and Tropicana? Seagram Wants Juice to Be Chinese Staple," *Wall Street Journal,* January 2, 1998, pp. A1, A4; "Coals to Newcastle, Ice to Eskimos; Now, Noodles to the Chinese," *Wall Street Journal,* November 17, 1997, pp. A1, A5; "Rethinking China," *Business Week,* March 4, 1996, Internet edition.

Helping Developing Nations: Aid or Trade?

Aid Is Better Than Trade

Many people throughout the world are concerned about improving living standards in developing countries. Some of this concern is prompted by humanitarian reasons, a desire to enrich the lives of poorer people. Some is based on a security rationale: improving living standards in poorer countries makes them less likely to threaten the lives and property of their neighbors. Some is based on economics: raising the income levels of these countries broadens the markets available to firms based in richer countries. Regardless of the motivation, what is the best means of accomplishing this task: aid or trade? That is, should the developed countries give developing countries resources (aid) or provide markets for their goods instead (trade)?

Many experts believe that the development of the less developed countries is dependent on aid. Richer nations annually provide some $60 billion in aid to poorer countries. Much of this aid is destined for infrastructure projects such as electrical generation, new roads, and telecommunications systems. As noted in Fig. 2.2, a strong correlation exists between per capita income and infrastructure. Adequate infrastructure is often a requirement for an MNC in deciding where to locate a factory or distribution facility. But private investors may be unwilling to lend funds for such public projects because of the financial weakness of a country's government. Therefore, aid may be the only way in which necessary improvements to the infrastructure can be financed. For example, $63 million of U.S. aid went to build roads in the southern Philippine island of Mindanao. This infrastructure improvement was a critical element in the development of the area's fishing industry.

Other aid may be used to alleviate human suffering directly. Gifts of food, medicines, and building materials help feed, heal, and house millions of people. Such aid is particularly beneficial when civil strife, such as the civil wars that have plagued Rwanda, Somalia, and Sudan, causes farmers to flee their homes, leaving crops rotting in the fields.

Aid may also be preferable to trade because it creates fewer political problems in the donor's country. Developing nations that successfully export often discover that importing countries raise barriers to their goods. For example, the developed nations willingly contribute $1 billion in aid to Bangladesh annually, but slap tariffs and import quotas on 80 percent of its exports.

Aid from the richer countries of North America, Western Europe, and Asia helps build roads, generate electricity, shelter families, and feed hungry children in developing countries.

The job of this Indonesian textile worker—and the continued economic development of her country—is dependent on access to the markets of the Quad countries.

An old Chinese proverb notes: "Give a man a fish and you feed him for a day. Teach a man to fish and you feed him for a lifetime." In line with this ancient wisdom, many development experts believe that it is better to base economic development on trade than on aid. Trade provides jobs for residents of less developed countries. The wages provided by these jobs get spent in the local economy, generating demand for local businesses and employment opportunities for local residents.

More important, as domestic firms expand their exports, their managers and employees learn new skills and techniques for producing and marketing these goods. They make contacts with foreign distributors, earn goodwill with foreign customers, develop credible reputations with foreign lenders, and learn the ins-and-outs of dealing with the customs services of foreign countries. This improvement in a country's stock of human capital inevitably gets transferred to other firms and industries as employees leave to start their own companies or get lured away by domestic competitors. The aggregate effect is to raise the competitiveness, productivity, and efficiency of the economy as a whole. The postwar economic successes of countries such as Singapore, Hong Kong, and Taiwan are based on this pattern of export-driven economic development. Other experts support trade-based economic development because of the failures of aid programs. Long-term food aid, for example, often depresses local crop prices so that farmers cannot make a living, forcing them to abandon their fields and seek work in urban areas. When U.S. and UN troops entered Somalia in 1992, for example, they brought so much food to feed the local population that Somalian farmers were unable to raise crops profitably. In the next growing season, fields remained unplanted, thereby making the country more dependent on outsiders. And far too often aid takes the form of large, ill-planned projects that do little to improve a country's living standard. For example, international donors, including the World Bank and Denmark, Norway, and Sweden, donated over $16 billion to Tanzania between 1961 and 1987. Much of this money was used to finance nationalization of the country's industries and relocation of 14 million peasants and their families to newly collectivized farms. Because of inefficiencies of the state-owned industrial sector and reductions in agricultural productivity at the collective farms, the net result of the aid was a halving of Tanzania's per capita income between 1980 and 1993.

Sources: "Food Crisis for 34m Africans," *Financial Times*, August 5, 1994, p. 3; "World Bank Attacked for Backing Nyerere," *Financial Times*, July 27, 1994, p. 12; "World Bank Laments Its Tanzania Role," *Financial Times*, July 27, 1994, p. 3; "Empty Promises," *The Economist*, May 7, 1994, pp. 11–12; "The Kindness of Strangers," *The Economist*, May 7, 1994, pp. 19–22; "Developed Nations Want Poor Countries to Succeed on Trade, But Not Too Much," *Wall Street Journal*, September 20, 1993, p. A10.

Wrap-up

1 In your judgment, which is better, trade or aid?

2 What alternatives, other than aid, are available to improve the infrastructures of developing countries?

3 Which should determine how foreign aid is spent, the donor countries or the recipient countries?

International Trade and Investment Theory

CHAPTER

3

After studying this chapter you should be able to:

Understand the motivation for international trade.

Discuss the differences among the classical, country-based theories of international trade.

Use the modern, firm-based theories of international trade to describe global strategies adopted by businesses.

Categorize the different forms of international investment.

Explain the reasons for foreign direct investment.

Summarize how supply, demand, and political factors influence foreign direct investment.

CATERPILLAR, INC., HEADQUARTERED IN PEORIA, ILLINOIS, IS THE world's largest producer of heavy earth-moving and construction equipment, with a 30 percent share of the global market. The company's complex involvement in international business is typical of most major firms today. Cat, as the company is widely known, manufactures engines and earth-moving, construction, and materials-handling equipment at 61 factories spread over five continents. Of its 57,026 employees, 32 percent work outside the United States. Almost half of its 1996 output of $16.5 billion was purchased by foreign customers: $5.5 billion as exports from the United States and $2.6 billion as output from Cat's 29 overseas factories. Caterpillar is no newcomer to international production. It established its first overseas factory in the United Kingdom in 1951. Its 1963 joint venture with Mitsubishi Heavy Industries was one of the first such investments by a U.S. firm in Japan. More recently, in February 1998 it purchased Perkins Engines, a British producer of small-to-medium size diesel engines, which had been a primary supplier of such engines to Cat. Caterpillar plans to leverage the Perkins acquisition to develop new products for the small and compact construction equipment market and for the agricultural market. ■ ■ Because down-time of a critical piece of equipment can halt construction, success in this industry depends on equipment reliability and after-sales support. Caterpillar has two competitive advantages that have enabled it to dominate the international heavy-equipment market:

Caterpillar: Making Money by Moving Mountains

1 A commitment to quality that makes the Caterpillar brand name a symbol of tough, reliable products

2 An effective network of 192 dealers worldwide who sell and service Caterpillar's products.

The importance of these two elements has been summed up by John Bibby, a typical Cat customer, who runs John Bibby Backhoe Hire, an excavating firm in a Melbourne, Australia suburb. Bibby is a small operator—he owns only one piece of equipment—so when his backhoe isn't operating, his business is essentially shut down.

> It was embarrassing before I got my Cat machine because something would break down every week. Now, that kind of thing just doesn't happen very often . . . and when it does, they send somebody out straight away and the blokes fix it right up.

> I'm happy with the parts you can get and the availability of them. And I know a lot of the boys now. You know, once you're in a good thing, you don't want to get out of it.[1]

Caterpillar engages in many forms of international business. It is an exporter, sending its well-known yellow earth-moving equipment to virtually every country in the world. It is an importer, purchasing parts from Asian, European, and North American suppliers. Cat is an international investor, owning and operating factories in 15 countries. It also is an international borrower, seeking short-term and long-term capital from investors and banks throughout the world. The company is involved in the international licensing of technology, both in purchasing the right to use innovative technology developed by foreign firms and in selling the use of its own technologies to other foreign firms. It also franchises the rights to sell its equipment to 65 U.S. dealers and 127 foreign dealers. ▌▌ Of course, given the fierceness of international competition, Caterpillar's future is no more assured than that of any other global enterprise. Its arch-rival, Komatsu Ltd., enjoyed lower labor costs in the 1980s and a reputation for producing innovative, high-quality products. In the early 1980s, Komatsu undercut Cat's prices to U.S. customers by as much as 40 percent, causing an 11 percent erosion in Cat's domestic market share. Slashing its own prices, Cat stopped the market-share losses, although its profitability suffered. Since 1987, Cat has invested $2.1 billion in plant modernization to improve manufacturing quality and flexibility and has developed new inventory control systems to cut inventory costs. Cat also is working with its 4000 suppliers to improve the quality of parts and supplies. The rise in the value of the yen from 1985 to 1995 helped these efforts by eroding Komatsu's cost advantage. Unfortunately for Cat, the yen has fallen in value since reaching a peak of 80 yen to the dollar in April 1995. With the yen now trading in the range of 120–130 yen to the dollar—making Japanese exports some 33 to 38 percent cheaper than they were in the spring of 1995—Cat's managers must accelerate their drive to become more cost-efficient. ▌▌ Cat also aggressively reined in its labor costs to maintain its worldwide dominance of the heavy earth-moving and construction equipment market, although this effort has come at a high price. In 1992 it fought a bitter five-month strike by the United Auto Workers in order to slow down wage increases, relax productivity-robbing work rules, and shrink its labor force. After the union called off this strike, the company suffered through 11 more union walkouts and 440 unfair labor practice complaints filed before the National Labor Relations Board. Only in March 1998 was the 1992 strike finally settled, and it is clear that not all the wounds from this struggle have been healed. Caterpillar faces the challenge of improving its labor relations because it must rely on these same workers to improve productivity and the quality of its output in the face of Komatsu's competition.[2] ▌▌▌▌▌

Caterpillar is a microcosm of the complex business relationships that bind firms and countries in the contemporary global marketplace. In this chapter we analyze the underlying economic forces that shape and structure the international business transactions conducted by Caterpillar and thousands of other firms. We discuss the major theories that explain and predict international trade and investment activity. These theories introduce you to the economic environment in which firms compete. They also help firms sharpen their global business strategies, identify promising export and investment opportunities, and react to threats posed by foreign competitors. These theories also can help you understand why a firm like Caterpillar can be simultaneously an exporter, importer, international investor, international borrower, franchiser, and licensor and licensee of technology.

International Trade and the World Economy

Trade is the voluntary exchange of goods, services, assets, or money between one person or organization and another. Because it is voluntary, both parties to the transaction must believe they will gain from the exchange, or else they would not complete it. **International trade** is trade between residents of two countries. The residents may be individuals, firms, nonprofit organizations, or other forms of associations. Why does international trade occur? The answer follows directly from our definition of trade: both parties to the transaction, who happen to reside in two different countries, believe they benefit from the voluntary exchange. Behind this simple truth lies much economic theory, business practice, government policy, and international conflict—topics we cover in this and the next four chapters.

Total international merchandise trade in 1996 was $5.1 trillion, or approximately 18 percent of the world's $29 trillion GDP; trade in services in that year amounted to $1.2 trillion.[3] The Quad countries accounted for almost two thirds of the world's merchandise exports (see Fig. 3.1). Such international trade has important direct and indirect effects on national economies. On the one hand, exports spark additional economic activity in the domestic economy. Caterpillar's $5.5 billion in exports generate orders for its U.S. suppliers, wages for its U.S. workers, and dividend payments for its U.S. shareholders, all of which in turn create income for local automobile dealers, grocery stores, and others that then add to their own payrolls. On the other hand, imports can pressure domestic suppliers to cut their prices and improve their competitiveness. Failure to respond to foreign competition may lead to shut-down factories and unemployed workers. Because of

---

FIGURE 3.1

Sources of the World's Merchandise Exports, 1996

Source: World Trade Organization, "After Two Outstanding Years, World Trade Growth Returned to Earlier Levels."

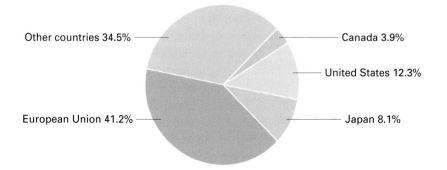

Other countries 34.5%

Canada 3.9%

United States 12.3%

Japan 8.1%

European Union 41.2%

international trade's obvious significance to businesses, consumers, and workers, scholars have attempted to develop theories to explain and predict the forces that motivate such trade. Governments use these theories when they design policies they hope will benefit their countries' industries and citizens. Businesses use them to identify promising markets and profitable internationalization strategies.

Classical Country-Based Trade Theories

The first theories of international trade developed with the rise of the great European nation-states in the sixteenth century. Not surprisingly, these early theories focused on the country in examining patterns of exports and imports. As we discuss in more detail later in this chapter, these country-based theories are particularly useful for describing trade in commodities—standardized, undifferentiated goods such as oil, sugar, or lumber that are typically bought on the basis of price rather than brand name. However, as MNCs rose to power in the middle of this century, scholars shifted their attention to the firm's role in promoting international trade. The firm-based theories developed after World War II are useful in describing patterns of trade in differentiated goods—those such as automobiles, consumer electronics, and personal care products, for which brand name is an important component of the customer's purchase decision. In this section we examine the classical, country-based theories of international trade; in the next section we explore the more modern, firm-based theories.

Mercantilism

Mercantilism is a sixteenth-century economic philosophy that maintains that a country's wealth is measured by its holdings of gold and silver. According to mercantilists, a country's goal should be to enlarge those holdings. To do this it should strive to maximize the difference between its exports and its imports by promoting exports and discouraging imports. The logic was transparent to sixteenth-century policy makers: if foreigners buy more goods from you than you buy from them, then the foreigners have to pay you the difference in gold and silver, enabling you to amass more treasure. Mercantilist terminology is still used today, for example, when television commentators and newspaper headlines report that a country suffered an "unfavorable" balance of trade—that is, its exports were less than its imports.

At the time mercantilism seemed to be sound economic policy—at least to the local king. Large gold and silver holdings meant he could afford to hire armies to fight other countries and thereby possibly expand his kingdom. Politically, mercantilism was popular with many manufacturers and their workers. Export-oriented manufacturers favored mercantilist trade policies, such as those establishing subsidies or tax rebates, that stimulated their sales to foreigners. Domestic manufacturers threatened by foreign imports endorsed mercantilist trade policies, such as those imposing tariffs or quotas, that protected them from foreign competition. These businesses, their workers, their suppliers, and the local politicians representing the communities in which the manufacturers had production facilities all praised the wisdom of the king's mercantilist policies.

However, most members of society are hurt by such policies. Governmental subsidies of the exports of certain industries are paid by taxpayers in the form of

Great Britain's mercantilist policy was a major contributor to the political unrest in its American colonies. Colonial merchants and manufacturers resented British taxes and regulations that hindered the growth of American firms and protected British industries. The Boston Tea Party and similar incidents led to armed conflict and ultimately to independence for the thirteen colonies.

Americans throwing the Cargoes of the Tea Ships into the River at Boston

higher taxes. Governmental import restrictions are paid for by consumers in the form of higher prices because domestic firms face less competition from foreign producers. During the Age of Imperialism, governments often shifted the burden of mercantilist policies onto their colonies. For example, under the Navigation Act of 1660 all European goods imported by the American colonies had to be shipped from Great Britain. The British prohibited colonial firms from exporting certain goods that might compete with those from British factories, such as hats, finished iron goods, and woolens. To ensure adequate supplies of low-cost inputs for British merchants, the British required some colonial industries to sell their output only to British firms. This output included rice, tobacco, and naval stores (forest products used in shipbuilding).[4] This particular mercantilist strategy ultimately backfired—it contributed to the grievances that led to the overthrow of the British Crown in the American colonies.

Because mercantilism does benefit certain members of society, mercantilist policies are still politically attractive to some firms and their workers. Modern supporters of such policies, called **neo-mercantilists**, or **protectionists,** include such diverse U.S. groups as the American Federation of Labor-Congress of Industrial Organizations, textile manufacturers, steel companies, sugar growers, and peanut farmers.

Such protectionist attitudes are not limited to the United States. North Americans and Europeans have long complained that Japan limits the access of foreign goods to its market. For example, it took forty years of negotiations before Japan grudgingly agreed in 1993 to allow the importation of foreign rice, and even then it limited rice imports to less than 10 percent of its market. And Asian and North American firms criticize the Europeans for imposing barriers against imported goods such as beef, automobiles, and video cassette recorders. Such finger pointing is amply justified: nearly every country has adopted some neo-mercantilist policies in order to protect key industries in its economy.

Absolute Advantage

Neo-mercantilism has superficial appeal, particularly to patriots who want to strengthen their country's economy. Why shouldn't a country try to maximize its holdings of gold and silver? According to Adam Smith, the Scottish economist who is viewed as the father of free-market economics, mercantilism's basic problem is that it confuses the acquisition of treasure with the acquisition of wealth. In *An Inquiry into the Nature and Causes of the Wealth of Nations* (1776), Smith attacked the intellectual basis of mercantilism and demonstrated that mercantilism actually *weakens* a country. He maintained that a country's true wealth is measured by the wealth of all its citizens, not just that of its king; thus a country's goal should be to maximize its citizens' wealth. In so doing the country will also become wealthy and strong, offering the king a larger base on which to levy taxes.

In Smith's view, mercantilism robs individuals of the ability to trade freely and to benefit from voluntary exchanges. Moreover, in the process of avoiding imports at all costs, a country must squander its resources producing goods it is not suited to produce. The inefficiencies caused by mercantilism reduce the wealth of the country as a whole, even though certain special-interest groups may benefit.

Smith advocated free trade among countries as a means of enlarging a country's wealth. As we explain later in this chapter, free trade enables a country to expand the amount of goods and services available to it by specializing in the production of some goods and services and trading for others. But which goods and services should a country export and which should it import? In answer to this question, Smith developed the **theory of absolute advantage,** which suggests that a country should export those goods and services for which it is more productive than other countries are and import those goods and services for which other countries are more productive than it is.

Absolute advantage can be demonstrated through a numerical example. Assume, for the sake of simplicity, that there are only two countries in the world, France and Japan; only two goods, wine and clock radios; and only one factor of production, labor. Table 3.1 shows the output of the two goods per hour of labor for the two countries. In France 1 hour of labor can produce either 2 bottles of wine or 3 clock radios. In Japan, 1 hour of labor can produce either 1 bottle of wine or 5 clock radios. France has an absolute advantage in the production of wine: 1 hour of labor produces 2 bottles in France but only 1 in Japan. Japan has an absolute advantage in the production of clock radios: 1 hour of labor produces 5 clock radios in Japan but only 3 in France.

If France and Japan are able to trade with one another, both will be better off. Suppose France agrees to exchange 2 bottles of wine for 4 clock radios. Only 1 hour of French labor is needed to produce the 2 bottles of wine bound for Japan. In return, France will get 4 clock radios from Japan. These 4 clock radios would have required 1.33 hours of French labor had France produced

TABLE 3.1

The Theory of Absolute Advantage: An Example

	OUTPUT PER HOUR OF LABOR	
	France	Japan
Wine	2	1
Clock radios	3	5

them itself rather than buying them from the Japanese. By trading with Japan rather than producing the clock radios itself, France saves 0.33 hour of labor. It can use this freed-up labor to produce more wine, which in turn can be consumed by French citizens or traded to Japan for more clock radios. By allocating its scarce labor to produce goods for which it is more productive than Japan and then trading them to Japan, France can consume more goods than it could have done in the absence of trade.

Japan is similarly better off. Japan uses 0.8 hour of labor to produce the 4 clock radios to exchange for the 2 bottles of French wine. Producing the 2 bottles of wine itself would have required 2 hours of labor. By producing clock radios and then trading them to France, Japan saves 1.2 hours of labor, which can be used to produce more clock radios that the Japanese can consume themselves or trade to France for more wine.

Comparative Advantage

The theory of absolute advantage makes intuitive sense. Unfortunately, it is flawed. What happens to trade if one country has an absolute advantage in both products? The theory of absolute advantage incorrectly suggests that no trade would occur. David Ricardo, an early nineteenth-century British economist, solved this problem by developing the **theory of comparative advantage,** which states that a country should produce and export those goods and services for which it is *relatively* more productive than are other countries and import those goods and services for which other countries are *relatively* more productive than it is.[5]

The difference between the two theories is subtle: absolute advantage looks at *absolute* productivity differences; comparative advantage looks at *relative* productivity differences. The distinction occurs because comparative advantage incorporates the concept of opportunity cost in determining which good a country should produce. The **opportunity cost** of a good is the value of what is given up in order to get the good. Most of us apply the principles of comparative advantage and opportunity cost without realizing it. For example, a brain surgeon may be better at both brain surgery and lawn mowing than her neighbor's teenaged son is. However, if the surgeon is comparatively better at surgery than at lawn mowing, she will spend most of her time at the operating table and pay the teenager to mow her lawn. The brain surgeon behaves this way because the opportunity cost of mowing the lawn is too high: time spent mowing is time unavailable for surgery.

Let's return to the example in Table 3.1 to contrast absolute and comparative advantage. Recall that France has an absolute advantage in wine and Japan has an absolute advantage in clock radios. The theory of absolute advantage says that France should export wine to Japan and Japan should export clock radios to France. As Table 3.1 shows, France also has a comparative advantage in wine: with 1 hour of labor it produces 2 times as much wine as does Japan, but only 0.6 times as many clock radios. Thus France is *relatively* more productive in wine. Japan has a comparative advantage in clock radios. With 1 hour of labor it produces 1.67 times as many clock radios as France does, but only 0.5 times as much wine. So Japan is *relatively* more productive in clock radios. The theory of comparative advantage says that France should export wine to Japan and Japan should export clock radios to France. For the example in Table 3.1, the

TABLE 3.2		
The Theory of Comparative Advantage: An Example		
	OUTPUT PER HOUR OF LABOR	
	France	**Japan**
Wine	4	1
Clock radios	6	5

theory of absolute advantage and the theory of comparative advantage both yield the same outcome.

Now let's change the facts some. Suppose productivity stays the same in Japan but doubles in France as the result of new job training programs. Table 3.2 shows this new situation. France now can produce 4 bottles of wine or 6 clock radios per hour of labor. France now has an absolute advantage in *both* wine and clock radios: for each hour of labor France can produce 3 more bottles of wine (4 minus 1) or 1 more clock radio (6 minus 5) than Japan can. According to the theory of absolute advantage, no trade should occur because France is more productive than Japan in producing both goods.

The theory of comparative advantage, on the other hand, indicates that trade should still occur. France is 4 times better than Japan is in wine production but only 1.2 times better in clock radio production. (Alternatively, Japan is only 0.25 as good as France in wine production but 0.83 as good in clock radio production.) France is comparatively better than Japan in wine production, while Japan is comparatively better than France in clock radio production.

By the theory of comparative advantage, France should export wine to Japan and Japan should export clock radios to France. If they do so, both will be better off. In the absence of trade, 1 bottle of wine will sell for 1.5 clock radios in France and for 5 clock radios in Japan. If Japan offers to trade 2 clock radios for 1 bottle of wine, France will be better off—*even though France has an absolute advantage in clock radio production*. Without trade, sacrificing 1 bottle of wine domestically would yield France only 1.5 clock radios in increased production. With trade, France could get 2 clock radios by giving up 1 bottle of wine to Japan. France gets more clock radios per bottle of wine given up by trading with Japan than by producing the clock radios domestically.

Japan also gains. Without trade, Japan has to give up 5 clock radios to get 1 more bottle of wine. With trade, Japan has to give up only 2 clock radios to obtain 1 more bottle. Japan gets more wine per clock radio given up by trading with France than by producing the wine domestically. Even though France has an absolute advantage in both wine and clock radio production, both countries gain from this trade. It is comparative advantage that motivates trade, not absolute advantage.

Comparative Advantage with Money

The lesson of the theory of comparative advantage is simple but powerful: *You're better off specializing in what you do relatively best. Produce (and export) those goods and services you are relatively best able to produce, and buy other goods and services from people who are relatively better at producing them than you are.*

TABLE 3.3				

The Theory of Comparative Advantage with Money: An Example

	COST OF GOODS IN FRANCE		COST OF GOODS IN JAPAN	
	French-Made	Japanese-Made	French-Made	Japanese-Made
Wine	Fr18	Fr40	¥450	¥1000
Clock radios	Fr12	Fr8	¥300	¥200

Note: For example, 1 hour's worth of French labor can produce 4 bottles of wine at a total cost of Fr72, or an average cost of Fr18 per bottle. At an exchange rate of 25 yen per franc, a bottle of French-made wine will cost ¥450 (450 = 18 × 25).

Of course, Tables 3.1 and 3.2 are both simplistic and artificial. The world economy produces more than two goods and services and is made up of more than two countries. Barriers to trade may exist, someone must pay to transport goods between markets, and inputs other than labor are necessary to produce goods. Even more important, the world economy uses money as a medium of exchange. Table 3.3 introduces money into our discussion of trade and incorporates these assumptions:

1 The output per hour of labor in France and Japan for clock radios and wine is as shown in Table 3.2.

2 The hourly wage rate in France is 72 francs (Fr).

3 The hourly wage rate in Japan is 1000 yen (¥).

4 One French franc is worth 25 yen.

Given these assumptions, in the absence of trade, a bottle of wine in France costs Fr18, the equivalent of ¥450, and clock radios cost Fr12, the equivalent of ¥300. In Japan a bottle of wine costs ¥1000 (Fr40), and clock radios cost ¥200 (Fr8).

In this case trade will occur because of the self-interest of individual entrepreneurs (or the opportunity to make a profit) in France and Japan. For example, buyers for Galeries Lafayette, a major Paris department store, observe that clock radios cost Fr12 in France and the equivalent of only Fr8 in Japan. To keep their cost of goods low, these buyers will order clock radios in Japan, where they are cheap, and sell them in France, where they are expensive. Accordingly, clock radios will be exported by Japan and imported by France, just as the law of comparative advantage predicts. Similarly, wine distributors in Japan observe that a bottle of wine costs ¥1000 in Japan but the equivalent of only ¥450 in France. To keep their cost of goods as low as possible, buyers for Japanese wine distributors will buy wine in France, where it is cheap, and sell it in Japan, where it is expensive. Wine will be exported by France and imported by Japan, as predicted by the law of comparative advantage.

Note that none of these businesspeople needed to know anything about the theory of comparative advantage. They merely looked at the price differences in the two markets and made their business decisions based on the desire to obtain supplies at the lowest possible cost. Yet they benefit from comparative advantage because prices set in a free market reflect a country's comparative advantage.

Relative Factor Endowments

The theory of comparative advantage begs a broader question: What determines the products for which a country will have a comparative advantage? To answer this question, two Swedish economists, Eli Heckscher[6] and Bertil Ohlin,[7] developed the **theory of relative factor endowments,** now often referred to as the **Heckscher-Ohlin theory.** These economists made two basic observations:

1 *Factor endowments (or types of resources) vary among countries.* For example, Argentina has much fertile land, Saudi Arabia has large crude oil reserves, and China has a large pool of unskilled labor.

2 *Goods differ according to the types of factors that are used to produce them.* For example, wheat requires fertile land, oil production requires crude oil reserves, and clothing requires unskilled labor.

From these observations Heckscher and Ohlin developed their theory: *a country will have a comparative advantage in producing products that intensively use resources (factors of production) it has in abundance.* Thus Argentina has a comparative advantage in wheat growing because of its abundance of fertile land; Saudi Arabia has a comparative advantage in oil production because of its abundance of crude oil reserves; and China has a comparative advantage in clothing manufacture because of its abundance of unskilled labor.

The Heckscher-Ohlin theory suggests a country should export those goods that use intensively those factors of production that are relatively abundant in the country. The theory was tested empirically after World War II by economist Wassily Leontief using input-output analysis, a mathematical technique for measuring the interrelationships among the sectors of an economy. Leontief believed the United States was a capital-abundant and labor-scarce economy. Therefore,

The Heckscher-Ohlin theory predicts that a country will have a comparative advantage producing goods that intensively use resources the country has in abundance. For example, Australia's abundance of land has given it a comparative advantage in the production of wool and mutton.

FIGURE 3.2

U.S. Imports and Exports, 1947: The Leontief Paradox

according to the Heckscher-Ohlin theory, he reasoned that the United States should export capital-intensive goods, such as bulk chemicals and steel, and import labor-intensive goods, such as clothing and footware.

Leontief used his input-output model of the U.S. economy to estimate the quantities of labor and capital needed to produce "bundles" of U.S. exports and imports worth $1 million in 1947 (see Fig. 3.2).[8] (Each bundle was a weighted average of all U.S. exports or imports in 1947.) He determined that in 1947 U.S. factories utilized $2.551 million of capital and 182.3 person-years of labor, or $13,993 of capital per person-year of labor, to produce a bundle of exports worth $1 million. He also calculated that $3.093 million of capital and 170.0 person-years of labor, or $18,194 of capital per person-year of labor, were used to produce a bundle of U.S. imports worth $1 million in that year. Thus U.S. imports were more capital-intensive than U.S. exports. Imports required $4201 ($18,194 – $13,993) more in capital per person-year of labor to produce than exports did.

These results were not consistent with the predictions of the Heckscher-Ohlin theory: U.S. imports were nearly 30 percent more capital-intensive than were U.S. exports. The economics profession was distraught. The Heckscher-Ohlin theory made such intuitive sense, and yet Leontief's findings were the reverse of what was expected. Thus was born the **Leontief paradox.**

In the past forty years numerous economists have repeated Leontief's initial study in an attempt to resolve the paradox. The first such study was performed by Leontief himself. He thought trade flows may have been distorted in 1947 because much of the world economy was still reeling from World War II. Using 1951 data he found that U.S. imports were 6 percent more capital-intensive than U.S. exports were. Although this figure was less than that in his original study, it still disagreed with the predictions of the Heckscher-Ohlin theory.[9]

Some scholars argue that measurement problems flaw Leontief's work. Leontief assumed there are two homogeneous factors of production: labor and capital. Yet other factors of production exist, most notably land, human capital, and technology—none of which were included in Leontief's analysis. Failure to include these other factors may have caused him to mismeasure the labor intensity of U.S. exports and imports. Many U.S. exports are intensive in either land (such as agricultural goods) or human knowledge (such as computers, aircraft, and services).[10] Consider the products sold by one of the leading U.S. exporters, Boeing Aircraft Company. Leontief's approach measures the physical capital—the plants, property, and equipment—and the physical labor used to construct Boeing aircraft but fails to gauge adequately the role of human capital and technology in the firm's operations. Yet human capital—the well-educated engineers who design the aircraft and highly skilled machinists who assemble it—and technology—the sophisticated management techniques that control the world's largest assembly lines—are more important to Boeing's success than mere physical capital and physical labor. Leontief's failure to measure the role that these other factors of production play in determining international trade patterns may account for his paradoxical results.

Modern Firm-Based Trade Theories

Since World War II, international business research has focused on the role of the firm rather than the country in promoting international trade. Firm-based theories have developed for several reasons:

1 The growing importance of MNCs in the postwar international economy

2 The inability of the country-based theories to explain and predict the existence and growth of intraindustry trade (defined below)

3 The failure of Leontief and other researchers to empirically validate the country-based Heckscher-Ohlin theory

Unlike country-based theories, firm-based theories incorporate factors such as quality, technology, brand names, and customer loyalty into explanations of trade flows. Because firms, not countries, are the agents for international trade, the newer theories explore the firm's role in promoting exports and imports.

Country Similarity Theory

Country-based theories, such as the theory of comparative advantage, do a good job of explaining interindustry trade among countries. **Interindustry trade** is the exchange of goods produced by one industry in country A for goods produced by a different industry in country B, such as the exchange of French wines for Japanese clock radios. Yet much international trade consists of **intraindustry trade,** that is, trade between two countries of goods produced by the same industry. For example, Japan exports Toyotas to Germany, while Germany exports BMWs to Japan. Intraindustry trade accounts for approximately 40 percent of world trade,[11] and it is not predicted by country-based theories.

In 1961 Swedish economist Steffan Linder sought to explain the phenomenon of intraindustry trade.[12] Linder hypothesized that international trade in manufactured goods results from similarities of preferences among consumers in countries that are at the same stage of economic development. In his view, firms initially manufacture goods in order to serve their domestic market. As they explore exporting opportunities, they discover that the most promising foreign markets are in countries in which consumers' preferences resemble those of their own domestic market. The Japanese market, for example, provides BMW with well-off, prestige- and performance-seeking automobile buyers similar to the ones who purchase its cars in Germany. The German market provides Toyota with quality-conscious and value-oriented customers similar to those found in its home market. As each company targets the other's home market, intraindustry trade arises. Linder's **country similarity theory** suggests that most trade in manufactured goods should be between countries with similar per capita incomes and that intraindustry trade in manufactured goods should be common. This theory is particularly useful in explaining trade in differentiated goods such as automobiles, expensive electronics equipment, and personal care products, for which brand names and product reputations play an important role in consumer decision making.

Product Life Cycle Theory

Product life cycle theory, which originated in the marketing field to describe the evolution of marketing strategies as a product matures, is a second firm-based theory of international trade (and, as we will see, of international investment). As developed in the 1960s by Raymond Vernon of the Harvard Business School, international product life cycle theory traces the roles of innovation, market expansion, comparative advantage, and strategic responses of global rivals in international production, trade, and investment decisions.[13]

According to Vernon's theory the international product life cycle consists of three stages (see Fig. 3.3):

1 New product

2 Maturing product

3 Standardized product

In Stage 1, the *new product stage,* a firm develops and introduces an innovative product, such as a photocopier or a personal computer, in response to a perceived need in the domestic market. Because the product is new, this innovating firm is uncertain whether a profitable market for it exists. The firm's marketing executives must closely monitor customer reactions to ensure the new product satisfies consumer needs. Quick market feedback is important, so the product is likely to be initially produced in the country in which its research and development occurred, typically a developed country like Japan, Germany, or the United States. Further, because the market size also is uncertain, the firm usually will minimize its investment in manufacturing capacity for the product. Most output initially is sold in the domestic market and export sales are limited.

For example, in the early days of the personal computer industry the small producers that populated the industry had their hands full trying to meet the burgeoning demand for their product. Apple Computer typified this problem. Founded on April Fool's Day in 1976, its initial assembly plant was located in cofounder Steve Jobs's garage. The first large order for its homemade computers— fifty units from a local computer hobbyist store that summer—almost bankrupted the firm because it lacked the financing to buy the necessary parts.[14] But Apple survived because of the nurturing environment in which it was born, California's

INNOVATING FIRM'S COUNTRY

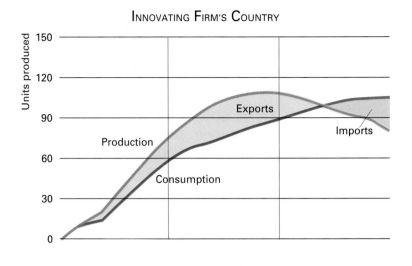

OTHER INDUSTRIALIZED COUNTRIES

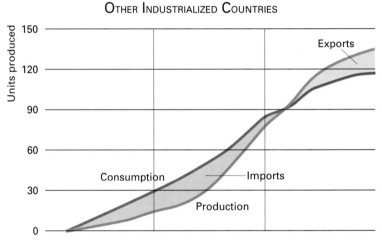

LESS-DEVELOPED COUNTRIES

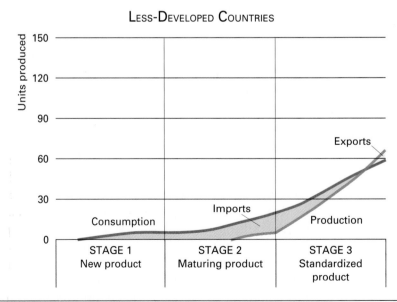

STAGE 1
New product

STAGE 2
Maturing product

STAGE 3
Standardized
product

FIGURE 3.3   **The International Product Life Cycle**   Source: Raymond Vernon/Louis T. Wells, Jr., *The Economic Environment of International Business*, 5th ed., © 1991, p. 85. Adapted by permission of Prentice Hall, Englewood Cliffs, NJ.

Silicon Valley. Home to major electronics firms such as Hewlett-Packard, Intel, and National Semiconductor, the Valley was full of electrical engineers who could design and build Apple's products and venture capitalists who were seeking the "next Xerox." It was the perfect locale for Apple's sales to grow from zero in 1976 to $7.8 million in 1978 and $7.1 billion in 1997.

In Stage 2, the *maturing product stage*, demand for the product expands dramatically as consumers recognize its value. The innovating firm builds new factories to expand its capacity and satisfy domestic and foreign demand for the product. Domestic and foreign competitors begin to emerge, lured by the prospect of lucrative earnings. In the case of Apple, the firm introduced a hand-assembled version of its second model, the Apple II, at a San Francisco computer fair in spring 1977. Within three years Apple had sold 130,000 units and expanded its production facilities beyond Jobs's garage. To serve domestic and foreign customers, Apple IIs were manufactured in California and Texas and distributed from warehouses in the United States and the Netherlands.

In Stage 3, the *standardized product stage*, the market for the product stabilizes. The product becomes more of a commodity, and firms are pressured to lower their manufacturing costs as much as possible by shifting production to facilities in countries with low labor costs. As a result, the product begins to be imported into the innovating firm's home market (by either the firm or its competitors). In some cases imports may result in the complete elimination of domestic production.

The personal computer industry is in the early phase of the standardized product stage. In the U.S. market low-priced brand-name imports from new producers such as South Korea's Hyundai and Samsung have threatened the more established U.S. manufacturers. Taiwanese manufacturers such as Tatung, Mitac International, First International, and TECO Information Systems—none of them household names in the United States—annually export to the United States millions of personal computers, many of which are produced under contract for foreign distributors. To meet the challenge of these new competitors Apple shifted some of its production to plants in Ireland and Singapore to take advantage of lower-priced labor. Apple also decided to squeeze more value out of its well-known brand name by broadening its product line, invading high-growth niches in the microcomputer market, expanding its distribution network, and slashing its overhead expenses in order to price its products more competitively.[15] Despite these efforts, Apple's economic survival is under siege as domestic and foreign competitors continue to eat away at its market share and profit margins, and the company is rapidly being relegated to a niche player in the industry it pioneered.

According to the international product life cycle theory, domestic production begins in Stage 1, peaks in Stage 2, and slumps in Stage 3. Exports by the innovating firm's country also begin in Stage 1 and peak in Stage 2. By Stage 3, however, the innovating firm's country becomes a net importer of the product. Foreign competition begins to emerge toward the end of Stage 1, as firms in other industrialized countries recognize the product's market potential. In Stage 2 foreign competitors expand their productive capacity, thus servicing an increasing portion of their home markets and perhaps becoming net exporters. But as competition intensifies in Stage 2, the innovating firm and its domestic and foreign rivals seek to lower their production costs by shifting production to low-cost sites in less developed countries. Eventually, in Stage 3, the less developed countries may become net exporters of the product.

Global Strategic Rivalry Theory

More recent explanations of the pattern of international trade, developed in the 1980s by such economists as Paul Krugman[16] and Kelvin Lancaster,[17] examine the impact on trade flows of global strategic rivalry between MNCs. According to this view, firms struggle to develop some sustainable competitive advantage, which they can then exploit to dominate the global marketplace. Like Linder's approach, global strategic rivalry theory predicts that intraindustry trade will be commonplace. However, it focuses on strategic decisions firms adopt as they compete internationally. These decisions affect both international trade and international investment.

For example, after deregulation in 1978 U.S. airlines created hub-oriented route systems and frequent flyer programs to lure passengers to their domestic and international flights. As a result, over the past decade European airlines have been losing market share in the transatlantic market to U.S. carriers. To reverse this decline, KLM entered into a strategic alliance with Northwest Airlines in 1992, allowing KLM to funnel traffic from Northwest's domestic flights onto its transatlantic flights, effectively turning Northwest's hubs and frequent flyer program from a competitive disadvantage into an advantage for KLM. Northwest gained similar advantages at KLM's hub at Amsterdam. To keep pace with Northwest and KLM, a variety of alliances between carriers from each side of the Atlantic soon sprung up.[18] British Airways paired up with USAir in 1993. It subsequently proposed an alliance with American Airlines, which caused its agreement with USAir to collapse. Delta allied with three smaller European carriers—Sabena, Swissair, and Austrian Air. United Airlines formed a strategic alliance with Lufthansa in 1994, which was broadened in 1997 to include Scandinavian Airlines System, Air Canada, and Thai Airways. Meanwhile, Air France, Virgin Atlantic, Czech Airways, and Alitalia entered into similar agreements with Continental. Other firms are playing similar games in their own industries as they attempt to leverage their own strengths and neutralize those of their rivals, as "Going Global" suggests.

This photo shop in Nagano, Japan prominently displays Kodak's official role in the 1998 Winter Olympics. Kodak used its Olympic sponsorship as a key element of its assault on the home market of its chief global rival, Fuji.

Firms competing in the global marketplace have numerous ways of obtaining a sustainable competitive advantage. The more popular ones are

♦ Owning intellectual property rights

♦ Investing in research and development

♦ Achieving economies of scale or scope

♦ Exploiting the experience curve

GOING GLOBAL

As visitors poured into Nagano, Japan during the 1998 Winter Olympics, one of the first things they saw as they entered the city were two billboards. The first, featuring the familiar gold tones of Eastman Kodak, the official film of the 1998 winter games, announced "Honored to Be Part of the Olympics." The second, sponsored by Kodak's chief rival, proclaimed "Fuji Film: It Captures the Moment of Truth."

Kodak and Fuji are bitter rivals around the globe. Kodak's share of the world film market in 1997 was estimated to be 39 percent, while Fuji's was 37 percent. Kodak owns the lion's share of the $2.7 billion U.S. film market, while Fuji enjoys similar dominance in the $2.0 billion Japanese market. In the late 1990s, however, Fuji intensified its assault on the U.S. market. It launched a pricing war there, cutting the price of multiple-roll packs of film by as much as 50 percent. Fuji's attack was successful, taking several points of market share away from Kodak and forcing its U.S. rival to cut its own prices and lay off thousands of employees. Global strategic rivalry theory suggests the wisdom of Fuji's offensive. The price war in the U.S. market did far more damage to Kodak's bottom line than to Fuji's. By forcing Kodak to hemorrhage red ink to stop its loss of U.S. market share, Fuji hoped to weaken Kodak's ability to compete with it elsewhere.

An Olympic-Sized Rivalry

Kodak has not yet thrown in the towel and surrendered. Rather, it vigorously counterattacked Fuji in the Japanese market. Kodak's status as an official Olympic sponsor was a key element of its strategy. For two years prior to the games, it built its presence in the Nagano market to ensure that the 1.2 million people who visited the Olympics were able to buy film in Kodak's gold boxes rather than Fuji's green ones. To bypass distributors loyal to Fuji, Kodak trucked film into Nagano and subsidized a local entrepreneur to open a Kodak store right next to Nagano's leading Fuji dealer. It installed its own film processing lab in Nagano to meet the needs of Olympic photographers and visitors. It flooded the town with Olympic-themed outdoor advertisements, outfitted local buses with photos of its products, and slashed its prices. Special promotions offering Olympic pins for purchasers of Kodak film provided further enticements for local Fuji-loyal shutterbugs to try Kodak film. Fuji was forced to cut its own prices in the area in response, something which it rarely does in the Japanese market. Through these efforts, Kodak increased its share of the Nagano market to 20 percent, double its share of the Japanese market as a whole.

Ironically, Kodak has been an official sponsor of every Olympic games since 1896, except one: the 1984 Summer Games in Los Angeles. At those games, Fuji was the official sponsor. Many industry experts trace Fuji's success in the U.S. market to its sponsorship of those games, which gave it instant visibility in the huge U.S. market and doubled its U.S. market share in the space of four years. Kodak obviously hopes that lightning will strike twice, and that it too can use the Olympic games to boost its profits and market share in the home market of its chief rival.

Sources: "Kodak and U.S. Government Team Up for New Drive on Japan's Film Market," *Wall Street Journal*, February 4, 1998, p. A4; "A Film War Breaks Out in Nagano," *Wall Street Journal*, February 3, 1998, p. B1; "A Dark Moment for Kodak," *Business Week*, August 4, 1997, p. 30.

Owning Intellectual Property Rights. A firm that owns an intellectual property right—a trademark, brand name, patent, or copyright—often gains advantages over its competitors. For example, copyright laws require foreign film distributors and movie theaters that want to show *Titanic* to buy the right to do so from Paramount and Twentieth Century Fox, the holders of the movie's distribution rights. Owning prestigious brand names enables Ireland's Waterford Wedgewood Company, France's Louis Vuitton, and Canada's Seagram Company to charge premium prices for their upscale products. And Coca-Cola and PepsiCo compete for customers worldwide on the basis of their trademarks and brand names.

Investing in Research and Development. Research and development (R&D) is a major component of the total costs of high-technology products. For example, Boeing spent $2 billion developing the 747 jet and $4.5 billion designing its new 777 aircraft.[19] Firms in the computer, pharmaceutical, and semiconductor industries also spend large amounts on R&D to maintain their competitiveness. Because of such large "entry" costs, other firms often hesitate to compete against these established firms. Thus the firm that acts first often gains a **first-mover advantage.**

However, knowledge does not have a nationality. Firms that invest up front and secure the first-mover advantage have the opportunity to dominate the world market for goods that are intensive in R&D. According to the global strategic rivalry theory, trade flows may be determined by which firms make the necessary R&D expenditures. Why is the United States a large exporter of commercial aircraft? Because Boeing is one of the few firms willing to spend the large sums of money required to develop new aircraft and because Boeing just happens to be headquartered in the United States.

Firms with large domestic markets may have an advantage over their foreign rivals in high-technology markets because they often are able to obtain quicker and richer feedback from customers. With this feedback they can fine-tune their R&D efforts, thus enabling them to better meet the needs of their domestic customers. This knowledge can then be utilized to serve foreign customers. For example, U.S. agricultural chemical producers such as Monsanto and Eli Lilly have an advantage over Japanese rivals in developing soybean pesticides because the U.S. market for such pesticides is large while the Japanese market is small. Knowledge gained in the U.S. pesticide market can be readily transferred to meet the needs of Japanese farmers. Often firms will locate their R&D and marketing facilities near important customers. For example, DuPont wanted to be closer to French farmers, who constitute Europe's largest market for pesticides and herbicides, so it moved the European headquarters of its agricultural chemicals division from Geneva to Paris.[20]

Achieving Economies of Scale or Scope. Economies of scale or scope offer firms another opportunity to obtain a sustainable competitive advantage in international markets. **Economies of scale** occur when a product's average costs decrease as the number of units produced increases. **Economies of scope** occur when a firm's average costs decrease as the number of different products it sells increases. Firms that are able to achieve economies of scale or scope enjoy low average costs, which give them a competitive advantage over their global rivals. For example, France's Michelin Company, the world's largest tire producer, has aggressively expanded its capacity in order to capture economies of scale in production, distribution, and marketing. Sony has sought economies of scope by broadening its consumer electronics product line. It uses its reputation as an innovative, high-quality producer of such goods as televisions to help sell camcorders, VCRs, and CD players.

Exploiting the Experience Curve. Another source of firm-specific advantages in international trade is exploitation of the experience curve. For certain types of products, production costs decline as the firm gains more experience in manufacturing the product. For example, the cost of constructing Liberty Ships in World War II declined as employees gained more experience in fabricating the ships. Boeing, with its vast experience in coordinating the manufacture of complex, sophisticated aircraft, benefits similarly from this phenomenon.

The presence of an experience curve may in fact govern global competition within an industry. For example, a strong experience curve exists in semiconductor chip production. Unit cost reductions of 25–30 percent with each doubling of a firm's cumulative chip production are not uncommon.[21] Any firm attempting to be a low-cost producer of so-called commodity chips—such as 16MB memory chips—can achieve that goal only if it moves further along the experience curve than its rivals do. Both U.S. and Asian chip manufacturers have often priced their new products below current production costs in order to capture the sales necessary to generate the production experience that will in turn enable them to lower future production costs. Because of their technological leadership in manufacturing and their aggressive, price-cutting pricing strategies, Asian semiconductor manufacturers such as NEC and Samsung dominate the production of low-cost, standardized semiconductor chips.[22] On the other hand, innovative U.S. semiconductor firms such as Intel and Motorola utilize the experience curve to maintain leadership in the production of higher-priced, proprietary chips, such as the Pentium II chips that form the brains of newer microcomputers.

Porter's National Competitive Advantage

The most recent contribution to international trade theory comes from Harvard Business School professor Michael Porter. In *The Competitive Advantage of Nations,* an influential book published in 1990, Porter develops the **theory of national competitive advantage,** which states that success in international trade comes from the interaction of four country- and firm-specific elements: factor conditions, demand conditions, related and supporting industries, and firm strategy, structure, and rivalry. Porter represents these four elements as the four corners of a diamond (see Fig. 3.4).

Factor Conditions. A country's endowment of factors of production affects its ability to compete internationally. While the importance of factor endowments was the centerpiece of the Hecksher-Ohlin theory, Porter goes beyond the basic factors considered by the classical trade theorists—land, labor, capital—to include more advanced factors such as the educational level of the work force and the quality of the country's infrastructure. His work stresses the role of factor creation through training, research, and innovation.

Demand Conditions. The existence of a large, sophisticated domestic consumer base often stimulates the development and distribution of innovative products, as firms struggle for dominance in their domestic market. But in meeting their domestic customers' needs firms continually develop and fine-tune products that also can be marketed internationally. Thus pioneering firms can stay ahead of their international competitors as well. For example, Japanese consumer electronics producers maintain a competitive edge internationally because of the willingness of Japan's large, well-off middle class to buy the latest electronic creations of Sony, Toshiba, and Matsushita. After being fine-tuned in the domestic market, new models of Japanese camcorders, big screen TVs, and VCRs are sold to eager European and North American consumers.

FIGURE 3.4

Porter's Diamond of National Competitive Advantage

Source: Reprinted by permission of *Harvard Business Review*. An exhibit from "The Competitive Advantage of Nations" by Michael E. Porter, March/April 1990. Copyright © 1990 by the President and Fellows of Harvard College; all rights reserved.

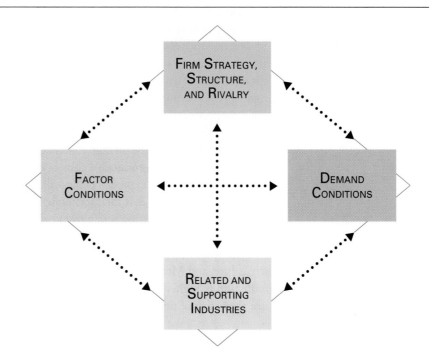

Related and Supporting Industries. The emergence of an industry often stimulates the development of local suppliers eager to meet that industry's production, marketing, and distribution needs. An industry located close to its suppliers will enjoy better communication and the exchange of cost-saving ideas and inventions with those suppliers. Competition among these input suppliers leads to lower prices, higher-quality products, and technological innovations in the input market, in turn reinforcing the industry's competitive advantage in world markets. For example, as we noted earlier, Apple's path-breaking personal computer was first made in Steve Jobs's California garage in the mid-1970s. As demand for personal computers exploded, supplier firms located in the Silicon Valley in order to be closer to Apple and other personal computer manufacturers. The local availability of sophisticated software, disk drive, and computer chip suppliers strengthened the competitive advantage of California personal computer manufacturers in world markets.

Ironically, the suppliers may outlive the original industry. For example, Houston, Texas, became the center of the oil industry after the discovery of oil at Spindletop in 1901. While Texas is no longer a leading oil producer, the technologies developed during boom times by Houston oilfield services firms in such diverse areas as seismological exploration, maritime drilling, and oilfield firefighting have enabled those firms to remain international leaders in these markets.

Firm Strategy, Structure, and Rivalry. The domestic environment in which firms compete shapes their ability to compete in international markets. To survive, firms facing vigorous competition domestically must continuously strive to reduce costs, boost product quality, raise productivity, and develop innovative products. Firms that have been tested in this way often develop the skills needed to succeed internationally. Further, many of the investments they made in order to succeed in the domestic market (for example, in R&D, quality control, brand image, and employee training) are transferable to international markets at low cost. Such firms have an edge as they expand abroad. Thus, according to Porter's theory, the international success of Japanese automakers and consumer electronics goods manufacturers and of U.S. personal computer manufacturers is aided by intense domestic competition in these firms' home countries.

Porter holds that national policies may also affect firms' international strategies and opportunities in more subtle ways. Consider the German automobile market. German labor costs are very high, so German automakers find it difficult to compete internationally on the basis of price. But, as most auto enthusiasts know, no speed limits exist on Germany's famed *autobahns.* So German automakers such as Daimler-Benz, Porsche, and BMW have chosen to compete on the basis of quality and high performance by engineering chassis, engines, brakes, and suspensions that can withstand the stresses of high-speed driving. Consequently these firms dominate the world market for high-performance automobiles.

Porter's theory is a hybrid: it blends the traditional country-based theories that emphasize factor endowments with the firm-based theories that focus on the actions of individual firms. Countries (or their governments) play a critical role in creating an environment that can aid or harm firms' ability to compete internationally, but firms are the actors that actually participate in international trade. Some firms succeed internationally; others don't. Porsche, Daimler-Benz, and BMW successfully grasped the opportunity presented by Germany's decision to allow unlimited speeds on its highways and captured the high-performance niche of the worldwide automobile industry. But Volkswagen and Opel chose to focus on the broader middle segment of the German automobile market, ultimately limiting their international success.

In summary, no single theory of international trade explains all trade flows among countries. The classical, country-based theories are useful in explaining interindustry trade of homogeneous, undifferentiated products such as agricultural goods, raw materials, and processed goods like steel and aluminum. The firm-based theories are more helpful in understanding intraindustry trade of heterogeneous, differentiated goods, such as Sony televisions and Caterpillar bulldozers, many of which are sold on the basis of their brand names and reputations. And, in many ways, Porter's theory synthesizes the features of the existing country-based and firm-based theories.

Overview of International Investment

As we have discussed, international business takes many forms, trade being the most obvious. The second major form of international business activity is international investment, whereby residents of one country supply capital to a second country. Sometimes trade and investment are *substitutes* for each other. For example, Honda's plants in the United States act as a substitute for international trade because they allow Honda to export fewer cars and parts from its Japanese plants to the United States, thereby reducing international trade. At other times, international trade and investment may be *complementary.* For example, in order to reduce production costs, Compaq Computer, headquartered in Houston, Texas, operates two factories in Scotland's "Silicon

Glen"—the region between Glasgow and Edinburgh where 10 percent of the world's personal computers are produced.[23] U.S.-bound exports from Compaq's Scottish factories illustrate the complementary relationship between international trade and investment.

Types of International Investments

International investment, as discussed in Chapter 1, is divided into two categories: portfolio investment and foreign direct investment (FDI). The distinction between the two rests on the question of control: does the investor seek an active management role in the firm or merely a return from a passive investment?

Portfolio investments represent passive holdings of securities such as foreign stocks, bonds, or other financial assets, none of which entail active management or control of the securities' issuer by the investor. Modern finance theory suggests that foreign portfolio investments will be motivated by attempts to seek an attractive rate of return as well as the reduction of risk that can come from geographically diversifying one's investment portfolio. Sophisticated money managers in New York, London, Frankfurt, Tokyo, and other financial centers are well aware of the advantages of international diversification. In 1996 private U.S. citizens purchased $108 billion of foreign securities, bringing their total holdings of such securities to $1.3 trillion. Foreign private investors purchased $307 billion of U.S. corporate, federal, state, and local securities, raising their total holdings of such securities to $1.8 trillion.[24]

Foreign direct investment (FDI) is acquisition of foreign assets for the purpose of controlling them. U.S. government statisticians define FDI as "ownership or control of 10 percent or more of an enterprise's voting securities . . . or the equivalent interest in an unincorporated U.S. business."[25] Perhaps the most historically significant FDI in the United States was the $24 Dutch explorer Peter Minuet paid local Native Americans for Manhattan Island.[26] The result: New York City, one of the world's leading financial and commercial centers.

FDI may take many forms, including purchase of existing assets in a foreign country, new investment in property, plant, and equipment, and participation in a joint venture with a local partner. An example of the first form is Ford's 1990 purchase of Jaguar Motor Company for $2.5 billion, after a takeover battle in which Ford fought for management and control of Jaguar's prestigious line of fine automobiles. The second form is illustrated by Toyota's $800 million investment in new property, plant, and equipment for its Georgetown, Kentucky, automobile assembly facility. The third form is demonstrated by Caterpillar's joint venture with Mitsubishi Heavy Industries to produce and sell earth-moving equipment in Japan.

Foreign Direct Investment and the United States

Like international trade, FDI mostly occurs among the developed countries (refer back to Table 1.2). The stock of FDI in the United States at the end of 1996 totaled $630 billion, with $77 billion of new investment occurring that year (see Table 3.4a). The United Kingdom was the most important source of this FDI, accounting for $142.6 billion, or 22.6 percent, of the total. The countries listed by name in Table 3.4a account for 88 percent of total FDI in the United States.

TABLE 3.4

Patterns of FDI for the United States, end of 1996 (billions of dollars)

a. Sources of FDI in the United States

United Kingdom	$142.6
Japan	118.1
Netherlands	73.8
Germany	62.2
Canada	53.8
France	49.3
Switzerland	35.1
Bermuda, the Bahamas, and other Caribbean islands	16.6
Other European countries	41.6
All other countries	36.9
Total	$630.0

b. Destinations of FDI from the United States

United Kingdom	$ 142.6
Canada	91.6
Bermuda, the Bahamas, and other Caribbean islands	52.5
Netherlands	44.7
Germany	44.3
Japan	39.6
Switzerland	35.8
France	34.0
Other European countries	98.2
All other countries	213.2
Total	$ 796.5

Source: *Survey of Current Business*, July 1997, pp. 36 and 39.

The stock of FDI by U.S. residents in foreign countries totaled $796.5 billion at the end of 1996, with $87.8 billion of new investment in that year (see Table 3.4b). Most of this FDI was in other developed countries, particularly the United Kingdom ($142.6 billion) and Canada ($91.6 billion). The countries listed by name in Table 3.4b account for 61 percent of total FDI from the United States.

Looking at Table 3.4, you may wonder why Bermuda, the Bahamas, and other small Caribbean islands are so important. They serve as offshore financial centers, which we'll discuss in Chapter 5. Many U.S. companies set up finance subsidiaries in such centers to take advantage of low taxes and business-friendly regulations. Similarly, many financial services companies from other countries establish such subsidiaries as the legal owners of their U.S. operations.

Over the past decade outward FDI has remained larger than inward FDI for the United States (see Fig. 3.5), but both categories have tripled in size. While inward and outward flows of FDI are not perfectly matched, the pattern is clear: most FDI is made by and destined for the most prosperous countries. In the next section we discuss how this pattern suggests the crucial role MNCs play in FDI.

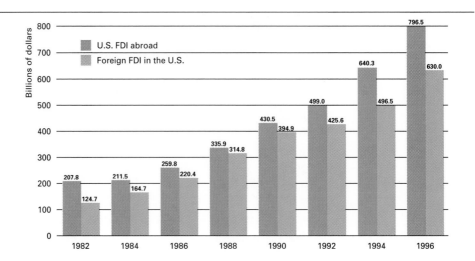

FIGURE 3.5

Outward and Inward U.S. FDI, 1982–1996

Source: *Survey of Current Business*, July 1997, p. 35.

International Investment Theories

Why does FDI occur? A sophomore taking his or her first finance course might answer with the obvious: average rates of return are higher in foreign markets. Yet given the pattern of FDI between countries that we just discussed, this answer is not satisfactory. Canada and the United Kingdom are both major sources of FDI *in* the United States and important destinations for FDI *from* the United States. Average rates of return in Canada and the United Kingdom cannot be simultaneously below that of the United States (which would justify inward U.S. FDI) and above that of the United States (which would justify outward U.S. FDI). The same pattern of two-way investment occurs on an industry basis. In 1996, for example, U.S. firms invested $123 million in the chemical industry in Belgium, while Belgian firms invested $223 million in the U.S. chemical industry. This pattern cannot be explained by national or industry differences in rates of return. We must search for another explanation for FDI.

Ownership Advantages

More powerful explanations for FDI focus on the role of the firm. Initially researchers explored how firm ownership of competitive advantages affected FDI. The **ownership advantage theory** suggests that a firm owning a valuable asset that creates a competitive advantage domestically can use that advantage to penetrate foreign markets through FDI. The asset could be, for example, a superior technology, a well-known brand name, or economies of scale.[27] This theory is consistent with the observed patterns of international and intraindustry FDI discussed earlier in this chapter. Caterpillar, for example, built factories in Asia, Europe, Australia, South America, and North America in order to exploit proprietary technologies and its brand name. Its chief rival, Komatsu, has constructed plants in Asia, Europe, and the United States for the same reason.

Internalization Theory

The ownership advantage theory only partly explains why FDI occurs. It does not explain why a firm would choose to enter a foreign market via FDI rather than exploit its ownership advantages internationally through other means, such as exporting its products, franchising a brand name, or licensing technology to foreign firms. For example, McDonald's has successfully internationalized by franchising its fast-food operations outside the United States, while Boeing has relied on exporting in order to serve its foreign customers.

Internalization theory addresses this question. In doing so it relies heavily on the concept of transaction costs. **Transaction costs** are the costs of entering into a transaction, that is, those connected to negotiating, monitoring, and enforcing a contract. A firm must decide whether it is better to own and operate its own factory overseas or to contract with a foreign firm to do this through a franchise, licensing, or supply agreement. **Internalization theory** suggests that FDI is more likely to occur—that is, international production will be *internalized* within the firm—when the costs of negotiating, monitoring, and enforcing a contract with a second firm are high. For example, Toyota's primary competitive advantages are its reputation for high quality and its sophisticated manufacturing techniques—neither of which are easily conveyed by contract. So Toyota has chosen to maintain ownership of its overseas automobile assembly plants. Conversely, the internalization theory holds, when transaction costs are low, firms are more likely to contract with outsiders and internationalize by licensing their brand names or franchising their business operations. For example, McDonald's is the premier expert in the United States in devising easily enforceable franchising agreements. Because McDonald's is so successful in reducing transaction costs between itself and its franchisees, it has continued to rely on franchising for its international operations.

Dunning's Eclectic Theory

Although internalization theory addresses why firms choose FDI as the mode for entering international markets, it ignores the question of why production, either by the company or a contractor, should be located abroad. That is, is there a location advantage to producing abroad? This issue was incorporated by John Dunning in his **eclectic theory,** which combines ownership advantage, location advantage, and internalization advantage to form a unified theory of FDI. This theory recognizes that FDI reflects both *international* business activity and business activity *internal* to the firm.[28] According to Dunning, FDI will occur when three conditions are satisfied:[29]

1 *Ownership advantage.* The firm must own some unique competitive advantage that overcomes the disadvantages of competing with foreign firms on their home turfs. This advantage may be a brand name, ownership of proprietary technology, the benefits of economies of scale, and so on. Caterpillar enjoys all three of these advantages in competing in Brazil against local firms.

2 *Location advantage.* Undertaking the business activity must be more profitable in a foreign location than undertaking it in a domestic location. For example, Caterpillar produces bulldozers in Brazil to enjoy lower labor costs and avoid high tariff walls on goods exported from its U.S. factories.

3 *Internalization advantage.* The firm must benefit more from controlling the foreign business activity than from hiring an independent local company to provide the service. Control is advantageous, for example, when it is expensive to monitor and enforce the contractual performance of the local company,[30] when the local company may misappropriate proprietary technology, or when the firm's reputation and brand name could be jeopardized by poor behavior by the local company. All these factors are important to Caterpillar.

Factors Influencing Foreign Direct Investment

Given the complexity of the global economy and the diversity of opportunities firms face in different countries, it is not surprising that numerous factors may influence a firm's decision to undertake FDI. These can be classified as supply factors, demand factors, and political factors (see Table 3.5).

Supply Factors

FDI may be motivated by a firm's efforts to control its own costs. Some of the most important supply factors that may influence a firm's decision to undertake FDI are production costs, logistics, availability of natural resources, and access to key technology.

Production Costs. Firms often undertake foreign direct investment in order to lower production costs. Foreign locations may be more attractive than domestic sites because of lower land prices, tax rates, or commercial real estate rents or because of better availability and lower cost of skilled or unskilled labor. For example, Germany's Freyunger Loeffler Kunststoffwerke invested $2 million to build a factory in the Czech town of Ckyne to produce plastic plant pots and bathroom fixtures, just 27 miles from its other factory in Bavaria. The advantage to this small family-owned company was lower labor costs; the company expects to pay its Czech workers only $220 per month, a tenth of what it pays its German labor force.[31] Similarly, GumSung Plastics, a small family-owned Korean firm, invested $8 million in a factory in Mexicali, Mexico, to produce plastic casings for

TABLE 3.5

Factors Affecting the FDI Decision

SUPPLY FACTORS	DEMAND FACTORS	POLITICAL FACTORS
Production costs	Customer access	Avoidance of trade barriers
Logistics	Marketing advantages	Economic development incentives
Resource availability	Exploitation of competitive	
Access to technology	advantages	
	Customer mobility	

TVs and computer monitors. By so doing, the company reduced its labor costs by two thirds.[32]

As communities grow (or shrink), their attractiveness or unattractiveness as potential production sites changes. For example, South Korea was once a production center for low-priced sneakers sold by the millions by discounters such as Kmart and Wal-Mart. But the rising prosperity and wages of South Koreans eliminated the country's ability to compete at the low end of the market. South Korea's sneaker industry has contracted and now concentrates on producing more expensive, fashion-oriented sneakers under license from Nike, Reebok, and other major companies. China now dominates the low end of the sneaker market.

Technological change also affects production costs and the attractiveness of FDI. McGraw-Hill moved the maintenance of the circulation files of its 16 magazines from the New York City area to Loughrea, Ireland, to take advantage of Ireland's low labor costs, English-speaking population, generous tax abatements, and sophisticated fiber-optic telephone network. Technology has permitted this back-office operation to be physically housed in Ireland but directly linked to McGraw-Hill's mainframe computers at its Hightstown, New Jersey, corporate headquarters. As an added benefit the Irish facility can utilize the corporate mainframe computers during off-peak times, since Ireland is five time zones ahead of New Jersey.[33]

Logistics. If transportation costs are significant, a firm may choose to produce in the foreign market rather than export from domestic factories. For example, Heineken has utilized FDI extensively as part of its internationalization strategy because its products are primarily water. It finds it cheaper to brew its beverages close to where its foreign consumers live than to transport them long distances from its Dutch breweries. International businesses also often make host-country investments in order to reduce distribution costs. For example, Citrovita, a Brazilian producer of orange-juice concentrate, operates a storage and distribution terminal at the Port of Antwerp rather than ship to European grocery chains directly from Brazil. It can take advantage of low ocean shipping rates to transport its goods in bulk from Brazil to the Belgian port. It then uses the Antwerp facility to repackage and distribute concentrate to its customers in France, Germany, and the Benelux countries.

Availability of Natural Resources. Firms may make FDI to access natural resources that are critical to their operations. For example, an integrated international oil company explores, produces, refines, and markets petroleum-based products. Because of the decrease in oil production in the United States, U.S.-based international oil companies have been forced to make significant investments worldwide in order to obtain new oil reserves. Often international businesses negotiate with host governments to obtain access to raw materials in return for FDI. For example, Manila's Ayala Corporation built tuna canneries on the northern Indonesian island of Sulawesi as part of a deal with the Indonesian government to allow Philippine tuna boats based in the southern Philippine island of Mindanao to fish its territorial waters (see Map 3.1). This deal in turn has benefited both countries: over 8000 people in the Philippines and Indonesia are now employed in nine canneries and on 600 fishing vessels, part of an operation that annually exports $34 million of tuna to North American and European consumers.[34]

MAP 3.1

The Tuna Industry in Indonesia and the Philippines

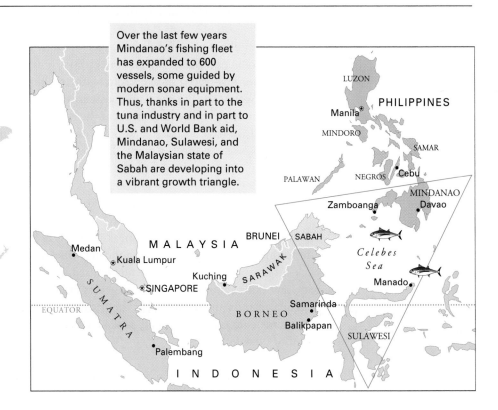

Over the last few years Mindanao's fishing fleet has expanded to 600 vessels, some guided by modern sonar equipment. Thus, thanks in part to the tuna industry and in part to U.S. and World Bank aid, Mindanao, Sulawesi, and the Malaysian state of Sabah are developing into a vibrant growth triangle.

Access to Key Technology. Another motive for FDI is to gain access to technology. Firms may find it more advantageous to acquire ownership interests in an existing firm than to assemble an in-house group of research scientists to develop or reproduce an emerging technology. For example, many Swiss pharmaceutical manufacturers have invested in small U.S. biogenetics companies as an inexpensive means of obtaining cutting-edge biotechnology. Similarly, Taiwan's Acer Inc., a manufacturer of personal computers and workstations, paid $100 million in the early 1990s for a pair of Silicon Valley computer companies in hopes of leveraging their technology and existing distribution networks to boost Acer's share of the U.S. personal computer market.[35]

Demand Factors

Firms also may engage in FDI in order to expand the market for their products. The demand factors that encourage FDI include customer access, marketing advantages, exploitation of competitive advantages, and customer mobility.

Customer Access. Many types of international business require firms to have a physical presence in the market. For example, fast-food restaurants and retailers must provide convenient access to their outlets for competitive reasons. KFC can't provide its freshly prepared fried chicken to Japanese customers from its restaurants in the United States; it must locate outlets in Japan to do so. Toys 'R' Us's success in broadening its customer base is due to its opening of a large number of new stores worldwide. Similarly, Aetna invested $390 million to create a joint venture with Brazil's largest insurance company, Sul America Seguros, to market life insurance to Brazil's growing middle class.[36]

Marketing Advantages. FDI may generate several types of marketing advantages. The physical presence of a factory may enhance the visibility of a foreign firm's products in the host market. If production costs are lower in the host market, the firm may be able to reduce the price of its products to host-country consumers, thereby expanding its sales. The foreign firm also gains from "buy local" attitudes of host-country consumers. For example, through ads in such magazines as *Time* and *Sports Illustrated*, Toyota has publicized the beneficial impact of its U.S. factories and input purchases on the U.S. economy (see Fig. 3.6). Firms may also engage in FDI to improve their customer service. Taiwan's Delta Products, which makes battery packs for laptop computers, was concerned that it could not respond quickly and flexibly to meet the changing needs of its U.S. customers from its factories in China and Thailand. As one of its executives noted, if you "build in the Far East, you're too far away. You can't do a last-moment modification while the product is on the ocean." Accordingly, Delta shifted some of its production to a Mexican factory just over the border from Nogales, Arizona, in order to better serve its U.S. customers.[37]

Exploitation of Competitive Advantages. FDI may be a firm's best means to exploit a competitive advantage that it already enjoys. An owner of a valuable trademark, brand name, or technology may choose to operate in foreign countries rather than export to them. Often this decision depends on the product's nature. For example, Pari Mutuel Urbain (PMU) operates 7000 off-track betting facilities in Europe. It developed an ingenious network of computers, on-site terminals, and satellite communications to make it France's seventh-largest service company with annual revenues of $6 billion. PMU's success in harnessing modern communications technology to meet the needs of horse-racing fans has boosted its French business by 25 percent and enabled it to expand its off-track betting operations into Switzerland and Monaco.[38]

Customer Mobility. A firm's FDI also may be motivated by FDI of its customers or clients. If one of a firm's existing customers builds a foreign factory, the firm may decide to locate a new facility of its own nearby, thereby enabling it to continue to supply its customer promptly and attentively. Equally as important, it reduces the possibility that some competitor in the host country will step in and steal the customer. For example, Japanese parts suppliers to the major Japanese automakers have responded to the construction of Japanese-owned automobile assembly plants in the United States by building their own factories, warehouses, and research facilities there. Their need to locate facilities in the United States is magnified by the automakers' use of JIT inventory management techniques, which minimize the amount of parts inventory held at an assembly plant, thus severely disadvantaging a parts-supply facility located in Japan. Likewise, after Samsung decided to construct and operate an electronics factory in northeast England, six of its Korean parts suppliers also established factories in the vicinity.[39]

Similar problems confront firms in the service sector. As manufacturing firms internationalize, service providers need to expand their horizons to meet their

Toyota Ad on the Economic Benefits of the Firm's FDI in the United States

Source: Toyota Motor Corporate Services of North America, Inc. Reprinted with permission.

customers' needs. For example, accounting giants Peat Marwick Mitchell and KMG merged in 1987. The merger produced KPMG, one of the world's largest accounting firms, with 6320 partners and annual revenues of $8.1 billion. KPMG operates 840 offices in 155 countries, so as its clients internationalize, it is ready to meet their local accounting requirements, no matter how far-flung their global operations.

Political Factors

Political factors may also enter into a firm's decision to undertake FDI. Firms may invest in a foreign country in order to avoid host-country trade barriers or to take advantage of host-government economic development incentives.

Avoidance of Trade Barriers. Firms often build foreign facilities in order to avoid trade barriers. In the late 1970s and early 1980s, for example, U.S. automakers lobbied Congress to limit Japanese automobile imports. Before Congress could act, the Japanese government announced in 1981 that it would impose a voluntary export restraint (VER) on the Japanese automakers, thereby limiting the number of Japanese autos imported into the United States. To get around the VER, the Japanese auto companies built assembly plants in the United States. This move also fractured the political coalition in the United States that was developing against them. U.S. workers employed in the Japanese-owned assembly plants now provide new political support in the United States for their employers. Similarly, in 1997 the Fuji Photo Film Company invested $200 million in its Greenwood, South Carolina, factory complex to begin manufacturing film for sale in the United States. Previously, the company supplied film to its U.S. customers from its factories in the Netherlands and Japan. By producing in the United States rather than exporting to it, Fuji avoided a 3.7 percent tariff on film imposed by the United States and deflected claims by Kodak that Fuji was unfairly "dumping" Japanese-made film in the U.S. market (dumping is explained in Chapter 6).[40]

Economic Development Incentives. Most democratically elected governments—local, state, and national—are vitally concerned with promoting the economic welfare of their citizens, many of whom are, of course, voters. Many governments offer incentives to firms to induce them to locate new facilities in the governments' jurisdictions. Governmental incentives that can be an important catalyst for FDI include reduced utility rates, employee training programs, infrastructure additions (such as new roads and railroad spurs), and tax reductions or tax holidays. Often MNCs benefit from bidding wars among communities eager to attract them and the jobs they bring. Siemens, for example, is investing $380 million to construct and operate a memory chip factory near Oporto, Portugal as a result of economic development incentives granted by Portugal and the European Union, which will cover approximately 40 percent of its investment and training costs. When fully operational, the factory will create 750 jobs and 150 million 16MB dynamic random access memory chips annually.[41] Likewise, Alabama provided Daimler-Benz with $253 million in incentives in order to capture that firm's new plant.

CHAPTER REVIEW

Summary

International trade is an important form of international business—over $6.3 trillion of goods and services were traded between residents of different countries in 1996. Most of this trade involved the wealthy Quad countries. International trade affects domestic economies both directly and indirectly. Exports stimulate additional demand for products, thus generating income and employment gains. Imports lower consumer prices and pressure domestic firms to become more efficient and productive.

Because of trade's importance to businesses and governments worldwide, scholars have offered numerous explanations for its existence. The earliest theories, such as absolute advantage, comparative advantage, and relative factor endowments, relied on characteristics of countries to explain patterns of exports and imports. These country-based theories help explain trade in undifferentiated goods such as wheat, sugar, and steel.

Coincident with the rise of the MNC, postwar research focused on firm-based explanations for international trade. Country similarity, product life cycle, and global strategic rivalry theories focus on the firm as the agent for generating trade and investment decisions. These firm-based theories help explain intraindustry trade and trade in differentiated goods such as automobiles, personal care products, and consumer electronics goods.

International investment is the second major way in which firms participate in international business. International investments fall into two categories: portfolio investments and FDI. FDI has risen in importance as MNCs have increased in size and number.

Dunning's eclectic theory suggests that FDI will occur when three conditions are met: (1) the firm possesses a competitive advantage that allows it to overcome the disadvantage of competing on the foreign firm's home turf, (2) the foreign location is superior to a domestic location, and (3) the firm finds it cheaper (because of high transaction costs) to produce the product itself rather than hire a foreign firm to do so.

Numerous factors can influence a firm's decision to undertake FDI. Some FDI may be undertaken to reduce the firm's costs. Such supply factors include production costs, logistics, availability of natural resources, and access to key technology. The decision to engage in FDI may be affected by such demand factors as developing access to new customers, obtaining marketing advantages through local production, exploiting competitive advantages, and maintaining nearness to customers as they internationalize their operations. Political considerations may also play a role in FDI. Often firms use FDI to avoid host-country trade barriers or to capture economic development incentives offered by host-country governments.

Review Questions

1. What is international trade? Why does it occur?

2. How do the theories of absolute advantage and comparative advantage differ?

3. Why are Leontief's findings called a paradox?

4. How useful are country-based theories in explaining international trade?

5. How do interindustry and intraindustry trade differ?

6. Explain the impact of the product life cycle on international trade and international investment.

7. What are the primary sources of the competitive advantages firms use to compete in international markets?

8. What are the four elements of Porter's diamond of national competitive advantage?

9. How do portfolio investments and FDI differ?

10. What are the three parts of Dunning's eclectic theory?

11. How do political factors influence international trade and investment?

Questions for Discussion

1. In our example of France's trading wine to Japan for clock radios, we arbitrarily assumed the countries would trade at a price ratio of 1 bottle of wine for 2 clock radios. Over what range of prices can trade occur between the two countries? (*Hint*: In the absence of trade what is the price of clock radios in terms of wine in France? In Japan?) Does your answer differ if you use Table 3.2 instead of Table 3.1?

2. In the public debate over NAFTA's ratification Ross Perot said he heard a "giant sucking sound" of U.S. jobs headed south because of low wage rates in Mexico. Using the theory of comparative advantage, discuss whether Perot's fears are valid.

3. Why is intraindustry trade not predicted by country-based theories of trade?

4. **a.** What factors do you think Siemens considered in deciding to build a new semiconductor chip factory in Portugal? In Oporto?

   b. Who benefits and who loses from the new plant in Portugal?

   c. Is the firm's decision to build the new plant consistent with Dunning's eclectic theory?

BUILDING GLOBAL SKILLS

The U.S. market for computers is dominated by U.S. firms such as IBM, Apple, Compaq, Dell, and Hewlett-Packard. The U.S. market for consumer electronics is dominated by Japanese firms and brands such as Sony, JVC, Panasonic, Mitsubishi, and Toshiba. However, the U.S. automobile market includes both strong domestic firms such as Ford and Chrysler and formidable Japanese competitors such as Toyota and Honda.

Your instructor will divide the class into groups of four or five and assign each group one of the three industries noted above. To begin, discuss within your group your individual views as to why the specific state of affairs described above exists.

Next analyze the industry assigned to your group from the standpoint of each country-based and firm-based theory of international trade discussed in this chapter. Try to agree on which theory is the best predictor and which is the worst predictor of reality for your specific industry.

Next reconvene as a class. Each group should select a spokesperson. Each spokesperson should indicate the industry that the person's group dis-

cussed and identify the best and worst theories selected. Note the points on which the groups who analyzed the same industries agree.

Finally, separate again into your small groups and discuss the areas of common disagreements. Also discuss the following questions:

1. Do some theories work better than others for different industries? Why?

2. What other industries can you think of that fit one of the three patterns noted in the opening paragraph?

3. Do the same theories work as well in making predictions for those industries?

4. Based on what you know about the Japanese market, decide whether the same pattern of competitiveness that exists in the United States for the computer, consumer electronics, and automobile industries also holds true for that market. Why or why not?

WORKING WITH THE WEB: Building Global Internet Skills

Export Data Web Sites: the Good, the Bad, and the Ugly

Information about trade and investment flows between countries is often of great use to market researchers. For example, a Canadian maker of machine tools who wishes to export to South America can gain insights into that market by examining the volume of machine tools imported to the region. Alternatively, this firm may specialize in outfitting new factories and have an existing customer base among Canadian, U.S., and U.K. auto parts firms. Accordingly, it needs to carefully monitor foreign investments made by auto parts firms from these three countries.

Numerous web sites, some of which can be accessed at the textbook's web site, provide informa-

tion about international trade and investment. Some of these web sites present highly aggregated data about trade and investment flows between countries. Others provide industry-level data. And others, quite frankly, are pretty useless.

The assignment: pick an industry and a product, such as automotive parts/mufflers or agriculture/cotton. Locate five web sites that contain data about trade or foreign investment in the industry and the product that you selected. Which ones would be the most useful to businesses? Which ones are of little use? Defend your answers.

CLOSING CASE

Komatsu's Challenge[42]

This chapter opened with a discussion of the international business activities of Caterpillar, Inc. But Cat's success has not gone unchallenged. For the past three decades its preeminence has been imperiled by well-designed, high-quality goods produced by Komatsu Ltd., a relative newcomer to the industry. Komatsu had virtually no presence in the key U.S. market in 1970. Within fifteen years it had captured almost 20 percent of Cat's home turf.

Komatsu is the parent corporation of a group of sixty-two affiliated companies that produce construction equipment and industrial machinery. Komatsu's 1996 sales amounted to $9.4 billion. Founded in 1921, it has focused on manufacturing high-quality products and offering strong product support. Until Komatsu decided to attack the construction equipment market dominated by Caterpillar, its main strength lay in the production of forklifts and other materials-handling equipment, for which Komatsu is generally recognized as the world leader.

Like many Japanese companies, Komatsu traditionally relied on exports rather than FDI to serve its foreign customers. During its initial assault on the U.S. market in the 1970s, it enjoyed lower wage rates than Caterpillar did. However, during the 1980s its labor-cost advantage began to shrink as wages rose in Japan. Anticipating a rise in the yen's value, which would reduce the profitability of export sales from its Japanese factories, Komatsu began to shift some of its production to overseas plants via FDI. Komatsu built overseas plants in Indonesia (in 1982), Mexico, the United Kingdom, and Brazil and in 1985 completed its first U.S. facility. The foreign plants aided communication with local customers, reduced delivery times, and improved delivery of parts to Komatsu's dealers. In a recent report to its shareholders Komatsu said the goal of its globalization strategies is "full localization" in its key markets of Asia, Europe, and North America.

Komatsu adopted several strategies as it grew from a specialist in forklift trucks to a broad-based pro-ducer of construction equipment. It systematically expanded its product line to help its dealers better compete against Caterpillar's well-established distributors. New products included innovations such as underground construction equipment and underwater robots. It also teamed up with foreign producers. For example, to penetrate the closed Indian market Komatsu established a long-term production arrangement with Bharat Earth Movers, Ltd., an Indian government-owned firm, to produce bulldozers, graders, and excavators. And it entered the Korean market by licensing Dong-A Motor Co. to produce Komatsu-designed dump trucks.

Komatsu is well positioned to exploit the large Japanese construction market. It recognized the growing shortage of skilled workers and so allocated R&D resources to develop labor-saving robots for use at construction sites and increased its production of prefabricated building materials. Komatsu has enjoyed steady growth in sales to the Japanese market. With annual domestic sales of $6.2 billion, it holds a comfortable lead over its chief domestic rival, the partnership between Cat and Mitsubishi Heavy Industries, which sold $3.7 billion of construction equipment in Japan in 1996.

Komatsu's position in the U.S. market is not as comfortable. Like most Japanese manufacturers, its initial postwar successes in North America were attributable to its skilled but low-paid work force that produced quality products at prices that undercut those of U.S. firms. However, Japanese economic growth created labor shortages that in turn forced domestic wages higher. Komatsu enjoyed booming sales in the U.S. market in the early 1980s because of the dollar's high value against the yen. But by the decade's end this exchange-rate advantage had disappeared, and increases in the yen's value relative to the dollar's eroded Komatsu's labor-cost advantage. As the yen continued to rise through the first half of the 1990s, labor costs at Komatsu's Japanese factories were higher than at Caterpillar's U.S. plants. Fortunately, Komatsu's executives had foreseen these difficulties, and had been systematically lessening the company's dependency on its Japanese factories through FDI and licensing arrangements mentioned above. In 1988 they made another important strategic move, forming a 50–50 joint venture with Dresser Industries, one of Caterpillar's primary U.S. rivals. To establish the new company, called Komatsu Dresser, Dresser contributed its existing plants, while Komatsu offered its more advanced machinery and sophisticated manufacturing technology.

Unfortunately, Komatsu was disappointed by Komatsu Dresser's initial performance. Its share of the U.S. construction equipment market quickly fell from 20 percent to 18 percent, while Caterpillar's rose from 34.5 percent to 36.4 percent. Both Komatsu Dresser and Cat were struck by the UAW in late 1991. Hoping to restore peaceful labor relations and output levels, Komatsu Dresser quickly yielded to the union's demands, while Cat's bitter five-month strike gained that firm more flexible work rules that promised improved productivity. In addition, Komatsu Dresser's $200 million program to modernize its factories was dwarfed by Cat's $2.1 billion investment in revitalizing its plants. Further, Komatsu Dresser's dealership network was weaker than Cat's. The net worth of Cat's 65 U.S. dealers is over $2.3 billion; that of Komatsu Dresser's 60 dealers, only $300 million. Consolidating Komatsu's dealers with Dresser's distributors also proved costly, as former Komatsu and former Dresser dealers with overlapping territories battled with each other rather than focusing on the threat from Caterpillar. And U.S.-born managers of Komatsu Dresser were resentful of being excluded from informal Friday evening management gatherings—conducted in Japanese—where key operating decisions often were made.

To remedy these problems, in 1993 Komatsu took over control of Komatsu Dresser, raising its share of the joint venture's equity to 81 percent. Later it renamed the company Komatsu America. This ownership change allowed Komatsu to better integrate Komatsu America's activities with those of the rest of the Komatsu group. For example, Komatsu America designed and produced, in conjunction with Komatsu engineers from Japan, a 150-ton off-highway truck targeted for the global mining industry, which is sold worldwide by Komatsu's local affiliates. Equally important, Komatsu entered into two joint ventures with

Cummins Engines, one of the world's leading producers of diesel engines. While Caterpillar builds and designs most of its own diesel engines, Komatsu did not. Because durable, efficient diesel engines are a critical component of most earth-moving machinery, the joint ventures with Cummins fill an important strategic gap for Komatsu. These efforts appear to be paying off: in 1992 Komatsu Dresser lost $110 million on sales of $844 million. In 1996, under Komatsu ownership and management, Komatsu America boosted its annual revenues to over $1.4 billion.

While Komatsu's management appears to have surmounted the problems caused by the 1985–1995 rise in the yen's value and the initial difficulties generated by the joint venture with Dresser Industries, Komatsu has a way to go before it matches Caterpillar's international success. Of its $9.4 billion in 1996 sales, only $3.2 billion were outside of Japan. Conversely, of Caterpillar's $16.5 billion in 1996 sales, $8.1 billion were outside of the United States. To increase its penetration of these markets, Komatsu will have to go head-to-head against Caterpillar and overcome Cat's stronger international dealership network.

Case Questions

1. How does Komatsu gain from manufacturing abroad rather than exporting from its Japanese plants?

2. How does the yen's decreased value against the dollar since 1995 affect Komatsu's ability to export?

3. This case argues that Komatsu's joint ventures with Cummins Engines are of great strategic significance. Do you agree with this assertion? Are there other ways that Komatsu could acquire diesel engine technology other than through such joint ventures?

4. Caterpillar enjoys a significant advantage over Komatsu in sales outside its home market. How important is it for Komatsu to close this gap in international sales? Would Komatsu be better off if it focused its resources on the Japanese market?

CHAPTER NOTES

1. Caterpillar Inc., *1990 Annual Report,* p. 15.

2. "Caterpillar, UAW Face Renewed Hurdles," *Wall Street Journal,* February 24, 1998, p. A2; Ronald Henkoff, "This Cat Is Acting like a Tiger," *Fortune,* December 19, 1988, pp. 69ff; "Cat vs. Labor: Hardhats, Anyone?" *Business Week,* August 26, 1991, p. 48; Caterpillar Inc., *1996 Annual Report;* "Union and company waging 'holy war,'" *Bryan–College Station Eagle,* August 7, 1994, p. C1.

3. World Trade Organization, "After Two Outstanding Years, World Trade Growth Returned to Earlier Levels."

4. Arthur M. Schlesinger, *The Colonial Merchants and the American Revolution 1763–1776* (New York: Facsimile Library, 1939), pp. 16–20.

5. David Ricardo, *The Principles of Political Economy and Taxation* (Homewood: Irwin, 1963). (Ricardo's book was first published in 1817.)

6. Eli Heckscher, "The Effect of Foreign Trade on the Distribution of Income," reprinted in *Readings in the Theory of International Trade,* eds. H. S. Ellis and L. A. Metzler (Homewood: Irwin, 1949). (Translated into English from the original 1919 Swedish article.)

7. Bertil Ohlin, *Interregional and International Trade* (Cambridge, Mass.: Harvard University Press, 1933).

8. Wassily Leontief, "Domestic Production and Foreign Trade; the American Capital Position Re-examined," reprinted in *Readings in International Economics,* eds. R. Caves and H. Johnson (Homewood: Irwin, 1968).

9. Wassily Leontief, "Factor Proportions and the Structure of American Trade: Further Theoretical and Empirical Analysis," *Review of Economics and Statistics,* Vol. 38 (November 1956), pp. 386–407.

10. Donald B. Keesing, "Labor Skills and Comparative Advantage," *American Economic Review,* Vol. 56 (May 1986), pp. 249–258.

11. F. Clairmonte and J. Cauvanagh, "TNCs: The Ever Grasping Drive," *Development Forum,* 1985.

12. S. B. Linder, *An Essay on Trade and Transformation* (New York: Wiley, 1961).

13. R. Vernon, "International Investment and International Trade in the Product Cycle," *Quarterly Journal of Economics,* Vol. 80 (May 1966), pp. 190–207.

14. Michael Moritz, *The Little Kingdom: The Private Story of Apple Computer* (New York: William Morrow, 1984).

15. Apple Computer, Inc., *1991 Annual Report,* p. 5.

16. P. Krugman, "Intraindustry Specialization and the Gains from Trade," *Journal of Political Economy,* Vol. 89 (October 1981), pp. 959–973.

17. K. Lancaster, "Intra-industry Trade under Perfect Monopolistic Competition," *Journal of International Economics,* Vol. 10 (May 1980), pp. 151–175.

18. Michael W. Pustay, "Toward a Global Airline Industry: Prospects and Impediments," *Logistics and Transportation Review,* Vol. 28, No. 1 (March 1992), pp. 103–128.

19. Laurence S. Kuter, *The Great Gamble: the Boeing 747* (University, Ala.: The University of Alabama Press, 1973), p. vii.

20. Michael E. Porter, "New Global Strategies for Competitive Advantage," *Planning Review,* May/June 1990, p. 14.

21. Andrew R. Dick, "Learning by Doing and Dumping in the Semiconductor Industry," *Journal of Law and Economics,* Vol. 34, No. 1 (April 1991), p. 134.

22. Fred Warshofsky, *The Chip War* (New York: Scribner's, 1989), pp. 131–132.

23. "Scotland becomes high-tech giant," *Houston Chronicle,* May 11, 1992, p. 4B.

24. The FDI statistics for this section are taken from the *Survey of Current Business,* July 1997, pp. 24 ff.

25. A. Quijana, "A Guide to BEA Statistics on Foreign Direct Investment in the United States," *Survey of Current Business,* February 1990, pp. 29–37.

26. Grant T. Hammond, *Countertrade, Offsets and Barter in International Political Economy* (St. Martin's Press: New York, 1990), p. 3.

27. The initial argument was presented in Stephen Hymer's 1960 doctoral dissertation. The full argument is presented in Hymer's *The International Operations of National Firms* (Cambridge, Mass.: M.I.T. Press, 1976).

28. P. Krugman and M. Obstfeld, *International Economics* (Glenview, Ill.: Scott, Foresman, 1988), p. 159.

29. J. Dunning, "Explaining Changing Patterns of International Production: In Defense of the Eclectic Theory," *Oxford Bulletin of Economics and Statistics,* Vol. 41 (November 1979).

30. O. Williamson, *Markets and Hierarchies* (New York: Free Press, 1983).

31. "Smaller Firms Lead German Push East; History Forces Low Profile on Investment," *Wall Street Journal,* June 14, 1995, p. A9.

32. "Asian Investment Floods into Mexican Border Region," *Wall Street Journal,* September 6, 1996, p. A10.

33. "American Firms Send Office Work Abroad to Use Cheaper Labor," *Wall Street Journal,* August 14, 1991, p. A1.

34. Rigoberto Tiglao, "Growth Zones," *Far Eastern Economic Review,* February 10, 1994, pp. 40ff.

35. "Acer Is Still Searching for the Password to the U.S.," *Business Week,* May 18, 1992, p. 129.

36. "Aetna Joins the Crowd of U.S. Insurers Making Investments in Latin America," *Wall Street Journal,* February 14, 1997, p. A15.

37. "Asian Investment Floods into Mexican Border Region," *Wall Street Journal,* September 6, 1996, p. A10.

38. Peter Mikelbank, "I've Got the Cheval Right Here," *Sports Illustrated,* November 11, 1991, pp. 9–10.

39. "Samsung attracts six Korean suppliers," *Financial Times,* April 24, 1996, p. 9.

40. "Fuji, Challenging Kodak, to Make Film in U.S.," *Wall Street Journal,* May 8, 1997, p. A3.

41. "Portugal wins Siemens' chip plant project," *Financial Times,* May 30, 1996, p. 5.

42. Komatsu Ltd., *Annual Report 1996;* "Going for the Lion's Share," *Business Week,* July 18, 1988, p. 71; Komatsu Ltd., *Annual Report 1991,* p. 2; "Maybe Caterpillar Can Pick Up Where It Left Off," *Business Week,* April 27, 1992, p. 35; "Komatsu Throttles Back on Construction Equipment," *Wall Street Journal,* May 13, 1992, p. B4; Larry Green, "Confidence in Tomorrow," *Equipment Management,* April 1990, pp. 30–36; "A Dream Marriage Turns Nightmarish," *Business Week,* April 29, 1991, pp. 94–95.

The International Monetary System and the Balance of Payments

Chapter Outline

History of the international monetary system

The gold standard
The collapse of the gold standard
The Bretton Woods era
The end of the Bretton Woods system
Performance of the international monetary system since 1971

The balance of payments accounting system

The major components of the balance of payments accounting system
The U.S. balance of payments in 1996
Defining balance of payments surpluses and deficits

After studying this chapter you should be able to:

Discuss the role of the international monetary system in promoting international trade and investment.

Explain the evolution and functioning of the gold standard.

Summarize the role of the World Bank Group and the International Monetary Fund in the postwar international monetary system established at Bretton Woods.

Explain the evolution of the flexible exchange-rate system in use since 1971.

Describe the function and structure of the balance of payments accounting system.

Differentiate among the various definitions of a balance of payments surplus and deficit.

WHAT'S HAPPENING IN THE INTERNATIONAL MONEY MARKET IS always a hot topic in the world's financial press. Consider these headlines and stories that appeared in the *Wall Street Journal* during one three-week period in early 1998. ▪▪ *Dollar Declines against Mark Again as Traders Refocus on Washington Risks*—The dollar maintained its downward path against the mark and the yen before recovering yesterday as currency traders refocused on political risks in Washington. Most traders said the dollar looks oversold and due to rebound, especially as the looming threat of U.S.-Iraq military conflict attracts "safe haven" dollar-buying.[1] ▪▪ *Exports Fail to Grow, Survey Indicates*—As 1998 got under way, Asia's financial crisis began to infect an otherwise healthy U.S. economy.

The Dollar is Front Page News

Asian countries are selling off their products at fire-sale prices, so U.S. factories are competing with low-priced imports. In Tecumseh, Mich., Tecumseh Products Co., which makes compressors for air-conditioning products, complained that currency devaluations have flooded the U.S. with low-priced compressors from Asian competitors. Yet, some companies will benefit—particularly if they import their goods from Asian countries. Vans Inc., the shoe maker in Santa Fe Springs, Calif., said it "looks forward" to "the prospect of better pricing from our Korean manufacturers," from which it gets 70% of its total production.[2] ▪▪ *Drift by Dollar Continues as Traders Seek Improving Yields in Japan, Europe*—Speculation over a budgetary stimulus package for Japan's moribund economy and references to future interest-rate increases intensified the yen's appeal to the market.[3] ▪▪ *Dollar Is Bid Up against Mark and Yen as Traders Focus on Economic Basics*—Traders focused on economic reasons to buy the U.S. dollar, bidding it sharply higher against the mark. Germany's exposure to external threats—from uncertainty over Europe's single currency to a potential devaluation of the Russian ruble and the credit risks of Asia—also hurt the mark. Meanwhile, as high-level resignations shook Japan's Ministry of Finance, the dollar regained some ground it had lost to the yen.[4] ▪▪ *Earnings Outlook for 1998 Could Jar Stocks*—The corporate profit outlook, already its darkest in two years, is probably going to get worse before it gets better, and that could add up to a rough ride for stocks. "We haven't seen the full effects of Asia," says the managing editor for Montreal-based *Bank Credit Analyst*. "That's going to show up as exchange-rate effects, lack of pricing power, or more competition from Asian companies." In the next six months, earnings will suffer from slowing sales to Asia and increased competition from Asian companies seeking markets to replace those they have lost at home. Mutual fund manager Edwin Walczak is troubled by how little companies know about the consequences of Asia's troubles. "If Asia impacts Latin

America, which it's got to, this thing seems likely to spread. Am I worried about McDonald's hamburger sales because of what's happened in Asia? Yes I am. Am I worried about Coca-Cola's sales in Latin America because of Asia? Yes."[5] ■ ■

Dollar Gains on Mark, Sags against Yen—The dollar zigged and zagged against its counterparts. Anticipation that the International Monetary Fund will reach agreement with Indonesia to hasten economic reform has cast a more becoming patina on Asia, helping bolster most regional currencies against the dollar and providing the yen with support against the U.S. currency.[6] ■ ■ ■ ■

Stories like these appear in the world's financial press daily. They are avidly read by managers, for they deal with topics vital to international businesspeople. What is the value of the dollar today? What will its value be next month? How will the latest disruption in the currency market, like the one that devastated Southeast Asia in 1997–1998, affect the competitiveness of our firm? Will foreign governments stimulate their economies, thereby increasing export opportunities next year? Will imports be a greater challenge in the future? Will trade wars break out, thereby damaging access to foreign markets?

Underlying these headlines are the operations of the international monetary system. An international monetary system arises because most countries have their own currencies. A means of exchanging these currencies is needed if business is to be conducted across national boundaries. The **international monetary system** establishes the rules by which countries value and exchange their currencies. It also provides a mechanism for correcting imbalances between a country's international payments and its receipts. Further, the cost of converting foreign money into a firm's home currency—a variable critical to the profitability of international operations—depends on the smooth functioning of the international monetary system.

International businesspeople also monitor the international monetary system's accounting system, the balance of payments. The **balance of payments (BOP) accounting system** records international transactions and supplies vital information about the health of a national economy and likely changes in its fiscal and monetary policies. BOP statistics can be used to detect signs of trouble that could eventually lead to governmental trade restrictions, higher interest rates, accelerated inflation, reduced aggregate demand, or general changes in the cost of doing business in any given country.

History of the International Monetary System

Today's international monetary system can trace its roots to the ancient allure of gold and silver, both of which served as media of exchange in early trade between tribes and in later trade between city-states. Silver, for example, was used in trade among India, Babylon, and Phoenicia as early as the seventh century B.C.[7] As the modern nation states of Europe took form in the sixteenth and seventeenth centuries, their coins were traded on the basis of their relative gold and silver content.

The Gold Standard

Ancient reliance on gold coins as an international medium of exchange led to the adoption of an international monetary system known as the gold standard. Under the **gold standard,** countries agree to buy or sell their paper currencies in exchange for gold on the request of any individual or firm and—in contrast to mercantilism's hoarding of gold—to allow the free export of gold bullion and coins.[8] In 1821 the United Kingdom became the first country to adopt the gold standard. During the nineteenth century, most other important trading countries—including Russia, Austria-Hungary, France, Germany, and the United States—did the same.

The gold standard effectively created a fixed exchange-rate system. An **exchange rate** is the price of one currency in terms of a second currency. Under a **fixed exchange-rate system,** the price of a given currency does not change relative to each other currency. The gold standard created a fixed exchange-rate system because each country tied, or **pegged,** the value of its currency to gold. The United Kingdom, for example, pledged to buy or sell an ounce of gold for 4.247 pounds sterling, thereby establishing the pound's **par value,** or official price in terms of gold. The United States agreed to buy or sell an ounce of gold for a par value of $20.67. The two currencies could be freely exchanged for the stated amount of gold, making £4.247 = 1 ounce of gold = $20.67. This implied a fixed exchange rate between the pound and the dollar of £1 = $4.867, or $20.67/£4.247.

As long as firms had faith in a country's pledge to exchange its currency for gold at the promised rate when requested to do so, many actually preferred to be paid in currency. Transacting in gold was expensive. Suppose Jardine Matheson, a Hong Kong trading company, sold £100,000 worth of tea to Twining & Company, a London distributor of fine teas. If it wanted to be paid in gold by Twining & Company upon delivery of the tea, Jardine Matheson had to bear the costs of loading the gold into the cargo hold of a ship, guarding it against theft, transporting it, and insuring it against possible disasters. Moreover, because of the slowness of sailing ships, Jardine Matheson would be unable to earn interest on the £100,000 payment while the gold was in transit from London to Hong Kong. On the other hand, if Jardine Matheson was willing to be paid in British pounds, Twining could draft a check to Jardine Matheson and give it to the firm's London agent. The London agent could then either immediately deposit the check in Jardine Matheson's interest-bearing London bank account or transfer the funds via telegraph to the firm's account at its Hong Kong bank.

From 1821 until the end of World War I in 1918, the most important currency in international commerce was the British pound sterling, a reflection of the United Kingdom's emergence from the Napoleonic Wars as Europe's dominant economic and military power. Most firms worldwide were willing to accept either gold or British pounds in settlement of transactions. As a result, the international monetary system during this period is often called a **sterling-based gold standard.**[9] The pound's role in world commerce was reinforced by the expansion of the British Empire. The Union Jack flew over so many lands (see Map 4.1)—for example, present-day Canada, Australia, New Zealand, Hong Kong, Singapore, India, Pakistan, Bangladesh, Kenya, Zimbabwe, South Africa, Gibraltar, Bermuda, and Belize—that the claim was made that "the sun never set on the British Empire." In each British colony,

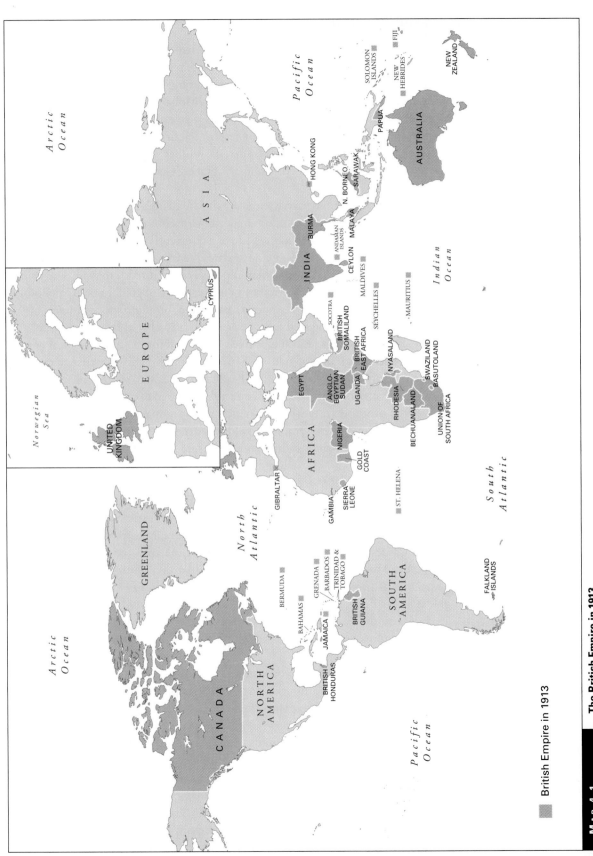

British Empire in 1913

MAP 4.1 The British Empire in 1913

British banks established branches and used the pound sterling to settle international transactions among themselves. Because of the international trust in British currency, London became a dominant international financial center in the nineteenth century, a position it still holds.[10] The international reputations and competitive strengths of such British firms as Barclays Bank, Thomas Cook, and Lloyd's of London stem from the role of the pound sterling in the nineteenth-century gold standard.

The Collapse of the Gold Standard

During World War I, the sterling-based gold standard unraveled. With the outbreak of war, normal commercial transactions between the Allies (France, Russia, and the United Kingdom) and the Central Powers (Austria-Hungary, Germany, and the Ottoman Empire) ceased. The economic pressures of war caused country after country to suspend their pledges to buy or sell gold at their currencies' par values. After the war, conferences at Brussels (1920) and Genoa (1922) yielded general agreements among the major economic powers to return to the prewar gold standard. Most countries, including the United States, the United Kingdom, and France, readopted the gold standard in the 1920s despite the high levels of inflation, unemployment, and political instability that were wracking Europe.[11]

The resuscitation of the gold standard proved to be short-lived, however. The standard was doomed by economic stresses triggered by the worldwide Great Depression. The Bank of England, the United Kingdom's central bank, was unable to honor its pledge to maintain the value of the pound. On September 21, 1931, it allowed the pound to **float,** meaning that the pound's value would be determined by the forces of supply and demand and the Bank of England would no longer guarantee to redeem British paper currency for gold at par value.[12]

After the United Kingdom abandoned the gold standard, a "sterling area" emerged as some countries, primarily members of the British Commonwealth, pegged their currencies to the pound and relied on sterling balances held in London as their international reserves.[13] Other countries tied the value of their currencies to the U.S. dollar or the French franc. The harmony of the international monetary system degenerated further as some countries—including the United States, France, the United Kingdom, Belgium, Latvia, the Netherlands, Switzerland, and Italy—engaged in a series of competitive devaluations of their currencies. By deliberately and artificially lowering (devaluing) the official value of its currency, each nation hoped to make its own goods cheaper in world markets, thereby stimulating its exports and reducing its imports. Any such gains were offset, however, when other countries also devalued their currencies. (If two countries each devalue their currency by 20 percent, neither gains an advantage because each currency's value relative to the other remains the same.) Most countries also raised the tariffs they imposed on imported goods in the hope of protecting domestic jobs in import-competing industries. Yet as more and more countries adopted these **beggar-thy-neighbor policies,** international trade contracted (see Fig. 4.1), hurting employment in each country's export industries. More ominously, this international economic conflict was soon replaced by international military conflict—the outbreak of World War II in 1939.

FIGURE 4.1

Down the Tube: The Contraction of World Trade, 1929–1933.

Note: Total imports of 75 countries (monthly values, millions of dollars)

Source: Charles Kindleberger, *The World in Depression*, Berkeley: University of California Press, 1986, p. 170.

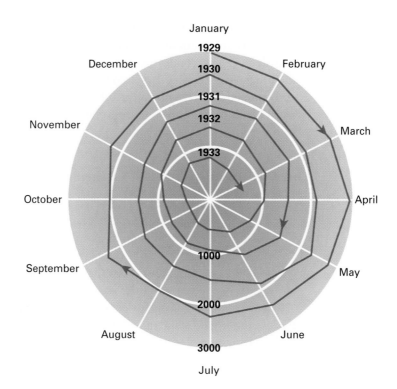

The Bretton Woods Era

Many politicians and historians believe the breakdown of the international monetary system and international trade after World War I created economic conditions that helped bring about World War II. Inflation, unemployment, and the costs of rebuilding war-torn economies created political instability that enabled fascist and communist dictators (Hitler, Mussolini, and Stalin) to seize control of their respective governments. Determined not to repeat the mistakes that had caused World War II, Western diplomats desired to create a postwar economic environment that would promote worldwide peace and prosperity. In 1944 representatives of forty-four countries met at a resort in Bretton Woods, New Hampshire, with that objective in mind. The Bretton Woods conferees agreed to renew the gold standard on a greatly modified basis. They also agreed to the creation of two new international organizations to assist the rebuilding of the world economy and the international monetary system: the International Bank for Reconstruction and Development and the International Monetary Fund.

The International Bank for Reconstruction and Development.
The **International Bank for Reconstruction and Development (IBRD)** is the official name of the **World Bank.** Established in 1945, the World Bank's initial goal was to help finance reconstruction of the war-torn European economies. With the assistance of the Marshall Plan, the World Bank accomplished this task by the mid-1950s. The Bank then adopted a new mission—to build the economies of the world's developing countries.

As its mission has expanded over time, the World Bank created three affiliated organizations:

The years after World War I were marked by international economic competition among countries, which many experts believe created economic hardships and political conditions that led to World War II. Western diplomats did not wish to make the same mistake twice. By creating the World Bank and the International Monetary Fund, the delegates to the 1944 Bretton Woods conference sought to promote world peace and prosperity through international economic cooperation.

1 The International Development Association

2 The International Finance Corporation

3 The Multilateral Investment Guarantee Agency

Together with the World Bank, these constitute the **World Bank Group** (see Fig. 4.2). The World Bank, which currently has $106 billion in loans outstanding, is owned by its 180 member countries. In reaching its decisions, the World Bank uses a weighted voting system that reflects the economic power and contributions of its members. The United States currently controls the largest bloc of votes (17 percent), followed by Japan (6 percent), Germany (5 percent), the United Kingdom (4 percent), France (4 percent), and six countries with 3 percent each: Canada, China, India, Italy, Russia, and Saudi Arabia. From time to time, the voting weights are reassessed as economic power shifts or as new members, such as Latvia, Slovenia, and Ukraine, join the World Bank. To finance its lending operations, the World Bank borrows money in its own name from international capital markets. Interest earned on existing loans it has made provides it with additional lending power. New lending by the World Bank averaged $13 billion per year from 1993 to 1997.[14]

According to its charter, the World Bank may lend only for "productive purposes" that will stimulate economic growth within the recipient country. An example of such a loan is the $150 million provided to Romania in 1997 to rehabilitate and modernize its national highways. The World Bank cannot finance a trade deficit, but it can finance an infrastructure project, such as a new railroad or harbor facility, that will bolster a country's economy. It may lend only to national governments or for projects that are guaranteed by a national government, and its loans may not be tied to the purchase of goods or services from any country. Most important, the World Bank must follow a **hard loan policy;** that is, it may make a loan only if there is a reasonable expectation that the loan will be repaid.[15]

FIGURE 4.2

Organization of the World Bank Group

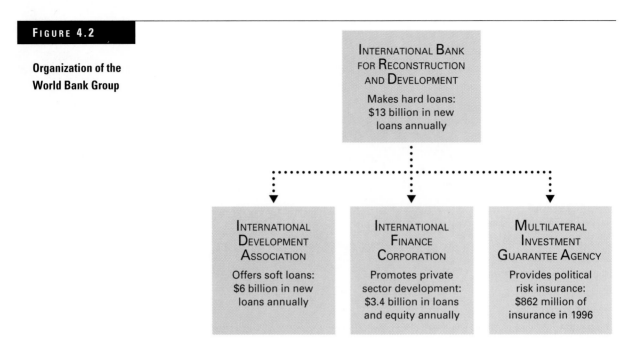

The hard loan policy was severely criticized in the 1950s by poorer countries, who complained it hindered their ability to obtain World Bank loans. In response, the World Bank established the **International Development Association (IDA)** in 1960. The IDA offers **soft loans,** loans that bear some significant risk of not being repaid. IDA loans carry no interest rate, although the IDA collects a small service charge (currently 0.75 percent) from borrowers. The loans also have long maturities (normally 35 to 40 years), and borrowers are often granted a 10 year grace period before they need to begin repaying their loans. Its lending efforts focus on the least-developed countries. A typical loan is the $80 million provided in 1997 to build a water treatment plant in Dhaka, Bangladesh. The IDA obtains resources from the initial subscriptions its members make when joining it, from transferred World Bank profits, and from periodic replenishments contributed by richer countries. From 1993 to 1997, IDA disbursements averaged $6 billion per year.[16]

The two other affiliates of the World Bank Group have narrower missions. The **International Finance Corporation (IFC),** created in 1956, is charged with promoting the development of the private sector in developing countries. Acting like an investment banker, the IFC, in collaboration with private investors, provides debt and equity capital for promising commercial activities. For example, in 1997 the IFC provided Mongolia's G&M Industrial Co. Ltd. with a $1.45 million loan and $300,000 in equity to help it construct a $3.5 million leather garment factory, which will tan and sew goat and sheep skins supplied from Mongolia's ample herds. Similarly, the IFC provided Orzunil, the Guatemalan affiliate of Israel's Ormat Industries, with $27 million in loans and $2.2 million in equity to build a geothermal power plant near Quetzaltenango, Guatemala's second largest city. In 1997 the IFC provided $3.4 billion of financing to supplement $14.6 billion of capital raised from other sources for private-sector projects.

The other World Bank affiliate, the **Multilateral Investment Guarantee Agency (MIGA),** was set up in 1988 to overcome private-sector reluctance to invest in developing countries because of perceived political riskiness—a topic covered

Kyrgyz Republic President Askar Akaev (second from left) celebrates the opening of the first soft drink bottling plant in his country, which was aided by political risk insurance supplied by MIGA. The new facility, which employs 180 workers, is a joint venture among the Coca-Cola Export Company, Efes (a Turkish company which operates other Coca-Cola franchises), and local investors.

more thoroughly in Chapter 8. MIGA encourages direct investment in developing countries by offering private investors insurance against noncommercial risks. For example, in 1996 MIGA issued the Wilken Group of the United Kingdom $1.1 million of political risk insurance to cover its investments in two satellite communications joint ventures that it had established with local investors in Tanzania and Uganda. MIGA's insurance protected the Wilken Group from expropriation, war, civil disturbances, and restrictions on currency transfer. Similarly, it issued Turkey's Efes Sinai Yatirim Ve Tiracaret $27.6 million in political risk insurance to protect its investment in two Coca-Cola bottling companies it was establishing in the Kyrgyz Republic and Kazakhstan with local joint venture partners. As a result of this insurance, Efes was protected against losses due to expropriation, war, or other civil disturbances.[17] In 1996 MIGA underwrote $862 million of political risk insurance.

The World Bank Group is often embroiled in international political controversy. For example, as part of its drive to promote private enterprise in developing countries, the U.S. government under President Bush lobbied the World Bank to make more direct loans to the private sector and to coordinate its lending policies more closely with the IFC. The U.S. position has been resisted by the World Bank's staff, as well as by the governments of European and developing countries, which fear that increased loans to the private sector may jeopardize the AAA credit rating of the World Bank's bonds.[18] Because the World Bank is a major source of capital to developing countries, such debates are of great interest to international businesses. World Bank loans fund major construction projects throughout less-developed economies, thereby providing business opportunities for international construction companies, steel manufacturers, cement makers, and others. Further, these loans generate economic activity in the recipient countries, thus boosting the market for foreign and domestically produced consumer goods and services.

Paralleling the efforts of the World Bank are the **regional development banks,** such as the African Development Bank, the Asian Development Bank, and the Inter-American Development Bank. These organizations promote the economic development of the poorer countries in their respective regions. The most recently created regional development bank is the European Bank for Reconstruction and Development. It was established by the Western countries to assist in the reconstruction of Central and Eastern Europe after the collapse of the region's communist regimes. The regional development banks and the World Bank often work together on development projects. In 1996, for example, the Asian Development Bank, in conjunction with the World Bank and several other agencies, helped fund and insure a 60-megawatt hydroelectric power plant near Kathmandu, Nepal, which when operational will supply 25 percent of Nepal's electrical power.[19]

The International Monetary Fund. The Bretton Woods attendees believed that the deterioration of international trade in the years after World War I was attributable in part to the competitive exchange-rate devaluations that plagued international commerce. To ensure that the post–World War II monetary system would promote international commerce, the Bretton Woods Agreement called for the creation of the **International Monetary Fund (IMF)** to oversee the functioning of the international monetary system. Article I of the IMF's Articles of Agreement lays out the organization's objectives:

1 To promote international monetary cooperation

2 To facilitate the expansion and balanced growth of international trade

3 To promote exchange stability, to maintain orderly exchange arrangements among members, and to avoid competitive exchange depreciation

4 To assist in the establishment of a multilateral system of payments

5 To give confidence to members by making the general resources of the Fund temporarily available to them and to correct maladjustments in their balances of payments

6 To shorten the duration and lessen the degree of disequilibrium in the international balances of payments of members

Membership in the IMF is available to any country willing to agree to its rules and regulations. As of February 1998, 182 countries were members. To join, a country must pay a deposit, called a **quota,** partly in gold and partly in the country's own currency. The quota's size primarily reflects the global importance of the country's economy, although political considerations may also have some effect. The size of a quota is important for several reasons.

1 A country's quota determines its voting power within the IMF. From time to time, quotas have been adjusted, which has led to much political bickering among members. For example, the quotas assigned to Russia and other former republics of the Soviet Union when they joined the IMF in 1992 totaled about 5 percent of the IMF's total quota. This reduced the voting strengths of the United States, the United Kingdom, Canada, Australia, and many others. Currently the United States controls 17.8 percent of the votes in the IMF. Germany and Japan each control the next-largest blocs (5.5 percent), followed by France (5.0 percent), the United Kingdom (5.0 percent), and Saudi Arabia (3.5 percent).

2 A country's quota serves as part of its official reserves (we discuss official reserves later in the chapter).

3 The quota determines the country's borrowing power from the IMF. Each IMF member has an unconditional right to borrow up to 25 percent of its quota from the IMF. IMF policy allows additional borrowings contingent on the member country's agreeing to IMF-imposed restrictions—called **IMF conditionality**—on its economic policies. For example, in return for an IMF loan of $21 billion, South Korea agreed in December 1997 to under-

The conditions imposed by the IMF on its loans to troubled countries are often controversial. Like many other Indonesians, these protestors objected to the elimination of government subsidies on food and fuel demanded by the IMF.

take major economic reforms, including permitting foreign banks to take over their Korean counterparts, closing insolvent merchant banks, reducing government favoritism toward the larger chaebol, and lowering its tariffs on many goods. The previous month the IMF consented to lend Indonesia $10 billion only after that country pledged to scrap state monopolies controlling certain foodstuffs, reform its banking industry, and cut trade barriers directed against imported goods.[20] Local politicians and interest groups often bitterly protest the IMF's conditionality requirements, arguing that foreigners, working through the IMF, are taking advantage of the country's short-term problems to extract changes favorable to them. At times, the situation can turn uglier. For example, in 1998 Indonesia was wracked by rioting after prices and unemployment soared as a result of the austerity measures demanded by the IMF, and long-time President Suharto was forced to resign his office.

A Dollar-Based Gold Standard. The IMF and the World Bank provided the institutional framework for the postwar international monetary system. The Bretton Woods participants also addressed the problem of how the system would function in practice. All countries agreed to peg the value of their currencies to gold. For example, the par value of the U.S. dollar was established at $35 per ounce of gold. However, only the United States pledged to redeem its currency for gold at the request of a foreign central bank. Thus the U.S. dollar became the keystone of the Bretton Woods system. Why this central role for the U.S. dollar? In the early postwar years, only the U.S. and Canadian dollars were convertible currencies, that is, ones that could be freely exchanged for other currencies without legal restrictions. Countries had faith in the U.S. economy and so were willing to accept U.S. dollars to settle their transactions. As the British pound sterling had been in the nineteenth century, the U.S. dollar became the preferred vehicle for settling most international transactions. The effect of the Bretton Woods conference was thus to establish a U.S. dollar-based gold standard.

Because each country established a par value for its currency, the Bretton Woods Agreement resulted in a fixed exchange-rate system. (Figure 4.3 shows the structure of exchange rates at the end of the Bretton Woods era.) Under the Agreement, each country pledged to maintain the value of its currency within ±1 percent of its par value. If the market value of its currency fell outside that range, a country was obligated to intervene in the foreign-exchange market to

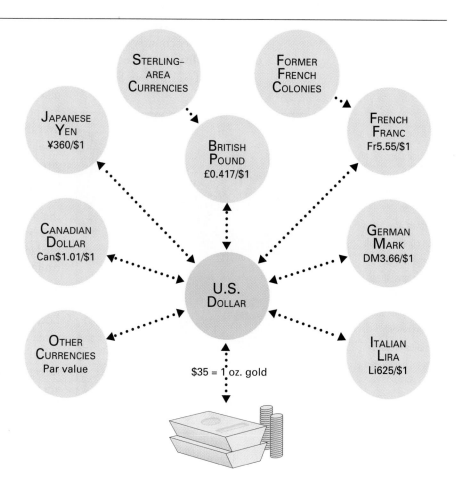

bring the value back within ±1 percent of par value. This stability in exchange rates benefited international businesses, since the Bretton Woods system *generally* provided an assurance that the value of each currency would remain stable.

Note the use of the qualifier *generally*. Under extraordinary circumstances, the Bretton Woods Agreement allowed a country to adjust its currency's par value. Accordingly, the Bretton Woods system is often described as using an **adjustable peg** because currencies were pegged to gold but the pegs themselves could be altered under certain conditions. For example, under the system the British pound's par value was first set at $2.80. (Technically, the par value was pegged to an ounce of gold, which then could be translated into dollars at a rate of $35.00 per ounce. Most businesspeople ignored this technicality and focused on the implicit par value of a currency in terms of the U.S. dollar.) Thus the Bank of England was obligated to keep the pound's value between $2.772 and $2.828 (±1 percent of $2.80). Suppose pessimism about the British economy caused the pound's market price to fall to $2.76. The Bank of England would be required to defend the value of the pound by selling some of its gold or U.S. dollar holdings to buy pounds. This move would increase the demand for pounds, and the market price would return to within the legal range—from $2.772 to $2.828.

This arrangement worked well as long as pessimism about a country's economy was temporary. But if a country suffered from structural macroeconomic problems, major difficulties could arise. For example, in the late 1960s, Labour governments striving for social justice dominated British politics, and British unions secured higher wages, better working conditions, and protective work rules. At the same time, however, British productivity decreased relative to that of its major international competitors, and the pound's value weakened. The Bank of England had to intervene continually in the foreign-currency market, selling gold and foreign currencies to support the pound. But in so doing, the Bank's holdings of official reserves, which were needed to back up the country's Bretton Woods pledge, began to dwindle. International currency traders began to fear the Bank would run out of reserves. As that fear mounted, international banks, currency traders, and other market participants became unwilling to hold British pounds in their inventory of foreign currencies. They began dumping pounds on the market as soon as they received them. A vicious cycle developed: as the Bank of England continued to drain its official reserves to support the pound, the fears of the currency-market participants that the Bank would run out of reserves were worsened.

The situation resembles a run on a bank. Banks never have enough cash on hand to honor all their liabilities. However, as long as everyone trusts that their bank will give them their money if they need it, no one worries. If people lose that trust and withdraw more of their money than the bank has on hand, the bank could be in trouble. The Bretton Woods system was particularly susceptible to speculative "runs on the bank," for there was little risk in betting against a currency in times of doubt. For example, speculators distrustful of the Bank of England's ability to honor the United Kingdom's Bretton Woods pledge could convert their pounds into dollars. If they guessed right and the pound were devalued, they could make a quick financial killing. If they guessed wrong and the Bank of England maintained the pound's par value, the speculators could always reconvert their dollar holdings back into pounds with little penalty.

The United Kingdom faced a "run on the bank" of this type in November 1967. The Bank of England could not counter the flood of pounds dumped on the market by speculators and was forced to devalue the pound by 14.3 percent (from $2.80 to $2.40 per pound). France faced a similar run in 1969 and had to devalue the franc. These devaluations tested the international business community's faith in the Bretton Woods system. But the system faced its true Waterloo when the dollar came under attack in the early 1970s.

The End of the Bretton Woods System

These runs on the British and French central banks were a precursor to a run on the most important bank in the Bretton Woods system—the U.S. Federal Reserve Bank. Ironically, the reliance of the Bretton Woods system on the dollar ultimately led to the system's undoing. Because the supply of gold did not expand in the short run, the only source of the liquidity needed to expand international trade was the U.S. dollar. Under the Bretton Woods system, the expansion of international liquidity depended on foreigners' willingness to continually increase their holdings of dollars. Foreigners were perfectly happy to hold dollars as long as they trusted the integrity of the U.S. currency, and during the 1950s and 1960s the number of dollars held by foreigners rose steadily.

As foreign dollar holdings increased, however, people began to question the ability of the United States to live up to its Bretton Woods obligation. This led to the **Triffin paradox,** named after the Belgian-born Yale University economist

Robert Triffin, who first identified the problem. The paradox arose because foreigners needed to increase their holdings of dollars to finance expansion of international trade. But the more dollars they owned, the less faith they had in the ability of the United States to redeem those dollars for gold. The less faith foreigners had in the United States, the more they wanted to rid themselves of dollars and get gold in return. But if they did this, international trade and the international monetary system might collapse because the United States didn't have enough gold to redeem all the dollars held by foreigners.

As a means of injecting more liquidity into the international monetary system while reducing the demands placed on the dollar as a reserve currency, IMF members agreed in 1967 to create **special drawing rights (SDRs)**. IMF members can use SDRs to settle official transactions at the IMF. Thus SDRs are sometimes called "paper gold." As of early 1998, approximately 21.4 billion SDRs, representing about 2 percent of the world's total reserves, had been distributed to IMF members in proportion to their IMF quotas. An SDR's value is currently calculated daily as a weighted average of the market value of five major currencies—the U.S. dollar, German mark, French franc, Japanese yen, and pound sterling—with the weights revised every five years.[21] As of February 1998, the SDR was worth $1.36 in U.S. dollars.

While SDRs did provide new liquidity for the international monetary system, they did not reduce the fundamental problem of the glut of dollars held by foreigners. By mid-1971, the Bretton Woods system was tottering, the victim of fears about the dollar's instability. In the first seven months of 1971, the United States sold one third of its gold reserves.[22] It became clear to the marketplace that the United States did not have sufficient gold on hand to meet the demands of those who still wanted to exchange their dollars for gold. In a dramatic address on August 15, 1971,

President Nixon's decision to end the U.S. dollar's central role in the Bretton Woods system was front-page news around the world.

President Richard M. Nixon announced that the United States would no longer redeem gold at $35 per ounce. The Bretton Woods system was ended.

In effect, the bank was closing its doors. After Nixon's speech, most foreign currencies began to float, their values being determined by supply and demand in the foreign-exchange market. The value of the U.S. dollar fell relative to most of the world's major currencies.

But the nations of the world were not yet ready to abandon the fixed exchange-rate system. At the **Smithsonian Conference**, held in Washington, D.C. in December 1971, central bank representatives from the Group of Ten (see Table 4.1) agreed to restore the fixed exchange-rate system but with restructured rates of exchange between the major trading currencies. The U.S. dollar was devalued to $38 per ounce but remained inconvertible into gold,

TABLE 4.1

The Groups of Five, Seven, and Ten

	GROUP OF FIVE	GROUP OF SEVEN	GROUP OF TEN*	PERCENTAGE OF WORLD GDP
	United States	United States	United States	25.0
	Japan	Japan	Japan	18.3
	Germany	Germany	Germany	8.7
	France	France	France	5.5
	United Kingdom	United Kingdom	United Kingdom	4.0
		Italy	Italy	3.9
		Canada	Canada	2.0
			Netherlands	1.4
			Switzerland	1.1
			Belgium	1.0
			Sweden	0.8
Cumulative Percentage of World GDP	61.5	67.4	71.7	

*The Group of Ten has eleven members.

and the par values of strong currencies such as the yen were revalued upward. Currencies were allowed to fluctuate around their new par values by ±2.25 percent, which replaced the narrower ±1.00 percent range authorized by the Bretton Woods Agreement.

Performance of the International Monetary System since 1971

Free-market forces disputed the new set of par values established by the Smithsonian conferees. Speculators, believing the dollar and the pound were overvalued, sold both and hoarded currencies they believed were undervalued, such as the Swiss franc and the German mark. The Bank of England was unable to maintain the pound's value within the ±2.25 percent band and in June 1972 had to allow the pound to float downward. Switzerland let the Swiss franc float upward in early 1973. The United States devalued the dollar by 10 percent in February 1973. By March 1973, the central banks (see Table 4.2 for a list of the most important of the central banks) conceded they could not successfully resist free-market forces and so established a flexible exchange-rate system. Under a **flexible (or floating) exchange-rate system,** supply and demand for a currency determine its price in the world market. Since 1973, exchange rates among many currencies have been established *primarily* by the interaction of supply and demand. We use the qualifier *primarily* because central banks sometimes try to affect exchange rates by buying or selling currencies on the foreign-exchange market. Thus the current arrangements are often called a **managed float** (or, more poetically, a **dirty float**), because exchange rates are not determined purely by private-sector market forces.

The new flexible exchange-rate system was legitimized by an international conference held in Jamaica in January 1976. According to the resulting **Jamaica**

TABLE 4.2	

Key Central Banks

COUNTRY	BANK
Canada	Bank of Canada
France	Bank of France
Germany	Bundesbank*
Italy	Bank of Italy
Japan	Bank of Japan
United States	Federal Reserve Bank
United Kingdom	Bank of England
European Union	European Central Bank**

*Although we have provided the English translation for most of these banks, by convention English-language news media use the term *Bundesbank* for the German central bank, rather than its English translation, "Federal Bank."
**Scheduled to begin operations in January 1999.

Agreement, each country was free to adopt whatever exchange-rate system best met its own requirements. The United States adopted a floating exchange rate. Other countries adopted a fixed exchange-rate by pegging their currencies to the dollar, the French franc, or some other currency.

The European Monetary System. Of particular note is the strategy adopted by EU members in the belief that flexible exchange rates would hinder their ability to create an integrated European economy. Dissatisfied with the outcome of the Smithsonian Agreement and freed by the Jamaica Agreement to do what they wanted, the EU members in 1979 created the **European Monetary System (EMS)** to manage currency relationships among themselves. Most EMS members chose to participate in the EU's **exchange-rate mechanism (ERM)**. ERM participants pledged to maintain fixed exchange rates among their currencies within a narrow range of ±2.25 percent of par value and a floating rate against the U.S. dollar and other currencies. Italy, however, was at first allowed a wider ±6 percent range. The United Kingdom initially chose not to join the ERM (it joined in 1990). The EMS members also created an index currency, the European Currency Unit. The **European Currency Unit (ECU)** is a weighted "basket" of the currencies of the EU members that is used for accounting purposes within the EU and in international financial markets. As of February 1998, the ECU is worth about $1.10 in U.S. currency.

The EMS has helped EU members fight inflation and promote intra-EU investment, in part because the zealous anti-inflation philosophy of the Bundesbank (Germany's central bank) has dominated EU monetary policy. However, the EMS is not flawless. During its first ten years, the fixed exchange rates established by the ERM had to be adjusted thirty-nine times because of differences in the monetary policies of EU members.[23] The ERM suffered several near fatal blows in September 1992: turmoil in the currency market forced the United Kingdom and Italy to abandon the ERM "temporarily," compelled Spain and Portugal to devalue their currencies drastically, and caused the remaining EMS members to broaden the currency fluctuation range from the original ±2.25 percent to ±15 percent. (See the opening case of Chapter 5 for insights into these events.) Despite the ERM's problems, most members of the European Union believe that the EU should further the integration of their economies by the creation of a single European currency. As we will discuss in Chapter 7, the creation of this currency, the *euro*, which is to become effective in January 1999, is the boldest and riskiest initiative that the EU has undertaken.

Table 4.3 shows the current status of the world's exchange-rate arrangements. The current international monetary system is based on flexible exchange rates, although some countries have chosen to maintain fixed rates. For example, as just discussed, most members of the EU have constructed a fixed exchange-rate system among themselves, while some other countries have voluntarily adopted a fixed exchange rate against the U.S. dollar, the French franc, or some other currency. Under the current international monetary system, currencies of one country grouping float against the currencies of other country groupings. For example, the U.S. dollar group floats against the yen, the deutsche mark, the Canadian dollar, the Australian dollar, and the French franc currency group.

Other Postwar Conferences. The international monetary system that has grown out of the Jamaica Agreement has not pleased all the world's central banks all the time. Since 1976, they have met numerous times to iron out policy conflicts among themselves. For example, U.S. complaints that an overvalued dollar was hurting the competitiveness of U.S. exports and allowing cheap imports to damage U.S. industries prompted finance ministers of the Group of Five (see Table 4.1) to meet in September 1985 at the Plaza Hotel in New York City. The meeting led to the **Plaza Accord,** whereby the central banks agreed to let the dollar's value fall on currency markets. And fall it did. From its peak in February 1985, it plummeted almost 46 percent against the deutsche mark and 41 percent against the yen by the beginning of 1987. Fearing that continued devaluation of the dollar would disrupt world trade, finance ministers from the Group of Five met again, this time at the Louvre in Paris in February 1987. The **Louvre Accord** signaled the commitment of these five countries to stabilizing the dollar's value. However, the foreign-exchange market was once again thrown into turmoil in 1990, in this case by the onset of the Persian Gulf hostilities. The values of key currencies have continued to fluctuate in the 1990s. Figure 4.4 shows changes in the dollar's value against the yen and the mark since the collapse of the Bretton Woods system.

These fluctuations in currency values are of great importance to international businesses. Depreciation in the value of a firm's home currency makes it easier for the firm to export and helps it defend itself from the threat of imports. Appreciation has the opposite effect. Recall from the discussion of the Caterpillar-Komatsu rivalry in Chapter 3 that the strong dollar caused Caterpillar problems in the early 1980s and the weak dollar (and strong yen) caused Komatsu problems in the late 1980s and early 1990s. The dollar's rise since mid-1995 has eased Komatsu's concerns but given Caterpillar fits. Currency

TABLE 4.3

Exchange-Rate Arrangements (as of January 1, 1998)*

			CURRENCY PEGGED TO		
U.S. Dollar	**French Franc**	**South African Rand**	**Other Currency**	**SDR**	**Other Composite†**
Angola	Benin	Lesotho	Bhutan	Latvia	Bangladesh
Antigua & Barbuda	Burkina Faso	Namibia	(Indian rupee)	Libya	Botswana
Argentina	Cameroon	Swaziland	Bosnia and	Myanmar	Burundi
Bahamas, The	Central African Republic		Herzegovina		Cape Verde
Barbados	Chad		(deutsche		Cyprus
Belize	Comoros		mark)		Fiji
Djibouti	Congo, Rep. of		Brunei Darussalam		Iceland
Dominica	Côte d'Ivoire		(Singapore		Jordan
Grenada	Equatorial Guinea		dollar)		Kuwait
Iraq	Gabon		Bulgaria		Malta
Lithuania	Guinea-Bissau		(deutsche		Morocco
Marshall Islands	Mali		mark)		Samoa
Micronesia,	Niger		Estonia		Seychelles
Fed. States of	Senegal		(deutsche		Slovak Republic
Nigeria	Togo		mark)		Solomon Islands
Oman			Kiribati		Tonga
Panama			(Australian		Vanuatu
St. Kitts & Nevis			dollar)		
St. Lucia			Nepal		
St. Vincent and			(Indian rupee)		
the Grenadines			San Marino		
Syrian Arab Republic			(Italian lira)		

* For members with dual or multiple exchange markets, the arrangement shown is that in the major market.
† Comprises currencies that are pegged to various "baskets" of currencies of the members' own choice, as distinct from the SDR basket.
‡ Exchange rates of all currencies have shown limited flexibility in terms of the U.S. dollar.
** Refers to the cooperative arrangement maintained under the European Monetary System.

Source: IMF, *International Financial Statistics*, March 1998, p. 8. Reprinted with permission.

fluctuations also affect international investment opportunities. For example, the appreciation of the mark against the dollar after 1985 made it more difficult for Bayerische Motoren Werke to sustain its sales of BMWs in the United States. The company's solution was to build an automobile assembly plant near Spartanburg, South Carolina, a move designed to lower the company's production costs and raise its visibility in the North American market. The mark's fall against the dollar since 1995 has eroded some of the cost advantages to BMW of its new South Carolina plant.

continued

Flexibility Limited in Terms of a Single Currency or Group of Currencies		More Flexible		
Single Currency‡	**Cooperative Arrangements****	**Other Managed Floating**		**Independently Floating**
Bahrain	Austria	Algeria	Macedonia, FYR of	Moldova
Qatar	Belgium	Belarus	Malaysia	Mongolia
Saudi Arabia	Denmark	Brazil	Maldives	Mozambique
United Arab	Finland	Cambodia	Mauritius	New Zealand
Emirates	France	Chile	Nicaragua	Papua New
	Germany	China, P.R.	Norway	Guinea
	Ireland	Colombia	Pakistan	Paraguay
	Italy	Costa Rica	Poland	Peru
	Luxembourg	Croatia	Russia	Philippines
	Netherlands	Czech Republic	Singapore	Romania
	Portugal	Dominican Republic	Slovenia	Rwanda
	Spain	Ecuador	Sri Lanka	São Tomé and
		Egypt	Sudan	Príncipe
		El Salvador	Suriname	Sierra Leone
		Georgia	Thailand	Somalia
		Greece	Tunisia	South Africa
		Honduras	Turkmenistan	Sweden
		Hungary	Turkey	Switzerland
		Iran, I.R. of	Ukraine	Tajikistan,
		Israel	Uruguay	Rep. of
		Kazakhstan	Uzbekistan	Tanzania
		Kyrgyz Rep.	Venezuela	Trinidad and
		Lao, P.D. Rep.	Vietnam	Tobago

(Independently Floating column, continued):
Afghanistan, Islamic State of
Albania
Armenia
Australia
Azerbaijan
Bolivia
Canada
Congo, Dem. Rep.
Eritrea
Ethiopia
Gambia, The
Ghana
Guatemala
Guinea
Guyana
Haiti
India
Indonesia
Jamaica
Japan
Kenya
Korea
Lebanon
Liberia
Madagascar
Malawi
Mauritania
Mexico

Uganda
United Kingdom
United States
Yemen, Rep. of
Zambia
Zimbabwe

The International Debt Crisis. The flexible exchange-rate system instituted in 1973 was immediately put to a severe test. In response to the Israeli victory in the Arab-Israeli War of 1973, Arab nations imposed an embargo on oil shipments to countries such as the United States and the Netherlands, which had supported the Israeli cause. As a result, the Organization of Petroleum Exporting Countries (OPEC) succeeded in quadrupling world oil prices from $3 a barrel in October 1973 to $12 a barrel by March 1974. This rapid increase in oil prices caused inflationary pressures in oil-importing countries. For example, in the

FIGURE 4.4

Exchange Rates of
the Dollar versus
the Yen and the
Deutsche Mark,
1960–1997

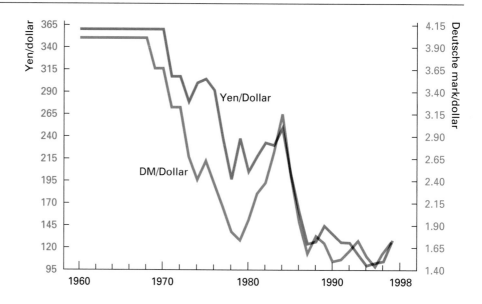

United States inflation rose from 6.1 percent in 1973 to 11.1 percent in 1974. In 1974 alone, $60 billion in wealth was transferred from oil-importing countries to oil-exporting countries. The new international monetary arrangements absorbed some of the shock caused by this upheaval in the oil market, as exchange rates adjusted to account for changes in the value of each country's oil exports or imports. The currencies of the oil exporters strengthened, while those of the oil importers weakened.

This enormous transfer of wealth raised certain economic concerns. The higher oil prices acted as a tax on the economies of the oil-importing countries. Some economists feared that worldwide depression would develop as consumer demand fell in the richer countries. Other economists worried that because trade in oil was denominated in dollars, international liquidity would dry up as dollars piled up in Arab bank accounts. Neither of these fears was realized. Many of the oil-exporting countries went on spending sprees, using their new wealth to improve their infrastructures or to invest in new facilities (such as petroleum refineries) to produce wealth for future generations. The unspent petrodollars were deposited in banks in international money centers such as London and New York City. The international banking community then recycled these petrodollars through its international lending activities to help revive the economies damaged by rising oil prices.

Unfortunately, the international banks were too aggressive in recycling these dollars. Many countries borrowed more than they could repay. Mexico, for example, borrowed $90 billion, while Brazil took on $67 billion in new loans. The financial positions of these borrowers became precarious after the oil shock of 1978–1979, which was triggered by the toppling from power of the Shah of Iran. The price of oil skyrocketed from $13 a barrel in 1978 to over $30 a barrel in 1980, triggering another round of worldwide inflation. Interest rates on these loans rose, as most carried a floating interest rate, further burdening the heavily indebted nations. The international debt crisis formally began when Mexico declared in August 1982 that it could not service its external debts. Mexico requested a rescheduling of its debts, a moratorium on repayment of principal, and a loan from the IMF to help it through its debt crisis. Mexico was soon joined by Brazil and Argentina. In total, more than forty countries in Asia, Africa, and Latin America sought relief from their external debts. Negotiations among the debtor countries, creditor countries, private banks, and international organizations continued throughout the rest of the 1980s.

Various approaches were used to resolve the crisis. The 1985 **Baker Plan** (named after then U.S. Treasury Secretary James Baker) stressed the importance of debt rescheduling, tight IMF-imposed controls over domestic monetary and fiscal policies, and continued lending to debtor countries in hopes that economic growth would allow them to repay their creditors. In Mexico's case, the IMF agreed to provide a loan package only if private foreign banks holding Mexican debt agreed to reschedule their loans and provide Mexico with additional financing. However, the debtor nations made little progress in repaying their loans. Debtors and creditors alike agreed that a new approach was needed. The 1989 **Brady Plan** (named after the Bush administration's treasury secretary, Nicholas Brady) focused on the need to reduce the debts of the troubled countries by writing off parts of the debts or by providing the countries with funds to buy back their loan notes at below face value.

The international debt crisis has receded in the 1990s as the debt servicing requirements of debtor countries have been made more manageable via a combination of IMF loans, debt rescheduling, and changes in governmental economic policies (see the discussion of economic reforms in Mexico, Argentina, and Brazil in Chapter 2). The impact of the crisis cannot be overstated. Many experts consider the 1980s the "lost decade" for economic development in Latin America.

The most recent crisis facing the international monetary system erupted in July 1997, when Thailand, which had pegged its currency to a dollar-dominated basket of currencies, was forced to unpeg its currency, the baht, after investors began to distrust the abilities of Thai borrowers to repay their foreign loans and of the Thai government to maintain the baht's value. Not wanting to hold a currency likely to be devalued, foreign and domestic investors converted their bahts to dollars and other currencies. The Thai central bank spent much of its official reserves desperately trying to maintain the pegged value of the baht. After Thailand was forced to abandon the peg on July 2, the baht promptly fell 20 percent in value. As investors realized that other countries in the region shared Thailand's overdependence on foreign short-term capital, their currencies also came under attack and their stock markets were devastated. Indonesia was hit the worst by the so-called "Asian contagion," as Fig. 4.5 shows. All told, the IMF and the Quad countries pledged over $100 billion in loans to help restore these countries to economic health. The closing case of Chapter 5 and the "Point-Counterpoint" that follows that chapter discuss this crisis in more detail.

These crises did not come as a surprise to those analysts who had been watching for danger signs. The BOP accounting system provided clear warning of the deteriorating performance of the countries in crisis and the increasing riskiness of their overextended external debt positions. A careful reading of BOP statistics could have protected international bankers from bad investments and risky loans. Because the BOP accounting system provides such valuable economic intelligence information, the next section discusses it in detail.

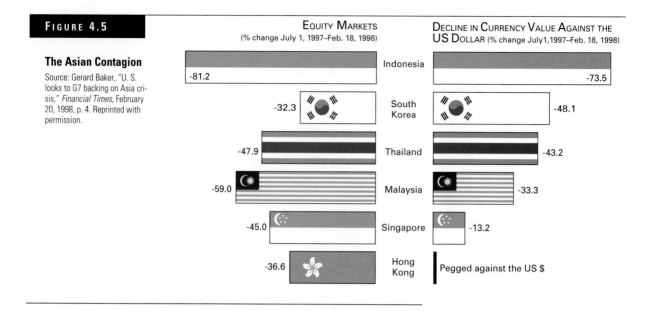

FIGURE 4.5

The Asian Contagion

Source: Gerard Baker, "U. S. looks to G7 backing on Asia crisis," *Financial Times*, February 20, 1998, p. 4. Reprinted with permission.

EQUITY MARKETS
(% change July 1, 1997–Feb. 18, 1998)

DECLINE IN CURRENCY VALUE AGAINST THE
US DOLLAR (% change July1,1997–Feb. 18, 1998)

Country	Equity Markets	Decline in Currency Value
Indonesia	-81.2	-73.5
South Korea	-32.3	-48.1
Thailand	-47.9	-43.2
Malaysia	-59.0	-33.3
Singapore	-45.0	-13.2
Hong Kong	-36.6	Pegged against the US $

The Balance of Payments Accounting System

Each year, countries purchase trillions of dollars of goods, services, and assets from each other. The BOP accounting system is a double-entry bookkeeping system designed to measure and record all economic transactions between residents of one country and residents of all other countries during a particular time period. It helps policy makers understand the performance of each country's economy in international markets. It also signals fundamental changes in the competitiveness of countries and assists policy makers in designing appropriate public policies to respond to these changes.

International businesspeople need to pay close attention to countries' BOP statistics for several reasons, including the following:

1 BOP statistics help identify emerging markets for goods and services.

2 They can warn of possible new policies that may alter a country's business climate, thereby affecting the profitability of a firm's operations in that country. For example, sharp rises in a country's imports may signal an overheated economy and portend a tightening of the domestic money supply. In this case, attentive businesspeople will shrink their inventories in anticipation of a reduction in customer demand.

3 They can indicate reductions in a country's foreign-exchange reserves, which may mean that the country's currency will depreciate in the future, as occurred in Thailand in 1997. Exporters to that country may find that domestic producers will become more price competitive.

4 As was true in the international debt crisis, BOP statistics can signal increased riskiness of lending to particular countries.

Four important aspects of the BOP accounting system need to be highlighted:

1 The BOP accounting system records international transactions made during some time period, for example, a year.

2 It records only economic transactions, those that involve something of monetary value.

3 It records transactions between *residents* of one country and residents of all other countries. Residents can be individuals, businesses, government agencies, or nonprofit organizations, but defining residency is sometimes tricky. Persons temporarily located in a country—tourists, students, and military or diplomatic personnel—are still considered residents of their home country for BOP purposes. Businesses are considered residents of the country in which they are incorporated. Firms often conduct international business by locating either a branch or a subsidiary in a foreign country. A branch, which by definition is an unincorporated operation and thus not legally distinct from its parent corporation, is a resident of the parent's home country. A subsidiary, which by definition is a separately incorporated operation, is a resident of the country in which it is incorporated. In most cases, the subsidiary is incorporated in the host country to take advantage of legally being a resident of the country in which it is operating.

4 It is a *double-entry system*. Each transaction produces a credit entry and a debit entry of equal size. In most international business dealings, the first entry in a BOP transaction involves the purchase or sale of something—a good, a service, or an asset. The second entry records the payment or receipt of payment for the thing bought or sold. Figuring out which is the BOP debit entry and which is the BOP credit entry is not a skill that most people are born with. Many experts compare a BOP accounting statement to a statement of sources and uses of funds. Debit entries reflect *uses* of funds; credit entries measure *sources* of funds. Under this framework, buying things creates debits, and selling things produces credits.

The Major Components of the Balance of Payments Accounting System

The BOP accounting system can be divided conceptually into four major accounts. The first two accounts—the current account and the capital account—record purchases of goods, services, and assets by the private and public sectors. The official reserves account reflects the impact of central bank intervention in the foreign-exchange market. The last account—errors and omissions—captures mistakes made in recording BOP transactions.

Current Account. The **current account** records four types of transactions among residents of different countries:

1 Exports and imports of goods (or merchandise)

2 Exports and imports of services

3 Investment income

4 Gifts

Table 4.4 summarizes debit and credit entries for transactions involving the current account.

For example, to Germany, the sale of a Mercedes-Benz automobile to a doctor in Marseilles is a **merchandise export,** and the purchase by a German resident

TABLE 4.4

BOP Entries, Current Account

	DEBIT	CREDIT
Goods	Buy	Sell
Services	Buy	Sell
Dividends and interest (investment income)	Pay	Receive
Gifts	Give	Receive

of Dom Perignon champagne from France is a **merchandise import.** (The British use the term **trade in visibles** to refer to merchandise trade.) The difference between a country's exports and imports of goods is called the **balance on merchandise trade.** For example, the United States, which has been importing more goods than it has been exporting, has a *merchandise trade deficit;* Japan, which has been exporting more goods than it has been importing, has a *merchandise trade surplus.*

The services account records sales and purchases of such services as transportation, tourism, medical care, telecommunications, advertising, financial services, and education. The sale of a service to a resident of another country is a **service export,** and the purchase by a resident of a service from another country is a **service import.** (The British use the term **trade in invisibles** to denote trade in services.) For example, for Germany, a German student spending a year studying at the Sorbonne in Paris is an import of services, and the telephone call home that an Italian tourist makes during the Oktoberfest in Munich represents a service export. The difference between a country's exports of services and its imports of services is called the **balance on services trade.**

The third type of transaction recorded in the current account is investment income. Income German residents earn from their foreign investments is viewed as an **export of the services of capital** by Germany. This income takes the form of either interest and dividends earned by German residents on their investments in foreign stocks, bonds, and deposit accounts or profits that are repatriated back to Germany from incorporated subsidiaries in other countries that are owned by German firms. On the other hand, foreigners also make investments in Germany. Income earned by foreigners from their investments in Germany is viewed as an **import of the services of capital** by Germany. This income includes interest and dividends paid by firms in Germany on stocks, bonds, and deposit accounts owned by foreign residents, as well as profits that are repatriated by foreign-owned incorporated subsidiaries in Germany back to their corporate parents.

The fourth type of transaction in the current account is **unilateral transfers,** or gifts between residents of one country and another. Unilateral transfers include private and public gifts. For example, a Pakistani-born resident of Kuwait who sends part of his earnings back home to feed his relatives is engaging in a private unilateral transfer. In contrast, governmental aid from the United Kingdom used for a flood control project in Bangladesh is a public unilateral transfer. In either case, the recipient need not provide any compensation to the donor.

The **current account balance** measures the net balance resulting from merchandise trade, service trade, investment income, and unilateral transfers. It is closely scrutinized by government officials and policy makers because it broadly reflects the country's current competitiveness in international markets.

Capital Account. The second major account in the BOP accounting system is the **capital account,** which records capital transactions—purchases and sales of assets—between residents of one country and those of other countries. Capital account transactions (summarized in Table 4.5) can be divided into two categories: foreign direct investment (FDI) and portfolio investment. (Recall that we discussed both of these in Chapter 1.)

FDI is any investment made for purpose of controlling the organization in which the investment is made, typically through ownership of significant blocks of common stock with voting privileges. Under U.S. BOP accounting standards, control is defined as ownership of at least 10 percent of a company's voting stock. A portfolio investment is any investment made for purposes other than control. Portfolio investments are divided into two subcategories: short-term and long-term. **Short-term portfolio investments** are financial instruments with maturities of one year or less. Included in this category are commercial paper; checking accounts, time deposits, and certificates of deposit held by residents of a country in foreign banks or by foreigners in domestic banks; trade receivables and deposits from international commercial customers; and banks' short-term international lending activities, such as commercial loans. **Long-term portfolio investments** are stocks, bonds, and other financial instruments issued by private and public organizations that have maturities greater than one year and that are held for purposes other than control. For example, when IBM invests excess cash balances overnight in a Paris bank to earn a higher interest rate than it could earn in New York, it is making a short-

---

TABLE 4.5

Capital Account Transactions

	MATURITY	MOTIVATION	TYPICAL INVESTMENTS
Portfolio (short-term)	One year or less	Investment income or facilitation of international commerce	Checking account balances Time deposits Commercial paper Bank loans
Portfolio (long-term)	More than one year	Investment income	Government bills, notes, and bonds Corporate stocks and bonds
Foreign direct investment	Indeterminate	Active control of organization (own at least 10 percent of voting stock)	Foreign subsidiaries Foreign factories International joint ventures

term portfolio investment. When the California Public Employers Retirement System Pension Fund buys stock in British Airways, it is making a long-term portfolio investment. When British Airways purchases 23 percent of the common stock of USAir, it is making an FDI.

Current account transactions invariably affect the short-term component of the capital account. Why? Well, as noted earlier in the chapter, the first entry in the double-entry BOP accounting system involves the purchase or sale of something—a good, a service, or an asset. The second entry typically records the payment or receipt of payment for the thing bought or sold. In most cases, this second entry involves a change in someone's checking account balance, which in the BOP accounting system is a short-term capital account transaction. "Building Global Skills" at the end of this chapter walks you through this linkage between the current account and the capital account in more detail.

Capital inflows are credits in the BOP accounting system. They can occur in two ways:

1. *Foreign ownership of assets in a country increases.* One highly publicized example of a capital inflow into the United States was the Mitsubishi Estate Co.'s purchase of 51 percent of the Rockefeller Group, owner of Rockefeller Center, for $846 million.[24] A capital inflow also occurs if a foreign firm deposits a check in a U.S. bank. In this case, the asset being purchased is a claim on a U.S. bank, which of course is all that a checking account balance represents.

2. *Ownership of foreign assets by a country's residents declines.* When K-Mart and a U.S. partner sold K-Mart's Canadian operations to Zeller's (a division of Canada's Hudson's Bay Company) for $168 million in early 1998, the United States experienced a capital inflow. Similarly, when IBM pays a Japanese disk drive supplier with a check drawn on IBM's account at a Tokyo bank, IBM's Japanese checking account balance declines and the United States experiences a capital inflow because IBM is partially liquidating its ownership of foreign assets.

Capital outflows are debits in the BOP accounting system. They also can occur in two ways:

1. *Ownership of foreign assets by a country's residents increases.* Ford's £1.5 billion purchase of the British firm Jaguar Motor Company represented a capital outflow from the United States. A U.S. capital outflow also occurs when Delta Air Lines deposits a check from a London businessperson into an account it holds in an English bank.

2. *Foreign ownership of assets in a country declines.* A German mutual fund that sells 100,000 shares of GM common stock from its portfolio to a U.S. resident causes a capital outflow from the United States. A U.S. capital outflow also occurs if Japan Air Lines writes a check drawn on its account at an Hawaiian bank to pay its fuel supplier at Honolulu Airport. In both cases, foreigners are liquidating a portion of their U.S. assets.

Table 4.6 summarizes the impact of various capital account transactions on the BOP.

TABLE 4.6

BOP Entries, Capital Account

	DEBIT (OUTFLOW)	CREDIT (INFLOW)
Portfolio (short-term)	Receiving a payment from a foreigner	Making a payment to a foreigner
	Buying a short-term foreign asset	Selling a domestic short-term asset to a foreigner
	Buying back a short-term domestic asset from its foreign owner	Selling a short-term foreign asset acquired previously
Portfolio (long-term)	Buying a long-term foreign asset (not for purposes of control)	Selling a domestic long-term asset to a foreigner (not for purposes of control)
	Buying back a long-term domestic asset from its foreign owner (not for purposes of control)	Selling a long-term foreign asset acquired previously (not for purposes of control)
Foreign direct investment	Buying a foreign asset for purposes of control	Selling a domestic asset to a foreigner for purposes of control
	Buying back from its foreign owner a domestic asset previously acquired for purposes of control	Selling a foreign asset previously acquired for purposes of control

Official Reserves Account. The third major account in the BOP account-ing system is the official reserves account. The **official reserves account** records holdings of the official reserves held by a national government. These reserves are used to intervene in the foreign-exchange market and in transactions with other central banks. Official reserves comprise four types of assets:

1 Gold
2 Convertible currencies
3 SDRs
4 Reserve positions at the IMF

Official gold holdings are measured using a par value established by the treasury or finance ministry. Convertible currencies are currencies that are freely exchange-able in world currency markets. The convertible currencies most commonly used as official reserves are the U.S. dollar, the deutsche mark, and the yen. The last two types of reserves—SDRs and reserve positions (quotas minus IMF borrow-ings) at the IMF—were discussed earlier in this chapter.

Errors and Omissions. The last account in the BOP accounting system is the errors and omissions account. One truism of the BOP accounting system is that the BOP must balance. In theory the following equality should be observed:

$$\text{Current Account + Capital Account + Official Reserves Account = 0.}$$

However, this equality is never achieved in practice because of measurement errors. The account called **errors and omissions** is used to make the BOP balance in accordance with the following equation:

$$\text{Current Account + Capital Account + Errors and Omissions} \\ \text{+ Official Reserves Account = 0.}$$

The errors and omissions account can be quite large. In 1996, for example, the U.S. errors and omissions account totaled $46.9 billion. Experts suspect that a large portion of the errors and omissions account balance is due to under-reporting of capital account transactions. Such innovations as instantaneous, round-the-clock foreign-exchange trading, sophisticated monetary swaps and hedges, and international money-market funds have made it difficult for government statisticians to keep up with the growing volume of legal short-term money flowing between countries in search of the highest interest rate. Sometimes, errors and omissions are due to deliberate actions by individuals who are engaged in illegal activities such as drug smuggling, money laundering, or evasion of currency and investment controls imposed by their home governments. Politically stable countries, such as the United States, are often the destination of **flight capital,** money sent abroad by foreign residents seeking a safe haven for their assets, hidden from the sticky fingers of their home governments. Given the often illegal nature of flight capital, persons sending it to the United States often try to avoid any official recognition of their transactions, making it difficult for government BOP statisticians to record such transactions. Residents of other countries who distrust the stability of their own currency may also choose to use a stronger currency, such as the dollar or the mark, to transact their business or keep their savings, as "Going Global" suggests. An estimated $26 billion of U.S. dollar bills flowed to Russia and the other former Soviet republics from 1994 to 1996, for example, as their citizens reacted to growing domestic economic and political uncertainties by converting their local currencies to U.S. dollars. Dollar holdings in this part of the world are so large and important that when the U.S. government introduced a new $100 banknote in 1996, it launched a special hotline to assure Russian citizens that the value of their holdings of old $100 bills was still intact.[25]

Some errors may crop up in the current account as well. Statistics for merchandise imports are generally thought to be reasonably accurate because most countries' customs services scrutinize imports to ensure that all appropriate taxes are collected. This scrutiny generates paper trails that facilitate the collection of accurate statistics. However, few countries tax exports, so customs services have less incentive to assess the accuracy of statistics concerning merchandise exports. Statistics for trade in services also may contain inaccuracies. Many service trade statistics are generated by surveys. For example, U.S. tourism exports are measured by surveying foreign tourists on how many days they spent in the United States and how many dollars they spent per day. If tourists underestimate their daily spending, then U.S. service exports are underestimated. To help you gain a better understanding of the BOP accounts, we next review the international transactions of the United States in 1996.

GOING GLOBAL

Ben Franklin, World Traveler

Who is the most well-known American outside the borders of the United States? . . . Bill Clinton? . . . Madonna? . . . Sylvester Stallone? A good argument can be made in favor of Ben Franklin, whose face adorns the U.S. $100 bill. Economists and accountants at the U.S. Federal Reserve Bank (FRB) have been trying for years to estimate how much U.S. currency is held by foreigners. Their best guess is that of the $398 billion in U.S. currency in circulation in 1996, $210 billion, or 53 percent, is held by foreigners. Most of this foreign-held currency is in the form of $100 bills, while U.S. consumers prefer to utilize smaller denomination bills.

Tracking down the total number of dollars held overseas is rather complex, and is based on a mixture of sophisticated economic modeling, consumer surveys, and educated guesswork. A 1995 FRB survey of U.S. households could account for only 3 percent of the $100 bills printed by the U.S. government, yet the number of such bills in circulation has increased by $143 billion since 1990. FRB staffers also know that the Los Angeles and New York City branches of the FRB distribute enormous numbers of $100 bills relative to the other branches. From 1990 to 1996 these two branches accounted for 84 percent of the new $100 bills placed in circulation. Experts believe that most of this currency flows to citizens of countries where economic and/or political unrest is high. Russia, other former Soviet Republics, the Middle East, and Latin America appear to be particularly important destinations for U.S. $100 dollar bills.

These foreign holdings of U.S. paper currency provide an important benefit to the U.S. Treasury and ultimately to the U.S. taxpayer, for effectively they serve as an interest-free loan. Normally, to fund the U.S. debt the U.S. Treasury must float loans in the form of bonds, notes, and bills. Currency holdings substitute for such loans, and reduce the amount the Treasury must borrow. If 30-year Treasury bonds bear an interest rate of 6.5 percent, then the U.S taxpayer saves $13.7 billion (6.5 percent times $210 billion) in interest payments annually as a result of foreign holdings of U.S. currency. This is one of the benefits American citizens receive as a result of the country's economic and political stability. Other countries—in particular, Germany—also benefit from large holdings of their paper currencies by residents of other countries.

Sources: "Dollar's Share of World Reserves Grows," *Wall Street Journal*, September 10, 1997, p. A2; *Survey of Current Business*, July 1997, p. 49; "Russia counts cost of change as US set to issue new $100 bill," *Financial Times*, January 16, 1996, p. 20; "Where's the buck? Dollars make the world go around, Fed says," *Houston Chronicle*, October 13, 1995, p. 2C.

The U.S. Balance of Payments in 1996

The first component of the current account is merchandise (goods) exports and imports. As shown in Table 4.7, U.S. merchandise exports totaled $612.1 billion in 1996, or approximately 8.0 percent of 1996's GDP of $7.6 trillion. Figure 4.6(a) presents a more detailed picture of the leading U.S. exports. Automobiles and auto parts were the largest component of U.S. merchandise exports, generating $65.0 billion in sales. Of U.S. automobile exports, 54 percent were to Canada, a reflection of the integrated nature of North American automobile production that resulted from the 1965 Auto Pact between the United States and Canada. (Canada—meaning primarily GM, Ford, and Chrysler plants that are located in Canada—exported $45.9 billion in automobiles and auto parts to the United States.) The six industries shown in Fig. 4.6(a) accounted for 46 percent of U.S. merchandise exports in 1996.

From Table. 4.7, you can see that U.S. merchandise *imports* totaled $803.3 billion in 1996. From Fig. 4.6(b), you can see that the leading import was automobiles

---

TABLE 4.7

U.S. BOP, 1996 (in billions of dollars)

Current Account

Goods		
Exports	+$612.1	
Imports	−803.3	
Balance on Merchandise Trade	−191.2	
Services		
Exports	+236.8	
Imports	−156.6	
Balance on Services Trade	+80.2	
Investment Income		
Received	206.4	
Paid	−203.6	
Balance on Investment Income	+2.8	
Unilateral Transfers (net)	−40.0	
(− means outward gifts greater than inward)		
Balance on Current Account		−148.2
Capital Account		
Portfolio, Short-Term (Net Outflow)	−116.1	
Portfolio, Long-Term		
New Foreign Investment in U.S.	+424.3	
New U.S. Investment Abroad	−109.0	
Foreign Direct Investment		
New FDI in U.S.	+77.0	
New U.S. FDI Abroad	−87.8	
Balance on Capital Account		+188.4
Official Reserves Account		+6.7
Errors and Omissions		−46.9
Net Balance		0

---

and auto parts, at $128.9 billion, or 16 percent of imports. Six industries accounted for $370.5 billion, or 46 percent of total U.S. merchandise imports.

The second component of the current account is trade in services. U.S. exports of services totaled $236.8 billion in 1996, with travel and tourism being the largest portion ($69.9 billion). U.S. service imports equaled $156.6 in 1996, with travel and tourism again being the largest portion ($48.7 billion). The United States had a positive balance on services trade of $80.2 billion (see Table 4.7).

Figure 4.7 shows exports and imports for the major trading partners of the United States. Unlike Figs. 4.6(a) and (b), this figure includes trade in both goods and services. While the United States tends to import more *goods* from its major

FIGURE 4.6

Leading U.S. Merchandise Exports and Imports, 1996

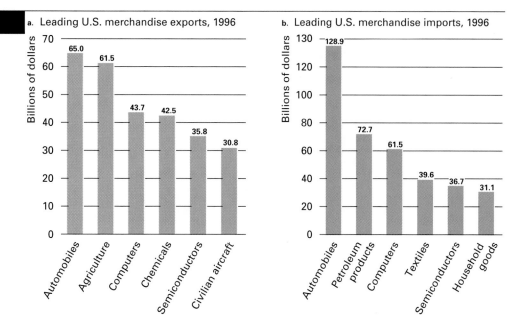

a. Leading U.S. merchandise exports, 1996

b. Leading U.S. merchandise imports, 1996

trading partners than it exports to them, Fig. 4.7 shows it tends to export more *services* to them than it imports from them.

The third component of the current account is investment income (see Table 4.7). In 1996 U.S. residents received $206.4 billion from foreign investments and paid out $203.6 billion to foreigners for a net balance on investment income of $2.8 billion. The United States had a net deficit of $40 billion in the fourth component of the current account, unilateral transfers. Summing up the four components yielded a 1996 current account deficit of $148.2 billion.

The capital account is the second major BOP account (see Table 4.7). In 1996 new U.S. FDI abroad (outflows) totaled $87.8 billion, while new FDI in the U.S. (inflows) totaled $77.0 billion. New U.S. long-term international portfolio investments were $109.0 billion in 1996, while new foreign long-term portfolio investments in the United States were $424.3 billion, resulting in a net long-term portfolio investment balance of $315.3 billion. There was also a net outflow of short-term portfolio investment from the United States, totaling $116.1 billion. The capital account balance was $188.4 billion in 1996, as foreigners bought more U.S. assets than U.S. residents did foreign assets.

U.S. official reserves account transactions were $6.7 billion, meaning the United States decreased its official holdings. (Although that may seem backward to you, the positive sign means that the U.S. government "sold" official reserves to other countries.) If the BOP statistical data net were perfect, the current account balance plus the capital account balance plus the official reserves account balance should equal zero. Any discrepancy is put into the errors and omissions account. In 1996 there was a discrepancy of $46.9 billion. So for the U.S. BOP in 1996, the following equation applies:

Current Account	Capital Account	Changes in Official Reserves	Errors and Omissions	
(−$148.2 billion)	+ (+$188.4 billion)	+ (+$6.7 billion)	+ (−$46.9 billion)	= 0.

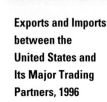

FIGURE 4.7

Exports and Imports between the United States and Its Major Trading Partners, 1996

Note: Data on services exports and imports are not available for Taiwan, China, and South Korea.

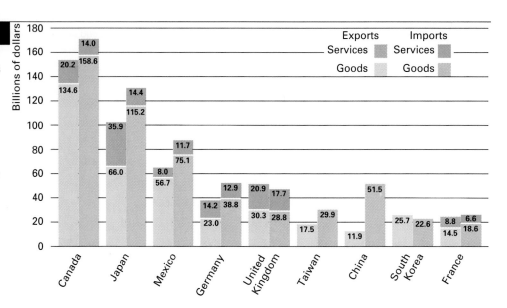

Defining Balance of Payments Surpluses and Deficits

Every month the federal government reports the performance of U.S. firms in international markets when it releases the monthly BOP statistics. In most months in the past decade, newscasters have solemnly reported on the evening news that the U.S. BOP is in deficit.

What do the newscasters mean? We just said that the BOP always balances (equals zero), so how can there be a BOP deficit? In reality, when knowledgeable people (or even newscasters) talk about a BOP surplus or deficit, they are referring only to a subset of the BOP accounts. Most newscasters are in fact reporting on the balance on trade in goods and services. When a country exports more goods and services than it imports, it has a trade surplus. When it imports more goods and services than it exports, it has a trade deficit.

Because the balance on trade in goods and services is readily understandable and quickly available to the news media, it receives the most public attention. But other balances also exist, for example, the balance on services, the balance on merchandise trade, and the current account balance. Another closely watched BOP balance is the official settlements balance. The **official settlements balance** reflects changes in a country's official reserves; essentially, it records the net impact of the central bank's interventions in the foreign-exchange market in support of the local currency.

Which of these BOP balances is *the* balance of payments? That's a trick question; there is no single measure of a country's global economic performance. Rather, as in the parable of the blind men touching the elephant, each balance presents a different perspective on the nation's position in the international economy. Which BOP concept to use depends on the issue confronting the international businessperson or government policy maker. The balance on merchandise trade reflects the competitiveness of a country's manufacturing sector. The balance on services reflects the service sector's global competitiveness. While the balance on merchandise trade often receives more publicity, the balance on services is growing in importance because of the expansion of the service sector in many national economies. The balance on goods and services reflects the combined international competitiveness of a

FIGURE 4.8

The U.S. BOP
According to Various
Reporting Measures

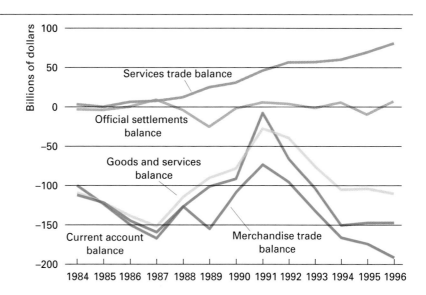

country's manufacturing and service sectors. The current account balance shows the combined performance of the manufacturing and service sectors and also reflects the generosity of the country's residents (unilateral transfers) as well as income generated by past investments. The official settlements balance reflects the net quantity demanded and supplied of the country's currency by all market participants, other than the country's central bank.[26] Figure 4.8 shows the U.S. balance of payments for the past decade according to these various measures.

CHAPTER REVIEW

Summary

In their normal commercial activities, international businesses often deal with currencies other than that of their home country. For international commerce to thrive, some system for exchanging and valuing different currencies, preferably at low cost, must exist. The international monetary system accomplishes this by establishing the rules for valuing and exchanging different currencies.

The economic growth of the nineteenth century is attributable in part to the success of the gold standard in providing a stable, reliable international monetary system based on fixed exchange rates. However, the gold standard broke down during World War I and could not be satisfactorily revived in the years between the two world wars.

The Bretton Woods Agreement of 1944 structured the post–World War II international monetary system. In addition to creating the International Bank for Reconstruction and Development (the World Bank) and the International Monetary Fund, it reinstituted a fixed exchange-rate system, with the dollar playing a key role in international transactions. However, as the number of dollars held by foreigners increased, the marketplace began to distrust the ability of the United States to redeem its currency at $35 per ounce of gold as required by the Bretton Woods Agreement. After fending off waves of speculation against the dollar, the United States abandoned the Bretton Woods Agreement in August 1971.

Since then, the international monetary system has relied on a flexible exchange-rate system, although certain countries, such as the EU members, have attempted to maintain fixed exchange rates among their currencies. The system has proven responsive to major shocks to the world economy, such as the shift of wealth from oil-consuming to oil-producing countries after the 1973–1974 oil embargo, the 1980s international debt crisis, and the 1997–1998 Asian currency crisis.

The BOP accounting system, which is used to record international transactions, is important to international businesspeople. The BOP system provides economic intelligence data about the international competitiveness of a country's industries, likely changes in its fiscal and monetary policies, and its ability to repay its international debts.

The BOP accounting system comprises four accounts. The current account reflects exports and imports of goods, exports and imports of services, investment income, and gifts. The capital account records capital transactions among countries and includes FDI and portfolio investments. Portfolio investments in turn can be divided into long-term and short-term investments. The official reserves account is a record of changes in a country's official reserves, which include central bank holdings of gold, convertible currencies, SDRs, and reserves at the International Monetary Fund. The errors and omissions account captures statistical discrepancies that often result from transactions that participants want to hide from government officials.

There are numerous ways to measure a balance of payments surplus or deficit. Each presents a different perspective on a country's global economic performance. The balance on merchandise trade measures the difference between a country's exports and imports of goods. The balance on services is growing in importance because of the rapid expansion of the service sector in many economies. The balance on goods and services measures the nation's trade in goods and services. The current account balance reflects both trade in goods and trade in services, as well as net investment income and gifts. The official settlements balance shows changes in the country's official reserves.

Review Questions

1. What is the function of the international monetary system?

2. Why is the gold standard a type of fixed exchange-rate system?

3. What were the key accomplishments of the Bretton Woods conference?

4. Why was the IFC established by the World Bank?

5. Why are quotas important to IMF members?

6. Why did the Bretton Woods system collapse in 1971?

7. Describe the differences between a fixed exchange-rate system and a flexible exchange-rate system.

8. List the four major accounts of the BOP accounting system and their components.

9. What factors cause measurement errors in the BOP accounts?

10. Differentiate among the different types of balance of payments surpluses and deficits.

Questions for Discussion

1. What parallels exist between the role of the British pound in the nineteenth-century international monetary system and that of the U.S. dollar since 1945?

2. Did the key role that the dollar played in the Bretton Woods system benefit or hurt the United States?

3. Under what conditions might a country devalue its currency today?

4. Are there any circumstances under which a country might want to increase its currency's value?

5. Can international businesses operate more easily in a fixed exchange-rate system or in a flexible exchange-rate system?

6. What connections exist between the current account and the capital account?

BUILDING GLOBAL SKILLS

This Building Global Skills exercise explains how governmental statisticians account for international transactions. You may want to refer back to Tables 4.4 and 4.6 and to the definitions of capital inflows and capital outflows on page 146.

Example 1

Suppose Wal-Mart imports $1 million worth of VCRs from the Sony Corporation of Japan. The debit entry is a merchandise import of $1 million. The import of the Japanese goods means the United States will observe an outflow (or a use) of foreign exchange.

Here's the tough part. What is the offsetting credit entry? The answer is a capital inflow affecting the short-term portfolio account. Recall that a capital inflow occurs because of either an increase in foreign-owned U.S. assets or a decrease of U.S.-owned foreign assets. If Wal-Mart pays Sony with a $1 million check that Sony deposits in its U.S. bank, foreign ownership of assets in the United States increases, which is a short-term capital inflow. If Wal-Mart pays Sony in yen by drawing down a Wal-Mart checking account balance at a Tokyo bank, a decrease of U.S.-owned assets in foreign countries occurs, which is also a short-term capital inflow. Either way, a short-term capital inflow occurs, since the VCRs are being exchanged for a change in a checking account balance.

What if Wal-Mart pays Sony with a $1 million check, but Sony wants yen? Sony will take the check to its U.S. bank and ask the bank to convert the $1 million check to yen. The U.S. bank can accommodate Sony in one of two ways:

1. Give Sony yen that the U.S. bank already owns—this represents a decrease of U.S.-owned foreign assets.
2. Pass the check along to a Japanese bank that keeps the $1 million but gives Sony the equivalent in yen—this represents an increase in U.S. assets owned by foreigners (the Japanese bank).

In either case, a capital inflow occurs.

Thus Wal-Mart's purchase of the VCRs from Sony enters the BOP accounts as follows:

	DEBIT	CREDIT
Merchandise imports account	$1 million	
Short-term portfolio account		$1 million

The merchandise import account is debited to reflect a use of funds. The payment itself is credited because effectively a foreigner has purchased a U.S. asset (either an increase in foreign claims on the United States or a decrease in U.S. claims on foreigners). Note the linkage between the current account and the capital account.

Example 2

An Iraqi restaurant owner in Los Angeles who escaped her homeland during the Gulf War in 1991 smuggles $1000 in cash back to her relatives in Baghdad. The U.S. BOP accounts *should* record this transaction as follows:

	DEBIT	CREDIT
Unilateral transfer account	$1000	
Short-term portfolio account		$1000

The transaction involves a unilateral transfer, since the $1000 is a gift. Because the gift is being given by a U.S. resident, it is a debit. The capital account is credited because foreigners have increased their claims on the United States. (A country's currency reflects a claim on its goods, services, and assets.) Had the restaurant owner sent a $1000 stereo system instead of cash, the credit entry would have been a merchandise export.

Note the use of the qualifier *should* in the previous paragraph. If U.S. governmental statisticians were omniscient, the transaction would be recorded as just explained. However, if the restaurant owner wished to hide their transaction from the government, it is unlikely U.S. statisticians would ever learn of it. When you consider the widespread usage of the dollar in countries suffering political turmoil, it is not surprising that the errors and omissions account is as large as it is.

Example 3

Mitsubishi buys 51 percent of Rockefeller Center for $846 million from a Rockefeller family trust. This transaction will be recorded in the U.S. BOP accounts as follows:

	DEBIT	CREDIT
Foreign direct investment account		$846 million
Short-term portfolio account	$846 million	

In this transaction, two assets are being exchanged. Japan is buying a long-term asset—Rockefeller Center—for purposes of control, and the United States is buying a short-term asset called an "increase of claims on foreigners or a decrease of foreign claims on the United States." The U.S. BOP is credited with a long-term FDI capital inflow of $846 million, because foreign ownership of U.S. assets (for purposes of control) has increased. But the actual payment of the $846 million is debited as a short-term capital outflow: either Japanese-owned checking account balances in the United States declined by $846 million or U.S.-owned checking account balances in Japan rose by $846 million.

Unlike Examples 1 and 2, this transaction does not involve a current account entry and a capital account entry. Both the debit entry and the credit entry affect the capital account. However, a balance in someone's checking account is affected by this transaction, as was the case in Example 1.

Do the following exercises on your own. How will the following transactions be recorded in the U.S. BOP accounts?

1. A Chicago entrepreneur seeking to sell souvenirs at the 2000 Summer Olympics in Sydney, Australia, pays Qantas, an Australian airline, $1400 for a Chicago-Sydney round-trip ticket.

2. The Chicago entrepreneur instead pays United Airlines (a U.S. airline) $1400 for a Chicago-Sydney round-trip ticket.

3. Ford Motor Company (U.S.) pays $2.5 billion for the Jaguar Motor Co. (U.K.).

4. The U.S. government gives Rwanda $500 million worth of food to feed starving refugees.

WORKING WITH THE WEB: Building Global Internet Skills

Doing Business with the World Bank

The web site of the World Bank provides a variety of information about the World Bank's mission, its current policies, and how and where it's spending its monies. Because the Bank loans billions of dollars a year, its web site is a treasure trove of marketing leads for a wide variety of companies that sell goods and services needed by the Bank's clients.

Assignment: You are currently employed by WaterPure, a company that manufactures water treatment machinery and hydroelectric generating technology. Most of its sales are to large, publicly owned water treatment facilities and public power authorities. WaterPure is currently examining whether it should place a sales office in Africa to take advantage of the political and economic reforms adopted by many countries in that continent. Because the World Bank finances many infrastructure projects in Africa, you are assigned the task of determining whether the World Bank is likely to fund any water treatment or hydroelectric projects there in the near future. Such information is contained in the Annual Report of the World Bank, which is accessible from its web site. If you recommend that Waterpure should place an office in Africa, in what city should the office be placed? (The textbook's web site provides a link to the World Bank's web site.)

CLOSING CASE

Recent U.S. BOP Performance: Is the Sky Falling or Not?

During much of the past decade, the U.S. BOP performance could be characterized as follows:

♦ The U.S. current account recorded large annual deficits.

♦ The U.S. capital account recorded large annual surpluses of roughly the same magnitude as the current account deficits.

♦ Changes in the official reserves account were small relative to the magnitude of the current account deficits.

Two scenarios can be developed from these three facts:

1. The sky is falling. U.S. industries are uncompetitive in international markets (as indicated by the first fact), and foreigners are taking over the country by buying up valuable U.S. assets and transforming the country into the largest debtor in international history (as indicated by the second fact).

2. Everything is wonderful. Foreigners are so enthralled with the future prospects of the U.S. market, which is a showcase of economic democracy, that they are eagerly investing in the U.S. economy (the second fact). But the only way they can do so is by running a current account surplus with the United States (the first fact).

Needless to say, these two scenarios conflict, *even though both are consistent with the data.* They reflect a policy war that is occurring between protectionists and free traders, between Rust Belt firms and Sunbelt firms, between liberals and conservatives, and between export-oriented firms and firms threatened by foreign imports.

People who believe the sky is falling argue that the United States must reduce its balance of trade deficit. They argue that U.S. firms are increasingly uncompetitive in global markets and must be strengthened via aggressive government policies, such as those calling for worker training programs, increased investment in infrastructure, and tax credits for R&D and investment expenditures. They assert that U.S. firms are victimized by the unfair trade practices of foreign firms and governments. They propose stiffer tariffs and quotas on imported goods and believe that the federal government should do more to promote U.S. exports and restrict foreign ownership of U.S. assets.

People who believe everything is wonderful say the best policy is to continue to make the United States an attractive economy in which to invest. By keeping tax rates low and governmental regulation modest, the United States will attract foreign capital. U.S. industries, consumers, and workers will then benefit from increased capital investment and the enhancements in productivity that will ensue from this investment. U.S. consumers will benefit from the availability of low-priced, high-quality imported goods and services. Moreover, U.S. firms will become "leaner and meaner" as they respond to foreign competitors.

A variant of this "everything is wonderful" argument has been offered by Nobel laureate Milton Friedman, the provocative free-market advocate from the University of Chicago. Friedman argues that Japanese workers have been busily producing VCRs, Toyota Camrys, and Sony Walkmans in return for dollar bills from U.S. consumers. If the Japanese are happy voluntarily exchanging their goods for pieces of paper (that is, dollar bills), and U.S. citizens are happy voluntarily exchanging pieces of paper for goods, why should anyone worry?

As you ponder these divergent perspectives, recognize that they have developed because of two very different views of what represents a BOP deficit. The "sky is falling" crowd is focusing on the balance on merchandise trade and assessing whether U.S. firms are able to sell as many goods to foreigners as foreigners buy from U.S. firms. The "everything is wonderful" folks are focusing on voluntary transactions in the marketplace. In their view, if U.S. citizens find it in their self-interest to be net buyers of foreign goods and foreigners find it in their self-interest to be net buyers of U.S. assets, then what's the problem?

Because BOP statistics affect the ongoing domestic political battle over international trade policy, they are important to virtually every U.S. firm. Export-oriented firms and workers benefit from the free-trade policies promoted by the "everything is wonderful" crowd, as do communities that benefit from jobs created by inward FDI. Firms and workers threatened by imported goods or by the output of new domestic factories built by foreign competitors are more likely to support the "sky is falling" view.

Case Questions

1. What is more important to an economy—exports or foreign capital inflows?

2. What is the connection between the U.S. current account deficit and capital account surplus?

3. Which of the following groups is likely to endorse the "sky is falling" view of the U.S. BOP?

   ♦ Import-threatened firms such as textile producers

   ♦ Textile workers

   ♦ A cash-starved California biotechnology company

   ♦ Merrill Lynch

   ♦ Boeing Aircraft, one of the country's largest exporters

   ♦ Consumers

CHAPTER NOTES

1. Passage quoted from "Dollar Declines against Mark Again as Traders Refocus on Washington Risks," *Wall Street Journal*, February 6, 1998, p. C20.

2. Passage quoted from "Exports Fail to Grow, Survey Indicates," *Wall Street Journal*, February 3, 1998, p. A2.

3. Passage quoted from "Drift by Dollar Continues as Traders Seek Improving Yields in Japan, Europe," *Wall Street Journal*, February 5, 1998, p. C23.

4. Passage quoted from "Dollar Is Bid Up against Mark and Yen as Traders Focus on Economic Basics," *Wall Street Journal*, January 30, 1998, p. C14.

5. Passage quoted from "Earnings Outlook for 1998 Could Jar Stocks," *Wall Street Journal*, January 26, 1998, p. C1.

6. Passage quoted from "Dollar Gains on Mark, Sags against Yen," *Wall Street Journal*, January 15, 1998, p. C19.

7. Del Mar, *A History of Money in Ancient Countries* (New York: Burt Franklin, 1968; originally published in 1885), p. 71.

8. I. Drummond, *The Gold Standard and the International Monetary System 1900–1939* (London: MacMillan Education Group, 1987), pp. 10–11.

9. At the turn of the century, the French franc and the German mark were used in addition to sterling for settling private international transactions. For more details, see P. Lindert, "Key Currencies and Gold 1900–1913," *Princeton Studies in International Finance* No. 24 (Princeton: Department of Economics, 1969), p. 1. See also D. Williams, "The Evaluation of the Sterling System," in *Essays in Money and Banking in Honor of R. S. Sayers*, eds. C. Whittlesley and J. Wilson (Oxford, 1968).

10. B. Cohen, *The Future of Sterling as an International Currency* (London: MacMillan, 1971), pp. 60–61.

11. Drummond, op. cit., p. 31.

12. Ibid., pp. 40ff.

13. Cohen, op. cit., p. 68.

14. The World Bank, *The World Bank Annual Report 1997*.

15. The World Bank, *The World Bank* (New York: World Bank, 1991), p. 17.

16. *The World Bank Annual Report 1997*, op. cit., Table 1.

17. *MIGA, 1996 Annual Report*, pp. 19, 20, and 28.

18. Stephen Riddell, "U.S. set to compromise on World Bank loan policy," *Financial Times*, June 10, 1991, p. 1; "U.S. Agrees to Capital Increase for IFC, Backing Down from Earlier Demands," *Wall Street Journal*, July 1, 1991, p. C14; "New Regime Forming at World Bank That Is Likely to Increase Role of U.S.," *Wall Street Journal*, September 17, 1991, p. B5; "Aid and enterprise," *The Economist*, May 25, 1991, p. 18.

19. *MIGA, 1996 Annual Report*, p. 22.

20. "South Korea Reaches Accord with IMF over Terms of Bailout," *Wall Street Journal,* December 1, 1997, p. A15; "Group offers Indonesia loans of up to $40 billion," *Houston Chronicle*, November 1, 1997, p. 1C.

21. International Monetary Fund, *1990 Annual Report*, p. 133.

22. David Eitemann, Arthur Stonehill, and Michael Moffett, *Multinational Business Finance*, 6th ed. (Reading, Mass.: Addison-Wesley, 1992), p. 30.

23. *The European Financial Common Market* (Luxembourg: Office for Official Publications of the European Communities, 1989), pp. 43ff; *The European Community in the Nineties* (Washington, D.C.: EC Delegation to the United States, 1992), pp. 12ff; Directorate-General for Economic and Financial Affairs, *European Economy*, No. 44 (October 1990), p. 42.

24. "Mitsubishi Estate Resembles Rockefeller," *Wall Street Journal*, November 1, 1989, p. A11.

25. *Survey of Current Business*, July 1997, p. 49; "Russia counts cost of change as US set to issue new $100 bill," *Financial Times*, January 16, 1996, p. 20.

26. "Basic truths," *The Economist*, August 24, 1991, p. 68.

Foreign Exchange and International Financial Markets

After studying this chapter you should be able to:

Describe how demand and supply determine the price of foreign exchange.

Analyze how balance of payments equilibrium is reached in a fixed exchange-rate system and a flexible exchange-rate system.

Discuss the role of international banks in the foreign-exchange market.

Assess the different ways firms can use the spot and forward markets to settle international transactions.

Summarize the role of arbitrage in the foreign-exchange market.

Discuss the important aspects of the international capital market.

NEW YORK—"IT'S BEEN BEDLAM—PEOPLE ARE TRYING TO GET prices and can't find them," says Paul Farrell, one of the senior currency traders at Chase Manhattan Bank, on one of the for-eign-exchange market's wildest days ever. ▌▌ Britain has just raised its interest rates twice to defend the pound, but it isn't working. The pound is slipping. The entire European exchange-rate system is in doubt. Rumors are flying, and the dollar is rallying. ▌▌ Thirty-five floors above Chase Manhattan Plaza yesterday morning, a small army of 50 traders and salespeople is trying to ride the billion-dollar waves sweeping across the currency markets. Hunched over banks of phones and green electronic quote screens, they bark out customer orders or price quotes as currency trading machines emit a series of ever-louder, high-pitched beeps, seeking prices from Chase.

Exchange-Rate Chaos[1]

▌▌ "We knew this week would be wild, but not like this," says Geoff Koestner, a European currency trader seated near Mr. Farrell. "It's all been unraveling." Now, Chase's traders want to avoid risks and mistakes at all costs. "The whole idea is just be square," Mr. Koestner explains. "Do the deal. Make the money and get out.". . . ▌▌ As one trader gets a substantial customer order, he stands up and shouts out for exchange-rate quotes from other Chase traders who specialize in the currencies involved. Then the other traders try to fill the customer's order as quickly as possible—before the market moves or the order is canceled. Usually, one or two traders will be stand-ing at any given time, swapping prices and orders. This day, seven or eight are standing at once; sometimes nearly the entire roomful of traders are on their feet. ▌▌ Chase . . . is doing twice its normal trading volume—and making more than twice a normal day's profits, says James Borden, Chase's head of foreign exchange. With the currency market so chaotic, the spread between bids and offering prices is far wider than usual. For Chase, that can be good news, as it makes much of its currency-trading profits from such bid-asked spreads, instead of betting heavily on the market's direction. ▌▌ At 11:15 a.m., a grave Mr. Farrell stands up and tells other traders: "The central banks are gone here"—meaning the world's central banks appear to have temporarily abandoned their efforts to support the wobbling British pound. A few moments later, Joseph Greene, a sandy-haired bespectacled "sterling-mark" trader, stands and announces that a customer wants to sell £100 million and buy German marks. "There are no prices!" shouts Arnold Neimanis, who trades marks and is on the phone con-stantly to other brokers who are making price quotes. . . . ▌▌ Instead of making a bid—and taking the risk of holding the pounds with the market so disorderly—the Chase traders persuade the customer to allow them to execute the order bit by bit. Over the next few minutes, Chase executes half the trade, £5 million at a time; but the customer decides to stop at £50 million. ▋▋ To veteran currency traders such as Mr. Farrell, the signs of turmoil are everywhere. Normally, he says, currency bid-asked spreads move in orderly progressions, for example, 10–20, then 15–25, then 20–30. The numbers denote the last two digits of a currency's price, such as 1.5220 marks per dollar. Dealers give price quotes without necessarily knowing whether the customer wants to buy or sell, and so must be prepared to buy or sell at the quoted price. At 10–20, the dealer would be offering to buy dollars at 1.5210 or sell at 1.5220. Today, the progression is more like 10–30, then 50–80. ▋▋ Around 11:45, Rick Walsh, a trader who sits opposite Mr. Neimanis, warns him urgently: "Don't be exposed. They're buying dollars on the floor"—meaning the dollar may be moving up sharply against the mark. A few moments later, Mr. Neimanis calls out: "Just buy it, just buy it." Seated next to him, Russell Lascala marvels, "This dollar is going to the moon!" ▋▋ Around noon, Seth Cohen, a salesman, approaches Mr. Neimanis to confer about a rumor that the German central bank is about to hold a news conference. The dollar keeps rising. As the U.S. currency rises through 1.52 marks per dollar, Mr. Neimanis cries out happily, "This thing is bid! I just got paid the figure [meaning 1.5200 exactly]! 152! We're over the figure!" ▋▋ At noon, Chase's traders normally troop outside the trading room for lunch; today, a trader hauls a stack of five large pizza boxes to the window sills. The traders stack pizza slices on paper plates precariously atop their quote machines. ▋▋ With the rumors flying and uncertainty at its peak, Mr. Neimanis gives an indication of an unusually wide market spread of 40–80. "It's so thin that people are afraid to make prices," he explains. When the customer decides to sell at 40, it suddenly appears that the dollar is falling back. "Really?" he says, incredulously. Seconds later, he says, "They just hit a quarter," meaning someone just bought at 25, indicating the dropoff is continuing. ▋▋▋▋

One factor that obviously distinguishes international business from domestic business is the involvement of more than one currency in commercial transactions. If Marks and Spencer, one of the U.K.'s leading department stores, purchases kitchen appliances from a British supplier, that is a domestic transaction that will be done entirely in pounds. But if Marks and Spencer chooses to purchase the appliances from Iowa-based Maytag Corporation, this international transaction will require some mechanism for exchanging pounds, Mark and Spencer's home currency, and U.S. dollars, Maytag's home currency. The foreign-exchange market exists to facilitate this conversion of currencies, thereby allowing firms to conduct trade more efficiently across national boundaries. The foreign-exchange market also facilitates international investment and capital flows. Firms can shop for low-cost financing in capital markets around the world and then use the foreign-exchange market to convert the foreign funds they obtain into whatever currency they require.

The Economics of Foreign Exchange

Foreign exchange is a commodity that consists of currencies issued by countries other than one's own. Like the prices of other commodities, the price of foreign exchange—given a flexible exchange-rate system—is set by demand and supply in the marketplace, as the opening case indicates. Let's look more closely at what this means by using the market between U.S. dollars and Japanese yen as an example.

The Demand for Foreign Exchange

Like every other textbook demand curve, the demand curve for yen is downward sloping. When the price of yen, P_1, is high, as it is at point A in Fig. 5.1(b), the quantity of yen demanded, Q_1, is low. As the price of yen falls to P_2—as you move from point A to point B in Fig. 5.1(b)—the quantity of yen demanded increases, to Q_2.

But what causes the demand for yen in the first place? Most foreigners don't want yen because they like pieces of colored paper with Japanese writing on them. Rather, the demand for yen derives from foreigners' demand for goods, services, and assets that Japanese residents offer for sale, as suggested by Fig. 5.1(a). For simplicity, we label these goods, services, and assets "Japanese products." When the price of Japanese products, P_1, is high, as it is at point A in Fig. 5.1(a), the quantity of Japanese products demanded by foreigners, Q_1, is low. The quantity of yen demanded, which is derived from foreigners' desires for Japanese products, also is low (see point A in Fig. 5.1(b)). As the price of Japanese products drops to P_2, the quantity of Japanese products demanded by foreigners rises to Q_2—as shown by a movement from point A to point B in Fig. 5.1(a). The quantity of yen demanded, derived from the demand for Japanese products, also rises—as shown by the movement from point A to point B in Fig. 5.1(b).

FIGURE 5.1

The Demand for Japanese Yen Is Derived from Foreigners' Demand for Japanese Products

a. Foreigners' demand for Japanese products

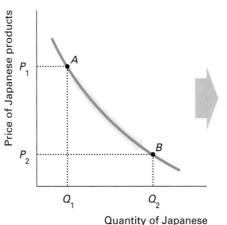

b. Foreigners' demand for yen

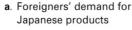
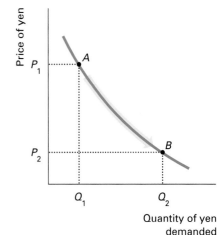

The Supply of Foreign Exchange

Similarly, the supply curve for yen is upward sloping. As with the prices of other goods, when the price of yen is low, the quantity of yen supplied is also low, represented by point *A* in Fig. 5.2(b). As the price of yen rises, the quantity supplied also rises, as you can see when you move from point *A* to point *B* in Fig. 5.2(b). The supply curve for yen thus behaves like most other supply curves: people offer more yen for sale as the price of yen rises.

As Fig. 5.2(a) shows, underlying the supply curve for yen is Japanese desire to buy foreign goods, services, and assets. To buy foreign products, Japanese need to obtain foreign currencies, which they do by selling yen and using the proceeds to buy the foreign currencies. Selling yen has the effect of supplying yen to the foreign-exchange market.

Figure 5.2(a) indicates that when the price of foreign products is *high* (as at point *A*), the quantity of foreign products Japanese demand is *low*. Correspondingly, point *A* in Fig. 5.2(b) indicates that the amount of yen the Japanese are willing to sell in order to buy the foreign goods is also *low*. As the price of foreign products *falls*, the quantity of those products that Japanese want to buy *rises*, shown as a movement from *A* to *B* in Fig. 5.2(a). The amount of yen the Japanese are willing to sell in order to buy the foreign products also *rises*, shown as the movement from *A* to *B* in Fig. 5.2(b). As with any well-behaved supply curve, the quantity of yen supplied rises as the price of yen rises.[2]

Determination of the Equilibrium Price

Figure 5.3 illustrates the market for yen. Points along the vertical axis show the price of yen in dollars—how many dollars one must pay for each yen purchased. Points along the horizontal axis show the quantity of yen. As in other markets, the intersection of the supply curve (*S*) and the demand curve (*D*) yields the market-clearing, equilibrium price ($.009/yen in this case) and the equilibrium quantity demanded and supplied (200 million yen). Recall from Chapter 4 that this equi-

---

FIGURE 5.2	**a.** Japanese demand for foreign products	**b.** Supply of yen

The Supply of Yen Is Derived from Japanese Demand for Foreign Products

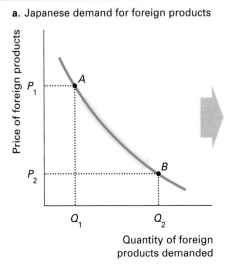

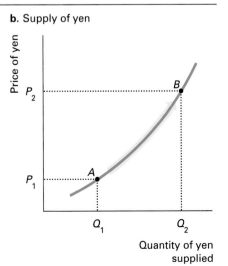

Quantity of foreign products demanded

Quantity of yen supplied

GOING GLOBAL

A Brief Hint

Not everyone reading this book is a finance major. Some readers may have difficulty with the concept of using money to buy money and what is meant by a currency's value rising or falling. If you are having trouble with this, here's a simple trick. In Fig. 5.3, replace the currency that is being bought and sold with the phrase loaf of bread (or the name of any other tangible good). If you do this, then the vertical axis is the price in dollars of one unit of bread and the horizontal axis is the quantity of bread sold—a standard supply and demand graph that you encountered in your basic economics course. Nothing has changed in the supply and demand graph except the label. Think about this until you feel comfortable with the notion that yen are merely a good like bread or widgets.

As you read the rest of the book, if you get confused about what is up and what is down when we say a currency is rising or falling in value, you can use the same trick. For example, suppose that on Monday the British pound is worth $1.73 and on Tuesday it is worth $1.74. From Monday to Tuesday, the pound rose in value, while the dollar fell in value. If that's obvious to you, fine. If it isn't, substitute *loaf of bread* for *pound*. A statement about this example would then read "On Monday a loaf of bread is worth $1.73, and on Tuesday a loaf of bread is worth $1.74." The conclusion is that a loaf of bread has gone up in value, because more dollars are needed to buy it on Tuesday. Or, you can say the dollar has gone down in value, because each dollar on Tuesday buys less bread.

librium price is called the *exchange rate,* the price of one country's currency in terms of another country's currency. (See "Going Global" for a better understanding of these processes.)

Although Fig. 5.3 illustrates the dollar-yen foreign-exchange market, a similar figure could be drawn for every possible pair of currencies in the world, each of which would constitute a separate market, with the equilibrium prices of the currencies determined by the supply of and demand for them. Foreign-exchange

---

FIGURE 5.3

The Market for Yen

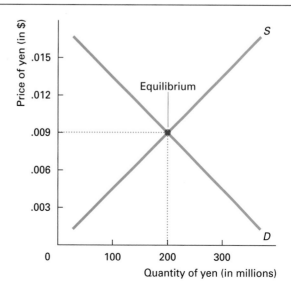

FIGURE 5.4

Direct and Indirect Exchange Rates

Source: *Wall Street Journal*, February 18, 1998, p. C21. Reprinted by permission of the *Wall Street Journal*, © 1998 Dow Jones & Company, Inc. All Rights Reserved Worldwide.

CURRENCY TRADING

EXCHANGE RATES
Wednesday, February 18, 1998

The New York foreign exchange selling rates below apply to trading among banks in amounts of $1 million and more, as quoted at 4 p.m. Eastern time by Dow Jones and other sources. Retail transactions provide fewer units of foreign currency per dollar.

Country	U.S. equiv. Wed	U.S. equiv. Tue	Currency per U.S. $ Wed	Currency per U.S. $ Tue
Argentina (Peso)	1.0001	1.0001	.9999	.9999
Australia (Dollar)	.6681	.6688	1.4968	1.4952
Austria (Schilling)	.07805	.07793	12.812	12.832
Bahrain (Dinar)	2.6518	2.6518	.3771	.3771
Belgium (Franc)	.02663	.02653	37.550	37.700
Brazil (Real)	.8864	.8865	1.1282	1.1281
Britain (Pound)	1.6380	1.6330	.6105	.6124
1-month forward	1.6356	1.6307	.6114	.6133
3-months forward	1.6304	1.6256	.6133	.6152
6-months forward	1.6229	1.6183	.6162	.6180
Canada (Dollar)	.6980	.6946	1.4326	1.4397
1-month forward	.6985	.6950	1.4317	1.4389
3-months forward	.6992	.6957	1.4303	1.4375
6-months forward	.6999	.6963	1.4288	1.4362
Chile (Peso)	.002257	.002264	443.05	441.75
China (Renminbi)	.1203	.1203	8.3100	8.3100
Colombia (Peso)	.0007406	.0007402	1350.23	1350.97
Czech. Rep. (Koruna)	....	....	....	....
Commercial rate	.02891	.02886	34.594	34.649
Denmark (Krone)	.1441	.1438	6.9420	6.9555
Ecuador (Sucre)	....	....	....	....
Floating rate	.0002200	.0002200	4545.00	4545.00
Finland (Markka)	.1812	.1806	5.5189	5.5368
France (Franc)	.1638	.1634	6.1045	6.1200
1-month forward	.1641	.1637	6.0946	6.1101
3-months forward	.1646	.1642	6.0737	6.0891
6-months forward	.1654	.1650	6.0450	6.0600
Germany (Mark)	.5491	.5479	1.8210	1.8253
1-month forward	.5500	.5487	1.8181	1.8224
3-months forward	.5521	.5506	1.8114	1.8161
6-months forward	.5546	.5533	1.8030	1.8074
Greece (Drachma)	.003481	.003476	287.30	287.65
Hong Kong (Dollar)	.1291	.1292	7.7465	7.7415
Hungary (Forint)	.004789	.004806	208.80	208.09
India (Rupee)	.02574	.02570	38.845	38.910
Indonesia (Rupiah)	.0001106	.0001061	9045.50	9425.00
Ireland (Punt)	1.3598	1.3641	.7354	.7331
Israel (Shekel)	.2774	.2777	3.6052	3.6011
Italy (Lira)	.0005571	.0005556	1795.00	1800.00
Japan (Yen)	.007910	.007901	126.43	126.57
1-month forward	.007940	.007932	126.94	126.07

Country	U.S. equiv. Wed	U.S. equiv. Tue	Currency per U.S. $ Wed	Currency per U.S. $ Tue
3-months forward	.008012	.008000	124.82	125.01
6-months forward	.008109	.008100	123.32	123.46
Jordan (Dinar)	1.4134	1.4134	.7075	.7075
Kuwait (Dinar)	3.2712	3.2733	.3057	.3055
Lebanon (Pound)	.0006561	.0006561	1524.25	1524.25
Malaysia (Ringgit)	.2628	.2584	3.8050	3.8700
Malta (Lira)	2.5316	2.4691	.3950	.4050
Mexico (Peso)	....	....	....	....
Floating Rate	.1170	.1181	8.5500	8.4640
Netherlands (Guilder)	.4870	.4862	2.0534	2.0566
New Zealand (Dollar)	.5779	.5789	1.7304	1.7274
Norway (Krone)	.1316	.1313	7.5983	7.6143
Pakistan (Rupee)	.02296	.02296	43.560	43.560
Peru (new Sol)	.3603	.3607	2.7751	2.7721
Philippines (Peso)	.02494	.02462	40.095	40.625
Poland (Zloty)	.2811	.2811	3.5575	3.5580
Portugal (Escudo)	.005363	.005352	186.47	186.83
Russia (Ruble) (a)	.1651	c.1652	6.0570	c6.0540
Saudi Arabia (Riyal)	.2666	.2666	3.7505	3.7505
Singapore (Dollar)	.6070	.6001	1.6475	1.6665
Slovak Rep. (Koruna)	.02803	.02831	35.675	35.322
South Africa (Rand)	.2022	.2025	4.9450	4.9380
South Korea (Won)	.0005853	.0005924	1708.50	1688.00
Spain (Peseta)	.006480	.006470	154.33	154.57
Sweden (Krona)	.1235	.1227	8.0995	8.1475
Switzerland (Franc)	.6798	.6791	1.4710	1.4725
1-month forward	.6823	.6816	1.4656	1.4672
3-months forward	.6875	.6868	1.4545	1.4561
6-months forward	.6952	.6944	1.4385	1.4401
Taiwan (Dollar)	.03041	.03037	32.887	32.926
Thailand (Baht)	.02191	.02172	45.650	46.050
Turkey (Lira)	.00000442	.00000404	226165.00	225240.00
United Arab (Dirham)	.2723	.2723	3.6730	3.6730
Uruguay (New Peso)	....	....	....	....
Financial	.1033	.1003	9.9750	9.9750
Venezuela (Bolivar)	.001944	.001939	514.38	515.80
SDR	1.3467	1.3494	.7425	.7411
ECU	1.0857	1.0838	....	....

Special Drawing Rights (SDR) are based on exchange rates for the U.S., German, British, French, and Japanese currency. Source: International Monetary Fund.

European Currency Unit (ECU) is based on a basket of community currencies.

a-fixing, Moscow Interbank Currency Exchange. c-Corrected. Ruble newly-denominated January 1998.

The Wall Street Journal daily foreign exchange data for 1996 and 1997 may be purchased through the Readers' Reference Service (413) 592-3600

---

rates are published daily in most major newspapers worldwide. For example, Fig. 5.4 presents rates for February 18, 1998, published in the *Wall Street Journal*. These rates are quoted in two ways. A **direct exchange rate** (or **direct quote**) is the price of the foreign currency in terms of the home currency. For example, from the perspective of a U.S. resident, the direct exchange rate between the U.S. dollar and the yen (¥) on Wednesday, February 18, was $.00791/¥1. An **indirect exchange rate** (or **indirect quote**) is the price of the home currency in terms of the foreign currency. From the U.S. resident's perspective, the indirect exchange rate on Wednesday, February 18, was ¥126.43/$1. Mathematically, the direct exchange rate and the indirect exchange rate are reciprocals of one another. By tradition—and sometimes for convenience—certain exchange rates are typically quoted on a direct basis and others on an indirect basis. For example, common U.S. practice is to quote British pounds on a direct basis but Japanese yen, German marks, and French francs on an indirect basis.

If you get confused about which is the direct rate and which is the indirect rate, just remember that you normally buy things using the direct rate. If you go to the store to buy bread, it is typically priced using the direct rate: a loaf of bread costs $.89. The indirect rate would be 1.12 loaves of bread per dollar.

Balance of Payments Equilibrium

As you saw in Chapter 4, the international monetary system has historically utilized two different types of exchange-rate systems: fixed and flexible. Next we discuss how the market for foreign exchange interacts with each of these exchange-rate systems to produce equilibrium in the balance of payments (BOP).

Fixed Exchange-Rate System

We begin by examining how BOP equilibrium was achieved under a fixed exchange-rate system, which existed under the gold standard (1821–1914) and under the Bretton Woods system (1945–1971). For ease of analysis, we assume that the market initially is in equilibrium at the fixed exchange rate, P_{fixed}. The foreign-exchange market for yen is shown in Fig. 5.5, where D represents the demand curve for yen and S the supply curve for yen. The intersection of D and S yields an equilibrium dollar price for yen of P_{fixed}.

Short-Run Equilibrium. Now suppose that as a result of quality improvements in U.S.-made multipurpose automobiles like Ford Explorers and Chrysler minivans, Japanese consumers increase their demand for U.S. automobiles. To obtain dollars to buy them, Japanese must sell more yen, thus shifting the supply curve for yen in Fig. 5.5 from S to S_1. But the new intersection of D and S_1 yields a new equilibrium price of P_1. This price, if allowed to stand, will violate the responsibility of both Japan and the United States to maintain a fixed exchange rate of P_{fixed}. Thus the central banks of Japan (the Bank of Japan) and the United States (the Federal Reserve Bank, or FRB) must act to restore P_{fixed} as the equilibrium price. They can do this in one of three ways:

FIGURE 5.5

Short-Run Equilibrium in a Fixed Exchange-Rate System

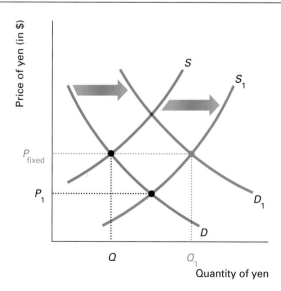

1 The Bank of Japan may act alone.

2 The FRB may act alone.

3 The Bank of Japan and the FRB may act together.

The Bank of Japan, acting alone, can sell gold or dollars from its official reserves and use the proceeds to buy yen. This transaction will cause the demand curve for yen in Fig. 5.5 to shift to the right. When the Bank of Japan sells enough gold (and/or dollars) and buys enough yen to shift the demand curve for yen from D to D_1, P_{fixed} will be restored as the equilibrium exchange rate. Or the FRB, acting alone, can sell enough gold and/or dollars and buy enough yen to shift the demand curve for yen from D to D_1. The new market price, P_{fixed}, would then equal the fixed exchange rate. Or the FRB and the Bank of Japan, acting together, could coordinate their policies to shift the demand curve for yen to D_1, again restoring market equilibrium at P_{fixed}. Thus short-run BOP equilibrium in a fixed exchange-rate system is reached through changes in official reserves.

Long-Run Equilibrium. For long-run equilibrium to occur, all changes in official reserves must fall to zero. Assuming no errors and omissions, capital account transactions and current account transactions will thus sum to zero at the fixed exchange rate.

Under the nineteenth-century gold standard, long-run equilibrium was reached through the effects of gold inflows or outflows on a country's money supply, which in turn affected domestic price levels and the international competitiveness of the country's products. In the previous example, the Bank of Japan's sale of gold to restore the fixed exchange rate, P_{fixed}, would cause a deflationary contraction in the Japanese money supply. As the Japanese economy deflated, the prices of Japanese products would fall relative to the prices for foreign goods. The lower prices of Japanese products would make them more attractive to foreigners, thereby increasing Japanese exports. The demand for yen would increase as foreigners desired more yen to buy the attractively priced Japanese products. Similarly, lower prices for Japanese products would make foreign goods less attractive to Japanese consumers, thereby reducing imports and reducing the supply of yen (Japanese consumers need to buy less foreign currency because they desire fewer foreign goods). The deflation-induced increase in exports and decrease in imports will eventually lead to sufficient shifts in the demand for and supply of yen to restore the exchange rate to P_{fixed}.

The process is reversed for a country enjoying gold inflows. The inflows should increase the domestic money supply, thereby causing inflation in the domestic economy. Higher domestic prices reduce the foreign demand for domestic goods—thus reducing the demand for the home currency in the foreign-exchange market—and increase the domestic demand for foreign goods—thus increasing the supply of the home currency in the foreign-exchange market. As long as the BOP imbalance remains, the inflation will continue until shifts in the supply and demand curves restore the exchange rate to P_{fixed}. When this occurs, the foreign-exchange market is in long-run equilibrium and the country's BOP surplus equals zero. Figure 5.6 summarizes these movements.

While this automatic adjustment process worked reasonably well under the nineteenth-century gold standard, it did not under the postwar Bretton Woods

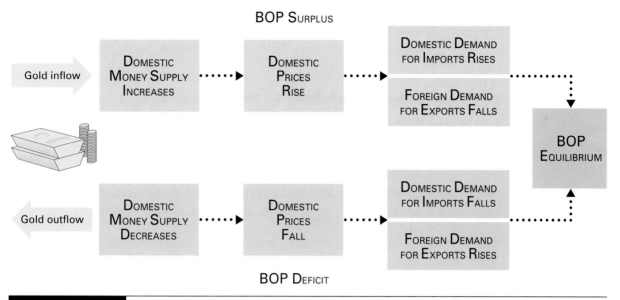

BOP SURPLUS

| Gold inflow → | DOMESTIC MONEY SUPPLY INCREASES | ⋯▶ | DOMESTIC PRICES RISE | ⋯▶ | DOMESTIC DEMAND FOR IMPORTS RISES / FOREIGN DEMAND FOR EXPORTS FALLS | ⋯▶ | BOP EQUILIBRIUM |

| ← Gold outflow | DOMESTIC MONEY SUPPLY DECREASES | ⋯▶ | DOMESTIC PRICES FALL | ⋯▶ | DOMESTIC DEMAND FOR IMPORTS FALLS / FOREIGN DEMAND FOR EXPORTS RISES |

BOP DEFICIT

FIGURE 5.6

Long-Run Adjustment under the Gold Standard

fixed exchange-rate system. Recall that gold played only a minor role in the Bretton Woods system. Only the United States agreed to convert its currency into gold. Other countries merely promised to maintain the par value of their currencies against the dollar. The Bretton Woods system did not rely on automatic gold inflows and outflows to correct BOP surpluses and deficits. Rather it relied on the willingness of national governments to use macroeconomic policies to deflate or inflate their economies to solve BOP adjustment problems. But often domestic political forces constrained a country's central bank from carrying out the necessary but unpopular economic deflation or inflation. On the one hand, correction of a BOP deficit required a contraction of the money supply, which led to domestic deflation, economic recession, job losses, high unemployment rates, and much political grief. So, politicians usually tried to avoid implementing policies that would lead to deflation. On the other hand, countries running a BOP surplus needed to inflate their economy to eliminate the surplus. But domestic voters, who dislike inflation, and export-dependent firms and their work forces, who dislike the prospect of losing their foreign markets, pressured local politicians to avoid an inflationary policy. Politicians looking forward to the next election often chose to minimize the economic difficulties imposed on their constituents, at least until the election was over.

In practice, the adjustment process under the Bretton Woods fixed exchange-rate system was asymmetric. A country with a BOP surplus did not need to do anything, provided it was willing to accumulate foreign exchange or gold. A country suffering a BOP deficit saw a continuing decrease in its official reserves. It had to cure its BOP problems well before it ran out of reserves. If the country did nothing, other countries (and investors), seeing its reserves dwindling, would begin to distrust its ability to honor its pledge to maintain its currency's par value. These foreigners would rush to sell their holdings of the currency, thereby worsening the drain on the country's reserves. Ultimately the government would have to renege on its promise to convert at the fixed rate and would resort to devaluing its currency. This is what happened to the United Kingdom in 1967, France in 1969, and the United States in 1971. Thus, in practice, the Bretton Woods adjustment burden fell more heavily on deficit countries than on surplus countries.

Flexible Exchange-Rate System

Since the collapse of the Bretton Woods system in 1971, the world economy has relied increasingly on the second type of exchange-rate system—the flexible system. Under a flexible exchange-rate system, the exchange rate is determined by the forces of supply and demand for each currency. Assuming a country's central bank is willing to live with the outcome of these market forces, its official reserves need not be depleted because consumers and investors are determining the currency's value through their self-interested transactions. As we noted in Chapter 4, the United States has run very large current account deficits over the past decade, yet has suffered very little change in its official reserves over the same period.

Consider Fig. 5.7, where D represents the initial demand for yen and S represents the supply of yen. The exchange rate between dollars and yen is determined by the intersection of D and S, which yields an equilibrium exchange rate of P. Now suppose U.S. demand for Japanese products increases. U.S. residents will need more yen in order to purchase those products, thus shifting the demand curve for yen from D to D_1. The equilibrium exchange rate between dollars and yen rises to P_1, where the new demand curve D_1 and the unchanged supply curve S intersect. If the FRB and the Bank of Japan choose not to intervene in the foreign-exchange market, the exchange rate will remain at its new level of P_1. But if one or both of the central banks are unhappy with the market-determined exchange rate, they are free to intervene by selling or buying foreign currency. Such transactions are observable as changes in the official reserves held by the central bank(s) and will shift either the supply or the demand curve, thereby altering the equilibrium price of yen.

BOP Adjustments in the 1990s. As discussed in Chapter 4, the existing international monetary system relies on a combination of fixed and flexible exchange-rate systems. Most members of the European Union, for example, have

---

FIGURE 5.7

Exchange-Rate Adjustments in the Market for Yen in a Flexible Exchange-Rate System

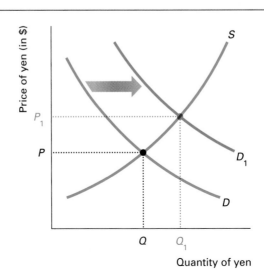

Quantity of yen

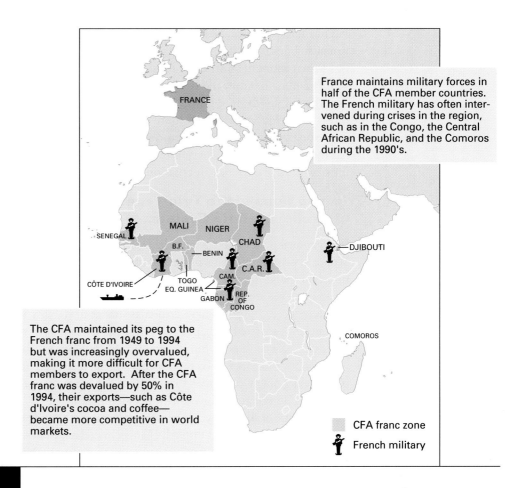

France maintains military forces in half of the CFA member countries. The French military has often intervened during crises in the region, such as in the Congo, the Central African Republic, and the Comoros during the 1990's.

The CFA maintained its peg to the French franc from 1949 to 1994 but was increasingly overvalued, making it more difficult for CFA members to export. After the CFA franc was devalued by 50% in 1994, their exports—such as Côte d'Ivoire's cocoa and coffee—became more competitive in world markets.

CFA franc zone
French military

MAP 5.1

Fourteen Countries That Use the CFA Franc Peg Their Currencies to the French Franc

tried to maintain a fixed exchange-rate system among themselves through their participation in the exchange-rate mechanism (ERM) of the European Monetary System (EMS), as Chapter 4 explained. In January 1999, most EU members will take this a step further by creating a single currency, the euro. (This change is discussed more fully in Chapter 7.) Other fixed exchange-rate arrangements exist between the U.S. dollar and the currencies of such countries as Panama (see Table 4.3) and between the French franc and the currencies of many of France's former African colonies. As Map 5.1 indicates, users of the CFA franc have maintained close political and economic ties to France. French firms often have the inside track for public sector projects in these countries.

Aside from these currency groupings, flexible exchange rates exist between the U.S. dollar and the currencies of major trading countries, including the Canadian dollar, the British pound, the German mark (and, presumably, the euro group when it comes into being), the Japanese yen, and the Australian dollar. As Fig. 4.4 showed, exchange rates have varied widely over time, thereby causing significant problems for international businesses. For example, as discussed in Chapter 3, the wild fluctuations in the yen-dollar exchange rate in the 1980s first favored Komatsu in its attempts to dethrone Caterpillar in the U.S. construction equipment market. When the value of the dollar fell from ¥251 in 1984 to ¥80 in April 1995, the shoe was on the other foot. Komatsu suffered erosion of its profit margins as each dollar of sales in the United States produced fewer yen to cover the costs of its Japanese production. But in the summer of 1995, the dollar began to rise in value; by February 1998 it took ¥126 to buy a dollar, easing the pressure on Komatsu but raising it for Caterpillar's managers.

When the value of the domestic currency increases because of changes in supply and demand in the foreign-exchange market, firms find it harder to export their goods, more difficult to protect their domestic markets from the threat of foreign imports, and more advantageous to shift their production from domestic factories to foreign factories. A decrease in the domestic currency's value has the opposite effects. Savvy international businesspeople are mindful of the impact of these currency fluctuations on their business opportunities.

Pros and Cons of the Two Types of Exchange-Rate Systems

International policy makers have debated the value of reconstructing the Bretton Woods system. Proponents of the system believe fixed exchange rates offer international businesses several advantages. Exchange rates are not subject to wide daily, weekly, and monthly fluctuations. The riskiness of international trade transactions is thus reduced, and firms have greater assurance of stability in the values of foreign currencies. Also, fixed exchange rates are an important anti-inflationary tool, since the loss of official reserves forces a country to counteract inflationary tendencies in its economy. Bretton Woods proponents also are distressed because the wild swings in the values of key currencies that occur in flexible exchange-rate systems can disrupt sound international investment decision making.

Advocates of flexible exchange rates look at the other side of the coin. If BOP equilibrium can be reached through changes in exchange rates, then domestic policy makers are free to focus on domestic economic concerns without worrying about the BOP consequences of their actions. Flexible exchange rates also reduce the need for international coordination of domestic economic policies and allow each country to follow its own economic destiny. For example, if Mexico's monetary authorities choose more inflationary, growth-oriented economic policies than those adopted by its major trading partners, changes in exchange rates will bring about BOP equilibrium. Flexible exchange rates can absorb the impact of damaging external economic events, such as occurred during the two oil embargoes in the 1970s. Proponents of flexible exchange rates also suggest that fixed exchange-rate systems are not invulnerable to disorderly changes in currency values and cite the depreciation of the pound in 1967, of the French franc in 1969, and of the U.S. dollar in 1971. Similarly, they point out the chaos and hardships created by the 1997–1998 collapse of the fixed exchange-rate systems used by Thailand, Indonesia, and other Southeast Asian countries, which is the focus of the chapter's Closing Case.

The Structure of the Foreign-Exchange Market

The foreign-exchange market comprises buyers and sellers of currencies issued by the world's countries. Anyone who owns money denominated in one currency and wants to convert that money to a second currency participates in the foreign-exchange market. Pakistani tourists exchanging rupees for deutsche marks at the Frankfurt airport utilize the foreign-exchange market, as does Toyota when it exports automobiles to Canada from its factory in Toyota City, Japan, and the British government when it arranges a multimillion-pound loan to

FIGURE 5.8

Currencies Involved in Foreign-Exchange Market Transactions

Percentage share of foreign-exchange transactions involving selected currencies. Since there are two currencies involved in each transaction, the percentages add up to 200 percent.

Source: Bank for International Settlements, *Central Bank Survey of Foreign Exchange and Derivatives Market Activity* (Basle, May 1996), p. 8.

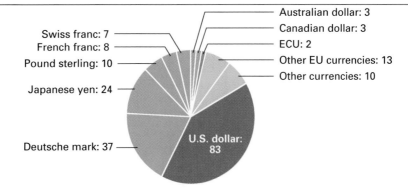

rebuild the monsoon-ravaged economy of Bangladesh. The worldwide volume of foreign-exchange trading is estimated at $1.2 trillion *per day*. Approximately 83 percent of the transactions involve the U.S. dollar, a dominance stemming from the dollar's role in the Bretton Woods system, as Fig. 5.8 indicates. Because the dollar is used to facilitate most currency exchange, it is known as the primary **transaction currency** for the foreign-exchange market.

Foreign exchange is traded by bankers, brokers, businesses, and speculators somewhere in the world every minute of the day (see Map 5.2). Traditionally, the trading day begins in Auckland, New Zealand, which lies just west of the International Date Line. As the earth rotates, foreign-exchange markets open in turn in Sydney, Tokyo, Hong Kong, Singapore, Bahrain, Frankfurt, Zurich, Paris, London, New York, Chicago, and San Francisco. The most important of these markets is in London, followed by New York and Tokyo. The British, U.S., and Japanese markets account for 56 percent of global foreign-exchange volume.[3]

The Role of Banks

Recall from the chapter opening that the foreign-exchange departments of large international banks such as Chase Manhattan in major financial centers such as New York, London, Frankfurt, and Tokyo play a dominant role in the foreign-exchange market. These banks stand ready to buy or sell the major traded currencies. They profit from the foreign-exchange market in several ways, but much of their profits comes from the spread between the bid and asked prices for foreign exchange. For example, if Chase Manhattan buys DM10 million from one customer at a price of DM1.5220/$1 and sells those marks to a second customer at DM1.5210/$1 (as it offered to do in the chapter opening), it makes $4319.73. (Get out your calculator and do the arithmetic! It buys the marks for 10,000,000 ÷ 1.5220, or $6,570,302.23, and sells them for 10,000,000 ÷ 1.5210, or $6,574,621.96, thereby earning a profit of $4319.73.) Sometimes international banks act as speculators, betting that they can guess which direction exchange rates are headed. Such speculation can be enormously profitable, although it is always risky. And, as discussed later in this chapter, banks also may act as arbitrageurs in the foreign-exchange market.

International banks are key players in the wholesale market for foreign exchange, dealing for their own accounts or on behalf of large commercial customers. Interbank transactions, typically involving at least $1 million (or the foreign-currency equivalent), account for the vast majority of foreign-exchange transactions. Banks may rely on the assistance of independent foreign-exchange brokers, who provide current information about the prices of different foreign currencies and who facilitate

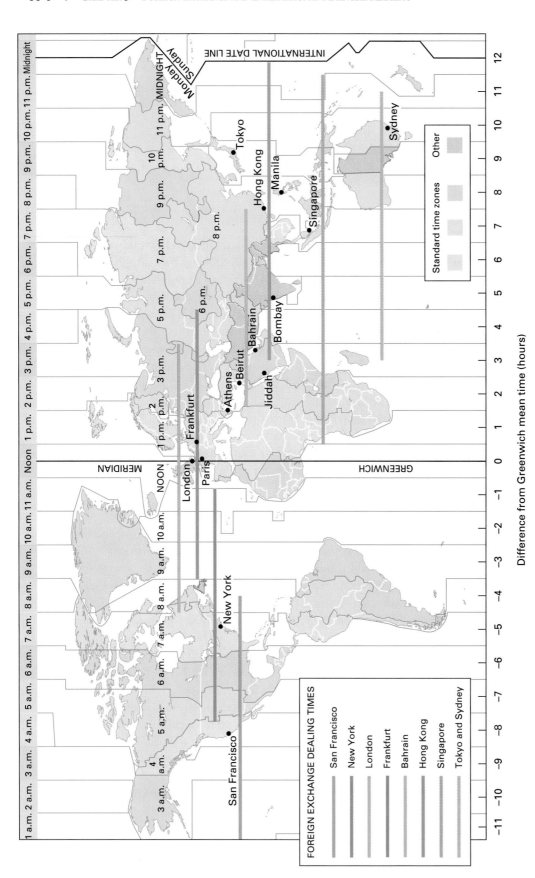

Difference from Greenwich mean time (hours)

A Day of Foreign-Exchange Trading

MAP 5.2

transactions by linking buyers and sellers of foreign exchange.[4] Using computers, telephones, telexes, e-mail, and fax machines, banks and brokers in one market are in constant contact with their counterparts in other markets in order to seek the best currency prices. Telecommunications link foreign-exchange markets world-wide into one global market.

International banks also play a key role in the retail market for foreign exchange, dealing with individual customers who want to buy or sell foreign currencies in large or small amounts. Typically, the price paid by retail customers for foreign exchange is the prevailing wholesale exchange rate plus a premium. The size of the premium is in turn a function of transaction size and the importance of the customer to the bank. For example, a Danish music store chain that needs $100,000 to pay for 20,000 compact discs of Celine Dion's or U2's latest release will pay a higher premium for its foreign currency than will General Motors when it needs £20 million to repay British investors. And, of course, foreign tourists cashing in a traveler's check for local currency at a bank or exchange office pay an even higher premium.

The clients of the foreign-exchange departments of banks fall into several categories:

♦ *Commercial customers* engage in foreign-exchange transactions as part of their normal commercial activities, such as exporting or importing goods and services, paying or receiving dividends and interest from foreign sources, and purchasing or selling foreign assets and investments. Some commercial customers may also use the market to hedge (reduce) their risks due to potential unfavorable changes in foreign-exchange rates for monies to be paid or received in the future.

♦ *Speculators* deliberately assume exchange-rate risks by acquiring positions in a currency, hoping that they can correctly predict changes in the currency's market value. Foreign-exchange speculation can be very lucrative if one guesses correctly, but it is also extremely risky.

♦ *Arbitrageurs* attempt to exploit small differences in the price of a currency between markets. They seek to obtain riskless profits by simultaneously buying the currency in the lower-priced market and selling it in the higher-priced market.

Countries' central banks and treasury departments are also major players in the foreign-exchange market. As discussed in Chapter 4, under the gold standard and the Bretton Woods system, a country's central bank was required to intervene in the foreign-exchange market in order to ensure that the market value of the country's currency approximated the currency's par value. Countries that have chosen to peg their currencies to that of another country must do the same. And, of course, central banks of countries that allow their currencies to float are free to intervene in the foreign-exchange market to influence the market values of their currencies if they so desire.

Active markets exist for relatively few pairs of currency other than those involving the U.S. dollar, the German mark, the British pound, and the Japanese yen.[5] (An active market in the euro is likely to develop as well when that currency becomes operational.) Suppose a Swedish knitting mill needs New Zealand dollars to pay for a purchase of 100,000 pounds of merino wool. The foreign-exchange market between the Swedish krona and the New Zealand dollar is very small—in fact, no active market exists for the direct exchange of these two currencies. Usually, the U.S. dollar would be used as an intermediary currency to facilitate this transaction. The knitting mill's Swedish banker would obtain the necessary New Zealand dollars by first selling Swedish krona to obtain U.S. dollars and then selling the U.S. dollars to obtain New Zealand dollars. Such transactions are routine for international banks.

Domestic laws may constrain the ability to trade a currency in the foreign-exchange market. Currencies that are freely tradable are called **convertible currencies.** Also called **hard currencies,** these include the various EU currencies, the Canadian dollar, the Japanese yen, and the U.S. dollar. Currencies that are not freely tradable because of domestic laws or the unwillingness of foreigners to hold them are called **inconvertible currencies,** or **soft currencies.** The currencies of many developing countries fall in the soft category.

Spot and Forward Markets

Many international business transactions involve payments to be made in the future. These include lending activities and purchases on credit. Because changes in currency values are common, such international transactions would appear to be risky in the post–Bretton Woods era. How can a firm know for sure the future value of a foreign currency? Fortunately, in addition to its geographical dimension, the foreign-exchange market also has a time dimension. Currencies can be bought and sold for immediate delivery or for delivery at some point in the future. The **spot market** consists of foreign-exchange transactions that are to be consummated immediately. ("Immediately" is normally defined as two days after the trade date, because of the time historically needed for payment to clear the international banking system.) Spot transactions account for 41 percent of all foreign-exchange transactions.

The **forward market** consists of foreign-exchange transactions that are to occur some time in the future. Organized markets exist for foreign exchange that will be delivered 30 days, 90 days, and 180 days in the future. For example, the following *Wall Street Journal* excerpt indicates that on Wednesday, February 18, 1998, the spot price of the British pound was $1.6380, while the forward price for pounds for delivery in 30 days was $1.6356 and for delivery in 180 days was $1.6229.

	U.S. $ equiv.		Currency per U.S. $	
	Wed.	Tues.	Wed.	Tues.
Britain (Pound)	1.6380	1.6330	.6105	.6124
30-Day Forward	1.6356	1.6307	.6114	.6133
90-Day Forward	1.6304	1.6256	.6133	.6152
180-Day Forward	1.6229	1.6183	.6162	.6180

Pure forward transactions account for 8 percent of total foreign-exchange volume.

Most users of the forward market engage in swap transactions. A **swap transaction** is a transaction in which the same currency is bought and sold simultaneously but delivery is at two different points in time. For example, in a typical "spot against forward" swap, a U.S. manufacturer borrowing £10 million from a British bank for 30 days will sell the £10 million in the spot market in order to obtain U.S. dollars and simultaneously buy £10 million (plus the number of pounds it owes in interest payments) in the 30-day forward market in order to repay its pound-denominated loan. Swaps account for 45 percent of all foreign-exchange transactions.

Normally an international business that wants to buy or sell foreign exchange on a spot or forward basis will contract with an international bank to do so. The bank will charge the firm the prevailing wholesale rate for the currency, plus a small premium for its services. Because of the bank's extensive involvement in the foreign-exchange market, it is typically willing and able to customize the spot, forward, or swap contract to meet the customer's specific needs. For example, if Chrysler expects to receive 10.7 million schillings from its Austrian affiliate in 42 days, its bank will usually agree to enter into a forward contract to buy those schillings from Chrysler with delivery in 42 days.

Computerized trading systems are used to improve the efficiency of the foreign-exchange market. The two leading systems, Dealing 2000 and Electronic Broking Service, generate almost 10 percent of the $1.2 trillion daily volume of the foreign-exchange market.

The foreign-exchange market has developed two other mechanisms to allow firms to obtain foreign exchange in the future. Neither, however, provides the flexibility in amount and in timing that international banks offer. The first mechanism is the currency future. Publicly traded on many exchanges worldwide, a **currency future** is a contract that resembles a forward contract. However, unlike the forward contract, the currency future is for a standard amount (for example, ¥12.5 million or SwF125,000) on a standard delivery date (for example, the third Wednesday of the contract's maturity month). As with a forward contract, a firm signing a currency-future contract must complete the transaction by buying or selling the specified amount of foreign currency at the specified price and time. This obligation is usually not troublesome, however; a firm wanting to be released from a currency-future obligation can simply make an offsetting transaction. In practice, 98 percent of currency futures are settled in this manner. Currency futures represent only 1 percent of the foreign-exchange market.

The second mechanism, the **currency option,** allows, but does not require, a firm to buy or sell a specified amount of a foreign currency at a specified price at any time up to a specified date. A **call option** grants the right to *buy* the foreign currency in question; a **put option** grants the right to *sell* the foreign currency. Currency options are publicly traded on organized exchanges worldwide. For example, put and call options are available for Canadian dollars on the Chicago Mercantile Exchange (in contract sizes of Can$100,000) and on the Philadelphia Exchange (in contract sizes of Can$50,000). Figure 5.9 lists some of the options available on the Chicago Mercantile Exchange on February 18, 1998. Because of the inflexibility of publicly traded options, international bankers often are willing to write currency options customized as to amount and time for their commercial clients. Currency options account for 5 percent of foreign-exchange market activity.

FIGURE 5.9

Foreign-Exchange Options on the Chicago Mercantile Exchange

Source: *Wall Street Journal*, February 19, 1998, p. C19. Reprinted by permission of the *Wall Street Journal*, © 1998 Dow Jones & Company, Inc. All Rights Reserved Worldwide.

JAPANESE YEN
12,500,000 yen; cents per 100 yen

Strike Price	Calls-Settle Mar	Apr	May	Puts-Settle Mar	Apr	May
7850	1.46	....	....	0.54	0.77	....
7900	1.14	0.00	....	0.73	0.93	....
7950	0.89	0.00	....	0.97	....	....
8000	0.68	1.75	....	1.26	1.34	....
8050	0.51	1.48	....	1.59	1.00	....
8100	0.38	1.26	....	1.96	1.85	....

Est vol 4,191 Tue 3,732 calls 4,671 puts
Op int Tue 58,816 calls 71,559 puts

DEUTSCHEMARK
125,000 marks; cents per mark;

Strike Price	Calls-Settle Mar	Apr	May	Puts-Settle Mar	Apr	May
5400	1.13	....	....	0.15	0.13	0.55
5450	.075	....	....	0.26	0.46	0.00
5500	0.27	0.69	....	0.78	0.91	....
5600	0.15	0.50	0.75	1.15	1.21	....
5650	0.08	0.35	....	1.59	....	....

Est vol 6,804 Tue 928 calls 1,316 puts
Op int Tue 25,234 calls 29,734 puts

CANADIAN DOLLAR
100,000 Can.$; cents per Can.$;

Strike Price	Calls-Settle Mar	Apr	May	Puts-Settle Mar	Apr	May
6900	0.94	....	....	0.12	0.24	....
6950	0.56	0.81	....	0.24	0.39	....
7000	0.28	0.52	....	0.46	0.60	....
7050	0.13	0.34	....	0.81	....	....
7100	0.06	0.22	0.00	1.24	....	....
7150	0.03	0.00	....	1.71	....	....

Est vol 660 Tue 636 calls 408 puts
Op int Tue 27,189 calls 8,091 puts

BRITISH POUND
62,500 pounds; cents per pound;

Strike Price	Calls-Settle Mar	Apr	May	Puts-Settle Mar	Apr	May
16200	2.29	2.68	0.00	0.50	1.62	....
16300	1.64	2.16	0.00	0.84	2.10	....
16400	1.10	1.70	0.00	1.30	2.64	....
16500	0.68	0.00	0.00	1.88	0.00	....
16600	0.40	0.00	1.60	2.60	0.00	....
16700	0.24	0.76	0.00	3.44	0.00	....

Est vol 547 Tue 373 calls 417 puts
Op int Tue 12,101 calls 11,792 puts

SWISS FRANC
125,000 francs; cents per franc;

Strike Price	Calls-Settle Mar	Apr	May	Puts-Settle Mar	Apr	May
6700	1.42	0.00	....	1.08	0.00	....
6750	1.03	....	....	0.28	0.42	....
6800	0.71	0.00	....	0.47	0.56	....
6850	0.47	....	....	0.73	0.00	....
6900	0.30	0.00	....	1.06	0.99	....
6950	0.18	....	....	1.44	0.00	....

Est vol 684 Tue 1,029 calls 156 puts
Op int tue 16,922 calls 12,604 puts

BRAZILIAN REAL
100,000 Braz. reais; $ per reais;

Strike Price	Calls-Settle Mar	Apr	May	Puts-Settle Mar	Apr	May
875	....	....	....	0.00	....	....
880	....	....	....	....	....	....
885	....	....	....	0.00	....	....
890	....	....	....	....	....	....
895	....	....	....	....	....	....
900	....	....	....	....	....	....

Est vol 0 Tue 0 calls 0 puts
Op int Tue 0 calls 6,337 puts

MEXICAN PESO
500,000 new Mex. pesos; $ per MP

Strike Price	Calls-Settle Mar	Apr	May	Puts-Settle Mar	Apr	May
1137	....	....	....	....	....	....
1150	1.72	....	....	1.05	....	....
1162	....	....	....	1.55	....	....
1175	0.45	....	....	2.27	....	....
1187	0.20	....	....	3.27	....	....
1200	0.05	....	....	4.37	....	....

Est vol 8 Tue 4 calls 7 puts
Op int Tue 8,968 calls 3,337 puts

The forward market, currency options, and currency futures facilitate international trade and investment by allowing firms to hedge, or reduce, the foreign-exchange risks inherent in international transactions. Suppose Toys 'R' Us wants to purchase Nintendo 64 game players for ¥140 million for delivery 90 days in the future, with payment due at delivery. Rather than having to buy yen today and hold them for 90 days, Toys 'R' Us can simply go to its bank and contract to buy the ¥140 million for delivery in 90 days. The firm's bank will in turn charge Toys 'R' Us for those yen based on the yen's current price in the 90-day forward wholesale market. Toys 'R' Us could also protect itself from increases in the yen's price by purchasing a currency future or a currency option. We discuss the advantages and disadvantages of these different hedging techniques more thoroughly in Chapter 18.

The forward price of a foreign currency often differs from its spot price. If the forward price (using a direct quote) is less than the spot price, the currency is selling at a **forward discount.** If the forward price is higher than the spot price, the currency is selling at a **forward premium.** For example, as Fig. 5.4 indicates, the *Wall Street Journal* reported that the spot price of the British pound on February 18, 1998, was $1.6380. On the same day, the 90-day forward price was $1.6304, indicating that the pound was selling at a forward discount. The annualized forward premium or discount on the pound can be calculated by using the following formula:

$$\text{Annualized forward premium or discount} = \frac{P_f - P_s}{P_s} \times n$$

where, using our example,

$$P_f = \text{90-day forward price} = \$1.6304$$

$$P_s = \text{spot price} = \$1.6380$$

$$n = \text{the number of periods in a year} = 4$$

(Because the example calls for a 90-day forward rate, n equals 4; there are four 90-day periods in a year.) Thus

$$\text{Annualized forward discount} = \frac{\$1.6304 - \$1.6380}{\$1.6380} \times 4$$

$$= -0.0186 = 1.86\%$$

Had the forward price of the pound been higher than the spot price (using the direct quote), the formula would have yielded the annualized forward premium for the pound.

The forward price represents the marketplace's aggregate prediction of the spot price of the exchange rate in the future.[6] Thus, the forward price helps international businesspeople forecast future changes in exchange rates. These changes can affect the price of imported components as well as the competitiveness and profitability of the firm's exports. If a currency is selling at a forward discount, the foreign-exchange market believes the currency will depreciate over time. Firms may want to reduce their holdings of assets or increase their liabilities denominated in such a currency. The currencies of countries suffering BOP trade deficits or high inflation rates often sell at a forward discount. Conversely, if a currency is selling at a forward premium, the foreign-exchange market believes the currency will appreciate over time. Firms may want to increase their holdings of assets and reduce their liabilities denominated in such a currency. The currencies of countries enjoying BOP trade surpluses or low inflation rates often sell at a forward premium. Thus the difference between the spot and forward prices of a country's currency often signals the market's expectations regarding that country's economic policies and prospects.

Arbitrage and the Currency Market

Another important component of the foreign-exchange market is arbitrage activities. **Arbitrage** is the riskless purchase of a product in one market for immediate resale in a second market in order to profit from a price discrepancy. We explore two types of arbitrage activities that affect the foreign-exchange market: arbitrage of goods and arbitrage of money.

Arbitrage of Goods—Purchasing Power Parity. Underlying the arbitrage of goods is a very simple notion: if the price of a good differs between two markets, people will tend to buy the good in the market offering the lower price, the "cheap" market, and resell it in the market offering the higher price, the "expensive" market. Under the *law of one price,* such arbitrage activities will continue until the price of the good is identical in both markets (excluding transactions costs, transportation costs, taxes, and so on). This notion induced purchasing agents for Galeries Lafayette to buy clock radios in Japan and export them to France in the example in Chapter 3.

The arbitrage of goods across national boundaries is represented by the theory of **purchasing power parity (PPP).** This theory states that the prices of tradable goods, when expressed in a common currency, will tend to equalize across countries as a result of exchange-rate changes. PPP occurs because the process of buying goods in the cheap market and reselling them in the expensive market affects the demand for, and thus the price of, the foreign currency. For example, assume the exchange rate between U.S. and Canadian dollars is U.S.$0.80 = Can$1. Suppose Levi's jeans sell for U.S.$24 in the United States and Can$30 in Canada. PPP would exist in this case. At the existing exchange rate,

$$\frac{U.S.\$0.80}{Can\$1} \times Can\$30 = U.S.\$24$$

Thus the Levi's jeans are the same price in both markets (expressed in either U.S. or Canadian dollars), and neither U.S. nor Canadian residents would have any reason to cross their shared border to purchase the jeans in the other country.

Now suppose Canada undergoes an inflation that raises all Canadian prices 20 percent. The Levi's jeans in Canada would now cost Can$36. PPP would no longer exist. At the current exchange rate of U.S.$0.80 = Can$1, Canadians could cross the border, exchange Can$30 for U.S.$24, and buy their Levis in the United States, thereby saving themselves Can$6. This behavior affects the foreign-exchange market. By buying their jeans in the United States, Canadians increase the supply of Canadian dollars in the foreign-exchange market, thereby lowering the exchange rate between the Canadian dollar and the U.S. dollar. This process will continue until the exchange rate falls to U.S.$0.67 = Can$1. At that exchange rate, PPP will be restored because the price of Levi's jeans will be the same in both countries:[7]

$$\frac{U.S.\$0.67}{Can\$1} \times Can\$36 = U.S.\$24$$

Does this really happen? Obviously, teenagers from Calgary, Alberta, don't fly to Miami, Florida, just to save Can$6 on a pair of jeans. But consider the residents of Sault Ste. Marie, Ontario, who in the early 1990s paid the equivalent of U.S.$25 for a case of Canadian-brewed Labatt's beer and U.S.$2.50 for a gallon of gasoline on their side of the border. They eagerly crossed the bridge to Sault Ste. Marie, Michigan, in order to buy a case of Labatt's for $12 and a gallon of U.S. gasoline for $1.20. It takes little imagination to predict the impact of such price differences on the health of the retail sector, on employment opportunities, and on the local tax bases of the two communities. Merchants in the Ontario Sault Ste. Marie lost an estimated Can$100 million in retail sales annually to Michigan stores because of PPP imbalances in the early 1990s.[8]

Of course, the Canadian-U.S. exchange rate is determined by much more than the relative price of jeans in the two countries and border trade between the two Sault Ste. Maries. Nonetheless, if PPP doesn't exist in the two countries for jeans (or any other tradable good), people will buy the good in the cheap market and transport it to the expensive market, thereby affecting supply and demand in the foreign-exchange market and influencing the equilibrium exchange rate. That's why the PPP theory states that prices of tradable goods will *tend* to equalize. Even if prices don't equalize, the effects can be significant. In 1991, for example—a year when the value of the Canadian dollar was high relative to the U.S. dollar, encouraging Canadians to shop in the U.S.—cross-border shopping is estimated to have siphoned Can$3.1 billion from the Canadian economy.[9]

International economists use PPP to help them compare standards of living across countries. Consider, for example, Japan and the United States. Converting Japan's 1996 per capita income measured in yen into U.S. dollars using the average 1996 exchange rate between the yen and the dollar would yield $40,726. U.S. per capita income for 1996 was $29,020. These figures suggest that the average Japanese citizen enjoys a higher income than the average American citizen. However, this comparison fails to take into account differences in price levels between the two countries. After adjusting for purchasing power, Japan's dollar-denominated per capita income falls to $21,795, indicating that the average Japanese is worse off than the average American. Because of such distortions due to price levels, international businesspeople who use international income data to make decisions, such as which market to enter or how to position a product, must pay close attention to whether the data are reported with or without PPP adjustments.

Foreign-exchange analysts also use the PPP theory to forecast long-term changes in exchange rates. They believe that broad purchasing power imbalances between countries signal possible changes in exchange rates. As a quick and dirty way of assessing misalignments in exchange rates, the British business weekly *The Economist* periodically reports the prices of McDonald's Big Macs around the world; see "Going Global." As the article suggests, even the prices of Big Macs may signal whether currencies are overvalued or undervalued in the foreign-exchange market.

Arbitrage of Money. While we do not want to diminish the long-run importance of the arbitrage of goods, its impact on the foreign-exchange market is dwarfed by that of the short-term arbitrage of money. Much of the demand and supply of foreign currencies stems from financial arbitrage. Professional traders employed by money-market banks and other financial organizations seek to profit from small differences in the price of foreign exchange in different markets. Although not all of the volume in currency markets reflects arbitrage activities, the importance of financial activities relative to real activities (purchases of goods and services) in foreign-exchange markets is indicated by the ratio of daily foreign-currency trading ($1.2 trillion) to daily international trade ($17 billion).

Whenever the foreign-exchange market is not in equilibrium, professional traders can profit through arbitraging money. Numerous forms of foreign-exchange

GOING GLOBAL

Big Mac Currencies

Can hamburgers provide hot tips about exchange rates? The Big Mac index is based upon the theory of purchasing-power parity (PPP)—the notion that a dollar should buy the same amount in all countries. In the long run, argue PPP fans, currencies should move towards the rate which equalizes the prices of an identical basket of goods in each country. Our "basket" is a McDonald's Big Mac, which is now produced in over 100 countries. The Big Mac PPP is the exchange rate that would leave hamburgers costing the same in America as abroad. Comparing actual exchange rates with PPP provides one indication of whether a currency is under- or over-valued. . . .

The first column in the table shows local-currency prices of a Big Mac; the second converts them into dollars. The average American price (including tax) is $2.42. China is the place for bargain hunters: a Beijing Big Mac costs only $1.16. At the other extreme, Big Mac fans pay a beefy $4.02 in Switzerland. In other words, the yuan is the most undervalued currency (by 52%), the Swiss franc the most over-valued (by 66%).

The third column calculates Big Mac PPPs. For example, dividing the German price by the American one gives a dollar PPP of DM2.02. The actual rate on April 7th was DM1.71, implying that the D-mark is 18% overvalued against the dollar. But over the past two years the dollar has risen nearer to its PPP against most currencies. The yen is now close to its PPP of ¥121. Two years ago the Big Mac index suggested that it was 100% overvalued against the dollar.

Some critics find these conclusions hard to swallow. Yes, we admit it, the Big Mac is not a perfect measure. Price differences may be distorted by trade barriers on beef, sales taxes, or large variations in the cost of nontraded inputs such as rents. All the same, the index tends to come up with PPP estimates that are similar to those based on more sophisticated methods.

Moreover, research by Robert Cumby, an economist at Georgetown University, suggests that a currency's deviation from Big Mac PPP can be a useful predictor of exchange rates. Over the past year, the Big Mac index has correctly predicted the direction of exchange-rate movements for eight of twelve currencies of large industrial economies. Of the seven currencies which changed by more than 10%, the Big Mac standard got the direction right in six cases. Better than some highly-paid currency forecasters. Investors who turned up their noses at the Big Mac index should now be feeling cheesed off.

---

arbitrage are possible, but we discuss three common examples: two-point, three-point, and covered-interest.

Two-point arbitrage, also called **geographic arbitrage,** involves profiting from price differences in two geographically distinct markets. Suppose £1 is trading for $2.00 in New York City and $1.80 in London. A profitable arbitrage opportunity is available. A foreign-exchange trader at Chase Manhattan, such as those depicted in the chapter opening, could take $1.80 and use it to buy £1 in London's foreign-exchange market. The trader could then take the pound and sell it for $2.00 in New York's foreign-exchange market. Through this two-point, or geographic, arbitrage, the trader at Chase Manhattan magically converts $1.80 into $2.00 at no risk whatsoever.

Of course, currency traders at other banks will also note the opportunity for quick profits. As arbitrageurs sell dollars and buy pounds in London, the dollar falls in value relative to the pound there. As arbitrageurs buy dollars and sell pounds in New York, the pound falls in value relative to the dollar in that market. This process will continue until the pound-dollar exchange rate is identical in

The Hamburger Standard

	BIG MAC PRICES		Implied PPP* of the Dollar	Actual Exchange Rate 4/7/97	Local Currency Under(–)/over(+) Valuation, %[†]
	In Local Currency	In Dollars			
United States[‡]	**$2.42**	**2.42**	—	—	—
Argentina	Peso2.50	2.50	1.03	1.00	–3
Australia	A$2.50	1.94	1.03	1.29	+20
Austria	Sch34.00	2.82	14.0	12.0	–17
Belgium	BFr109	3.09	45.0	35.3	–28
Brazil	Real2.97	2.81	1.23	1.06	–16
Britain	£1.81	2.95	1.34[‡‡]	1.63[‡‡]	–22
Canada	C$2.88	2.07	1.19	1.39	+14
Chile	Peso1,200	2.88	496	417	–19
China	Yuan9.70	1.16	4.01	8.33	+52
Czech Republic	CKr53.0	1.81	21.9	29.2	+25
Denmark	DKr25.75	3.95	10.6	6.52	–63
France	FFr17.5	3.04	7.23	5.76	–26
Germany	DM4.90	2.86	2.02	1.71	–18
Hong Kong	HK$9.90	1.28	4.09	7.75	+47
Hungary	Forint271	1.52	112	178	+37
Israel	Shekel11.5	3.40	4.75	3.38	–40
Italy	Lire4,600	2.73	1,901	1,683	–13
Japan	¥294	2.34	121	126	+3
Malaysia	M$3.87	1.55	1.60	2.50	+36
Mexico	Peso14.9	1.89	6.16	7.90	+22
Netherlands	Fl5.45	2.83	2.25	1.92	–17
New Zealand	NZ$3.25	2.24	1.34	1.45	+7
Poland	Zloty4.30	1.39	1.78	3.10	+43
Russia	Rouble11,000	1.92	4,545	5,739	+21
Singapore	S$3.00	2.08	1.24	1.44	+14
South Africa	Rand7.80	1.76	3.22	4.43	+27
South Korea	Won2,300	2.57	950	894	–6
Spain	Pta375	2.60	155	144	–7
Sweden	SKr26.0	3.37	10.7	7.72	–39
Switzerland	SFr5.90	4.02	2.44	1.47	–66
Taiwan	NT$68.0	2.47	28.1	27.6	–2
Thailand	Baht46.7	1.79	19.3	26.1	+26

*Purchasing-power parity: local price divided by price in United States. [†]Against dollar
[‡]Average of New York, Chicago, San Francisco, and Atlanta [‡‡]Dollars per pound

Source: *The Economist*, April 12, 1997, p. 71; © 1997 The Economist Newspaper Group, Inc. Reprinted with permission. Further reproduction prohibited.

both markets. Only when there is no possibility of profitable arbitrage will the foreign-exchange market be in equilibrium.

We add one caveat: if the costs of making an arbitrage transaction were large, there would be differences in the exchange rates in the two markets that reflected the size of the transaction costs. However, for major currencies, foreign exchange is sold in large amounts by very large, well-known international banks. Accordingly, transaction costs are extremely small, and two-point arbitrage generally will cause exchange rates between any two major currencies to be identical in all markets.

FIGURE 5.10

Three-Point Arbitrage

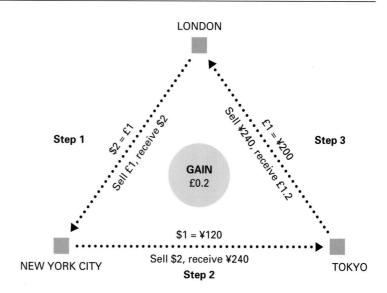

Consider another example. Suppose that £1 can buy $2 in New York, Tokyo, and London, $1 can buy ¥120 in those three markets, and £1 can buy ¥200 in all three. Because the exchange rate between each pair of currencies is the same in each country, no possibility of profitable two-point arbitrage exists. However, profitable three-point arbitrage opportunities exist. **Three-point arbitrage** is the buying and selling of three different currencies to make a riskless profit. Figure 5.10 shows how this can work:

Step 1: Convert £1 into $2.

Step 2: Convert the $2 into ¥240.

Step 3: Convert the ¥240 into £1.2.

Through these three steps, £1 has been converted into £1.2, for a riskless profit of £0.2.

Professional currency traders can make profits through three-point arbitrage whenever the price of buying a currency directly (such as using pounds to buy yen) differs from the cross rate of exchange. The **cross rate** is an exchange rate between two currencies calculated through the use of a third currency (such as using pounds to buy dollars and then using the dollars to buy yen). Because of the depth and liquidity of dollar-denominated currency markets, the U.S. dollar is the primary third currency used in calculating cross rates. In the earlier example, the direct quote between pounds and yen is £1/¥200, while the cross rate is

$$\frac{£1}{$2} \times \frac{$1}{¥120} = \frac{£1}{¥240}$$

The difference between these two rates offers arbitrage profits to foreign-exchange market professionals. The market for the three currencies will be in equilibrium only when arbitrage profits do not exist, which occurs when the direct quote and the cross rate for each possible pair of the three currencies are equal.

The real significance of three-point arbitrage is that it links together individual foreign-exchange markets. Changes in the pound/dollar market will affect the yen/pound market and the dollar/yen market because of the direct quote–cross rate equilibrium relationship. But these changes will in turn affect other markets, such as the dollar/franc market, the yen/franc market, and the pound/franc market. Because of three-point arbitrage, changes in any one foreign-exchange market can affect prices in all other foreign-exchange markets.

The third form of arbitrage we discuss here is covered-interest arbitrage. **Covered-interest arbitrage** is arbitrage that occurs when the difference between two countries' interest rates is not equal to the forward discount/premium on their currencies. In practice, it is the most important of the three types of arbitrage discussed here. Because of the globalization of capital markets resulting from telecommunications and information management innovations, international bankers, insurance companies, and corporate treasurers can scan money markets worldwide to obtain the best returns on their short-term excess cash balances and the lowest rates on short-term loans. But in so doing, they often want to protect, or *cover* (hence the term *covered-interest arbitrage*), themselves from exchange-rate risks.

A simple example demonstrates how covered-interest arbitrage works. Suppose the annual interest rate for 90-day deposits is 12 percent in London and 8 percent in New York. New York investors will be eager to earn the higher returns available in London. To do so, they must convert their dollars to pounds today in order to invest in London. However, the New York investors ultimately want dollars, not pounds, so they must reconvert the pounds back to dollars at the end of 90 days. But what if the pound's value were to fall during that period? The extra interest the New Yorkers will earn in London might then be wiped out by losses suffered when they exchange pounds for dollars in 90 days.

The New York investors can capture the higher London interest rates but avoid exchange-rate dangers by covering in the forward market their exposure to potential drops in the pound's value. Suppose they have $1 million to invest, the spot pound is selling for $1.60, and the 90-day forward pound is selling for $1.59. They have two choices:

1 They can invest their money in New York at 8 percent interest.

2 They can convert their dollars into pounds today, invest in London at 12 percent interest, and in 90 days liquidate their London investment and convert it back to dollars.

If the New York investors choose the first option and invest their funds in the New York money market for 90 days at 8 percent annual interest (or 2 percent for 90 days), at the end of the 90 days their investment will be

$$\$1,000,000 \times 1.02 = \$1,020,000.$$

Or they can invest their money in London for 90 days. To do so, they first convert their $1,000,000 into £625,000 at the spot rate of $1.60/£1. At the 12 percent annual interest rate available in London (or 3 percent for 90 days), their investment will grow in 90 days to

$$£625,000 \times 1.03 = £643,750.$$

If they want to avoid exposure to exchange-rate fluctuations, they can sell the £643,750 today in the 90-day forward market at the current 90-day forward rate of $1.59/£1, thereby yielding at the end of 90 days:

$$£643,750 \times \$1.59/£1 = \$1,023,562.50.$$

The New Yorkers thus earn more money by investing in London than they would at home ($23,562.50 versus $20,000). Covered-interest arbitrage allows them to capture the higher interest rate in London while covering themselves from exchange-rate fluctuations by using the forward market. So, short-term investment money, seeking the higher, covered return, will flow from New York to London.

What happens in the two lending markets and the foreign-exchange market when such arbitrage occurs? Because funds are transferred from New York to London, interest rates will rise in New York, since the supply of loanable money in New York decreases. Interest rates will fall in London, since the supply of loanable money increases there. In the spot market, the demand for pounds increases, thereby raising the spot price of pounds. In the 90-day forward market, the supply of pounds increases, thereby lowering the forward price of pounds. Loanable funds will continue to flow from New York to London until the return on the covered investment is the same in London as it is in New York. Only then will all possibilities for profitable covered-interest arbitrage be exhausted.

Returns to international investors will be equal—and arbitrage-driven, short-term international capital flows will end—when the interest-rate difference between the two markets equals the 90-day forward discount on the pound. Said another way, covered-interest arbitrage will end if the gains investors capture from the higher interest rates in the London market are just offset by the exchange-rate losses they suffer from the conversion of their dollars to pounds today and reconversion of their pounds back to dollars in 90 days. (Note that the pound's forward discount measures the exchange-rate loss on this "spot against forward" swap transaction.)

The short-term capital flows that result from covered-interest arbitrage are so important to the foreign-exchange market that in practice the short-term interest-rate differential between two countries determines the forward discount or forward premium on their currencies.[10]

This last statement raises another question: why should interest rates vary among countries in the first place? Addressing this question in 1930, Yale economist Irving Fisher demonstrated that a country's nominal interest rate reflects the real interest rate plus expected inflation in that country. National differences in expected inflation rates thus yield differences in nominal interest rates among countries, a phenomenon known as the **international Fisher effect.** Because of the international Fisher effect and covered-interest arbitrage, an increase in a country's expected inflation rate will lead to higher interest rates in that country. This in turn will lead to either a shrinking of the forward premium or a widening of the forward discount on the country's currency in the foreign-exchange market. Because of this linkage between inflation and expected changes in exchange rates, international business-people and foreign-currency traders carefully monitor countries' inflation trends. The connection between inflation and exchange rates also impacts the international monetary system. For example, a fixed exchange-rate system functions poorly if inflation rates vary widely among countries participating in the system.

In summary, arbitrage activities are important for several reasons. Arbitrage constitutes a major portion of the $1.2 trillion in currencies traded globally each working day. It affects the supply and demand for each of the major trading currencies. It also ties together the foreign-exchange markets, thereby overcoming differences in geography (two-point arbitrage), currency type (three-point arbitrage), and time (covered-interest arbitrage). Arbitrage truly makes the foreign-exchange market global.

The International Capital Market

Not only are international banks important in the functioning of the foreign-exchange market and arbitrage transactions, but they also play a critical role in financing the operations of international businesses, acting as both commercial bankers and investment bankers (as local law permits). As commercial bankers, they finance exports and imports, accept deposits, provide working capital loans, and offer sophisticated cash management services for their clients. As investment bankers, they may underwrite or syndicate local, foreign, or multinational loans and broker, facilitate, or even finance mergers and joint ventures between foreign and domestic firms.

Major International Banks

The international banking system is centered in large money-market banks headquartered in the world's financial centers—Japan, the United States, the United Kingdom, Germany, and France. These banks are involved in international commerce on a global scale. Of the world's thirty largest banks, eleven are located in Japan (see Table 5.1), a reflection in part of that country's global financial power and in part of the key role Japanese banks play in financing the business needs of members of Japanese keiretsu.

International banking takes many forms. Originally, most international banking was done through reciprocal correspondent relationships among banks located in different countries. A **correspondent relationship** is an agent relationship whereby one bank acts as a correspondent, or agent, for another bank in the first bank's home country. For example, a U.S. bank could be the correspondent for a Danish bank in the United States, while the Danish bank could be the U.S. bank's correspondent in Denmark. Services performed by correspondent banks include paying or collecting foreign funds, providing credit information, and honoring letters of credit. To facilitate these transactions, each bank maintains accounts at the other that are denominated in the local currency.

As the larger banks have internationalized their operations, they have increasingly provided their own overseas operations, rather than utilizing correspondent banks, in order to improve their ability to compete internationally. A bank that has its own foreign operations is better able to access new sources of deposits and profitable lending opportunities. Equally as important, as its domestic clients internationalize, it can better meet those clients' international banking needs. Thus, it retains the international business of its domestic clients and reduces the risk that some other international bank will steal them away.

TABLE 5.1

The World's 30 Largest Banks

RANK BY ASSETS 1996	1995		ASSETS ($ MILLIONS)
1	6/35	Bank of Tokyo-Mitsubishi (Japan)	$752,318
2	4	Deutsche Bank (Germany)	575,693
3	1	Sumitomo Bank (Japan)	513,781
4	2	Dai-Ichi Kangyo Bank (Japan)	476,696
5	5	Fuji Bank (Japan)	474,371
6	3	Sanwa Bank (Japan)	470,336
7	14	ABN Amro Holdings (Netherlands)	444,410
8	7	Sakura Bank (Japan)	436,687
9	10	Industrial & Commercial Bank (China)	435,723
10	13	HSBC Holdings (U.K.)	405,037
11	8	Norinchukin Bank (Japan)	400,031
12	11	Industrial Bank (Japan)	399,509
13	15	Dresdner Bank (Germany)	389,626
14	19	Banque Nationale de Paris (France)	358,187
15	18	Societe Generale (France)	342,760
16	49	Chase Manhattan (U.S.)	336,099
17	16	Union Bank of Switzerland (Switzerland)	325,082
18	25	Commerzbank (Germany)	320,419
19	29	Barclays Bank (U.K.)	318,551
20	30	National Westminster Bank (U.K.)	317,411
21	12	Credit Lyonnais (France)	312,926
22	17	Mitsubishi Trust & Banking (Japan)	312,223
23	23	Westdeutsche Landesbank (Germany)	305,879
24	22	Tokai Bank (Japan)	296,895
25	27	Cie. Financiere de Paribas (France)	293,437
26	26	Bank of China (China)	292,554
27	32	Citicorp (U.S.)	277,653
28	33	Swiss Bank (Switzerland)	268,161
29	20	Sumitomo Trust & Banking (Japan)	266,035
30	34	Bayerische Vereinsbank (Germany)	256,371

Source: From "The 100 Largest Banks," *Wall Street Journal*, Sept. 18, 1997, p. R27. Reprinted by permission of the *Wall Street Journal*, © 1997 Dow Jones & Company, Inc. All Rights Reserved Worldwide.

An overseas banking operation can take several forms. If it is separately incorporated from the parent, it is called a **subsidiary bank;** if it is not separately incorporated, it is called a **branch bank.** Sometimes an international bank may choose to create an **affiliated bank,** an overseas operation in which it takes part ownership in conjunction with a local or foreign partner.

U.S. banks may also use either of the following two techniques to establish international banking operations while operating in the United States:

1   The Edge Act of 1919 allows U.S. banks to establish an **Edge Act corporation,** a bank set up outside of the parent bank's home state (thus circumventing federal regulations restricting interstate banking) for the sole purpose of providing international banking services. Because much of the international financial services infrastructure is located in large cities, Edge Act corporations are an attractive way for banks headquartered outside of financial centers to participate in international lending. For example, an Ohio bank can, through an Edge Act corporation, locate its international operations in New York City, continue to serve its local clients in Cleveland, and yet not violate interstate banking restrictions. Use of the Edge Act is likely to decline over time, however, for federal regulations against interstate banking are in the process of being eliminated.

2   A bank can create an international banking facility. This alternative is discussed in detail later in this chapter.

Commercial Banking Services. Tourists utilize international banking services when they exchange their home currency or traveler's checks for local currency. While the physical exchange of one country's paper currency for another's is part of international banking operations, a far more important part involves financing and facilitating everyday commercial transactions. For example, when J.C. Penney orders $10 million worth of high-tech running shoes from Adidas, the German footwear manufacturer, with payment due in 90 days, J.C. Penney may require any of the following:

♦ Short-term financing of the purchase

♦ International electronic funds transfer

♦ Forward purchases of deutsche marks

♦ Advice about proper documentation for importing and paying for the athletic shoes

The international department of the firm's bank will provide any or all of these services as part of its normal commercial banking operations.

Investment Banking Services. In addition to commercial banking services, most international banks also provide investment banking services. Corporate clients hire investment bankers to package and locate long-term debt and equity funding and to arrange mergers and acquisitions of domestic and foreign firms. As the capital market has internationalized, competition has forced investment bankers to globalize their operations in order to secure capital for their clients at the lowest possible cost.

In most of the world, international banks provide both commercial banking services and investment banking services. In the United States, however, the 1934 Glass-Stegall Act limits the ability of commercial banks to provide investment banking services. As a result, investment banking services in the United States are supplied predominantly by securities firms, such as Salomon Brothers, Goldman Sachs, and Merrill Lynch. The foreign subsidiaries of U.S.-based banks are free to provide investment banking services outside the United States, however.

The Eurocurrency Market

Another important facet of the international financial system is the Eurocurrency market. Originally called the Eurodollar market, the Eurocurrency market originated in the early 1950s when the communist-controlled governments of Central and Eastern Europe needed dollars to finance their international trade but feared the U.S. government would confiscate or block their holdings of dollars in U.S. banks for political reasons. The communist governments solved this problem by using European banks that were willing to maintain dollar accounts for them.[11] Thus the Eurodollar was born—U.S. dollars deposited in European bank accounts. As other banks worldwide, particularly in Canada and Japan, began offering dollar-denominated deposit accounts, the term **Eurodollar** evolved to mean U.S. dollars deposited in any bank account outside the United States. As other currencies became stronger in the postwar era—particularly the yen and the deutsche mark—the Eurocurrency market broadened to include Euroyen, Euromarks, and other currencies. Today a **Eurocurrency** is defined as a currency on deposit outside of its country of issue. Some $6 trillion worth of Eurocurrencies are on deposit in banks worldwide; roughly two thirds of these deposits are in the form of Eurodollars.[12]

The Euroloan market has grown up with the Eurocurrency market. The Euroloan market is extremely competitive, and lenders operate on razor-thin margins. Euroloans are often quoted on the basis of the **London Interbank Offer Rate (LIBOR),** the interest rate that London banks charge each other for short-term Eurocurrency loans. The Euroloan market is often the low-cost source of loans for large, creditworthy borrowers, such as governments and large MNCs, for three reasons. First, Euroloans are free from costly government banking regulations, such as reserve requirements, that are designed to control the domestic money supply but that drive up lending costs. Second, Euroloans involve large transactions, so the average cost of making the loans is less. And, third, since only the most creditworthy borrowers use the Euroloan market, the risk premium that lenders charge also is less.

In the 1970s U.S. banks complained that reserve requirements and other expensive regulations imposed by the Federal Reserve Board prevented them from competing with European and Asian banks in issuing dollar-denominated international loans. These loans account for 60 percent of the Euroloan market. Foreign banks lending in Eurodollars were not subject to the regulations. To counter this problem, the Federal Reserve Board in 1981 authorized the creation of international banking facilities. An **international banking facility (IBF)** is an entity of a U.S. bank that is legally distinct from the bank's domestic operations and that may offer only international banking services. IBFs do not need to observe the numerous U.S. domestic banking regulations. Of course, the Federal Reserve Board has issued various regulations to ensure IBFs do not engage in domestic banking services. For example, IBFs may only accept deposits from or make loans to non-U.S. residents. Nonetheless, they enable U.S. banks to compete with other international bankers on a more equal footing in the critical Euroloan market.

The International Bond Market

The international bond market represents a major source of debt financing for the world's governments, international organizations, and larger firms. This market has traditionally consisted of two types of bonds: foreign bonds and Eurobonds.

FIGURE 5.11

International Bond Issues, 1996, by Currency (U.S. Dollar Equivalents)

Source: Bank for International Settlements, "International Banking and Financial Market Developments" (Basle, August 1997), p. 41.

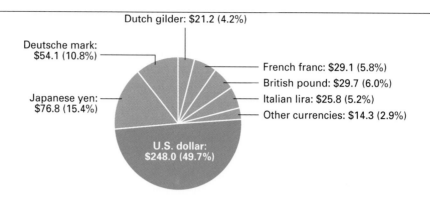

Foreign bonds are bonds issued by a resident of country A but sold to residents of country B and denominated in the currency of country B. For example, the Nestlé Corporation, a Swiss resident, might issue a foreign bond denominated in yen and sold primarily to residents of Japan. A **Eurobond** is a bond issued in the currency of country A but sold to residents of other countries. For example, American Airlines could borrow $500 million to finance new aircraft purchases by selling Eurobonds to residents of Denmark and Germany. The U.S. dollar is the dominant currency in the international bond market (see Fig. 5.11).

As the global capital market has evolved, the international bond market has grown increasingly sophisticated. Syndicates of investment banks, securities firms, and commercial banks put together complex packages of international bonds to serve the borrowing needs of large, creditworthy borrowers, such as major MNCs, national governments, and international organizations. For example, in 1989 the World Bank lowered its borrowing costs by issuing a new type of financing instrument, the global bond. A **global bond** is a large, liquid financial asset that can be traded anywhere at any time. The World Bank simultaneously sold $1.5 billion of U.S.-dollar denominated global bonds in North America, Europe, and Japan and succeeded in lowering its interest costs on the bond issue by about 0.225 percentage points. While 0.225 percentage points may not seem much, multiplying that amount by $1.5 billion reveals that the Bank reduced its annual financing costs by $3,375,000. Attracted by the World Bank's success, other large organizations, such as Matsushita Electric, the Province of Ontario, Citicorp, and Household Finance, have also issued global bonds recently.[13]

Other innovative opportunities exist in the bond market. For example, at the borrower's option, bond interest may be paid in one currency with the principal paid in a second. Or the borrower may secure a lower interest rate by offering inflation protection through pegging the principal repayment to the value of gold or the SDR.

Like the Euroloan market, the international bond market is highly competitive and borrowers are often able to obtain funds on very favorable terms. Large transaction sizes, creditworthy borrowers, and freedom from annoying regulations imposed on domestic capital markets all lower the interest rates charged on such loans.

Global Equity Markets

The growing importance of multinational operations and improvements in telecommunications technology have also made equity markets more global. Start-up companies are no longer restricted to raising new equity solely from domestic sources. For example, Swiss pharmaceutical firms are a major source of equity capital for new U.S. biotechnology firms. Established firms also tap into the global equity market. When expanding into a foreign market, a firm may choose to raise capital for its foreign subsidiary in the foreign market. For example, the Walt Disney Company initially sold 51 percent of its Disneyland Paris project to French investors. Numerous MNCs also cross-list their common stocks on multiple stock exchanges. British Airways, for example, is listed on both the London Stock Exchange and the New York Stock Exchange, thereby enabling both European and American investors to purchase its shares conveniently. Another innovation is the development of country funds. A **country fund** is a mutual fund that specializes in investing in a given country's firms.

The globalization of equity markets has been facilitated by the globalization of the financial services industry. Most major financial services firms, such as Merrill Lynch, Daiwa Securities, and Deutsche Bank, have expanded their operations from their domestic bases into the major international financial centers. These financial services firms are eager to raise capital, provide investment advice, offer stock market analyses, and put together financing deals for clients anywhere around the world.

Offshore Financial Centers

Offshore financial centers focus on offering banking and other financial services to nonresident customers. Many of these centers are located on island states, such as the Bahamas, Bahrain, the Cayman Islands, Bermuda, the Netherlands Antilles, and Singapore. Luxembourg and Switzerland, although not islands, are also important "offshore" financial centers.

MNCs often use offshore financial centers to obtain low-cost Eurocurrency loans. Many MNCs locate financing subsidiaries in these centers to take advantage of the benefits they offer: political stability, a regulatory climate that facilitates international capital transactions, communications links to other major financial centers, and availability of legal, accounting, financial, and other expertise needed to package large loans. The efficiency of offshore financial centers in attracting deposits and then lending these funds to customers worldwide is an important factor in the growing globalization of the capital market.[14]

CHAPTER REVIEW

Summary

A currency's price in the foreign-exchange market is determined by the interaction of the demand for and supply of the currency. Underlying the demand is foreigners' desire to buy goods, services, and assets of the country. Underlying the supply is residents' desire to purchase goods, services, and assets owned by foreigners.

Two types of exchange-rate systems exist: fixed and flexible. BOP equilibrium is achieved differently in the two types of systems. In a fixed exchange-rate system, short-run equilibrium is achieved via changes in the official reserves owned by central banks. Long-run equilibrium results from the inflationary or deflationary consequences of changes in the domestic money supply on the competitiveness of the country's exporters. Under a flexible exchange-rate system, equilibrium is reached by allowing a currency's price to change until the quantity of currency demanded equals the quantity supplied.

Major international banks in financial centers such as London, Frankfurt, Tokyo, and New York City play a critical role in the functioning of the foreign-exchange market. Key players in the wholesale market, they account for the vast majority of foreign-exchange transactions. In servicing their clients' needs, they are also an important component of the retail market. Banks assist commercial customers, speculators, and arbitrageurs in acquiring foreign currency on both the spot and forward markets.

An important feature of the foreign-exchange market is its time dimension. International businesses may buy currency in the spot market for immediate delivery or in the forward market for future delivery. The forward market, currency futures, and currency options enable firms to protect themselves from unfavorable future exchange-rate movements.

Arbitrage activities affect the demand for and supply of foreign exchange. The theory of purchasing power parity says the prices of tradable goods will tend to equalize among countries. Arbitrage of foreign exchange itself is even more important. Two-point arbitrage implies that the exchange rate between two currencies will be the same in all geographic markets. Three-point arbitrage links individual foreign-exchange markets together. Covered-interest arbitrage causes geographic differences in interest rates to equal differences between spot and forward exchange rates.

The international capital market is growing in sophistication as a result of technological advances in telecommunications and computers. Major international banks still utilize their traditional correspondent relationships, but are increasingly engaged in overseas bank operations themselves. The development of the Eurocurrency market allows banks of any country to conduct lending operations in whatever currencies their clients require. MNCs now commonly raise capital, both debt and equity, on a global basis, wherever its cost is lowest.

Review Questions

1. How are prices established in the foreign-exchange market?

2. How is equilibrium achieved in a fixed exchange-rate system?

3. How is equilibrium reached in a flexible exchange-rate system?

4. What are the advantages and disadvantages of the two types of exchange-rate systems?

5. What is the role of international banks in the foreign-exchange market?

6. Explain the different techniques firms can use to protect themselves from future changes in exchange rates.

7. List the major types of arbitrage activities that affect the foreign-exchange market.

8. Describe the various forms a bank's overseas operations may take.

9. What are Eurocurrencies?

10. What are the major characteristics of offshore financial centers?

Questions for Discussion

1. Suppose the Federal Reserve Board unexpectedly raises interest rates in the United States. How will this impact the foreign-exchange market?

2. How important is communications and computing technology to the smooth functioning of the foreign-exchange market? If the technological advances of the past four decades were eliminated—for example, no PCs or satellite telecommunications—how would the foreign-exchange market be affected?

3. Chapter 4 mentions the attempt by EU members to create a single currency, the euro. Once the euro has been established, do you expect the U.S. dollar to maintain its position as the dominant currency in the foreign-exchange market? Why or why not?

4. Suppose the spot pound and the 90-day forward pound are both selling for $1.65, while U.S. interest rates are 10 percent and British interest rates are 6 percent. Using covered interest arbitrage theory, describe what will happen to the spot price of the pound, the 90-day forward price of the pound, interest rates in the U.S., and interest rates in the U.K. when arbitrageurs enter this market.

5. How important is the creation of international banking facilities to the international competitiveness of the U.S. banking industry?

6. What would be the impact on world trade and investment if there were only one currency based on the SDR?

BUILDING GLOBAL SKILLS

Please refer back to Fig. 5.4 in order to answer the following questions:

1. What is the spot rate for the British pound on Wednesday in terms of the U.S. dollar? (Or, stated differently, how many dollars does a pound cost? Or, from the U.S. perspective, what's the direct quote on pounds?)

2. What is the spot price for the dollar on Wednesday in terms of the Swiss franc? (Or, from the U.S. perspective, what is the indirect rate on Swiss francs?)

3. Calculate the cross rate of exchange between the British pound and the Swiss franc.

4. Calculate the annualized forward premium or discount on 180-day yen.

5. If you're planning to go to Japan this summer, should you buy your yen today? Why or why not?

6. According to covered-interest arbitrage theory, is the United States or Japan expected to have higher interest rates?

7. According to covered-interest arbitrage theory, what is the expected difference between interest rates in the United States and Japan?

8. According to the international Fisher effect, is expected inflation higher in Japan or the United States?

9. Did the value of the Canadian dollar rise or fall between Tuesday and Wednesday?

WORKING WITH THE WEB: Building Global Internet Skills

What Will the Zloty Be Worth in a Year?

You are the head of marketing for a small U.S. producer of innovative, high-quality computer-controlled machine tools called Machine Solutions. Machine Solutions has bid on a contract to supply four stamping machines over the next twelve months to one of Poland's leading and fastest growing auto parts manufacturers. The bidding is likely to be extremely competitive. Winning this contract is important to Machine Solutions for several reasons. First, it gains the company access to the growing auto parts industry in Central and Eastern Europe. Second, the Polish company has been experiencing rapid growth, and is likely to need additional stamping machines in the future. Third, the contract will increase Machine

Solutions' annual sales by 25 percent. Fourth, because Machine Solutions was started only two years ago, it is experiencing growing pains and cash flow problems.

Machine Solutions offers to sell the Polish company four machines at $1 million each, payable on delivery. In accord with the Polish company's request, Machine Solutions agrees to deliver two machines in 90 days, one in 180 days, and the last one a year from now. After you submit your bid, the purchasing manager of the Polish company says that he is extremely interested in your offer, but Machine Solutions can win the contract only if it agrees to invoice the company in its home currency, zlotys. Because he is asking Machine Solutions to accept the foreign-exchange risk in the transaction, the purchasing manager says there may be some "wiggle room" on the price, but that there are other companies who he will buy from if the price in zlotys is too high.

You present this news to Machine Solutions' other executives. The firm's treasurer hits the roof, arguing that he knows nothing about Polish sausages or zlotniks or whatever the money is called, and is afraid that changes in the value of the currency will rob the sale of its profits. You respond that this sale is vital to Machine Solutions' future health, allowing it to get its foot in the door at a growing company in a growing market. After listening to the argument, the CEO tells you to rework the proposed contract, agreeing to accept zlotys in payment but to protect Machine Solutions from foreign exchange risk.

Your first thought is to go to the *Wall Street Journal* and look up the price of Polish zlotys in the spot and forward market. Unfortunately, only a spot price is published because currently no forward market exists for the zloty. Accordingly, you have to develop some means of forecasting what the zloty will be worth in 90 days, 180 days, and a year from now, when the machines are to be paid for. You know that the value of the zloty over this period will be influenced by a variety of factors, such as interest rates, inflation rates, balance of payments performance, the stability of Poland's economic and political policies, and other factors. You are also aware that many banks and consulting firms scrutinize such markets for their clients.

Here's your task: determine the prices in zlotys that Machine Solutions should propose to charge for the four stamping machines as they are delivered over the course of the year. You can use whatever criteria you wish to establish these prices, but you must defend how you arrived at them. The textbook's web site provides hot-links to some useful sources of information, although of course you are free to use other sources as you see fit.

CLOSING CASE

A Bad Case of Bahtulism[15]

On February 3, 1997, Goldman Sachs & Co., the large New York-based international investment banking house, announced that it feared that Thailand's currency, the *baht*, might be devalued in the next six months. Goldman Sachs' warnings followed on the heels of reports that Thailand's government had suffered a budget deficit and that foreign investors were withdrawing some of their short-term investments from the country in fear of a devaluation. Goldman Sachs executives were also concerned about the impact of the rising value of the U.S. dollar on the international competitiveness of Thailand's exports. The country's central bank, the Bank of Thailand, relied on a variant of a fixed exchange-rate system in which it pegged the value of the baht to a bundle of currencies, with the U.S. dollar comprising about 80 percent of the bundle. Because of the fixed relationship between the baht and the U.S. dollar, the dollar's rise in value from its nadir in summer 1995 meant that Thai exports were becoming increasingly expensive relative to goods produced in other locales.

But the Bank of Thailand felt confident that it could maintain the baht's value in the foreign-exchange market. To counteract the short-term capital outflows, the Bank raised interest rates, making Thai investments more attractive to foreign investors. If that proved inadequate, the Bank pledged to spend its $38.7 billion in foreign-currency reserves to support the baht's value.

Unfortunately, that's not how it turned out. Goldman Sachs' February warning proved accurate. Foreign-currency speculators sold their baht, believing that the Thai government would be forced to devalue the currency because of the increasing uncompetitiveness of Thai exports and the long-term domestic economic damage that would be caused by high interest rates. The Bank of Thailand spent almost $10 billion of its foreign-currency reserves defending the fixed value of the baht before throwing in the towel. On July 2, 1997, it unpegged the baht, which promptly fell 20 percent on the foreign-exchange market, rewarding all those speculators who believed such an action was inevitable. The devaluation baht-ered the domestic economy. Secure in the belief—false, as it turned out—that the Bank of Thailand would maintain a fixed rate with the U.S. dollar, many Thai companies had borrowed dollars to fund their domestic capital needs. This had seemed to be a reasonable approach, because interest rates on dollar-denominated loans secured in the international lending market were lower than the interest rates charged for locally procured baht-denominated loans. Some had even used the borrowed dollars to relend in the domestic capital market. Unfortunately, these dollar-denominated loans became much more expensive due to the devaluation—more baht would be needed to pay each dollar of interest and principal— creating cash flow problems for the borrowers and raising the likelihood that they might default on their loans and declare bankruptcy. Thai financial services firms were particularly vulnerable, for many of them had funded property speculators who had trouble meeting payments as commercial real estate prices in Bangkok and other Thai cities tumbled. But even the profits of otherwise healthy companies like Siam Cement were wiped out due to the difficulty of servicing their foreign debts.

The currency crisis has also hurt foreign MNCs doing business in Thailand. Goodyear's subsidiary in Thailand, for example, was hit with a double whammy. First, its primary customer, the Thai new-car market, was in free fall due to the devaluation-created economic crisis. Second, its profit margins shrank significantly, for while it sells its tires for baht, many of its costs are denominated in dollars. The company estimated its costs increased by 20 percent as a result of the baht's devaluation.

Thailand's problems soon spread to its neighbors. The so-called bahtulism epidemic (or "Asian contagion") infected neighboring countries such as Indonesia, Malaysia, and the Philippines, all of which compete with Thailand for FDI from international businesses looking to build factories to tap the region's abundant hard-working, low-cost labor supply. With the devaluation of the baht, Thai exports suddenly became 20 percent cheaper, making Indonesian, Malaysian, and Philippino exports relatively more expensive. Speculators turned their attention to these countries, believing that they too would have to devalue their currencies in order to remain competitive with Thailand. By early September 1997, the baht had devalued 26 percent relative to its value against the dollar a year earlier, the Indonesian rupiah by 21 percent, the Malaysian ringgit by 14 percent, and the Philippino peso by 13 percent. The epidemic then spread eastward, wracking the South Korean economy. The Korean won plummeted, as bankers realized that many Korean firms were threatened by overborrowing and devaluation-induced price cutting by regional rivals.

The currency crisis affected more than the foreign-exchange market. Area stock markets were hit hard as well, since investors feared that the burden of paying back dollar-denominated debt with the depreciated local currencies would hurt the earnings of regional corporations. By early September 1997, the average Thai stock lost 60 percent of its dollar value, the average Philippino stock 45 percent, the average Malaysian stock 40 percent, and the average Indonesian stock 30 percent relative to their year-earlier values. Even foreign stocks were hurt by the crisis. The prices of so-called "global consumer" stocks such as Coca-Cola, Gillette, and Whirlpool fell as investors realized that a slowdown in the growth of these emerging Southeast Asian markets would cost them sales.

As fear of a worldwide recession arose, the International Monetary Fund (IMF) and the governments of the Quad countries hurriedly assembled financial aid packages to help Thailand, Malaysia, Indonesia, the Philippines, and South Korea. Over $100 billion has been pledged to restore these countries to economic health and, hopefully, to end the spread of the Asian contagion. Whether the IMF's aid will prove successful is as yet unknown. What is known, however, is that its aid package has proven to be quite controversial, as the "Point-Counterpoint" following the chapter suggests.

Case Questions

1. How can a central bank use its currency reserves to support the value of its country's currency in the foreign-exchange market?

2. Would Thailand have been better off using a flexible exchange-rate system instead of the fixed system it did use?

3. If you were a manager of an international business in Thailand in February 1997, what could you have done to protect your company against the possibility of a devaluation of the baht?

4. There's an old saying that "it's an ill wind that blows no good." Can you think of anyone who benefited from Thailand's currency crisis?

5. How does the Asian contagion affect other regions, such as Latin America or the European Union?

CHAPTER NOTES

1. "European Exchange Rate Chaos Is Bedlam for Currency Traders at Chase Manhattan," *Wall Street Journal,* September 17, 1992, p. C1. Reprinted by permission of the *Wall Street Journal,* © 1992 Dow Jones & Company, Inc. All Rights Reserved Worldwide.

2. To simplify the exposition, we assumed the foreign-exchange supply curve is upward-sloping like most supply curves. Unfortunately, foreign-exchange supply curves may bend backward, a complication that can be left for graduate students in economics and finance to deal with.

3. Bank for International Settlements, *Central Bank Survey of Foreign Exchange Market Activity in April 1995* (Basle, 1996) is the source of this and subsequent market share data.

4. Rudi Weisweiller, *How the Foreign Exchange Market Works* (New York: New York Institute of Finance, 1990), p. 12.

5. *Euromoney, The 1991 Guide to Currencies* (London: Euromoney, 1991), p. 105.

6. Boris Antl and Richard Ensor, *Management of Foreign Exchange Risk* (London: Euromoney Publications, 1982), p. 43.

7. To simplify our example, we assumed the domestic price of the jeans in Canada and in the United States remained constant. But consider the market for Levis in Canada. As Canadians travel to the United States to buy their jeans, the demand for jeans in Canada decreases, which should decrease the price of jeans in Canada. Similarly, the demand for jeans in the United States should increase, which should increase the price of jeans in the United States. Thus, PPP might occur as a result of changes in the price of the product as well as changes in the price of foreign exchange.

8. "Canada Suffers Exodus of Jobs, Investment and Shoppers to U.S.," *Wall Street Journal,* June 20, 1991, p. A1.

9. "Canadians' Shopping Trips to U.S. Decline," *Wall Street Journal,* July 15, 1992, p. A2.

10. Antl and Ensor, op. cit., p. 112.

11. Paul Einzig, *The Euro-Dollar System* (New York: St. Martin's Press, 1973), p. 3.

12. Paul R. Krugman and Maurice Obstfeld, *International Economics,* 3rd ed. (New York: HarperCollins, 1994), p. 642f.

13. "Matsushita Electric's Planned $1 Billion Issue May Open Up Access to Issuance of Global Bonds," *Wall Street Journal,* June 8, 1992, p. C1.

14. Eiteman, Stonehill, and Moffett, op. cit., p. 281.

15. "Goodyear's Thai Subsidiary Sees Bad Year," *Wall Street Journal,* September 5, 1997, p. A9; "The real lesson from Asia," *Financial Times,* September 2, 1997, p. 15; "Asia's endangered tigers," *Financial Times,* August 30/August 31, 1997, p. 6; "Thais count cost of baht defence," *Financial Times,* August 29, 1997, p. 5; "The IMF: Immune from (Frequent) Failure," *Wall Street Journal,* August 25, 1997, p. A18; "Thais face slow economic climb," *USA Today,* August 12, 1997, p. 4B; "Southeast Asia Seems Still on Track to Grow Despite Currency Slide," *Wall Street Journal,* August 5, 1997, p. A1; "Economic Troubles in Thailand Stoke Betting Against the Baht," *Wall Street Journal,* February 10, 1997, p. A14.

Should the IMF Bail Out Asia?

International Monetary Fund aid to Asia can be justified solely on humanitarian grounds. For example, when Thailand shuttered 56 of its 58 investment banks as a result of its currency crisis, 20,000 white-collar employees were put out of work. Without international assistance, other Thai firms would have followed suit and the Thai people would have faced economic disaster. The IMF's actions can also be justified on more pragmatic grounds. In today's global economy, economic troubles in one country are quickly transmitted to others. Thailand's problems triggered similar crises in Indonesia, Malaysia, the Philippines, and South Korea. Their crises in turn threaten to damage economies around the world. Stock markets in London, Frankfurt, and New York weakened as investors realized that recession in Indonesia, the Philippines, and other far-off lands would reduce demand for North American and European products. Communities in Brazil, France, and Mexico were devastated when Korean chaebol announced the cancellation or delay of new factories that had promised to bring jobs and prosperity to their citizens. By getting the battered Asian economies back on their feet, the IMF is ensuring that not only will Asian jobs be saved, but also jobs in the other five inhabited continents.

In the long run, the IMF's intervention often improves the productivity of the recipient countries and the lives of their citizens. Conditions imposed by the IMF (so-called IMF conditionality) lead to necessary economic and political reforms. Consider the problem of crony capitalism, typified by companies owned by the family of former Indonesian President Suharto, which benefited from a variety of tax and tariff concessions, subsidized loans, and preferential treatment from their father's ministers. As part of Indonesia's agreement with the IMF, Suharto was forced to revoke these privileges. Their elimination will make the Indonesian economy more productive and give businesses not connected to the Suharto family a chance to thrive. Similarly, Korea has been required to impose more control over the borrowing and investment policies of the chaebol, relax its import regulations, and permit foreign entry into

IMF intervention will help curb Indonesia's crony capitalism, which has benefited Tommy Suharto and other Suharto children.

Korea's financial services markets. These reforms will boost the efficiency of the Korean economy and bolster opportunities for other firms, domestic and foreign alike, to compete for the Korean market.

Critics like to point out that the IMF's actions bail out bad bankers and corrupt governments. Even if that's true, does it make any sense to let their mistakes drag down the entire global economy? A little IMF money, well spent and with appropriate conditions attached, is the best means available to restore these countries as productive members of the global economy.

No, IMF aid rewards governments, banks, and businesses for making bad decisions

IMF bailouts undermine the efficiency of the global economy. Under a free market system, capital is supplied by investors who carefully analyze risks and rewards. If investors know the IMF will bail them out if their investments go sour, they are more likely to invest in risky projects. If their investments prove successful, they won't share their profits with the taxpayers who fund the IMF. Why then should these taxpayers share their losses?

International competition is also disrupted by IMF bailouts. Consider Idaho's Micron Technology, a memory chip manufacturer. Micron's profitability has been harmed by competition from Korean rivals like Samsung, LG, and Hyundai, who Micron believes have senselessly expanded their chip-making capacity, fueled by cheap loans from Korean banks. Output from their factories has caused the market price of 16 MB DRAM chips to fall by 94 percent in the space of two years, severely damaging Micron and other chip manufacturers. If IMF funds—supplied by taxpayers around the world like Micron—are used by the Korean government to help these firms, then Micron is effectively subsidizing its foreign rivals for their mistakes and helping get them back on their feet so that they can better compete against Micron in the future. Needless to say, Micron objects to such a policy.

Many Indonesians protested against the elimination of food and fuel subsidies demanded by the IMF. But is the IMF the villain, or their own government?

The mere existence of the IMF encourages governments to ignore economic problems when they first arise. Instead of taking quick action that creates some short-term pain, they prefer to maintain monetary and spending policies in hopes that the problem will go away. But delaying the day of reckoning until major economic surgery is required inevitably worsens the situation. Delay has an important political benefit to the government, however. When the IMF steps in and imposes conditions on the country, its leaders can blame the IMF for the ensuing hardships that its people must inevitably suffer.

The IMF's bailout of Asia may cost the world's taxpayers over $100 billion. And what's the result of this philanthropy? International bankers who made risky loans will get their money back. Government officials who lined their pockets, or spent money their countries did not have, will not have to pay for their sins. Who's left holding the bag? Taxpayers from the contributing countries, and the average citizen of the receiving countries, who inevitably will suffer a decline in their standards of living.

Source: "Who needs the IMF?" *Wall Street Journal,* February 3, 1998, p. A22; "Suharto family benefits in peril from spirit of reform," *Financial Times,* January 16, 1998, p. 16; "Fingerprints of Korea's Cash Woes Cover Globe," *Wall Street Journal,* December 15, 1997, p. A16; "S. Korean economy tells cautionary tale," *Houston Chronicle,* December 5, 1997, p. 1C; "Micron Technology Opposes U.S. Role in Korean Bailout," *Wall Street Journal,* December 2, 1997, p. B6.

Wrap-up

1 If Indonesia had been unwilling to abandon its policies favoring firms linked to the Suharto family, should the IMF still have assisted the country?

2 If you were the official U.S. delegate to the IMF's board of governors, how would you have responded to Micron's complaint?

3 Some Koreans believe the IMF has taken unfair advantage of Korea's financial problems to force it to make concessions in its trade and FDI regulations. Do you agree with this complaint? Why or why not?

PART 3

The National Environment

Formulation of National Trade Policies

6

Chapter Outline

Rationales for trade intervention

Industry-level arguments
National trade policies

Barriers to international trade

Tariffs
Nontariff barriers

Promotion of international trade

Subsidies
Foreign trade zones
Export financing programs

Controlling unfair trade practices

Countervailing duties
Antidumping regulations
Super 301

After studying this chapter you should be able to:

Present the major arguments in favor of and against governmental intervention in international trade.

Discuss the advantages and disadvantages of adopting an industrial policy.

Analyze the role of domestic politics in formulating a country's international trade policies.

Describe the major tools countries use to restrict trade.

Specify the techniques countries use to promote international trade.

Explain how countries protect themselves against unfair trade practices.

At first glance, Desmarais & Frère, Ltd. (Desmarais), a Longueuil, Quebec, manufacturer founded in 1951, would appear to be in an enviable position. It employs as many as 400 workers during peak production periods and is Canada's largest producer of photo albums that have self-adhesive pages. Its albums retail at $15 to $50 and are sold through mass marketers such as Wal-Mart, Zellers, and Metropolitan. In fact, ten customers account for 70 percent of Desmarais's annual sales, keeping its marketing costs low. And all but one small domestic competitor has fallen by the wayside. Thus Desmarais captured 50 to 90 percent of the Canadian market for these photo albums in the 1970s and 1980s—

Desmarais Is Tired of Being Dumped On[1]

an enviable market share level in any industry. ▮▮ But in truth the firm's situation is not so rosy. For twenty years, it has been plagued by import competition from low-priced photo albums produced in Asia. One response Desmarais considered to counter this threat was to focus on quality. Yet its major discount-chain customers pride themselves on providing the lowest possible prices for consumers and are willing to use whatever supplier is cheapest, whether foreign or domestic. Further, the photo albums are typically shrink-wrapped in clear plastic, which makes it impossible for a retail customer to compare the quality of different producers' albums. Also, such albums are bought infrequently by the average consumer, so developing brand loyalty among consumers is difficult. ▮▮ Desmarais believed it was being victimized by a practice known as dumping. **Dumping** is the selling by a firm of its products outside its domestic market at prices below those it charges in its domestic market. Fortunately for Desmarais, Canadian law protects Canadian businesses from dumping. In 1975 Desmarais petitioned the Canadian Import Tribunal (CIT), which had jurisdiction over such cases, for relief from the low prices charged by Japanese and Korean photo album manufacturers. The CIT determined that firms from these two countries were indeed dumping their albums in Canada, thereby causing material injury to Desmarais and its smaller Canadian rivals. The CIT then imposed an **antidumping duty**—a tax on the dumped imported goods—on Korean and Japanese photo albums. This duty was equivalent to the difference between the lower price the Asians were charging in the Canadian market and the higher prices they charged in their home markets. In theory, the duty would eliminate any price advantage the Asian producers gained from the dumping. ▮▮ However, the new duty did not solve Desmarais's problem because it applied only to Japanese and Korean producers. The production of photo albums simply shifted to other Asian locations, which were not covered by the duty. By 1984 Desmarais's share of the Canadian market had fallen to an all-time low of 50 percent. The foreign competition had hurt the company's profit margins, profits, and financial performance, for it could not raise its prices to compensate for increases in its costs. In 1985 it filed a second successful complaint with the CIT against dumping by Hong Kong, South Korea, and the United States. (The United States entered the picture because Korean manufacturers were shipping the photo albums to the United States and then re-exporting them from there to Canada.) Desmarais then filed dumping complaints against China in 1986, against Singapore, Malaysia, and Taiwan in 1987, and against Indonesia, Thailand, and the Philippines in 1991. ▌▌ In all these cases, the CIT or its successor, the Canadian International Trade Tribunal (CITT), determined that dumping had occurred. Desmarais's case was reviewed again in 1996, and the CITT found Desmarais still vulnerable to dumping by its foreign competitors. The antidumping duties imposed by the CIT and the CITT were not trivial. For example, as a result of the 1991 complaint, antidumping duties were imposed ranging from 35.1 percent (on self-adhesive pages) to 78 percent (on photo albums with self-adhesive pages). Yet Desmarais cannot rest easy. For twenty years, its home market has been targeted by Asian producers. As soon as the firm obtains relief from the CIT or the CITT, production of photo albums shifts to a country not covered by an antidumping duty. Desmarais has little reason to be optimistic that it will be able to raise its prices to recover its cost increases over the past two decades. ▌▌▌▌▌

In today's global economy, firms must deal with both domestic and foreign competitors. The problem facing Desmarais & Frère, Ltd., exemplifies the plight of domestic manufacturers threatened by competition from low-priced foreign producers. And its reaction typifies that of similar firms: it asked its national government for protection against the foreigners. However, many firms benefit from international trade, finding foreign markets a rich source of additional customers. Exports generate domestic jobs, so many national governments promote the success of their countries' domestic firms in international markets. In this chapter we discuss the development of national trade policies that protect domestic firms from foreign competition and help promote the country's exports. We also explore the rationale for these policies and how governments implement them.

Rationales for Trade Intervention

Politicians, economists, and businesspeople have been arguing for centuries over government policy toward international trade. Two principal issues have shaped the debate on appropriate trade policies:

1 Whether a national government should intervene to protect the country's domestic firms by taxing foreign goods entering the domestic market or constructing other barriers against imports

2 Whether a national government should directly help the country's domestic firms increase their foreign sales through export subsidies, government-to-government negotiations, and guaranteed loan programs

These two issues are the subject of this chapter.

In the United States, the trade policy debate has recently focused on the issue of whether the government should promote "free" trade or "fair" trade. **Free trade** implies that the national government exerts minimal influence on the exporting and importing decisions of private firms and individuals. **Fair trade**, sometimes called **managed trade**, suggests that the national government should actively intervene to ensure that exports of domestic firms receive an equitable share of foreign markets and that imports are controlled to minimize losses of domestic jobs and market share in specific industries. Some participants in this debate argue that the government should ensure a "level playing field" on which foreign and domestic firms can compete on equal terms. While sounding reasonable, the "level playing field" argument is often used to justify policies that restrict foreign competition.

The outcome of this debate is critical to firms. The policies individual countries adopt affect the size and profitability of foreign markets and investments, as well as the degree to which firms are threatened by foreign imports in their domestic markets. Governments worldwide are continually pressured by successful and efficient firms that produce goods for export, as well as by their labor forces and the communities in which their factories are located, to adopt policies supporting freer trade. Companies such as Sony (consumer electronics), Daimler-Benz (automobiles), and Caterpillar (earth-moving equipment) gain increased sales and investment opportunities in foreign markets when international trade barriers are lowered. At the same time governments are petitioned by firms beleaguered by foreign competitors, as well as by their labor forces and the communities in which their factories are located, to raise barriers to imported goods by adopting fair-trade policies. Companies such as Desmarais and French automakers Renault and Peugeot gain increased sales opportunities in their domestic markets when international trade barriers exist. The outcome of this debate also affects consumers in every country, influencing the prices they pay for automobiles, clothing, televisions, and thousands of other goods. Barriers erected by the U.S. government against free trade in textiles and sugar, for example, raise the prices that parents must pay to clothe and feed their children.

Industry-Level Arguments

The argument for free trade follows Adam Smith's analysis outlined in Chapter 3: voluntary exchange makes both parties to the transaction better off and allocates goods to their highest valued use. In Smith's view, the welfare of a country and its citizens is best promoted by allowing self-interested individuals, regardless of where they reside, to exchange goods, services, and assets as they see fit. However, many businesspeople, politicians, and policy makers believe that, under certain circumstances, deviations from free trade are appropriate. In this section we review the primary arguments against free trade and for government intervention and we discuss trade policies that focus on the needs of individual industries. In the next section we explore broader, national-level policies aimed at meeting the needs of the economy and society as a whole.

The National Defense Argument. National defense has often been used as a reason to support governmental protection of specific industries. Since world events can suddenly turn hostile to a country's interests, the **national defense argument** holds that a country must be self-sufficient in critical raw materials, machinery, and technology or else be vulnerable to foreign threats. For example, the vulnerability of Japan's supply lines was demonstrated by the extensive damage done to its merchant marine fleet by Allied submarines in World War II. After the war Japan banned the importation of rice as a means of promoting domestic self-sufficiency in its dietary staple. Similarly, the United States, to retain shipbuilding skills and expertise within the country in case of war, has developed numerous programs to support its domestic shipbuilding industry. For example, all U.S. naval vessels must be built in U.S. shipyards, and ocean transportation between U.S. ports must be conducted by U.S.-built ships. Many of the 120,000 jobs in the U.S. shipbuilding industry would be lost without these federal protections, for U.S. shipyards are not competitive with those of Japan, Korea, Norway, Denmark, or Germany. One federal study found that the average bid by U.S. shipyards on commercial contracts was 97 percent higher than the lowest foreign bid.[2]

The national defense argument appeals to the general public, which is concerned that its country will be pushed around by other countries that control critical resources. Many special-interest groups have used this politically appealing argument to protect their industries from foreign competition. For example, the U.S. mohair industry produces wool that was once used in military uniforms. It benefited from federal subsidies after the passage of the 1954 National Wool Act, which protected the industry purportedly in the country's strategic interest. Even though the military has long since replaced mohair garments with synthetic ones, the subsidy remained in effect until 1995. Other U.S. industries receiving favorable treatment for national defense reasons include steel, electronics, machine tools, and the merchant marine.[3]

The Infant Industry Argument. Alexander Hamilton, the first U.S. Secretary of the Treasury, articulated the **infant industry argument** in 1791. He believed that the newly independent country's infant manufacturing sector possessed a comparative advantage that would ultimately allow it to thrive in international markets. However, he feared that the young nation's manufacturers would not survive their infancy and adolescence because of fierce competition from more mature European firms. Hamilton thus fought for the imposition of tariffs on numerous imported manufactured goods to give U.S. firms temporary protection from foreign competition until they could fully establish themselves. His philosophy has since been adopted by countries worldwide. Japan, for example, has been particularly effective in nurturing its domestic industries. Despite its lack of significant natural resources, Japan has developed since the end of World War II thriving metal fabrication industries (iron and steel, aluminum, copper, and zinc) by eliminating tariffs on imports of raw ores and ore concentrates while imposing high tariffs on processed and fabricated metals. For example, in 1970 no tariff was imposed on copper ore imported in Japan, but fabricated copper products bore tariffs as high as 22 percent. As its metal fabrication industry matured, Japan reduced the level of import protection. Today its tariffs on copper products are negligible.[4]

Governmental nurturing of domestic industries that will ultimately have a comparative advantage can be a powerful economic development strategy, as Japan's postwar economic success indicates. However, determining which industries deserve infant industry protection is often done on a political, rather than an economic, basis. Firms, workers, and shareholders are not shy about using the infant industry argument to bolster support for import protection or export subsidies for their industries. Moreover, once an industry is granted protection, it may be reluctant to give it up. Many infant industries end up being protected well into their old age.

Maintenance of Existing Jobs. Well-established firms and their workers, particularly in high-wage countries, are often threatened by imports from low-wage countries, as shown in the case of Desmarais. To maintain existing employment levels, firms and workers often petition their governments for relief from foreign competition. Government officials, eager to avoid the human and economic misery inflicted on workers and communities when factories are shut down, tend to lend a sympathetic ear to such pleas. Assistance may come in the form of tariffs, quotas, or other barriers that we discuss in more detail in the next section. The assistance may be temporary in nature, as was the case when Harley-Davidson received tariff protection from Japanese imports for five years in the mid-1980s to allow the firm to revamp its operations and restore its image in the marketplace. Or it may be long-lived, as in the case of governmental protection of the U.S. commercial shipbuilding industry, which has extended that industry's life by over thirty years.

Strategic Trade Theory. When firms and labor union officials plead for government intervention to help them compete internationally, their efforts are usually criticized by economists, who claim that such intervention ultimately harms the economy. The economists base that claim on the theoretical predictions of the classical trade theories—absolute advantage and comparative advantage—discussed in Chapter 3. But these trade theories assume that firms operate in perfectly competitive markets of the sort that exist only in economics textbooks. They also assume that each country's consumers are able to buy goods and services at the lowest possible prices from the world's most efficient producers. According to the classical theories, any governmental intervention that denies consumers these buying opportunities will make the country as a whole worse off, although it could make certain groups within the society better off.

In the early 1980s, however, new models of international trade—known collectively as **strategic trade theory**—were developed. These models provide a new theoretical justification for government trade intervention, thereby supporting firms' requests for protection. Strategic trade theory makes very different assumptions about the industry environment in which firms operate than do the

FIGURE 6.1

**Payoff Matrix:
Profits from
Developing a
Nuclear Power
Plant Design (in bil-
lions of dollars)**

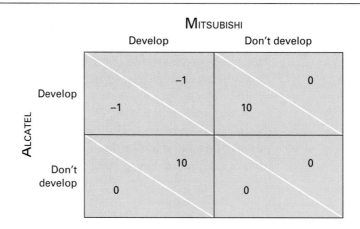

classical theories. Strategic trade theory considers those industries capable of supporting only a few firms worldwide, perhaps because of high product development costs or strong experience curve effects. A firm can earn monopoly profits if it can succeed in becoming one of the few firms in such a highly concentrated industry. Strategic trade theory suggests that a national government can make its country better off if it adopts trade policies that improve the competitiveness of its domestic firms in such oligopolistic industries.[5]

For example, consider the potential market for a new nuclear power plant design, one that could safely and cheaply supply electrical energy. Assume that because of economies of scale, the market will be extremely profitable if one—and only one—firm decides to enter it. Further assume that only two firms, France's Alcatel Alsthom and Japan's Mitsubishi, have the engineering talent and financial resources to develop the new plant design and both are equally capable of successfully completing the project. Figure 6.1 shows the payoff matrix for the two firms. If Mitsubishi decides to develop the plant design and Alcatel decides not to (see the lower left-hand corner), Mitsubishi profits by $10 billion, while Alcatel makes nothing. If Alcatel decides to develop the plant design and Mitsubishi doesn't, Alcatel profits by $10 billion, while Mitsubishi makes nothing (see the upper right-hand corner). If neither firm chooses to develop the design, they both make nothing (see the lower right-hand corner). If both decide to develop the design, both will lose $1 billion, for the market is too small to be profitable for both of them. Neither firm has a strategy that it should follow regardless of what its rival does.

Now suppose the French government learns of the large profits that one of its country's firms could earn if that firm were the sole developer of the new plant design. If France were to offer Alcatel a subsidy of $2 billion to develop the new nuclear technology, the payoff matrix would change to that shown in Fig. 6.2. Because of the subsidy, Alcatel's payoff is increased by $2 billion if and *only* if it develops the technology (see the first row). With the subsidy, Alcatel will develop the technology regardless of what Mitsubishi does, because it makes more money by developing than by not developing. If Mitsubishi chooses to develop, Alcatel makes nothing if it doesn't develop and $1 billion if it does develop. If Mitsubishi doesn't develop, Alcatel makes nothing if it doesn't develop and $12 billion if it does develop. Thus Alcatel will always choose to develop. But if Mitsubishi knows Alcatel will always choose to develop, then the best strategy for Mitsubishi is not to develop.

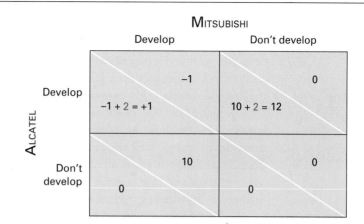

FIGURE 6.2

Payoff Matrix: Profits Resulting from a $2 Billion Subsidy to Alcatel (in billions of dollars)

What has the French government accomplished with its $2 billion subsidy?

1 It has induced Alcatel to develop the new nuclear power plant technology.

2 It has induced the Japanese firm to stay out of the market.

3 It has succeeded in allowing a French firm to make a $12 billion profit at a cost to French taxpayers of only $2 billion.

By adopting a strategic trade policy in a market where monopoly profits are available, the French government has made French residents as a group better off by $10 billion ($12 billion in profits minus $2 billion in subsidies).

However, strategic trade theory applies only to markets that are incapable of supporting more than a handful of firms on a worldwide basis. Most global industries are more competitive than this. A country's wholesale adoption of strategic trade policies to cover a broad group of industries may actually reduce the country's overall international competitiveness, since favoring certain industries inevitably hurts others. For example, if the French government chooses to subsidize the nuclear power industry, the demand for and salaries paid to the mechanical engineers, computer programmers, and systems analysts needed by the nuclear power industry will rise, thereby reducing the international competitiveness of other French industries requiring such skilled personnel. Further, the benefit of the subsidy could be neutralized if another country adopts a similar strategy. If Japan responded to France's $2 billion subsidy by giving a $3 billion subsidy to Mitsubishi, the payoff matrix would change: Mitsubishi would be encouraged to develop the power plant as well. Any anticipated monopoly profits might be dissipated if the two countries engaged in an all-out subsidy war.[6]

National Trade Policies

The policies just discussed address the needs of individual industries. A national government also may develop trade policies that begin by taking a broader perspective on the needs of the economy and society as a whole. After assessing these needs, the government then adopts industry-by-industry policies to promote the country's overall economic agenda.

Economic Development Programs. An important policy goal of many governments, particularly those of developing countries, is economic development. International commerce can play a major role in economic development programs. Countries dependent on a single export often choose to diversify their economies in order to reduce the impact of, say, a bad harvest or falling prices for the dominant export. For example, the West African country of Ghana, which once depended heavily on cocoa, began an industrialization program to protect itself from fluctuations in cocoa prices. Also, Kuwait chose to diversify from its heavy dependency on oil sales, electing to do so through investment rather than trade. It used cash from its oil revenues to build up its investment portfolio, a strategy so successful that much of its resistance to the 1990 Iraqi invasion was financed by its overseas investments.

As discussed in Chapter 2, some countries, such as Japan, Korea, and Taiwan, based their post–World War II economic development on heavy reliance on exports. According to this **export-promotion strategy**, a country encourages firms to compete in foreign markets by harnessing some advantage the country possesses, such as low labor costs. Other countries, such as Australia, Argentina, India, and Brazil, adopted an **import-substitution strategy** after World War II; such a strategy encourages the growth of domestic manufacturing industries by erecting high barriers to imported goods. Many MNCs responded by locating production facilities within these countries in order to avoid the costs resulting from the high barriers. In general, the export-promotion strategy has been more successful than the import-substitution strategy, as Chapter 2 indicated.

Industrial Policy. In many countries, the government plays an active role in managing the national economy. Often an important element of this task is determining which industries should receive favorable governmental treatment. Bureaucrats within Japan's Ministry of International Trade and Industry (MITI), for example, identify emerging technologies and products and, through subsidies, public statements, and behind-the-scenes maneuvering, encourage Japanese firms to enter those markets. During the 1950s and 1960s, MITI actively diverted scarce credit and foreign exchange from low-value-added, labor-intensive industries such as textiles into high-value-added, capital-intensive heavy industries such as steel and automobiles. In the 1970s and 1980s, MITI targeted industries with high growth potential, such as semiconductors, aerospace, biotechnology, and ceramics. The Taiwanese and Korean governments patterned their economic development strategies after the successful Japanese model.

Because of the postwar economic successes of these Asian countries, the governments of most other Quad countries face the major issue of whether to adopt **industrial policy**, by which the national government identifies key domestic industries critical to the country's future economic growth and then formulates programs that promote their competitiveness. Ideally, industrial policy assists a country's firms in capturing large shares of important, growing global markets, as MITI has done for Japanese MNCs.

Many experts, however, do not view industrial policy as a panacea for improving the global competitiveness of a country's firms. They argue that government bureaucrats cannot perfectly identify the right industries to favor under such policy. As an example, they cite France, where industrial policies targeting automobiles, computers, military and commercial aircraft, and telecommunications have created some spectacularly unprofitable enterprises that require large government subsidies. These industries became a drag on the French economy rather than a generator of new wealth. Even Japan has not been infallible. In the early 1980s, MITI bureaucrats encouraged domestic consumer electronics firms to develop high-definition television (HDTV) that relied on Japan's lead in analog-based TV technology. Although HDTV is viewed as the wave of the future for television, the technical transmission standards for HDTV products adopted by U.S. and European regulators rely on more sophisticated digital technology being developed by Western firms rather than the dated analog technology imposed on Japanese firms by MITI. Consequently, the multibillion-dollar investment of the leading Japanese consumer electronics firms in analog-based HDTV turned out to be a total loss.

Opponents of industrial policy also fear that the determination of which industries will receive governmental largesse will depend on the domestic political clout of those industries rather than on their potential international competitiveness. Instead of future winners in the international marketplace being selected, opponents say, industrial policy will become a more sophisticated-sounding version of pork-barrel politics.

At the heart of the industrial policy debate is the question of what is the proper role of government in a market economy. The Reagan and Bush administrations chose not to adopt formally a strategy of industrial policy on the grounds that the government should limit its role in the economy.[7] Yet others disagree, including key players in the Clinton administration such as former Labor Secretary Robert Reich. These advocates argue that improving the global competitiveness of the country's firms is too important to be left to the private sector. In furtherance of this belief, the Clinton administration announced in April 1994 five emerging technologies for which it would increase federal R&D support: genetics, health care information systems, electronics, automobiles and highway systems, and computer software.[8]

Public Choice Analysis. While many arguments favoring governmental trade intervention are couched in terms of national interest, such intervention typically helps some special-interest groups but invariably hurts other domestic interests and the general public. For example, the CIT's decision to impose antidumping duties helped Desmarais and its Quebec workforce. However, it reduced the work available to dockworkers who unload foreign cargos in British Columbia's Port of Vancouver and raised the prices that Canadian consumers had to pay for photo albums.

Why do national governments adopt public policies that hinder international business and hurt their own citizenry overall, even though the policies may benefit small groups within their societies? According to **public choice analysis**, a branch of economics that analyzes public decision making, the special interest will often dominate the general interest on any given issue because special-interest groups are willing to work harder for the passage of laws favorable to their interests than the general public is willing to work for the defeat of laws unfavorable to its interest. For example, under the 1920 Jones Act the United States restricts foreign ships from providing transportation services between U.S. ports. This restriction is supported by owners of U.S. ocean-going vessels, who gain increased

MAP 6.1

An Effect of the Jones Act

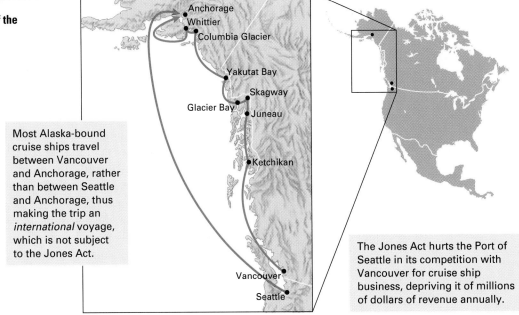

Most Alaska-bound cruise ships travel between Vancouver and Anchorage, rather than between Seattle and Anchorage, thus making the trip an *international* voyage, which is not subject to the Jones Act.

The Jones Act hurts the Port of Seattle in its competition with Vancouver for cruise ship business, depriving it of millions of dollars of revenue annually.

profits estimated at $630 million per year. But the Jones Act is also estimated to increase the transportation costs consumers pay by $10.5 billion annually, or $40 per person. Further, like other restrictions on free trade, the Jones Act has had unintended consequences, as Map 6.1 suggests.

Public choice analysis suggests few consumers will be motivated either to learn about the impact of the Jones Act on them or to write or call their elected officials to save a trivial sum like $40. The special interests, such as shipowners and members of U.S. maritime unions, however, are motivated to know all the ins and outs of the Jones Act and to protect it from repeal, because the gains to them make it worth their while to do so. As a result, members of Congress constantly hear from special-interest groups about the importance of preserving the Jones Act, while the average consumer is silent on the issue.[9] Knowing that they will be harmed by the special-interest groups and will not be rewarded by the general public if they repeal the Jones Act, members of Congress will rationally vote with the special interests on this issue.

According to public choice analysis, domestic trade policies that affect international business do not stem from some grandiose vision of a country's international responsibilities but rather from the mundane interaction of politicians trying to get elected. And who elects the politicians? The people in their legislative districts. Hence former Speaker of the House of Representatives Tip O'Neill's brilliant insight: "All politics is local." For example, Japan's unwillingness to open its markets to imported rice stems from the need of Japan's ruling party in parliament to retain the votes of local farmers. Similarly, French politicians restrict the importation of Japanese automobiles in order to win the votes of workers at Renault and Peugeot factories. The impact of these policies on Texas rice farmers, Yokohama autoworkers, or the world economy is of little concern to the domestic politicians.

Smart international businesspeople recognize these political realities. Often a foreign firm needs to find domestic political allies to run interference for it. For

example, Nissan and Toyota received much criticism for the size of their exports to the U.S. market, so in the 1980s they began building new factories in the United States. The congressional delegations of Indiana, West Virginia, Tennessee, and Kentucky, where these factories are located, can now be expected to support the firms legislatively in order to protect the jobs of constituents working for the Japanese firms. The not-so-subtle political message of the advertisement depicted in Fig. 6.3 is that if you mess with Toyota, you mess with the jobs, lives, and votes of thousands of U.S. workers. Clearly, Toyota understands that "all politics is local."

Barriers to International Trade

As the previous section indicated, domestic politics often causes countries to try to protect their domestic firms from foreign competitors by erecting barriers to trade. Such forms of government intervention can be divided into two categories: tariffs and nontariff barriers. Countries have been erecting trade barriers since the creation of the modern nation-state in the sixteenth century in hopes of increasing national income, promoting economic growth, and/or raising their citizens' standards of living. Sometimes, as you just saw, national trade policies that benefit special-interest groups are adopted at the expense of the general public or society at large.

Tariffs

A **tariff** is a tax placed on a good involved in international trade. Some tariffs are levied on goods either as they leave the country (an **export tariff**) or as they pass through one country bound for another (a **transit tariff**). Most, however, are collected on imported goods (an **import tariff**). Three forms of import tariffs exist:

I An **ad valorem tariff** is assessed as a percentage of the market value of the imported good. For example, in Table 6.1 (which is drawn from the existing U.S. tariff code) a 2.8 percent ad valorem tariff is levied against imported pineapples preserved by sugar.

TABLE 6.1

A Section of the Harmonized Tariff Schedule of the United States

HEADING/ SUBHEADING	STAT. SUFFIX	ARTICLE DESCRIPTION	UNITS OF QUANTITY	RATES OF DUTY
2006.00		Fruit, nuts, fruit-peel and other parts of plants, preserved by sugar (drained, glacé or crystallized):		
2006.00.20	00	Cherries	kg	12.7¢/kg + 8.2%
2006.00.30	00	Ginger root	kg	3.9%
2006.00.40	00	Pineapples	kg	2.8%
		Other, including mixtures:		
2006.00.50	00	Mixtures	kg	18%
2006.00.60	00	Citrus fruit; peel of citrus or other fruit	kg	6.8¢/kg
2006.00.70	00	Other fruit and nuts	kg	9%
2006.00.90	00	Other	kg	18%

Source: U.S. International Trade Commission, *Harmonized Tariff Schedule of the United States* (Washington, D.C.: ITC Trade Data Base as of October 29, 1997).

2 A **specific tariff** is assessed as a specific dollar amount per unit of weight or other standard measure. As Table 6.1 shows, imported citrus fruit preserved by sugar bears a specific tariff of 6.8¢ per kilogram.

3 A **compound tariff** has both an ad valorem component and a specific component. Imported cherries preserved in sugar are levied an 8.2 percent ad valorem tariff and a 12.7¢ per kilogram specific tariff.

In practice, most tariffs imposed by developed countries are ad valorem in nature. The tariff applies to the product's value, which is typically the sales price at which it enters the country. For example, suppose Kmart buys a large shipment of canned pineapples preserved by sugar from a Filipino food processor at $400 a ton. When the pineapples are delivered to the Port of Los Angeles, Kmart will have to pay the U.S. Customs Service a duty of 2.8 percent of $400, or $11.20, for each ton it imports, a cost Kmart will pass on to its customers.

Most countries have adopted a detailed classification scheme for imported goods called the **harmonized tariff schedule (HTS)**. Because of its complexity, the HTS can sometimes be difficult to use. The first problem facing an importer is anticipating what customs officials will decide is the appropriate tariff classification for an imported good. For example, leather ski gloves imported into the United States are assessed a 5.5 percent ad valorem tariff. But if the leather ski gloves are specifically designed for cross-country skiing, then the ad valorem tariff is only 3.5 percent. Porcelain figurines imported into the United States generally bear no tax. But if they are valued at over $2.50 and are produced by professional sculptors, they fall into a separate tariff classification and carry a 1.3 percent ad valorem tariff.

An importer's expected profit margin on a transaction can shrink or disappear if a customs official subjects the imported good to a higher tariff rate than the importer expected. To reduce this risk, U.S. importers can request an advance tariff classification on prospective importations by writing the U.S. Customs Service. Figure 6.4 reproduces parts of a letter from the Customs Service in response to such a request from a small importer, Dan Dee, as to the tariff to be paid on the "Reindeer Caps" that it wants to import from China. These caps come with a full set of fabric antlers; when the proper button is pushed, lights sewn into the antlers flash, Christmas music is played, and a voice shouts "Merry Christmas." Dan Dee wanted to know whether this item would be classified as a toy, a hat, or a festive article. After pondering the question for four months, customs officials determined that the item was indeed a hat for reasons

Like tariffs, questions of what products fall under specific quotas cause difficulties for international businesses. The EU imposed a quota on imports of nonhuman dolls from China but allowed unlimited human dolls to be imported. Soon the best legal minds in Europe had to wrestle with the question of whether Mr. Spock was human or nonhuman. As any Trekkie knows, while Spock claims Vulcan origins, his mother, Amanda, was in fact an earthling. However, trade bureaucrats ruled that Spock dolls fell under the nonhuman quota, noting that "You don't find a human with ears that size." While others may find it humorous, such decisions by customs officials can cause havoc for international businesses, disrupting supplier relationships and raising the costs of doing business. (See page 218 for a further discussion of quotas.)

December 19, 1995

Michele R. Markowitz, Esquire
Sharretts, Paley, Carter & Blauvelt, P.C.
67 Broad Street
New York, New York 10004

Dear Ms. Markowitz:

This letter is in response to your request of July 25, 1995, on behalf of your client, Dan Dee, concerning the classification of items identified as "Reindeer Caps" imported from China. Two sample caps were submitted with your request. . . .

FACTS: The sample articles identified by item nos. X53081 and X53082 are hats/caps composed of plush, knit, man-made fibers. Extending from the top of each cap is a pair of antlers, within which are contained electrical wires and light emitting diodes (LEDs). A textile patch on the front of each cap displays the words "PRESS HERE." When pressed, a switch activates a battery powered module sewn into the interior top of each cap. The device causes the LEDs to flash and produces the sounds of Christmas carols and the words "Merry Christmas" or "Happy New Year." . . . The items are said to be designed, bought, sold, advertised, marketed, and primarily used as festive articles.

ISSUE: Whether the items are classified in heading 9505, HTSUS, as festive articles; in heading 9503, HTSUS, as other toys; or in heading 6505, HTSUS, as hats and other headgear.

LAW AND ANALYSIS:
* * *
In general, merchandise is classifiable in heading 9505, HTSUS, as a festive article when the article, as a whole: 1. Is of non-durable material or, generally, is not purchased because of its extreme worth, or intrinsic value; 2. Functions primarily as a decoration (e.g., its primary function is not utilitarian); and 3. Is traditionally associated or used with a particular festival (e.g., stockings and tree ornaments for Christmas, decorative eggs for Easter).

Although we find the reindeer hats to be made of durable material, they are not likely to be purchased for their extreme worth or value. As is the case with hats in general, these items are both decorative and utilitarian and neither function clearly predominates. In addition to decorating the head in a humorous fashion, the hats are sturdy and warm. . . . Since the hats do not function primarily as decorations, they do not satisfy the second criterion.

Upon examination of the third criterion, we do not find reindeer or reindeer hats to be traditionally associated or used with a particular festival. . . . Reindeer are associated with cold climates and snow-filled regions of the world where they are often domesticated, trained to pull sleds, raced, hunted, eaten, etc. North American reindeer (caribou) are occasionally associated with controversy due to the effects of wolf populations on their numbers. We do not find that the reindeer hats would only be worn during the Christmas/New Year holidays. It is not uncommon to see hats of a similar nature being worn to keep the head warm, get attention, and provoke responses throughout the colder months at ski slopes, skating rinks, sports events, etc.
* * *
We next consider your alternative assertion that the hats are toys. . . . Customs will classify [an item as] a stuffed toy representing an animal or non-human creature . . . if the toy is a reasonably full-figured depiction of the animal's or creature's anatomy that the toy seeks to represent. The representation must be constructed in a sculpted, three dimensional form. Since the reindeer hats represent only the head or part of the head of a reindeer, they are not classifiable as stuffed toy animals.

The American College Dictionary (1970) defines "hat" in pertinent part as "1. a shaped covering for the head, usually with a crown and a brim, worn outdoors." Although this definition comfortably fits the reindeer hats, it does little to indicate whether or not the goods are classifiable as toy hats. . . . As previously noted, the reindeer hats are not only amusing but are also fully functional. Not all merchandise that amuses is properly classified in a toy provision and we find that the play value of the reindeer hats is secondary to their utilitarian purpose. . . .

HOLDING: The "Reindeer Caps," identified by item nos. X53081 and X53082, are properly classified in subheading 6505.90.6090, HTSUSA, textile category 659, the provision for "hats and other headgear, knitted or crocheted, or made up from lace, felt or other textile fabric . . ." The applicable duty rate is 37.7 cents per kilogram plus 13.4 percent ad valorem.

Sincerely,

John Durant
Director, Tariff Appeals Division

FIGURE 6.4 **U.S. Customs Service Letter to Dan Dee, Inc.**

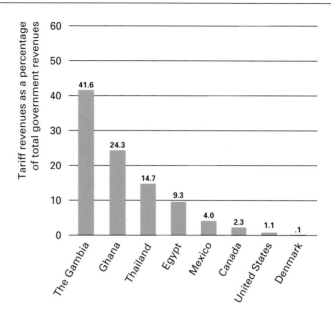

FIGURE 6.5

Tariff Revenues as a Percentage of Total Government Revenues for Selected Countries, 1995

stated in the letter. Discreet as good civil servants should be, they made no comment about the good taste or sobriety of potential purchasers and wearers of these caps. Based on this written decision of the Customs Service, Dan Dee can import its goods with full knowledge of their landed cost.

Tariffs historically have been imposed for two reasons:

I Tariffs raise revenue for the national government. As Fig. 6.5 shows, tariff revenues account for a significant portion of government revenues of developing countries such as The Gambia and Ghana. Such countries depend heavily on subsistence agriculture and so find it difficult to collect significant tax revenues from domestic sources. Customs duties, however, are reasonably easy to collect. Further, imported goods tend to be purchased by the wealthier members of society, so heavy reliance on import tariffs adds progressivity to the domestic tax system. Conversely, taxes on international trade form a relatively small percentage of government revenues in more developed economies that have broader tax bases such as Thailand, Egypt, and Mexico. Of course, like most taxes, people try to avoid paying tariffs when they can, as "Going Global" indicates.

2 A tariff acts as a trade barrier. Because tariffs raise the prices paid by domestic consumers for foreign goods, they increase the demand for domestically produced substitute goods.

Tariffs affect both domestic and foreign special-interest groups. For example, suppose the U.S. government imposes a $2000 specific tariff on imported minivans. Foreign producers of minivans will be forced to raise their U.S. prices, thereby reducing their U.S. sales. But foreign-made minivans and U.S.-made minivans are substitute goods. Thus the higher prices of foreign minivans will increase the demand for U.S.-made minivans, as is shown in Fig. 6.6 by the shift in the demand

FIGURE 6.6

Impact of an Import Tariff on Demand for U.S.-made Minivans

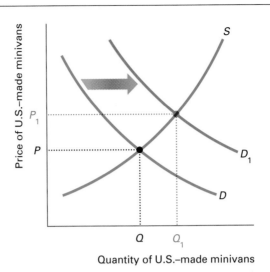

for U.S.-made minivans from D to D_1, resulting in more domestic vehicles being sold at higher prices. The $2000 specific tariff creates both gainers and losers. Gainers include GM, Ford, and Chrysler automobile dealerships selling domestic minivans; suppliers to domestic producers; workers at domestic GM, Ford, and Chrysler minivan assembly plants; and the communities in which domestic minivan factories are located. Domestic consumers are losers because they pay higher prices for both domestic and foreign minivans. Foreign producers also lose, as well as people and firms that depend on them including Toyota and Mazda automobile dealerships in the United States, workers and suppliers in Japan, and communities in Japan in which the minivans are manufactured.

Nontariff Barriers

Nontariff barriers are the second category of governmental controls on international trade. Any government regulation, policy, or procedure other than a tariff that has the effect of impeding international trade may be labeled a **nontariff barrier (NTB)**. In this section we discuss three kinds of NTBs: quotas, numerical export controls, and other nontariff barriers.

Quotas. Countries may restrain international trade by imposing quotas. A **quota** is a numerical limit on the quantity of a good that may be imported into a country during some time period, such as a year. Quotas have traditionally been used to protect politically powerful industries, such as agriculture, automobiles, and textiles, from the threat of competition, as in the case of Japan's and the Philippines' use of quotas to limit imports of rice. However, as a result of trade agreements such as the Uruguay Round (see Chapter 7), many countries have replaced quotas with tariff-rate quotas (TRQs). A **tariff-rate quota** imposes a low tariff rate on a limited amount of imports of a specific good into the country, but then subjects all imports of the good above that threshold to a prohibitively high tariff. Canada, for example, has substituted a tariff-rate quota for its previous quotas on imports of eggs, dairy products, and poultry. Imports of these goods above the threshold may pay tariffs of as much

GOING GLOBAL

A Loophole Big Enough To Drive Through

Few people like to pay taxes, and Poles are no exception. Polish tariffs on imported automobiles are sky-high: the duty is $1900 or 33 percent of the vehicle's value—whichever is higher. In addition, Poland levies a 22 percent value-added tax on the vehicles. However, the tariffs on automobile parts are much lower. So a common sight at border crossings between Germany and Poland are late model cars, minus their engines, tires, and other easily removable parts, being towed on open trailers. Ten or fifteen places back in the customs queue is the vehicle's engine, being transported by a friend of the owner of the chassis up ahead. The remaining parts will be found even further back in the line in a third vehicle. German officials don't care, as long as the vehicles aren't stolen. Polish customs officials understand what's going on, but are powerless to do anything about it as long as the vehicles are for personal use. Complains one government official, "Sometimes a Pole would tell me he just picked up a body of a new car, as if it fell out of the sky. Can I believe that?" The Polish customs service can still levy taxes on the automobile parts, but these run about half of the tariffs paid for a fully-assembled vehicle. For many Poles, this is a sufficient savings to go through the hassle of disassembling their newly-purchased vehicles on the German side of the border and reassembling them on the Polish side.

Source: "Car importers take apart customs regulations," *Financial Times*, June 29/30, 1996, p. 2.

as 350 percent. In the short run, such high tariffs have the same effect as a quota: they normally limit imports of a good to the threshold level. However, at least in concept exporters are allowed to increase their sales to the country as long as they are willing to pay the high tariff. And because tariffs are more visible than quotas, most experts believe that converting quotas to tariff-rate quotas makes it easier to eliminate this type of trade barrier over time through diplomatic negotiations.

A quota or tariff-rate quota helps domestic producers of the good in question but invariably hurts domestic consumers. Consider, for example, the impact of the sugar tariff-rate quota on the U.S. market. The U.S. government effectively restricts the amount of foreign sugar that can be imported to about 2 million tons annually by slapping a 17-cent specific tariff on each pound of sugar imported into the United States above that amount. (Domestic producers normally produce about 8 million tons per year.) The price of sugar in the United States is higher than that elsewhere in the world because the tariff-rate quota prevents more imports from flowing into the U.S. market to equalize the prices. In March 1998, for example, the U.S. price for sugar was 21.6¢ per pound, while the average world price was only 10.2¢ per pound.

Who gains from the tariff-rate quota? Domestic sugar producers, such as sugar cane growers in Louisiana and sugar beet growers in North Dakota, benefit because domestic production is increased and the price that domestic suppliers receive rises. Producers of sugar substitutes, such as Archer Daniels Midland, the largest domestic producer of corn-based fructose sweeteners, and corn-belt farmers who supply the corn for the fructose sweeteners also gain as manufacturers of sweetened products substitute lower-cost fructose sweeteners for sugar. Losers from the policy include domestic candy manufacturers and soft-drink makers, which must pay higher prices for sugar, as well as U.S. consumers, who pay a higher price—an estimated $1.4 billion a year—for all goods containing sugar. U.S. firms such as San Francisco's Ghiardelli Chocolate Company (premium chocolates) or Corsicana, Texas's Collin Street Bakery (fruitcakes) that export goods with high sugar content become less competitive in world markets because the sugar quota increases the cost of their ingredients.

The Collin Street Bakery attracts over 250,000 visitors a year to the small Texas town of Corsicana. International sales are an important component of the Bakery's success. Twenty-five percent of the 1.5 million fruitcakes it makes each year are sold overseas, many to repeat customers. But U.S. quotas on sugar and tariffs on imported inputs raise the Bakery's costs, making it more difficult for it to compete in international markets.

Anyone with the right to import sugar into the United States within the 2 million ton threshold also gains, since the holder of such rights can buy sugar at the lower world price and resell it in the United States at the higher U.S. price. For this reason, the U.S. government uses these rights as an instrument of foreign policy and foreign aid. Countries that are politically sympathetic to the United States or that the United States is trying to woo often receive generous rights, while countries hostile to the United States find their rights reduced or eliminated.

Numerical Export Controls. A country also may impose quantitative barriers to trade in the form of numerical limits on the amount of a good it will export. A **voluntary export restraint (VER)** is a promise by a country to limit its exports of a good to another country to a prespecified amount or percentage of the affected market. Often this is done to resolve or avoid trade conflicts with an otherwise friendly trade partner. For example, the United States and Canada have been squabbling since 1982 over whether the latter has been subsidizing its lumber industry by charging low stumpage fees (rights to harvest timber) in government-owned forests. To end the conflict, Canada agreed in 1996 to adopt a VER, limiting its annual exports to the United States of softwood lumber from Alberta, British Columbia, Ontario, and Quebec to 14.7 billion board feet. Canada also pledged to levy a substantial tax on any exports above that level bound for the United States. In return, the United States agreed it would not initiate any investigations of Canadian softwood lumber exports for five years.

Export controls may also be adopted to punish the country's political enemies. An **embargo**—an absolute ban on the exporting (and/or importing) of goods to a particular destination—is adopted by a country or international governmental authority to discipline another country. For example, after Iraq invaded Kuwait in 1990, the United Nations imposed an embargo on trade with Iraq.

Other Nontariff Barriers. Countries also use various other NTBs to protect themselves from foreign competition. Some NTBs are adopted for legitimate domestic public policy reasons but have the effect of restricting trade. Most NTBs, however, are blatantly protectionist in nature. As we discuss in Chapter 7, international negotiations in the post–World War II era have reduced the use of tariffs and quotas. For this reason, nonquantitative NTBs have now become major impediments to the growth of international trade. These NTBs are more difficult to eliminate than tariffs and quotas because they often are embedded in bureaucratic procedures and are not quickly changeable. Among the most common forms of nonquantitative NTBs are the following:

- Product and testing standards
- Restricted access to distribution networks
- Public-sector procurement policies
- Local-purchase requirements
- Regulatory controls
- Currency controls
- Investment controls

We discuss these in the following subsections.

Product and Testing Standards. A common form of NTB is a requirement that foreign goods meet a country's domestic product standards or testing standards before they can be offered for sale in that country. Foreign firms often claim these standards discriminate against their products. For example, under purity laws that date back to 1516, beer marketed in Germany could be made only with water, yeast, barley, and hops. As most other beers have additional ingredients, the effect was to restrict imports of foreign beer (this law was overturned by the EU in the 1980s).[10] While this purity law was not originally explicitly designed as an NTB, such is not the case for many other product-testing regulations. Taiwan, for example, uses more extensive and costly purity testing for imported fruit juices than for domestically produced juices. China requires foreign pesticide and agricultural chemical manufacturers to undergo elaborate testing procedures that may cost as much as $5 million per product, but imposes no such regulation on domestic manufacturers of these products. Manufacturers wishing to export pressure boilers to China must pay for Chinese inspectors to visit their factories and the factories of all their suppliers to ensure that the boilers meet Chinese safety standards, which are not well spelled out. Not only does the average cost of these inspections approach $100,000, but most of the inspectors are linked to research institutes tied to Chinese manufacturers of these goods.[11] Japan similarly requires that imported horticultural products be inspected at the production site in the exporting country by Japanese government inspectors prior to their shipment. U.S. exporters of goods like cherries, apples, and nectarines complain that inspectors are expensive and often not available when needed.[12]

Restricted Access to Distribution Networks. Restricting access of foreign goods to the normal channels of distribution may also act as an NTB. Indonesia, for example, for many years allowed retail distribution to be provided only by Indonesian companies or individuals. Indonesian factories owned by foreigners were eligible to provide their own wholesale distribution; the wholesale distribution of all other foreign goods was reserved for Indonesians. Taiwan allows only thirty-one prints of a given movie to be imported into the country and limits the number of theaters that can simultaneously show the same movie to eleven in the cities of Taipei and Kaoshiung and six in all other cities. This policy helps protect the local film industry.[13]

Japan has borne the brunt of world criticism over the issue of access to distribution networks. Foreigners' access to Japan's networks is often restricted because of the tight corporate and cultural ties among domestic manufacturers, wholesalers, and retailers. For example, Michigan-headquartered Guardian Industries, one of the world's largest producers of flat glass, has had trouble penetrating the Japanese market despite offering prices 25 percent less than those of its Japanese competitors. Guardian's problem has been finding Japanese intermediaries to handle its product line. Often, Japanese glass fabricators and wholesalers fear retribution from the three large Japanese flat glass producers, which dominate the domestic market, if they handle a competitor's products.[14] In several cases, Japan's keiretsu system has been explicitly blamed for restricting foreigners' access to the Japanese market. For example, AIG, a leading multinational insurance company, has been selling consumer-oriented insurance in the Japanese market since 1946 but still finds it difficult to sell industrial risk insurance because most major Japanese firms buy such insurance from an insurance company affiliated with their keiretsu. Of course, these close corporate ties, while acting as an NTB, may not be discriminatory, since they hurt both foreign and domestic newcomers in the Japanese market.

Public-Sector Procurement Policies. Public-sector procurement policies that give preferential treatment to domestic firms are another form of NTB. In the United States, "Buy American" restrictions are common at the federal, state, and local levels. The City of Los Angeles, for example, biased its procurement of mass transit equipment in favor of U.S. producers.[15] And the federal government generally requires that international air travel paid for by U.S. government funds occur on U.S. carriers.

Despite its own discriminatory policies, the U.S. government has loudly criticized similar policies in other countries. For example, the United States has fought a long battle with the Japanese government over the right of U.S. construction firms to bid on public construction projects in Japan. The U.S. claimed that the Japanese policy of excluding foreign firms from the bidding process unless they had previous construction experience in Japan created a burdensome chicken-or-egg dilemma for U.S. firms.[16] The United States has also complained about comparable policies in Taiwan, which requires government agencies to procure goods and services locally if such products are available. Firms bidding on major construction projects must demonstrate their competence by showing that they have similar experience in Taiwan; non-Taiwanese experience does not count.[17]

Public-sector procurement policies are particularly important in countries that have extensive state ownership of industry and in industries in which state ownership is common. If a national government adopts procurement policies that favor local firms, then foreigners are locked out of much of the market. The large size of the state-controlled sector in Brazil, for example, coupled with the country's "Buy Brazilian" policies, deters imports in such industries as computers, computer software, and telecommunications. Bidders for government contracts that meet the criteria for preferential treatment—either Brazilian-owned, using Brazilian technology or products, or meeting local content thresholds—are given bidding preferences of up to 12 percent. Belarus follows a similar procedure, giving its local companies a 20 percent bidding preference for government contracts.[18]

Local-Purchase Requirements.   Host governments may hinder foreign firms from exporting to or operating in their countries by requiring them to purchase goods or services from local suppliers. For example, the Italian government requires foreign air carriers to purchase ground-handling services from a subsidiary of Alitalia, the government-owned Italian airline. Foreign carriers, unhappy about having to buy these essential services from their main rival at Italian airports, complain bitterly that they are overcharged for the poor service they receive. The French government requires local TV services, such as privately owned TF1 or Canal Plus SA, a pay-TV channel, to show French-made films at least 40 percent of the time and European-made films at least 60 percent of the time, thus restricting the market available to non-European films.[19] Such quotas were extended to radio broadcasting in 1996. During prime time, at least 40 percent of the songs played on France's 1700 AM and FM stations must be written or sung by French or Francophone artists.[20] Similarly, the EU requires that the majority of programming broadcast by European television stations be of European origin. The U.S. government has strongly protested the French and EU requirements, arguing that they are designed to restrict competition from U.S. movie and television producers.[21] Local-purchase requirements also plague MNCs' attempts to develop global advertising campaigns using commercials that can be played in any market. For example, Australia limits imported TV ads to 20 percent of the total shown on television, thus forcing many firms to reshoot ads in Australia using local actors, directors, and film crews.[22]

Regulatory Controls.   Governments can create NTBs by adopting regulatory controls, such as conducting health and safety inspections, enforcing environmental regulations, requiring firms to obtain licenses before beginning operations or constructing new plants, and charging taxes and fees for public services that affect the ability of international businesses to compete in host markets. For example, Taiwan's Department of Health often refuses to grant import licenses for generic drugs that are also produced locally. In India, a Central Board of Film Certification controls the importation of foreign films, checking to make sure that their content is deemed appropriate for import. In Turkmenistan, all imports of consumer goods must be approved by the State Standards Committee. The slowness of this approval process discourages the import of perishable goods. And U.S. exporters believe that South Korea's food labeling laws, which are controlled by three separate agencies and often change arbitrarily without warning or notification to foreign food producers, are a deliberate attempt to discourage imports of foreign agricultural goods.[23]

Seemingly innocent laws may affect international trade. For example, in the early 1990s Ontario imposed a 10¢ per bottle fee on all beer sold in nonrefillable containers. Although this regulation might appear to be part of the pro-environment movement, Anheuser-Busch and the Miller Brewing Company believed it was designed to hurt the sales of imported U.S. beers, most of which are sold in recyclable aluminum cans, in favor of Canadian beers, most of which are bottled. Noting that the 10¢ tax did not apply to all beverages sold in aluminum cans (such as soft drinks), the United States retaliated by imposing a 50 percent duty on Canadian exports of beer to the United States, triggering a round of trade negotiations between the two countries.[24]

Currency Controls. Many countries, particularly developing countries and those with centrally planned economies, raise barriers to international trade through currency controls. Exporters of goods are allowed to exchange foreign currency at favorable rates, so as to make foreign markets attractive sales outlets for domestic producers. Importers are forced to purchase foreign exchange from the central bank at unfavorable exchange rates, thus raising the domestic prices of foreign goods. Tourists may be offered a separate exchange rate that is designed to extract as much foreign exchange as possible from free-spending foreigners.

Syria, for example, utilizes five official and two unofficial exchange rates. The most favorable rate is reserved for repayment of official government loans. Another favorable rate is used for public sector exports of petroleum and all imports by the government. Less favorable rates are used for Syrian students studying abroad, payment of fees to the government, tourists, capital inflows, and other international transactions. Other countries using dual or multiple exchange rate systems include Cambodia, Guinea-Bissau, Iran, Nigeria, and Zambia.[25]

Investment Controls. Controls on foreign investment and ownership are common, particularly in key industries like broadcasting, utilities, air transportation, defense contracting, and financial services. Such controls often make it difficult for foreign firms to develop an effective presence in such markets. Taiwan, for example, limits foreign ownership in such industries as freight forwarding (50 percent limit), mining (50 percent), cement (50 percent), trust companies (40 percent), and air transport (33.3 percent). The Philippines imposes barriers to foreign ownership in advertising (30 percent) and public utilities (40 percent). Indonesia requires foreign banks, securities firms, and insurance companies wishing to enter that country to form joint ventures with Indonesian partners. The United States similarly restricts foreign ownership of airlines and broadcast stations.

These NTBs are now more important impediments to international trade than tariffs are. And because they are sometimes imposed for sound domestic policy reasons but affect the competitiveness of foreign firms, NTBs can quickly cause intense international conflicts. International businesses whose operations are affected by NTBs often need the support of their home govern-

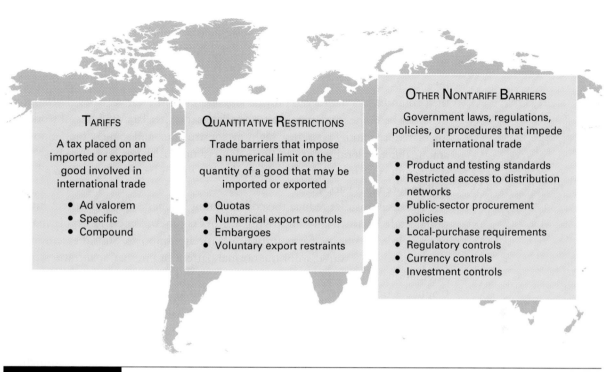

TARIFFS

A tax placed on an imported or exported good involved in international trade

- Ad valorem
- Specific
- Compound

QUANTITATIVE RESTRICTIONS

Trade barriers that impose a numerical limit on the quantity of a good that may be imported or exported

- Quotas
- Numerical export controls
- Embargoes
- Voluntary export restraints

OTHER NONTARIFF BARRIERS

Government laws, regulations, policies, or procedures that impede international trade

- Product and testing standards
- Restricted access to distribution networks
- Public-sector procurement policies
- Local-purchase requirements
- Regulatory controls
- Currency controls
- Investment controls

FIGURE 6.7

Types of Barriers to International Trade: A Summary

ments to help resolve these problems. "Building Global Skills" at the end of the chapter will acquaint you with some of the U.S. government agencies that can help such firms.

Figure 6.7 summarizes the various forms that trade barriers can take.

Promotion of International Trade

The previous section discussed techniques that governments use to restrict foreign business activity. In this section we discuss government policies to promote international business, including subsidies, establishment of foreign trade zones, and export financing programs. Typically, these programs are designed to create jobs in the export sector or to attract investment to economically depressed areas.

Subsidies

Countries often offer a variety of subsidies to firms operating within their borders in order to increase economic activity and job creation. These subsidies are generally designed to stimulate the country's exports or to promote investment in the country (from both domestic and foreign sources) or both. Exports are generally stimulated by government actions that reduce the firm's cost of doing business. Brazil, for example, exempts imported inputs that are used to produce goods for export from taxes and tariffs. Domestically produced goods used to manufacture goods for export may similarly be exempted from taxation. Kenya frees exporters from paying tariffs and other taxes on imported inputs, while India exempts export earnings from income taxes. Australia has adopted similar schemes to encourage automotive, textile, clothing, and footware exports.[26]

National, state, and local governments often provide economic development incentives—another type of subsidy—to entice firms to locate or expand facilities in their communities in order to provide jobs and increase local tax bases. These incentives may be in the form of property tax abatements, free land, training of work forces, reduced utility rates, new highway construction, and so on. Competition among different localities can be fierce. For example, Alabama beat out a host of states competing to attract a new Mercedes-Benz plant by offering the firm a $253 million incentives package.

Because subsidies reduce the cost of doing business, they may affect international trade by artificially improving a firm's competitiveness in export markets or by helping domestic firms to fight off foreign imports. Subsidies, however, can grow so large as to disrupt the normal pattern of international trade. The international wheat market is a notorious example. The International Wheat Council estimates that governmental export subsidies influence two thirds of international wheat sales. Thus wheat exports often reflect the size of a country's subsidies, not the forces of comparative advantage. In the early 1990s, for example, the EU captured 20 percent of the international wheat market through its extensive sales of heavily subsidized wheat. In retaliation, the U.S. government sold wheat to China for $75 a ton and to Algeria for $65 a ton, even though U.S. production costs averaged $125 a ton. Even a desert country can compete in the wheat market when the game includes subsidies: Saudia Arabia sold wheat to New Zealand for $100 a ton, even though its production costs were $600 a ton. In the past decade, the United States has spent over $6 billion subsidizing its wheat exports, as has the EU. The big losers in the subsidy wars are farmers in wheat-exporting countries that lack large-scale subsidies, such as Argentina, Canada, and Australia.[27]

Foreign Trade Zones

A **foreign trade zone (FTZ)** is a geographical area in which imported or exported goods receive preferential tariff treatment. An FTZ may be as small as a warehouse or a factory site (such as Caterpillar's diesel engine facility in Mossville, Illinois) or as large as the entire city of Shenzhen, China (which neighbors Hong Kong).[28] FTZs are used by governments worldwide to spur regional economic development. For example, an FTZ has played a key role in the economic development of the small African island nation of Mauritius (see Map 6.2). Through utilization of an FTZ a firm typically can reduce, delay, or sometimes totally eliminate customs duties. Generally a firm can import a component into an FTZ, process it further, and then export the processed good abroad and avoid paying customs duties on the value of the imported component.

In the United States, FTZs are extremely popular. Their numbers have grown from approximately 25 in the early 1970s to 293 active zones and subzones today. Of particular importance is the growth of FTZs that specialize in assembling automobiles, which now account for 85 percent of all goods produced in U.S. FTZs and for most U.S. automobile production. The automobile-based FTZs developed from an inverted tariff structure in which tariffs on

MAP 6.2

Foreign Trade Zone on Mauritius

Mauritius, which was once a French naval base, is a tropical island, roughly 10½ times the area of Washington, D.C. For much of its history, Mauritius's 1.1 million residents depended on sugar cane, and even today 90 percent of its cultivated land is devoted to this crop.

Mauritius has created a foreign trade zone to diversify its economy and encourage manufacturing. Today the country exports over $1.5 billion of textiles, apparel, and other goods to Europe and the U.S. Because of the FTZ's success, the country's economy has enjoyed a 4.9 percent annual growth in the 1990's.

imported auto parts, ranging from 4 percent to 11 percent, are higher than the 2.5 percent tariff on imported assembled automobiles. A manufacturer can import parts to the FTZ duty-free and assemble them into an automobile. When the assembled automobile leaves the FTZ and enters the jurisdiction of the U.S. Customs Service, the firm pays a tariff on the foreign parts used in the automobile at the lower 2.5 percent rate. Chrysler, GM, and Ford are estimated to save customs duties of $5 to $10 on each automobile assembled in a U.S. FTZ, while the savings of Japanese-owned automobile factories in U.S. FTZs range from $40 to $50 per auto.[29] (Japanese-owned assembly plants enjoy higher FTZ savings because they tend to use more imported components than do U.S.-owned plants.) As one might expect, automakers are pleased with this arrangement. However, U.S. auto parts producers view this use of FTZs as a means of avoiding the high tariffs on imported auto parts.[30]

The maquiladora system represents another important use of FTZs. A **maquiladora** is a factory located in an FTZ in Mexico; most are situated near the U.S. border. These factories import unfinished goods or component parts, further process the goods or parts, and re-export them. The goods produced by maquiladoras enjoy preferential customs and tax treatment. Mexico levies no customs duties on unfinished goods imported by a maquiladora, provided the goods are re-exported after having been further processed in Mexico. Machinery imported into Mexico used by a maquiladora is also exempt from customs duties. U.S. customs duties on maquiladoras' exports are applied only to the value of the processing performed in Mexico.

The maquiladora industry, which was established in 1965 as part of Mexico's Border Industrialization Program, takes advantage of Mexico's low labor costs and its proximity to the United States. Today the maquiladora industry is the second-largest sector of the Mexican economy (after oil production) and the second-largest source of Mexico's foreign-exchange earnings.

However, many ethical issues have been raised regarding the maquiladora industry. The maquiladoras have been criticized by environmentalists, who claim the factories allow firms to escape tough U.S. environmental laws by shifting their operations to Mexico, where enforcement of environmental regulations is lax. U.S. union officials object to maquiladoras because they threaten the jobs of the unions' members and the health of the union movement. Critics also complain that firms utilizing maquiladoras have ignored the social disruption that the maquiladora program has created. The rapid influx of workers into the border area has placed heavy demands on the public infrastructure of Mexico's northern states, overburdening the area's roads, utilities, schools, and housing facilities.

Ironically, the biggest threat to the maquiladoras may be the North American Free Trade Agreement (NAFTA). As a result of NAFTA, many tariff advantages once enjoyed only by the maquiladoras are now available to factories throughout Mexico. Thus interior cities such as Monterrey and Saltillo have been put on a more even footing with border communities such as Nuevo Laredo and Matamoros in terms of attracting new plants to serve the North American market.

Export Financing Programs

For many big-ticket items such as aircraft, supercomputers, and large construction projects, success or failure in exporting depends on a firm's producing a high-quality product, providing reliable repair service after the sale, and—often the critical factor—offering an attractive financing package. For example, Boeing competes with Airbus Industrie to sell Singapore Airlines 200-seat short-range aircraft. When Singapore Airlines is deciding which firm's aircraft to buy, it carefully weighs price, after-sale technical support, aircraft operating costs, and financing expenses. All other things being equal, the financing terms offered it may be critical in its decision of which firm wins the contract.

Because of the importance of the financing package, most major trading countries have created government-owned agencies to assist their domestic firms in arranging financing of export sales, both large or small. The **Export-Import Bank of the United States (Eximbank)** provides financing for U.S. exports through direct loans and loan guarantees; in 1997, it supplied financing for over 2000 export transactions worth $12.2 billion. Large firms like Boeing are important clients, but the Eximbank also services small U.S. exporters. For example, it guaranteed $7.9 million in bank loans for the family-owned De Francisci Machine Corporation, thereby allowing this small New York manufacturer of food-processing equipment to export noodle-drying and pasta-making equipment to two factories in Poland. But government aid often goes beyond mere financing. Eximbank or its subcontractors also provide routine commercial insurance services for Eximbank-supported exports.[31] Another U.S. government-sponsored organization, the **Overseas Private Investment Corporation (OPIC)**, provides a very different type of insurance—political-risk insurance—a subject we cover in Chapter 8. If a foreign country confiscates an insured firm's goods or assets, OPIC will compensate the firm for its losses. Other countries have similar organizations that provide export financing, commercial insurance, and political-risk insurance.

Controlling Unfair Trade Practices

With governments around the world adopting programs designed to protect domestic industries from imports and other programs to promote their exports, it should not be surprising that competitors often cry foul. In response to these complaints, many countries have implemented laws protecting their domestic firms from unfair trade practices.

In the United States, complaints from firms affected by alleged unfair trade practices are first investigated by the International Trade Administration (ITA), a division of the U.S. Department of Commerce, which determines whether an unfair trade practice has occurred. The Department of Commerce transfers confirmed cases of unfair trading to the U.S. International Trade Commission (ITC), an independent government agency. If a majority of the six ITC commissioners decide that U.S. producers have suffered "material injury," the ITC will impose duties on the offending imports to counteract the unfair trade practice. The ITC, like Canada's CITT in the case of Desmarais and like similar government agencies worldwide, focuses on two types of unfair trade practices: government subsidies that distort trade and unfair pricing practices.

Countervailing Duties

Most countries protect local firms from foreign competitors that benefit from subsidies granted by their home governments. A **countervailing duty (CVD)** is an ad valorem tariff on an imported good that is imposed by the importing country to counter the impact of foreign subsidies. The CVD is calculated to just offset the advantage that the exporter obtains from the subsidy. In this way, trade can still be driven by the competitive strengths of individual firms and the laws of comparative advantage rather than by the level of subsidies governments offer their firms.

Not all government subsidies give a foreign firm an unfair advantage in the domestic market. Most countries impose CVDs only when foreign subsidization of a product leads to a distortion of international trade.[32] For example, the U.S. government, in administering its CVD rules, tries to determine whether a particular subsidy is generally available to all industries in a country, in which case CVDs will not be applied, or restricted to a specific industry, in which case CVDs may be imposed. If a foreign government grants a tax credit to all employers for training handicapped workers, a CVD will not be applied, for the tax credit is available to all the country's firms. If the tax credit is restricted to the footware industry, however, a CVD may be imposed on imported footware equal to the value of the tax credit.

CVD complaints are often triggered as a result of some governmental action designed to overcome some other governmental action. For example, the European Union's common agricultural policy has had the effect of raising the prices paid to European grain farmers. Unfortunately, the high cost of feed grains raised the costs of European swine producers and made their meat products uncompetitive in world markets. To undo the damage caused swine producers by high grain prices, the EU agreed to provide an export subsidy for canned hams and other processed

TABLE 6.2											
Antidumping Cases Initiated, 1983–1993											
	1983–84	1984–85	1985–86	1986–87	1987–88	1988–89	1989–90	1990–91	1991–92	1992–93	TOTAL
Australia	70	63	54	40	20	19	23	46	76	61	472
Canada	26	35	27	24	20	14	15	12	16	36	225
EU	33	34	23	17	30	29	15	15	23	33	252
U.S.	46	61	63	41	31	25	24	52	62	78	483
Other developed countries	1	0	2	5	9	12	5	9	21	8	72
Developing countries	0	0	3	4	13	14	14	41	39	38	166
TOTAL	176	193	172	131	123	113	96	175	237	254	1670

Source: From "Negotiations down in the dumps over U.S. draft," *Financial Times*, November 25, 1993. Reprinted with permission.

meat products. With the aid of this subsidy, Danish and Dutch pork processors were able to capture 25 percent of the Canadian canned ham and canned luncheon meat market. As a result, Canadian pork-packing houses successfully petitioned the Canadian International Trade Tribunal to impose a countervailing duty on Danish and Dutch canned pork products.

Economic development incentives may also trigger complaints of unfair trade. For example, in the early 1990s, the Austrian government (at the time, Austria was not an EU member) wanted to attract a Chrysler minivan assembly plant to a depressed region in the country. It offered $96 million in economic development incentives to Eurostar Automobil Fabrik GmbH, a joint venture between Austria's Steyr-Daimler Puch AG and a European subsidiary of Chrysler. In response, the EU threatened to impose a 10 percent CVD on Eurostar minivans exported to its members. It argued that the incentives were an unfair subsidy that lowered the cost of producing minivans in Austria and therefore distorted trade. After many months of negotiations, Austria agreed to lower the incentives offered to Eurostar and the EU agreed not to impose the CVD.[33]

Antidumping Regulations

Many countries are also concerned about their domestic firms being victimized by discriminatory or predatory pricing practices of foreign firms, such as dumping. Recall from the chapter opening that dumping occurs when a firm sells its goods in a foreign market at a price below what it charges in its home market. This type of dumping is a form of international price discrimination. Another type of dumping involves the firm's selling its goods below cost in the foreign market, in which case the dumping is a form of predatory pricing. Antidumping laws protect local industries from dumping by foreign firms. As Table 6.2 shows, in the decade ending June 1993, Australia, the United States, Canada, and the EU initiated over 1400 legal actions against dumping, including that discussed in the Desmarais case.[34]

Determining whether the first type of dumping—price discrimination—has actually occurred is not always easy. For example, many Western politicians incorrectly accuse Japanese automakers of dumping, noting that Japanese automobiles retail for higher prices in Tokyo than in New York City. Retail prices, however, are irrelevant in determining whether dumping has occurred. The comparison should be between the prices charged foreign customers and domestic customers at the factory gate; these prices are often difficult to obtain. The higher retail prices in Tokyo might reflect the inefficient Japanese distribution system or higher costs of doing business rather than dumping by the automaker.

In the second type of dumping—predatory pricing—defining costs is complicated, particularly when dealing with a large, multidivisional MNC such as Toyota or Nissan. For example, when the ITA is determining the "cost" of a Toyota Sienna minivan, should it measure cost as the marginal cost of producing one more Sienna? Should it include some of Toyota's minivan-related R&D expenses, or should it simply recognize that these R&D costs would have been incurred whether or not the U.S. market existed? Should it include charges for Toyota's corporate overhead? Foreigners' guilt or innocence in dumping cases often turns on the answers to such accounting questions.

Super 301

Another weapon available to the U.S. government to combat unfair trading practices of foreign countries is Section 301—so-called Super 301—of the 1974 Trade Act. **Super 301** requires the U.S. trade representative, a member of the executive branch, to publicly list those countries engaging in the most flagrant unfair trade practices. The U.S. trade representative is then required to negotiate the elimination of the alleged unfair trade practices with the listed countries. If the negotiations are unsuccessful, the executive branch must impose on the recalcitrant offenders appropriate retaliatory restrictions such as tariffs or import quotas. Super 301 gives U.S. negotiators a big club in their dealings with foreign governments. For example, the U.S. government determined in the early 1990s that U.S. firms were having difficulty obtaining contracts for large-scale construction projects in Japan, despite their success and experience in managing major construction projects around the world. The then U.S. Trade Representative, Carla Hills, threatened to prohibit Japanese firms from bidding on federally funded construction projects in the United States. The Japanese government agreed to improve the access of U.S. construction firms to major Japanese building projects.[35]

Section 301 technically expired in 1994. However, President Clinton resuscitated it via executive order, and it remains a powerful, though controversial, weapon in the U.S. trade arsenal. The use of Super 301 has not won the United States many friends internationally. Because Super 301 provides relief solely for U.S. firms, EU members have been particularly displeased with it, arguing that it hinders the development of global trade and promotes unilateral, rather than multilateral, attempts to redress problems facing international commerce. Many targets of Super 301 actions are similarly resentful. They believe its use represents bullying by the United States and pandering to those special-interest groups that have the ear of Congress at any point in time.[36]

CHAPTER REVIEW

Summary

Formulating trade policies that advance the economic interests of their citizens is an important task facing most national governments. While some policy makers suggest that free trade is the most appropriate policy, numerous firms, government bureaucrats, and other interested parties argue for active governmental intervention in international trade.

Some rationales for governmental intervention focus on the specific needs of an industry (national defense, infant industry, maintenance of existing jobs, and strategic trade arguments), while others focus on the country's overall needs (economic development and industrial policy).

Over the centuries, governments have developed a variety of trade barriers. Import tariffs raise revenues for the government as well as help domestically produced goods compete with imported goods. Quotas and VERs place a numerical limitation on the amount of a good that can be imported or exported. Other NTBs may also disadvantage foreign products in the market. These barriers include product and testing standards, restricted access to distribution systems, public procurement policies that favor local firms, local-purchase requirements, regulatory powers, and currency and investment controls.

National governments also seek to promote the interests of domestic firms in international trade through other programs. They may subsidize local production of goods and services in order to make them more competitive in international markets. They also may authorize the establishment of FTZs to help domestic firms export goods. Export financing programs have been developed to assist exporters in marketing their goods.

National governments protect local producers from unfair foreign competition by enacting unfair trade laws. CVDs are imposed on foreign products that benefit from government subsidies that distort international trade. Antidumping laws protect domestic producers from being victimized by predatory pricing policies of foreign firms. Super 301 strengthens the bargaining power of U.S. negotiators in international trade conflicts.

Review Questions

1. What is free trade? Who benefits from it?

2. What is the infant industry argument?

3. What is the difference between the export-promotion and import-substitution economic development strategies?

4. What are the different types of tariffs?

5. Why is it useful for an importer to seek out an advance tariff classification from the U.S. Customs Service?

6. Why might a country adopt a VER?

7. What are the major forms of NTBs?

8. What is an FTZ?

9. What is the role of the Eximbank?

10. What is the purpose of a CVD?

11. Which U.S. government agencies administer laws regarding unfair trade practices?

Questions for Discussion

1. What are the advantages and disadvantages of an industrial policy?

2. Because of Japan's success in competing in international markets, it has been the target of numerous complaints that it restricts foreign access to its local markets. As Japan reduces its barriers to imported goods, who is likely to gain from lowered barriers? Who is likely to lose from them?

3. The U.S. Congress authorized the creation of FTZs in order to stimulate U.S. exports. Given the discussion of FTZs in the text, do you believe FTZs are accomplishing Congress's goal? Does the FTZ law need to be changed?

4. Are the ethical issues raised by the critics of maquiladoras valid? To what extent should managers of international businesses consider these issues in deciding whether or not to operate a maquiladora factory?

5. Strategic trade theory applies to industries that are composed of only a few firms worldwide. List as many industries as possible that fit this description.

6. Since 1992 Indonesia has imposed high export taxes on the export of raw wood and sawn timber. Why would they do this? (Hint: What is the impact of these export tariffs on the domestic market for wood and timber? Which domestic industries would benefit from this impact?) Who is hurt by these high export taxes?

BUILDING GLOBAL SKILLS

In the United States, at least 18 separate government agencies have some responsibility for promoting exports of U.S. firms. The ITA coordinates the export development efforts of these federal agencies. The U.S. and Foreign Commercial Service (US&FCS), a branch of the ITA, staffs offices throughout the United States and in foreign countries with international trade experts available to help U.S. firms export their products. These experts can help firms assess their products' export potential, identify the most likely markets for their goods, and locate promising overseas partners and distributors. To promote exports, US&FCS experts also work with 51 District Export Councils, 107 field offices of the Small Business Administration (SBA), the Foreign Agricultural Service (part of the Department of Agriculture), commercial banks, chambers of commerce, and state governments. These groups provide seminars on exporting and information about exporting opportunities in different countries and product lines. A quick listing of these services can be found in the Department of Commerce's accurately titled publication, *A Basic Guide to Exporting*, which provides an informative overview of the exporting process.

Assignment

The U.S. government has so many sources of information available to help first-time exporters that managers are often overwhelmed by deciding where to begin. Put yourself in the shoes of a neophyte exporter who wants to learn about the exporting process.

1. Find out which branch office of the US&FCS serves your local market. You can do this by using *A Basic Guide to Exporting* in your library, looking in your local phone book, calling your congressperson's office (the staff there are experts about the federal bureaucracy), asking a local banker, or chatting with local chambers of commerce. Ask the local US&FCS office to send you literature on its activities and a list of its "Country Desk Officers" (experts knowledgeable about the markets in specific countries) and "Industry Desk Officers" (experts knowledgeable about the international markets for individual products).

2. Find out which state agencies in your state are responsible for promotion of exports from local firms. Ask them about their export development programs.

3. Identify the SBA district office in your area. Ask how it can help local firms identify promising export markets.

4. Locate any private organizations in your area (profit and nonprofit) that provide trade development services. Ask them about the types of services they offer their members and newcomers like yourself.

Much of this information is available on the Internet as well. The textbook's web site provides links to other web sites of use for this assignment.

WORKING WITH THE WEB: Building Global Internet Skills

Assessing Trade Barriers

The ability of firms to market their products in foreign countries is often affected by trade barriers imposed by individual countries. Your assignment is to pick an industry or product, and report on the barriers to trade or investment that five countries impose on this industry or product. Since the members of the European Union have common trade policies, only one of the five countries can be an EU member.

Fortunately, there are numerous sources of useful information available in published form and on the Internet. The Office of the U.S. Trade Representative publishes annually an analysis of trade barriers imposed by other nations entitled the *National Trade Estimate Report on Foreign Trade Barriers.* This study also provides a detailed description of the evolution of existing trade conflicts between the U.S. and the rest of the world. The EU publishes a similar report. The U.S. Customs Service's web site provides information on tariffs imposed by the United States. Other groups, such as the World Trade Organization and industry trade associations, also publish useful information. The textbook's web site for Chapter 6 provides links to web sites you may find of use for this assignment.

CLOSING CASE

Regulatory Warfare[37]

As you may recall from Chapter 3, one of the bitterest battles being fought today involves the struggle between Kodak and Fuji for dominance in the world film market. Both companies are arguing that they are being victimized by unfair trade practices in the other's country. Kodak has moved aggressively to bolster its position by appealing to the U.S. government for relief from what it claims are unfair Japanese practices.

Kodak enjoys a 70 percent share of the U.S. film market; Fuji has a mere 11 percent, and the remaining 19 percent is divided among firms like Polaroid, Japan's Konica, Germany's Agfa-Gavaert, and a handful of private label brands. The numbers are reversed in Japan, where Fuji owns 67 percent of the market, Kodak 11 percent, and other firms the remainder. The rest of the world is split almost evenly between these three groups: Kodak has 36 percent of the market outside Japan and the United States, Fuji 33 percent, and all other firms 31 percent.

Fuji developed into a powerhouse brand in its home market due to high tariffs—40 percent ad valorem—on imported film that freed it from competition from Kodak and other non-Japanese brands.

Since 1980, however, these tariffs have been cut and in 1990 were totally eliminated. Ironically, it is the United States that now has the higher tariff on imported film, albeit a modest 3.7 percent tariff.

Kodak believes that its poor showing in the Japanese market is due to trade barriers erected by Japan, not due to any lack of effort or commitment on its part—Kodak has invested some $750 million in Japan. Taking Kodak's side, the U.S. government has complained that Japan's government has promoted exclusive wholesaling arrangements that favor Fuji, hindered the growth of large discount stores that would stock foreign goods, and restricted the use of price competition and price promotions that would allow Kodak to underprice Fuji. Of particular concern is the Japanese film distribution system, which is dominated by four distributors who together control 70 percent of the film market. These four distributors have signed exclusive dealing contracts with Fuji, effectively locking Kodak and other film manufacturers out of these important distribution channels. These distributors are particularly important suppliers to Japan's camera stores and film shops, which market to skilled amateurs and professionals. At such shops, profit margins are high because these stores compete primarily on service, not price.

Allegedly, Fuji grants these retailers secret rebates based on their sales of its film, further discouraging them from stocking competitive brands. Kodak, Agfa, and other manufacturers like Konica are forced to focus most of their competitive energies at discount outlets where profit margins are lower.

Kodak also filed a complaint before the U.S. Department of Commerce (DOC), claiming that Fuji was dumping film in the U.S. market. Officials at DOC's International Trade Administration and the International Trade Commission agreed with Kodak's charges, and levied antidumping duties on Fuji film manufactured at its facilities in Japan and the Netherlands. But this tactic seems to have backfired on Kodak. Fuji expanded its manufacturing complex in Greenwood, South Carolina, allowing it to begin manufacturing film in the United States. By so doing, Fuji avoided the 3.7 percent tariff on imported film. More important, Fuji shortened its supply lines and rendered Kodak's antidumping complaint moot. It can now respond to changing circumstances in the U.S. market more quickly because the film is produced locally, not thousands of miles away.

Fuji has engaged Kodak in a war of words, arguing that the Japanese market is more open than the U.S. market. Japan imposes no tariffs on imported film, and discounters and supermarkets are among the fastest growing segments of Japanese retailing. Fuji points to Agfa's success in capturing 5 percent of the Japanese film market since 1990 by focusing on selling private-label film. Fuji also claims that Kodak uses a variety of techniques in the United States to discourage retailers from selling other brands of film. For example, Kodak offers many retailers a 3 percent rebate if their sales of Kodak film meet the previous year's level. Fuji notes that Kodak has systematically purchased wholesale photofinishers, which allows it to control 70 percent of the U.S. wholesale photofinishing market.

Kodak counters that it has access to only 15 percent of the Japanese market because of the exclusive contracts that the big four distributors have with many Japanese film retailers; conversely, it says that Fuji film is available at retail outlets that generate 65 percent of U.S. film sales. Kodak also notes that the openness of the U.S. market gives Fuji more maneuvering room in the United States than Kodak has in Japan. For example, in August 1996 Fuji bought six photofinishing labs from Wal-Mart, giving its film the inside track at thousands of Wal-Mart and Sam's Club stores.

Kodak then successfully lobbied the U.S. government to file a complaint before the World Trade Organization (WTO), an international agency charged with promoting world trade that will be discussed in the next chapter. The U.S. government filed over 20,000 pages of documents detailing, it believes, covert measures by the Japanese government to restrict foreign access to the Japanese film market. Unfortunately for Kodak, in December 1997 the WTO ruled in Fuji's favor, rejecting all of the U.S. charges.

Despite its loss, Kodak claimed the millions of dollars it spent preparing the case before the WTO were monies well spent. The Japanese government was forced to rebut Kodak's case point-by-point rather than dismiss its claims with vague language. In so doing, it made promises to the WTO that, if kept, will help Kodak compete in the Japanese film market. For example, prior to the filing of the case before the WTO, the Japanese government restricted Kodak's ability to gain market share through price discounting, disallowing 2-for-1 offers and other promotional techniques that would encourage loyal Fuji users to try Kodak film. (As the "Going Global" in Chapter 3 reported, such price discounting has been an important means by which Fuji has gained market share in the United States.) In its WTO filings, the Japanese government pledged to not stand in the way of price discounting, a decision that Kodak, as the underdog in the Japanese market, believes favors its interests.

In response to the WTO's decision, Kodak and the U.S. government announced a new strategy in February 1998. The Japanese government had asserted in its filing before the WTO that it does not permit anticompetitive behavior, that it encourages the importing of film, and that the Japanese film market is open. The U.S. government plans to monitor the Japanese government to check whether its actions are consistent with these assertions. For example, it will enumerate the number of Japanese retail photo outlets that carry foreign film brands to see if such brands have reasonable access to Japanese consumers. It will also observe whether the Japanese government imposes restrictions on pricing promotions that Kodak may adopt to woo Japanese customers to purchase its products.

Case Questions

1. Fuji's success seems to be a good example of the application of the infant industry argument for intervening in free trade. Do you think that Fuji would have been able to dominate Japan's film market if Japan had not initially imposed tariffs on photo film?

2. Kodak's strategy seems to be to use the regulatory process to accomplish what it has not been able to do through normal competitive processes. Do you agree with this strategy? Are there dangers to it?

3. Consider Fuji's argument that it does to Kodak in Japan what Kodak does to it in the U.S. market. If true, does this weaken Kodak's case?

4. How significant for Kodak is the Japanese government's pledge to not stand in the way of price competition?

CHAPTER NOTES

1. Information for this case was obtained from various decisions of the Canadian Import Tribunal and the Canadian International Trade Tribunal, including: "Photo Albums Originating in or Exported from Singapore, Malaysia, and Taiwan," Inquiry No. CIT-5–87; CITT Review No. RR-89–012; and CITT Inquiry No. NQ–90–003.

2. U.S. International Trade Commission, *Shipbuilding Trade Reform Act of 1992: Likely Economic Effects of Enactment*, USITC Publication 2495 (June 1992), Washington, D.C. The U.S. shipbuilding industry is so uncompetitive in world markets that from 1960 to 1994 the industry exported no commercial oceangoing vessels (p. 6).

3. "The trough," *The Economist*, June 27, 1992, p. 22.

4. Edward J. Lincoln, *Japan's Unequal Trade* (Washington, D.C.: The Brookings Institution, 1990), p. 112.

5. Brander and Spencer, "International R&D Rivalry and Industrial Strategy," *Review of Economic Studies,* Vol. 50 (1983), pp. 707–722. See also Paul R. Krugman and Maurice Obstfeld, *International Economics* (Glenview, Ill.: Scott, Foresman/Little Brown College Division, 1988), pp. 261ff.

6. Paul R. Krugman, "Is Free Trade Passe?" *Economic Perspectives* (Fall 1987), pp. 131–144.

7. Krugman and Obstfeld, op. cit., Chapter 11.

8. "U.S. Picks Areas of Technology It Wants to Back," *Wall Street Journal*, April 26, 1994, p. A4.

9. "Torpedo Shipping Protectionism," *Wall Street Journal*, November 26, 1991, p. A14.

10. European Court Reporter (1987–3 at 1227), *Commission of the European Communities v. Federal Republic of Germany*.

11. "China Hinders Its Own Bid for WTO, Adding Trade Barriers as Old Ones Fall," *Wall Street Journal*, May 20, 1997, p. A15; Office of the U.S. Trade Representative, *National Trade Estimate Report on Foreign Trade Barriers 1997,* p. 351.

12. Office of the U.S. Trade Representative, ibid., pp. 49 and 189.

13. Ibid., p. 357.

14. "Japan Glass Market Proves Hard to Crack," *Wall Street Journal*, August 7, 1991, p. A4.

15. "Los Angeles Proposal Gives Preference to Local Bids," *Wall Street Journal*, February 7, 1992, p. A7.

16. "White House Again Says Japan Uses Unfair Tactics to Aid Building Industry," *Wall Street Journal*, November 24, 1989, p. 2A.

17. Office of the U.S. Trade Representative, *National Trade Estimate Report on Foreign Trade Barriers 1997*, pp. 160 and 352.

18. Ibid., pp. 23–24 and 273.

19. "France Eases Film Quota," *Wall Street Journal*, July 23, 1992, p. A6.

20. Office of the U.S. Trade Representative, *National Trade Estimate Report on Foreign Trade Barriers 1997*, p. 101.

21. "U.S. Criticizes EC's TV-Content Stance, Seeks Arbitration," *Wall Street Journal*, October 11, 1989, p. A15.

22. "Global Ad Campaigns, After Many Missteps, Finally Pay Dividends," *Wall Street Journal*, August 27, 1992, p. A1.

23. Office of the U.S. Trade Representative, *National Trade Estimate Report on Foreign Trade Barriers 1997*, pp. 159, 237, 275, and 351.

24. "Beer Blast," *Wall Street Journal*, August 4, 1992, p. A14.

25. International Monetary Fund, *Exchange Arrangements and Exchange Restrictions Annual Report 1997*. Washington, D.C.: IMF, 1997.

26. Office of the U.S. Trade Representative, *National Trade Estimate Report on Foreign Trade Barriers 1997*, pp. 17, 24, 161, and 230.

27. "Arable parable," *The Economist*, August 24, 1991, p. 60; Laurie Morse, "U.S./China wheat deal shows trade war is still on," *Financial Times*, January 11, 1994, p. 30.

28. Committee on Ways and Means, *Operation of the Foreign Trade Zones Program of the United States and Its Implications for the U.S. Economy and U.S. International Trade*, October 1989, Serial 101–56, pp. 281 and 326.

29. Ibid., pp. 75 and 166.

30. Ibid., p. 327.

31. Export-Import Bank of the United States, 1997 *Annual Report* (Washington, D.C.: Eximbank, 1998); *1992 Annual Report* (Washington, D.C.: Eximbank, 1993); *1994 Annual Report* (Washington, D.C.: Eximbank, 1995).

32. Richard Boltuck and Robert E. Litan, "America's 'Unfair' Trade Laws," in Boltuck and Litan, eds., *Down in the Dumps* (Washington, D.C.: The Brookings Institution, 1991), p. 9.

33. "EC Delays Ruling on Grants by Austria for Minivan Plant," *Wall Street Journal*, August 4, 1992, p. B9; *Wall Street Journal*, July 30, 1992, p. A8.

34. Nancy Dunne, "Brisk Business for U.S. anti-dumping agencies," *Financial Times*, August 16, 1991, p. 3.

35. "U.S., Japan Failing in Talks to Expand Construction Trade," *Wall Street Journal*, May 24, 1991, p. A8.

36. "EC Criticizes U.S. on Trade Barriers in War of Words," *Wall Street Journal*, May 4, 1989, p. A3.

37. "Kodak and U.S. Government Team Up for New Drive on Japan's Film Market," *Wall Street Journal,* February 4, 1998, p. A4; Fuji Photo Film Co., Ltd. Annual Report 1997; "WTO weighs up Fuji-Kodak dispute," *Financial Times,* April 18, 1997, p. 9; "Exposed: Kodak's path to the WTO," *Financial Times,* June 16, 1996, p. 5;" Fuji Invests $100 Million in U.S. Plant," *Wall Street Journal,* February 21, 1996, p. A3; "Kodak says Fuji response a diversionary tactic," *Business Wire,* July 31, 1995, p. 1; "Kodak Boosts Pressure on Washington to Force Tokyo to Open Photo Market," *Wall Street Journal,* June 1, 1995, p. A4; "Kodak exposes Fuji's market grip," *Financial Times,* June 1, 1995, p. 7.

Should Unfair Trade Laws Be Enforced?

They provide important advantages to the world and national economies

Advocates of strong CVD and antidumping policies believe that government subsidies and dumping reduce the efficiency of the global economy by distorting international trade flows and rewarding inefficient firms. According to the country-based and firm-based trade theories discussed in Chapter 3, international trade not only makes both parties better off but also allocates resources efficiently across national economies because goods are (1) bought by those consumers that value them most highly, and (2) produced by those firms that can produce them at lowest cost. Unfair trade practices thus reduce global economic efficiency because the level of government subsidy or the degree of dumping, not efficiency, will determine which firms will produce which goods.

Enforcement of unfair trade laws also protects domestic jobs and firms. Subsidies by foreign governments and dumping by foreign firms will cause price reductions in the domestic market and lower the profits of domestic producers. Domestic producers will be forced to cut their costs in order to survive. Workers may bear the brunt of these cost-cutting measures as the affected firms reduce wages, fire workers, and/or close down factories. To restore their profitability, domestic firms may be forced to relocate their factories to other countries where wages are lower or to go out of business entirely.

Other experts believe foreign firms may use unfair trade practices to gain a long-run competitive advantage. A firm may dump output in the home markets of its worldwide competitors in order to weaken those competitors and thereby gain a strategic edge in the global competitive battle. For example, the three major U.S. automakers filed a complaint in 1992 against Mazda and Toyota, claiming that they were dumping minivans in the U.S. market. Chrysler, which made a majority of its profits from selling minivans, charged that Toyota's and Mazda's minivan pricing was designed to rob Chrysler of the cash flow it needed to regain its status as a world-class competitor in automotive markets. (However, the ITC ruled that Japan had not dumped minivans in the U.S. market.)

Advocates of aggressive enforcement of unfair trade laws also believe unfair trade practices hurt consumers. Without such laws, they fear, foreign firms will adopt predatory pricing practices, forcing down domestic prices by dumping their goods in the domestic market and driving domestic firms out of the market. The foreigners will then raise prices, earn monopoly profits, and gouge domestic consumers.

U.S. consumers benefit from price competition among U.S. and Japanese manufacturers. But U.S. automakers argued that Toyota dumped Previa vans on the U.S. market to cripple the long-run viability of the U.S. automobile industry.

Advocates of free trade argue that unfair trade laws do more damage than good: while they sound reasonable in theory, in practice they are thinly concealed attempts to promote protectionism. Free trade advocates maintain that Department of Commerce (DOC) and ITC procedures are biased against foreign firms. For example, a foreign firm typically has only 30 days to reply to a DOC information request, which may run 100 pages. By the deadline it must supply comprehensive documents detailing in English its pricing and cost accounting procedures. Its failure to do so means that the DOC can use the costs of its U.S. competitors to construct an estimate of its direct costs. To calculate the foreign firm's average costs, the DOC adds in an allowance for overhead costs and a profit margin, the size of which are often derived from an industry-wide average. As a result of these bureaucratic procedures, foreign firms often find it difficult to win unfair trade practices cases and are forced to raise their prices. This benefits domestic producers but harms domestic consumers.

Some economists go even further in their disdain for unfair trade laws. They believe the laws make no sense either in theory or in practice because of the harm to consumers. These economists are skeptical of the predatory pricing argument, contending that decades of economic research have failed to find many real examples of such behavior.

Other critics argue that unfair trade laws may damage the U.S. economy. For example, in 1991 the federal government received a complaint from seven small U.S. manufacturers of active-matrix liquid crystal displays (LCDs) that

Japanese manufacturers of this product were dumping it in the U.S. market. The ITC imposed a 62.67 percent duty on the imported active-matrix LCDs. However, imported displays account for as much as 30 percent of the cost of a laptop computer. Not surprisingly, the ITC's action was vigorously resisted by U.S. computer manufacturers such as Apple, IBM, and Compaq, which feared that the duty would dramatically increase the costs of U.S.-made laptops, thereby giving imported Japanese laptops a huge advantage in the U.S. market. They also claimed that saving a few hundred jobs in the U.S. active-matrix LCD industry by imposing the duty would jeopardize thousands of jobs in the U.S. laptop computer industry.

Sources: Lisa Zagaroli, "U.S. Rules Japan Not Dumping Minivans," *Boston Globe,* June 25, 1992, p. 33; "ITC, in Big Blow to U.S. Laptop Makers, Tacks Steep Duties on Japanese Screens," *Wall Street Journal,* August 16, 1991, p. B3; "Laptops: U.S. Pulls Plug on a Domestic Industry," *Wall Street Journal,* August 12, 1992, p. A10; Hiroshi Matsumoto, "Legal Harassment of Foreign Firms: The Case of the U.S. Steel Industry," *Pacific Basin Quarterly,* No. 20 (Fall 1993), p. 31; Tracy Murray, "The Administration of the Antidumping Duty Law by the Department of Commerce," in Richard Boltuck and Robert E. Litan, eds., *Down in the Dumps* (Washington, D.C.: Brookings Institution, 1991), pp. 23–63.

Wrap-up

1 The case involving imported active-matrix LCDs posed a dilemma for the ITC: it could protect jobs in the small LCD industry at the cost of threatening a much larger number of jobs in the laptop computer industry. Was the ITC's decision correct?

2 Do you agree that enforcing unfair trade laws hurts the economy, rather than helps it? Why or why not?

Apple shifted production of laptops from Colorado to Ireland to avoid the 62.67 percent duty on imported active-matrix LCDs, which did not apply to imported laptops containing such displays. The result was a loss of U.S. jobs.

International Cooperation among Nations

After studying this chapter you should be able to:

Explain the importance of the GATT and the WTO to international businesses.

Contrast the different forms of economic integration among cooperating countries.

Analyze the opportunities for international businesses created by completion of the EU's internal market.

Describe the other major trading blocs in today's world economy.

Discuss the role of commodity cartels in international trade.

I F ALL GOES AS PLANNED, EUROPE IS ABOUT TO DEMOLISH THE one European economic institution that works well: Germany's central bank, the Bundesbank. In its place is to be the world's first supranational central bank, with the world's first supranational currency. But no one, even the architects, is quite sure how all this is going to work. ▮▮ Will the European Central Bank, or ECB, be tougher on inflation than the German Bundesbank, to earn credibility with financial markets? Or will it be more susceptible to political pressure than the fiercely independent Bundesbank? Will it push the new European currency, the euro, down to foster exports? Or up to resist inflation? Who will set the exchange-rate policy? Will this be a historic achievement or a historic mess? ▮▮ Although the scheduled day of creation is near, Jan. 1, 1999, those who usually answer such questions are just beginning to ask them seri-

One Currency, One Central Bank, One Big Question[1]

ously. "Few people have stepped back and asked what the policies will be once the Bundesbank is dead," says David Soskice, an Oxford University political economist. ▮▮ Even fans of the European central bank idea concede that the Maastricht Treaty, which established conditions for monetary union, is largely mum about how the ECB will work in practice. It says the ECB should aim for "price stability," but nothing about how to achieve that goal. . . . ▮▮ The ECB could be a bonanza for the Europeans. A strict central bank, optimists argue, might force governments to revamp inflexible labor-market rules and reform social-welfare programs so their economies can prosper. With one currency making intra-European trade easier and one stern central bank keeping inflation at bay, Europe could create a rival for the dollar as a world currency, spawn a sizable pan-European financial market, and lure lots of investment. In short, Europe would have more economic clout with the U.S. ▮▮ Another question is, who calls the shots? The Maastricht Treaty provides that between four and six people will be appointed to an ECB executive board by the member nations' heads of state. Monetary-policy decisions will be made, by majority vote, by these six and up to 15 governors of the weakened national central banks. ▮▮ But in practice, asks Edwin M. Truman, the Fed's top international economist, "What will be the European equivalent of the weekly breakfast between the U.S. Secretary of the Treasury and the chairman of the Federal Reserve Board?" That's the informal setting for coordination between the elected government, which controls taxes and spending, and the independent central bank, which sets interest rates. Mr. Truman's view: "Europe has not yet answered this question or, more precisely, different Europeans have different answers." ▌▌That's for sure. The French are pushing a "stability council" where finance ministers would consult one another, and the ECB, about government-spending plans. But the Germans and the Dutch have resisted formalizing the sessions, fearing political influence will weaken the central bank's inflation-fighting resolve. ▌▌Balancing the French tradition of overt political influence on the central bank and the German tradition of central-bank independence remains a challenge. While the elected government in Bonn enjoys a right to interfere on exchange-rate policy, it never has. The Maastricht Treaty says heads of state will be responsible for guiding exchange-rate policy. "That's a right they'll be only too happy to use," said Ravi Bulchandant, currency analyst for Morgan Stanley & Co. in London. ▌▌Some Clinton administration officials fear the political role in swaying currency rates will translate into a weak euro; politicians, they reason, will seek to stimulate Europe's economy by weakening the currency and thus making European exports more price-competitive. Indeed, Paul Marchelli, a member of the council of France's central bank, has said publicly that "if the currency is less strong than [Bundesbank governor Hans] Tietmeyer hopes, that would be an excellent thing." ▌▌But Europe could wind up pursuing a strong euro. A strong currency could help investors in Europe by guaranteeing a secure return on euro-denominated securities, and might be the byproduct of a central bank that boosts interest rates to maintain the credibility of the new currency. No one can know in advance. ▌▌On crucial nuts-and-bolts matters, such as exchange-rate technicalities, supporters of monetary union say the central bank will be run by technocrats who are free to act in Europe's best interest. But views about what is in Europe's economic interest often diverge. ▌▌The Bundesbank's inflation-fighting world view already has permeated the staff of the European Monetary Institute. "Whether Italian or Dutch," one U.S. official observes, "they have bought into the Bundesbank mantra. Their culture is the Bundesbank culture." At Germany's insistence, the EMI, like the Bundesbank, is located in Frankfurt and will remain there when the EMI becomes Europe's central bank. ▌▌The EMI also has a University of Chicago influence. The university is known for its free-market, small-government approach to economic policy and a Bundesbank-like emphasis on the importance of controlling the money supply to resist inflation. Neither view is popular among the economic intelligentsia of France or Italy. But the EMI's highest-ranking Italian, the head of the policy division, earned his Ph.D. from Chicago. So did the EMI's French chief economist. ▌▌No matter how well-designed the new central bank proves to be, it will face still another enormous challenge. Interest-rate policy will still be uniform across Europe, but tax-and-spending policy will still be under the control of national governments. ▌▌"How do you maintain stability in an economy that may have different regions that behave differently, when you don't have a national, overarching fiscal policy?" asks Alice Rivlin, vice-chairwoman of the U.S. Federal Reserve. Europe lacks the U.S. practice of temporarily shifting money from booming states to those that are in recession. If, say, food prices suddenly plummet and send Nebraska into a recession because it is highly dependent on agriculture, the Fed doesn't do much. But Washington automatically sends more farm-support payments and unemployment benefits to Nebraska. ▐ ▐ While the European Union has a regional-development fund, it is limited in size, rigidly planned, and doesn't act as an economic stabilizer. After monetary union, any national government that tries to boost its deficit to jump-start its economy will be subject to penalties. The ECB thus could have a tougher time dealing with sovereign nations than the Fed has dealing with American states. ▐ ▐ Pro-ECB bureaucrats say the economies of Europe are converging more rapidly than critics realize, particularly among countries likely to be part of the initial monetary union. Already, they insist, there is a meeting of minds on the importance of price stability. ▐ ▐ History suggests otherwise, warns Karl Haeuser, a retired finance professor from Frankfurt University. At a 1997 conference, he presented the dismal history of the efforts to unify currencies before political union. Attempts at currency union without prior political unity have failed, he said, citing the Latin currency union attempt in the 1860s, the Scandinavian union attempt in the 1970s, and the German-Austrian attempts of the 1850s and 1860s, which ended in 1867, a year after the two powers went to war with each other. These failures resulted from conflicts arising from different macro-economic conditions. "I fear the euro will see similar problems," he concluded. ▐ ▐ ▐ ▐ ▐

In Chapter 6, we explored the ways in which national governments intervene in international trade and investment. When a country adopts restrictions on international commerce, it can benefit at least some of its producers and workers. But other countries may retaliate with similar restrictions, thinking that they, too, will gain. As restrictions proliferate, international trading opportunities decline and all countries end up losing. They often then realize that each is better off if they cooperate and agree to forswear trade restrictions. This chapter is about the outcomes of those realizations.

International cooperative agreements form a major part of the economic environment in which international businesses operate. To be successful, international businesspeople must be knowledgeable about these agreements and use them to create business opportunities for their firms and to counteract competitors' actions. Of particular importance is the growth of regional trading blocs, such as the Mercosur Accord and NAFTA, which are designed to reduce trade barriers among their members. And by far the boldest of these regional economic integration efforts is that of the European Union, which, as the opening case indicates, is trying to replace marks, francs, guilders, and lira with a single currency, the euro.

The General Agreement on Tariffs and Trade and the World Trade Organization

The collapse of the international economy between the two world wars has been blamed in part on countries' imposing prohibitive tariffs, quotas, and other protectionist measures on imported goods. Trading and investment opportunities for international businesses dried up as country after country adopted such "beggar-thy-neighbor" policies. By raising tariff and quota barriers, each nation believed that it could help its own industries and citizens, even though in doing so it might harm the citizens and industries of other countries. For example, in 1930 the United States sought to protect domestic industries from import competition by raising tariffs under the Smoot-Hawley Tariff Act to an average of 53 percent.[2] However, as other countries, such as the United Kingdom, Italy, and France, constructed similarly high tariff walls, the cumulative effect was that each country was worse off rather than better off. None gained a competitive advantage over another, and as international trade declined, all suffered from the contraction of export markets.

To ensure that the post–World War II international peace would not be threatened by such trade wars, representatives of the leading trading nations met in Havana, Cuba, in 1947 to create the International Trade Organization (ITO). The ITO's mission was to promote international trade; however, it never came into being because of a controversy over how extensive its powers should be. Instead the ITO's planned mission was taken over by the General Agreement on Tariffs and Trade (GATT), which had been developed as part of the preparations for the Havana Conference. From 1947 to 1994 the signatories to the GATT (the GATT was technically an agreement, not an organization) fought to reduce barriers to international trade. The GATT provided a forum for trade ministers to discuss policies and problems of common concern. In January 1995, it was replaced by the World Trade Organization (WTO), which adopted the GATT's mission.

How the GATT Worked

Many MNCs strongly supported the GATT's objectives, for its goal was to promote a free and competitive international trading environment benefiting efficient producers. The GATT accomplished this by sponsoring international negotiations to reduce tariffs, quotas, and other non-tariff barriers (NTB). Because high tariffs were initially the most serious impediment to world trade, the GATT first focused on reducing the general level of tariff protection. It sponsored a series of eight negotiating "rounds," generally named after the location where each round of negotiations began (see Table 7.1), during its lifetime. The cumulative effect of the GATT's eight rounds was a substantial reduction in tariffs. Tariffs imposed by the developed countries fell from an average of over 40 percent in 1948 to approximately 3 percent in 1995.[3] As Fig. 7.1 shows, the GATT negotiations led to dramatic growth in world trade over the past fifty years.

To help international businesses compete in world markets regardless of their nationality, the GATT sought to ensure that international trade was conducted on a

TABLE 7.1			
GATT Negotiating Rounds			
ROUND	DATES	NUMBER OF PARTICIPANTS	AVERAGE TARIFF CUT (%)
Geneva	1947	23	35
Annecy	1949	13	NA
Torquay	1950–1951	38	25
Geneva	1956	26	NA
Dillon	1960–1962	45	NA
Kennedy	1964–1967	62	35
Tokyo	1973–1979	99	33
Uruguay	1986–1994	117	36

nondiscriminatory basis. This was accomplished through use of the most favored nation principle. The **most favored nation (MFN) principle** requires that any preferential treatment granted to one country must be extended to all countries. Under GATT rules, all members were required to utilize the MFN principle in dealing with other members. For example, if the United States cut the tariff on imports of British trucks to 20 percent, it had to also reduce its tariffs on imported trucks from all other members to 20 percent. Because of the MFN principle, multilateral, rather than bilateral, trade negotiations were encouraged, thereby strengthening GATT's role.

There are two important exceptions to the MFN principle:

I To assist poorer countries in their economic development efforts, the GATT permitted members to lower tariffs to developing countries without lowering them for more developed countries. In the U.S. tariff code such reduced rates offered to developing countries are known as the **Generalized System of Preferences (GSP).** Other developed countries have similar exemptions. Obviously, by reducing these tariffs, the GSP increases the pressures on domestic firms that are vulnerable to import competition from the developing countries. In contrast, MNCs can reduce their input and production costs by locating factories and assembly facilities in countries benefiting from the GSP.

2 The second exemption is for regional arrangements that promote economic integration, such as the EU and NAFTA, both of which we discuss soon.[4]

While GATT's underlying principles were noble, its framers recognized that domestic political pressures often forced countries to retreat from pure free trade policies. The GATT permitted countries to protect their domestic industries on a nondiscriminatory basis, although under GATT rules countries were supposedly restricted to the use of tariffs only. Quotas and other NTBs can often be applied discriminatorily, and they are less "transparent"—that is, it is often hard to judge their impact on competition. However, there were loopholes in these rules, so many countries adopted quotas and other NTBs and yet remained in compliance with the GATT. For example, U.S. quotas

VOLUME OF WORLD TRADE IN GOODS: 1950 = 100 (semi-log scale)

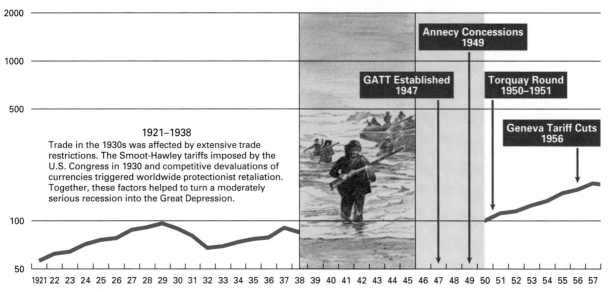

1921–1938
Trade in the 1930s was affected by extensive trade restrictions. The Smoot-Hawley tariffs imposed by the U.S. Congress in 1930 and competitive devaluations of currencies triggered worldwide protectionist retaliation. Together, these factors helped to turn a moderately serious recession into the Great Depression.

Annecy Concessions 1949

GATT Established 1947

Torquay Round 1950–1951

Geneva Tariff Cuts 1956

FIGURE 7.1

The History of GATT's Effect on World Trade in Goods

Sources: From *Financial Times*, December 16, 1993, p. 5. Reprinted with permission. Also: World Trade Organization, "After Two Outstanding Years, World Trade Growth Returned to Earlier Levels," 1997.

restricting imports of peanuts, sugar, and other agricultural products that were granted a "temporary" waiver from GATT rules in 1955 remained in effect for decades.[5] Countries were allowed exemptions to preserve national security or to remedy balance of payments (BOP) problems. The GATT also permitted them in certain circumstances to protect themselves against "too much" foreign competition.

The Uruguay Round

The eighth, and final, round of GATT negotiations began in Uruguay in September 1986. Ratified by GATT members in Morocco in March 1994, the Uruguay Round agreement took effect in 1995. Like its seven predecessors, the Uruguay Round cut tariffs on imported goods—in this case, from an average of 4.7 percent to 3 percent. But as average tariff rates declined, most countries recognized that NTBs had become a more important impediment to the growth of world trade, and so the Uruguay Round also addressed them as well (see Table 7.2). For example, the participants made substantial progress in abolishing quotas by encouraging countries to convert existing quotas to tariff-rate quotas (see Chapter 6). More important, Uruguay Round participants agreed to create the World Trade Organization, established its initial agenda, and granted it more power to attack trade barriers than the GATT had possessed.

The World Trade Organization

The World Trade Organization (WTO) came into being on January 1, 1995. Headquartered in Geneva, Switzerland, the WTO is comprised today of 132 members and 34 observer countries. Members are required to open their markets to international trade and to follow the WTO's rules. (See "Going Global," p. 250) The WTO has three primary goals:

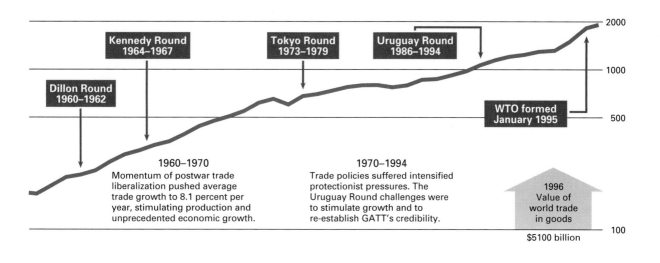

- Promote trade flows by encouraging nations to adopt nondiscriminatory, predictable trade policies. (Figure 7.2 details the WTO's principles for the world trading system.)

- Reduce remaining trade barriers through multilateral negotiations. During the first three years of its existence, the WTO has emphasized sectoral negotiations. For example, the WTO sponsored 1996's Information Technology Agreement, which will eliminate tariffs on such products as computers, software, fax machines, and pagers by the year 2000. Similar agreements covering financial services and telecommunications were signed in 1997.

- Establish impartial procedures for resolving trade disputes among members.

The WTO was clearly designed to build on and expand the successes of the GATT; indeed, the GATT agreement was incorporated into the WTO agreement. The WTO differs from the GATT in several important dimensions. First, the GATT focused on promoting trade in goods. The WTO's mandate is much broader. It is responsible for trade in goods, trade in services, international intellectual property protection, and trade-related investment. Second, the WTO's enforcement powers are much stronger than those possessed by the GATT.

Problem Sectors. Needless to say, the WTO faces a variety of challenges. One is dealing with sectors of the economy that seemingly receive government protection in every country. Two such sectors are agriculture and textiles. Trade in many agricultural products has been distorted by export subsidies, import restrictions, and other trade barriers. The **Cairns Group,** a group of major agricultural exporters led by Argentina, Australia, Brazil, Canada, and Thailand, has pressured the WTO to ensure that the Uruguay Round agreements (see Table 7.2) dealing with agricultural trade are implemented according to schedule. Similarly, since 1974 trade in textiles has been governed by the **Multifibre Agreement (MFA),**

TABLE 7.2			

What the Uruguay Round Accomplished

AREA	STATUS PRIOR TO URUGUAY ROUND	PROVISIONS OF URUGUAY ROUND	MAIN IMPACT
Industrial Tariffs	This is the backbone of previous GATT rounds. Tariffs on manufactures average 4.7 percent in rich countries, down from 40 percent in the late 1940s.	Tariffs on industrial goods cut by rich countries by more than one third. Over 40 percent of imports enter duty-free. Key traders scrap duties for pharmaceuticals, construction equipment, medical equipment, steel, beer, furniture, farm equipment, spirits, wood, paper, and toys.	Easier access to world markets for exporters of industrial goods. Lower prices for consumers. Higher-paying jobs through promotion of competitive industries.
Agriculture	High farm subsidies and protected markets in Europe and the United States lead to overproduction and dumping of cut-price surpluses, thereby squeezing exports of more efficient producers. Farm supports by OECD countries amount to $354 billion in 1992.	Trade-distorting subsidies and import barriers cut over six years. Domestic farm supports reduced 20 percent. Subsidized exports sliced 36 percent in value and 21 percent in volume. All import barriers converted to tariffs and cut 36 percent. Japan's and South Korea's closed rice markets gradually open.	Restraint of farm subsidies war. Lower food prices for consumers in currently protected countries. Better market opportunities for efficient producers. Special treatment for developing countries, although higher world prices could hurt poor food-importers.
Services	No international trade rules cover services such as banking and insurance, transportation, tourism, consultancy, telecommunications, construction, accountancy, films and television, and labor. Countries protect industries from foreign competition.	Rules framework set for basic fair-trade principles such as nondiscrimination. Special provisions made for financial services, telecommunications, air transportation, and labor movement. Individual countries pledge market opening in wide range of sectors.	Boost for trade in services, currently worth $1.2 trillion a year in cross-border trade and another $3.0 trillion in business of foreign subsidiaries. Further liberalization to be negotiated.
Intellectual Property	Standards of protection for patents, copyrights, and trademarks vary widely. Trade in counterfeit goods reaches alarming levels.	Extensive agreement reached on patents, copyright, performers' rights, trademarks, geographical indications (wine, cheese, etc.), industrial designs, microchip layout designs, trade secrets. International standards of protection, and requirements for effective enforcement.	Boost for foreign investment and technology transfer, though poor countries with weak patent protection fear higher prices for drugs and seeds.

which created a complex array of quotas and tariffs that affected 65 percent of the annual $248 billion trade in textile and apparel products. Developing countries are monitoring the WTO's dismantling of the MFA to ensure that their goods will have freer access to the markets of developed countries.

Table 7.2 continued

AREA	STATUS PRIOR TO URUGUAY ROUND	PROVISIONS OF URUGUAY ROUND	MAIN IMPACT
Textiles and Clothing	Rich countries restrict since 1974 imports of textiles and clothing through bilateral quotas under Multifibre Arrangement (MFA). Countries maintain high textile import tariffs. Protection raises prices but fails to protect jobs.	MFA quotas progressively dismantled over ten years and tariffs reduced. Developing countries reduce trade barriers. Normal GATT rules apply at end of ten years.	Developing countries able to sell more textiles and clothing abroad. Reduced prices for consumers worldwide because of fairer textiles and clothing trade (worth $248 billion in 1992).
Anti-dumping	Countries allowed to combat dumping (exports priced below domestic prices) with anti-dumping duties. Anti-dumping actions proliferate and are increasingly seen as disguised form of protectionism.	Clearer rules for conduct of investigations and criteria for determining dumping and injury to industry. Duties lapse after five years. Rules covering circumvention of anti-dumping duties by relocating production.	More difficult to use anti-dumping actions for trade harassment. Harder to dodge duties by relocating.
Subsidies	Subsidized exports can be met with countervailing duties but these, like anti-dumping duties, are cause of growing trade tensions and increased disputes.	Definition of which subsidies are legal or not: some prohibited, some nonactionable (e.g., research or regional development). Others actionable if they harm competitors.	Tighter curbs on subsidy use, especially for exports. More difficult to use anti-subsidy actions for trade harassment.
Technical Barriers	Product regulations and standards are extensively used by governments to ensure products are safe for consumers and the environment. Varying standards can be disguised trade barriers.	Better rules to ensure that technical norms and testing and certification procedures do not create unnecessary obstacles to trade and to encourage harmonization around international standards but not preclude governments' opting for higher standards.	Reduction in costs of complying with different standards and regulations. Environmental and consumer groups fear higher standards than international norms may be discouraged.
World Trade Organization	GATT originally envisaged as part of the International Trade Organization (third pillar of Bretton Woods institutions alongside World Bank and IMF). ITO not ratified and GATT still applied provisionally.	World Trade Organization implements results of Uruguay Round. It becomes permanent world trade body covering goods, services, and intellectual property rights with a common disputes procedure.	Boost to the status of international trading rules, and more effective advocacy and policing of the open trading system.

Source: Adapted from *Financial Times*, December 16, 1993. Reprinted with permission.

The General Agreement on Trade in Services (GATS). Another challenge facing the WTO is reducing barriers to trade in services. The Uruguay Round developed a set of principles under which such trade should be conducted. For example, government controls on service trade should be adminis-

GOING GLOBAL

The World Trade Organization, Richard Gere, and China

The World Trade Organization currently operates without the presence of two of the world's most populous nations, China and Russia. Russia's accession has been held up by its revenue crisis and its need for tariff revenues. Once its tariffs meet WTO standards, it will join the organization with little controversy. Such is not the case for China, however.

China began lobbying to become a member of the World Trade Organization as soon as Uruguay Round negotiators announced its creation. The United States and the EU have blocked the Chinese efforts to join the WTO, arguing that China has not sufficiently opened its markets to imported goods. China, for example, restricts the importation of automobiles and forbids most foreign banks from conducting business using the local currency. It also requires Chinese firms to obtain government permission before purchasing goods from foreign firms, a slow and cumbersome process. China has offered to let its firms import goods directly from foreign companies within three years of joining the WTO, a delay not acceptable to Western trade officials.

Complicating the problem is the distaste of many Westerners for a variety of Chinese policies. For example, many Hollywood figures, including Richard Gere and Harrison Ford, have protested China's control of Tibet and systematic destruction of Tibetan culture. After the release of three movies in 1997 critical of its policies regarding Tibet and other issues—*Seven Years in Tibet*, *Red Corner*, and *Kundun*—the Chinese government made it clear to the films' distributors that it was unhappy with foreign meddling in what it believes is a purely internal matter and that it might retaliate against the distributors. But trade officials interpreted the Chinese temper tantrum as indicating that the Chinese were not yet ready to assume the obligations of being a WTO member.

Another element of this problem is the grant of most-favored-nation (MFN) treatment to China. Because China is not a WTO member, its imports do not automatically qualify for MFN treatment. The United States often extends MFN status to non-WTO members as part of its overall trade policy. The ethical implications of continued granting of MFN status to China have been the subject of vigorous debate in the United States. Human rights advocates accuse China of exploiting prison labor and squelching democracy. They argue that the United States should withdraw China's MFN status because of these violations of human rights. In the eyes of human rights activists, China's profitable trade with the United States strengthens the political popularity of the existing regime. Withdrawing MFN status

tered in a nondiscriminatory fashion. One nondiscriminatory approach is the use of **national treatment,** in which a country treats foreign firms the same as it treats domestic firms. If, for example, national insurance regulators require domestic firms to maintain reserves equal to 10 percent of their outstanding policies, then the identical requirement should be imposed on foreign firms operating in that country. However, service industries are very diverse, and few concrete agreements regarding specific service industries were included in the Uruguay Round. The WTO members have agreed to begin negotiating a new GATS agreement by 2000.

Agreement on Trade-Related Aspects of Intellectual Property Rights (TRIPS). **Intellectual property rights** include patents, copyrights, trademarks, and brand names. Entrepreneurs, artists, and inventors have been hurt

would raise the tariffs on many Chinese exports and shrink China's trade surplus with the United States, putting pressure on the Beijing government to reform its policies. For example, China is the primary source of low-priced toys for the U.S. market, which enter the country duty-free. If China's MFN status were revoked, the tariffs imposed on Chinese toys would soar to 70 percent ad valorem. Chinese toys would be knocked out of the U.S. market, to the benefit of toy producers based in other low labor-cost countries and/or at the North Pole.

Defenders of the status quo argue that the United States has more leverage with Beijing policy makers if trading relations between the two countries remain friendly. These defenders note that countries often are more likely to honor human rights when their economic futures look prosperous. Thus, over the long run, human rights are more likely to improve in China if the United States adopts policies that aid that country's economic growth. U.S. firms eager to tap the Chinese market, such as Ford, Caterpillar, and Boeing, also claim that unilateral withdrawal of MFN status by the U.S. government would do little to promote human rights. Rather, the Chinese would simply shift their business to EU, Japanese, and Korean firms, accomplishing little but the loss of U.S. jobs and profits.

China threatened to retaliate against several U.S. movie studios after three films critical of its policies were released in 1997. Chinese government officials denounced Brad Pitt's *Seven Days in Tibet* (seen here relaxing on location) for meddling in its internal affairs. But the controversy has delayed China's admission to the World Trade Organization.

Sources: "China Puts Heat on U.S. Firms to Lobby for 'Most Favored-Nation' Trade Status," *Wall Street Journal,* June 24, 1997, p. A24; "China Is Optimistic on WTO Admission; Boeing Corp. Argues for MFN Renewal," *Wall Street Journal,* April 24, 1997, p. B24; "China Agrees to Let Firms Deal Directly with Foreigners in Bid to Enter WTO," *Wall Street Journal,* March 7, 1997, p. A3; "Can China deliver the goods?," *The Economist,* February 15, 1997, pp. 67–68.

by inadequate enforcement by many countries of laws prohibiting illegal usage, copying, or counterfeiting of intellectual property. These problems are particularly widespread in the music, filmed entertainment, and computer software industries. The Uruguay Round agreement substantially strengthened the protection granted to owners of intellectual property rights and developed enforcement and dispute settlement procedures to punish violators. However, because most such owners reside in the developed countries and many violators live in developing countries, the Uruguay Round negotiators agreed to phase in intellectual property protections over a decade. Not all industries were happy with this concession. For example, the Pharmaceutical Manufacturers Association believes that it grants developing countries carte blanche to continue pirating patented drugs for another ten years.[6]

Trade-Related Investment Measures Agreement (TRIMS).

WTO members are well aware of the relationship between trade and investment: approximately one third of the $6.3 billion of annual trade in goods and services

WTO's TRADING SYSTEM PRINCIPLES

WITHOUT DISCRIMINATION

Members should not discriminate between their trading partners (all are granted "most favoured nation status") nor discriminate between their own and foreign products, services, or nationals (who receive "national treatment").

FREER

Members lower trade barriers through negotiations.

PREDICTABLE

Members agree not to arbitrarily raise trade barriers (including tariffs and non-tarif barriers) against foreign companies, investors, and governments.

MORE COMPETITIVE

The WTO's discourages "unfair" practices such as export subsidies and dumping products below cost to gain market share.

BENEFICIAL FOR LESS DEVELOPED COUNTRIES

The WTO gives less developed nations more time to adjust, greater flexibility, and special privileges.

is between subsidiaries of a parent organization. However, the developing countries believe FDI can be an important mechanism for promoting economic growth, technology transfer, and industrialization, and thus were unwilling to yield much control over it. Accordingly, the TRIMS agreement in the Uruguay Round is but a modest start toward eliminating national regulations on FDI that may distort or restrict trade. The TRIMS agreement affects:

♦ *trade-balancing rules.* Countries may not require foreign investors to limit their imports of inputs to an amount equal to their exports of local production.

♦ *foreign-exchange access.* Countries may not restrict foreign investors' access to foreign exchange.

♦ *domestic sales requirements.* Countries may not require the investor to sell a percentage of a factory's output in the local market.[7]

Under certain circumstances, however, developing countries are able to waive these requirements.

Enforcement of WTO Decisions. The enforcement power of the GATT was notoriously weak. A country found to have violated its GATT obligations by an arbitration panel was in effect asked, "Is it OK if we punish you?" Most countries, as you might expect, answered "no," and there the matter ended. Under WTO rules, a country failing to live up to the agreement—for

GOING GLOBAL

The Slippery Path to Free Trade

The staff of the World Trade Organization had little time to enjoy its creation before they were confronted with a host of very slippery and meaty trade disputes that they were suddenly responsible for solving. Many of these arose because national laws designed to promote some legitimate public purpose had an impact on the ability of other countries to export their goods. Consider the following examples:

Dollar Bananas: The United States and Europe, neither of which produces bananas, have waged a bitter trade war over this tropical fruit for over a decade. To promote the economic development of certain African, Caribbean, and Pacific countries, the EU gives preferential access to bananas grown in these countries. Several U.S. firms, such as Chiquita Brands, which own banana plantations in Guatemala and Honduras, argue that the EU's economic development program discriminates against their so-called "dollar bananas" in violation of the EU's WTO obligations.

Hormone-Treated Beef: Many Canadian and U.S. beef producers boost the productivity of their operations by feeding their cattle fodder laced with hormones that stimulate growth. EU regulations ban the sale of meat from cattle treated with such hormones for health reasons. North American cattlemen argue that there is no scientific basis for the EU's action; rather, they claim, the ban is imposed to protect EU farmers from competition from the more efficient Canadian and U.S. ranching operations.

Protecting Cultural Values: Fearing domination by the broadcast and print media of its southern neighbor, Canada has attempted to protect Canadian broadcasters, filmmakers, newspapers, and magazines. For example, it imposed an 80 percent excise tax on advertising contained in Canadian editions of U.S. magazines that are packed with Canadian advertisements but U.S. editorial content. The U.S. government views this policy as discriminating against U.S. magazines like *Sports Illustrated* or *Reader's Digest.* Similarly, Canada levied a tax on blank tapes, and dedicated the proceeds to a fund to support Canadian artists. The Canadians view these efforts as legitimate attempts to preserve Canada's identity and national pride, while the United States views them as pure protectionism.

How Cheesy Can You Get?: The United States has tried to eliminate imports of unpasteurized soft cheeses, such as Camembert, claiming that such foodstuffs are sources of food poisoning. European cheese makers dismiss the U.S. claims as protectionist; one European delicatessen owner was even more outspoken, denouncing the U.S. actions as a "grave threat to our cultural traditions."

Source: "Cheesed-off producers take battle to U.S." *Financial Times,* September 5, 1997, p. 4.

example, by imposing a nontariff barrier contrary to the WTO agreement—may have a complaint filed against it. If a WTO panel finds the country in violation of the rules, the panel will likely ask the country to eliminate the trade barrier. If the country refuses, the WTO will allow the complaining country to impose trade barriers on the offending country equal to the damage caused by the nontariff barrier. Furthermore, under the rules, the offending country is not allowed to counter-retaliate by imposing new trade barriers against the complainant. "Going Global" reports some trade disputes before the WTO, most of which were unable to be resolved by the GATT because of its lack of enforcement powers.

Although barriers to international trade and investment remain, no one believed that they would come tumbling down like the walls of Jericho as soon as the WTO arrived on the scene. Most experts give the WTO high marks for its accomplishments during its first three years of existence. The WTO's initial actions, such as the sectoral agreements in telecommunications, information technology, and financial services, are laying the foundations for the continued elimination of impediments to international commerce.

Regional Economic Integration

Regional alliances to promote liberalization of international trade are an important feature of the postwar international landscape. Over 100 such agreements are in existence, although not all have had much practical impact. They present international businesses with myriad opportunities and challenges. The past decade in particular has seen a rise in the number and strengthening of trading blocs, as countries seek to integrate their economies more closely in order to open new markets for their firms and lower prices for their consumers. Regional trading blocs are designed to stimulate trade among their members, although some experts are concerned that such increased trade comes at the expense of trade among the world's regions.

Forms of Economic Integration

Regional trading blocs differ significantly in form and function. The characteristic of most importance to international businesses is the extent of economic integration among a bloc's members, because this affects exporting and investment opportunities available to firms from member and nonmember countries. There are five different forms of regional economic integration: free trade area, customs union, common market, economic union, and political union. We next discuss these in order of ascending degree of economic integration.

Free Trade Area. A **free trade area** encourages trade among its members by eliminating trade barriers (tariffs, quotas, and other NTBs) among them. An example of such an arrangement is NAFTA, which reduces tariff and nontariff barriers to trade among Canada, Mexico, and the United States.

Although a free trade area reduces trade barriers among its members, each member is free to establish its own trade policies against nonmembers. As a result, members of free trade areas are often vulnerable to the problem of **trade deflection,** in which nonmembers reroute (or deflect) their exports to the member nation with the lowest external trade barriers. Canada, for example, may use high tariffs or quotas to discourage imports of a given product from nonmembers, while the United States may impose few restrictions on imports of the same good from nonmembers. Taking advantage of the latter's low barriers, nonmembers may deflect their Canada-destined exports by first shipping the good to the United States and then re-exporting it from the United States to Canada. In Chapter 6 we noted that Desmarais & Frère, well before NAFTA was signed, was victimized by trade deflection as Korean manufacturers first shipped photo albums to the United States and then re-exported them from the United States to Canada in order to avoid Canada's antidumping duty on Korean photo albums. To prevent trade deflection from destroying their members' trade policies toward nonmembers, most free trade agreements specify **rules of origin**, which detail the conditions under which a good is classified as a member good or a nonmember good. For example, under NAFTA rules of origin, photo albums qualify for preferential treatment as a North American product only if they undergo substantial processing or assembly in Mexico, Canada, or the United States.

Customs Union. A **customs union** combines the elimination of internal trade barriers among its members with the adoption of common external trade policies toward nonmembers. Because of the uniform treatment of products from nonmember countries, a customs union avoids the trade deflection problem. A firm from a nonmember country pays the same tariff rate on exports to any member of the customs union.

Historically the most important customs union was the *Zollverein,* created in 1834 by several independent principalities in what is now Germany. The eventual unification of Germany in 1870 was hastened by this customs union, which tightened the economic bonds among the Germanic principalities and facilitated their political union. A more contemporary example of a customs union is the Mercosur Accord, an agreement signed by Argentina, Brazil, Paraguay, and Uruguay to promote trade among themselves.

Common Market. A **common market** is a third step along the path to total economic integration. As in a customs union, members of a common market eliminate internal trade barriers among themselves and adopt a common external trade policy toward nonmembers. A common market goes a step further, however, by eliminating barriers that inhibit the movement of factors of production—labor, capital, and technology—among its members. Workers may move from their homeland and practice their profession or trade in any of the other member nations. Firms may locate production facilities, invest in other businesses, and utilize their technologies anywhere within the common market. Productivity within the common market is expected to rise because factors of production are free to locate where the returns to them are highest.

The best example of a common market is the EU, which achieved this status in the 1990s as a result of a 35-year struggle to end barriers to the free movement of labor, capital, and technology. (We discuss the EU in the next section.)

Economic Union. An **economic union** represents full integration of the economies of two or more countries. In addition to eliminating internal trade barriers, adopting common external trade policies, and abolishing restrictions on the mobility of factors of production among members, an economic union requires its members to coordinate their economic policies (monetary policy, fiscal policy, taxation, and social welfare programs) in order to blend their economies into a single entity.

The Belgium-Luxembourg Economic Union, founded in 1922, is the best existing example of this form of economic integration. The economic union of these two European neighbors has been facilitated by the tight bonds between their two currencies. The two nations coordinate their monetary policies and maintain a fixed exchange rate of one Luxembourg franc to one Belgian franc; the Belgian franc is commonly used to conduct business in Luxembourg. However, a much larger economic union is struggling to be born. As the opening case indicates, the EU is in the process of converting its common market into an economic union that will feature the use of a single currency by all participants.

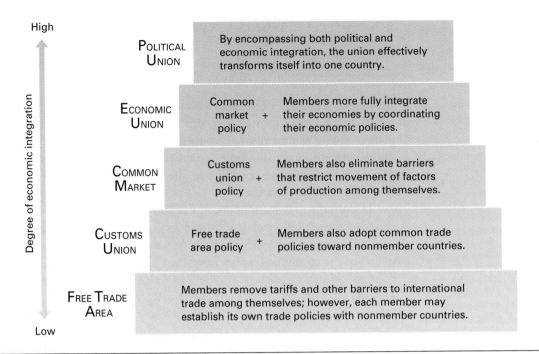

High

Degree of economic integration

POLITICAL UNION — By encompassing both political and economic integration, the union effectively transforms itself into one country.

ECONOMIC UNION — Common market policy + Members more fully integrate their economies by coordinating their economic policies.

COMMON MARKET — Customs union policy + Members also eliminate barriers that restrict movement of factors of production among themselves.

CUSTOMS UNION — Free trade area policy + Members also adopt common trade policies toward nonmember countries.

FREE TRADE AREA — Members remove tariffs and other barriers to international trade among themselves; however, each member may establish its own trade policies with nonmember countries.

Low

FIGURE 7.3

Forms of Economic Integration

Political Union. A political union is the complete political as well as economic integration of two or more countries, thereby effectively making them one country. An example of a political union is the integration of the thirteen separate colonies operating under the Articles of Confederation into a new country, the United States of America. Figure 7.3 summarizes the five forms of economic integration.

The Impact of Economic Integration on Firms

From the viewpoint of an individual firm, regional integration is a two-edged sword. Consider elimination of internal trade barriers, a feature common to all five forms of economic integration. Lowering tariffs within the regional trading bloc opens the markets of member countries to all member country firms. Firms can lower their average production and distribution costs by capturing economies of scale as they expand their customer base within the trading bloc. The lower cost structure will also help the firms compete internationally outside the trading bloc. For example, many Canadian manufacturers supported their country's free trade agreements with the United States. They believed that improved access to the large U.S. market would allow longer production runs in Canadian factories, thereby lowering their average costs and making Canadian goods more competitive in international markets inside and outside the free trade area. However, elimination of trade barriers also exposes a firm's home market to competition from firms located in other member countries, thus threatening less efficient firms. A regional trading bloc may also attract FDI from nonmember countries, as firms outside of the bloc seek the benefits of insider status by establishing manufacturing facilities within the bloc. Most non-European MNCs, including General Mills, Toyota, and Samsung, have invested heavily in the EU to take advantage of Europe's increased economic integration. These investments bolster the productivity of European workers and increase the choices available to European consumers but threaten established European firms such as Unilever, Renault, and Siemens.

Typically each form of economic integration confers benefits on the national economy as a whole but often hurts specific sectors and communities within the economy. As a result, negotiating any form of economic integration is not easy. The special-interest groups that will be damaged will lobby against any agreement. For example, U.S. and Canadian auto workers lobbied against NAFTA, fearing that Ford, GM, and Chrysler would shift production to Mexico to take advantage of its lower-cost labor. As a result of such internal political pressures, few economic integration treaties are "pure"; most contain some exemptions to quiet politically powerful domestic special-interest groups.

The growth of regional trading blocs has been controversial because of their uncertain impact on the global market. Trading blocs promote the efficiency of the world economy to the extent that they reallocate production from high-cost producers to lower-cost producers within the trading bloc, a phenomenon called **trade creation.** Efficiency is hurt, however, by **trade diversion,** the shifting of production to higher-cost internal producers from lower-cost external producers, whose products become uncompetitive in the internal market after the higher-cost internal producers are no longer subjected to tariffs within the trading bloc. The extent of trade creation relative to trade diversion determines whether the regional trading bloc benefits international trade.[8]

For example, suppose that prior to the formation of the EU, apples grown in French orchards cost $1.00 a kilogram, while those grown in German orchards cost $1.20. If Germany were to impose a $0.25 per kilogram specific tariff on imported apples, lower-cost French apples would be excluded from the German market because there they would cost $1.25 a kilogram ($1.00 + $0.25 for the tariff). Under the EU, however, the German tariff would be abolished. Trade would be created because apple production would shift from high-cost Germany to lower-cost France.

But to complicate matters, assume Chilean orchards can produce apples for only $0.85 a kilogram, thereby making Chile a lower-cost producer than either France or Germany. Prior to the formation of the EU, Chilean apples would thus be cheaper than French apples in the German market. (For simplicity, we assume transportation costs are zero.) Chile's crop could be successfully sold in the German market; it would cost $1.10 a kilogram ($0.85 + $0.25 for the tariff), or $0.10 less than German-grown apples and $0.15 less than French-grown apples. Under the EU, however, Germany's tariff on French apples would be eliminated but not its tariff on Chilean apples. As a result, French apples would be cheaper in the German market (at $1.00 a kilogram) than would Chilean apples (at $1.10 a kilogram). Trade would be diverted from the low-cost external producer, Chile, to a higher-cost internal producer, France, thereby reducing the overall efficiency of the global economy.

The European Union

The most important regional trading bloc in the world today is the European Union (EU). The EU's fifteen member countries, with a combined population of 372 million, compose the world's richest market, which has a total GDP of $8.4 trillion, or 30 percent of the world economy. (See Table 7.3 and Map 7.1.)

TABLE 7.3

The European Union, 1995 Data

MEMBERS	POPULATION (MILLIONS)	GDP (BILLIONS)	PER CAPITA GDP*	DATE OF ENTRY
Original Six				
Belgium	10.1	$ 269.1	$21,660	1957
France	58.1	1,536.1	21,030	1957
Luxembourg	0.4	16.6	37,930	1957
Germany	81.9	2,415.8	20,070	1957
Italy	57.2	1,086.9	19,870	1957
Netherlands	15.5	395.9	19,950	1957
Later Entrants				
Denmark	5.2	172.2	21,230	1973
Ireland	3.6	60.8	15,680	1973
United Kingdom	58.5	1,105.8	19,260	1973
Greece	10.5	90.6	11,710	1981
Spain	39.2	558.6	14,520	1986
Portugal	9.9	102.3	12,670	1986
Recent Entrants				
Austria	8.1	$ 233.4	$21,250	1995
Finland	5.1	125.4	17,760	1995
Sweden	8.8	228.7	18,540	1995
Total, 15 Members	372.1	$8,398.2	$19,033	

*GDP per capita adjusted by World Bank for purchasing power parity.
Source: World Bank, *World Development Report,* 1997.

The EU's beginnings stem from the 1952 creation of the European Coal and Steel Community, which was designed to restore those two industries to profitability after World War II. The European Economic Community (EEC) was established in 1957 when six countries (see Table 7.3) signed the **Treaty of Rome.** Under the treaty, they pledged to create a common market by eliminating internal trade barriers, developing common external trade policies, and improving mobility of labor, capital, and technology within the EEC. A third organization, the European Atomic Energy Community, was created in 1958. Officially these three communities formed the European Communit*ies* (EC), although the singular form of the noun was often used unofficially. In November 1993, the name of the EC was changed to the European Union (EU) as a result of the Maastricht Treaty.

Completing the Common Market—EC '92

For most of the EU's history, the Treaty of Rome's vision of a common market permitting free movement of goods, services, labor, and capital was nothing more than a cruel mirage. The reality through the 1980s was that most firms wanting to serve the entire EU market continued to have to meet numerous, and sometimes contradictory, sets of national laws and regulations. In practice, the member

MAP 7.1

The European Union

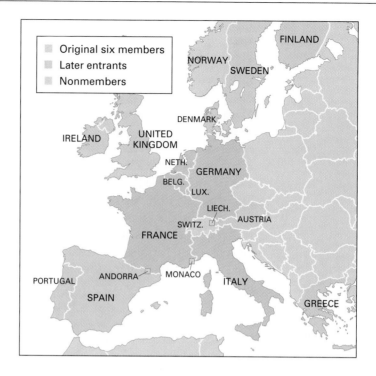

Original six members
Later entrants
Nonmembers

FINLAND
NORWAY
SWEDEN
DENMARK
IRELAND
UNITED KINGDOM
NETH.
GERMANY
BELG.
LUX.
LIECH.
SWITZ.
AUSTRIA
FRANCE
ANDORRA
MONACO
ITALY
PORTUGAL
SPAIN
GREECE

nations moved cautiously in implementing the common market because of political pressures from domestic special-interest groups.

As a result, numerous conflicting regulations adopted by the members, which affected nearly every good and service purchased by Europeans, hindered trade and the completion of the common market. For example, Spain required that keyboards sold there contain a "tilde" key, an accent mark commonly used in the Spanish language. Italy required pasta to be made of durum wheat, a requirement not imposed by other EU members. And Belgium allowed yogurt to be colored with dyes extracted from beetroot, but cherries in the yogurt could not be so colored; Germany, in contrast, allowed the cherries to be colored using beetroot dyes, but not the yogurt. The conflicting regulations restricted the ability of Belgian yogurt producers to sell cherry yogurt in Germany and German producers to sell cherry yogurt in Belgium unless a producer established two different production processes to sell yogurt in the two countries.

The EU initially relied on a process of **harmonization** to eliminate such conflicting national regulations. The EU encouraged member countries to voluntarily adopt common, EU-wide ("harmonized") regulations affecting intra-EU trade in goods and services and movement of resources. The harmonization process moved slowly, however, as domestic political forces within the member states resisted change. For example, Belgian yogurt manufacturers balked at Belgium's agreeing to adopt Germany's yogurt regulations; such a concession would raise the level of competition they would face in the domestic yogurt market and force them to bear the cost of retooling their production processes to meet German regulatory standards. German yogurt manufacturers were unwilling to adopt Belgian regulatory standards, because they would have to bear the costs incurred in changing their production processes as well as increased competition in their home market. EU producers of all goods spent an estimated $260 billion (in 1988 dollars) annually to comply with the different national regulations.[9] These increased costs raised the prices European consumers had to pay and reduced the global competitiveness of European manufacturers.

Displeased with the slow progress toward the creation of the common market envisioned by the Treaty of Rome, in 1985 the European Commission (one of the EU's four governing bodies) issued the *White Paper on Completing the Internal Market.* The *White Paper* called for accelerated progress on ending all trade barriers and restrictions on the free movement of goods, services, capital, and labor among members. Accepting the vision of the *White Paper*, the members in February 1986 signed the Single European Act, which took effect on July 1, 1987. The act was intended to help complete the formation of the internal market by December 31, 1992, a goal labeled by the popular press **EC '92.** (At the time, the EU was called the European Community, hence EC '92.) In the act, the internal market was defined as "an area without internal frontiers in which the free movement of goods, persons, services, and capital is ensured." The implications of completing the internal market were more directly expressed by Ernest Bevin, former British Foreign Secretary. When asked about his vision of Europe without frontiers, he replied: "To be able to take a ticket at Victoria Station and go anywhere I damn well please."[10]

Under the Single European Act, 282 broad regulatory changes had to be made to complete the internal market. While not all have been completely implemented, substantial progress toward EC '92 has been made. These changes can be grouped in three categories: physical barriers, technical barriers, and fiscal barriers.

Physical Barriers. The first goal of EC '92 was the removal of physical barriers to the free flow of goods, services, capital, and people. Prior to EC '92, shipments among members were stopped at each national border for tax collection, statistics collection, confirmation of compliance with national quotas, administrative checks for plant and animal diseases, and other bureaucratic necessities. On New Year's Day 1993, these requirements were eliminated for intra-EU trade. Abolishing these border formalities is estimated to have saved Europeans between $15 and $27 billion a year. Substantial progress has also been made in freeing the movement of people. In 1990, Germany, France, and the Benelux countries signed the **Schengen Agreement,** abolishing passport controls at their common borders. EC '92 and the Treaty of Amsterdam (discussed later in the chapter) further extended the reach of the Schengen Agreement to most other EU countries. However, Ireland and the United Kingdom continue to scrutinize passports in order to control immigration, terrorism, and illegal activities.

Technical Barriers. According to the Treaty of Rome, goods, services, labor, and capital were supposed to move freely among members. But differing national product standards restricted trade because manufacturers had to either abandon certain markets or modify their products to meet members' conflicting regulations. The harmonization of technical standards resulting from EC '92 means that a manufacturer has to meet only one set of standards in order to legally sell its goods in each member country. For example, Belgian cherry yogurt can now be sold anywhere within the EU. However, some controversies still remain. For example, the EU has not yet resolved what products can be marketed as chocolates. At issue is the milk content of "true" chocolates, as well as whether vegetable fats can be used as substitutes for cocoa butter. Belgium's chocolatiers believe that British and Irish confections containing vegetable fats and high milk content should be labeled "household milk chocolates," presumably so that consumers will not be duped into thinking they are buying "real" chocolates of the sort for which Belgium is world famous. British chocolate manufacturers, like Cadbury, dismiss these claims, arguing that their products are not inferior, just different, and should be allowed to be marketed as chocolates.[11]

The technical standards being adopted by the EU are important to firms of nonmember countries. These firms may be shut out of the European market or face expensive modifications if they fail to meet EU product standards. The EU is working through several European standards-setting organizations, such as the European Committee for Standardization, to establish EU-wide product certification and testing standards. The process is open: representatives of other international organizations, such as the Geneva-based International Standards Organization, and national organizations, such as the American National Standards Institute, may make presentations to the EU's standards setters. Nonmember countries, such as the United States, are also trying to ensure that the standards adopted do not limit their firms' access to the EU market. However, governmental negotiators are often unaware of the impact of technical standards and act only if affected firms notify them of prospective problems. Firms that ignore the EU's deliberations now may pay the price later if standards are imposed that are expensive to meet. One survey of medium-sized U.S. firms, for example, indicated that 48 percent had not even heard of ISO 9000, a set of quality standards adopted by the EU and commonly used in Asia as well. Only 8 percent were planning to adopt these standards. The remaining 92 percent will have difficulty marketing their goods internationally because of their ignorance and inattention.[12]

Fiscal Barriers. European countries rely on value-added taxes (VAT) as a primary source of revenue. In assessing a VAT, a country taxes each firm in the production-distribution process based on the value it adds to the product. The EU has been concerned that if VAT rates differ substantially among members, consumers will travel to buy goods in countries with lower VAT rates, thereby eroding the tax base of the high-tax country. For example, because French alcohol and tobacco prices are lower than British prices because of tax differences, British citizens have been flocking to Calais and other French ports to stock up on low-priced liquor and cigarettes, to the chagrin of British Inland Revenue officials who are losing nearly $3 million daily in taxes. Unless the gaps between VAT rates are reduced, border controls may need to be reinstituted in high-VAT countries in order to collect additional VAT taxes from their residents, thereby defeating EC '92's goal of

Pressure by the EU to raise value-added taxes on art imported from non-EU countries threatens the profitability of prestigious London auctioneers like Sotheby's and Christie's, who are fearful that owners of fine art will shift their business to New York City.[13]

eliminating physical barriers among members. The EU is proposing that all national VAT taxes fall within certain narrow bands: 14 to 20 percent for most goods and a reduced rate of 4 to 9 percent for basic necessities. Controlling VATs in this way would reduce the incentives for EU residents to travel to countries with lower VAT rates to purchase goods.[14] However, harmonization of taxes has proceeded rather slowly, because any EU-mandated rules regarding fiscal matters must receive unanimous approval by its members. Since tax policies often reflect a complex interaction of national cultural, social, and political forces, achieving EU-wide agreement on tax policy has been most difficult.[15]

The Benefits of EC '92. The EU's substantial progress toward completing its internal market offers the opportunity for firms both in Europe and elsewhere to sell their goods in a large, rich market. While firms in EU member countries have gained improved access to a larger market, they also face increased competition in their home markets from other members' firms. This increased competition benefits consumers throughout the EU. Marketing, production, and R&D costs have been reduced, since firms generally have to comply with only one, EU-wide set of regulations instead of fifteen separate sets of national regulations. Many firms have been able to restructure their European manufacturing operations to capture economies of scale and lower their production costs. For example, Samsung shifted its European color television production, which was previously split between factories in Portugal and Spain, to its plant in Billingham, England. It dedicated its Spanish factory to producing VCRs for the entire EU market and its Portuguese factory to supplying parts for all of its European operations. Also, in 1992 the firm purchased an East German picture tube manufacturer, Werk für Fernsehelektronik, to supply its European operations. Samsung determined that the economies of scale obtained by this realignment of its operations would lower its manufacturing costs, improve the quality of its products, and create new jobs for European workers.[16] And the EU has been a magnet for new investment from other foreign firms eager to enter the lucrative European market and benefit from EC '92. U.S. FDI in the EU has risen from $84 billion in 1985, when the *White Paper* was first issued, to $390 billion in 1996. Similarly, over 500 Japanese companies have established operations in the EU since 1985.[17]

From Common Market to Economic Union

Going beyond the initial concept of the EU as a common market, many Europeans argued for the creation of an economic union with common defense and foreign policies.[18] Heeding this call, the EU's Council of Ministers met in the Dutch city of Maastricht in December 1991 to discuss the EU's economic and political future. The result was a new treaty that amended the Treaty of Rome; this new treaty was known formally as the **Treaty on European Union** and informally as the **Maastricht Treaty.** After ratification by the then twelve EU members, the Maastricht Treaty came into force on November 1, 1993.

The Maastricht Treaty rests on three "pillars" designed to further Europe's economic and political integration:

I A new agreement to create common foreign and defense policies among members

2 A new agreement to cooperate on police, judicial, and public safety matters

3 The old familiar EC, with new provisions to create an economic and monetary union among member states

In recognition of the increasing integration of Europe, the treaty changed the name of the European Community to the European Union. Additionally, the Maastricht Treaty granted citizens the right to live, work, vote, and run for election anywhere within the EU and strengthened the powers of the EU's legislative body, the European Parliament, in budgetary, trade, cultural, and health matters. The treaty also created a new **cohesion fund,** a means of funneling economic development aid to countries whose per capita GDP is less than 90 percent of the EU average (these countries are Greece, Ireland, Portugal, and Spain).

Without a doubt, the most important aspect of the Maastricht Treaty is the creation of the **economic and monetary union (EMU).** The goal of the EMU is to create a single currency for the EU, thereby eliminating exchange-rate risks and the costs of converting currencies for intra-EU trade. EU officials believe the creation of a single currency, which will be called the *euro*, will save Europeans $25 to $30 billion annually in such costs. Companies expect to capture significant savings, which should flow right to their bottom lines. Germany's Bosch Company estimates that its annual currency conversion costs will fall by $28.5 million due to the single currency, although it also expects its one-time costs of converting its accounting and financial systems to the euro may run as much as $30 million. Imperial Chemical Industries, the U.K.'s largest chemical manufacturer, expects to save almost $90 million in currency conversion costs annually once the euro is in place.[19] European financial services firms hope that the euro will become as important in international commerce as the U.S. dollar or the yen.

Creation of a single currency is not without controversy, however. Its development implies members will lose the ability to control their own domestic money supplies and economic destinies. National governments facing depressions will be deprived of one tool for reviving their economies and will become more vulnerable to losing elections because of short-term pocketbook issues. Conversely, some Europeans are concerned that the EU's central bankers will adopt inflationary policies, a fear that is particularly noticeable among the German electorate.

Creation of the EMU is proceeding in three steps:

1 Full membership in the exchange-rate mechanism (ERM) of the European Monetary System by all EU members. This step is deemed to have been reached, even though the United Kingdom and Italy were forced to withdraw "temporarily" from the ERM in September 1992.

2 The creation of the European Monetary Institute in January 1994. The **European Monetary Institute (EMI)** is charged with overseeing members' monetary policies to ensure that they promote the eventual creation of a single currency. In 1998, the EMI will be transformed into the European Central Bank, and given responsibility for conducting monetary policy and exchange-rate policy for all EMU members in conjunction with the national central banks. To allay symbolically the fears that its policies might be inflationary, the European Central Bank (ECB) has been located in Frankfurt, the home of the strongly anti-inflationary

Bundesbank. However, as the opening case indicates, financial experts are divided over whether the ECB will adopt the Bundesbank's tight, anti-inflationary monetary policies or the more expansionary, jobs-oriented policies of the French.

3 Complete economic and monetary union, which is to occur on January 1, 1999. At this time "the rates of conversion between the euro and the participating national currencies will be irrevocably fixed and the euro will become a currency in its own right."[20] For the next three years, businesses and the banking system will gradually convert to using the euro for accounting and settlement purposes. At the beginning of 2002, euro banknotes and coins will be placed into circulation. Current plans are for national currencies to be withdrawn from circulation six months after the introduction of euro banknotes and coins.

In order to participate in the EMU, EU members must meet certain **convergence criteria,** which include the following:

1 A country's inflation rate must be no more than 1.5 percentage points higher than that of the average of the three EU countries with the lowest inflation rates.

2 A country's long-term interest rates must be no more than 2 percentage points higher than that of the average of the three EU countries with the lowest long-term interest rates.

3 In the two years prior to joining the EMU, a country's exchange rate must have remained within the normal fluctuation margins of the exchange-rate mechanism of the European Monetary System and it must not have devalued its currency.

4 A country's government budget deficit must be no more than 3 percent of its GDP.

5 A country's outstanding government debt must be trending toward no more than 60 percent of its GDP.

Effectively, these conditions require convergence of the monetary and fiscal policies of the participating countries. This is a necessary condition for the long-term survival of any fixed exchange-rate system. Only those EU members that meet these criteria are allowed to join the EMU. However, Denmark, Sweden, and the United Kingdom chose not to become charter members of the single currency bloc. Greece did not meet the convergence criteria. As a result, in May 1998 the EU announced that eleven of its members would participate in the EMU on January 1, 1999.

The latest step the EU has taken toward integration is the **Treaty for Europe** (more popularly known as the **Treaty of Amsterdam**), which was signed in 1997. Among the more important components of the Treaty of Amsterdam are

♦ A strong commitment to attack the EU's chronic high levels of unemployment, particularly among younger citizens

♦ Strengthening the role of the EU Parliament by expanding the number of areas that require use of the "co-decision" procedure (discussed below)

◆ Establishment of a two-track system, allowing groups of members to proceed with economic and political integration faster than the EU as a whole.

Governing the European Union

The EU members have created a supranational and intergovernmental government that develops, implements, and administers its programs and resolves conflicts among members' diverse interests. The EU is governed by four organizations that perform its executive, administrative, legislative, and judicial functions:

- ◆ The Council of the European Union (headquartered in Brussels)
- ◆ The European Commission (also Brussels-based)
- ◆ The European Parliament (which normally meets in Strasbourg, France)
- ◆ The European Court of Justice (sitting in Luxembourg)

Because these governmental bodies establish the rules by which international businesses compete within the EU, we discuss them in some detail.

The Council of the European Union. The **Council of the European Union** (sometimes called the Council of Ministers) is composed of fifteen representatives, each selected directly by and responsible to his or her home government. Normally, a country's foreign minister represents his or her country at the Council meetings. However, a country's representative may differ depending on the Council's agenda. For example, if the Council is dealing with farm policies, each country may send its minister of agriculture to the Council meeting. The Council presidency rotates among the members every six months. In Council decisions, France, Germany, Italy, and the United Kingdom have 10 votes each; Spain has 8; Belgium, Greece, the Netherlands, and Portugal, 5 each; Austria and Sweden, 4 each; Denmark, Finland, and Ireland, 3 each; and Luxembourg, 2. The allocation of votes is in rough proportion to the population and economic importance of the members.

The Council is the EU's most powerful decision-making body. Each representative pursues the interests of his or her home government. The Council's strong powers reflect the hesitancy of the member states to surrender power to Brussels (shorthand for the EU government) on issues they view as vital to their national interests. As a result, some Council decisions require unanimous approval. On matters perceived to be less threatening to national interests, Council decisions require only a qualified majority (62 out of a total 87 votes) for passage. Effectively, a coalition of two large countries and three smaller countries can block a decision. However, the EU strives to create consensus on all issues and often slows its deliberations in order to develop compromises amenable to all the members, even when unanimity is not required. In 1994, for example, 86 percent of Council decisions were made unanimously.

The European Commission. The **European Commission** is composed of twenty people selected for five-year terms. The smaller EU countries each nominate one citizen to serve on the Commission; the larger countries select two. However, once these individuals are in office, their loyalty is to the EU itself, not to their home countries. The Commission's primary mandate is to be the "guardian of the Treaties." The Commission also acts as the EU's administrative branch and manages the EU's $100 billion annual budget. Its functions include the following:

- ♦ It proposes legislation to be considered by the Council.
- ♦ It implements the provisions of the Treaty of Rome and other EU treaties.
- ♦ It protects the EU's interests in political debates, particularly in Council deliberations.
- ♦ It has extensive powers in implementing the EU's customs union, the Common Agricultural Policy (CAP), and the completion of the internal market.
- ♦ It administers the EU's permanent bureaucracy, which employs about 15,000 people—popularly known as "Eurocrats"—two thirds of whom work at Commission headquarters in Brussels. (Because the EU has eleven official languages, one fifth of the Commission's employees are engaged in translation services!)

The European Parliament. The **European Parliament** comprises 626 representatives elected in national elections to serve five-year terms. Seats are allocated in rough proportion to a country's population, but the allocation also reflects political jockeying among members. For example, Germany has 99 seats, while France, Italy, and the United Kingdom are allocated 87 seats each, even though Germany's population is at least 40 percent larger than that of any of the other three (see Table 7.3). Of the EU's governing bodies, the Parliament was originally the weakest. Initially it possessed only a consultative role in EU policy making. However, it has used its budgetary powers to enlarge its influence within the EU's governing institutions, and it also gained additional powers under the Maastricht Treaty. On many issues, such as health, culture, education, and consumer protection, the Parliament shares decision-making power with the Council through the **co-decision procedure** (see Fig. 7.4). If the Council and the Parliament cannot agree on a common policy in these areas, the Parliament can veto any Council decision. The Treaty of Amsterdam, when ratified by the member states, will expand the use of the co-decision procedure, thereby strengthening the Parliament's power.

The European Court of Justice. The **European Court of Justice** consists of fifteen judges who serve six-year terms. It interprets EU law and ensures that members follow EU regulations and policies. Because national governments carry out the EU's policies, many cases reaching the Court are referred from national courts asking it to interpret EU law. For example, as noted in Chapter 6, the Court declared Germany's 450-year-old beer purity law regulating beer additives illegal, ruling that the law unreasonably restricted imports into Germany.

The Legislative Process. The legislative process in the EU has never been simple, although it was once understandable, as captured in the catchphrase "the Commission proposes, the Parliament advises, and the Council disposes." As the Parliament has gained increased powers, the complexity of passing legislation has

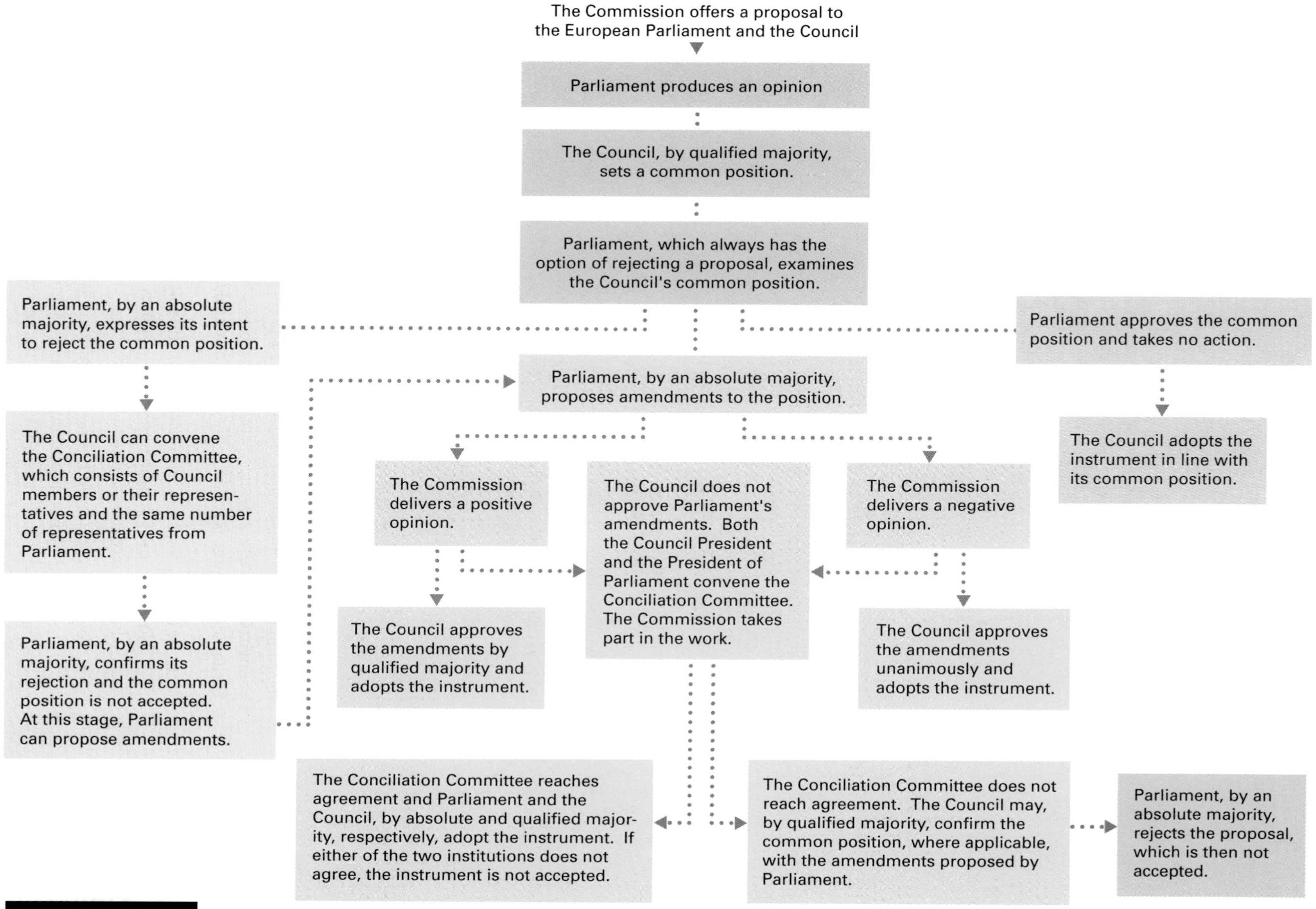

The Co-Decision Procedure (Article 189b of the Treaty on European Union)

Source: *The European Union*, Luxembourg: Office for Official Publications of the European Communities, 1997, pp 24–25.

Figure 7.4

GOING GLOBAL

Lobbying the European Union

The EU's government is engaged in many activities that affect international businesses. For example, the EU has decided that at least 50 percent of the programs broadcast on TV stations in its member countries must be European in origin. The effect of this regulation is to shrink the market for movies and TV shows produced in the United States, Mexico, Australia, and other countries. Because of the impact of the EU's decisions on the opening or closing of the enormous European market to international businesses, most countries maintain diplomatic relationships with the EU to ensure the EU does not disregard their economic interests. The United States, for example, maintains a United States Mission to the European Union, led by a senior State Department official with ambassadorial status.

But savvy international businesspeople do not rely solely on their home governments to protect them from adverse EU regulations. The first step is understanding the power relationships within the EU—particularly between the Council, which defends national interests, and the Commission, which promotes the interests of an integrated Europe. Firms threatened by pending EU regulations can adopt two strategies:

1 They may lobby the Commission and its elaborate bureaucracy to adopt regulations more beneficial to their interests. Because the Commission must continually balance the often diverse interests of EU members, firms can often influence the Commission to add their interests to the long list of other factors that it will consider in proposing legislation to the Council. Because of the commitment of the Commission to the completion of the EU's internal market, firms have found that arguments promoting increased European integration are particularly well received by Eurocrats. For example, the Commission dropped proposed franchising regulations after U.S. firms convinced its staff that the pending regulations would hinder European integration.

2 Firms may lobby an ally on the Council. For example, remembering that "all politics is local," Japanese automakers that built assembly plants in the United Kingdom were able to enlist the help of the British representative on the Council—who was interested in preserving jobs in his country—when French and Italian automakers were urging the EU to adopt regulations prejudicial to those U.K. assembly plants.

Sources: James N. Gardner, "Lobbying, European-Style," *Europe*, November 1991 (Number 311), pp. 29–30; "European Bureaucrats Are Writing the Rules Americans Will Live By," *Wall Street Journal*, May 17, 1989, p. A1; "Lobbying Brussels in Anticipation of 1992," *Wall Street Journal*, March 6, 1989, p. A12.

increased exponentially, as Fig. 7.4, which depicts decision-making under the co-decision process, shows. On issues where the co-decision process is not used (such as environmental, research, or transport issues), the process is simpler and the Parliament's power is weaker. This is summarized by the following five steps:

I In most cases, the Commission has the sole right to initiate legislation. Normally, the Commission's staff proposes legislation to the Commission, which it may adopt, amend, or kill.

2 Legislation approved by the Commission is sent to the Parliament and a broad-based labor and industry advisory group, the Economic and Social Committee, for their opinions on the matter. The Commission may amend its proposal based on the opinions of these two bodies.

3 The legislation is sent to the Council of Ministers. Each representative sends the proposed legislation to senior officials of his or her home government to determine if the legislation is in the member's best interests.

4 Having heard all the diverse views on the proposed legislation, the Council then votes on the issue. Depending on the nature of the proposal, unanimity or a qualified majority of the Council's votes is needed to pass new legislation.

5 Each member's government must pass national legislation to implement the new EU policy.

Because the EU prefers to develop a strong consensus on issues among its members before it adopts new legislation, transforming a Commission proposal into an EU law and then implementing that law into national legislation often takes years. The complicated governance arrangements of the EU reflect the ongoing struggle between the members' desire to retain their national sovereignty and their desire to create a supranational government with an international political and economic stature equal to those of the United States and Japan. (As "Going Global" suggests, many MNCs exploit this power struggle to their benefit.) The member countries have granted EU governing bodies power over trade and agricultural policy. The EU and its members share responsibility for formulating transportation policy and environmental policy. Many other areas of responsibility remain with members' governments. The debate over national sovereignty versus supranational government is manifested in another way: while EU policies are formulated supranationally, they must be implemented by members at a national level.[21]

Other EU Controversies. The members of the European Union have made remarkable progress in implementing the goals of the Treaty of Rome. Political conflicts still remain, of course. One divisive issue is state aid to industry. Under EU rules, national governments may not provide subsidies to firms that "distort" competition. Yet many governments are loath to let domestic firms go bankrupt, especially if local jobs are threatened. This is a particular problem in the airline industry, where privately owned carriers like British Airways, Lufthansa, and KLM are outraged by the continuation of state subsidies to state-owned Air France, Alitalia, Iberia, TAP, and Olympic Airlines, whom they compete with in intra-EU markets. A similar problem is plaguing the auto industry: state aid to firms like SEAT, Renault, and Alfa-Romeo adds to overcapacity in Europe's auto industry, making it more difficult for unsubsidized firms like BMW or Ford of Europe to compete profitably. In another conflict, the poorer members, led by Spain, successfully argued for increasing the EU's spending on economic development in its poorer regions, against the wishes of the United Kingdom. And France and the United Kingdom continue to squabble over the EU's Common Agricultural Policy, which disproportionately benefits French farmers to the detriment of British interests and hurts European MNCs by poisoning relationships between the United States and the EU. Other countries, such as Denmark, are concerned about the paucity of democracy within the EU. They believe more power should be given to the EU's only directly elected governing body, the European Parliament.[22]

Perhaps the most important issue, however, is whether, how, and when the membership of the EU should be expanded. A dozen countries have applied for membership in the EU. In the negotiations leading to the signing of the Treaty of

Amsterdam, EU members agreed that the first group of countries to be considered for admission to the EU would be Cyprus, the Czech Republic, Estonia, Hungary, Poland, and Slovenia. Consideration of the applications of Turkey and five other former Soviet Bloc countries was deferred. The members remain divided on many other aspects of expansion. Some members believe that the EU should broaden its scope quickly, while others believe the EU should move slowly. Another group believes that the governance of the EU will have to change to accommodate the larger number of members, perhaps by curtailing the powers of the Council of Ministers, which protects national interests. Others assert that the EU will have to slash its aid to farmers and poorer regions if these new—and poorer—countries are added to the EU.[23] At the core of the disagreement is the **"wider vs. deeper"** question. "Wider" proponents argue that the EU should rapidly broaden its membership, even if that makes it more difficult for the EU to fully integrate the economies of its members and to develop common foreign and defense policies. "Deeper" proponents believe that the EU should expand more slowly, carefully making sure that each new member is ready to participate in all of the EU's economic and political initiatives. At the heart of the wider vs. deeper controversy are competing visions of the future of the EU: is the primary mission of the EU to promote trade and investment or is its primary mission to promote the political integration of Europe?

Other Regional Trading Blocs

The EU's success in enriching its members through trade promotion has stimulated the development of other regional trading blocs. Every inhabited continent now contains at least one regional trading group. Europe, for example, has many other smaller trading blocs, such as the **European Free Trade Association (EFTA).** Its members are Iceland, Liechtenstein, Norway, and Switzerland. The first three of these countries have joined with the European Union to create a common market known as the **European Economic Area,** which promotes the free movement of goods, services, labor, and capital among its eighteen members. Members of the Commonwealth of Independent States have created a free trade area as well. Russia, Belarus, Kazakhstan, and Kyrgyzstan have gone one step further, forming a customs union in 1995.

The North American Free Trade Agreement

Another important example of regional economic integration is the North American Free Trade Agreement (NAFTA). Implemented in 1994 to reduce barriers to trade and investment among Canada, Mexico, and the United States, NAFTA builds on the 1988 Canadian-U.S. Free Trade Agreement. Canada and the United States enjoy the world's largest bilateral trading relationship, with two-way trade totaling $327.5 billion in 1996. The United States is Mexico's largest trading partner, while Mexico is the third-largest trading partner of the United States (after Canada and Japan). However, trade between Canada and Mexico, while growing, is rather small.

NAFTA reflects the continuation of a decade-long process of opening up the economies of Canada and Mexico. Former Canadian Prime Minister Brian Mulroney worried in the 1980s that Canada's small domestic market limited the ability of Canadian firms to capture economies of scale, raised their costs, and hurt their international competitiveness. In 1985 he sought to strengthen economic ties between Canada and the United States. After several years of negotiation, Mulroney and President Ronald Reagan signed the Canadian-U.S. Free Trade Agreement on January 2, 1988. While U.S. and Canadian negotiators were hammering out the details of this agreement, President Carlos Salinas de Gortai of Mexico was undertaking substantial reforms of the Mexican economy after his election in 1988, including dismantling the high tariff walls that had protected Mexican manufacturers and promoting foreign investment. Salinas also undertook massive privatization of state-owned businesses, selling off key firms in the transportation, banking, and telecommunications industries. As part of this economic development and modernization program, Salinas proposed broadening the Canadian-U.S. Free Trade Agreement to include Mexico. After three years of negotiations and then ratification by the participating governments, NAFTA became effective in January 1994.

The agreement promises an increasing integration of the North American economies. Over fifteen years, tariff walls will be lowered, NTBs reduced, and investment opportunities increased for firms located in the three countries. Table 7.4 shows NAFTA's main features. However, note from the table that many industries have received special treatment in the agreement. Negotiators from all three countries recognized the political sensitivity of certain issues and industries and chose to compromise on their treatment within NAFTA to ensure the agreement's ratification. For example, because Canada fears being dominated by U.S. media, NAFTA allows Canada to continue to bar foreign investments in its culture industries (publishing, music, television, radio, cable, and film). Similarly, Mexico may maintain control over foreign investments in its energy sector, while the United States may bar foreign ownership in its airline and broadcasting industries.

U.S. and Canadian negotiators also were concerned that firms from nonmembers might locate so-called screwdriver plants in Mexico as a means of evading U.S. and Canadian tariffs. A **screwdriver plant** is a factory in which very little transformation of the product is undertaken. Speaking metaphorically, in such factories the only tool workers need is the screwdriver they use to assemble a product. So the negotiators developed detailed rules of origin that defined whether a good was North American in origin and thus qualified for preferential tariff status. In the automobile industry, for example, U.S. and Canadian labor unions worried that European and Asian automakers would exploit the treaty by producing major components elsewhere and then establishing a North American factory merely to assemble motor vehicles, thereby causing the loss of jobs at Canadian and U.S. parts-producing factories. To diminish this problem, NAFTA specifies that for an automobile to qualify as a North American product, 62.5 percent of its value must be produced in Canada, Mexico, or the United States. Similarly, to protect textile industry jobs, clothing and other textile products must use North American–produced fibers in order to benefit from NAFTA's preferential tariff treatment.

Most experts believe that NAFTA has benefited all three countries, although the gains have been more modest than most NAFTA advocates expected. For example, some studies have indicated that during its first three years, NAFTA by itself raised the U.S. GDP by $13 billion, U.S. exports to Mexico by $12 billion, and U.S. imports from Mexico by $5 billion annually. However, isolating the direct impact of NAFTA is difficult, because of other economic changes that occurred during this time period, such as the reduction in trade barriers mandated by the Uruguay Round, the drastic devaluation of the Mexican peso in December

TABLE 7.4

What Is NAFTA?

GENERAL PROVISIONS	INDUSTRIES	SIDE AGREEMENTS	OTHER DEALS
Tariffs reduced over fifteen years, depending on sector.	Agriculture: Most tariffs between the United States and Mexico to be removed immediately. Tariffs on 6 percent of products—corn, sugar, and some fruits and vegetables—fully eliminated only after fifteen years. For Canada, existing agreement with the United States applies.	Environment: The three countries can be fined, and Mexico and the United States sanctioned, if a panel finds a repeated pattern of their not enforcing environment laws.	The United States and Mexico to set up a North American Development Bank to help finance clean-up of the U.S. border.
Investment restrictions lifted in most sectors, with the exception of oil in Mexico, culture in Canada, and airline and broadcasting in the United States.			
Immigration excluded, except some movement of white-collar workers to be eased.	Cars: Tariffs removed over ten years. Mexico's quotas on imports lifted over the same period. Cars eventually to meet 62.5 percent local content rule to be free of tariff.	Labor: Countries are liable for penalties for nonenforcement of child, minimum wage, and health and safety laws.	The United States to spend about $90 million in the first eighteen months retraining workers who lost their jobs because of the treaty.
Any country can leave the treaty with six months' notice.	Energy: Mexican ban on private-sector exploration continues, but procurement by state oil firm opened up to the United States and Canada.		
Treaty allows for the inclusion of any additional country.			
Government procurement opened up over ten years, mainly affecting Mexico, which reserves some contracts for Mexican firms.	Financial Services: Mexico gradually to open financial sector to United States and Canadian investment, eliminating barriers by 2007.		
Dispute resolution panels of independent arbitrators to resolve disagreements arising out of treaty.	Textiles: Treaty eliminates Mexican, U.S., and Canadian tariffs over ten years. Clothes eligible for tariff breaks to be sewn with fabric woven in North America.		
Some snap-back tariffs if surge of imports hurts a domestic industry.	Trucking: North American trucks could drive anywhere in the three countries by the year 2000.		

Source: Adapted from "What is NAFTA?" *Financial Times*, November 17, 1993. Reprinted with permission.

1994 and the ensuing recession in Mexico, and the strengthening of the U.S. dollar in the foreign-exchange market.[24]

Expansion of NAFTA to include other countries in the Americas has been endorsed by leaders of the three members. The United States has been unable to proceed, however, because the Congress's grant to the president of **fast-track authority** expired during President Clinton's first term in office. (Fast-track authority allows the president to negotiate trade treaties with other countries. Although the resultant treaties need the approval of both the House of Representatives and the Senate, they may not be amended by Congress.) While President Clinton has requested that his fast-track authority be renewed, Democrat leaders are unwilling to grant his request unless the ensuing trade treaties contain language protecting the environment, workers rights, and human rights; Republican legislators believe that environmental policy, workers rights, and human rights should not be linked to trade policy. Accordingly, both Canada and Mexico have negotiated bilateral free trade agreements with Chile, which is the most likely candidate to be the fourth member of NAFTA, while the United States has not yet done so.

Other Free Trade Agreements in the Americas

Many other countries are negotiating or implementing free trade agreements on a bilateral or multilateral basis. For example, Mexico, Venezuela, and Colombia hammered out a trilateral agreement that called for relaxing trade barriers against each other's goods in 1991. Mexico has also negotiated free trade pacts with its five Central American neighbors.[25]

The Caribbean Basin Initiative. In 1983 the United States established the Caribbean Basin Initiative in order to facilitate the economic development of the countries of Central America and the Caribbean Sea. The **Caribbean Basin Initiative (CBI)** overlaps two regional free trade areas: the Central American Common Market (CACM) and the Caribbean Community and Common Market (CARICOM), the members of which are listed in Table 7.5 and shown in Map 7.2. The CBI, which acts as a uni-directional free trade agreement, permits duty-free import into the United States of a wide range of goods that originate in Caribbean Basin countries or that have been assembled there from U.S.-produced parts. However, numerous politically sensitive goods, many of which are traditional exports of the area, have been excluded from the CBI, including textiles, canned tuna, luggage, apparel, footware, petroleum, and petroleum products. Through this pattern of duty-free access to the U.S. market, the United States hopes to stimulate investment by domestic, U.S., and other foreign firms in new industries in the Caribbean Basin countries.[26]

The Mercosur Accord. In March 1991, the governments of Argentina, Brazil, Paraguay, and Uruguay signed the **Mercosur Accord** (*Mercosur* is Spanish for "southern cone"), an agreement to create a customs union among themselves. They agreed to establish common external tariffs and to cut over four years their internal tariffs on goods that account for 85 percent of intra-Mercosur trade. Full implementation of the customs union began in 1995. Chile and Bolivia later joined Mercosur as associate members, allowing them to participate in the free trade area component of Mercosur. Firms from the six countries have preferential access to a combined market of 224 million people and a total GDP

TABLE 7.5

Major Regional Trade Associations

ACRONYM	FULL NAME/MEMBERS
AFTA	ASEAN Free Trade Area Brunei, Indonesia, Malaysia, Myanmar, Philippines, Singapore, Thailand, Vietnam
ANCOM	Andean Pact Bolivia, Colombia, Ecuador, Peru, Venezuela
APEC	Asia-Pacific Economic Cooperation Australia, Brunei, Canada, Chile, China, Hong Kong, Indonesia, Japan, Malaysia, Mexico, New Zealand, Papua New Guinea, Philippines, Singapore, South Korea, Taiwan, Thailand, United States
CACM	Central American Common Market Costa Rica, El Salvador, Guatemala, Honduras, Nicaragua
CARICOM	Caribbean Community and Common Market Antigua and Barbuda, Bahamas, Barbados, Belize, Dominica, Grenada, Guyana, Jamaica, Montserrat, St. Kitts and Nevis, St. Lucia, St. Vincent and the Grenadines, Suriname, Trinidad and Tobago
CEEAC	Economic Community of Central African States Burundi, Cameroon, Central African Republic, Chad, Democratic Republic of the Congo, Republic of the Congo, Equatorial Guinea, Gabon, Rwanda, Sao Tome and Principe
CER	Australia–New Zealand Closer Economic Trade Relations Agreement Australia, New Zealand
ECOWAS	Economic Community of West African States Benin, Burkina Faso, Cape Verde, Gambia, Ghana, Guinea, Guinea-Bissau, Ivory Coast, Liberia, Mali, Mauritania, Niger, Nigeria, Senegal, Sierra Leone, Togo
EU	European Union Austria, Belgium, Denmark, Finland, France, Germany, Greece, Ireland, Italy, Luxembourg, Netherlands, Portugal, Spain, Sweden, United Kingdom
EFTA	European Free Trade Association Iceland, Liechtenstein, Norway, Switzerland
GCC	Gulf Cooperation Council Bahrain, Kuwait, Oman, Qatar, Saudi Arabia, United Arab Emirates
MERCOSUR	Southern Cone Customs Union Argentina, Brazil, Paraguay, Uruguay; Associate Members: Bolivia, Chile
NAFTA	North American Free Trade Agreement Canada, Mexico, United States
SADC	Southern African Development Community Angola, Botswana, Lesotho, Malawi, Mauritius, Mozambique, Namibia, South Africa, Swaziland, Tanzania, Zambia, Zimbabwe

UNITED STATES

BERMUDA

BAHAMAS
MEXICO
HAITI
CUBA
BELIZE
DOMINICAN REPUBLIC
PUERTO RICO
HONDURAS JAMAICA
GUATEMALA
EL SALVADOR
NICARAGUA
GUYANA
COSTA RICA
VENEZUELA
SURINAME
PANAMA
COLOMBIA
FRENCH
GUIANA
ECUADOR

PERU
BRAZIL

BOLIVIA

PARAGUAY
CHILE

URUGUAY
ARGENTINA

ANTIGUA AND
BARBUDA

BARBADOS

DOMINICA

GRENADA

MONTSERRAT

ST. KITTS
AND NEVIS

ST. LUCIA

ST. VINCENT AND
THE GRENADINES

TRINIDAD AND
TOBAGO

Andean Pact

CACM

CARICOM

MERCOSUR

MAP 7.2

Free Trade Agreements in Central and South America and the Caribbean

of $1.1 trillion. In Mercosur's first six years, trade among its members increased from $4 billion in 1990 to $14 billion in 1996.

The Mercosur Accord is a direct response to the growth of other regional trading blocs. But it is also a key element of the free-market–oriented economic reforms adopted by the Argentinian and Brazilian governments elected in 1989 to revitalize their stagnating economies. By opening up their countries' economies, these governments hope to stimulate new flows of FDI, which will enhance the productivity of their work forces and make their goods more competitive in world markets. As noted by Argentina's President Carlos Menem, "There aren't many options. Either we work out a joint strategy in line with our development needs, or we will be the objects of outside strategies."[27] To date, the Mercosur nations have been a magnet for FDI. Particularly noticeable is the expansion of the area's automotive industry, which has attracted $18 billion in new FDI from the world's leading car manufacturers since Mercosur was founded.[28]

Andean Pact. The **Andean Pact** is a 1969 agreement to promote free trade among five small South American countries—Bolivia, Chile, Colombia, Ecuador, and Peru—in order to make them more competitive with the continent's larger countries. Venezuela joined the Pact in 1973, but Chile dropped out in 1976. During its first twenty years, the agreement was not very successful; trade among members totaled only 5 percent of their total trade. Geography played a role in this failure: the Andes mountain range, from which the agreement got its name, makes land transportation of goods between some members costly. More important, most members adopted protectionist, import-substitution policies that hindered trade.

The Andean Pact members agreed in 1991 to reinvigorate their agreement. The new resolve resulted from Chile's economic successes that followed its adoption of free-market, export-oriented economic policies in the 1980s and from the threat posed by the Mercosur Accord. In January 1992, the members established a customs union that provided for phased elimination of tariffs among themselves on most goods, a common external tariff, and harmonized regulations on capital movements, immigration, and agriculture. However, this liberalization has not gone smoothly. Creation of a common external tariff was stalled by political squabbling over the appropriate tariff level and structure.[29] Peru suspended its membership in the group after judging that the customs union agreement permitted too many loopholes that allowed members to subsidize local firms and erect barriers to imported goods. Despite these setbacks, trade in the region is likely to become freer over time. Indicative of this, the leaders of every country in the Americas except Cuba have pledged to create a Free Trade Area of the America (FTAA) by 2005.

Trade Arrangements in the Asia-Pacific Region

Trade groups are also growing in importance in the Asia-Pacific region. One of the longest standing groupings is the Closer Economic Relations agreement between Australia and New Zealand. More recently the Association of Southeast Asian Nations has initiated a free trade agreement. And members of APEC (Asia-Pacific Economic Cooperation) have begun to reduce trade barriers among themselves as well.

The Australia–New Zealand Agreement. The Australia–New Zealand Closer Economic Relations Trade Agreement, known as **ANZCERTA** or more simply as **CER,** took effect on January 1, 1983. For most of their histories Australia and New Zealand have been trade rivals, for they are both commodities producers. As members of the British Commonwealth, both enjoyed preferential access to the U.K. market. After the United Kingdom joined the European Union, however, both countries lost their privileged status in the British market. This change was particularly damaging to their agricultural sectors.

The ensuing poor performance by both the New Zealand and Australian economies in the 1970s, and the flow of human capital from the more depressed New Zealand to Australia, led to calls for closer economic ties. The CER agreement came into effect in 1983, and established schedules for eliminating tariff and non-tariff barriers between the two countries. The CER also sought to strengthen and foster links and cooperation in fields as diverse as investment, marketing, the movement of people, tourism, and transport. Although some areas have been excluded from the CER, such as broadcasting, postal services, and air traffic control, most analysts believe the CER has been one of the world's most successful free trade agreements.

Association of Southeast Asian Nations. The Association of Southeast Asian Nations was established in August 1967 to promote regional political and economic cooperation (see Map 7.3). Its founding members were Brunei, Indonesia, Malaysia, Philippines, Singapore, and Thailand. Vietnam was admitted in 1995 and Myanmar in 1997. These countries are by no means homogeneous: oil-rich Brunei had a 1996 per capita income of over $16,000, while Vietnam's was only $240. Nonetheless, the ASEAN economy has been developing rapidly because some of its poorer members—particularly Indonesia, Malaysia, Philippines, and Thailand— provide large pools of low-cost labor, receive preferential tariff rates under the U.S.

MAP 7.3

The ASEAN Members

Generalized System of Preferences and those of other WTO members, and have attracted significant Japanese, European, and North American direct investments.

To promote intra-ASEAN trade, members established the ASEAN Free Trade Area (AFTA), effective January 1, 1993. AFTA members will slash their tariffs to between 0 percent and 5 percent on most manufactured goods by 2003, and then on all goods by 2010. As with the Mercosur Accord and the Andean Pact, the desire for creation of the ASEAN trading bloc stems from two factors: a decrease in government control of national economies that has stimulated local entrepreneurs and attracted FDI and a defensive response to the growth of other regional trading blocs such as the EU and NAFTA.

Intra-ASEAN trade currently represents about 20 percent of total trade for the group as a whole, and it is growing quickly. Paralleling the history of the WTO, recent meetings of ministers in ASEAN have increasingly addressed trade in services and considered an "ASEAN Free Investment Area." They also intend to remove non-tariff barriers over time. As with other new trading blocs, firms have reacted quickly to take advantage of opportunities created by AFTA. For example, shortly after the agreement was negotiated, Filipino brewer San Miguel, which controls 90 percent of its home market, purchased Jakarta-based Delta brewery, which controls 40 percent of the Indonesian beer market. By moving quickly, San Miguel hoped to dominate the entire ASEAN market prior to the fall of tariff rates triggered by AFTA.[30]

The Asia-Pacific Economic Cooperation Initiative. The **Asia-Pacific Economic Cooperation (APEC)** initiative commenced at a 1989 meeting in Canberra, Australia. APEC, whose membership is comprised of 18 countries from both sides of the Pacific Ocean (see Map 7.4), developed in response to the growing interdependence of the Asia-Pacific economies.[31] In 1996, merchandise exports from APEC members were valued at a little over $2.3 trillion, and represented about 40 percent of total world exports. In addition, over the five years to 1995, APEC exports grew at over 9 percent per annum. During the same period imports grew at a similar rate and exceeded $2.4 billion.[32]

In its early years, APEC was a very informal group. At a meeting in Bangkok in 1992, APEC ministers agreed to establish a small permanent secretariat in Singapore, and formed ten sectoral-based working groups in areas such as trade and investment, energy, and telecommunications. In 1993 APEC held an economic

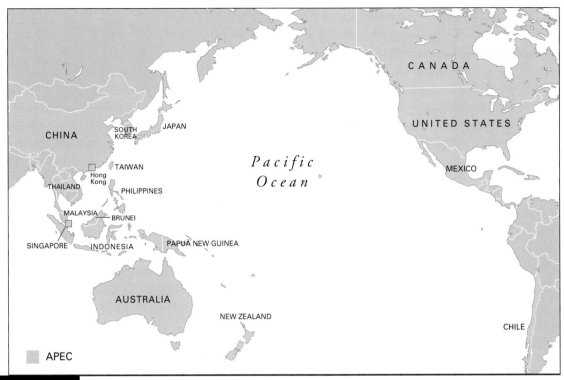

CANADA

UNITED STATES

CHINA

SOUTH KOREA · JAPAN

Pacific Ocean

TAIWAN

MEXICO

Hong Kong

THAILAND

PHILIPPINES

MALAYSIA — BRUNEI

SINGAPORE · INDONESIA · PAPUA NEW GUINEA

AUSTRALIA

NEW ZEALAND

CHILE

APEC

MAP 7.4

Asia-Pacific Economic Cooperation Initiative (APEC)

summit in Seattle. At this meeting various national leaders expressed their vision for APEC, which reflected the work of the working groups. A 1994 meeting in Indonesia led to a declaration committing members to the objective of achieving free trade in goods, services, and investment among member governments by 2010 for developed economies, and by 2020 for developing economies.[33] This objective was furthered at APEC's 1996 meeting in Manila, where many countries made explicit pledges to reduce barriers to Asia-Pacific trade, as Table 7.6 indicates.

African Initiatives. Many African countries have also established regional trading blocs. As shown in Table 7.5 and Map 7.5, the most important of these groups are the Southern African Development Community (SADC), the Economic Community of Central African States (CEEAC), and the Economic Community of West African States (ECOWAS). While these groups were established during the 1970s and early 1980s, they have not had a major impact on regional trade to date because of inadequate intra-regional transportation facilities and the failure of most domestic governments to create economic and political systems that encourage significant regional trade. Intra-Africa trade to date accounts for less than 7 percent of the continent's total exports.[34]

International Commodity Arrangements

Countries may also cooperate with one another to control the production, pricing, and sale of goods that are traded internationally. A **commodity cartel** is a group of producing countries that want to protect themselves from the wild fluctuations that often occur in prices of some commodity that is

---

TABLE 7.6

What the Manila APEC Meeting Means for Business

Reduction in tariffs
- Indonesia will reduce its applied tariff from 13% in 1996 to 5% or 10% on nearly all industrial products by 2003.
- Chile will reduce most tariffs to zero by 2010.
- China will reduce its simple average applied tariff from 23% in 1996 to 15% by 2000.
- Hong Kong will expand the percentage of tariff lines bound at zero from 35% in 1996 to 50% by 2000, 75% by 2005, and 100% by 2010.
- Thailand will reduce its average applied tariff from 30% in 1994 to 17% in 1996.
- New Zealand will reduce its simple average applied tariff from 6% in 1996 to 3% by 2000 and to zero by 2010.
- Philippines plans to reduce its applied tariff from 16% in 1996 to 5% for most products by 2004.
- Singapore will bind all tariffs at 6.5% by 2005 and zero by 2010.
- Currently 75% of tariffs are bound at 5.5%.

Reduction in nontariff measures
- Import restrictions on coal will be eliminated in the Philippines by 2000.
- Hong Kong will relax import controls on rice by 1997 and on meat and poultry by 2000.
- Japan will revise administrative arrangements to facilitate the entry of plant and animal imports.
- Korea provides further detail on its commitment to liberalize shelf life restrictions by 1998.
- Thailand will expand its tariff-rate quotas on skim milk powder and soybean products.

Reductions to barriers to trade in services
- Korea to review restrictions on foreign accounting firms and improve access for foreign lawyers.
- Singapore to remove restrictions on engineers, architects, and medical doctors.
- Hong Kong to consider establishing criteria for foreign lawyers to practice as barristers by 2000 and remove preferential arrangements for recognizing qualifications applying to veterinary surgeons, medical laboratory technicians, and occupational therapists by 1997.
- Japan will review liberalizing its laws relating to foreign lawyers operating in Japan.
- China will increase the number of licenses for foreign banks, insurance, and securities organizations and devise a program to comply with international rules for trade in telecommunications.
- Singapore will gradually open its domestic banking sector to foreign banks.

Source: Michael Dwyer, "What the Manila APEC meeting means for business," The *Australian Financial Review*, November 27, 1996, p. 4.

---

traded internationally, such as crude oil, coffee, rubber, or cocoa. Cartel members may also seek higher, as well as more stable, prices for their good. By assigning production quotas to individual countries and limiting overall output, a commodity cartel can raise the price of its good in international markets. A **commodity agreement** is an agreement among representatives from both producing and consuming countries who jointly negotiate production levels and target prices for the

MAP 7.5

**Free Trade
Agreements in
Africa**

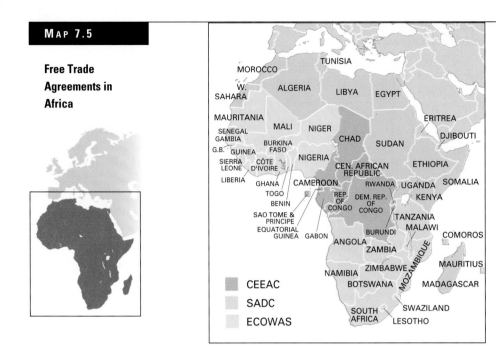

CEEAC
SADC
ECOWAS

commodity. Membership in a commodity agreement is voluntary, but to be successful it normally must include representatives from countries that produce most of the good in question.

The **Organization of Petroleum Exporting Countries (OPEC)** is the most important and successful commodity cartel in the world's history. OPEC is composed of eleven members, which account for 40 percent of the world's oil production. OPEC attempts to control the price of oil in world markets by assigning to its members production quotas that limit the overall amount of crude oil supplied internationally. OPEC first rose to prominence as a result of the Arab oil embargo that followed the 1973 Arab-Israeli War. By restricting the flow of oil to the market, OPEC succeeded in tripling the price of oil from $4 a barrel to $12 a barrel in a few short months in 1973–1974. OPEC stabilized world oil prices at these higher levels until the fall of the Shah of Iran in 1978, when it took advantage of the ensuing political chaos to elevate crude oil prices further. By 1981, crude oil was selling for $35 a barrel on world markets.

However, OPEC's control over the world crude oil market gradually lessened during the 1980s. Higher prices for petroleum products motivated consumers to reduce their consumption of such goods, thereby lessening the demand for crude oil. Higher crude oil prices also prompted a shift to other forms of energy, including natural gas, coal, nuclear energy, and renewable sources such as wind and geothermal power. Finally, the higher prices for crude oil attracted increased production from non-OPEC countries, such as Mexico, Norway, and Russia. OPEC's control over oil prices was further weakened by political infighting among its members for increased production quotas in the face of falling prices, as well as by claims that members were producing more than their assigned quotas. By early 1998, crude oil prices had fallen to less than half their 1981 peak.

CHAPTER REVIEW

Summary

Countries have joined to create numerous international organizations to promote their joint interests in international commerce. One of the most important was the GATT. The goal of this 1947 agreement was to promote global prosperity by reducing international trade barriers. Through a series of negotiating rounds over 47 years, the GATT significantly reduced the average level of tariffs facing exporters. The most recent series of GATT negotiations, the Uruguay Round, continued the trend of reductions in tariffs and NTBs. In 1995 the GATT's mission was taken over by a successor organization, the World Trade Organization.

Countries may also band together in various ways to integrate their economies regionally. Free trade areas promote economic integration by abolishing trade barriers among their members. Members of a customs union carry regional economic integration a step further by adopting common external trade barriers as well as abolishing internal barriers to trade. A common market combines the characteristics of a customs union with the elimination of controls on the free movement of labor, capital, and technology among its members. An economic union adds to the features of a common market the coordination of economic policies in order to promote regional economic integration. A political union involves complete political as well as economic integration of two or more countries.

The most important example of a regional trading bloc is the EU, a market of 372 million consumers and a combined GDP of $8.4 trillion. Spurred by the passage of the Single European Act of 1987, EU members dismantled most of the physical, technical, and fiscal trade barriers among themselves in an initiative labeled EC '92. Under the Maastricht Treaty, the EU is attempting to create a true economic union, an effort that goes beyond the common market originally envisioned by the 1957 Treaty of Rome.

A second, but much newer, regional integration effort is occurring in North America. The United States, Mexico, and Canada have instituted NAFTA, which came into effect in January 1994. NAFTA's implementation signals a commitment to tightening the economic bonds among the North American countries.

The development of regional trading blocs in Europe and North America has stimulated efforts to promote regional economic integration on other continents. South America is home to two such agreements, the Mercosur Accord and the Andean Pact. The chances of their future success have been increased by the economic reforms many South American countries have adopted, which have increased the competitiveness of their products in international markets. Australia and New Zealand and the ASEAN countries have similarly created free trade areas to promote regional economic integration. Several regional economic integration agreements negotiated by various African countries have yet to show much promise.

International agreements have also been made to manage trade in individual commodities. OPEC has attempted to control the price and production of crude oil. While successful in raising oil prices in the 1970s, OPEC has found its influence over the oil market reduced in the 1980s and 1990s because of energy conservation efforts and increased production from non-OPEC countries.

Review Questions

1. What were the major issues facing GATT negotiators during the Uruguay Round?

2. How does the WTO differ from the GATT?

3. How do the various forms of economic integration differ?

4. Why do free trade areas develop rules of origin?

5. What was the goal of the Treaty of Rome?

6. Describe the four major organizations governing the EU.

7. What are NAFTA's major provisions?

8. What is the Caribbean Basin Initiative? What is its goal?

9. What efforts have South American countries made to regionally integrate their economies?

10. What are the goals of international commodity agreements?

Questions for Discussion

1. How does the WTO affect the operations of large MNCs? Did MNCs benefit from the successful completion of the Uruguay Round?

2. Should international businesses promote or fight the creation of regional trading blocs?

3. What strategies can North American and Asian firms adopt to ensure access to the enormous EU market?

4. Is the abandonment of import-substitution policies by South American governments a necessary condition for the success of the Andean Pact and the Mercosur Accord?

5. Do regional trading blocs help or hurt world trade?

6. Of what importance are rules of origin to international businesses?

7. Why does the MFN principle promote multilateral, rather than bilateral, negotiations among WTO members?

BUILDING GLOBAL SKILLS

NAFTA has been lauded by some as creating a major new market opportunity for U.S. businesses, and criticized by others because of the potential loss of domestic jobs as firms relocate production to Mexico to take advantage of lower-cost labor. This exercise will help you to learn more about the effects of NAFTA on various firms.

Your instructor will divide the class up into groups of four to five students each. Working with your group members, identify four products made by firms in each of the three countries that are part of NAFTA. The four products should include two that would seem to benefit from NAFTA and two that would seem to face increased threats from competitors in the other countries as a result of NAFTA. For example, identify two Canadian-made products that have considerable market potential in the United States and/or Mexico and two other Canadian-made products that would seem to face new competition from U.S. and/or Mexican firms. Each group should identify a total of twelve different products.

Next, work with your group members to determine and assess the appeal of each product in the NAFTA market. Investigate for each the current market share, domestic competitors, foreign competitors, and so forth. Research how well each was doing before and since NAFTA's passage. Carefully discuss exactly how NAFTA has and/or may potentially affect each product.

Follow-up Questions

1. Has NAFTA provided new market opportunities for some of the products you identified? Why or why not?

2. Has it increased competition from other producers?

3. Have the effects of NAFTA on each product been consistent with what either advocates or critics of NAFTA might have predicted?

WORKING WITH THE WEB: Building Global Internet Skills

Evaluating New EU Entrants

The next group of countries to be considered for membership in the European Union consists of Cyprus, the Czech Republic, Estonia, Hungary, Poland, and Slovenia. Pick one of these countries. What would the impact of this country's entry be on the country itself and on the existing EU members? For example, how much would the country pay in taxes to the EU? Would it receive any cohesion fund payments? Are there any EU programs that the country would benefit from? How many votes would it have in the EU Parliament? Does the country meet

the EMU's convergence criteria? Do you foresee any problems with this country's entering the EU?

Visiting the European Union's web site is a good way to start this assignment. It provides an enormous amount of information about how the EU works, the composition and responsibilities of its governing organizations, the EU's policy initiatives, and so forth. The textbook's web site provides links to the EU's web site and to other web sites of use for this exercise.

CLOSING CASE

Will Whirlpool Clean Up in Europe?[35]

For years, international businesses have looked forward to the EU's emergence as a single, integrated market. Among these are firms that produce so-called white goods, or appliances such as refrigerators, dishwashers, ovens, washers, and dryers. (In the past, these kitchen and laundry room appliances predominantly came in white, hence the industry's name. Consumer electronics such as radios, televisions, and stereos came in brown, so these consumer durables are called *brown goods*. The widespread use of color in appliances today makes these labels somewhat anachronistic.)

While the European market has always been large—an estimated $20 billion in 1998—the peculiarities of each European country kept the white goods market fragmented into many different, often relatively small, markets. For example, different countries use different outlets for plugging in electrical appliances, and there are also differences in the voltage supplied to homes. Consumer tastes vary as well. For example, French consumers tend to prefer top-loading washing machines, whereas many others in Europe prefer front-loading machines. German cooks prefer different types of burner arrangements and heat sources on stoves than French cooks do. And

many European homemakers still like to hang their wash out to dry.

About the only constant across Europe is product size. U.S. consumers are used to large appliances; homebuilders there usually construct separate utility rooms with plenty of room for washers and dryers. But homes in Europe are much smaller, with much more limited appliance space. Moreover, many Europeans buy fresh foods daily, thereby decreasing the need for refrigerated storage. As a result, home appliances in Europe are much smaller than their U.S. counterparts. And in some product lines, the European market is underdeveloped by U.S. standards. For example, fewer than 20 percent of European homes have a dishwasher or clothes dryer. Even as consumer tastes change, size still remains an issue. In the United Kingdom, for example, one popular appliance is a combined clothes washer and dryer.

White goods manufacturers believe the emergence of a single market in Europe will change the way they will (and must) do business. Previously, they had to customize their products to meet the often conflicting standards of the EU's fifteen national governments. Harmonized product standards resulting from EC '92 allow them to standardize their products, thus permitting them to cut product development and production costs. Reduced barriers to internal trade allow them to concentrate production in one factory that can serve markets throughout the EU. Reduced impediments to cross-border advertising make it easier to develop pan-European brands, which in turn reduce marketing and distribution costs. And EC '92's elimination of physical barriers at border crossing points and restrictions on trucking competition by national governments leads to productivity gains in logistics and physical distribution management.

But the challenges of operating in the EU's single, integrated white goods market are not for the faint-hearted. Firms that fail to adjust are doomed. One of the most aggressive firms seeking to conquer the new European market is Whirlpool, the world's largest white goods manufacturer. Whirlpool currently controls twelve percent of the European white goods market. The firm's managers have a clearly defined view of this market:

> Among the truths about the European home-appliance market, there are two whose net effect Whirlpool has a particular interest in: first, consumers in Europe spend up to twice as many days of household income for appliances as do their U.S. counterparts, creating . . . a consumer "value gap"; second, industry profit margins in the region are traditionally much lower than those of North American manufacturers. The reason for this truth is cultural: historically, the industry was organized to do business in individual, national markets, an approach with inherent cost inefficiencies. Now, however, with barriers to pan-European business disappearing, Whirlpool believes that it can use its unique regional position to deliver greater home-appliance value to customers and, in turn, establish a competitive advantage for itself. A strategy to do so suggests that the opportunity to eliminate costs which do not add to consumers' perceptions of value—and invest some of the savings into product and service characteristics that *do* add perceived value—will be substantial.[36]

For the past decade, Whirlpool's managers have been attacking the European white goods market by translating these words into concrete actions. One key element of the firm's strategy was the purchase of the appliance business of Philips Industries, the large Netherlands-based MNC. Whirlpool acquired a 53 percent interest in Philips' European white goods operations in 1989 and the remainder in 1991, thereby obtaining control over Philips' European

white goods production facilities and distribution systems. To build brand recognition among European consumers, Whirlpool initially marketed its appliances using the brand name Philips Whirlpool. It is gradually phasing out the Philips label on its products, as its rights to use that name terminate in 1999.

But Whirlpool has also sought many other operating and marketing economies:

1. It produces and markets three well-established pan-European brands purchased from Philips: Bauknecht, a premium upscale product; Philips Whirlpool, for the broad middle segment of the white goods market; and Ignis, its low-price "value" brand aimed at price-sensitive consumers. This comprehensive product strategy allows Whirlpool to fully utilize its European production facilities and distribution systems and market its goods to Europeans at all income levels.

2. It consolidated thirteen separate national sales offices for these three product lines into five regional operations in order to cut costs, coordinate pan-European promotional campaigns, and enhance the productivity of its sales force.

3. It centralized Whirlpool Europe's logistics, information technology, and consumer services operations to take advantage of EC '92. For example, reduced barriers to free trade in trucking services ease the task of warehousing products and distributing them throughout the EU.

4. It has redeployed its manufacturing capacity to take advantage of the elimination of national trade barriers. For example, it concentrates its production of refrigerators for its European customers in Trento, Italy, and that of automatic washers in Schondorf, Germany, thus allowing it to achieve significant manufacturing economies of scale.

5. It has encouraged technology transfer between its European and North American operations, a task made easier by the centralization of its European operations. For example, Whirlpool Europe now produces a line of clothes dryers that feature easier loading and unloading and gentler treatment of clothes, features first developed by Whirlpool's

Marion, Ohio, division. Conversely, European engineers are helping Whirlpool's U.S. engineers adapt energy-efficient horizontal-axis washing machines, which are common in Europe, for the North American market in order to meet pending federal energy-efficiency standards. Clearly Whirlpool is leveraging its European operations in ways that substantiate the benefits of globalization suggested by Kenichi Ohmae and others.

Despite these initiatives, Whirlpool has found the European market a tougher nut to crack than it had anticipated. Since 1989, Whirlpool has spent $2 billion implementing its European strategy, and plans to expend an additional $1 billion over the next five years. While its European operations generated $2.5 billion in sales in 1996—about 29 percent of the firm's total revenues—its European sales have increased only 13 percent since 1990. Its return on sales in Europe is less than a quarter of that earned by its U.S. operations.

Whirlpool characterizes its problems as temporary, and due to overcapacity in the industry. Europe is home to over 170 factories churning out over 200 different brands of household appliances. Moreover, its EU competitors have not stood still while Whirlpool has invaded their home markets. Germany's Bosch-Siemens, for example, has poured money into R&D to maintain the innovativeness of its appliances. It has dramatically increased the efficiency of its dishwashers, reducing their energy usage by 62 percent and their water usage by 34 percent compared to the machines it made two decades previously. It has also spent $350 million automating its production facilities in Germany and built new factories in Poland, Spain, and the Czech Republic to reduce its dependence on high-cost German labor. Sweden's Electrolux, which vies with Whirlpool for the title of the world's largest white goods manufacturer, purchased the appliance business of AEG Hausgerate from Daimler-Benz. Already controlling a 20 to 25 percent market share in Europe, Electrolux increased its market share by about 6 percentage points through this acquisition. Electrolux is also aggressively moving to control its costs, by closing twenty-five factories and reducing its payrolls by 12,000.

Nonetheless, Whirlpool remains optimistic that its European strategy will be successful. The 1995 addition of Austria, Finland, and Sweden to the EU means that its European factories can easily access millions of new middle-class consumers with substantial disposable incomes. The proposed addition to the EU of several former Soviet bloc countries in the next decade raises the importance of its European factories as production platforms to serve this growing market. And in the second half of 1997 Whirlpool's European sales rose 4 percent, contributing $60 million in operating profits to the company's 1997 results—a potential indicator that Whirlpool's European strategy may be finally paying off.

Case Questions

1. What are the advantages of consolidating production of product lines at single factories in the EU? What are the disadvantages?

2. Should Whirlpool continue to produce and market in Europe its three product lines (Bauknecht, Whirlpool Philips, and Ignis), which span the entire white goods market, or should it focus on one market niche?

3. What benefits will Whirlpool gain by broadening the Whirlpool brand name from a North American brand to a global one?

4. In light of the aggressive responses of Electrolux and Bosch-Siemens, should Whirlpool revise or abandon its European strategy?

5. Do you think it is possible to design and sell the same basic appliance around the world?

CHAPTER NOTES

1. Matt Marshall and David Wessel, "One Currency, One Central Bank, One Big Question," *Wall Street Journal,* May 2, 1997, p. A10. Reprinted by permission of the *Wall Street Journal* ©1997 Dow Jones & Company, Inc. All Rights Reserved Worldwide.

2. H. Grubel, *International Economics* (Homewood, Ill.: Richard D. Irwin, 1981), p. 172.

3. B. Zepter, "Prospects for the Uruguay Round: the Declaration of Punta del Este," in R. Rode, ed., *GATT and Conflict Management* (Boulder, Colo.: Westview, 1990), p. 103.

4. S. Golt, *The GATT Negotiations 1986–90: Origins, Issues & Prospects* (London: British-North American Committee, 1988), p. 4.

5. J. Schott, "U.S. Policies towards the GATT: Past, Present, Prospective," in Rode, ed., *GATT and Conflict Management,* op. cit., p. 26.

6. John Maggs and Keith M. Rockwell, "Hollywood Scuffle: US Concession Stuns Experts," *Journal of Commerce,* December 16, 1993.

7. United Nations Conference on Trade and Development, *The Outcome of the Uruguay Round: An Initial Assessment (Supporting Papers to the Trade and Development Report, 1994).* New York: United Nations, 1994, p. 143.

8. Jacob Viner, *The Customs Union Issue* (New York: Carnegie Endowment for International Peace, 1950).

9. *Consumer Policy in the Single Market* (Luxembourg: Office for Official Publications of the European Communities, 1991), pp. 7–8.

10. *Europe Without Frontiers—Completing the Internal Market* (Luxembourg: Office for Official Publications of the European Communities, 1989), p. 29.

11. "MEPs vote for 'pure' chocolate," *Financial Times,* October 24, 1997, p. 3.

12. Delegation of the European Communities, *Sources for Standards* (mimeo, November 1991); Mary Saunders, "EC Testing and Certification Procedures: How Will They Work?" *Business America,* February 25, 1991, p. 27; "Not Many Firms Stand Up," *Wall Street Journal,* September 17, 1992, p. A1.

13. "London falling out of the picture," *Financial Times,* July 19/20, 1997, p. 7.

14. *Taxation in the Single Market* (Luxembourg: Office for Official Publications of the European Communities, 1990), p. 14; *Opening Up the Internal Market* (Luxembourg: Office for Official Publications of the European Communities, 1991), p. 51.

15. "The big catch," *Financial Times,* July 29, 1997, p. 11.

16. "Daewoo, Samsung, and Goldstar: Made in Europe?" *Business Week,* August 24, 1992, p. 43.

17. *Opening Up the Internal Market,* op. cit., p. 6.

18. "France, Germany Initiate EC Plan for Defense Role," *Wall Street Journal,* October 18, 1991, p. A18.

19. "Emu 'boost for Bosch,' " *Financial Times,* July 8, 1997, p. 2; "Coin Toss: Pan-European Currency Divides British Firms," *Wall Street Journal,* April 24, 1997, p. A15; The European Commission, *Economic and Monetary Union*

(Luxembourg: Office for Official Publications of the European Communities, 1996), p. 13.

20. The European Commission, *Economic and Monetary Union,* op. cit., p. 19.

21. Richard Hay, *The European Commission and the Administration of the Community* (Luxembourg: Office for Official Publications of the European Communities, 1989), p. 26.

22. Leonard Bierman, James Kolari, and Michael Pustay, "Denmark and the Maastricht Treaty: A Market Analysis," *Duke Journal of Comparative & International Law,* Vol. 3, No. 1 (Fall 1992), pp. 147–171; "The Battle of 1992," *Wall Street Journal,* March 16, 1989, p. A16.

23. "No turning back from brave new Europe," *Financial Times,* July 17, 1997, p. 3; "Enlargement may test EU's treaty," *Financial Times,* June 19, 1997, p. 2.

24. Office of the U.S. Trade Representative, *Study on the Operation and Effect of the North American Free Trade Agreement* (Washington, D.C., 1997), pp. 2, 3, and 14; "Experts' View of NAFTA's Economic Impact: It's a Wash," *Wall Street Journal,* June 17, 1997, p. A20.

25. "Mexico and Chile to sign free trade agreement next month," *Financial Times,* August 2, 1991, p. 3; "Chile and Mexico display the pioneer spirit," *Financial Times,* September 19, 1991, p. 8; "Mexico, Venezuela and Colombia conclude free trade pact," *Financial Times,* December 7, 1993, p. 10.

26. Maritza Castro-Gershberg, *Global Trade Talk,* Vol. 1, No. 4 (July–August 1991), pp. 13ff; U.S. International Trade Commission, *U.S. Market Access in Latin America: Recent Liberalization Measures and Remaining Barriers,* USITC Publication 2521 (June 1992), pp. 4–6.

27. In an address to the Brazilian Congress, as reported by the *Houston Chronicle,* November 6, 1989, p. B1.

28. "Latin auto sales drive investment," *Houston Chronicle,* May 15,1997, p. 1C.

29. "Andean Pact still split on outside tariff," *Financial Times,* May 12, 1994, p. 6; "Andean five put common back into market," *Financial Times,* May 30, 1991, p. 4; "Andean Trade Zones Formed," *Wall Street Journal,* December 6, 1991, p. A5; "Bolivia puts Andean pact in doubt," *Financial Times,* July 7, 1992, p. 5.

30. "San Miguel's Purchase of Delta Brewery Gives Firm a Stronghold in Indonesia," *Wall Street Journal,* September 11, 1992, p. B14.

31. Russell Trood and Deborah McNamara, *The Asia-Australia Survey 1995–96,* (Hong Kong: Centre of Australia-Asia Relations, 1995), pp. 516–517.

32. Department of Foreign Affairs and Trade, *The APEC Region: Trade and Investment: November 1995,*

Commonwealth of Australia, 1995, p. 1; Economist Intelligence Unit, *Fact Sheet—Global Economy 1996*, 1st quarter, 1997; International Monetary Fund, *Direction of Trade Statistics,* IMF, March 1997.

33. Ibid., p. 1.

34. The General Agreement on Tariffs and Trade, *International Trade Statistics 1993* (GATT: Geneva, 1993), p. 8; "African Nations Act on Trade," *Wall Street Journal*, February 3, 1992, p. A6.

35. Thomas A. Stewart, "A Heartland Industry Takes on the World," *Fortune*, March 12, 1990, pp. 110–112; "Whirlpool Goes Off on a World Tour," *Business Week*, June 3, 1992, pp. 98–100; "A chance to clean up in European white goods," *Financial Times*, December 13, 1993, p. 23; "If You Can't Stand the Heat, Upgrade the Kitchen," *Business Week*, April 25, 1994, p. 35; Rahul Jacob, "The Big Rise," *Fortune*, May 30, 1994, pp. 74–90; "Whirlpool to Build Washing Machines with European, Fuel-Efficient Design," *Wall Street Journal*, August 19, 1994; Maytag, *1993 Annual Report*, p. 20; "Rough and tumble industry," *Financial Times*, July 2, 1997, p. 13; "Whirlpool Expected Easy Going in Europe, And It Got A Big Shock," *Wall Street Journal*, April 10, 1998, p. A1. "Despite Setbacks, Whirlpool Pursues Overseas Markets," *Wall Street Journal*, December 9, 1997, p. B4; "Whirlpool Net Doubled in 4th Quarter; Gains in Europe, Revamping Are Cited," *Wall Street Journal*, February 4, 1998, p. A6.

36. Whirlpool Corporation, *1993 Annual Report*, p. 15.

Legal and Political Forces

After studying this chapter you should be able to:

Describe the major types of legal systems confronting international businesses.

Explain how home country laws can affect the international marketplace.

Describe the impacts MNCs may have on a host country.

Discuss the major types of controls that host countries place on international businesses.

List the ways firms can resolve international business disputes.

Explain how firms can protect themselves from political risk.

Analyze the risks facing international firms doing business in emerging market economies.

N 1948 CHARLES LAZARUS INVESTED $4000 TO START A CHILDREN'S furniture store in Washington, D.C. But the budding enterprise began to catch on only after Lazarus added a line of toys to the store's merchandise mix. Finally realizing that his fortune lay in toys rather than furniture, he opened in 1958 the first "superstore" devoted solely to toys and related merchandise. And the rest (as they say) is history. Renamed Toys 'R' Us, the firm grew rapidly through the next three decades, eventually becoming the largest toy retailer in the United States. Lazarus's firm proved so successful that stock market analysts developed a new term to describe Toys 'R' Us: *category killer,* a niche retailer so successful that few opportunities remain for other merchants selling the same category of goods. ▌▌The Toys 'R' Us formula for success is really quite simple. The firm builds large, free-standing stores in the suburbs,

Toys 'R' Us Takes on the World[1]

maintains a large inventory of virtually every toy available, and sells the toys at discount prices. The firm also sells baby products such as disposable diapers at a very low price as a way of building the loyalty of new parents (who will soon be buying toys). ▌▌By 1984, prime locations in the U.S. market were getting harder to find. Lazarus and his managers realized that they needed to venture outside the United States if the firm was to continue to grow and prosper. The firm opened its first foreign store in Canada, where it met a receptive Canadian government and a marketplace that was familiar with the firm, since Canadians were used to traveling to Detroit, Buffalo, and other U.S. border cities to buy discounted Barbie dolls and Nintendo Game Boys at Toys 'R' Us stores. As a result, Toys 'R' Us encountered few problems in successfully utilizing its money-making formula in its first international venture, and today operates sixty-one stores from its Canadian headquarters in Concord, Ontario. ▌▌The firm's first tough international test came when it decided to expand its operations to the United Kingdom. Its market research found that British customers were accustomed to excellent service, did not want to travel far to shop, and distrusted discounting because they thought it indicated poor quality. But the real roadblocks were legal. Small retailers throughout the country had long before fought for and won passage of regulations that prohibit most retailers from being open in the evenings and on Sundays. Even tougher were the zoning laws. The United Kingdom has some of the world's most complex zoning requirements, and local firms are often able to take advantage of them to keep foreign competitors from setting up shop. For example, apparel retailers have used zoning laws in some areas of England to keep new Toys 'R' Us stores from selling children's clothing. Still, the firm has cornered 10 percent of the British market, and continues aggressively and successfully to pursue opportunities not only in the United Kingdom but in other European countries. ▋▋ But the United Kingdom was a cakewalk compared to Japan. For several years, Toys 'R' Us was thwarted in its efforts to build in Japan. That country's Large-Store Law gives the Ministry of International Trade and Industry (MITI) and local communities the ability to slow or stop the building of large stores that threaten to take business from smaller ones. The part of the law that really hurt foreign firms was the ten-year application process it requires. Local Japanese toy retailers, wary of the reputation of Toys 'R' Us as a category killer, exploited every provision of the Large-Store Law to deny the firm access to their market. ▋▋ In the late 1980s, two events turned the tide for the firm. The first was the signing of the Structural Impediments Initiative, one of several agreements between the U.S. and Japanese governments designed to help U.S. firms enter the Japanese market and therefore ease the U.S.-Japanese trade imbalance. The other was the partnership Toys 'R' Us formed with savvy Japanese entrepreneur Den Fujita. ▋▋ Fujita is president of McDonald's Corporation (Japan). Several years earlier, he had gained vast experience in dealing with the Japanese government when he helped McDonald's launch its Japanese restaurants. In return for Fujita's assistance to Toys 'R' Us, McDonald's was given a 20 percent stake in the Toys 'R' Us Japanese operation. Fujita fiercely lobbied his Japanese contacts and took advantage of the Structural Impediments Initiative. As a result, he was able to drastically shorten the application process for the firm. ▋▋ Toys 'R' Us opened its first store in Japan in 1991. President George Bush attended the ribbon-cutting ceremony, and over 60,000 customers made purchases during the first three days. Other stores opened soon after, and today Toys 'R' Us is a major player in the Japanese market, operating fifty-one stores there. ▋▋ But the firm still has hurdles to overcome in Japan. Its stores must close every evening by 8:00 p.m. and must remain closed all day for twenty days each year. Further, many Japanese toymakers have been unwilling to sell to the firm. Of course, U.S. toymakers greet this news gleefully, because it means new export opportunities for them. Although it no doubt has to weather other legal and political storms, Toys 'R' Us is well on its way to becoming an important force in the global toy retailing industry. Its international division manages 396 stores in twenty-six countries, generating 28 percent of Toys 'R' Us's $10 billion annual revenues. ▋▋▋▋▋

A domestic firm must follow the laws and customs of its home country. An international business faces a more complex task: it must obey the laws not only of its home country but also of all the host countries in which it operates, as Toys 'R' Us has discovered. Both home and host country laws can critically affect the profitability of international commercial transactions. They determine the markets firms may serve, the prices they can charge for their goods, and the cost of necessary inputs such as labor, raw materials, and technology. This chapter focuses on the impact of home and host country laws and political processes on international business operations. We begin by discussing the different types of legal systems and then examine the rules and regulations that home and host countries may impose on domestic and foreign firms—and the problems created for international managers when these laws conflict. Next we talk about the approaches that international businesses may take in resolving disputes with host countries. Finally, we discuss political risk assessment and explore the opportunities and challenges international businesses face in the risky but emerging markets of China and Central and Eastern Europe.

Differences in Legal Systems

National legal systems vary dramatically. The rule of law, the role of lawyers, the burden of proof, the right to judicial review, and, of course, the laws themselves differ from country to country for historical, cultural, political, and religious reasons. International businesspeople must be aware of the legal systems of the host countries in which their firms operate, for the firms' legal obligations in those countries will likely differ from those in their home countries. In the United States, for example, in times of economic distress firms can lay off workers with minimal notice and severance pay. In Belgium, however, firms wishing to trim their white-collar work forces must provide each worker with three months' notice, three months' severance pay, or some combination of the two for every five years (or fraction of five years) the employee has worked for the firm. And woe to those who bounce a check in the United Arab Emirates! According to its laws, people who commit such a crime remain in jail—sleeping on concrete benches and dining on camel meat—until they repay their debtors, even if they have completed their sentence, as one poor British woman whose day-care center there had gone bankrupt found out.[2] Access to the legal system also may vary from country to country, as suggested by Fig. 8.1. While many people in the United States believe their country has too many lawyers (it is blessed with about 39 percent of the world's lawyers), availability of lawyers and nondiscriminatory access to the host country's legal system are important to international businesses in settling disputes with suppliers and customers.[3] South Korea, in contrast, suffers from a shortage of lawyers because of its tough bar exam—only 2 percent of the candidates taking it pass. Thus, many international businesses are forced to resolve disputes privately rather than utilize South Korea's courts. Similarly, the Indian court system has a backlog of over three million cases. Many attorneys advise their clients to settle conflicts out of court, because resolving common business disputes such as breach of contract can take as long as ten years to be heard in a court of law.[4]

Common Law

Common law is the foundation of the legal systems in the United Kingdom and its former colonies, including the United States, Canada, Australia, India, New

FIGURE 8.1

Lawyers per 100,000 Population

Source: University of Wisconsin, Institute for Legal Studies, from *The Economist*, March 5, 1994, p. 36. © The Economist Newspaper Group, Inc. Reprinted with permission. Further reproduction prohibited.

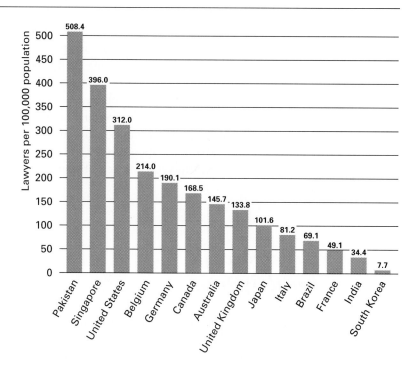

Zealand, Barbados, Saint Kitts and Nevis, and Malaysia. **Common law** is law based on the cumulative wisdom of judges' decisions on individual cases through history. These cases create legal precedents, which other judges use to decide similar cases. Because common law is based on the cumulative effect of judicial decisions over centuries, it has evolved differently in each common law country. Thus laws affecting business practices vary somewhat among these countries, creating potential problems for the uninformed international businessperson. For example, manufacturers of defective products are more vulnerable to lawsuits in the United States than in the United Kingdom as a result of evolutionary differences in the two countries' case law.

In addition to evolutionary differences in case law, **statutory laws**—those enacted by legislative action—also vary among the common law countries. For example, many business transactions between firms and the British government are shielded from public scrutiny—and the prying eyes of competitors—by that country's Official Secrets Act. In contrast, more information about transactions between firms and the U.S. federal government is publicly available because of that country's Freedom of Information Act. Even the administration of the law may vary. For example, in the United States the plaintiff and the defendant in a lawsuit generally pay their own legal fees. Often, defendants agree to quick settlements regardless of the strength of their cases in order to avoid expensive litigation. In the United Kingdom, the losers in trials pay the legal expenses of both parties. Thus the British have less incentive to file frivolous lawsuits. By lowering the amount and overall cost of litigation, the British system reduces the legal costs of firms operating in the United Kingdom.[5]

Civil Law

Civil law, the world's most common form of legal system, is law based on a codification, or detailed listing, of what is and is not permissible. The civil law system originated with the Romans in biblical times, who spread it throughout the Western world. Its dominance was reinforced by the imposition of the Napoleonic Code on territories conquered by French emperor Napoleon Bonaparte during the early nineteenth century.

One important difference between common law and civil law systems concerns the roles of judges and lawyers. In a common law system, the judge serves as a neutral referee, ruling on various motions by the opposing parties' lawyers. These lawyers are responsible for developing their clients' cases and choosing which evidence to submit on their clients' behalf. In a civil law system, the judge takes on many of the tasks of the lawyers, determining, for example, the scope of evidence to be collected and presented to the court.

Religious Law

Religious law is law based on the officially established rules governing the faith and practice of a particular religion. A country that applies religious law to civil and criminal conduct is called a **theocracy.** In Iran, for example, a group of mullahs, or holy men, determine legality or illegality through their interpretation of the Koran, the holy book of Islam. Religious laws can create interesting problems for firms. Consider the impact of the Koran on the capital market. It denounces charging interest on loans as an unfair exploitation of the poor; thus Muslim firms and financial institutions have had to develop alternative financing arrangements. For example, Muslim businesses often rely on leasing arrangements, rather than borrowing money, to obtain long-term assets.[6] In Iran, banks charge up-front fees that act as a substitute for loan interest payments, and owners of bank deposits receive shares of the bank's profits rather than interest payments. Family-owned firms are often influential in legal systems based on the Koran, since members of the owners' extended family may be the best available source of capital, given the costs of circumventing the prohibition on interest.

But countries relying on religious law often have other features that should make outsiders cautious, such as an absence of due process and appeals procedures. In Saudi Arabia, for example, all foreign firms must have a local representative or sponsor, typically a government agency or a person well connected to the royal family. Should a commercial dispute arise between a foreign businessperson and the local representative, the local representative can have the foreigner detained by the local police. Because no independent judiciary exists in the country to protect the foreigner's rights, the foreigner is in a weak bargaining position.[7]

Bureaucratic Law

The legal system in communist countries and in dictatorships is often described as bureaucratic law. **Bureaucratic law** is whatever the country's bureaucrats say it is, regardless of the formal law of the land. Contracts can be made or broken at the whim of those in power. The collapse of Zairean dictator Mobutu Sese Seko's government in 1997, for example, threatened the viability of all existing contracts

International businesspeople often find dealing with bureaucratic legal systems a frustrating experience. In such a system many of the laws seem to be arbitrary and capricious, and appeal procedures may be nonexistent. The moral dilemma faced by actress Michelle Pfeiffer while filming *The Russia House* in Moscow (see "Going Global") typifies the problems encountered by many foreigners when working in countries that use bureaucratic law.

signed by foreign companies and triggered a mad scramble to revalidate old contracts and negotiate new ones with the new government of Laurent Kabila.[8] Protections that may appear in the country's constitution—such as the right to an attorney and the right to hear witnesses against one—may be ignored if government officials find them inconvenient. For example, under the regime of terror of dictator Idi Amin in the 1970s, the formalities of Ugandan law afforded Ugandans and foreigners little protection. Similarly, the elaborate protections detailed in the constitution of the former Soviet Union offered little solace to the victims of Joseph Stalin's political purges in the 1930s.

In countries relying on bureaucratic law, an MNC's ability to manage its operations is often compromised by bureaucrats. International managers are often confronted with arbitrary rules or decisions that have the force of law. Steven Spielberg, for example, received permission from Shanghai city officials to film parts of *Empire of the Sun* in that city's dirty, rundown downtown area. However, these same officials later arbitrarily fined Spielberg's movie company $10,000, claiming that smoke from the movie's battle scenes had degraded Shanghai's environment.[9] Thus Spielberg, like numerous international businesspeople before him, learned that an unfortunate by-product of bureaucratic law is the lack of consistency, predictability, and appeal procedures.

International businesspeople must be aware of these general differences in legal systems to avoid unfortunate misunderstandings, as "Going Global" illustrates. They should also rely on the expertise of local lawyers in each country in which they operate to help them comply with the specific requirements of local laws and to counsel them on substantive differences in due process, legal liabilities, and procedural safeguards.

GOING GLOBAL

International businesspeople are often forced to operate in legal and political settings that they may find personally offensive. When actress Michelle Pfeiffer was in Moscow for the filming of the John Le Carré spy novel *The Russia House* a year before the collapse of the former Soviet Union, she was outraged that the U.S. film crew could gorge themselves at tables full of food while the Soviet extras hungrily watched, forbidden by Soviet law from joining in. Eager to help their plight, Pfeiffer walked off the set, vowing not to return until the extras were fed. The result of her protest? Nothing. After receiving a lecture from Soviet film commission officials, the actress realized that her efforts would not help; Soviet law would not change merely because it offended a foreigner's sense of fairness or ethics. Pfeiffer nicely summed up the dilemma facing many international businesspeople dealing with different laws, ethical standards, cultures, and political systems when she said, "I realized . . . this is so typically American. . . .This is what, as a country, we're accused of all the time. Now, whether I was right or wrong isn't the issue. The issue was, do I have the right, as an outsider, to come in and force my sensibilities on this culture?"

The Law Is the Law

Source: Hal Hinson, "Michelle Pfeiffer as a Work in Progress," *Esquire*, December 1990, p. 122.

Home Country Laws

Home country laws affect all facets of a firm's domestic operations: managing its workforce (recruitment, compensation, and labor relations laws); financing its operations (securities, banking, and credit laws); marketing its products (advertising, distribution, and consumer protection laws); and developing and utilizing technology (patent, copyright, and trademark laws).

But home country laws may also affect a firm's international operations as well as those of its international competitors. Home country laws may

- ◆ Directly regulate international business activities that originate inside the country's borders
- ◆ Indirectly affect the ability of domestic firms to compete internationally
- ◆ Directly or indirectly affect business activities occurring outside the country's borders

Restrictions on Trading with Unfriendly Countries

Many home country laws are explicitly designed to regulate international business activities originating within the home country's borders. Such laws are often politically motivated and designed to promote the country's foreign policy or military objectives. A country may attempt to induce a second country to change an undesirable policy by imposing **sanctions**—restraints against commerce with that country. Sanctions may take many forms, such as restricting access to high-technology goods,

MAP 8.1

Northern India and Neighboring Countries

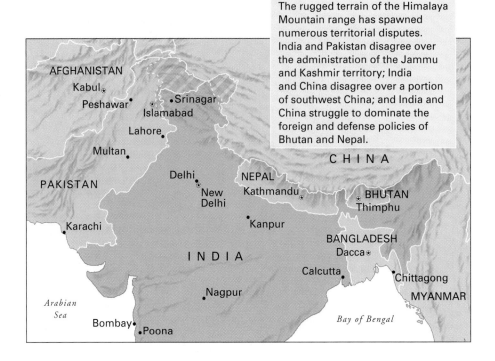

The rugged terrain of the Himalaya Mountain range has spawned numerous territorial disputes. India and Pakistan disagree over the administration of the Jammu and Kashmir territory; India and China disagree over a portion of southwest China; and India and China struggle to dominate the foreign and defense policies of Bhutan and Nepal.

withdrawing preferential tariff treatment, boycotting the country's goods, and denying new loans. For example, the United States imposed sanctions against China in 1989 to protest the Tienanmen Square massacre and against Haiti in 1994 as part of its program to restore to power the democratically elected government of Jean-Bertrand Aristide. In May 1998, it applied sanctions against India and Pakistan after they conducted underground nuclear testing in violation of U.S. nuclear non-proliferation laws. An **embargo**—a comprehensive sanction against commerce with a given country—may be imposed by countries acting in unison or alone. For example, the United Nations embargoed trade with Iraq after its 1990 invasion of Kuwait. Most countries embargoed goods to or from South Africa in the 1980s to protest its apartheid policies. The United States has unilaterally embargoed trade with Cuba since 1961, when the attempted U.S.-supported overthrow of Fidel Castro died on the beaches of the Bay of Pigs. Similarly, India acted alone in the early 1990s when it embargoed trade with Nepal because it believed that country's prime minister was favoring China's interests over India's (see Map 8.1).

A particularly important form of sanction is export controls on high-technology goods. Typically such controls are imposed multilaterally. For example, seventeen Western countries established the **Coordinating Committee for Multilateral Export Controls (COCOM)** in 1949 to prevent exportation to the Soviet Union and its military allies of Western goods and technology that could be used to give the Soviets a military advantage. COCOM also required that firms secure a license to export high-technology goods to neutral countries in order to prevent such goods from being re-exported to the Soviets.[10] After the Soviet Union broke apart and tensions between the East and West diminished, COCOM's mission ended and the organization was dissolved.[11]

Although the Cold War is over, many technologically advanced countries continue to control the export of so-called **dual use** products that may be used for both civilian and military purposes. The United States, for example, requires export licenses for computers if they are capable of more than two billion calculations per second to ensure that they are used for nonmilitary purposes. Silicon Graphics found itself in hot water when it exported four supercomputers to the All-Russian Scientific Research Institute for Technical Physics without the required licenses. Although the purchaser stated that the machines would be used for analyzing air and water pollution caused by radioactive substances, Silicon Graphics was unaware that the Research Institute was best known for being the primary designer of Soviet nuclear warheads.[12]

The United States also controls the export of encryption technology embedded in computer software and hardware. Without such controls, it fears that terrorists, narcotraficantes, money launderers, and other international bad guys will be better able to evade the surveillance of police and antidrug officers around the world. Yet merchants, banks, and other financial institutions require advanced encryption technology to foil electronic embezzlers and scam artists. U.S. software exporters like Netscape and Microsoft believe that limiting the encryption capabilities of U.S. software exports is of little value: at best, they claim that many foreign users will patch stronger foreign-made encryption programs into their software; at worst, foreign purchasers will simply buy foreign-made software not subject to U.S. encryption regulations. Accordingly, the U.S. government has begrudgingly begun to relax its controls. Exported software used by financial institutions, for example, can now incorporate the latest encryption techniques free from controls. In most cases, however, the Bureau of Export Administration permits the export of high-powered encryption software only if the appropriate U.S. government agency is given the "keys" needed to decode electronic messages sent using that software should the need arise. As you can imagine, this policy makes many foreign users of U.S. software very uneasy, and U.S. software producers are concerned that they will lose sales to foreign companies not burdened by this encryption policy.[13]

Indirect Effects on International Competitiveness

Domestic laws may also indirectly affect the abilities of domestic firms to compete internationally by increasing their costs, thus reducing their price competitiveness relative to foreign firms. For example, labor costs for manufacturers in Germany, France, and the Benelux countries are among the world's highest as a result of government-mandated benefits packages. Thus those manufacturers find that their products are less price-competitive in export markets; many of them that compete internationally stress their products' quality rather than their price.

Many experts are particularly concerned about the impact of U.S. tort laws, particularly regarding product liability, on the international competitiveness of U.S. goods. **Tort laws** cover wrongful acts, damages, and injuries caused by an action other than a breach of contract. The costs imposed by tort laws include payments made by negligent parties to injured parties as well as the costs of pursuing such cases and defending oneself from lawsuits. Various features of the U.S. legal system encourage numerous lawsuits and large awards. These include easy availability of lawyers, the use of contingency fees, generous compensation for pain and suffering and punitive damages, strict liability standards, and opportunities to file class action suits. Tort costs as a percentage of GNP are in fact three to four times higher in the United States than in other developed countries (see Fig. 8.2).

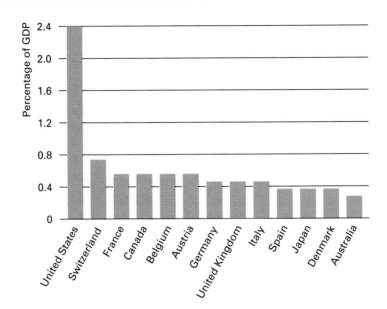

FIGURE 8.2

Tort Costs Relative to GNP

Source: Tillinghast, from *The Economist*, July 18, 1992, p. 13. © The Economist Newspaper Group, Inc. Reprinted with permission. Further reproduction prohibited.

Some U.S. manufacturers fear being driven out of their markets, despite their technological superiority, because of their vulnerability to product liability suits. The small-aircraft manufacturing industry is a good example of this phenomenon. U.S. juries have tended to make large awards to plaintiffs in crashes of small aircraft, regardless of whether the product itself was defective. As a result, the cost of aircraft liability insurance has skyrocketed. For example, the price of each aircraft sold by Cessna Aircraft now includes over $90,000 to cover insurance costs. Non-U.S. aircraft manufacturers are less vulnerable to product liability lawsuits than are U.S. firms, for reasons we discuss later in the chapter. As a result, Beech, Cessna, and other leading U.S. small aircraft manufacturers all but abandoned the low end of this market to non-U.S. firms. U.S. manufacturers produced only 613 small aircraft in 1991, down from 17,000 in 1978.[14] Only after the Congress passed the General Aviation Revitalization Act in 1994, which limits product liability lawsuits against small aircraft over 18 years of age, did companies like Cessna and Piper Aircraft return to building single-engine aircraft.[15]

Extraterritoriality

Countries often attempt to regulate business activities that are conducted outside their borders, a practice known as **extraterritoriality.** For example, many countries monitor international **transfer prices**—prices that one subsidiary of a firm pays for goods purchased from a second subsidiary—to ensure that firms are not evading income taxes owed them. How could a firm use transfer prices to evade taxes? Suppose subsidiary A, located in a country that imposes low corporate income taxes, deliberately overcharges subsidiary B, located in a country that imposes high corporate income taxes, for goods transferred between the two subsidiaries. As a result, reported profits are raised in the low-tax country and lowered in the high-tax country. By manipulating these transfer prices, the parent corporation lowers its overall tax bill. Most countries, including Japan and the United States, claim the right to reject the transfer prices used by a parent corporation to calculate its tax bill, even if they are associated with transactions outside of the country's borders.

Antitrust laws may be applied in an extraterritorial manner. Firms are vulnerable to antitrust lawsuits if they engage in activities outside the United States that diminish competition in the U.S. market. For example, the United States successfully sued Pilkington PLC, the British owner of the most important patents for producing flat glass, for limiting the ability of its U.S. licensees to use the technology in international markets. U.S. authorities claimed that Pilkington's policies hurt U.S. exports and reduced the incentive of U.S. flat glass producers to invest in R&D, thereby lessening competition.[16]

Antiboycott provisions in U.S. trade law also have an extraterritorial reach. U.S. antiboycott law prohibits U.S. firms from complying with any boycott ordered by a foreign country that prohibits trade with a country friendly to the United States. This law is primarily directed against a 1954 resolution adopted by the League of Arab States that calls for a boycott of any firm that does business with Israel. Briggs and Stratton, a U.S. small-engine manufacturer, typifies the plight of firms caught in the middle of this political struggle. Because of the Arab boycott, Briggs was blacklisted in 1977 from doing business in Syria because it had previously done business in Israel. However, U.S. antiboycott law prevented Briggs and Stratton from complying with Syrian law and refusing to do business with Israel.[17] Baxter International, one U.S. MNC that did get dropped from the Arab blacklist, found itself in deep trouble after a U.S. grand jury investigated it for selling discounted hospital supplies to Syria, allegedly as a bribe for being delisted. Baxter pleaded guilty to violating the antiboycott law and paid a fine of $6.6 million.[18]

The Helms-Burton Act is probably the most controversial application of extraterritoriality affecting international business today. This act, which sailed through both houses of the U.S. Congress after the Cuban air force shot down two small aircraft operated by a Miami exile group in early 1996, is directed against international firms that "traffic" in the assets of U.S. companies that were confiscated by the Cuban government when Fidel Castro took over that country in 1959. After their initial seizure, these confiscated assets were turned over to state-owned Cuban enterprises, which were beyond the reach of the U.S. owners and the U.S. court system. However, over time the Cuban government has leased or sold many of these assets to foreign companies, many of which do operate in the United States. The Helms-Burton Act authorizes the U.S. government and the former U.S. owners of the confiscated assets to take action against their new foreign owners. For example, the U.S. government can deny entrance into the United States of officers of companies who benefit from the use of these confiscated assets; such a fate has befallen executives of Canada's Sherritt Corporation, which is producing nickel and cobalt from a mine formerly owned by Freeport McMoRan, a New Orleans-based natural resources company. Companies can avoid such problems by compensating the former U.S. owners of Cuban assets for their losses. For example, ITT operated the telephone system in Cuba prior to Castro's takeover. The Cuban government confiscated ITT's property, but later allowed Stet, an Italian telecommunications conglomerate, to use that property. To avoid violating the Helms-Burton Act, Stet agreed to compensate ITT for the loss of its Cuban property. In the eyes of the U.S. government, the Helms-Burton Act is simply designed to ensure that foreign companies do not profit from Cuban property that was stolen from U.S. owners. In the eyes of many other countries, such as Canada and the European Union, the Helms-Burton Act is an ill-conceived policy of trying to bludgeon them into joining the U.S. anti-Castro crusade. Since by some

GOING GLOBAL

In many countries a small payment to government officials such as customs officers, immigration authorities, and building inspectors is an accepted part of doing business. If they want to succeed in such countries, international businesspeople are often faced with the ethical problem of whether or not to make such payments. Such payoffs to government officials are often frowned on in the Quad countries. In other countries, however, if a firm's employees fail to make such payments, its goods may face long delays in customs, its newly hired employees may be unable to obtain work permits, or building inspections and telephone installations may be delayed for months. Such payments are often justified on the basis that civil servants are underpaid, that "that's the way things are done here," or that they don't affect government policy. Less benign by any ethical standard, however, are large payments—often on the order of 10 to 20 percent of the contract amount—made to well-connected politicians and government officials designed to allow a firm to win major contracts.

Should Bribes Be a Competitive Weapon?

The U.S. Congress, in another application of the principle of extraterritoriality, passed in 1977 the **Foreign Corrupt Practices Act (FCPA)** to regulate payments to government officials in other countries. The FCPA prohibits U.S. firms, their employees, and agents acting on their behalf from paying or offering to pay bribes to any foreign government official in order to influence the official actions or policies of that official to gain or retain business. This prohibition applies even if the transaction occurs entirely outside U.S. borders. However, the FCPA does not outlaw routine payments, regardless of their size, made to government officials to expedite normal commercial transactions, such as issuance of customs documents or permits, inspection of goods, or provision of police services.

After the FCPA was passed, many U.S. MNCs argued that this law would put them at a substantial disadvantage in competing for international sales, since many of their rivals headquartered in other Quad countries are not burdened by similar antibribery laws. For example, only one third of the OECD countries (including Canada, Japan, the United Kingdom, and the United States) forbid firms from deducting foreign bribes from their income tax calculations as a cost of doing business. A U.S. Department of Commerce study suggested that U.S. firms lost $20 billion in international sales in 1996 to foreign companies that were able to pay bribes.

The damage to the global economy extends beyond the loss of sales by U.S. businesses. As one *Wall Street Journal* editorial noted:

estimates 85 percent of all foreign-owned private property in pre-Castro Cuba was owned by U.S. interests, it is easy to see why the disposition of confiscated property in Cuba is more important to the United States than to other countries.[19]

The Iran-Libya Sanctions Act, which authorizes the U.S. government to impose penalties on companies making new investments exceeding $20 million in the energy sector of those two countries, is creating similar problems. The first companies to run afoul of this act were Total, a French energy company, which proposed to invest $2 billion to develop a major Iranian gas field in conjunction with Russia's largest natural gas supplier, Gazprom, and Thailand's Petronas. Many U.S. trading partners disagree with U.S. foreign policy toward Iran and Libya and reject the U.S. attempt to impose its foreign policy views on foreign companies through application of this extraterritorial law. Some have even passed "blocking laws," which make it illegal for their home firms—including local subsidiaries of U.S. multinational corporations—to comply with U.S. sanctions.[20] Another important example of extraterritoriality is the Foreign Corrupt Practices Act, the purpose of which is explained in "Going Global."

Corruption distorts decision-making, which hurts competition, market efficiency, and economic development. For any who've watched as sleaze corrodes a country's economic engine—say in China, Vietnam, or Russia—this is obvious. Less obvious, but equally important, is the fact that corrosion makes its way around the globe. Slush funds set up to pay for palm-greasing in Timbuktu can as easily be dipped into for purposes closer to home.

Unfortunately, there is plenty of evidence to suggest that the *Wall Street Journal* is right. Montedison of Italy, for example, has been sued by the U.S. Securities and Exchange Commission for misleading U.S. investors by writing off $272 million of bribes as a bad loan on its financial statements. Similarly, $460,000 bribes to their presidents induced Korea First Bank and Cho Hung Bank to lend $1.84 billion to Hanbo Steel, which later declared bankruptcy in January 1997. The resulting scandal caused other banks to raise their credit standards, threatening the ability of thousands of small Korean businesses to acquire short-term financing to meet their legitimate business needs. Official corruption has destroyed the infrastructure and economy of developing countries such as Zaire (now renamed the Democratic Republic of the Congo), while the economic development of many other countries has been slowed by the inefficiencies created by choosing suppliers based on the size of the bribe rather than on the quality of the product or the price being charged.

Leaders of the world economic community have begun to acknowledge the seriousness of the problem. The World Bank and the International Monetary Fund have threatened to cut off aid and loans to countries unwilling to battle official corruption. Perhaps more important—since bribery takes both a briber and a bribee—in 1997 the OECD members agreed to a bribery ban that would apply to firms headquartered or located in member states. Symptomatic of the growing interest in this issue, the annual reports of Transparency International, a Berlin-based anticorruption group, are receiving increased publicity. According to its latest rankings, the Nordic countries of Denmark, Finland, Sweden, and Norway rank among the least corrupt countries, as do Australia, Canada, the Netherlands, and New Zealand. Unfortunately, some politicians still want to play by the old rules: despite all the publicity given to the corruption issue, in December 1997 President Suharto of Indonesia decreed that all companies and individuals earning over $42,000 should "donate" 2 percent of their salaries to a private charity controlled by Suharto and his political allies. Suharto was forced from office in May 1998 as a result of this and similar policies.

Sources: "Momentum Builds for Corporate-Bribery Ban," *Wall Street Journal,* September 23, 1997, p. A16; "Nigeria seen as most corrupt nation," *Financial Times,* August 1, 1997, p. 4; "Germany Says Business Bribes on the Rise," *Wall Street Journal,* April 14, 1997, p. A12; "Corruption destroys Zaire's infrastructure," *Houston Chronicle,* April 3, 1997, p. 24A; "Bribery Arrests at Hanbo Steel Creditors Add to Pressure on South Korean Banks," *Wall Street Journal,* February 6, 1997, p. A10; "Anticorruption Drive Starts to Show Results," *Wall Street Journal,* January 27, 1997, p. A1; "Commercial Corruption," *Wall Street Journal,* January 2, 1997, p. 6; "Charity in Indonesia," *Wall Street Journal,* December 27, 1997, p. A6; "Montedison of Italy Is Sued by the SEC over Scandal That Nearly Sank Firm," *Wall Street Journal,* November 22, 1996; "Kantor calls for bribery action," *Financial Times,* July 26, 1996, p. 3; "Foreigners Use Bribes to Beat U.S. Rivals in Many Deals, New Report Concludes," *Wall Street Journal,* October 12, 1995, p. A3. Quote from "Competitive Bribing," *Wall Street Journal,* April 19, 1996, p. A12.

Domestic laws may also inadvertently affect the business practices of foreign firms operating outside the country's borders. For example, firms whose products are geared to the export market often alter their production techniques to meet the regulations of the importing countries, even though their operations are legal within their home country. For example, Ceramica Santa Anita, a china manufacturer in Saltillo, Mexico, exports 30 percent of its output to the United States. Because of the importance of the U.S. market, the firm adheres in its manufacturing processes to the more restrictive U.S. regulations regarding the lead content of dishware.[21] Similarly, Grupo Herdez was forced to alter its production processes in Mexico in order to sell its goods in the U.S. market. Grupo Herdez is one of Mexico's largest producers of mole, a spicy but sweet sauce made from chocolate and chili peppers. The firm's traditional way of preparing the chilies for production—laying them out to dry in the sun for several days—failed to meet hygiene standards of the U.S. Food and Drug Administration (FDA). To receive the necessary FDA approval and benefit from the growing U.S. market for Mexican foods,

Grupo Herdez had to develop a new technology that uses electronic dryers to prepare the chilies for mole production.[22]

The Impacts of MNCs on Host Countries

Firms establishing operations beyond the borders of their home country affect and are affected by the political, economic, social, and cultural environments of the host countries in which they operate. To compete effectively in these markets and maintain productive relationships with the host country governments, managers of MNCs must recognize how they and their firms should interact with the national and local environments.[23]

Economic and Political Impacts

MNCs affect every local economy in which they compete and operate. Many of their effects are positive. They may make direct investments in new plants and factories, thereby creating local jobs. In 1995 U.S. subsidiaries of foreign MNCs employed 4.9 million people, while foreign subsidiaries of U.S. MNCs employed 6.0 million workers.[24] Such investments provide work for local contractors, builders, and suppliers. MNCs also pay taxes, which benefit the local economy, helping to improve educational, transportation, and other municipal services. For example, when Toyota began operating in Georgetown, Kentucky, the $1.5 million in property taxes it paid represented almost one quarter of the town's municipal budget. Technology transfer can also have positive local effects. For example, a main benefit to the Beijing municipal government of its joint venture with American Motors was access to the latest U.S. automotive technology. And General Electric raised the productivity of Hungary's largest light bulb manufacturer by transferring technological knowledge to the Hungarian firm.

However, MNCs may also have negative effects on the local economy. To the extent MNCs compete directly with local firms, they may cause those firms to lose both jobs and profits. Also, as the local economy becomes more dependent on the economic health of an MNC, the financial fortunes of that firm take on increasing significance. When retrenchment by the MNC is accompanied by layoffs, cutbacks, or a total shutdown of local operations, the effects can be devastating to the local economy.

MNCs also may have a significant political impact, either intentionally or unintentionally. Their sheer size, for example, often gives them tremendous power in each country in which they operate. And, as is always the case, there is the possibility that this power may be misused. Even when it is not, MNCs are often able to counter efforts by host governments to restrict their activities. They simply threaten to shift production and jobs to other locations. For example, when Spain passed new laws in the early 1990s that raised labor costs, MNCs such as Colgate-Palmolive, S.C. Johnson & Son, Kubota, and Volkswagen closed some of their Spanish factories and/or slashed payrolls. The result was soaring unemployment that reached 24.5 percent in the mid-1990s.[25]

Cultural Impacts

MNCs also can exert a major influence on the cultures in which they operate. As they raise local standards of living and introduce new products and services previously unavailable locally, people in the host cultures develop new norms, standards, and behaviors. Some of these changes are positive, such as the introduction of safer equipment and machinery, better health care and pharmaceuticals, and purer and more sanitary food products. Others are not. While Toyota's locating a plant in Kentucky induced local grocers to stock bean curd and tempura batter, it also encouraged a local entrepreneur to open the "Osaka Health Spa," a massage parlor located within a block of city hall.[26] A more important example is Nestlé's heavy promotion of infant formulas in the world's developing countries. Mothers in such countries were allegedly enticed into buying the products but were not trained in their proper use. They diluted the formula in order to make it go further and often were unable to follow adequate sanitation procedures. As a result, critics argue, infant mortality in those countries increased significantly.

Host Country Laws

Countries have broad discretion to pass and enforce within their borders whatever laws they want, free from legal interference by other countries. While most laws adopted by a host country affect both domestic and foreign firms equally, some are explicitly directed against foreign firms. Because countries are sovereign entities, international businesses have little recourse except to abide by local laws.

Ownership Issues

In most countries, there is ongoing debate between the political left and right regarding the appropriate balance between governmental control of the economy and reliance on market forces to allocate resources. Often when leftist governments obtain power, they choose to transfer ownership of resources from the private to the public sector, a process known as **nationalization.** Most vulnerable to such actions are industries that lack mobility: natural resource industries such as crude oil production and mining and capital-intensive industries such as steel, chemicals, and oil refining. When the host government compensates the private owners for their losses, such a transfer is called **expropriation.** When the host government offers no compensation, the transfer is called **confiscation.** Most governments, including that of the United States, recognize the right of other national governments to mandate the transfer of private property within their borders to the public sector, although they do expect that foreign owners will receive suitable compensation for their lost property. For example, many Arab oil-producing countries nationalized the properties of Western oil firms after 1973. However, they offered those firms a combination of compensation, continuing operating agreements, and future drilling rights that the firms found acceptable. Conversely, a key element in the U.S. conflict with Cuba is Cuba's lack of compensation for assets seized from U.S. firms.

Privatization. **Privatization** is the conversion of state-owned property to privately owned property. Although not strictly an issue of host country control, it is the opposite of nationalization and creates opportunities for international businesses. Most state-owned enterprises sold to the private sector are unprofitable, undercapitalized, and overstaffed. Nevertheless, they are often attractive to international businesses seeking to expand their operations into new markets located in key sectors of a national economy, such as telecommunications, transportation, and manufacturing.

Privatization, which gained momentum in the 1980s, stems from two primary forces: political ideology and economic pressure. Political ideology prompted Margaret Thatcher, the prime minister of the United Kingdom from 1979 to 1990, who is widely seen as the "mother of privatization," to call for diminishing the role of the state in the economy. During the 1980s, the British government sold off its interests in British Airways, British Telecom, the British Airport Authority, and British Petroleum. Brian Mulroney, head of Canada's Progressive Conservative Party, followed a similar agenda during his tenure as Canada's prime minister from 1984 to 1993, as have the leaders of Argentina, Brazil, Chile, Mexico, and many other countries in the past decade.[27]

Privatization has also resulted from competitive pressures that firms face in global markets. The telecommunications industry provides a perfect example of this phenomenon. That industry has benefited from rapid technological change. Yet many national governments, facing enormous budgetary pressures and deficits, have found it difficult to raise the capital required to upgrade and expand state-owned telecommunications systems. As a result, countries such as Argentina, Mexico, Chile, Venezuela, and the United Kingdom have privatized telecommunications services.[28]

Constraints on Foreign Ownership. Many governments limit foreign ownership of domestic firms in order to avoid control of their economies or key industries by foreigners. For example, Mexico restricts foreign ownership in its energy industry, believing that the benefits of its oil reserves, which it views as part of its "national patrimony," should accrue only to its citizens. Foreign firms are often excluded from the radio and television broadcasting industries. For example, the United States limits foreigners to 25 percent ownership of U.S. television and radio stations. Similar rules exist in Europe. Alternatively, a country's government may restrict foreign ownership because of a fear that a large community of foreign-owned firms with easy access to foreign capital could undermine its industrial policy. South Korea used this rationale to restrict foreign ownership of its firms for almost half a century. South Korea also has controlled foreign participation in its economy via its banking policies, which helped the government to funnel credit at preferential interest rates to the country's largest chaebols, the family-centered conglomerates that account for much of Korea's GNP. These barriers hindered the ability of foreign firms to expand their Korean operations or act independently of the government's industrial policy.[29]

Countries can also constrain foreign MNCs by imposing restrictions on their ability to **repatriate,** or return to their home countries, profits earned in the host country. Such restrictions were common in the 1980s, but many countries, such as Botswana and Ethiopia, have abolished their repatriation controls in the 1990s as they have adopted more free market-oriented policies.

Intellectual Property Rights

Intellectual property—patents, copyrights, trademarks, brand names—is an important asset of most MNCs. The value of intellectual property can be quickly damaged unless countries enforce firms' ownership rights. Several international treaties exist to promote protection of such rights, including the International Convention for the Protection of Industrial Property Rights (more commonly known as the Paris Convention), the Berne Convention for the Protection of Literary and Artistic Works, the Universal Copyright Convention, and the Trade-Related Intellectual Property Rights agreement (part of the Uruguay Round). These treaties provide some protection to owners of intellectual property rights. However, not all countries have signed them. Further, their enforcement by many signatories is lax. Generally, countries that are net exporters of intellectual property protect it strongly, while net importing countries protect it weakly, if at all.

Weak protection for intellectual property rights can have high costs for international businesses. For example, piracy of computer software written for business and professional applications cost U.S. software developers an estimated $11.2 billion in annual revenue in 1997. Music companies estimate their losses to illegal duplication of cassettes and CDs run $2.2 billion annually. China is a particular sore point to the music industry. Experts believe that it is the source of 60 percent of the estimated 200 million CDs that are illegally duplicated annually in the world. After years of promising to close down pirate CD factories and then failing to do so—in part because many of the factories were owned by Chinese government ministries—Chinese officials began to crack down on these rogue operations after signing an intellectual property protection agreement with the United States in 1996. Although they have closed down dozens of pirate CD factories, new ones have sprung up elsewhere in China or migrated to nearby areas like Macao. Bulgaria is another major source of illegal CDs, shipping an estimated 1 million CDs per month to Moscow, where they are distributed throughout Russia and the other former Soviet republics.[30]

Enforcement of intellectual property rights is weak in many areas, such as Serbia. This Belgrade seller of CDs is obviously making no attempt to hide the source of his merchandise from the local police.

International conflicts may also develop because intellectual property laws are not consistent. The United States follows a "first to invent" patent policy, as do Canada and the Philippines.[31] The U.S. system focuses on protecting the rights of the "true" inventor. Unfortunately, it also encourages much litigation as competing patent applicants attempt to prove they were the first to invent the product. The "first to file" system adopted by other countries avoids this litigation by unambiguously assigning rights to the first patent applicant. However, it also puts a premium on speed in applying and favors larger firms with deeper pockets.

Differences in patent practices can also lead to conflicts. For example, Japanese firms tend to file numerous patents, each of which may reflect only a minor modification of an existing patent. Conversely, U.S. patent law requires that patentable inventions be new, useful, and nonobvious. Accordingly, U.S. firms tend to file far fewer patents than Japanese companies. This had led to trade disputes between the United States and Japan over the use of so-called "patent flooding" by Japanese firms, in which a company files a series of patent applications protecting narrow, minor technical improvements to a competitor's existing patents. Patent flooding makes it difficult for the competitor to improve its own technology without infringing on the intellectual property of the patent flooder. CyberOptics, a small Minneapolis developer of LaserAlign, a software and laser-based technology that helps robots position miniature components on circuit boards, provides an example of a firm that believes it has been harmed by patent flooding by a much larger company. It had worked closely with Yamaha for five years to incorporate CyberOptics technology on the pick-and-place robots Yamaha used to produce its motorcycles and other products. Both companies agreed that neither would file for patent protection for technology they had developed jointly without each other's consent. However, CyberOptics discovered that Yamaha had filed twenty-six patent applications in Japan, Europe, and the United States for technology it believes was developed collaboratively based on the LaserAlign system, and that Yamaha was allegedly warning potential CyberOptics customers that they might be in violation of Yamaha's patents if they purchased CyberOptics' services. Consequently, the Minneapolis firm sued Yamaha for breach of contract and infringement of its patents.[32]

Registration of trademarks and brand names can also cause problems for international businesses. Generally, most countries follow a "first to file" approach, which often lends itself to abuses against foreigners. A firm may popularize a brand name or trademark in its home market, only to find when it attempts to export its product to a second country that some opportunistic entrepreneur has already applied for the intellectual property rights in that country. For example, Nike, while preparing its marketing campaign for the 1992 Summer Olympics in Barcelona, discovered to its horror that its trademarks in Spain applied only to footware, not to sports apparel. Cidesport, the Spanish firm that possessed the rights to use the Nike name on wearing apparel, generously offered to sell those rights to Nike—for $30 million.[33] Similarly, J.C. Penney, which had registered its trademark in most markets to avoid such blackmail, lost the rights to its name in Singapore to a small entrepreneur who adopted the name "J C Penney Collections" for her two clothing stores. The High Court of Singapore, while acknowledging that J.C. Penney had validly registered its trademark in that country, determined that the U.S. firm had lost the right to its company name for failure to exercise its use there.[34]

Administrative delays may also hurt the rights of intellectual property owners. In Japan, approval of a trademark application often takes four times as long for a foreign firm as for a Japanese firm.[35] Approval of foreign patent applications may also take a long time. For example, three decades elapsed before Japanese courts in 1989 recognized Texas Instruments' (TI) original patents on integrated circuits, substantially reducing the value of TI's royalty payments from Japanese licensees. Some firms, such as Fujitsu, have been able to avoid paying TI any royalties at all, arguing that their circuit designs rely on newer, more improved technology rather than on TI's original patents. In essence, the slowness of Japan's judicial process allowed companies like Fujitsu to benefit from TI's technology during the early days of the semiconductor industry without having to compensate TI for its intellectual property.[36]

Dispute Resolution in International Business

As in purely domestic transactions, conflicts often arise in international business. Resolving disputes in international commerce can be very complicated. Typically, four questions must be answered for an international dispute to be resolved:

1 Which country's law applies?
2 In which country should the issue be resolved?
3 What technique should be used to resolve the conflict—litigation, arbitration, mediation, or negotiation?
4 How will the settlement be enforced?

Many international business contracts specify answers to these questions in order to reduce uncertainty and expense in resolving disputes. The courts of most of the major trading countries will honor and enforce the provisions of these contracts, as long as they are not contrary to other aspects of the country's public policy. For example, a contract could not include a waiver of the right of a third party to seek damages for injuries caused by a product defect in his or her home country. If a contract contains no answer to the first two questions above, each party to the transaction may seek to hear the case in the court system most favorable to its own interests—a process known as **forum shopping.** Forum shopping is alleged to place some U.S. manufacturers, such as Cessna, at a disadvantage in international markets. Monetary awards are higher in U.S. courts, so many plaintiffs' lawyers attempt to use those courts to adjudicate foreign lawsuits for product defects in U.S.-made goods sold internationally. In contrast, a foreign manufacturer of a good sold outside the United States would not face the threat of having to defend its product in a U.S. court because of the lack of a tie to that forum.

The leakage of poisonous gas at Union Carbide's Indian affiliate in Bhopal, India, in December 1984 led to an instance of attempted forum shopping. Negligence at a plant owned by Union Carbide–India, which was 51 percent owned by the U.S. MNC Union Carbide, was allegedly responsible for the death of 2800 people and injury to thousands more (22 percent of the Indian firm's stock was owned by the Indian government and the remaining 27 percent by thousands of Indian investors). After hearing of the accident, several U.S. trial lawyers flew to India, signed up Indian clients, rushed back to the United

States, and filed a class action lawsuit against Union Carbide in U.S. courts, arguing that the U.S. parent effectively controlled the Indian affiliate and that therefore U.S. courts were the appropriate forum in which to try the case. Union Carbide claimed that, as only part owner of Union Carbide–India, it did not have effective control of the Indian operations. It therefore countered that Indian courts were the appropriate forum to adjudicate responsibility and damages for the accident. Both Union Carbide and the U.S. trial lawyers (who typically get a **contingency fee** equal to one third of all monetary damages awarded) were fully aware that U.S. courts would be likely to award higher monetary damages than Indian courts. However, both U.S. and Indian courts determined that damage suits against the firm should be heard in Indian courts. The settlements ultimately received by the Indian plaintiffs were small by U.S. judicial standards.[37]

Whether a foreign court order is enforced is determined by the principle of comity. The **principle of comity** provides that a country will honor and enforce within its own territory the judgments and decisions of foreign courts, with certain limitations. For the principle to apply, countries commonly require three conditions to be met:

1 Reciprocity is extended between the countries; that is, country A and country B mutually agree to honor each other's court decisions.

2 Proper notice is given the defendant.

3 The foreign court judgment does not violate domestic statutes or treaty obligations.[38]

Because of the costs and uncertainties of litigation, many international businesses seek less expensive means of settling disputes over international transactions. Often business conflicts will be resolved through alternative dispute resolution techniques, such as arbitration. **Arbitration** is the process by which both parties to the conflict agree to submit their cases to a private individual or body whose decision they will honor. Because of the speed, privacy, and informality of such proceedings, disputes can often be resolved more cheaply than through the court system. For example, a five-year-old conflict between IBM and Fujitsu over the latter's unauthorized use of proprietary IBM software that was moving slowly through the U.S. judicial system was settled quickly with the help of two neutral arbitrators from the American Arbitration Association.[39]

Another set of issues arises when an international business is in a dispute with a national government. The legal recourse available to international businesses in such disputes is often limited. For example, the **Foreign Sovereign Immunities Act of 1976** of the United States provides that the actions of foreign governments against U.S. firms are generally beyond the jurisdiction of U.S. courts. Thus if France chose to nationalize IBM's French operations or to impose arbitrary taxes on IBM computers, IBM could not use U.S. courts to seek redress against the sovereign nation of France. However, the Foreign Sovereign Immunities Act does not grant immunity for the *commercial* activities of a sovereign state. For example, if the French government contracted to purchase 2000 personal computers from IBM and then repudiated the contract, IBM could sue France in U.S. courts.

Countries, including the United States, often seek to protect their firms from arbitrary actions by host country governments by negotiating bilateral treaties. These treaties commonly require the host country to agree to arbitrate investment disputes involving that country and citizens of the other country. For example, the United States and Jamaica have such a treaty. When the Jamaican government announced an increase in taxes on Alcoa's aluminum refining plant despite a contract between that government and Alcoa that prohibited such an increase, Alcoa was able to force the Jamaican government to submit its decision to arbitration.[40]

The Political Environment

An important part of any business decision is assessing the political environment in which the firm operates. Laws and regulations passed by governments at any level can affect the viability of a firm's operations in the host country. For example, minimum wage laws affect the price the firm must pay for labor, zoning regulations affect the way in which it can use its property, and environmental protection laws affect the production technology it can use as well as the costs of disposing of waste materials. Adverse changes in tax laws can slowly destroy a firm's profitability. But civil wars, assassinations, or kidnappings of foreign businesspeople and expropriation of a firm's property are equally as dangerous to the viability of a firm's foreign operations.

Political Risk

Most firms are comfortable assessing the political climate in their home countries. However, assessing the political climate in other countries is far more problematic. Experienced international businesses engage in **political risk assessment,** a systematic analysis of the political risks they face in foreign countries. **Political risks** are defined as any changes in the political environment that may adversely affect the value of the firm's business activities. Most political risks can be divided into three categories:

♦ Ownership risk, where the property of the firm is threatened through confiscation or expropriation

♦ Operating risk, in which the ongoing operations of the firm and/or the safety of its employees are threatened through changes in laws, environmental standards, tax codes, terrorism, armed insurrection, etc.

♦ Transfer risk, in which the government interferes with the firm's ability to shift funds into and out of the country

As Table 8.1 shows, political risks may result from governmental actions such as passage of laws that expropriate private property, raise operating costs, devalue the currency, or constrain the repatriation of profits. They may also arise from nongovernmental actions, such as kidnappings, extortion, and acts of terrorism.

TABLE 8.1

Examples of Political Risks

TYPE	IMPACT ON FIRMS
Expropriation	Loss of future profits
Confiscation	Loss of assets Loss of future profits
Campaigns against foreign goods	Loss of sales Increased costs of public relations campaigns to improve public image
Mandatory labor benefits legislation	Increased operating costs
Kidnappings, terrorist threats, and other forms of violence	Disrupted production Increased security costs Increased managerial costs Lower productivity
Civil wars	Destruction of property Lost sales Disruption of production Increased security costs Lower productivity
Inflation	Higher operating costs
Repatriation	Inability to transfer funds freely
Currency devaluations	Reduced value of repatriated earnings
Increased taxation	Lower after-tax profits

Political risks may affect all firms equally or focus on only a handful. A **macropolitical risk** affects all firms in a country; examples are the civil wars that tore apart Zaire, Bosnia, and Rwanda in the mid-1990s. A **micropolitical risk** affects only a specific firm or firms within a specific industry. Saudia Arabia's nationalization of its oil industry in the 1970s is an example of a governmentally imposed micropolitical risk. Nongovernmental micropolitical risks are also important. For example, Disneyland Paris has been the target of numerous symbolic protests by French farmers, who view it as a convenient target for venting their disgust with U.S. international agricultural policies.

Any firm contemplating entering a new market should acquire basic knowledge of that country, learning, for example, about its political and economic structure in order to control the firm's political risks. The firm needs answers to such questions as:

- Is the country a democracy or a dictatorship? Is power concentrated in the hands of one person or one political party?

- Does the country normally rely on the free market or on government controls to allocate resources? How much of a contribution is the private sector expected to make in helping the government achieve its overall economic objectives? Does the government view foreign firms as a means of promoting or hindering its economic goals?

- Are the firm's customers in the public or private sector? If public, does the government favor domestic suppliers? Are its competitors in the public or private sector? If public, will the government allow foreigners to compete with the public firms on even terms?

- When making changes in its policies, does the government act arbitrarily or does it rely on the rule of law?

- How stable is the existing government? If it leaves office, will there be drastic changes in the economic policies of the new government?

Many experts believe that political risks increase when the gap between citizens' current welfare levels and their expectations widens. When this gap between reality and expectations grows large, politicians may impose new burdens on businesses in an attempt to deflect citizens' frustrations from themselves. In such instances, foreign firms are particularly vulnerable to becoming the scapegoat for domestic economic problems. Alternatively, governments failing to meet the basic necessities of their citizens may trigger armed insurgencies or terrorist activities. Needless to say, the greater the level of political instability in the country, the more likely that changes will be forthcoming and that they will be drastic in nature.

Most MNCs continually monitor the countries in which they do business for changes in political risk. Often the best sources of information are internal to the firm. Employees of a foreign subsidiary, whether they are citizens of the home country or of the host country, possess firsthand knowledge of the local political environment and are a valuable source of political risk information. The views of local staff should be supplemented by those of outsiders. Embassy officials and international chambers of commerce are often rich sources of information. Governments themselves can supply vital information. Most governments signal their economic and political agendas during the political campaigns that lead to their elections or during the military campaigns that lead to the overthrow of their opponents; once in office, they continue to provide useful information about their current and future plans. Moreover, numerous consulting firms specialize in political risk assessment to help firms evaluate the risks of doing business in a particular country. And several international business publications annually print surveys of political risk around the world. Map 8.2 depicts the results of one such survey published in *Euromoney* magazine.

The types of information and the level of detail firms need to assess political risk depend on the type of business and its likely duration in the host country. The greater and longer-lived a firm's investment, the broader its risk assessment should be. A Singapore toy manufacturer that subcontracts with a Chinese firm to assemble toy trucks needs to know about politically influenced factors such as trends in exchange rates, reliability of customs procedures, and the legal recourse available to it in the event the Chinese subcontractor fails to deliver products that meet con-

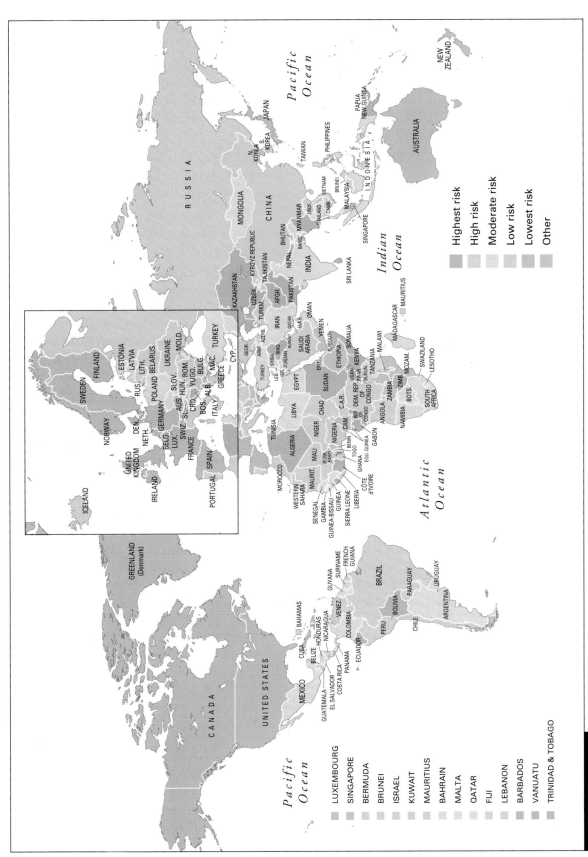

MAP 8.2   **Countries' Relative Political Riskiness, 1998**   Source: Euromoney's Annual Survey of Country Risk, *Euromoney*, December 1997, p. 60 ff.

tract specifications and deadlines. If the Singapore toy manufacturer wants to build and operate its own toy factory in China, its political risk assessment must be broadened. It needs to scrutinize its vulnerability to changes in laws dealing with labor relations, environmental protection, currency controls, and profit repatriation, as well as the likelihood the Chinese government may nationalize foreigners' property or split into warring factions and trigger a civil war.

Some degree of political risk exists in every country. But obviously the nature and importance of these risks change by country. The French farmers' protests merely inconvenienced Disneyland Paris's managers, whereas bombardment of Bosnia's capital of Sarajevo by Serbian nationalists destroyed the economic viability of firms operating there. In political risk assessment, as in most business decisions, it is a matter of matching risks with rewards. A firm considering an investment in an environment high in political risk should be sure that it can obtain sufficiently offsetting high rates of return if it decides to enter that market. Firms already operating in a high-risk country may choose to take steps to reduce their vulnerability to political risks. For example, a firm can reduce its financial exposure by reducing its net investment in the local subsidiary, perhaps by repatriating the subsidiary's profits to the parent through dividend payments, by selling shares in the subsidiary to host country citizens, or by utilizing short-term leases to acquire new capital equipment rather than purchasing it outright. Alternatively, a firm may build domestic political support in the host country by being a good corporate citizen, for example, by purchasing inputs from local suppliers where possible, employing host country citizens in key management and administrative positions, and supporting local charities.

To reduce the risk of foreign operations, most developed countries have created government-owned or government-sponsored organizations to insure firms against political risks. As we mentioned in Chapter 6, the **Overseas Private Investment Corporation (OPIC)** insures U.S. overseas investments against nationalization, insurrections or revolutions, and foreign-exchange inconvertibility. For example, it sold Texaco $28 million in insurance to cover its investment in 150 oil wells in western Siberia in the mid-1990s.[41] However, OPIC insurance is limited to firms operating in countries with which the United States has signed a bilateral investment treaty. The **Multilateral Investment Guarantee Agency (MIGA),** a subsidiary of the World Bank established in 1988, provides similar insurance against political risks. Private insurance firms, such as Lloyd's of London, also underwrite political risk insurance, although the premiums they charge are often higher than those of OPIC or MIGA.[42]

The Emerging Market Economies

Political risk assessment is particularly important when a country is undergoing substantial political, economic, and legal changes, such as is the case in the former centrally planned economies of Eastern and Central Europe and of the People's Republic of China. (A centrally planned economy (CPE) is one in which government planners determine prices and production levels for individual firms.) The changes are more dramatic in the case of the former Soviet bloc countries, for they have abandoned communism both economically and politically as a result of political revolutions that swept the area in 1989 and 1990. China continues to be ruled by its Communist Party; however, the party adopted a series of pro-free market reforms beginning in 1982 that have allowed a vibrant private sector to develop and coexist alongside many inefficient, highly subsidized state-owned enterprises.

Creating a modern market economy from the remains of a centrally planned system is an enormous and complex challenge. It produces concomitant micropolitical and macropolitical risks for international businesses. A primary source of political risk in most of these countries is the instability of their political systems. Democratic traditions are weakly rooted in many of the countries of Central and Eastern Europe, particularly those that emerged from the former Soviet Union and its Czarist history of one-person rule. While some former Soviet bloc countries, such as the Czech Republic, Hungary, and Poland, have quickly established functioning democracies, others, such as Azerbaijan, Belarus, and Kazakhstan, have not. The situation in Russia is more complex. Because the Russian presidency has extensive powers, an important source of political risk lies in who will replace Boris Yeltsin when his term of office expires. Ethnic conflicts also permeate the region. For example, the province of Chechnya fought a well-publicized, bloody war of independence from Russia. A similar struggle has allowed ethnic Armenians to carve out their homeland of Nagorno-Karabakh from Azerbaijan.

Government unpredictability is another cause of political risk. One source is the continued employment of Soviet-era bureaucrats, who often use their control over required licenses and permits to frustrate the plans of private businesses. For example, Motorola spent $2 million on feasibility studies for establishing a mobile-phone network after receiving assurances from the Ukrainian Ministry of Communication that no fees would be charged to obtain an exclusive frequency for its service. Later the Ministry changed its mind, proposing to assess a fee of $65 million annually, jeopardizing the $500 million project. Similarly, Monsanto found itself under investigation by a branch of the Ukrainian Ministry of Agriculture after it began to sell its agricultural chemicals to private distributors and farmers directly, instead of through another branch of the Ministry of Agriculture.[43]

Another problem faced by these countries is establishing tax codes and tax collection systems that raise necessary revenues but still encourage economic growth. Such a problem has plagued Russia. By some estimates, it collected only 50 to 60 percent of those taxes due it in 1996. This creates several difficulties. First, low collection rates discourage many firms and individuals from paying their taxes, in the belief if nobody else is paying taxes, then why should I? Facing shortages of tax revenues, the government then imposes new taxes to make up the revenue shortfall. The cumulative burden of these taxes would likely bankrupt any firm that tried to pay them all. IBM, for example, announced in 1996 that it would pull out of a joint production venture for just this reason.[44] The net effect is that the tax code discourages many firms, both domestic and foreign, from investing in Russia. Instead, many Russian firms are busily establishing subsidiaries in tax havens to avoid taxes. From 1993 to 1996, an estimated $65 billion in Russian capital has been deposited in Cyprus and other tax havens such as Belize, the Cayman Islands, Lichtenstein, and Luxembourg. In 1996 alone, Russian firms established 16,000 subsidiaries in Cyprus. Second, shortfalls in tax collections mean that the government has been unable to pay its employees, military forces, and pensioners, which in turn has made it difficult for them to obtain goods or repay their creditors. By one estimate, overdue payables in 1996 reached a level equal to 21 percent of the country's GDP. This in turn has increased the prevalence of small bribes as a means of paying for the bureaucracy. Government agencies are expected to generate "nonbudget" funds, such as arbitrarily imposed fines that may look like bribes to the cynical, to fund the salaries that the central government is unable to pay. At least one Russian entrepreneur has received a request from a government agency, faxed on its letterhead, for a bribe to allow her restaurant to open. The breakdown in public services has also allowed organized crime to thrive. Rather than deal with criminal groups, many foreign companies have resorted to hiring security services, often operated by former KGB or police officials, to protect their interests and steer them out of sticky situations.[45]

Firms operating in China avoid some of these risks because of the continuing control of its government by the Communist Party. Yet the party's control creates other problems for international businesses operating there. For example, government procurement decisions often reflect the warmness or coldness of diplomatic relations between the Chinese government and a company's home government. To show its displeasure with U.S. protests of China's human rights policies, for example, the Chinese government shifted a large aircraft order from Boeing to Airbus Industrie. The Chinese government also often exploits the eagerness of foreign firms to gain access to the world's largest market to its advantage. For example, by imposing a 100 percent tariff on automobile imports and controlling FDI in that industry, China creates bidding wars among U.S., Asian, and European car companies wishing to build assembly factories there. Often the winner must agree to help train Chinese engineers, set up research centers, produce parts locally, and transfer technology to their local joint venture partner.

A further complication is that many government agencies have responded to China's promarket reforms by hatching new for-profit businesses. For example, the largest business conglomerate in China—some 20,000 firms—is controlled by the People's Liberation Army, which owns and operates such diverse enterprises as mines, construction firms, warehouses, karaoke bars, massage parlors, and Baskin-Robbins ice cream parlors.[46] Similarly, many municipalities have created for-profit companies. By some estimates, these hybrid public-private firms number in the millions and account for 40 percent of China's manufacturing output.[47] These firms can be suppliers, joint venture partners, or competitors to international firms doing business in China. Needless to say, given their political connections, they often must be dealt with gingerly.

Foreign firms participating in the transition of former communist economies to a free market system have also encountered operational difficulties. The public infrastructures of these countries have been neglected for the past forty years. Highways, airports, and distribution systems for electricity, water, and natural gas are often overtaxed and unreliable. Deficiencies in communications systems have proven to be particularly troublesome to Western firms used to telephone conference calls and overnight package deliveries—remember, the communist governments wanted to control communication among their populations, not encourage it.

The executive education and management training needs of these countries are also huge. Under the old communist system, capital was allocated to businesses according to a central plan. Production quotas were assigned to factories, whose output was distributed to state-owned retail stores. Given the scarcity of consumer goods, the stores quickly sold whatever was given them to sell. Under this system, there was no need for entrepreneurs or specialists in finance or marketing. Accounting and management information systems were designed to monitor production, not costs or sales or inventory levels. As a result, multiple layers of managers must be trained in the skills needed to run a business in a competitive market economy.

These training needs extend below the managerial level. Many communist factories were plagued by low production levels. Workers' attitudes could be summed up by this remark: "They pretend to pay us and we pretend to work." Attitudes in service industries were anything but service-oriented. Because of the lack of consumer goods, most sales personnel treated customers as beggars pleading for the right to buy what few goods were available. As a result, international businesses beginning operations in these countries must thoroughly train their employees in the behaviors and attitudes required in a competitive market economy. Fortunately, many of these employees are eager to learn about the free market system and to work for Western firms. For example, when McDonald's was preparing to open its first Moscow restaurant, it received 27,000 job applications. McDonald's put the 600 applicants it hired through a thorough training program to teach them its systems and procedures.

Nonetheless, many Western firms have recognized the potentially rich market the region offers. The consumer goods market is particularly attractive for Western firms because of the poor quality and scarcity of such goods under state control. As one businessperson noted, "The late Soviet Union could awe the world by putting men in space, but it couldn't make decent detergents, soaps, and shampoos."[48] And while the risks are high, so are the potential rewards, for the market is indeed huge. China and the former Soviet Union encompass a market of 1.5 billion people with a total GDP of $1.2 trillion.

CHAPTER REVIEW

Summary

The legal systems used by the world's countries vary dramatically. The former British colonies follow the common law tradition of the United Kingdom, while most other Western countries use the civil law system that originated with the Romans. A few countries, such as Iran and Saudia Arabia, use religious law, while centrally planned economies use bureaucratic law.

Laws adopted by the home countries of international businesses can influence the global marketplace in many ways. The home country can impose restrictions on the ability of firms to conduct business internationally, as well as indirectly affect their competitiveness by raising their costs of doing business. Home country laws may also have extraterritorial reach, that is, affecting transactions conducted beyond the country's borders.

MNCs operating in a host country can influence that country's economic, political, and cultural environments. Often these changes are positive. For example, FDI generates new employment opportunities and raises the productivity of local workers. But MNCs can also impact the host country negatively by increasing

competition for workers or introducing products or practices incompatible with the local culture.

Host countries also shape the environment in which international businesses must operate. A host country can control ownership of firms within its borders and enforce (or fail to enforce) the intellectual property rights of foreign firms. The host country may also control the ability of MNCs to repatriate their profits home.

Resolution of international disputes is also important to international businesses. Because of the costliness of international litigation, firms often attempt to resolve disputes through dispute resolution techniques such as arbitration. When U.S. MNCs are dealing with sovereign countries, however, their ability to resolve conflicts is often hindered by the terms of the Foreign Sovereign Immunities Act.

International businesses operating in foreign environments are also subject to political risks. To protect themselves from changes in the political environment, firms should continually monitor the political situations in the countries in which they operate by consulting with local staff, embassy officials, and, where appropriate, consulting firms specializing in political risk assessment.

Firms doing business in the emerging market economies of China and the former Soviet bloc countries face particularly high levels of political risk. In many of these countries, democratic traditions are weakly rooted or nonexistent. Ethnic conflicts still plague the area. These countries often fail to understand the importance of designing stable economic policies and have not yet developed sound tax codes that encourage the prosperity of their private sectors. The lack of skills necessary to operate a business in a free market economy is also an impediment to the revitalization of these economies, as are deficiencies in the public infrastructures.

Review Questions

1. Describe the four different types of legal systems with which international businesses must deal.

2. What is extraterritoriality?

3. How does forum shopping affect the competitiveness of U.S. firms in international markets?

4. How can an MNC affect its host country?

5. How do expropriation and confiscation differ?

6. Why do countries impose restrictions on foreign ownership of domestic firms?

7. What is the difference between "first to invent" and "first to file" patent systems?

8. How do restrictions on repatriation of profits affect MNCs?

9. What is political risk? What forms can it take?

10. What is OPIC's role in promoting international business activity?

11. What difficulties do countries with centrally planned economies have in transforming them into free market economies?

Questions for Discussion

1. What options do firms have when caught in conflicts between home country and host country laws?

2. What is the impact of vigorous enforcement of intellectual property rights on the world economy? Who gains and who loses from strict enforcement of these laws?

3. Consider the following transactions. Which of these would you consider to be bribes that should be outlawed by international agreements?

    a. A payment to a customs inspector to allow your goods to clear customs more quickly

    b. Hiring a law firm that employs the son of the president of the country

    c. Making a $1 million donation of equipment to the local university, one of whose alumni is an important government minister (would your answer change if the amount were $30 million?)

    d. Creating a joint venture with a local company controlled by a close relative of the country's president

    e. Donating 2 percent of your company's profits to a private charity controlled by the country's president

4. Do you agree with the U.S. government's policies restricting the export of encryption technology? Why or why not? (You may wish to check out the Bureau of Export Administration's web site, which details how the Bureau operates.)

5. Map 8.2 presents countries' relative political riskiness at the beginning of 1998. For which countries has political riskiness changed significantly since then?

6. Union Carbide's U.S. managers fought to have the Bhopal case decided in Indian courts, knowing that plaintiffs would receive lower damage awards than if the case were adjudicated in the United States. Was such behavior ethical?

BUILDING GLOBAL SKILLS

This exercise will help you better understand the influence of legal and political forces on a firm that is entering a foreign market. Your instructor will divide the class into groups of four or five members each and then assign a different type of firm to each group. Example firm types include food retailers, general merchandisers, auto parts makers, steel producers, paper recyclers, computer manufacturers, beer manufacturers, cigarette makers, filmmakers, and petroleum refineries.

Assume your group is a top management team of a foreign firm of the type you've been assigned. Your firm has decided to expand into the United States and has selected the local community as its first point of entry. Your task is to find out what legal and political barriers the firm may encounter and to develop a general strategy for dealing with them. Use whatever resources are available. For example, you could interview a member of the city council or a representative from the area's economic development committee. You could also identify potential competitors and discuss what strategies they might adopt to block your entry. As

you identify potential barriers, try to determine if they are industry-specific or applicable only to foreign firms.

Finally, carefully assess each potential political or legal barrier and determine how difficult or easy it might be to address it.

Follow-up Questions

1. How easy or difficult was it to identify political or legal forces affecting your firm's proposed entry?

2. What other political or legal barriers might exist that you were unable to identify?

3. Are the potential barriers so great as to keep your firm out altogether? Why or why not?

4. Do different levels of government (city, state, and federal) pose different political and legal barriers to your firm? If so, describe these differences.

WORKING WITH THE WEB: Building Global Internet Skills

Assessing Political Risks

As the chapter amply illustrates, firms are confronted with assessing political risks in any market in which they operate, although some markets are more risky than others. Suppose you are employed by a pension fund that has been asked to lend $100 million to build one of the pipelines discussed in the closing case, "Baku Oil, Beaucoup Problems." The project sponsors are willing to pay an interest rate 8 percent above that currently being paid by U.S. treasury bills, so your boss is definitely interested in examining their proposal. Your boss assigns you the task of conducting a political risk assessment of the project. (For

purposes of this assignment, pick one of the pipeline routes discussed in the closing case.)

You may wish to begin this assignment by first listing all the possible types of political risks that may affect the ability of your pension fund to receive interest payments and the return of its principal in a timely fashion. Having developed this list, you then need to assess the likelihood that these problems will arise and affect the pipeline route you have selected. The textbook's web site provides links to other web sites that may be of help in this assignment.

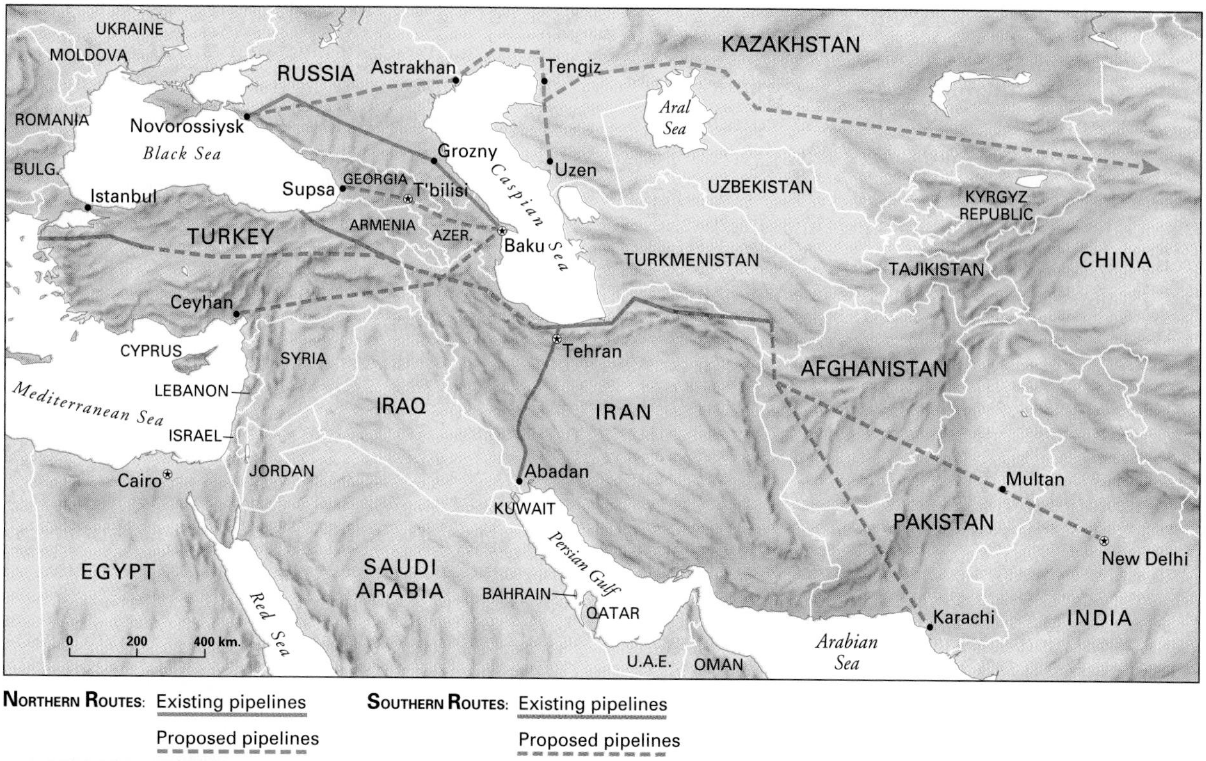

NORTHERN ROUTES: Existing pipelines   **SOUTHERN ROUTES:** Existing pipelines

Proposed pipelines   Proposed pipelines

MAP 8.3

**Possible Pipeline
Routes**

CLOSING CASE

Baku Oil, Beaucoup Problems[49]

If you're looking to find a perfect example of the importance of political risk analysis, you can't find a better example than the conundrum facing foreign oil companies trying to exploit the oil and gas riches of the Caspian Sea and the Central Asian Republics. Baku, the capital of Azerbaijan, is the center of the oil industry operating in the Caspian Sea region. Home to nearly 40 percent of Azerbaijan's 7.5 million citizens, Baku is also the Caspian's main port (see Map 8.3). The Caspian Sea in turn sits on a sea of oil, which virtually every oil company in the world is eager to exploit. They know where the oil is; they know how to get it out of the ground. There's just one catch: they need to get the oil to market, and all

the possible transportation routes traverse territory marked by political instability.

The problem is most acutely felt by the Azerbaijan International Operating Company (AIOC), which is owned by a consortium of oil companies (including British Petroleum, Amoco, Exxon, Unocal, Pennzoil, and Russia's Lukoil). AIOC expects to spend $8 to $10 billion over the next three decades to develop and produce four billion barrels of Caspian Sea oil. AIOC will ship the oil to Western markets by two pipelines from Baku to the Black Sea. The first route, 850 miles in length, goes from Baku to Russia and thence to the Black Sea port of Novorossiysk. The second route goes from Baku through Georgia to the Black Sea port of Supsa, a mere 550-mile journey. Unfortunately, the first route goes through Grozny, the capital of the breakaway Russian province of Chechnya. Chechnyian rebels fought the Russian army to a standstill during a bloody revolt from 1994 to 1996 and have proclaimed their independence from Moscow's control. However, Russia has not acknowledged the area's sovereignty, and armed conflict could break out again at any time. The second route, which bypasses Russia, goes through rough mountainous terrain where security is difficult. Local residents routinely tap into an existing pipeline in the area, siphoning off oil to heat their homes. Moreover, some Russian politicians have indicated their displeasure with the second route, claiming that it threatens the "energy security" of the country. (A less charitable interpretation is that Russia doesn't wish to lose its monopoly over the transportation of Caspian Sea oil and the lucrative transit fees that it generates.) While the Yeltsin government has not blockaded its development, should Russian nationalists capture control of the government in the next election, they might adopt a more bellicose pipeline policy. Turkish officials, concerned about traffic jams and possible collisions of oil tankers heading through the narrow Straits of Bosporus on their way to Western markets, prefer a new pipeline from Baku to Ceyhan. While this 1236-mile route would be very expensive—an estimated $2.9 billion—Turkish officials fear that one collision between loaded tankers at the Bosporus would make the *Exxon Valdez* disaster seem like a minor slipup in comparison.

Azerbaijan has problems of its own. While business is thriving at bars like the Ragin' Cagin or Margaritaville that cater to slaking the thirst of free-spending American oilfield workers, the oil boom has not as yet benefited the average citizen: annual per capita income is only $420. The country is run, Soviet-style, by a former KGB general, Geidar Aliev, who is not a poster boy for democracy. After taking office in a 1993 coup, Aliev suppressed political dissent, stifled freedom of the press, and imposed a blockade on neighboring Armenia. Moreover, after Azerbaijan declared its independence from the Soviet Union, the ethnic Armenians of its Nagorno-Karabakh province declared their independence from Azerbaijan. A bloody, as yet unresolved, civil war ensued, sending hundreds of thousands of refugees into Baku and other cities.

Meanwhile, oil companies operating on the other side of the Caspian Sea in Turkmenistan and Kazakhstan face similar problems. California-based Unocal, which owns production rights in Turkmenistan, is proposing to build an oil pipeline and a gas pipeline from Turkmenistan to Pakistan. The only problem is that the proposed route goes through Afghanistan, which has been ripped apart by insurrections and civil wars since the mid-1970s. Even Sylvester Stallone (remember *Rambo III*?) has been unable to bring political stability and peace to the Afghanis. Another possible route for Turkmen oil is via pipeline through Iran to the Persian Gulf or through Iran and Turkey to the Black Sea. However, as we noted earlier in the chapter, the United States has exerted diplomatic pressure that discourages companies from doing business with Iran. While the U.S. government has tentatively granted a waiver for this project, the volatility in diplomatic relations between the United States and Iran should make company executives think twice about this project. Moreover, Russian companies like Gazprom are unhappy that such a routing would limit their access to Turkmen reserves.

Kazakh oil has a similar set of options and a similar set of problems. One potential pipeline route is to go around the northern coast of the Caspian Sea to Novorossiysk. While avoiding Chechnya, the Kazakhs would be at the mercy of a Russian government that has a reputation for imposing new tax burdens on foreign companies whenever it faces a revenue shortfall. Alternatively, its oil could tap into the Turkmen pipelines to Pakistan or Iran.

A route through China is another possibility. In 1997 the Chinese National Petroleum Company purchased a 60 percent stake in Aktobemunaigaz, a leading Kazakh oil company, which controls reserves containing one billion barrels of high-quality crude oil and 220 billion cubic meters of natural gas. In conjunction with Korean and Japanese firms, China also agreed to finance and construct a new 1800-mile pipeline to Karamay in the western Chinese province of Xinjiang, which would then tap into China's existing pipeline grid and allow Kazakh oil access to the Chinese, Japanese, and Korean markets and generate huge transit fees for China's government. Unfortunately, Xinjiang, a vast desert province, is the subject of a small but tense rebellion by native Uighur separatists. The Uighurs, who are ethnic cousins to the Turkic populations of the Central Asian republics, resent the growing influx of the Han Chinese in the province, which has risen from 5 percent of the province's population in 1949 to 38 percent of Xinjiang's 18 million population today. The Uighurs claim that the Han (the main ethnic group in China) have flooded the province and reserved the best jobs for themselves. So far the attacks of the poorly trained and poorly armed separatists have had little impact on Chinese control of the province, although local residents fear the situation could worsen. Duing 1997 riots in the border city of Gulja, the army had to escort 1200 Han settlers out of town to safety.

Needless to say, each of these choices poses problems for the oil companies operating in the region. Nonetheless, they are ready for the challenge, in large part because the potential rewards are so large. Proven reserves in the region are estimated to reach 15 to 20 billion barrels of oil; based on the area's geology, some experts believe as much as 160 billion barrels lie underground waiting to be discovered.

Case Questions

1. Characterize the types of investments that are most vulnerable to political risk. Characterize those that are least vulnerable. Oil and natural gas pipelines are immobile and long-lived. They are also very expensive. On a scale of one to ten (ten being highest), how vulnerable are they to political risks?

2. Which of the pipeline routes discussed in the case offers the least political risk? Which offers the greatest political risk? (You may wish to refer to the "Working with the Web" exercise for help in answering this question.)

3. In his novel *Kim*, Rudyard Kipling introduced the phrase "The Great Game" to describe the struggle between the Russian czars and the British Empire to control the wealth of Central Asia and the Caspian Sea. Clearly, the great game is being replayed as countries fight to control access to the area's oil and natural gas reserves. What can international businesses do to protect themselves from the geopolitical struggles of Russia, China, Iran, the United States, and other nations in this region?

CHAPTER NOTES

1. Toys 'R' Us Annual Report, 1997, p. 2; "Guess Who's Selling Barbies in Japan?" *Business Week*, December 9, 1991, pp. 72–76; "Toys 'R' Us Goes Overseas—And Finds That Toys 'R' Them, Too," *Business Week*, January 26, 1987, pp. 71–72; "A New Game Plan: Toys 'R' Us Ups Ante in Global Market," *Atlanta Constitution*, June 27, 1993, p. R1; "U.S. Discount Retailers Are Targeting Europe and Its Fat Margins," *Wall Street Journal*, September 20, 1993, pp. A1, A4.

2. "British Debtor Ill in Abu Dhabi Jail," *Daily Telegraph*, March 11, 1996, p. 5.

3. *The Economist*, August 14, 1993; *The Economist*, July 18, 1992, Survey, p. 4.

4. "India's Laws a Mixed Blessing for Investors," *Wall Street Journal*, July 11, 1997, p. A10.

5. Joseph Flom, " 'Home Court' is best advantage," *Financial Times*, June 27, 1991, p. 12; "American Competitiveness," *Wall Street Journal*, August 14, 1991, p. A8.

6. Ken Brown, "Banking on laws of Islam," *Houston Chronicle*, April 10, 1994, p. 4F.

7. Peter Waldman, "Alleged Victims of Saudi Brutality Think the U.S. Brushes Aside Charges," *Wall Street Journal*, October 26, 1992, p. A10.

8. "Mining executives woo rebels with billion-dollar mineral deals," *Houston Chronicle*, April 17, 1997, p. 20A; "As Zaire's War Wages, Foreign Businesses Scramble for Inroads," *Wall Street Journal*, April 14, 1997, p. A1.

9. Jim Mann, *Beijing Jeep* (New York: Simon and Schuster, 1989, p. 267).

10. Alison Maltland, "COCOM eases rules on hi-tech exports," *Financial Times*, August 13, 1991, p. 15; "Licensing Regulations in Exports Are Lifted for Four Countries," *Wall Street Journal*, May 22, 1991, p. A4.

11. "Sales to Soviets of Technology Are Broadened," *Wall Street Journal*, May 28, 1991, p. A8.

12. "U.S. Investigates Silicon Graphics's Computer Sale," *Wall Street Journal*, February 18, 1997, p. A4.

13. "U.S. Loosens Export Policy on Encryption," *Wall Street Journal*, June 25, 1997, p. B6; "Netscape gets approval to export secure software," *Houston Chronicle*, June 25, 1997, p. 12C.

14. Nikki Tait, "Textron takes the controls of an overhauled Cessna," *Financial Times*, February 18, 1992, p. 21.

15. "Cessna Says It Will Make Small Airplanes," *Wall Street Journal*, March 14, 1995, p. B1.

16. George Graham, "Pilkington bows to U.S. pressure on process licensing," *Financial Times*, May 27, 1994, p. 1; George Graham, "Washington's new anti-trust vigor," *Financial Times*, May 27, 1994, p. 6.

17. *Briggs and Stratton Corp. v. Baldrige*, 539 F. Supp. 1307 (E.D. Wis. 1982), aff'd, 728 F.2d 915 (1984), United States Court of Appeals (7th Cir.).

18. Thomas M. Burton, "Baxter Agreed to Cut-Rate Shipments of Supplies to Syria, U.S. Probe Finds," *Wall Street Journal*, December 22, 1992, p. A3; "How Baxter Got Off the Arab Blacklist and How It Got Nailed," *Wall Street Journal*, March 23, 1993, p. A1.

19. "Keeping the lid on Helms-Burton," *Financial Times*, July 31, 1997, p. 4; "Stet avoids Helms-Burton sanctions," *Financial Times*, July 24, 1997, p. 1; "Property issue harks back to old Cuba," *Houston Chronicle*, October 3, 1996, p. 1C.

20. "Total's Oil Pact Clouds Talks Between U.S., EU," *Wall Street Journal*, October 1, 1997, p. C24; "Iranian trade ban forms balancing act," *Houston Chronicle*, May 4, 1995, p. 1B.

21. "Foreign industries may strain Saltillo's services," *Bryan-College Station Eagle*, January 28, 1992, p. A1.

22. "U.S. Appetite for Mexican Food Grows, Cooking Up Hotter Sales for Exporters," *Wall Street Journal*, February 5, 1992, p. A6.

23. Richard J. Barnet and Ronald E. Muller, *Global Reach—The Power of the Multinational Corporation* (New York: Simon and Schuster, 1974).

24. *Survey of Current Business*, June 1997, p. 48, and October 1997, p. 45.

25. "With Boom Gone Bust, Spain's Social Agenda Still Haunts Economy," *Wall Street Journal*, June 13, 1994, p. A1.

26. "To Georgetown, Ky., Toyota Plant Seems a Blessing and a Curse," *Wall Street Journal*, November 26, 1991, p. A1.

27. Christina Lamb, "Brazil's sell-off gathers pace as field widens," *Financial Times*, January 21, 1992, p. 24.

28. John Barham, "Argentina scours the world for investors," *Financial Times*, August 22, 1991, p. 17; "The Deals Are Good, but the Dial Tone Isn't," *Business Week*, April 6, 1992, p. 86.

29. "Spoiled rotten," *Financial Times*, June 8, 1991, p. 76.

30. "Asian Region Reduces Piracy of Software," *Wall Street Journal*, June 27, 1997, p. B9; "Russian Copyright Lawyer Is Leading Crackdown on Piracy in Music Industry," *Wall Street Journal*, June 10, 1997, p. C13; "CD Piracy Flourishes in China, and West Supplies Equipment," *Wall Street Journal*, April 24, 1997, p. A1.

31. Masaaki Kotabe, "A Comparative Study of U.S. and Japanese Patent Systems," *Journal of International Business Studies*, Vol. 23, No. 1 (First Quarter 1992), p. 150.

32. "Patent Suit Shows Small U.S. Firms' Fears," *Wall Street Journal*, June 5, 1996, p. A10.

33. Peter Bruce, "Spanish ban means Nike can't just do it," *Financial Times*, July 17, 1992, p. 4.

34. "Trademark Piracy at Home and Abroad," *Wall Street Journal*, May 7, 1991, p. A20.

35. "Blue Bell frosted as Japanese freeze trademark," *Houston Chronicle*, September 5, 1991, p. 1B.

36. "Fujitsu backed in patent dispute," *Financial Times*, September 11, 1997, p. 8.

37. *In re Union Carbide Corporation Gas Plant Disaster at Bhopal*, 809 F.2d 195 (1987), United States Court of Appeals (2d Cir.).

38. Richard Schaffer, Beverley Earle, and Filiberto Agusti, *International Business Law and Its Environment* (St. Paul, Minn.: West Publishing, 1990), p. 196.

39. Ibid., pp. 196–197.

40. Ibid., pp. 429–430.

41. "Texaco Receives U.S. Assistance for Russian Project," *Wall Street Journal*, September 3, 1993, p. A3.

42. Schaffer, Earle, and Agusti, op. cit., pp. 410–421.

43. "Regulatory Surprises in Ukraine Lead Motorola to Pull Investment," *Wall Street Journal*, March 28, 1997, p. A12; "Ukraine's Bureaucrats Stymie U.S. Firms," *Wall Street Journal*, November 4, 1996, p. A14.

44. "IBM to Close Two-Year-Old Venture in Russia, Citing Onerous Taxes for Step," *Wall Street Journal*, February 29, 1996, p. A10.

45. "Foreigners Learn to Play by Russia's Rules," *Wall Street Journal*, August 14, 1997, p. A10; "Some Russian officials consider bribery just a part of job," *Houston Chronicle*, August 2, 1997, p. 30A.

46. "Chinese Army Fashions Major Role for Itself as a Business Enterprise," *Wall Street Journal*, May 24, 1994, p. A1.

47. "Municipal-Run Firms Helped Build China; Now, They're Faltering," *Wall Street Journal*, October 8, 1997, p. A1.

48. "Ukraine's Women Love These Two Firms," *Wall Street Journal*, February 6, 1992, p. A10.

49. "Oil firms eye Caspian area," *Houston Chronicle*, November 28, 1997, p. 1C; "Unocal to route Turkmenistan pipeline through Afghanistan," *Houston Chronicle*, November 11, 1997, p. 4C; "Older oil city enjoys new boom," *Houston Chronicle*, October 7, 1997, p. 1C; "Texaco, Mobil Expect Deals with Kazakhstan," *Wall Street Journal*, October 3, 1997, p. A6; "China's rebellious province," *The Economist*, August 23, 1997, p. 29; "Superpowers circle Caspian," *Financial Times*, August 8, 1997, p. 4; "Resourceful competitors," *Wall Street Journal*, July 28, 1997, p. A18; "Oil Companies Rush into the Caucasus to Tap the Caspian," *Wall Street Journal*, April 25, 1997, p. A1; "The combustible Caspian," *The Economist*, January 11, 1997, p. 45.

The Role of Culture

After studying this chapter you should be able to:

Discuss the primary characteristics of culture.

Describe the various elements of culture and provide examples of how they influence international business.

Identify the means by which members of a culture communicate with each other and how international businesses can prevent intercultural communication problems.

Discuss how religious and other values affect the domestic environments in which international businesses operate.

Explain Hofstede's primary findings about differences in cultural values.

Describe the major cultural clusters and their use to international businesspeople.

Explain how ethical conflicts may arise when international businesspeople conduct business with persons from other cultures.

As almost everyone in the United States knows, Nike rules the athletic shoe market. The Beaverton, Oregon, firm has taken an aggressive, winner-take-all, no-holds-barred approach to marketing that has paid off handsomely. Nike's media persona has been one that snipes at authority (the firm helped pay Tonya Harding's legal fees following her alleged attack on rival Nancy Kerrigan preceding the 1994 Olympics), worships athletes (its spokespersons include Michael Jordan and Tiger Woods), and elevates the lowly sneaker to mystical levels (its commercials often have a Zen-like quality about them, and Nike has worked to make its famous "Swoosh" emblem as much an icon as the McDonald's golden arches and the shape of a Coke bottle). ▌▌ This strategy has worked well in the United States. The centerpiece of Nike's efforts has been basketball, a very popular sport in its domestic market. Recently, however, Nike has decided that it needs a stronger international presence if it is to continue to grow. And while basketball has a strong following in some foreign countries, it is soccer—or football, as it's called virtually everywhere outside the United States—that is the true international sport. Indeed, to be seen as a big player in most countries, an athletic apparel company has to have connections to soccer. Thus, Nike recently determined to take a more aggressive approach to its international marketing efforts and to create a more visible link between its products and soccer. ▌▌ Nike thought it had taken the first big step in this direction when it paid the staggering sum of $200 million to sponsor Brazil's national soccer federation. But many Brazilians saw the relationship as tainted by the "money will get you everything" strategy they generally associate with the United States. Further, Brazilians saw a big multinational corporation trying to buy their passion and history and pass them off as its own. Things only got worse when Nike announced that it would be taking the Brazilian team on an annual five-game global tour. That action prompted Pele, the country's greatest living sports legend, to file a lawsuit alleging that Nike was forcing the country's national team to play unnecessary exhibition games. ▌▌ Further, the in-your-face advertising attitude that has worked so well in Nike's home court has hit some serious potholes in the firm's quest to extend its reach into more and more foreign markets. For example, Nike recently produced a television commercial featuring Satan and his demons playing soccer against a team of Nike endorsers. The commercial was a big hit in the United States, but some European stations refused to broadcast it because they thought it was too scary and offensive to show during prime time when children were watching. And in France, Nike launched a commercial showing a soccer bad boy bragging about how spitting on a fan and insulting his coach caused him to

A Clash of Cultures[1]

win a big contract from the shoe manufacturer. So insulting was this commercial that Nike was reviled in a scathing editorial published in the newsletter of soccer's international governing federation. ▌▌ One clash after another with foreign cultures has caused Nike to rethink its strategy for global expansion. Nike managers now have a clearer sense of their challenge: they need to keep the hip edge that has appealed to the sneaker-buying public in the United States while playing to the more tradition-bound cultures in Europe and Asia. The trick, of course, is how to pull it off. Nike is recognizing the importance of respecting foreign cultures, a concept it ignored in one of its early commercials in an international soccer magazine that proclaimed: "Europe, Asia, and Latin America: Barricade your stadiums. Hide your trophies. Invest in some deodorant. Here comes Nike." ▌▌ Nike does seem to be getting the message. For one thing, it's softened its approach to marketing in most countries. Rather than bulldozing its way in with its U.S. style and mentality, Nike now takes more time to learn about the local culture and to be at least a bit more respectful of local customs, attitudes, and values. And it relies more on local designers and managers as barometers of cultural norms and nuances in different countries. While this approach signals a clear retreat for Nike, most of its competitors know that the sneaker war is far from over. ▌▌▌▌▌

Firms and businesspeople venturing beyond their familiar domestic markets soon recognize that foreign business customs, values, and definitions of ethical behavior differ vastly from their own. Indeed, Nike's difficulties are all too common among firms that ignore cultural differences among the world's people. Virtually all facets of an international firm's business—including contract negotiations, production operations, marketing decisions, and human resource management policies—may be affected by cultural variations. Reliance on a firm's familiar culture to compete in a new culture can seriously harm its international success. This chapter highlights some of the kinds of cultural differences among countries and explains how familiarity with those differences can prove invaluable for international businesspeople.

Characteristics of Culture

Business, like all other human activities, is conducted within the context of society. **Culture** is the collection of values, beliefs, behaviors, customs, and attitudes that distinguish a society. A society's culture determines the rules that govern how firms operate in the society. As firms expand their sales into foreign markets, locate production facilities abroad, and search the world for the most productive and talented employees, they are increasingly challenged by the cultural differences among countries and among the people with whom they do business. Improvements in communications technology and reductions in transportation costs have raised the frequency of cross-cultural contacts and increased the importance of a firm's understanding the role of culture in business activities if it wants to remain competitive internationally.

Several characteristics of culture are worth noting:

- Culture reflects *learned behavior* that is transmitted from one member of a society to another. Some elements of culture are transmitted intergenerationally, as when a father teaches his child table manners. Other elements are transmitted intragenerationally, as when upperclassmen educate incoming freshmen about a school's traditions.

- The elements of culture are *interrelated*. For example, as "Going Global" indicates, Japan's group-oriented, hierarchical society stresses harmony, which historically translated into lifetime employment and little job switching.

- Because culture is learned behavior, it is *adaptive;* that is, the culture changes in response to external forces that affect the society. For example, after World War II, Germany was divided into free-market–oriented West Germany and communist-controlled East Germany. Despite a common heritage developed over centuries, this division created large cultural differences between *Ossis* (East Germans) and *Wessis* (West Germans). The differences resulted from adaptions of the East German culture to the dictates of communist ideology regarding attitudes toward work, risk taking, and fairness of reward systems.

- Culture is *shared* by members of the society and indeed *defines the membership* of the society. Individuals who share a culture are members of a society; those who do not are outside the boundaries of the society.

Elements of Culture

A society's culture determines how its members communicate and interact with each other. The basic elements of culture (see Fig. 9.1) are social structure, language, communication, religion, and values and attitudes. The interaction of these elements affects the local environment in which international businesses operate.

Social Structure

Basic to every society is its social structure, the overall framework that determines the roles of individuals within the society, the stratification of the society, and individuals' mobility within the society.

Individuals, Families, and Groups. All human societies involve individuals living in family units and working with each other in groups. Societies differ, however, in how the family is defined and in the relative importance they place on the individual's role within groups. The U.S. view of family ties and responsibilities focuses on the nuclear family (father, mother, and offspring). In other cultures, the extended family is far more important. Arabs, for example, consider uncles, brothers, cousins, and in-laws as parts of their family unit to

GOING GLOBAL

Let's briefly review some key elements of Japanese culture and how the culture affects Japanese business practices. Note how this culture is learned, interrelated, and shared and how it defines group membership.

The first cultural element that plays a major role in Japanese business practices is the *hierarchical structure* of Japanese society. The social hierarchy strictly defines how people deal with each other. In fact, speaking the Japanese language requires that one know one's position relative to the person to whom one is talking. Different forms of language are used depending on whether one is conversing with a superior or a subordinate. Thus, when two Japanese businesspeople meet, they immediately exchange business cards, in part to determine their relative status so that they can know which form of address to use.

A second cultural element is *groupism*. A person is identified as a member of a group rather than as an individual. This group identity is ingrained in Japanese children at an early age. Watching the differences between children in a U.S. preschool and those in a Japanese preschool is interesting. The U.S. school focuses on nurturing the individual by praising individual accomplishments and working to raise the child's self-esteem. The Japanese school concentrates on transforming spoiled preschoolers, whose every wish to date has been met by their doting mothers, into members of a cohesive group. Strong group identity is reinforced by Japan's ethnic homogeneity and its relative isolation from the rest of the world until the 1850s.

A third element of Japanese culture is *wa*, or social harmony. The goal of each group member is to promote harmony, or consensus, within the group. Decisions are not made within Japanese organizations by upper-management fiat, for that would upset the *wa*. Rather, group members must discuss and negotiate until consensus is reached. The need to preserve *wa* is one reason many Japanese firms encourage after-work socializing and partying by Japanese salarymen. These parties are a means of building trust among group members and allowing them to develop consensus on issues facing their firm. Similarly, many firms compensate their employees based upon seniority, rather than on their individual performance, in order to preserve *wa*.

A fourth cultural element is *obligation,* or duty. The individual, once hired, becomes indebted to the firm. The debt owed the firm for agreeing to employ the person is so great that the person can never extinguish it. The person owes everything to the firm, and the firm's needs come first, even before personal and familial needs. The strong cultural disapproval of an employee's moving to another firm stems from this facet of Japanese culture. At the same time, the firm accepts certain responsibilities toward the employee, much as a feudal lord accepted the obligation to protect the peasants, serfs, craftsmen, and merchants in the lord's realm. The traditional lifetime (until age 55) employment practices of many major Japanese firms stem from this cultural element, which in turn affects other Japanese business practices. Because of the lifetime employment relationship, Japanese firms take considerable care in selecting employees and force job applicants to undergo rigorous testing and interviewing prior to being hired. Once hired, employees recognize that their jobs depend on the long-term survival of their employer, but also that their jobs are secure as long as the firm is secure.

A handful of Japanese firms are beginning to scrap some of these culturally-based business practices in response to the slowdown of the Japanese economy in the 1990s. Fujitsu, for example, announced in 1998 that it would abandon its seniority-oriented compensation approach and instead adopt a merit-based pay and performance philosophy. Other firms have quietly trimmed their commitment to lifetime employment. Nonetheless these traditional practices remain the norm in most Japanese firms.

The Impact of Japanese Culture on Business

Sources: Richard G. Newman and K. Anthony Rhee, "Self-Styled Barriers Inhibit Transferring Management Methods," *Business Horizons*, May–June 1989, pp. 17–21; "Fujitsu to Institute Merit-Based Pay For All Employees," *Wall Street Journal*, March 26, 1998, p. B5.

FIGURE 9.1

Elements of Culture

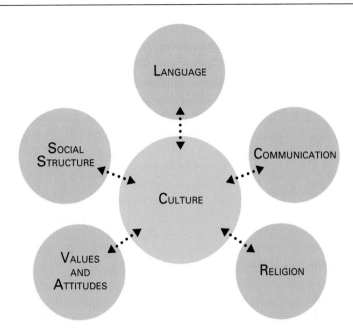

whom they owe obligations of support and assistance. Other societies utilize an even broader definition of family. For example, Somalia's society is organized in clans, each of which comprises individuals of the same tribe who share a common ancestor.

These social attitudes are reflected in the importance of the family to business. In the United States, firms forbid nepotism, and the competence of a man who married the boss's daughter is routinely questioned by coworkers. But in Arab-owned firms, family ties are crucial, and hiring relatives is a common, accepted practice. Similarly, in Chinese-owned firms, family members fill critical management positions and supply capital from personal savings to ensure the firm's growth.[2]

Cultures also differ in the importance of the individual relative to the group. U.S. culture, for example, promotes individualism. Schools try to raise the self-esteem of each child and encourage each one to develop individual talents. Because respect for individual authority and responsibility is so strong in the United States, children are trained to believe their destinies lie in their own hands. Conversely, in group-focused societies such as China and Japan and in Israel's kibbutzim, children are taught that their role is to serve the group (see "Going Global"). Virtues such as unity, loyalty, and harmony are highly valued in such societies. These characteristics often are more important in hiring decisions than are personal accomplishments or abilities.[3]

Social Stratification. Societies differ in their degree of **social stratification.** All societies categorize people to some extent on the basis of their birth, occupation, educational achievements, and/or other attributes. But the importance of these categories in defining how individuals interact with each other within and between these groups varies by society. For instance, in medieval Europe the roles and obligations of peasants, craftsmen, tradesmen, and nobles were carefully delineated by custom and law. The British class structure and the Indian caste system provide more recent examples of the same phenomenon, in which one's social position affects all facets of one's dealings with other people. In other societies, social stratification is less important. For example, a U.S. bank president may haughtily bark orders at his janitorial staff on the job yet willingly take orders from those same individuals when cleaning up after a church fundraiser.

MNCs operating in highly stratified societies often must adjust their hiring and promotion procedures to take into account class or clan differences among supervisors and workers. Hiring members of one group to do jobs traditionally performed by members of another group may lower workplace morale and productivity. In less stratified societies, firms are freer to seek out the most qualified employee, regardless of whether that person went to the right school, goes to the proper church, or belongs to all the best clubs. In highly stratified societies, advertisers must more carefully tailor their messages to ensure that those messages reach only the targeted audience and do not spill over to another audience that may be offended by receiving a message intended for the first group. In less stratified societies, such concerns may be less important.

Social mobility is the ability of individuals to move from one stratum of society to another. Social mobility tends to be higher in less stratified societies. It is higher in the United States, for example, than in the United Kingdom or India. Social mobility (or the lack thereof) often affects individuals' attitudes and behaviors toward such factors as labor relations, human capital formation, risk taking, and entrepreneurship. The U.K.'s formerly rigid class system and relatively low social mobility created an "us versus them" attitude among many British industrial workers, causing them to eye suspiciously any management efforts to promote workplace cooperation. Until relatively recently, some British working-class youth dropped out of school, believing that their role in society was preordained and thus investment in education a waste of time. In more socially mobile societies, such as those of the United States, Singapore, and Canada, individuals are more willing to seek higher education or to engage in entrepreneurial activities, knowing that if they are successful, they and their families are free to rise in society.

Language

Language is a primary delineator of cultural groups because it is an important means by which a society's members communicate with each other. Experts have identified some 3000 different languages and as many as 10,000 distinct dialects worldwide (see Map 9.1).[4]

Language organizes the way members of a society think about the world. It filters observations and perceptions and thus affects unpredictably the messages that are sent when two individuals try to communicate. In one famous experiment in Hong Kong, 153 undergraduate students, bilingual in English and Chinese, were divided into two groups. One group was given a class assignment written in English; the second was given the same assignment written in Chinese. The professor in charge of the experiment took every precaution to ensure that the translations were perfect. Yet the answers given by the two groups differed significantly, indicating that the language itself altered the nature of the information being conveyed.[5]

In addition to shaping one's perceptions of the world, language provides important clues about the cultural values of the society and aids acculturation.

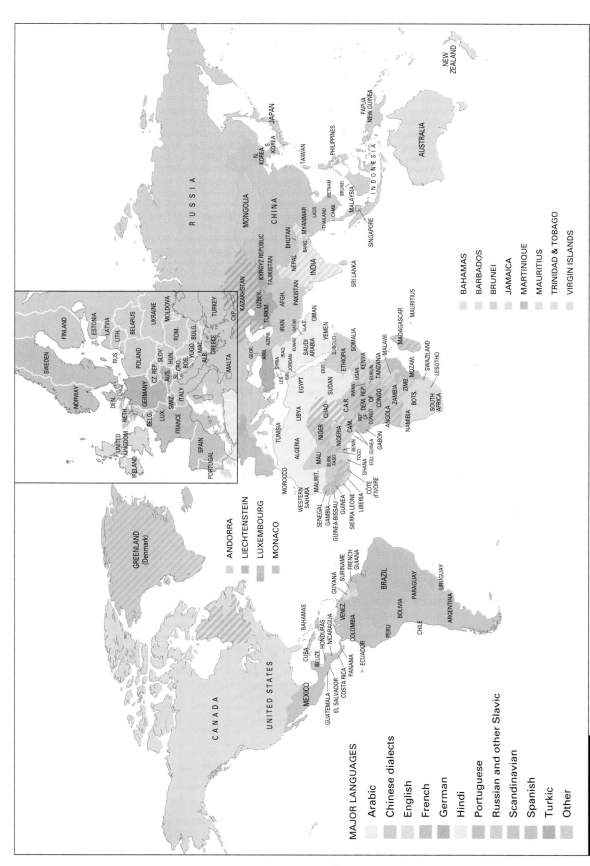

MAJOR LANGUAGES

- Arabic
- Chinese dialects
- English
- French
- German
- Hindi
- Portuguese
- Russian and other Slavic
- Scandinavian
- Spanish
- Turkic
- Other

ANDORRA
LIECHTENSTEIN
LUXEMBOURG
MONACO

BAHAMAS
BARBADOS
BRUNEI
JAMAICA
MARTINIQUE
MAURITIUS
TRINIDAD & TOBAGO
VIRGIN ISLANDS

MAP 9.1 **World Languages**

For example, many languages, including French, German, and Spanish, have informal and formal forms of the word for "you," the use of which depends on the relationship between the speaker and the person addressed.[6] Existence of these language forms provides a strong hint that one should take care in maintaining an appropriate level of formality when dealing with businesspeople from countries in which those languages predominate.

The presence of more than one language group is an important signal about the diversity of a country's population and suggests that there may also be differences in income, work ethic, and/or educational achievement. For example, India recognizes 16 official languages, and approximately 3000 dialects are spoken within its boundaries, a reflection of the heterogeneity of its society. In several mountainous countries of South America, such as Bolivia and Paraguay, most of the poor rural population speak local Indian dialects and have trouble communicating with the Spanish-speaking urban elites. Generally, countries dominated by one language group tend to have a homogeneous society, in which nationhood defines the society. Countries with multiple language groups tend to be heterogeneous, with language providing an important means of identifying cultural differences within the country.

Savvy businesspeople operating in heterogeneous societies adapt their marketing and business practices along linguistic lines to account for cultural differences among their prospective customers. For example, market researchers discovered that English Canadians favor soaps that promise cleanliness, while French Canadians prefer pleasant- or sweet-smelling soaps. Thus Procter & Gamble's English-language Canadian ads for Irish Spring soap stress the soap's deodorant value, while its French-language ads focus on the soap's pleasant aroma.[7] Generally, advertisers should seek out the media—newspapers, radio, cable television, and magazines—that allow them to customize their marketing messages to individual linguistic groups. For example, in the United States the development of Spanish-language cable television channels such as Univision has allowed advertisers to more easily customize their advertisements to reach the Hispanic market, without confusing their marketing messages to the larger English-speaking audience.

The presence of multiple major linguistic groups within a country should also alert international businesspeople to potential political conflicts within the country that may threaten the stability of a firm's investments or affect its hiring practices. For example, political conflict exists between Canada's Francophone (French-speaking) province of Quebec and the rest of Canada, which speaks English predominantly. Also, for the past century a political fault line has existed between Belgium's Flemish (Dutch-speaking) citizens in the north and its Walloon (French-speaking) citizens in the south. Unfortunately, linguistic differences may boil over into actual conflict, which sadly has been the case in the former Soviet Union and Yugoslavia.

Same Language, Same Business Culture? Differences in language within a country signal cultural differences among its populace, but one cannot conclude that countries that share a language also share a culture. It is often said, for example, that the United States and the United Kingdom are two countries divided by a common language. Sometimes the meanings of words in British English differ from those in American English. For example, in American English, tabling an item on a business agenda means the group chooses to delay taking action, often because its members were unable to reach a consensus. In British English, tabling an item means the exact opposite—that action was taken on it.

National differences in laws, political systems, social structure, and economic wealth create differences in culture (and vice versa) among countries that share a language. For example, the current British culture has been influenced by a strong class system, which was developed in feudal times. The country's governmental structure reflects the quality of noblesse oblige expected among the upper classes and concentrates much political power in the hands of one person, the prime minister. U.S. culture has rejected the British class system and stresses instead the importance of individual achievement. The checks and balances contained in the U.S. Constitution embody the distrust U.S. citizens have of concentrating power in any one person or institution.

However, researchers have found that countries that share a language often are culturally similar, although not identical. (See the section titled "Cultural Clusters" later in this chapter). Because cultural similarities ease the task of doing business internationally, a domestic firm's initial efforts to expand abroad often focus on countries that speak the firm's home language. For example, the U.S. and British markets are often the first export targets of Canadian firms.

Language as a Competitive Weapon. Linguistic ties often create important competitive advantages because the ability to communicate is so important in conducting business transactions. Commerce among Australia, Canada, New Zealand, the United Kingdom, and the United States is facilitated by their common use of English. For example, Giro Sport Design, a Soquel, California, manufacturer of bicycle helmets, decided in the early 1990s to manufacture its product in Europe rather than export it from the United States. The firm told the consultants hired to find a plant location that the plant had to be located in an English-speaking country. William Hanneman, Giro's president, noted, "With all the problems you have in running a business abroad, we didn't want to be bothered by language."[8] The firm located its European production facilities in Ireland, where it has enjoyed a plentiful supply of low-cost English-speaking labor, economic development incentives, and tax benefits. Similarly, Spain's Telefonica de Espana SA has moved aggressively into Latin America as part of its internationalization strategy. Benefiting from the region's privatization programs, it has bought controlling interests in the formerly state-owned telephone monopolies of Argentina, Chile, and Peru. Spanish banks such as Banco Santander, Banco Bilbao Vizcaya, and Banco Central Hispano have adopted a comparable approach, investing heavily in Argentina, Chile, Mexico, Peru, Puerto Rico, and Uruguay.[9] And Turkey is fast becoming the jumping-off point to do business in the Turkic areas of the former Soviet Union, such as Azerbaijan, Kazakhstan, and Turkmenistan.

The linguistic legacy of colonialism also affects international business today. For example, French firms possess competitive advantages in former French colonies in Africa (see Map 9.2), such as Algeria, Chad, and Côte d'Ivoire, because much of the local business elite has been taught French as a second language and because government officials often receive their undergraduate and graduate training in French universities. Also, the infrastructures of these countries were developed using French technology, creating a demand for French-made spare parts. Strong banking, communications, and transportation links remain from the colonial period. For similar reasons, British firms possess competitive advantages in former British colonies such as Kenya, India, and Zimbabwe.

MAP 9.2

Africa's Colonial Heritage

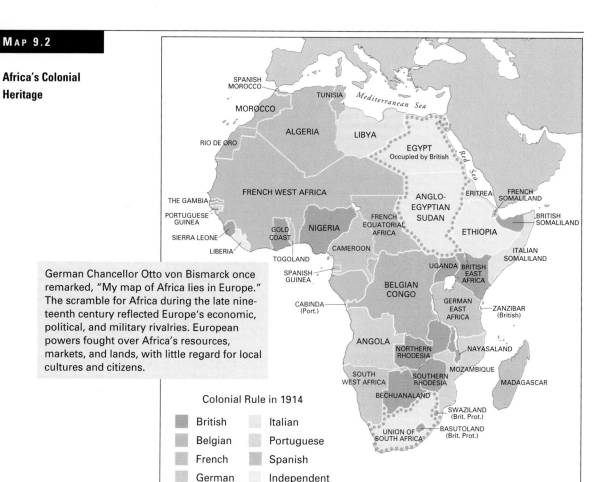

German Chancellor Otto von Bismarck once remarked, "My map of Africa lies in Europe." The scramble for Africa during the late nineteenth century reflected Europe's economic, political, and military rivalries. European powers fought over Africa's resources, markets, and lands, with little regard for local cultures and citizens.

Colonial Rule in 1914

British	Italian
Belgian	Portuguese
French	Spanish
German	Independent

Lingua Franca. To conduct business, international businesspeople must be able to communicate. As a result of British economic and military dominance in the nineteenth century and U.S. dominance since World War II, English has emerged as the predominant common language, or **lingua franca,** of international business. Most European and Japanese public school students study English for many years. Some countries that have many linguistic groups, such as India and Singapore, have adopted English as an official language in order to facilitate communication among the diverse groups. Similarly, firms with managers from many different countries may use English as the official corporate language. For example, Philips, the Dutch-based electronics MNC, has used English for intracorporate communications since 1983. Switzerland's Brown Boveri and Sweden's Asea adopted English as their corporate language after their merger in 1987. And the Board of Directors of SKF, a Swedish ball bearing manufacturer, conducts its meetings in English, for its Board is composed of 11 Swedes, one Italian, one German, and a Swiss.[10]

The dominance of English seemingly confers an advantage on native English speakers in international commerce, particularly when transactions are done in Canada, the United Kingdom, or the United States. However, failure by English speakers to learn a second language puts them and their firms at a decided disadvantage when negotiating or operating on foreign turf. For example, a few years ago Lionel Train Company moved its manufacturing facilities to Mexico to take advantage of lower labor costs. But it could not find enough bilingual managers to run the plant. As a result, the firm eventually shut down the plant and moved its operations back to the United States.[11]

Because language serves as a window onto the culture of a society, many international business experts argue that students should be exposed to foreign languages, even if they are unable to master them. Although mastery is best, even modest levels of language training provide students with clues about cultural norms and attitudes that prove helpful in international business.

Translation. Of course, some linguistic differences may be overcome through translation. An area in which most international businesses must adjust their practices to account for cultural differences is the translation of advertising, operating instructions, and other printed material. While companies sometimes will hire local specialists to develop new materials for the local market, they often choose simply to translate written materials created in the home country into the language of the host country. Yet the translation process requires more than merely substituting words of one language for those of a second. Translators must be sensitive to subtleties in the connotations of words and focus on the translating of ideas, not the words themselves. Far too often, translation problems create marketing disasters. A classic case is KFC's initial translation of "Finger Lickin' Good" into Chinese, which came out as the far less appetizing "Eat Your Fingers Off." Similarly, the original translation of Pillsbury's Jolly Green Giant for the Saudi Arabian market was "intimidating green ogre"—a very different image from what the firm intended (although it still might encourage children to eat their peas).

Some translation problems can be eliminated by hiring local native speakers as translators. However, problems may remain if the translators have not mastered all the idioms and connotations of the two languages involved. Firms can reduce the chances that they are sending the wrong message to their customers by using a technique known as backtranslation. In **backtranslation,** after one person translates a document, a second person is hired to translate the translated version back into the original language. This technique provides a check that the intended message is actually being sent, thus avoiding communication mistakes.

When communications to non–native speakers must be made in the home country language, speakers and writers should use common words, use the most common meanings of those words, and try to avoid idiomatic phrases. For example, Caterpillar is faced with the problem of communicating with the diverse international users of its products. It developed its own language instruction program called Caterpillar Fundamental English (CFE), which it uses in its overseas repair and service manuals. CFE is a simplified, condensed version of English that can be taught to non-English speakers in 30 lessons. It consists of 800 words that are necessary to repair Cat's equipment: 450 nouns, 70 verbs, 100 prepositions, and 180 other words.[12] The following "Going Global" presents some other hints for communicating internationally.

Saying No. Another cultural difficulty international businesspeople face is that words may have different meanings to persons with diverse cultural backgrounds. North Americans typically translate the Spanish word *mañana* literally to mean "tomorrow." But in parts of Latin America, the word is used to mean "soon—within the next several days."

GOING GLOBAL

International Communication: A Primer

Conversational Principle #1: Recognize that many cultures need to know as much as possible about you and the firm you represent. Always remember when you are in Latin America, Asia, and parts of Western Europe that even the most seemingly casual, insignificant conversations have a level of significance far beyond that dictated by the content being discussed. Conversations about your family, your firm, or current events are used to "warm up relationships," just as one might warm a car engine on a cold day. You should also give your hosts insights into you as a person and recognize their need to find out what makes you "tick."...

Conversational Principle #2: Speak slowly, clearly, and simply. Avoid jargon, slang, clichés, and idiomatic usage. When foreigners learn English, they learn a "correct" version of formal English. When they listen to people from the United States (or Australia, Canada, or the United Kingdom) lapsing into slang or idiom, they become confused. We must realize that even an everyday expression such as "Let's get rolling" or "I'm all ears" can be perplexing if the foreigner tries to translate it literally....

Conversational Principle #3: Sprinkle your conversation with at least some words and phrases in the language of your listeners. It is regarded as "good manners" to make at least an attempt to learn a few phrases in your host's language....

Conversational Principle #4: Be careful about what your body language and your tone of voice communicate. When listeners cannot follow what is being said, they will pay far greater attention to body language. And if they do understand English, they will look for contradictions between what is said and how it is said....Tone of voice also plays an important role when communicating internationally. There are vast cultural differences at play here: notice, for example, how softly people from most Asian cultures speak. People from the United States often seem loud and aggressive in negotiations and vigorous in arguments. And negotiations in Latin American, Mediterranean, and Central European countries are far louder, often including heated, arm-waving exchanges of opinion that rarely mean anything personal....

Presentation Principle #1: Respect many foreign audiences' desire for greater formality of presentation. U.S. businesspeople generally like presentations that seem natural and spontaneous, not "canned" or overly rehearsed. Most other countries...expect more formality. "Natural" presentations...give the impression that the speaker has not respected the audience sufficiently....

*Presentation Principle #2: Allow for differences in behavior of foreign audiences....*Japanese audiences, for example, usually sit and nod their heads (which means they understand, not that they agree) and say nothing. However, on some occasions, they may start frenzied talking among themselves. Or, in open discussions, they may suddenly become evasive. What this usually means is that something said is disturbing to them....

Presentation Principle #3: Have patience; design your presentation's length, completeness, and "interruptability" with the audience's culture in mind. U.S. businesspeople are impatient and are used to fast-paced, efficient presentations. Most foreigners, with the probable exceptions of Germans and the Swiss, prefer slower, more deliberate efforts....Japanese, Latin American, and Arabic audiences expect a presentation to be in short, separate segments that allow time for questions and digestion of what has been presented....

Presentation Principle #4: Match rank and age of presenter to rank and age of important members of foreign audiences. In many American companies, meritocracy is dominant and fairly young executives rise rapidly to powerful positions early in their career. In other cultures, however, age (or seniority) is a major indicator of status. Therefore, sending young executives, regardless of their rank, to negotiate important contracts with businesspeople in those cultures can be a disaster.

Sources: Ronald E. Dulek, John S. Fielden, and John S. Hill, "International Communication: An Executive Primer." Reprinted from *Business Horizons*, January–February 1991. Copyright © 1991 by the Foundation for the School of Business at Indiana University. Used with permission.

Even the use of *yes* and *no* differs across cultures. In contract negotiations, Japanese businesspeople often use *yes* to mean "Yes, I understand what is being said." Foreign negotiators often assume that their Japanese counterparts are using *yes* to mean "Yes, I agree with you" and are disappointed when the Japanese later fail to accept contract terms the foreigners had assumed were agreed to. Misunderstandings can be compounded because directly uttering *no* is considered very impolite in Japan. Japanese negotiators who find a proposal unacceptable will, in order to be polite, suggest that it "presents many difficulties" or requires "further study."[13] Foreigners waiting for a definitive no may have to wait a long time. Such behavior may be considered evasive in U.S. business culture, but it is the essence of politeness in Japanese business culture.

Communication

Communicating across cultural boundaries, whether verbal or nonverbal, is a particularly important skill for international managers. While communication can often go awry between people who share a culture, the chances of miscommunication increase substantially when the people are from different cultural backgrounds. In such cases, the sender encodes a message using her cultural filters and the receiver decodes the same message using his cultural filters. The result of using different cultural filters is that misunderstandings are common and often expensive to resolve. For example, a contract between Boeing and a Japanese supplier called for the delivery of fuselage panels for Boeing's 767 aircraft to have a "mirror finish." Labor costs for the part were higher than expected because the Japanese supplier polished and polished the panels to achieve what it believed to be the desired finish, when all Boeing wanted was a shiny surface.[14]

The context in which a discussion occurs may also play a role in cross-cultural communication. Experts distinguish between high-context and low-context cultures.[15] A **low-context culture** is one in which the words used by the speaker explicitly convey the speaker's message to the listener. Anglo-Saxon countries, such as Canada, the United Kingdom, and the United States, and Germanic countries are good examples of low-context cultures (see Fig. 9.2). A **high-context culture** is one in which the context in which a conversation occurs is just as important as the words that are actually spoken, and cultural clues are important in understanding what is being communicated. Examples are Japan and Arab countries. Business behaviors in high-context cultures often differ from those in low-context cultures. For example, German advertising is typically fact-oriented, while Japanese advertising is more emotion-oriented.[16] High-context

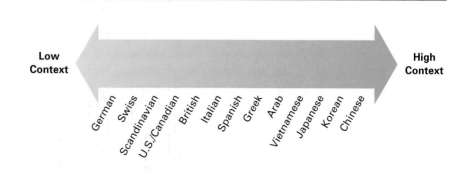

FIGURE 9.2

High- and Low-Context Cultures

Source: From Edward T. Hall, "How Cultures Collide," *Psychology Today*, July 1976, pp. 67–74. Reprinted with permission from *Psychology Today* Magazine, Copyright © 1976 (Sussex Publishers, Inc.).

Low Context   High Context

German Swiss Scandinavian U.S./Canadian British Italian Spanish Greek Arab Vietnamese Japanese Korean Chinese

cultures place higher value on interpersonal relations in deciding whether to enter into a business arrangement. Low-context cultures place more importance on the specific terms of a transaction.[17] In low-context cultures like Canada, the United Kingdom, and the United States, lawyers are often present at negotiations to ensure that their clients' interests are protected. In contrast, in high-context cultures such as those of Saudi Arabia, Japan, and Egypt, the presence of a lawyer, particularly at the initial meeting of the participants, would be viewed as a sign of distrust. Because these cultures value long-term relationships, an assumption by a potential partner that one cannot be trusted may be sufficient grounds to end the negotiations. Table 9.1 provides additional information about differences in negotiating styles across cultures.

In addition to the challenge of differing cultural contexts, managers of international firms in different parts of the world find communication hindered by physical barriers of time and distance. The normal working day for managers in Canada and the United States overlaps by only a few hours that of managers in Europe. Thus a manager in Montreal may reach a colleague in London or Rome only by calling first thing in the morning. His colleague is likely still to be at work, although her work day is drawing to an end. Calls to managers in the Far East are much more difficult to schedule because the time differences are so much greater.

Another mode of business communication is the face-to-face meeting. Distance makes this mode more difficult for MNCs than for domestic firms. But international travel is a necessity in many cases. For example, when Ford and Mazda worked together to design the new Ford Escort, Ford managers on the project made over 150 trips to Japan within a three-year period for meetings.

Nonverbal Communication. Members of a society communicate with each other using more than words. In fact, some researchers believe 80 to 90 percent of all information is transmitted among members of a culture by means other than language.[18] This nonverbal communication includes facial expressions and hand gestures, intonation, eye contact, body positioning, and body posture. While most members of a society quickly understand nonverbal forms of communication common to their society, outsiders may find these difficult to comprehend. Table 9.2 lists some of the many common forms of nonverbal communication.

Because of cultural differences, nonverbal forms of communication often can lead to misunderstandings. For example, in the United States, people discussing business at a party typically stand 20 inches from each other. In Saudi Arabia, the normal conversational distance is only 9 to 10 inches. A U.S. businessperson conversing with a Saudi counterpart at a party will respond to the Saudi's polite attempts to move in closer by politely moving back. Each is acting politely within the context of his or her own culture—and insulting the other in the context of that person's culture.[19]

Differences in the meanings of hand gestures and facial expressions also exist among cultures. Nodding one's head means "yes" in the United States but "no" in Bulgaria. Joining the thumb and forefinger in a circle while extending the remaining three fingers is the signal for "okay" in the United States. However, it symbolizes money to the Japanese, worthlessness to the French, male homosexuals to the Maltese, and a vulgarity in many parts of Eastern Europe.[20] Needless to say, international businesspeople should avoid gesturing in a foreign culture unless they are sure of the gesture's meaning in that culture.

TABLE 9.1

Differences in Negotiating Styles across Cultures

JAPANESE	NORTH AMERICAN	LATIN AMERICAN
Emotional sensitivity highly valued.	Emotional sensitivity not highly valued.	Emotional sensitivity valued.
Hiding of emotions.	Dealing straightforwardly or impersonally.	Emotionally passionate.
Subtle power plays; conciliation.	Litigation not as much as conciliation.	Great power plays; use of weakness.
Loyalty to employer. Employer takes care of its employees.	Lack of commitment to employer. Breaking of ties by either if necessary.	Loyalty to employer (who is often family).
Group decision-making consensus.	Teamwork provides input to a decision maker.	Decisions come down from one individual.
Face-saving crucial. Decisions often made on basis of saving someone from embarrassment.	Decisions made on a cost-benefit basis. Face-saving does not always matter.	Face-saving crucial in decision making to preserve honor, dignity.
Decision makers openly influenced by special interests.	Decision makers influenced by special interests but this often not considered ethical.	Execution of special interests of decision maker expected, condoned.
Not argumentative. Quiet when right.	Argumentative when right or wrong, but impersonal.	Argumentative when right or wrong; passionate.
What is down in writing must be accurate, valid.	Great importance given to documentation as evidential proof.	Impatient with documentation as obstacle to understanding general principles.
Step-by-step approach to decision making.	Methodically organized decision making.	Impulsive, spontaneous decision making.
Good of group is the ultimate aim.	Profit motive or good of individual ultimate aim.	What is good for the group is good for the individual.
Cultivate a good emotional social setting for decision making. Get to know decision makers.	Decision making impersonal. Avoid involvements, conflicts of interest.	Personalism necessary for good decision making.

Source: From Pierre Casse, *Training for the Multicultural Manager: A Practical and Cross-Cultural Approach to the Management of People*. Washington, D.C.: SIETAR International, © 1982. Reprinted with permission of the author.

Even silence has meaning. People in the United States tend to abhor silence at meetings or in private conversation, believing that silence reflects an inability to communicate or to empathize. In Japan, silence may indicate nothing more than that the individual is thinking or that additional conversation would be disharmonious. U.S. negotiators have often misinterpreted the silence of their Japanese counterparts and offered contract concessions when none were needed, simply to end the lull in the discussion.[21] Attitudes toward silence also affect

TABLE 9.2

Forms of Nonverbal Communication

Hand gestures, both intended and self-directed, such as nervous rubbing of hands

Facial expressions, such as smiles, frowns, and yawns

Posture and stance

Clothing and hair styles (hair being more like clothes than like skin, both subject to the fashion of the day)

Walking behavior

Interpersonal distance

Touching

Eye contact and direction of gaze, particularly in "listening behavior"

Architecture and interior design

"Artifacts" and nonverbal symbols, such as lapel pins, walking sticks, and jewelry

Graphic symbols, such as pictures to indicate "men's room" or "handle with care"

Art and rhetorical forms, including wedding dances and political parades

Smell (olfaction), including body odors, perfumes, and incense

Speech rate, pitch, inflection, and volume

Color symbolism

Synchronization of speech and movement

Taste, including symbolism of food and the communication function of chatting over coffee or tea; oral gratification, such as smoking or gum chewing

Cosmetics: temporary, such as powder and lipstick; permanent, such as tattoos

Drum signals, smoke signals, factory whistles, police sirens

Time symbolism: what is too late or too early a time to telephone or visit a friend or too long or too short a time to make a speech or stay for dinner

Timing and pauses within verbal behavior

Silence

Source: Reprinted with permission of Simon & Schuster Inc. from the Macmillan College text *An Introduction to Intercultural Communication* by John C. Condon and Fathi Yousef. Copyright © 1975 by Macmillan College Publishing Company, Inc.

management styles. In the United States, good managers solve problems. Thus U.S. managers often attempt to dominate group discussions in order to signal their competence and leadership abilities. In Japan, good managers encourage their subordinates to seek solutions that are acceptable to all parties involved. A Japanese manager therefore will demonstrate leadership by silence, thereby encouraging full participation by subordinates attending the meeting and promoting group consensus.[22]

Cross-cultural differences also are reflected in the spatial arrangements and furnishings of offices. In a typical U.S. firm, large, windowed corner offices on the highest floors of the firm's headquarters are the most prestigious. Most U.S. offices are partitioned to allow each employee private space and to restrict socializing with coworkers. In Japan, the group orientation of the society results in private offices being nonexistent for all but the most senior managers. Japanese offices are open and public with double rows of desks to encourage cooperation and communication between members of a group. The desk of the group leader is positioned at one end of the row to facilitate supervision and group cohesion.[23] In Germany, offices are designed for privacy. The closed-door policy adopted by many German managers suggests their belief that subordinates may be trusted to do their jobs competently without constant monitoring by their supervisor.[24]

Gift Giving and Hospitality. Gift giving and hospitality are important means of communication in many business cultures. Japanese business etiquette requires solicitous hospitality. Elaborate meals and after-hours entertainment serve to build personal bonds and group harmony among the participants. These personal bonds are strengthened by the exchange of gifts, which vary according to the occasion and the status of the giver and the recipient. However, business gifts are opened in private, so as not to cause the giver to lose face should the gift be too expensive or too cheap relative to the gift offered in return.[25] As the rules for gift giving can be quite complicated, even to native Japanese, etiquette books are available that detail the appropriate gift for each circumstance.[26]

Arab businesspeople, like the Japanese, are very concerned about their ability to work with their proposed business partners; the quality of the people one deals with is just as important as the quality of the project. Thus the business culture of Arab countries also includes gift giving and elaborate and gracious hospitality as a means of assessing these qualities. Unlike in Japan, however, business gifts are opened in public so that all may be aware of the donor's generosity.[27]

Norms of hospitality even affect the way bad news is delivered in various cultures. In the United States, bad news is typically delivered as soon as it is known. In Korea, it is delivered at day's end so it will not ruin the recipient's whole day. Further, in order not to disrupt personal relationships, the bad news is often only hinted at. In Japan, maintaining harmony among participants in a project is emphasized. Bad news often is communicated informally from a junior member of one negotiating team to a junior member of the other team. Even better, a third party may be used to deliver the message in order to preserve the harmony within the group.[28]

Religion

Religion is an important aspect of most societies. It affects the ways in which members of a society relate to each other and to outsiders. Approximately 80 percent of the world's 5.7 billion people claim some religious affiliation. As reflected in Map 9.3, 69 percent of the world's population adheres to one of four religions: Christianity, comprising Roman Catholic (18.8 percent), Protestant (10.1 percent), and Eastern Orthodox (3.1 percent); Islam (17.7 percent); Hinduism (13.3 percent); and Buddhism (5.7 percent).

Religion shapes the attitudes its adherents have toward work, consumption, individual responsibility, and planning for the future. Sociologist Max Weber, for example, has attributed the rise of capitalism in Western Europe to the **Protestant ethic,** which stresses individual hard work, frugality, and achievement as means of glorifying God. The Protestant ethic makes a virtue of high savings rates, constant striving for efficiency, and reinvestment of profits to improve future productivity, all of which are necessary for the smooth functioning of a capitalist economy.

In contrast, Hinduism emphasizes spiritual accomplishment rather than economic success. The goal of a Hindu is to achieve union with Brahma, the universal spirit, by leading progressively ascetic and pure lives as one's reincarnated soul goes through cycles of death and rebirth. The quest for material possessions may delay one's spiritual journey. Thus Hinduism provides little support for capitalistic

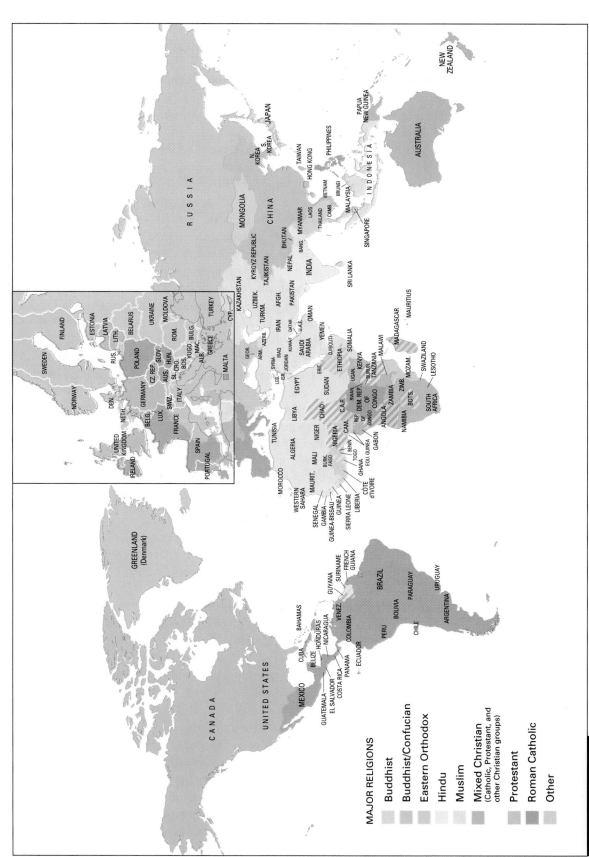

MAJOR RELIGIONS

- Buddhist
- Buddhist/Confucian
- Eastern Orthodox
- Hindu
- Muslim
- Mixed Christian
  (Catholic, Protestant, and
  other Christian groups)
- Protestant
- Roman Catholic
- Other

MAP 9.3 **Major World Religions**

activities such as investment, wealth accumulation, and the constant quest for higher productivity and efficiency.

Islam, while supportive of capitalism, places more emphasis on the individual's obligation to society. According to Islam, profits earned in fair business dealings are justified, but a firm's profits may not result from exploitation or deceit, for example, and all Muslims are expected to act charitably, justly, and humbly in their dealings with others. The Islamic prohibition against payment or receipt of interest noted in Chapter 8 results from a belief that the practice represents exploitation of the less fortunate.

Religion affects the business environment in other important ways. Often religions impose constraints on the roles of individuals in society. For example, the caste system of Hinduism traditionally has restricted the jobs individuals may perform, thereby affecting the labor market and foreclosing business opportunities. For example, only members of the Dom subcaste may provide cremation services.[29] Countries dominated by strict adherents to Islam, such as Saudi Arabia and Iran, limit job opportunities for women, in the belief that their contact with adult males should be restricted to relatives.

Religion also affects the types of products consumers may purchase as well as seasonal patterns of consumption. In most Christian countries, for example, the Christmas season represents an important time for gift giving, yet very little business is done on Christmas Day itself. While consumption booms during the Christmas holidays, production plummets as employees take time off to visit friends and family.

The impact of religion on international businesses varies from country to country, depending on the country's legal system, its homogeneity of religious beliefs, and its toleration of other religious viewpoints. Consider Saudi Arabia, home of the holy city of Mecca, to which all Muslims are supposed to make a pilgrimage sometime in their lives. The teachings of the Koran form the basis of the country's theocratic legal system, and 99 percent of the Saudi population is

Firms often adapt their products to meet the needs of local cultures. Blonde-haired Barbie dolls are a popular item in any North American toy store. But Barbie's features change from market to market. The dark-haired Barbie dolls produced by these Indonesian workers will be marketed to little girls throughout Asia.

Muslim. Strong political pressure exists within the country to preserve its religious traditions. It is impossible to overstate the importance to foreign businesspeople of understanding the tenets of Islam as they apply to exporting, producing, marketing, or financing goods in the Saudi market. For example, work stops five times a day when the faithful are called to pray to Allah. A non-Muslim manager would be foolish to object to the practice even though it seemingly leads to lost production. Foreigners must also be considerate of their Saudi hosts during the holy month of Ramadan, when the Muslim faithful fast from sunrise to sunset. Female executives of Western firms have additional obstacles because of Saudi attitudes toward the appropriate roles for women, which stem from their religion. Even actions taken outside of Saudi borders may affect commercial relations with the country. For example, McDonald's made a major faux pas when, as part of its British marketing campaign during the 1994 World Cup, it printed the flags of the twenty-four participating soccer teams, including that of Saudi Arabia, on its paper takeout bags. But the Saudi flag includes a sacred inscription that reads, "There is no God but Allah, and Mohammed is His Prophet." Muslims in Saudi Arabia and in other countries were outraged by McDonald's actions, believing that Islam had been insulted by including the name of Allah on a container that would be thrown into garbage cans. McDonald's quickly apologized and pledged to stop using the bags, thereby diffusing a controversy that would have otherwise affected its business in Saudi Arabia and other Muslim countries. Nike made a similar gaffe when Muslim groups protested that the logo designed for a line of athletic shoes it was introducing in summer 1997 resembled the Arabic word for God, Allah. Nike quickly pulled the footwear from production and redesigned the offending logo.[30]

In many other countries, however, religion, while important, does not permeate every facet of life. For example, in many South American countries most of the population is Roman Catholic. But other religions are also practiced, and tolerance of those religions is high. The Catholic Church is an important pillar of these societies, but only one of many institutions that affect and shape the daily lives of the citizens. Yet public holidays reflect Christian theology (Easter, Christmas), as does the work week (Sunday is the day of rest). A firm operating in these countries thus needs to adjust its production and employee scheduling to meet the expectations of its workers and customers. Firms operating in Sweden, which is 97 percent Lutheran, must make similar adjustments.

Ironically, countries characterized by religious diversity may offer even greater challenges. Firms that operate in the cosmopolitan cities of London and New York, such as Barclays Bank, Hoffman-LaRoche, and IBM, must accommodate the religious needs of their Jewish, Christian, Muslim, and Hindu employees and customers by taking into account differences in religious holidays, dietary restrictions or customs, and sabbath days. Firms that fail to adjust to these needs will suffer from absenteeism, low morale, and lost sales.

Values and Attitudes

Culture also affects and reflects the values and attitudes of members of a society. Values are the principles and standards accepted by members of a society; attitudes encompass the actions, feelings, and thoughts that result from those values. Cultural values often stem from deep-seated beliefs about the individual's position in relation to his or her deity, the family, and the social hierarchy that we discussed earlier. Cultural attitudes about such factors as time, age, education, and status reflect these values and in turn shape the behavior of and opportunities available to international businesses operating in a given culture.

Time. Attitudes about time differ dramatically across cultures. In Anglo-Saxon cultures, the prevailing attitude is "time is money." U.S. and Canadian business-people expect meetings to start on time. Keeping a person waiting is considered extremely rude. This cultural attitude toward time is interrelated with other aspects of these cultures. In these North American countries, pay is linked to time and to one's productivity, so it is not surprising that time is valued highly. Time represents the opportunity to produce more and to raise one's income, so it is not to be wasted. Underlying this attitude is the Protestant ethic, which encourages one to better one's position in life through hard work, and the puritanical belief that "idle hands are the Devil's workshop."

In Latin American cultures, however, few participants would think it unusual if a meeting began 45 minutes after the appointed time.[31] In Arab cultures, meetings not only often start later than the stated time, but they also may be interrupted by family and friends who wander in to exchange pleasantries. Westerners may interpret their host's willingness to talk to these unscheduled visitors as a sign of rudeness and as a subtle device to undermine their dignity. Nothing could be further from the truth. This open-door policy reflects the hospitality of the host and the respect he offers to all guests—just the sort of person with whom the Arab presumes the Westerner wants to do business.[32]

Even the content of business meetings can vary by country. If a meeting is scheduled for 2:00 p.m., U.S., Canadian, and British businesspeople arrive at 1:55 p.m. and expect the meeting to start promptly at 2:00 p.m. After exchanging a few pleasantries, they then get down to business, following a well-planned agenda that has been distributed in advance to the participants. At the meeting, the positions of the parties are set forth and disagreement is common. In contrast, in high-context cultures like those of Japan and Saudi Arabia the agenda of an initial meeting will be quite different. Time must be expended to determine whether the parties can trust each other and work together comfortably. The initial meeting does not necessarily focus on the details of the proposed business at hand but rather on assessing the character and integrity of the potential business partners. But note that this time is not being wasted. Because these cultures value personal relationships so highly, time is being utilized for an important purpose—assessing the qualities of potential business partners.

Age. Important cultural differences exist in attitudes toward age. Youthfulness is considered a virtue in the United States. Many U.S. firms devote much time and energy to identifying young "fast-trackers" and providing them with important, tough assignments, such as negotiating joint ventures with international partners. However, in Asian and Arab cultures, age is respected and a manager's stature is correlated with age. These cultural differences can lead to problems. For example, many foreign firms mistakenly send younger, fast-track executives to negotiate with government officials of China. The Chinese, however, prefer to deal with older and more senior members of the firm, and thus may be offended by this approach.

In Japan's corporate culture, age and rank are highly correlated. Yet senior (and by definition, older) managers will not grant approval to projects until they have achieved a consensus among junior managers. Many foreign firms mistakenly focus their attention in negotiations on the senior Japanese managers, failing to realize that their goal should be to persuade the junior managers. Once the junior managers consent to the project, the senior manager will grant his approval as well.

Education. A country's formal system of public and private education is an important transmitter and reflection of the cultural values of its society. For example, U.S. primary and secondary schools emphasize the role of the individual and stress the development of self-reliance, creativity, and self-esteem. The United States prides itself on providing widespread access to higher education. Research universities, liberal arts colleges, and community colleges coexist in order to meet the educational needs of students with disparate incomes and intellectual talents. In contrast, the United Kingdom, reflecting its class system, historically provided an elite education to a relatively small number of students. And Germany has well-developed apprenticeship programs that train new generations of skilled craftspeople and machinists for its manufacturing sector. The Japanese and French educational systems share a different focus. Their primary and secondary schools concentrate on rote memorization to prepare students to take a nationwide college entrance exam. The top-scoring students gain entry to a handful of prestigious universities—such as Tokyo University or Kyoto University in Japan and the five *grandes écoles* in France—which virtually guarantee their graduates placement in the most important corporate and governmental jobs in their societies.[33]

Status. The means by which status is achieved also vary across cultures. In some societies, status is inherited as a result of the wealth or rank of one's ancestors. In others, it is earned by the individual through personal accomplishments or professional achievements. In some European countries, for example, membership in the nobility ensures higher status than does mere personal achievement, and persons who inherited their wealth look down their noses at the *nouveau riche.* In the United States, however, hard-working entrepreneurs are honored, and their children are often disdained if they fail to match their parents' accomplishments.

In Japan, a person's status depends on the status of the group to which he or she belongs. Thus Japanese businesspeople often introduce themselves by announcing not only their name but also their corporate affiliation. Attendance at elite universities such as Tokyo University or employment in elite organizations such as Toyota Motor Corporation or the Ministry of Finance grant one high status in Japanese society.

In India, status is determined by one's caste. The caste system, on which much of India's social hierarchy is based, divides the society into various groups such as Brahmins (priests and intellectuals), kshatriyas (soldiers), vaishyas (businesspeople), sudras (farmers and workers), and untouchables, who perform the dirtiest and most unpleasant jobs. According to Hinduism, one's caste reflects the virtue (or lack of virtue) that one exhibited in a previous life. Particularly in rural areas, caste affects every facet of life, from the way a man shapes his mustache to the food the family eats to the job a person may hold.[34]

Individual Differences, Culture, and Business Behavior

These elements of national culture affect the behavior and expectations of managers and employees in the workplace. Psychologists who study the impact of these behaviors and expectations on business focus primarily on the relationship between culture and personality traits and need structures. International businesspeople, who face the challenge of managing and motivating employees with different cultural backgrounds, need to understand what these personality traits and need structures are and how they differ across cultures. Fortunately, an increasing number of studies by industrial psychologists and organizational behavior specialists are identifying these cultural differences, thereby helping international business managers to manage their people more effectively.

Among the most influential of these studies is that performed by Geert Hofstede, a Dutch researcher who studied 116,000 people working in dozens of different countries.[35] (Hofstede's research has been criticized for methodological weaknesses and his own cultural biases but remains the largest and most comprehensive work of its kind.) Hofstede's work identified five important dimensions along which people seem to differ across cultures. These dimensions are shown in Fig. 9.3. Note that these dimensions do not represent absolutes, but instead reflect tendencies within cultures. Within any given culture, there are likely to be people at every point on each dimension.

Social Orientation

The first dimension identified by Hofstede is social orientation.[36] (We have altered Hofstede's terminology a bit for the sake of clarity.) **Social orientation** is a person's beliefs about the relative importance of the individual and the groups to which that person belongs. The two extremes of social orientation, summarized in Table 9.3, are individualism and collectivism. **Individualism** is the cultural belief that the person comes first. People who hold this belief tend to put their own interests and those of their immediate families ahead of those of others. Key values of individualistic people include a high degree of self-respect and independence. These people often put their own career interests before the good of their organizations, and they tend to assess decisions in terms of how those decisions affect them as individuals. Hofstede's research suggested that people in the United States, the United Kingdom, Australia, Canada, New Zealand, and the Netherlands tend to be relatively individualistic.

Collectivism, the opposite of individualism, is the belief that the group comes first. Societies that tend to be collectivistic are usually characterized by well-defined social networks, including extended families, tribes, and coworkers. People are expected to put the good of the group ahead of their own personal welfare, interests, or success. Individual behavior in such cultures is strongly influenced by the emotion of shame; when a group fails, its members take that failure very personally and experience shame. In addition, group members try to fit into their group harmoniously, with a minimum of conflict or tension. Hofstede found that people from Mexico, Greece, Hong Kong, Taiwan, Peru, Singapore, Colombia, and Pakistan tend to be relatively collectivistic in their values.

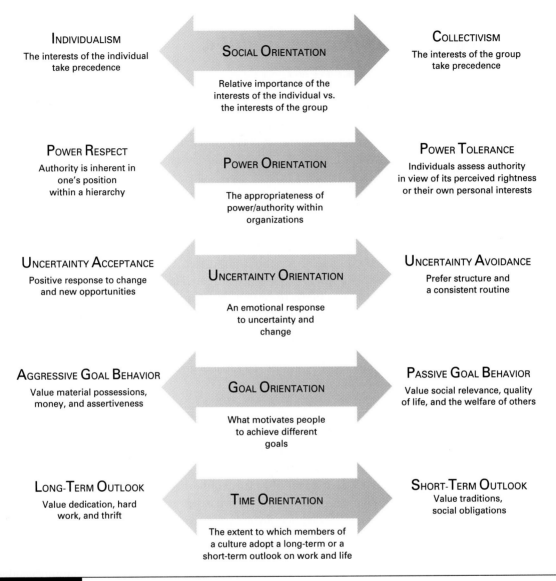

INDIVIDUALISM
The interests of the individual take precedence

SOCIAL ORIENTATION

Relative importance of the interests of the individual vs. the interests of the group

COLLECTIVISM
The interests of the group take precedence

POWER RESPECT
Authority is inherent in one's position within a hierarchy

POWER ORIENTATION

The appropriateness of power/authority within organizations

POWER TOLERANCE
Individuals assess authority in view of its perceived rightness or their own personal interests

UNCERTAINTY ACCEPTANCE
Positive response to change and new opportunities

UNCERTAINTY ORIENTATION

An emotional response to uncertainty and change

UNCERTAINTY AVOIDANCE
Prefer structure and a consistent routine

AGGRESSIVE GOAL BEHAVIOR
Value material possessions, money, and assertiveness

GOAL ORIENTATION

What motivates people to achieve different goals

PASSIVE GOAL BEHAVIOR
Value social relevance, quality of life, and the welfare of others

LONG-TERM OUTLOOK
Value dedication, hard work, and thrift

TIME ORIENTATION

The extent to which members of a culture adopt a long-term or a short-term outlook on work and life

SHORT-TERM OUTLOOK
Value traditions, social obligations

FIGURE 9.3

Individual Differences across Cultures

International firms must be aware of differences in the cultural orientations of countries along the social orientation dimension. Nepotism is often frowned on in individualistic cultures but may be a normal hiring practice in collectivist ones. In countries such as the United States, where individualism is a cultural norm, many workers believe they should be compensated according to their individual achievements. They judge the fairness of any compensation system by whether it achieves this objective. U.S. firms thus spend much time and resources assessing individual performance in order to link pay and performance. A firm that fails to do this will likely lose its more productive employees to firms that do.

Because of its group-oriented culture, prevailing compensation practices in Japan are very different. In most Japanese corporations, a person's compensation reflects the group to which he or she belongs, not personal achievements. For example, all individuals who joined Toshiba's engineering staff in 1996 receive the same compensation, regardless of their individual talents, insights, and efforts.

TABLE 9.3

Extremes of Social Orientation

	COLLECTIVISM	INDIVIDUALISM
In the family	Education toward "we" consciousness	Education toward "I" consciousness
	Opinions predetermined by group	Private opinion expected
	Obligations to family or in-group: ♦ Harmony ♦ Respect ♦ Shame	Obligations to self: ♦ Self-interest ♦ Self-actualization ♦ Guilt
At school	Learning is for the young only	Continuing education
	Learn how to do	Learn how to learn
At the workplace	Value standards differ for in-group and out-groups: particularism	Same value standards apply to all: universalism
	Other people seen as members of their group	Other people seen as potential resources
	Relationship prevails over task	Task prevails over relationship
	Moral model of employer-employee relationship	Calculative model of employer-employee relationship

Source: Reprinted from Geert Hofstede, "The Business of International Business Is Culture," *International Business Review*, Copyright 1994, page 3, with kind permission from Elsevier Science Ltd., The Boulevard, Langford Lane, Kidlington OX5 1GB, UK.

The salaries received by each cohort within the corporation reflect seniority: engineers who joined Toshiba in 1996 receive higher salaries than do engineers who joined the firm in 1997 but lower salaries than engineers who started in 1995. This compensation structure, which lasts for the first six to eight years the employee works for the firm, encourages employees to focus on group goals. While a handful of Japanese corporations have begun to abandon these group-oriented approaches in favor of more merit-oriented ones, individual-oriented approaches remain the exception, not the rule.

These cultural differences help explain the widely publicized differences in CEO pay between the United States and Japan. In group-oriented Japan, the CEO's pay symbolically reflects the performance of the group. In the United States, the CEO's pay is presumed to measure the CEO's contribution to the firm. Even the way the issue is framed reflects the cultural values of the United States: the question "How can President Smith of the XYZ Corporation be worth $10 million?" implicitly assumes that the CEO's pay should measure his or her individual contribution to the organization.

A similar pattern characterizes the career progression and job mobility of employees. In individualistic societies, a person's career path often involves switching employers in a search for higher-paying and more challenging jobs so that the person can prove his or her capabilities in new and changing circumstances. Indeed, in the United States, a person's failure to accept a better paying job at another firm raises suspicions about the person's ambition, motivation, and dedication to his or

---

TABLE 9.4

Extremes of Power Orientation

	POWER TOLERANCE	POWER RESPECT
In the family	Children encouraged to have a will of their own	Children educated toward obedience to parents
	Parents treated as equals	Parents treated as superiors
At school	Student-centered education (initiative)	Teacher-centered education (order)
	Learning represents impersonal "truth"	Learning represents personal "wisdom" from teacher (guru)
At the workplace	Hierarchy means an inequality of roles, established for convenience	Hierarchy means existential inequality
	Subordinates expect to be consulted	Subordinates expect to be told what to do
	Ideal boss is resourceful democrat	Ideal boss is benevolent autocrat (good father)

Source: Reprinted from Geert Hofstede, "The Business of International Business Is Culture," *International Business Review*, Copyright 1994, page 3, with kind permission from Elsevier Science Ltd., The Boulevard, Langford Lane, Kidlington, OX5 1GB, UK.

---

her career. But in collectivistic cultures, such as Japan, a person's changing jobs is often interpreted as reflecting disloyalty to the collective good (the firm) and may brand the person as unworthy of trust.[37] Because of this stigma, job switchers traditionally have had difficulties finding appropriate jobs in other Japanese companies. Although this norm is slowly changing, job mobility is much lower in Japan than in the United States.

Power Orientation

The second dimension Hofstede proposed is power orientation. **Power orientation** refers to the beliefs that people in a culture hold about the appropriateness of power and authority differences in hierarchies such as business organizations. The extremes of the dimension of power orientation are summarized in Table 9.4.

Some cultures are characterized by **power respect.** This means that people in a culture tend to accept the power and authority of their superiors simply on the basis of the superiors' positions in the hierarchy and to respect the superiors' right to that power. People at all levels in a firm accept the decisions and mandates of those above them because of their implicit belief that those higher-level positions carry with them the right to make those decisions and issue those mandates. Hofstede found people in France, Spain, Mexico, Japan, Brazil, Indonesia, and Singapore to be relatively power respecting.

In contrast, people in cultures characterized by **power tolerance** attach much less significance to a person's position in the hierarchy. These people are more willing to question a decision or mandate from someone at a higher level or perhaps even refuse to accept it. They are willing to follow a leader when that leader is perceived to be right or when it seems to be in their own self-interest to do so, but not because of the leader's intangible right to issue orders. Hofstede's work suggested that people in the United States, Israel, Austria, Denmark, Ireland, Norway, Germany, and New Zealand tend to be more power tolerant.

Persons from power-tolerant cultures believe that hierarchies exist in order to solve problems and organize tasks within organizations. Power-respecting business cultures, such as those in Indonesia and Italy, assume that hierarchies are developed so that everyone knows who had authority over whom. In approaching a new project, power-tolerating Americans would first define the tasks at hand and then assemble the project team. Conversely, power-respecting Indonesians would first determine who would be in charge and then assess whether the project would be feasible under that manager's leadership.

These cultural differences regarding the role of hierarchies were highlighted in a survey that asked international managers to respond to the following statement: "In order to have efficient work relationships, it is often necessary to bypass the hierarchical line." Swedish, British, and U.S. managers agreed with the statement. They believed that superiors do not necessarily have all the information subordinates need to make decisions and that it is efficient for the subordinate to seek out the person who has the relevant information regardless of the firm's formal hierarchy. Italian managers, on the other hand, disagreed: bypassing a superior is a sign of insubordination, not efficiency, in the Italian business culture. The managers were also asked whether they should be able to provide precise answers to most questions raised by subordinates. French, Italian, and Indonesian managers said yes; most Swedish, British, and U.S. managers said no. The former group viewed the manager as an expert, while the latter viewed the manager as a problem solver. To a U.S. businessperson, a manager who failed to refer a subordinate to a more knowledgeable authority would be viewed as an egomaniac. To an Indonesian, a manager who referred a subordinate to someone else would be demonstrating incompetence.[38]

Differing cultural attitudes toward power orientation can lead to misunderstandings in business. For example, when firms are negotiating with each other, a firm from a power-tolerant country will often send a team composed of experts on the subject, without concern for rank or seniority. But a team composed of junior employees, no matter how knowledgeable they are about the problem at hand, may be taken as an insult by managers from a power-respecting culture, who expect to deal with persons of rank equal to their own. Also, the quick adoption of informalities by U.S. managers—for example, calling a counterpart by that person's first name—may be misinterpreted by managers from power-respecting cultures as an insulting attempt to diminish another's authority. Similarly, the willingness of a U.S. manager to roll up his or her sleeves and pitch in on the factory floor in an emergency is likely to win praise from U.S. production workers. Conversely, an Indian manager would find performance of such a menial task beneath his dignity. Worse, a manager so lacking in self-respect would be deemed unworthy of respect or obedience from his peers and subordinates.[39]

We can gain a different perspective on Hofstede's dimensions by viewing them in combinations. For example, when social orientation and power orientation are superimposed, individualistic and power-tolerant countries seem to cluster, as do collectivistic and power-respecting countries (see Fig. 9.4).

FIGURE 9.4

Social Orientation and Power Orientation Patterns for Forty Countries

Source: Geert Hofstede, "Motivation, Leadership, and Organization: Do American Theories Apply Abroad?" Reprinted by permission of the publisher from *Organizational Dynamics* Summer 1980 © 1980. Dr. Geert Hofstede, et al. American Management Association, New York. All rights reserved.

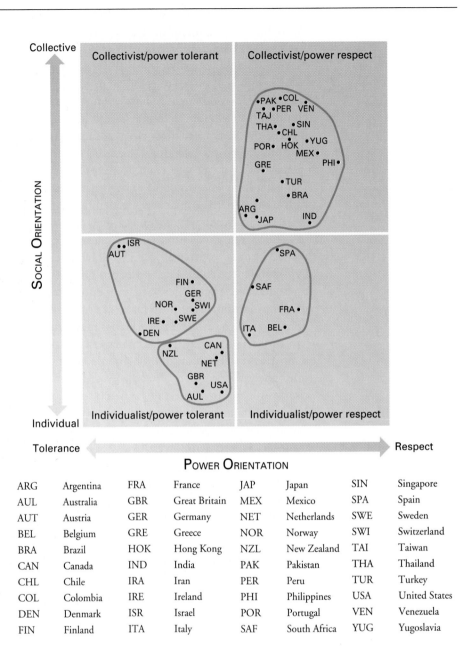

ARG	Argentina	FRA	France	JAP	Japan	SIN	Singapore
AUL	Australia	GBR	Great Britain	MEX	Mexico	SPA	Spain
AUT	Austria	GER	Germany	NET	Netherlands	SWE	Sweden
BEL	Belgium	GRE	Greece	NOR	Norway	SWI	Switzerland
BRA	Brazil	HOK	Hong Kong	NZL	New Zealand	TAI	Taiwan
CAN	Canada	IND	India	PAK	Pakistan	THA	Thailand
CHL	Chile	IRA	Iran	PER	Peru	TUR	Turkey
COL	Colombia	IRE	Ireland	PHI	Philippines	USA	United States
DEN	Denmark	ISR	Israel	POR	Portugal	VEN	Venezuela
FIN	Finland	ITA	Italy	SAF	South Africa	YUG	Yugoslavia

Uncertainty Orientation

The third basic dimension of individual differences Hofstede studied is uncertainty orientation. **Uncertainty orientation** is the feeling people have regarding uncertain and ambiguous situations. The extremes of this dimension are summarized in Table 9.5.

People in cultures characterized by **uncertainty acceptance** are stimulated by change and thrive on new opportunities. Ambiguity is seen as a context within which an individual can grow, develop, and carve out new opportunities.

TABLE 9.5

Extremes of Uncertainty Orientation

	UNCERTAINTY ACCEPTANCE	UNCERTAINTY AVOIDANCE
In the family	What is different is ridiculous or curious	What is different is dangerous
	Ease, indolence, low stress	Higher anxiety and stress
	Aggression and emotions not shown	Showing of aggression and emotions accepted
At school	Students comfortable with ♦ Unstructured learning situations ♦ Vague objectives ♦ Broad assignments ♦ No timetables Teachers may say "I don't know"	Students comfortable with ♦ Structured learning situations ♦ Precise objectives ♦ Detailed assignments ♦ Strict timetables Teachers should have all the answers
At the workplace	Dislike of rules, written or unwritten	Emotional need for rules, written or unwritten
	Less formalization and standardization	More formalization and standardization

Source: Reprinted from Geert Hofstede, "The Business of International Business Is Culture," *International Business Review*, Copyright 1994, page 3, with kind permission from Elsevier Science Ltd., The Boulevard, Langford Lane, Kidlington OX5 1GB, UK.

In these cultures, certainty carries with it a sense of monotony, routineness, and overbearing structure. Hofstede suggested that many people from the United States, Denmark, Sweden, Canada, Singapore, Hong Kong, and Australia are uncertainty accepting.

In contrast, people in cultures characterized by **uncertainty avoidance** dislike and will avoid ambiguity whenever possible. Ambiguity and change are seen as undesirable. These people tend to prefer a structured and routine, even bureaucratic, way of doing things. Hofstede found that many people in Israel, Austria, Japan, Italy, Colombia, France, Peru, and Germany tend to avoid uncertainty whenever possible.

Uncertainty orientation affects many aspects of managing international firms. Those operating in uncertainty-avoiding countries, for example, tend to adopt more rigid hierarchies and more elaborate rules and procedures for doing business. Conversely, uncertainty-accepting cultures are more tolerant of flexible hierarchies, rules, and procedures. Risk taking ("nothing ventured, nothing gained") is highly valued in uncertainty-accepting countries such as the United States and Hong Kong, whereas preserving the status and prestige of the firm through conservative, low-risk strategies is more important in uncertainty-avoiding countries such as Spain, Belgium, and Argentina.

It is interesting to consider uncertainty orientation along with the social orientation dimension. For example, job mobility is likely to be higher in uncertainty-accepting countries than in those characterized by uncertainty avoidance. Some Japanese firms have traditionally used lifetime employment practices partly in response to the uncertainty-avoiding and collectivistic tendencies of the Japanese culture. Yet lifetime employment—as well as the seniority-based pay and promotion policies traditionally used by Japanese firms—may not be an effective policy when transplanted to individualistic and uncertainty-accepting countries. For example, Japanese firms operating in uncertainty-accepting Canada and the United States have been forced to modify their pay and promotion policies because North American workers are more oriented toward an individualistic "pay me what I'm worth" attitude and are less worried about job security than are their counterparts in Japan.

Goal Orientation

The fourth dimension of cultural values Hofstede measured is goal orientation. In this context, **goal orientation** is the manner in which people are motivated to work toward different kinds of goals. One extreme on the goal orientation continuum is aggressive goal behavior (see Table 9.6). People who exhibit **aggressive goal behavior** tend to place a high premium on material possessions, money, and assertiveness. At the other extreme, people who adopt **passive goal behavior** place a higher value on social relationships, quality of life, and concern for others.

According to Hofstede, cultures that value aggressive goal behavior also tend to define gender-based roles somewhat rigidly, whereas cultures that emphasize passive goal behavior do not. For example, in cultures characterized by extremely aggressive goal behavior, men are expected to work and to focus their careers in traditionally male occupations; women are generally expected not to work outside the home and to focus more on their families. If they do work outside the home, they are usually expected to pursue work in areas traditionally dominated by women. According to Hofstede's research, many people in Japan tend to exhibit relatively aggressive goal behavior, whereas many people in Germany, Mexico,

The uncertainty avoidance aspect of German culture spills over into politics. In the most recent campaign for the EU Parliament, both major parties stressed security. The Socialist Party (SPD) poster on the left focuses on providing jobs for German workers so that they can enjoy economic "security instead of fear." The Christian Democratic Union (CDU) poster on the right stresses a future secure against threats of war, violence, and terrorism.

TABLE 9.6		
Extremes of Goal Orientation		
	PASSIVE GOAL BEHAVIOR	**AGGRESSIVE GOAL BEHAVIOR**
In the family	Stress on relationships	Stress on achievement
	Solidarity	Competition
	Resolution of conflicts by compromise and negotiation	Resolution of conflicts by fighting them out
At school	Average student is norm	Best students are norm
	System rewards students' social adaptation	System rewards students' academic performance
	Student's failure at school is relatively minor problem	Student's failure at school is disaster; may lead to suicide
At the workplace	Assertiveness ridiculed	Assertiveness appreciated
	Undersell yourself	Oversell yourself
	Stress on life quality	Stress on careers
	Intuition	Decisiveness

Source: Reprinted from Geert Hofstede, "The Business of International Business Is Culture," *International Business Review*, Copyright 1994, page 3, with kind permission from Elsevier Science Ltd., The Boulevard, Langford Lane, Kidlington OX5 1GB, UK.

Italy, and the United States exhibit moderately aggressive goal behavior. Men and women in passive goal behavior cultures are more likely both to pursue diverse careers and to be well represented within any given occupation. People from the Netherlands, Norway, Sweden, Denmark, and Finland tend to exhibit relatively passive goal behavior.

These cultural attitudes affect international business practices in many ways. For example, one study showed that decisions made by Danish managers (a passive goal behavior culture) incorporate societal concerns to a greater extent than those made by more profit-oriented U.S., British, and German executives (from more aggressive goal behavior cultures).[40] Similarly, studies of the Swedish work force indicate that that country's egalitarian traditions, as well as workers' desires to maintain comfortable work schedules, often make promotions less desirable than in other countries. Many Swedish workers prefer more fringe benefits rather than higher salaries.[41] Or consider the impact of the role of women in business. In Sweden, the high proportion of dual-career families makes it difficult for many workers to accept a promotion if it entails moving. And, not surprisingly, Swedish firms are among the world's leaders in providing fringe benefits such as maternity and paternity leave and company-sponsored child care.

Differences in goal orientation may also affect production techniques. For example, Volvo sought to maintain its product quality and competitiveness by pioneering the use of flexible work groups to produce automobiles. This technique is a means of promoting job satisfaction and reflects Sweden's passive goal behavior, as well as its uncertainty acceptance. Japanese manufacturers, on the other hand, developed quality circles. This practice, inaugurated to promote quality, mirrors the more aggressive goal behavior and the collectivistic aspects of Japanese culture.[42]

Time Orientation

Hofstede recently introduced a fifth dimension into his framework.[43] This dimension, called **time orientation,** is the extent to which members of a culture adopt a long-term versus a short-term outlook on work, life, and other aspects of society. Some cultures, such as those of Japan, Hong Kong, Taiwan, and South Korea, have a long-term, future orientation that values dedication, hard work, perseverance, and thrift. Other cultures, including Pakistan and West Africa, tend to focus on the past and present, emphasizing respect for traditions and fulfillment of social obligations. Hofstede's work suggests that the United States and Germany tend to have an intermediate time orientation.

International Management and Cultural Differences

Given the complexities of culture, how should an international manager go about trying to conduct business across national borders? Three specific concepts that need acknowledgment include cultural clusters, how to better understand new cultures, and the role of ethics in different cultures.

Cultural Clusters

Cultural differences provide challenges to international businesspeople in marketing products, managing work forces, and dealing with host country governments. Fortunately, similarities do exist among many cultures, thereby reducing some of the need to customize business practices to meet the demands of local cultures. Anthropologists, sociologists, and international business scholars have analyzed such factors as job satisfaction, work roles, and interpersonal work relations in an attempt to identify clusters of countries that share similar cultural values that can affect business practices. Map 9.4 shows the eight country clusters developed by one such team of researchers, Ronen and Shenkar. (In their study, four countries—Brazil, India, Israel, and Japan—were not placed in any cluster.) A **cultural cluster** comprises countries that share many cultural similarities, although differences do remain. Many clusters are based on language similarities, as is apparent in the Anglo, Germanic, Latin American, and Arab clusters and, to a lesser extent, in the Nordic and Latin European clusters. Of course, one can disagree with some placements of countries within clusters. Israel, for example, shares many cultural values with the United States, as do Spain and the countries of Latin America.

Many international businesses instinctively utilize the country-clustering approach in formulating their internationalization strategies. Many U.S. firms' first exporting efforts focus on Canada and the United Kingdom. Hong Kong and Taiwanese firms have been very successful in exploiting China's markets. And we noted earlier in this chapter how Spain's Telefonica de Espana has chosen to focus its international expansion efforts on Spanish-speaking areas in the Americas.

Closeness of culture may affect the form firms use to enter foreign markets. Recent research has found, for example, that Canadian firms are more likely to enter the British market by establishing joint ventures with British firms, while

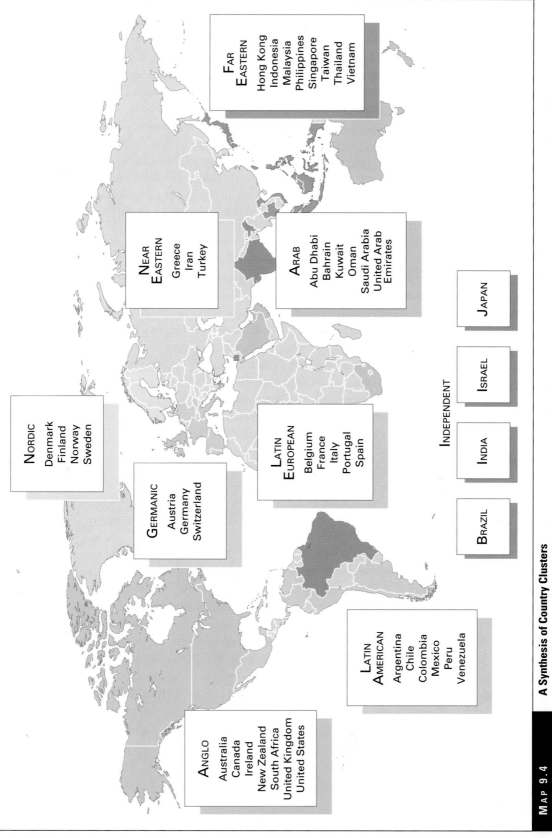

A Synthesis of Country Clusters

Source: From Simcha Ronen and Oded Shenkar, "Clustering Countries on Attitudinal Dimensions: A Review and Synthesis," *Academy of Management Review*, Vol. 10, No. 3 (1985), p. 449. Reprinted with permission.

MAP 9.4

Japanese firms are more likely to enter the British market via a **greenfield investment,** that is, a brand new one. The likely reason for the difference? Because of the relative closeness of their national cultures, Canadian firms are more comfortable working with British partners than are Japanese firms.[44]

Some experts believe the world's cultures are growing more similar as a result of improvements in communication and transportation. Thanks to MTV and CNN, teenagers worldwide have been able to enjoy the wit and wisdom of Beavis and Butthead, while their parents can learn about politics, scandals, disasters, and culture in other countries. Lower airfares generated by increased airline competition mean that more tourists can learn about other cultures firsthand. MNCs facilitate this process of **cultural convergence,** for better or worse, through their advertisements that define appropriate lifestyles, attitudes, and goals and by bringing new management techniques, technologies, and cultural values to the countries in which they operate.

Understanding New Cultures

Nonetheless, cultural differences do exist. When dealing with a new culture, many international businesspeople make the mistake of relying on the **self-reference criterion,** the unconscious use of one's own culture to help assess new surroundings. For example, a U.S. salesperson who calls on a German customer in Frankfurt and asks about the customer's family is acting politely according to U.S. culture—the salesperson's reference point—but rudely according to German culture, thereby generating ill will and the potential loss of a customer.[45] In behaving as expected in the United States, the salesperson forgot the answer to a critical question: "Who is the foreigner?"

The successful international businessperson traveling abroad must remember that he or she is the foreigner and must attempt to behave according to the rules of the culture at hand. There are numerous ways to obtain knowledge about other cultures in order to achieve **cross-cultural literacy.** The best and most common means, not surprisingly, is personal experience that results from conducting business abroad—as part of either a business trip or a long-term assignment—or from nonbusiness travel.[46] Many firms, such as Motorola, offer cross-cultural training programs to their employees headed for foreign assignments.[47] Information about specific cultures can also be obtained from various published sources. For example, Brigham Young University publishes a series of highly regarded *Culturegrams* on over 125 countries, and the U.S. government publishes detailed descriptions and analyses of the economies, political systems, natural resources, and cultures of the world's countries in a series of volumes called *Country Studies.*

Cross-cultural literacy is the first step in **acculturation,** the process by which a person not only understands a foreign culture but also modifies and adapts his or her behavior to make it compatible with that culture. Acculturation is of particular importance to home country managers who frequently interact with host country nationals—for example, a home country plant manager or marketing director working overseas at a foreign subsidiary.

To complicate matters further, many countries have more than one culture, although the level of such cultural diversity varies by country. Japan, with a population consisting of 99.4 percent ethnic Japanese, is extremely homogeneous. The

United States, on the other hand, is culturally heterogeneous, with significant Caribbean, Latin American, Middle Eastern, Hispanic, African, and Asian communities complementing the dominant Anglo-Saxon culture. Successful international businesspeople must recognize the attributes of the primary national culture as well as any important subcultures in culturally heterogeneous societies.

Cultural Differences and Ethics

Cultural differences often create ethical problems. Acceptable behavior in one culture may be viewed as immoral in another. For example, in many poorer countries low-paid workers often expect a small payment in return for stamping a passport or finding a "lost" hotel reservation. Such behavior may appear inappropriate to members of richer countries like the United States or Germany, where such a payment would be considered a bribe. And recall Michelle Pfeiffer's dilemma presented in Chapter 8: should she have stood her ground and refused to return to the set until the Soviet extras were fed, or did she do the right thing by obeying local law and custom?

Consider the following scenarios:

♦ To assist the sale of your products in a particular foreign market, it is suggested that you pay a 10 percent commission to a "go-between" who has access to high-ranking government officials in that market. You suspect, but do not know, that the go-between will split the commission with the government officials who decide which goods to buy. Should you do it? Does it make a difference if your competitors routinely pay such commissions?

♦ You have a long-standing client in a country that imposes foreign-exchange controls. The client asks you to pad your invoices by 25 percent. For example, you would ship the client $100,000 of goods, but would invoice the client for $125,000. On the basis of your invoice, the client would obtain the $125,000 from the country's central bank. He then would pay you $100,000 and have you put the remaining $25,000 in a Swiss bank account in his name. Should you do it? Would it make a difference if your client is a member of a politically unpopular minority who may have to flee the country at a moment's notice?

Needless to say, your answers to these questions will reflect your culture as well as your personal circumstances.

A Final Word

Parts 1, 2, and 3 of this book have discussed the external environments in which international businesses operate. Part 1 provided a general introduction to the world economy. Parts 2 and 3 described the international environment and host country environments, respectively, as the framework in which international business occurs. Part 4, which begins with the next chapter, focuses on the firm itself. Part 5 examines the functional areas within the firm—marketing, operations management, finance, accounting, and human resource management.

As you read Parts 4 and 5, note how often the external environment shapes the opportunities available to international businesses. A firm's strategic choices and operating decisions are often influenced by such external factors as the international monetary system, international treaties, national trade policies, domestic laws, and cultural values. Particularly striking is the importance of politics and culture. As you read the rest of this book, note how often political and cultural factors influence the opportunities available to and the decisions made by international businesses.

CHAPTER REVIEW

Summary

Understanding cultural differences is critical to the success of firms engaging in international business. A society's culture affects the political, economic, social, and ethical rules a firm must follow in its business dealings within that society.

A society's culture also reflects its values, beliefs, behaviors, customs, and attitudes. Culture is learned behavior that is transmitted from one member of a society to another. The elements of culture are interrelated and reinforce each other. These elements are adaptive, changing as outside forces affect the society. Culture not only is shared by the society's members but also defines the society's membership.

A society's culture comprises numerous elements. The social structure reflects the culture's beliefs about the individual's role in society and the importance of mobility within that society.

Language is another important cultural element, for it allows members of the society to communicate with each other. Communication can also take nonverbal forms, such as facial expressions and hand gestures, voice intonation, and use of space. These nonverbal forms of communication are often difficult for outsiders to master.

Approximately 80 percent of the world's population claims some religious affiliation. Religion influences attitudes toward work, investment, consumption, and responsibility for one's behavior. Religion may also influence the formulation of a country's laws.

A society's culture reflects and shapes its values and attitudes, including those toward time, age, status, and education. These affect business operations in numerous ways, such as in hiring practices, job turnover, and the design of compensation programs.

The pioneering research of Geert Hofstede has identified five basic cultural dimensions along which people may differ: social orientation, power orientation, uncertainty orientation, goal orientation, and time orientation. These differences affect business behavior in numerous ways and often lead to cross-cultural misunderstandings.

Cultural differences often create ethical dilemmas for international businesspeople. Behaviors that are acceptable in the home country culture may be deemed inappropriate by the host country culture. Such cultural conflicts commonly arise among persons from different cultural backgrounds, and international businesspeople must be prepared to deal with any resultant ethical conflicts.

The existence of cultural clusters eases to some extent the difficulties of doing business internationally. Researchers have discovered that many countries share similar attitudes toward work roles, job satisfaction, and other work-related aspects of life. Often countries within a cultural cluster share a common language.

Review Questions

1. What is culture?

2. What are the primary characteristics of culture?

3. How does *wa* affect Japanese business behavior?

4. What is a *lingua franca*? Why has English become a lingua franca?

5. What is backtranslation? What problem is it designed to solve?

6. Describe the difference between high-context and low-context cultures.

7. What are individualism and collectivism? How do they differ?

8. What is power orientation?

9. What is uncertainty orientation?

10. What are aggressive and passive goal behaviors? How do they differ?

11. How do differences in attitudes toward time affect international businesspeople?

12. Discuss the differences in pay systems between U.S. and Japanese firms. To what extent are these differences culturally determined?

13. What are cultural clusters?

14. What is the self-reference criterion?

15. What is acculturation? Why is it important to international businesspeople?

Questions for Discussion

1. How can international businesspeople avoid relying on the self-reference criterion when dealing with people from other cultures?

2. How important is it for native English speakers to learn a second language? Should all business students whose native tongue is English be required to learn another language? Why or why not?

3. U.S. law protects women from job discrimination, but many countries do not offer women such protection. Suppose several important job opportunities arise at overseas factories owned by your firm. However, these factories are located in countries that severely restrict the working rights of women. You fear that female managers thus will be ineffective there. Should you adopt gender-blind selection policies for these positions? Does it make a difference if you have good reason to fear for the physical safety of your female managers? Does it make a difference if the restrictions are cultural rather than legal in nature?

4. Under what circumstances should international businesspeople impose the ethics of their culture on foreigners with whom they do business? Does it make a difference if the activity is conducted in the home or the host country?

5. Is nonverbal communication more important or less important when two people speak different languages? What are the pitfalls of trying to use only nonverbal communication to "talk" to someone from another country?

6. How would you evaluate yourself on each of Hofstede's dimensions?

7. Assume you have just been transferred by your firm to a new facility in a foreign location. How would you go about assessing the country's culture along Hofstede's dimensions? How would you incorporate your findings into conducting business there?

BUILDING GLOBAL SKILLS

This exercise will help give you insights into how cultural and social factors affect international business decisions. Your instructor will divide the class into groups of four or five people. Each group then picks any three products from the first column of the following list and any three countries from the next column. (Or, your instructor may assign each group three products and three countries.)

Products	*Countries*
swimsuits	France
CD players	Singapore
desks and bookcases	Poland
men's neckties	Saudi Arabia
women's purses	Taiwan
throat lozenges	Italy
film	South Africa
shoes	Russia

Assume that your firm already markets its three products in the United States. It has a well-known trademark and slogan for each product, and each product is among the market leaders. Assume further that your firm has decided to begin exporting each product to each of the three countries. Research the cultures of those three countries to determine how, if at all, you may need to adjust packaging, promotion, advertising, and so forth in order to maximize your firm's potential for success. Do not worry too much about whether a market truly exists (assume that market research has already determined one does). Focus instead on how your product will be received in each country given that country's culture.

Follow-up Questions

1. What were your primary sources of information about the three countries? How easy or difficult was it to find information?

2. Can you think of specific products that are in high demand in the United States that would simply not work in specific other countries because of cultural factors?

3. How do you think foreign firms assess American culture as they contemplate introducing their products into the U.S. market?

WORKING WITH THE WEB: Building Global Internet Skills

Learning about Cultural Values

A variety of Internet sites provide useful information about cultural differences among countries. (Check out the textbook's web site for linkages to some of the most interesting ones.) Pick three countries that Hofstede studied. Visit several of these web sites and review the material provided for your three countries.

Relate the material you find to Hofstede's work. For example, does the material about each country on the web site seem consistent or inconsistent with Hofstede's findings about that country? If relationships between the web site and Hofstede's analysis are not obvious, can you speculate as to why this is true?

CLOSING CASE

The Benefits of Foreign Exchange[48]

The international hotel industry is so hugely competitive that it is heartening to hear that the general managers of two very different hotels recently acknowledged that they might learn something from each other.

The Athenaeum Hotel and Apartments in London's Piccadilly is a small privately owned hotel which has business travellers from the U.S. as the majority of its guests. Sally Bulloch, general manager, says one way of finding out if the hotel was giving customers what they wanted was to compare it with what they are offered in the U.S.

She suggested swapping jobs for a week with Valerie Ferguson, general manager of the Ritz-Carlton in Atlanta, Georgia, and secretary of the American Hotel and Motel Association. . . .

Ferguson decided to take up Bulloch's offer and go ahead with the swap. She says: "I had no idea what I would get out of it but I saw it was an opportunity to gain an insight into how I could further develop my product. About 35 percent to 40 percent of our guests are international and I wanted to walk away with a better idea of how to service that business and how to build it up."

Business travel is increasingly based on the notion of servicing global travellers with similar wants and needs. Ms. Ferguson says, however, that there can be enormous differences.

"One thing that has left an indelible impression is that European travellers are not as vocal as Americans—you have to take more time to pull the information out. In America, a guest might go to the front desk and say 'my breakfast was terrible,' but the

British are just not going to do that. We've got to find a way of getting that feedback, rather than make the assumption that everything is OK."

One way might be to contact visitors after they have left the hotel. "I don't think they will speak to you unless something major happens but once they get home or to the office, they might," she says.

Guests with limited English could be inhibited by language difficulties, and Ms. Ferguson believes one of her achievements over the past five years at the Ritz-Carlton is to ensure that staff speaking a number of languages are available at all times.

She is impressed by the efforts made at the Athenaeum to make guests feel at home. "There are all these reminders that you are at home—whether it's a bowl of apples or wonderful nick-nacks in the lobby. We like to think you can get a homey atmosphere in a Ritz-Carlton—we have afternoon teas and a special breakfast for Japanese guests—but customers don't want it so comfortable that it's like an old pair of shoes."

For her part, Sally Bulloch of the Athenaeum believes there is a difference in attention to detail. "It's higher over here. For instance, I've often found that if there is a bowl of fruit in an American hotel, it tends to stay there all week, whereas we change it every day." But she admires the informality of U.S. hospitality, and would like to incorporate more of it in the hotel. "We can sometimes be too British," says Ms. Bulloch. "It took me 10 years to get a hamburger on our room-service menu. I kept suggesting that was what our guests wanted but kept being told 'that is not what we do at the Athenaeum'."

She adds: "Many travellers want a quick tea or coffee but do not want to sit at a table. At the Ritz-Carlton outside the breakfast room they had this wonderful silver urn and attractive cups, not paper cups, so people could just have some coffee. It's very American but then why not give our American guests what they want rather than . . . what we think they should have?"

Despite the difference in size between the two hotels—the Ritz-Carlton has 457 rooms and the Athenaeum has 157—Ms. Ferguson says the day-to-day management is very similar. "It's the same, except for the British accent." But decisions can be made more quickly in a smaller hotel, she says. "Product development is managed quite differently in an independent hotel than from a chain. While our standards are very similar and our company is decentralized with

a lot of decisions made at the hotel, the decision-making process here is faster—we're trying to regain that entrepreneurial spirit."

Ms. Bulloch says she has been struck by the amount of time spent by senior staff in U.S. hotels on administration. "My impression has always been that senior staff tend to be in meetings or handling paperwork. But you don't know what's going on unless you are on the floor, and guests often want to meet the managers," she says.

Ms. Ferguson says she is going back to Atlanta with "an increased awareness of the importance of face-to-face contact. Each employee here tries to establish a relationship with the guest; they try and remember the guest's name."

Both would like to extend the swap to other staff. "I would eventually like some of our housekeepers and reception staff to do the swap and to experience what it's like to travel as a guest—especially when you are jet-lagged," says Ms. Bulloch. "There's nothing worse than arriving at 7:30 a.m. and a smiling girl at reception says, 'Sorry, your room won't be ready till 11' and you want to kill her. Since lots of people leave early, we get the maids to start at 6 a.m. instead of at 8 a.m. With three maids, a room can be ready in eight minutes."

She goes on: "We ought to be able to understand our guests' needs. For example, when you are in the U.S., you notice how people will give detailed orders in a restaurant. I don't want our staff not to know what a guest is talking about if they ask for a low-sodium meal."

Ms. Ferguson would like to use the idea of a swap as an incentive to staff by offering it to the hotel's employee of the year. "A lot of our people don't get to travel."

Case Questions

1. What lesson might an international manager learn from this case?

2. What business characteristics lend themselves most to organizational learning from using this practice? What characteristics are least conducive to learning from this practice?

3. What are the advantages and disadvantages of using the method described in the case?

CHAPTER NOTES

1. "Nike Being Polite in Nagano," *USA Today,* February 16, 1998, p. 6B; "Nike Plans to Swoosh into Sports Equipment But It's a Tough Game," *Wall Street Journal,* January 16, 1998, pp. A1, A10; "In Global Drive, Nike Finds Its Brash Ways Don't Always Pay Off," *Wall Street Journal,* May 5, 1997, pp. A1, A10.

2. "The Overseas Chinese: A Driving Force," *The Economist,* July 18, 1992, pp. 21–24.

3. Nancy Adler, *International Dimensions of Organizational Behavior* 3rd Ed. (Cincinnati: South-Western College Publishing, 1997), pp. 15–16.

4. Vern Terpstra and Kenneth David, *The Cultural Environment of International Business* (Cincinnati: South-Western College Publishing, 1985), p. 20.

5. John R. Schermerhorn, Jr., "Language Effects in Cross-Cultural Management Research: An Empirical Study and a Word of Caution," *Proceedings of the Academy of Management,* 1987, p. 103.

6. John C. Condon and Fathi Yousef, *An Introduction to Intercultural Communication* (New York: Bobbs-Merrill, 1975), p. 174; Jon P. Alston, *The American Samurai: Blending American and Japanese Business Practices* (New York: Walter de Gruyter, 1986), p. 325.

7. Adler, op. cit., p. 16.

8. Julie Amparano Lopez, "Going Global," *Wall Street Journal,* October 16, 1992, p. R20.

9. "Spanish Firms Discover Latin American Business as New World of Profit," *Wall Street Journal,* May 23, 1996, p. A1.

10. Trenholme J. Griffin and W. Russell Daggatt, *The Global Negotiator* (New York: Harper Business, 1990), p. 40; "Mother of all Tongues," *Financial Times,* April 4/April 5, 1998, p. 25.

11. "Some Firms Resume Manufacturing in U.S. after Foreign Fiascoes," *Wall Street Journal,* October 14, 1986, pp. 1, 27.

12. Terpstra and David, op. cit., p. 37.

13. Alston, op. cit., p. 331.

14. Henry W. Lane and Joseph J. DiStefano, *International Management Behavior* (Boston: PWS-Kent Publishing, 1992), p. 214.

15. Edward T. Hall, *Beyond Culture* (Garden City, N.Y.: Anchor Press, 1976).

16. Edward T. Hall and Mildred Reed Hall, *Understanding Cultural Differences* (Yarmouth, Me.: Intercultural Press, 1990), pp. 72–73.

17. Edward T. Hall and Mildred Reed Hall, *Hidden Differences* (Garden City, N.Y.: Doubleday, 1987), pp. 9–10.

18. Ibid., p. 3.

19. Gary P. Ferraro, *The Cultural Dimension of International Business* (Englewood Cliffs, N.J.: Prentice Hall, 1990), p. 82.

20. Ferraro, op. cit., p. 76.

21. "For Japanese, silent negotiation is golden," *Houston Chronicle,* December 14, 1992, p. 2B.

22. Alston, op. cit., pp. 305–306.

23. Ibid., pp. 162–163.

24. Hall and Hall, *Understanding Cultural Differences,* p. 41.

25. Gavin Kennedy, *Doing Business Abroad* (New York: Simon and Schuster, 1985), p. 92.

26. Hall and Hall, *Hidden Differences,* p. 109.

27. Marlene L. Rossman, *The International Businesswoman* (New York: Praeger Publishers, 1986), p. 40.

28. Jon P. Alston, "Wa, Guanxi, and Inhwa: Managerial Principles in Japan, China, and Korea," *Business Horizons,* March–April 1989, pp. 26–31.

29. "The reincarnation of caste," *The Economist,* June 8, 1991, pp. 21–23.

30. "Nike tries to quell two of its disputes," *Houston Chronicle,* June 25, 1997, p. 5C.

31. Ferraro, op. cit., p. 99.

32. Kennedy, op. cit., pp. 97–98.

33. "Miyazawa, Making Waves, Seeks to Cut the Clout of Tokyo University's Alumni," *Wall Street Journal,* March 5, 1992, p. A12.

34. "The reincarnation of caste," *The Economist,* op. cit.

35. Geert Hofstede, *Culture's Consequences: International Differences in Work Related Values* (Beverly Hills, Calif.: Sage, 1980).

36. We have taken the liberty of changing the actual labels Hofstede applied to each dimension. The terms we have chosen are more descriptive, simpler, and more self-evident in their meaning.

37. Ferraro, op. cit., p. 157.

38. Adler, op. cit., pp. 45–46; Andre Laurent, "The Cultural Diversity of Western Conceptions of Management," *International Studies of Management and Organization,* Vol. XIII, No. 1–2 (Spring–Summer 1983), pp. 75–96.

39. Ferraro, op. cit., p. 162.

40. B. Bass and L. Eldridge, "Accelerated Managers' Objectives in Twelve Countries," *Industrial Relations*, Vol. 12 (1973), pp. 158–171.

41. Susan C. Schneider, "National versus Corporate Culture: Implications for Human Resource Management," *Human Resource Management,* Vol. 27, No. 2 (Summer 1988), pp. 231–246.

42. Nancy Adler, *International Dimensions of Organizational Behavior,* 2nd ed. (Boston: PWS-Kent, 1991), p. 43.

43. Geert Hofstede, "The Business of International Business Is Culture," *International Business Review*, Vol. 3, No. 1 (1994), pp. 1–14.

44. Bruce Kogut and Harbir Singh, "The Effect of National Culture on the Choice of Entry Mode," *Journal of International Business Studies*, Fall 1988, pp. 411–432.

45. Kathleen K. Reardon, "It's the thought that counts," *Harvard Business Review*, September–October 1984, pp. 136–141.

46. Stephen Kobrin, *International Expertise in American Business* (New York: Institute of International Education, 1984), p. 38.

47. "Firms Grapple with Language," *Wall Street Journal,* November 7, 1989, pp. B1, B10.

48. "The Benefits of Foreign Exchange," *Financial Times,* January 15, 1996, p. 12.

PART 4

Managing in the International Environment

International Strategic Management

After studying this chapter you should be able to:

Describe the challenges of international strategic management.

Identify and describe basic strategic alternatives.

Identify and discuss the components of international strategy.

Describe the international strategic management process.

Identify and describe levels of international strategies.

To MANY PEOPLE AROUND THE WORLD, MICKEY MOUSE IS A PURELY American icon. But Mickey's corporate parent, The Walt Disney Company, is a $23 billion MNC pursuing the world market. For years the firm, founded in 1923, was best known for its animated movies such as *Snow White*, *Pinocchio*, and *Fantasia*. From the firm's beginning, Disney creations proved to be as popular abroad as in the United States. Disney movies attract huge audiences worldwide, and merchandise featuring Mickey and other Disney characters generates over $150 million annually in royalties and licensing fees for the company. ■■ Another critical component of the Disney organization is its theme park operations. The firm's first theme park, Disneyland, opened in Anaheim, California, in 1955 and was soon generating huge profits. Indeed, in 1957 *Time* magazine dubbed Disneyland the biggest tourist attraction in the United States.

Global Mickey[1]

The firm's next major theme park development, Walt Disney World, opened near Orlando, Florida, in 1971; it also was a major success. Because the two parks generate enormous profits, Disney has continued to invest in them by building new attractions and on-site hotels and by opening new parks adjacent to the existing ones. For example, Epcot Center opened in 1982, the Disney–MGM Studios Theme Park in 1988, Blizzard Beach in 1995, and the Animal Kingdom in 1998. ■■ Given the enormous popularity of Disney characters abroad, the firm saw opportunities to expand its theme park operations there. Its first venture into a foreign market, Tokyo Disneyland, opened in 1984. The Japanese have always been keen fans of Disney characters, and many Japanese tourists visit Disneyland and Disney World. Market research showed the Japanese enthusiastically supported the idea of a Disney park in Japan. To limit its risk, the firm did not directly invest in the park. Instead, a Japanese investment group called the Oriental Land Company financed and owns Tokyo Disneyland entirely. Disney oversaw the park's construction and manages it, but receives only royalty income from it. Tokyo Disneyland has been an enormous success from the day it opened its gates: it greeted its 100 millionth visitor after only eight years, a milestone that Disneyland took twice as long to reach. ■■ The success of Tokyo Disneyland inspired the firm to seek other foreign market opportunities. This time, though, Disney decided to participate more fully in both the park's ownership and profits. Disney officials also knew where the next foreign park belonged— Europe. After careful consideration of sites throughout the continent, they narrowed their choice to two: one in France (just outside Paris) and one in Spain (close to Barcelona). The Spanish site held the advantage of a more favorable climate, similar to Florida's. However, the French site, although subject to harsher winter weather conditions, is closer to Europe's major population centers. Three hundred and fifty million people live within a two-hour plane ride of Paris. After careful consideration of the two locations, Disney chose the French site and made its plans for Euro Disney public in 1988. ❚❚ The French government's offer of numerous economic incentives also played a role in Disney's decision. The government sold the land for the park to Disney at bargain-basement prices and agreed to extend the Parisian rail system to the proposed park's front door. The government also decreed that Disney could own up to 49 percent of the stock in its new venture, with the remaining 51 percent made available for trade on European stock exchanges. (The French government had traditionally mandated greater local ownership of projects when it was providing economic incentives.) ❚❚ But as Euro Disney took shape, storm clouds loomed. The cultural elite in Paris lambasted the project as an affront to French cultural traditions. One vocal critic called the project "a cultural Chernobyl," as threatening to French culture as that disastrous nuclear power plant meltdown was to the health and environment of Europe. Farmers protested the manner in which the French government

As part of an incentive package to convince The Walt Disney Company to build its European theme park near Paris, the French government condemned farmland and sold it to Disney at a bargain-basement price. Resenting the manner in which their land had been taken, French farmers protested by blockading entrances to the park shortly after it opened.

condemned their land so that it could be sold to Disney. And the firm found itself defending its conservative employee dress codes, regimented training practices, and plans to ban alcohol from park facilities. ❚❚ Amid the controversy, Euro Disney opened its doors to the public on April 12, 1992. Early visitors seemed happy with their experience, and the park's attendance was generally in line with Disney's planning projections—approximately 11 million visitors a year. But, to the surprise of many observers, Euro Disney's initial financial performance was so bad that it tarnished Disney's reputation for astute management and the park actually came close to being closed within its first year of operation! Among other things, Disney's quest for perfection had raised construction costs. For example, CEO Michael Eisner had ordered the removal, at a cost of $300,000, of two steel staircases that obscured the view of the Star Tours ride. ❚❚ Bad timing also played a part. An economic recession swept through Europe just as Euro Disney was opening. As a result, the firm scotched its plan to reduce its debt by selling off to local developers land it owned near the park. And the carrying cost of its debt rose further as French interest rates climbed. The 1992 collapse of the EU's exchange rate mechanism added to the problem, since the devaluation of the British pound, the Italian lira, and the Spanish peseta raised the cost of vacationing in France for citizens from those countries. As a result, visitors spent 12 percent less on food and souvenirs than expected. ❚❚ Particularly troublesome was the lower than planned occupancy rates at Disney-owned hotels. Disney planners had presumed hotel guests would stay an average of three days, as they do in Orlando. But Euro Disney visitors typically stayed at most only two days. These shorter stays lowered occupancy rates and placed an unanticipated burden on the hotel's computer operations because of the unexpectedly high volume of check-in and check-out activity. Disney had to add new computer terminals and staff to handle the flow of guests. Further, the firm had planned to sell the hotels shortly after the park's opening and to use the proceeds to finance expansion in other areas. Unfortunately, the low occupancy rates made the properties less attractive, and Disney found no eager buyers. ▌▌ After 18 months of operation, Euro Disney faced a major financial crisis. The park was not earning enough revenue to cover its expenses, and the bad press about these financial problems was hurting its stock price. The banks that financed the project feared that the park would default on its loans. Everyone agreed new capital was needed to keep the park in operation, but Disney was unwilling to put up new funds without concessions from the local banks, and vice versa. In March 1994, Disney and the banks finally agreed to a complex rescue package that included injection of new capital by Disney, suspension of royalty payments and management fees due the parent corporation from Euro Disney, forgiveness on interest payments to the banks for 18 months, a new public rights offering, and the sale and lease-back of the Temple of Doom and Discovery Mountain attractions. These efforts halved Euro Disney's debt burden to Fr10 billion and saved the park Fr800 million in interest payments. Finally, in the summer of 1994 Prince Al-Walid bin Talal of Saudi Arabia bought $400 million in Euro Disney stock. His investment gave him about 20 percent ownership and provided Euro Disney with much needed capital. ▌▌ Fortunately, these measures, along with a revitalized European economy, appear to have saved the day. In 1995 the park's financial condition stabilized, and attendance began to grow. Attendance was given another boost in 1996 when rail links via the Channel Tunnel were completed from London to the park's main gate. That same year the park's name was also changed to Disneyland Paris, apparently to distance it from its disastrous start-up. By 1997 Disneyland Paris had finally lived up to its dream, becoming the number one tourist destination in Europe. That year, almost 12 million people visited Mickey, Donald, and Blanche Neige et les Sept Nains (Snow White and the Seven Dwarfs). And indeed, Disney has become so bullish on its international growth potential that the firm has contracted to build a second theme park, Tokyo DisneySea, adjacent to Tokyo Disneyland, in conjunction with the Oriental Land Company. By the end of 2001, visitors to Disney's newest park will be able to explore a South Pacific volcano, play with the Little Mermaid in a Mermaid Lagoon, retrace Sinbad's journeys along the Arabian Coast, wander through old Cape Cod, and pour even more yen into the Disney Company's coffers. ▌▌▌▌▌

To survive in today's global marketplace, firms must be able to quickly exploit opportunities presented them anywhere in the world and respond to changes in domestic and foreign markets as they arise. This requires them to fully understand why, how, and where they intend to do business. They need a cogent definition of their corporate mission, a vision for how they intend to achieve that mission, and an unambiguous understanding of how they intend to compete with other firms. To obtain this understanding, they must carefully compare their strengths and weaknesses to those of their worldwide competitors; assess likely political, economic, and social changes among their current and prospective customers; and analyze the impact of new technologies on their ways of doing business.

Disney's decisions to build Tokyo Disneyland and Disneyland Paris are consistent with its strategy to be a global entertainment firm. So, too, is its lucrative worldwide licensing of its characters for T-shirts, school lunchboxes, toys, and other items. While these ventures have generally been successful—Disney has enjoyed a 20 percent compound annual growth rate over the past several years—the firm stumbled badly in its initial efforts with Disneyland Paris. Further, Disney knows its competitors will continue to fight for market share. European vacationers can enjoy other amusement parks, such as Denmark's Legoland or France's Cipal–Parc Asterix. Mickey Mouse lunchboxes compete for the attention of the world's schoolchildren with those featuring England's Paddington Bear, France's Babar the Elephant, and Belgium's Smurfs. Disney's top managers know that they are in a continuous battle for the entertainment dollars (and yen and marks) of the world's consumers and that it is up to them to deploy the firm's resources to achieve desired levels of profitability, growth, and market share.

The Challenges of International Strategic Management

Disney's managers, like those of other international businesses, utilize strategic management to address these challenges. More specifically, **international strategic management** is a comprehensive and ongoing management planning process aimed at formulating and implementing strategies that enable a firm to compete effectively internationally. The process of developing a particular international strategy is often referred to as **strategic planning.** Strategic planning is usually the responsibility of top-level executives at corporate headquarters and senior managers in domestic and foreign operating subsidiaries.[2] Most larger firms also have a permanent planning staff to provide technical assistance for top managers as they develop strategies. Disney's five-person planning staff, for example, gathered demographic and economic data that the firm's decision makers used to select the French site for its European theme park.

International strategic management results in the development of various **international strategies,** which are comprehensive frameworks for achieving a firm's fundamental goals. Conceptually, there are many similarities between developing a strategy for competing in a single country and developing one for competing in multiple countries. In both cases, the firm's strategic planners must answer the same fundamental questions:

- What products and/or services does the firm intend to sell?
- Where and how will it make those products or services?
- Where and how will it sell them?
- Where and how will it acquire the necessary resources?
- How does it expect to outperform its competitors?[3]

C + 4P

But developing an international strategy is far more complex than developing a domestic one. Managers developing a strategy for a domestic firm must deal with one national government, one currency, one accounting system, one political and legal system, and, usually, a single language and a comparatively homogeneous culture. But managers responsible for developing a strategy for an international firm must understand and deal with multiple governments, multiple currencies, multiple accounting systems, multiple political systems, multiple legal systems, and a variety of languages and cultures. These and other differences in domestic and international operations and how they affect a firm's strategy are summarized in Table 10.1.

Moreover, managers in an international business must also coordinate the implementation of their firm's strategy among business units located in different parts of the world with different time zones, different cultural contexts, and different economic conditions, as well as monitor and control their performance. But managers usually accept these complexities as acceptable trade-offs for the additional opportunities that come with global expansion. Indeed, international businesses have the ability to exploit three sources of competitive advantage unavailable to domestic firms:

(i)

- *Global efficiencies.* International firms can improve their efficiency through several means unaccessible to domestic firms. They can capture *location efficiencies* by locating their facilities anywhere in the world that yields them the lowest production or distribution costs or that best improves the quality of service they offer their customers. Production of athletic shoes, for example, is very labor intensive, and Nike, like many of its competitors, centers its manufacturing in countries where labor costs are especially low.[4] Similarly, by building factories to serve more than one country, international firms may also lower their production costs by capturing *economies of scale.* For example, rather than splitting production of its new sports utility vehicle among several factories, Mercedes-Benz has decided to produce this vehicle only at its new assembly plant in Alabama to benefit from economies of scale in production.[5] Finally, by broadening their product lines in each of the countries they enter, international firms may enjoy *economies of scope,* lowering their production and marketing costs and enhancing their bottom lines. When Nissan first started selling cars in the United States, it introduced a single model and sold the car through dealerships owned by other companies. In relative terms, the costs of distributing a single vehicle model in this manner were quite high. Over time, however, as the firm's reputation became established, it gradually introduced other models and today has its own North American sales and distribution network selling a wide range of cars and trucks. As a result, its distribution costs per vehicle model are much lower than when it first entered the U.S. market.[6]

For e.g., China has low labour cost.
Product: shoes
Rockport: Produce shoes in China to take advantage of location efficiencies

• To take advantage of economies of scale, produce a very large quantity in a factory in China.

TABLE 10.1

Differences between Domestic and International Operations That Affect Strategic Management for U.S. Firms

FACTOR	U.S. OPERATIONS	INTERNATIONAL OPERATIONS
Language	English used almost universally.	Use of local language required in many situations.
Culture	Relatively homogeneous.	Quite diverse, both between countries and within countries.
Politics	Stable and relatively unimportant.	Often volatile and of decisive importance.
Economy	Relatively uniform.	Wide variations among countries and among regions within countries.
Governmental interference	Minimal and reasonably predictable.	Often extensive and subject to rapid change.
Labor	Skilled labor available.	Skilled labor often scarce, requiring training or redesign of production methods.
Financing	Well-developed financial markets.	Often poorly developed financial markets; capital flows subject to government control.
Market Research	Data easy to collect.	Sometimes data difficult and expensive to collect.
Advertising	Many media available; few restrictions.	Media limited; many restrictions; low literacy rates rule out print media in some countries.
Money	U.S. dollar used universally.	Must change from one currency to another; problems created by changing exchange rates and governmental restrictions.
Transportation/ communication	Among the best in the world.	Often inadequate.
Control	Always a problem, but centralized control will work.	A worse problem; must walk a tightrope between overcentralizing and losing control through too much decentralizing.
Contracts	Once signed, are binding on both parties even if one party makes a bad deal.	Can be voided and renegotiated if one party becomes dissatisfied.
Labor relations	Collective bargaining; layoff of workers easy.	Layoff of workers often not possible; may have mandatory worker participation in management; workers may seek change through political process rather than collective bargaining.

Source: Adapted from R. G. Murdick, R. C. Moor, R. H. Eckhouse, and T. W. Zimmerer, *Business Policy: A Framework for Analysis* (Columbus, Ohio: Grid, 1984), p. 275; as found in Pearce and Robinson, *Strategic Management: Formulation, Implementation, and Control*, 5th ed., © 1994 (Burr Ridge, Ill.: Richard D. Irwin, Inc.). Reprinted with permission.

 ◆ *Multinational flexibility.* As we discussed in Chapters 8 and 9, there are wide variations in the political, economic, legal, and cultural environments of countries. Moreover, these environments are constantly changing: new laws are passed, new governments are elected, economic policies are changed, new competitors may enter (or leave) the national market, and so on. International businesses thus face the challenge of responding to these multiple diverse and changing environments. But unlike domestic firms, which operate in and respond to changes in the context of a single domestic environment, international businesses may also respond to a change in one country by implementing a change in another country. Chicken processor Tyson Foods, for example, has benefited over the past decade from the

[Handwritten margin notes, left side:]

whole chicken

white meat   dark meat   chicken feet

Instead of selling all 3 parts in the US mrkt. & charge 3 diff. prices, sell dark meat to Russia, chicken feet to feet & sell them at a high price.

→ Use price discrimination.

increased demand by health-conscious U.S. consumers for chicken breasts. In producing more chicken breasts, Tyson also produced more chicken legs and thighs, which are considered less desirable by U.S. consumers. Tyson capitalized on its surplus by targeting the Russian market, where dark meat is preferred over light, and the Chinese market, where chicken paws are considered a tasty delicacy. Tyson now exports over $250 million worth of chicken thighs and legs to hungry Russians and Chinese.[7] In a variety of ways similar to this, international businesses are better able to exploit and respond to changes and differences in their operating environments than purely domestic firms.

Worldwide learning. The diverse operating environments of MNCs may also contribute to organizational learning. Differences in these operating environments may cause the firm to operate differently in one country than another. An astute firm may learn from these differences and transfer this learning to its operations in other countries.[8] For example, McDonald's U.S. managers believed that its restaurants should be freestanding entities located in suburbs and small towns. A Japanese franchisee convinced McDonald's to allow it to open a restaurant in an inner-city office building. That restaurant's success caused McDonald's executives to rethink their store location criteria. Nontraditional locations—office buildings, Wal-Mart superstores, even airplanes—are now an important source of new growth for the firm.

General Motors provides an even more dramatic example of the benefits of worldwide learning. In the 1980s the company was suffering from high production costs, deterioration in the quality of its vehicles, and a loss of market share to its domestic and foreign rivals. In 1984 General Motors entered into a joint venture with Toyota to establish a new company called NUMMI. GM's goal in creating NUMMI was to learn more about how Toyota's lean manufacturing, kaizen (continuous improvement), and just-in-time inventory controls systems worked. GM then used this new knowledge in developing its newest U.S. automotive division, Saturn. Later, the lessons learned from NUMMI were adopted by GM's Germany subsidiary, Adam Opel AG, when it built its new factory in the East German town of Eisenach in the early 1990s. The Eisenach operation is now not only Europe's most efficient auto assembly plant, it is also GM's: its productivity is double GM's average. And GM is now incorporating the lessons learned from its Eisenach/Saturn/NUMMI experiences into three new factories it is building in Argentina, China, and Poland.[9]

[Handwritten margin note, lower left:]

Global efficiency requires prod^n concentrates in 1 location which reduce flexibility.

Unfortunately, it is difficult to exploit these three factors simultaneously. Global efficiencies can be more easily obtained when a single unit of a firm is given worldwide responsibility for the task at hand. BMW's engineering staff at headquarters in Munich, for example, is responsible for the research and design of the company's new automobiles. By focusing its R&D efforts at one location, BMW engineers designing new transmissions are better able to coordinate their activities with their counterparts designing new engines. However, centralizing control of its R&D operations hinders the firm's ability to customize its product to meet the differing needs of customers in different countries. Consider the simple question of whether to include cupholders in its cars. In designing cars to be driven safely at the prevailing high speeds of Germany's autobahn, the company's engineers decided that cupholders were both irrelevant and dangerous. Driving speeds in the United States, however, are much lower, and cupholders are an important comfort feature in autos sold to U.S. consumers. Lengthy battles were fought between BMW's German engineers and its U.S. marketing managers over this seemingly trivial issue. Only in the mid-1990s did cupholders finally become a standard feature in the firm's automobiles sold in North America.

As this example illustrates, if too much power is centralized in one unit of the firm, it may ignore the needs of consumers in other markets. Conversely, multinational flexibility is enhanced when firms delegate much responsibility to the managers of local subsidiaries. Vesting power in local managers allows each subsidiary to tailor its products, personnel policies, marketing techniques, and other business practices to meet the specific needs and wants of potential customers in each market the firm serves. However, this increased flexibility will reduce the firm's ability to obtain global efficiencies in such areas as production, marketing, and R&D.

Furthermore, the unbridled pursuit of global efficiencies and/or multinational flexibility may stifle the firm's attempts to promote worldwide learning. Centralizing power in a single unit of the firm in order to capture global efficiencies may cause it to ignore lessons and information acquired by other units of the firm. Moreover, these other units may have little incentive or ability to acquire such information if they know that the "experts" at headquarters will ignore them. Decentralizing power in the hands of local subsidiary managers may create similar problems. A decentralized structure may make it difficult to transfer learning from one subsidiary to another. Local subsidiaries may be disposed to reject any outside information out of hand as not being germane to the local situation. Firms wishing to promote worldwide learning must utilize an organizational structure that promotes knowledge transfer among its subsidiaries and corporate headquarters. They must also create incentive structures that motivate managers at headquarters and in subsidiaries to acquire, disseminate, and act upon worldwide learning opportunities.

For example, consider the success of Nokia, headquartered in Helsinki, Finland, which is among the world's leaders in the cellular telephone and telecommunications industries. In 1995 Nokia, like other telecommunications equipment manufacturers, was struggling to keep pace with rapid shifts in its worldwide markets. Managers in different regions had little idea what their counterparts in other markets were doing, and Nokia factories were grappling with excess inventories of some products and inventory shortages of others. In some instances, Nokia factories in one country would shut down for a lack of a critical part that a Nokia factory in another country had in surplus. In early 1996 the firm's CEO, Jorma Ollila, established what he called "commando teams" to attack these problems. The teams were charged with improving efficiency throughout the firm. Using a new worldwide information system, Nokia managers now monitor global, regional, and local sales and inventory on a real-time basis. This allows them to make internal transfers of parts and finished goods efficiently. More important, this approach has allowed Nokia to spot market trends and new product developments that arise in one region of the world and transfer this knowledge to improve its competitiveness in other areas and product lines.[10]

Strategic Alternatives

Multinational corporations typically adopt one of four strategic alternatives in their attempt to balance these three goals.

The first of these strategic alternatives is the *international strategy*. In this approach, a firm utilizes the core competency or firm-specific advantage it developed at home as its main competitive weapon in the foreign markets that it enters. That is, it takes what it does exceptionally well in its home market and attempts to duplicate it in foreign markets. Mercedes-Benz's internationalization strategy, for example, relies on its well-known brand name and its reputation for engineering excellence. It is a world leader in building luxurious cars capable of traveling safely at very high speeds. It is this market segment that it has chosen to exploit internationally, despite the fact that only a very few countries have both the high income levels and the high speed limits appropriate for its products. Yet consumers in Asia, the rest of Europe, and the Americas, attracted by the car's German mystique, eagerly buy it, knowing that they too could drive their new car 150 miles per hour, if only the local police would let them.

The *multidomestic strategy* is a second alternative available to international firms.[11] A multidomestic corporation views itself as a collection of relatively independent operating subsidiaries, each of which focuses on a specific domestic market. In addition, each of these subsidiaries is free to customize its products, its marketing campaigns, and its operations techniques to best meet the needs of its local customers. The multidomestic approach is particularly effective when there are clear differences among national markets, when the economies of scale for production, distribution, and marketing are low, and when there are high coordination costs between the parent corporation and its various foreign subsidiaries. Because each subsidiary in a multidomestic corporation must be responsive to the local market, the parent company usually delegates considerable power and authority to managers of its subsidiaries in various host countries. MNCs operating in the years prior to World War II often adopted this approach because of difficulties of controlling distant foreign subsidiaries given the communication and transportation technologies of those times.

The *global strategy* is the third alternative philosophy available for international firms. A global corporation views the world as a single marketplace and has as its primary goal the creation of standardized goods and services that will address the needs of customers worldwide. The global strategy is almost the exact opposite of the multidomestic strategy. Whereas the multidomestic firm believes that its customers in every country are fundamentally different and must be approached from that perspective, a global corporation assumes that customers are fundamentally the same regardless of their nationalities. Thus, the global corporation views the world market as a single entity as it develops, produces, and sells its products. It tries to capture economies of scale in production and marketing by concentrating its production activities in a handful of highly efficient factories and then creating global advertising and marketing campaigns to sell those goods. Since the global corporation must coordinate its worldwide production and marketing strategies, it usually concentrates power and decision-making responsibility at a central headquarters location.

The international strategy and the global strategy share an important similarity: under either approach, a firm conducts business the same way anywhere in the world. There is an important difference between the two approaches, however. A firm utilizing the international strategy takes its domestic way of doing business and uses that approach in foreign markets as well. In essence, a firm using this strategy believes that if its business practices work in its domestic market, then they should also work in foreign markets as well. Conversely, the starting point for a firm adopting a global strategy has no such home-country bias. In fact, the concept of a home market is irrelevant, for the global firm thinks of its market as a global one, not one divided into domestic and foreign segments. The global firm tries to figure out the best way to serve all of its customers in the global market, and then does so.

A fourth approach available to international firms is the *transnational strategy*. The transnational corporation attempts to combine the benefits of global scale efficiencies, such as those pursued by a global corporation, with the benefits and advantages of local responsiveness, which is the goal of a multidomestic corporation. To do so, the transnational corporation does not automatically centralize or decentralize authority. Rather, it carefully assigns responsibility for various organizational tasks to that unit of the organization best able to achieve the dual goals of efficiency and flexibility.

A transnational corporation may choose to centralize certain management functions and decision making, such as research and development and financial operations, at corporate headquarters. Other management functions, such as human resource management and marketing, however, may be decentralized, allowing managers of local subsidiaries to customize their business activities to better respond to the local culture and business environment. Microsoft, for example, locates most of its product development efforts in the United States, while responsibility for marketing is delegated to its foreign subsidiaries. Oftentimes transnational corporations locate responsibility for one product line in one country and responsibility for a second product line in another. To achieve an interdependent network of operations, transnational corporations focus considerable attention on integration and coordination among their various subsidiaries.

Figure 10.1 assesses these four strategic approaches against two criteria, the need for local responsiveness and the need to achieve global integration. Firms must pay particular attention to local conditions when consumer tastes or preferences vary widely across countries, when large differences exist in local laws, economic conditions, and infrastructure, or when host-country governments play a major role in the particular industry. Pressures for global integration arise when the firm is selling a standardized commodity with little ability to differentiate its products through features or quality, such as agricultural goods, bulk chemicals, ores, and low-end semiconductor chips. If trade barriers and transportation costs are low, such firms must strive to produce their goods at the lowest possible cost. Conversely, if the product features desired by consumers vary by country or if firms are able to differentiate their products through brand names, after-sales support services, and quality differences, the pressures for global integration are lessened.

The international strategy is often adopted by firms when both the pressures for global integration and the need for local responsiveness are low, as the lower left-hand cell in Fig. 10.1 shows. Toys 'R' Us, for example, has adopted this

FIGURE 10.1

Strategic Alternatives for Balancing Pressures for Global Integration and Local Responsiveness

Source: Adapted from Sumantra Ghoshal and Nitin Nohria, "Horses for Courses: Organizational Forms for Multinational Corporations," *Sloan Management Review,* Winter 1993, pp. 27 and 31.

approach to internationalizing its operations. It continues to use the marketing, procurement, and distribution techniques developed in its U.S. retail outlets in its foreign stores as well. The company's managers believe that the firm's path to success internationally is the same as it was domestically: build large, warehouse-like stores, buy in volume, cut prices, and take market share from smaller, high-cost toy retailers. Accordingly, they see little reason to adjust the firm's basic domestic strategy as they enter new international markets.

The multidomestic approach is often used when the need to respond to local conditions is high, but the pressures for global integration are low. Many companies selling brand-name food products have adopted this approach. While not unmindful of the benefits of reducing manufacturing costs, such marketing-driven companies as Kraft, Unilever, and Cadbury Schweppes are more concerned with meeting the specific needs of local customers, thereby ensuring that these customers will continue to pay a premium price for the brand-name goods these companies sell. Moreover, they often rely on local production facilities to ensure that local consumers will readily find fresh, high-quality products on their supermarket shelves.

The global strategy is most appropriate when the pressures for global integration are high but the need for local responsiveness is low. In such cases, the firm can focus on creating standardized goods, marketing campaigns, distribution systems, and so forth. This strategy has been adopted by many Japanese consumer electronics firms such as Sony and Matsushita, which design their products with the world in mind. Aside from minor adaptions for differences in local electrical systems, these firms' portable disc players, VCRs, camcorders, and stereo systems are sold to consumers throughout the Quad countries with little need for customization. Thus, these firms are free to seek global efficiencies by capturing economies of scale in manufacturing and concentrating their production in countries offering low-cost manufacturing facilities.

The transnational strategy is most appropriate when pressures for global integration and local responsiveness are both high. The Ford Motor Company has been attempting to employ this strategy. For example, Ford now has a single manager responsible for global engine and transmission development. Other managers have similar responsibilities for product design and development, production, and marketing. But each manager is also responsible for ensuring that Ford products are tailored to meet local consumer tastes and preferences. For instance, Ford products sold in the United Kingdom must have their steering wheels mounted on the right side of the passenger compartment. Body styles may also need to be slightly altered in different markets to be more appealing to local customer tastes.

Not addressed to this point has been the issue of worldwide learning. Worldwide learning requires the multidirectional transfer of information and experiences from the parent to each subsidiary, from each subsidiary to the parent, and among subsidiaries. The international, multidomestic, and global strategies are not explicitly designed, however, to accomplish such learning transfer. The international strategy is predicated on the parent company's transferring the firm's core competencies to its foreign subsidiaries. The multidomestic strategy decentralizes power to the local subsidiaries so that they can respond easily to local conditions. The global strategy centralizes decision making so that the firm can achieve global integration of its activities.

The transnational strategy would, therefore, appear to be better able to promote global learning with its mix of centralization of certain functions and decentralization of others—a primary reason for adopting the transnational strategy in the first place. Transnational corporations utilize such techniques as matrix organizational designs, project teams, informal management networks, and corporate cultures to help promote transfer of knowledge among their subsidiaries. Such approaches to promote worldwide learning are also available to firms adopting the international, multidomestic, and global approaches as well. The point, however, is that they may need to make a conscious decision and a systematic effort to successfully make use of these techniques.

Components of an International Strategy

After determining the overall international strategic philosophy of their firm, managers who engage in international strategic planning then need to address the four basic components of strategy development. These components are distinctive competence, scope of operations, resource deployment, and synergy.[12] It is important that the firm's planners consider each of these elements in designing the firm's strategies.

Distinctive Competence

Distinctive competence, the first component of international strategy, answers the question "What do we do exceptionally well, especially as compared to our competitors?" A firm's distinctive competence may be cutting-edge technology, efficient distribution networks, superior organizational practices, or well-respected brand names. As our discussion of Dunning's eclectic theory in Chapter 3 suggested, a firm's possession of a distinctive competence (what Dunning called an ownership advantage) is thought by many experts to be a necessary condition for a firm to compete successfully outside its home market.

Without a distinctive competence, a foreign firm will have difficulty competing with local firms that are presumed to know the local market better. The Disney name, image, and portfolio of characters, for example, is a distinctive competence that allows the firm to succeed in foreign markets. Similarly, the ready availability of software programs compatible with Windows 95 gives Microsoft an advantage in competing with local firms outside the United States.

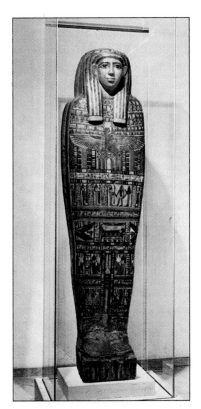

For 150 years Frankfurt's Glasbau Hahn has produced high-quality display cases for the world's museums, which are willing to pay premium prices to show and protect priceless artifacts and treasures. Airtight, climate-controlled cases like the one preserving this mummy at the Rheinisches Landesmuseum in Trier are bought by museums in London, New York, Tokyo, and other cultural centers.

Whatever its form, this distinctive competence represents an important resource to the firm. Having developed a distinctive competence, a firm often then wishes to exploit this advantage by expanding its operations into as many markets as its resources allow. To a large degree, the internationalization strategy adopted by a company reflects the interplay between its distinctive competence and the business opportunities available in different countries.[13]

For example, Stuttgart-based Robert Bosch GmbH, the world's largest automotive electronic equipment supplier, was the first company to develop and sell electronic fuel injection and antilock brake systems. This head start resulted in a distinctive competence that other firms have found difficult to match. Bosch still enjoys a 50 percent share of these lucrative markets, selling to automobile manufacturers in all six inhabited continents.[14] Similarly, Frankfurt's Glasbau Hahn constructs glass showcases with self-contained climate controls and fiber optic lighting. Because the showcases are perceived to be the world's best, museums pay Glasbau Hahn as much as $100,000 for a case in which to display priceless art, sculpture, or artifacts. Exploiting its distinctive competence in this specialized market, Glasbau Hahn has built a $12 million international business.[15]

Scope of Operations

The second component, the **scope of operations,** answers the question "Where are we going to conduct business?" Scope may be defined in terms of geographical regions, such as countries, regions within a country, and/or clusters of countries. Or it may focus on market or product niches within one or more regions, such as the premium-quality market niche, the low-cost market niche, or other specialized market niches. Because all firms have finite resources and because markets differ in their relative attractiveness for various products, managers must decide which markets are most attractive to their firm. The question of the scope is, of course, tied to the firm's distinctive competence: if the firm possesses a distinctive competence only in certain regions or in specific product lines, then its scope of operations will focus on those areas where the firm enjoys the distinctive competence.

For example, the geographical scope of Disney's theme park operations consists of the United States, Japan, and France, while the geographical scope of its movie distribution and merchandise sales operations is more than one hundred countries. Other companies have chosen to participate in many lines of business, but narrow their geographic focus, such as Grupo Luksics, a family-owned conglomerate with interests in beer, copper, banking, hotels, railroads, telecommunications, and ranching in Chile and neighboring countries. Conversely, Ballantyne, a small ($12 million in annual revenues) Nebraska-based company, is sharply focused, just like its primary product: feature-film projectors, in which it enjoys a 65 percent share of the U.S. market and a 30 percent market share elsewhere.[16] Similarly, in the semiconductor industry, many firms have chosen to limit their operations to specific product niches. Asian semiconductor manufacturers like Samsung, NEC, and Toshiba dominate the global memory chip market. California-based Intel focuses on producing the microprocessors that power most IBM-compatible personal computers. Lucent Technologies and Texas Instruments specialize in digital signal processors, which convert analog signals into digital signals. Such chips have many uses, from computer modems to stereo systems to cellular phones. Siemens concentrates on chips that have automotive applications, and Philips specializes in the development of multimedia semiconductors, which bridge consumer electronics and computers.[17] Thus, strategic planning results in some international businesses choosing to compete in only a few markets, some to compete in many, and others (such as Disney) to vary their operations across the different types of business operations in which they are involved.

Resource Deployment

Resource deployment answers the question "Given that we are going to compete in these markets, how will we allocate our resources to them?" For example,

The enormous R&D costs of designing cutting-edge semiconductor chips and building state-of-the art fabrication facilities have led many semiconductor producers to focus their resources in specific market niches. For example, Samsung, relying on its manufacturing prowess, has specialized in the production of memory chips, such as its new 64-megabyte DRAM chip.

even though Disney has theme park operations in three countries, the firm does not have an equal resource commitment to each market. Disney invested nothing in Tokyo Disneyland and limited its original investment in Disneyland Paris to 49 percent of its equity. But it continues to invest heavily in its U.S. theme park operations and in filmed entertainment.

Resource deployment might be specified along product lines, geographical lines, or both. This part of strategic planning determines relative priorities for a firm's limited resources. Disney could have easily solved Disneyland Paris's financial difficulties without outside assistance. However, additional investment would have taken the firm's commitment far beyond the level it thought viable for its resource deployment goals and perhaps jeopardized its ability to build the Animal Kingdom in Orlando or to purchase Capital Cities/ABC.

Some large MNCs choose to deploy their resources worldwide. For example, Osaka-based Sharp Corporation manufactures its electronic goods in 33 plants in 26 countries. Other firms have opted to focus their production in one. Boeing, the leading U.S. exporter, concentrates final assembly of commercial aircraft in the Seattle, Washington region. And Daimler-Benz concentrates production of Mercedes-Benz automobiles in Germany; although its newest plant is in Alabama, nine out of ten Mercedes are still German-built.[18] Although these firms have a global scope regarding the markets in which they buy materials and sell products, they have limited most of their production resource deployment to their home countries.

Synergy

The fourth component of international strategy, synergy, answers the question "How can different elements of our business benefit each other?" The goal of synergy is to create a situation where the whole is greater than the sum of the parts. The world's acknowledged master in generating synergy is Disney. People know the Disney characters from television, so they plan vacations to Disney theme parks. At the parks they are bombarded with information about the newest Disney movies, and they buy merchandise featuring Disney characters, which encourage them to watch Disney characters on TV, starting the cycle all over again. "Going Global" provides more information about the latest step Disney has taken to generate synergy, its acquisition of Capital Cities/ABC.

Developing International Strategies

Developing international strategies is not a one-dimensional process. In fact, firms generally carry out international strategic management in two broad stages. These stages into which international strategic management is divided are strategy formulation and strategy implementation:

1 In *strategy formulation*, the firm establishes its goals and the strategic plan that will lead to the achievement of those goals. In international strategy formulation, managers develop, refine, and agree on which markets to enter (or exit) and how best to compete in each. Much of what we discuss in the rest

GOING GLOBAL

Disney: Master of Synergy

Disney has a long and proven record of creating synergy by leveraging one part of its operation with another part in ways that benefit both. For example, most summers the company issues a new animated movie: *Mulan* (in 1998), *Hercules* (in 1997), *The Hunchback of Notre Dame* (1996), *Pocohontas* (1995), *The Lion King* (1994), and so on. Months before the movie's release, Disney has licensed toy companies, book publishers, lunch box manufacturers, and T-shirt producers to reproduce the movie's characters on their wares. Visitors to Disneyland, Disney World, Tokyo Disneyland, and Disneyland Paris are treated to advertisements extolling the new film as they tour the parks. Meanwhile, these theme parks, Disney's retail chain, The Disney Store, and other retailers are busy selling the movie's licensed merchandise, further building demand for the new animated feature. After the movie's theatrical run is finished, the company continues to exploit its investment by releasing the film on video and selling the film's original artwork to art and Disneyana collectors. A successful movie like *Aladdin* or *The Lion King* may also be turned into a video game, a Broadway play, an afternoon series, a Saturday morning cartoon show, or a sequel. As part of a corporate family, Disney's movie, theme park, and licensing operations are each stronger than they would be if they were stand-alone operations.

Disney's synergy opportunities took a dramatic leap in early 1996 when it acquired Capital Cities/ABC, thereby creating the world's largest media and entertainment company. This acquisition made Disney the first media company to control distribution channels in broadcast, cable, film, and telephone media (through a joint venture with three regional Bell telephone companies in the United States). The addition of ABC's extensive distribution network, 225 affiliated television stations, cable programming (ESPN, A&E, Lifetime), and international syndication to its ongoing operations has enhanced Disney's access to consumers of all ages and incomes. Disney quickly seized the opportunity to generate additional synergy: for example, the ABC network featured a prime-time special on *The Making of Hercules* just before the movie was released in movie theaters, creating even more publicity for the film among its target audience.

Strategically, the most important advantage of the acquisition for Disney may lay overseas, where Capital Cities has built a strong distribution network to rival that of Rupert Murdoch's News Corp. (which owns the Fox television network in the United States, the Twentieth Century-Fox movie studio, newspapers on three continents, and satellite broadcasting operations throughout the world) and Time-Warner (which controls Warner Brothers, HBO, the Time-Life magazine empire, and extensive cable TV holdings). Like Disney, News Corp. and Time-Warner are attempting to capture synergies among their entertainment and communications enterprises.

The Capital Cities/ABC merger has bolstered Disney's position vis-à-vis these rivals. The four most important programming platforms that enable media and entertainment companies to compete successfully in domestic and foreign markets are news, sports, movies, and family entertainment. Without ABC, Disney only owned two. Now it has all four to use to create synergies. For example, as Tokyo DisneySea approaches its scheduled opening in Autumn 2001, you can be sure that each branch of the Disney empire will help publicize the birth of the latest member of the Disney family. With the addition of Capital Cities/ABC, Disney is better positioned to compete for the huge global entertainment market of the twenty-first century, which can only get larger with the deregulation of television in many countries, rising incomes, and population growth in developed and developing countries alike.

of this chapter and in the next two chapters primarily concerns international strategy formulation.

2 In *strategy implementation*, the firm develops the tactics for achieving the formulated international strategies. Disney's decisions to build Disneyland Paris

FIGURE 10.2

**Steps in International
Strategy Formulation**

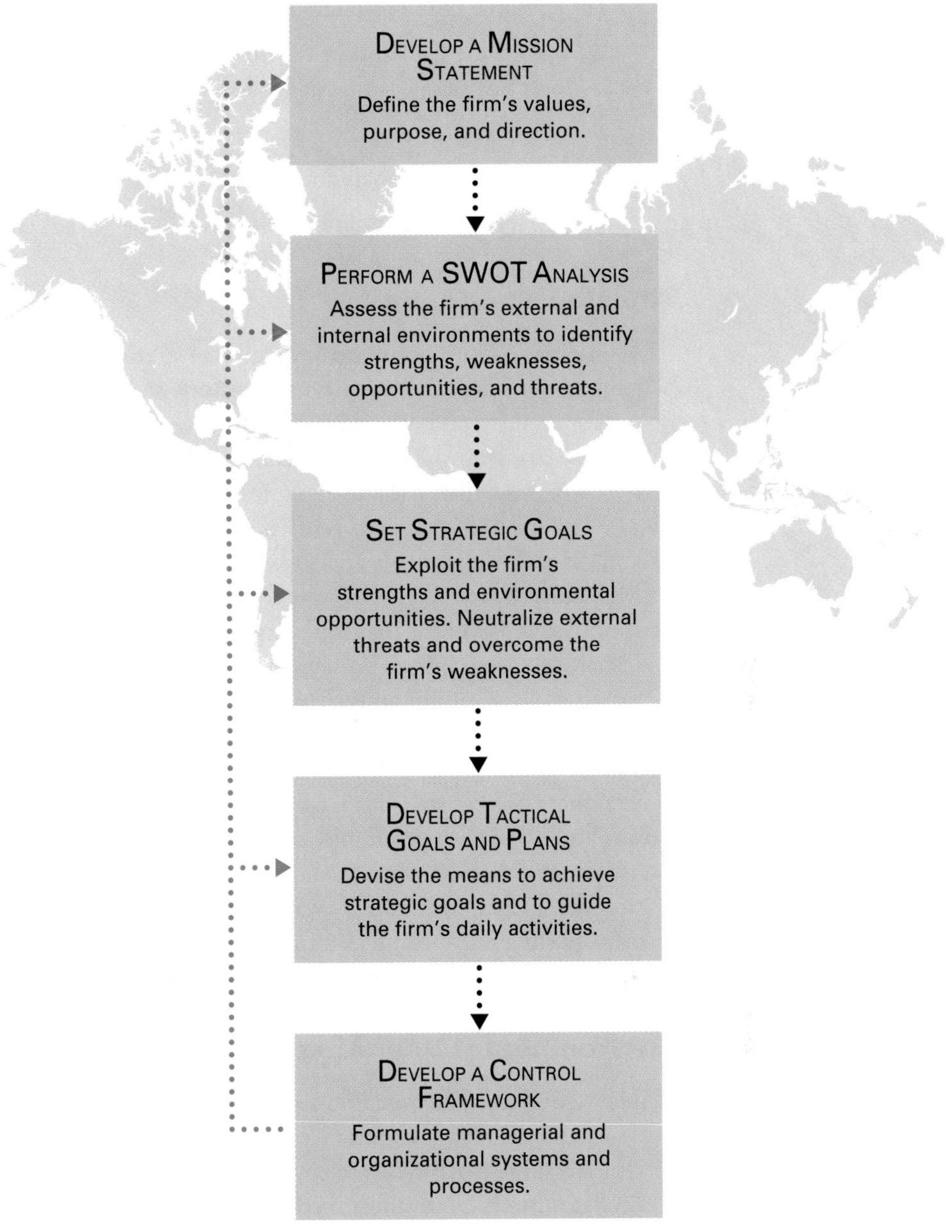

**DEVELOP A MISSION
STATEMENT**
Define the firm's values,
purpose, and direction.

PERFORM A SWOT ANALYSIS
Assess the firm's external and
internal environments to identify
strengths, weaknesses,
opportunities, and threats.

SET STRATEGIC GOALS
Exploit the firm's
strengths and environmental
opportunities. Neutralize external
threats and overcome the
firm's weaknesses.

**DEVELOP TACTICAL
GOALS AND PLANS**
Devise the means to achieve
strategic goals and to guide
the firm's daily activities.

**DEVELOP A CONTROL
FRAMEWORK**
Formulate managerial and
organizational systems and
processes.

and to build it in France were part of strategy formulation. But deciding which attractions to include, when to open, and what to charge for admission is part of strategy implementation. In essence, strategy formulation is deciding what to do and strategy implementation is actually doing it. Strategy implementation is usually achieved via the organization's design, the work of its employees, and its control systems and processes. Chapters 13 through 15 deal primarily with implementation issues.

While every strategic planning process is in many ways unique, there are nevertheless a set of general steps that managers usually follow as they set about developing international strategies. These steps, shown in Fig. 10.2, are as follows:

1 Develop a mission statement.

2 Analyze the firm and its environment to determine its strengths, weaknesses, opportunities, and threats (called a **SWOT analysis**).

3 Set strategic goals.

4 Develop tactical goals and plans.

5 Develop a strategic control framework.

Mission Statement

Most organizations begin the international strategic planning process by creating a mission statement. A **mission statement** attempts to clarify the organization's purpose, values, and directions. The process of developing a mission statement helps clarify what the firm's distinctive competence is and what business it is in. AT&T, for example, defines itself as a communications company, not a telephone company.

The mission statement is often used as a way of communicating with internal and external constituents and stakeholders about the firm's strategic direction. Mission statements, which many firms include in their annual reports, generally specify such factors as the firm's target customers and markets, principal products or services, geographical domain, core technologies, concerns for survival, plans for growth and profitability, basic philosophy, and desired public image.[19] For example, the mission statement of Hershey Foods includes the goal of being the "No. 1 confectionery company in North America, moving toward worldwide confectionery market share leadership," and Carpenter Technology specifies its mission to be a "major, profitable, and growing international producer and distributor of specialty alloys, materials, and components." MNCs may have multiple mission statements, one for the overall firm, as well as one for each of its various foreign subsidiaries. Of course, a firm that has multiple mission statements must ensure that they are compatible.

Environmental Scanning and the SWOT Analysis

The second step in developing a strategy is conducting a SWOT analysis. SWOT is an acronym for "Strengths, Weaknesses, Opportunities, and Threats." A firm typically initiates its SWOT analysis by first performing an environmental scan. **Environmental scanning** involves the systematic collection of data about all elements of the firm's external and internal environments, including data about markets, regulatory issues, competitors' actions, production costs, and labor productivity.

When members of a planning staff scan the external environment, they try to identify both *opportunities* (the O in SWOT) and *threats* (the T in SWOT) confronting the firm. They obtain data about economic, financial, political, legal, social, and competitive changes in the various markets the firm serves or might want to serve. (Such data are also used for political risk analysis, discussed in Chapter 8, as well as the country market analysis discussed in Chapter 11.) For example, Boeing continuously monitors changes in political and economic forces that affect air travel. In China, political shifts in the early 1990s to allow more competition in the air travel market led the government to split the giant state-owned carrier CAAC into competing regional carriers and to allow Hong Kong's Cathay Pacific airline to offer air travel within China. Boeing's environmental scanning suggested that booming demand for air travel would make the

Chinese market a particularly appealing opportunity. Accordingly, the firm chose to locate a new sales office in Beijing. So far, the move has paid off: China has become one of Boeing's most important markets, accounting for $757 million in sales in 1996.

Disney's original decision to build Disneyland Paris was also the result of environmental scanning that suggested that many Europeans were interested in the sort of vacation opportunities the firm provides. Bayerische Motoren Werke (BMW), the manufacturer of BMW cars and motorcycles, took advantage of such external factors as the then weak U.S. dollar, low U.S. labor costs, and NAFTA when it decided to build a new automobile assembly plant near Spartanburg, South Carolina.

External environmental scanning also yields data about environmental threats to the firm, such as shrinking markets, increasing competition, the potential of new government regulation, political instability in key markets, and the development of new technologies that could make the firm's manufacturing facilities or product lines obsolete. Threats to Disney include increased competition in the U.S. market from Universal Studios, Six Flags, and other theme parks, potential competition in Europe from theme parks there, potential French resentment of U.S. intrusion in France, and fluctuating exchange rates. Threats to BMW include changing U.S. automobile fuel-efficiency standards, increased competition from Japanese producers in the luxury car market, and high German labor costs. The threats Federal Express faces include not only competition in the international express package delivery market from firms such as DHL Worldwide and TNT, but also the rapidly growing usage of e-mail and fax machines to send messages internationally.

In conducting a SWOT analysis, a firm's strategic managers must also assess the firm's internal environment, that is, its *strengths* and *weaknesses* (the S and W in SWOT). Organizational strengths are skills, resources, and other advantages the firm possesses relative to its competitors. Potential strengths, which form the basis of a firm's distinctive competence, might include an abundance of managerial talent, cutting-edge technology, well-known brand names, surplus cash, a good public image, and strong market shares in key countries. Disney's strengths include low corporate debt and the international appeal of its characters. BMW's strengths include its skilled workforce, innovative engineers, and reputation for producing high-quality automobiles.

A firm also needs to acknowledge its organizational weaknesses. These weaknesses reflect deficiencies or shortcomings in skills, resources, or other factors that hinder the firm's competitiveness. They may include poor distribution networks outside the home market, poor labor relations, a lack of skilled international managers, or product development efforts that lag behind competitors'. Disney's organizational weaknesses regarding Disneyland Paris include high capital costs, negative publicity, and underutilized hotel capacity. BMW's weaknesses include its extremely high domestic labor costs, which make it difficult for it to compete on the basis of price.

One technique for assessing a firm's strengths and weaknesses is the value chain. Developed by Harvard Business School Professor Michael Porter, the **value chain** is a breakdown of the firm into its important activities—production, marketing, human resource management, and so forth—to enable its strategists to identify its competitive advantages and disadvantages. Each primary and support activity depicted in Fig. 10.3 can be a source of an organizational strength (distinctive competence) or weakness. For example, the quality of Caterpillar's

FIGURE 10.3

The Value Chain
Source: Adapted with the permission of The Free Press, a Division of Simon & Schuster, from *Competitive Advantage: Creating and Sustaining Superior Performance,* by Michael E. Porter. Copyright © 1985 by Michael E. Porter.

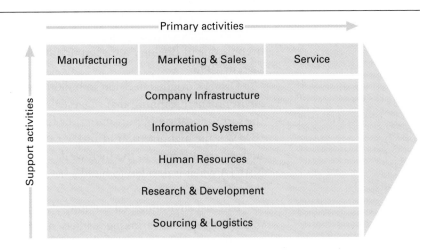

products (Research and Development in the figure) and the strength of its worldwide dealership network (Marketing, Sales, and Service in the figure) are among its organizational strengths, but poor labor relations (Human Resources in the figure) represent one of its organizational weaknesses.

Managers use information derived from the SWOT analysis to develop specific effective strategies. Effective strategies are ones that exploit environmental opportunities and organizational strengths, neutralize environmental threats, and protect or overcome organizational weaknesses. For example, BMW's decision to build automobiles in South Carolina took advantage of its strong brand image in the United States. This decision also neutralized the firm's internal weakness of high German labor costs and its vulnerability to loss of U.S. customers if the deutsche mark were to rise in value relative to the U.S. dollar.

Strategic Goals

With the mission statement and SWOT analysis as context, international strategic planning is largely framed by the setting of strategic goals. **Strategic goals** are the major objectives the firm wants to accomplish through pursuing a particular course of action. By definition, they should be measurable, feasible, and time-limited (answering the questions "how much, how, and by when?"). For example, Disney set strategic goals for Disneyland Paris for projected attendance, revenues, and so on. But, as the Scottish poet Robert Burns noted, "the best laid plans of mice and men" often go awry. Part of the park's resultant problems arose from the firm's goals not being met. Disney's strategic managers had to revise the firm's strategic plan and goals, taking into account the new information painfully learned from the first years of the park's unprofitable operation.

Tactics

As shown in Fig. 10.2, after a SWOT analysis is performed and strategic goals are set, the next step in strategic planning is to develop specific tactical goals and plans, or **tactics**. Tactics usually involve middle managers and focus on the details of how to implement strategic plans. For example, Grand Metropolitan, a huge British food company, and Guinness, a major British spirits maker, recently merged to create Diageo PLC, the world's fifth largest consumer products company with revenues of $34 billion. The factors underlying the merger reflected strategic decisions by the two companies. But after plans for the merger were announced, middle managers in both companies were faced with the challenges of integrating various components of the two original companies into a single new one. For example, tactical issues such as the integration of the firms' accounting and information systems, human resource procedures involving hiring, compensation, and career paths, and distribution and logistics questions ranging from shipping and transportation to warehousing all had to be addressed and synthesized into one new way of doing business.[20]

Control Framework

The final aspect of strategy formulation is the development of a control framework. A **control framework** is the managerial and organizational processes used to keep the firm on target toward its strategic goals. For example, Disneyland Paris had a first-year attendance goal of 12 million visitors. When it became apparent that this goal would not be met, the firm increased its advertising to help boost attendance and temporarily closed one of its hotels to cut costs. Had attendance been running ahead of the goal, the firm might have decreased advertising and extended its operating hours. Each set of responses stems from the control framework established to keep the firm on course. As shown by Fig. 10.2's feedback loops, the control framework can prompt revisions in any of the preceding steps in the strategy formulation process. We discuss control frameworks more fully in Chapter 15.

Levels of International Strategy

Given the complexities of international strategic management, many international businesses—especially MNCs—find it useful to develop strategies for three distinct levels within the organization. These levels of international strategy, illustrated in Fig. 10.4, are corporate, business, and functional.[21]

Corporate Strategy

Corporate strategy attempts to define the domain of businesses the firm intends to operate. Consider three Japanese electronics firms: Sony competes in the global market for consumer electronics and entertainment but has not broadened its scope into home and kitchen appliances. Archrival Matsushita competes in all these industries, while Pioneer Electronic Corporation focuses only on electronic audio and video products. Each firm has answered quite differently the question of what constitutes its business domain. Their divergent answers reflect their differing corporate strengths and weaknesses, as well as their differing assessments of the opportunities and threats produced by the global economic and political environments. A firm might adopt any of three forms of corporate strategy. These are called a single-business strategy, a related diversification strategy, or an unrelated diversification strategy.

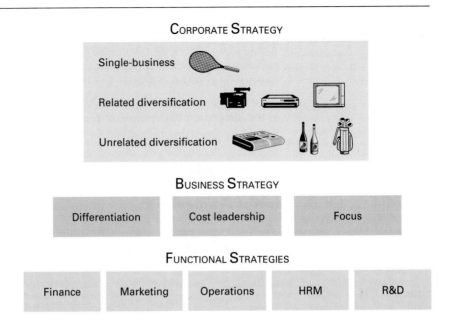

FIGURE 10.4

**Three Levels of
Strategy for MNCs**

The Single-Business Strategy. The **single-business strategy** calls
for a firm to rely on a single business, product, or service for all its revenue.
The most significant advantage of this strategy is that the firm can concentrate
all its resources and expertise on that one product or service. However, this
strategy also increases the firm's vulnerability to its competition and to changes
in the external environment. For example, for a firm producing only phono-
graph players, a new innovation such as the CD player makes the firm's single
product obsolete, and the firm may be unable to develop new products quickly
enough to survive.

Nonetheless, many MNCs have found the single-business strategy a rewarding one, for they can focus all of their corporate energies and resources on their
chosen business. For example, Pennsylvania's Carpenter Technology Corporation
has earned an average rate of return on shareholder's equity of 19 percent over the
past three years while specializing in the manufacture and distribution of stain-
less steel, titanium alloys, and other specialty metals throughout the world. Air
Canada, McDonald's, and Dell have similarly expanded globally while utilizing a
single-business strategy, respectively focusing on the air transportation, fast-food,
and personal computer markets.

Related Diversification. **Related diversification**, the most common corporate strategy, calls for the firm to operate in several different businesses, industries, or markets at the same time. However, the operations are related to each
other in some fundamental way. This strategy allows the firm to leverage a distinctive competence in one market in order to strengthen its competitiveness in others. The goal of related diversification and the basic relationship linking various
operations are often defined in the firm's mission statement.

Disney uses the related diversification strategy. Each of its operations is linked
to the others via Disney characters, the Disney logo, a theme of wholesomeness,
and a reputation for providing high-quality family entertainment. Disney movies
and TV shows, many of which are broadcast over Disney-owned networks, help
sell Disney theme parks, which in turn help sell Disney merchandise. Accor SA,

the world's second-largest hotel operator, also uses a related diversification strategy. Originally the operator of a chain restaurant, this Paris-based firm began acquiring luxury hotel chains such as Sofitel and budget chains such as Motel 6 (see Map 10.1). To keep its dining rooms and hotel beds full, Accor then branched out into the package tour business and the rental car business. To promote tourism, the firm even opened its own theme park north of Paris based on the French cartoon character Asterix the Gaul.[22]

Related diversification has several advantages. First, the firm depends less on a single product or service, so it is less vulnerable to competitive or economic threats. For example, if Disney faces increased competition in the theme park business, its movie, television, and licensing divisions can offset potential declines in theme park revenues. Moreover, these related businesses may make it more difficult for an outsider to compete with Disney in the first place. For example, non-Disney animated movies have trouble competing against new animated releases from the Disney Studios. Makers of these movies must buy advertising at commercial rates, while Disney can inexpensively promote its new releases to families waiting in line at its theme parks and to viewers of shows on ABC or the Disney Channel. Similar problems confront rival theme park operators, who have to contend with the constant exposure that Disney's theme parks receive on network television and the Disney Channel and on T-shirts and caps worn by kids of all ages worldwide.

Second, related diversification may produce economies of scale for a firm. For example, The Limited, Inc., takes advantage of its vast size to buy new clothing lines at favorable prices from Far Eastern manufacturers and then divides the purchases among its Limited, Express, Lerner, and other divisions.

Third, related diversification may allow a firm to use technology or expertise developed in one market to enter a second market more cheaply and easily. For example, Pirelli SpA used its expertise in producing rubber products and insulated cables, refined over 100 years ago, to become the world's fifth largest producer of automobile tires. Pirelli has also transferred its knowledge of rubber cables to become a major producer of fiber optic cables. More recently, Casio Computer Company transferred the knowledge it gained in making hand-held electric calculators in the 1970s to the production of inexpensive electronic digital watches, musical synthesizers, and pocket televisions. Such potential synergies are a major advantage of the related diversification strategy.

One potential disadvantage of related diversification is the cost of coordinating the operations of the related divisions. A second is the possibility that all the firm's business units may be affected simultaneously by changes in economic conditions. For example, Accor can create synergies by steering travel customers to its hotels and restaurants. Yet all of Accor's divisions are vulnerable to a downturn in tourism. If another oil crisis erupts or an increase in terrorist actions keeps travelers at home, all Accor businesses will suffer.

Unrelated Diversification. A third corporate strategy international businesses may use is **unrelated diversification**, whereby a firm operates in several unrelated industries and markets. For example, Pearson PLC, a British firm, owns publishing companies, Madame Tussaud's Wax Museum, and a merchant banking business.[23] Similarly, General Electric (GE) owns such diverse business units as a television network (NBC), a lighting manufacturer, a medical technology firm, an aircraft engine producer, a semiconductor manufacturer, and an investment bank.

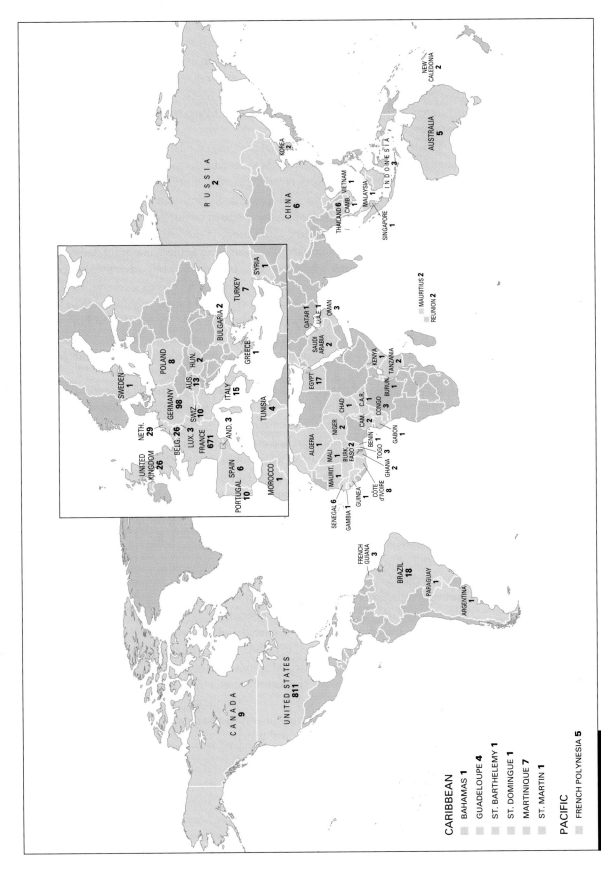

NEW CALEDONIA 2

AUSTRALIA 5

KOREA 2

RUSSIA 2

CHINA 6

VIETNAM 1
THAILAND 6
CAMB. 1
MALAYSIA 1
SINGAPORE 1
INDONESIA 3

MAURITIUS 2
REUNION 2

SYRIA 1
TURKEY 7
BULGARIA 2
GREECE 1

QATAR 1
U.A.E. 1
OMAN 3
SAUDI ARABIA 2

SWEDEN 1
POLAND 8
HUN. 2
AUS. 13
ITALY 15
TUNISIA 4

GERMANY 98
SWIZ. 10
AND. 3

NETH. 29
BELG. 26
LUX. 3
FRANCE 671

UNITED KINGDOM 26
PORTUGAL 10
SPAIN 6
MOROCCO 1

EGYPT 17
KENYA 1
TANZANIA 2
BURUN. 1

ALGERIA 1
NIGER 2
CHAD 2
C.A.R. 1
CAM. 2
CONGO 3
GABON 1

MALI 1
BURK. FASO 2
BENIN 2
TOGO 3
GHANA 2

MAURIT. 1
SENEGAL 6
GUINEA 1
GAMBIA 1
CÔTE d'IVOIRE 8

FRENCH GUIANA 3
BRAZIL 18
PARAGUAY 1
ARGENTINA 1

UNITED STATES 811

CANADA 9

CARIBBEAN
BAHAMAS 1
GUADELOUPE 4
ST. BARTHELEMY 1
ST. DOMINGUE 1
MARTINIQUE 7
ST. MARTIN 1

PACIFIC
FRENCH POLYNESIA 5

MAP 10.1   Accor's Worldwide Chain of Hotels

These operations are unrelated to each other, and there is little reason to anticipate synergy among such diverse operations and businesses.

During the 1960s, unrelated diversification was the most popular investment strategy. Many large firms, such as ITT, Gulf and Western, LTV, and Textron became **conglomerates**, the term used for firms comprising unrelated businesses. The unrelated diversification strategy yields several benefits. First, the corporate parent may be able to raise capital more easily than any of its independent units can separately. The parent can then allocate this capital to the most profitable opportunities available among its subsidiaries. Second, overall riskiness may be reduced because a firm is less subject to business cycle fluctuations. For example, temporary difficulties facing one business might be offset by success in another. Third, a firm is less vulnerable to competitive threats, since any given threat is likely to affect only a portion of the firm's total operations. Fourth, a firm can more easily shed unprofitable operations because they are independent. It also can buy new operations without worrying about how to integrate them into existing businesses.

Nonetheless, the creation of conglomerates through the unrelated diversification strategy is out of favor today primarily because of the lack of potential synergy across unrelated businesses. Since the businesses are unrelated, any one operation cannot regularly sustain or enhance the others. For example, GE managers cannot use any of the competitive advantages they may have developed in the lighting business to help offset low ratings at the firm's television network. Further, it is difficult for staff at corporate headquarters to effectively manage diverse businesses because it must understand a much wider array of businesses and markets than if operations are related. This complicates the performance monitoring of individual operations. As a result, while some conglomerates, such as GE and Textron, have thrived, many others have changed their strategy or disappeared altogether.

Business Strategy

Whereas corporate strategy deals with the overall organization, business strategy focuses on specific businesses, subsidiaries, or operating units within the firm. Business strategy seeks to answer the question "How should we compete in each market we have chosen to enter?"

Firms that pursue corporate strategies of related diversification or unrelated diversification tend to bundle sets of businesses together into **strategic business units (SBUs)**. In firms that follow the related diversification strategy, the products and services of each SBU are somewhat similar to each other. For example, Disney defines its SBUs as Theme Parks and Resorts, Creative Content (filmed entertainment, character licensing, Disney Stores), and Broadcasting (ABC, the Disney Channel, ESPN). In firms that follow unrelated diversification strategies, products and services of each SBU are dissimilar. Textron, for example, has created four SBUs: aircraft, automotive products, financial services, and industrial products.

By focusing on the competitive environment of each business or SBU, business strategy helps the firm improve its distinctive competence for that business or unit. Once a firm selects a business strategy for an SBU, it typically uses that strategy in all geographical markets the SBU serves. The firm may develop a unique business strategy for each of its SBUs, or it may pursue the same business strategy for all of them. The three basic forms of business strategy are differentiation, overall cost leadership, and focus.

Differentiation. **Differentiation strategy** is a very commonly used business strategy. It attempts to establish and maintain the image (either real or perceived) that the SBU's products or services are fundamentally unique from other products or services in the same market segment. Many international businesses today are attempting to use quality as a differentiating factor. If successful at establishing a high-quality image, they can charge higher prices for their products or services. For example, Rolex sells its timepieces worldwide for premium prices. The firm limits its sales agreements to only a few dealers in any given area, stresses quality and status in its advertising, and seldom discounts its products. Other international firms that use the differentiation strategy effectively include Coca-Cola (soft drinks), Nikon (cameras), Calvin Klein (fashion apparel), and Waterford Wedgewood (fine china and glassware).

Other firms adopt value as their differentiating factor. They compete on the basis of charging reasonable prices for quality goods and services. Marks and Spencer has used the value factor to thrive in the department store market in the United Kingdom. Lands' End, a Wisconsin mail-order clothing seller, has also used this differentiation strategy to grow into a billion dollar company. It has established operations in the United Kingdom, Germany, and Japan. By translating its catalogs into the local language, providing local mailing addresses and telephone numbers, and accepting local currencies, its international operations account for almost 10 percent of its sales. Ironically, this effort puts Marks and Spencer and Lands' End in direct competition with each other, with each stressing the value factor. The differentiation factor they may have to switch to then is distribution mode—catalog versus retail outlet sales.

Overall Cost Leadership. The **overall cost leadership strategy** calls for a firm to focus on achieving highly efficient operating procedures so that its costs are lower than its competitors'. This allows it to sell its goods or services for lower prices. A successful overall cost leadership strategy may result in lower levels of unit profitability due to lower prices but higher total profitability due to increased sales volume. For example, France's Bic Pen Company makes approximately three million pens every day. By concentrating on making those pens as cheaply as possible, the firm is able to sell them for a very low price. Taken together, volume production and a worldwide distribution network have allowed Bic to flourish. Other firms that use this strategy are Timex (watches), Fuji (film), Hyundai (automobiles), the LG Group (consumer electronics), and NEC (semiconductors). Sometimes a business may find it prudent to switch from one business strategy to another. For example, the "Going Global" feature discusses how Volkswagen is trying to shift from a cost leadership to a differentiation strategy.

Focus. A **focus strategy** calls for a firm to target specific types of products for certain customer groups or regions. Doing this allows the firm to match the features of specific products to the needs of specific consumer groups. These groups might be characterized by geographical region, ethnicity, purchasing power, tastes in fashion, or any other factor that influences their purchasing patterns. For example, Cadbury Schweppes PLC markets Hires Root Beer only in the United States because root beer does not appeal to people elsewhere. In other countries, Cadbury sells other flavors of soft drinks, including Solo (mixed-fruit–flavored) and Trina (grapefruit-flavored), that do not appeal to U.S. consumers. Honda sells

GOING GLOBAL

The 1960s were tumultuous times, and the icons of that era remain instantly recognizable symbols to those who lived through those counterculture years. Bell-bottom pants, wire-rimmed tinted glasses, and long straight hair are among the more memorable. Another is the Volkswagen Beetle, a funky, cheap, and reliable car driven by hippies and hippy wannabes everywhere.

But that image continues to cause problems for Volkswagen today as it attempts to gain market share and increase profitability in the United States. The problem is that virtually everyone in North America associates Volkswagen with the characteristics it once relished and that caused the Beetle to be so successful in earlier times. And indeed, during that era Volkswagen was using a cost leadership strategy very effectively in dozens of markets.

Volkswagen Tries to Shift Gears

In recent times, however, the German carmaker has been trying to change its image, and its strategy, to that of a premium automobile company like BMW and Mercedes. With the largest market share of any company in Europe, Volkswagen has been pushing its more expensive cars such as the Passat and the Vento. Volkswagen also owns Audi, a brand that has historically been in the luxury end of the market.

But North American consumers simply don't seem to buy it! They often ignore Volkswagen's higher-priced cars, and instead concentrate on the lower-priced cars on Volkswagen lots. For all its marketing efforts, Volkswagen is still associated with low-priced Beetles in the minds of many U.S. and Canadian customers. So what's a company to do? Well, Volkswagen is trying an interesting approach—it's bringing back the Beetle, albeit one with a bit more contemporary styling. Critics worry that the new model will only further confuse the Volkswagen image. But Volkswagen believes that the new Beetle will attract new customers, some of whom will gravitate up to the firm's premium cars. Of course, only time will tell.

Sources: "New Bug Goes Upscale but Draws on Nostalgia," *USA Today,* January 6, 1998, p. 1B; "VW Longs for Life in Luxury Lane," *USA Today,* July 11, 1997, pp. 1B, 2B; "VW's U.S. Comeback Rides on Restyled Beetle," The *Wall Street Journal,* May 6, 1997, pp. B1, B2.

Accord station wagons primarily in the United States because U.S. consumers like station wagons more than do consumers in other countries. It concentrates on selling its low-priced Civic in less-developed countries because consumers there have less discretionary income and emphasizes its faster Prelude in Europe because highways there tend to have higher speed limits. Sony's business strategy for its Consumer Electronics SBU focuses on continually upgrading and refining the products through extensive R&D while maintaining its reputation for producing high-quality products.

Disney has different business strategies for each of its SBUs. For its Theme Parks and Resorts SBU, strategies include making the businesses comprehensive destination resorts, stressing quality and cleanliness, and continually upgrading and adding to them. For its Creative Content SBU, strategies include targeting children with movies with the Buena Vista imprint and adults with the Touchstone and Hollywood Pictures imprints and making at least one new animated movie per year. This SBU also strives to make sure that kids everywhere can show off lunch boxes and sweatshirts emblazoned with Mickey Mouse's smiling face, and that harried parents on business trips can purchase high-quality Disney souvenirs at The Disney Store for their children waiting at home. The Broadcasting SBU seeks to televise a variety of entertaining and informative programs for diverse audiences, including families, younger children, and sports fans. When possible, it also tries to close the corporate loop by showcasing Disney-produced cartoons, films, and products.

Functional Strategies

Functional strategies attempt to answer the question "How will we manage the functions of finance, marketing, operations, human resources, and research and development (R&D) in ways consistent with our international corporate and business strategies?" We briefly introduce each common functional strategy here, but leave more detailed discussion to later chapters.

International *financial* strategy deals with such issues as the firm's desired capital structure, investment policies, foreign-exchange holdings, risk-reduction techniques, debt policies, and working-capital management. Typically, an international business develops a financial strategy for the overall firm as well as for each SBU. We cover international financial strategy more fully in Chapter 18.

International *marketing* strategy concerns the distribution and selling of the firm's products or services. It addresses questions of product mix, advertising, promotion, pricing, and distribution. International marketing strategy is the subject of Chapter 16.

International *operations* strategy deals with the creation of the firm's products or services. It guides decisions on such issues as sourcing, plant location, plant layout and design, technology, and inventory management. We return to international operations management in Chapter 17.

International *human resource* strategy focuses on the people who work for an organization. It guides decisions regarding how the firm will recruit, train, and evaluate employees and what it will pay them, as well as how it will deal with labor relations. International human resource strategy is the subject of Chapter 20.

Finally, a firm's international *R&D* strategy is concerned with the magnitude and direction of the firm's investment in creating new products and developing new technologies.

The next steps in formulating international strategy involve determining which foreign markets to enter and which to avoid. Having determined which markets to enter, the firm's managers must then decide how to enter those markets. These two issues are the subject of Chapters 11 and 12.

CHAPTER REVIEW

Summary

International strategic management is a comprehensive and ongoing management planning process aimed at formulating and implementing strategies that enable a firm to compete effectively in different markets. While there are many similarities in developing domestic and international strategies, international firms have three additional sources of competitive advantages unavailable to domestic firms. These are global efficiencies, multinational flexibility, and worldwide learning.

Firms participating in international business usually adopt one of four strategic alternatives: the international strategy, the multidomestic strategy, the global strategy, or the transnational strategy. Each of these strategies has advantages and disadvantages in terms of its ability to help firms be responsive to local circumstances and to achieve the benefits of global efficiencies.

A well-conceived strategy has four essential components:

1. Distinctive competence—what the firm does exceptionally well

2. Scope of operations—the array of markets in which the firm plans to operate

3. Resource deployment—how the firm will distribute its resources across different areas

4. Synergy—the degree to which different operations within the firm can benefit each other

International strategy formulation is the process of creating a firm's international strategies. The process of carrying out these strategies via specific tactics is called international strategy implementation. In international strategy formulation, a firm follows three general steps:

1. Develop a mission statement that specifies its values, purpose, and directions.

2. Thoroughly analyze its strengths and weaknesses, as well as the opportunities and threats that exist in its environment.

3. Set strategic goals, outline tactical goals and plans, and develop a control framework.

Most firms develop strategy at three levels:

1. Corporate strategy answers the question "What businesses will we operate?" Basic corporate strategies are single-business, related diversification, and unrelated diversification.

2. Business strategy answers the question "How should we compete in each market we have chosen to enter?" Fundamental business strate-

gies are differentiation, overall cost leadership, and focus.

3. Functional strategy deals with how the firm intends to manage the functions of finance, marketing, operations, human resources, and R&D.

Review Questions

1. What is international strategic management?

2. What are the three sources of competitive advantage available to international businesses that are not available to purely domestic firms?

3. Why is it difficult for firms to exploit these three competitive advantages simultaneously?

4. What are the four basic philosophies that guide strategic management in most MNCs?

5. How do international strategy formulation and international strategy implementation differ?

6. What are the steps in international strategy formulation? Are these likely to vary among firms?

7. Identify the four components of an international strategy.

8. Describe the role and importance of distinctive competence in international strategy formulation.

9. What are the three levels of international strategy? Why is it important to distinguish among the levels?

10. Identify and distinguish among three common approaches to corporate strategy.

11. Identify and distinguish among three common approaches to business strategy.

12. What are the basic types of functional strategies most firms use? Is it likely that some firms have different functional strategies?

Questions for Discussion

1. What are the basic differences between a domestic strategy and an international strategy?

2. Should the same managers be involved in both formulating and implementing international strategy, or should each part of the process be handled by different managers? Why?

3. Successful implementation of the global and the transnational approaches requires high levels of coordination and rapid information flows between corporate headquarters and subsidiaries. Accordingly, would you expect to find many companies adopting either of these approaches in the nineteenth century? Prior to World War II? Prior to the advent of personal computers?

4. Study mission statements from several international businesses. How do they differ, and how are they similar?

5. How can a poor SWOT analysis affect strategic planning?

6. Why do relatively few international firms pursue a single-product strategy?

7. How are the components of international strategy (scope of operations, resource deployment, distinctive competence, and synergy) likely to vary across different types of corporate strategy (single-business, related diversification, and unrelated diversification)?

8. The scheduled opening for Tokyo DisneySea is in autumn 2001. Develop a list of at least five ways other units of the Disney corporation can help promote and publicize DisneySea's opening.

9. Is a firm with a corporate strategy of related diversification more or less likely than a firm with a corporate strategy of unrelated diversification to use the same business strategy for all its SBUs? Why or why not?

10. Identify products you use regularly that are made by international firms that use the three different business strategies.

11. Related and unrelated diversification represent extremes of a continuum. Discuss why a firm might want to take a mid-range approach to diversification, as opposed to being purely one or the other.

12. What are some of the issues that a firm might need to address if it decides to change its corporate or business strategy? For example, how would an MNC go about changing from a strategy of related diversification to a strategy of unrelated diversification?

BUILDING GLOBAL SKILLS

Form a group with three or four of your classmates. Your group represents the planning department of a large U.S. manufacturer that has been pursuing a domestic corporate strategy of unrelated diversification. Currently, the firm makes four basic products, as follows:

1. *All-terrain recreational vehicles.* This product line consists of small two- and three-wheeled recreational vehicles, the most popular of which is a gasoline-powered mountain bike.

2. *Color televisions.* The firm concentrates on high-quality large-screen projection-type televisions.

3. *Luggage.* This line is aimed at the low end of the market and comprises pieces made from inexpensive aluminum frames covered with ballistics material (high-strength, tear-resistant fabric). Backpacks are especially popular.

4. *Writing instruments.* The firm makes a full line of mechanical pens and pencils pitched to the middle-market segment, between low-end products such as Bic and high-end ones such as Montblanc.

Your firm's CEO is contemplating international expansion. However, the CEO also thinks that in order to raise its profitability the corporation should begin pursuing a strategy of related diversification. This may mean selling off some businesses and perhaps buying or starting new ones. The CEO has instructed you to develop alternatives, evaluate those alternatives, and then make recommendations as to how the company should proceed. With this in mind, follow these steps:

1. Characterize the current business strategies the company appears to be following with each of its four existing businesses.

2. Evaluate the extent to which there are any bases of relatedness among any of the four existing businesses.

3. Using any criterion your group prefers, select any single existing business and assume that you will recommend that it be kept and the other three sold.

4. Identify existing competitors for the business you chose to keep, including both domestic and international firms.

5. Identify three other countries where there might be potential for business expansion. Explain why.

6. Think of at least two other businesses that are related to the business you will keep and that might be targets for acquisition.

WORKING WITH THE WEB: Building Global Internet Skills

Assessing the Strategic Content of Web Sites

The chapter notes four different strategic alternatives that a firm might pursue in an effort to globalize. These are the international, multidomestic, global, and transnational strategies. In addition, the chapter also points out that businesses usually adopt a competitive strategy based on differentiation, cost leadership, or focus.

To start this exercise, locate, visit, and study the web sites for the following companies (you may find it convenient to go to the textbook's web site for hotlinks to them):

♦ Groupe Danone SA

♦ BASF AG

♦ Textron

♦ Mitsubishi Group

♦ Tata Enterprises

Based on the information you locate, see if you can classify each company in terms of both its strategy for internationalization and the business strategy it seems to use.

Follow-Up Questions

1. How much confidence can you place in your interpretation?

2. What are the advantages and disadvantages to a firm that follow from its using a web site to promote its internationalization and competitive strategies?

3. Might a company use its web site in ways to deceive its competitors regarding its internationalization and competitive strategies? Are there risks in doing this?

CLOSING CASE

The Kerry Group[24]

The Kerry Group is not exactly a household brand name. Indeed, few people outside of Hong Kong have even heard of it. But a closer inspection reveals an enormous company with major holdings across Asia and with growing operations in a number of different industries. With businesses ranging from bottling to shipping to food processing and a presence from China to Canada, the company is on its way to becoming a global powerhouse.

The Kerry Group was founded—and is still owned and run—by Robert Kuok. Kuok was born in British Malaya in 1923 and started his career with Mitsubishi at the age of 18. Within a few years he was heading up the company's rice importing business in Malaya. After World War II, Kuok left Mitsubishi and set up his own company specializing in food distribution.

As the years passed, Kuok's business expanded and prospered. By the mid-1950s the company was a major player in sugar as well as rice and as early as 1960 had extensive operations in China. Today this part of Kuok's business extends to grains, edible oils, and animal feed, although sugar refining is still its biggest operation. A brief but fortuitous period of speculating in the commodities futures markets in the mid-1960s also provided Kuok with enough extra revenue to seek new business opportunities.

After careful research, he decided to launch a hotel business. His travels to Europe and his visits to luxury hotels in that continent's major cities led him to believe that well-planned and managed luxury hotels could represent an attractive investment.

Working with local investors, both to reduce risk and to tap into local expertise, the Kerry Group began opening luxury hotels in Vancouver, Fiji, Indonesia, Malaysia, China, the Philippines, Thailand, and Singapore. The hotel chain was named Shangri-La to conjure up images of paradise. Because no one in the Kerry Group was knowledgeable in hotel management, the first few properties were developed in conjunction with Westin Hotels. Today, the Shangri-La chain is the largest and most profitable in Asia with an estimated worth of $4 billion.

As the Kerry Group continued to grow, it also began to branch out into other businesses. Expanding to real estate from the hotel business, for example, the company now owns major stakes in numerous clubs, luxury residential buildings, parking structures, office buildings, and shopping malls. Other businesses either launched or bought over the last 30 years include several magazines, television stations, and newspapers in China, a trading company in France, a rubber glove manufacturing concern in Indonesia, a supermarket chain, a discount grocery chain, and several manufacturing concerns in Malaysia, and a shipping business in Singapore.

The Kerry Group's newest business venture, however, is the one that may bring it a bit more public awareness. When the Coca-Cola Company decided to establish a major presence in China in 1993, it knew that it needed a strong local partner to manage its bottling and distribution operations. Since experts predicted that the deal would one day be worth as much as $8 billion, virtually every business in China and Hong Kong sought the contract. But it was the Kerry Group that won.

Kerry Beverages, the name given to the new enterprise, is 87.5 percent owned by the Kerry Group, with Coca-Cola owning the rest. The new business owns and operates ten Coke bottling plants in China. In addition, in order to grow this portion of its business even more quickly, the Kerry Group also made a major investment in Coca-Cola Amatil, the largest bottler outside the United States, which also has major operations throughout Southeast Asia.

Interestingly, the Kerry Group has kept its activities focused in Asia, and has expressed little interest in expanding to Europe or the United States. The firm's big presence in Vancouver might, therefore, seem at first to be a bit out of line. As it turns out, however, many of Vancouver's residents are of Chinese heritage, and many of the firm's luxury condos there have been sold to Chinese living in Asia. But since no one can predict the future with certainty, there may someday be a Shangri-La in every corner of the globe.

Case Questions

1. Which strategic philosophy does the Kerry Group seem to follow?

2. Identify and describe the components of the Kerry Group's strategy.

3. Analyze the Kerry Group in terms of its strengths, weaknesses, opportunities, and threats.

4. Discuss the Kerry Group's corporate and business strategies.

CHAPTER NOTES

1. "Euro Disney's Sales Climb 17%," *Wall Street Journal*, January 22, 1998, p. A15; "Euro Disney—Oui or Non?" *Travel & Leisure*, August 1992, pp. 80–115; "An American in Paris," *Business Week*, March 12, 1990, pp. 60–64; "Mouse Fever Is About to Strike Europe," *Business Week*, March 30, 1992, p. 32; "The Mouse Isn't Roaring," *Business Week*, August 24, 1992, p. 38; The Walt Disney Company *1993 Annual Report*, p. 6; "Fans Like Euro Disney But Its Parent's Goofs Weigh the Park Down," *Wall Street Journal*, March 10, 1994, p. A1; "Walt Disney prepares to share the pain," *Financial Times*, March 15, 1994, p. 25; "Euro Disney Rescue Package Wins Approval," *Wall Street Journal*, March 15, 1994, p. A3; "How Disney Snared a Princely Sum," *Business Week*, June 20, 1994, pp. 61–62; "Euro Disney's Prince Charming?" *Business Week*, June 13, 1994, p. 42.

2. Daniel Sullivan and Alan Bauerschmidt, "The 'Basic Concepts' of International Business Strategy: A Review and Reconsideration," *Management International Review*, Vol. 31, 1991, pp. 111–121.

3. See Charles W. L. Hill and Gareth R. Jones, *Strategic Management: An Analytical Approach*, 4th ed. (Boston: Houghton Mifflin, 1998), for an overview of strategy and strategic management.

4. Kasra Ferdows, "Making the Most of Foreign Factories," *Harvard Business Review*, March-April 1997, pp. 73–88.

5. "Mercedes Bends Rules," *USA Today*, July 16, 1997, pp. B1, B2.

6. "Nissan's Slow U-turn," *Business Week*, May 12, 1997, pp. 54–55.

7. "Russian Bans U.S. Chicken Shipments, Inspiring Fears of Tough Trade Battle," *The Wall Street Journal*, February 23, 1996, p. A2.

8. Christopher A. Bartlett and Sumantra Ghoshal, *Transnational Management*, 2nd ed. (Chicago, Illinois: Richard D. Irwin, 1995), pp. 237–242.

9. "GM Is Building Plants in Developing Nations to Woo New Markets," *Wall Street Journal*, August 4, 1997, p. A1.

10. "At Nokia, A Comeback—And Then Some," *Business Week*, December 2, 1996, p. 106.

11. Bartlett and Ghoshal label this strategy the *multinational strategy*. We have altered their terminology to avoid confusion with other uses of the term *multinational*.

12. See Hill and Jones, *Strategic Management*.

13. Bruce Kogut, "Designing Global Strategies: Comparative and Competitive Value-Added Chains," *Sloan Management Review* (Summer 1985), pp. 15–28.

14. *Hoover's Handbook of World Business 1997* (Austin, Texas: Hoover's Business Press, 1996), pp. 430–431.

15. "Think Small," *Business Week*, November 4, 1991, p. 58.

16. "Producer of Feature-Film Projectors Reels in Fat Profit as Cinemas Expand," *Wall Street Journal*, October 22, 1996, p. B5; "Chile's Luksics: Battle-Tested and on the Prowl," *Wall Street Journal*, December 1, 1995, p. A10.

17. Stephen Kreider Yoder, "Intel, Backing Its Bets with Big Chips, Wins," *Wall Street Journal*, September 24, 1992, p. B1; Michiyo Nakamoto, "Looking for smaller worlds to conquer," *Financial Times*, September 2, 1992.

18. "European Auto Makers Show Signs of Bouncing Back," *Wall Street Journal*, September 15, 1994, p. B4.

19. John A. Pearce II and Fred David, "Corporate Mission Statements: The Bottom Line," *The Academy of Management Executive*, May 1987, pp. 109–115.

20. "Grand Met, Guinness to Form Liquor Colossus," *The Wall Street Journal*, May 13, 1997, pp. B1, B8.

21. Hill and Jones, op. cit.

22. "Accor SA, Europe's Biggest Hotel Firm, Takes on a New Look Under a New CEO," *Wall Street Journal*, January 30, 1998, p. B6A.

23. *Hoover's Handbook of World Business 1997*, op. cit., pp. 382–383.

24. "The Amazing Mr. Kuok," *Forbes*, July 28, 1997, pp. 90–96.

Strategies for Analyzing and Entering Foreign Markets

CHAPTER

11

Chapter Outline

Foreign market analysis
Assessing alternative foreign markets
Evaluating costs, benefits, and risks

Choosing a mode of entry

Exporting to foreign markets
Forms of exporting
Additional considerations
Export intermediaries

International licensing
Basic issues in international licensing
Advantages and disadvantages of
    international licensing

International franchising
Basic issues in international franchising
Advantages and disadvantages of
    international franchising

**Specialized entry modes for
international business**
Contract manufacturing
Management contract
Turnkey project

Foreign direct investment
The greenfield strategy
The acquisition strategy
Joint ventures

After studying this chapter you should be able to:

Discuss how firms go about analyzing foreign markets.

Analyze the process by which firms choose their mode of entry into a foreign market.

Describe forms of exporting and the types of intermediaries available to assist firms in exporting their goods.

Identify the basic issues in international licensing and discuss the advantages and disadvantages of licensing.

Identify the basic issues in international franchising and discuss the advantages and disadvantages of franchising.

Describe contract manufacturing, management contracts, and turnkey projects as specialized entry modes for international business.

Discuss greenfield strategies and acquisition strategies as forms of FDI.

EINEKEN NV IS THE WORLD'S SECOND-LARGEST BEER PRODUCER, after Anheuser-Busch and slightly ahead of Miller. But these two large U.S. brewers have a relatively small international presence: more than 90 percent of their sales are made to U.S. customers. Heineken sells more beer outside the United States than either of them. Of its $7.1 billion in 1996 sales, only 12 percent were in its home market of the Netherlands. Not only is Heineken a market leader in every European country, it also sells its products throughout North and South America, Africa, and Asia—170 countries in all. ▋▋ Heineken was started in Amsterdam by Gerald Heineken in 1864. Almost from the start, the firm was successful. Within a few years of its founding, it was export-

Heineken Brews Up a Global Strategy[1]

ing beer to France, Italy, Spain, Germany, and even the Far East. In 1889 its lager won a gold medal at the World's Fair in Paris. In 1914 Heineken's managers decided to export beer to the United States. Gerald Heineken's son Henri, who was running the firm at the time, sailed to the United States to set up the operation. On board the ship, he met a young bartender named Leo van Munching. Impressed with van Munching's knowledge of beer, Heineken contracted with him to import and distribute the firm's products in North America under the name Van Munching & Company. ▋▋ Despite Heineken's success, it ceased its U.S. operations during Prohibition. After Prohibition's repeal in 1933, it reestablished those operations, again granting Van Munching & Company of New York exclusive rights to import Heineken products into the United States. After World War II, Henri Heineken sent his son, Alfred, to New York to study marketing and advertising from Van Munching. Alfred returned to the Netherlands in 1948 with knowledge he used to help launch Heineken into other foreign markets worldwide. ▋▋ Heineken has continued to grow steadily. It has breweries in over 50 countries. Some of the largest are in Canada and France; however, the firm also produces in New Guinea, Australia, and Brazil. Its joint venture with a leading Japanese brewer, Kirin, gives it a strong presence in that key market. Heineken bought its largest Dutch competitor, Amstel, in 1968. In the early 1970s, seeing its bottling technology and global distribution networks as distinctive competencies, the firm entered the soft drink and wine businesses. For example, Heineken is licensed to manufacture and sell Pepsi-Cola and Seven-Up in the Netherlands. ▋▋ Recently Heineken has stepped up its European expansion plans in order to compete more effectively as the EU completes the formation of its internal market. The firm wants to establish the same sort of overwhelming market dominance in Europe that Anheuser-Busch has in the United States. Thus, during the 1980s Heineken bought breweries in France, Greece, Ireland, Italy, and Spain as a way of expanding its product lines and facilitating distribution throughout Europe. It also bought controlling interests in the Hungarian brewer Komaromi Sorgyar and the Slovak Zlaty Bazont Brewery. Further, to cut its operating costs, it closed ten of its older breweries and modernized six others. To help manage its complex international distribution system, Heineken has invested heavily in new Internet-based technology. The firm uses the Internet to keep distributors informed about sales, promotions, and so forth, and distributors can use the Internet to supply sales figures and place orders.[2] ▮▮ Interestingly, Heineken has refused to establish a brewery in the United States. Why? Consider a case in point. Several years ago Miller, owner of rights to distribute Lowenbrau in the United States, was selling as much of that Munich-brewed beer in the United States as it could import from Germany. To help keep pace with demand, Miller renegotiated its contract with Lowenbrau and began brewing the beer in Texas under license. Sales soon began to drop, in part because the beer was no longer an import and was perceived to have lost its cachet as an authentic Bavarian beer. To avoid Lowenbrau's mistake and retain its product's image as a true "imported" beer, Heineken continues to ship its beer into the U.S. market even though it might be cheaper to make it there. ▮▮ Heineken has recently made one important strategic decision regarding the U.S. market: it bought Van Munching & Company, changed its name to Heineken USA, and now owns its U.S. distribution arm outright. Its being under Heineken's control has helped cut costs and added additional profit to each bottle of beer sold in the United States. Heineken also can now more easily coordinate its U.S. marketing campaigns with its global promotional efforts for its world-famous beer. ▮▮▮▮

Chapter 10 focused on the process by which a firm formulates its international strategy. This chapter discusses the next steps in the implementation of strategy: choosing the markets the firm will enter and the modes of entry it will use to compete in these markets. As the opening case indicates, MNCs such as Heineken are free to choose among the world's markets and are not restricted to using a single method for participating in international business. For example, Heineken exports its products to a variety of markets. In other markets, it uses licensing agreements with independent firms to promote its business interests. And in New Guinea, Australia, and Brazil, Heineken-owned subsidiaries produce, distribute, and sell Heineken beer. As we discuss in this chapter, in deciding whether and how to enter a market, a well-managed firm will match its internal strengths and weaknesses to the unique opportunities and needs of that market. Heineken has successfully done this in each of the national markets in which it participates.

Foreign Market Analysis

Regardless of their strategies, most international businesses have the fundamental goals of expanding market share, revenues, and profits. They often achieve these goals by entering new markets or by introducing new products into markets in which they already have a presence. A firm's ability to do this effectively hinges on its developing a thorough understanding of a given geographical or product market.[3] To successfully increase market share, revenue, and profits, firms must normally follow three steps: (1) assess alternative markets, (2) evaluate the respective costs, benefits, and risks of entering each, and (3) select those that hold the most potential for entry or expansion.

Assessing Alternative Foreign Markets

In assessing alternative foreign markets, a firm must consider a variety of factors, including the current and potential sizes of these markets, the levels of competition the firm will face, their legal and political environments, and sociocultural factors that may affect the firm's operations and performance.[4] Table 11.1 summarizes some of the most critical of these factors.

Information on some of these factors is relatively objective and easy to obtain. For example, a country's currency stability is important to a firm contemplating exporting to or importing from that country or analyzing investment opportunities there. Information about this topic can be objectively assessed and can be easily obtained from various published sources in the firm's home country. Other information about foreign markets is much more subjective and may be quite difficult to obtain. For example, information on the honesty of local government officials or on the process of obtaining utility permits may be very hard to acquire in the firm's home country. Obtaining such information often entails visiting the foreign location early in the decision-making process to talk to local experts, such as embassy staff and chamber of commerce officials, or contracting with a consulting firm to obtain the needed data.[5]

Market Potential. The first step in foreign market selection is assessing market potential. Many publications, such as those listed in "Building Global Skills" in Chapter 2, provide data on population, GDP, per capita GDP, public infrastructure, and ownership of such goods as automobiles and televisions. Such data permit firms to conduct a preliminary "quick and dirty" screening of various foreign markets. If the population is highly concentrated in urban areas, has strong purchasing power, and shows high usage of products such as automobiles and televisions, the market may be highly attractive to a firm selling consumer goods such as stereo equipment. But if most of the country's population is rural, has weak purchasing power, and purchases few consumer durables, the market may be much more attractive to a manufacturer of low-cost farm tools and equipment than to stereo equipment manufacturers. The firm must also consider the positioning of its products relative to those of its competitors. A firm producing high-quality products at premium prices will find richer markets attractive but may have more difficulty penetrating a poorer market. Conversely, a firm specializing in low-priced, lower-quality goods may find the poorer market even more

TABLE 11.1

Critical Factors in Assessing New Market Opportunities

TOPIC OF APPRAISAL	ITEMS TO BE CONSIDERED
Product-market dimensions	How big is the product market in terms of unit size and sales volume?
Major product-market "differences"	What are the major differences relative to the firm's experience elsewhere in terms of customer profiles, price levels, national purchase patterns, and product technology?
	How will these differences affect the transferability of the firm's capabilities to the new business environment and their effectiveness?
Structural characteristics of the national product market	What links and associations exist between potential customers and established national competitors currently supplying these customers?
	What are the major channels of distribution (discount structure, ties to present producers, levels of distribution separating producers from final customers, links between wholesalers, links between wholesalers and retailers, finance, role of government)?
	What links exist between established producers and their suppliers?
	Do industry concentration and collusive agreements exist?
Competitor analysis	What are major competitor characteristics (size, capacity utilization, strengths and weaknesses, technology, supply sources, preferential market arrangements, and relations with the government)?
	What is competitor performance in terms of market share, sales growth, and profit margins?
Potential target markets	What are the characteristics of major product-market segments?
	Which segments are potential targets upon entry?
Relevant trends (historic and projected)	What changes have occurred in total size of product market (short-, medium-, and long-term)?
	What changes have occurred in competitor performance (market share, sales, and profits)?
	What is the nature of competition (e.g., national or international)?
	What changes have occurred in market structure?
Explanation of change	Why are some firms gaining and others losing?
	Are foreign firms already operating here gaining or losing?
	Is there some general explanation of observed change, for example, product life cycle, change in overall business activity, and shift in nature of demand?
	What is the future outlook?
Success factors	What are the key factors behind success in this business environment, the pressure points that can shift market share from one firm to another?
	How are these different from those we have experienced in other countries?
	How do these success factors relate to our firm?
Strategic options	What elements emerge from the above analysis that point to possible strategies for this country?
	What additional information is required to identify our options more precisely?

Source: Reprinted with the permission of Lexington Books, an imprint of The Free Press, a Division of Simon & Schuster, from *Multinational Corporate Strategy: Planning for World Markets* by James C. Leontiades. Copyright © 1985 by Lexington Books.

lucrative than the richer market.[6] For example, consider the market differences between the two Chinas—the Peoples' Republic of China and the Republic of China (Taiwan)—highlighted in Map 11.1. Although China's population dwarfs that of Taiwan, per capita income in Taiwan is quite high and ownership of various consumer durable goods is widespread, while the reverse is the case in China. Nonetheless, rapid economic growth in China portends a booming market for

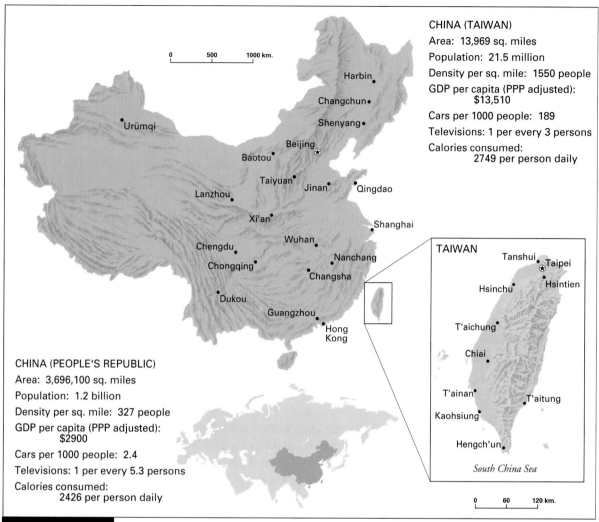

CHINA (TAIWAN)
Area: 13,969 sq. miles
Population: 21.5 million
Density per sq. mile: 1550 people
GDP per capita (PPP adjusted):
    $13,510
Cars per 1000 people: 189
Televisions: 1 per every 3 persons
Calories consumed:
    2749 per person daily

TAIWAN

Tanshui
Taipei
Hsinchu
Hsintien
T'aichung
Chiai
T'ainan
T'aitung
Kaohsiung
Hengch'un

South China Sea

0   60   120 km.

CHINA (PEOPLE'S REPUBLIC)
Area: 3,696,100 sq. miles
Population: 1.2 billion
Density per sq. mile: 327 people
GDP per capita (PPP adjusted):
    $2900
Cars per 1000 people: 2.4
Televisions: 1 per every 5.3 persons
Calories consumed:
    2426 per person daily

0   500   1000 km.

Harbin
Changchun
Shenyang
Urümqi
Beijing
Baotou
Taiyuan
Jinan
Qingdao
Lanzhou
Xi'an
Shanghai
Chengdu
Wuhan
Chongqing
Nanchang
Changsha
Dukou
Guangzhou
Hong Kong

MAP 11.1

A Tale of Two Chinas

such goods there. A firm attempting to sell its products in both of these markets would clearly have a very different set of considerations to address for each.

A firm must then collect data relevant to the specific product line under consideration. For example, if Pirelli SpA is contemplating exporting tires to Thailand, its strategic managers must collect data about that country's transportation infrastructure, transportation alternatives, gasoline prices, and growth of vehicle ownership. Pirelli would also need data on the average age of motor vehicles and the production of automobiles in Thailand in order to assess whether to focus its marketing efforts on the replacement market or the OEM (original equipment manufacturer) market. In some situations, a firm may have to resort to using proxy data. For example, Whirlpool, in deciding whether to enter the dishwasher market in South Korea, could examine sales of other household appliances, per capita electricity consumption, or the number of two-income families.

But such data reflect the past, not the future. Firms must also consider the potential for growth in a country's economy by using both objective and subjective measures. Objective measures include changes in per capita income, energy consumption, GDP, and ownership of consumer durables such as private automobiles. More subjective considerations must also be taken into account when assessing potential growth. For example, following the collapse of communist economies in Central and Eastern Europe, many Western firms ignored the data indicating negative economic growth in these countries. Instead they focused on the prospects for future growth as these countries adopted new economic policies and programs. As a result, firms such as Procter & Gamble and Unilever established production facilities, distribution channels, and brand recognition in order to seize first-mover advantages as these economies recovered from the process of adjusting to capitalism.

Levels of Competition. Another factor a firm must consider in foreign market selection is the level of competition in the market—both the current level and the likely future level. For a firm to assess its competitive environment, it should identify the number and sizes of firms already competing in the target market, their relative market shares, their pricing and distribution strategies, and their relative strengths and weaknesses, both individually and collectively. It must then weigh these factors against actual market conditions. For example, a small market already characterized by severe competition may not be able to sustain new competitors. However, a market that is large and prosperous may still hold opportunities for new entrants, particularly if they can identify underserved market niches to exploit. For example, the poor-quality image of U.S.-made small cars in the 1970s made GM, Ford, and Chrysler vulnerable to a competitor such as Honda that offered a product of superior quality. Honda's successful entry into the U.S. automobile market was based on its exploiting this vulnerability by offering a high-quality product at a low cost. However, a foreign automaker entering the U.S. market today would be faced with enormous competition not only from the three dominant U.S. automakers but also from such well-entrenched Japanese and European firms as Toyota, Nissan, and BMW.

Most successful firms continually monitor major markets in order to exploit opportunities as they become available. This is particularly critical for industries undergoing technological or regulatory changes. The telecommunications industry provides an important example of this phenomenon. Once the sinecure of inefficient, plodding state-owned monopolies, this industry is in the epicenter of the convergence of a variety of new technologies—fiber optics, personal pagers, cellular service, satellite networks, and so on. Many of these firms—particularly in Europe and Latin America—have been or are being privatized. Privatization has been coupled with the tumbling of regulatory barriers to entry and innovation, allowing firms to enter new geographic and product markets. To hasten their ability to expand globally, several consortia have been created, as Map 11.2 indicates.

Legal and Political Environment. A firm contemplating entry into a particular market also needs to understand the host country's trade policies and its general legal and political environments, which we discussed in Chapters 6 and 8.[7] For example, a firm may choose to forgo exporting its goods to a country that has high tariffs and other trade restrictions in favor of exporting to one that has fewer or less significant barriers.[8] Conversely, trade policies and/or

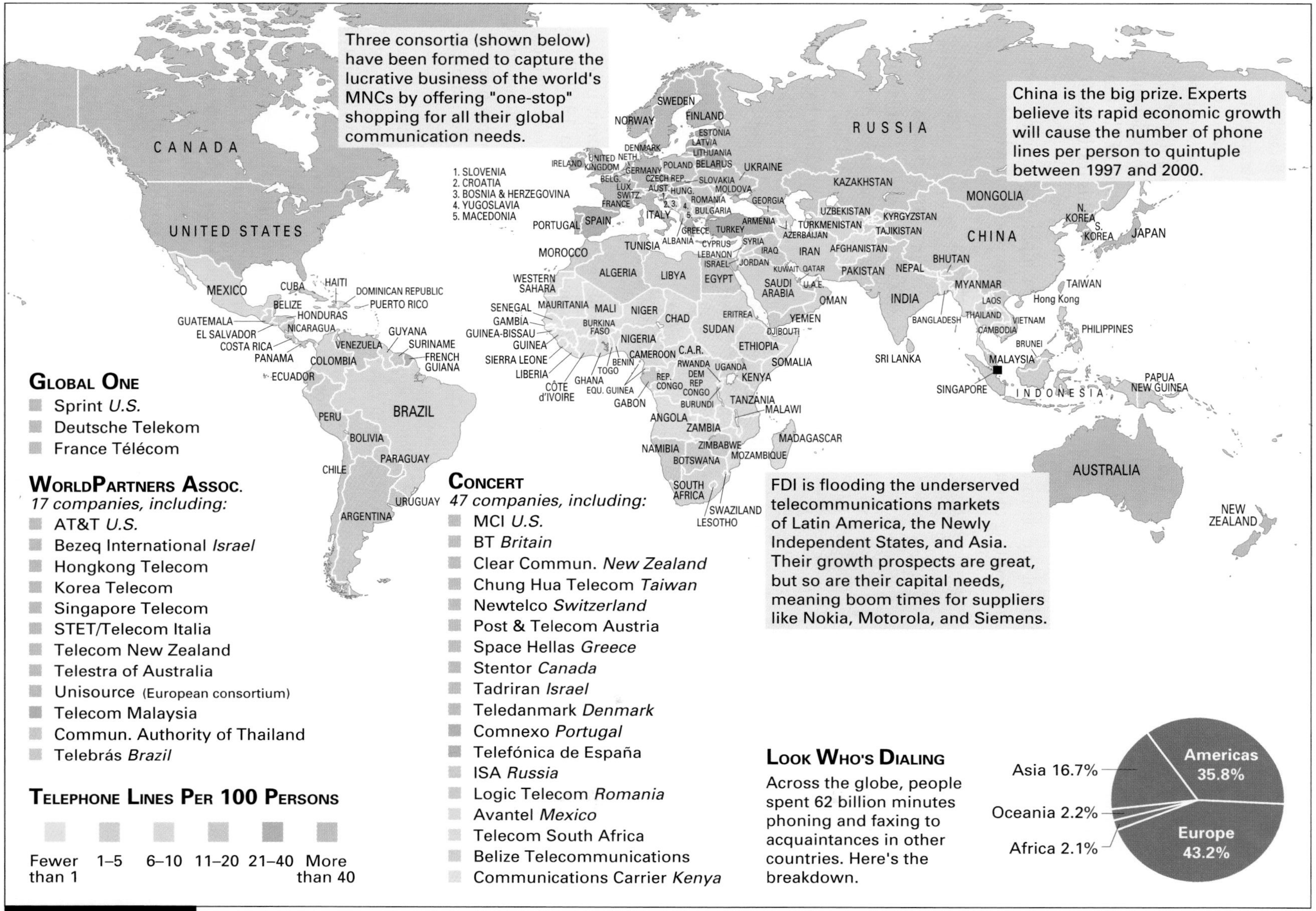
Three consortia (shown below) have been formed to capture the lucrative business of the world's MNCs by offering "one-stop" shopping for all their global communication needs.
China is the big prize. Experts believe its rapid economic growth will cause the number of phone lines per person to quintuple between 1997 and 2000.
FDI is flooding the underserved telecommunications markets of Latin America, the Newly Independent States, and Asia. Their growth prospects are great, but so are their capital needs, meaning boom times for suppliers like Nokia, Motorola, and Siemens.
GLOBAL ONE
Sprint U.S.
Deutsche Telekom
France Télécom
WORLDPARTNERS ASSOC.
17 companies, including:
AT&T U.S.
Bezeq International Israel
Hongkong Telecom
Korea Telecom
Singapore Telecom
STET/Telecom Italia
Telecom New Zealand
Telestra of Australia
Unisource (European consortium)
Telecom Malaysia
Commun. Authority of Thailand
Telebrás Brazil
CONCERT
47 companies, including:
MCI U.S.
BT Britain
Clear Commun. New Zealand
Chung Hua Telecom Taiwan
Newtelco Switzerland
Post & Telecom Austria
Space Hellas Greece
Stentor Canada
Tadriran Israel
Teledanmark Denmark
Comnexo Portugal
Telefónica de España
ISA Russia
Logic Telecom Romania
Avantel Mexico
Telecom South Africa
Belize Telecommunications
Communications Carrier Kenya
TELEPHONE LINES PER 100 PERSONS
Fewer than 1
1–5
6–10
11–20
21–40
More than 40
LOOK WHO'S DIALING
Across the globe, people spent 62 billion minutes phoning and faxing to acquaintances in other countries. Here's the breakdown.
Americas 35.8%
Europe 43.2%
Asia 16.7%
Oceania 2.2%
Africa 2.1%
1. SLOVENIA
2. CROATIA
3. BOSNIA & HERZEGOVINA
4. YUGOSLAVIA
5. MACEDONIA
CANADA
UNITED STATES
MEXICO
CUBA
HAITI
DOMINICAN REPUBLIC
PUERTO RICO
BELIZE
HONDURAS
GUATEMALA
EL SALVADOR
NICARAGUA
COSTA RICA
PANAMA
VENEZUELA
GUYANA
SURINAME
FRENCH GUIANA
COLOMBIA
ECUADOR
PERU
BRAZIL
BOLIVIA
PARAGUAY
CHILE
URUGUAY
ARGENTINA
RUSSIA
SWEDEN
NORWAY
FINLAND
ESTONIA
LATVIA
LITHUANIA
DENMARK
IRELAND
UNITED KINGDOM
NETH.
BELG.
LUX.
GERMANY
POLAND
BELARUS
UKRAINE
CZECH REP.
SLOVAKIA
AUST.
HUNG.
MOLDOVA
SWITZ.
FRANCE
ROMANIA
BULGARIA
GEORGIA
PORTUGAL
SPAIN
ITALY
GREECE
TURKEY
ARMENIA
AZERBAIJAN
ALBANIA
CYPRUS
SYRIA
LEBANON
ISRAEL
JORDAN
IRAQ
IRAN
KUWAIT
QATAR
U.A.E.
SAUDI ARABIA
OMAN
YEMEN
KAZAKHSTAN
UZBEKISTAN
TURKMENISTAN
KYRGYZSTAN
TAJIKISTAN
AFGHANISTAN
PAKISTAN
NEPAL
BHUTAN
INDIA
BANGLADESH
SRI LANKA
MONGOLIA
CHINA
N. KOREA
S. KOREA
JAPAN
TAIWAN
Hong Kong
MYANMAR
LAOS
THAILAND
VIETNAM
CAMBODIA
PHILIPPINES
BRUNEI
MALAYSIA
SINGAPORE
INDONESIA
PAPUA NEW GUINEA
AUSTRALIA
NEW ZEALAND
MOROCCO
WESTERN SAHARA
ALGERIA
TUNISIA
LIBYA
EGYPT
MAURITANIA
MALI
NIGER
CHAD
SUDAN
ERITREA
DJIBOUTI
ETHIOPIA
SOMALIA
SENEGAL
GAMBIA
GUINEA-BISSAU
GUINEA
SIERRA LEONE
LIBERIA
CÔTE d'IVOIRE
BURKINA FASO
GHANA
TOGO
BENIN
NIGERIA
CAMEROON
EQU. GUINEA
GABON
C.A.R.
REP. CONGO
DEM REP CONGO
RWANDA
BURUNDI
UGANDA
KENYA
TANZANIA
MALAWI
ANGOLA
ZAMBIA
ZIMBABWE
MOZAMBIQUE
MADAGASCAR
NAMIBIA
BOTSWANA
SOUTH AFRICA
SWAZILAND
LESOTHO

MAP 11.2 **Look Who's Talking** Source: "The Race to wire the World," *Fortune*, October 17, 1997.

trade barriers may induce a firm to enter a market via FDI. For example, Ford, GM, Audi, and Mercedes-Benz are building auto factories in Brazil to avoid that country's high tariffs and to use Brazil as a production platform to access other Mercosur members.[9] Care also often needs to be taken to avoid offending the political sensibilities of the host nation. For example, consider the political implications of Map 11.1. The leadership of the Peoples' Republic of China (PRC) refuses to recognize the Republic of China (ROC) as an independent nation, viewing Taiwan as a breakaway province. Our labeling of Taiwan in Map 11.1 as the Republic of China might discourage sales of this textbook in the PRC; failure to do so might hurt sales in the ROC/Taiwan.

A firm must carefully evaluate the legal and political environment of a foreign market in order to control risk. While Russia provides tremendous opportunities, its legal and political environment also carries considerable risk. Thus Mars has entered the market carefully through the use of kiosks and other low-cost facilities. It now sells $300 million worth of candy bars annually in Russia. It has been so successful that its products have become a symbol of the so-called "Snickerization" of the Russian economy: a concern that Western products are becoming too dominant and hurting Russian firms.[10]

Other legal and political issues relate to ownership. Some countries require foreign firms wanting to establish local operations to work with a local joint-venture partner; this requirement may reduce the attractiveness of such a strategy. Barriers to the repatriation of profits may also limit the appeal of operating local production facilities.

Tax policies are also important. Some countries tax foreign firms at a higher rate than they do domestic firms. Others, wanting to promote domestic economic development, are willing to offer economic incentives to firms to locate within their borders. For example, in December 1997 Toyota agreed to construct a $668 million assembly plant in northern France, which will create 2000 jobs in the area, after receiving a variety of economic incentives from local and national governments. Similarly, the state of Alabama lured Mercedes-Benz to build its new factory in Tuscaloosa with an incentive package worth an estimated $253 million.

Government stability is also an important factor in foreign market assessment, as our discussion of political risk analysis in Chapter 8 indicated. Governmental transitions in the Quad countries are relatively smooth, so stability is not an issue. But in some less developed countries prone to military coups and similar disruptions, it is a serious problem. Government regulation of pricing and promotional activities also creates important legal and political issues to consider. For example, many governments restrict advertising for tobacco and alcohol products, so foreign manufacturers of those products must understand how those restrictions will affect their ability to market their goods in those countries. Still another important legal and political factor to consider is the extent to which the government establishes and enforces health and safety standards for both consumers and employees.[11]

Sociocultural Influences. Managers assessing foreign markets must also consider sociocultural influences. We discussed the role of culture in international business in Chapter 9. To reduce the uncertainty associated with sociocultural factors, firms often focus their initial internationalization efforts in countries culturally similar to their home markets.[12] As with legal and political factors, firms must carefully assess relevant sociocultural factors in deciding whether to enter a particular market. Because of their subjective nature, these factors are often difficult to quantify.

If the proposed strategy is to produce goods in another country and export them to the market under consideration, the most relevant sociocultural factors are those associated with consumers. Firms that fail to recognize the needs and preferences of host country consumers often run into trouble. For example, Denmark's Bang & Olufsen, a well-known stereo system manufacturer, has floundered in some markets because its designers stress style rather than function. Japanese competitors, meanwhile, stress function and innovation over style and design. Bang & Olufsen's Danish managers have failed to realize that consumers in markets such as the United States are generally more interested in function than in design and that they are more willing to pay for new technology than for an interesting appearance.[13]

A firm considering FDI in a factory or distribution center must also evaluate sociocultural factors associated with potential employees.[14] It must understand the motivational basis for work in that country, the norms for working hours and pay, and the role of labor unions. By hiring—and listening to—local managers, foreign firms can often avoid or reduce cultural conflicts.

Evaluating Costs, Benefits, and Risks

The next step in foreign-market assessment is a careful evaluation of the costs, benefits, and risks associated with doing business in a particular foreign market.

Costs. Two types of costs are relevant at this point: direct and opportunity. Direct costs are those the firm incurs in entering a new foreign market and include costs associated with setting up a business operation (leasing or buying a facility, for example), transferring managers to run it, and shipping equipment and merchandise. The firm also incurs opportunity costs. Because a firm has limited resources, entering one market may preclude or delay its entry into another. The profits it would have earned in that second market are its opportunity costs—the organization has forfeited or delayed its opportunity to earn those profits by choosing to enter another market first. Thus the firm's planners must carefully assess all the alternatives available to it.

Benefits. Entering a new market presumably offers a firm many potential benefits; otherwise, why do it? Among the most obvious potential benefits are the expected sales and profits from the market. Others include lower acquisition and manufacturing costs (if materials and/or labor are cheap), foreclosing of markets to competitors (which limits competitors' ability to earn profits), competitive advantage (which allows the firm to keep ahead of or abreast with its competition), access to new technology, and the opportunity to achieve synergy with other operations.

Risks. Of course, few benefits are achieved without some degree of risk. Many of the earlier chapters provided overviews of the specific types of risks facing international businesses. Generally, a firm entering a new market incurs the risks of exchange rate fluctuations, additional operating complexity, and direct financial losses due to misassessment of market potential. In extreme cases, it also faces the risk of loss through government seizure of property or due to war or terrorism.

This list of factors a firm must consider when assessing foreign markets may seem onerous. Nonetheless, successful international businesses carefully analyze these factors in order to uncover and exploit any and all opportunities available to them. At best, poor market assessments may rob a firm of profitable opportunities. At worst, a continued inability to reach the right decisions may threaten the firm's existence.

Choosing a Mode of Entry

Having decided which markets to enter, the firm is now faced with another decision: which mode of entry should it use? Dunning's eclectic theory, discussed in Chapter 3, provides useful insights into the factors that affect the choice among either home country production (exporting), host country production in firm-owned factories (FDI and joint venture), or host country production performed by others (licensing, franchising, and contract manufacturing). Recall that the eclectic theory considers three factors: ownership advantages, location advantages, and internalization advantages.[15] Other factors a firm may consider include the firm's need for control, the availability of resources, and the firm's global strategy. The role of these factors in the entry mode decision is illustrated in Fig. 11.1.

Ownership advantages are resources owned by a firm that grant it a competitive advantage over its industry rivals. These firm-specific ownership advantages may be tangible or intangible. For example, the ownership by Toronto-based Inco, Ltd., of rich, nickel-bearing ores has allowed the firm, formerly known as International Nickel, to dominate the production of both primary nickel and nickel-based metal alloys. The luxury appeal of Dom Perignon champagne and Christian Dior perfumes—both products of France's LVMH Moet Hennessy Louis Vuitton—although a more intangible resource than a nickel ore mine, similarly grants the Parisian firm a competitive advantage over its rivals in international markets. Assuming that local firms know more about their home turf than foreigners do, a foreign firm contemplating entry into a new market should possess some ownership advantage in order to overcome the information advantage of local firms. As discussed later in this chapter, the nature of the firm's ownership advantage affects its selection of entry mode. Imbedded technology, for example, is often best transferred through an equity mode, while firms whose competitive advantage is based on a well-known brand name sometimes enter foreign markets through a licensing or franchising mode. Further, firm advantages are primary determinants of bargaining strength; thus they can influence the outcome of entry mode negotiations.

Location advantages are those factors that affect the desirability of host country production relative to home country production. Firms routinely com-

FIGURE 11.1

**Choosing a Mode
of Entry**

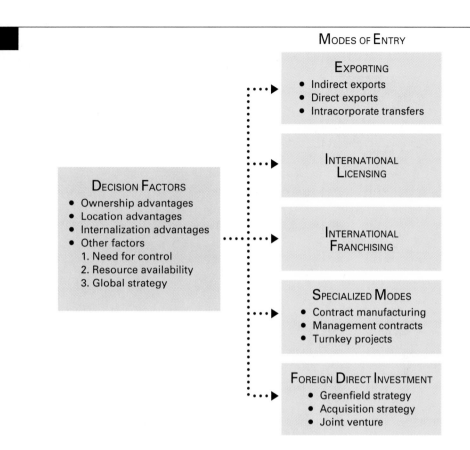

Figure 11.1

Choosing a Mode of Entry

pare economic and noneconomic characteristics of the home market with those of the foreign market in determining where to site their production facilities. If home country production is found to be more desirable than host country production, the firm will choose to enter the host country market via exporting. For example, Siam Cement, one of the world's lowest-cost producers, has relied on exports from its modern Thailand factories to serve the Cambodian, Vietnamese, and Laotian markets rather than setting up production facilities in those countries.[16] But if host country production is more desirable, the firm may invest in foreign facilities or license the use of its technology and brand names to existing host country producers.

The desirability of home country versus host country production is affected by many factors. Relative wage rates and land acquisition costs in the countries are important, but firms may also consider surplus or unused capacity in existing factories, access to R&D facilities, logistical requirements, the needs of customers, and the additional administrative costs of managing a foreign facility. Political risk must also be considered. The presence of civil war, official corruption, or unstable governments will discourage many firms from devoting significant resources to a host country. Government policies can also have a major influence.[17] For example, high tariff walls discourage exporting and encourage local production, while high corporate taxes or government prohibitions against repatriation of profits inhibit FDI. Even government inaction may affect locational decisions. McDonald's, for example, built a bakery in Cairo in 1996 to supply its regional restaurants in part because of its frustration in dealing with Egyptian customs

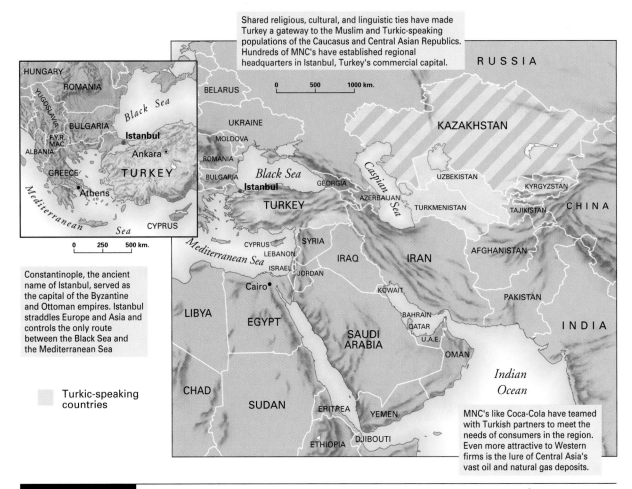

Shared religious, cultural, and linguistic ties have made Turkey a gateway to the Muslim and Turkic-speaking populations of the Caucasus and Central Asian Republics. Hundreds of MNC's have established regional headquarters in Istanbul, Turkey's commercial capital.

Constantinople, the ancient name of Istanbul, served as the capital of the Byzantine and Ottoman empires. Istanbul straddles Europe and Asia and controls the only route between the Black Sea and the Mediterranean Sea

Turkic-speaking countries

MNC's like Coca-Cola have teamed with Turkish partners to meet the needs of consumers in the region. Even more attractive to Western firms is the lure of Central Asia's vast oil and natural gas deposits.

MAP 11.3

Turkey: The Gateway to the Central Asian Republics and the Caucasus

Source: "Istanbul's Location Gives It a Crucial Role," The *Wall Street Journal,* March 27, 1997, p. A10.

bureaucrats, who required the company to obtain more than a dozen signatures each time it wished to import hamburger buns into the country.[18] Location advantages may also be culture-bound. Turkey, for example, has benefited from its geographic, religious, linguistic, and cultural ties to the Central Asian and Caucasus republics of the former Soviet Union (see Map 11.3). MNCs like Siemens, Chase Manhattan, and Goodyear have based their regional headquarters and export operations in Istanbul, viewing it as the ideal jumping-off point for doing business in the entire Eurasian region.[19]

Internalization advantages are those factors that affect the desirability of a firm's producing a good or service itself rather than contracting with a local host country firm to produce the product. As noted in Chapter 3, the amount of transaction costs (costs of negotiating, monitoring, and enforcing an agreement) is critical to this decision. If contracts are difficult to negotiate, monitor, and enforce, the firm may rely on FDI and joint ventures as entry modes. If transaction costs are low and the firm believes local firms can more efficiently produce the good or service without jeopardizing its interests, the firm may use franchising, licensing, or contract manufacturing as entry modes. In deciding, the firm must consider both the nature of the ownership advantage it possesses and its ability to ensure productive and harmonious working relations with any local firm with which it does business. Toyota, for example, possesses two important ownership advantages: efficient manufacturing techniques and a reputation for producing high-quality automobiles. Neither asset is readily saleable or transferable to other firms; thus Toyota has used FDI and joint ventures rather than franchising and licensing for its foreign production of automobiles.

Pharmaceutical firms routinely use licensing as their entry mode. In this industry, two common ownership advantages are the ownership of a patented drug that has unique medical properties and the ownership of local distribution networks. Obtaining either is expensive; researching, developing, and testing a new wonder drug can cost several hundred million dollars, while distribution networks must be large to be effective. In Japan, for example, a sales force of at least 1000 employees is necessary to efficiently market prescription drugs.[20] Once a pharmaceutical firm has developed and patented a new drug, it is eager to amortize its R&D costs in both domestic and foreign markets. Many such firms prefer to forgo the expensive and time-consuming process of setting up overseas production facilities and foreign distribution networks. Instead they grant existing local firms the right to manufacture and distribute the patented drug in return for royalty payments. For example, Merck licensed Israel's Teva Pharmaceutical Industries to manufacture and market its pharmaceutical products in Israel, saving it the expense of establishing its own Israeli sales force. Licensing is also attractive because the risk that the local licensee will cheat the pharmaceutical firm or damage its reputation is minimal, since the costs of monitoring the sales and product quality of patented drugs sold in the host country are relatively low.

Other factors may also affect the choice of entry mode. For example, a firm is likely to consider its need for control and the availability of resources.[21] A firm's lack of experience in a foreign market may cause a certain degree of uncertainty. To reduce this uncertainty, some firms may prefer an initial entry mode that offers them a high degree of control.[22] However, firms short on capital or thin in executive talent may be unable or unwilling to commit themselves to the large capital investments this control entails; they may prefer an entry mode that economizes on their financial and managerial commitments, such as licensing. Cash-rich firms may view FDI more favorably, believing that it offers high profit potential and the opportunity to more fully internationalize the training of their young, fast-track managers.

A firm's overall global strategy also may affect the choice of entry mode. Firms such as Ford that seek to exploit economies of scale and synergies between their domestic and international operations may prefer ownership-oriented entry modes. Conversely, firms such as Microsoft and Compaq, whose competitive strengths lie in flexibility and quick response to changing market conditions, are more likely to use any and all entry modes warranted by local conditions in a given host country.[23] A firm's choice may also be driven by its need to coordinate its activities across all markets as part of its global strategy. For example, IBM has for this reason traditionally favored ownership-oriented entry modes as part of its globalization strategy.[24]

In short, like most business activities, the choice of entry mode is often a trade-off between the level of risk borne by the firm, the potential rewards to be obtained from a market, the magnitude of the resource commitment necessary to compete effectively, and the level of control the firm seeks.[25]

The first entry modes we discuss, which require no firm ownership of foreign assets, are exporting, licensing, franchising, contract manufacturing, management contracts, and turnkey projects. We then discuss two types of FDI—greenfield strategy and acquisition strategy—and touch on a third type—joint venture—that is covered in more detail in Chapter 12. Table 11.2 summarizes the advantages and disadvantages of these modes of entry.

Exporting to Foreign Markets

Perhaps the simplest mode of internationalizing a domestic business is exporting, the most common form of international business activity. Recall from Chapter 1 that exporting is the process of sending goods or services from one country to other countries for use or sale there. In that chapter we noted that merchandise exports in the world economy totaled $5.1 trillion in 1996, or 18 percent of the world's total economic activity. Service exports amounted to $1.2 trillion in 1996.

Exporting offers a firm several advantages. First, the firm can control its financial exposure to the host country market as it deems appropriate. Little or no capital investment is normally needed as long as the firm chooses to hire a host country firm to distribute its products. In this case, the firm's financial exposure is often limited to start-up costs associated with market research, locating and choosing its local distributor, and/or local advertising plus the value of the goods and services involved in any given overseas shipment. Alternatively, the firm may choose to distribute its products itself to better control their marketing. If the firm opts for this approach, it is then able to raise its selling prices because a middleman has been eliminated. However, its investment costs and its financial exposure may rise substantially, for the firm will have to equip and operate its own distribution centers, hire its own employees, and market its products.

Second, exporting permits a firm to enter a foreign market gradually, thereby allowing it to assess local conditions and fine-tune its products to meet the idiosyncratic needs of host country consumers. If its exports are well received by foreign consumers, the firm may use this experience as a basis for a more extensive entry into that market. For example, the firm may choose to take over distribution of its product from the host country distributor or to build a factory in the host country to supply its customers there, particularly if it finds it can reduce its production and distribution costs or improve the quality of its customer service. "Going Global" describes how a British company has started exporting jams to Japan. Its current arrangement is a classic example of the advantages of exporting, but the door is open for changes in the way it operates in Japan as it learns more about that market.

Firms may have proactive or reactive motivations for exporting. Proactive motivations are those that *pull* a firm into foreign markets as a result of opportunities available there. For example, San Antonio's Pace, Inc., a maker of Tex-Mex food products, began exporting proactively to Mexico in the early 1990s after discovering that Mexican consumers enjoy its picante sauce as much as its U.S. customers do.[26]

TABLE 11.2

Advantages and Disadvantages of Different Modes of Entry

MODE	PRIMARY ADVANTAGES	PRIMARY DISADVANTAGES
Exporting	Relatively low financial exposure Permit gradual market entry Acquire knowledge about local market Avoid restrictions on foreign investment	Vulnerable to tariffs and NTBs Logistical complexities Potential conflicts with distributors
Licensing	Low financial risks Low-cost way to assess market potential Avoid tariffs, NTBs, restrictions on foreign investment Licensee provides knowledge of local markets	Limits market opportunities/profits Dependency on licensee Potential conflicts with licensee May be creating future competitor
Franchising	Low financial risks Low-cost way to assess market potential Avoid tariffs, NTBs, restrictions on foreign investment Maintain more control than with licensing Franchisee provides knowledge of local market	Limits market opportunities/profits Dependency on franchisee Potential conflicts with franchisee May be creating future competitor
Contract manufacturing	Low financial risks Minimize resources devoted to manufacturing Focus firm's resources on other elements of the value chain	Reduced control (may affect quality, delivery schedules, etc.) Reduced learning potential Potential public relations problems—may need to monitor working conditions, etc.
Management contracts	Focus firm's resources on its area of expertise Minimal financial exposure	Potential returns limited by contract May unintentionally transfer proprietary knowledge and techniques to contractee
Turnkey projects	Focus firm's resources on its area of expertise Avoid all long-term operational risks	Bear financial risks (cost overruns, etc.) Bear construction risks (delays, problems with suppliers, etc.)
Foreign direct investment	High profit potential Maintain control over operations Acquire knowledge of local market Avoid tariffs and NTBs	High financial and managerial investments Higher exposure to political risk Vulnerable to restrictions on foreign investment Greater managerial complexity

GOING GLOBAL

Jumping on a Japanese Jam Deal

Managers at Chivers Hartley recently scored a major coup by landing a big order from Jusco, one of Japan's largest retailers. Chivers is a UK firm that makes a variety of fruit preserves—jellies, jams, and marmalades. Because its domestic market has matured, Chivers sees exports as an important growth opportunity. The firm currently obtains 15 percent of its revenues from exports, with France, Germany, and Holland its largest foreign markets.

Chivers spent two years cultivating the deal with Jusco. A senior marketing manager from the company initially established a contact with Jusco, which expressed interest in selling the firm's products. Jusco executives then visited Chivers' factory near Cambridge, England, and laid out for officials there exactly what Chivers would need to do to compete in the Japanese market.

Based on this feedback, Chivers began developing a new product line just for the Japanese market. First, product formulas were altered to include more fruit and less sugar. In addition, Chivers also developed blueberry as a flavor, since it is popular among Japanese consumers. The firm also switched to smaller jars because Japanese consumers are accustomed to making more frequent trips to market, use jams more sparingly than British consumers do, and have less storage space. Chivers also created an exclusive new brand name just for Jusco called Cambridgeshire. The jar labels have a sepia picture of King's College, Cambridge, taking advantage of Japanese respect for British universities.

Chivers was rewarded for its efforts when Jusco placed an order for 2900 cases and promised to promote the product in 300 of its stores. Chivers and Jusco expect Cambridgeshire to compete with the number one local brand, Blue Flag. And Chivers also hopes that this is just the first step toward Japan's becoming the firm's fourth largest export market.

Source: "Japanese Jam Deal Set to Boost Preserves Group," *Financial Times*, November 3, 1997, p. 8.

A firm also may export proactively in order to exploit a technological advantage or to spread fixed R&D expenses over a wider customer base, thereby allowing it to price its products more competitively in both domestic and foreign markets. For example, the break-even price of commercial airliners produced by Boeing and Airbus Industrie would skyrocket if these firms limited their sales to either domestic or foreign customers.

Reactive motivations for exporting are those that *push* a firm into foreign markets, often because opportunities are decreasing in the domestic market. Some firms turn to exporting because their production lines are running below capacity or because they seek higher profit margins in foreign markets in the face of downturns in domestic demand. For example, Space-Lok, Inc., a small, 40-person Burbank, California manufacturer of high-stress fasteners for the aerospace industry, began to internationalize its operations only after the U.S. defense budget began to shrink as a result of the end of the Cold War. Similarly, Toto Ltd. dominated Japan's porcelain bathroom fixtures market but paid little attention to export markets until the Japanese economy slowed down in the early 1990s. While Toto has managed to carve out a 15 percent share of the market for imported commodes in such key markets as China, its late start has put it at a disadvantage vis-à-vis other foreign competitors like American Standard.[27]

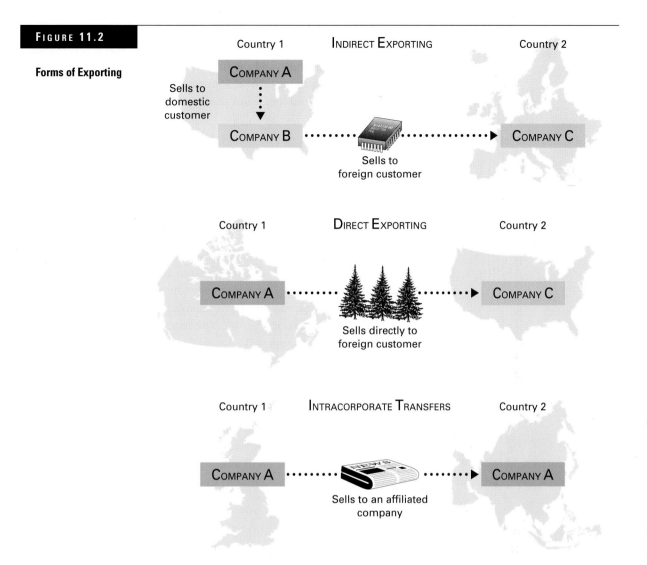

FIGURE 11.2

Forms of Exporting

Forms of Exporting

Export activities may take several forms (see Fig. 11.2), including indirect exporting, direct exporting, and intracorporate transfers.

Indirect Exporting. Indirect exporting occurs when a firm sells its product to a domestic customer, which in turn exports the product, in either its original form or a modified form. For example, if Hewlett-Packard (a U.S. firm) buys microchips from Intel (also a U.S. firm) to use in manufacturing computers, and then exports those completed computers to Europe, Intel's chips have been indirectly exported. Or, a firm may sell goods to a domestic wholesaler who then sells them to an overseas firm. A firm also may sell to a foreign firm's local subsidiary, which then transports the first firm's products to the foreign country.

Some indirect exporting activities reflect conscious actions by domestic producers. For example, the Association of Guatemala Coffee Producers sells bags of coffee to passengers boarding international flights in Guatemala City in order to gain export sales and to build consumer awareness of its product. In most cases, however, indirect exporting activities are not part of a conscious internationalization strategy by a firm. Thus they yield the firm little experience in conducting international business. Further, for firms that passively rely on the actions of others, the potential short-term and long-term profits available from indirect exporting are often limited.

Direct Exporting. Direct exporting involves sales to customers—either distributors or end-users—located outside the firm's home country. Research suggests that in one third of cases, a firm's initial direct exporting to a foreign market is the result of an unsolicited order. However, its subsequent direct exporting typically results from deliberate efforts to expand its business internationally. In such cases, the firm actively selects the products it will sell, the foreign markets it will service, and the means by which its products will be distributed in those markets. Through direct exporting activities, the firm gains valuable expertise about operating internationally and specific knowledge concerning the individual countries in which it operates. And export success often breeds additional export success. Increasing experience with exporting often prompts a firm to become more aggressive in exploiting new international exporting opportunities.[28] Such experience also often proves useful if the firm later engages in FDI. Baskin-Robbins, for example, followed this deliberate approach in entering the Russian market. It began by shipping ice cream to that country in 1990 from company-owned plants in Canada and Texas. Over a five-year period, the company opened up 74 retail outlets with Russian partners, carefully observing the likes and dislikes of local consumers. Finally, in 1995 Baskin-Robbins invested $30 million in a new ice cream plant in Moscow, ensuring a constant flow of Jamoca Almond Fudge and (at least) 30 other flavors to please Russian appetites.[29]

Intracorporate Transfers. A third form of export activity is the intracorporate transfer, which has become more important as the sizes of MNCs have increased. An **intracorporate transfer** is the selling of goods by a firm in one country to an affiliated firm in another. For example, when British Petroleum ships crude oil from its storage facilities in Kuwait to its Australian subsidiary, the transaction is counted as a Kuwaiti export and an Australian import, but the revenues for the transaction remain within the same firm.

Intracorporate transfers are an important part of international trade. They account for about 40 percent of all U.S. merchandise exports and imports.[30] Many MNCs constantly engage in such transfers, importing and exporting semifinished products and component parts in order to lower their production costs. By so doing, they use the productive capacity of both their domestic and foreign factories more efficiently by concentrating production of individual inputs at specific factories and shipping these inputs to other factories as needed. (We discuss these factors more thoroughly in Chapter 17 when we analyze the global sourcing strategies of MNCs.) For example, consider the Ford Crown Victoria automobile. Ford's U.S. assembly plant imports the automobiles' fuel tank, windshield, instrument panel, and seats from Ford factories in Mexico, their wheels from a Ford factory in England, their electronic engine control system from a Ford factory in Spain, and their electronic con-

Baskin-Robbins' decision to build a new plant in Moscow was the result of a careful, well-thought out entry strategy. The factory not only provides jobs for its workers, but also free ice cream!

trol system for their antilock brakes from a Ford factory in Germany.[31] Ford's intricate meshing of inputs produced at various locations is typical of the behavior of many MNCs.

Such transfers are also common in the service sector. For example, the Dow-Jones Company publishes both Asian and European versions of the *Wall Street Journal* in addition to its U.S. edition. Although some of the stories in each edition are written locally and are intended for local audiences, others are written in one location and printed in all editions of the newspaper. The usage of stories first published by a Dow-Jones subsidiary in one country by Dow-Jones affiliates in other countries is an intracorporate transfer of services.

Additional Considerations

In considering exporting as its entry mode, a firm must consider many other factors besides which form of exporting to use, including (1) government policies, (2) marketing concerns, (3) logistical considerations, and (4) distribution issues.

Government Policies. Government policies may influence a firm's decision to export. Export promotion policies, export financing programs, and other forms of home country subsidization encourage exporting as an entry mode. Host countries, however, may impose tariffs and NTBs on imported goods, thereby discouraging the firm from relying on exports as an entry mode. Similarly, Japan's imposition of voluntary export restraints (VERs) on Japanese automobiles reduced Japanese exports, but also encouraged Japanese automakers to construct assembly plants in the United States.

Marketing Concerns. Marketing concerns, such as image, distribution, and responsiveness to the customer, may also affect the decision to export. Often foreign goods have a certain product image or cachet that domestically produced goods cannot duplicate. For example, buyers of Dom Perignon champagne are purchasing, at least in part, the allure of France's finest champagne. This allure would be lost should LMVH choose to produce the product in Lubbock, Texas, even though Lubbock vineyards yield a regionally acclaimed wine, Llano Estacado. Also, recall Lowenbrau's U.S. marketing disaster, described in the opening case. Produced in Munich, Lowenbrau was a premium product to U.S. consumers; produced in the United States, it was just another beer. Swiss watches, German automobiles, Italian shoes, Cuban cigars, and Scottish wool are among the other product groups whose allure is closely associated with specific countries.

The choice of exporting is also influenced by a firm's need to obtain quick and constant feedback from its customers. Such feedback is less important for standardized products whose designs change slowly, if at all, such as toothbrushes and coffeemakers. On the other hand, producers of goods such as personal computers must continually monitor the marketplace to ensure that they are meeting the rapidly changing needs of their customers. For example, Korean manufacturer Hyundai shifted its production of personal computers from Korea to the United States because it needed to be closer to its U.S. customer base.

Logistical Considerations. Logistical considerations also enter into the decision to export. The firm must consider the physical distribution costs of warehousing, packaging, transporting, and distributing its goods, as well as its inventory carrying costs and those of its foreign customers. Typically, such logistical costs will be higher for exported goods than for locally produced goods. But logistical considerations go beyond mere costs. Because exporting means longer supply lines and increased difficulties in communicating with foreign customers, firms choosing to export from domestic factories must ensure that they maintain competitive levels of customer service for their foreign customers.

Distribution Issues. A final issue that may influence a firm's decision to export is distribution. A firm experienced in exporting may choose to establish its own distribution networks in its key markets. For example, Japanese consumer electronics manufacturers like Sony, Minolta, and Hitachi typically rely on wholly owned host country subsidiaries to distribute their products to wholesalers and retailers in the Quad countries. Although the firms bear the costs of establishing and operating these distribution networks, they benefit in two ways from this approach. First, they capture additional revenues generated by performing the distribution function. Second, they maintain control over the distribution process, thereby avoiding the problems that we discuss in the following paragraphs.

However, a firm—particularly a smaller business or one just beginning to export—often lacks the expertise to market its products abroad, so it will seek a local distributor to handle its products in the target market. Critical to the firm's success is the selection of this distributor. The distributor must have sufficient expertise and resources (capital, labor, facilities, and local reputation) to successfully market the firm's products. However, often the best local distributors already handle the products of existing firms. Consequently, the firm must decide between an experienced local distributor and a less-experienced one that will handle the firm's products exclusively.

The profitability and growth potential of exporting to a foreign market will be affected by the firm's agreement with the local distributor. The local distributor must be compensated for its services, of course. This compensation will potentially reduce the exporter's profit margin. Further, the exporter and its local distributor depend on each other to ensure that a satisfactory business relationship is established and maintained. For example, if the host country distributor inadequately markets, distributes, and/or services the exporter's products, it is the exporter that will suffer lost sales and damaged reputation. Apple's initial share of the Japanese personal computer market was hurt by the performance of a Canon subsidiary hired to market and distribute the firm's products in Japan. Apple took over these tasks in the early 1990s and quickly quintupled its market share.[32]

The business judgments of the local distributor and the exporter may differ. The exporter and the importer may differ on pricing strategies, with the exporter preferring lower retail prices to stimulate sales and the distributor favoring higher prices that fatten its profit margins. The exporter may want its distributor to market its products more aggressively in hopes of building sales volume; the distributor may believe that the additional sales generated by this strategy will not cover the increased expenses incurred. For example, GM set the goal of increasing European sales of its products made in North America from 17,500 vehicles in 1991 to 250,000 vehicles by 2000. But it was concerned that paperwork and red tape discouraged its European dealers from buying North American–made GM vehicles. Thus in 1992 it shifted the responsibility of importing such cars from its individual dealers in Europe, which predominantly handle vehicles produced by GM's German subsidiary, Adam Opel AG, to a new GM subsidiary, General Motors Import & Distribution Company GmbH. The new subsidiary, in turn, was responsible for distributing the North American–made vehicles to European GM dealerships. GM believed that easing the administrative burden on individual dealerships was critical to encouraging them to sell more of its North American–made products.[33]

Because of the importance of distributors in the exporting process, many governments assist their domestic firms in the selection of foreign distributors. For example, overseas officers of the U.S. and Foreign Commercial Service regularly report back to the U.S. Department of Commerce about foreign firms interested in acting as distribution agents for U.S. exporters. The National Trade Data Bank, discussed in the Building Global Skills section of Chapter 2, incorporates a list of potential distributors in its data files.

Export Intermediaries

An exporter may also market and distribute its goods in international markets by using one or more **intermediaries**, third parties that specialize in facilitating imports and exports.[34] These specialists may offer limited services such as handling only transportation and documentation. Or they may perform more extensive roles, including taking ownership of foreign-bound goods and/or assuming total responsibility for marketing and financing exports.[35] Types of intermediaries that offer a broad range of services include the following:

- Export management companies
- Webb-Pomerene associations
- International trading companies

Export Management Company. An **export management company (EMC)** is a firm that acts as its client's export department. Smaller firms often use an EMC to handle their foreign shipments. Several thousand EMCs operate in the United States. Most are small operations that rely on the services of a handful of professionals. An EMC's staff typically is knowledgeable about the legal, financial, and logistical details of exporting and so frees the exporter from having to develop this expertise in-house. The EMC may also provide advice about consumer needs and available distribution channels in the foreign markets the exporter wants to penetrate.

EMCs usually operate in one of two ways:

1 Some act as commission agents for exporters. They handle the details of shipping, clearing customs, and document preparation in return for an agreed-upon fee. In this case, the exporter normally invoices the client and provides any necessary financing it may need.

2 Others take title to the goods. They make money by buying the goods from the exporter and reselling them at a higher price to foreign customers. Such EMCs may offer customer financing and design and implement advertising and promotional campaigns for the product.

Webb-Pomerene Association. A **Webb-Pomerene association** is a group of U.S. firms that operate within the same industry and that are allowed by law to coordinate their export activities without fear of violating U.S. antitrust laws. First authorized by the Export Trade Act of 1918, a Webb-Pomerene association engages in market research, overseas promotional activities, freight consolidation, contract negotiations, and other services for its members. It may also directly engage in exporting by buying goods domestically from members and selling the goods in foreign markets on the association's behalf. Although such associations were originally designed to allow smaller, related firms to cooperate in promoting exports, most are now dominated by larger firms. In general, Webb-Pomerene associations have not played a major role in international business. Fewer than 25 such associations exist today, and they tend to be concentrated in raw materials such as wood pulp, sulfur, and phosphate rock.

International Trading Company. An **international trading company** is a firm directly engaged in importing and exporting a wide variety of goods for its own account. It differs from an EMC in that it participates in both importing and exporting activities. By buying goods in one country and selling them in a second, an international trading company provides the gamut of necessary exporting and importing services. These include market research, customs documentation, international transportation, and host country distribution, marketing, and financing. Typically, international trading companies have agents and offices worldwide. The economic intelligence information they glean from these far-flung operations is one of their most potent competitive weapons.

The most important international trading companies in the global marketplace are Japan's sogo sosha. Recall from Chapter 2 that sogo sosha acquire goods by importing them from other countries or by having the goods manufactured and then reselling them in both domestic and foreign markets. The sogo sosha are an integral part of Japan's keiretsu system, often providing exporting, importing, marketing, distribution, and financial services for fellow keiretsu members. The Mitsubishi Corporation, for example, is the trading arm of the Mitsubishi Group, Japan's largest keiretsu. It works with the Mitsubishi Bank (the banking arm of the Mitsubishi keiretsu) to provide trading services for the keiretsu's 160 affiliates, including Mitsubishi Motors, Nikon, Kirin Brewery, Mitsubishi Electric, Asahi Glass, and the Mitsubishi Estate Company.[36] The sogo sosha also provide trading services for numerous firms that are not keiretsu members.

The sogo sosha have prospered for several reasons. Because of their far-flung operations, they continuously obtain information about economic conditions and business opportunities in virtually every corner of the world. As part of a keiretsu, a sogo sosha enjoys ready access to financing (from the keiretsu's lead bank) and a built-in source of customers (its fellow keiretsu members). This customer base reduces the sogo sosha's costs of soliciting clients and builds up its business volume, thereby allowing it to reap economies of scale in its transportation and information-gathering roles. Nonmembers of the keiretsu are then attracted to doing business with the sogo sosha because of its low cost structure and international expertise. Japan's international trading companies have been so successful that, measured by sales volume, the world's five largest service companies are all sogo sosha.[37] These five are featured in Table 11.3.

As is normal in business, the sogo sosha's success has attracted imitators. In the mid-1970s, South Korea's government ordered its chaebol to create their own trading companies in order to promote Korean exports. This effort has been successful: as discussed in Chapter 2, chaebol such as Samsung, Hyundai, and the LG Group are now a major presence in the world market. Similarly, in 1982, under the Export Trading Company Act, the United States authorized the creation of export trading companies to stimulate exports from smaller U.S. firms. An **export trading company (ETC)** is a firm that may engage in various cooperative business practices without fear of violating U.S. antitrust laws. Members of an industry may create an ETC to provide necessary exporting services, such as market research, warehousing, and/or foreign distribution. ETCs may be organized on a product basis or on a geographical basis. U.S. commercial banks also may create ETCs to facilitate the financing of U.S. exports. ETCs may engage in importing services and help U.S. firms arrange international barter transactions. So far, however, ETCs have been only modestly successful. It remains to be seen whether they will become an important component of the importing and exporting sector of the U.S. economy.

Other Intermediaries. In addition to the intermediaries that provide a broad range of services to international exporters and importers, numerous other types of intermediaries, including the following, offer more specialized services:

- **Manufacturers' agents** solicit domestic orders for foreign manufacturers, usually on a commission basis.

- **Manufacturers' export agents** act as a foreign sales department for domestic manufacturers, selling those firms' goods in foreign markets.

TABLE 11.3

The Five Largest Sogo Sosha

RANK	FIRM	1996 SALES ($ Millions)	KEY SUBSIDIARIES AND AFFILIATES
1	Mitsui & Company	144,943	Japan Steel Works, Ltd. (steel manufacturing) Mitsui Construction Company, Ltd. (construction) Mitsukoshi, Ltd. (department stores) Mitsui Mutual Life Insurance Company, Ltd. Onoda Cement Company, Ltd. (construction materials) Sakura Bank
2	Mitsubishi Corporation	140,204	Kirin Brewery (alcoholic beverages) The Mitsubishi Bank, Ltd. Mitsubishi Heavy Industries, Ltd. (construction) Mitsubishi Motor Corporation (automobiles) Nikon Corporation (cameras and video equipment) The Tokyo Marine and Fire Insurance Company
3	Itochu Corporation	135,542	American Isuzu Motors (wholesaling) ATR Wires & Cable Company (steel tire cords) Century 21 Real Estate of Japan, Ltd. (real estate brokerage) Dunhill Group Japan, Inc. (men's clothing and accessories) Mazda Motor of America (wholesaling) Time Warner Entertainment of Japan (25 percent limited partnership) VIDEOSAT, Inc. (satellite transmission of video signals)
4	Marubeni	124,027	Archer Pipe and Tube Company (steel pipe sales) Bactec Corporation (insecticides) Columbia Grain International (grain trading) Fremont Beef Company (meat processing) Kubota Tractor Company (farm equipment) Precision Tools Service, Inc. (machine tools)
5	Sumitomo Group	119,281	Asahi Breweries, Ltd. (alcoholic beverages) NEC Corp. (electronics) Nippon Sheet Glass Company The Sumitomo Bank, Ltd. Sumitomo Cement Company, Ltd. Sumitomo Chemical Company, Ltd. Sumitomo Coal Mining Company, Ltd. Sumitomo Forestry Company, Ltd. Sumitomo Metal Industries, Ltd. Sumitomo Realty & Development Company, Ltd.

- **Export and import brokers** bring together international buyers and sellers of such standardized commodities as coffee, cocoa, and grains.

- **Freight forwarders** specialize in the physical transportation of goods, arranging customs documentation and obtaining transportation services for their clients.

This list is by no means complete. Indeed, specialists are available to provide virtually every service needed by exporters and importers in international trade.

International Licensing

Another means of entering a foreign market is **licensing**, in which a firm, called the **licensor**, leases the right to use its intellectual property—technology, work methods, patents, copyrights, brand names, or trademarks—to another firm, called the **licensee**, in return for a fee. This process is illustrated in Fig. 11.3. The use of licensing as an entry mode may be affected by host country policies. Firms are not advised to use licensing in countries that offer weak protection for intellectual property, since they may have difficulty enforcing licensing agreements in the host country's courts. On the other hand, the use of licensing may be encouraged by high tariffs and NTBs, which discourage imports, or by host country restrictions on FDI or repatriation of profits.

Licensing is a popular mode for entering foreign markets. Many international firms choose it because it involves little out-of-pocket costs. A firm has already incurred the costs of developing the intellectual property to be licensed; thus revenues received through a licensing agreement often go straight to the firm's bottom line. Licensing also allows a firm to take advantage of any locational advantages of foreign production without incurring any ownership, managerial, or investment obligations.

For example, as the popularity of Japanese foods such as sushi and tempura increased and the number of Japanese expatriates worldwide rose, Kirin Brewery,

---

FIGURE 11.3

The Licensing Process

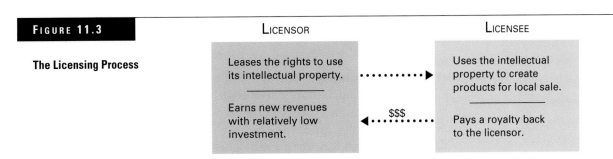

LICENSOR

Leases the rights to use its intellectual property.
_____
Earns new revenues with relatively low investment.

$$$

LICENSEE

Uses the intellectual property to create products for local sale.
_____
Pays a royalty back to the licensor.

BASIC ISSUES
1. Set the boundaries of the agreement.
2. Establish compensation rates.
3. Agree on the rights, privileges, and constraints conveyed in the agreement.
4. Specify the duration of the agreement.

Japan's largest beer producer, decided to expand internationally. Kirin wanted to maintain the beer's freshness, so exporting the beer from Japan was not an option. Its solution was to sign licensing agreements with host country producers. Molson now produces Kirin beer for the Canadian market, and the Charles Wells brewery does the same for the British market.[38]

Basic Issues in International Licensing

Of course, as in any international business arrangement, a firm involved in licensing negotiations must carefully consider the terms of the proposed license as well as its advantages and disadvantages. The terms of a licensing agreement usually reflect the relative bargaining power and negotiating skills of the licensor and the licensee. Nearly every international licensing arrangement is unique because of variations in corporate strategy, the levels of competition, the nature of the product, and the interests of the licensor and licensee. However, each licensing arrangement must also address a number of basic issues. Because of the complexities and uncertainties associated with licensing, such arrangements are usually specified in a detailed legal contract. Issues this contract typically addresses include (1) specifying the boundaries of the agreement, (2) determining compensation, (3) establishing rights, privileges, and constraints, (4) defining dispute resolution methods, and (5) specifying the duration of the contract.

Specifying the Agreement's Boundaries. The first step in negotiating a licensing contract is to specify the boundaries of the agreement. The firms involved must determine which rights and privileges are and are not being conveyed in the agreement. For example, Heineken is exclusively licensed to manufacture and sell Pepsi-Cola in the Netherlands. To implement this agreement, PepsiCo must either provide Heineken with the formula for its soft drink or supply concentrated cola syrup. Heineken is then allowed to add carbonated water to create the beverage, package it in appropriate containers, and distribute and sell it in the Netherlands. But PepsiCo cannot withhold both the formula and the syrup and cannot enter into a competing licensing agreement with another firm to sell Pepsi-Cola in the Netherlands. Similarly, Heineken cannot begin duplicating other products owned by PepsiCo (such as Lays Potato Chips) without a separate agreement. Nor can it alter PepsiCo's formula, market the firm's products as its own, or ship them outside the Netherlands.

Determining Compensation. Compensation is another basic issue that is specified in a licensing contract. Obviously, the licensor wants to receive as much compensation as possible, while the licensee wants to pay as little as possible. Yet each also wants the agreement to be profitable for the other so that both parties will willingly perform their contractual obligations. Licensees must be careful to ensure that they can reach their target levels of profitability after paying licensing fees; the licensor will attempt to establish a rate that allows it to recoup its variable costs of negotiating and enforcing the licensing agreement plus recover at least part of its fixed investment in the intellectual property being licensed. Of course, from the licensor's perspective, the license fee, after deducting these variable costs, should also exceed its opportunity costs—i.e., the profits it would have earned had it entered the market via a different entry mode.

Compensation under a licensing agreement is called a **royalty**. The royalty is usually paid to the licensor in the form of a flat fee, a fixed amount per unit sold, or, most commonly, a percentage of the sales of the licensed product or service. Although the royalty amount is often determined by prevailing market forces, royalties of 3–5 percent of sales are typical and have long been viewed as reasonable and appropriate. Some licensing agreements also guarantee a minimum royalty payment to ensure that the foreign licensee will take full advantage of the market value of whatever has been licensed rather than merely acquiring and then shelving it to keep domestic rivals from obtaining it.

Establishing Rights, Privileges, and Constraints. Another basic issue to be addressed in licensing agreements concerns the rights and privileges given to the licensee and the constraints imposed on it by the licensor. For example, if a licensee began using inferior (and hence cheaper) materials as a way to boost its profit margin, the image of the licensor's product could be severely damaged. Similarly, if the agreement involved the transfer of technology, production processes, or work methods, the licensee might be tempted to sell this information to another firm, thereby harming the licensor. Or the licensee could simply underreport licensed sales as a means of reducing its licensing fees.

To prevent these practices, licensing agreements usually limit the licensee's freedom to divulge information it has obtained from the licensor to third parties, specify the type and form of records the licensee must keep regarding sales of the licensed products or services, and define standards that will be adhered to regarding product and service quality.

Resolving Disputes. The licensing agreement should also detail how the parties will resolve disputes and disagreements. For example, suppose the licensor feels the materials the licensee uses are inferior but the licensee argues that they meet minimum quality standards. It could be expensive and time-consuming for the two parties to reconcile their differences if they wind up in court. The costs of such conflicts can be reduced if the licensing agreement requires, for example, that disagreements be resolved through the use of a third-party mediator.

Specifying the Agreement's Duration. The last part of the licensing agreement usually specifies its duration. The licensor may view the licensing agreement as a short-term strategy designed to obtain knowledge about the foreign market at low cost and with little risk. If sales of its products and services are strong, it may want to enter the market itself after the agreement has ended. Thus the licensor may seek a short-term agreement. However, if the contract's duration is too short, the licensee may be unwilling to invest in necessary consumer research, distribution networks, and/or production facilities, believing that it will be unable to amortize its investment over the life of the licensing contract. Normally the licensor wants the licensee to undertake these market development efforts. Accordingly, the greater the investment costs incurred by the licensee, the longer is the likely duration of the licensing agreement. For example, the licensees that built Tokyo Disneyland insisted on a

100-year licensing agreement with The Walt Disney Company before agreeing to invest the millions of dollars necessary to build the park. However, in most cases the term of the licensing agreement is far shorter than this.

Licensing is an important element of the strategies of many international firms. Consider the Nintendo Company. The firm manufactures electronic video game players and game cartridges. It also licenses dozens of firms worldwide to design and, in some cases, to manufacture game cartridges to be used in its game players. As part of its licensing arrangements, Nintendo provides game designers with technical specifications for how its game players work. The design firms create the games and then pay Nintendo a fee to manufacture those games. A few firms manufacture the games themselves, but they must still pay a licensing fee to Nintendo. Through licensing, Nintendo not only generates new revenues; it also inspires the development of new video games, which in turn stimulate demand for Nintendo game players. Similar arrangements are used by many video game and software firms.[39]

Another firm that relies on a licensing strategy is Cantab Pharmaceuticals PLC, a biotech firm founded in 1989 by a scientist at Cambridge University. Cantab specializes in immunogenics, a branch of medicine that uses genetically engineered vaccines and drugs to repair and rejuvenate the body's immune system to fight such diseases as herpes, genital warts, and cervical cancer. Preferring to focus its energies on developing new immunogenic drugs and lacking the resources to quickly and effectively manufacture and distribute its cutting-edge products on its own, the young British company has chosen to license its technology to pharmaceutical giants like Glaxo Wellcome, Pfizer, and SmithKline Beecham.[40]

Advantages and Disadvantages of International Licensing

Like exporting, licensing has its advantages and disadvantages. One advantage is that licensing carries relatively low financial risk, provided the licensor fully investigates its market opportunities and the abilities of its licensees. It also allows the licensor to learn more about the sales potential of its products and services in a new market without significant commitment of financial and managerial resources. Licensees benefit through the opportunity to make and sell, with relatively little R&D cost, products and services that have been successful in other international markets. Nintendo game designers, for example, have the relative safety of knowing there are millions of game system units available that will play their games.

However, licensing does have opportunity costs. Licensing agreements limit the market opportunities for both parties. For example, as long as the licensing agreement between PepsiCo and Heineken is in effect, PepsiCo cannot enter the soft-drink market in the Netherlands and Heineken cannot sell competing soft drinks such as Coca-Cola. Further, licensor and licensee mutually depend on each other to maintain product quality and to promote the product's brand image. Improper actions by one party can damage the other party. For example, if the licensor damages the image and reputation of its products as a result of bad publicity, the licensee will also suffer. If the licensee damages the product's reputation in its market through poor quality control, the adverse publicity can spill over into the licensor's other markets. Further, if the licensee or licensor does not adhere to the agreement, costly and tedious litigation may hurt both parties.

No matter how carefully worded a licensing agreement may be, there is always the risk of problems and misunderstandings. For example, several years ago Oleg Cassini licensed Jovan, the U.S. subsidiary of Beecham of Great Britain, to market the Cassini beauty products line in the United States. After signing the agreement, Jovan was approached by Diane Von Furstenberg Cosmetics with a similar proposal but better terms. Jovan subsequently signed a licensing agreement with Von Furstenberg to make and market its products instead of Cassini's. Cassini was left without a licensee in the United States. To complicate things even further, a clause in the contract between Jovan and Cassini prevented Cassini from licensing its name to any other U.S. firm. Cassini sued Jovan for $789 million. The dispute was eventually settled out of court, but it was more than three years beyond Cassini's original target date before the firm finally got its products into the United States.[41]

A final concern involves the long-term strategic implications of licensing a firm's technology. Many firms are concerned that sharing their technology will inadvertently create a future competitor. The licensee, by producing under the licensing agreement, may be able to learn the manufacturing secrets of the licensor or to develop new production tricks of its own. The licensee can also build an independent reputation for manufacturing quality and service excellence while operating under the contract. Although the licensing agreement may restrict the geographical area in which the licensee can manufacture and sell the product, once the licensing agreement expires, the former licensee may choose to expand its operations into the licensor's existing territory. This is a risk the licensor must take if it chooses to license its product.

International Franchising

Still another popular strategy for internationalizing a business is franchising. Essentially a special form of licensing, **franchising** allows the franchisor more control over the franchisee and provides for more support from the franchisor to the franchisee than is the case in the licensor-licensee relationship. International franchising is among the fastest-growing forms of international business activity today. A franchising agreement allows an independent entrepreneur or organization, called the **franchisee**, to operate a business under the name of another, called the **franchisor**, in return for a fee. The franchisor provides its franchisees with trademarks, operating systems, and well-known product reputations, as well as continuous support services such as advertising, training, reservation services (for hotel operations), and quality assurance programs.

Basic Issues in International Franchising

International franchising is likely to succeed when certain market conditions exist:

♦ The franchisor has been successful domestically because of unique products and advantageous operating procedures and systems. McDonald's was successful initially because it provided a popular menu that was consistently prepared and service that was quick and efficient.

♦ The factors that contributed to domestic success should be transferable to foreign locations. For McDonald's, "American" food is popular in other countries, efficiency and lower prices are valued by consumers worldwide, and foreign visitors to the United States usually seem to want to visit a McDonald's restaurant.

♦ The franchisor has already achieved considerable success in franchising in its domestic market. For example, there were hundreds of franchised McDonald's restaurants in the United States before the first was built abroad.

♦ There must be foreign investors who are interested in entering into franchise agreements. For well-established franchisors like McDonald's, this is typically not a problem.

Like licensing agreements, franchising agreements are spelled out in formal contracts with terms typically as follows:

♦ The franchisor receives a fixed payment plus a royalty based on the franchisee's sales for the rights to use the franchisor's name, trademarks, formulas, and operating procedures.

♦ The franchisee agrees to adhere to the franchisor's requirements for appearance, financial reporting, and operating procedures. However, franchisors are likely to allow some degree of flexibility in order to meet local customs and tastes. In fact, as with other licensing arrangements, one of the services the franchisee offers the franchisor is knowledge about the local market's culture and customs. For example, McDonald's restaurants sell beer in Germany and Switzerland and wine in France.

♦ The franchisor helps the franchisee establish the new business, provides expertise, advertising, and a corporate image, and is usually able to negotiate favorable arrangements with suppliers.

Franchising is more common in the United States than in other countries, and U.S. firms are among the leaders in international franchising. One out of three U.S.-based franchisors have at least one foreign franchisee, and half of those without foreign units plan to grow internationally in the next five years.[42] Fast-food firms such as McDonald's, Dairy Queen, Domino's, Pizza Hut, and KFC have franchised restaurants worldwide. Hotels such as Hilton and Marriott and rental car firms such as Hertz and Avis are also successful international franchisors. U.S. franchisors heavily populate Canada, the European Union, and Japan.

Of course, a number of non-U.S. firms have also been successful in franchising. Accor SA has spread its chain of Ibis, Sofitel, and Novotel hotels throughout Europe. It entered the North American market in 1979 and boosted its presence there with the $1.3 billion purchase of Motel 6 in 1990.[43] Benetton, the Italian clothing manufacturer, has franchised outlets in many countries. Allied-Lyons PLC, a British firm, owns and franchises Baskin-

Fast-food restaurants like McDonald's have been very successful in franchising their operations in foreign markets. As this German menu shows, McDonald's food looks the same just about everywhere. But beer is sold in McDonald's German restaurants and wine in its French ones.

Robbins 31 Flavors and Dunkin' Donuts. And Bridgestone Corporation, a Japanese firm, franchises both Bridgestone and Firestone tire retail outlets in the United States as well as several other countries.

Advantages and Disadvantages of International Franchising

International franchising has both advantages and disadvantages. On the plus side, franchisees can enter a business that has an established and proven product and operating system, and franchisors can expand internationally with relatively low risk and cost. A franchisor also can obtain critical information about local market customs and cultures from host country entrepreneurs that it otherwise might have difficulty obtaining. It further can learn valuable lessons from franchisees that apply to more than the host country. McDonald's, for example, benefited from this worldwide learning phenomenon (see Chapter 10). Its U.S. managers once believed that the firm's restaurants would be successful only if they were free-standing entities located in suburbs and smaller towns. A Japanese franchisee convinced the firm to allow him to open a restaurant in an inner-city office building. It quickly became one of the firm's most popular restaurants. Because of the insight of its Japanese franchisee, McDonald's now has restaurants in downtown locations in many cities throughout the world.

On the negative side, as with licensing, both parties to a franchising agreement must share the revenues earned at the franchised location. International franchising may also be more complicated than domestic franchising. For example, when McDonald's expanded to Moscow, it had to teach local farmers how to grow potatoes that met its standards. Moreover, control is also an issue in international franchising. McDonald's was once forced to revoke the franchise it had awarded a French investor because his stores were not maintained according to McDonald's standards.

Specialized Entry Modes for International Business

A firm may also use any of several specialized strategies to participate in international business without making long-term investments. Such specialized modes include contract manufacturing, management contracts, and turnkey projects.

Contract Manufacturing

Contract manufacturing is used by firms, both large and small, who outsource most or all of their manufacturing needs to other companies. By so doing, these firms reduce the amount of their financial and human resources devoted to the physical production of their products. Nike, for example, has chosen to focus its corporate energies on marketing its products and has contracted with numerous factories throughout Southeast Asia to produce its athletic footwear. Mega Toys, a $30 million Los Angeles-based company started by Charlie Woo, an immigrant from Hong Kong, similarly contracts with Chinese plants to produce the firm's inexpensive toys and party favors, allowing Mega Toys to concentrate on marketing its products. By using this approach, international businesses can focus on that part of the value chain where their distinctive competence lies and yet benefit from any locational advantages generated by host country production. However, they also surrender control over the production process, which can lead to quality problems or other unexpected surprises. Nike, for example, has suffered a string of blows to its public image—including a series of unflattering *Doonesbury* cartoons—because of reports of unsafe and harsh working conditions in Vietnamese factories churning out Nike footware.[44]

Management Contract

A **management contract** is an agreement whereby one firm provides managerial assistance, technical expertise, or specialized services to a second firm for some agreed-upon time in return for monetary compensation. For its services the first firm may receive either a flat fee or a percentage of sales. The management contract may also specify performance bonuses based on profitability, sales growth, or quality measures. Often such contracts arise as a result of governmental activities. For example, after the Saudi Arabian government nationalized Aramco in the 1970s, it hired Aramco's former owners to manage the firm. Exxon and the other former owners of Aramco, eager to maintain good ties with the Saudi government and access to Saudi oil reserves, were happy to oblige. Sometimes, a government may forbid foreign ownership of firms in certain industries but lack the technical expertise to manage those firms. Major airlines such as Delta, Air France, and KLM often sell their management expertise to small state-owned airlines headquartered in developing countries.

Management contracts allow firms to earn additional revenues without incurring any investment risks or obligations. A subsidiary of Hilton Hotels, for example, offers hotel management and reservation services to hotels that bear the Hilton logo but that are not company-owned. The benefits of Hilton's approach were so pronounced that in the early 1990s the Marriott Corporation decided to separate its hotel management operations (Marriott International) from its hotel ownership activities (Host Marriott). Marriott believed that doing this would increase its market value because professional investors would recognize the high profitability and low risks associated with its global hotel management services.[45] Similarly, in the 1990s Italy's ENI (Ente Nazionale Idrocarburi) used its knowledge of the European energy industry to aid the Algerian national oil firm, which sought to increase its presence in the European petroleum market. Under a management contract, ENI agreed to construct a network of pipelines for the Algerians and to oversee the distribution of Algerian petroleum in Europe for a predetermined but undisclosed number of years.[46]

Turnkey Project

Another specialized strategy for participating in international business is the turnkey project. A **turnkey project** is a contract under which a firm agrees to fully design, construct, and equip a facility and then turn the project over to the purchaser when it is ready for operation. The turnkey contract may be for a fixed price, in which case the firm makes its profit by keeping its costs below the fixed price. Or the contract may provide for payment on a cost plus basis, which shifts the risk of cost overruns from the contractor to the purchaser.

International turnkey contracts often involve large, complex, multiyear projects such as construction of a nuclear power plant, an airport, or an oil refinery. Managing such complex construction projects requires special expertise. As a result, most are administered by large construction firms such as Bechtel, Brown and Root, Hyundai Group, New Zealand's Fletcher Challenge Ltd., and Germany's Friedrich Krupp GmbH. The awarding of lucrative turnkey projects is often based on the availability of home government financing, such as through the Eximbank of the United States, or on political ties between the host and home countries. U.S. construction engineering firms have secured many contracts in Saudi Arabia because of the friendly relations between the two countries, while French construction companies have done well in Francophone Africa.

Turnkey projects also may be used when a firm fears that difficulties may arise in procuring resources locally. For example, when PepsiCo wanted to open its first bottling plant in the Soviet Union, it was concerned about its ability to deal with local suppliers, local building regulations, and the pervasive government bureaucracy. To get around these problems, it contracted with the Soviet government to build the plant to PepsiCo's specifications. When the plant was completed and ready for start-up, PepsiCo managers took over.

An increasingly popular variant of the turnkey project is the so-called **B-O-T project**, in which the firm *builds* a facility, *operates* it, and later *transfers* ownership of the project to some other party. Through this approach, the contractor profits from operation and ownership of the project for some period of time but bears any financial risks associated with it during this period. For example, the government of Gabon wished to upgrade the quality of electrical service and fresh water delivered to its citizens. Aided by the International Finance Corporation, a branch of the World Bank Group discussed in Chapter 4, Gabon contracted in 1997 with two foreign companies, the Electricity Supply Board International of Ireland and France's Compagnie Generale des Eaux, to operate the country's electrical and water systems for twenty years. The two companies plan to invest $600 million to improve these basic services. After the twenty-year contract expires, ownership of these assets will be transferred to the government of Gabon.

Foreign Direct Investment

Exporting, licensing, franchising, and the specialized strategies just discussed all allow a firm to internationalize its business without investing in foreign factories or facilities. However, many firms prefer to enter international markets through ownership and control of assets in host countries. Other firms may first establish themselves in a foreign market through exporting, licensing, franchising, or contract manufacturing. After gaining knowledge of and expertise in operating in the host country, they may then want to expand in the market through ownership of production or distribution facilities, as was Baskin-Robbins' strategy in Russia. The "Point-Counterpoint" feature on pages 446–447 summarizes some interesting issues involving government policies and FDI.

Such FDI affords the firm increased control over its international business operations, as well as increased profit potential. Control is particularly important to the firm if:

1 It needs to closely coordinate the activities of its foreign subsidiaries to achieve strategic synergies, as IBM has long done; or

2 It determines that the control is necessary in order to fully exploit the economic potential of proprietary technology, manufacturing expertise, or some other intellectual property right.

In one study, for example, British subsidiaries of U.S.-headquartered MNCs were found to be more effective and successful competitors in the United Kingdom than a matched set of British-owned firms, primarily because the U.S. parents were able to transfer their technological and managerial expertise to their British affiliates.[47]

FDI is also beneficial if host country customers prefer dealing with local factories. Many firms and governments participate in programs that favor locally made products—e.g., "Buy American" or "Buy Korean"—in order to promote their local economies. Equally as important, many purchasing managers perceive that local production implies greater supply certainty, faster service, and better communication with their suppliers.

On the other hand, FDI carries with it much greater risk and far more complexity than the other modes of entry. It exposes the firm to greater economic and political risks, as well as the potential erosion of the value of its foreign investments if exchange rates change adversely. A firm's decision to engage in FDI may also be influenced by government policies. As noted in Chapter 8, host countries may discourage FDI through direct controls on foreign capital, bans on the acquisition of local companies by foreigners, or restrictions on repatriation of dividends and capital; home countries can promote FDI through such devices as political risk insurance. Firms using FDI must also meet the standard challenges of managing, operating, and financing their foreign subsidiaries while facing the additional hurdle of doing so in political, legal, and cultural milieus different from their own.

There are three methods for FDI: (1) building new facilities (called the **greenfield strategy**), (2) buying existing assets in a foreign country (called the **acquisition strategy** or the **brownfield strategy**), and (3) participating in a joint venture.

The Greenfield Strategy

The greenfield strategy involves starting a new operation from scratch (the word *greenfield* arises from the image of starting with a virgin green site and then building on it). The firm buys or leases land, constructs new facilities, hires and/or transfers in managers and employees, and then launches the new operation. Fuji's recently opened film production factory in South Carolina represents a greenfield investment, as does the Mercedes-Benz automobile assembly plant in Alabama and Nissan's factory in Sunderland, England.

The greenfield strategy has several advantages:

♦ The firm can select the site that best meets its needs and construct modern, up-to-date facilities. Local communities often offer economic development incentives to attract such facilities because they will create new jobs; these incentives lower the firm's costs.

♦ The firm starts with a clean slate. Managers do not have to deal with existing debts, nurse outmoded equipment, or struggle to modify ancient work rules protected by intransigent labor unions. For example, GM's managers consider a major advantage of its new Eisenach factory in former East Germany to be its ability to implement Japanese-style production techniques and labor policies without having to battle workers wedded to the old way of doing things.

♦ The firm can acclimate itself to the new national business culture at its own pace, rather than having the instant responsibility of managing a newly acquired, ongoing business. Recent research, for example, indicates that the greater the cultural differences between the home and host countries, the more likely a firm is to choose to build a new factory rather than purchase an existing firm.[48]

However, the greenfield strategy has some disadvantages:

♦ Successful implementation takes time and patience.

♦ Often land in the desired location is unavailable or very expensive.

♦ In building the new factory, the firm must comply with various local and national regulations and oversee the factory's construction.

♦ The firm must recruit a local workforce and train it to meet the firm's performance standards.

♦ The firm, by constructing a new facility, may be more strongly perceived as a foreign enterprise.

Disney managers faced several of these difficulties in building Disneyland Paris. Although the French government sold the necessary land to Disney at bargain prices, Disney was not fully prepared to deal with French construction contractors. For example, Disney executives had numerous communications difficulties with a painter that applied 20 different shades of pink to a hotel be-fore the firm approved the color. The park's grand opening was threatened when local contractors demanded an additional $150 million for extra work allegedly requested by Disney. And Disney clashed with its French employees, who resisted the firm's attempt to impose its U.S. work values and grooming standards on them.[49]

The Acquisition Strategy

A second FDI strategy is acquisition of an existing firm conducting business in the host country. Although the actual transaction may no doubt be very complex—involving bankers, lawyers, regulators, and mergers and acquisitions specialists from several countries—the basic motivation for this strategy is quite simple. By acquiring a going concern, the purchaser quickly obtains control over the acquired firm's factories, employees, technology, brand names, and distribution networks. The acquired firm can continue to generate revenues as the purchaser integrates it into its overall international strategy. And, unlike the greenfield strategy, the acquisition strategy adds no new capacity to the industry. In times of overcapacity, this is an obvious benefit of the latter approach. Of course, in times of underca-pacity, this benefit disappears.

Sometimes international businesses acquire local firms simply as a means of entering a new market. For example, in 1997 Procter & Gamble chose to enter the Mexican tissue products market by purchasing Loreto y Pena Pobre from its owner, Grupo Carso SA. By so doing, it acquired Loreto's manufacturing facilities, its well-known tissue and toilet paper brand names, and its existing distribution system.[50] Similarly, Cementos Mexicanos SA (commonly known as Cemex), the dominant cement producer in Mexico, expanded its position in the global cement industry during the 1990s by buying up competitors in Europe, the United States, South America, and the Caribbean.[51]

At other times, acquisitions may be undertaken by a firm as a means of implementing a major strategic change. For example, the state-owned Saudi Arabian Oil Co. has tried to reduce its dependence on crude oil production by purchasing "downstream" firms, such as Petron Corporation, the largest petro-leum refiner in the Philippines, and South Korea's Ssangyong Oil Refining Company. It also owns half of Star Enterprise, which distributes Texaco's petro-leum products in the United States.[52] Similarly, after its privatization in 1994, Koninklijke PTT Netherland, the Netherlands' formerly state-owned postal and telephone company, determined that it would need to expand interna-tionally if it were to survive in the European Union's deregulated market. To further its goal of being the world's largest mail company and to improve its competitiveness against such firms as Federal Express, DHL Worldwide Express, and United Parcel Service, it purchased Australia's TNT Ltd. in 1996, allowing it to combine its postal operations with TNT's express package deliv-ery services.[53]

The acquisition strategy does have some disadvantages, however. The acquiring firm assumes all the liabilities—financial, managerial, and otherwise—of the acquired firm. For example, if the acquired firm has poor labor relations, unfunded pension obligations, or hidden environmental cleanup liabilities, the acquiring firm becomes financially responsible for solving the problem. The acquiring firm usually must also spend substantial sums up front. For example, when Matsushita purchased U.S. entertainment conglomerate MCA for $6.6 billion in the early 1990s, it had to pay out this vast sum shortly after the deal was closed. The greenfield strategy, in contrast, may allow a firm to grow slowly and spread its investment over an extended period. For example, Honda developed its Ohio operations gradually, beginning with a motorcycle factory in 1972 and adding an automobile assembly plant in 1982. Since 1984, Honda has added an engine factory and expanded its manufacturing capacity as its strategy for succeeding in the U.S. market has evolved. An international acquisition may also reveal unexpected local issues that must be subsequently resolved. For example, after Matsushita bought MCA, it discovered that one of MCA's subsidiaries operated concessions at several U.S. national parks, including Yosemite National Park. Some U.S. government officials expressed concerns that such activities should not be controlled by foreigners. MCA eventually sold the subsidiary to a U.S. firm in order to placate critics.

Joint Ventures

Another form of FDI is the joint venture. **Joint ventures** are created when two or more firms agree to work together and create a jointly owned separate firm to promote their mutual interests. The number of such arrangements is burgeoning as rapid changes in technology, telecommunications, and government policies outstrip the ability of international firms to exploit opportunities on their own. Because of the growing importance of international intercorporate cooperation, as well as the unique set of challenges it offers international firms, we devote Chapter 12 to this subject.

CHAPTER REVIEW

Summary

An important aspect of international strategy formulation is determining which markets to enter. To make this decision, a firm must consider many factors, including market potential, competition, legal and political environments, and sociocultural influences. It must also carefully assess the costs, benefits, and risks associated with each prospective market. Once a firm has decided to expand its international operations and assessed potential foreign markets, it must decide how to enter and compete most effectively in the selected foreign markets. An array of strategic options is available for doing this. Choosing an entry mode involves careful assessment of firm-specific ownership advantages, location advantages, and internalization advantages.

Exporting, the most common initial entry mode, is the process of sending goods or services from one country to other countries for use or sale there. Exporting continues to grow rapidly. There are several forms of exporting, including indirect exporting, direct exporting, and intracorporate transfer. In deciding whether to export, a firm must consider such factors as government policies, marketing concerns, consumer information needs, logistical considerations, and distribution issues. Export intermediaries are often used to facilitate exporting. These include export management companies, Webb-Pomerene associations, international trading companies, and export trading companies.

International licensing, another popular entry mode, occurs when one firm leases the right to use its intellectual property to another firm. Basic issues in international licensing include negotiating mutually acceptable terms, determining compensation, defining the rights and privileges of and the constraints imposed on the licensee, and specifying the duration of the agreement.

International franchising is also growing rapidly as an entry mode. International franchising is an arrangement whereby an independent organization or entrepreneur operates a business under the name of another. Several market conditions must exist in order for a firm to successfully franchise. As with licensing agreements, the terms of a franchising agreement are usually quite detailed and specific.

Three specialized entry modes are contract manufacturing, the management contract, and the turnkey project. Contract manufacturing permits a firm to outsource physical production of its product and focus its energies on some other element of the value chain. A management contract calls for one firm to provide managerial assistance, technical assistance, or specialized services to another firm for a fee. A turnkey project involves one firm agreeing to fully design, construct, and equip a facility for another.

The most complex entry mode is FDI. FDI involves the ownership and control of assets in a foreign market. The greenfield strategy for FDI calls for the investing firm to start a totally new enterprise from scratch. The acquisition strategy, in contrast, involves buying an existing firm or operation in the foreign market. In joint ventures, a third form of FDI, ownership and control are shared by two or more firms.

Review Questions

1. What are the steps in conducting a foreign market analysis?

2. What are some of the basic issues a firm must confront when choosing an entry mode for a new foreign market?

3. What is exporting? Why has it increased so dramatically in recent years?

4. What are the primary advantages and disadvantages of exporting?

5. What are three forms of exporting?

6. What is an export intermediary? What is its role? What are the various types of export intermediaries?

7. What is international licensing? What are its advantages and disadvantages?

8. What is international franchising? What are its advantages and disadvantages?

9. What are three specialized entry modes for international business, and how do they work?

10. What is FDI? What are its three basic forms? What are the relative advantages and disadvantages of each?

Questions for Discussion

1. Do you think it is possible for someone to make a decision about entering a particular foreign market without having visited that market? Why or why not?

2. How difficult or easy do you think it is for managers to gauge the costs, benefits, and risks of a particular foreign market?

3. How does each advantage in Dunning's eclectic theory specifically affect a firm's decision regarding entry mode?

4. Why is exporting the most popular initial entry mode?

5. What specific factors could cause a firm to reject exporting as an entry mode?

6. What conditions must exist for an intracorporate transfer to be cost-effective?

7. Your firm is about to begin exporting. In selecting an export intermediary, what characteristics would you look for?

8. Do you think trading companies like Japan's sogo sosha will ever become common in the United States? Why or why not?

9. What factors could cause you to reject an offer from a potential licensee to make and market your firm's products in a foreign market?

10. Under what conditions should a firm consider a greenfield strategy for FDI? An acquisition strategy?

BUILDING GLOBAL SKILLS

When Heineken enters a new market, it follows a basic set of steps designed to maximize its potential profits in that market:

1. It often begins to export its beer into that market as a way to boost brand familiarity and image.

2. If sales look promising, it then licenses its brands to a local brewer. Doing this allows Heineken to build its sales further while simultaneously becoming more familiar with local distribution networks.

3. If this relationship also yields promising results, Heineken then either buys partial ownership of the local brewer or forms a new joint venture with that brewer.

The end result is a two-tier arrangement with the more expensive Heineken label at the top end of the market and the lower-priced local brands at the bottom, all sharing a common brewery, sales force, and distribution network.

After reading and thinking about Heineken's approach, break up into groups of four or five people each and proceed as follows:

1. Identify at least five products or brands you are familiar with that could use the same three-step approach perfected by Heineken for entering foreign markets. Develop a clear rationale to support each example.

2. Identify at least five products or brands that probably could not use that strategy. Develop a clear rationale to support each example.

3. Randomly list the ten examples you identified, keeping the rationale for each hidden. Exchange lists with another group. Each group should discuss the list given to it by the other group and classify the various products or brands into one of two categories: "can copy Heineken's approach" and "cannot copy Heineken's approach." Be sure to have some rationale for your decision.

4. Each pair of groups that exchanged lists should form one new group. Compare lists and note areas in which the smaller groups agreed and disagreed on their classifications. Discuss the reasons for any disagreements in classification.

Follow-up Questions

1. What are the specific factors that enable Heineken to use the approach described and simultaneously make it difficult for some other firms to copy it? What types of firms are most and least likely to be able to use this approach?

2. What does this exercise teach you about international business?

WORKING WITH THE WEB: Building Global Internet Skills

Assessing Foreign Market Entry Conditions

A variety of useful information about domestic and foreign markets is available on the Internet. Statistics about population, per capita income, consumption of different products, and other relevant information are provided by national governments, international organizations, and private companies. Similarly, information about national laws affecting business activity are available from a variety of sources. For example, the U.S. State Department's *Country Commercial Guides* are posted on its web site. (Links to its web site, and others that may be of use for this assignment, are available at the textbook's web site.)

Now, assume that you own a chain of computer accessory stores, which sell such items as software, speakers, keyboards, anti-glare screens, mouse pads,

and so forth. Some of your stores are company-owned, while others are franchised. You have a total of 300 retail outlets, located in most major U.S. cities, and you see only limited opportunities for future growth in the U.S. market.

You have recently decided to look into the possibility of expanding into foreign countries. Start by making a list of ten countries that would seem like logical candidates for foreign expansion. Then visit the country guides mentioned above and any other relevant sources and research their business regulations. Rank in order the countries on the basis of apparent ease of entry and determine which mode of entry would be most appropriate to use in each country.

CLOSING CASE

GE Picks Its Markets Well[54]

For years now the world's major companies have tried to figure out how to play the global game. Some have sought a "one-size-fits-all" strategy. They select a country for entry, build a huge factory, and then churn out their products in cookie-cutter fashion for distribution throughout the region.

In 1992 General Electric was also pursuing this same strategy. That year it dispatched a senior executive named Bruce Albertson to China. His mission? To find a huge existing facility that could be used to produce GE appliances and owned by a company suitable for partnership with the elite American firm. The goal was to develop a facility that could be used to supply appliances throughout Southeast Asia.

But Albertson found that he was spinning his wheels. He would find a potential partner, bring the details back home, and get shot down because some aspect of the partnership did not meet GE's rigid

financial goals. He would then return to China and line up another prospect, only to find out that it, too, failed to measure up.

He and other managers at GE eventually figured out the problem. For one thing, China already had surplus capacity for making appliances, with over 100 air conditioner manufacturers in the Guangdong province alone. For another, most companies in China used outdated technology. And for yet another, distribution was a nightmare. These and other problems simply made it impossible for GE to find a single partner that could help it meet all of its requirements.

So, instead of using a single giant factory to supply all of Asia, GE decided instead to evaluate each country and each region separately and make smaller deals that best fit each local situation. For example, GE used this approach when it decided to partner with the Shanghai Communication & Electrical Appliance Commercial Group—but only for distribution. Another partner was found for the actual construction of refrigerators while another was selected for stoves.

General Electric has subsequently taken this approach to ever higher levels of sophistication. In India and the Philippines, for example, single partners with the manufacturing, marketing, and financial standards desired by GE were identified and locked up in traditional arrangements. But in Indonesia, like China, a patchwork matrix of firms is involved, each with its own strengths and weaknesses.

When GE is considering a specific market, it examines every aspect of that market under the keenest of microscopes. For example, managers look at the quality and strength of local competitors, the market's growth potential, and the availability of skilled labor. The firm then tailors a mix of products, brands, manufacturing facilities, marketing, and retail approaches best suited for the market.

General Electric is also pioneering new methods for doing business in foreign markets. In Japan, for example, normal distribution channels call for products to pass through myriad intermediaries, each of which adds a markup to the product as it is passed on to the next intermediary. But GE recently struck a deal with Japan's biggest discount chain, Kojima, that eliminates all intermediaries—appliances are shipped directly from GE factories to Kojima stores. As a result, a refrigerator that sold for $10,000 under the previous system now carries a price tag of $4,000. And GE sold over 20,000 during the first month of the new deal.

How has this strategy affected GE's bottom line? While Whirlpool has lost millions in Asia and Maytag and Electrolux have maybe broken even, experts peg GE's annual Asian appliance profits at over $320 million.

Case Questions

1. What are the advantages and disadvantages of GE's approach?

2. Why don't more firms use GE's approach to market selection and entry?

3. What kinds of products would seem to be most suited to a "one-size-fits-all" approach, and what kinds are likely to be customized for local use?

CHAPTER NOTES

1. "Heineken's Battle to Stay Top Bottle," *Business Week*, August 1, 1994, pp. 60–62; Gary Hoover, Alta Campbell, Alan Chai, and Patrick J. Spain (eds.), *Hoover's Handbook of World Business 1994* (Austin, Tex.: Reference Press, 1993), p. 250; Brett Duval Fromson, "Cheers to Heineken," *Fortune*, November 19, 1990, p. 172.

2. "Replacing Inventory with Information," *Forbes*, March 24, 1997, pp. 54–58; "Heineken finds strong global brew," *Financial Times*, February 7, 1996, p. 16.

3. Anoop Madhok, "Cost, Value, and Foreign Market Entry Mode: The Transaction and the Firm," *Strategic Management Journal*, Vol. 18, 1997, p. 37.

4. See George S. Yip and George A. Coundouriotis, "Diagnosing Global Strategy Potential: The World Chocolate Confectionery Industry," *Planning Review*, January–February 1991, pp. 4–14, for an example of how this can be done.

5. William H. Davidson, "The Role of Global Scanning in Business Planning," *Organizational Dynamics*, Winter 1991, pp. 4–16.

6. John H. Dunning, "Governments, Markets and Multinational Enterprises: Some Emerging Issues," *The International Trade Journal*, Vol. 7, No. 1 (Fall 1992), pp. 1–14.

7. Peter Smith Ring, Stefanie Ann Lenway, and Michele Govekar, "Management of the Political Imperative in International Business," *Strategic Management Journal*, Vol. 11, 1990, pp. 141–151.

8. C. Fred Bergsten and Edward M. Graham, "Needed: New International Rules for Foreign Direct Investment," *The International Trade Journal*, Vol. 7, No. 1 (Fall 1992), pp. 15–44.

9. "Ford plans $800m Brazil plant," *Financial Times*, October 3, 1997, p. 6; "GM plans to develop car in Brazil," *Financial Times*, June 3, 1997, p. 5.

10. "Russia falls to 'Snickerization' Campaign," *Houston Chronicle*, October 8, 1995, p. 5D.

11. J. Behrman and R. Grosse, *International Business and Governments* (Columbia, S.C.: University of South Carolina Press, 1990).

12. M. Krishna Erramilli, "The Experience Factor in Foreign Market Entry Behavior of Service Firms," *Journal of International Business Studies*, Vol. 22, No. 3 (Third Quarter 1991), pp. 479–501.

13. "A Beautiful Face Is Not Enough," *Forbes*, May 13, 1991, pp. 105–106.

14. Susan C. Schneider and Arnoud De Mayer, "Interpreting and Responding to Strategic Issues: The Impact of National Culture," *Strategic Management Journal*, Vol. 12 (1991), pp. 307–320.

15. John H. Dunning, "Trade, Location of Economic Activity and the MNE: A Search for an Eclectic Approach," in Bertil Ohlin et al., eds., *The International Allocation of Economic Activity* (London: Macmillan, 1977); Alan M. Rugman, "A New Theory of the Multinational Enterprise: Internation-alization versus Internalization," *Columbia Journal of World Business*, 1980, pp. 23–29.

16. "Siam Cement Looks Solid to Analysts Despite Building Slump, New Rivalry," *Wall Street Journal*, October 13, 1992, p. C21.

17. Jean J. Boddewyn, "Political Aspects of MNE Theory," *Journal of International Business Studies*, Vol. 19, No. 1 (1988), pp. 341–363; Thomas L. Brewer, "Effects of Government Policies on Foreign Direct Investment as a Strategic Choice of Firms: An Expansion of Internalization Theory," *The International Trade Journal*, Vol. 7, No. 1 (Fall 1992), pp. 111–129.

18. "Egypt Suddenly Is a Magnet for Investors," *Wall Street Journal*, April 10, 1997, p. A6.

19. "Istanbul's Location Again Makes It Crucial to the Entire Region," *Wall Street Journal*, March 27, 1997, p. A1.

20. Kenichi Ohmae, "The Global Logic of Strategic Alliances," *Harvard Business Review*, March–April 1989, p. 151.

21. John M. Stopford and Louis T. Wells, *Managing the Multinational Enterprise: Organization of the Firm and Ownership of the Subsidiaries* (New York: Basic Books, 1972).

22. M. Krishna Erramilli, "The Experience Factor in Foreign Market Entry Behavior of Service Firms," *The Journal of International Business Studies*, Vol. 22, No. 3 (Third Quarter 1991), pp. 479–502.

23. Bruce Kogut, "Designing Global Strategies: Profiting from Operational Flexibility," *Sloan Management Review*, Fall 1985, pp. 27–38; Edward W. Desmond, "Byting Japan," *Time*, October 5, 1992, pp. 68–69.

24. W. Chan Kim and Peter Hwang, "Global Strategy and Multinationals' Entry Mode Choice," *Journal of International Business Studies*, Vol. 23, No. 1 (First Quarter

1992), pp. 29–54; see also Sumantra Ghoshal, "Global Strategy: An Organizing Framework," *Strategic Management Journal*, Vol. 8 (1987), pp. 425–440.

25. Sanjeev Agarwal and Sridhar N. Ramaswami, "Choice of Foreign Market Entry Mode: Impact of Ownership, Location, and Internalization Factors," *Journal of International Business Studies*, Vol. 23, No. 1 (First Quarter 1992), pp. 1–28.

26. "Latin Links," *Wall Street Journal*, September 24, 1992, p. R6.

27. "Top Toilet Makers from U.S. and Japan Vie for Chinese Market," *Wall Street Journal*, December 19, 1996, p. A1.

28. Geir Gripsud, "The Determinants of Export Decisions and Attitudes to a Distant Market: Norwegian Fishery Exports to Japan," *The Journal of International Business Studies*, Vol. 21, No. 3 (Third Quarter 1990), pp. 469–494.

29. "Baskin-Robbins to open plant in Moscow," *Bryan College Station Eagle*, August 14, 1995, p. A1.

30. F. Steb Hipple, "Multinational Companies and International Trade: The Impact of Intrafirm Shipments on U.S. Foreign Trade 1977–1982," *Journal of International Business Studies*, Vol. 21, No. 3 (Third Quarter 1990), pp. 495–504.

31. Alex Taylor III, "Do You Know Where Your Car Was Made?" *Fortune*, June 17, 1991, pp. 52–56.

32. Desmond, op. cit.

33. "German Unit Is Established for Importing, Distribution," *Wall Street Journal*, October 8, 1992, p. C15.

34. See *A Basic Guide to Exporting* (Washington, D.C.: U.S. Department of Commerce, 1986) and *Importing into the United States* (Washington, D.C.: U.S. Department of the Treasury, 1986) for general introductions to exporting and importing.

35. For a discussion of the theory of export intermediaries, see Anne C. Perry, "The Evolution of the U.S. International Trade Intermediary in the 1980s: a Dynamic Model," *Journal of International Business Studies*, Vol. 21, No. 1 (First Quarter 1990), pp. 133–153.

36. "The World's 100 Largest Banks," *Wall Street Journal*, September 24, 1992, p. R27; Hoover et al., op. cit., p. 238.

37. *Fortune*, August 4, 1997, pp. F2–F3. Because sogo sosha are involved primarily in buying and selling goods on very small profit margins, they are often excluded from lists of the world's largest firms.

38. "Creating a worldwide yen for Japanese beer," *Financial Times*, October 7, 1992, p. 20.

39. "Nintendo to Ease Restrictions on U.S. Game Designers," *Wall Street Journal*, October 22, 1991, pp. B1, B4.

40. "Cantab Bounces Back with a Fierce Immune Response," *Wall Street Journal*, March 31, 1997, p. B4.

41. "Oleg Cassini, Inc., Sues Firm over Licensing," *Wall Street Journal*, March 28, 1984, p. 5.

42. *Wall Street Journal*, November 13, 1992, p. 132.

43. Hoover et al., op. cit., p. 145.

44. "Unsafe conditions at Nike factory in Vietnam revealed in '96 audit," *Houston Chronicle*, November 10, 1997, p. 18A.

45. "Hospitality Split," *Time*, October 19, 1992, p. 22.

46. "Can a Pumped-Up ENI Get into Fighting Trim?" *Business Week*, May 27, 1991, pp. 76–77.

47. J. H. Dunning, *American Investment in British Manufacturing Industry* (London: George Allen and Unwin, 1958).

48. Bruce Kogut and Harbir Singh, "The Effect of National Culture on the Choice of Entry Mode," *Journal of International Business Studies*, Vol. 19 (Fall 1988), pp. 411–432.

49. "Disney's Rough Ride in France," *Fortune*, March 23, 1992, p. 14.

50. "Carso Unit Provides Entry to Mexican Tissue Market," *Wall Street Journal,* July 22, 1997, p. A13.

51. "Model Cross-Border Deal Proves Costly," *Wall Street Journal*, December 7, 1995, p. A10.

52. "Saudis Hope to Jump-Start Oil Industry," *Wall Street Journal*, December 6, 1995, p. A12.

53. "KPN Grows to Challenge Delivery Giants," *Wall Street Journal*, December 17, 1996, p. A14.

54. Linda Grant, "GE's 'Smart Bomb' Strategy," *Fortune*, July 21, 1997, pp. 109–110; *Hoover's Handbook of American Business 1997* (Austin, Tex.: Hoover's Business Press, 1996), pp. 632–633.

Should Nations Encourage Foreign Direct Investment?

Yes, it provides important advantages to the world and national economies

The economic benefits of foreign direct investment (FDI) are numerous. From a global perspective, FDI is an important means of promoting economic efficiency. Encouraging FDI allows capital to flow where it is most valuable. Moreover, FDI facilitates the production of goods and services in locations that have a comparative advantage for such production.

FDI also provides many economic benefits to national economies. FDI in the form of new factories generates employment opportunities in the communities where the factories are built. These newly hired individuals in turn spend their paychecks in the local community, boosting sales and government tax revenues and inducing auto dealers, grocery stores, retailers, and others to add to their own payrolls.

But the benefits of FDI go beyond increased employment. Like any other form of capital investment, FDI enhances labor productivity. Increases in labor productivity in turn lead to higher wage rates, improved overall productivity, and lower inflation rates. Increasing the supply of capital available within a country lowers domestic interest rates, leading to lower borrowing costs for businesses and consumers. In short, attracting foreign capital is one way a national government can improve the living standard of its people.

FDI also brings with it new ways of doing business that improve the efficiency of the national economy. The transfer of technology often accompanies FDI, as foreign firms introduce new technologies and management techniques to the host country. For example, the Japanese companies Honda and Toyota brought their lean manufacturing and JIT inventory systems to the United States when they built assembly plants in Ohio, California, and Kentucky. U.S. manufacturers such as Harley-Davidson and General Motors have adapted these techniques to their factories, boosting their productivity and profitability.

FDI also may raise the level of competition in the national economy to the benefit of consumers, providing new or higher-quality products at lower prices. In many industries, foreign

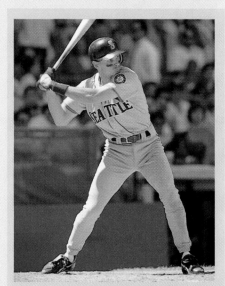

Does it make any difference to the players, the fans, or the country that the Seattle Mariners are owned by Japanese investors?

entrants often ignore "the way things have always been done" and introduce more consumer-friendly ways of doing business. For example, Swedish furniture retailer IKEA has pioneered new ways of selling furniture in Europe and North America, lowering prices in the process.

Many critics believe FDI is a Trojan horse—it looks good on the outside but carries the seeds of national destruction.

FDI may result in foreign control of the national economy. Foreigners' ownership of natural resources such as crude oil, coal, or mineral deposits may mean that these nonrenewable assets are exploited for the short-term gain of the foreigners, not the long-term benefit of the host country's citizens. Tropical rain forests in Papua New Guinea and the Solomon Islands, for example, currently are threatened by heavy logging by Malaysian firms that care little about utilizing sound reforestation practices to help future generations of islanders.

Some fear that FDI may also be used to seize a country's advanced technologies. Foreign venture capitalists are often able to buy struggling high-tech firms for a song and thereby acquire emerging technologies cheaply. Other experts believe that FDI may lead to a reduction in a country's R&D efforts. Often, when a foreign MNC buys a domestic firm, the foreign parent consolidates corporate R&D activities back at its headquarters, drying up research opportunities and jobs for domestic scientists and engineers. Similarly, FDI may lead to a reduction in the development of human capital in the host country. Companies often reserve the best jobs in their foreign affiliates for home-country managers, reducing opportunities for host-country citizens to obtain high-level training and experience.

Foreign companies also are more likely to disturb the national culture and social system. For example, U.S. and European investment bankers and securities brokers operating in Japan have disrupted decades-old pay and promotion practices in that country. Japanese firms presume that their employees will be loyal, lifelong workers and pay them based on seniority. These firms have been shocked that their Western rivals operating in Japan encourage job-hopping and base their employees' compensation on individual performance.

Sources: "Cause for Concern Behind the South Pacific Smiles," *Financial Times*, August 8, 1994, p. 3; Sun Bae Kim, "Foreign Direct Investment: Gift Horse or Trojan Horse," *Weekly Letter* (Federal Reserve Bank of San Francisco), March 20, 1992.

FDI provides these Mexican workers jobs, but will it negatively affect their culture and values?

Wrap-up

1 What are the benefits of FDI? What are the costs?

2 Should governments create agencies to review proposed FDI in their countries?

3 Should FDI be excluded from certain industries? If yes, identify those industries and explain why you believe they should remain locally owned.

International Strategic Alliances

After studying this chapter you should be able to:

Compare joint ventures and other forms of strategic alliances.

Discuss the benefits of strategic alliances.

Describe the scope of strategic alliances.

Discuss the forms of management used for strategic alliances.

Describe the limitations of strategic alliances.

THE BREAKFAST CEREAL MARKET IN EUROPE HOLDS ENORMOUS potential. Consumption of cereal is increasing rapidly, and the reduction of trade barriers makes it easier than ever to do business there. Some experts predict that the market could quadruple in the next decade. Thus it is extremely attractive, with the potential to generate enormous profits for firms wise enough to seize the opportunity. ▌▌ Kellogg virtually created the market for breakfast cereals in Europe. The maker of such popular brands as Kellogg's Corn Flakes, Rice Krispies, and Frosted Flakes, Kellogg began introducing its products in the United Kingdom in the 1920s and on the continent in the 1950s. However, Europeans traditionally favored bread, fruit, eggs, and meats for breakfast, so the firm had a tough sell on its hands. Indeed, it has taken decades for Europeans to accept cereals as a viable breakfast choice.

The European Cereal Wars[1]

▌▌ During the last several years, demand for breakfast cereals in Europe has begun to increase faster as European consumers have become more health-conscious and started looking for breakfast alternatives to eggs and meat. Also, the busy schedules of the increasing numbers of dual-career families have spurred demand for prepackaged foods. Another contributing factor has been the emergence of supermarkets in Europe. Traditionally most food products in Europe were sold at small specialty stores. Those stores were often reluctant to stock cereals because they take up so much shelf space. In recent years, however, more full-line supermarkets have opened in Europe, and shelf space is now available for a wider array of products. Finally, the growth of commercial TV outlets in Europe has helped firms increase demand through advertising. Thus the stage was set for Kellogg's competitors to move into the European breakfast cereal market. ▌▌ One of Kellogg's biggest competitors in the United States is General Mills. General Mills, which makes Cheerios, Golden Grahams, and other popular brands, has traditionally concentrated on the North American market. But in 1989 General Mills's managers decided it was time to enter the European market. However, they also recognized that taking on Kellogg, which controlled 50 percent of the worldwide cereal market and dominated the European market, would be a monumental battle. ▌▌ After careful consideration, General Mills's CEO Bruce Atwater decided that the firm could compete most effectively in Europe if it worked with a strategic ally located there. And it didn't take him long to choose one: Nestlé, the world's largest food-processing firm. Nestlé is a household name in Europe, has a well-established distribution system, and owns manufacturing plants worldwide. One major area in which Nestlé had never succeeded, however, was the cereal market. Thus Atwater reasoned that Nestlé would be a logical and willing partner. ▌▌ When he approached his counterpart at Nestlé, he was amazed to discover that that firm had already been considering approaching General Mills about just such an arrangement. From Nestlé's perspective, General Mills could contribute its knowledge of cereal technology, its array of proven cereal products, and its expertise in marketing cereals to consumers, especially children. ▌▌ Top managers of the two firms met and quickly outlined a plan of attack. Each firm contributed around $80 million to form a new firm called Cereal Partners Worldwide (CPW). General Mills agreed to install its proprietary manufacturing systems in existing Nestlé factories, oversee the production of cereals, and help develop advertising campaigns. Nestlé, in turn, agreed to use its own corporate name on the products and to handle sales and distribution throughout Europe. The two partners set two major goals for CPW: they wanted CPW to be generating annual sales of $1 billion and to be a strong number 2 in market share outside of North America by the year 2000. ▌▌ By almost any measure, CPW has been a big success and appears on track to meet its goals. Among its first triumphs was to strike a deal with Disneyland Paris to supply breakfast cereals to the restaurants and hotels at the French theme park and use Disney characters to promote the firm's cereals. The firm quickly established itself as a major player in the European cereal market and became a formidable competitor with Kellogg. Having established its beachhead in Europe, CPW then expanded its operations to Latin America and Asia. ▌▌ By 1996 CPW had achieved annual sales of $610 million and established operations in 60 countries. Interestingly, itself a joint venture (JV), CPW often uses joint ventures with local partners when entering new markets. For example, it created JVs with local partners in both Brazil and South Korea to facilitate entry into those markets. But other modes of entry have also been used. For example, CPW bought an existing cereal manufacturer in Poland as its primary mechanism for entering that Central European nation. ▌▌▌▌▌

As should be obvious by now, firms throughout the world are globalizing. But globalization can be a very expensive process, particularly when a firm must perfectly coordinate R&D, production, distribution, marketing, and financial decisions throughout the world in order to succeed. A firm may discover that it lacks all the necessary internal resources to effectively compete against its rivals internationally. The high costs just for researching and developing new products often stretch corporate budgets. Thus a firm may seek partners to share these costs. For example, Boeing enlisted the support of Japanese partners to help offset the high development costs of its latest generation of jumbo jets. Or a firm may develop a new technology but lack a distribution network or production facilities in all the national markets it wants to serve. Accordingly, the firm may seek out other firms with skills or advantages that complement its own and negotiate agreements to work together. As the chapter opener indicates, General Mills possesses extensive manufacturing knowledge and valuable brand names for breakfast cereals. It wanted to enter the European cereal market but lacked distribution networks and marketing clout with European grocery retailers. Nestlé, on the other hand, has well-established distribution and marketing expertise in Europe but lacked General Mills's extensive knowledge about manufacturing ready-to-eat cereals.

International Corporate Cooperation

Cooperation between international firms can take many forms, such as cross-licensing of proprietary technology, sharing of production facilities, cofunding of research projects, and marketing of each other's products using existing distribution networks. Such forms of cooperation are known collectively as **strategic alliances,** business arrangements whereby two or more firms choose to cooperate for their mutual benefit.[2] The partners in a strategic alliance may agree to pool R&D activities, marketing expertise, and/or managerial talent.

American Motors Corporation (now a part of Chrysler) was able to enter the Chinese market through a joint venture with the municipally owned Beijing Automotive Works. The joint venture, called Beijing Jeep, produces Jeeps and other vehicles for the Chinese market.

For example, beginning in 1992, Kodak and Fuji—two fierce competitors in the film market—formed a strategic alliance with camera manufacturers Canon, Minolta, and Nikon to develop a new standard for cameras and film, the Advanced Photo System, to make picture taking easier and more goof-proof.[3]

A **joint venture** is a special type of strategic alliance in which two or more firms join together to create a new business entity that is legally separate and distinct from its parents. Joint ventures are normally established as corporations and owned by the founding parents in whatever proportions they negotiate. Many are owned equally by the founding firms, although unequal ownership is also common. The joint venture agreement may even provide for changes in ownership shares. For example, initial ownership of the joint venture Beijing Jeep was divided equally between its owners, American Motors Corporation and the municipally owned Beijing Automotive Works. However, the joint venture agreement allows American Motors to increase its ownership stake in Beijing Jeep to 70 percent by using its share of the profits to purchase additional shares.

A strategic alliance is only one method by which a firm can enter or expand its international operations. As Chapter 11 discussed, other alternatives exist: exporting, licensing, franchising, and FDI. Each of these alternatives, however, involves a firm acting alone or hiring a second individual or firm—often one further down the distribution chain—to act on its behalf. In contrast, a strategic alliance results from cooperation among two or more firms. Each participant in a strategic alliance is motivated to promote its own self-interest but has determined that cooperation is the best way to achieve its goals.

Some means for managing any cooperative agreement is required. For example, a joint venture, as a separate legal entity, must have its own set of managers and board of directors. A joint venture may be managed in any of three ways. First, the founding firms may jointly share management, with each appointing key personnel who report back to officers of the parent. Second, one parent may assume primary responsibility. And third, an independent team of managers may be hired to run it. The third approach is often preferred, for independent managers focus on what is best for the joint venture rather than attempting to placate bosses from the founding firms.[4] Other types of strategic alliances, on the other hand, may be managed more informally—for example, by a coordinating committee, composed of employees of each of the partners, which oversees the alliance's progress.

Creation of a formal organization to manage a joint venture allows the venture to be broader in purpose, scope (or range of operations), and duration than other types of strategic alliances. A non–joint venture strategic alliance may be formed merely to allow the partners to overcome a particular hurdle that each faces in the short run. A joint venture will be more helpful if the two firms plan a more extensive and long-term relationship. A typical non-joint venture strategic alliance has a narrow purpose and scope, such as marketing a new videophone system in Canada. A joint venture might be formed if firms wanted to cooperate in the design, production, and sale of a broad line of telecommunications equipment in North America. Non-joint venture strategic alliances are often formed for a specific purpose that may have a natural ending. For example, the agreement among the camera manufacturers Canon, Minolta, and Nikon and the film manufacturers Fuji and Kodak to jointly create the Advanced Photo System for cameras and film terminated in 1996, after the new standards were developed. Each participant then marketed the resulting products on its own: Kodak called its new film Advantix, while Minolta labeled its new cameras Vectis and Nikon chose the name Nuvis.[5] But because joint ventures are separate legal entities, they generally have a longer duration.

Because of their narrow mission and lack of a formal organizational structure, non-joint venture strategic alliances are relatively less stable than joint ventures. For example, in 1988 United Airlines and British Airways entered into an agreement to form a strategic marketing alliance involving their North American and European routes. At the time, United was offering limited service to Europe and was losing market share to archrivals Delta and American Airlines, both of which offered more extensive service there. To solve its problem, United agreed to coordinate its flight schedules with British Airways, thereby making it more convenient for a Europe-bound U.S. traveler to board a domestic United flight and then transfer to a transatlantic British Airways flight. United and British Airways both prominently described the arrangement in their marketing campaigns and in the visits of their marketing reps to U.S. and European travel agencies. Within a year, however, Pan Am's routes to London were placed on the auction block. United quickly purchased those routes from Pan Am and severed relations with its strategic ally. British Airways was of little use to United once United could operate in London on its own. Needing a transatlantic partner, British Airways then entered into a similar strategic alliance with US Air in 1993. To cement the relationship, British Airways purchased a minority interest in the U.S. carrier. However, in 1996 American Airlines and British Airways agreed to form a separate strategic alliance. US Air, believing that it would be the odd man out in a three-way alliance, promptly sued British Airways and terminated their alliance.

Benefits of Strategic Alliances

Firms that enter into strategic alliances usually expect to benefit in one or more ways. As summarized in Fig. 12.1, there are four potential benefits that international business may realize from strategic alliances: ease of market entry, shared risk, shared knowledge and expertise, and synergy and competitive advantage.[6]

Ease of Market Entry

Chapter 11 discussed some of the basic factors a firm must consider when assessing potential foreign markets. Even if those factors are all favorable and the firm decides to enter a particular market, it may still face major obstacles, such as entrenched competition and hostile government regulations. Choosing a strategic alliance as the entry mode may overcome some of these obstacles or reduce the costs of entry.

Advances in telecommunications, computerization, and transportation have made it easier for international firms to enter new foreign markets. Further, economies of scale and scope in marketing and distribution confer benefits on firms that aggressively and quickly enter numerous markets.[7] Yet the costs of doing this are often large and beyond the capabilities of a single firm. Strategic alliances may allow a firm to achieve the benefits of rapid entry while keeping costs down.

For example, Warner Brothers, a movie distribution subsidiary of Time Warner, recently targeted Europe as an important growth market. To speed its entry, in 1997 it entered into several joint ventures with European movie theater chains. It established a joint venture with Lusomundo, a leading Portuguese media company, to build 20 multiplex theaters in Spain by the end of the century. It will also build 23 new multiplex theaters in the United Kingdom in partnership with Village Roadshow, an Australian-based company with extensive theater holdings in Europe.[8] A similar meshing of strengths is illustrated by a 1997 joint venture between Cigna, the U.S. insurance giant, and Banco Excel Economico, one of

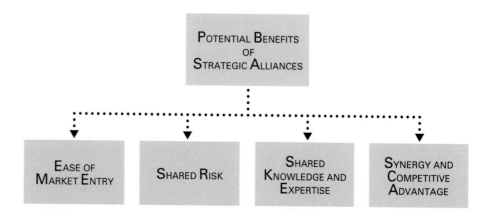

FIGURE 12.1

Benefits of Strategic Alliances

POTENTIAL BENEFITS OF STRATEGIC ALLIANCES

EASE OF MARKET ENTRY

SHARED RISK

SHARED KNOWLEDGE AND EXPERTISE

SYNERGY AND COMPETITIVE ADVANTAGE

Namibia's government has promoted development of the country's fishing industry by requiring foreign investors who wish to fish its waters to join with local partners in establishing onshore fish-processing plants. As a result, joint ventures have created jobs, both onshore and offshore, for some 10,000 Namibians.

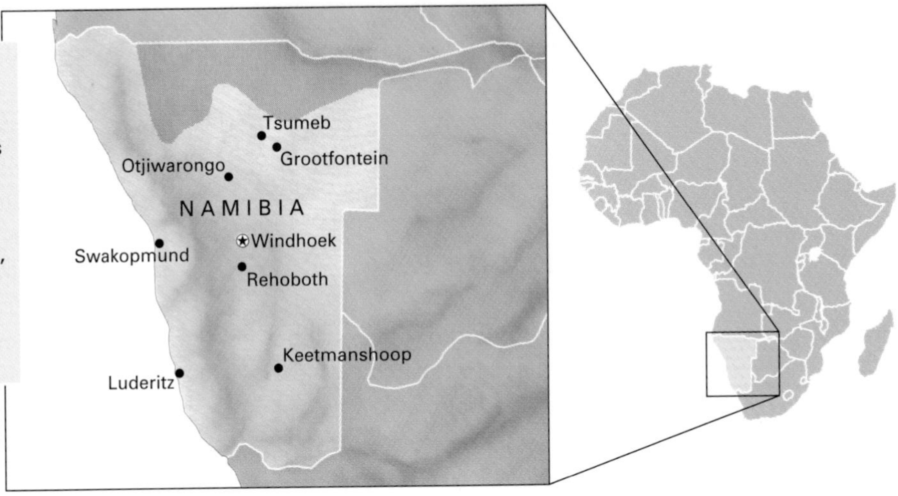

Desert and desert shrub

Wooded savanna

MAP 12.1

Namibia and Joint Ventures

Brazil's largest privately owned banks, to sell personal insurance in Brazil. Cigna provides expertise in selling life, accident, and credit insurance to consumers, while Banco Excel supplies its knowledge of the Brazilian financial service industry, as well as access to its existing retail customer base. Each partner is contributing half of the $19 million invested in the new company, Excel Cigna Seguradora.[9]

Regulations imposed by national governments also influence the formation of joint ventures. For example, many countries are so concerned about the influence of foreign firms on their economies that they require MNCs to work with a local partner if they want to operate in these countries.[10] For example, the government of Namibia, an African nation, requires foreign investors operating fishing fleets off its coast to work with local partners (see Map 12.1). At other times governments strongly encourage foreign companies to participate in joint ventures in order to promote other policy goals. A case in point is China, which has been concerned about the disappearance of local brands from store shelves since many Chinese consumers prefer Western products to often shoddy goods produced by state-owned factories. Recognizing the importance of local brands, the Coca-Cola company established a joint venture with a local company to create a noncarbonated line of drinks, Heaven and Earth, which is tailored to Chinese tastes.[11]

Many Western firms have chosen to enter the markets of the formerly communist Central and Eastern European countries in cooperation with existing domestic firms, in order to obtain information about local customers, distribution networks, and suppliers. For example, Bristol-Myers Squibb joined with the Akrihin Chemical Company in 1992 to create a joint venture that uses Akrihin's existing plant in Kupavna, Russia, to produce and package pharmaceuticals.[12] And Bestfoods (formerly known as CPC International, Inc.), a food-processing firm that sells such brands as Hellmann's mayonnaise and Mazola corn oil, has several cooperative arrangements with firms in Eastern European countries to market its products there.[13]

Shared Risk

Another common rationale for entering into cooperative arrangements is risk sharing. Today's major industries are so competitive that no firm has a guarantee of success when it enters a new market or develops a new product. Strategic alliances can be used to either reduce or control individual firms' risks. For example, a firm that independently undertakes a new venture requiring an investment of $10 million stands to lose its entire investment if the venture fails. But if it undertakes the same size project as a joint venture instead, with a 50/50 split of the $10 million investment, its greatest potential loss is equal to only $5 million. The $5 million not spent enables the firm to expand in other areas or diversify into other, lower-risk activities, thereby reducing its average risk.

For example, as mentioned earlier in the chapter, Boeing developed a strategic alliance with several Japanese firms to reduce its financial risk in the development and production of its new widebody jet, the Boeing 777. Researching, designing, developing, and safety-testing a new aircraft model costs billions of dollars, much of which must be spent before the manufacturer can establish how well the airplane will be received in the marketplace. Even though Boeing is the world's most successful commercial aircraft manufacturer, it wanted to reduce its financial exposure on the 777 project. Thus it collaborated with three Japanese partners—Fuji, Mitsubishi, and Kawasaki—agreeing to let them build 20 percent of the airframe for the new jet. Boeing, the controlling partner in the alliance, also hoped its allies would help sell the new aircraft to large Japanese customers such as Japan Air Lines and All Nippon Airways.

Or consider the strategic alliance involving Kodak and Fuji and three Japanese camera firms. At face value, it might seem odd for Kodak to agree to collaborate with Fuji, its biggest competitor, to develop a new film that both will make and sell. Closer scrutiny, however, suggests that the arrangement reduces Kodak's risks considerably. Kodak managers realized that if they developed the film alone, Fuji would aggressively fight the innovation in the marketplace and Kodak would have to work hard to gain consumer acceptance of its new standard for film. Still worse, Fuji might have decided to develop its own new standard film, thereby jeopardizing Kodak's R&D investment should the Japanese-dominated camera-manufacturing industry adopt Fuji's approach rather than Kodak's. Mindful of the financial losses incurred by Sony when VHS rather than Betamax became the standard format for VCRs, Kodak chose to include Fuji in the deal. Through this strategic alliance, Kodak reduced its risks. It also can compete on a playing field of its own choosing, free to harness its marketing clout, distribution networks, and formidable brand name against the efforts of its rivals.

Shared risk is an especially important consideration when a firm is entering a market that has just opened up or that is characterized by much uncertainty and instability. "Going Global" discusses how one international business, Otis Elevator, uses joint ventures to slash its risks in such situations.

Shared Knowledge and Expertise

Still another common reason for strategic alliances is the potential for the firm to gain knowledge and expertise that it lacks. A firm may want to learn more about how to produce something, how to acquire certain resources, how to deal with local governments' regulations, or how to manage in a different environment—information that a partner often can offer.[14] The firm can then use the newly acquired information for other purposes.

GOING GLOBAL

The Ups and Downs of Market Entry

Entering a new market is always a risky proposition, but when a firm is the first foreigner to enter, its risks are even greater. That's why many foreign firms who try to be first often look for a local partner for help. A good case in point is Otis Elevator.

A division of United Technologies, Otis has a strategy of trying to be the first foreign elevator manufacturer to enter emerging markets. For example, the firm entered China in 1984. The morning after the Berlin Wall fell, Otis executives began negotiating with prospective local partners in Central and Eastern Europe. And more recently, it was among the very first U.S. companies to announce plans to enter Vietnam when President Clinton lifted the trade embargo with that country.

Otis always looks for one or more local partners to ease its entry and reduce its risks. For example, the firm currently has five different joint ventures in China (see Map 12.2). Total investments by Otis in China now exceed $70 million, and the firm has about 25 percent of the market. Otis's sales in China are about $260 million and growing at a rapid pace. And its Vietnam deal involved two local partners, and expectations for sales and profits there are running high.

Otis sees local partners as an important mechanism for reducing its risks. These partners know the local landscape and can help the company avoid problems. They also aid the marketing of Otis's products. For example, Otis won the lucrative contract to provide 158 escalators for the Shanghai metro system thanks in part to its Chinese partners. On the other hand, Otis also often has to work hard to get its partners "up to speed." For example, it took Otis three years to get its first Chinese partner to phase out its own antiquated product line and replace it with newer Otis equipment. And convincing the partner about the benefits of customer service took even longer. To instill the service-oriented spirit vital to its success, Otis now spends over $2 million a year training its 5000 Chinese managers and employees.

Otis's strategy seems to be a sound one. Providing its local partner with cutting-edge technology, equipment, and training often yields high returns. Yet often low-tech solutions are equally as valuable. For example, the simple act of providing its new Russian work force with vans boosted productivity; previously, these workers often transported spare parts by carrying them on the Moscow subway. Otis now services over 118,000 elevators throughout Russia and Ukraine. All told, 88 percent of Otis's revenues are earned outside the United States. Perhaps more important, the company is perfectly positioned to benefit from the elevated growth prospects of many large emerging markets.

Sources: "The Pioneers," *Wall Street Journal*, September 26, 1996, pp. R1, R14; "Overseas, Otis and Its Parent Get In on the Ground Floor," *Wall Street Journal*, April 21, 1995, p. A6.

One of the more successful joint ventures in the United States has been that between Toyota and GM. In 1982 GM closed an old automobile manufacturing plant in Fremont, California, because it was inefficient. In 1984 Toyota agreed to reopen the plant and manage it through a joint venture called Nummi (New United Motor Manufacturing, Inc.). Although Nummi is owned equally by the two partners, Toyota manages the facility and makes automobiles for both. Each firm entered into the deal primarily to acquire knowledge. Toyota wanted to learn more about how to deal with labor and parts suppliers in the U.S. market; GM wanted to observe Japanese management practices firsthand.[15] Toyota used its newly acquired information when it opened its own manufacturing plant in Georgetown, Kentucky, in 1988. GM used lessons learned from Nummi in developing and operating its newest automotive division, Saturn, and in organiz-

MAP 12.2

Otis Elevators' Joint Ventures in China (Shown in Red)

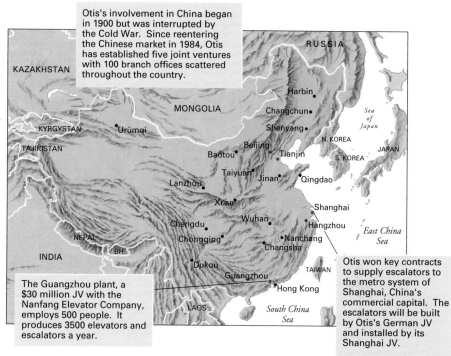

Otis's involvement in China began in 1900 but was interrupted by the Cold War. Since reentering the Chinese market in 1984, Otis has established five joint ventures with 100 branch offices scattered throughout the country.

The Guangzhou plant, a $30 million JV with the Nanfang Elevator Company, employs 500 people. It produces 3500 elevators and escalators a year.

Otis won key contracts to supply escalators to the metro system of Shanghai, China's commercial capital. The escalators will be built by Otis's German JV and installed by its Shanghai JV.

ing its new assembly plant in Eisenach, Germany. As a result, productivity in this plant is double that of GM's plants in the United States.

Synergy and Competitive Advantage

Firms may also enter into strategic alliances in order to attain synergy and competitive advantage. These related advantages reflect combinations of the other advantages discussed in this section: the idea is that through some combination of market entry, risk sharing, and learning potential, each collaborating firm will be able to achieve more and to compete more effectively than if it had attempted to enter a new market or industry alone.[16]

For example, creating a favorable brand image in consumers' minds is an expensive, time-consuming process, as is creating efficient distribution networks and obtaining the necessary clout with retailers to capture shelf space for one's products. These factors led PepsiCo, the world's second-largest soft drink firm, to establish a joint venture with Thomas J. Lipton Co., a division of Unilever, to produce and market ready-to-drink teas in the United States. Lipton, which has a 50 percent share of the $400 million worldwide market for ready-to-drink teas, provides the joint venture with manufacturing expertise and brand recognition in teas. PepsiCo supplies its extensive and experienced U.S. distribution network.[17] Similarly, Siemens and Motorola established a joint venture in 1995 to produce 64-megabyte and 256-megabyte DRAM computer chips. Motorola teamed with Siemens in part to help finance the new $1.5 billion factory the partners agreed to build, while Siemens sought to benefit from Motorola's manufacturing expertise and to improve its access to the U.S. market, which typically accounts for 40 percent of the worldwide market for DRAM memory chips.[18]

FIGURE 12.2

The Scope of Strategic
Alliances

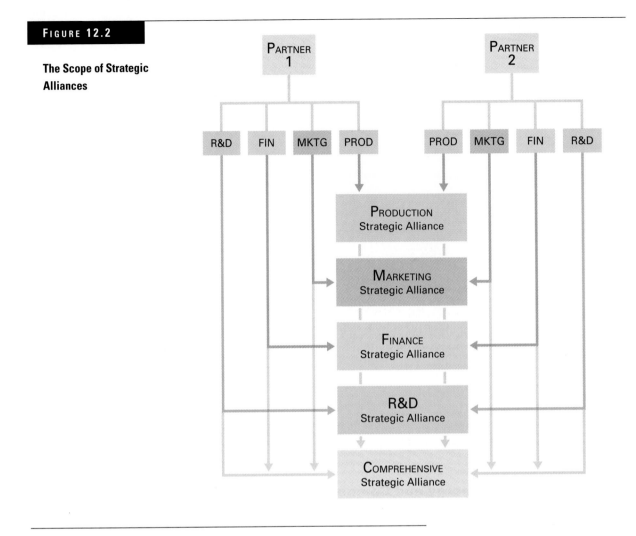

FIGURE 12.2

The Scope of Strategic
Alliances

Scope of Strategic Alliances

The scope of cooperation among firms may vary significantly, as Fig. 12.2 illustrates. For example, it may consist of a comprehensive alliance, in which the partners participate in all facets of conducting business, ranging from product design to manufacturing to marketing. Or it may consist of a more narrowly defined alliance that focuses on only one element of the business, such as R&D. The degree of collaboration will depend on the basic goals of each partner.

Comprehensive Alliances

Comprehensive alliances arise when the participating firms agree to perform together multiple stages of the process by which goods or services are brought to the market: R&D, design, production, marketing, and distribution. Because of the broad scope of such alliances, the firms involved must establish common procedures for intermeshing such functional areas as finance, production, and marketing for the alliance to succeed. Yet integrating the different operating procedures of the parents over a broad range of functional activities is difficult in the absence of a formal organizational structure. As a result, most comprehensive alliances are organized as joint ventures. As an independent entity, the joint venture can adopt operating procedures that suit its specific needs, rather than attempting to accommodate the often incompatible procedures of the parents, as might be the case with another type of strategic alliance.

Moreover, by fully integrating their efforts, participating firms in a comprehensive alliance are able to achieve greater synergy through sheer size and total resources. For example, General Mills would still have had a major uphill battle in the European cereal market if its joint venture with Nestlé had involved only a single function such as marketing. But a complete meshing of each firm's relative strengths (General Mills's cereal-making expertise and Nestlé's European distribution network and name recognition) resulted in a business unit that has emerged as a formidable competitor for Kellogg from its beginning.

Functional Alliances

Strategic alliances may also be narrow in scope, involving only a single functional area of the business. In such cases, integrating the needs of the parent firms is less complex. Thus functionally based alliances often do not take the form of a joint venture, although joint ventures are still the more common form of organization. Types of functional alliances include production alliances, marketing alliances, financial alliances, and R&D alliances.

Production Alliances. A **production alliance** is a functional alliance in which two or more firms each manufacture products or provide services in a shared or common facility. A production alliance may utilize a facility one partner already owns. For example, as we discussed earlier, the Nummi joint venture between Toyota and GM is housed in a former GM assembly plant in California, which the company had closed down. Alternatively, the partners may choose to build a new plant, as was the case in a $500 million joint venture Chrysler and BMW formed to build small, 1.4 liter four-cylinder engines in South America in 1996. Both companies believed they needed to develop this size engine if they were to compete effectively in South America and in the emerging countries of Asia. Each company determined independently that to capture economies of scale an efficient engine factory would need to produce 400,000 engines annually, yet each believed it could sell only half that number of cars powered by a 1.4 liter engine. Creation of the joint venture readily solved their problem, and, as an added bonus, allowed them better access to the rapidly growing Mercosur countries.[19]

Marketing Alliances. A **marketing alliance** is a functional alliance in which two or more firms share marketing services or expertise. In most cases, this involves one partner introducing its products or services into a market in which the other partner already has a presence. The established firm helps the newcomer by promoting, advertising, and/or distributing its products or services. The established firm may negotiate a fixed price for its assistance or may share in a percentage of the newcomer's sales or profits. Alternatively, the firms may agree to market each others' products on a reciprocal basis. For example, Mallinckrodt, a St. Louis maker of chemicals and pharmaceuticals, established a strategic marketing alliance with India's Cadila Pharmaceuticals Ltd. in 1997. Each company markets the other's medical, pharmaceutical, and laboratory products in its home market.[20] However, when forming a marketing alliance, partners must take care to ensure that their

GOING GLOBAL

Culture Clash at GM and Toyota

It seemed like a marketing marriage made in heaven, at least for General Motors. Long constrained in its ability to sell its cars in Japan, GM recently negotiated a deal with Toyota wherein the Japanese firm would market the GM Chevrolet Cavalier under a Toyota nameplate in its domestic market. But the deal has fallen on hard times, in part due to cultural clashes between the firms at both the corporate and the national levels.

Both parties, of course, knew going in that the GM car would have to be modified to fit the Japanese market. Major changes included moving the steering wheel from the left side of the car to the right and redesigning the front fenders to cover the tires (a legal requirement in Japan).

But problems surfaced when Toyota began to mandate additional changes beyond the scope of the original agreement. For example, the gas pedal needed to be moved forward to accommodate shorter drivers. And the hand brake and steering wheel had to be covered in leather to meet local consumer tastes. Toyota also found major quality problems with the GM cars, requiring rework on 80 to 90 percent of them.

From its perspective, GM sees things a bit differently. For example, it argued that too much luxury was being added, driving up the price unnecessarily and making its cars less competitive with Japanese-produced vehicles. Defects were also overstated by Toyota, charged GM. And GM managers also came to believe that their Japanese counterparts were simply looking for problems to reinforce their perceptions about lower quality in U.S. products. Thus, while the marketing venture is still in place, it has thus far proven to be a big disappointment for both partners.

Sources: "Is Cavalier Japanese for Edsel?" *Business Week*, June 24, 1996, p. 39; "Shaking Up an Old Giant," *Forbes*, May 20, 1996, pp. 68–80.

expectations and needs are mutually understood. As "Going Global" indicates, failure to reach such an understanding can reduce the success of the alliance.

Financial Alliances. A **financial alliance** is a functional alliance of firms that want to reduce the financial risks associated with a project. Partners may share equally in contributing financial resources to the project, or one partner may contribute the bulk of the financing while the other partner (or partners) provides special expertise or makes other kinds of contributions to partially offset its lack of financial investment. The strategic alliance between Boeing and its three Japanese partners was created primarily for financial purposes—Boeing wanted the other firms to help cover R&D and manufacturing costs. Those firms, in turn, saw a chance to gain valuable experience in commercial aircraft manufacturing as well as profits.

Similarly, financial concerns were also an important factor in the creation of a joint venture among Mills Corp., a Virginia-based mall operator, Kan Am International, a German investment group, and the Simon DeBartolo Group, a U.S. real estate developer, to construct the huge 1.7 million-square-foot Ontario Mills mall in San Bernadino County, California (complete with high tech video arcades, a wildlife preserve, 30 movie screens, and 214 stores) in 1996. In this joint venture, the Simon DeBartolo Group contributed its expertise in developing and constructing complex real estate projects, Mills its mall management talents, and Kan Am its financial clout.[21] And 20th Century Fox and Paramount Pictures were financial allies in producing *Titanic*, the most successful movie in history.

Titanic was filmed and marketed through a financial alliance between Paramount and Twentieth Century Fox. Although it became the highest-grossing movie in history in the U.S. and international markets, prior to its release many experts believed that both studios would take a financial bath because of *Titanic's* estimated $200 million production cost.

Research and Development Alliances. Rapid technological change in high-technology industries and the skyrocketing cost of staying abreast of that change have prompted an increasingly common type of functional alliance that focuses on R&D. In an **R&D alliance,** the partners agree to undertake joint research to develop new products or services. An example of a typical R&D alliance is one formed among Siemens, Motorola, IBM, and Toshiba in 1995 to design a one-gigabyte DRAM semiconductor chip, which they expected to be ready by the year 2001.[22] Similarly, in 1997 SGS-Thomson Microelectronics joined with Hitachi to develop a new generation of 64-bit microprocessors. SGS-Thomson agreed to transfer its knowledge of 64-bit technology, while Hitachi contributed its SuperH microprocessor design, on which it had earlier based four generations of microprocessors.[23] These alliances are usually not formed as joint ventures, since scientific knowledge can be transmitted among partners through private research conferences, the exchange of scientific papers, and laboratory visits. Moreover, forming a separate legal organization and staffing it with teams of researchers drawn from the partners' staffs might disrupt ongoing scientific work in each partner's laboratory. Instead each partner may simply agree to cross-license whatever new technology is developed in its labs, thereby allowing its partner (or partners) to use its patents at will. Each partner then has equal access to all technology developed by the alliance, an arrangement that guarantees the partners will not fall behind each other in the technological race. Partners also are freed from legal disputes among themselves over ownership and validity of patents. For example, the alliance among Kodak, Fuji, and the three Japanese camera makers focused solely on R&D. Both Kodak and Fuji are licensed to make the new film they developed; the three camera makers are free to market the cameras to use it.

Because of the importance of high-tech industries to the world economy, many countries are supporting the efforts of R&D consortia as part of their industrial policies. An **R&D consortium** is a confederation of organizations that band together to research and develop new products and processes for world markets. It represents a special case of strategic alliance in that governmental support plays a major role in its formation and continued operation. The EU has developed a wide array of joint research efforts with clever acronyms—such as ESPRIT,

RACE, BRITE, EURAM, JOULE, and SCIENCE—to ensure that its firms can compete against U.S. and Japanese firms in high-tech markets. Until the past decade, R&D consortia were virtually forbidden in the United States because of antitrust concerns. However, a new federal law passed in 1984 makes it easier for U.S. firms to create such consortia. For example, in cooperation with the U.S. Department of Defense, ten U.S. semiconductor manufacturers, including Hewlett-Packard, Intel, and Lucent Technologies, participate in SEMATECH, an Austin, Texas-based R&D consortium founded in 1987. SEMATECH's goal is to conduct and sponsor research to promote the global competitiveness of the U.S. semiconductor industry. The success of SEMATECH has caused other U.S. industries to consider creating research consortia to share R&D costs.

Japanese firms have successfully practiced this type of arrangement for many years. For example, over two decades ago the Japanese government, Nippon Telephone and Telegraph, Mitsubishi, Matsushita, and three other Japanese firms agreed to work together to create new types of high-capacity memory chips. They were so successful that they now dominate this market. However, such consortia are not always successful. A similar consortium formed in 1981, called the Fifth Generation Computer Systems Project, has yet to dislodge U.S. firms from their leadership in the high end of the supercomputer market.[24]

Implementation of Strategic Alliances

The decision to form a strategic alliance should develop from the firm's strategic planning process, discussed in Chapter 10. After a firm's top managers analyze the firm's goals, strengths and weaknesses, and market opportunities, they may decide that a strategic alliance with one or more other firms is the preferred mode for entering a foreign market. Having made this decision, they then must address several significant issues, which set the stage for how the arrangement will be managed. Some of the most critical of these issues are the selection of partners, the form of ownership, and joint management considerations.

Selection of Partners

The success of any cooperative undertaking depends on choosing the appropriate partner(s). Research suggests that strategic alliances are more likely to be successful if the skills and resources of the partners are complementary—each must bring to the alliance some organizational strength the other lacks.[25] A firm contemplating a strategic alliance should consider at least four factors in selecting a partner (or partners): (1) compatibility, (2) the nature of the potential partner's products or services, (3) the relative safeness of the alliance, and (4) the learning potential of the alliance.[26]

Compatibility. The firm should select a compatible partner with which it can work effectively and that it can trust. Without mutual trust, a strategic alliance is unlikely to succeed.[27] But incompatibilities in corporate operating philosophies may also doom an alliance. For example, an alliance between General Electric Corporation (a U.K. firm unrelated to the U.S. firm of the same name) and the German firm Siemens failed because of incompatible management styles. The former firm is run by financial experts and the latter by engineers. General Electric

Corporation's financial managers continually worried about bottom-line issues, short-term profitability, and related financial considerations. Siemens's managers, in contrast, wanted to worry less about financial issues and pay more attention to innovation, design, and product development.[28] In contrast, a key ingredient in CPW's success is the high level of compatibility between General Mills and Nestlé.

Nature of a Potential Partner's Products or Services. Another factor to consider is the nature of a potential partner's products or services. It is often hard to cooperate with a firm in one market while doing battle with that same firm in a second market. Under such circumstances, each partner may be unwilling to reveal all its expertise to the other partner for fear that the partner will use that knowledge against the firm in another market. Most experts believe a firm should ally itself with a partner whose products or services are complementary to but not directly competitive with its own. The joint venture between General Mills and Nestlé is an example of this principle in action: both are food-processing firms, but Nestlé does not make cereal, the product on which it is collaborating with General Mills. Similarly, PepsiCo and Lipton complement but do not compete with one another, thus raising the likelihood that their joint venture to market ready-to-drink tea in the United States will succeed.

Sometimes, however, a firm may receive a rude surprise. For example, JVC, a subsidiary of the Japanese firm Matsushita, wanted to enter the European VCR market. It formed a joint venture with a small German firm. The new venture, a 50/50 partnership, had only limited success because the German firm lacked the necessary marketing expertise to help JVC gain a foothold. Thomson SA, a large French electronics firm, bought out the German firm and learned the tricks for producing VCRs from JVC. JVC was unconcerned about the potential transfer of its technology to Thomson, however, because its worldwide sales totaled over 5 million VCRs compared to a mere 800,000 units for its European joint venture. Then, in the late 1980s, Thomson purchased General Electric's consumer electronics business. That purchase boosted its VCR sales to 5 million a year—making the access to JVC's technology gained through the joint venture a very valuable commodity indeed.[29]

The Relative Safeness of the Alliance. Firms should move carefully in selecting, negotiating with, and contracting with a partner. Strategic alliances should be undertaken cautiously and deliberately as part of the firm's strategic plan. Given the complexities and potential costs of failed agreements, managers should gather as much information as possible about a potential partner before proceeding with an agreement.[30] For example, managers should assess the success or failure of previous strategic alliances formed by the potential partner. Also, it often makes sense to analyze the prospective deal from the other firm's side. What does the potential partner hope to gain from the arrangement? What are the partner's strengths and weaknesses? How will it contribute to the venture? Does the proposed arrangement meet its strategic goals? The probability of success rises if the deal makes good business sense for both parties.[31]

For example, Corning, Inc., created a joint venture—Asahi Video Products Company—by integrating its television glass production with the operations of Asahi Glass, a producer of large television bulbs. Corning believed this joint venture would be a sound one for several reasons:

◆ Asahi Glass's expertise in large television bulb technology complemented Corning's strength in other bulb sizes.

+ The joint venture would benefit from Asahi Glass's ongoing business connections with the increasing number of Japanese television manufacturers that were establishing North American facilities.

+ The combined strengths of the two firms would help both keep abreast of technological innovations in the video display industry.

+ Asahi Glass would benefit from Corning's technology and marketing clout in the U.S. market.

+ Corning had successfully operated another joint venture with Asahi Glass since 1965.

In fact, Corning is so good at developing joint ventures that almost half its profits are generated by joint ventures with PPG, Dow Chemical, Samsung, Siemens, Ciba-Geigy, IBM, and, of course, Asahi Glass.[32]

The Learning Potential of the Alliance. Before establishing a strategic alliance, partners should also assess the potential to learn from each other. Areas of learning can range from the very specific—for example, how to manage inventory more efficiently or how to train employees more effectively—to the very general—for example, how to modify corporate culture or how to manage more strategically. At the same time, however, each partner should carefully assess the value of its own information and not provide the other partner with any that will result in competitive disadvantage for itself should the alliance dissolve—a point we revisit in the next section.

Form of Ownership

Another issue in establishing a strategic alliance is the exact form of ownership that is to be used. Recall from earlier in the chapter that a common type of strategic alliance is the joint venture.[33] A joint venture almost always takes the form of a corporation, and a joint venture is usually incorporated in the country in which it will be doing business. In some instances, it may be incorporated in a different country, such as one that offers tax or legal advantages. The Bahamas, for example, are sometimes seen as a favorable tax haven for the incorporation of joint ventures.

The corporate form enables the partners to arrange a beneficial tax structure, implement novel ownership arrangements, and better protect their other assets. This form also allows the joint venture to create its own identity apart from those of the partners. Of course, if either or both of the partners have favorable reputations, the new corporation may choose to rely on those, perhaps by including the partners' names as part of its name.

A new corporation also provides a neutral setting in which the partners can do business. As we discuss later in the chapter, strategic alliances sometimes lead to conflict among partners. The probability of conflict and related problems increases if the partners are doing business within the facilities or organization of one of them. However, the potential for conflict may be reduced if the interaction between the partners occurs outside their own facilities or organizations. It may also be reduced if the corporation does not rely on employees identified with either partner and instead hires its own executives and work force whose first loyalty is to the joint venture. For example, a joint venture formed by Corning and Genentech was not performing as well as expected. Corning soon discovered one source of the difficulties: managers contributed by Genentech to the joint venture were actually on leave from Genentech. To ensure that these managers' loyalties were not divided between Genentech and the joint venture, Corning requested that they resign from Genentech. Once they did, the performance of the joint venture improved rapidly.[34]

In isolated cases, incorporating a joint venture may not be possible or desirable. For example, local restrictions on corporations may be so stringent or burdensome that incorporating is not optimal. The partners in these cases usually choose to operate under a limited partnership arrangement. In a limited partnership, one firm, the managing partner, assumes full financial responsibility for the venture, regardless of the amount of its own investment. The other partner (or partners) has liability limited to its own investment. Obviously, such arrangements are riskier for the managing partner.

Public-Private Venture. A special form of joint venture, a **public-private venture,** is one that involves a partnership between a privately owned firm and a government. Such an arrangement may be created under any of several circumstances:

I When the government of a country controls a resource it wants developed, it may enlist the assistance of a firm that has expertise related to that resource. For example, South American countries have used several foreign lumber firms, such as Weyerhaeuser, to assist in the development of their rain forests and surrounding lands. A similar pattern exists in the discovery, exploration, and development of oil fields. National governments that control access and ownership of oil fields may lack the technical expertise to drill for and manage the extraction of crude oil reserves. International oil firms, on the other hand, possess the requisite knowledge and expertise but may lack the necessary drilling rights. A common result is a joint venture for which the government grants drilling rights and private oil firms provide capital and expertise. For example, in late 1997 the government of the Ivory Coast formed a venture with Canada's Ranger Oil Ltd. and Gulf Canada to explore and develop prospective oil fields in its coastal waters.[35]

2 A firm may pursue a public-private venture if a particular country does not allow wholly owned foreign operations. If the firm cannot locate a suitable local partner, it may invite the government itself to participate in a joint venture. Or, the government may request an ownership share. Public-private ventures are typical in the oil industry. In assessing the opportunities and drawbacks to such a venture, a firm should consider and evaluate the various aspects of the political and legal environment it will be facing. Foremost among these is the stability of the government. In a politically unstable country, the current government may be replaced with another, and the firm may face serious challenges. At best, the venture will be considered less important by the new government because of its association with the old government. At worst, the firm's investment may be completely wiped out, its assets seized, and its operation shut down. However, if negotiations are handled properly and if the local government is relatively stable, public-private ventures can be quite beneficial. The government may act benignly and allow the firm to run the joint venture. It may also use its position to protect its own investment—and therefore that of its partner—by restricting competing business activity.

3 A firm entering a centrally planned economy may have no choice but to enlist governmental support, because these governments often limit the freedom of both domestic and foreign firms. In this case, the firm should ensure that it thoroughly understands the expectations and commitments of both the host country's government and its prospective business partner. These concerns are most obvious in China. Because of the vast size (over a billion people) and growth prospects of the Chinese market, many firms are interested in investment opportunities there, and joint ventures with state-owned firms have been the most common mode of entry for MNCs. Many Western firms have prospered through such arrangements. For example, Alcatel's joint venture with the Ministry of Post and Telecommunications, Shanghai Bell, has captured more than half the market for switching equipment in the booming Chinese telecommunications market, much to the chagrin of its traditional rivals, Siemens and Lucent Technologies. Volkswagen's and Chrysler's long-standing joint ventures with local companies have also proved profitable.

However, other Western firms have had their share of troubles with these arrangements, prompting a bitter joke among expatriates in China: "What qualities should you look for in a joint-venture partner?" "One who never comes to the office." For example, Unilever's joint venture partner in Shanghai not only continued to sell its own brand of detergent, White Cat, in competition with the Unilever product (Omo) produced by the joint venture, but also copied Omo's formula and packaged its detergent in a box that copycatted Omo's. Similarly, Daimler-Benz signed an agreement in 1995 to establish a joint venture with state-owned Nanfang South China Motor Corporation to build minivans. Two years later, nothing had been done as the two partners bickered over a variety of issues. Nanfang, for example, wanted to assemble the minivans at two plant sites, while Daimler-Benz officials fought for a single plant so as to capture economies of scale.[36]

Public-private joint ventures were also an important part of the strategies of many Western firms entering the markets of Central and Eastern Europe after the collapse of the Soviet bloc in the late 1980s and early 1990s. A joint venture with a state-owned firm often gave the Western firm access to that firm's existing customers—and these have often dealt exclusively with the state-owned firm. For example, Glavunion, a joint venture formed in 1990 between Glaverbel, Belgium's largest glass manufacturer, and Sklo Union, the Czech Republic's largest glass manufacturer, inherited all of Sklo Union's domestic customers. This investment proved to be a bonanza for Glaverbel. Glavunion has benefited from increased vehicle production by VW-Skoda, itself a joint venture between Volkswagen and the Czech Republic's monopolist automaker under the old communist system. Glavunion's production costs are much lower than Glaverbel's costs in its Belgian factories or those of its main rivals—St. Gobain, Pilkington, and Guardian Glass. Because its main factories are located in Bohemia, near the German border, Glavunion has also benefited from eastern Germany's postunification building boom.[37] Although such public-private ventures are declining in importance in Central and Eastern Europe over time, they represented a popular way of entering these promising but often chaotic markets.

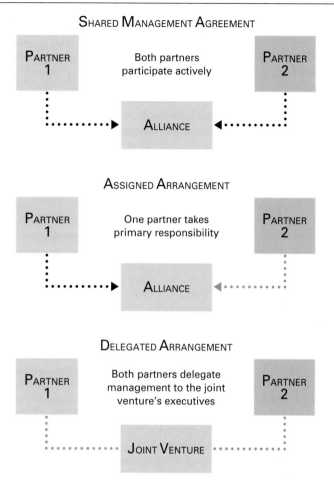

FIGURE 12.3

Managing Strategic Alliances

SHARED MANAGEMENT AGREEMENT

PARTNER 1 — Both partners participate actively — PARTNER 2

ALLIANCE

ASSIGNED ARRANGEMENT

PARTNER 1 — One partner takes primary responsibility — PARTNER 2

ALLIANCE

DELEGATED ARRANGEMENT

PARTNER 1 — Both partners delegate management to the joint venture's executives — PARTNER 2

JOINT VENTURE

Joint Management Considerations

Further issues and questions are associated with how a strategic alliance will be managed. In general, there are three obvious means that may be used to jointly manage a strategic alliance (see Fig. 12.3): shared management agreements, assigned arrangements, and delegated arrangements.

Under a **shared management agreement,** each partner fully and actively participates in managing the alliance. The partners run the alliance, and their managers regularly pass on instructions and details to the alliance's managers. The alliance managers have limited authority of their own and must defer most decisions to managers from the parent firms. This type of agreement requires a high level of coordination and near-perfect agreement between the participating partners. Thus it is the most difficult to maintain and the one most prone to lead to conflict among the partners. An example of a joint venture operating under a shared management agreement is one formed by Coca-Cola and France's Groupe Danone in 1996 to distribute Coke's Minute Maid orange juice in Europe and Latin America. This joint venture combines Danone's distribution network and production facilities—Danone supplies between 15 and 30 percent of the dairy products sold by supermarkets in these countries—with the Minute Maid brand name. The joint venture operates under a shared management arrangement: each company supplies three members of the JV's board of directors. Danone is responsible for the JV's operations, while Coke controls its marketing and finance.[38]

Under an **assigned arrangement,** one partner, such as that owning the majority of a joint venture's stock, assumes primary responsibility for the operations of the strategic alliance. For example, GM, with a 67 percent stake in a joint venture with Raba, a Hungarian truck, engine, and tractor manufacturer, has assumed management control over the venture's operations.[39] Boeing controls the overall operations of its strategic alliance with Fuji, Mitsubishi, and Kawasaki for the design and production of its new 777 commercial aircraft. Under an assigned arrangement, management of the alliance is greatly simplified because the dominant partner has the power to set its own agenda for the new unit, break ties among decision makers, and even overrule its partner(s). Of course, these actions may create conflict, but they keep the alliance from becoming paralyzed, which may happen if equal partners cannot agree on a decision.

Under a **delegated arrangement,** which is reserved for joint ventures, the partners agree not to get involved in ongoing operations and so delegate management control to the executives of the joint venture itself. These executives may be specifically hired to run the new operation or may be transferred from the participating firms. They are responsible for the day-to-day decision making and management of the venture and for implementing its strategy. Thus they have real power and the autonomy to make significant decisions themselves and are much less accountable to managers in the partner firms (at least in the short term). For example, both American Motors and the Beijing Automotive Works contributed experienced managers to the operation of Beijing Jeep so that its management team could learn both modern automobile assembly operations and operating conditions in China. Moreover, these managers were given responsibility for the joint venture's operations.

Pitfalls of Strategic Alliances

Regardless of the care and deliberation a firm puts into constructing a strategic alliance, it still must consider limitations and pitfalls. Figure 12.4 summarizes five fundamental sources of problems that often threaten the viability of strategic alliances: incompatibility of partners, access to information, distribution of earnings, potential loss of autonomy, and changing circumstances.

Incompatibility of Partners

Incompatibility among the partners of a strategic alliance is a primary cause of the failure of such arrangements. At times, incompatibility can lead to outright conflict, although typically it merely leads to poor performance of the alliance. We noted earlier in the chapter the example of the conflict between Siemens's engineering-oriented management and General Electric Corporation's financially oriented management. Incompatibility can stem from differences in corporate culture, national culture, goals and objectives, or virtually any other fundamental dimension linking the two partners.

In many cases, incompatibility problems can be anticipated if the partners carefully discuss and analyze the reasons why each is entering into the alliance in the first place. For example, a useful starting point may be a meeting between top

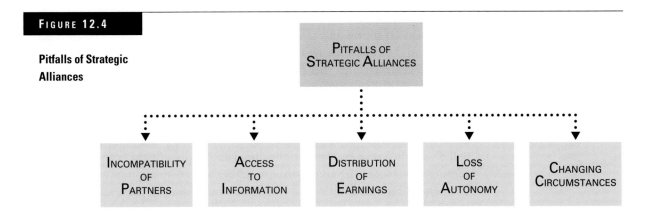

FIGURE 12.4

Pitfalls of Strategic Alliances

managers of the two partners to discuss their mutual interests, goals, and beliefs about strategy. The manner in which the managers are able to work together during such a meeting may be a critical clue to their ability to cooperate in a strategic alliance. Obviously, if the partners cannot agree on such basic issues as how much decision-making power to delegate to the alliance's business unit, what the alliance's strategy should be, how it is to be organized, or how it should be staffed, compromise will probably be difficult to achieve and the alliance is unlikely to succeed. For example, a marketing alliance between AT&T and Italy's Olivetti announced with great fanfare in the mid-1990s quickly failed after the firms could not reach agreement on a marketing strategy, what they wanted the alliance to accomplish, and how they planned to work together.

Access to Information

Access to information is another drawback of many strategic alliances. For a collaboration to work effectively, one partner (or both) may have to provide the other with information it would prefer to keep secret. It is often difficult to identify information needs ahead of time; thus a firm may enter into an agreement not anticipating having to share certain information. When the reality of the situation becomes apparent, the firm may have to be forthcoming with the information or else compromise the effectiveness of the collaboration.[40]

For example, Unisys, a U.S. computer firm, negotiated a joint venture with Hitachi, a Japanese electronics firm. Only after the venture was well underway did Unisys realize that it would have to provide Hitachi with most of the technical specifications it used to build computers. Although Unisys managers reluctantly gave Hitachi the information, they feared they were potentially compromising their own firm's competitiveness. And an alliance between Ford and Mazda to work on the design of the new Ford Escort almost stalled when Mazda officials would not allow their Ford counterparts to visit their research laboratory. After several weeks of arguing, a compromise was eventually reached whereby Ford engineers could enter the facility but only for a limited time.

Distribution of Earnings

An obvious limitation of strategic alliances relates to the distribution of earnings. Because the partners share risks and costs, they also share profits. For example,

General Mills and Nestlé split the profits from their European joint venture on a 50/50 basis. Of course, this aspect of collaborative arrangements is known ahead of time and is virtually always negotiated as part of the original agreement.

However, there are other financial considerations beyond the basic distribution of earnings that can cause disagreement. For example, the partners must also agree on the proportion of the joint earnings that will be distributed to themselves as opposed to being reinvested in the business, the accounting procedures that will be used to calculate earnings or profits, and how transfer pricing will be handled. For example, in the mid-1990s Rubbermaid ended its joint venture to manufacture and distribute rubber and plastic houseware products throughout Europe, North Africa, and the Middle East because its local partner, the Dutch chemical company DSM Group NV, resisted reinvesting profits to develop new products to expand the joint venture's sales as Rubbermaid preferred.[41]

Potential Loss of Autonomy

Another pitfall of a strategic alliance is the potential loss of autonomy. Just as firms share risks and profits, they also share control, thereby limiting what each can do. Most attempts to introduce new products or services, change the way the alliance does business, or introduce any other significant organizational change first must be discussed and negotiated. For example, as part of its contract with General Mills, Nestlé had to agree that if the joint venture is ever terminated, it cannot enter the North American cereal market for at least ten years. Similarly, Fuji Xerox, the long-lived and successful joint venture between Rank Xerox and Fuji Photo Film, was originally limited to selling copiers only in Indonesia, Japan, South Korea, the Philippines, Taiwan, and Thailand, although that restriction was later eliminated.[42]

At the extreme, a strategic alliance may even be the first step toward a takeover. In the early 1980s, the Japanese firm Fujitsu negotiated a strategic alliance with International Computers, Ltd. (ICL), a British computer firm. After nine years of working together, Fujitsu bought 80 percent of ICL. One survey of 150 terminated strategic alliances found that over three fourths ended because a Japanese firm had taken over its non-Japanese partner.[43] In other cases, partners may accuse each other of opportunistic behavior, that is, trying to take advantage of each other. For example, a joint venture between the Walt Disney Company and Sky Television, a British pay-TV channel operator, broke down after Sky accused Disney of deliberately delaying the supply of promised programming. Disney, in turn, accused Sky of proceeding too hastily and without consulting it.[44]

Changing Circumstances

Changing circumstances may also affect the viability of a strategic alliance. The economic conditions that motivated the cooperative arrangement may no longer exist, or technological advances may have rendered the agreement obsolete. For example, in 1994 Ford Motor Co. and Volkswagen disbanded their 1987 joint venture, Autolatina, which was the biggest car manufacturer in South America at the time. When Autolatina was established, the economies of Brazil and its main regional trading partners were being battered by inflation and the debt crisis of the

1980s. Both companies thought they could best weather these economic storms by combining their South American operations. However, economic reforms in Brazil and Argentina and the reduction in trade barriers due to the Mercosur Accord and the Uruguay Round boosted the demand for cars in the region in the 1990s. Ford executives increasingly viewed Autolatina as an impediment to implementation of Ford's new globalization strategy. Since Volkswagen executives also believed that they could do better if they were free of their partnership, the joint venture was terminated by mutual consent.[45]

CHAPTER REVIEW

Summary

Strategic alliances, in which two or more firms agree to cooperate for their mutual benefit, are becoming increasingly popular in international business. A joint venture, a common type of strategic alliance, involves two or more firms joining together to create a new entity that is legally separate and distinct from its parents.

Strategic alliances offer several benefits to firms that use them. First, they facilitate market entry. Second, they allow the partners to share risks. Third, they make it easier for each partner to gain new knowledge and expertise from the other partner(s). Finally, they foster synergy and competitive advantage among the partners.

The scope of strategic alliances can vary significantly. Comprehensive alliances involve a full array of business activities and operations. Functional alliances involving only one aspect of the business, such as production, marketing, finance, or R&D, are also common.

The decision to form a strategic alliance needs to be based on a number of different considerations. Selecting a partner is, of course, critically important and must take into account compatibility, the nature of the potential partner's products or services, the relative safety of the alliance, and the learning potential of the alliance. Selecting a form of organization is also very important to the success of the alliance. A special form of strategic alliance involves public and private partners. The management structure of the strategic alliance must also be given careful consideration.

Partners in a strategic alliance must be aware of several pitfalls that can undermine the success of their cooperative arrangement. These include incompatibility of the partners, access to information, distribution of earnings, potential loss of autonomy, and changing circumstances.

Review Questions

1. What are the basic differences between a joint venture and other types of strategic alliances?

2. Why have strategic alliances grown in popularity in recent years?

3. What are the basic benefits partners are likely to gain from their strategic alliance? Briefly explain each.

4. What are the basic characteristics of a comprehensive alliance? What form is it likely to take?

5. What are the four common types of functional alliances? Briefly explain each.

6. What is an R&D consortium?

7. What factors should be considered in selecting a strategic alliance partner?

8. What are the three basic ways of managing a strategic alliance?

9. Under what circumstances might a strategic

alliance be undertaken by public and private partners?

10. What are the potential pitfalls of strategic alliances?

Questions for Discussion

1. What are the relative advantages and disadvantages of joint ventures compared to other types of strategic alliances?

2. Assume you are a manager for a large international firm, which has decided to enlist a foreign partner in a strategic alliance and has asked you to be involved in the collaboration. What effects, if any, might the decision to structure the collaboration as a joint venture have on you personally and on your career?

3. What factors could conceivably cause a sharp decline in the number of new strategic alliances formed?

4. Could a firm conceivably undertake too many strategic alliances at one time? Why or why not?

5. Can you think of any foreign products you use that may have been marketed in this country as a result of a strategic alliance? What are they?

6. What are some of the issues involved in a firm's trying to learn from a strategic alliance partner without giving out too much valuable information of its own?

7. Why would a firm decide to enter a new market on its own rather than using a strategic alliance?

8. What are some of the similarities and differences between forming a strategic alliance with a firm from your home country and forming one with a firm from a foreign country?

9. The joint venture between General Mills and Nestlé was worked out in only 23 days. Most experts, however, argue that a firm should spend a long time getting to know a prospective partner before proceeding with an alliance. What factors might account for CPW being an exception to this general rule?

10. Otis Elevator has sought to obtain first-mover advantages by quickly entering emerging markets with the help of local partners. This strategy has proven very successful for Otis. Should all firms adopt this strategy? Under what conditions is this strategy most likely to be successful?

BUILDING GLOBAL SKILLS

Break into small groups of four to five people. Assume your group is the executive committee (that is, the top managers) of Resteaze, Inc. Resteaze is a large manufacturer of mattresses, box springs, and waterbeds. The publicly traded firm is among the largest in the U.S. bedding market. It operates 15 factories, employs over 10,000 people, and last year generated $20 million in profits on sales of $380 million. Resteaze products are sold through department stores, furniture stores, and specialty shops and have the reputation of being of good quality and medium-priced.

Your committee is thinking about entering the European bedding market. You know little about the European market, so you are thinking about forming a joint venture. Your committee has identified three possible candidates for such an arrangement.

One candidate is Bedrest. Bedrest is a French firm that also makes bedding. Unfortunately,

Bedrest products have a poor reputation in Europe and most of its sales stem from the fact that its products are exceptionally cheap. However, there are possibilities for growth in Eastern Europe. The consultant who recommended Bedrest suggests that your higher-quality products would mesh well with Bedrest's cheaper ones. Bedrest is known to be having financial difficulties because of declining sales. However, the consultant thinks the firm will soon turn things around.

A second candidate is Home Furnishings, Inc., a German firm that manufactures high-quality furniture. Its line of bedroom furniture (headboards, dressers, chests, and so on) is among the most popular in Europe. The firm is also known to be interested in entering the U.S. furniture market. Home Furnishings is a privately owned concern that is assumed to have a strong financial position. Because of its prices, however, the firm is not expected to be able to compete effectively in Eastern Europe.

Finally, Pacific Enterprises, Inc., is a huge Japanese conglomerate that is just now entering the European market. The firm does not have any current operations in Europe but has enormous financial reserves to put behind any new undertaking it might decide to pursue. Its major product lines are machine tools, auto replacement parts, communications equipment, and consumer electronics.

Your task is to assess the relative advantages and disadvantages of each of these prospective partners for Resteaze. The European market is important to you, this is your first venture abroad, and you want the highest probability for success. After assessing each candidate, rank the three in order of their relative attractiveness to your firm.

Follow-up Questions

1. How straightforward or ambiguous was the task of evaluating and ranking the three alternatives?

2. Determine and discuss the degree of agreement or disagreement among the various groups in the class.

WORKING WITH THE WEB: Building Global Internet Skills

Implementing Strategic Alliances

This exercise will give you Internet experience in learning more about foreign government regulation of strategic alliances and sources of information regarding potential strategic partners. As a first step, read the exercise scenario that follows.

Exercise Scenario

You are the marketing manager for a medium-size computer company. Your firm buys components from other suppliers, assembles computers using those components, and then markets the computers directly to small businesses using print advertising, telephone sales, and direct mail. One of the keys to your firm's success is that the company has developed its own software packages. The software works with existing products like those marketed by Microsoft, but provides extra applications for small

businesses, independent contractors, professional specialists like lawyers and doctors, and so forth.

Your CEO wants to begin a slow expansion into foreign markets. She believes that England, Canada, or Australia would be the best bet to start so as to minimize language difficulties. Her idea is to locate an existing company in one of those countries that also sells computers and discuss with its owners the idea of a strategic alliance. Your firm would modify its existing software for the foreign market and provide it to your partner in exchange for the partner agreeing to help you market your computers there as well.

With this information as context, do the following:

1. Using the Internet, learn as much as possible about government regulations in each of the

three countries that (a) may affect your business and (b) may affect the relative attractiveness of each market.

2. Using the information gathered above, select a market for entry.

3. Now use the Internet again and see if you can locate one or more potential strategic partners in the country you have chosen to enter.

CLOSING CASE

Microsoft Wants the World[46]

It's no secret, of course, that Microsoft dominates the software industry in the United States. Its Windows operating system and Microsoft Office application programs are the most widely used in industry. Moreover, each is considered the standard against which other software is measured. But Microsoft and its leader, Bill Gates, think that the firm's future growth potential really lies in other countries.

Gates believes that countries like China and India, as well as those in Eastern Europe, will provide much of the firm's growth over the next few years. And given that those countries do not have a long-standing history of using other kinds of equipment or operating systems, Gates believes that Microsoft can amass even larger market shares there than it has in its domestic market. Microsoft already derives over half of its annual revenues from overseas operations, but much of it comes from the European Union and Japan. Thus, the potential in these emerging markets is substantial.

Microsoft has developed an interesting—and highly effective—strategy for entering new foreign markets. Whenever the firm enters a new market it hires a local manager to head up the operation. Gates thinks this is important both in terms of familiarity with local conditions and for symbolic purposes. This manager, in turn, then creates a small, lean staff comprised almost exclusively of other local managers. Indeed, out of Microsoft's 6200 foreign employees, only five are expatriates.

Once the foreign operation is up and running, it then seeks smaller local companies to become strategic allies with Microsoft. An ideal partner for Microsoft is a firm that is knowledgeable about the local market and has expertise and visibility in the local computer and/or software industry. Microsoft then sets up an exclusive partnership with that firm that allows it to market Microsoft products such as Windows, Windows NT, and Office. These local partners, in turn, are also encouraged to enlist other partners and to gradually spread their presence throughout the country. The immediate benefit to the partner is access to the popular Microsoft products.

But Microsoft is hoping to do more than simply create a network of strategic allies in each country where it does business. Instead, it hopes to create local software industries especially keyed to local circumstances. For example, Microsoft will help support independent distributors and encourage them to sell not only Microsoft products but competing software as well. Moreover, it also encourages other firms to write software that is compatible with Microsoft products. In China alone, Microsoft is working with hundreds of start-up software companies and has a network of over 15,000 distribution companies.

Microsoft is finding this strategy to be effective not only for product distribution and sales purposes, but for local language issues as well. For example, each Microsoft product must be adapted to support different languages, writing and formatting conventions, and so forth in each foreign market where it does business. In some countries, this adaptation is especially complicated. In India, for example, Microsoft must contend with the country's multiple official languages and 3000 local dialects. But the firm is also finding it easier than ever to handle this daunting task by relying on its local partners to help it line up other local businesses to provide translation services.

Another benefit to Microsoft's strategy is its impact on pirating. In Eastern Europe, China, and many other parts of Asia, more than 90 percent of software in use are illegal copies made and sold without Microsoft's permission. One cause for this has been high import tariffs. Up until recently in India, for example, the import tariff on high-tech products like software was 112 percent. This tariff, of course, raised the costs of imported software to very high levels and encouraged pirating. Another cause has been either weak copyright laws or weak enforcement of existing laws.

Like other high-tech firms, Microsoft believes that the 1996 pact sponsored by the World Trade Organization to reduce barriers to trade in information technology will help it boost its global sales. But Microsoft has also been working diligently to convince local governments to lower tariffs to more competitive levels and to more aggressively enforce copyright and related legislation. In India, for example, Microsoft and its local partners have succeeded in reducing the piracy rate from 90 percent to 75 percent and "legitimate" sales are soaring.

Still, some critics worry that Microsoft's strategy will end up causing problems. They warn, for

example, that its reliance on diffused local partners will eventually erode the Microsoft culture and lead to product quality and distribution problems. For now, however, Microsoft looks unbeatable.

Case Questions

1. What are the relative advantages and disadvantages of using multiple small local partners (like Microsoft) versus using a single large local partner (like General Mills)?

2. Are there countries where Microsoft's strategy might not work?

3. What other kinds of businesses might find Microsoft's strategy to be effective?

4. How might Microsoft need to change its strategy once it has established a strong position in a foreign market?

CHAPTER NOTES

1. Christopher Knowlton, "Europe Cooks Up a Cereal Brawl," *Fortune*, June 3, 1992, pp. 175–179; "Cafe au Lait, A Croissant—and Trix," *Business Week*, August 24, 1992, pp. 50–52; "General Mills Reports Record Earnings of 78 Cents Per Share for Fiscal 1997 Third Quarter," *PR Newswire*, March 12, 1997; "Cereal Partners Venture Shakes Up Kellogg's," *Eurofood*, July 1995, p. 24.

2. Refik Culpan, *Multinational Strategic Alliances* (New York: International Business Press, 1993). See also Richard N. Osborn and John Hagedoorn, "The Institutionalization and Evolutionary Dynamics of Interorganizational Alliances and Networks," *Academy of Management Journal*, Vol. 40, No. 2 (1997), pp. 261–278.

3. "For Kodak's Advantix, Double Exposure as Company Relaunches Camera System," *Wall Street Journal*, April 23, 1997, p. B1; "Camera System Is Developed but Not Delivered," *Wall Street Journal*, August 7, 1996, p. B1; "Kodak Joins Fuji, Others for Project," *USA Today*, March 26, 1992, p. B1.

4. Peter J. Killing, "How to Make a Global Joint Venture Work," *Harvard Business Review* (May–June 1982), pp. 120–127.

5. "Camera System Is Developed but Not Delivered," op. cit.

6. David Lei and John W. Slocum, Jr., "Global Strategic Alliances: Payoffs and Pitfalls," *Organizational Dynamics* (Winter 1991), pp. 44–62.

7. Michael E. Porter, *Competitive Strategy* (New York: Free Press, 1980), p. 275.

8. "Time Warner to attack Spain's cinema market," *Financial Times*, April 8, 1997, p. 19.

9. "Cigna enters retail alliance in Brazil," *Financial Times*, March 21, 1997, p. 18.

10. Farok J. Contractor, "Ownership Pattern of U.S. Joint Ventures Abroad and the Liberalization of Foreign Government Regulations in the 1980s: Evidence from the Benchmark Surveys," *Journal of International Business Studies*, Vol. 21, No. 1 (First Quarter 1990), pp. 55–73.

11. "Chinese Government Struggles to Rejuvenate National Brands," *Wall Street Journal*, June 24, 1996, p. B1.

12. Gregg Laskoski, "U.S. pharmaceutical companies compete for CIS foothold," *We*, September 7–20, 1992, p. 7.

13. Maile Hulihan, "Into the Fray," *CFO, The Magazine for Senior Financial Executives* (June 1992), pp. 18–26.

14. Bruce Kogut, "Joint Ventures: Theoretical and Empirical Perspectives," *Strategic Management Journal*, Vol. 9 (1988), pp. 319–332; Andrew C. Inkpen and Paul W. Beamish, "Knowledge, Bargaining Power, and the Instability of International Joint Ventures," *Academy of Management Review*, Vol. 22, No. 1 (1997), pp. 177–202.

15. Jeremy Main, "Making a Global Alliance Work," *Fortune*, December 17, 1990, pp. 121–126.

16. Kenichi Ohmae, "The Global Logic of Strategic Alliances," *Harvard Business Review* (March–April 1989), pp. 143–154.

17. "PepsiCo Planning Tea-Drink Venture with Unilever Unit," *Wall Street Journal*, December 4, 1991, p. B8.

18. "Siemens, Motorola Plan U.S. Chip Plant," *Wall Street Journal*, October 26, 1995, p. A18.

19. "Chrysler and BMW Team Up to Build Small-Engine Plant in South America," *Wall Street Journal*, October 2, 1996, p. A4.

20. "Five-Year Alliance Is Set with Company in India," *Wall Street Journal*, June 11, 1997, p. B5.

21. "Huge Mall Bets on Formula of Family Fun and Games," *Wall Street Journal*, June 11, 1997, p. B1.

22. "Siemens, Motorola Plan U.S. Chip Plant," *Wall Street Journal*, October 26, 1995, p. A18.

23. "Alliance Set with Hitachi to Develop Microprocessors," *Wall Street Journal*, December 10, 1997, p. A24.

24. Herbert I. Fusfield and Carmela S. Haklisch, "Cooperative R&D for Competitors," *Harvard Business Review* (November–December 1985), pp. 60–76.

25. J. Michael Geringer, "Strategic Determinants of Partner Selection Criteria in International Joint Ventures," *Journal of International Business Studies,* Vol. 22, No. 1 (First Quarter 1991), pp. 41–62; Kathryn R. Harrigan, *Strategies for joint venture success* (Lexington, Mass.: Lexington, 1985); Keith D. Brouthers, Lance Eliot Brouthers, and Timothy J. Wilkinson, "Strategic Alliances: Choose Your Partners," *Long Range Planning*, Vol. 28, No. 3 (1995), pp. 18–25.

26. Main, op. cit.

27. The question of trust reflects a larger class of issues revolving around the size of transaction costs. See Paul W. Beamish and John C. Banks, "Equity Joint Ventures and the Theory of the Multinational Enterprise," *Journal of International Business Studies*, Vol. 18 (Summer 1987), pp. 1–16.

28. Main, op. cit.

29. Ibid.; Joseph E. Pattison, "Global Joint Ventures," *Overseas Business* (Winter 1990), pp. 24–29.

30. Peter Lorange and Johan Roos, "Why Some Strategic Alliances Succeed and Others Fail," *The Journal of Business Strategy* (January/February 1991), pp. 25–30.

31. Stephen J. Kohn, "The Benefits and Pitfalls of Joint Ventures," *The Bankers Magazine* (May/June 1990), pp. 12–18.

32. Corning, Inc., *1988 Annual Report*, p. 7.

33. Richard N. Osborn and C. Christopher Baughn, "Forms of Interorganizational Governance for Multinational Alliances," *Academy of Management Journal* (September 1990), pp. 503–519.

34. Joseph E. Pattison, "Global Joint Ventures," *Overseas Business* (Winter 1990), pp. 24–29.

35. "Ivory Coast oil exploration pact signed," *Houston Chronicle*, December 28, 1997, p. 4E.

36. "Daimler-Benz May Pull Out of Venture to Build Cars with Chinese Company," *Wall Street Journal*, May 23, 1997, p. A8; "Going it alone," *The Economist*, April 19, 1997, pp. 54–55; "Ford Hopes Small Investment in China Will Pay Off Big," *Wall Street Journal*, November 9, 1995, p. B3.

37. Anthony Robinson, "Czech deal with clear attractions," *Financial Times*, June 5, 1992, p. 18.

38. "Coke in Venture with France's Danone to Distribute Orange Juice Overseas," *Wall Street Journal*, September 25, 1996, p. B8.

39. Nicholas Denton, "GM puts further DM100m into its Hungary venture," *Financial Times*, November 6, 1991, p. 7.

40. Karen J. Hladik and Lawrence H. Linden, "Is an International Joint Venture in R&D for You?" *Research Technology Management* (July–August 1989), pp. 11–13.

41. "Rubbermaid Ends Venture in Europe, Signalling Desire to Call Its Own Shots," *Wall Street Journal*, June 1, 1994, p. A4.

42. "An angry young warrior," *Financial Times*, September 19, 1994, p. 11.

43. Main, op. cit.

44. "Murdoch Firm Sues Disney, Alleges Violation of Pact for Pay TV in Britain," *Wall Street Journal*, May 17, 1989, p. B6.

45. "Bruised in Brazil: Ford Slips as Market Booms," *Wall Street Journal*, December 13, 1996, p. A10.

46. Brent Schlender, "Microsoft—First America, Now the World," *Fortune*, August 18, 1997, pp. 214–217; David Kirkpatrick, "He Wants All Your Business—And He's Starting to Get It," *Fortune*, May 26, 1997, pp. 58–68; Brent Schlender, "On the Road With Chairman Bill," *Fortune*, May 26, 1997, pp. 72–81.

Organization Design for International Business

Chapter Outline

The nature of international organization design

Initial impacts of international activity on organization design

The corollary approach
The export department
The international division

Global organization designs

Global product design
Global area design
Global functional design
Global customer design
Global matrix design
Hybrid global designs

Related issues in global organization design

Centralization versus decentralization
Role of subsidiary boards of directors
Coordination in the global organization

Corporate culture in international business

Creating the corporate culture in
    international business
Managing the corporate culture in
    international business

Managing change in international business

Reasons for change in international
    business
Types of change in international business

After studying this chapter you should be able to:

Summarize the nature of international organization design.

Identify and describe the initial impacts of international business activity on organization design.

Identify and describe five advanced forms of international organization design and discuss hybrid global designs.

Identify and summarize related issues in global organization design.

Discuss the role of corporate culture in international business.

Describe the management of change in international business.

NILEVER IS THE WORLD'S SECOND LARGEST PACKAGED CONSUMER goods company; with $57 billion in annual sales, it trails only U.S. giant Procter & Gamble in this industry. Among its best-known brand names are Lipton, Dove, Helene Curtis, Vaseline, and Q-tips. Unilever's major product groups include margarine and oils, frozen foods, drinks, and personal care products. In addition, Unilever is also the largest maker of ice cream in the world. ■ ■ The firm's ownership and management structure are unique. Unilever is jointly headquartered in London and Rotterdam. It is operated by two different holding companies, one based in each of these two cities. These holding companies have separate stock listings but identical boards of directors. A single management team runs the entire enterprise. ■ ■ Over the years Unilever has occasionally set up other businesses to support its consumer products operations. For example, the firm established a

Unilever Matches Strategy and Structure[1]

chemical unit to process the oils it uses to make margarine. At the time, managers believed that this route provided them with a predictable and controllable source of materials. Fragrances and food flavorings operations were created for the same reason. In similar fashion, Unilever has often grown by acquiring other consumer products businesses, many of which had supporting operations as well. ■ ■ Unilever evolved to the point where it was structured around five basic business groups: food products, personal products, soap/laundry products, cosmetics/perfume/hair products, and specialty chemicals. As the company continued to expand, however, this arrangement grew increasingly unwieldy. The methods and operations used to package, distribute, and promote the products and brands in the four consumer products groups are all very similar. Managers could be transferred across businesses easily, and knowledge about local market conditions in different countries was freely exchanged. ■ ■ But the specialty chemical group was an altogether different story. Since it had no consumer products, only indirect linkages existed between its operations and those in the consumer products groups. For example, in some markets the chemical companies made chemicals that were then "sold" to Unilever's consumer products businesses. These businesses, in turn, used the chemicals to create their consumer products for resale around the world. ■ ■ By 1997 Unilever's board of directors had grown concerned about the firm's seeming inability to compete with Procter & Gamble. In market after market, Procter & Gamble brands had the largest share, and Unilever was a solid but consistent number 2. A new CEO, Niall FitzGerald, was hired to remedy this situation and to improve Unilever's financial performance. ■ ■ After carefully studying Unilever's operations, FitzGerald concluded that the firm's specialty chemical businesses were a big part of the problem. For one thing, they did not meet the firm's profitability targets. For another, some of the chemicals they were making could actually be bought on the open market for the same—and sometimes lower—prices. And third, the firm had higher administrative costs due to the unrelated nature of the chemical units relative to the consumer products groups. ■ ■ Accordingly, Unilever made the decision in mid-1997 to sell its specialty chemical units. This would eliminate the inefficiencies created by the firm's structure. It would also generate cash that could be used to reduce debt and to finance new acquisitions in Unilever's core business areas. FitzGerald argued that the new structure would allow Unilever to focus all of its attention on competing with Procter & Gamble and other firms in the consumer products markets. Accordingly, in late 1997 Unilever negotiated the sale of its specialty chemical group to Britain's Imperial Chemical Industries PLC for a price of approximately $8 billion. ■ ■ ■ ■

Unilever's efforts to sell its specialty chemical operations represent an important strategic decision. But the underlying basis for that decision was the firm's organization design. Developed over time in somewhat piecemeal fashion, the firm's design came to represent a burden in the marketplace and a barrier to effective competition. Thus, the new CEO decided to change the firm's design in order to improve the organization's ability to compete in international markets.

In this chapter, we describe the various organization designs that international businesses use to achieve their strategic goals. Because these designs typically evolve along a well-defined path as firms become more international, we first discuss the initial forms of organization design firms use as they begin to internationalize their operations.[2] We then analyze the more advanced forms of organization design adopted as firms broaden their participation in international business to become true MNCs. Next we discuss several related issues in global organization design. We conclude by describing two other aspects of organization design: corporate culture and change.

The Nature of International Organization Design

Organization design (sometimes called *organization structure*) is the overall pattern of structural components and configurations used to manage the total organization. Organization design is the basic vehicle through which strategy is ultimately implemented and through which the work of the organization is actually accomplished.

A firm cannot function unless its various structural components are appropriately assembled.[3] Through its design, the firm:

♦ Allocates organizational resources

♦ Assigns tasks to its employees

♦ Instructs those employees concerning the firm's rules, procedures, and expectations about their job performances

♦ Collects and transmits information necessary for problem solving and decision making.[4]

This last task is of particular importance for large MNCs, which must manage the sharing of vast amounts of information between corporate headquarters and subsidiaries and staff spread worldwide.[5]

Early studies of organization design sought to identify the single best design that all organizations should use. The pioneering work of the German sociologist Max Weber, for example, described a so-called **bureaucratic design,** which was based on rational rules, regulations, and standard operating procedures.[6] Later research, however, suggested that there was no one best way to design an organization. Eventually managers, stimulated by British researchers Joan Woodward, Tom Burns, G. M. Stalker, Derek Pugh, and David Hickson, came to learn there are many different ways to effectively design organizations.[7] Managers must carefully assess their situation and context and then develop an appropriate design to fit both. Certain key elements determine the appropriate design for any given organization, including the firm's size, strategy, technology, environment, and the cultures of the countries in which it operates. That is, various theories and research suggest that the appropriate form of organization design for any particular company is contingent on one or more of these factors.[8]

For example, often a firm that sells brand-name consumer goods customized for markets in different host countries will structure itself geographically so that regional managers knowledgeable about the idiosyncratic needs of local customers will be empowered with appropriate decision-making authority. Procter & Gamble is an example of a firm with this type of structure. In contrast, a firm that seeks manufacturing efficiencies may organize itself along product lines in order to utilize its lowest-cost production facilities, regardless of their geographical location. Black & Decker has done this.

However, an organization's structure is not created and then left alone; organization design is an ongoing process. Indeed, managers change the design of their firms almost continually. For example, shortly after Unilever sold off its specialty chemical operations, it combined the U.S. operations of its Cheesebrough-Pond's, Helene Curtis, and Lever Brothers affiliates to form a new subsidiary, Unilever Home & Personal Care USA. By so doing, Unilever believed it could achieve economies of scale and scope in marketing and distributing its products in the U.S. market.[9] One study found that most firms and divisions of large firms make moderate design changes about once a year and one or more major design changes every four to five years.[10] These changes often result from changes in the firm's strategy, since an important characteristic of a successful firm is its ability to match its strategy with a compatible organization design, as Unilever has sought to do.[11]

Initial Impacts of International Activity on Organization Design

As a domestic firm expands internationally, it will change its organization design to accommodate its increased international activities. To see how this happens, we'll start by considering a domestic firm that has no international sales. This is not an unreasonable starting point. Many entrepreneurs, particularly in larger economies such as those of the United States, Japan, and Germany, start new firms in response to some perceived need in the local market; they give little immediate thought to the international marketplace. And many small, domestically oriented firms enter international markets passively through indirect exporting, as discussed in Chapter 11. Such a firm may sell its product to a domestic customer, and that customer then incorporates the product into a good that it distributes in foreign markets. Or, a domestic customer may purchase the firm's product for one of its foreign subsidiaries, or a domestic purchasing agent of a foreign wholesaler may order the firm's product. Because such indirect exporting occurs as a routine part of the firm's domestic business, the firm's organization design need not change at all.

The Corollary Approach

Now assume that this firm begins to engage in direct exporting on a modest level. Such a firm often initially responds to international sales and orders by following the **corollary approach**, whereby it delegates responsibility for processing such orders to individuals within an existing department, such as finance or marketing. Under this approach, the firm continues to use its existing domestic organization design. This approach is typical of a firm that has only a very small level of international activity.

For example, Texas-based O.I. International was started in 1969 to produce highly specialized equipment to analyze and monitor oil-drilling activities. In its early years, it had little need to think internationally because oil-drilling activity in Texas and elsewhere in the United States was booming. However, as oil field activity slowed in the United States, O.I. needed new sources of revenue. One day, CEO John Huey was reading a trade magazine and noticed an announcement of an industrial exhibition in Japan. He quickly made arrangements to attend the show to promote O.I. products. During the show, he contracted with JASKO International, a Japanese equipment firm, to distribute O.I. products in Pacific Asia. Because initial sales were relatively small, and because Huey had negotiated the agreement himself, he initially handled sales to JASKO through his own office. There was certainly no need to overhaul the firm's structure in order to deal with this level of international involvement.

The Export Department

As a firm's export sales become more significant, its next step is usually to create a separate export department. The export department takes responsibility for overseeing international operations, marketing products, processing orders, working with foreign distributors, and arranging financing when necessary. Initially, the head of the export department may report to a senior marketing or finance executive. As exports grow in importance, however, the export department may achieve equality on the organization chart with finance, marketing, human resources, and the other functional areas of the firm. O.I., for example, eventually created a small export department—comprising one manager and an assistant—to handle its exports to Japan. Figure 13.1 illustrates how an export department fits into a typical small firm.

The International Division

At first, where selling to foreign customers may not be fundamentally different from selling to domestic ones, the export department may get by with little familiarity with foreign markets. However, as international activities further increase, firms often find that an export department no longer serves their needs.

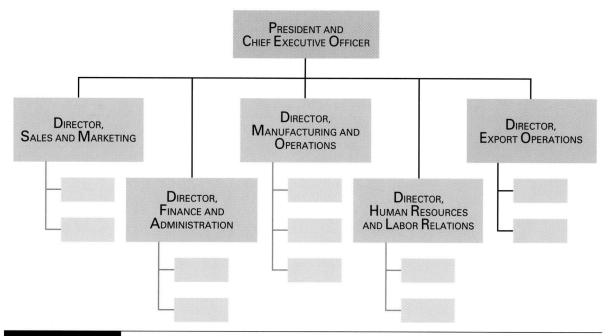

FIGURE 13.1

An Export Department in a Small Manufacturing Firm

Once a firm begins to station employees abroad or establish foreign subsidiaries to produce, distribute, and/or market its products, managerial responsibilities, coordination complexities, and information requirements all swell beyond the export department's capabilities and expertise. Familiarity with foreign markets becomes more important and new methods for organizing may be required.

Firms respond to the challenges of controlling their burgeoning international business by changing their organization design through the creation of an international division that specializes in managing foreign operations.[12] The international division allows the firm to concentrate resources and create specialized programs and activities targeted on international business activity while simultaneously keeping that activity segregated from the firm's ongoing domestic activities.

For example, Brazil's Banco Economico SA, the oldest private bank in Latin America, uses the international division approach. As Fig. 13.2 shows, Banco Economico's organization design emphasizes its product lines—corporate finance and nonfinancial investments, retail banking, and corporate banking. The international banking division has equal status with each of these product groups on the organization chart. International division managers are responsible for operating the bank's international branches and foreign-exchange operations and for providing corporate banking and corporate financial services to meet the needs of foreign customers, as well as the international needs of domestic customers.[13]

Global Organization Designs

As a firm evolves from being domestically oriented with international operations to becoming a true multinational corporation with global aspirations, it typically abandons the international division approach. In

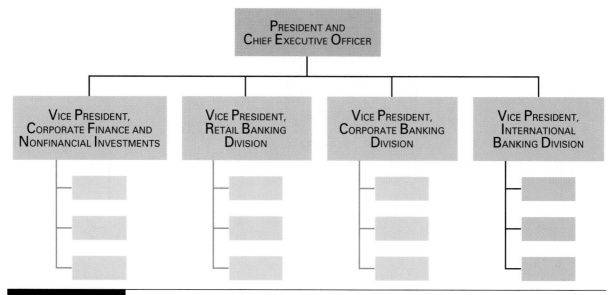

FIGURE 13.2

**Banco Economico
S.A.'s International
Division Design**

place of that division, it usually creates a global organization design to achieve synergies among its far-flung operations and to implement its organizational strategy.[14] The global design adopted by the firm must deal with its need to integrate three types of knowledge to compete effectively internationally:

♦ *Area knowledge:* managers must understand the cultural, commercial, social, and economic conditions in each host country market the firm does business in.

♦ *Product knowledge:* managers must comprehend such factors as technological trends, customer needs, and competitive forces affecting the goods the firm produces and sells.

♦ *Functional knowledge:* managers must have access to coworkers with expertise in basic business functions such as production, marketing, finance, accounting, human resource management, and MIS.

The five most common forms of global organization design are product, area, functional, customer, and matrix. As we will discuss, each of these design types allows the firm to emphasize one type of knowledge yet perhaps makes it more difficult to incorporate the other types of knowledge in its decision-making. Accordingly, the global design the MNC chooses will reflect the relative importance of each of the three types of knowledge in its operations as well as its need for coordination among its units, the source of its firm-specific advantages, and its managerial philosophy about its position in the world economy.[15] MNCs typically adopt one of three managerial philosophies that guide their approach to such functions as organization design and marketing. The **ethnocentric approach** is used by firms that operate internationally the same way they do domestically. The **polycentric approach** is used by firms that customize their operations for each foreign market they serve. Finally, the **geocentric approach** is used by firms that analyze the needs of their customers worldwide and then

FIGURE 13.3

Shougang Corp.'s
Global Product Design

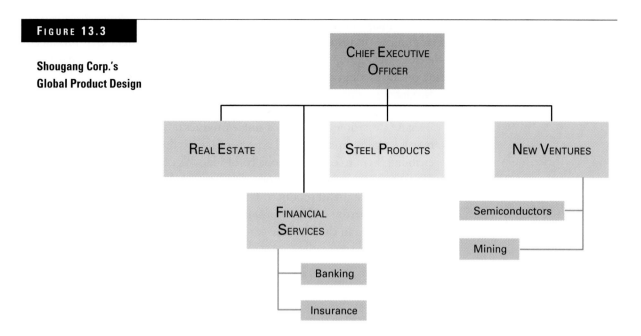

adopt standardized operations for all markets they serve. (We discuss these concepts more fully in Chapter 16.)

Global Product Design

The most common form of organization design adopted by MNCs is the global product design. The **global product design** assigns worldwide responsibility for specific products or product groups to separate operating divisions within a firm.[16] This design works best when the firm has diverse product lines or when its product lines are sold in diverse markets, thereby rendering the need for coordination between product lines relatively unimportant. If the products are related, the organization of the firm takes on what is often called an **M-form design**; if the products are unrelated, the design is called an **H-form design**.[17] The M in M-form stands for "multidivisional"—the various divisions of the firm are usually self-contained operations with interrelated activities. The H in H-form stands for "holding," as in "holding company"—the various unrelated businesses function with autonomy and little interdependence. After selling its specialty chemicals group, Unilever has become an M-form business since the businesses it chose to retain are all somewhat related to one another.

Shougang Corp., one of the largest and oldest state-owned companies in China, provides an example of an H-form organization using a global product design. For over fifteen years Shougang has been pursuing a strategy of unrelated diversification, which has, in turn, resulted in the organization design shown in Fig. 13.3. Shougang's core business is the production of various steel products, and steel remains a central product group within the company. Shougang also has several operations in various financial markets, and groups these together in its financial products group. Examples include Canadian Eastern Life Assurance and Huaxia Bank. Another product group consists of various real estate projects and developments. Finally, its new ventures group includes such businesses as a semiconductor joint venture with Japan's NEC and a mining operation.[18]

Pennsylvania's Harsco Corporation, too, is organized according to its major product groups—industrial services and building products, engineered products, and defense. Each group is responsible for managing domestic and international production, marketing, and distribution for its individual product lines.[19]

The global product design has several advantages:

1 Because a division focuses on a single product or product group, the division managers gain expertise in all aspects of the product or products, better enabling them to compete globally. In Harsco's case, one of the firm's competitive advantages lies in its specialized knowledge of how to convert steel mill waste into useful products. Using the global product design, Harsco can focus this expertise within its industrial services and building products group, which can then use this knowledge to compete internationally for contracts with steel mills.

2 It facilitates efficiencies in production because managers are free to manufacture the product wherever manufacturing costs are the lowest.

3 It allows managers to coordinate production at their various facilities, shifting output from factory to factory as global demand or cost conditions fluctuate.

4 Because managers have extensive product knowledge, they are more able to incorporate new technologies into their product(s) and respond quickly and flexibly to technological changes that affect their market.

5 It facilitates global marketing of the product. The firm gains flexibility in how it introduces, promotes, and distributes each product or product group. Rather than being tied to one marketing plan that encompasses the whole firm, individual product-line managers may pursue their own plans.

6 Because the global product design forces managers to think globally, it facilitates geocentric corporate philosophies. This is a useful mind-set as firms work to develop greater international skills internally.

The global product design also has disadvantages:

1 It may encourage expensive duplication, since each product group needs its own functional-area skills such as marketing, finance, and information management and sometimes even its own physical facilities for production, distribution, and R&D.

2 Each product group must develop its own knowledge about the cultural, legal, and political environments of the various regional and national markets in which it operates.

3 It makes coordination and corporate learning across product groups more difficult. If such coordination is an important part of the firm's international strategy, it may want to adopt a different global design, such as the global area design.

Thus, businesses must carefully consider the relative advantages and disadvantages of using the global product design when deciding the best form of organization design for their particular circumstances.

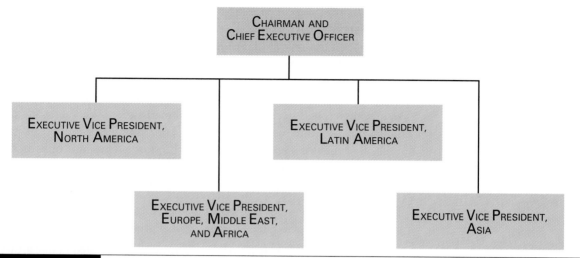

FIGURE 13.4

Procter & Gamble's
Global Area Design

Global Area Design

The second most common form of global design is the global area design. The **global area design** organizes the firm's activities around specific areas or regions of the world. This approach is particularly useful for firms with a polycentric or multidomestic corporate philosophy.[20] Figure 13.4 illustrates the global area approach adopted by Procter & Gamble. Four executive vice presidents responsible for a region of the world—North America; Europe, the Middle East, and Africa; Asia; and Latin America—report to the CEO's office. Although not shown in this figure, senior managers responsible for various product lines (like Beauty Care, Health Care, Laundry and Cleaning Products, and Paper and Beverage Products) within each region report to the appropriate executive vice president for their region.

A global area design is most likely to be used by a firm whose products are not readily transferable across regions. For example, Bertelsmann AG is one of the world's largest media firms; it publishes newspapers and magazines and records music and video materials. Because of language differences and cultural preferences, however, a Bertelsmann magazine published in the United States cannot be exported in large quantities for sale in Germany or Japan. Thus the firm has separate headquarters in each country in which it operates. The U.S. headquarters, for example, oversees publication of books under the mastheads of Bantam, Dell, and Doubleday and of magazines such as *Parents* and *Young Miss* and records music under such labels as Arista and RCA. Similarly, Bertelsmann's German operation publishes books under the label Bertelsmann Club, publishes magazines such as *Der Spiegel*, and records music under the label BMG Ariola.

Cadbury Schweppes PLC, a British soft drink and candy firm, also uses the global area design. Cadbury owns such brand names as Canada Dry, Hires, Holland House, Cadbury Chocolate, and Beechnut. The firm has five basic divisions, each representing a different area of the world—the United Kingdom, Other Europe, the Pacific Rim, North and South America, and Other Countries. Managers in each area division handle distribution, promotion, advertising, and other functions for all Cadbury Schweppes products in their particular markets.[21]

The global area design is particularly useful for a firm whose strategy is marketing-driven rather than predicated on manufacturing efficiencies or technological innovation or a firm whose competitive strength lies in the reputation of its brand-name products. Both conditions apply to Cadbury Schweppes. Further, the geographical focus of this design allows a firm to develop expertise about the local market. Area managers can freely adapt the firm's products to meet local needs and can quickly respond to changes in the local marketplace. They also can tailor the product mix they offer within a given area. For example, Cadbury managers do not sell all of the firm's products in all areas but instead promote only those that match local tastes and preferences.

The global area design does have disadvantages, however:

1 By focusing on the needs of the area market, the firm may sacrifice cost efficiencies that might be gained through global production.

2 Diffusion of technology is slowed, for innovations generated in one area division may not be adopted by all the others. Thus this design may not be suitable for product lines undergoing rapid technological change.

3 The global area design results in duplication of resources because each area division must have its own functional specialists, product experts, and, in many cases, production facilities.

4 It makes coordination across areas expensive and discourages global product planning.

Global Functional Design

The **global functional design** calls for a firm to create departments or divisions that have worldwide responsibility for the common organizational functions—finance, operations, marketing, R&D, and human resources management. This design is used by MNCs that have relatively narrow or similar product lines.[22] It results in what is often called a **U-form organization,** where the U stands for "unity." An example of the global functional design is that used by British Airways, shown in Fig. 13.5. This firm is essentially a single-business firm—it provides air transport services—and has company-wide functional operations dedicated to marketing and operations, public affairs, engineering, corporate finance, human resources, and other basic functions. "Going Global" describes how the Body Shop has also come to use this form of organization design.

The global functional design offers several advantages:

1 The firm can easily transfer expertise within each functional area. For example, Exxon uses the global functional design, so that production skills learned by Exxon's crews operating in the Gulf of Mexico can be used by its offshore operations in Malaysia's Jerneh field, and new catalytic cracking technology tested at its Baton Rouge, Louisiana, refinery can be adopted by its refineries in Singapore and Trecate, Italy.[23]

2 Managers can maintain highly centralized control over functional operations. For example, the head of Exxon's refinery division can rapidly adjust the production runs or product mix of refineries to meet changes

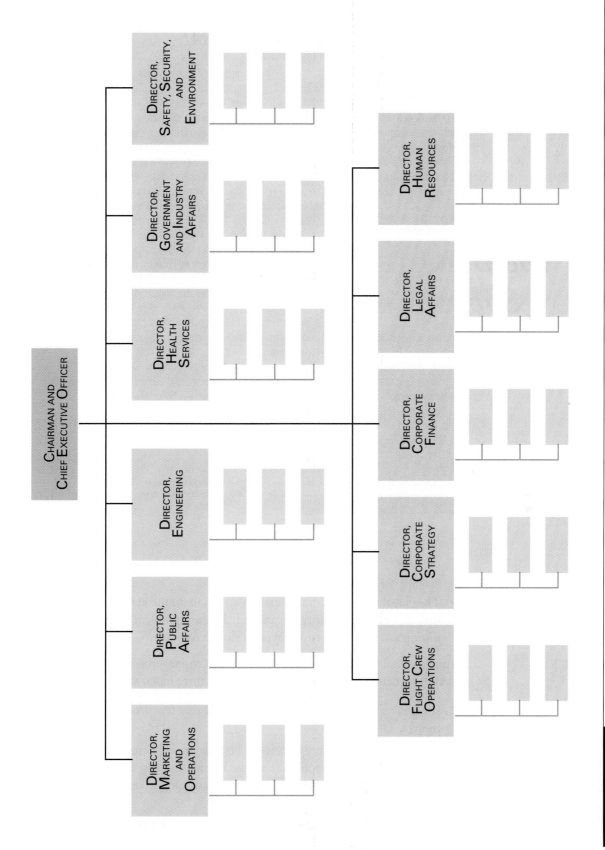

FIGURE 13.5   British Airways' Global Functional Design

Blunders at the Body Shop

The Body Shop is a unique company. Founded in England in 1976 by Anita Roddick, the firm sells cosmetics and toiletries. Roddick has always had a strong social agenda, and applied that agenda to her firm. For example, all of the products made for and sold at the Body Shop are environmentally friendly. The products use all-natural ingredients, avoid testing on animals, and rely heavily on recycled materials. Roddick also tries to use suppliers from less developed countries whenever possible.

Growing from a single store, the Body Shop eventually became England's largest international retailer with over 1000 stores worldwide. But with growth came serious problems. Roddick was so focused on her social agenda that she did not pay adequate attention to the actual management of her firm. Indeed, she never developed any sort of formal organization design for the Body Shop. As a result, when the firm grew too large for her to manage alone, she simply allowed operations and activities to evolve with no formal forethought. For example, reporting relationships were seldom defined, and communication between different parts of the organization was nonexistent.

Not surprisingly, the Body Shop began to suffer. Profit margins began to slip, and a new competitor, Bath & Body Works (a division of The Limited, a U.S. retailer), took away big chunks of market share. Finally, in 1995 Roddick was forced to admit that her firm needed more professional management. She subsequently appointed Stuart Rose, a retailing industry veteran, to run the firm.

One of Rose's first steps was to create a formal organization design for the Body Shop. To get things back on track as quickly as possible, he implemented a U-form functional design, centralizing finance, marketing, new product development, and other functions at company headquarters. This step has served to improve inventory control, streamline operations, improve communication, and lower costs. Of course, the firm must still sharpen its strategy and do some fine-tuning of its design. But on balance, actually having an organization design—really for the first time—is helping to turn things around at the Body Shop.

Sources: Charles P. Wallace, "Can the Body Shop Shape Up?" *Fortune*, April 15, 1996, pp. 118–120; "Key Success Factors from Leading Innovative Retailors," *International Journal of Retail and Distribution Management*, June–July, 1997, pp. 6–7.

in worldwide demand, thereby achieving efficient usage of these very expensive corporate resources.

3 The global functional design focuses attention on the key functions of the firm. For example, managers can easily isolate a problem in marketing and distinguish it from activities in other functional areas.

Despite these advantages, however, this design is inappropriate for many businesses. In particular, this organization design has three major shortcomings:

1 It is practical only when the firm has relatively few products or customers.

2 Coordination between divisions can be a major problem. For example, the manufacturing division and the marketing division may become so differentiated from each other that each may start pursuing its own goals to the detriment of the firm as a whole.

3 There may be duplication of resources among managers. For example, the finance, marketing, and operations managers may each hire an expert on

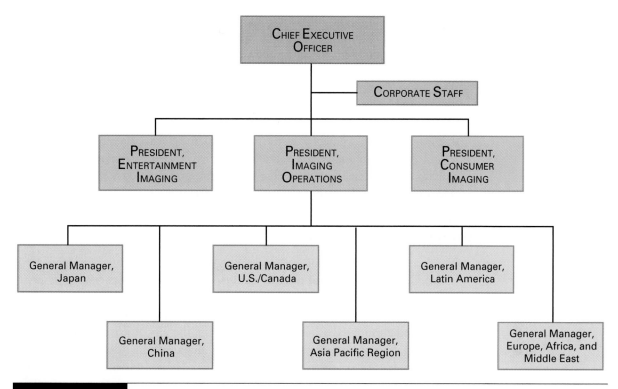

FIGURE 13.6

**Eastman Kodak's
Global Customer
Design**

Japanese regulation, when a single expert could have served all three functional areas just as effectively.

Because of these problems, the global functional design has limited applicability. It is used by many firms engaged in extracting and processing natural resources, such as in the mining and energy industries, because in their case the ability to transfer technical expertise is important. Firms that need to impose uniform standards on all of their operations may also adopt this approach. For example, to ensure safety, British Airways standardizes its maintenance and flight procedures regardless of whether a flight originates in London, Hong Kong, or Sydney.

Global Customer Design

The **global customer design** is used when a firm serves different customers or customer groups, each with specific needs calling for special expertise or attention. For example, Kodak has adopted a global customer design, as is shown in Fig. 13.6. Its Entertainment Imaging Group focuses on selling high-quality film to studios in Hollywood, London, Munich, Hong Kong, Toronto, and other centers for filmed entertainment. Its Consumer Imaging Group sells to professional and amateur photographers, while its Imaging Operations Group targets businesses and the medical community, selling scanners, copier-printers, and high-tech medical film and imaging systems throughout the world.

Japan's Bridgestone Corporation, the world's third-largest tire manufacturer, uses the global customer design in selling tires worldwide under its brand names Bridgestone and Firestone. One division deals with automobile manufacturers such as Ford, Nissan, and BMW, which buy tires as original equipment for new automobiles. Another deals with individual consumers and markets tires through the firm's network of automotive retail outlets. Still another division markets tires to agricultural users through firms such as Deere and Case.

This design is useful when the various customer groups targeted by the firm are so diverse as to require totally distinct marketing approaches. For example, selling four replacement tires to an individual is a completely different task from selling 4 million tires to an automaker. The global customer approach allows the firm to meet the specific needs of each customer segment and track how well its products or services are doing among those segments. On the other hand, the global customer design may lead to a significant duplication of resources, if each customer group needs its own area and functional specialists. Coordination between the different divisions is also difficult, since each is concerned with a fundamentally different market.

Global Matrix Design

The most complex form of international organization design is the global matrix design.[24] A **global matrix design** is the result of superimposing one form of organization design on top of an existing, different form. The resulting design is usually quite fluid, with new matrix dimensions being created, downscaled, and eliminated as needed. For example, the global matrix design shown in Fig. 13.7 was created by superimposing a global product design (shown down the side) on an existing global functional design (shown across the top). Using a global matrix design, a firm can form specific product groups comprising members from existing functional departments. These product groups can then plan, design, develop, produce, and market new products with appropriate input from each functional area. In this way, the firm can draw on both the functional and the product expertise of its employees. After a given product development task is completed, the product group may be dissolved; its members will then move on to new assignments. And, of course, other matrix arrangements are possible. For example, an area design could be overlaid on a functional design, thereby allowing area specialists to coordinate activities with functional experts.

The global matrix design has the advantage of helping to bring together the functional, area, and product expertise of the firm into teams that develop new products or respond to new challenges in the global marketplace. For example, Texas Instruments (TI) often uses a global matrix design for new product development, although its underlying organization design is based on function. At any time, it has several product development groups in operation. Within any given country in which TI operates, the groups draw members from relevant functional groups and work toward creating new products or new uses for existing ones. When and if such breakthroughs are achieved, matrix-based product groups are used to transfer the new technology throughout the rest of the firm.[25] After the task assigned to the product group is completed (for example, after the new product is launched), the group may be dissolved.

The global matrix design thus promotes organizational flexibility. It allows firms to take advantage of functional, area, customer, and product organization designs as needed while simultaneously minimizing the disadvantages of each. Members of a product development team can be added or dropped from the team as the firm's needs change. The global matrix design also promotes coordination and communication among managers from different divisions.

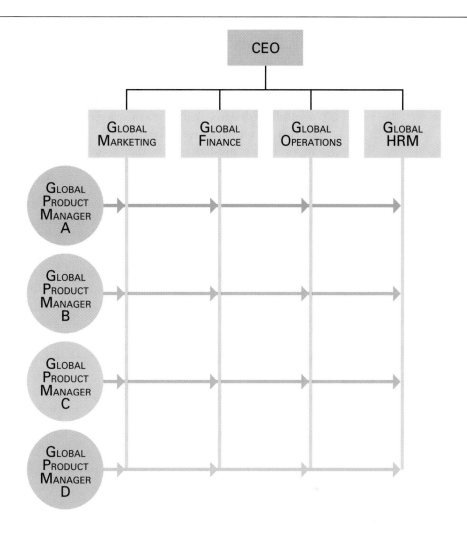

FIGURE 13.7

A Global Matrix Design

The global matrix design has disadvantages, however:

1 It is not appropriate for a firm that has few products and that operates in relatively stable markets.

2 It often puts employees in the position of being accountable to more than one manager. For example, at any given time an employee may be a member of his or her functional, area, or product group as well as of two or three product development groups. As a result, the individual may have split loyalties—caught between competing sets of demands and pressures as the area manager the employee reports to wants one thing and the product-line manager wants another.

3 The global matrix design creates a paradox regarding authority. On the one hand, part of its purpose is to put decision-making authority in the hands of those managers most able to use it quickly. On the other hand, because reporting relationships are so complex and vague, getting approval for major decisions may actually be slower.

4 It tends to promote compromises or decisions based on the relative political clout of the managers involved.[26]

Hybrid Global Designs

A final point to consider is that each global form of international organization design described in this section represents an ideal. Most firms create a hybrid design that best suits their purposes, as dictated in part by size, strategy, technology, environment, and culture. Most MNCs are likely to blend elements of all these designs. A firm may use a global product design as its overall approach, but it may have different levels of functional orientation or area focus in some of its product groups than in others. In fact, if it were possible to compare the designs used by the world's 500 largest MNCs, no two would look exactly the same. A firm's managers start with the basic prototypes discussed here, merge them, throw out bits and pieces, and create new elements unique to their firm as they respond to changes in the organization's strategy and competitive environment.

Figure 13.8 illustrates how Nissan Motor Corporation uses a hybrid design to structure its U.S. operations. At the top level of the firm, Nissan has some managers dedicated to products (such as the vice president and general manager for the Infiniti division) and others dedicated to functions (such as the vice president and chief financial officer). The marketing function for Nissan automobiles is broken down by product, with specific units responsible for sedans, sports cars, and trucks and utility vehicles. Both the Infiniti and Nissan divisions also have regional general managers organized by area. In similar fashion, all large international firms mix and match forms of organization in different areas and at different levels to create hybrid organization designs that their managers believe best serve the firm's needs.

Related Issues in Global Organization Design

In addition to the fundamental issues of organization design we have already addressed, MNCs also face a number of related organizational issues that must be carefully managed. We discuss several of these issues next:

- Centralization versus decentralization
- The role of subsidiary boards of directors
- Coordination among the firm's various operations

Centralization versus Decentralization

When designing its organization, an MNC must make a particularly crucial decision, one that involves the level of autonomy, power, and control it wants to grant its subsidiaries. Suppose it chooses to decentralize decision making by allowing individual subsidiaries great discretion over strategy, finance, production, and marketing decisions, thereby allowing those decisions to be made by managers closest to the market. These managers may then focus only on the subsidiary's needs rather than the firm's overall needs. An MNC can remedy this deficiency by tightly centralizing decision-making authority at corporate headquarters. Decisions made by the corporate staff can then take into account the firm's overall

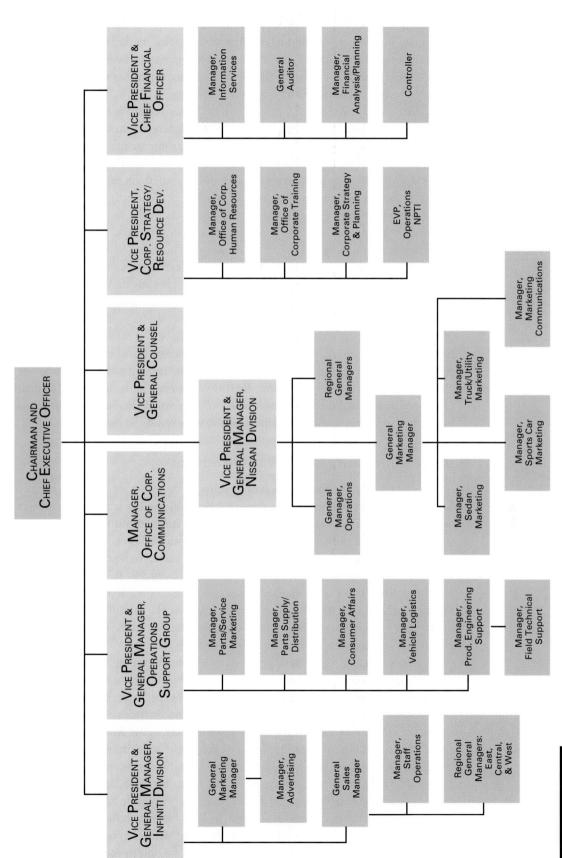

FIGURE 13.8 **Nissan USA's Hybrid Design**

needs. However, these decisions often hinder the ability of subsidiary managers to quickly and effectively respond to changes in their local market conditions. Because both centralization and decentralization offer attractive benefits to the MNC, most firms use a blend of the two and constantly tinker with the blend to achieve the best outcome in terms of overall strategy.

There seems to be a trend among some MNCs toward greater centralization. While the need to address local factors in different markets is best handled by decentralizing control to local managers, some managers have come to believe it is more important to address the specific needs of different customer groups across many markets, a task best handled via centralization. For example, Europcar International SA, Europe's largest car-rental firm, used to be very decentralized. High-ranking local managers in the nine countries it served held great authority and ran their local operations with virtual autonomy. However, the firm's new CEO decided that business customers, tourists, and local individual renters each represented a clear market segment whose needs could better be handled via centralization. He thus fired the country managers—replacing them with lower-level managers—and centralized operations at headquarters.[27]

Advancements in electronic communications have also made it easier for firms to centralize more of their operations. For example, workers at Sun Microsystems who want to change their employee benefits can log onto the corporate web site and fill out forms electronically from anywhere. This allows Sun to maintain a single centralized benefits coordination unit, rather than having many such units attached to each of its subsidiaries scattered around the world.[28]

Role of Subsidiary Boards of Directors

An MNC typically incorporates each of its subsidiaries in that subsidiary's country of operation in order to limit the subsidiary's liability and to allow it to attain legal status as a local citizen. Most countries require each corporation, including a wholly owned subsidiary of a foreign MNC, to have a board of directors. This board is elected by corporate shareholders (which is the MNC), is responsible to those shareholders for the effective management of the subsidiary (which is owned by the MNC), and oversees the activities of top-level managers (who are hired by the MNC). The issue facing most MNCs, then, is whether to view the creation of a subsidiary board of directors as a pro forma exercise and therefore give the board little real authority or to empower the board with substantial decision-making authority.

Empowering the subsidiary's board has a primary advantage of promoting decentralization. Foreign subsidiaries may need the authority to act quickly and decisively without having to always seek the parent's approval. Also, if the MNC decentralizes authority to local levels, an active board provides a clear accountability and reporting link back to corporate headquarters. Some MNCs have also found that appointing prominent local citizens to the subsidiary's board is helpful in conducting business in a foreign country. These members can help the subsidiary integrate itself into the local business community and can be an effective source of information for both parent and subsidiary about local business and political conditions. For example, prominent local business officials on the board of Apple's Japanese subsidiary were key to the firm's success in the Japanese market in the early 1990s. They enhanced the credibility of Apple's products in a market in which corporate connections and status are an important marketing tool, while their appointment demonstrated Apple's long-term commitment to the Japanese market.[29] A subsidiary board also can help monitor the subsidiary's ethical and social responsibility practices. Among the MNCs that make frequent use of such boards are Honda, Matsushita, Hewlett-Packard, and Dow.

A potential disadvantage of empowering a subsidiary's board is that the subsidiary may become too independent as its board assumes too much authority and thereby fails to maintain the desired level of accountability to the parent. This chapter's closing case discusses how this problem arose among the subsidiaries of Royal Dutch/Shell.

In general, a subsidiary board is most useful when the subsidiary has a great deal of autonomy, its own self-contained management structure, and a business identity separate from the parent's. Active subsidiary boards are particularly useful in H-form organizations, since a holding company's subsidiaries are typically run independently of one another. For example, Nestlé's U.S. subsidiary, Carnation, meets each of the three criteria noted above. Not surprisingly, therefore, Carnation also has a very active board of directors.

Coordination in the Global Organization

Finally, as part of creating an effective design for itself, an international firm must also address its coordination needs. In this sense, **coordination** is the process of linking and integrating functions and activities of different groups, units, or divisions. Coordination needs vary as a function of interdependence among the firm's divisions and functions.[30] That is, the higher the level of interdependence among divisions and functions, the more coordination is necessary among them. There are three levels of interdependence:

1 Organizations that have less need for coordination have *pooled interdependence;* that is, each division or activity functions with relatively little dependence on the others because it does its own work and its results are pooled with the others' at the corporate level. Examples are H-form organizations and firms that use the global product design.

2 Firms with moderate coordination needs are characterized by *sequential interdependence;* that is, each division or activity is dependent on only some of the others because work flows between divisions in a one-way or sequential fashion. Examples are M-form organizations and firms that use global area or customer designs.

3 The highest coordination needs are found in organizations that have *reciprocal interdependence;* that is, each division or activity is dependent on all other divisions or activities because work flows back and forth between divisions in a reciprocal fashion. Examples are U-form organizations and firms that use global functional and matrix designs.

MNCs use any of several strategies to achieve and manage their desired level of coordination. The organizational hierarchy itself is one way to manage interdependence and promote coordination. An organization design that clearly specifies all reporting relationships and directions of influence facilitates coordination because each manager knows how to channel communications, decision making, and so on. Rules and procedures also facilitate coordination. For example, a standard operating procedure that requires the reporting of monthly and quarterly revenue, cost, and profit data to headquarters allows corporate staff to coordinate the firm's cash flows and to quickly identify troublesome markets.

MNCs may also adopt somewhat more temporary or ad hoc coordination techniques.[31] Using employees in liaison roles is one such technique. For example, suppose two divisions of an MNC are collaborating on an activity or function. Each may designate a specific manager as its liaison with the other. If any manager in one unit has information or questions that involve the other unit, it is channeled through the liaison to the appropriate person or unit. Toyota, for example, frequently uses this technique for managing relatively small-scale joint efforts.

When the magnitude of the collaboration is significant, task forces may be used for coordination. Here, each participating unit or division assigns one or more representatives to serve on the task force. The assignment may be either full-time or part-time. Ford and Mazda, for example, used a task force when they collaborated on the design of the Ford Escort. Each firm designated members of its design, engineering, operations, and finance departments to serve on the task force. Employees of the two firms rotated on and off the task force depending on its needs and the stage of development of the automobile. When the final design was complete and the automobile was put into production, the task force was dissolved.

Task forces may also be used to resolve intraorganizational conflicts or to build commitment to new projects. For example, in the early days of the personal computer industry (the early 1980s), Toshiba had to decide which operating system its personal computers would use. To the managers of its U.S. affiliate, Toshiba America, there was only one choice: IBM-compatible. However, the firm's Japanese engineers and marketing staff resisted this choice. So Toshiba created a task force composed of Toshiba America managers, Japanese R&D staff, and Japanese marketers, who, with the aid of a consulting firm, interviewed computer users, distributors, and dealers. In the end, the task force decided that Toshiba's personal computers should be IBM-compatible. Although this decision was obvious to the U.S. managers, the task force was still invaluable because it resulted in the Japanese employees' being fully committed to the use of the IBM-compatible operating system.[32]

Many international firms also rely heavily on informal coordination mechanisms. Informal management networks can be especially effective. An **informal management network** is simply a group of managers from different parts of the world who are connected to one another in some way. These connections often form as a result of personal contact, mutual acquaintances, and interaction achieved via travel, training programs, joint meetings, task force experiences, and so on. Informal management networks can be very powerful for short-circuiting bureaucracy that may delay communication and decision making. They also can be effective for getting things done more quickly and more effectively than if normal and routine procedures were always followed.[33]

Corporate Culture in International Business

While the structural components of an organization design can be somewhat objectively specified and drawn in an organizational chart, there also are informal elements of an organization that are more subjective and amorphous. This informal organization, which also plays a critical role in coordination, is called the corporate culture. **Corporate culture** is the set of shared values that defines for its members what the organization stands for, how it functions, and what it considers important.[34] Most managers agree that it is important to develop a clearly defined and consistent culture to help guide the behavior of managers. Such a culture not only helps managers make sense of the organization and facilitates their understanding of their own jobs but also contributes to overall competitiveness.[35]

Creating such a culture is difficult for any organization. Success in doing so is considerably more important for an MNC, however, than for a purely domestic firm. Each unit within the MNC will naturally have its own culture. This unit culture will be partially defined by the national culture within which that unit functions. At the same time, however, there also needs to be an overall corporate culture that permeates the entire organization. At Sony, for example, the firm's Japanese units have one culture, while its U.S. units have a different one. Each culture was developed from the context of the national culture of the units. But there is also the overall culture—"Sony's Way"—that permeates the entire firm.

Creating the Corporate Culture in International Business

The creation of a corporate culture for an MNC usually starts with the firm's mission statement. As discussed in Chapter 10, the mission statement spells out the firm's values, goals, and basic operating philosophy. But managers throughout the firm must also accept and enact the corporate culture if it is to become a reality. Contributing to the development of a strong and accepted corporate culture are symbols (such as the corporate logo), heroes (usually successful and distinctive managers), legends (including stories about past successes and failures that get passed from manager to manager), and shared experiences (such as working together toward shared goals). For example, Sony's former chairman, Akio Morita, was one of the firm's founders, and his personal values and beliefs still permeate the entire organization. He is given credit for much of the firm's success today and is revered by many of the firm's employees. Because of his integrity, loyalty to his employees, and exemplary managerial acumen, his influence is indelibly felt throughout the firm.

Many MNCs have found that changing their culture is an important element in improving their global competitiveness. For example, when Helmut Maucher became CEO of Nestlé, he soon decided that the firm was too bureaucratic and not sufficiently interested in innovation. Maucher is a tough-minded executive who abhors bureaucracy. He hates to read reports and thinks most firms spend too much time processing paperwork instead of carrying out their business. He adopted the slogan "Let's have more pepper and less paper" to let people know he wanted them to spend less time on paperwork and more time communicating,

GOING GLOBAL

Philips Tries to Change Its Culture

Philips Electronics is Europe's largest manufacturer of such electronics products as light bulbs, televisions, shavers, and dictation machines. For years, however, the firm has been performing at disappointing levels. For example, in 1996 Philips generated $37 billion in sales with its 262,500 employees. Sony, however, which is Philips' most direct competitor, used its 151,000 employees to generate $43 billion in sales.

One reason critics cite for Philips' mediocre performance is that for years its top managers have been too inbred—starting their careers at the company at an early age, working up through the ranks, and not really understanding other ways of doing business. But this pattern recently changed when Cor Boonstra was hired to run the company. Boonstra, originally from the Netherlands, had spent the previous twenty years at Sara Lee, a major U.S. consumer products firm.

Boonstra quickly decided that Philips' biggest problems were related to its organization design. Specifically, he felt that the firm was too bureaucratic. It had too many layers of management, too many rules and procedures, and was too slow in getting things done. Consequently, he drew up a blueprint for organization change based on flattening the organization, eliminating unnecessary rules, and allowing managers at lower levels of the organization to make more significant decisions.

Boonstra also sold off twenty subsidiaries that did not fit into Philips' strategic plan or that were unlikely to meet his target of a 24 percent rate of return on equity, including Grundig, a TV manufacturer, and a subsidiary making car navigation systems. To lower input costs, Boonstra shifted some of Philips' parts production to Asia. To better position Philips in the cellular telephone market, he teamed with Lucent Technologies to create a $2.5 billion joint venture that combined their existing consumer communication operations.

Perhaps the most dramatic symbol that Philips could no longer operate the way it has for a century was announced by Boonstra in late 1997: the company's headquarters would be shifted from the small Dutch city of Eindhoven to the country's bustling commercial capital, Amsterdam.

While it is too soon to assess the results of these steps, insiders believe that Boonstra's actions may be just what the doctor ordered to ignite new growth at the firm.

Sources: Charles P. Wallace, "Can He Fix Philips?" *Fortune*, March 31, 1997, pp. 98–100; "Philips' Outlook Revisal to Stable; Ratings Affirmed," *PR Newswire*, August 29, 1997, p. 829. "Ultimatum at Philips," *Business Week*, November 17, 1997, p. 134; "Philips and Lucent late at the party," *Financial Times*, June 19, 1997, p. 16.

stimulating innovation, and generating new ideas. He repeatedly used this slogan in conversations and meetings with Nestlé managers worldwide. As a result, it gradually became embedded in the firm's corporate culture. "Going Global" shows how another major European company, Philips, is currently trying to change its culture to improve its competitiveness.

Of course, there is no one best culture toward which international firms should aspire. For example, TI, Honda, and Daimler-Benz each have a distinctive corporate culture that helps everyone understand how the firm functions. TI has what its managers call a "shirt sleeve" culture in which people "roll up their sleeves" and work hard; there are few status differences among its managers. Honda, on the other hand, has a culture that stresses teamwork and togetherness. Each Honda employee understands that he or she is to take responsibility for doing whatever is necessary to enhance quality. Daimler-Benz's culture centers around technology. The firm and its managers have always focused on applying technology as efficiently and effectively as possible. As a result, Daimler-Benz managers put a premium on technological innovation and refinement. The firm also considers its German operations to be superior to its operations in other countries, and so it concentrates its highest-profile and highest-profit activities in its German factories.

Managing the Corporate Culture in International Business

Managing the corporate culture is best approached from the standpoints of consistency and communication. Managers should take every opportunity to communicate the firm's culture to others so as to keep it in the forefront of decision making and other activities. Frequent contact and interaction between managers and other employees are also useful for transmitting and reinforcing the corporate culture. Still another way to spread the culture throughout the organization is to transfer key managers to different units.

A strong corporate culture can help transmit a firm's values and beliefs to operations around the world. For example, Pizza Hut worked hard to ensure that its foreign restaurants would have the same entrepreneurial culture as its successful outlets in the United States. The firm discovered how well it had succeeded when the manager of the Moscow Pizza Hut passed out free food to demonstrators fighting a failed coup attempt, winning the firm much goodwill among Russians.

When corporate culture is not properly managed, the firm is likely to stumble and its effectiveness diminish. For example, Bond Corporation Holdings, Inc., once a high-flying Australian conglomerate, suffered serious setbacks in the last few years, in part because of its disjointed and vague culture. During the 1980s, Bond amassed a collection of businesses ranging from breweries to newspapers to banks to resorts. Some units thought cost control was paramount; others thought they were supposed to expand aggressively with little regard for the bottom line; still others believed their mandate was to earn profits regardless of the methods employed. Because of such diverse approaches and the poorly articulated corporate vision, the Bond empire crumbled and its various units self-destructed. Today, Bond is a shell of its former self, in large part because its managers failed to develop a strong, clearly defined culture.[36]

In contrast, Merrill Lynch works hard at spreading its corporate culture to its new operations as it expands around the world. The financial services firm wants to be known for doing business in a straightforward and honest way with few of the elaborate trappings used by many other Wall Street brokerage firms. Whenever the firm opens a branch in another country, it hires local managers to run it. But those managers are first brought to the firm's U.S. training center to learn the Merrill Lynch system, including not only operating procedures but the company's values and culture as well. And each office contains a sign in the local language reflecting Merrill Lynch's philosophy—"Integrity: No one's personal bottom line is more important than the reputation of the firm."[37]

Managing Change in International Business

Another critical facet of organization design in international firms is change management. In this context, **organization change** is any significant modification or alteration in the firm's strategy, organization design, technology, and/or employees. The process of internationalizing the firm's design, discussed earlier in the chapter, is an important example of organization change. Because the international environment in which a firm operates is never static, managing change in ways that enhance the firm's productivity and profitability is a continual challenge confronting international managers. Because managing change is both complex and important, international managers must understand the reasons for change, the varieties of change they may confront, and how to implement change most effectively.[38]

Reasons for Change in International Business

Change in the firm may be necessitated by any number of factors.[39] Among the most significant forces for organization change are changes in the environment in which the firm operates. As new markets open or existing markets shrink, for example, the firm must develop appropriate responses. Consider the completion of the EU's internal market in 1992. Literally thousands of firms changed their strategy for doing business in that market. Some rearranged production among their existing factories, hoping to benefit from economies of scale. Unilever, for example, restructured its detergent product line by replacing autonomous, nearly independent national operations with a new subsidiary, Lever Europe, which was charged with treating Europe as one big market.[40] Other firms bought out their competitors in order to broaden their presence within the EU. For example, Air France prepared for the EU's deregulation of air services by purchasing Air Inter, the leading provider of internal air services in France. Firms headquartered outside the EU, such as Samsung, Toshiba, Whirlpool, and Procter & Gamble, increased their direct investments in that area. But as non-EU firms increased their presence, existing firms were forced to respond as well. For example, entrenched European automakers such as Fiat, BMW, and Ford of Europe have had to improve their productivity and quality in the face of increased competition from non-EU firms such as Toyota, Nissan, and Mitsubishi.

Organization change can also result from changes in technology. New technology may redefine work roles and reporting relationships among employees. For example, the spread of personal computers in the workplace has reduced the need for mainframe computers, altered the role of corporate MIS staff, and offered customer service employees far more information than their counterparts possessed two decades ago, thereby raising their stature as well as their educational requirements. Advances in telecommunications technology have also affected organization design. U.S. computer firms, for example, have established joint ventures in Ireland and India to supply software, which is then transported electronically via satellite to program developers in the United States.

Changes in cultural values and mores also can prompt organization change. For example, decreased consumption of tobacco products in the United States has caused makers of such products to diversify into other products. Philip Morris purchased General Foods in 1985 and Kraft in 1988. It is now aggressively attacking the European market, acquiring chocolate and coffee marketer Jacob Suchard as well as the leading cigarette company in former East Germany. However, Philip Morris has had to admit to at least one failure: it cannot get French consumers to buy Kraft Velveeta cheese.[41]

Types of Change in International Business

Change in a firm can take many forms. One significant change occurs when a firm alters its corporate strategy, which results when an international firm moves among the single-product, related diversification, and unrelated diversification strategies discussed in Chapter 10. A firm entering a new market is undertaking strategic change, as is one that adopts a new entry mode such as FDI or a joint venture. Even more dramatic strategic changes include acquiring or being acquired by another firm.[42]

As such changes in corporate strategy develop, compensating changes in organization design are often necessary in order to implement the new strategy successfully.[43] Design changes may involve how the firm configures itself, how it delegates authority to its subsidiaries abroad, how it engages in coordination, and how it establishes reporting relationships. Market conditions may also prompt changes in organization design. For example, Siemens Nixdorf had trouble attaining profitability in its core computer businesses, in part because it could not keep pace with rapid technological and marketing changes in this industry. In order to improve profits and innovation, in 1992 the firm split its computer operations into three autonomous divisions: personal computer, computer printer, and corporate computer systems. By so doing, Siemens Nixdorf made each division more responsive to changes in the competitive environment.[44]

A final type of organization change involves a firm's employees. A firm sometimes wants to change the attitudes of its employees—for example, enhance their morale or improve their job satisfaction. It also may find it useful to improve its employees' ability or performance levels. For example, Collins & Aikman implemented a systematic program of improving its employees' reading and math skills to ensure they can efficiently operate the firm's increasingly sophisticated textile machinery.

In other cases, the firm effects employee change via transfers, promotions, terminations, or the hiring of more qualified people. For example, the board of directors of Beecham Group PLC, a British consumer products firm, wanted a CEO who had a strong commitment to and understanding of global competitiveness. However, it did not think any current Beecham executive had those qualities, so it hired an experienced U.S. manager, Robert P. Bauman, who had demonstrated his abilities in several previous positions.[45] Similarly, in the early 1990s GM became increasingly concerned that its automobiles' old-fashioned appearance was endangering its short-term profitability and long-term viability. So it transferred the chief designer at its German subsidiary to Detroit to head its worldwide design programs.[46]

CHAPTER REVIEW

Summary

Organization design is the overall pattern of structural components and configurations used to manage the total organization. Early attempts to identify the one best way to design organizations included the bureaucratic design. However, managers now realize that the most appropriate design of an organization depends on its situation. Managers today also realize that organization design is an evolutionary process.

When a firm first begins to operate internationally, it usually must change its design in one or more ways. Such change may involve following the corollary approach, then establishing an export department, and then creating an international division.

After a firm has established a significant international presence, however, it will usually develop a global organization design. The most common approaches to global organization design are the global product design, the global area design, the global functional design, the global customer design, and the global matrix design. Each of these approaches has unique advantages and disadvantages, and one or more may be more appropriate for some firms than for others. Indeed, many firms actually use a hybrid global design best suited to their needs.

MNCs also must make other decisions related to organization design. Particularly important are those regarding centralization versus decentralization, the role of subsidiary boards of directors, and which coordination mechanisms to use. Informal management networks are especially powerful mechanisms for coordination.

Whereas a firm's design is relatively formal and objective, its culture is more informal and subjective. Corporate culture is the set of values that defines for members what the firm stands for, how it functions, and what it considers important. Culture is shaped by such things as the firm's mission statement, symbols, heroes, legends, past successes and failures, and shared experiences. A strong, clearly defined, and well-managed culture can be a major contributor to the firm's success.

Organization change is any significant modification or alteration in the firm's strategy, organization design, technology, and/or employees. Most firms find they must change regularly for various reasons. The key is to keep change properly focused on specific objectives and in line with other aspects of the firm.

Review Questions

1. What is organization design?

2. What are some of the initial impacts of international activity on organization design?

3. What is the global product design? What are its strengths and weaknesses?

4. What is the global area design? What are its strengths and weaknesses?

5. What is the global functional design? What are its strengths and weaknesses?

6. What is the global customer design? What are its strengths and weaknesses?

7. What is the global matrix design? What are its strengths and weaknesses?

8. What are three issues related to organization design that MNCs face?

9. What is corporate culture? Why is it important in international business?

10. What is organization change? Why do managers of international firms need to understand organization change?

Questions for Discussion

1. Why does a firm's organization design depend on its situation? Why is the design evolutionary?

2. If a new organization starts out with a global perspective, will it necessarily experience any of the initial impacts of international activity on organization design? Why or why not?

3. Do managers of international firms need to approach organization design differently from their counterparts in domestic firms? Why or why not?

4. How do the global product, area, functional, and customer approaches to organization design differ? How are they similar?

5. Why is a global matrix design almost always transitional in nature?

6. Why do international firms need to develop a unique organization design rather than simply model themselves after other firms?

7. Why is coordination important in international business?

8. Can a strong corporate culture be bad? If not, why? If so, give an example.

9. How are national culture and corporate culture likely to be related?

10. Under what circumstances might a firm need to change its design from one of the global designs to a different one?

BUILDING GLOBAL SKILLS

Form small groups of three or four students. Assume that your group is the board of directors of a large firm, Unipro Incorporated, which for many years followed a single-product strategy. It manufactured small jet aircraft and sold them worldwide. Its products are market leaders in North America, Asia, and Europe and also sell well in South America and Africa. Because of the single-product strategy, Unipro set up a global functional organization design, which it still uses.

The board has been concerned about the firm's dependence on a single product, so several years ago it decided to diversify the firm. Over four years, the firm has bought several other businesses:

♦ General Chemical (based in England; almost 90 percent of its revenues come from Europe)

♦ Total Software (based in Canada; most of its revenues come from North America and Europe)

♦ Pleasure Park (an amusement park in Japan)

♦ Fundamental Foods (a large food-processing firm with strong operations in the United States, Europe, and Japan)

Now that Unipro's diversification strategy has been fully implemented, the board (your group) sees that it needs to change the firm's organization design to better fit the new business mix. Based solely on the information you have, sketch a new organization design for the firm. When you are finished, draw your organization design on the blackboard.

Follow-up Questions

1. How is your group's organization design similar to and different from those of other groups?

2. What do you see as the biggest advantages and disadvantages of your group's organization design?

3. What additional information would have made it easier for you to develop a new organization design for Unipro?

WORKING WITH THE WEB: Building Global Internet Skills

Matching Intranets and Organization Design

Most larger companies today make use of what they call an "intranet." An intranet is similar to the Internet but is specific to a single company. Various web pages are developed for different divisions, functions, and operations within the company, and users move through the system using a browser such as Netscape. There is also a "security screen" around most intranets—usually called a *firewall*—that keeps unauthorized users from accessing the system. The system itself is used for communication and coordination among people in the organization.

On a sheet of paper draw a 2 × 5 matrix. Label each of the "5" cells to correspond to the five basic global organization designs (exclude the hybrid design). Label the "2" cells "centralized" and "decentralized." Inside each cell, note one or two especially important criteria for the effective use of an intranet for that particular situation.

For example, an intranet for a centralized/global product design might require local product managers frequently to report and share information with authorities at corporate headquarters. Likewise, an intranet for a decentralized/global matrix design might need to focus more on multiple-directional communication capabilities.

After you have completed filling in your matrix, form small groups with three or four of your classmates. Compare and contrast the criteria you each developed individually, and then develop a group matrix.

Questions for Discussion

1. What are the similarities and differences that need to be kept in mind when developing intranet and Internet web sites?

2. What role might an intranet play in an international company beyond communication and coordination, as addressed in this exercise?

CLOSING CASE

Shell Shifts Its Structure[47]

Royal Dutch/Shell represents an interesting enigma. On the one hand, it is one of the world's most profitable firms and invariably provides its investors with one of the highest returns in the petroleum industry. On the other hand, its senior managers have concluded that the firm needs a major overhaul if it is to remain competitive.

Like Unilever, Royal Dutch/Shell is headquartered in two countries. London-based Shell Transport & Trading owns 40 percent of the firm, while Royal Dutch Petroleum, based in The Hague, controls 60 percent. Overall, the company has over 100,000 employees, owns 54 refineries and 47,000 gasoline stations, and operates in 130 countries.

Royal Dutch/Shell has traditionally been very decentralized. Its two headquarters together comprise an entity called—oddly enough—the Centre. Executives at the Centre coordinate a network of global shared services such as research and planning. But the firm's 100 or so operating companies have been almost totally independent in terms of how they manage their operations.

Each one is led by a CEO and virtually all have their own boards of directors. Each local business built up such strong local ties over the years that many saw their counterparts in other countries as competitors rather than allies. And a long history had created a culture whereby loyalty to the local operating company was more valued and rewarded than loyalty to the parent firm.

In 1994 Royal Dutch/Shell's CEO, Cornelius Herkstroter, became concerned that the firm was not performing up to its true potential. To figure out why, he assembled the company's top fifty managers for a meeting. Amazingly, while several of these managers knew one another, they had never before been assembled in one place for a meeting.

Almost from the beginning of the meeting, Herkstroter realized that the problems were more severe than he had feared. The Centre, for example, had gradually been taken over by risk-averse bureaucrats who took months to approve the budgets of the operating companies. And the operating companies were not performing efficiently and were highly inconsistent in their profitability. Herkstroter decided that he had to shake things up if Royal Dutch/Shell was to maintain its lofty position in the petroleum industry.

His first step was to reduce the staff at the Centre by 30 percent. He then consolidated power at corporate headquarters into five basic oversight committees that were given global responsibilities for exploration and production, oil products, gas and coal, chemicals, and central staff functions such as the human resources and legal departments. Meanwhile, the operating companies' control and power in these areas were substantially reduced.

At first, the operating company CEOs rebelled at what they saw as a reduction in their influence. And several left the firm. But those who stayed began to see the benefits of this new way of doing things. For example, Royal Dutch/Shell is now able to use its massive size to buy things like gasoline additives for prices significantly lower than those paid by the various individual operating companies acting alone.

Herkstroter's next move was to change Royal Dutch/Shell's corporate culture. This culture was previously tied to entitlements based on seniority, educational background, and personal contacts. Herkstroter, however, believed that to remain competitive the firm needed to focus more attention on rewarding performance, fostering creativity and innovation, and being flexible and responsive. People throughout the firm also needed to recognize the value of working together and develop loyalties to the parent company.

To enact these changes, the CEO has relied heavily on outside consultants. Using techniques ranging from team-building exercises to personality assessment scales, managers at Royal Dutch/Shell are becoming more focused on interpersonal relations and the advantages of teamwork. Of course, a culture change of this magnitude is a big project, and the experts believe that it will take several more years before the work is done.

Case Questions

1. Describe Royal Dutch/Shell's old and new organization designs in terms of the forms discussed in this chapter.

2. What are the risks Royal Dutch/Shell is running in making the changes discussed in the case?

3. What future events might dictate another major change in Shell's organization design?

CHAPTER NOTES

1. "Unilever to Sell Specialty-Chemical Unit to ICI of the U.K. for About $8 Billion," *Wall Street Journal,* May 7, 1997, pp. A3, A12; "Unilever Sells Off Four Chemical Units," *USA Today,* May 8, 1997, p. 3B; *Hoover's Handbook of World Business 1997* (Austin, Texas: Hoover's Business Press, 1997).

2. J. M. Stopford and L. T. Wells, *Managing the Multinational Enterprise* (New York: Basic Books, 1972).

3. Alfred Chandler, Jr., *Strategy and Structure* (Cambridge, Mass.: MIT Press, 1962).

4. Gareth Jones, *Organizational Theory* 2nd ed. (Reading, Mass.: Addison-Wesley, 1998).

5. William G. Egelhoff, "Strategy and Structure in Multinational Corporations: An Information Processing Approach," *Administrative Science Quarterly,* Vol. 27 (1982), pp. 435–458.

6. Max Weber, *Theory of Social and Economic Organizations,* translated by T. Parsons (New York: Free Press, 1947).

7. See John Woodward, *Industrial Organization: Theory and Practice* (London: Oxford University Press, 1965); Tom Burns and G. M. Stalker, *The Management of Innovation* (London: Tavistock, 1961); Derek S. Pugh and David J. Hickson, *Organization Structure in Its Context: The Aston Program* (Lexington, Mass.: D.C. Heath, 1976).

8. See Jones, op. cit., for a review.

9. *Drug Store News*, Nov. 3, 1997, p. 21.

10. John P. Kotter and Leonard A. Schlesinger, "Choosing Strategies for Change," *Harvard Business Review* (March-April 1979), pp. 106–119.

11. Chandler, op. cit.

12. John D. Daniels, Robert A. Pitts, and Marietta J. Tretter, "Strategy and Structure of U.S. Multinationals: An Exploratory Study," *Academy of Management Journal*, Vol. 27, No. 2 (1984), pp. 292–307.

13. Banco Economico, *1991 Annual Report* (Salvador, Brazil: Banco Economico, 1992).

14. Anant K. Sundaram and J. Stewart Black, "The Environment and Internal Organization of Multinational Enterprises," *Academy of Management Review*, Vol. 17, No. 4 (1992), pp. 729–757.

15. Kendall Roth, David M. Schweiger, and Allen J. Morrison, "Global Strategy Implementation at the Business Unit Level: Operational Capabilities and Administrative Mechanisms," *The Journal of International Business Studies*, Vol. 22, No. 3 (Third Quarter 1991), pp. 369–402.

16. Arvind V. Phatak, *International Dimensions of Management*, 3rd ed. (Boston: PWS-Kent, 1992).

17. Bruce T. Lamont, Robert J. Williams, and James J. Hoffman, "Performance During 'M-Form' Reorganization and Recovery Time: The Effects of Prior Strategy and Implementation Speed," *Academy of Management Journal*, Vol. 37, No. 1 (1994), pp. 153–166.

18. "Dinosaur Rescue," *Business Week*, October 20, 1997, pp. 52–53.

19. Harsco Corporation, *1991 Annual Report* (Camp Hill, Pa.: Harsco Corporation, 1992).

20. Christopher A. Bartlett, "Organizing for Worldwide Effectiveness: The Transnational Solution," *California Management Review* (Fall 1988), pp. 54–74.

21. Alan Chai, Alta Campbell, and Patrick J. Spain (eds.), *Hoover's Handbook of World Business 1993*, op. cit., pp. 178–179.

22. Phatak, op. cit.

23. The Exxon Corporation, *1990 Annual Report* (Irving, Tex.: Exxon, 1991).

24. Christopher A. Bartlett and Sumantra Ghospal, "Matrix Management: Not a Structure, A Frame of Mind," *Harvard Business Review* (July-August 1990), pp. 138–145.

25. Jeremy Main, "How to Go Global—And Why," *Fortune,* August 28, 1989, pp. 70–76.

26. Lawton R. Burns and Douglas R. Wholey, "Adoption and Abandonment of Matrix Management Programs: Effects of Organizational Characteristics and Interorganizational Networks," *Academy of Management Journal,* Vol. 36, No. 1 (1993), pp. 105–138.

27. "Power at Multinationals Shifts to Home Office," *Wall Street Journal,* September 9, 1994, pp. B1, B4.

28. "Building a New Home," *Wall Street Journal*, September 26, 1997, p. 1B.

29. Edmund W. Desmond, "Byting Japan," *Time,* October 5, 1992, pp. 68–69.

30. James Thompson, *Organizations in Action* (New York: McGraw-Hill, 1967).

31. Jon I. Martinez and J. Carlos Jarillo, "The Evolution of Research on Coordination Mechanisms in Multinational Corporations," *The Journal of International Business Studies,* Vol. 20 (Fall 1989), pp. 489–514.

32. John Rehfeld, "What Working for a Japanese Company Taught Me," *Harvard Business Review* (November-December 1990), pp. 167–176.

33. Sumantra Ghoshal and Christopher A. Bartlett, "The Multinational Corporation as an Interorganizational Network," *Academy of Management Review,* Vol. 15, No. 4 (1990), pp. 603–625.

34. See Terrence E. Deal and Allan A. Kennedy, *Corporate Culture: The Rites and Rituals of Corporate Life* (Reading, Mass.: Addison-Wesley, 1982), for one of the most influential treatments of corporate culture.

35. Jay Barney, "Organizational Culture: Can It Be a Source of Sustained Competitive Advantage?" *Academy of Management Review* (July 1986), pp. 656–665.

36. Chai, Campbell, and Spain, op. cit., p. 154.

37. "Merrillizing the World," *Forbes*, February 10, 1997, pp. 146–151.

38. See Roy McLennan, *Managing Organizational Change* (Englewood Cliffs, N.J.: Prentice-Hall, 1989).

39. Rosabeth Moss Kanter, "Transcending Business Boundaries—12,000 World Managers View Change," *Harvard Business Review* (May-June 1991), pp. 151–164.

40. Guy de Jonquieres, "Unilever adopts a clean sheet approach," *Financial Times,* October 21, 1991, p. 13.

41. Patricia Sellars, "Can He Keep Philip Morris Growing?" *Fortune*, April 6, 1992, pp. 86–92.

42. Kotter and Schlesinger, op. cit.

43. William G. Egelhoff, *Organizing the Multinational Enterprise* (Cambridge, Mass.: Ballinger, 1988).

44. "Siemens AG," *Wall Street Journal,* October 9, 1992, p. B6.

45. "Beecham's Chief Imports American Ways," *Wall Street Journal,* October 27, 1988, p. B9.

46. "GM Selects Cherry as Vice President of Company's World-Wide Design Staff," *Wall Street Journal,* September 16, 1992, p. B9.

47. Janet Guyon, "Why Is the World's Most Profitable Company Turning Itself Inside Out?" *Fortune*, August 4, 1997, pp. 120–125; *Hoover's Handbook of World Business 1997*, op. cit., pp. 442–443.

Managing Behavior and Interpersonal Relations

Chapter Outline

Individual behavior in international business

Personality differences across cultures
Attitudes across cultures
Perception across cultures
Stress across cultures

Motivation in international business

Needs and values across cultures
Motivational processes across cultures
Need-based models across cultures
Process-based models across cultures
The reinforcement model across cultures

Leadership in international business

Decision making in international business

Models of decision making
The normative model across cultures
The descriptive model across cultures

Groups and teams in international business

The nature of group dynamics
Managing cross-cultural teams

After studying this chapter you should be able to:

Identify and discuss basic perspectives on individual differences in different cultures.

Discuss basic views of employee motivation in international business.

Describe basic views of managerial leadership in international business.

Discuss the nature of managerial decision making in international business.

Describe group dynamics and discuss how teams are managed across cultures.

T HE EARTH'S POPULATION TODAY IS APPROACHING 6 BILLION PEOPLE. While this figure is staggering on its own absolute terms, it becomes even more amazing when we consider the fact that no two of these people are exactly the same. Each one of us has a unique set of physical, intellectual, emotional, and psychological traits that sets us apart from everyone else. ▌▌ Consider, for example, the story of Emiko Muto, a young Japanese woman who has followed a difficult career path in pursuit of her dreams. After Ms. Muto's father died when she was six, her mother, who had never before been employed outside the home, had to work two menial jobs to support the family. The mother thus learned firsthand the pitfalls of having no job skills or other preparation for the working world and encouraged her daughter to attend college. Taking her mother's advice, Ms. Muto studied elementary education, accounting, and English at a two-year college and then earned a four-year degree through correspondence. ▌▌ Her first job was as the "Office Lady" in a real-estate developer's office. Such positions are common in Japan and are the most frequent entry-level jobs for women. She was instructed to wear a "uniform" each day consisting of a mint-green skirt and blouse. One of the first daily duties assigned to her was to serve coffee or tea to the sixty men who worked in the office, remembering exactly how much sugar and milk each one used. ▌▌ Ms. Muto quickly became disillusioned with this work. She soon quit her job and used her savings to journey to the United States for a year. While there she became very impressed with the freedom and career opportunities available to women. During this period she traveled widely throughout the country and also improved her English skills. Then she returned home again, determined to launch a new and more promising career. ▌▌ She quickly found a new job back in Japan with a French-owned start-up firm. Ms. Muto was pleased to see that the sexism so common in most Japanese companies did not exist in this firm. She was especially happy to avoid the weekend trips and late-night parties that were part of normal business practices in most other firms in Japan. ▌▌ Unfortunately, her new firm subsequently hired a senior Japanese manager to take over its human resources department. He soon began to incorporate more traditional Japanese practices and approaches into the firm's management. For example, Ms. Muto and other women were systematically excluded from important meetings, and he began to give them increasingly menial jobs to do. She saw the handwriting on the wall, and left. ▌▌ Her next job was with an advertising agency. She quickly demonstrated that she was a talented employee and was soon managing individual accounts, including one

It Takes All Kinds[1]

large account for a cosmetics firm. But then Ms. Muto encountered another big setback. The agency eliminated her position as a full-time employee and redefined it as a contractual position. Under this arrangement, while she maintained the same work load and obligations to the company, her salary was cut by 30 percent. ▮▮ Ms. Muto has maintained the job as a way of supporting herself. But she has also launched her own part-time business in conjunction with an acupuncturist friend. This business runs classes in yoga-like relaxation techniques to help harried Japanese managers cope with stress. If the business succeeds, she intends to quit her other job and further establish her autonomy and independence as a business owner. She has also become somewhat of a political activist, helping to organize rallies and teach Japanese women more about their legal rights. ▮▮▮▮

The story of Emiko Muto illustrates two very important messages for all managers, but especially those who work in international businesses. First, as detailed more fully back in Chapter 9, culture can be a powerful determinant of human behavior. In Japan, for example, cultural norms prescribe very explicit career paths and limitations for women. At the same time, however, just because two people are from the same culture does not necessarily mean that they are alike in all respects. Ms. Muto is a unique human being partially shaped by her Japanese cultural background but also strongly influenced by other personal forces as well, including the hardships borne by her mother and her own struggle to find a fulfilling career.

People differ in terms of their personalities, goals, and motives and in how they perceive and interpret their environments. They differ in terms of their values, emotions, and priorities and in what they want from their work. They differ in terms of how they respond to various types of supervision, rewards, feedback, and work settings. And they exhibit different levels of job satisfaction, commitment, absenteeism, turnover, and stress. People also behave differently when they are put into groups. Take a group of five people with a well-developed and understood set of behavioral profiles. Remove one member, add another, and the behavior of each member shifts, if only a little.[2]

Managers who operate in a domestic firm must understand and contend with a complex set of behavioral and interpersonal processes. Managers in a multicultural firm have the additional complexity of managing people with even more diverse frames of reference and perspectives on work and organizations. International managers who develop insights into dealing with people from different cultural backgrounds will be far ahead of those who do not.

In Chapter 9, we discussed national culture and its implications for firms with international operations. We now look more closely at the actual behaviors of managers and employees in different cultures and how those behavioral differences affect the conduct of international business. We start by discussing the nature of individual differences in different cultures. Then we introduce and discuss four aspects of behavior that are especially important for international businesses: motivation, leadership, decision making, and groups and cross-cultural teams.

Individual Behavior in International Business

ndividual behavior in organizations is strongly influenced by a variety of individual differences—specific dimensions or characteristics of a person that influence that person.[3] Most patterns of individual differences are, in turn, based on personality. Other important dimensions that relate to individual behavior are attitudes, perception, creativity, and stress.

Personality Differences across Cultures

Personality is the relatively stable set of psychological attributes that distinguishes one person from another.[4] A long-standing debate among psychologists—often referred to as the question of "nature versus nurture"—is the extent to which personality attributes are biologically inherited (the "nature" argument) or shaped by the social and cultural environment in which people are raised (the "nurture" argument). In reality, both biological factors and environmental factors play important roles in determining personalities.[5] While the details of this debate are beyond the scope of our discussion here, international managers should recognize the limitations of sweeping generalizations about people's behavior based on their cultural backgrounds, and acknowledge that individual differences also exist within any given cultural group. That is, while culture may lead to certain behavioral tendencies, as outlined in Chapter 9, individual behavior within any given culture can also vary significantly. Ms. Muto's behavior, for example, clearly lies outside the norms of the Japanese culture she grew up in.

The "Big Five" Personality Traits. Psychologists have identified literally thousands of personality traits and dimensions that differentiate one person from another. But in recent years, researchers have identified five fundamental personality traits that are especially relevant to organizations. Because these five traits are so important and because they are currently the subject of so much attention, they are commonly referred to as the **"big five" personality traits** (see Fig. 14.1).[6]

Agreeableness refers to a person's ability to get along with others.[7] Agreeableness causes some people to be gentle, cooperative, understanding, and good-natured in their dealings with others, but its absence results in those who are irritable, short-tempered, and uncooperative toward other people. **Conscientiousness** refers to the order and precision a person imposes on activities. This trait measures whether one is organized, systematic, responsible, and self-disciplined, or, conversely, disorganized, careless, and irresponsible. The third of the "big five" personality dimensions is **emotional stability,** which causes some individuals to be poised, calm, resilient, and secure; those who have less emotional stability will be excitable, insecure, reactive, and subject to extreme mood swings. **Extroversion,** a person's comfort level with relationships, indicates that some people are sociable, talkative, and assertive, whereas others are less sociable and more introverted. Finally, **openness** measures a person's rigidity of beliefs and range of interests. This trait results in some people being willing to listen to new ideas and to change their own ideas, beliefs, and attitudes as a result of new information. Those who are less open are less receptive to new ideas and less willing to change their minds.

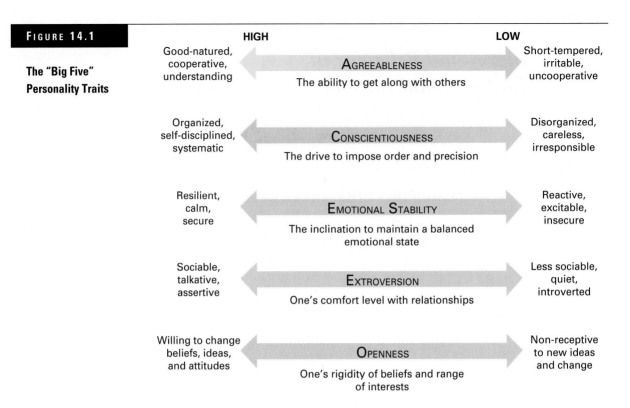

FIGURE 14.1

The "Big Five" Personality Traits

A growing body of research has emerged on the big-five framework in the United States. In general, this work focuses on using one or more of the five traits to predict performance in various kinds of jobs. Recently this research has been extended to other countries. For example, researchers have found that in the European Union, as in the United States, conscientiousness and emotional stability appear to be reasonable predictors of performance across a variety of job criteria and occupational groups. That is, Europeans with high conscientiousness and emotional stability are likely to perform at a higher level than those with low conscientiousness and less emotional stability. Similarly, extroversion is a useful predictor of managerial performance in China and among certain occupational groups in the European Union, most notably managers in sales and marketing. Openness and agreeableness predict performance across more occupational types, but only for certain performance criteria, most notably training proficiency.[8] Thus, when selecting individuals for job assignments in different countries, managers should take advantage of any valid and reliable personality measures that might help with their choices, but should also be sure to not overgeneralize the validity and reliability of such measures across cultures.

Other Personality Traits at Work. Besides the "big five," there are also several other personality traits that influence behavior in organizations. Among the most important are locus of control, self-efficacy, authoritarianism, and self-esteem.

Locus of control is the extent to which people believe that their behavior has a real effect on what happens to them.[9] Some people, for example, trust that if they work hard they will succeed. They also may believe that people who fail do so because they lack ability or motivation. People who maintain that individuals are in control of their lives are said to have an *internal locus of control*. Other people think that fate, chance, luck, or other people's behavior determines what happens to them. For example, an employee who fails to get a promotion may attribute that failure to a politically motivated boss or just bad luck, rather than to his own lack of skills or poor performance record. People who think that forces beyond their control dictate what happens to them are said to have an *external locus of control.*

While not yet demonstrated by research, it seems reasonable to suggest that people from relatively individualistic and power-tolerant cultures are more likely to have an internal locus of control, whereas people from relatively collectivistic and power-respecting cultures may be more likely to have an external locus of control. Similarly, an external locus of control is likely to be prevalent among Moslems, whereas an internal locus of control is more consistent with Protestantism. One study has found that samples of people in New Zealand and Singapore seem to be relatively internal in their orientation, as are many people in the United States.[10] It also seems likely, however, that locus of control will vary significantly across cultures.

Self-efficacy is a related but subtly different personality characteristic. Self-efficacy indicates a person's beliefs about his or her capabilities to perform a task.[11] People with high self-efficacy believe that they can perform well on a specific task, while people with low self-efficacy tend to doubt their ability to perform that task. While self-assessments of ability contribute to self-efficacy, so too does the individual's personality. Some people simply have more self-confidence than do others. This belief in their ability to perform a task effectively results in their being more self-assured and more able to focus their attention on performance.[12] In one interesting recent study, the self-efficacy of senior managers was found to be positively related to the performance of international joint ventures. That is, joint venture managers who have confidence in their abilities to meet the goals and objectives of the business are more likely to do so than are managers in joint ventures with lower confidence in their abilities.[13] Based on her actions so far, Ms. Muto also appears to have a lot of self-efficacy, evidenced by her continued quest for fulfilling and rewarding work.

Another important personality characteristic is **authoritarianism,** the extent to which an individual believes that power and status differences are appropriate within hierarchical social systems like business organizations.[14] For example, a person who is highly authoritarian may accept directives or orders from someone with more authority purely because the other person is "the boss." On the other hand, while a person who is not highly authoritarian may still carry out appropriate and reasonable directives from the boss, he or she is also more likely to question things, express disagreement with the boss, and even to refuse to carry out orders if they are for some reason objectionable. A highly authoritarian manager may be relatively autocratic and demanding, and highly authoritarian subordinates will be more likely to accept this behavior from their leader. On the other hand, a less authoritarian manager may allow subordinates a bigger role in making decisions, and less authoritarian subordinates will respond positively to this behavior.[15] This trait is obviously quite similar to the concept of power orientation discussed in Chapter 9.

Self-esteem is the extent to which a person believes that he or she is a worthwhile and deserving individual.[16] A person with high self-esteem is more likely to seek higher status jobs, be more confident in her ability to achieve higher levels of performance, and derive greater intrinsic satisfaction from her accomplishments. In contrast, a person with less self-esteem may be more content to remain in a lower-level job, be less confident of his ability, and focus more on extrinsic rewards.[17]

Among the major personality dimensions, self-esteem is the one that has been most widely studied in other countries. While more research is clearly needed, the published evidence does suggest that self-esteem is an important personality trait in most Western European countries, throughout North America and South America, and in Australia. However, it has not been found to exist as a separate personality trait among people in Africa and the Middle East. Self-esteem has not yet been studied in most Asian countries. In those societies where self-esteem does emerge as a meaningful personality trait, those individuals with high levels of self-esteem seem to be more motivated and to perform at a higher level than those with lower levels of self-esteem.[18]

Attitudes across Cultures

Another dimension of individuals within organizations is their attitudes. Attitudes are complexes of beliefs and feelings that people have about specific ideas, situations, or other people. While some attitudes are deeply rooted and long-lasting, others can be formed or changed quickly. For example, attitudes toward political parties or major social issues, such as pollution control or abortion, evolve over an extended period of time. But attitudes about a new restaurant may be formed immediately after eating there for the first time. Attitudes are important because they provide a way for most people to express their feelings. An employee's statement that he is underpaid by the organization reflects his feelings about his pay. Similarly, when a manager endorses the new advertising campaign, she is expressing her feelings about the organization's marketing efforts.

Job Satisfaction. One especially important attitude in most organizations is job satisfaction. **Job satisfaction** or **dissatisfaction** is an attitude that reflects the extent to which an individual is gratified by or fulfilled in his or her work. Extensive research conducted on job satisfaction has indicated that personal factors such as an individual's needs and aspirations determine this attitude along with group and organizational factors such as relationships with coworkers and supervisors and working conditions, work policies, and compensation.[19] A satisfied employee also tends to be absent less often, to make positive contributions, and to stay with the organization. In contrast, a dissatisfied employee may be absent more often, may experience stress that disrupts coworkers, and may be continually looking for another job. However, high levels of job satisfaction do not necessarily lead to higher levels of performance.

Research has shown, at least in some settings, that expatriates who are dissatisfied with their jobs and foreign assignments are more likely to leave their employers than are more satisfied managers.[20] One survey measured job satisfaction among 8300 workers in 106 factories in Japan and the United States. Contrary to what many people believe, this survey found that Japanese workers in general are less satisfied with their jobs than are their counterparts in the United States.[21] Some of the more interesting results of this study are summarized in Table 14.1. Another survey found that managers in the former USSR are relatively dissatisfied with their jobs, especially in terms of their autonomy to make important decisions.[22] Ms. Muto, profiled in our opening case, has left several of her previous jobs because of her apparent dissatisfaction with them.

TABLE 14.1

Job Satisfaction Differences Between Japanese and U.S. Workers

JOB SATISFACTION QUESTION	JAPANESE MEAN	U.S. MEAN
All in all, how satisfied would you say you are with your job? (0 = not at all, 4 = very)	2.12*	2.95
If a good friend of yours told you that he or she was interested in working at a job like yours at this company, what would you say? (0 = would advise against it, 1 = would have second thoughts, 2 = would recommend it)	0.91	1.52
Knowing what you know now, if you had to decide all over again whether to take the job you now have, what would you decide? (0 = would not take job again, 1 = would have some second thoughts, 2 = would take job again)	0.84	1.61
How much does your job measure up to the kind of job you wanted when you first took it? (0 = not what I wanted, 1 = somewhat, 2 = what I wanted)	0.43	1.20

*The differences in average response to each question are statistically significant, which means that the differences between U.S. and Japanese responses are large enough that they do not appear to be chance results.

Source: Adapted from J.R. Lincoln, "Employee work attitudes and management practice in the U.S. and Japan: Evidence from a large comparative survey," Copyright © 1989 by the Regents of the University of California. Reprinted from the *California Management Review*, Fall 1989, p. 91 by permission of the Regents.

Organizational Commitment. Another important job-related attitude is **organizational commitment,** which reflects an individual's identification with and loyalty to the organization. One comparative study of Western, Asian, and local employees working in Saudi Arabia found that the expatriate Asians reported higher levels of organizational commitment than did the Westerners and local Saudis.[23] Another found that U.S. production workers reported higher levels of organizational commitment than did Japanese workers.[24] More recently, a large study of organizational commitment among U.S. expatriates in four Asian and four European countries found that if those expatriates had a long service history with the firm, received extensive pretransfer training, and adjusted easily to the foreign culture after transfer, they retained high levels of commitment to their parent company. But expatriates with shorter service histories, who had less pretransfer training, and who had a more difficult adjustment period actually developed stronger levels of commitment toward the foreign affiliate.[25] These findings seem reasonable: the first group of employees had made major personal investments in the parent organization and, because of the ease of their transfer, had less need to invest themselves emotionally in their new assignments. The second group had less attachment to their domestic employers, but needed to make larger personal investments in their new assignments to overcome the difficulties they were encountering. Similar "bonding" is observed among people who undergo stressful situations together, such as basic training in the military, initiation week in a fraternity or sorority, or the "ropes" course commonly used by many corporate trainers.

Perception across Cultures

One important determinant of an attitude is the individual's perception of the object about which the attitude is formed. **Perception** is the set of processes by which an individual becomes aware of and interprets information about the environment. Perception obviously starts when we see, hear, touch, smell, or taste something. Each individual, however, then interprets that awareness through filtering processes that are unique to that person. For example, two people supporting different teams can watch the same play on a soccer or rugby field and "see" very different realities. Ms. Muto's experiences are detailed in the opening case from her perspective, but others involved in her experiences—former bosses or coworkers, for example—might describe some of the events very differently because they perceived things in different ways. And a Canadian or Danish reader of her story might have a very different impression of Ms. Muto than a Japanese student. An individual's cultural background obviously plays a role in shaping how the person's filtering mechanisms work.

Stereotyping is one common perceptual process that affects international business. *Stereotyping* occurs when we make inferences about someone because of one or more characteristics they possess. For example, some people in the United States hold stereotypes that Japanese managers work all the time, that Swiss managers are well organized, and that French managers are elitist. And some people in those countries stereotype U.S. managers as greedy. While such stereotypes may sometimes be useful as cultural generalizations, all managers should be aware that each individual is unique and may or may not fit preconceived impressions. To demonstrate some of the pitfalls of stereotyping, "Going Global" describes a variety of stereotypes held by some Chinese about Americans.

Aside from stereotyping, perception can affect international business in many other ways. For example, as described in Chapter 8, international managers must assess political and other forms of risk in foreign markets. However, there may be differences across cultures as to how risk is perceived. As illustrated in one recent study, managers from six Latin American countries perceived common business risks (such as political, commercial, and exchange-rate risks) very differently from one another.[26] For example, managers in Costa Rica saw risk as a definable and manageable part of the environment, whereas managers from Guatemala saw risk as an abstract force that was determined almost by chance.

Similarly, another study of Japanese expatriates and British locals working together in Japanese-owned banks in London found that the two groups perceived each other in very different ways.[27] The Japanese expatriates saw their British

GOING GLOBAL

More than 90% of Americans lie frequently. Some Americans so love guns that they sleep with them. Others are habitually sadomasochistic. And when they die, many Americans leave their estates to their pets, not their children.

That, at least, is a view of Americans Chinese can glean from reading the country's state-controlled press. While Beijing is ratcheting up a campaign against the Western media for biased reporting of China, Chinese media aren't entirely innocent when it comes to screwy depictions of the other side of the Pacific. Just as some Western reports about China may paint a distorted view of China, some of China's portrayals of the U.S. speak volumes about the misperceptions that color the two countries' ties.

Consider these recent findings from the Chinese press:

The U.S. Is Crowded with Liars Who Prefer Pets to Kids

- ◆ The Beijing Youth Daily reported Nov. 22 that three out of 10 people killed by police in the U.S. threw themselves in the line of fire to commit suicide.
- ◆ Many Americans are addicted to lying. A state newspaper reported in October a survey showing that 79% of Americans admit to giving fake names and phone numbers to strangers on airplanes; 91% often lie, and 20% say they can't get through a day without lying. People lie most about their weight, age, money, and hair color, the newspaper said.
- ◆ "Survival of the fittest" best describes relations between employers and employees in the U.S., and there is no need to curry favor, as bosses never want lasting relations with staff, the Sichuan Workers' News told readers.
- ◆ One newspaper asserted that Americans like to leave inheritances to their pets, instead of their children. After all, a third newspaper found, incidents of mothers abusing or even killing their children occur often. "No doubt, the world that American children live in is full of darkness, violence, and cruelty."

Qian Ning, son of China's Foreign Minister Qian Qichen and author of a best-selling book about Chinese studying in the U.S., says he only learned that "the U.S. is very normal—American masses are like [China's] masses, its farmers are . . . down-to-earth like [our] farmers, and its businessmen are more savvy, like [our] businessmen"—after living in the U.S. for six years. Growing up in China and reading its newspapers, he recalls, "I had gotten the impression that the U.S. was a very strange country."

The negative tone of many news stories on the U.S. also may reflect the attitude of Chinese leaders, who often use the state-run news outlets to push their own propaganda. When Sino-U.S. ties plunged to new lows in 1995 and 1996, the official Chinese media were filled with stories about how the U.S. dominated other nations. During the 1996 Summer Olympics in Atlanta, Beijing ordered Chinese reporters to play down U.S. medal wins and positive aspects of U.S. life in their articles.

But with relations now on the upswing and after two decades of economic reforms, Chinese media coverage of the U.S. increasingly consists of a confusing mixture of begrudging admiration, outright stereotyping and—as with media everywhere—a healthy dose of titillation.

Despite the Chinese media's odd depictions of the U.S., many Chinese still retain a glowing—indeed, overly rosy—impression of life in America. Many believe the U.S. government is a bully and U.S. crime rates are frighteningly high, but they also cherish the U.S. as a land of opportunity.

Source: "To China's Press, the U.S. Is Crowded With Liars Who Prefer Pets To Kids," by Kathy Chen, *Wall Street Journal*, February 15, 1997, p. A15 Reprinted by permission of the *Wall Street Journal*, © 1997 Dow Jones and Co., Inc. All rights reserved worldwide.

coworkers as being most interested in protecting their jobs and maintaining their income whereas the British locals saw the Japanese as being most interested in profit and group harmony. And, finally, another study found that senior executives in the United States, the United Kingdom, Germany, and Austria perceived ethical situations very differently from one another.[28] Clearly, then, international managers must consider the role of perception as they conduct business in different countries.

Stress across Cultures

Another important element of behavior in organizations is stress. **Stress** is an individual's response to a strong stimulus.[29] This stimulus is called a **stressor.** We should note that stress is not all bad. In the absence of stress, we may experi-

Stress is often an unfortunate by-product of the intense competitiveness of today's global economy. How individual workers deal with stress is influenced by their personalities and their national cultures.

ence lethargy and stagnation. An optimal level of stress, on the other hand, can result in motivation and excitement. Too much stress, however, can have negative consequences. It is also important to understand that stress can be caused by "good" as well as "bad" things. Excessive pressure, unreasonable demands on our time, and bad news can all cause stress. But receiving a bonus and then having to decide what to do with the money can also be stressful. So, too, can receiving a promotion, gaining recognition, and similar "good" things.

There are two different perspectives on stress that are especially relevant for international managers. One, managing stress resulting from international assignments, is covered in Chapter 20. The other is recognizing that people in different cultures may experience different forms of stress and then

handle that stress in different ways. For example, one study looked at stress patterns across ten countries. The study found that Swedish executives experienced the least stress. Executives from the United States, the United Kingdom, and the former West Germany reported relatively moderate stress, and that they were managing this stress effectively. But managers from Japan, Brazil, Egypt, Singapore, South Africa, and Nigeria reported that they were experiencing very high levels of stress and/or that they were having difficulties managing stress.[30] More recently, another study reported that managers in Germany do a better job of maintaining a healthy balance between work and nonwork activities and managing stress than do managers in the United Kingdom.[31]

Motivation in International Business

All international businesses face the challenge of motivating their work forces to reduce costs, develop new products, enhance product quality, and improve customer service. **Motivation** is the overall set of forces that causes people to choose certain behaviors from a set of available behaviors.[32] Yet the factors that influence an individual's behavior at work differ across cultures. An appreciation of these individual differences is an important first step in understanding how managers can better motivate their employees to promote the organization's goals. "Going Global" illustrates how Sony has used its highly motivated work force for long-term competitive advantage.

GOING GLOBAL

Sony Corporation is among the best known Japanese firms in the world today. It seems that virtually everybody has a Walkman and the Sony Trinitron is among the best selling televisions in the United States, Europe, and Asia. But relatively few people understand how Sony's unique approach to dealing with its employees has contributed so much to the firm's success. Indeed, the firm's ability to motivate its workers has been a major ingredient in Sony's ability to grow and prosper.

Like other Japanese electronics firms, Sony recruits most of its new employees from the engineering schools at major Japanese universities. But unlike those firms, Sony doesn't always seek out the top graduates (a common practice not only in Japan but in many other countries as well). Instead, the firm looks for innovators, people who are *neyaka*—optimistic, open-minded, and wide-ranging in their interests. Sony believes that the employees most likely to thrive in its culture are those who want to move around in different product groups and who are interested in working in areas they didn't study in school.

Another ingredient in Sony's success is how it treats people after they are hired. Most other firms—including U.S., European, and other Japanese companies—are very rigid in their approach to transferring people to different jobs. Employees who want a transfer must first convince their boss to find new positions and then work with the head of that department to expedite the transfer. At Sony, however, individuals are encouraged to seek out new projects and convince the head of that department to accept them as a transfer. Only after the details have been worked out does the employee's present boss learn of the impending move. Sony believes that this allows employees to gravitate to projects they will be most motivated by and encourages managers to maintain stimulating, challenging, and enjoyable projects so as to attract new people.

The Sony Way

Sony also believes that people can make greater contributions to the organization if they are kept fully informed as to what the organization is doing, why, and how it expects to succeed. Thus, the firm goes to great lengths to provide information to everyone in the organization. While most firms provide information to those managers and employees who clearly need it, Sony goes far beyond that minimal level and broadly disseminates information to everyone, whether or not they have a clear and immediate "need to know."

An insightful example of how people contribute to Sony's success comes from its recent breakthroughs in computer technology. A few years ago the firm began to assemble a group of engineers to develop the firm's first entry into the computer market. The group's leader, Toshi T. Doi, was concerned that the firm had grown too large and bureaucratic to function as quickly as he would like. Thus, he chose a group of highly individualistic engineers who were not fitting in well with the rest of the firm. He gave them a separate work area, gave them their general charge, and left them alone. For six months they worked day and night to develop the computer prototype. Team members literally moved into the office and most slept in chairs at night. When they finished the job—two days ahead of schedule—everyone in the firm applauded their efforts. And the new computer quickly captured a big chunk of the Japanese market.

These and many other similar experiences and stories have resulted in a strong Sony culture. People are hired and promoted on the basis of their talents and skills. No one advances because of their personal contacts or their university pedigrees (again, unlike organizational practices in many firms). Everyone is expected to work for the benefit of the organization. But people can still maintain their individuality. Encouraging people to be entrepreneurial within the organizational umbrella creates a big challenge for the firm but also helps maintain enthusiasm, motivation, and drive. Although they may not know about the abstract concept of a "corporate culture," most employees do know exactly what is meant when the firm's internal slogan "Sony's Way" is invoked.

Sources: "A New World at Sony," *Time*, November 17, 1997, pp. 56–62; "Sony's Idei Finds Winning Path," *Wall Street Journal*, May 14, 1997, p. A18; Brenton R. Schlender, "How Sony Keeps the Magic Going," *Fortune*, February 24, 1992, pp. 76–84; "How Sony Pulled Off Its Spectacular Computer Coup," *Business Week*, January 15, 1990, pp. 76–77.

Needs and Values across Cultures

The starting point in understanding motivation is to consider needs and values. **Needs** are the things an individual must have or wants to have.[33] **Values,** meanwhile, are the things that people believe to be important. Not surprisingly, most people have a large number of needs and values. Primary needs are things that people require in order to survive, such as food, water, and shelter. Thus, they are instinctive and physiologically based. Secondary needs, on the other hand, are more psychological in character and are learned from the environment and culture in which the individual lives. Examples of secondary needs include the needs for achievement, autonomy, power, order, affiliation, and understanding. Secondary needs often manifest themselves in organizational settings. For example, if an individual is to be satisfied with her psychological contract, the inducements offered by the organization must be consistent with her needs. Offering a nice office and job security may not be sufficient if the individual is primarily seeking income and promotion opportunities. Values, meanwhile, are learned and developed as a person grows and matures. These values are influenced by one's family, peers, experiences, and culture.

Motivational Processes across Cultures

Most modern theoretical approaches to motivation fall into one of three categories. *Need-based models of motivation* are those that attempt to identify the specific need or set of needs that results in motivated behavior. *Process-based models of motivation* focus more on the conscious thought processes people use to select one behavior from among several. Finally, the *reinforcement model* deals with how people assess the consequences of their behavioral choices and how that assessment goes into their future choice of behaviors. This model incorporates the roles of rewards and punishment in maintaining or altering existing behavioral patterns.

Need-Based Models across Cultures

Hofstede's work, discussed in Chapter 9, provides some useful insights into how need-based models of motivation are likely to vary across cultures.[34] Common needs incorporated in most models of motivation include the needs for security, for being part of a social network, and for opportunities to grow and develop. By relating these need categories to four of Hofstede's dimensions—social orientation, power orientation, uncertainty orientation, and goal orientation—several inferences can be drawn about differences in motivation across cultures.

For example, managers and employees in countries that are individualistic may be most strongly motivated by individually based needs and rewards. Opportunities to demonstrate personal competencies and to receive recognition and rewards as a result may be particularly attractive to such people. In contrast, people from collectivistic cultures may be more strongly motivated by group-based needs and rewards. Indeed, they may be uncomfortable in situations in which they are singled out for rewards apart from the group with which they work.

Conflicts can easily arise when an international firm's mechanisms for motivating workers clash with cultural attitudes. For example, many U.S. managers working for Japanese MNCs have difficulty with the seniority-based, group-performance–oriented compensation systems of their employers. Similarly, Michigan autoworkers resisted the attempts by Mazda officials to get them to "voluntarily" wear Mazda baseball caps as part of their work uniforms.[35] Tom Selleck's 1992 movie *Mr. Baseball* depicted still other aspects of the cultural clashes arising from these motivational differences between the individual-oriented U.S. culture and the group-oriented Japanese culture. In particular, U.S. baseball players, accustomed to the "star system" that accords them status, prestige, and special privileges, are often shocked by the team-based approach in Japan, which discourages attention to individuals.

Power-respecting individuals are those who accept their boss's right to direct their efforts purely on the basis of organizational legitimacy. As a consequence of this power respect, they may be motivated by the possibility of gaining their boss's approval and acceptance. Thus they may willingly and unquestioningly accept and attempt to carry out directives and mandates. In contrast, power-tolerant people attach less legitimacy to hierarchical rank. Thus they may be less motivated by gaining their boss's approval than by opportunities for pay raises and promotions.

The use of management by objectives also reflects the importance of cultural differences. **Management by objectives (MBO)** is a motivational technique whereby subordinates and managers agree on the subordinates' goals over some period of evaluation. Developed in the United States, a power-tolerant country, it appeals to the U.S. cultural value of individualism in that the employee is made responsible for achieving goals agreed to by the employee and the employee's boss. Exported to Japan, MBO shifted from a focus on individual goals to an evaluation of group goals. However, the MBO concept was a failure in France; it was not compatible with the strong hierarchical nature of French bureaucracy, in which superiors dictate orders to their subordinates.[36]

Managers and employees in uncertainty-avoiding cultures may be highly motivated by opportunities to maintain or increase their perceived levels of job security and job stability. Any effort to reduce or eliminate that security or stability may be met with resistance. In contrast, people in uncertainty-accepting cultures may be less motivated by security needs and less inclined to seek job security or stability as a condition of employment. They also may be more motivated by change and by new challenges and opportunities for personal growth and development. For example, recent studies comparing U.S. and German workers reveal substantial differences in their preferences regarding job values. Job security and shorter work hours were valued more highly by the German workers than the U.S. workers. Income, opportunities for promotion, and the importance of one's work were much more highly valued by the U.S. workers than by their German counterparts.[37]

Finally, people from more aggressive goal behavior cultures are more likely to be motivated by money and other material rewards. They may pursue behavioral choices that they perceive as having the highest probability of financial payoff. They also may be disinclined to work toward rewards whose primary attraction is mere comfort or personal satisfaction. In contrast, workers in passive goal behavior cultures may be more motivated by needs and rewards that can potentially enhance the quality of their lives. They may be less interested in behavioral choices whose primary appeal is a higher financial payoff. For example, Swedish firms provide generous vacations and fringe benefits, while many firms operating in China, where wage rates are low by world standards, provide workers with housing, medical care, and other support services.

Various studies have tested specific motivation theories in different cultural settings. The theory receiving the most attention has been Abraham Maslow's hierarchy of five basic needs: physiological, security, social, self-esteem, and self-actualization.[38]

International research on Maslow's hierarchy provides two different insights. First, managers in many different countries, including the United States, Mexico, Japan, and Canada, usually agree that the needs included in Maslow's hierarchy are all important to them. Second, the relative importance and preference ordering of the needs vary considerably by country.[39] For example, managers in less developed countries such as Liberia and India place a higher priority on satisfying self-esteem and security needs than do managers from more developed countries.[40]

Results from research based on another motivation theory, David McClelland's learned needs framework, have been slightly more consistent. In particular, the need for achievement (to grow, learn, and accomplish important things) has been shown to exist in many different countries. McClelland has also demonstrated that the need for achievement can be taught to people in different cultures.[41] However, given the role of Hofstede's cultural differences, it follows that McClelland's needs are not likely to be constant across cultures. In particular, individualistic, uncertainty-accepting, power-tolerant, and aggressive goal behavior cultures seem more likely to foster and promote the needs for achievement and power (to control resources) than the need for affiliation (to be part of a social network). In contrast, collectivistic, uncertainty-avoiding, power-respecting, and passive goal behavior cultures may promote the need for affiliation more than the needs for achievement and power.[42]

Frederick Herzberg's two-factor theory is another popular need-based theory of motivation.[43] This theory suggests that one set of factors affects dissatisfaction and another set affects satisfaction. It, too, has been tested cross-culturally with varied results. For example, research has found different patterns of factors when comparing U.S. managers with managers from New Zealand and Panama.[44] Results from U.S. employees suggested that supervision contributed to dissatisfaction but not to satisfaction. But supervision did contribute to employees' satisfaction in New Zealand. Unfortunately, Herzberg's theory often fails to yield consistent results even within a single culture.[45] Thus, even though the theory is well known and popular among managers, managers should be particularly cautious in attempting to apply it in different cultural contexts.

Process-Based Models across Cultures

In contrast to need-based theories, expectancy theory takes a process view of motivation.[46] The theory suggests that people are motivated to behave in certain ways to the extent that they perceive that such behaviors will lead to outcomes they find personally attractive. The theory acknowledges that different people have different needs—one person may need money, another recognition, another social satisfaction, and still another prestige. But each will be willing to improve his or her performance if he or she believes the result will be fulfillment of the needs he or she finds most important.

There has been relatively little research that explicitly tests expectancy theory in countries other than the United States. It does seem logical, however, that the basic framework of the theory should have wide applicability. Regardless of where people work, they are likely to work toward goals they think are important. However, cultural factors will partially determine both the nature of those work goals and people's perceptions of how they should most fruitfully pursue them.

One particularly complex factor that is likely to affect the expectancy process is the cultural dimension of social orientation. The expectancy theory is essentially a model of individual decisions regarding individual behavioral choices targeted at individual outcomes. Thus it may be less able to explain behavior in collectivistic cultures, but otherwise may be one of the most likely candidates for a culturally unbiased explanation of motivated behavior. For example, expectancy theory helps explain the success Sony has enjoyed. As noted in "Going Global," people who go to work for Sony know they will be able to pursue diverse opportunities and will be kept informed about what is happening in the firm. People who see these conditions as especially important will be most strongly motivated to work for Sony.

The Reinforcement Model across Cultures

Like the expectancy theory, the reinforcement model has undergone relatively few tests in different cultures. Basically, this model says that behavior that results in a positive outcome (reinforcement) will be likely to be repeated under the same circumstances in the future. Behavioral choice that results in negative consequences (punishment) will result in a different choice under the same circumstances in the future. As this model makes no attempt to specify what people will find reinforcing or punishing, it may also be generalizable to different cultures.

Like expectancy theory, the reinforcement model may have exceptions. In Muslim cultures, for example, people tend to believe that the consequences they experience are the will of God rather than a function of their own behavior. Thus reinforcement and punishment are likely to have less effect on their future behavioral decisions. Aside from relatively narrow exceptions such as this, however, the reinforcement model, like expectancy theory, warrants careful attention from international managers, provided they understand that what constitutes rewards and punishment will vary across cultures.

Leadership in International Business

Another important behavioral and interpersonal consideration in international business is leadership. **Leadership** is the use of noncoercive influence to shape the goals of a group or organization, to motivate behavior toward reaching those goals, and to help determine the group or organizational culture.[47] Some people mistakenly equate management and leadership. But as Table 14.2 demonstrates, there are clear and substantive differences between these two important processes. Management tends to rely on formal power and authority and to focus on administration and decision making. Leadership, in contrast, relies more on personal power and focuses more on motivation and communication. Leadership has been widely studied by organizational scientists for decades. Early studies attempted to identify physical traits or universal behaviors that most clearly distinguished leaders from nonleaders. More recently, attention has focused on matching leadership with situations.[48] Although some studies still focus on traits, most leadership models suggest that appropriate leader behavior depends on situational factors.[49]

Contemporary leadership theories recognize that leaders cannot succeed by always using the same set of behaviors in all circumstances. Instead, leaders must carefully assess the situation in which they find themselves and then tailor one or more behaviors to fit that situation. Common situational factors that affect appropriate leader behavior include individual differences among subordinates;

TABLE 14.2

Differences Between Leadership and Management

ACTIVITY	MANAGEMENT	LEADERSHIP
Creating an agenda	Planning and budgeting. Establishing detailed steps and timetables for achieving needed results; allocating the resources necessary to make those needed results happen	Establishing direction. Developing a vision of the future, often the distant future, and strategies for producing the changes needed to achieve that vision
Developing a human network for achieving the agenda	Organizing and staffing. Establishing some structure for accomplishing plan requirements, staffing that structure with individuals, delegating responsibility and authority for carrying out the plan, providing policies and procedures to help guide people, and creating methods or systems to monitor implementation	Aligning people. Communicating the direction by words and deeds to all those whose cooperation may be needed to influence the creation of teams and coalitions that understand the vision and strategies and accept their validity
Executing plans	Controlling and problem solving. Monitoring results vs. plan in some detail, identifying deviations, and then planning and organizing to solve these problems	Motivating and inspiring. Energizing people to overcome major political, bureaucratic, and resource barriers to change by satisfying very basic, but often unfulfilled, human needs
Outcomes	Produces a degree of predictability and order and has the potential to consistently produce major results expected by various stakeholders (e.g., for customers, always being on time; for stockholders, always being on budget)	Produces change, often to a dramatic degree, and has the potential to produce extremely useful change (e.g., new products that customers want, new approaches to labor relations that help make a firm more competitive)

Source: Reprinted with permission of The Free Press, a Division of Simon & Schuster Inc. from *A Force for Change: How Leadership Differs from Management*, by John P. Kotter. Copyright © 1990 by John P. Kotter, Inc.

characteristics of the group, the organization, and the leader; and subordinates' desire to participate.

Clearly, cultural factors will affect appropriate leader behavior, and the way in which managers spend their workday will vary among cultures.[50] For example, Figure 14.2 summarizes some interesting findings from an early international study of leadership. Managers were asked to indicate the extent to which they agreed with the statement, "It is important for a manager to have at hand precise answers to most of the questions that subordinates may raise about their work." As shown in the figure, about three quarters of the managers in Japan and Indonesia agreed with this statement, whereas a much smaller percentage of managers in Sweden, the Netherlands, and the United States did so. In general, agreement with the statement would suggest that managers and leaders are conceived as experts who should know all the answers. Those who disagree with the statement believe that managers and leaders are supposed to be problem solvers who may not know the answer to a question but can figure it out or know how to find the answer. In the United

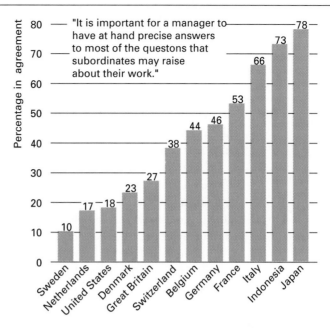

FIGURE 14.2

The Role of Managers Varies across Cultures

Source: Reprinted from *International Studies of Management and Organization*, Vol. XIII, No. 1–2, Spring-Summer 1983, by permission of M. E. Sharpe, Inc., Armonk, N.Y. 10504.

States, therefore, a manager who failed to refer a subordinate to a more knowledgeable authority would be seen as arrogant. But in Indonesia, a manager who refers a subordinate to someone else for answers is likely to be seen as incompetent.

Several implications for leaders in international settings can be drawn from the cultural factors identified in Hofstede's work. For example, in individualistic cultures, leaders may need to focus their behavior on individual employees rather than the group. The development of MBO in the United States reflects this characteristic of individualistic cultures. MBO promotes employee involvement and participation by allowing each employee to set individual goals that he or she is best suited to pursue.

In contrast, in a collectivistic culture, leader behaviors will clearly need to focus on the group rather than on individual group members. In a group-oriented culture such as that of Japan, an effective leader must guide subordinates while preserving group harmony. At Sony, for example, managers are expected to allow their employees to transfer at will to more interesting job settings because such transfers are believed to be in the firm's overall best interests. The Japanese management system focuses on consensus-building efforts to ensure that both leader and subordinates reach a common decision. A leader would destroy group harmony if he dictatorially commanded his subordinates to implement his decisions. One problem that may develop, however, is that junior managers attempt to anticipate what their boss's preferred strategy is and then offer it as their own. A leader confronted with such a strong tendency toward conformity must seek ways to encourage creative solutions from subordinates to new problems as they arise. A Japanese manager may thus distance himself from pending decisions, thereby encouraging subordinates to discuss a variety of options among themselves. Only then will the manager lead by dropping subtle hints regarding what he sees as the correct solution to an issue.[51]

Power orientation carries even more direct implications for situational leadership. In power-respecting cultures employees may expect leaders to take charge, to make decisions, and to direct their efforts. Leaders may therefore need to concentrate on performance-oriented behaviors (direct, structured, and goal-oriented behaviors), avoid employee-oriented behaviors (caring, concern, and interpersonally oriented behaviors), and make little attempt to foster participation. But if power tolerance is the more pervasive cultural value, a leader should spend less time on performance-oriented behaviors. Instead, employee-oriented behaviors and more employee participation may result in higher levels of effectiveness.

Attempts at blurring the distinctions between managers and workers may not be well received in more authoritarian, hierarchical societies. For example, one U.S. firm exported the "company picnic" concept to its Spanish subsidiary, complete with company executives serving food to the Spanish employees. However, this informality was not well received by the employees, who were embarrassed at being served by their "superiors."[52]

Uncertainty orientation is also an important situational factor to consider. Where uncertainty avoidance is the rule, employees will have a strong desire for structure and direction. Thus performance-oriented behaviors are likely to be more successful, whereas employee-oriented behaviors and attempts to use participation may be less so. For example, German managers tend to be autocratic and task-oriented, making decisions with reference to existing corporate rules and procedures. Having determined departmental objectives, they then confidently delegate tasks to subordinates, whom they expect to competently carry out the tasks necessary to achieve the objective.[53]

In contrast, employees more prone toward uncertainty acceptance may respond more favorably to opportunities for participation. They may even prefer participative behaviors on the part of their leaders. But performance-oriented leadership may be undesirable or unnecessary, while employee-oriented leadership may have little impact. That is, employees may have such a strong desire to participate and be involved in their work that they see performance-oriented or employee-oriented behaviors from their supervisor as being redundant with or even negating their own opportunities for participation.

Finally, differences in goal orientation will affect leader behavior. Recall that people in aggressive goal behavior cultures tend to value money and other material rewards. If performance-oriented leadership or higher levels of participation are perceived by followers to result in higher rewards, those behaviors will be more acceptable. In contrast, outcomes enhancing quality of life are more desirable in passive goal behavior cultures. To the extent that employee-oriented leader behaviors may cause followers to feel more satisfied with their work and the organization, such behaviors may be more effective in these settings.

The overriding lesson is that leaders in international settings need to consider a wide array of situational factors that may determine how effective their behavior will be. For example, when Bridgestone (a Japanese firm) bought Firestone (a U.S. firm), it wanted Firestone's CEO, John Nevin, to stay on and run the operation. Nevin's leadership style was blunt and straightforward, with little time wasted on subtleties. His new Japanese bosses, unfortunately, did not react very well to these behaviors. In their country, leaders are expected to be more polite and reserved. Even though both sides appear to have made an honest effort to adjust, Nevin eventually had to leave the firm.[54]

Cultural factors are among the most difficult and complex to assess and understand. They may also be among the most critical in determining leader effectiveness. It is important that leaders attempt to match their behaviors with the context—the people they are leading and the organization in which they are functioning. For example, one study analyzed the productivity of U.S. and Mexican factories owned by the same MNC. Cultural differences clearly exist between the two countries. Mexico ranks high on power respect relative to the United States. U.S. residents are far more individualistic than those of Mexico, while the family is more highly valued in Mexico than in the United States. Mexican cultural values translate into the paternalistic, authoritarian management style adopted by managers of the MNC's Mexican facilities. Managers of its U.S. facilities, however, adopted less paternalistic and more participative styles in managing their employees. By allowing management styles to adapt to national culture, the MNC enjoyed equally high levels of productivity from both facilities.[55]

Decision Making in International Business

Another area of international business in which large cultural differences exist is how decisions are made. **Decision making** is the process of choosing one alternative from among a set of alternatives in order to promote the decision maker's objectives.

Models of Decision Making

There are two very different views of how managers go about making decisions (see Fig. 14.3). The *normative model of decision making* suggests that managers apply logic and rationality in making the best decisions.[56] In contrast, the *descriptive model of decision making* argues that behavioral processes limit a manager's ability to always be logical and rational.[57]

The normative model suggests that decision making starts when managers recognize that a problem exists and a decision has to be made. For example, a Shell refinery manager recently noticed that turnover among a certain group of workers had increased substantially. The second step is for the manager to identify potential alternatives for addressing the problem. The Shell manager determined that since turnover can be caused by low wages, poor working conditions, or poor supervision, his alternatives included raising wages, improving working conditions, or changing the group's supervisor.

The third step in the normative model is to evaluate each alternative in light of the original problem. The Shell manager knew that the group's wages were comparable to what others in the refinery were making. He also realized that the group's work area had recently been refurbished, so he assumed working conditions were not a problem. In addition, he also discovered that a new supervisor had recently been appointed for the group. Using this information, the manager proceeded to step four in the normative process, selecting the best alternative. He felt that the problem was one of poor supervision, so he looked more closely at that particular part of the situation.

After scrutinizing the new supervisor's records, the plant manager saw that he had been promoted during a very hectic period and had not gone through the refinery's normal supervisory training program. Since step five of the normative model suggests that the chosen alternative be implemented, the plant manager arranged for the new supervisor to complete his training. After six months, turnover in the group had dropped significantly and the plant manager was certain from this follow-up and evaluation that his chosen course of action was the correct one.

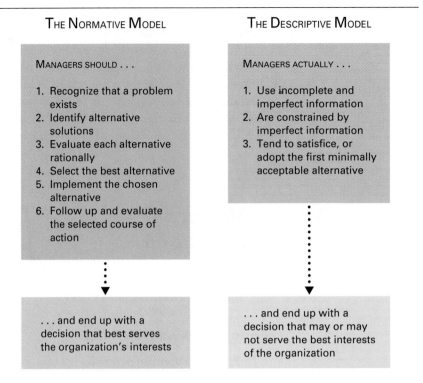

FIGURE 14.3

Models of the Decision-Making Process

THE NORMATIVE MODEL

MANAGERS SHOULD . . .

1. Recognize that a problem exists
2. Identify alternative solutions
3. Evaluate each alternative rationally
4. Select the best alternative
5. Implement the chosen alternative
6. Follow up and evaluate the selected course of action

. . . and end up with a decision that best serves the organization's interests

THE DESCRIPTIVE MODEL

MANAGERS ACTUALLY . . .

1. Use incomplete and imperfect information
2. Are constrained by imperfect information
3. Tend to satisfice, or adopt the first minimally acceptable alternative

. . . and end up with a decision that may or may not serve the best interests of the organization

The descriptive model acknowledges that this is perhaps how managers should make their decisions. But the descriptive model notes that, in reality, managers are actually affected by two important behavioral processes. The first is called bounded rationality. *Bounded rationality* suggests that decision makers are constrained in their ability to be objective and rational by limitations of the human mind. Thus, they often use incomplete and imperfect information. Notice that the Shell manager in the example above did not consult with the members of the group to find out why turnover had increased. Had he done so, he might have gained additional information. The other behavioral process is called satisficing. *Satisficing* suggests that managers sometimes adopt the first minimally acceptable alternative they identify, when a further search might suggest an even better alternative. For example, since the supervisor had an opportunity to gain some experience, he might have been able to improve his skills with an abbreviated or accelerated training program.

The Normative Model across Cultures

Several possible implications can be drawn from applying a basic understanding of the normative and descriptive models to decision making in other cultures.[58] To explore those implications, we first walk through the steps in the normative model.

Step 1: Problem Recognition. People from different cultures are likely to recognize and define problem situations in very different ways. For example, in individualistic cultures, problems are likely to be defined in terms of individual scenarios and consequences. In collectivistic cultures, the focus will be more on group-related issues and situations. In an uncertainty-accepting culture, managers are more likely to take risks in solving problems and making decisions. In uncertainty-avoiding cultures, they may be much more cautious and strive to reduce uncertainty as much as possible before making a decision. As a result, they may fall back on firm policies and rules to provide a course of action ("We can't do that because it's against company policy").

Step 2: Identifying Alternatives. The processes through which alternatives are identified will also vary across cultures. For example, in power-respecting cultures, managers may be much less willing to consider an alternative that potentially threatens the hierarchy—for example, that a suggestion from a subordinate might be valid or that a problem might exist at a higher level in the organization. But in power-tolerant cultures, such hierarchical issues are more likely to be considered possible remedies to organizational problems.

In collectivistic societies, the desire for group harmony and conflict avoidance may be so strong that decision making is approached in unique ways. For example, the Japanese concern for maintaining group harmony has given rise to the ringi system for identifying alternatives and making decisions. The **ringi system** provides that decisions cannot be made unilaterally; doing that would be too individualistic and therefore destructive of group harmony. To encourage creative solutions, a manager may draw up a document, called the *ringisho*, which defines the problem and sets out a proposed solution. The Japanese corporate belief is that those who implement a solution should be those most affected by the problem, since they understand the problem and are motivated to solve it. Thus most ringisho originate from middle managers. Although the ringisho originates from an individual, it is soon subsumed by the group. The document is circulated to all members of the originator's work group, as well as to other groups affected by it. As the ringisho passes through the workplace, it may be accepted, rejected, or modified. Only a document that is approved by all its reviewers is passed to a more senior manager for approval or disapproval. But before the ringisho reaches this stage, any senior manager worth his salt will have already dropped hints if he had any objections to any parts of it. Appropriate changes then would have been incorporated into the document by some subordinate before the ringisho arrived at the senior manager's desk. Through the ringi system, creativity, innovation, and group harmony are all promoted.[59]

In contrast, the German business structure is both strongly hierarchical and compartmentalized. Decision making tends to be slow and drawn out, designed to build consensus within a department of a firm. Data are painstakingly gathered, then communicated to the appropriate employees within the hierarchy. However, information often does not flow easily between departments, and a decision, once reached, may be difficult to change. Also, established operating procedures are followed carefully. These factors substantially reduce the firm's flexibility and responsiveness to rapidly changing conditions. The resulting inflexibility often hinders the performance of foreign subsidiaries of German MNCs, which have difficulty getting the home office to acknowledge that their operating conditions may differ from those in Germany.[60]

Step 3: Evaluating Alternatives. Evaluating alternatives can also be affected by cultural phenomena. For example, an alternative that results in financial gain may be more attractive in an aggressive goal behavior culture than in a passive goal behavior culture, which may prefer an alternative that results in improved quality of work life. Uncertainty avoidance will also be a consideration; alternatives with varying levels of associated uncertainty may be perceived to be more or less attractive.

Evaluating alternatives is further complicated in countries where people tend to avoid taking responsibility for making decisions. China's economic policies, for example, have changed so quickly and drastically over the past five decades that those supporting today's economic policies may find themselves in political difficulties tomorrow. A Chinese proverb, "The tall tree gets broken off in the wind," suggests the tendency of many Chinese officials to avoid association with any decision that could haunt them later. Group decision making reduces the potential blame an individual bureaucrat may suffer.[61]

Step 4: Selecting the Best Alternative. Cultural factors can affect the actual selection of an alternative. In an individualistic culture, for example, a manager may be prone to select an alternative that has the most positive impact on him or her personally; in a collectivistic culture, the impact of the alternative on the total group will carry more weight. Not surprisingly, a manager trained in one culture will often use the same techniques when operating in a different culture, even though they may be ineffective there. In one recent study comparing U.S. managers operating in the United States with U.S. managers operating in Hong Kong, the managerial behaviors of the two groups were found to be the same. These behaviors included managerial supportiveness of subordinates, problem solving, openness of communication, disciplining of subordinates, and so on. However, although these behaviors positively affected firm performance in the United States, they had no effect on firm performance in Hong Kong.[62]

Cultural differences in problem solving and decision making may be particularly troublesome for partners in a joint venture or other strategic alliance because they must develop mutually acceptable decisions. U.S. managers often deliberately use conflict (in the form of devil's advocate or dialectical inquiry techniques) as a means of improving the decision-making process. Managers from more consensus-oriented societies, such as Japan, find this disharmonious approach very distasteful and unproductive.[63]

Step 5: Implementation. In a power-respecting culture, implementation may be mandated by a manager at the top of the organization and accepted without question by others. But in a power-tolerant culture, participation may be more crucial in order to ensure acceptance. In an uncertainty-avoiding culture, managers may need to carefully plan every step of the implementation before proceeding so that everyone knows what to expect. In an uncertainty-accepting culture, however, managers may be more willing to start implementation before all the final details have been arranged.

Step 6: Follow-Up and Evaluation. Follow-up and evaluation also have cultural implications, most notably regarding power orientation. In a power-respecting culture, a manager may be unwilling to find fault with an alternative suggested by a higher-level manager. Also, too much credit may be given to a higher-level manager purely on the basis of his or her position in the hierarchy. But in a power-tolerant culture, responsibility, blame, and credit are more likely to be accurately attributed.

The Descriptive Model across Cultures

The behavioral processes of bounded rationality and satisficing are more difficult to relate to cultural differences. Few research efforts have specifically explored these phenomena in different cultures, and their very nature makes it hard to draw reasonable generalizations. Thus, while it is likely that they do have some impact on business decisions made in different cultures and therefore need to be understood by managers, more research needs to be conducted on their precise influence. In particular, all managers need to understand the potential limitations of applying different modes of decision making in different cultural settings. For example, a few years ago the Japanese owners of the Dunes Hotel and Casino in Las Vegas tried to implement a variety of Japanese management practices in the casino operation. One was decision making by consensus. They quickly recognized, however, that it was far too slow for the intensely competitive, fast-changing casino industry.[64]

The Dunes Hotel and Casino is owned by a group of Japanese investors. A few years ago, they tried to implement the methodical, consensus-oriented approach to decision making that works so well in Japan. They soon discovered, however, that their U.S. workers found this approach ineffective for the dynamic and fluid environment in which they worked.

Groups and Teams in International Business

Other important behavioral processes that international managers should understand are those associated with groups and teams. Regardless of whether a firm is a small domestic company or a large MNC, much of its work is accomplished by people working together as a part of a team, task force, committee, or operating group.

The Nature of Group Dynamics

Firms use groups frequently because, in theory, people working together as a group can accomplish more than they can working individually. While organizations use a wide array of different kinds of groups, teams are especially popular today. Indeed, many managers now refer to all their groups as teams. Technically, a *group* is any collection of people working together to accomplish a common purpose, while a *team* is a specific type of group that assumes responsibility for its own work. Because teams are so ubiquitous today and the term is so common among managers, we will use this term in our discussion.

A mature team in a firm generally has certain characteristics:

1 It develops a well-defined role structure; each member has a part to play on the team, accepts that part, and makes a worthwhile contribution.

2 It establishes norms for its members. Norms are standards of behavior, such as how people should dress, when team meetings or activities will begin, the consequences of being absent, how much each member should produce, and so on.

3 It is cohesive. That is, team members identify more and more strongly with the team, and each member respects, values, and works well with the others.

4 Some teams identify informal leaders among their members—individuals whom the team accords special status and who can lead and direct the team without benefit of formal authority.

If a team's role structure promotes efficiency, its norms reinforce high performance, it truly is cohesive, and its informal leaders support the firm's goals, then it can potentially reach maximum effectiveness. Sony's computer development group took on all of these characteristics, which no doubt helped contribute to the group's ability to reach its goal ahead of schedule. However, if the team's role structure is inefficient, its performance norms are low, it is not cohesive, and/or its informal leaders do not support the firm's goals, then it may become very ineffective from the firm's standpoint.

Managing Cross-Cultural Teams

The composition of a team plays a major role in the dynamics that emerge from it. A relatively homogeneous team generally has less conflict, better communication, less creativity, more uniform norms, higher cohesiveness, and clear informal leadership. A more heterogeneous team often has more conflict, poorer communication, more creativity, less uniform norms, a lower level of cohesiveness, and more ambiguous informal leadership.

Managers charged with building teams in different cultures need to assess the nature of the task to be performed and, as much as possible, match the composition of the team to the type of task. For example, if the task is relatively routine and straightforward, a homogeneous team may be more effective. Similarities in knowledge, background, values, and beliefs can make the work go more smoothly and efficiently. But if the task is nonroutine, complex, and/or ambiguous, a heterogeneous team may be more effective because of members' diverse backgrounds, experiences, knowledge, and values.

Other cultural factors may also play a role in team dynamics. For example, in an individualistic culture, establishing shared norms and cohesiveness may be somewhat difficult, while in a collectivistic culture, team cohesiveness may emerge naturally. In a power-respecting culture, team members should probably be from the same level of the organization, since members from lower levels may be intimidated and subservient to those from higher levels. In a power-tolerant culture, variation in organizational level may be less of a problem. Uncertainty avoidance and team dynamics may also interact as a function of task. If a task is vague, ambiguous, or unstructured, an uncertainty-avoiding group may be unable to function effectively; in contrast, an uncertainty-accepting group may actually thrive. Finally, teams in an aggressive goal behavior culture may work together more effectively if their goal has financial implications, whereas teams in a passive goal behavior culture may be more motivated to work toward attitudinal or quality-of-work outcomes. "Going Global" provides some additional interesting insights into cross-cultural teams.

Matching business behavior with the cultural values of the work force is a key ingredient to promoting organizational performance. Much of the competitive

GOING GLOBAL

The Best and the Brightest

A few years ago, IBM, Siemens, and Toshiba entered into a strategic alliance to develop an advanced new type of computer chip. Each firm identified a set of research scientists for the project and the total group of around 100 people assembled for work at an IBM facility in East Fishkill, a small Hudson River Valley town in New York. The idea was that the best and brightest minds from three diverse companies would bring such an array of knowledge, insight, and creativity to the project that it was bound to succeed.

Unfortunately, things didn't start out well, and it took much longer than expected for the firms to really figure out how to work together. The biggest reasons cited for the early difficulties related to the cultural differences and barriers that existed among the group members. For example, the Japanese scientists were accustomed to working in one big room where everyone could interact with everyone else and it was easy to overhear what others were saying. The IBM facility, in contrast, had small, cramped offices that could only hold a few people at a time. The Germans were unhappy because most of their offices lacked windows—they claimed that back home no one would be asked to work in a windowless office.

Interpersonal styles also caused conflict at times. Both the U.S. and Japanese scientists criticized their German colleagues for planning and organizing too much, while the Japanese were criticized for their unwillingness to make clear decisions. The German and Japanese scientists felt that their U.S. hosts did not spend enough time socializing with them after work. There were also problems with employee privacy and workplace rights. The office doors at the IBM facility all had small windows that visitors could use to peek in to see if the occupant was busy before knocking. Both the Germans and Japanese, however, saw this as an invasion of their privacy and often hung their coats over the windows. And they also objected to IBM's strict no-smoking policy that mandated that people go outside to smoke, regardless of weather conditions.

Because of these problems, the group's initial lack of progress was discouraging. Managers felt that a big part of the problem was that they did not do an adequate job of training the group members before transferring them to the project, and that better cultural training in particular would have been useful. Fortunately, the group eventually began to essentially train and socialize itself about how to overcome the cultural differences. Indeed, after the early rough spots, the new venture is off and running, and all three partners are again optimistic about the alliance's success.

Sources: "Computer Chip Project Brings Rivals Together, But the Cultures Clash," *Wall Street Journal*, May 3, 1994, pp. A1, A8; Alan Chai, Alta Campbell, and Patrick J. Spain (eds.), *Hoover's Handbook of World Business 1993* (Austin, Tex.: The Reference Press, 1993), pp. 440, 478; Gary Hoover, Alta Campbell, and Patrick J. Spain (eds.), *Hoover's Handbook of American Business 1994* (Austin, Tex.: The Reference Press, 1993), p. 640.

strength of Japanese firms, for example, is due to their incorporation of Japanese cultural norms into the workplace. Japanese culture emphasizes the importance of group harmony and respect for superiors. "Silent leaders," ones who guide rather than command subordinates and who preserve group harmony, are more admired than are authoritarian managers. The ringi system ensures that new approaches are granted group approval before being implemented. The traditional lifetime employment practices that some major Japanese firms use promote employee loyalty to the organization. All these features are reinforced by careful selection of new employees. Only those persons who are willing to subordinate their individual goals to the needs of the group are hired. This corporate philosophy carries over to foreign operations of Japanese MNCs. For example, many U.S. newspapers have reported on the extraordinary amounts of testing and interviewing that such firms operating in North America do before hiring an employee.

CHAPTER REVIEW

Summary

Behavioral and interpersonal processes are vitally important in any organization. Both their importance and their complexity are magnified in international firms. Individual differences provide the cornerstone for understanding behavioral patterns in different cultures. Personality traits, attitudes, perceptions, and stress are all important individual differences that international managers should understand.

Motivation is the overall set of forces that causes people to choose certain behaviors from a set of available behaviors. Need-based, process-based, and reinforcement models of motivation each explain different aspects of motivation. While none of these models is generalizable to all cultures, each can provide insights into motivation in similar cultures.

Leadership is the use of noncoercive influence to shape the goals of a group or organization, to motivate behavior toward reaching those goals, and to help determine the group or organizational culture. People from different cultures react in different ways to each type of leadership behavior. These different reactions are determined partially by cultural dimensions and partially by the individuals themselves.

Decision making is the process of choosing an alternative from among a set of alternatives designed to promote the decision maker's objectives. People from different cultures approach each step in the decision-making process differently. Again, variation along cultural dimensions is a significant determinant of variations in decision-making processes.

Groups and teams are part of all organizations. A team's role structure, cohesiveness, norms, and informal leadership all contribute to its success or failure. Culture plays a major role in determining the team's degree of heterogeneity or homogeneity, which in turn helps determine its overall level of effectiveness.

Review Questions

1. Define personality and explain how personality differences affect individual behavior.

2. Explain how attitudes vary across cultures.

3. Discuss the basic perceptual process and note how it differs across cultures.

4. Explain how attitudes and perception can affect each other.

5. Discuss stress and how it varies across cultures.

6. Identify some of the basic issues managers must confront when attempting to motivate employees in different cultures.

7. How do needs and values differ in different cultures?

8. Summarize the steps in the normative model of decision making and relate each to international business.

9. Why are teams so important? What are the basic implications of teams for an international business?

Questions for Discussion

1. Which do you think is a more powerful determinant of human behavior—cultural factors or individual differences?

2. Think of two or three personality traits that you believe are especially strong in your culture, and two or three that are especially weak. Relate these to Hofstede's cultural dimensions.

3. Assume that you have just been transferred by your company to a new facility in a foreign location. Which of your own personal dimensions do you think will be most effective in helping you deal with this new situation? Does your answer depend on which country you're sent to?

4. How might perception affect motivation in different cultures?

5. How might organizations in different cultures go about trying to enhance leadership capabilities?

6. Do you think it will ever be possible to develop a motivation framework that is applicable in all cultures? Why or why not?

7. How do motivation and leadership affect corporate culture?

8. What advice would you give a Japanese, an Australian, and an Italian manager just transferred to the United States?

9. Assume that you are leading a team composed of representatives from British, Mexican, Brazilian, and Egyptian subsidiaries of your firm. The team must make a number of major decisions.

   a. What guidelines might you develop for yourself for leading the team through its decision-making process?

   b. What steps might you take to enhance the team's cohesiveness? How successful do you think such an effort would be?

BUILDING GLOBAL SKILLS

Select a country in which you have some interest and about which you can readily find information (for example, Japan as opposed to Bhutan). Go to your library and learn as much as you can about the behavior of people from the country you selected. Concentrate on such culturally based social phenomena as the following:

♦ The meaning people from the country attach to a few common English words
♦ The meaning they attach to common gestures
♦ How they interpret basic colors
♦ The basic rules of business etiquette they follow
♦ Their preferences regarding personal space
♦ How the country is characterized along Hofstede's dimensions

Team up with a classmate who chose a different country. Each of you should pick a product or commodity that is produced in the country you studied (such as stereos, bananas, oil, or machine parts). Attempt to negotiate a contract for selling your product or commodity to the other. As you negotiate, play the role of someone from the country you studied as authentically as possible. For example, if people from that culture are offended by a certain gesture and your counterpart happens to make that gesture while negotiating, act offended!

Spend approximately fifteen minutes negotiating. Then spend another fifteen minutes discussing with your classmate how the cultural background each of you adopted affected (or could have affected) the negotiation process.

Follow-up Questions

1. How easy or difficult is it to model the behavior of someone from another country?

2. What other forms of advance preparation might a manager need to undertake before negotiating with someone from another country?

WORKING WITH THE WEB: Building Global Internet Skills

Preparing for an International Expansion

Assume that you are a senior human resource manager with a large food products firm. Your company has recently decided to increase its international activities and is aggressively seeking new market opportunities abroad. As a first step, your firm is exploring joint venture or strategic alliance partnerships in Sweden, Denmark, Italy, Indonesia, and Japan.

One of your responsibilities will be to train your firm's managers as they prepare to relocate to foreign settings to represent your firm in the partnerships being negotiated. You know that each set of managers destined for specific locations will need specialized language training. You are less sure, however, about the leadership and cultural training that you need to develop. That is, you are unsure as to whether each set of managers will need unique training, whether they can all go through common training together, or if there is some optimal combination of training for certain sets of managers together.

Use the Internet to learn as much about individual behavior and interpersonal relations in these countries as you can. Specifically, see if you can locate useful information about individual differences, motivation, leadership, decision making, and group processes in these countries. Next, using the information that you have located, make a tentative decision about the number of leadership and cultural training programs you will need to develop and whether sets of managers destined for certain countries can be combined or need to be trained separately. Finally, form small groups with two or three of your classmates and compare notes. How similar or dissimilar are the training strategies you each developed? Why did these similarities and differences emerge?

CLOSING CASE

Adidas Runs to Catch Up[65]

Adidas AG, a German apparel company, once dominated the athletic sportswear business. But a long series of missteps and mistakes caused the firm to lose its dominant position in the industry to U.S. upstarts Nike and Reebok. Only now is Adidas beginning to turn itself around and to show signs of life.

Adidas was founded in 1948 by Adi Dassler, a Bavarian shoe designer. For years Adidas dominated the athletic shoe market. For example, when U.S. discus thrower Al Oerter won the first of his four Olympic gold medals in 1956, he was wearing Adidas shoes. And basketball hall-of-famer Kareem Abdul-Jabbar wore Adidas shoes throughout his career.

But with success sometimes come trials and tribulations. The first big problem for Adidas came when Adi Dassler's brother, Rudolf, grew frustrated playing second fiddle to Adi and left to form his own company, Puma. Adi's son, Horst, also left Adidas and started his own company as well. Horst and Adi eventually reconciled, and Horst took over the man-

agement of the firm when Adi retired in 1985. While the family travails had taken a toll on the company's performance, Horst did seem to understand the problems and have a vision for straightening them out. But when Horst died two years later, there was no one else in line to run the firm.

Horst Dassler's two sisters, who inherited ownership of the firm, sold Adidas to a French financier named Bernard Tapie in 1989 for $320 million. By this time, however, the firm was going downhill fast. For example, its share of the U.S. athletic shoe market had dropped from an amazingly strong 70 percent to an amazingly weak 2 percent. This drop was due in part to new competition from Nike and Reebok, but also in part to neglect and mismanagement.

Tapie promised to inject $100 million of new money into the firm but never carried through. He was so involved in left-wing politics in his native France that he paid little attention to the firm and ignored its growing losses. Tapie was eventually indicted in a soccer-fixing scandal while serving as the country's Urban Affairs Minister, sentenced to eighteen months in jail, and declared bankruptcy. Adidas, meanwhile, was taken over by its creditors in 1993. At the time, the company was losing $100 million a year.

These creditors knew that they needed an astute manager, a strong leader, and an extraordinary turnaround artist if Adidas was to regain its competitiveness. And fortunately for them, they found all three in a single person—Robert Louis-Dreyfuss, another French financier. At the time, Louis-Dreyfuss was 42, had pocketed $10 million from previous turnarounds, and was restlessly retired. He quickly jumped at the opportunity to take on another interesting challenge.

Louis-Dreyfuss began to appreciate the size of his task on his first day at work when he saw that he was required to approve a salesperson's expense account for $300. He subsequently identified many of the problems as resulting from an old-line rigid bureaucracy based on rank, title, and status and a belief in slow, calculated decision making. He quickly realized that these were perhaps not the best traits to compete in the fast-moving athletic footwear market where the hottest style one month may be a loser the next, particularly among urban teenagers who represent the most profitable niche in this market.

Within a matter of weeks, Louis-Dreyfuss had fired the firm's entire top management team—all German—and set in motion plans for streamlining the company. He brought in a French friend to head up sales, a Swede to run marketing, and an Australian as finance director. He also changed the firm's official language to English.

Next up was manufacturing. Louis-Dreyfuss shut down the firm's high-cost factories in Germany, Austria, and France, moving production to Asian countries with lower labor costs. At the same time, he also began to invest heavily in marketing and advertising. Under previous management teams, marketing was cut regularly as a way of slashing costs. But Louis-Dreyfuss knew that more—not less—marketing was necessary if Adidas was to get back on track. Following the model established by Nike, Adidas is now rapidly signing up big-name athletes to wear and endorse its shoes.

Louis-Dreyfuss also stressed that decision making was going to occur much faster than before. A good example of his imprint came when the New York Yankees let it be known that they were looking to make a "deal" with an athletic shoe company. While Nike and Reebok were calculating and reviewing the financial details of making such an arrangement with the best-known baseball team in the world, Adidas put together a package very quickly and won the contract.

Under Louis-Dreyfuss's leadership, Adidas is again becoming a force with which to be reckoned. Its market share is growing, for example, and more and more Adidas shoes are showing up on the basketball courts and soccer fields of the world. Nike is still growing at a faster clip, primarily due to its expansion into sportswear and other athletic equipment. But Adidas is gaining ground on number 2 Reebok in the athletic shoe market and has both Reebok and Nike taking an occasional look over their shoulders to see who's gaining on them.

Case Questions

1. What role has leadership played in both the decline and recovery at Adidas?

2. Contrast Adidas's former and current approaches to decision making to what you now know about the normal German approach.

3. How do you think Adidas's current success is affecting the motivation of its employees?

CHAPTER NOTES

1. "She Is Free, Yet She's Alone in Her World," *Wall Street Journal*, July 26, 1995, pp. B1, B8.

2. For a review of behavioral processes in organizations, see Gregory Moorhead and Ricky W. Griffin, *Organizational Behavior*, 5th ed. (Boston: Houghton Mifflin, 1998).

3. Ibid.

4. Lawrence Pervin, "Personality," in Mark Rosenzweig and Lyman Porter, eds., *Annual Review of Psychology*, Vol. 36 (Palo Alto, Calif.: Annual Reviews, 1985), pp. 83–114.

5. Jennifer George, "The Role of Personality in Organizational Life: Issues and Evidence," *Journal of Management*, Vol. 18 (1992), pp. 185–213.

6. L. R. Goldberg, "An Alternative 'Description of Personality': The Big Five Factor Structure," *Journal of Personality and Social Psychology*, Vol. 59 (1990), pp. 1216–1229; M. R. Barrick and M. K. Mount, "The Big Five Personality Dimensions and Job Performance," *Personnel Psychology,* Vol. 44 (1991), pp. 1–26.

7. Pierce J. Howard and Jane M. Howard, "Buddy, Can You Paradigm?" *Training & Development* (September 1995), pp. 28–34.

8. Jesus F. Salgado, "The Five Factor Model of Personality and Job Performance in the European Community," *Journal of Applied Psychology,* Vol. 82, No. 1 (1997), pp. 30–43.

9. J. B. Rotter, "Generalized Expectancies for Internal vs. External Control of Reinforcement," *Psychological Monographs*, Vol. 80 (1966), pp. 1–28; Bert De Brabander and Christopher Boone, "Sex Differences in Perceived Locus of Control," *The Journal of Social Psychology*, Vol. 130 (1990), pp. 271–276.

10. Colleen Ward and Antony Kennedy, "Locus of Control, Mood Disturbance, and Social Difficulties During Cross-Cultural Transitions," *International Journal of Intercultural Relations*, Vol. 16 (1992), pp. 175–194.

11. Marilyn E. Gist and Terence R. Mitchell, "Self-Efficacy: A Theoretical Analysis of Its Determinants and Malleability," *Academy of Management Review* (April 1992), pp. 183–211.

12. Peg Thoms, Keirsten S. Moore, and Kimberly S. Scott, "The Relationship Between Self-Efficacy for Participating in Self-Managed Work Groups and the Big Five Personality Dimensions," *Journal of Organizational Behavior*, Vol. 17 (1996), pp. 349–362; Cynthia Lee and Philip Bobko, "Self-Efficacy Beliefs: Comparison of Five Measures," *Journal of Applied Psychology*, Vol. 79, No. 3 (1994), pp. 364–369.

13. J. Michael Geringer and Colette A. Frayne, "Self-Efficacy, Outcome Expectancy and Performance of International Joint Venture General Managers," *Canadian Journal of Administrative Sciences*, Vol. 10, No. 4 (1993), pp. 322–333.

14. T. W. Adorno, E. Frenkel-Brunswick, D. J. Levinson, and R. N. Sanford, *The Authoritarian Personality* (New York: Harper & Row, 1950).

15. "Who Becomes an Authoritarian?" *Psychology Today* (March 1989), pp. 66–70.

16. Jon L. Pierce, Donald G. Gardner, and Larry L. Cummings, "Organization-Based Self-Esteem: Construct Definition, Measurement, and Validation," *Academy of Management Journal*, Vol. 32 (1989), pp. 622–648.

17. Roy J. Blitzer, Colleen Petersen, and Linda Rogers, "How to Build Self-Esteem," *Training & Development* (February 1993), pp. 58–65.

18. Michael Harris Bond and Peter B. Smith, "Cross-Cultural Social and Organizational Psychology," in Janet Spence, ed., *Annual Review of Psychology,* Vol. 47 (Palo Alto, Calif.: Annual Reviews, 1996), pp. 205–235.

19. Patricia C. Smith, L. M. Kendall, and Charles Hulin, *The Measurement of Satisfaction in Work and Behavior* (Chicago: Rand-McNally, 1969).

20. Meg G. Birdseye and John S. Hill, "Individual, Organizational/Work and Environmental Influences on Expatriate Turnover Tendencies: An Empirical Study," *Journal of International Business Studies* (Fourth Quarter 1995), pp. 787–813.

21. James R. Lincoln, "Employee Work Attitudes and Management Practice in the U.S. and Japan: Evidence from a Large Comparative Study," *California Management Review* (Fall 1989), pp. 89–106.

22. Daniel J. McCarthy and Sheila M. Puffer, "Perestroika at the Plant Level—Managers's Job Attitudes and Views of Decision-Making in the Former USSR," *The Columbia Journal of World Business* (Spring 1992), pp. 86–99.

23. Abdul Rahim A. Al-Meer, "Organizational Commitment: A Comparison of Westerners, Asians, and Saudis," *International Studies of Management and Organization,* Vol. 19, No. 2 (1989), pp. 74–84.

24. Janet Near, "Organizational Commitment among Japanese and U.S. Workers," *Organization Studies,* Vol. 10, No. 3 (1989), pp. 281–300.

25. Hal B. Gregersen and J. Stewart Black, "Antecedents to Commitment to a Parent Company and a Foreign Operation," *Academy of Management Journal*, Vol. 35, No. 1 (1992), pp. 65–90.

26. Kent D. Miller, "Industry and Country Effects on Managers' Perceptions of Environmental Uncertainties," *Journal of International Business Studies* (Fourth Quarter 1993), pp. 693–714.

27. Satoko Watanabe and Ryozo Yamaguchi, "Intercultural Perceptions at the Workplace: The Case of the British Subsidiaries of Japanese Firms," *Human Relations,* Vol. 48, No. 5 (1995), pp. 581–607.

28. Bodo B. Schlegelmilch and Diana C. Robertson, "The Influence of Country and Industry on Ethical Perceptions of Senior Executives in the U.S. and Europe," *Journal of International Business Studies* (Fourth Quarter 1995), pp. 859–881.

29. For a recent overview of the stress literature, see Frank Landy, James Campbell Quick, and Stanislav Kasl, "Work, Stress, and Well-Being," *International Journal of Stress Management*, Vol. 1, No. 1 (1994), pp. 33–73.

30. "Executive Stress: A Ten-Country Comparison," *The Chicago Tribune*, March 31, 1988.

31. Bruce D. Kirkcaldy and Cary L. Cooper, "Stress Differences Among German and U.K. Managers," *Human Relations*, Vol. 46, No. 5 (1993), pp. 669–680.

32. Craig Pinder, *Work Motivation* (Glenview, Ill.: Scott, Foresman, 1984).

33. H. A. Murray, *Explorations in Personality* (New York: Oxford University Press, 1938).

34. Geert Hofstede, "Motivation, Leadership, and Organization: Do American Theories Apply Abroad?" *Organizational Dynamics* (Summer 1980), pp. 42–63.

35. Joseph J. Fucini and Suzy Fucini, *Working for the Japanese: Inside Mazda's American Auto Plant* (New York: Free Press, 1990).

36. Vern Terpstra and Kenneth David, *The Cultural Environment of International Business*, 2nd ed. (Cincinnati: South-Western, 1985), p. 180.

37. Charles Weaver and Michael Landeck, "Cross-National Differences in Job Values: A Segmented Comparative Analysis of United States and West German Workers" (Laredo State University, 1991), mimeo.

38. Abraham Maslow, "A Theory of Human Motivation," *Psychological Review* (July 1943), pp. 370–396.

39. Nancy Adler, *International Dimensions of Organizational Behavior*, 3rd ed. (Cincinnati: South-Western, 1997), pp. 130–138.

40. P. Howell, J. Strauss, and P. F. Sorenson, "Research Note: Cultural and Situational Determinants of Job Satisfaction among Management in Liberia," *Journal of Management Studies* (May 1975), pp. 225–227.

41. David McClelland, *The Achieving Society* (Princeton, N.J.: Van Nostrand, 1961).

42. Adler, op. cit.

43. Frederick Herzberg, Bernard Mausner, and Barbara Snyderman, *The Motivation to Work* (New York: Wiley, 1959).

44. G. H. Hines, "Achievement, Motivation, Occupations and Labor Turnover in New Zealand," *Journal of Applied Psychology*, Vol. 58, No. 3 (1973), pp. 313–317.

45. Pinder, op. cit.

46. Victor Vroom, *Work and Motivation* (New York: Wiley, 1964).

47. Gary Yukl, *Leadership in Organizations*, 2nd ed. (Englewood Cliffs, N.J.: Prentice-Hall, 1989).

48. Bernard M. Bass, *Bass & Stogdill's Handbook of Leadership*, 3rd ed. (Riverside, N.J.: Free Press, 1990).

49. David A. Ralston, David J. Gustafson, Fanny M. Cheung, and Robert H. Terpstra, "Differences in Managerial Values: A Study of U.S., Hong Kong, and PRC Managers," *Journal of International Business Studies* (Second Quarter 1993), pp. 249–275.

50. Robert H. Doktor, "Asian and American CEOs: A Comparative Study," *Organizational Dynamics*, Vol. 18, No. 3 (1990), pp. 46–56.

51. Jon P. Alston, *The American Samurai* (New York: Walter de Gruyter, 1986), pp. 103–113.

52. "The Spanish-American Business Wars," *Worldwide P & I Planning* (May–June 1971), pp. 30–40.

53. Arvin Parkhe, "Interfirm Diversity, Organizational Learning, and Longevity in Global Strategic Alliances," *Journal of International Business Studies*, Vol. 22, No. 4 (Fourth Quarter 1991), pp. 592–593; Edward T. Hall and Mildred Reed Hall, *Understanding Cultural Differences* (Yarmouth, Maine: Intercultural Press, 1990), pp. 55–62.

54. David Ricks, *Blunders in International Business* (Cambridge, Mass.: Blackwell, 1993).

55. Tom Morris and Cynthia M. Pavett, "Management Style and Productivity in Two Cultures," *Journal of International Business Studies*, Vol. 23, No. 1 (First Quarter 1992), pp. 169–179.

56. George P. Huber, *Managerial Decision Making* (Glenview, Ill.: Scott, Foresman, 1980).

57. Herbert A. Simon, *Administrative Behavior*, 3rd ed. (New York: Free Press, 1976).

58. Adler, op. cit.

59. Alston, op. cit., pp. 181–186.

60. Hall and Hall, op. cit., pp. 33–84.

61. Lawrence C. Wolken, "Doing Business in China," *Texas A&M Business Forum* (Fall 1987), pp. 39–42.

62. J. Stewart Black and Lyman W. Porter, "Managerial Behaviors and Job Performance: A Successful Manager in Los Angeles May Not Succeed in Hong Kong," *Journal of International Business Studies*, Vol. 22, No. 1 (First Quarter 1991), pp. 99–113.

63. Parkhe, op. cit., pp. 579–601.

64. Ricks, op. cit.

65. Charles P. Wallace, "Adidas—Back in the Game," *Fortune*, August 18, 1997, pp. 176–182; "Adidas is Dropping the Other Shoe," *International Herald Tribune*, March 20, 1998, pp. 15, 18.

Controlling the International Business

After studying this chapter you should be able to:

Describe the general purpose of control and the levels of control in international business.

Discuss how international firms manage the control function.

Describe the meaning of productivity and discuss how international firms work to improve it.

Describe how firms control quality and discuss total quality management in international business.

Discuss how international firms control the information their managers need to make effective decisions.

FOR YEARS TYCO TOYS INC. TRIED TO PLAY CATCH-UP AGAINST TOY industry leaders Mattel and Hasbro. In 1986 Tyco was only the 22nd largest toy maker in the United States. But through aggressive new product launches and acquisitions, Tyco had advanced to the number 3 spot by 1990, behind only the two industry giants. At the same time, however, Tyco executives realized that further gains against its larger competitors would be much harder to achieve. ▌▌ Mattel and Hasbro had already slowly and systematically built up their international market shares over an extended period of time, while Tyco had remained essentially a U.S. business. In 1990 Tyco was earning less than 13 percent of its sales from outside the United States. Tyco executives subsequently concluded that if they wanted their firm to gain an equal standing with the industry giants, they needed a stronger international presence. Their logic was

Tyco Loses Control[1]

two-fold: international expansion would allow Tyco to gain market share at lower costs than other competitive options and better enable Tyco to service its large retail customers like Toys 'R' Us that were also expanding aggressively into foreign markets. ▌▌ In 1992, therefore, Tyco's annual report—featuring a multiethnic group of children linking hands over a many-hued earth—announced a much ballyhooed international expansion strategy. The strategy outlined in the report indicated that Tyco was going to open one European subsidiary a year, with each expected to start showing a profit twelve months later. The company also set a goal of achieving 50 percent of its total sales from outside the United States within a four-year period. ▌▌ Unfortunately, however, Tyco executives quickly lost sight of this plan and ended up moving too far too quickly. First, they bought Universal Matchbox Group, Ltd., a Hong Kong-based manufacturer of die-cast toy vehicles that dominated the market in Germany and Great Britain. Next, the firm opened not one—as planned—but four European subsidiaries in 1992. This unusually rapid and essentially unplanned international expansion created a context for chaos. ▌▌ Compounding the problem was Tyco's relative inexperience in foreign markets. For example, only one senior Tyco executive had ever lived outside the United States. Top managers were also accustomed to running a highly centralized operation out of the corporate offices where all key decision makers were arrayed along a single hallway. Tyco promoted a key Matchbox executive to run Tyco Europe and gave him a 50 percent increase in salary, but also stipulated that he had to move from London to New Jersey, site of Tyco's corporate headquarters. ▌▌ Problems began to bubble to the surface almost immediately. Other key Matchbox executives left because Tyco stripped them of their decision-making authority. The firm's distribution system virtually collapsed because of mismanagement. For example, products that were supposed to be shipped in 72 hours were often taking 45 days. And Tyco executives still seemed to think they could run their foreign subsidiaries from New Jersey with an occasional long distance call to Europe. As a result of these mistakes, the company lost $70 million in 1993 and another $35 million in 1994. ▌▌ Within a couple of years, even corporate headquarters conceded that it had created a hopeless morass. The Italian subsidiary was liquidated altogether, a Belgian factory was shut down, the remaining three European subsidiaries were combined, and one third of the European staff was dismissed. Tyco's CEO was also replaced. Despite having the hottest-selling, hardest-to-get toy during the 1996 Christmas season—Tickle Me Elmo—the end came in mid-1997 when Tyco agreed to be purchased by Mattel for $755 million, less than half of what it had been valued at five years before. ▌▌▌▌▌

Tyco's executives failed at one of the most important and fundamental management tasks: controlling the things the firm is trying to do and how it is trying to do them. Because of the complexity of dealing with different cultures, laws, and currencies, control in international firms is obviously more challenging than in purely domestic ones. The Tyco case reflects this elementary truth: while it was a reasonably well-managed domestically oriented firm, Tyco obviously failed to recognize and respond to the challenges of controlling a large international operation.

For an international firm, control can be focused on activities within a given market, within several markets, or across the entire organization. **Control** is the process of monitoring and regulating activities in a firm so that some targeted measure of performance is achieved or maintained.[2] The control process begins with the establishment of a goal or other performance target (for example, meeting sales goals or cost limits). Managers then monitor progress toward meeting that goal or target and take appropriate actions to keep the firm on track. Control activities may focus on direct financial performance (such as the profit margin achieved by an individual manager, business unit, or foreign subsidiary) or on some other aspect of performance (such as cutting labor costs, improving quality, or reducing parts inventories).

For example, suppose the European purchasing manager of a Canadian manufacturing firm has an annual travel budget of $36,000. Based on previous experience, the manager expects travel costs to be spread evenly throughout the year, or around $3000 per month. So travel expenses of $2900 in January lead her to assume that costs are about where they should be. However, if her February travel expenses are $6000, she may need to cut back in March or, if she feels more travel is needed, request an increase in her travel budget from headquarters. The manager is controlling her travel costs by monitoring her monthly expenses to keep them within an expected range and then taking action if they fall too far outside that range.

In this chapter we introduce the three basic levels in international firms at which control systems may be used: strategic, organizational, and operational. We also discuss some methods by which control can be more effectively managed. Then we describe three important aspects of international management that are in fact forms of control systems: the management of productivity, quality, and information.

FIGURE 15.1

**Levels of
International
Control**

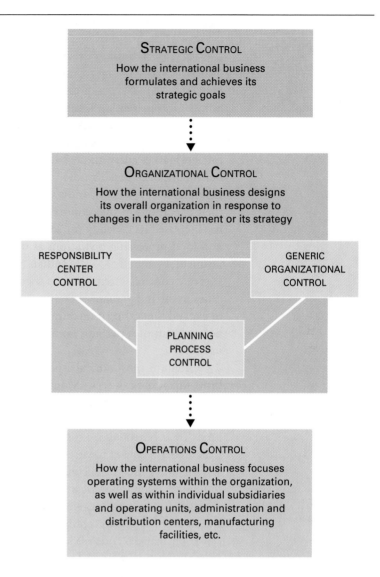

STRATEGIC CONTROL

How the international business
formulates and achieves its
strategic goals

ORGANIZATIONAL CONTROL

How the international business designs
its overall organization in response to
changes in the environment or its strategy

RESPONSIBILITY
CENTER
CONTROL

GENERIC
ORGANIZATIONAL
CONTROL

PLANNING
PROCESS
CONTROL

OPERATIONS CONTROL

How the international business focuses
operating systems within the organization,
as well as within individual subsidiaries
and operating units, administration and
distribution centers, manufacturing
facilities, etc.

Levels of Control in International Business

As illustrated in Fig. 15.1, there are three main levels at which control can be implemented and managed in an international business. These three key levels of control are the strategic, organizational, and operations levels. While each is important on its own merits, they are also important collectively as an organizing framework for managers to use in approaching international control from a comprehensive and integrated perspective.

Strategic Control

Strategic control is intended to monitor both how well an international business formulates strategy and how well it goes about implementing it.[3] Thus strategic control focuses on how well the firm defines and maintains its desired strategic alignment with its environment and how effectively it is setting and achieving its strategic goals. For example, Tyco's purchase of Matchbox represented a logical and attractive acquisition. Tyco was looking to expand internationally, and Matchbox had a strong reputation and profitable operation in major European markets. The initial acquisition thus represented a strategy of related diversification. Unfortunately, as detailed earlier, poor operationalization of this strategy contributed to the firm's eventual demise.

Strategic control also plays a major role in the decisions firms make about foreign-market entry and expansion. This is especially true when the market holds both considerable potential and considerable uncertainty and risk. For example, in the wake of India's overtures for FDI, many firms are expanding their operations in that country. Hindustan Lever, Unilever's Indian subsidiary, has increased its capacity for soap and detergent manufacturing and launched new food-processing operations as well. These steps represent a strategic commitment by the firm to the Indian market. As this strategy is implemented, strategic control systems will be used to ensure a smooth process.[4] If opportunities in the Indian market continue to unfold, Unilever will no doubt continue to expand there. But if uncertainty and risk become too great, the firm may become cautious, perhaps even going so far as to reduce its involvement in India.

Often the most critical aspect of strategic control is control of an international firm's financial resources. Money is the driving force of any organization, whether it is in the form of profits or of cash flow to ensure that ongoing expenses can be covered. And if a firm has surplus revenues, managers must ensure that those funds are invested wisely in order to maximize their payoff for the firm and its shareholders. Thus it is extremely important that an international firm develop and maintain effective accounting systems. Such systems should allow managers to fully monitor and understand where the firm's revenues are coming from in every market in which it operates, to track and evaluate all its costs and expenses, and to see how its parts contribute to its overall profitability.

Poor financial control can cripple a firm's ability to compete globally. For example, Mantrust, an Indonesian firm, bought Van Camp Seafood, packager of Chicken of the Sea tuna, for $300 million. Most of that money was borrowed from Indonesian banks. But Mantrust's owner was unskilled at managing debt, and the firm had difficulties making its loan payments. Both Mantrust and Van Camp struggled for years until finally in 1997 Mantrust sold Van Camp to Tri-Union Seafood, a limited partnership owned by investors in the United States and Thailand. "Going Global" provides another vivid illustration of the problems poor financial control can create.

Financial control is generally a separate area of strategic control in an international firm. Most firms create one or more special managerial positions to handle financial control. Such a position is usually called *controller*. Large international firms often have a corporate controller responsible for the financial resources of the entire organization. Each division within the firm is likely to have a divisional controller who is based in a country in which the division operates and who oversees local financial control. Divisional controllers are usually responsible both to the heads of their respective divisions and to the corporate controller. These control relationships are managed primarily through budgets and financial forecasts.

GOING GLOBAL

The Importance of Control

Control is an important management responsibility in any organization. In an international business with far-flung operations, however, the need for effective control becomes even more important. The recent financial disaster at Baring Brothers provides a vivid illustration of this fact.

Baring Brothers is one of the oldest and most respected banks in England. During its 233-year history, the venerable firm financed the Napoleonic Wars for Great Britain and the Louisiana Purchase for the United States and was banker to the House of Windsor. Like many major banks, Baring Brothers opened offices in many major cities around the world in recent years.

One of the bank's subsidiaries was Baring Futures PLC, an investment firm specializing in complex futures trading. In 1992, Baring Futures sent a young broker named Nick Leeson to work in its Singapore office. Leeson performed admirably for the firm, earning vast sums of money with his impressive understanding of Asian financial markets and winning accolades from his superiors for his ability to run a tight operation.

In early 1995, however, disaster struck. Leeson had made a number of questionable, highly leveraged investments in 1994, which would have been very profitable had the Tokyo stock market remained stable. However, the earthquake that struck Kobe, Japan, clobbered Japanese stock prices and Leeson's deals fell apart—bringing Baring to its knees and forcing it into bankruptcy.

The reason Leeson was able to inflict so much damage singlehandedly was that Baring allowed him to function with virtually no controls over his actions. In most investment houses, one person or group handles all trading, and another person or group serves as overseer. This latter function is for control—to ensure that the traders are not taking unnecessary risks and that they have financial backing to cover any losses they might incur.

Leeson, however, was allowed to perform both functions. He made trades, confirmed them himself, and then authorized the funds to cover them. As his deals went sour following the Kobe disaster, he made riskier and riskier investments in a desperate attempt to recoup the losses. Without anyone checking on his work, he eventually suffered trading losses of $1.4 billion.

After the disaster was discovered, Leeson fled but was soon apprehended in Germany. Baring, meanwhile, could find no investors to cover its losses and was taken over by the Bank of England. It was eventually sold to a Dutch finance group, Internationale Nederlanden Groep, which agreed to inject $1.3 billion to return the firm to solvency. And Leeson was sent to prison.

Sources: "Busted!" *Newsweek*, March 13, 1995, pp. 36–47; "The Lesson from Barings' Straits," *Business Week*, March 13, 1995, pp. 30–32; "Barings Debacle: High-Finance Thriller Laced with Greek Tragedy," *Associated Press News Story*, March 5, 1995; "Barings Is Back in Business," *USA Today*, March 7, 1995, p. 2B.

A special concern of an international controller is managing the inventory of various currencies needed to run the firm's subsidiaries and to pay its vendors.[5] For example, Coca-Cola has to manage its holdings of over 150 currencies as part of its daily operations. Each foreign subsidiary of an international firm needs to maintain a certain amount of local currency for its domestic operations. Each also needs access to the currency of the parent corporation's home country in order to remit dividend payments, reimburse the parent for the use of intellectual property, and pay for other intracorporate transactions. The subsidiary further must be able to obtain other currencies in order to pay suppliers of imported raw materials and component parts as their invoices are received.

Given the possibility of exchange-rate fluctuations, as discussed in Chapter 5, the controller needs to oversee the firm's holdings of diverse currencies in order to avoid losses if exchange rates change. Many MNCs centralize the management of exchange-rate risk at the corporate level. However, others, such as the Royal Dutch/Shell Group, allow their foreign affiliates to use both domestic and international financial and commodity markets to protect their costs and prices against exchange-rate fluctuations. Firms that decentralize this task need to maintain adequate financial controls on their subsidiaries or face financial disaster. For example, in the early 1990s Shell's Japanese affiliate, Showa Shell Seikiyu KK, engaged in widespread speculative trading in foreign-currency markets, a practice forbidden by Shell. That is, rather than trying to hedge against exchange-rate fluctuations, the Japanese affiliate was trying to earn profits through exchange-rate fluctuations. Knowledge of this speculative trading was brought to light only when the Japanese group reported a loss of over $1 billion. Clearly, Shell's internal controls had broken down and failed to detect the speculative activities. As a result, corporate officials implemented new procedures and tighter controls to better manage the firm's financial resources.[6]

Managers in international firms must have access to the information they need to engage in strategic control. Information networks and systems should be designed to provide as much relevant, current, and accurate information as possible to managers so they can make informed decisions. Failure to do so can lead to expensive mistakes. For example, the Mitsui Construction Company was seeking a site in London on which to build a new office complex. Rather than gather their own information on potential sites, Mitsui managers relied on a British consulting firm. The consultants convinced Mitsui to bid on the site of an old building, indicating that the property would sell for no more than $250 million and that the old building could be cheaply demolished. After Mitsui bought the property, it discovered that its bid of $255 million was $90 million more than the next highest bid. Even worse, a few days later the British government declared the building a historic site, so it could not be demolished. Clearly, Mitsui had acted on inaccurate and misleading information.[7]

Another type of strategic control that is increasingly important to international firms is control of joint ventures and other strategic alliances.[8] As we discussed in Chapter 12, strategic alliances, particularly joint ventures, are being used more often by and becoming more important to international firms. It follows then that strategic control systems must also account for the performances of such alliances. Because by definition a joint venture or other strategic alliance is operated as a relatively autonomous enterprise, most partners agree to develop an independent control system for each one in which they participate. The financial control of these alliances then becomes an ingredient in the overall strategic control system for each partner firm. That is, the alliance maintains its own independent control systems, but the results are communicated not only to the managers of the alliance but also to each partner.

Organizational Control

Organizational control focuses on the design of the organization itself. As discussed in Chapter 13, there are many different forms of organization design that an international firm can use. But selecting and implementing a particular design does not necessarily end the organization design process. For example, as a firm's environment or strategy changes, managers may need to alter the firm's design to better enable it to function in the new circumstances. Adding new product lines, entering a new market, or opening a new factory—all can dictate the need for a change in design.

International firms generally use one or more of three types of organizational control systems: responsibility center control, generic organizational control, and planning process control.[9] The first two types are based on the **locus of authority,** or where the power to make various decisions resides within the organization. If it is appropriate for individual subsidiaries to call the shots in an MNC, then many of their controls logically can be decentralized. In other cases, it may be more appropriate for headquarters or some other centralized location to maintain more direct control over various decisions. The third type of control system is based on the planning process.

Responsibility Center Control. The most common type of organizational control system is a decentralized one called **responsibility center control.** Using this system, the firm first identifies fundamental responsibility centers within the organization. Strategic business units are frequently defined as responsibility centers, as are geographical regions or product groups. Regardless of how the firm specifies and defines them, however, it then evaluates each center on the basis of how effectively it meets its strategic goals. Thus a unique control system is developed for each responsibility center. These systems are tailored to meet local accounting and reporting requirements, the local competitive environment, and other circumstances.

For example, Nestlé uses responsibility center control for each of its units, such as Poland Springs, Alcon Labs, and Nestlé-Rowntree (see Map 15.1). These subsidiaries regularly provide financial performance data to corporate headquarters. Managers at Poland Springs, for example, file quarterly reports to Nestlé headquarters in Switzerland so that headquarters can keep abreast of how well its U.S. subsidiary is doing. By keeping each subsidiary defined as a separate and distinct unit and allowing each to use the control system that best fits its own competitive environment, corporate managers in Switzerland can see how each unit is performing within the context of its own market. Each report must contain certain basic information, such as sales and profits, but each also has unique entries that best reflect the individual subsidiary and its market.

Generic Organizational Control. A firm may prefer to use **generic organizational control** across its entire organization; that is, the control systems used are the same for each unit or operation, and the locus of authority generally resides at the firm's headquarters. Generic organizational control is most commonly used by international firms that pursue similar strategies in each market in which they compete. Because there is no strategic variation between markets, responsibility center control would be inappropriate. The firm is able to apply the same centralized decision making and control standards to the strategic performance of each unit or operation. Moreover, because international firms that use the same strategy in every market often have relatively stable and predictable operations, the organizational control system they use can also be relatively stable and straightforward. For example, United Distillers PLC markets its line of bourbon products in the United States, Japan, and throughout Europe. But because the

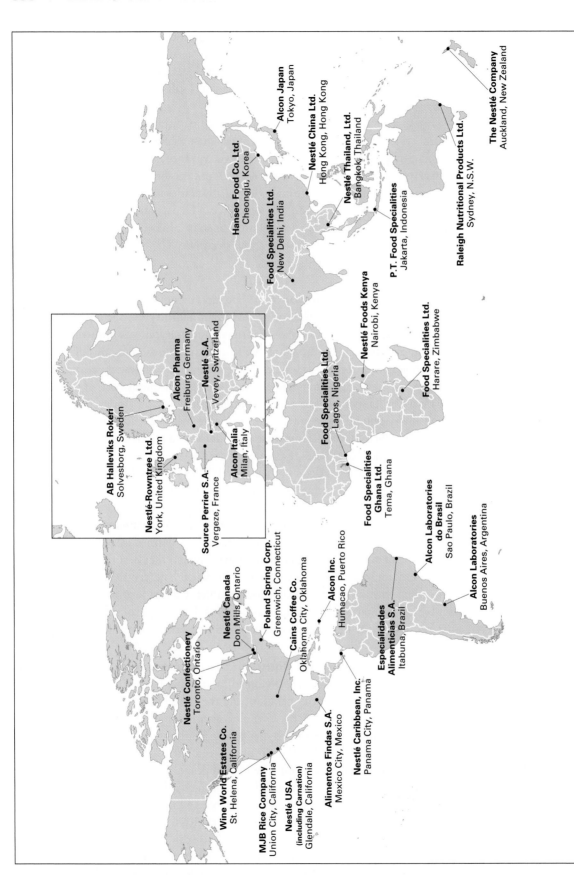

MAP 15.1   **A Sampling of Nestlé's Global Holdings, Subsidiaries, and Affiliates**

Starbucks's dedication to quality has been an important component of its success in the U.S. market. In internationalizing its operations, Starbucks managers face the challenge of transferring its control systems to national environments that differ substantially from that of its home market.

product line is essentially the same in every market and the characteristics of its consumers vary little across markets, the firm uses the same control methods for each market.[10] Similarly, Starbucks has achieved success by practicing rigid quality control throughout every aspect of its operations. As the firm starts to expand internationally—it opened two stores in Japan and one in Singapore in 1997 and acquired U.K.-based Seattle Coffee in 1998—it intends to use exactly the same control standards and methods it has been using in the United States for twenty-five years.[11]

Planning Process Control. A third type of organizational control, which could be used in combination with either responsibility center control or generic organizational control, focuses on the strategic planning process itself rather than on outcomes. **Planning process control** calls for a firm to concentrate its organizational control system on the actual mechanics and processes it uses to develop strategic plans. This approach is based on the assumption that if the firm controls its strategies, desired outcomes are more likely to result. And each business unit may then concentrate more on implementing its strategy, rather than worrying as much about the outcomes of that strategy.

For example, Northern Telecom uses this approach for part of its organizational control process. Whenever a unit fails to meet its goals, the head of that unit meets with the firm's executive committee. The meeting focuses on how the original goals were set and why they were not met. Throughout the meeting, the emphasis is on the process that was followed that led to the unsuccessful outcome. The goal, therefore, is to correct shortcomings in the actual process each unit uses. For example, a unit might have based its unmet sales goals on outdated market research data because there were insufficient funds for new market research. Planning process control would focus not on correcting the sales shortfall, but on enabling more accurate forecasting in the future.

There are clear and important linkages between strategic control and organizational control in an international firm. When a firm adopts a centralized form of organization design, strategic control is facilitated as a logical and complementary extension of that design. But when a firm uses a decentralized design, strategic control is not as logically connected with that design.[12] A decentralized design gives foreign affiliates more autonomy and freedom while making it more difficult for the parent to maintain adequate control. The challenge facing managers of the parent, then, is to foster the autonomy and freedom that accompany a decentralized design while simultaneously maintaining effective parent control of operating subsidiaries.

For a large international firm, organizational control must be addressed at multiple levels. At the highest level, the appropriate form of organization design must be maintained for the entire firm. At a lower level, however, the appropriate form of organization design also must be maintained for each subsidiary or operating unit. The firm also must ensure that these designs mesh with each other. Consider, for example, France's Cap Gemini S.A., the world's third-largest computer services firm. Cap Gemini uses organizational control as an overarching framework for managing its entire array of control systems scattered across twenty countries. The firm's founder and CEO, Serge Kampf, has structured Cap Gemini as a holding company. This structure allows each subsidiary in the various countries in which Cap Gemini operates to create a unique design that works most effectively in the particular country. Each subsidiary is run by a top manager who reports directly to Kampf and who is responsible for maintaining effective control within the unit while still being accountable to the parent corporation. Thus Kampf can maintain tight control over all the firm's operations by isolating group performance, growth, and costs within clearly defined operating units. Each unit manager is also instructed to create a control network within the unit so that the manager can report to Kampf on any aspect of the business at any time.[13] "Going Global" also illustrates how even smaller businesses must insure that the level of control matches the situation.

Operations Control

The third level of control in an international firm is operations control. **Operations control** focuses specifically on operating processes and systems within both the firm and its subsidiaries and operating units. Thus a firm needs an operations control system within each business unit and within each country or market in which it operates. It may also need an operations control system for each of its manufacturing facilities, distribution centers, administrative centers, and so on.

Strategic control often involves time periods of several years, while organizational control may deal with periods of only a few years or months. But operations control involves relatively short periods of time, dealing with components of performance that need to be assessed on a regular—perhaps even daily or hourly—basis. An operations control system is also likely to be much more specific and focused than are strategic and organizational control systems.

For example, a manufacturing firm may monitor daily output, scrappage, and worker productivity within a given manufacturing facility, while a retail outlet may measure daily sales. A firm that wants to increase the productivity of its work force or enhance the quality of its products or services will primarily use operations control to pursue these goals. Operations control usually focuses on the lower levels of a firm, such as first-line managers and operating employees.

Consider Aldi, a German grocery chain. While people in the United States are

GOING GLOBAL

Choosing the Right Level of Control

Azon, Inc. is a small Michigan-based supplier of machinery and chemicals used by makers of aluminum windows. Azon first began exporting its products to Europe in the 1980s. In 1986 the firm's owner and CEO, James Dunstan, established a sister company, Azon UK Ltd., in Wales and assigned a former Azon sales representative to run it. This executive has run the company effectively, and has grown accustomed to having a great deal of autonomy.

Dunstan believes that the arrangement has worked very well since its inception. He visits Wales once a year and the Wales executive visits Azon headquarters in Kalamazoo once a year as well. In between, brief quarterly reports are the only other normal contact between the two units. And Dunstan reports that the Wales unit continues to grow in terms of both sales and profits.

Because European sales were growing rapidly, Dunstan decided to open another sales office on the continent in 1990. And because the control framework he used in Wales had been working so well, he assumed that he could use the same approach with his new operation. He hired a new sales manager from outside the firm to run this operation, and gave him the same autonomy as his counterpart in Wales. Unfortunately, the arrangement with this new manager produced far different results.

For example, Dunstan understood that his new sales manager would need to travel extensively in order to generate new business. But he eventually learned that the manager was traveling far more than was necessary. And when he was on the road, the manager stayed only in premium hotels and dined lavishly, but generated little new business. Dunstan finally became alarmed at his losses in Europe and decided to take a closer look. He was distressed to learn that the European office had lost $750,000 over a five-year span.

Faced with this reality, Dunstan shut down the operation and fired the manager. In looking back, he admits that he underestimated the importance of effective control in international business. His first experience in Wales had worked so well that he simply assumed that he could use the same approach as he expanded into other countries. Now he recognizes that his initial experience was unique, and that stronger and more formal controls will be necessary if and when he decides to expand again into new international markets.

Source: "Small Firms, Big Hurdles," *Wall Street Journal*, September 26, 1996, pp. R4, R5.

used to sprawling, full-line supermarkets that carry everything from apples to zippers, typical European grocery stores tend to be smaller and less service-oriented, to carry fewer product lines, and to charge higher prices. Aldi has prospered in Europe through an elaborate operations control system that relies heavily on cost control and efficiency. Aldi stores do not advertise or even list their numbers in telephone directories. Products are not unpacked and put on shelves but are instead sold directly from crates and boxes. These no-frills stores are located in low-rent districts. Customers bring their own sacks (or pay Aldi 4 cents each for sacks) and bag their own purchases. Aldi does not accept checks or coupons and provides little customer service. But this austere approach allows the firm to charge rock bottom prices—25 cents for a loaf of bread and 90 cents for a six-pack of cola, for example. Aldi has effectively transferred its control methods to its U.S. operation. The result? Aldi's net profit margins in the United States run about 1.5 percent of sales, double the industry norm, and sales average $350 per square foot, compared to an industry norm of $275. With over 450 stores operating in the United States, Aldi has become one of the country's most profitable grocery chains.[14]

Managing the Control Function in International Business

Given the obvious complexities in control, it should come as no surprise that international firms must address a variety of issues in managing the control function. To effectively manage control, managers in such firms need to understand how to establish control systems, what the essential techniques for control are, why some people resist control, and what managers can do to overcome this resistance.

Establishing International Control Systems

As illustrated in Fig. 15.2, control systems in international business are established through four basic steps: set control standards for performance, measure actual performance, compare performance against standards, and respond to deviations. There obviously will be differences in specificity, time frame, and sophistication, but these steps are applicable to any area and any level of control.

Set Control Standards for Performance. The first step in establishing an international control system is to define relevant control standards. A **control standard** in this context is a target, a desired level of the performance component the firm is attempting to control. For example, if a firm anticipates selling 10,000 units of a new product in a particular market next year, 10,000 units sold becomes the control standard for which managers in that market become accountable. Similarly, as part of a worldwide program to lower costs and become more productive, managers at Ford Motor Company established a control standard of cutting costs by $1 billion during calender year 1997. Ford of Europe was specifically charged with the task of cutting its costs by $500 million, half of the company's worldwide total.[15]

Control standards need to be objective and consistent with the firm's goals. Suppose a firm is about to open its first manufacturing facility in Thailand. It might set the following three control standards for the plant:

1 Productivity and quality in the new plant will exceed the levels in the firm's existing plants.

2 After an initial break-in period, 90 percent of all key management positions in the plant will be filled by local managers.

3 The plant will obtain at least 80 percent of its resources from local suppliers.

These control standards help provide a roadmap for managers involved in opening and running the new plant. Managers can readily see that productivity and quality are critical and that the firm expects them to hire and buy locally. Where did these standards come from? The firm set them on the basis of its objectives for the new plant, its experience with similar operations, and its overall goals.[16] The second and third goals may have resulted from a conscious strategy of reducing political risk or the parent firm's desire to be a good corporate citizen in each country in which it operates.

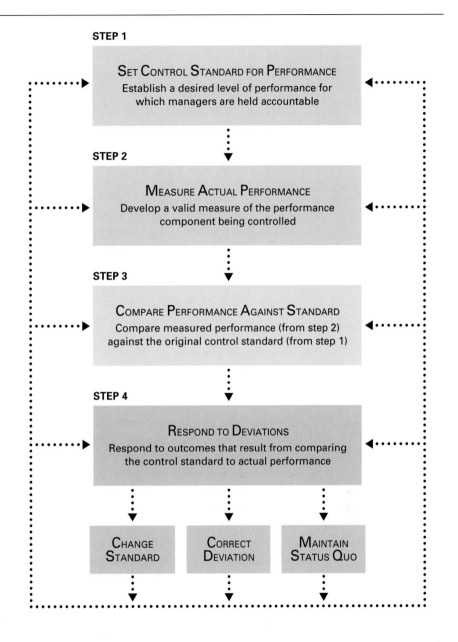

FIGURE 15.2

Steps in International Control

Measure Actual Performance. The second step in creating an international control system is to develop a valid measure of the performance component being controlled. For the firm introducing a new product in a foreign market, performance is based on the actual number of units sold. For the new plant in Thailand used as an example earlier, performance would be assessed in terms of productivity, quality, and hiring and purchasing practices. Similarly, using its existing accounting and financial reporting systems, Ford measured its costs regularly throughout 1997, taking an especially close look at the end of each quarter. For example, at the end of the first quarter of the year, the firm's costs had already been reduced by $800 million.

Some elements of performance are relatively easy and straightforward to measure; examples are actual output, worker productivity, product quality, unit sales, materials waste, travel expenses, hiring practices, and employee turnover. Considerably more difficult is measuring the effectiveness of an advertising campaign to improve a firm's public image, ethical managerial conduct, or employee attitudes and motivation.

Compare Performance Against Standards. The next step in establishing an international control system is to compare measured performance (obtained in step 2) against the original control standards (defined in step 1). Again, when control standards are straightforward and objective and performance is relatively easy to assess, this comparison is easy. For example, comparing actual sales of 8,437 units against a target sales level of 10,000 is simple. Likewise, comparing the actual hiring of twenty Thai managers against a target of hiring 19 Thai managers is also straightforward. And in Ford's case, because it was dealing with objective and straightforward financial data, Ford's comparisons were relatively easy to assess. For example, if the firm had expected its cost cutting to be spread evenly across the year, its first quarter cuts of $800 million clearly and dramatically exceeded the $250 million that, at the time, would have indicated that the firm was precisely on track toward meeting its goal. But when control standards and performance measures are less concrete, comparing one against the other is considerably more complicated. Suppose a manager established a control standard of "significantly increasing market share" and now finds that market share has increased by 4 percent. Is this significant? Obviously, this comparison is ambiguous and difficult to interpret. Managers are advised to use specific and objective standards and performance measures whenever possible.

Responding to Deviations. The final step in establishing an international control system is responding to deviations observed in step 3. Three different outcomes can result when comparing a control standard and actual performance: the control standard has been met, it has not been met, or it has been exceeded. For example, if the standard is sales of 10,000 units, actual sales of 9,998 units probably means the standard has been met, while sales of only 6,230 means it has not. But actual sales of 14,329 clearly surpasses the standard.

Depending on the circumstances, managers have many alternative responses to these outcomes. If a standard has not been met and the manager believes it is because of performance deficiencies on the part of employees accountable for the performance, the manager may mandate higher performance, increase incentives to perform at a higher level, or discipline or even terminate those employees.[17] Of course, the actual course taken depends on the nature of the standard versus performance expectations, the context within which the failure has occurred, and myriad other factors.

But sometimes standards are not met for unforeseen reasons, such as unexpected competition, an unexpected labor strike, unpredictable raw material shortages, or local political upheavals. Or the original control standard may have been set too high to begin with, in which case it may be possible to adjust the standard downward or to make additional allowances.

Finally, actual performance occasionally exceeds the control standard. Again, there may be multiple explanations: managers and employees may have expended extra effort, the original standard may have simply been too low, or competitors may have bungled their own opportunities. In this case, managers may need to provide additional rewards or bonuses, adjust their control standards upward, or aggressively seize new opportunities.

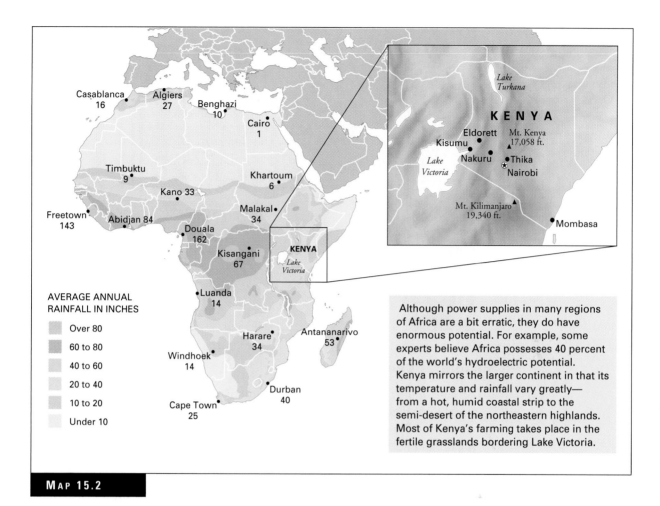

MAP 15.2

Kenyan Rainfall

Average annual rainfall in inches:
- Over 80
- 60 to 80
- 40 to 60
- 20 to 40
- 10 to 20
- Under 10

Although power supplies in many regions of Africa are a bit erratic, they do have enormous potential. For example, some experts believe Africa possesses 40 percent of the world's hydroelectric potential. Kenya mirrors the larger continent in that its temperature and rainfall vary greatly—from a hot, humid coastal strip to the semi-desert of the northeastern highlands. Most of Kenya's farming takes place in the fertile grasslands bordering Lake Victoria.

When Ford's managers realized at the end of the first quarter of 1997 that the firm was running far ahead of its cost-cutting goals, the firm raised its performance goal to a year-end target of $2 billion. Throughout the year, however, cost reductions continued to exceed expectations. By the end of the third quarter, the firm reported cost reductions of $2.3 billion, and again raised its goal for the year to $3 billion. Meanwhile, Ford of Europe also did quite well, easily exceeding its own goal of trimming $500 million in costs for the year.

Kenya Power & Lighting (KP&L) often finds it must react to deviations between control standards and actual performance in its distribution of electric power throughout Kenya. Businesses and municipalities in Kenya are more heavily dependent on hydroelectric power than are those in most other countries. Whenever the country experiences inadequate rain or prolonged dry spells (see Map 15.2), KP&L's water-powered electric plants have to ration electricity. Twice in the last decade, the government-run utility has been forced to enact nationwide rationing to ensure adequate power. It has also used smaller-scale rationing on numerous other occasions. During each rationing period, continued supplies of electricity were guaranteed to hospitals and security installations, while big businesses were required to cut energy consumption by 30 percent and home-owners were subjected to two-hour black-out periods each day. As soon as energy supplies reached an acceptable limit, rationing was phased out.[18]

These workers are helping to monitor power usage in Kenya so that Kenya Power & Lighting can effectively control the distribution of electricity throughout the country. Some degree of rationing must be implemented when a dry spell adversely affects hydroelectric generation of power.

Essential Control Techniques

Because of the complexities of both the international environment and international firms themselves, those firms rely on a wide variety of different control techniques. We do not describe them all here but introduce a few of the most important ones.

Accounting Systems. Accounting is a comprehensive system for collecting, analyzing, and communicating data about a firm's financial resources. Accounting procedures are heavily regulated and must follow prescribed methods dictated by national governments. Because of these regulations, investors, government agencies, and other organizational stakeholders within a given country can better compare the financial performance of different organizations, have a common understanding of what various kinds of information mean, and place reasonable trust in the accuracy and meaning of that information.

International firms face more difficulties in establishing their accounting procedures than do purely domestic firms. International businesses must develop accounting systems to control and monitor the performance of the overall firm and each division, operating unit, or subsidiary. These systems enable managers to keep abreast of the financial performance of every part of the firm. Dickson Poon, a Hong Kong investor, uses accounting systems to maintain tight financial control over poor performing retailers that he buys and then revitalizes. For example, he bought the struggling Harvey Nichol's department store in London a few years ago, implemented a stronger accounting system (along with other changes, of course), and has turned the store into a money-maker. More recently, he has been attempting to purchase the bankrupt Barney's chain in the United States; if successful, he will utilize the same strategy to return that retailer to profitability.[19]

But problems can arise when the accounting standards or procedures of the countries in which a firm operates are incompatible with each other, as is frequently the case. Each subsidiary must maintain its accounting records in accordance with local procedures and denominate its accounts in the local currency, in order to satisfy local government regulations and meet the needs of local managers. Yet the parent needs the local accounting records of each subsidiary translated into the parent's currency using accounting procedures dictated by the parent's home country in order to meet the needs of investors, regulators, and tax collectors in that country. The parent further must decide whether it will evaluate the performance of its subsidiaries and the subsidiaries' managers on the basis of their performance using the local accounting system, the parent's home country accounting system, or some combination of the two. We discuss international accounting in more detail in Chapter 19.

Procedures. Firms also use various procedures to maintain effective control. Policies, standard operating procedures, rules, and regulations all help managers carry out the control function. For example, as part of a manufacturing firm's political agreement with its host country, the firm may establish a policy that at least 75 percent of the raw materials it buys must be obtained from local suppliers. This policy guides plant managers in making purchasing decisions and allocations. A firm also could have a rule that each employee transferred to a foreign unit must attain basic proficiency in the local language within six months. This rule would serve as an ongoing and easily referenced measure of what is expected.

Firms often alter their procedures in the face of adversity. For example, consider Singapore Technologies Holdings (STH), a government-controlled R&D firm. STH incurred huge losses on several high-risk ventures. Following accepted practice, the firm's management had undertaken those ventures without getting the government's authorization. The government of Singapore traditionally gave the managers of its state-owned businesses considerable latitude in making decisions on their own. But the losses at STH, plus similar ones at other government-controlled firms, caused government officials to rethink this approach. They created a new set of policies, rules, regulations, and standard operating procedures that such firms must now follow. For example, any capital expenditure over $5 million must now be approved by a government official.[20]

Performance Ratios. International firms also use various performance ratios to maintain control. A **performance ratio** is a numerical index of performance that the firm wants to maintain. A common performance ratio used by many firms is inventory turnover. Holding excessive inventory is dysfunctional because the inventory ties up resources that could otherwise be used for different purposes and because the longer materials sit in inventory, the more prone they are to damage and loss. Based on a firm's unique circumstances, it may decide that it does not want anything to sit in inventory for more than 30 days. That is, it wants to turn its inventory over 12 times a year, and the performance ratio for inventory management, then, is 12. For example, Laura Ashley uses inventory turnover ratios to more effectively manage its stock of garments and household design accessories. But the ratio is likely to differ among different types of retailers and among different countries depending on the amount of floor space, the sophistication of inventory management systems, and the reliability of suppliers. For example, because rents are so high in Tokyo, convenience stores like 7-11 have little room for storage. They must maintain high inventory turnover ratios to remain profitable. Often vendors resupply the 7-11s four or five times a day to ensure that goods are available for customers. Sophisticated electronic linkages allow the stores to communicate their inventory needs to suppliers on a real-time basis.

British Airways also uses performance ratios to maintain control of its airline operations. One key ratio for an airline is the percentage of seats filled on specified flights. If this ratio falls below a set minimum, the firm looks into alternative ways to generate passenger demand, such as discounts or additional promotional activity. Another ratio of interest to British Airways is the percentage of its flights that arrive and depart on time. If this ratio slips too much, managers try to identify and eliminate the reasons for delays.[21]

Behavioral Aspects of International Control

Regardless of how well formulated and implemented a control system may be, managers must understand that human behavior plays a fundamental role in how well control works. Essential to this understanding is the awareness that some people resist control. Also essential is the recognition that resistance can be minimized. While resistance to control is likely to exist within most cultures, its magnitude will vary across cultures.

Resistance to Control. People in international firms may resist control for various reasons. One potential reason is overcontrol, whereby the firm tries to exert more control over individuals than they think is appropriate. By definition, control regulates and constrains behavior. And most people accept this within what they perceive to be reasonable limits (with the limits being partially determined by the cultural context). But if attempts to control behavior begin to exceed those perceived limits, people may balk and begin to resist. For example, when Disney first opened Disneyland Paris, it attempted to apply the same grooming standards for its employees there that it uses in the United States. It banned beards and mandated trimmed hair. However, French employees saw this as overcontrol. They complained about the standards, vented their grievances in the media, and occasionally ignored the standards altogether. The resistance grew to the point where Disney eventually backed off and developed standards that were more acceptable to its European employees.

Organizations that exert too much control over their employees are likely to encounter resistance and other behavioral problems. Because the government of Venezuela heavily restricts the actions of managers at its national oil company, PDV, those managers experience frustration as they attempt to make the company globally competitive.

Another firm that has to deal with problems of overcontrol is Petroleos de Venezuela (PDV), the state-owned national oil enterprise of Venezuela. Experts see PDV as an efficient and well-run organization capable of competing with private-sector rivals from other countries. But the government of Venezuela has restricted the firm's plans to expand, to invest in capital equipment, and to enter new markets. As a result, managers at PDV feel overly constrained and frustrated in their efforts to compete internationally.[22]

People may also resist control because it may be inappropriately focused; that is, the firm may be inadvertently trying to control the wrong things. For example, if a firm places so much emphasis on lowering costs that quality is compromised and employee morale suffers, employees may become indignant and attempt to circumvent the control system. Whistler Radar, a U.S. firm, encountered this problem in its assembly of radar detectors. Its control system focused on quality control only at the end of the assembly process. When managers discovered that 100 of the firm's 250 employees were doing nothing more than reworking defective units assembled by the other 150, they realized that control should have been focused on quality throughout the assembly process.

Finally, people may resist control because control increases their accountability. In the absence of an effective control system, employees may be able to get by with substandard performance because managers do not understand what the employees are doing relative to what they should be doing. For example, if a foreign branch manager has to submit financial performance data only annually, the manager may not be doing as good a job on a day-to-day basis as the firm would like. This lack of control was at the heart of Azon's trouble with its European sales manager, as recounted in the "Going Global" feature on page 553. If the firm were to request performance reports more frequently, it could increase the manager's accountability. At the same time, of course, if the firm demands too much reporting, it becomes prone to overcontrol. Thus it is important to strike a balance between appropriate and acceptable levels of accountability without edging over into a condition of overcontrol.

Foster's Brewing Group, an Australian conglomerate, once suffered because of a clear lack of accountability. Philip Morris Company's Miller Brewing unit bought 20 percent of Foster's Canadian joint venture with Molson. Japan's Asahi Breweries Ltd. already owned a stake in Foster's. Several banks on whose loans Foster's had failed to make payments made substantial claims against the firm's assets. The Australian government, too, made claims against Foster's assets because of past-due taxes, and it began to monitor and regulate the firm's activities. This complex network of ownership linkages and financial claims created a situation in which no one at Foster's home office knew who was in charge or how to proceed. It was hard to tell who made a particular decision, since Philip Morris, Molson, Asahi, banks, and the Australian government were all making decisions about different aspects of the organization. But when Edward T. Kunkel, formerly a Molson executive, took over Foster's, he began to set things straight. One of his first actions was to define accountability by clarifying reporting relationships among the firm's top executive team and establishing clear performance benchmarks against which managers would be evaluated.[23] Since that change the firm's performance has improved significantly and today Foster's is in the process of buying back its stock from Asahi.

People from different cultures will respond in different ways to control. Using the framework discussed in Chapter 9, for example, individuals from power-tolerant cultures may be more likely to resist control, since they are inclined to discount power relationships within their organization. Conversely, people from power-accepting cultures may perceive control to be a normal part of organizations. Uncertainty acceptance will also be important. People who want to avoid uncertainty may accept more control than will people who do not mind uncertainty.

Overcoming Resistance to Control. Although there are no guaranteed methods for eliminating resistance to control, there are a few that can help minimize it. The appropriate method, as well as its likely effectiveness, will vary by culture.

For many settings—especially those with low power acceptance—a particularly important method is to promote participation. Involving employees who are going to be affected by control in its planning and implementation will enable them to better understand the goal of the control system, how and why the system works, and how their jobs fit into the system. They may as a result be less prone to resist it.

Another obvious method to reduce resistance that works well in most cultures is to create a control system that has a clearly appropriate focus and creates reasonable accountability without overcontrolling. Glaxo Wellcome, Great Britain's largest pharmaceutical firm and the world's second largest, uses this method. The firm is very receptive to allowing scientists to explore ideas and possibilities for new prescription drugs, thereby motivating those scientists to pursue ideas and creating an atmosphere of creativity and innovation. At the same time, Glaxo managers carefully monitor the progress of new product development. If costs start becoming excessive or if development begins to lag too far behind the competition, managers may choose to curtail a given project. Employees see this as a viable strategy because it gives them the opportunity to pursue their scientific interests while simultaneously keeping costs in check.[24]

A firm may also overcome resistance to control by providing a diagnostic mechanism for addressing unacceptable deviations. Suppose a plant manager reports productivity levels far below those expected by headquarters. Top managers should avoid jumping to a potentially wrong conclusion, such as simply assuming the manager has done a poor job and reprimanding him, or worse. Instead they should first learn why the poor performance occurred. For example, it may have resulted from the corporate purchasing manager's having bought inferior materials for the plant.

Again, it is important to account for cultural factors when planning how to deal with resistance to control. People from power-accepting cultures, for example, may be reluctant to actively participate in planning and implementing control because they view such activities as the domain of management.

Finally, behavioral aspects of control can be approached and managed from a cultural perspective. The firm may attempt to replace behaviors resulting from national culture with those more consistent with its corporate culture. Being careful to hire people with values, experiences, work habits, and goals that are consistent with the firm's can go a long way toward this goal. Managers of Japanese-owned automobile factories in the United States, for example, spend thousands of dollars per worker selecting U.S. employees who will be receptive to the Japanese way of working. Further refinements in behavior can be expedited through training and management development programs designed to help impart the firm's cultural values and business methods.

Controlling Productivity in International Business

A key consideration in the control systems of many international firms is productivity. Productivity is distinct from control, yet it is also closely related in that the ultimate aim of most control systems is to ensure high levels of productivity. An understanding of productivity allows a better grasp of all the means of attaining it. Thus, in this section we define productivity, examine productivity around the world, and discuss how firms manage productivity.

At its simplest level, **productivity** is an economic measure of efficiency that summarizes the value of outputs relative to the value of the inputs used to create them.[25] Productivity is important for various reasons. For one thing, it helps determine a firm's overall success and contributes to its long-term survival. For another, productivity contributes directly to the overall standard of living of people within a particular country. If the firms within a country are especially productive, the country's citizens will have more products and services to consume. And the firm's goods and services can be exported to other countries, thereby bringing additional revenues back into the country of origin. Each of these factors positively impacts GDP and thus benefits the whole country.

Productivity can be measured in many ways. **Overall productivity** (also called **total factor productivity**) is determined by dividing total outputs by total inputs. But this summary index is often of little direct value to managers, who are likely to be more interested in productivity relative to specific outputs and/or specific inputs. For example, **labor productivity,** a measure of how efficiently the firm is using its work force, is determined by dividing output by direct labor (either hours or dollars). Comparing labor productivity for different subsidiaries may help managers identify problems before they become excessively costly. For example, because it was previously a monopoly, Japan's Nippon Telegraph & Telephone (NTT) did not worry too much about labor productivity. But since its industry is now undergoing deregulation, NTT has had to take a closer look at this measure of its performance. As it turns out, NTT's labor productivity is only about one third of that of AT&T. As a result of this comparison, managers at NTT are seeking ways to boost their labor productivity.[26]

Productivity around the World

While calculating productivity is relatively easy, finding the data to use in the calculations is another matter altogether. Few firms divulge their productivity statistics, and countries often report their data in such different terms that comparisons are difficult. Nevertheless, there is good evidence regarding productivity in the United States, Japan, Germany, and most other Quad countries. Among these countries, clear differences exist between absolute levels of productivity and productivity growth rates. In absolute terms, the United States is the world's most productive major economy.[27] But while U.S. workers are more productive than their foreign counterparts, U.S. productivity growth has fluctuated. For example, throughout the 1980s productivity growth rates were greater in both Germany and Japan than in the United States. More recently, productivity growth in the United States has begun to accelerate again, while productivity growth in Japan has stalled, due at least in part to that country's economic recession. Germany's productivity growth also slowed due to the difficulties of integrating the previously independent economies and political systems of East Germany and West Germany. While the United States maintains a clear lead, that lead is shrinking.[28]

Managing Productivity

Regardless of where a firm operates, one of its fundamental goals must be to continue to monitor and control its productivity. There are several general strategies it can pursue in its efforts to maintain and/or boost productivity. Three approaches in particular often help firms become more productive: spend more on R&D, improve operations, and increase employee involvement.[29]

Spend More on R&D. The starting point in improving productivity is often to invest more heavily in R&D. Through R&D, firms identify new products, new uses for existing products, and new methods for making products. Each of these outcomes, in turn, contributes directly to higher productivity. U.S. firms spend more on R&D than do their foreign competitors, but the gap is narrowing as more foreign firms increasingly invest in R&D.[30] Moreover, U.S. firms have a long and painful history of achieving significant scientific breakthroughs but then being ineffective in getting them to market.

Improve Operations. Another important way to increase productivity is to improve operations. This is where control comes in; a firm seeking to increase productivity needs to examine how it does things and then look for ways to do them more efficiently.[31] Replacing outmoded equipment, automating selected tasks, training workers to be more efficient, and simplifying manufacturing processes are all ways to improve operations and boost productivity. Japanese manufacturers have been especially successful at increasing productivity through improved operations. JIT manufacturing and inventory control techniques, consistent investments in technology, and a concentration on efficiency have paid big dividends for many of them. U.S. firms are also paying more attention to operations. For example, until recently General Electric required three weeks to fill an order for a custom-made industrial circuit-breaker box. Further, the firm had six plants making the boxes. Through improved operations—more efficient manufacturing methods and product simplification, among other improvements—the firm can now fill such an order in only three days and makes all its circuit-breaker boxes in a single facility.[32]

Boliviana de Energia Electrica SA, known in the United States as Bolivia Power, has worked continuously for years to improve its operations. As one of the few foreign-owned utility firms in Latin America (it is a subsidiary of a British utility), Bolivia Power has repeatedly escaped attempts at nationalization by demonstrating that it produces electricity more efficiently as a privately owned firm than it could if it were state-owned. Its managers have consistently sought ways to be more efficient, cut costs, and boost output. For example, they have always stressed the value of using the newest technology. By continuing to invest in new equipment and machinery, they have consistently increased productivity. This strategy and their attention to other areas of operations have streamlined the firm's operations to the point that it is among the world's most productive utility firms.[33]

Increase Employee Involvement. Finally, productivity can be improved by increasing employee involvement, particularly in power-tolerant cultures. The idea is that if managers give employees more say in how they do their jobs, those employees will become more motivated to work and more committed to the firm's goals. Further, because they are the ones actually doing the jobs, the employees probably have more insights than anyone else into how to do them better. Increased involvement is generally operationalized through the use of self-managed teams. Groups of workers are formed into teams, each of which has considerable autonomy over how it does its job. Self-managed teams were pioneered in Sweden and the United Kingdom, refined in Japan, and are now used extensively worldwide.[34]

For example, Lufthansa currently uses employee participation in its efforts to cut costs. The firm's overhead had grown out of control, and it needed to be reduced for the firm to remain competitive. Lufthansa wanted to cut its payroll in Germany but was stymied because of two strong national unions. So the firm enlisted the assistance of the unions to meet its cost-cutting goals. Representatives from the firm and both unions now meet regularly to devise ways to trim payroll costs without resorting to massive layoffs. So far, the cuts have focused on reducing work rules and eliminating jobs through attrition and early retirement.[35]

Controlling Quality in International Business

Control also helps firms maintain and enhance the quality of their products and/or services. Indeed, quality has become such a significant competitive issue in most industries that control strategies invariably have quality as a central focus.[36] The American Society for Quality Control has defined **quality** as the totality of features and characteristics of a product or service that bear on its ability to satisfy stated or implied needs.[37] The International Organization for Standardization (ISO) has been working to develop and refine an international set of quality guidelines. These guidelines, called collectively ISO 9000, provide the basis for a quality certification that is becoming increasingly important in international business. Indeed, major companies in more than fifty countries, including the United States and all EU members, have agreed to adopt ISO 9000 guidelines as they are developed.[38]

Quality is of vital importance for several reasons. First, many firms today compete on the basis of quality. Firms whose products or services have a poor reputation for quality are unlikely to succeed. For example, Daewoo, Samsung, and the LG Group, three Korean firms, have had some difficulty competing in Europe because their products are not perceived by Europeans as being of the same quality as those made by European firms. As we explain in Chapters 16 and 17, such country-of-origin factors play a major role in the marketing and location decisions of international firms. The South Korean chaebols are attempting to overcome this shortcoming by opening plants in Europe, establishing strategic alliances with European firms, and working to meet ISO 9000 guidelines and standards.[39]

Second, quality is important because it is directly linked with productivity. Higher quality means increased productivity because of fewer defects, fewer resources devoted to reworking defective products, and fewer resources devoted to quality control itself. Recall, for example, how Whistler Radar, by improving its product quality, also improved the productivity of its workers. Higher quality also serves to lower the costs associated with customer returns and warranty service.

Finally, higher quality helps firms develop and maintain customer loyalty. Customers who buy products and services they feel fulfill their quality expectations are more likely to buy again from the same firm.[40]

Quality consists of eight dimensions:[41]

1 **Performance** comprises the product's primary operating characteristics, such as an automobile's ability to transport its driver.

2 **Features** include supplementary characteristics, such as power windows on an automobile.

3 Reliability refers to the dependability of a product, such as the probability of an automobile's starting.

4 Conformance is how well the product meets normal standards.

5 Durability refers to the product's expected lifespan.

6 Serviceability refers to how fast and easily the product can be repaired.

7 Aesthetics refers to how the product looks, feels, tastes, and/or smells.

8 Perceived quality is the level of quality as seen by the customer. Perceived quality can be viewed in terms of price and expectations. For example, Sony manufactures and sells a variety of color televisions ranging in price from as little as $200 to well over $2000. For $200 a customer might expect a fairly reliable, small-screen television with basic features and good picture clarity. But for $2000 the same customer is likely to expect an extremely reliable, big-screen television with numerous features and exceptional picture clarity. It is difficult to compare the quality of the two televisions without understanding the price and expectations for each. That is, they may be of equal perceived quality based on actual quality adjusted for price and expectations.

Quality around the World

As with productivity, measuring quality may seem to be a reasonably straightforward task, but obtaining valid and reliable data is not as easy as might be imagined. Nevertheless, two recent studies provide insights into quality in different countries. One surveyed perceptions of managers; the other focused on consumers' perceptions.

Managerial Perceptions of International Quality. A major study of managers' perceptions of international quality was conducted by Ernst & Young and the American Quality Foundation.[42] This study involved teams of executives from more than 500 firms in the automotive, banking, computer, and health care industries in Canada, Germany, Japan, and the United States. Table 15.1 summarizes the study's major findings.

Two findings are particularly noteworthy. First, the Japanese firms studied indicated that they do not use work teams nearly as much as many people think, but *overall* more of their employees participated in decision making. This suggests that Japanese firms have done a better job of institutionalizing participation throughout their organizations, whereas firms in other countries still tend to use structural dimensions like work teams to achieve participation. Second, the Japanese are far ahead of the rest of the world in using process simplification (finding easier and simpler ways of doing things) and cycle time reduction (doing things faster). These activities are a part of improving operations, which was identified earlier in this chapter as a method for boosting productivity. German firms, however, use these practices far less than do U.S. and Canadian firms.

Consumers' Perceptions of International Quality. The consumer quality survey was conducted by the Gallup organization and the American Society for Quality Control.[43] The survey results are based on interviews with

TABLE 15.1

Management Perceptions of International Quality

1. Japanese firms do not organize the majority of their work force into teams that focus on quality programs, but they do have the highest rate of employee participation in regularly scheduled meetings about quality.

2. Firms in Canada, Germany, and the United States expect to increase their involvement of employees in quality-related teams. Firms in Japan expect little change in their use of quality teams.

3. More than half the firms in all four countries evaluate the business consequences of quality performance at least monthly. However, almost 20 percent of the U.S. firms review quality less than annually or not at all.

4. Although quality performance was used only on a limited basis in the past, its use as a criterion for compensating senior management is expected to increase substantially in all four countries; in the United States, more than half the firms plan to use this measure.

5. About 40 percent of firms in Canada, Japan, and the United States place primary importance on customer satisfaction in strategic planning; 22 percent of German firms do so.

6. German and Japanese firms are far ahead of Canadian and U.S. firms in incorporating customer expectations into the design of new products and services.

7. Japanese firms currently use technology twice as much as U.S. firms in meeting customer expectations. Although firms in all four countries expect to substantially increase the use of technology in meeting customer expectations over the next three years, Japanese firms will still lead the others.

8. German firms rarely place primary emphasis on competitors in the strategic planning process; however, almost one third of Japanese and U.S. firms do. In Canada, only one fourth do.

9. Japan dramatically leads the other countries in the routine use of process simplification and cycle time reduction. About half of Japanese firms use both of these practices more than 90 percent of the time.

10. About 20 percent of Canadian and U.S. firms always or almost always use process simplification techniques or process cycle time analyses to improve business processes; only 6 percent of German firms do so.

Source: Data from the Ernst & Young and American Quality Foundation study of managerial perceptions of international quality among U.S., Japanese, Canadian, and German executives. Adapted from Karen Bemowski, "The International Quality Study," *Quality Progress* (November 1991), pp. 33–37.

1008 U.S. consumers, 1446 Japanese consumers, and 1000 German consumers. Each consumer was asked various questions about his or her understanding of the meaning of quality and was asked to evaluate the quality of various products from each of the three countries. Table 15.2 summarizes some of the survey findings.

One clear finding is that domestic consumers in each country generally perceive the quality of products from their own country to be superior to the quality of products from the other two countries. Indeed, "TVs and VCRs" and "personal computers" were the only categories in which consumers picked products from another country (Japan) as being of higher quality than those made domestically.

Beyond these basic findings, the survey also revealed other interesting patterns. For one thing, Japanese and German consumers generally believe U.S.

TABLE 15.2

Consumer Perceptions of International Quality

	PERCENTAGES OF RESPONDENTS CHOOSING EACH COUNTRY		
	U.S. Consumers	Japanese Consumers	German Consumers
Best-quality autos			
United States	41	1	2
Japan	36	71	18
Germany	18	23	78
Don't know	5	5	2
Best-quality personal computers			
United States	48	12	14
Japan	39	80	45
Germany	1	1	33
Don't know	12	7	8
Best-quality TVs and VCRs			
United States	28	2	2
Japan	66	91	59
Germany	1	1	37
Don't know	5	6	2
Best-quality clothing			
United States	89	17	7
Japan	3	75	3
Germany	2	2	87
Don't know	6	6	3
Best-quality cosmetics			
United States	81	21	23
Japan	2	68	4
Germany	2	3	67
Don't know	15	8	6
Best-quality financial services			
United States	79	21	12
Japan	8	63	7
Germany	2	4	75
Don't know	11	12	6
Best-quality health care services			
United States	75	23	8
Japan	6	52	4
Germany	9	12	84
Don't know	10	13	4
Number of interviews	1008	1446	1000

Source: From "Looking for Quality in a World Marketplace," 1991 ASQC/Gallup survey. © 1991 American Society for Quality Control. Reprinted with permission.

FIGURE 15.3

The Essential
Components of Total
Quality Management

FIGURE 15.3

The Essential
Components of Total
Quality Management

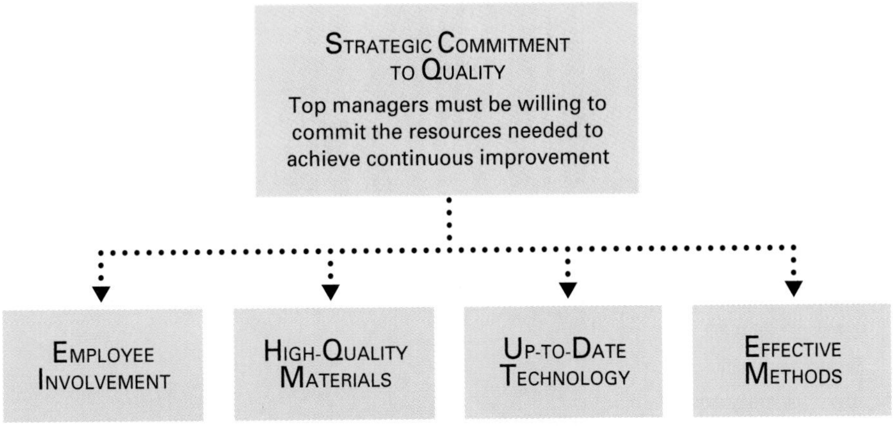

workers are not committed to quality. For another, U.S. firms have a better reputation abroad for services and soft goods than they do for hard goods. While U.S. firms do lag in quality, they are seen as the world's style leader—consumers in both Japan and Germany agreed that products made or introduced by U.S. firms tended to be more visually appealing than those made in their own countries. Finally, consumers in all three countries indicated that they are willing to pay higher prices for higher-quality products and services.

Total Quality Management

Because of the increasing importance of quality, firms worldwide are putting more and more emphasis on improving the quality of their products and services. Many of those firms call their efforts total quality management. **Total quality management (TQM)** is an integrated effort to systematically and continuously improve the quality of an organization's products and/or services.[44]

Components of TQM. TQM programs vary by firm and must be adapted to fit each firm's unique circumstances. As shown in Fig. 15.3, TQM must start with a strategic commitment to quality. This means the quality initiative must start at the top of the firm, and top managers must be willing to commit the resources necessary to achieve continuous improvement. Firms that only pay lip service to quality and try to fool employees and customers into believing they care about it are almost certain to fail.[45]

With a strong strategic commitment as a foundation, TQM programs rely on four operational components to implement quality improvement. Employee involvement is almost always cited as a critical requirement in quality improvement. All employees must participate in helping to accomplish the firm's quality-related objectives. Materials must also be scrutinized. Firms can often improve the quality of their products by requiring higher-quality parts and materials from their suppliers and procuring inputs only from suppliers whose commitment to quality matches their own. The firm also must be willing to invest in new technology in order to become more efficient and to achieve higher-quality manufacturing processes. And, finally, the firm must be willing to adopt new and improved methods of getting work done.[46]

Ford's commitment to quality has created new business opportunities. Ford has developed a profitable market reconditioning used Ford cars and re-selling them as premium used cars, complete with a full one-year warranty. The program's success rests on Ford's ability to produce high quality, trouble-free vehicles, as well as the skills of these workers at its Essex, England facility.

Quality Improvement Tools. Firms using TQM have a variety of tools and techniques they can draw on, including statistical process control and benchmarking. **Statistical process control** is a family of mathematically-based tools for monitoring and controlling quality. Its basic purposes are to define the target level of quality, specify an acceptable range of deviation, and then ensure that product quality is hitting the target. For example, Source Perrier SA uses statistical process control to monitor its bottling operations. Managers there have determined that a large bottle of Perrier water should contain 23 fluid ounces. Of course, regardless of how careful managers are, few bottles will have exactly 23 ounces—some will have a bit more, some a bit less. However, if too many bottles are filled with either too much or too little, adjustments must be made. An acceptable range for this situation might be an actual content of between 22.8 and 23.2 ounces, with a target of 99.9 percent of all bottles having content within this range. Samples of finished products are taken, and their actual content measured. As long as 99.9 percent of all samples have between 22.8 and 23.2 ounces, production continues. But if only 97 percent of one sample falls within the acceptable range, managers may stop production and adjust their bottling equipment.

Another important TQM technique is benchmarking. **Benchmarking** is the process of legally and ethically studying how other firms do something in a high-quality way and then either imitating or improving on their methods.[47] The managerial quality perception study summarized earlier in the chapter found that 31 percent of all U.S. firms engage in regular benchmarking, while only 7 percent never use benchmarking. Japanese and German firms also engage in benchmarking, but not to the same extent as U.S. firms.

Xerox started the benchmarking movement in the United States as a result of competitive pressures from foreign rivals. Canon, a Japanese firm, once introduced a mid-sized copier that sold for less than $10,000. Xerox was sure that Canon was selling below cost in order to gain market share. To learn more about what was going on, Xerox sent a team of managers to Japan to work with Fuji-

Xerox, a joint venture that a Xerox affiliate had established with Fuji to make copiers in Asia. While there, the managers bought a Canon copier and took it apart. To their surprise, they found the Canon copier to be of both higher quality and lower cost than those Xerox was making. By imitating Canon's materials and methods, Xerox was able to begin making its own higher-quality and lower-cost equipment. But Xerox did not stop there. It has subsequently benchmarked L.L. Bean's warehousing and distribution operation, Disney's equipment maintenance operation, and Corning's employee involvement program. As a result, the firm has regained its global competitive position and is again a formidable competitor against Japanese firms.[48]

Controlling Information in International Business

A final and increasingly important aspect of control in international business involves information. **Information** is data in a form that is of value to a manager in making decisions and performing related tasks.[49]

The Role of Information

Information is vitally important to any firm. Managers use it in every phase of their work, since it is necessary to the decision-making process. Obtaining accurate and timely information is of particular importance to international firms. Managers use information to better understand their firm's environment—its customers, competitors, and suppliers; the government policies that affect its hiring, producing, and financing decisions; and virtually every other element of its environment.

Managers also use information to help them decide how to respond to the environment. Meetings, reports, data summaries, telephone calls, and electronic mail messages are all used as managers set strategic goals and map out strategic plans. Information is also critical to implementing those strategic plans. For example, top managers must communicate their goals and expectations to managers of their foreign operations. Information is needed continually as managers make decisions daily and provide feedback to others in the firm about the consequences of those decisions. And, finally, information is an important part of the control process itself as managers monitor and assess how well they are meeting goals and executing plans. No manager likes to be taken by surprise. Having ready access to information that can be used to gauge ongoing performance and actual accomplishments is an important part of a manager's ability to function effectively.

The importance of information management depends on the type of strategy and organization design the firm uses. For example, if a firm is using related diversification, it is very important that various parts of the firm be able to communicate with other parts so that the firm can most effectively capitalize on the potential synergies of this strategy. If the firm is highly centralized, information systems are vital for top managers so that they can maintain the control they seek from using this particular design.[50] On the other hand, if a firm is using unrelated diversification, its information systems needs will be quite different. For example, communication among the various businesses within the firm will be far less important. And if the firm uses a decentralized form of organization design, its top managers will need and expect somewhat less information reporting by managers of various divisions and units.

Managing Information

The nature of international business adds considerable complexity to information and its role in a firm. In a domestic firm, information is almost certain to be in a common language, within the same legal context (the same accounting standards, financial reporting requirements, and so on will apply), and stored, manipulated, and accessible through common computer software and hardware configurations. But in an international firm, information is likely to be in different languages and subject to different legal contexts. For example, foreign partners and foreign governments may constrain the flow of information into and/or out of their countries. And computer software and hardware configurations are not always compatible. Thus managing information is not only very important for an international firm; it also is more complex than for a domestic firm.

Firms increasingly are working to develop integrated information systems in order to more effectively manage their information.[51] An **information system** is a methodology created by a firm to gather, assemble, and provide data in a form or forms useful to managers. Most information systems are computerized, although they do not necessarily have to be—routing slips, files, and file storage systems can effectively manage information in small firms. But larger firms today almost always use computerized systems to manage their information.[52] For example, managers at Laura Ashley, a British fashion and home furnishings chain, use a computerized information system to help the firm manage its information more effectively. Each sale is electronically recorded and used by managers to make decisions about reordering hot-selling merchandise.

To the extent possible, international firms would like to use information systems to link their operations so that their managers in any part of the world can access information and communicate with counterparts from any of the firm's operations.[53] The sheer size of this undertaking, however, along with computer software and hardware limitations, makes it difficult for firms to achieve true global integration of their information systems. Thus most firms develop information subsystems for specific functional operations or divisions.[54]

Texas Instruments (TI) is farther along the path toward a truly global system than most firms are. One of its subsidiaries, Tiris (Texas Instruments Registration and Identification Systems), is headquartered in the United Kingdom; its product development units are in Germany and the Netherlands; and its manufacturing facilities are in Japan and Malaysia. Managers and engineers at each facility communicate with each other over an integrated computer-based information system that enables them to function as if they were across the hall from each other rather than thousands of miles apart. For example, a manager in England might respond to a new customer order by sending a request electronically to a designer in Germany to make a small modification in a part to meet the customer's specifications. After the modification is made, the design specifications and order information can be sent electronically to Japan where the products will be manufactured. The original manager in England receives verification that the parts have been made and shipped and can call the customer with the news. And at any time during the entire process, any manager or designer can electronically monitor what is being done with the order and where it will be sent next. This approach helps TI compete internationally by enabling it to reduce its costs and meet differing needs of customers in different countries.

CHAPTER REVIEW

Summary

Control is the process of monitoring and regulating activities of a firm so that some targeted component of performance is achieved or maintained. For an MNC, control must be managed both at the corporate level and within each subsidiary.

Most MNCs usually address control at three levels. Strategic control monitors how well an international firm formulates strategy and then goes about trying to implement it. Financial control is an especially important area of strategic control in international business. Poor financial control can cripple a firm's ability to compete globally. Most MNCs have a corporate controller as well as controllers within each subsidiary. Organizational control involves the design of the firm. Three basic forms of organizational control are responsibility center control, generic strategic control, and planning process control. Operations control focuses specifically on operating procedures and systems within the firm.

When international firms establish control systems, they first set control standards, then measure actual performance. Next they compare performance against the standards and respond to deviations. Essential control techniques include accounting systems, procedures, and performance ratios. International managers also need to understand behavioral aspects of control, such as why people resist control and how to overcome that resistance. Cultural factors are an important ingredient in addressing behavioral aspects of control.

Productivity is an economic measure of efficiency that summarizes the value of outputs relative to the value of inputs used to create them. Productivity can be assessed at a variety of levels and in many different forms. U.S. workers are the world's most productive, but Japan and Germany have had greater productivity growth rates until recently. Experts agree that a firm can improve productivity by spending more on R&D, improving operations, and increasing employee involvement.

Quality is the total set of features and characteristics of a product or service that bears on its ability to satisfy stated or implied needs. Quality has become a critical factor in both domestic and global competition. Most domestic consumers in the Quad countries see products made in their own country as being of high quality. To improve quality, many firms are relying on TQM. TQM starts with a strategic commitment and is based on employee involvement, high-quality materials, up-to-date technology, and effective methods. Quality improvement tools include statistical process control and benchmarking.

Information is data in a form that is of value to a manager. It plays a major role in international business. Managers use information to understand their environment and to make decisions. It is also an important element in effective control. Managing information in an international firm is complex, and many firms use sophisticated electronic information systems to do so more effectively.

Review Questions

1. What are the three levels of control in international business?

2. Why is financial control so important?

3. What are three types of organizational control? Describe them.

4. What is the basic difference between responsibility center control and generic strategic control?

5. What is the basic focus of organizational control in international business?

6. What are the four basic steps in establishing an international control system?

7. Identify and discuss several essential control techniques.

8. Why is it important for organizations to control productivity?

9. What is quality? Why is it an important area of control for international firms?

10. How do firms manage information as part of control?

Questions for Discussion

1. Why is control an important management function in international business?

2. Do you think the three common types of international organizational control are mutually exclusive? Why or why not?

3. What are the advantages and disadvantages of each type of international organizational control?

4. Which form of control system would you most and least prefer for your own work? Why?

5. Which control techniques are most likely to be tailored to international settings? Which can be merely extensions of domestic operations?

6. What role does ethics play in control?

7. Why is it more common for developing countries to report dramatic increases in productivity, while more developed countries usually report much smaller increases?

8. List ten products you use for which quality is important in your purchasing decision. Which countries, if any, have reputations (good or bad) for each of those particular products?

9. Which of the findings in Table 15.1 do you think are most expected? Which are least expected?

10. What types of information are particularly important to an international firm?

BUILDING GLOBAL SKILLS

This exercise is to help you learn more about control in international business. To begin, read the following introduction about your firm and your role in it. Then complete the small-group exercise that follows.

Wahner, Inc., is a moderately large international holding company with subsidiaries in eight countries. Until recently the firm was managed by its founder, Pete Wahner, who got his start by using his inheritance to buy an importing firm. Over the years, Wahner bought and sold various businesses until he accumulated the current set of subsidiaries.

In total, Wahner, Inc., consists of fifteen subsidiaries operating around the world. Wahner died of cancer two years ago, and the firm has been run by his former assistant, Thomas Henderson. However, Wahner's heirs have become concerned that the firm is not being effectively managed and that Henderson may not have the skills necessary to manage a complex international business. An audit of the firm revealed several significant problems, and your consulting firm has been hired to straighten things out. After four weeks of learning the business, you have developed the following impressions:

♦ A French subsidiary that exports wine has been operating at a loss for three years. Because the firm was required to report revenues only annually, no one paid much attention to what was happening until recently. You now see that the losses are escalating.

♦ An Australian subsidiary that makes beer containers has been steadily losing market share because of deteriorating product quality. Three of its largest customers recently took their business to alternative suppliers.

♦ A manager at an Argentinean subsidiary has allegedly been stealing money from the firm, although this allegation is only in the form of a confidential report submitted by two of his subordinates. These subordinates are known to be trustworthy, however, and you believe the allegations are true.

♦ A German subsidiary has been enormously profitable but has several millions of surplus marks sitting idly in checking accounts. These funds are not drawing interest and have been accumulating for at least three years.

♦ Two subsidiaries in the United States, as well as one in Mexico and one in Egypt, have been performing effectively. Each is making a good profit and seems to be effectively managed.

♦ The audits of the remaining seven subsidiaries have not yet been completed, but a preliminary report suggests that there are few major problems in any of them. All seven of these subsidiaries are based in Canada and report to a single executive vice-president, Nancy Gleason. Gleason is currently considering leaving Wahner for the top position in another firm.

Your task is to develop a control framework for getting Wahner, Inc., back on track. Working in small groups, do the following:

1. Develop preliminary ideas as to why and how the current state of affairs has emerged.

2. Outline control-related issues that need to be addressed.

3. Determine how you will go about establishing control at Wahner.

WORKING WITH THE WEB: Building Global Internet Skills

Quality Certification

Quality is becoming an increasingly important aspect of international competition. Many organizations and governments are assisting firms in their quest to improve the quality of their products and customer service.

Suppose an important customer of your company has decided that it wishes to purchase inputs only

from companies that are ISO certified. The manager of your group has no idea what the customer is talking about and assigns you the task of learning about the ISO certification process. He also asks you to report back on how your company can use quality certification as a marketing tool.

To begin with, explore the web site of the ISO to

find out what it does and how it operates. You should also do a search for various other organizations that help firms improve their commitment to quality and for consultants that are available to guide a firm through the ISO's procedures. Then write a brief memo to your boss reporting what you have learned. (The textbook's web site provides links to some web sites that may be of use for this assignment.)

CLOSING CASE

Daimler-Benz Takes Control[55]

Several years ago Daimler-Benz executives embarked on a new grand strategy of diversification. Their goal was to create an organization that relied less on its motor vehicle business and instead generated revenues across a variety of product groups and businesses. To facilitate the implementation of this strategy, they created a new organization design for the company, closely resembling a holding company comprised of several divisions. The firm's core business, Mercedes-Benz, was set up as a near-autonomous entity run by its own CEO. This was done in part because Mercedes-Benz was contributing about two thirds of the firm's revenues.

The other subsidiaries were Debis (Daimler-Benz Interservices, which included computing and communication, financial, insurance, trading, and marketing services), AEG (which included automation, rail systems, domestic appliances, electrotechnical systems and components, microelectronics, and office and communication systems businesses), and Deutsche Aerospace (consisting of aircraft, space systems, defense systems, and propulsion systems businesses and related activities). Each of these divisions was also given considerable autonomy, but was run by a president (instead of a CEO) who reported directly to Daimler-Benz's CEO. These presidents had less power than did Mercedes Benz's CEO and needed more approvals from the parent company before making significant capital expenditures, changing business strategies, and launching other major initiatives.

Unfortunately, this strategy never produced the results that company executives had envisioned. The new organization design proved to be so unwieldy that the firm's performance actually began to decline. Profits from Mercedes-Benz had to be used to cover losses in other Daimler-Benz businesses, costs were going up throughout the firm, and productivity was suffering. Jurgen Schrempp was appointed CEO of the company in 1994 and given a mandate to clean things up. In 1996 this mandate was clarified even further: he was given two years to restore the company's profitability or he was out of a job.

As a starting point, Schrempp spent several months studying every aspect of the company. Though he had previously headed up one of Daimler-Benz's business units, he did not have a complete understanding of the entire company. But it soon became apparent to him how problems should be corrected. Specifically, he decided to fold Mercedes-Benz back into the core of the business.

Unfortunately, this decision prompted a firestorm of problems. Chief among them was the popularity of Mercedes-Benz's CEO, Helmut Werner, and his displeasure with this plan. He saw it as a reduction of his own power within the company and argued that since Mercedes-Benz was the only profitable part of the firm, it really made more sense to leave it alone to function as an independent entity. Werner himself had turned around the struggling carmaker earlier by cutting back on spending and moving factories out of Germany to lower-cost places.

But Schrempp was not to be deterred. One of his first steps was to commission Goldman, Sachs & Company to study the world's fifty largest conglomerates and critique their organization designs. This study found that loosely organized holding companies like Daimler-Benz were indeed less efficient than companies with more tightly controlled subsidiaries. That is, firms that retained control at the top of the organization in a centralized fashion generally outperformed those firms that delegated more control to operating companies in a more decentralized manner.

Schrempp also became more "hands on" in his management style, often visiting Mercedes-Benz facilities and meeting with Mercedes managers without Werner's knowledge. Finally, in late 1996 Schrempp forced the issue at a Daimler-Benz directors' meeting and won approval of his reorganization plans. Werner, the clear loser in this struggle, left the company quickly thereafter.

With his adversary out of the picture, Schrempp was then able to move more quickly. For example, his plans eliminated 40,000 jobs at Daimler-Benz and resulted in the sale of twelve unprofitable businesses. It also centralized virtually all key decision-making power in his hands. The CEO position at Mercedes-Benz was also eliminated and replaced with a president. This president, in turn, was given less power and autonomy than had been enjoyed by Werner. Schrempp orchestrated his boldest move yet in May 1998—a proposed merger with U.S.–based Chrysler Corporation to form a new company, Daimler-Chrysler. If approved by shareholders and various regulatory agencies on both sides of the Atlantic Ocean, the new company will become the third largest automaker in the world.

But Schrempp still faces significant challenges. For example, productivity in Daimler's aerospace division is lower than at its competitors. There are still major business units within the company that are chronic money losers. And of course, if the merger with Chrysler is approved, Schrempp faces the daunting task of integrating and controlling the operations of two of the world's premier automobile producers.

Case Questions

1. Describe how Daimler-Benz is using control to correct its business problems.

2. Develop one specific control framework that could be used to assess productivity at Daimler-Benz's aerospace division.

3. What measures of productivity and quality are most relevant for a firm like Daimler-Benz?

4. What control issues does the proposed merger of Chrysler and Daimler-Benz create?

CHAPTER NOTES

1. "Too Much, Too Fast," *Wall Street Journal*, September 26, 1996, pp. R1, R10; *Hoover's Handbook of American Business 1997* (Austin: Hoover's Business Press, 1997), pp. 876–877.

2. Robert N. Anthony, *The Management Control Function* (Boston: Harvard Business School Press, 1988).

3. David Asch, "Strategic Control: A Problem Looking for a Solution," *Long Range Planning* (February 1992), pp. 120–132.

4. Rahul Jacob, "India Is Open for Business," *Fortune*, November 16, 1992, pp. 128–130.

5. Lane Daley, James Jiambalvo, Gary Sundem, and Yasumasa Kondon, "Attitudes Toward Financial Control Systems in the United States and Japan," *Journal of International Business Studies* (Fall 1985), pp. 91–110.

6. "Royal Dutch/Shell Posts Profit Despite Japanese Affiliate's Loss," *Houston Chronicle*, February 26, 1993, p. 2B.

7. Carla Rapoport, "Great Japanese Mistakes," *Fortune*, February 13, 1989, pp. 108–111.

8. Hans Mjoen and Stephen Tallman, "Control and Performance in International Joint Ventures," *Organization Science,* (May-June 1997), pp. 257–268.

9. Asch, op. cit., pp. 120–132.

10. "Sweet Sales for Sour Mash—Abroad," *Business Week*, July 1, 1991, p. 62.

11. Jennifer Reese, "Inside the Coffee Cult," *Fortune,* December 9, 1996, pp. 190-200.

12. Michael Goold, "Strategic Control in the Decentralized Firm," *Sloan Management Review* (Winter 1991), pp. 69–81.

13. "The Napoleon of Software," *Forbes*, June 24, 1991, pp. 112–116. See also *Hoover's Handbook of World Business 1997* (Austin: Hoover's Business Press, 1997), pp. 148–149.

14. "Bag Your Own," *Forbes*, February 1, 1993, p. 70.

15. "Ford Triples Its Billion-Dollar Cost-Cutting Goal," *USA Today*, December 15, 1997, p. B1.

16. Robert S. Kaplan and David P. Norton, "The Balanced Scoreboard—Measures That Drive Performance," *Harvard Business Review* (January-February 1992), pp. 71–79.

17. Robert H. Schaffer, "Demand Better Results—and Get Them," *Harvard Business Review* (March-April 1991), pp. 142–149.

18. "Elaborate Plans for Power Cut-Back," *The Weekly Review*, April 10, 1992, pp. 19–20.

19. "Luxury's Mandarin," *Newsweek*, August 25, 1997, p. 43.

20. "Call to Account," *Far Eastern Economic Review*, March 1992, pp. 45–46.

21. "When the Dust Settles," *Far Eastern Economic Review*, February 27, 1992, pp. 36–37.

22. "How not to run an oil company," *The Economist*, January 11, 1992, pp. 65–66.

23. "Soap Opera Down Under," *Forbes*, February 15, 1993, pp. 140–146.

24. "Why to Kill New Product Ideas," *Fortune*, December 14, 1992, pp. 91–94.

25. John W. Kendrick, *Understanding Productivity: An Introduction to the Dynamics of Productivity* (Baltimore: Johns Hopkins, 1977).

26. "This Gorilla Wants to Dance," *Forbes,* September 22, 1997, pp. 97–102.

27. Thomas A. Stewart, "U.S. Productivity: First But Fading," *Fortune*, October 21, 1992, pp. 54–57.

28. "The Good Life Isn't Only in America," *Business Week*, November 2, 1992, p. 34.

29. "How to Regain the Productive Edge," *Fortune*, May 22, 1989, pp. 92–104.

30. Gene Bylinsky, "Turning R&D into Real Products," *Fortune*, July 2, 1990, pp. 72–77.

31. Jeremy Main, "Manufacturing the Right Way," *Fortune*, May 21, 1990, pp. 54–64.

32. Brian Dumaine, "How Managers Can Succeed Through Speed," *Fortune*, February 13, 1989, pp. 54–59.

33. "Stiff Upper Lip," *Forbes*, February 15, 1993, pp. 54–56.

34. Brian Dumaine, "Who Needs a Boss?" *Fortune*, May 7, 1990, pp. 52–60; Brian Dumaine, "The Trouble with Teams," *Fortune*, September 5, 1994, pp. 86–92.

35. "Even Lufthansa Is Carrying Too Much Baggage," *Business Week*, September 7, 1992, p. 80.

36. Richard J. Schonberger, "Total Quality Management Cuts a Broad Swath—Through Manufacturing and Beyond," *Organizational Dynamics* (Spring 1992), pp. 16–28.

37. Ross Johnson and William O. Winchell, *Management and Quality* (Milwaukee: American Society for Quality Control, 1989).

38. Ronald Henkoff, "The Hot New Seal of Quality," *Fortune*, June 28, 1993, pp. 116–120.

39. "Daewoo, Samsung, and Goldstar: Made in Europe?" *Business Week*, August 24, 1992, p. 43.

40. Genichi Taguchi and Don Clausing, "Robust Quality," *Harvard Business Review* (January-February 1990), pp. 65–75.

41. David A. Garvin, "Competing on the Eight Dimensions of Quality," *Harvard Business Review* (November-December 1987), pp. 101–109.

42. Karen Bemowski, "The International Quality Study," *Quality Progress* (November 1991), pp. 33–37; Stephen L. Yearout, "The International Quality Study Reveals Which Countries Lead the Race for Total Quality," *The Journal of European Quality* (March/April 1992), pp. 27–30.

43. *Looking for Quality in a World Marketplace* (Milwaukee: American Society for Quality Control, 1991).

44. "Quality," *Business Week*, November 30, 1992, pp. 66–75.

45. Marshall Sashkin and Kenneth J. Kiser, *Putting Total Quality Management to Work* (San Francisco: Berrett-Koehler, 1993).

46. Charles C. Poirier and William F. Houser, *Business Partnering for Continuous Improvement* (San Francisco: Berrett-Koehler, 1993).

47. Jeremy Main, "How to Steal the Best Ideas Around," *Fortune*, October 19, 1992, pp. 102–106.

48. "Beg, Borrow—and Benchmark," *Business Week*, November 30, 1992, pp. 74–75.

49. George W. Reynolds, *Information Systems for Managers* (St. Paul, Minn.: West, 1988).

50. Raja K. Iyer, "Information and Modeling Resources for Decision Support in Global Environments," *Information & Management*, Vol. XX (1988), pp. 67–73.

51. Albert L. Lederer and Raghu Nath, "Making Strategic Information Systems Happen," *The Academy of Management Executive* (August 1990), pp. 76–83.

52. Carolyn V. Woody and Robert A. Fleck Jr., "International Telecommunications: The Current Environment," *Journal of Systems Management* (December 1991), pp. 32–36.

53. Jeremy Main, "Computers of the World, Unite!" *Fortune*, September 24, 1990, pp. 113–122.

54. Charlene A. Dykman, Charles K. Davis, and August W. Smith, "Turf Wars: Managing the Implementation of an International Electronic Mail System," *Journal of Systems Management* (October 1991), pp. 10–35.

55. "The Bulldozer at Daimler-Benz," *Business Week*, February 10, 1997, p. 52; "Dustup at Daimler," *Business Week*, February 3, 1997, pp. 52–53; "A Tough Deadline," *Forbes*, April 22, 1996, pp. 165–173; "Chrysler Approves Deal with Daimler-Benz; Big Questions Remain," *Wall Street Journal*, May 7, 1998, pp. A1, A11.

PART 5

Managing International Business Operations

International Marketing

Chapter Outline

International marketing management
International marketing and business strategies
The marketing mix
Standardization versus customization

Product policy
Standardized products or customized products?
Legal forces
Cultural influences
Economic factors
Brand names

Pricing issues and decisions
Pricing policies
Market pricing

Promotion issues and decisions
Advertising
Personal selling
Sales promotion
Public relations

Distribution issues and decisions
International distribution
Channels of distribution

After studying this chapter you should be able to:

Characterize the nature of marketing management in international business.

Discuss the basic kinds of product policies and decisions made in international business.

Identify and describe pricing issues and decisions in international business.

Identify and describe promotion issues and decisions in international business.

Discuss the basic kinds of distribution issues and decisions in international business.

AT FIRST GLANCE IT SEEMS LIKE A SMALL DAVID FIGHTING THE international Goliaths—Sixt, a German car rental outfit taking on international car rental giants like Hertz and Avis. But ever since Erich Sixt took over his father's two small car rental offices in 1969, he has pushed and prodded the firm toward higher and higher levels of growth and has held the bigger companies at bay. Today, his firm controls almost one quarter of the car rental business in Germany, with annual sales of almost $1.5 billion. ▌▌The key to Sixt's success has been astute advertising and aggressive marketing. He spends far more on advertising than his competitors. Sixt ads show up on everything from billboards to more than 5000 airport luggage carts. Sixt is also known for novel advertising schemes. For example, passengers disembarking at Cologne's airport recently encountered a dirty, mud-encrusted Ford Explorer 4x4 with a

Spreading Sixt Across Europe[1]

sign on its hood proclaiming: "Sixt fulfills your dirtiest fantasies." ▌▌Sixt has also developed some highly effective marketing alliances with other German companies, most notably Lufthansa (Germany's biggest airline) and Deutsche Bahn (the German railroad operation). Travelers can rent Sixt cars at Deutsche Bahn ticket offices or even in the air on Lufthansa flights. And they can make future air or rail reservations at Sixt rental offices. ▌▌Sixt has now set its sights on the rest of Europe. The firm started its international expansion by opening a few offices in neighboring Austria and Switzerland. Its biggest splash, however, was buying controlling interest of a large French rental car operation and converting its offices to Sixt outlets, instantly giving the firm 120 rental offices in France. Sixt's next target is the United Kingdom, Europe's second largest car rental market. ▌▌But international expansion won't be a cakewalk for Sixt. For one thing, the firm probably caught its bigger rivals a bit by surprise in Germany, a mistake they vow will not happen again. Europcar, a joint venture between Volkswagen and the French hotel group Accor, is especially anxious to protect its market share in other parts of Europe and to avoid losing customers to its upstart rival. ▌▌Another question is the extent to which Sixt's marketing and advertising strategies will work as well in other cultures. For example, one of its recent effective ads in the German magazine *Der Spiegel* pictured four men weeping under a large headline that proclaimed "No rental company makes its customers unhappier." Only by reading a smaller caption underneath the picture did consumers see the point—the men were unhappy because they had to return the exciting cars they had been renting from Sixt. Some observers question whether or not this brand of humor will be well received in other countries. ▌▌It is also unlikely that Sixt will be able to establish the kinds of marketing alliances in other countries that it has struck with

Lufthansa and Deutsche Bahn. So Sixt's future outside of Germany remains an open question, at least for the time being. But visitors to London's Gatwick airport may one day soon see the same Sixt ads on their baggage carts as do so many visitors to Germany. ▌▌▌▌▌

Erich Sixt has achieved a strong position in the car rental business in his native Germany by aggressive and innovative marketing. He is now seeking to transfer this same formula to markets outside of Germany. As we will discuss throughout this chapter, marketing is a key ingredient in the success of any international business. But marketing can also be a significant stumbling block for the misinformed manager.

Marketing is "the process of planning and executing the conception, pricing, promotion, and distribution of ideas, goods, and services to create exchanges that satisfy individual and organizational objectives."[2] **International marketing** is the extension of these activities across national boundaries. Firms expanding into new markets in foreign countries must deal with differing political, cultural, and legal systems, as well as unfamiliar economic conditions, advertising media, and distribution channels. For example, an international firm accustomed to promoting its products on television will have to alter its approach when entering a less developed market in which relatively few people have televisions. Advertising regulations also vary by country. French law, for example, discourages advertisements that disparage competing products; comparative advertisements must contain at least two significant, objective, and verifiable differences between products.[3] New Zealand regulators may ban ads for a variety of reasons. A Nike ad featured a coach telling his players to "visualize your opponent as your worst enemy," who then gets tackled by the team; it was banned for being too violent by New Zealand's regulators, as was a Coca-Cola ad featuring aboriginal dancers for being "culturally insensitive."[4]

In addition to dealing with national differences, international marketing managers have two tasks their domestic counterparts do not face: capturing synergies among various national markets and coordinating marketing activities in those markets. Synergies are important because they provide opportunities for additional revenues and for growth and cross-fertilization. Coordination is important because it can help lower marketing costs and create a unified marketing effort.

International Marketing Management

An international firm's marketing activities are often organized as a separate and self-contained function within the firm. Yet that function both affects and is affected by virtually every other organizational activity, as shown in Fig. 16.1. Because of these interrelationships, international marketing management, which encompasses a firm's efforts to ensure that its international marketing activities comply with the firm's corporate strategy, business strategy, and other functional strategies, is a critical component of international business success.

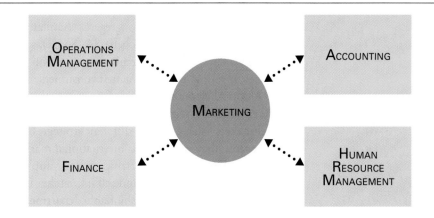

FIGURE 16.1

International Marketing as an Integrated Functional Area

International Marketing and Business Strategies

A key challenge for a firm's marketing managers is to adopt an international marketing strategy that supports the firm's overall business strategy.[5] As discussed in Chapter 10, business strategy can take one of three forms: differentiation, cost leadership, or focus.

A business strategy of differentiation requires marketing managers to develop products and pricing, promotional, and distribution tactics that differentiate the firm's products or services from those of its competitors in the eyes of customers. Differentiation can be based on perceived quality, fashion, reliability, or other salient characteristics, as the marketing managers of such products as Rolex watches, BMW automobiles, and Montblanc pens have successfully shown. Assuming that the differentiation can be adequately communicated to customers, the firm will be able to charge higher prices for its product or insulate itself from price competition from lesser brands. For example, Rolex, which follows a successful differentiation strategy, does not need to cut the price for its diamond-encrusted $15,000 watches whenever Kmart features Timex quartz watches for $39.95.

Alternatively, a firm may adopt an international business strategy that stresses its overall cost leadership. Cost leadership can be pursued and achieved through systematic reductions in production and manufacturing costs, reductions in sales costs, the acceptance of lower profit margins, the use of less expensive materials and component parts, or other means. Marketing managers for a firm adopting this strategy will concentrate their promotional efforts on advertising the low prices of the product and will utilize channels of distribution that allow the firm to keep the retail price low—for example, by selling through discounters rather than through fashionable boutiques. Texas Instruments calculators, Hyundai automobiles, and Bic pens are all marketed using a cost leadership strategy. And Timex's cost leadership approach has allowed it to thrive in the large market for low-price watches.

A firm also may adopt a focus strategy. In this case, marketing managers will concentrate their efforts on particular segments of the consumer market or on particular areas or regions within a market. International marketing managers will therefore need to concentrate on getting the appropriate message regarding the firm's products or services to the various selected target markets. For example, many U.S. cigarette makers focus their marketing efforts on young people in other countries;

they advertise and promote their products at high schools, video arcades, and other places where young people congregate.[6] Similarly, the Swiss watchmaker Ste. Suisse Microelectronique et d'Horlogerie SA (SMH), which manufactures the popular Swatch watches, focuses its marketing efforts on selling this inexpensive line of watches to young, fashion-oriented consumers in Europe, North America, and Asia.

A critical element for a firm's success is the congruency of its international marketing efforts with its overall business strategy. Timex, Rolex, and SMH—all watchmakers—have chosen different strategies, yet all are successful internationally because they match their international marketing efforts with their business strategies. Timex's cost leadership strategy implies that the firm must seek out low-cost suppliers globally and sell its watches in discount stores such as Wal-Mart and Target rather than in fashionable department stores such as Saks Fifth Avenue and Harrod's. Rolex's differentiation strategy, based on its carefully nurtured worldwide image, might collapse if it distributed its watches through armies of street corner vendors stationed in front of subway stations throughout the world instead of through a handful of very expensive and very chic horologists located on the most fashionable avenues of the world's most glamorous cities. Similarly, SMH does not advertise Swatch watches to the upper-class, middle-aged audiences of *Town and Country* and *Architectural Digest* in the United States while simultaneously marketing to young, fashion-oriented Parisian readers of *Elle,* for that would confuse Swatch's brand image. It does advertise its wares in the U.S., Chinese, and French editions of *Elle,* which are read by demographically similar young, trendy female audiences—the target of its focus strategy.

Having adopted an overall international business strategy, a firm must assess where it wants to do business. Decisions about whether to enter a particular foreign market are derived from and must be consistent with the firm's overall business strategy. For example, the steady growth in the past decade of such low-to-middle income countries as Costa Rica, Namibia, Poland, and Turkey offers exciting new business opportunities for Timex, but not necessarily for Rolex.

Chapter 11 discussed the techniques used by international managers to analyze the potential of foreign markets. Because of budget and resource limitations, international firms must carefully assess countries and rank them according to which will offer the greatest potential markets for their products. Influencing this process may be factors such as culture, levels of competition, channels of distribution, and availability of infrastructure. Depending on the nature of the product and other circumstances, a firm may choose to enter simultaneously all markets that meet certain acceptability criteria. For example, consumer goods marketers like Nike and Coca-Cola often introduce new products broadly throughout North America or Europe in order to maximize the impact of their mass media advertising campaigns. Or, a firm may choose to enter markets one by one, in an order based on their potential to the firm. Caterpillar, for example, uses this approach, since its marketing strategy is based on the painstaking development of strong local dealerships, not glitzy TV campaigns highlighting the endorsements of the latest music and sports stars.

The Marketing Mix

After an international firm has decided to enter a particular foreign market, further marketing decisions must be made.[7] In particular, international marketing managers must address four issues:

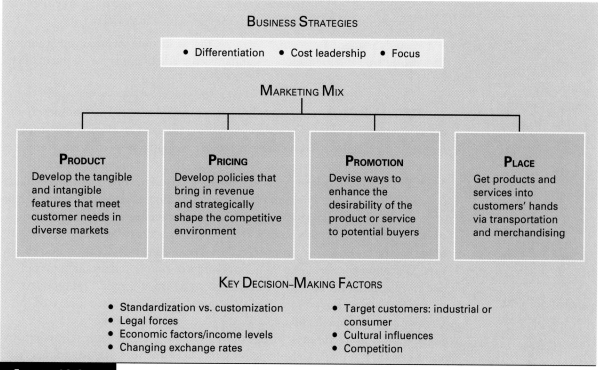

BUSINESS STRATEGIES

• Differentiation   • Cost leadership   • Focus

MARKETING MIX

PRODUCT
Develop the tangible and intangible features that meet customer needs in diverse markets

PRICING
Develop policies that bring in revenue and strategically shape the competitive environment

PROMOTION
Devise ways to enhance the desirability of the product or service to potential buyers

PLACE
Get products and services into customers' hands via transportation and merchandising

KEY DECISION-MAKING FACTORS

- Standardization vs. customization
- Legal forces
- Economic factors/income levels
- Changing exchange rates

- Target customers: industrial or consumer
- Cultural influences
- Competition

FIGURE 16.2

The Elements of the Marketing Mix for International Firms

1 How to develop the firm's product(s)

2 How to price those products

3 How to sell those products

4 How to distribute those products to the firm's customers

These elements are collectively known as the **marketing mix** and colloquially referred to as the *four P's of marketing:* product, pricing, promotion, and place (or distribution). The marketing mix reflects the firm's decisions regarding how it will actually market its goods. The role of the four P's in international marketing is illustrated in Fig. 16.2.

International marketing-mix issues and decisions parallel those of domestic marketing in most ways, although they are more complex. The array of variables international marketing managers must consider is far broader, and the interrelationships among those variables far more intricate, than is the case for domestic marketing managers. Before we discuss these complexities, however, we need to focus on another important issue in international marketing—the extent to which an international firm should standardize its marketing mix in all the countries it enters.

Standardization versus Customization

A firm's marketers usually choose among three basic approaches in deciding the extent to which they wish to standardize their firm's marketing mix:

♦ Should the firm adopt an *ethnocentric approach*, that is, simply market its goods internationally the same way it does domestically?

♦ Should it adopt a *polycentric approach*, that is, customize the marketing mix to meet the specific needs of each foreign market it services?

♦ Should it adopt a *geocentric approach*, that is, analyze the needs of customers worldwide and then adopt a standardized marketing mix for all the markets it serves?[8]

The **ethnocentric approach** is relatively easy to adopt. The firm simply markets its goods in international markets using the same marketing mix it uses domestically, thereby avoiding the expense of developing new marketing techniques to serve foreign customers. When some firms first internationalize, they adopt this approach, believing that a marketing mix that worked at home should be as successful abroad. For example, when Lands' End targeted the German mail-order market in the mid-1990s—which on a per capita basis is the largest in the world—it deliberately replicated its U.S. marketing strategy. Stressing its "down home" roots, the company trumpets to its U.S. consumers its location next to a rural Wisconsin cornfield, the friendliness of its operators and production staff, and its generous return policy—consumers can return all Lands' End products, even if they are used or worn out, with no questions asked. When it entered the German market, Lands' End established its local headquarters in an old schoolhouse in the tiny, picturesque village of Mettlach on the Saar River. The company spent months training its telephone operators to ensure that they would meet its standards for friendly, helpful service. And it transplanted its "no questions asked" return service, much to the consternation of its German competitors, whose policy was to accept returns only if the goods were flawed or inaccurately described in their catalogs and then only if the goods were unused and in good condition.[9] The ethnocentric approach may not be desirable, however, if as a result the firm loses sales because it failed to take into the account the idiosyncratic needs of its foreign customers. Should this be the case, successful firms will modify their marketing mixes to meet local conditions and needs after they learn more about the local market.

The **polycentric approach** is far more costly because the international marketers attempt to customize the firm's marketing mix in each market it enters in order to meet the idiosyncratic needs of customers in that market. However, while more expensive, customization may increase the firm's revenues if its marketers successfully match its marketing mix with the needs of local customers. Firms that adopt this approach believe that customers will be more willing to buy and more willing to pay a higher price for a product that exactly meets their needs than one that does not. Often, international firms that view themselves as multidomestic adopt this approach.

The **geocentric approach** calls for standardization of the marketing mix, thereby allowing the firm to provide essentially the same product or service in different markets and to use essentially the same marketing approach to sell that product or service globally. Coca-Cola was one of the first international businesses to adopt this approach. It sells its popular soft drink worldwide and uses essentially the same packaging, product, and advertising themes everywhere. Indeed, the contoured shape of a Coca-Cola bottle is one of the world's most recognized images. The firm has even gone so far as to add the contour shape to its plastic bottles.[10]

Standardization became a popular buzz word in the 1980s, as proponents such as Kenichi Ohmae (then managing director of McKinsey & Company's Tokyo office) argued that customers in the Triad are becoming increasingly so much alike, with similar incomes, educational achievements, lifestyles, and aspirations, that expensive customization of the marketing mix by country is less necessary.[11] Similarly, Harvard Business School marketing guru Theodore Levitt believes that standardization of a firm's products and other elements of its marketing mix creates huge economies of scale in production, distribution, and promotion. By transforming these cost savings into reduced world prices, Levitt argues, a firm that adopts standardization can easily outperform its international competitors.[12]

The trade-offs between standardization and customization are clear. Standardization allows a firm to achieve manufacturing, distribution, and promotional efficiencies and to maintain simpler and more streamlined operations.[13] However, the firm may suffer lost sales if its products fail to meet the unique needs of customers in a given market. Customization allows a firm to tailor its products to meet the needs of customers in each market, although it may sacrifice cost efficiencies by so doing. In essence, standardization focuses on the cost side of the profit equation; by driving down costs, the firm's profits are enhanced. Customization focuses on the revenue side of the profit equation; by attending to the unique customer needs in each market, the firm is able to charge higher prices and sell more goods in each market. In practice, most firms avoid the extremes of either approach.[14] Many successful firms have adopted a strategy of "think globally, act locally" in order to gain the economies of scale of a global marketing mix while retaining the ability to meet the needs of customers in differing national markets.

The home appliance market provides a useful example of this strategy. U.S. kitchens tend to be large and spacious, and consumers prefer large stoves, refrigerators, and washing machines. But the smaller kitchens of Europe and Japan dictate the use of much smaller appliances. Further, within Europe there are marked differences in power supply characteristics and in consumer preferences for various design features and alternatives. Thus appliance manufacturers must develop specific and unique product lines for each country in which they do business. Whirlpool has tried to reduce some of the costs of customization by designing its products to meet the needs of market niches that cross national boundaries. For example, Whirlpool designers have developed a "World Washer"—a small, stripped-down automatic washing machine targeted to meet the needs of the emerging middle classes in such countries as Brazil, Mexico, and India. But Whirlpool stands ready to customize even the World Washer when needed. For example, the agitators of World Washers sold in India have been modified to ensure that the machines won't shred or tangle the delicate saris traditionally worn by Indian women.[15]

The degree of standardization or customization a firm adopts depends on many factors, including product type, the cultural differences between the home country and the host countries, and the host countries' legal systems. The firm may adopt one approach for one element of the marketing mix and another for a second element. Often firms standardize product designs to capture manufacturing economies of scale but customize advertisements and the channels of distribution to meet specific local market needs. The degree of standardization may also be influenced by the firm's perception of the global marketplace—which is similar to the conundrum "Is the glass half full or half empty?" A firm tilting toward standardization assumes that consumers around the world are basically similar but then adjusts for differences among them. A firm tilting toward customization assumes that consumers are different but then adjusts for similarities among them.

In deciding where to locate on the standardization/customization spectrum, an international firm also must consider organizational structure and organizational control implications. Standardization implies that power and control should be centralized, often at the firm's headquarters, while customization suggests that headquarters must delegate considerable decision-making power to local managers. Thus a strongly centralized firm (see Chapter 13) can more easily standardize its international marketing mix than can a decentralized one. Often international firms address these organizational issues by adopting a two-step process:

1 The decision to standardize some elements of the marketing mix, such as product design, brand name, packaging, and product positioning, is made centrally.

2 Then local managers are called on to critique the global marketing program and to develop plans to implement customized elements of the marketing mix, such as promotion and distribution.[16]

Table 16.1 summarizes some factors that may lead a firm to adopt standardization or customization for all or part of its international marketing efforts.

TABLE 16.1

Advantages and Disadvantages of Standardized and Customized International Marketing

STANDARDIZED INTERNATIONAL MARKETING	
Advantages	**Disadvantages**
1. Reduces marketing costs	1. Ignores different conditions of product use
2. Facilitates centralized control of marketing	2. Ignores local legal differences
3. Promotes efficiency in R&D	3. Ignores differences in buyer behavior patterns
4. Results in economies of scale in production	4. Inhibits local marketing initiatives
5. Reflects the trend toward a single global marketplace	5. Ignores other differences in individual markets

CUSTOMIZED INTERNATIONAL MARKETING	
Advantages	**Disadvantages**
1. Reflects different conditions of product use	1. Increases marketing costs
2. Acknowledges local legal differences	2. Inhibits centralized control of marketing
3. Accounts for differences in buyer behavior patterns	3. Creates inefficiency in R&D
4. Promotes local marketing initiatives	4. Reduces economies of scale in production
5. Accounts for other differences in individual markets	5. Ignores the trend toward a single global marketplace

Product Policy

The first P of the international marketing mix is the product itself. Here, **product** comprises both the set of tangible factors (the physical product and its packaging) that the consumer can see or touch and numerous intangible factors (such as image, installation, warranties, and credit terms). Critical to a firm's ability to compete internationally is its success in developing products with tangible and intangible features that meet the wants and needs of customers in diverse national markets.[17] For example, Toyota's success in selling its automobiles in Europe, Asia, and the Americas reflects its product-related achievements in designing and producing mechanically reliable vehicles, offering competitive warranties, building a solid brand name for its products, providing spare parts and repair manuals, and furnishing financing to its dealers and retail customers.

Standardized Products or Customized Products?

A key product policy decision facing international marketers is the extent to which their firm's products should be standardized across markets or customized within individual markets. For example, Toyota, like many international firms, has adopted a blend of customization and standardization. It has standardized its corporate commitment to build high-quality, mechanically reliable automobiles and to maintain the prestige of the Toyota brand name. But it customizes its products and product mix to meet the needs of local markets. For example, it sells right-hand-drive motor vehicles in Japan, Australia, and the United Kingdom and left-hand-drive vehicles in the Americas and continental Europe. It also adjusts its warranties from country to country based on those offered by its competitors. The name under which it sells a product also may vary by country. For example, the automobile sold as a Lexus Sports Coupe in the United States is sold as a Toyota Soarer in Japan. Toyota will even adjust the products it sells in order to meet local market conditions. For example, its initial entry into the U.S. minivan market suffered from poor handling and a lack of power and therefore failed to make a dent in Chrysler's dominance of this growing market. The firm corrected these problems in its Previa van, which it rushed to the U.S. market in 1990. However, because Chrysler's sales in Asian markets were limited and of little threat, Toyota continued to sell its original van model for several years in those markets.

Sometimes firms learn they have customized their products not by design but by accident. For example, in the late 1980s Unilever discovered to its horror that for no apparent reason it was using eighty-five different recipes for its chicken soups and fifteen different shapes for cones for its Cornetto ice creams in Europe. Once the problem was detected, Unilever quickly standardized its ice cream cone design and slashed the number of chicken soup flavors it offered European customers, thereby reducing its production and inventory costs and simplifying its distribution requirements.[18]

The extent to which products should be customized to meet local needs varies according to several factors. One is the nature of the product's target customers—are they industrial users or are they individual consumers? While some industrial products are customized and some consumer products are standardized, generally speaking, industrial products are more likely to be standardized than consumer products.

For example, Caterpillar's bulldozers and front-end loaders are sold throughout the world with only minor modifications to meet local operating and regulatory requirements. Products sold as commodities are also typically standardized across different markets, for example, agricultural products, petroleum, 16MB computer memory chips, and chemicals. A general rule of thumb is that the closer to the body a product is consumed, the more likely it will need to be customized. Consider food, for example. McDonald's tailors its menus to local markets—selling pork sandwiches and beer in its German restaurants, wine in its French restaurants, and fish and rice in its Japanese restaurants. Even Coca-Cola modifies the sweetness and flavoring of its soft drinks to meet consumer preferences in different markets.

Legal Forces

The laws and regulations of host countries may also affect the product policies adopted by international firms. For example, countries often impose detailed labeling requirements and health standards on consumer products that firms, both foreign and domestic, must follow strictly. International firms must adjust the packaging and even the products themselves to meet these consumer protection regulations. For example, Grupo Modelo SA, the brewer of Corona beer, had to move product content listings from the back of the Corona bottle to the front in order to comply with German law. It also had to reduce the nitrosamine levels of the beer it sells in Germany, Austria, and Switzerland in order to meet those countries' health standards.[19] Countries also may regulate the design of consumer products in order to simplify purchase and replacement decisions. For example, Saudi Arabia requires electrical connecting cords on consumer appliances to be two meters long. GE suffered the embarrassment (and a loss of profits) of having its goods turned back at a Saudi port when an inspector determined its connecting cords were only two yards long.[20] Widely varying technical standards adopted by countries for such products as electrical appliances and broadcasting and telecommunications equipment also force firms to customize their products. For example, the electrical plugs of home appliances sold in Europe must be modified on a country-by-country basis to fit the array of electrical outlets found there. A country's legal requirements also may substantially affect the way a firm can do business. For example, the central bank of Singapore sought to control consumer spending in the early 1990s by imposing regulations specifying the minimum annual income needed to qualify for a credit card and capping the allowable credit limit on credit cards at two months' salary. These regulations hindered the ability of foreign firms such as American Express and Visa International to market their financial services to Singaporeans.[21]

Cultural Influences

International firms often must adapt their products to meet the cultural needs of local markets. One typical adaptation is to change the labeling on the product's package into the primary language of the host country. However, in some cases, a foreign language may be used to connote quality or fashion. For example, Procter & Gamble adds German words to the labels of detergents sold in the Czech Republic. Market researchers had determined that products in packages labeled in English or German are viewed by Czechs as being of higher quality than those whose packages are labeled in Czech.[22] Often the ingredients of food products are modified to better please local palates. Gerber, for example, customizes its baby food to meet the requirements of the local culture. It found that Polish mothers refused to purchase Gerber's mashed bananas for their infants, for that fruit was viewed as an expensive luxury. Instead they favor such Gerber delicacies as Vegetable and Rabbit Meat to help nurture their infants, while Japanese mothers choose Gerber's Freeze Dried Sardines and Rice for their children.[23] Pepsi's Frito-Lay division has also modified its snack foods to better meet the needs of foreign consumers, offering, for example, paprika-flavored chips to Poles and Hungarians and shrimp-chips to Koreans. Its food scientists are also busily working on a squid-peanut snack food that it believes will be very successful among Southeast Asians.[24] Presumably for cultural reasons, neither company has as yet made plans to market these items in North America.

Culture may affect product policy in other ways. For example, foreign automobile makers have learned that Japanese consumers are extremely quality conscious. For many Japanese consumers, an automobile is more a status symbol than a mode of transportation—the average car in Japan is driven only 5000 miles per year, about one third of the U.S. average. Thus how the car looks is often more important than how it drives. A Japanese customer may reject a car if the paint underneath the hood is uneven or the gas tank cover fits loosely.[25] Many German consumers are very environmentally conscious. As a result, firms often must redesign products they sell in Germany to allow for easier disposal and recycling. In another example, Mattel allowed its Japanese subsidiary to make Barbie dolls more Japanese in appearance. This move boosted the annual sales of Barbie dolls in Japan by 2 million units.[26]

Economic Factors

Economic factors also may induce an international firm to customize its products to meet local market needs. A country's level of economic development may affect the desired attributes of a product. Consumers in richer countries often favor products loaded with extra performance features; more price-sensitive consumers in poorer countries typically opt for stripped-down versions of the same products. Sometimes a firm may have to adjust package size or design to meet local conditions. For example, firms selling toothpastes or shampoos in poorer countries often package their goods in single-use sizes in order to make the products more affordable to local citizens. The quality of a country's infrastructure also may affect the customization decision. For example, manufacturers may reinforce the suspension systems of motor vehicles sold in countries where road maintenance is poor. The availability and cost of repair services can affect product design. For example, most automobiles sold in North America use electronic fuel injectors rather than carburetors. In poorer countries, the reverse is true, primarily because of maintenance considerations. Maintaining fuel injectors requires sophisticated electronic test equipment backed up by highly trained technicians; any mechanic can tune up a carburetor.

Brand Names

One element international firms often like to standardize is the brand name of a product. A firm that does this can reduce its packaging, design, and advertising production costs. It also can capture spillovers of its advertising messages from one market to the next. For example, Avon's entry into the China market was made easier because millions of consumers had seen its products advertised on Hong Kong television.[27] Mars, Inc., sought to capture the benefits of standardization by dropping its successful local brand names for the Marathon bar in the British market and the Raider chocolate biscuit on the Continent in favor of the more universally known Snickers and Twix brands.[28] However, sometimes legal or cultural factors force a firm to alter the brand names under which it sells its products. For example, Grupo Modelo SA markets Corona beer in Spain as Coronita because a Spanish vineyard owns the Corona brand name.[29] And Coca-Cola calls its low-calorie soft drink Diet Coke in weight-conscious North America but Coca-Cola Light in other markets.

Pricing Issues and Decisions

The second P of the international marketing mix is pricing. Developing effective prices and pricing policies is a critical determinant of any firm's success.[30] Pricing policies directly affect the size of the revenues earned by the firm. But they also serve as an important strategic weapon by allowing the firm to shape the competitive environment in which it does business. For example, Toys 'R' Us has achieved enormous success in Germany, Japan, the United States, and other countries by selling low-priced toys in low-cost warehouse-like settings. Its low prices have placed enormous pressure on its competitors to slash their costs, alter their distribution systems, and shrink their profit margins. The firm's aggressive pricing strategy has effectively forced its competitors to fight the battle for Asian, European, and American consumers on terms dictated by Toys 'R' Us.

Both domestic and international firms must strive to develop pricing strategies that will produce profitable operations. But the task facing an international firm is more complex than that facing a purely domestic firm. To begin with, a firm's costs of doing business vary widely by country. Differences in transportation charges and tariffs cause the landed price of goods to vary by country. Differences in distribution practices also affect the final price the end customer pays. For example, intense competition among distributors in the United States minimizes the margin between retail prices and manufacturers' prices. In contrast, Japan's inefficient multilayered distribution system, which relies on a chain of distributors to distribute goods, often inflates the prices Japanese consumers pay for goods. Exchange-rate fluctuations can also create pricing problems. If an exporter's home currency rises in value, the exporter must choose between maintaining its prices in the home currency (which makes its goods more expensive in the importing country) and maintaining its prices in the host currency (which cuts its profit margins by lowering the amount of home-country currency it receives for each unit sold).

International firms must consider these factors in developing their pricing policies for each national market they serve. They must decide whether they want to apply consistent prices across all those markets or customize prices to meet the needs of each. In reaching this decision, they must remember that competition, culture, distribution channels, income levels, legal requirements, and exchange-rate stability may vary widely by country.

Pricing Policies

International firms generally adopt one of three pricing policies:[31]

1 Standard price policy

2 Two-tiered pricing

3 Market pricing

An international firm following a geocentric approach to international marketing will adopt a **standard price policy,** whereby it charges the same price for its products and services regardless of where they are sold or the nationality of the customer. Firms that sell goods that are easily tradable and transportable often adopt this pricing approach out of necessity. For example, if a firm manufacturing DRAM memory chips charged different customers vastly different prices, some of its favored customers might begin to resell the chips to less favored ones—an easy task, given the small size and high value of the chips. Similarly, firms that sell commodity goods in competitive markets often use this pricing policy. For example, producers of crude oil, such as Aramco, Kuwait Oil, and Pemex, sell their products to any and all customers at prices determined by supply and demand in the world crude oil market. Other commodities produced and traded worldwide, such as coal and agricultural goods, are also sold at competitive prices (with suitable adjustments for quality differentials and transportation costs) with little regard to the purchaser's nationality.

An international firm that follows an ethnocentric marketing approach will use a **two-tiered pricing policy,** whereby it sets one price for all its domestic sales and a second price for all its international sales. A firm that adopts a two-tiered pricing policy commonly allocates to domestic sales all accounting charges associated with R&D, administrative overhead, capital depreciation, and so on. The firm can then establish a uniform foreign sales price without having to worry about covering these costs. Indeed, the only costs that need to be covered by the foreign sales price are the marginal costs associated with foreign sales, such as the product's unit manufacturing costs, shipping costs, tariffs, and foreign distribution costs.

Two-tiered pricing is often used by domestic firms that are just beginning to internationalize. In the short run, charging foreign customers a price that covers only marginal costs may be an appropriate approach for such firms. But the strong ethnocentric bias of two-tiered pricing suggests it is not a suitable long-run pricing strategy. A firm that views foreign customers as marginal to its business—rather than as integral to it—is unlikely to develop the international skills, expertise, and outlook necessary to compete successfully in the international marketplace.

Firms that adopt a two-tiered pricing policy are also vulnerable to charges of dumping. Recall from Chapter 6 that dumping is the selling of a firm's products in a foreign market for a price lower than that charged in its domestic market—an outcome that can easily result from a two-tiered pricing system. Most OECD countries have issued regulations intended to protect domestic firms from dumping by foreign competitors. For example, in the mid-1990s Toyota and Mazda were charged with dumping minivans in the U.S. market. Although the Japanese automakers were not penalized in this case, both subsequently raised their minivan prices in order to avoid future dumping complaints.

a. Finding the profit-maximizing price

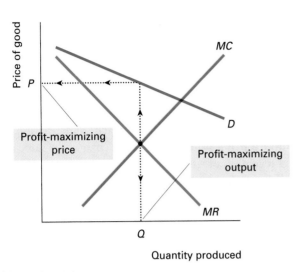

b. Finding the profit-maximizing price for two markets

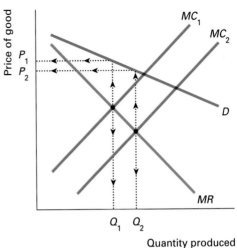

FIGURE 16.3

Determining the Profit-Maximizing Price

An international firm that follows a polycentric approach to international marketing will use a **market pricing policy.** Market pricing is the most complex of the three pricing policies and the one most commonly adopted. A firm utilizing market pricing customizes its prices on a market-by-market basis to maximize its profits in each market. Because of the importance and the complexity of this approach, we discuss it in more detail next.

Market Pricing

As you may remember from your microeconomics class, the profit-maximizing output (the quantity the firm must produce to maximize its profit) occurs at the intersection of the firm's marginal revenue curve and its marginal cost curve. The profit-maximizing price is found by reading across from the point on the firm's demand curve where the profit-maximizing output occurs. In Fig. 16.3(a), the intersection of the marginal revenue curve (MR) and the marginal cost curve (MC) occurs at Q, which is the profit-maximizing output. If you read straight up from Q until you reach the demand curve (D), then move left to the y-axis, you find the profit-maximizing price, P, the maximum price at which quantity Q of the good can be sold.

With market pricing, the firm calculates and charges the profit-maximizing price in each market it serves. Figure 16.3(b) shows two markets in which a firm has identical demand and marginal revenue curves but faces different marginal cost curves. The firm faces higher marginal costs (MC_1) in country 1 than in country 2 (MC_2). Accordingly, its profit-maximizing price in country 1 (P_1) must be higher than that in country 2 (P_2).

Two conditions must be met if a firm is to successfully practice market pricing:

I The firm must face different demand and/or cost conditions in the countries in which it sells its products. This condition is usually met, since taxes, tariffs, standards of living, levels of competition, infrastructure costs and availability, and numerous other factors vary by country.

2 The firm must be able to prevent arbitrage, a concept discussed in Chapter 5. The firm's market pricing policy will unravel if customers are able to buy the firm's products in a low-price country and resell them profitably in a high-price country. Because of tariffs, transportation costs, and other transaction costs, arbitrage is usually not a problem if country-to-country price variations are small. But if prices vary widely by country, arbitrage can upset the firm's market pricing strategy.

Assuming these conditions are met, the advantages of this polycentric approach are obvious. For example, the firm can set higher prices where markets will tolerate them and lower prices where necessary in order to remain competitive. It also can directly allocate relevant local costs against local sales within each foreign market, thereby allowing corporate strategists and planners to better allocate the firm's resources across markets. But such flexibility comes with a cost. To capture the benefits of market pricing, local managers must closely monitor sales and competitive conditions within their markets so that appropriate and timely adjustments can be made. Also, the corporate staff must be willing to delegate authority to local managers to allow them to adjust prices within their markets.

Firms most likely to use this approach are those that both produce and market their products in many different countries. For example, Samsung uses market pricing for its line of consumer electronics products. It operates production facilities in almost two dozen countries and sells its products in close to a hundred markets. Samsung has found that market pricing actually makes it easier to export and market its products within such a complex context.[32]

A market pricing policy can, however, expose a firm to dumping complaints (as discussed earlier) as well as to three other risks: damage to its brand name, development of a gray market for its products, and consumer resentment against discriminatory prices.

The firm needs to ensure that the prices it charges in one market do not damage the brand image it has carefully nurtured in others. For example, suppose Seagram encouraged its North American and European brand managers to market Johnny Walker Red as a premium scotch whiskey sold at a premium price but allowed its Japanese brand managers to peddle it as a nonprestigious brand sold at rock-bottom prices. Because of its marketing approach in Japan, Seagram would risk deterioration of Johnny Walker Red's premium brand image in North America and Europe. Thus any international firm that sells brand-name products and adopts market pricing should review the prices charged by local managers to ensure that the integrity of its brand names and its market images is maintained across all of its markets.

A firm that follows a market pricing policy also risks the development of gray markets for its products as a result of arbitrage. A **gray market** is a market that results when products are imported into a country legally but outside the normal channels of distribution authorized by the manufacturer. (This phenomenon is also known as *parallel importing*.) A gray market may develop when the price in one market is sufficiently lower than the price the firm charges in another that entrepreneurs can buy the good in the lower-price market and resell it in the higher-price market. Thus the firm that has large price differences among markets is vulnerable to having these differentials undercut by gray markets. Gray markets frequently arise when firms fail to adjust local prices after major fluctuations in exchange rates. Coca-Cola, for example, faced such a problem in 1994 after the yen strengthened relative to the U.S. dollar. Japanese discounters were able to purchase and import Coke made in the United States for 27 percent less than the price of Coke made in Japan, thereby disrupting the firm's pricing strategy in both countries.[33] Merck had a similar problem in 1997 when the British pound rose relative to other European Union currencies. The company was forced to cut the price in the United Kingdom of many of its drugs, such as the recently developed AIDS drug Crixivan, because of parallel importing from other EU countries.[34]

Products commonly influenced by gray markets include big-ticket items such as automobiles, cameras, computers, ski equipment, and watches. Gray markets are also more prevalent in free-market economies, where fewer government regulations make it easier for them to emerge. One recent estimate suggests that gray market sales in the United States approach $130 billion each year.[35] Many MNCs have attempted to eliminate or control gray markets through legal action, but few have had much success.

Gray market sales undermine a firm's market pricing policy and often lower its profits. They also cause friction between the firm and its distributors, who lose sales but are often stuck with the costs of either providing customer support and honoring product guarantees on gray market goods or explaining to unhappy customers why they will not do so. For example, Charles of the Ritz reports that over 10,000 retailers sell its Opium perfume, although the firm has authorized only 1,300 to do so. The prices its authorized dealers charge are continually being undercut by those offered by gray market sellers, thereby making it difficult for the authorized dealers to adhere to the firm's suggested pricing schedule. Charles of the Ritz has sought to smooth over the resulting friction by helping its authorized dealers to compete with the gray marketers through additional advertising allowances and special price reductions. This practice, however, harms the firm's profit margins. "Going Global" provides another example of the conflict between keeping customers happy and keeping distributors happy that manufacturers face when gray markets develop in their goods.

A third danger lies in consumer resentment. Consumers in the high-priced country may feel that they are being gouged by such pricing policies. Estee Lauder, for example, charges $40 for Clinique facial soap in Tokyo that sells for only $10 in the United States, while J. Crew charges Japanese customers $130 for wool sweaters that sell for $48 in the states. Japanese newspapers and television stations have highlighted this issue, claiming that foreign companies take advantage of Japanese consumers. While various company spokespersons have argued that the price differences are due to the high cost of doing business in Japan, the ill will engendered by the controversy has not helped their sales.[36]

Promotion Issues and Decisions

The third P of the international marketing mix is promotion. **Promotion** encompasses all efforts by an international firm to enhance the desirability of its products among potential buyers. While many promotional activities are specifically targeted at buyers, successful firms recognize that they must also communicate with their distributors and the general public to ensure favorable sentiment toward themselves and their products. Because promotion involves communication with audiences in the host country, it is the most culture-

GOING (GLOBAL

"Keep On Truckin'"

Gray markets often arise for high-priced, high-status goods. And because the Japanese distribution system often is very inefficient, gray markets are not uncommon there. One of the most unlikely products for which a gray market has developed in Japan, however, is the Chevrolet Astro Van. The Astro Van is one of the least popular and poorest-selling minivans available in the U.S. market. Most consumers shun the vehicle, preferring minivans produced by Chrysler, Ford, and Toyota; most U.S. sales are to commercial enterprises that use the Astro Van for deliveries and other mundane purposes.

In Japan, however, the Astro Van has achieved near cult status among Japanese yuppies who customize the vans with fog lights, exotic paint jobs, running boards, raised roofs, and the like. Despite its left-hand-drive status (like the British, the Japanese drive on the left-hand side of the road and thus prefer right-hand-drive vehicles) and a body design that hasn't been changed in over a decade, it is the best selling U.S.-made vehicle in Japan, with annual sales volume of about 14,000 units. An estimated 80 percent of the sales of the Astro Van in Japan are made through the gray market. The base price of an Astro Van sold through authorized Japanese dealers is about $41,000, while the gray market price for a base vehicle is only $35,000, although a tenacious bargainer can cut that price by another 10 percent or so.

The Astro Van's success is something of a mixed blessing to General Motors. While it is happy to boost the sales of the vehicle, like many other manufacturers whose products are sold through gray markets, it is concerned about upsetting its Japanese dealers who lose sales to gray market sellers. Moreover, General Motors is afraid that its reputation among Japanese consumers will be damaged because factory warranties do not apply to vehicles sold through the gray market, upsetting many Japanese owners of Astro Vans.

Source: "The Cult of the Astro Van," *Fortune*, August 18, 1997, pp. 44-45.

bound of the four P's. Thus a firm must take special care to ensure that the message host-country audiences receive is in fact the message the firm intended to send. International marketing managers must therefore effectively blend and utilize the four elements of the **promotion mix**—advertising, personal selling, sales promotion, and public relations—to motivate potential customers to buy their firm's products.

Advertising

The first element of the promotion mix is advertising. For most international firms, especially those selling consumer products and services, advertising is the most important element in the promotion mix. As a firm develops its advertising strategy, it must consider three factors:

1 The message it wants to convey

2 The media available for conveying the message

3 The extent to which the firm wants to globalize its advertising effort

At the same time, the firm must take into account relevant cultural, linguistic, and legal constraints found in various national markets.

Message. The message of an advertisement refers to the facts or impressions the advertiser wants to convey to potential customers. An automaker may want to convey a message of value (low price), reliability (quality), and/or style (image and prestige). The choice of message is an important reflection of how the firm sees its own products and services and how it wants them to be seen by customers. Coca-Cola, for example, believes that its products help consumers enjoy life, and its advertising messages consistently stress this theme worldwide. Products that are used for different purposes in different areas will need to be marketed differently. For example, in the United States motorcycles are seen primarily as recreational products, but in many other countries they are seen mainly as a means of transportation. Thus Honda's and Kawasaki's ads in the United States stress the fun and excitement of riding. In poorer countries, they stress the reliability and functionalism of motorcycles as a mode of inexpensive transportation.[37]

The country of origin of a product often serves as an important part of the advertising message.[38] For example, among fashion-conscious teenagers and young adults in Europe and Japan, U.S. goods are often viewed as being very trendy. Thus Levi Strauss, Harley-Davidson, Gibson guitars, Stetson hats, and the National Basketball Association, among others, highlight the U.S. origins of their products. Japanese products, on the other hand, are often perceived to be of high quality, so international marketers stress the Japanese origin of such products as Toyota automobiles and Sony electronics goods.

Medium. The **medium** is the communication channel used by the advertiser to convey a message. A firm's international marketing manager must alter the media used to convey its message from market to market based on availability, legal restrictions, standards of living, literacy rates, the cultural homogeneity of the national market, and other factors. In bilingual or multilingual countries such as Belgium, Switzerland, and Canada, international firms must adjust their mix of media outlets in order to reach each of the country's cultural groups. For example, Swissair communicates to its French-speaking Swiss audience by advertising in French-language newspapers, and to its German-speaking Swiss audience via ads in German-language newspapers.

A country's level of economic development may also affect the media firms use. For example, in many less developed countries, television ownership may be limited and literacy rates low. This eliminates television, newspapers, and maga-

International firms planning advertising campaigns must be attuned to how consumers in different countries will use their products. For example, in the United States, Honda markets its motorcycles as sports and recreation equipment, because that is how they are most often used. But in other countries, motorcycles are a basic form of transportation, and Honda must use a different advertising message there.

zines as useful media but raises the importance of radio advertising. To address this problem, firms may need to develop innovative solutions. For example, Colgate-Palmolive wished to increase its sales in rural India. Unfortunately, only one third of rural Indians own television sets, and more than half are illiterate. To reach these customers, the company's marketers outfitted "video vans" to tour the rural countryside. After showing rural villagers a half-hour long infomercial extolling the virtues of the company's oral hygiene products, sales representatives handed out samples of Colgate toothpaste and toothbrushes. This technique has proved successful, doubling toothpaste consumption in rural areas in the past five years.[39] "Going Global" illustrates another unusual, but innovative, approach to developing advertising media customized for the local market.

International marketers may need to develop nontraditional media to reach their customers. Colgate's use of "video vans" in rural India has successfully boosted sales of its oral hygiene products.

Legal restrictions may also prompt the use of certain media. Most national governments limit the number of TV stations as well as the amount of broadcast time sold to advertisers. Countries often outlaw the use of certain media for the advertising of products that may be harmful to their societies. For example, South Korea, Malaysia, Hong Kong, China, and Singapore ban cigarette advertising on television. South Korea has extended this ban to magazines read primarily by women and by persons under the age of 20; Hong Kong to radio; China to radio, newspapers, and magazines; and Singapore to all other media.[40] As in the United States, however, this ban has prompted tobacco firms to sponsor athletic events and to purchase display ads at stadiums that will be picked up by TV cameras.[41] Legal restrictions on the advertising of alcoholic products also are common throughout the world.

To help deal with issues related to message and media, many international firms use multinational advertising agencies, which have branch offices or affiliates in various national markets. As listed in Table 16.2, the world's largest advertising agencies are the WPP Group, the Omnicon Group, and the Interpublic Group—all headquartered in the United Kingdom or the United States.[42] International firms sometimes use local advertising agencies, too. Of course, a firm that wants to use a local advertising agency is advised to select a reputable, qualified one. Advertising has become so popular in Russia, for example, that there are as many as 800 agencies in Moscow alone. Many of them, however, are low-rent operations staffed by people with little skill in professional advertising. Firms that use them are likely to be overcharged and/or represented by poor-quality advertising campaigns.[43]

Global versus Local Advertising. A firm must also decide whether advertising for its product or service can be the same everywhere or must be tailored to each local market it serves.[44] Some products, such as Coca-Cola soft drinks, Bic pens, Levi jeans, and McDonald's hamburgers, have almost universal appeal. Such

GOING GLOBAL

Up until recently, advertising media in Egypt usually took one of two forms: dancing women pitching products on static-filled television ads and poor-quality billboards haphazardly thrown up along highways. But catching the attention of the 61 million residents of this North African country has recently led international advertisers to search for newer media to hook the consumer.

The advertising medium that has attracted the most attention has been the felucca—ancient sailboats that travel up and down the Nile. Feluccas have been used for transportation and recreation along the Nile River since the days of the pharaohs. Companies use them to transport merchandise up and down the river, and families frequently rent them for an evening's gathering. Tourists also queue up for rides.

New Advertising Media in Egypt

Feluccas are propelled by large, triangular white sails. Coca-Cola recently decided to see if it could place its ads on some of the sails. The firm signed a two-year deal with one of Egypt's largest felucca operators for 27,000 Egyptian pounds (around $8,000) plus new sails. At first, Coca-Cola wanted to use red sails to better display its trademark. But because felucca sails have always been white, the firm had to resort to white sails emblazoned with Coke's red logo.

Perrier quickly followed Coke's lead and now has its own advertising agreement with another large felucca operator. And Egypt's own recently privatized Al Ahram Beverages Co. of Cairo is also planning to use feluccas to promote its products as well. Still, it is sometimes hard to shape tradition. Even though the Coca-Cola-sponsored feluccas come equipped with complimentary Coke beverages, most Egyptians opt for their traditional favorite instead—apple juice!

Source: "Advertising Breezes Along the Nile River with Signs for Sails," *Wall Street Journal,* July 18, 1997, pp. A1, A11.

companies frequently advertise globally, utilizing the same advertising campaign in all of the markets they serve. For example, in 1997 Coca-Cola introduced a series of ads shown globally that featured its "Always Coca-Cola" slogan.[45] As Map 16.1 indicates, despite being the world's number one soft drink, Coca-Cola still has significant opportunities for growth.

Sometimes globally-oriented international firms may choose to make subtle adaptations to meet the needs of the local market. Unilever applied this approach to a recent advertising campaign for Dove soap. Its TV commercials were identical in each market, but the actors were not. On the same stage and set, U.S., Italian, German, French, and Australian models were filmed in succession, each stating in her own language, "Dove has one-quarter cleansing cream."[46] Nestlé used one theme in promoting Kit Kat candy to its European customers—"Have a break, have a Kit Kat"—but changed the backgrounds to better appeal to customers across national markets.

Other firms have opted for a regionalization strategy. IBM, for example, began advertising its PCs in European markets by creating a pan-European advertising campaign. Instead of customizing its ads by country, IBM featured the same text and visual images in all its European ads, altering only the language used for its broadcast and print ads. IBM determined that this approach saved $22–30 million in creative and production expenses (out of a total advertising budget of $150 million). However, maintaining uniformity of the product's image was of paramount concern. The

TABLE 16.2

The 20 Largest Advertising Organizations in the World (1995 Sales)

1995 RANK	COMPANY	HEADQUARTERS	1995 SALES ($ MIL.)
1	WPP Group	London	3,129.7
2	Omnicom Group	New York	2,576.7
3	Interpublic Group of Companies	New York	2,337.2
4	Dentsu	Tokyo	1,998.6
5	Cordiant	London	1,377.8
6	Young & Rubicam	New York	1,197.5
7	Hakuhodo	Tokyo	958.6
8	Havas Advertising	Levallois-Perret, France	909.4
9	Grey Advertising	New York	896.5
10	Leo Burnett Co.	Chicago	803.9
11	True North Communications	Chicago	758.7
12	D'Arcy Masius Benton & Bowles	New York	645.6
13	Publicis Communications	Paris	606.3
14	Bozell, Jacobs, Kenyon & Eckhardt	New York	404.5
15	BDDP Group	Paris	278.5
16	Asatsu Inc.	Tokyo	254.1
17	Tokyu Agency	Tokyo	238.5
18	Daiko Advertising	Tokyo	211.1
19	Dai-Ichi Kikaku Co.	Tokyo	168.4
20	Dentsu, Young & Rubicam Partnerships	Tokyo/Singapore	160.6

Source: Excerpted with permission from *Hoover's Handbook of World Business 1997*, p. 32. Data from *Advertising Age*, April 15, 1996.

campaign was designed specifically to ensure that IBM's European clients, regardless of the country in which they were located, received the same message regarding its product.[47] Similarly, Levi Strauss used the same TV ad to sell its 501 jeans in six European markets. Since each of its commercials costs about $500,000 to shoot, Levi Strauss would have spent about $3 million on six ads and thus saved $2.5 million in production costs alone by adopting this regional strategy.[48]

Of course, many firms find it useful to use both standard and localized approaches to advertising. Unilever, for example, generally follows a standardized advertising strategy. Thus it developed a national advertising campaign to promote its products in China, calling for the same basic message using the same basic media throughout the country. But Unilever found that clear differences exist within different regions of the country regarding perceptions of soap. Thus it developed fifty specialized commercials for its Lux soap for use in separate markets within China.[49]

Whether to choose a standardized or a specialized advertising campaign also is a function of the message the firm wants to convey. Standardized advertisements tend to contain less concrete information than do more specialized advertisements. Ads for products such as candy and soft drinks often can be standardized because the ads stress the warm, emotional aspects of consuming the good, while ads for products like credit cards, automobiles, and airline services tend to be customized to meet the needs of local consumers.[50]

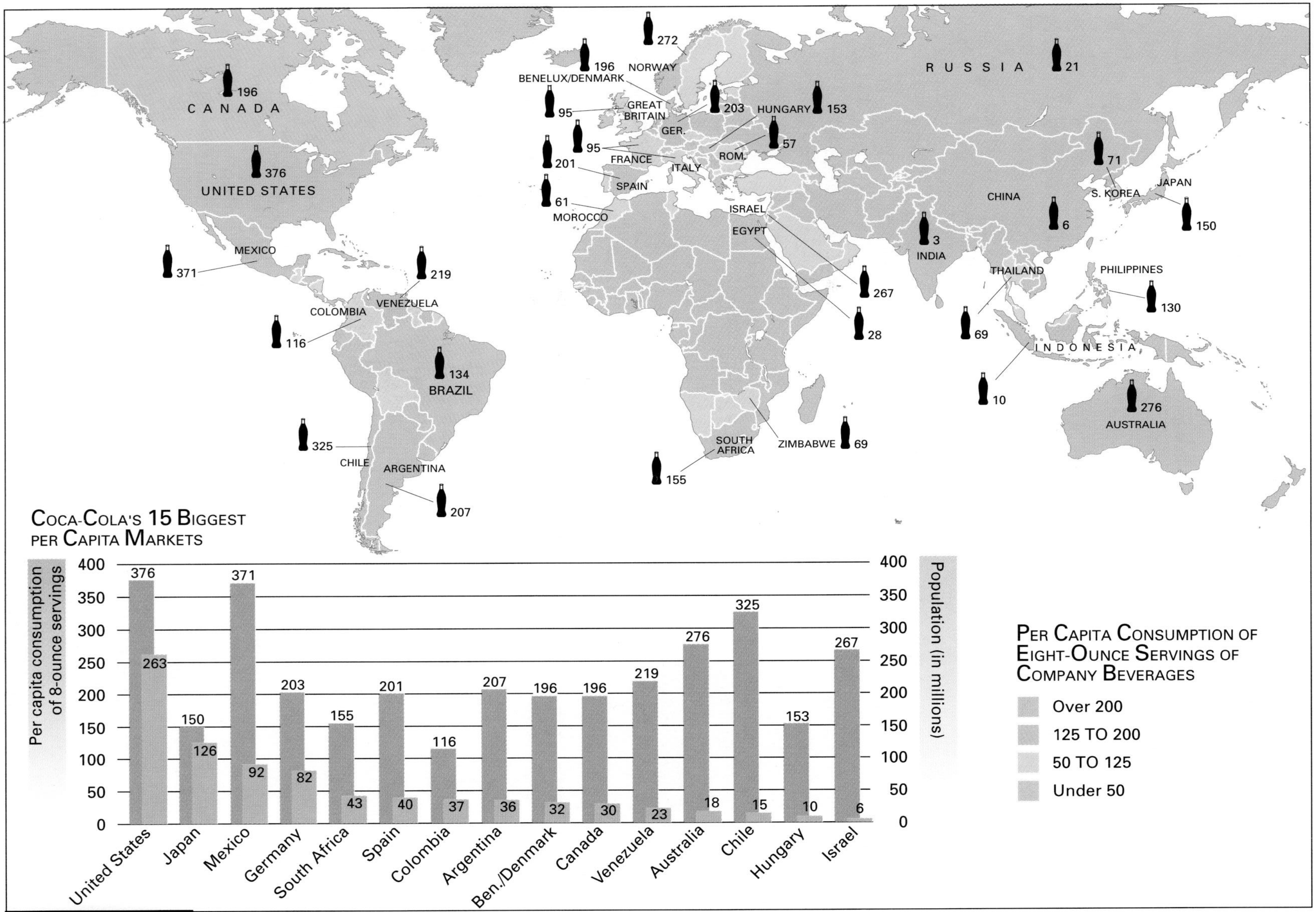

PER CAPITA CONSUMPTION OF EIGHT-OUNCE SERVINGS OF COMPANY BEVERAGES

- Over 200
- 125 TO 200
- 50 TO 125
- Under 50

Map labels (per capita consumption of 8-ounce servings):
- RUSSIA 21
- JAPAN 150
- S. KOREA 71
- PHILIPPINES 130
- AUSTRALIA 276
- CHINA 6
- THAILAND 69
- INDONESIA 10
- INDIA 3
- HUNGARY 153
- ROM. 57
- NORWAY 272
- BENELUX/DENMARK 196
- GREAT BRITAIN 95
- GER. 203
- FRANCE 95
- ITALY 201
- SPAIN 61
- MOROCCO
- ISRAEL 267
- EGYPT 28
- ZIMBABWE 69
- SOUTH AFRICA 155
- CANADA 196
- UNITED STATES 376
- MEXICO 371
- VENEZUELA 219
- COLOMBIA 116
- CHILE 325
- BRAZIL 134
- ARGENTINA 207

COCA-COLA'S 15 BIGGEST PER CAPITA MARKETS

Per capita consumption of 8-ounce servings

Country	Per capita consumption	Population (in millions)
United States	376	263
Japan	150	126
Mexico	371	92
Germany	203	82
South Africa	155	43
Spain	201	40
Colombia	116	37
Argentina	207	36
Ben./Denmark	196	32
Canada	196	30
Venezuela	219	23
Australia	276	18
Chile	325	15
Hungary	153	10
Israel	267	6

Per Capita Consumption of Coca-Cola

Source: Based on *The Coca-Cola Company Annual Report 1998.*

MAP 16.1

Personal Selling

The second element of the promotion mix is **personal selling**—making sales on the basis of personal contacts. The use of sales representatives, who call on potential customers and attempt to sell a firm's products or services to them, is the most common approach to personal selling.[51] Because of the close contact between the salesperson and the potential customer, sellers are likely to rely on host-country nationals to serve as their representatives. For a firm just starting international operations, personal selling is often subcontracted to local sales organizations that usually handle product lines from several firms. As the firm grows and develops a sales base in new markets, however, it is likely to establish its own sales force. Colgate-Palmolive, for example, made very effective use of personal selling to gain market share in Central Europe. The firm opened a sales office in Warsaw after the Iron Curtain fell and used it to develop a well-trained professional sales staff. That staff has made Colgate-Palmolive the consumer products market leader in Poland.[52]

The importance of personal selling as an element of the promotion mix differs for industrial products and for consumer products. For industrial products (such as complex machinery, electronic equipment, and customized computer software), customers often need technical information about product characteristics, usage, maintenance requirements, and availability of after-sales support. Well-trained sales representatives are often better able to convey information about the intricacies of such products to customers than are print or broadcast media. For consumer products, personal selling is normally confined to selling to wholesalers and to retail chains. Most consumer products firms find that advertising, particularly in print and broadcast media, is a more efficient means of communicating with consumers than is personal selling. However, personal selling can be used to market some goods, usually in the form of door-to-door selling. Avon and Amway, for example, have successfully exported to the Asian and European markets the personal selling techniques they developed in the United States. Similarly, American International Group (AIG) carefully built its 5,000 person sales force in Shanghai over a four-year period; today AIG enjoys a 90 percent share of the life insurance market in that city.[53] In Amway's case, personal selling and the ethnic ties of its existing distributors have played a critical role in the firm's internationalization strategy. When Amway decided to enter the Philippines in 1997, for example, it encouraged distributors from the United States, New Zealand, and Australia of Filipino heritage to act as "ambassadors," recruiting new distributors there. Because the ambassadors receive a percentage of the sales generated by the persons they recruit, over 100 existing distributors eagerly traveled to the Philippines at their own expense to develop Amway's sales force there. The company has used a similar approach to crack the Korean and Chinese markets.[54] "Going Global" describes another interesting and unexpected situation encountered by Amway in China.

Personal selling has several advantages for an international firm:

♦ Firms that hire local sales representatives can be reasonably confident that those individuals understand the local culture, norms, and customs. For example, a native of India selling products in that country will be better informed about local conditions than will someone sent from Spain to sell products in India.

♦ Personal selling promotes close, personal contact with customers. Customers see real people and come to associate that personal contact with the firm.

GOING GLOBAL

Taking Amway to the Cleaners in China

Capitalism is still an unfamiliar concept in China, as Amway Asia Pacific Ltd. has discovered. For months, being an Amway distributor was the best game in town among the rising ranks of Shanghai's unemployed: An $84 investment bought a box of soaps and cosmetics that the city's down-at-heel could peddle. And if customers were dissatisfied, they could get a full refund at any time, no questions asked—even if the returned bottles were empty.

Word of this no-lose proposition quickly spread, with some people repackaging the soap, selling it and turning in the containers for a refund. Others dispensed with selling altogether and scoured garbage bins instead—showing up at Amway's Shanghai offices with bags full of bottles to be redeemed.

One "salesman" got nearly $10,000 for eight sacks full of all kinds of empty Amway containers. And at least one barbershop started using Amway shampoo for free—getting a full refund on each empty bottle. Amway's Shanghai chief, Percy Chin, says refunds in recent weeks totaled more than $100,000 a day. "Perhaps we were too lenient," he says.

Late last month, Amway decided enough was enough and changed the policy, only to have hundreds of angry Amway distributors descend on the company's offices to complain. "We were cheated out of our money," frothed one woman on the sidewalk outside.

Amway security guards worked to mollify the crowd and the company called in local journalists to spread the word that it wasn't changing its refund policy, simply raising the standard for what is deemed "dissatisfaction." "If someone returns half a bottle, fine, but for empties we'll check our records to see if the person has a pattern of returns," says Mr. Chin.

Amway's refund policy—a courtesy to customers and testament that it stands behind its products—is the same all over the world, he says. But the company didn't anticipate the unusual sense of entitlement it engendered in China. "The satisfaction-guaranteed policy doesn't spell out specifically what dissatisfaction means, but people in the Western world understand," says Mr. Chin. "We thought that it was understood here, too."

Now, the change in policy has left many people dissatisfied. Railed one protesting distributor, "Don't open a company if you can't afford losses."

Source: From "In China, Some Distributors Have Really Cleaned Up with Amway," by Craig S. Smith, *Wall Street Journal*, August 4, 1997, p. B1. Reprinted by permission of the *Wall Street Journal*, © 1997 Dow Jones and Co., Inc. All Rights reserved worldwide.

♦ Personal selling makes it easier for the firm to obtain valuable market information. Knowledgeable local sales representatives are an excellent source of information that can be used to develop new products and/or improve existing ones for the local market.

On the other hand, personal selling is a relatively high-cost strategy. Each sales representative must be adequately compensated, but each may also reach relatively few customers. An industrial products sales representative, for example, may need a full day or more to see just one potential customer. And after a sale is closed, the sales representative may still find it necessary to spend large blocks of time with the customer explaining how things work and trying to generate new business. Most larger international firms also find it necessary to establish regional sales offices staffed by sales managers and other support personnel, which add still more sales-related costs.

Sales Promotion

The third element of the promotion mix is sales promotion. **Sales promotion** comprises specialized marketing efforts such as coupons, in-store promotions, sampling, direct mail campaigns, cooperative advertising, and trade fair attendance. Sales promotion activities focused on wholesalers and retailers are designed to increase the number and commitment of these intermediaries working with the firm. Many international firms, for example, participate in international trade shows such as the Paris Air Show or the Tokyo Auto Mart in order to generate interest among existing and potential distributors for their products. Participation in international trade shows is often recommended as a first step for firms wanting to internationalize their sales. The U.S. Department of Commerce will often help U.S. small firms participate in overseas trade shows as part of its export promotion efforts. Firms may also develop cooperative advertising campaigns or provide advertising allowances to encourage retailers to promote their products.

Sales promotion activities may be narrowly targeted to consumers and/or offered for only a short time before being dropped or replaced with more permanent efforts. This flexible nature of sales promotions makes them ideal for a marketing campaign tailored to fit local customs and circumstances. For example, British American Tobacco, Rothmans, Philip Morris, and RJR/Nabisco compete in the Taiwanese market by handing out free cigarettes, a practice not utilized in the U.S. market. Also, Philip Morris and RJR/Nabisco built market share by offering Korean consumers free cigarette lighters and desk diaries emblazoned with the firms' logos in return for cigarette purchases.[55] U.S. airlines have effectively used direct mail to lure international travelers away from foreign airlines. By carefully analyzing the travel habits of members of their frequent flyer programs, carriers like American and Continental can target their mailings (and customize the incentives, such as the awarding of bonus frequent flyer miles) to those customers who are most likely to respond to such lures.

Public Relations

The fourth element of the promotion mix is public relations. **Public relations** consists of efforts aimed at enhancing a firm's reputation and image with the general public, as opposed to touting the specific advantages of an individual product or service. The consequence of effective public relations is a general belief that the firm is a good "corporate citizen," that it is reputable, and that it can be trusted. Ineffective public relations can often lead to a public perception that the firm cannot be trusted or that it cares little for the community.

Savvy international firms recognize that money spent on public relations is money well spent because it earns them political allies and makes it easier to communicate their needs to the general public. They also recognize that as "foreigners," they often are appealing political targets; thus they attempt to reduce their exposure to political attacks. Toyota provides a case in point. Japanese firms, unlike their U.S. counterparts, do not have a tradition of corporate philanthropy. Toyota received large financial incentives from the state of Kentucky to build its first wholly-owned U.S. auto assembly plant in Georgetown. During the first few years it operated that plant, Toyota received a fair amount of criticism for its lack of community concern. The firm eventually realized that it had to adapt its corporate attitudes to local customs if it wanted to maintain the good will of local politicians. Toyota subsequently became a model corporate citizen, providing grants to local charities, funding college scholarships to graduating high school students, and sponsoring local youth sports teams.

The impact of maintaining good public relations is hard to quantify, but over time an international firm's positive image and reputation are likely to benefit it in a host country. Consumers are more likely to resist "buy local" pitches when the foreign firm is also perceived to be a good guy. Good public relations can also help the firm when it has to negotiate with a host-country government for a zoning permit or an operating license or when it encounters a crisis or unfavorable publicity. For example, Toshiba found itself in deep trouble in 1986 when a Toshiba subsidiary was discovered to have been illegally selling to the Soviet Union advanced technology designed to make the detection of nuclear submarines harder. Normally, few citizens would be aware of the importance of such a breach of security. Unfortunately for Toshiba, one of the best-selling novels of the 1980s, Tom Clancy's *The Hunt for Red October*, had educated U.S. readers about the technological nature of submarine warfare. Fortunately for Toshiba, the firm had been a good corporate citizen in the United States. Relying on the good will it had previously fostered with local government officials, community leaders, and its work force, it was able to avoid trade sanctions that would have jeopardized its stature in the United States. But this example offers a clear lesson: an international firm cannot rely on good will to bail it out of a crisis if it has no good will with important stakeholders to begin with.

Distribution Issues and Decisions

The fourth P of the international marketing mix is place—more commonly referred to as distribution. **Distribution** is getting products and services from the firm into the hands of customers. (As we discuss in Chapter 17, distribution is one component of international logistics management.) An international firm faces two important sets of distribution issues:

1 Addressing the problems of physically transporting its goods and services from where they are created to the various markets in which they are to be sold

2 Selecting the means by which it will merchandise its goods in the markets it wants to serve

International Distribution

The most obvious issue an international firm's distribution managers must address is the selection of mode(s) of transportation for shipping its goods from their point of origin to their destination. This choice entails a clear trade-off between time and money, as Table 16.3 indicates. Faster modes of transportation, such as air freight and motor carrier, are more expensive than slower modes, such as ocean shipping, railroad, pipeline, and barge. However, the transportation mode selected affects the firm's inventory costs and customer service levels, as well as the prod-

TABLE 16.3			

Advantages and Disadvantages of Different Modes of Transportation for Exports

TRANSPORTATION MODE	ADVANTAGES	DISADVANTAGES	SAMPLE PRODUCTS
Train	Safe Reliable Inexpensive	Limited to rail routes Slow	Automobiles Grains
Airplane	Safe Reliable	Expensive Limited access	Jewelry Medicine
Truck	Versatile Inexpensive	Size	Consumer goods
Ship	Inexpensive Good for large products	Slow Indirect	Automobiles Furniture
Electronic media	Fast	Unusable for many products	Information

uct's useful shelf life, exposure to damage, and packaging requirements. International air freight, for example, scores high on each of these dimensions, while ocean shipping ranks very low.

Consider the impact of transportation mode on the firm's inventory expenses and the level of customer service. If the firm relies on slower modes of transportation instead of faster ones, it can maintain a given level of inventory at the point of sale only by maintaining higher levels of inventory in transit. If it selects unreliable modes that make it difficult to predict when shipments will actually arrive, it will have to increase buffer stocks in its inventory in order to avoid stock-outs that will lead to disappointed customers. Choosing slower modes of transportation also increases the firm's **international order cycle time**—the time between the placement of an order and its receipt by the customer—for any given level of inventories. Longer order cycle times lower the firm's customer service levels and may induce its customers to seek alternative supply sources.

The product's shelf life affects the selection of transportation mode. Goods that are highly perishable because of physical or cultural forces—such as cut flowers or fashionable dresses—are typically shipped by air freight because of their short shelf life. Less perishable products, such as coal, crude oil, or men's socks, are shipped using less expensive modes. In some cases the transportation mode may affect the product's packaging requirements. For example, goods sent on long ocean voyages may need special packaging to protect them from humidity infiltration and damage due to rough seas; the firm could avoid the extra costs of such packaging if it chose a faster mode such as air freight. Of course, a simple solution is sometimes available: when Calpis, a Colorado-based agricultural goods processor, entered the Japanese orange juice market, it switched its packaging from glass bottles to cans in order to reduce breakage.[56]

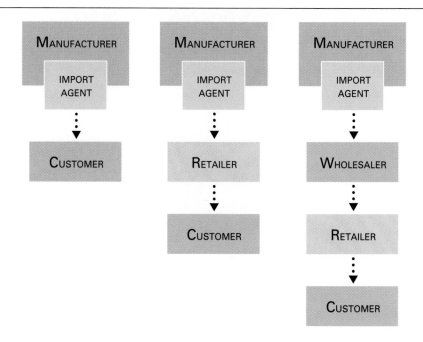

FIGURE 16.4

Distribution Channel Options

Channels of Distribution

An international firm's marketing managers must also determine which distribution channels to use to merchandise the firm's products in each national market it serves. Figure 16.4 shows the basic channel options used by most international manufacturing firms. Note that a distribution channel can consist of as many as four basic parts:

1 The manufacturer that creates the product or service

2 A wholesaler that buys products and services from the manufacturer and then resells them to retailers

3 The retailer, which buys from wholesalers and then sells to customers

4 The actual customer, who buys the product or service for final consumption.

Import agents (discussed in Chapter 11) may also be used as intermediaries, especially by smaller firms.

One important factor illustrated by Fig. 16.4 is channel length. **Channel length** is the number of stages in the distribution channel. A firm that sells directly to its customers, which then pay the business directly, bypasses wholesalers and retailers and therefore has a very short distribution channel. This approach is called **direct sales** because the firm is dealing directly with its final consumer. Dell Computer started out as a direct sales business, taking customer orders over toll-free, 24-hour telephone lines. The advantage of this approach is that the firm maintains control over retail distribution of its products and retains any retailing profits it earns. Unfortunately, the firm also bears the costs and risks of retailing its products.

A slightly longer channel of distribution involves selling to retailers, which then market and sell the products to customers. This is easiest to do when retailers in a given market are heavily concentrated. When there are relatively few large retailers, selling directly to each is easier for manufacturers; when a larger number of smaller retailers are present, selling to each is more complex. For example, huge supermarkets with vast selections of foods and toiletries exist throughout the United States. But in Europe, many consumers still buy food from small neighborhood stores, and few of these carry toiletries. A consumer products firm, therefore, will have to use very different approaches to distributing its products in the two markets. For example, in the United States, Procter & Gamble (P&G) may sell directly to Kroger or Safeway, which will routinely stock several hundred tubes of toothpaste of various sizes on its shelves and store cartons of inventory in its warehouses. But a European retailer may have retail space for only a few tubes and little storage space for backup inventory, thereby making it more difficult for P&G to sell directly to such outlets.

The longest distribution channel involves the use of wholesalers. Wholesalers are separate businesses that buy from manufacturers and then resell to retailers or, in some cases, to other wholesalers. For example, small farmers cannot easily sell their produce to large grocery chains because those chains find it inefficient to deal with large numbers of small suppliers. Instead, farmers sell their produce to wholesalers, which then sell it to grocery stores; thus the grocery stores must deal with only a few large suppliers. Similarly, in markets with little retail concentration, a consumer products firm like P&G generally finds it easier to sell to a few wholesalers rather than attempt to deal with a huge number of small retailers. The use of wholesalers makes it easier to market in countries with little retail concentration and also allows the firm to maintain a smaller sales staff. On the other hand, profit margins tend to be smaller because there are more businesses involved, each of which expects to make a profit. Rather than keeping all the profits for itself, as in the case of direct sales, a firm must share them with wholesalers and retailers.

The challenge for international marketing managers is to find the optimal distribution channel to match the firm's unique competitive strengths and weaknesses with the requirements of each national market it serves. In practice, as with other elements of international marketing, most international firms develop a flexible distribution strategy—they may use a short channel in some markets and a longer channel in others.

The firm's distribution strategy may also be an important component of its promotion strategy. For example, SMH manufactures not only relatively inexpensive Swatch watches but also high-priced watches such as Omega and Tissot. It distributes its expensive watches through exclusive jewelry stores and its Swatch watches through department stores like Macy's and Dillard's.[57] Toyota adopted different distribution strategies for its luxury cars in the United States and Japan. In the United States it named the model Lexus and set up an independent dealership network to strengthen the prestige of that brand name. But in Japan, where the firm had less need to bolster its image, the same model is sold under the Toyota name through existing Toyota dealerships.

As noted in Chapter 11, some international firms, particularly producers of more specialized products, may hire a sales or import agent to distribute their goods. For example, the National Football League contracted with Japan Marketing Services to promote NFL-licensed goods in Japan. Annual Japanese sales of T-shirts, sweatshirts, and other clothing bearing the names of U.S.

football teams exceed $50 million.[58] Many governments, as part of their efforts to stimulate exports, have developed programs to help firms locate suitable international import agents. For example, the U.S. and Foreign Commercial Service, a branch of the Department of Commerce, provides lists of foreign firms that have expressed a willingness to distribute given products in their market areas. These data can be obtained by contacting local offices of the U.S. and Foreign Commercial Service or through the National Trade Data Bank.

Firms should exercise caution when selecting a foreign distributor. The distributor *is* the firm as far as local customers are concerned, so a poor distributor jeopardizes the firm's reputation and performance in that market, often for a very long time. Further, local laws may make it difficult for a firm to terminate the distributor. In Saudi Arabia, for example, a foreign firm must hire a local national to represent it and firing that agent is virtually impossible without his consent.

Finding an appropriate distributor is a particular challenge in China, as many distributors are state-owned with little knowledge or incentive to market foreign consumer products appropriately. For example, the primary distributors of Wrigley gum are controlled by the China National Cereal & Oils Import & Export Corporation, a state-owned trading company. Its managers believe it is a waste of time to deliver goods to smaller wholesalers and retail outlets, preferring that these smaller customers come to its warehouses. While this tactic may lower China National's transportation costs, it makes it more costly for small wholesalers and retailers to stock Wrigley's gum, which drives down Wrigley's sales.[59] Firms like Amway and Avon, however, have been very successful in China because their sales force, relying on in-home parties and door-to-door sales, bypasses such distributor-created bottlenecks.[60]

Some international firms attempt to transfer to international markets the distribution systems developed in their home countries. McDonald's, for example, gained its status as the leading food service company in the United States by taking great care in selecting its franchisees and by nurturing their enterprises to the mutual benefit of both the franchisees and McDonald's. The firm has followed a similar distribution strategy to capture fast-food dollars in Europe, Asia, and Central and South America. Similarly, Coca-Cola utilizes a network of subsidiaries and bottlers (in some of which Coca-Cola has an equity stake) to market its soft drinks in virtually every country—a distribution strategy identical to that used by the firm in its home market. This extensive network has allowed Coca-Cola to respond quickly to new market opportunities. For example, to exploit the formerly communist Central European markets, the firm relied on its regional bottlers to help. Coca-Cola Amatil, which bottles Coke in Austria, was given responsibility for developing the Hungarian, Czech, and Slovak markets, while the firm's Greek bottler took charge of its Bulgarian and Romanian distribution.[61]

At other times, a firm may adapt its distribution practices to match local customs. In Russia, for example, many goods are sold at streetside kiosks; so Pepsi-Cola and Coca-Cola are sold at hundreds of these stands in Moscow alone.[62] Local laws also affect distribution strategies. For example, for many years the ability of foreigners to establish distribution systems was limited in India, Mexico, and China. As a result, most MNCs established joint ventures with local firms in order to distribute their products in those countries. Also, the complexities of Japan's culture and the complicated nature of its distribution networks have prompted many Western firms to seek joint venture partners to help them penetrate the Japanese market. KFC, for example, teamed up with Mitsubishi to create a joint venture to market its products in Japan. Mitsubishi contributed chicken (one of its subsidiaries is a major chicken producer), distribution networks, and an understanding of the cultural nuances of dealing with Japanese consumers. KFC contributed its brand name, an American image that appealed to fashion-conscious Japanese, and its technology and trade secrets—including, of course, the secret spices that make its product so finger-lickin' good.

CHAPTER REVIEW

Summary

International marketing is the process of planning and executing the conception, pricing, promotion, and distribution of ideas, goods, and services across national boundaries to create exchanges that satisfy individual and organizational objectives.

International marketing management is a critical organizational operation that should be integrated with other basic functions such as operations and human resource management. International marketing is generally based on one of three business strategies: differentiation, cost leadership, or focus. Determining the firm's marketing mix involves making decisions about product, pricing, promotion, and place (distribution). A related basic issue that marketing managers must address is the extent to which the marketing mix will be standardized or customized for different markets. A variety of factors must be considered in making their decision.

Product policy focuses on the tangible and intangible factors that characterize the product itself. Standardization versus customization is again a consideration. Industrial products and consumer products usually require different types of product policies. Legal, cultural, and economic forces also affect product policy and must be carefully evaluated.

Pricing issues and decisions constitute the second element of the marketing mix. The three basic pricing philosophies are standard pricing, two-tiered pricing, and market pricing. Market pricing, the most widely used and complex policy, involves setting different prices for each market. Basic economic analyses are used to arrive at the prices. Concerns related to gray markets, dumping, and potential consumer resentment must be addressed by firms that use this approach. Otherwise, serious problems may result.

Promotion issues and decisions generally concern the use of advertising and other forms of promotion. The promotion mix is a blend of advertising, personal selling, sales promotion, and public relations. Each of these elements is usually carefully tailored for the market in which it will be used and implemented accordingly.

Finally, international marketing managers must also plan for distribution—getting products and services from the firm to customers. International distribution may involve a variety of transportation modes, each with its own unique set of advantages and disadvantages. A firm must also develop appropriate distribution channels, which may involve wholesalers and retailers in addition to the firm and its customers. Effective distribution can have a significant impact on a firm's profitability.

Review Questions

1. What is international marketing?

2. What is the marketing mix?

3. What are the basic factors involved in deciding whether to use standardization or customization?

4. How do legal, cultural, and economic factors influence product policy?

5. Why are brand names an important marketing tool for international business?

6. What are the three basic pricing policies?

7. What are the problems that a firm using market pricing might encounter?

8. What are the four elements of the international promotion mix?

9. What are some of the fundamental issues that must be addressed in international advertising?

10. What is a distribution channel? What options does an international firm have in developing its channels?

Questions for Discussion

1. What are the similarities and differences between domestic and international marketing?

2. Are the four P's of international marketing of equal importance to all firms? What factors might cause some to be more or less important than others?

3. Identify several products you think could be marketed in a variety of foreign markets with

little customization. Identify other products that would clearly require customization.

4. How do legal, cultural, and economic factors in the United States affect product policy for foreign firms?

5. What are the pros and cons of trying to use a single brand name in different markets, as opposed to creating unique brand names for various markets?

6. What are the advantages and disadvantages of each pricing policy? Why do most international firms use market pricing?

7. The ethnocentric approach and the geocentric approach both suggest standardization of the marketing mix. What is the difference between these two approaches, if both lead to standardization?

8. What are some basic differences you might expect to see in TV ads broadcast in France, Japan, Saudi Arabia, and the United States?

9. Why is the public relations function important to an international firm?

10. What are the advantages and disadvantages of short versus long channels of distribution?

BUILDING GLOBAL SKILLS

Ajax Alarms is a medium-sized U.S. firm that sells alarm clocks. It licenses the production of its clocks to a Korean electronics firm, which handles complete production based on Ajax designs and specifications and then ships the clocks directly to the Ajax warehouse in Kansas. Ajax markets and distributes the clocks throughout the United States and Canada. The clocks themselves are brightly colored novelty items. For example, one of the firm's biggest

sellers is a plastic rooster that crows in the morning. Last year Ajax reported profits of around $5 million on total revenues of slightly more than $50 million.

Ajax managers have determined that the firm has few growth opportunities in the United States and so must sell its products internationally if it is to continue to expand. They have decided to start by selling in Mexico. They have hired you, an internationally famous marketing consultant, to advise them.

Your assignment here is to briefly outline a marketing plan for Ajax. (Your instructor may ask you to do this exercise as an outside-of-class assignment, either alone or in a group.) Essentially, Ajax wants you to consider product policy, pricing, promotion, and distribution issues. In developing your marketing plan, be sure to consider the factors discussed in this chapter, including standardization versus customization, legal forces, cultural influences, economic factors, and brand name questions. Note specific areas where you can make recommendations to your client. For example, if you believe that a certain advertising medium will be beneficial to Ajax, make that recommendation (be sure to provide some rationale or justification). If you feel you lack sufficient information to make a recommendation in some area, identify the factors that must be addressed by Ajax in that particular area. For example, if you cannot recommend a pricing policy, describe the information Ajax needs to acquire and evaluate when making that decision.

WORKING WITH THE WEB: Building Global Internet Skills

Nestlé Around the World

Nestlé S.A. is one of the world's foremost marketers, promoting and selling its products in more than 100 countries. Indeed, Nestlé's aggressive international marketing has led to more than one problem for the Swiss food company. One of the most significant criticisms that has been directed at Nestlé involves how the firm has marketed its infant products, such as baby formula, in different countries. Some observers, for example, claim that Nestlé has overstated the nutritional benefits of its infant formula in less developed countries, thus deceptively convincing mothers there to use the processed formula instead of breast-feeding their babies.

Use the Internet to do two things. First, locate and visit several Nestlé web sites in different countries. Use the information you obtain from these web sites to develop a description of Nestlé products and policies, pricing strategies, promotion strategies, and distribution strategies. Second, as you search for Nestlé web sites, also be on the alert for web sites for individuals and/or activist groups using the Internet to criticize Nestlé's marketing practices. Visit several of these sites and note your findings.

Follow-up Questions

1. Does Nestlé appear to be using a standardized or customized strategy for its international marketing?

2. Do Nestlé's critics appear to have a legitimate claim? Why or why not?

3. How effective do you think the Internet is as a forum for criticizing and/or influencing a multinational giant like Nestlé?

CLOSING CASE

P&G's Joy Makes an Unlikely Splash in Japan[63]

Anyone who thinks Japan doesn't offer opportunities for U.S consumer products should look at how quickly Procter & Gamble Co. has cleaned up in the country's dish-soap market.

Until 1995, P&G didn't sell dish soap in Japan at all. Now it has Japan's best-selling brand, Joy, which commands a fifth of the nation's $400 million dish-soap market. That's astounding progress, given that the market had appeared to be classically "mature"—both shrinking and dominated by giant Japanese companies.

"Joy surprised us all," says Tatsuo Ishii, dish-soap brand manager for one of those giants, Kao Corp. "It was brilliant."

How the Cincinnati company executed its coup provides lessons that transcend the kitchen sink. One big lesson: "Mature" Japanese markets can be surprisingly complacent. P&G offered new technology, something the two incumbents hadn't bothered to do for years. It developed packaging that let stores make more money. And it spent heavily on oddball commercials that created a buzz among consumers.

Joy offers "potent lessons" for foreign companies, says Hiroshi Tanaka, a marketing professor at Tokyo's Josai University. "At the least, Joy should tell you that Japan's got a lot more good opportunities for foreign companies than they might assume," he says. "Those opportunities are often disguised as unattractive markets suffering from saturation and oligopoly."

Just two years ago, two powerful consumer-product concerns, Kao and Lion Corp., each controlled nearly 40% of the kitchen-soap market with several brands and had essentially declared a truce. The rest of the market was cornered by private brands at chain stores. Meanwhile, the Japanese were cooking less at home and thus buying less dish soap every year.

P&G actually washed out of the Japanese kitchen-detergent market during an earlier attempt. It withdrew in the late 1970s after failing to make a dent with Orange Joy, a product that it transplanted from the U.S. But by 1992, it had succeeded in marketing other products, such as Pampers, in Japan. The home office told its Japanese unit to find new markets for products in which P&G was strong elsewhere in the world.

So that year P&G sent out researchers to study Japanese dish-washing rituals. They discovered one odd habit: Japanese homemakers, one after another, squirted out more detergent than needed. It was "a clear sign of frustration" with existing Japanese products, says Robert A. McDonald, head of P&G's Japanese operations. He saw the research as a sign that an "unarticulated consumer need" was more powerful soap. "We knew we had something to go after," he says.

Some P&G executives were concerned about entering such a mature market, says Mr. McDonald. But P&G's lab in Kobe went to work to create a highly concentrated soap formula, based on a new technology developed by the company's scientists in Europe, specifically for Japan.

The first hint that Joy was a hit came in March 1995 in the region around Hiroshima, 400 miles west of Tokyo, where P&G started test-marketing it. Four weeks into the test, Joy had become the most popular dish soap in the region with a 30% market share.

P&G's marketing pitch was deceptively simple: A little bit of Joy cleans better, yet it's easier on the hands. The message hit a chord, says Ayumi Osaki, a 31-year-old homemaker who rushed off to buy Joy after seeing pilot commercials. "Grease on Tupperware, that's the toughest thing to wash off," says Ms. Osaki, a mother of three in Hiroshima. "I had to try it."

Emboldened, P&G finished a nationwide introduction in March 1996, when Joy had attained a 10% market share. Three months later it had a 15% share. A year later it had 18%, and now its share is up to 20%, according to industry statistics. The results astounded even P&G. "Everybody in Japan wanted it," says P&G's Mr. McDonald. "Every retailer in Japan wanted to get his hands on Joy."

Retailers clamored for Joy because P&G had built in "fat margins," explains Masaharu Kubo, a buyer for Daiei Inc., which operates 383 supermarkets in Japan. P&G had exploited a weakness in the Japanese giants' products: Their long-necked bottles wasted space. P&G's containers were compact cylinders that took less space in stores, warehouses and delivery trucks. Joy improved the efficiency of Daiei's distribution by about 40%, Mr. Kubo estimates.

"Before Joy, dish soap was a sleepy category; [the containers] were bulky and took up a lot of shelf space, and their unit prices were falling every year," he says. "Joy freed up a lot of space for other products, pushed up prices of dish soaps as a whole, and gave us bigger margins. It was revolutionary."

P&G's advertising binge also delighted retailers, Mr. Kubo says. To look for ideas, P&G marketers had watched more than a hundred commercials from around the world from P&G and its rivals. They settled on a documentary-style TV ad used in Britain by P&G for a laundry soap called Daz.

P&G's advertising agency, Dentsu Inc., created commercials in which a famous comedian dropped in on homemakers, unannounced, with a camera crew to test Joy on the household's dirty dishes. The camera homed in on a patch of oil in a pan full of water. Then, after a drop of Joy, the oil dramatically disappeared.

Japanese soap makers were alarmed by the campaign. Kao's Mr. Ishii says he ordered up research into Joy and concluded that more than 70% of Joy users began using it because of the commercials. "We had mistakenly assumed Japanese didn't care much about grease-fighting power in dish soaps," Mr. Ishii says. "The reality was people are eating more meat and fried food and are frustrated about grease stains on their plastic dishes and storage containers."

Kao and Lion are now playing catch-up, turning out products that unabashedly mimic Joy, from its package and color (green) to its grease-fighting technology.

Successes like Joy have given P&G a change of heart about Japan. "For a long time, P&G's approach was to dump in Japan what sells in the U.S.," says a P&G manager who declined to be named. Now, he says, P&G generates ideas in Japan that it uses in other markets. It has begun selling Joy, for example, in the Philippines and is considering it for other Asian markets. It has also started to use a leak-free cap in the U.S. that it designed for Joy in Japan.

The Japanese consumer is "among the world's most educated and the most perceptive and articulate evaluators," says P&G's Mr. McDonald. "I've worked in a lot of countries but never been anywhere else where I can have a scientific discussion with the consumer like I can do here about dish soaps."

Case Questions

1. What lessons can international marketers learn from Procter & Gamble's experiences in Japan?

2. Identify and describe the roles of product policy, pricing, promotion, and distribution in marketing Joy in Japan.

3. What lessons from Japan might benefit Procter & Gamble in other markets?

CHAPTER NOTES

1. "Gearing up for the Grand Tour," *Business Week,* September 15, 1997, p. 95.

2. From "AMA Board Approves New Marketing Definition," *Marketing News,* March 31, 1985, p. 1.

3. "France retreats from 'knocking' adverts," *Financial Times,* August 14, 1995, p. 3.

4. "New Zealand Bans Reebok, Other Ads It Deems Politically Incorrect for TV," *Wall Street Journal,* July 25, 1995, p. A12.

5. David Lei, "Strategies for Global Competition," *Long Range Planning,* Vol. 22, No. 1 (1989), pp. 102–109. See also Yoram Wind and Susan Douglas, "International Portfolio Analysis and Strategy: The Challenge of the 1980s," *Journal of International Business Studies* (Fall 1981), pp. 69–82.

6. "America's New Merchants of Death," *Reader's Digest* (April 1993), pp. 50–57.

7. Nicholas Papadopoulos and Louise A. Heslop (eds.), *Product-Country Images—Impact and Role in International Marketing* (New York: International Business Press, 1993).

8. For an overview, see David McCutcheon, Amitabh Raturi, and Jack Meredith, "The Customization-Responsiveness Squeeze," *Sloan Management Review* (Winter 1994), pp. 89–100.

9. "U.S. Catalog Firms Go After Europeans," *Wall Street Journal,* January 6, 1998, p. A15.

10. "Behemoth on a Tear," *Business Week,* October 3, 1994, pp. 54–55.

11. Kenichi Ohmae, "The Triad World View," *Journal of Business Strategy,* Vol. 7, No. 4 (Spring 1987), pp. 8–19.

12. Theodore Levitt, "The Globalization of Markets," *Harvard Business Review* (May-June 1983), pp. 92–102.

13. Aysegul Ozsomer, Muzzafer Bodur, and S. Tamer Cavusgil, "Marketing Standardisation by Multinationals in an Emerging Market," *European Journal of Marketing,* Vol. 25, No. 12 (1991), pp. 50–63.

14. John A. Quelch and Edward J. Hoff, "Customizing Global Marketing," *Harvard Business Review* (May-June 1986), pp. 59–68.

15. "The Right Way to Go Global: An Interview with Whirlpool CEO David Whitwam," *Harvard Business Review* (March-April 1994), pp. 134–145; "A Little Washing Machine That Won't Shred a Sari," *Business Week*, June 3, 1991, p. 100.

16. Quelch and Hoff, op. cit.

17. Judie Lannon, "Developing Brand Strategies Across Borders," *Marketing and Research Today* (August 1991), pp. 160–167.

18. Guy de Jonquieres, "Just One Cornetto," *Financial Times*, October 28, 1991.

19. "Mexico's Corona Brew Wins Back Cachet Lost During the Late '80s," *Wall Street Journal*, January 19, 1993, p. B6.

20. "U.S. Firms Are Letting Saudi Market Slip," *Wall Street Journal*, January 20, 1994, p. A10.

21. "Credit-Card Firms Woo Singaporeans with Cars, Condos," *Wall Street Journal*, January 6, 1993, p. C10.

22. "Eastern Europe Poses Obstacles for Ads," *Wall Street Journal*, July 30, 1992, p. B6.

23. "It's Goo, Goo, Goo, Goo Vibrations at the Gerber Lab," *Wall Street Journal*, December 4, 1996, p. A1.

24. "Pepsi Mounts Effort to Make Potato Chips International Snack," *Wall Street Journal*, November 30, 1995, p. B10.

25. "Adapting a U.S. Car to Japanese Tastes," *Wall Street Journal*, June 26, 1995, p. B1.

26. Philip Kotler, "Global Standardization—Courting Danger," *The Journal of Consumer Marketing*, Vol. 3, No. 2 (Spring 1986), p. 14.

27. "U.S. Companies in China Find Patience, Persistence and Salesmanship Pay Off," *Wall Street Journal*, April 3, 1992, p. B1.

28. "In Pursuit of the Elusive Euroconsumer," *Wall Street Journal*, April 23, 1992, p. B1.

29. "Mexico's Corona Brew Wins Back Cachet," op. cit.

30. Clive Sims, Adam Phillips, and Trevor Richards, "Developing a Global Pricing Strategy," *Marketing and Research Today* (March 1992), pp. 3–14.

31. William Pride and O. C. Ferrell, *Marketing*, 9th ed. (Boston: Houghton Mifflin, 1995).

32. "The Korean Tiger Is Out for Blood," *Business Week*, May 31, 1993, p. 54.

33. "Coca-Cola Faces a Price War," *Wall Street Journal*, July 7, 1994, p. A1; "Cola Price War Breaks Out in Japan," *Financial Times*, July 14, 1994, p. 1.

34. "Merck cuts price of AIDS drug," *Financial Times*, March 20, 1997, p. 8.

35. "Copyrights Can't Stop Gray Markets," *Houston Chronicle*, March 10, 1998, p. 1C.

36. "Luxury Prices for U.S. Goods No Longer Pass Muster in Japan," *Wall Street Journal*, February 8, 1996, p. B1.

37. "World Marketing: Going Global or Acting Local? Five Expert Viewpoints," *Journal of Consumer Marketing* (Spring 1986), pp. 5–26.

38. Martin S. Roth and Jean B. Romeo, "Matching Product Category and Country Image Perceptions: A Framework for Managing Country-of-Origin Effects," *Journal of International Business Studies*, Vol. 23, No. 3 (Third Quarter 1992), pp. 477–498; John R. Darling and Van R. Wood, "A Longitudinal Study Comparing Perceptions of U.S. and Japanese Consumer Products in a Third/Neutral Country: Finland 1975 to 1985," *Journal of International Business Studies*, Vol. 21, No. 3 (Third Quarter 1990), pp. 427–450.

39. "In Rural India, Video Vans Sell Toothpaste and Shampoo," *Wall Street Journal*, January 10, 1996, p. B1.

40. "U.S. Cigarette Firms Are Battling Taiwan's Bid to Stiffen Ad Curbs Like Other Asian Nations," *Wall Street Journal*, May 5, 1992, p. C25.

41. General Accounting Office, *Advertising and Promoting U.S. Cigarettes in Selected Asian Countries*, Report GAO/GGD-93-38 (December 1992), p. 38f.

42. "World's Top 50 Advertising Organizations," *Advertising Age*, April 15, 1996.

43. "Signs of the times," *Financial Times*, September 22, 1994, p. 8.

44. Barbara Mueller, "Multinational Advertising: Factors Influencing the Standardised vs. Specialised Approach," *International Marketing Review*, Vol. 8, No. 1 (1991), pp. 7–18.

45. "Coke Global Image Ads," *Wall Street Journal*, April 29, 1997, p. B15.

46. "Global Ad Campaigns, After Many Missteps, Finally Pay Dividends," *Wall Street Journal*, August 27, 1992, p. A1.

47. "IBM Strives for a Single Image in Its European Ad Campaign," *Wall Street Journal*, April 16, 1991, p. B12.

48. "A universal message," *Financial Times*, May 27, 1993.

49. "This Time It's for Real," *Forbes*, August 2, 1993, pp. 58–61.

50. Barbara Mueller, "An Analysis of Information Content in Standardized vs. Specialized Multinational Advertisements,"

Journal of International Business Studies, Vol. 22, No. 1 (First Quarter 1991), pp. 23–40.

51. For a review of the issues involved, see Sudhir H. Kale and John W. Barnes, "Understanding the Domain of Cross-National Buyer-Seller Interactions," *Journal of International Business Studies*, Vol. 23, No. 1 (First Quarter 1992), pp. 101–132.

52. "Colgate-Palmolive Is Really Cleaning Up in Poland," *Business Week*, March 15, 1993, pp. 54–56.

53. "AIG Reshapes China's Insurance Industry," *Wall Street Journal*, February 9, 1996, p. A8.

54. "Amway Grows Abroad, Sending 'Ambassadors' To Spread the Word," *Wall Street Journal*, May 14, 1997, p. A1.

55. General Accounting Office, *Advertising and Promoting U.S. Cigarettes in Selected Asian Countries*, op. cit., pp. 37ff.

56. Ashley Blaker, "For global assistance, Dyal a marketer," *San Antonio Business Journal*, August 7, 1989, p. 8.

57. "SMH Leads a Revival of Swiss Watchmaking Industry," *Wall Street Journal*, January 20, 1992, p. B4.

58. Jean Downey, "Touchdown!" *Business Tokyo*, March 1992, p. 34.

59. "Doublemint in China: Distribution Isn't Double the Fun," *Wall Street Journal*, December 5, 1995, p. B1.

60. "Cosmetic Makers Offer World's Women an All-American Look with Local Twists," *Wall Street Journal*, May 8, 1995, p. B1.

61. Guy de Jonquieres, "A new red flag flies over eastern Europe," *Financial Times*, June 2, 1992, p. 19.

62. "Coca-Cola to Open Plant in Moscow," *Wall Street Journal*, January 17, 1992, p. A3.

63. Norihiko Shirouzu, "P&G's Joy Makes an Unlikely Splash in Japan," *Wall Street Journal*, December 10, 1997, pp. B1, B8, Reprinted by permission of the *Wall Street Journal*, © 1997 Dow Jones and Company, Inc. All rights reserved worldwide.

International Operations Management

Chapter Outline

The nature of international operations management

The strategic context of international operations management

Complexities of international operations management

Production management

Sourcing and vertical integration

Location decisions

International logistics and materials management

International service operations

Characteristics of international services

The role of government in international services trade

Managing service operations

After studying this chapter you should be able to:

Characterize the nature of international operations management.

Describe the sourcing and vertical integration decisions facing international production managers.

Identify and discuss the basic location decisions in international production management.

Discuss the basic issues in international logistics and materials management.

Identify and discuss the basic issues in international service operations.

BENETTON GROUP SPA, THE TRENDY ITALIAN CLOTHING CHAIN, HAS grown from a one-knitter operation to a multinational clothing empire. It started in 1955 near Venice, Italy, when Luciano Benetton convinced his sister, Giuliana, to let him sell the brightly colored sweaters she knit. The low-priced, stylish sweaters sold quickly. Their popularity convinced Luciano to sell his accordion and his younger brother's bicycle to buy his sister a knitting machine so that she could knit even faster. ▮▮ Over the next few years, Luciano and Giuliana worked together managing their rapidly growing operation. In the beginning, they rented production space in an empty warehouse and hired Giuliana's friends to help produce sweaters as well as other garments. Eventually, demand for Benetton products grew beyond what this small work force could handle. The Benetton family built a new factory near Venice and set up operations as a full-line apparel maker. ▮▮ The

Coloring the World[1]

first Benetton retail store opened in a fashionable ski resort in the Italian Alps in 1968. Others quickly followed in the leading fashion capitals of Europe. Between the early 1980s and 1993, the firm opened a new retail store somewhere in the world every day. When the Iron Curtain came down in the early 1990s, Benetton was among the first Western European retailers to set up shop in Central and Eastern Europe. It now has hundreds of stores throughout the former communist bloc, as well as stores in such far-flung locations as Turkey, Japan, and Egypt. And Benetton is opening stores in China at a frantic pace, hoping to have more than 500 outlets there by the year 2000. In total, Benetton distributes its goods through 7000 outlets in some 120 countries. Almost all Benetton outlets are independently owned; Benetton licenses its name to these shop owners, who in turn must carry only Benetton goods. While Benetton provides advertising and marketing support for its licensees, the shop owners provide the capital necessary to acquire their stores, fixtures, and inventory. ▮▮ Benetton's greatest problem has been cracking the U.S. market, where fashion is more faddish than in Europe, and retail competition from such rivals as The Gap and The Limited is more fierce. Although there were almost 1000 Benetton stores in the United States in the mid-1980s, today that number has shrunk considerably. Benetton is estimated to have lost some $10 to $15 million in the U.S. market in 1996, although the company hopes that its U.S. operations will return to profitability quickly. But in Europe, Benetton remains a leading force in the fashion industry. Using the profits supplied by its clothing goods empire, the Benetton Group has expanded into a variety of other areas, including sporting goods, venture capital, and Formula 1 racing. ▮▮ What are the keys to Benetton's success? Italian styling and reasonable prices are certainly two of the main ones. Reliance on licensees to distribute its apparel has cut

Benetton's capital costs and allowed it to benefit from the licensees' superior knowledge of the needs and habits of local customers. But it is Benetton's operations management that has enabled it to stay a world-class competitor in the fashion industry. Benetton has a commitment to achieving quality and meeting customer needs through its manufacturing and distribution systems. Design and production are centralized in Italy so that the firm can maintain tight control over manufacturing costs, quality, and related considerations. ▮▮ The starting point in the Benetton system involves information technology. Each retail transaction in a Benetton store is electronically coded and transmitted to a central information-processing center in Italy. Managers there can constantly track which products are selling where. In particular, they can track three vital pieces of information that are critical to success in any retailing operation: absolute sales levels, sales trends and patterns, and inventory distributions. This information can also be analyzed for individual stores, for clusters of stores in a given city or region, by country, or on a global basis. ▮▮ Managers use this sales information to plan and adjust production activity. Whenever a new sweater or other garment is designed, its creators try to plan for possible variations and alterations. For example, a new shirt will be designed so that it can be produced with short, mid-length, or full-length sleeves and with or without a collar. Early production runs and shipments will include all six possible styles. But a portion of those runs will be devoted to making shirt bodies without sleeves or collars. As sales figures begin to arrive, managers can very quickly tailor production adjustments to these inventoried shirt bodies to finish them out according to customer demand. If shirts with mid-length sleeves and a collar sell much faster than do other variations, more of this type of shirt can quickly be finished and shipped to stores. The same approach is also used for colors. If blue shirts sell twice as quickly as red ones, managers can easily tilt production toward finishing more blue shirts and fewer red shirts. ▮▮ Bar codes and scanners are used throughout Benetton factories and warehouses. Using fully networked computer workstations, managers can plan and initiate production runs based on style and color demand. Partially completed products are pulled from shelves by robots and placed on final production lines. As those products are finished out, bar codes are attached and they are automatically wrapped, packaged, and shipped to those stores that need inventory replenishment. Through the use of this sophisticated system, Benetton can fill an order from any of its 7000 stores spread throughout the globe in thirteen to twenty-seven days. ▮▮▮▮▮

Benetton has flourished for various reasons. Among them are its abilities to track demand for each of its various products and then to take the appropriate steps to satisfy that demand promptly and efficiently. By centralizing its design and manufacturing systems in its home country of Italy, Benetton is able to maintain tight control over those and related functions. By building flexibility into design, production, and distribution, the firm is able to get new inventory to its stores around the world much faster than most of its competitors can. The basis for planning and implementing these activities is operations management.

Some firms, such as Shell, Exxon, and British Petroleum, are concerned with physically transforming natural resources into various products through complex refining processes. Others, such as Compaq, Sony, and Philips, purchase completed component parts from suppliers and then assemble those into electronics products. Still others, such as Air France and JAL, use a global travel network to provide transportation services to people. Regardless of a firm's product, however, the goal of its international operations managers is to design, create, and distribute goods or services that meet the needs and wants of customers worldwide—and to do so profitably.[2]

The Nature of International Operations Management

Operations management is the set of activities an organization uses to transform different kinds of inputs (materials, labor, and so on) into final goods and services. **International operations management** refers to the transformation-related activities of an international firm. Figure 17.1 illustrates the international operations management process. As shown, a firm's strategic context provides a necessary backdrop against which it develops and then manages its operations functions. Flowing directly from the strategic context is the question of standardized versus customized production. The positioning of a firm along this continuum, in turn, helps dictate the appropriate strategies and tactics for other parts of the operations management process. The next part of international operations management is the activities and processes connected with the acquisition of the resources the firm needs to produce the goods or services it intends to sell. Location decisions—where to build factories and other facilities—are also important. Finally, international operations managers are concerned with logistics and materials management—the efficient movement of materials into, within, and out of the firm. We use this framework to organize this chapter's discussion of international operations management.

Operations management is closely linked with both quality and productivity. (Chapter 15 described how product quality and productivity have become two key elements in international competitiveness.) A firm's operations management system largely determines how inputs are transformed into goods or services. Properly designed and managed operating systems and procedures play a major role in determining product quality and productivity. For example, Benetton is able to squeeze extra measures of productivity from its distribution centers because of its highly efficient and flexible design. Conversely, poorly designed operating systems are a major cause of poor quality and lower productivity. They promote inefficiency and can contribute in various ways to higher costs and suboptimal profit performance, as "Going Global" indicates.[3]

GOING GLOBAL

"Where's the Factory? This Is a Warehouse."

While Porsche may be a car enthusiast's dream, in the early 1990s it was a production manager's nightmare. In 1991 it took 120 hours of very expensive German labor to build a single Porsche 911. In contrast, Japanese automakers routinely use less than thirty hours of labor to build their high-quality vehicles. The rising value of the mark and the growing Japanese share of the high end of the auto market were threatening the very existence of the company. By 1993, the company was near death—not because its cars weren't any good; they were just too expensive to build.

In desperation, the company's chairman, Wendelin Wiedeking, swallowed his pride and called in a team of Japanese auto consultants. Upon entering Porsche's main assembly plant for the first time and observing bins full of parts reaching to the ceiling, the Japanese consultants asked, "Where's the factory? This is a warehouse." The first task the consultants tackled was controlling Porsche's inventory. To send the message that things had to change, they insisted that Wiedeking himself take a circular saw and decapitate the 10-foot-tall shelves, crammed with parts, that circled the assembly line. They were appalled to learn that Porsche obtained its parts from 950 separate suppliers. Keeping track of shipments from this flock of vendors and ensuring their quality overburdened the purchasing staff. Thirty percent of the parts shipments were in error, and one fifth were delivered at least three days late. Worse, the rate of defective parts was too high, so Porsche spent too much time and energy rebuilding cars to ensure that they met the company's exacting standards. By reorganizing the parts operation—cutting the number of suppliers by two thirds, working with them to improve product quality, designing parts to ease the assembly process, and requiring just-in-time deliveries—Porsche has been able to cut the hours needed to build its autos. To further improve productivity, the company boosted its investment in equipment, spending $150 million on new tools. It also boosted its investment in people, from an appalling 12 minutes of annual training per employee in 1993 to 45 to 50 hours per employee in 1996, to ensure that all its workers understood the company's commitment to quality and efficiency. The company also took an important symbolic step, changing the award for the best employee idea of the year: instead of a Harley-Davidson motorcycle, the winning employee gets a year's use of a Porsche 911.

These efforts have paid off. By 1996, it took only 70 hours to build a Porsche 911, and the company finally returned to profitability after losing $270 million from 1992 to 1995. By incorporating these changes in the production line for its newest car, the Boxster, the company estimates this roadster will only require 45 hours of labor to build, allowing the company to sell the car for about $40,000, roughly half of what they were forced to charge for a 911.

Sources: "Porche calls 911, Boxster Japanese to the rescue," *USA Today*, April 8, 1997, p. 1B; "Here come the Germans again," *Forbes*, November 18, 1996, p. 218.

Successful firms recognize that to survive they must continually adapt and respond to changes in their environments. These include technological advancements, regional and/or local changes in consumer tastes and preferences, shifting pricing levels, and the actions of their competitors in a constantly changing global arena. An operations management system that is properly designed can help managers respond more effectively to these changes. For example, automakers used to shut down for an entire month when they changed equipment to produce a new model or make of automobile. Today, the most efficient automakers can enact that same shift in a matter of hours, thereby losing only a small amount of production time. This capability, in turn, makes it easier and less costly for them to

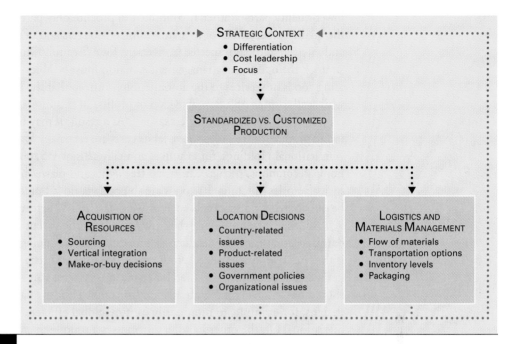

FIGURE 17.1

**The International
Operations
Management
Process**

change models or shift production from a low-profit line to a high-profit line. And as already noted, Benetton uses its operating systems to make timely adjustments to sales patterns and consumer preferences. The result is a competitive advantage over many of the firm's rivals around the world.

The Strategic Context of International Operations Management

The central role of operations management is to create the potential for achieving superior value for the firm. That is, operations management is a value-added activity intended to create or add new value to the organization's inputs in ways that directly impact outputs. If operations management can take $2 worth of inputs and create $10 worth of goods or services from them, it has created considerable value. But if it requires $9 worth of inputs to create the same $10 worth of goods or services, it has created very little value.

From Fig. 17.1 you can see that international operations management must be closely aligned with a firm's business strategy. Indeed, the business strategy set by top managers both at the corporate and regional levels of a firm will affect all facets of the planning and implementation of operations management activities, such as sourcing strategies, location decisions, facilities design, and logistics management.[4] For example, for a firm pursuing a differentiation strategy, the operations management function must be able to create goods or services that are clearly different from those of its competitors. For a firm like Porsche that wants to compete on the basis of product performance and status, costs will be less important than product quality and design. As a result, production facilities may need to be located where there is a skilled labor force, even if the cost of employing that labor is relatively high.[5] For example, despite its problems discussed in "Going Global," Porsche never considered shifting its production from Stuttgart to a lower labor-cost locale, for its highly skilled work force is vital to producing its high-quality cars. And while it recognized that its parts operation needed revamping, the company never considered using lower-quality parts. Rather, it continued to procure only parts capable of meeting the quality expectations of its status-conscious buyers and of performing durably and safely at autobahn speeds. Conversely, for a firm following a cost leadership strategy, the operations management function must be able to shave the costs of creating goods or services to the absolute minimum so that the firm can lower its prices while still earning an acceptable level of profits. In this case, cost and price issues are central, while quality may be less critical. As a result, it may be highly appropriate to locate production facilities where labor costs are especially low. Hong Kong's Roly International Holdings, for example, annually sells over $200 million of low-priced home decorations, such as Christmas tree lights and plaster bird baths, churned out by its factories in China. Its goods are shipped via slow, but low-cost, cargo ships to be distributed by discounters such as Wal-Mart and Walgreens.[6]

Another factor affecting the firm's choices is the extent to which it uses standardized or customized production processes and technologies. On the one hand, if the firm uses standardized production processes and technologies in every market where it does business, then its operations systems can—and almost certainly should be—globally integrated. Such firms may choose to adopt global product designs, for example, to more easily capture global efficiencies generated by their operations. On the other hand, if a firm uses a unique operations system in each market where it does business, such global integration is not only unnecessary but also likely to be impossible. Often such firms adopt a global area design to promote responsiveness of their operations managers to local conditions.

For example, Toyota uses a standardized operations management strategy in that it makes the same cars using the same manufacturing processes around the world. Thus, it can share technology between plants and freely ship component parts between factories in different countries. But Nestlé tailors its mix of products, as well as their ingredients and packaging, across markets. Thus, while there may be some sharing of production technology, Nestlé tends to operate each production facility as more of a self-contained unit.

Complexities of International Operations Management

International operations management presents one of the most complex and challenging set of tasks managers face today. The basic complexities inherent in operations management stem from the production problem itself—where and how to produce various goods and services. Operations managers typically must decide important and complex issues in three areas:

1 *Resources.* Managers must decide where and how to obtain the resources the firm needs to produce its products. Key decisions relate to sourcing and vertical integration.

2 *Location.* Managers must decide where to build administrative facilities, sales offices, and plants, how to design them, and so on.

3 *Logistics.* Managers must decide on modes of transportation and methods of inventory control.

All firms, whether domestic or international, must address these issues. However, resolving them is far more complicated for international firms. A domestic manufacturer may deal with only local suppliers, be subject to one set of government regulations, compete in a relatively homogeneous market, have access to an integrated transportation network, and ship its goods relatively short distances. An international manufacturer, in contrast, is likely to deal with suppliers from different countries and confront different government regulations wherever it does business, as well as very heterogeneous markets, disparate transportation facilities and networks, and relatively long distances. International operations managers must choose the countries in which to locate production facilities, taking into account factors such as costs, tax laws, resource availability, and marketing considerations. They also must consider potential exchange-rate movements and noneconomic factors such as government regulations, political risk, and predictability of a country's legal system. Further, they must consider the impact of facilities' locations on the firm's ability to respond to changes in customer tastes and preferences. Finally, they must factor in logistical problems. Just as long supply lines doomed Napoleon's invasion of Russia, locating factories far from one's suppliers may impede timely access to resources and materials.

Production Management

While some similarities exist between creating goods and creating services for international markets, there are also major fundamental differences. Operations management decisions, processes, and issues that involve the creation of tangible goods are called **production management**, and those involving the creation of intangible services are called **service operations management**. This section focuses on production management; service operations management is addressed later in the chapter.

Manufacturing involves the creation of goods by transforming raw materials and component parts in combination with capital, labor, and technology. Some examples of manufacturing activities are Sony's production of stereo equipment, BMW's production of automobiles, and Bridgestone's production of tires. BMW, for example, takes thousands of component parts, ranging from sheet metal to engine parts to upholstery to rubber molding, and combines them to make different types of automobiles.

Most successful manufacturers use many sophisticated techniques to produce high-quality goods efficiently. These techniques are best covered in more advanced and specialized production management courses, so we focus here on three important dimensions of international production management: international sourcing, international facilities location, and international logistics.

Sourcing and Vertical Integration

Because the production of most manufactured goods requires a variety of raw materials, parts, and other resources, the first issue an international production manager faces is deciding how to acquire those inputs.[7] **Sourcing** is the set of processes and steps a firm uses to acquire the various resources it needs to create its own products (some managers use the term *procuring* instead of *sourcing*).[8] Sourcing clearly affects product cost, product quality, and internal demands for capital. Because of these impacts, most international firms approach sourcing as a strategic issue to be carefully planned and implemented by top management.[9]

The first step in developing a sourcing strategy is to determine the appropriate degree of vertical integration.[10] **Vertical integration** is the extent to which a firm either provides its own resources or obtains them from other sources. At one extreme, firms that practice relatively high levels of vertical integration are engaged in every step of the operations management process as goods are developed, transformed, packaged, and sold to customers. Various units within the firm can be seen as suppliers to other units within the firm, which in turn can be viewed as the customers of the supplying units. At the other extreme, firms that have little vertical integration are involved in only one step or just a few steps in the production chain. They may buy their inputs and component parts from other suppliers, perform one operation or transformation, and then sell their outputs to other firms or consumers.[11]

British Petroleum is an excellent example of a vertically integrated international business. One unit of the firm is engaged in the worldwide exploration for natural gas and crude oil. After oil is discovered, another unit is responsible for its extraction. The oil is then transported through company-owned pipelines and on company-owned tanker ships to company-owned refineries. Those refineries transform the crude oil into gasoline, processed petroleum, and other petroleum-based fuels. Next, the fuel is transported by company-owned trucks to company-owned service stations and convenience stores, where it is sold to individual consumers. Thus British Petroleum's exploration and extraction business supplies its pipeline business, which supplies its refinery business, which supplies its retailing business. While the firm occasionally uses third-party suppliers and may sometimes sell its products to other firms, it primarily seeks to maintain an unbroken and efficient chain of vertically integrated operations from the beginning of the production process to the final sale of the product to individual consumers.[12]

In contrast, Heineken NV, the world's second-largest beer producer, practices relatively little vertical integration. The firm buys the grains and chemicals it needs to brew beer from local farmers and agricultural cooperatives. From various container suppliers it buys the bottles, labels, and cartons it uses to package its beers.

Logistics and materials management are important for international business. The Alaskan Pipeline provides a case in point. The pipeline was undertaken amid controversy regarding its negative environmental impact and the size of the necessary financial investment. The pipeline, however, has made the transport of petroleum from isolated regions of Alaska much more efficient and cost-effective.

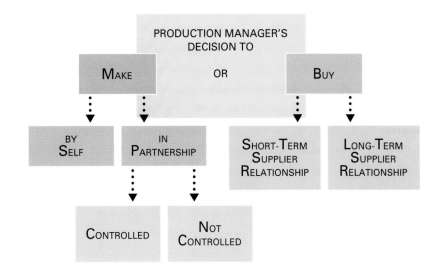

After brewing and bottling its beers, Heineken sells them to distributors, which subsequently resell them to retailers, which, in turn, resell them to consumers.

The extent of a firm's vertical integration is the result of a series of sourcing decisions made by production managers.[13] In deciding how to acquire the components necessary to manufacture a firm's products, its production managers have two choices: the firm can make the inputs itself, or it can buy them from outside suppliers. This choice is called the **make-or-buy decision**. The basic make-or-buy options available to an international firm are shown in Fig. 17.2. Note, in particular, that the make-or-buy decision carries with it other decisions as well. For example, a decision to buy rather than make dictates the need to choose between long-term and short-term supplier relationships. A decision to make rather than buy leaves open the option of making by self or making in partnership with others. And if partnership is the choice, yet another decision relates to the degree of control the firm wants to have.

The make-or-buy decision can be influenced by a firm's size, scope of operations, and technological expertise and by the nature of its product. For example, because larger firms are better able to benefit from economies of scale in the production of inputs, larger automakers such as GM and Fiat are more likely to make their parts themselves, while smaller ones such as Saab or BMW are more likely to buy them from outside suppliers. Components embodying relatively new technologies, such as satellite navigation systems and hands-free cellular telephones, are more likely to be purchased from outside suppliers, while more standardized components, such as conventional braking systems and AM/FM automotive radios, are more likely to be produced in-house. At other times, the make-or-buy decision will depend on existing investments in technology and manufacturing facilities. For example, personal computer manufacturers such as Dell and IBM must decide whether they want to make or buy microprocessors, memory chips, disk drives, motherboards, and power supplies. Because of its extensive manufacturing expertise with mainframe computers, IBM is more likely to make a PC component in-house, while Dell is more likely to rely heavily on outside suppliers.

All else being equal, a firm will choose to make or buy simply on the basis of whether it can obtain the resource cheaper by making it internally or by buying it

FIGURE 17.3

Competitive Advantage versus Strategic Vulnerability in the Make-or-Buy Decision

Source: Reprinted from "Strategic Outsourcing" by James Brian Quinn and Frederick G. Hilmer, *Sloan Management Review*, Summer 1994, p. 48, by permission of the publisher. Copyright 1994 by the Sloan Management Review Association. All rights reserved.

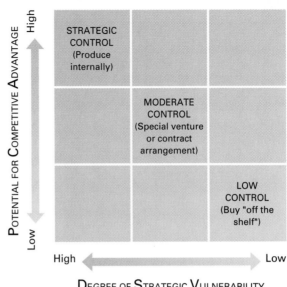

from an external supplier. But since "all else being equal" seldom actually occurs, strategic issues must also be considered. Figure 17.3 highlights the need to balance competitive advantage against strategic vulnerability when resolving the make-or-buy decision. For example, if a high potential for competitive advantage exists along with a high degree of strategic vulnerability, the firm is likely to maintain strategic control by producing internally. But if the potential for competitive advantage and the degree of strategic vulnerability are both low, the firm will need less control and will therefore be more likely to buy "off the shelf." Finally, when intermediate potential for competitive advantage and moderate degree of strategic vulnerability call for moderate control, special ventures or contract arrangements may be most appropriate.

In addition to these strategic considerations, other factors may play a role with respect to the make-or-buy decision. In particular, international firms typically must make trade-offs between costs and control, risk, investment, and flexibility.

Control. Making a component has the advantage of increasing the firm's control over product quality, delivery schedules, design changes, and costs. A firm that buys from external suppliers may become overly dependent on those suppliers. If a given supplier goes out of business, raises its prices, or produces poor-quality materials, the firm will lose its source of inputs, see its costs increase, or experience its own quality-related problems.

Another issue of control relates to the ability to enforce contracts with outside suppliers. Enforcing contracts with foreign suppliers may be difficult or costly because of differences in national legal systems. For example, if laws protecting intellectual property of foreigners are weak in a certain country, entertainment firms such as Sony Records and Warner Brothers may be unwilling to license firms in that country to duplicate their CDs and videotapes. When such considerations are important, a firm may prefer to make rather than buy necessary inputs. One strength of the Japanese keiretsu system, for example, is its ability to reduce the problem of enforcing contracts between a firm and its suppliers. Cross-owner-

GOING GLOBAL

Suppliers: Friend or Foe?

Relations between manufacturers and their suppliers can be vitally important to each. Manufacturers depend on their suppliers to provide them with high-quality parts and supplies on a timely basis, while suppliers depend on their manufacturing customers for revenue. But the nature of this relationship often varies between countries. Consider, for example, two examples from the auto industry, one in the United States and the other in Japan.

When Ford recently redesigned and re-engineered its popular Taurus automobile, the firm intended to copy the Japanese approach to managing supplier relations. Ford wanted its suppliers to make substantive commitments to delivering parts at low costs and to work with the company toward their mutual best interests. However, senior Ford managers in charge of the Taurus project had a fundamental distrust of suppliers, viewing them as antagonists rather than as partners. This attitude, in turn, crept into many different areas of how Ford treated its suppliers. The result was strained relations and each party sticking strictly to what it was contractually bound to do—and being unwilling to do anything more.

In contrast, Toyota has thrived in the Japanese keiretsu system. The level of trust created by its cooperative relationships with its suppliers has helped it become the world's most efficient automobile manufacturer and to respond quickly to unexpected challenges. For example, in 1997 a fire destroyed the factory of Aisin Seiki Co., the sole supplier to Toyota of a brake valve used in many of its cars. Since Toyota, like most Japanese manufacturers, uses a just-in-time inventory system, it had only four hours' worth of parts on hand. Its other suppliers, however, quickly recognized that Toyota, as well as their own companies, of course, would suffer immeasurably if the auto giant were shut down too long.

Consequently, these other suppliers went to heroic efforts to get Toyota back up and running. For example, one prevailed on one of its own suppliers, a sewing-machine maker, to retool itself to make some of the brake valves. All told, 36 suppliers and more than 150 additional subcontractors had over 50 separate lines making the brake valves for Toyota within a matter of days. As a result, rather than being out of commission for the several weeks experts originally predicted, Toyota was up and running again in less than five days.

Sources: "Toyota's Fast Rebound After Fire at Supplier Shows Why It Is Tough," *Wall Street Journal*, May 8, 1997, pp. A1, A6; "Toyota Factories in Japan Grind to a Halt," *Wall Street Journal*, February 4, 1997, p. A14; Mary Walton, "When Your Partner Fails You …," *Fortune*, May 26, 1997, pp. 151–154.

ship of shares among keiretsu members, which strengthens trust among members, increases their willingness to enter into long-term contracts and to share intellectual property with each other.[14] "Going Global" provides another illustration of the importance of good supplier relations.

By making rather than buying, the firm may also be able to develop new business opportunities. British Petroleum, for example, has a chemical division that relies in part on petroleum-based ingredients for the production of certain chemical products. This chemical unit has a relatively dependable and cooperative "built-in" supplier for its petroleum needs. This arrangement allows it to more effectively address future price, availability, and delivery schedule questions as it develops its strategic and operational plans.

Risk. Buying a component from an external supplier has the advantage of reducing the firm's financial and operating risks. British Petroleum, for example, has risk associated with its drilling platforms, pipelines, and every other stage in its production chain. If the firm simply bought crude oil from other firms, it would not have to worry about drilling platform injuries or equipment failure because those risks would be assumed by the supplier. It would also not have to worry about earning an adequate rate of return on those assets. Equally important, the firm that buys rather than makes can reduce its political risk in a host country. For example, British Petroleum runs the risk that politicians elected on anti-British or antiforeigner platforms in the United States, Nigeria, Colombia, or elsewhere may some day expropriate its refineries. Indeed, this did happen in 1951, when Iran's rulers seized a major British Petroleum operation in that country.

Investments in Facilities, Technology, and People. Buying from others lowers the firm's level of investment. By not having to build a new factory or learn a new technology, a firm can free up capital for other productive uses. Benetton, for example, primarily uses licensees to retail its goods, allowing the firm to concentrate on what it does best, manufacturing. Honda provides another example of this approach. As production at Honda's U.S. manufacturing plant in Ohio grew, the firm needed an increased supply of mirrors for its cars. It convinced a local supplier, Donnelly Corp., to build a new factory to assemble mirrors for its automobiles. Thus Honda obtained a convenient and dependable supplier without having to invest its own money in building a mirror factory.[15] Of course, by buying rather than making the mirrors, Honda surrendered the profits of mirror manufacturing to Donnelly.

Buying from others also reduces a firm's training costs and expertise requirements. By contracting with Donnelly, Honda avoided having to develop expertise in designing, manufacturing, and marketing automobile mirrors. British Petroleum, in contrast, needs a wide range of expertise and talent among the ranks of its managers to take full advantage of its highly vertically integrated global operations.

Flexibility. A firm that buys rather than makes retains the flexibility to change suppliers as circumstances dictate. This is particularly helpful in cases in which technology is rapidly evolving or delivered costs can change as a result of inflation or exchange-rate fluctuations. Most personal computer manufacturers, for example, have chosen to buy disk drives, CD-ROM units, and microprocessors from outside suppliers. By so doing, they avoid the risk of product obsolescence and the large R&D expenditures needed to stay on the cutting edge of each of the technologies embedded in the component parts of personal computers. Similarly, Dallas's Peerless Manufacturing buys components from numerous European subcontractors that produce filters and separators. Peerless can shift its sourcing around the Continent depending on currency fluctuations and flows of orders from its customers.[16]

Of course, sometimes a firm must make trade-offs that reduce flexibility. In the case of Honda and Donnelly, Donnelly was concerned that it would be at Honda's mercy once it invested in the new mirror factory. To induce Donnelly to agree to build the new factory, the automaker had to assure Donnelly managers that the firm would get all of Honda's mirror business for at least ten years. By so doing, Honda reduced its capital investment but sacrificed the flexibility of changing suppliers during the ten-year period. This example also illustrates a major trend in buyer-supplier relationships. Not long ago, managers assumed that it was useful to use a variety of suppliers in order to avoid becoming too dependent on a single one. A drawback of this approach, however, is the complexity associated with dealing with a large network of suppliers, especially if that network is global. More recently, some firms have come to realize that by engaging in exclusive or semi-exclusive long-term relationships with fewer suppliers, they can better benefit from these suppliers' experience and product knowledge. In the automobile industry many manufacturers are relying on so-called "first tier" suppliers such as Johnson Controls or Magna International to work with their engineers to design component systems, such as seating systems or dashboard assemblies, for new vehicles. For example, in designing its LH models, Chrysler worked closely with its first-tier suppliers, enabling it to cut its design staff by two thirds and its expected development time by 28 percent. Its suppliers offered nearly 4000 manufacturing and design suggestions, saving Chrysler an additional $156 million.[17] And companies are saving additional monies by relying on the first-tier suppliers to manage and monitor the acquisition of parts and subassemblies from second-tier suppliers.

Location Decisions

An international firm that chooses to make rather than buy inputs faces another decision: where should it locate its production facilities? In reaching a location decision, the firm must consider country-related issues, product-related issues, government policies, and organizational issues.

Country-Related Issues. Several features of countries can influence the decision about where to locate an international facility. Chief among these are resource availability and cost, infrastructure, and country-of-origin marketing effects.

Resource availability and cost constitute a primary determinant of whether an individual country is a suitable location for a facility. As suggested by the classical trade theories and the Heckscher-Ohlin theory (see Chapter 3), countries that enjoy large, low-cost endowments of a factor of production will attract firms needing that factor of production. For example, China has attracted toy, footwear, and textile manufacturers eager to take advantage of its vast army of low-cost labor. And British Petroleum has little choice but to situate drilling platforms where crude oil reserves are located.

Infrastructure also affects the location of production facilities. Most facilities require at least some minimal level of infrastructural support. To build a facility requires construction materials and equipment as well as materials suppliers and construction contractors. More important, electrical, water, transportation, telephone, and other services are necessary to utilize the facility productively. And access to medical care, education, adequate housing, entertainment, and other related services are almost certain to be important for the employees and managers who will work at the facility and their families.

Country-of-origin effects may also play a role in locating a facility. Certain countries have "brand images" that affect product marketing. For example, Japan has a reputation for manufacturing high-quality products, while Italy is often credited with stylishly designed ones. In one interesting experiment, a researcher found that consumer preference for Timex watches fell by only 6 percent when interviewees were told the watches were made in Pakistan rather than Germany. However, when consumers were confronted with an unfamiliar brand called "Tempomax," their willingness to buy the watches fell by 74 percent when they were told the watches were made in Pakistan instead of Germany. All else being equal, it obviously is easier to sell watches made in Germany than ones made in Pakistan to consumers in industrialized countries, particularly if the product is not backed by a strong brand name. Firms must take into account these country-of-origin effects in deciding where to site a production facility. A firm interested in marketing its product as high-quality might choose to locate in Japan or Germany rather than in Pakistan or Indonesia, while a firm competing on the basis of low costs and prices might make the opposite choice.[18]

Product-Related Issues. Product-related characteristics may also influence the location decision. Among the more important of these are the product's value-to-weight ratio, the required production technology, and the importance of customer feedback.[19]

The product's value-to-weight ratio affects the importance of transportation costs in the product's delivered price. Goods with low value-to-weight ratios, such as iron ore, cement, coal, bulk chemicals, and raw sugar and other agricultural goods, tend to be produced in multiple locations in order to minimize transportation costs. Conversely, goods with high value-to-weight ratios, such as microprocessors or diamonds, can be produced in a single location or handful of locations without loss of competitiveness. For example, transportation costs are a trivial part of the cost of producing and distributing Intel's Pentium II chips, so Intel is free to locate the chips' production on the basis of nontransportation factors.

The production technology used to manufacture the good may also affect facility location. A firm must compare its expected product sales with the efficient size of a facility in the industry. If a firm's sales are large relative to an efficient-sized facility, the firm is likely to operate many facilities in various locations. If its sales are small relative to an efficient-sized facility, it will probably utilize only one plant. For example, the minimum efficient size of a petroleum refinery is about 200,000 barrels per day. Thus British Petroleum, which can produce up to 5 million barrels per day, has chosen to operate 17 refineries located in such countries as the United Kingdom, Spain, and Colombia.

The relative importance of customer feedback may also influence the location decision. Products for which firms desire quick customer feedback are often produced close to the point of final sale. For example, a general rule of thumb in the U.S. apparel industry is that, all else being equal, the more fashionable the item, the more likely it is that its production will occur near or in the United States so that the manufacturer can quickly respond to market trends. At the beginning of each selling season, women's sportswear buyers for Macy's, Nordstrom's, and Dillards carefully monitor which new items are hot sellers. They quickly reorder the hot items and mercilessly dump goods that fashion-conscious shoppers ignore. Because the selling season for such goods may last only two or three months—and no one can predict with certainty what the fashion fanatics will buy—apparel manufacturers in the United States are better able to respond to the sportswear buyers' demands than are producers in Taiwan or Indonesia. Conversely, low-fashion items are more likely to be produced outside the United States to take advantage of lower production costs. For example, J.C. Penney can predict with great certainty how many athletic socks and white cotton briefs it will sell each summer. And if for some reason it overestimates summer sales of these items, it can continue to sell them in the fall. Accordingly, Penney's menswear buyers often enter into long-term contracts with Asian knitting mills. In this case, cost is a more important variable than speed or flexibility of delivery.

Government Policies. Government policies may also play a role in the location decision. Especially important are the stability of the political process, national trade policies, economic development incentives, and the existence of foreign trade zones.

The stability of the political process within a country can clearly affect the desirability of locating a factory there. Firms like to know what the rules of the game are so that they can make knowledgeable investment, production, and staffing decisions. A government that alters fiscal, monetary, and regulatory policies seemingly on whim and without consulting the business community raises the risk and uncertainty of operating in a country. Unforeseen changes in taxation policy, exchange rates, inflation, and labor laws are particularly troublesome to international firms.

National trade policies may also affect the location decision. To serve its customers, a firm may be forced to locate a facility within a country that has high tariff walls and other trade barriers. For example, Toyota, Nissan, and Mazda built factories in the United States to evade a VER imposed by the Japanese government to limit the exports of Japanese-built automobiles to the United States. Similarly, Compaq Computer located a personal computer manufacturing facility in Sao Paulo to avoid Brazilian import taxes.[20]

Economic development incentives may influence the location decision. Communities eager to create jobs and add to the local tax base often seek to attract new factories by offering international firms inexpensive land, highway improvements, job training programs, and discounted water and electric rates. For example, the government of France offered to sell the Walt Disney Company suburban land on which to build Disneyland Paris at a greatly discounted rate. And Tuscaloosa, Alabama, outbid dozens of North American cities for a new Mercedes-Benz factory in 1993, offering the firm a multimillion-dollar package of incentives.[21]

An international firm may also choose a site based on the existence of a foreign trade zone (FTZ). As discussed in Chapter 6, an FTZ is a specially designated and controlled geographical area in which imported or exported goods receive preferential tariff treatment. A country may establish FTZs near its major ports of entry and/or major production centers. It then allows international firms to import products into those zones duty-free for specified purposes, sometimes with express limitations, for example, about allowable types and value of products and the kind of work that may be performed.

A firm may decide to locate in a particular area because the existence of an FTZ gives it greater flexibility regarding importing or exporting and creates avenues for lowering costs.[22] For example, the Port of Houston operates a large FTZ used primarily for storage by non-U.S. automakers. Toyota and Nissan can ship all their automobiles bound for sale in the southern part of North America to Houston, where they are stored without any payment of import tariffs being required. Only when specific automobiles are removed from the zone and shipped to dealerships must the manufacturers pay the duty. However, some automobiles are eventually shipped to Mexico or various Caribbean countries. The firms then pay only whatever duty those countries levy and avoid payment of U.S. duties altogether.

Costs can be lowered through the creative use of FTZs. For example, a firm may be able to import component parts, supplement them with other component parts obtained locally, and assemble them all into finished goods. The duty paid on the imported components incorporated into the products assembled in the FTZ may be lower than the duty imposed on imported components in general. For this reason, most automobiles produced in the United States are assembled in FTZs. Further, some duties are calculated on the basis of the good's total weight, including packaging. So a firm may lower its duties by bringing goods into the FTZ in lightweight, inexpensive packaging, and then, after duties have been paid, repackaging them with heavier, more substantial materials obtained locally.

Organizational Issues. An international firm's business strategy and its organizational structure may also affect the location decision. Inventory management policies are also important considerations.

A firm's business strategy may affect its location decisions in various ways. A firm that adopts a price leadership strategy must seek out low-cost locations, while one that focuses on product quality must locate facilities in areas that have adequate skilled labor and managerial talent. A firm may choose to concentrate production geographically in order to better meet organizational goals. Benetton does this with its Italian production facilities so as to better control product design and quality. Similarly, Boeing has concentrated its final aircraft assembly operations in the Seattle area in order to take advantage of the skilled machinist and engineering talent in the area. Other firms find that strategic goals can be better met by dispersing facilities in various foreign locations. Most electronics firms take this approach. For example, Intel has manufacturing plants in the United States, Ireland, Puerto Rico, Israel, Malaysia, and the Philippines to take advantage of the relatively low-cost resources available in each of these markets. Further, shipping the firm's computer chips to distant markets from those manufacturing facilities is relatively easy and inexpensive. Multiple production facilities also protect a firm against exchange-rate fluctuations. FMC, for example, often shifts orders for its food-packaging machinery from plants in Chicago to plants in Italy or vice versa, depending on the relative values of the dollar and the lira.

A firm's organizational structure also influences the location of its factories. For example, as noted in Chapter 13, adoption of a global area structure decentralizes authority to area managers. These managers, seeking to maintain control over their area, are likely to favor siting factories within their area to produce goods sold within the area. For example, until 1994 Ford was structured into three area groups: North America, Europe, and Asia Pacific. The firm exported few automobiles from these regions; rather, each area focused on producing automobiles to meet the needs of consumers in its area. (Ford abandoned this organizational structure in 1994, believing that it hindered its ability to truly globalize its automobile production.[23]) Conversely, a firm having a global product structure will locate factories anywhere in the world in order to meet its cost and quality performance goals.

A firm's inventory management policies are affected by plant location decisions. Inventory management is a complex task all operations managers must confront. They must balance the costs of maintaining inventory against the costs of running out of materials and/or finished goods. The costs of maintaining inventory include those associated with storage (operating a warehouse, for example), spoilage and loss (some stored inventory gets ruined, damaged, or stolen), and opportunity costs (an investment in inventory cannot be put to other business uses).

Factory location affects the level of inventory that firms must hold because of the distances and transit times involved in shipping goods. For example, if Wal-Mart purchases private-label televisions for its U.S. stores from a Taiwanese factory, its inventory levels will be higher than if it purchases them from a Mexican factory. Compaq Computer has chosen to locate its primary assembly plants in Houston, Scotland, Singapore, and Brazil in order to improve service to its North American, European, Asian, and South American customers, respectively, while cutting overall inventory levels.

Factory location becomes particularly critical when the popular just-in-time (JIT) inventory management system is adopted. With this approach a firm's suppliers deliver their products directly to the firm's manufacturing center, usually in frequent small shipments, just as they are needed for production. The JIT system requires careful coordination between a firm and its internal and external suppliers. Often parts suppliers locate their facilities near the factories of their major customers in order to meet the JIT requirements of their customers. For example, many car-part makers, such as Toyota Machine Works, TRW Steering Systems, Eagle-Picher, and Orbseal, have located in Wales or the West Midlands region of England to better serve major customers like Jaguar and BMW's Range Rover division.[24] Parts manufacturers have also gravitated to the midwestern United States, Ontario, Brazil, Thailand, and other areas where auto assembly plants are clustered.

International Logistics and Materials Management

Regardless of the location of an international firm's factories, its operations managers must address issues involving international logistics.[25] **International logistics** is the managing of the flow of materials, parts, supplies, and other resources from suppliers to the firm; materials, parts, supplies, and other resources within and between units of the firm itself; and finished products, services, and goods from the firm to customers.[26]

The first two sets of activities are usually called **materials management**, while the third is often called physical distribution, or, more simply, distribution. Recall that we discussed distribution issues in Chapter 16 because they are often managed as a part of the firm's marketing function. Thus our focus here is on the materials management area of logistics. The role of logistics is particularly important for firms that have developed integrated, but geographically dispersed, manufacturing and distribution networks where parts may be made in one country for assembly in a second country for sale in a third country.[27] "Going Global" describes how several firms are benefiting from the growing demand for international logistics services.

Three basic factors differentiate domestic and international materials management functions. The first is simply the distance involved in shipping. Shipments within even the largest countries seldom travel more than a couple of thousand miles, and many travel much less. For example, the road distance between New York City and Los Angeles is around 2800 miles. But the distances between New York and Warsaw, Tokyo, and Sydney are 4300 miles, 6700 miles, and 9900 miles, respectively.[28] Thus assembling component parts in Kansas City, Chicago,

GOING GLOBAL

The Booming Market in Logistics Services

As firms globalize, logistics becomes more important and more sophisticated. This in turn has created new market opportunities for logistics experts. To most people, for example, Caterpillar is a leading earth-moving equipment manufacturer. But as the opening case in Chapter 3 indicated, Caterpillar has achieved this lofty position because of the quality of service it provides its customers. Construction sites may be shut down if a part breaks on a vital piece of equipment. To minimize downtime and keep its customers happy, Caterpillar has developed one of the world's best parts distribution systems. It is normally capable of getting any of the 550,000 spare parts that go into Caterpillar products to any customer within hours. (In contrast, a typical automobile manufacturer only has to deal with a piddling 70,000 spare parts.) Having developed this expertise, Caterpillar has been only too happy to solve other companies' distribution problems by handling their spare parts operations. Caterpillar is estimated to generate an additional $200 to $300 million in revenue annually by providing logistical services for other companies.

Another emerging logistical market is "one-stop" shipping, in which a customer contracts with one transportation company to handle all of its shipments from door to door. For example, Viking Technical Services, a small Florida exporter of machine parts, has contracted with Roadway Express to transport parts from the fifty domestic factories it deals with to the twenty countries it exports to. Roadway Express, using either its own equipment or equipment provided by other firms, is responsible for picking up the deliveries at the factory gate, transporting them from the United States to their foreign port of entry, clearing customs, and arranging transportation to the foreign customer. Not only does this arrangement save Viking money and hassle but, if a transportation problem arises, Viking knows who to call: Roadway. Of course, Roadway, like many of its competitors, has invested heavily in the latest information technology so it can track the whereabouts of any shipment instantaneously. By shifting the transportation responsibilities to an expert like Roadway, Viking can focus on what it does best.

Sources: "A moving story of spare parts," *Financial Times*, August 29, 1997, p. 7; "More Firms Rely on 'One-Stop' Shopping," *Wall Street Journal*, April 29, 1997.

and St. Louis and then shipping them to Cincinnati for final assembly is much easier than assembling component parts in San Diego, Montreal, and Cairo and then shipping them to Singapore for final assembly.

The second basic difference between domestic and international materials management functions is the sheer number of transport modes that are likely to be involved. Shipments within the same country often use only a single mode of transportation, such as truck or rail. But shipments that cross national boundaries, and especially those traveling great distances, almost certainly involve multiple modes of transportation. For example, a shipment bound from Kansas City to Berlin may use truck, rail, ship, and then rail and truck again.

Third, the regulatory context for international materials management is much more complex than for domestic materials management. Most countries regulate many aspects of their internal transportation systems—price, safety, packaging, and so on. Shipments that cross through several countries are subject to the regulations of each of those countries. While various economic trade agreements and groups such as NAFTA and the EU have sought to streamline international shipping guidelines and procedures, transporting goods across national boundaries is still complex and often involves much red tape.

Seemingly simple logistics and materials management issues often become much more complex in an international context. Packaging issues, which might at first glance seem minor, are in reality a significant consideration in managing international logistics. Packaging protects the goods in transit, helps make the goods easier to handle, and facilitates delivery and/or sale of finished goods at their final destination. International shipping complicates packaging decisions, however, because of the use of multiple modes of transportation as well as the variation in conditions that will be encountered.[29]

For example, consider the problems confronted by a firm that wants to ship a large quantity of delicate electronics equipment from a plant in California, where the equipment was produced, to a facility in Saudi Arabia, where it will be used. During the course of shipment, the equipment will likely be on trucks, railcars, and a ship. These transport settings will have variations in humidity, temperature, and amount of dust. And each time the equipment is loaded and unloaded, it will be handled with varying degrees of roughness or delicacy. Thus the equipment must be packaged to handle everything it will encounter during its travels.

The weight of the packaging itself is also a consideration, especially for finished goods en route to customers. As noted earlier in the chapter, weight sometimes determines the amount of import duty; so firms frequently repackage goods after shipment. Sometimes customers even go so far as to specify precise total weights they will accept, including packaging, and may require that packaging meet certain preset specifications.

Logistical considerations may play a critical role in the decision of where to locate a factory. Production costs may be lower in a domestic factory than in a foreign one. However, the firm must also consider the materials management costs of warehousing, packaging, transporting, and distributing its goods, as well as its inventory carrying costs and those of its foreign customers. Typically, such logistical costs will be higher for exported goods than for locally produced goods.

One of the most basic elements of managing international business operations is handling the actual movement of products across national boundaries. Ports of entry such as this one are extremely complex and busy facilities as boxcars of goods arrive from trains to be loaded onto ships or arrive by ship to be loaded onto railcars. Considerable amounts of paperwork accompany each shipment, and government inspections are commonplace as well.

And there are logistical considerations other than costs. Because of longer supply lines and increased difficulties in communicating with foreign customers, a firm that chooses to export from domestic factories must ensure that it maintains competitive levels of service for its foreign customers.

Needless to say, the ongoing globalization of the world's economy has magnified the importance of international logistics. Globalization would be much less extensive and much slower to develop had it not been for rapid changes in information technology (IT). While development of personal computers, fax machines, electronic mail, and the like are widely known, less visible IT breakthroughs such as satellite communications, electronic data interchange, and bar coding have been equally significant. By integrating such technological changes into their logistical operations, firms are able to increase their productivity and enhance customer satisfaction. Firms such as Benetton that have aggressively and innovatively harnessed these new information technologies have improved the efficiency of their overall operations as well as their logistical operations. Cost savings can be huge: Volkswagen, for example, believes that it can trim its overall operating costs by 1 percent using electronic data interchange for all of its internal and external transactions. IT has also promoted a reconceptualization of the logistics process and a rethinking of the supplier-customer relationship. By harnessing IT, firms are able to analyze how to promote the efficiency and productivity of the entire supply chain, rather than just their particular component of it. For example, Kay-Bee Toy Stores' IT system monitors sales at its 1300 retail outlets and inventory levels at the company's distribution centers. When store inventories of a hot item like Nintendo 64 game players or Tickle Me Elmo run low, replacements can automatically be sent from the company's distribution centers; when inventory runs low at the distribution centers, new orders can be placed with the manufacturers. By using IT creatively, Kay-Bee and other companies not only enhance their own productivity but also raise the satisfaction of their customers. IT has other advantages as well. Investments in IT can act as substitutes for investments in inventory and warehousing capacity, reducing capital costs and improving rates of return on assets. Moreover, IT helps firms monitor their progress toward attainment of their strategic goals.[30]

International Service Operations

The service sector has emerged in recent years as an increasingly important part of many national economies, especially those of developed countries.[31] For example, the service sector accounts for almost three fourths of the U.S. GNP and is the source of most new U.S. jobs.[32] It should therefore come as no surprise that services are becoming a more integral part of international trade and of the global economy. An **international service business** is a firm that transforms resources into an intangible output that creates utility for its customers. Examples of international services are British Airways's transporting of passengers from London to India, Price Waterhouse's assistance with the accounting and auditing functions of firms such as Amoco, Baxter, and IBM, and Dai-Ichi Kangyo Bank's handling of international corporate business accounts.

Characteristics of International Services

Services have several unique characteristics that create special challenges for firms that want to sell them in the international marketplace. In particular, services often are intangible, are not storable, require customer participation, and are linked with tangible goods.

Services are intangible. A consumer who goes to a store and buys a Sony Walkman has a tangible product, one that can be held, manipulated, used, stored, damaged, and/or returned. But a customer who goes to an accountant and gets financial advice leaves with intangible knowledge that cannot be held or seen. (The pieces of paper sometimes associated with services—tax statements, insurance policies, and so on—while tangible themselves, are actually just symbols or representations of the service product itself.) Because of this intangibility, assessing a service's value or quality is often more difficult than assessing that of a good.

Services are also generally not storable. Often they cannot be created ahead of time and inventoried or saved for future usage. A service call to repair a broken washing machine can occur only when the technician is physically transported to the site of the broken appliance—and is wasted if no one is home to unlock the door. An empty airline seat, an unused table in a restaurant, an unsold newspaper—all lose their economic value as soon as their associated window of opportunity closes—that is, after the plane takes off, the restaurant kitchen closes, and the next day's newspaper is printed. The high degree of perishability of services makes capacity planning a critical problem for all service providers. **Capacity planning** is deciding how many customers a firm will be able to serve at a given time. Failure to provide sufficient capacity often means permanently lost sales, while provision of too much capacity raises the firm's costs and lowers its profits.

Services often require customer participation. International services such as tourism cannot occur without the physical presence of the customer. Because of customer involvement in the delivery of the service, many service providers need to customize the product to meet the purchaser's needs. Thomas Cook, for example, can sell more bus tours in London if it provides Spanish-speaking guides for its Mexican, Venezuelan, and Argentinean clients and Japanese-speaking guides for its Japanese customers. Further, an identical service can be perceived quite differently by each of its customers, thereby creating strategic and marketing problems. The London bus tour, for example, may be viewed with great excitement by Japanese honeymooners on their first trip outside of Osaka but with boredom by a harried Toshiba executive who has visited the city many times.

Many services are tied to the purchase of other products. Many firms offer **product-support services**—assistance with operating, maintaining, and/or repairing products for customers. Such services may be critical to the sale of the related product. For example, Swedish appliance maker AB Electrolux manufactures vacuum cleaners, refrigerators, washing machines, and other appliances under such names as Eureka, Frigidaire, Tappan, and Weed Eater. It also has service operations set up to repair those products for consumers who buy them, to provide replacement parts, and so on. The firm's ability to sell its appliances would be substantially harmed if it did not offer these related services. And it must not only offer them at its corporate home in Stockholm, Sweden. If AB Electrolux wants to compete in the U.S., Canadian, and British markets, it must provide repair and parts distribution services there as well.

The Role of Government in International Services Trade

An important dimension of the international services market is the role of government. Many governments seek to protect local professionals and to ensure that domestic standards and credentials are upheld by restricting the ability of foreigners to practice such professions as law, accounting, and medicine. Government regulations often stipulate which firms are allowed to enter service markets and the prices they may charge. For example, in the United States, foreign banks and insurance firms are heavily regulated and must follow the directives of numerous state and federal regulatory agencies. In many countries, telecommunications, transportation, and utility firms typically need governmental permission to serve individual markets. For example, airline routes between the United States and France are spelled out by a bilateral agreement between those two countries. Air France can fly passengers from Paris to Dallas and from Paris to New York, but it cannot board passengers in New York and fly them to Dallas. U.S. carriers are given similar rights to routes between U.S. and French cities.

On the other hand, the past decade has seen a reduction in domestic and international regulation of many service industries. Continued reductions in barriers to service trade is a high priority of the World Trade Organization. This deregulation has created opportunities for firms in industries such as banking and telecommunications and spurred them to aggressively seek new domestic markets and expand their operations to foreign markets. For example, in the early 1980s the U.S. government began to relax its regulation of AT&T, thereby giving that firm the opportunity to expand its operations into new markets. In 1985, Japan followed suit by deregulating its largest telephone company, Nippon Telegraph and Telephone. Many governments, particularly in South America and Europe, privatized their previously state-owned telephone monopolies in the 1990s. These changes have triggered numerous strategic alliances, cross-border investments, and new start-up companies in every corner of the globe. A new round of such initiatives has been generated by the European Union's dismantling of barriers to competition for telecommunication services within its borders, which took effect in January 1998. Table 17.1 illustrates the dramatic effect on the telecommunications market of these regulatory changes.

Managing Service Operations

The actual management of international service operations involves a number of basic issues, including capacity planning, location planning, facilities design and layout, and operations scheduling.

Recall that capacity planning is deciding how many customers the firm will be able to serve at one time. Because of the close customer involvement in the purchase of services, capacity planning affects the quality of the services provided to customers. For example, McDonald's first restaurant in Russia was considerably larger than many of its other restaurants in order to accommodate an anticipated higher level of sales volume. Despite this larger size, customer waiting times at the Moscow restaurant are much longer than those in the United States. The lack of

---

TABLE 17.1

Impact of Deregulation on Long Distance Telephone Service

	YEARS SINCE DEREGULATION	MARKET SHARE LOST BY MONOPOLY CARRIER	PRICE DECLINE
United Kingdom	14	30%	73%
Sweden	5	5	39
United States	14	47	48
Australia	6	15	18
Japan	11	12	60

Source: "Firms Vie to Ring in New Year in Europe," by Gautam Naik, *Wall Street Journal*, December 18, 1997, p. A18. Reprinted by permission of the *Wall Street Journal* © 1997 Dow Jones and Co., Inc. All rights reserved worldwide.

restaurant alternatives makes Muscovites more willing to stand in long lines for their "Big Mek." In contrast, if customers had to wait a half-hour to be served in Boulder, Columbus, or even Paris, McDonald's would lose much of its business.

As with production management, location planning is important for international service operations. By definition, most service providers must be close to the customers they plan to serve (exceptions might be information providers that rely on electronic communication). Indeed, most international service operations involve setting up branch offices in each foreign market and then staffing each with locals.

International service facilities must also be carefully designed so that the proper look and layout are established. U.S. firms operating internationally typically try to create a look that blends their American heritage with the local culture. At Disneyland Paris, for example, signs are in both English and French. Many foreign firms, however, try to blend their facilities into the local environment so as to look local. For example, most guests at a Motel 6 in the United States have no idea that the chain is foreign-owned.

Finally, international service firms must schedule their operations to best meet the customers' needs. For example, airlines transporting passengers from the United States to Europe generally depart late in the evening. Doing this gives passengers the opportunity to spend some of the day working before they depart, and they arrive around mid-morning the next day. In contrast, westbound flights usually leave Europe in mid-morning and arrive in the United States late that same afternoon. This scheduling provides an optimal arrangement because it factors in customer preferences, time zones, jet lag, and aircraft maintenance requirements.

CHAPTER REVIEW

Summary

International operations management is the set of activities used by an international firm to transform resources into goods or services. Effective operations management is a key ingredient in any firm's success. A firm's business strategy provides the major direction it will take regarding its operations management activities.

Production management refers to the creation of tangible goods. One of the first decisions production managers must make concerns sourcing and vertical integration. Sourcing, also called procuring, encompasses the set of processes and steps used in acquiring resources and materials. Vertical integration refers to the extent to which a firm either provides its own resources or obtains them externally.

A key decision is whether to make or buy inputs. Several options exist. Production managers attempting to select from among them must consider strategic issues as well as risks, flexibility, investments in facilities, and questions of control.

Location decisions are also of paramount importance to effective international operations management. Country-related considerations include resource availability and costs, infrastructure, and country-of-origin marketing effects. Product-related issues are the value-to-weight ratio, production technology, and the importance of customer feedback. Governmental factors that must be considered include stability of the political process, tariffs and other trade barriers, economic development incentives, and the existence of FTZs. Finally, organizational issues include the firm's strategy, its structure, and its inventory management policies.

International logistics and materials management are also a basic part of production management. Several factors differentiate international from domestic materials management, including shipping distance, transportation modes, and the regulatory context. Packaging, weight, and factory location must also be considered.

Technological changes in information technology are revolutionizing logistics and redefining relationships between suppliers and end-users.

Service operations management is concerned with the creation of intangible products. The service sector is an increasingly important part of the global economy. International services are generally characterized as being intangible, not storable, requiring customer participation, and linked with tangible goods. The basic issues involved in managing service operations include capacity planning, location planning, design and layout, and operations scheduling.

Review Questions

1. What is international operations management and how is it accomplished?

2. Why is effective operations management important for an international firm?

3. How does a firm's corporate strategy affect its operations management?

4. How do production management and service operations management differ?

5. What is sourcing? What is vertical integration?

6. What factors must a firm consider when addressing the make-or-buy decision?

7. What basic set of factors must a firm consider when selecting a location for a production facility?

8. How do materials management and physical distribution differ?

9. What basic factors must be addressed when managing international service operations?

Questions for Discussion

1. How does international operations management relate to international marketing (discussed in Chapter 16)?

2. How are a firm's strategy and operations management interrelated?

3. What constraints do operations impose on strategic options?

4. How do each of the basic business strategies (differentiation, cost leadership, and focus) relate to operations management?

5. In the mid-1990s Jaguar, the producer of expensive motor cars, threatened to shut down its British factory and produce its cars in Portugal. If it were cheaper to produce Jaguars in Portugal, would you advise the company to shift its production there? Can you think of any reason why it shouldn't make such a move? (P.S.: As it turned out, the British government agreed to provide Jaguar with some economic development incentives if it would modernize its existing factory, and Jaguar kept its British factory open.)

6. What are the basic similarities and differences between production management and service operations management?

7. What are the advantages and disadvantages of being vertically integrated?

8. What are the steps a manager might follow in selecting a site for a new factory?

9. Why are services most closely associated with developed, industrialized economies?

BUILDING GLOBAL SKILLS

Begin by reading the following, which is adapted from a *Harvard Business Review* case study titled "The Plant Location Puzzle."[33]

Ann Reardon made her way across the crowded trade-show floor, deep in thought and oblivious to the noisy activity all around her. As CEO of The Eldora Company (EDC) for the previous 13 years, she had led her organization through a period of extraordinary success. While larger bicycle makers had moved their manufacturing operations overseas to take advantage of lower labor costs, Eldora had stuck with a domestic manufacturing strategy, keeping its plant on the same campus as its corporate offices in Boulder, Colorado. Ann felt that her strategy of keeping all the parts of the company in the same location, while unconventional, had contributed greatly to cooperation among various departments and, ultimately, to the company's growth: EDC had become the largest and most profitable bicycle company in the United States. Yet her manufacturing vice president, Sean Andrews, was now urging her to build a plant in China.

"Look at the number of companies here," he had said that morning, as they helped several EDC staffers stack brochures on the exhibit table and position the company's latest models around the perimeter of their area. "There are too many players in this market," he had said. "I've been saying this for two months now, and you know the forecasters' numbers back me up. But if they weren't enough to convince you, just look around. The industry is reaching the saturation point here in the States. We have to break into Asia."…

Ann thought about what Sean had said about the U.S. market. In 1997, EDC's sales and earnings had hit record levels. The company produced almost 30 percent of the bicycles sold in the United States. But U.S. mass-market bicycle sales were growing by only 2 percent per year, while the Asian market for those same bikes was nearly doubling on an annual basis. And Eldora could not competitively serve those markets from its U.S. manufacturing facility. Two of the largest bike manufacturers in the world, located in rapidly growing Asian markets, enjoyed a significant labor and distribution cost advantage.…

One of the reasons the company had been so successful was that Boulder, Colorado, was a bicyclists' mecca. Eldora employees at all levels shared a genuine love of bicycling and eagerly pursued knowledge of the industry's latest trends and styles. Someone was always suggesting a better way to position the hand brakes or a new toe grip that allowed for better traction and easier dismounts. And Eldora never had a shortage of people willing to test out the latest prototypes.

Another reason was that all marketing staff, engineers, designers, and manufacturing personnel worked on one campus, within a ten minute walk of one another. Ann had bet big on that strategy, and it had paid off. Communication was easy, and changes in styles, production plans, and the like could be made quickly and efficiently. Mountain bikes, for example, had gone from 0 percent to more than 50 percent of the market volume since 1991, and Eldora had met the increased demand with ease. And when orders for cross-bikes—mountain/road bike hybrids that had enjoyed a spurt of popularity—began to fall off, Eldora had been able to adjust its production run with minimal disruption.…

Ann's satisfaction was quickly tempered with thoughts of foreign sales performance. Between 1990 and 1995, EDC's foreign sales had grown at an annual rate of over 80 percent. But during the previous two years, they had been flat.

Sean appeared at Ann's side, jolting her out of her thoughts and into the reality of her surroundings. "Dale just finished up the first round of retailers' meetings," he said. "We'd like to get some lunch back over at the hotel and talk about our options." Dale Stewart was Eldora's marketing vice president. His views of what was best for the company often differed from Sean's, but the two had an amiable working relationship and enjoyed frequent spirited verbal sparring matches.…

Over sandwiches, Sean made his case. "Our primary markets in North America and Western Europe represent less than a quarter of the worldwide demand. Of the 200 million bicycles made in the world last year, 40 million were sold in China, 30 million in India, and 9 million in Japan. Historically, bikes sold in Asia's developing markets were low-end products used as primary modes of transportation. But the economic picture is changing fast. There's a growing middle class. Suddenly people have disposable income. Many consumers there are now seeking higher quality and trendier styles. Mountain bikes with suspension are in. And cross-bikes are still holding their own. In fact, the demand in those markets for the product categories we produce has been doubling annually, and the growth rates seem sustainable.

"If we're going to compete in Asia, though, we need a local plant. My staff has evaluated many locations there. We've looked at wage rates, proximity to markets, and materials costs, and we feel that China is our best bet. We'd like to open a plant there as soon as possible, and start building our position."

Dale jumped in. "Two of our largest competitors, one from China, one from Taiwan, have been filling the demand so far," he said. "In 1993, 97 percent of the volume produced by these companies was for export. In 1999, they are projecting that 45 percent of their production will be for local markets. We can't compete with them from here. About 20 percent of our product cost is labor, and the hourly wages of the manufacturing workforce in these countries are between 5 percent and 15 percent of ours. It also costs us an additional 20 percent in transportation and duties to get our bicycles to these markets."

He glanced at Sean quickly and continued. "But here's where I disagree with Sean. I think we need a short-term solution. These companies have a big lead on us, and the more I think about it, the more I believe we need to put a direct sales operation in Asia first."

"Dale, you're crazy," Sean said, pouring himself some ice water from the pitcher on the table. "What good would an Asian sales operation do without a manufacturing plant? I know we source components in Asia now, but we could save another 10 percent on those parts if we were located there. Then we would really be bringing Eldora to Asia. If we want to compete there, we have to play from our greatest strength—quality. If we did it your way, you wouldn't be selling Eldora bikes. You'd just be selling some product with our label on it. You wouldn't get the quality. You wouldn't build the same kind of reputation we have here. It wouldn't really be Eldora. Over the long term, it couldn't work."

"We're building bicycles, not rocket ships," Dale countered. "There are lots of companies in Asia that could provide us with a product very quickly if we gave them our designs and helped them with their production process. We could outsource production in the short term, until we made more permanent arrangements." He turned to Ann. "We could even outsource the product permanently, despite what Sean says. What do we know about building and running a plant in China? All I know is we're losing potential share even as we sit here. The trading companies aren't giving our products the attention they deserve, and they also aren't giving us the information we need on the features that consumers in those markets want. A sales operation would help us learn the market even as we're entering it. Setting up a plant first would take too long. We need to be over there now, and opening a sales operation is the quickest way."

Ann cut in. "Dale has a good point, Sean," she said. "We've been successful here in large part because our entire operation is in Boulder, on one site. We've

had complete control over our own flexible manufacturing operation, and that's been a key factor in our ability to meet rapid change in the local market. How would we address the challenges inherent in manufacturing in a facility halfway around the world? Would you consider moving there? And for how long?

"Also, think about our other options. If the biggest issue keeping us out of these markets right now is cost, then both of you are ignoring a few obvious alternatives. Right now, only our frame-building operation is automated. We could cut labor costs significantly by automating more processes. And why are you so bent on China? Frankly, when I was there last month touring facilities, a lot of what I saw worried me. You know, that day I was supposed to tour a production facility, there was a power failure. Judging by the reactions of the personnel in the plant the next day, these outages are common. The roads to the facility are in very poor condition. And wastewater and cleaning solvents are regularly dumped untreated into the waterways. We could operate differently if we located there, but what impact would that have on costs?

"Taiwan has a better developed infrastructure than China. What about making that our Asian base? And I've heard that Singapore offers attractive tax arrangements to new manufacturing operations. Then there's Mexico. It's closer to home, and aside from distribution costs, the wage rates are similar to Asia's and many of the other risks would be minimized. You both feel strongly about this, I know, but this isn't a decision we can make based on enthusiasm."...

Walking back to the convention center with Dale and Sean, Ann realized that she wasn't just frustrated because she didn't know which course EDC should pursue. She was concerned that she really didn't know which aspects of the decision were important and which were irrelevant. Should she establish a division in China? If so, which functions should she start with? Manufacturing? Marketing? And what about engineering? Or should she consider a different location? Would China's low labor costs offset problems caused by poor infrastructure?

Growth had always been vitally important to Eldora, both in creating value to shareholders and in providing a work environment that could attract and retain the most talented people. Now it appeared that Ann would have to choose between continued growth and a domestic-only manufacturing strategy that had served her well.

Now that you have read the case study, you are ready to participate in the exercise related to it. First, make sure you completely understand the details of the case. Next, form groups of six people each. One person should adopt the role of Ann Reardon, one the role of Sean Andrews, and one the role of Dale Stewart. The other three group members will constitute the board of directors of The Eldora Company. If the number of people in the class doesn't divide evenly by six, the board of directors can be increased in size. Ann, Sean, and Dale should each summarize for the board—in two minutes or less—the basic issues each sees regarding the firm's potential entry into the Asian market.

The board of directors should then use its own understanding of the background material (in the case itself) to discuss and debate whether to build a new plant in Asia. Your instructor will then ask each group to summarize its deliberations and report on its final decision.

Follow-up Questions

1. How similar or different were the reports from each group?

2. Why do you think this pattern of similarities or differences occurred?

WORKING WITH THE WEB: Building Global Internet Skills

Obtaining International Logistic Service

Assume that you are the marketing manager of a small valve manufacturer trying to export to Egypt for the first time. Make a list of the logistical issues that you are likely to face in exporting to Egypt. Now check out the web sites of providers of international logistics services. (Chapter 17's section of the text-book's web site provides links to some web sites you may find helpful). Which of these web sites is the most useful to you? What information provided on these web sites is of the most value to you? What information is missing? Based on the information contained in its web site, which company would you call first? Why? Would your answers change if you were an experienced exporter?

CLOSING CASE

International Operations at General Motors[34]

For years General Motors dabbled with the idea of becoming a truly global business. While the firm exported its cars to several other countries for years and had a few plants outside the United States, it remained predominantly a North American enterprise. Just a few years ago, for example, 80 percent of the firm's vehicles were made in North America. And cars made elsewhere were often retreads of older GM models no longer in demand in its domestic market. GM's older South American plants, for example, were still churning out Chevy Chevettes well into the 1990s.

But all that has changed dramatically in recent years since GM has made a bold and public commitment to becoming a global automaker. New products are being designed and manufactured in other countries, and GM is striving aggressively to reach a goal of having 50 percent of its capacity outside of North America. And at the center of this effort is an innovative approach to designing and manufacturing its automobiles in the four corners of the world.

General Motors is essentially emulating its Japanese rival Toyota. Through a series of partnerships and alliances, GM has gained important insights into the payoffs that Toyota has achieved through its strategies of plant standardization and lean manufacturing. At Toyota, a change in a car being made in Japan can easily be replicated throughout other Toyota plants around the world, and Toyota is the acknowledged master and pioneer of cutting costs by managing parts inventory and other aspects of its logistics more efficiently.

In contrast, U.S. automakers have traditionally designed each automobile factory as a unique and autonomous facility. While this sometimes makes a given plant especially productive—since it was designed for one specific purpose—it also constrains flexibility and makes it more difficult to transfer new technologies and methods between factories.

GM is now using Toyota's strategy in its newest factories. These factories are located in Argentina, Poland, and China. (Completion of a fourth plant in Thailand has been postponed because of the Asian currency crisis.) The plants look so much alike that a visiting GM executive might forget which country she or he is in. This strategy allows GM to launch global products, such as a new "world car," more easily. Equally as important, if one factory develops a glitch or problem, it might easily be solved by simply calling one of the others. Similarly, if a manager at one factory discovers a new way of achieving a productivity gain, this information can be easily passed on and implemented in the other factories.

GM's new factories have been designed with flexibility and efficiency in mind. Each factory can be easily expanded should demand warrant higher production. Each is constructed in a large "U" shape so that suppliers can deliver component parts and accessories directly to the assembly lines, cutting down on warehouse costs and improving productivity.

But while the plants are as similar to one another as possible, GM also found it necessary to make adjustments in each to meet unique conditions in each country. In China, for example, managing the plant's just-in-time inventory system will present unique challenges, for suppliers will be delivering many parts on carts and bicycles due to that country's poor road system. Despite such minor accommodations to local conditions, GM nonetheless believes that its standardized plants will cut its production costs substantially and allow it to succeed in the world's emerging markets.

Case Questions

1. What are the advantages and disadvantages of General Motors' strategy for plant construction?

2. In what businesses is this strategy appropriate, and in which businesses might it be less appropriate?

3. What operations management issues are illustrated in this case?

CHAPTER NOTES

1. "Fashionable Tech: How Benetton Keeps Costs Down," *Information Week*, February 12, 1990, pp. 24–25; Alan Chai, Alta Campbell, and Patrick J. Spain (eds.), *Hoover's Handbook of World Business 1997* (Austin, Tex.: Reference Press, 1997), pp. 110–111; "The Faded Colors of Benetton," *Business Week*, April 10, 1995, pp. 87–90; "Even when you fail, you learn a lot," *Forbes*, March 11, 1996, p. 58; "Retailers Rely on High-Tech Distribution," *Wall Street Journal*, December 19, 1996, p. A2; "Rollerblade, Inc. Returns to Grass Roots with Global Partner," *PR Newswire*, November 14, 1997, p. 1114.

2. Barrie James, "Reducing the Risks of Globalization," *Long Range Planning*, Vol. 23, No. 1 (1990), pp. 80–88.

3. Scott Young, K. Kern Kwong, Cheng Li, and Wing Fok, "Global Manufacturing Strategies and Practices: A Study of Two Industries," *International Journal of Operations & Production Management*, Vol. 12, No. 9 (1992), pp. 5–17.

4. Robert H. Hayes and Gary P. Pisano, "Beyond World-Class: The New Manufacturing Strategy," *Harvard Business Review* (January–February 1994), pp. 77–87.

5. Michael McGrath and Richard Hoole, "Manufacturing's New Economies of Scale," *Harvard Business Review* (May–June 1992), pp. 94–103.

6. "Roly's Products Deck the Halls in U.S., Asia," *Wall Street Journal*, December 27, 1996, p. A3B.

7. Masaaki Kotabe and Janet Y. Murray, "Linking Product and Process Innovations and Modes of International Sourcing in Global Competition: A Case of Foreign Manufacturing

Firms," *Journal of International Business Studies* (Third Quarter, 1990), pp. 383–408.

8. Ravi Venkatesan, "Strategic Sourcing: To Make or Not To Make," *Harvard Business Review* (November–December 1992), pp. 98–108.

9. James Brian Quinn and Frederick G. Hilmer, "Strategic Outsourcing," *Sloan Management Review* (Summer 1994), pp. 43–55.

10. James A. Welch and P. Ranganath Nayak, "Strategic Sourcing: A Progressive Approach to Make-or-Buy Approach," *The Academy of Management Executive* (February 1992), pp. 23–31.

11. Stephen J. Kobrin, "An Empirical Analysis of the Determinants of Global Integration," *Strategic Management Journal*, Vol. 12 (1991), pp. 17–31.

12. Peter Siddall, Keith Willey, and Jorge Tavares, "Building a Transnational Organization for British Petroleum," *Long Range Planning*, Vol. 25, No. 1 (1992), pp. 18–26.

13. Welch and Nayak, op. cit.

14. David Flath, "Keiretsu Shareholding Ties: Antitrust Issues," *Contemporary Economic Issues*, Vol. 12, No. 1 (January 1994), pp. 24–36.

15. Myron Magnet, "The New Golden Rule of Business," *Fortune*, February 21, 1994, pp. 60–64.

16. "U.S. Companies Move to Limit Currency Risk," *Wall Street Journal*, August 3, 1993, p. A10.

17. Lorraine Eden, Kaye G. Husbands, and Maureen Appel Molot, "Shocks and Responses: Canadian Auto Parts Suppliers Adjust to Free Trade and Lean Production," mimeo, 1997.

18. Victor V. Cordell, "Effects of Consumer Preferences for Foreign Sourced Products," *Journal of International Business Studies*, Vol. 23, No. 2 (Second Quarter 1992), pp. 251–270; Paul Chao, "Partitioning Country of Origin Effects: Consumer Evaluations of a Hybrid Product," *Journal of International Business Studies*, Vol. 24, No. 2 (Second Quarter 1993), pp. 291–306; Frederick W. Schroath, Michael Y. Hu, and Haiyang Chen, "Country-of-Origin Effects of Foreign Investments in the People's Republic of China," *Journal of International Business Studies*, Vol. 24, No. 2 (Second Quarter 1993), pp. 277–290.

19. Andrew D. Bartmess, "The Plant Location Puzzle," *Harvard Business Review* (March–April 1994), pp. 20–22.

20. Dwight Silverman, "Compaq plans to build $15 million Brazil plant," *Houston Chronicle*, March 23, 1994, p. 1B.

21. "'The Exodus of German Industry Is Under Way,'" *Business Week*, May 25, 1994, pp. 42–43.

22. Patriya S. Tansuhaj and George C. Jackson, "Foreign Trade Zones: A Comparative Analysis of Users and Non-Users," *Journal of Business Logistics*, Vol. 10, No. 1 (1989), pp. 15–30.

23. "Ford Is Expected to Name President of Global Auto Operations This Week," *Wall Street Journal*, April 19, 1994, p. B10.

24. "The supplier moves next door," *Financial Times*, July 24, 1997, p. IV.

25. John H. Roberts, "Formulating and Implementing a Global Logistics Strategy," *The International Journal of Logistics Management*, Vol. 1, No. 2 (1990), pp. 53–58.

26. William C. Capacino and Frank F. Britt, "Perspectives on Global Logistics," *The International Journal of Logistics Management*, Vol. 2, No. 1 (1991), pp. 35–41.

27. Stanley E. Fawcett, Linda L. Stanley, and Sheldon R. Smith, "Developing a Logistics Capability to Improve the Performance of International Operations," *Journal of Business Logistics,* vol. 18, no. 2 (1997), p. 102.

28. Walter Zinn and Robert E. Grosse, "Barriers to Globalization: Is Global Distribution Possible?" *The International Journal of Logistics Management*, Vol. 1 (1990), pp. 13–18.

29. Clyde E. Witt, "Packaging: From the Plant Floor to the Global Customer," *Material Handling Engineer* (October 1992), pp. 3–31.

30. "EDI data exchange spreads its wings," *Financial Times,* March 21, 1997, p. 7; "Retailers Rely on High-Tech Distribution," *Wall Street Journal*, December 19, 1996, p. A2; J. M. Masters and B. J. LaLonde, "Driven by New Information Technologies," *Distribution*, Vol. 92, No. 11 (1993), pp. 62–9.

31. Ronald Henkoff, "Service Is Everybody's Business," *Fortune*, June 27, 1994, pp. 48–60.

32. Richard B. Chase and Warren J. Erikson, "The Service Factory," *The Academy of Management Executive* (August 1988), pp. 191–196.

33. Reprinted by permission of *Harvard Business Review*. An excerpt from "The Plant Location Puzzle" by Andrew D. Bartmess, March/April 1994. Copyright © 1994 by the President and Fellows of Harvard College; all rights reserved.

34. "GM Is Building Plants in Developing Countries to Woo New Markets," *Wall Street Journal*, August 4, 1997, pp. A1, A4; "Can GM Stop Its European Skid?," *Business Week*, November 3, 1997, pp. 60–62.

Should International Businesses Promote Human and Worker Rights?

International Businesses Have a Moral Obligation to Protect Human and Worker Rights

It is a common business practice today for firms to move their manufacturing facilities to countries in which production costs are low or to subcontract production to local firms in those countries. Unfortunately, the reasons for the low production costs may be inadequate wages, unsafe or unhealthy working conditions, and disregard for worker rights. For example, two hundred people died in a 1993 fire in a Thai toy factory that lacked basic safety precautions such as fire extinguishers and sprinkler systems.

Businesses that set up shop in foreign countries have an obligation to make the proper treatment of local employees a high priority. Just because an MNC might be able to get away with paying substandard wages and providing poor working conditions by no means suggests that it should do so. Indeed, today's international businesses have a social obligation to improve the quality of life for their employees and those of their subcontractors worldwide.

To do so makes good business sense for several reasons. First, it is simply good public relations. Firms that allow their foreign workers to be treated poorly fare badly themselves when their practices receive media attention. For example, in recent years the reputations of Nike, Wal-Mart, and TV personality Kathie Lee Gifford have been damaged as a result of such publicity.

Second, human rights advocates argue that to treat employees poorly violates human rights. This simple premise becomes even more persuasive when it is augmented with stories and examples detailing such abhorrent practices as using what amounts to slave labor and physically abusing workers.

Third, international businesses can make a difference in the world by practicing more humanitarian HRM policies. Levi Strauss is an excellent example of a firm that has taken to heart the importance of treating its foreign workers with dignity and providing them with the proper rewards and working conditions. This firm mandates that all its foreign plants, including those of its subcontractors, must maintain safety and health practices comparable to those in the United States. For example, drinking water purity and bathroom conditions must meet U.S. standards.

When businesses set up operations in foreign countries, they should have the same regard for their workers as they have at home. These IBM workers in Brazil, for example, have safety equipment and procedures comparable to those used by IBM workers around the world.

Often the only comparative advantage that developing countries have in the international marketplace is low wage rates. International businesses locating in these countries should be allowed to exploit fully these countries' low-cost production opportunities as long as they adhere to local customs and norms.

If foreign MNCs were required to pay above-market wages or to provide working conditions equal to those in developed countries, the economic development of poorer countries might be crippled. If an international giant moves into a low-cost region and pays higher-than-normal wages, workers will no longer be willing to work for the prevailing wage rate. Thus costs for local businesses increase. In addition, requiring foreign firms to pay above-market wages and benefits will discourage them from locating in developing countries. Such countries need to lure more foreign capital and technology, not drive it away.

Some government officials in developing countries believe the sentiments expressed by worker rights advocates in richer countries are thinly disguised attempts at protectionism. In their view, public pressure to force Western retailers to buy goods only from factories that pay wages and offer working conditions equivalent to those in the Quad countries acts as an NTB against goods from developing countries.

These officials also often resent these pressures as a form of cultural imperialism by Westerners who have little first-hand knowledge of the often harsh economic alternatives facing workers in developing countries. When Levi Strauss recently discovered that one of its Bangladeshi factories was employing young children, it demanded that the factory's practices be changed. The manager pointed out that most of the children were their families' only source of income and to deprive them of a job would bring hardship on entire families. In some regions of Southeast Asia, the situation is far worse: children who are unable to obtain jobs are often sold into prostitution by their families. Critics argue that given these alternatives, foreign MNCs should stick to providing jobs for developing countries and leave the social engineering to local governments.

Sources: "Levi Tries to Make Sure Contract Plants in Asia Treat Workers Well," *Wall Street Journal,* July 28, 1994, pp. A1, A6; "Levi's Law," *Far Eastern Economic Review,* April 14, 1994, p. 60; Tim Smith, "The Power of Business for Human Rights," *Business & Society Review* (Winter 1994), pp. 36–38.

One of the most controversial issues in international business today is how different firms around the world treat their workers. In Bangladesh, for example, children are often used to perform difficult jobs under adverse working conditions while being paid minimal wages.

Wrap-up

1 What ethical responsibilities do MNCs have to their workers in developing countries? Do their ethical responsibilities differ for workers employed at a firm-owned factory and workers employed at a subcontractor's factory?

2 Do you agree that attempts to impose Western-style wage rates and working conditions in factories in developing countries constitute an NTB? Why or why not?

International Financial Management

Chapter Outline

Financial issues in international trade

Choice of currency
Credit checking
Method of payment
Financing trade

Managing foreign-exchange risk

Transaction exposure
Translation exposure
Economic exposure

Management of working capital

Minimizing working capital balances
Minimizing currency conversion costs
Minimizing foreign-exchange risk

International capital budgeting

Net present value
Internal rate of return
Payback period

Sources of international investment capital

Internal sources of investment capital
External sources of investment capital

After studying this chapter you should be able to:

Discuss the major forms of payment in international trade.

Identify the primary types of foreign-exchange risk faced by international businesses.

Describe the techniques used by firms to manage their working capital.

Evaluate the various capital budgeting techniques used for international investments.

Discuss the primary sources of investment capital available to international businesses.

KLM ROYAL DUTCH AIRLINES (KLM) LIVES OR DIES IN THE international market. It has virtually no domestic market because the physical size of the Netherlands does not lend itself to extensive airline travel: the country is smaller than West Virginia, and its two major cities, Amsterdam and Rotterdam, are only 40 miles apart. Although the Dutch government owns 11 percent of the company's common stock, KLM operates as a profit-seeking, privately owned firm. As the world's fifteenth-largest airline, it competes head-to-head against other major international carriers, including American, United, Delta, British Airways, Lufthansa, Air France, Japan Air Lines, Qantas, and Singapore Airlines. ■■ The foundation of KLM's global

KLM's Worldwide Financial Management[1]

success is its reputation for providing high-quality service. Its service has lured passengers of all nationalities to its flights, particularly highly valued business travelers, who are willing to pay a premium for luxurious and reliable service. Only 27 percent of its business is done on the friendly turf of Europe. Asian operations account for 22 percent of its revenues, and the critical U.S.-Netherlands market accounts for over 23 percent. ■■ KLM is one of a handful of European carriers that has held its own against the mighty U.S. airlines in the transatlantic market. In 1995, U.S. carriers held 64 percent of the U.S.-France market, 59 percent of the U.S.-Spain market, and 56 percent of the U.S.-Germany market. However, they captured only 34 percent of the U.S.-Netherlands market. KLM's success in this transatlantic market is due in part to its strategic alliance with Minneapolis-based Northwest Airlines, the world's seventh-largest airline. KLM and Northwest coordinate their flight schedules to entice U.S.-Europe travelers to use KLM on the transatlantic leg and Northwest on the U.S. leg of their trips. To heighten their appeal to quality-sensitive passengers, the two airlines jointly market their premium-priced World Business Class service throughout their two route networks. ■■ A truly international carrier, KLM flies to more than 150 cities on six continents. But its international success brings a major financial challenge—managing its holdings of the 80 or so currencies it uses in the normal conduct of business. KLM receives from its customers a rainbow of currencies, including francs (Belgian, French, and Swiss), crowns (Czech, Danish, Norwegian, Slovak, and Swedish), dollars (Australian, Canadian, Hong Kong, New Zealand, and U.S.), as well as yen, marks, and, of course, Dutch guilders. It also must pay in local currency for local services—landing fees, ground handling services, travel agent commissions, and so on—in each country in which it does business. ■■ Further, the firm has had to obtain over $5 billion to pay for aircraft from U.S. and European manufacturers. To fund its aircraft purchases and other operational needs, KLM has borrowed the equivalent of $3.8 billion from international sources, including 38 billion yen, 780 million Swiss francs, 194 million French francs, 160 million deutsche marks, 412 million U.S. dollars, 900,000 ECUs, and 695 million Dutch guilders. ▌▌ Managing the firm's revenues, expenses, assets, and liabilities, all denominated in various foreign currencies, is a major task for KLM's financial officers. To pay local expenses, they must maintain local-currency cash balances in each country. They also must search worldwide for sources of low-cost capital in order to modernize the firm's aircraft fleet and thereby maintain its reputation for high-quality service. In addition, they must protect KLM from exchange-rate fluctuations, which will change the value in guilders that it receives for its services and the cost in guilders that it pays for aircraft, fuel, flight services, and ground handling. These officers must thoroughly understand how the contemporary international monetary system operates. They must monitor changes in the foreign-exchange market, be knowledgeable about potential shifts in government economic policies in their major markets, and constantly shop for the best credit terms in such capital markets as Amsterdam, London, Frankfurt, New York, and Tokyo. ▌▌▌▌

In most business transactions, the receipt of goods by the buyer and the receipt of payment by the seller in a form the seller can use immediately do not coincide. Even when a customer pays for goods with a check, the seller will not have access to the funds until the check clears. Until then, the seller risks having the check returned because of insufficient funds. Thus some type of financing and some degree of trust between buyer and seller are necessary to allow business transactions to occur.

While these problems affect both domestic and international business, the problems of financing and credit checking are far greater for international transactions. Differences in laws, customs, financial practices, and currency convertibility among countries mean that an international firm must know the practices both of its home country and of each country in which it does business—or else hire experts who do. A firm also must acquire specific credit information about the foreign firms with which it wants to deal. On top of these problems is that of transacting in a foreign currency—a problem that either the buyer or the seller must face. Financial officers of international businesses like KLM are well aware of the challenges created by using different currencies. How international businesses address these myriad problems is the subject of this chapter.

Financial Issues in International Trade

We begin by considering the problems associated with financing international trade. In any business transaction, the buyer and the seller must negotiate and reach agreement on such basic issues as price, quantity, and delivery date. However, when the transaction involves a buyer and seller from two countries, several other issues arise:

- Which currency to use for the transaction
- When and how to check credit
- Which form of payment to use
- How to arrange financing

Choice of Currency

One problem unique to international business is choosing the currency to use to settle a transaction. Exporters and importers usually have clear and conflicting preferences as to which currency to use. The exporter typically prefers payment in its home currency so that it can know the exact amount it will receive from the importer. The importer generally prefers to pay in its home currency so that it can know the exact amount it must pay the exporter. Sometimes an exporter and an importer may elect to use a third currency. For example, if both parties are based in countries with relatively weak or volatile local currencies, they may prefer to deal in a more stable currency such as the deutsche mark, the Japanese yen, or the U.S. dollar. By some estimates, over 70 percent of the exports of less developed countries and 85 percent of the exports of Latin American countries are invoiced using the U.S. dollar.[2] In some industries, one currency is customarily used to settle commercial transactions. For example, in the oil industry, the U.S. dollar serves this function. Among the major exporting countries, the most common practice is for the exporter to invoice foreign customers using its home currency.[3] However, smaller exporting countries may choose to use the currency of a major trading partner: 91 percent of Thailand's exports are invoiced in U.S. dollars, for example.

Credit Checking

Another critical financial issue in international trade concerns the reliability and trustworthiness of the buyer. If an importer is a financially healthy and reliable company and one with whom an exporter has had previous satisfactory business relations, the exporter may choose to simplify the payment process by extending credit to the importer. But if the importer is financially troubled or known to be a poor credit risk, the exporter may demand a form of payment that reduces its risk.

In commercial transactions, it is wise to check customers' credit ratings. For most domestic business transactions, firms have simple and inexpensive mechanisms for doing this. In the United States, for example, firms may ask for credit references or contact established sources of credit information such as Dun & Bradstreet. Similar sources are available in other countries; however, many first-time exporters are unaware of them. Fortunately, an exporter's domestic banker often can obtain credit information on foreign customers through the bank's foreign banking operations or through its correspondent bank in a customer's country. Most national government agencies in charge of export promotion also offer credit-checking services. For example, the International Trade Administration, a branch of the U.S. Department of Commerce, provides financial information about foreign firms for a fee. Numerous commercial credit-reporting services are also available. Country desk officers of the U.S. and Foreign Commercial Service are available to steer new exporters to these services.

The firm that ignores the credit-checking process may run into serious payment problems. In the early 1990s, for example, one small U.S. manufacturer exported $127,000 worth of fan blades to a new customer in Africa. However, it failed to first contact any of the customer's credit references. Frustrated by the subsequent lack of payment, the manufacturer turned the account over to a collection agency, which discovered that the supposed customer had vanished and its credit references were nonexistent.[4]

Implicit in this discussion is an important lesson that many successful international businesspeople have learned the hard way. Because the physical and cultural gaps between the exporter and the importer are often large, finding partners, customers, and distributors with whom to build long-term, trusting relationships is invaluable to any international business.

Method of Payment

As with domestic transactions, firms engaged in international transactions must select the method of payment carefully.[5] The parties to the transaction negotiate a method of payment based on the exporter's assessment of the importer's creditworthiness. Many forms of payment have been developed over the centuries, including payment in advance, open account, documentary collection, letters of credit, credit cards, and countertrade. As with most aspects of finance, each form involves different degrees of risk and cost.

Payment in Advance. From the exporter's perspective, the safest method of payment in international trade is payment in advance: the exporter receives the importer's money prior to shipping the goods. Using this method, the exporter can reduce its risk and also receive payment quickly, which may be important if its working capital balance is low. Exporters prefer payments in advance to be made by wire transfer, which allows immediate use of the funds. Payment by ordinary check may take four to six weeks to clear the banking systems of the two countries involved, depending on the size and sophistication of their financial services sectors.

From the importer's perspective, payment in advance is very undesirable. The importer must give up the use of its cash prior to the receipt of the goods. The importer also bears the risk that the exporter will fail to deliver the goods in accordance with the sales contract. For these reasons, exporters that insist on payment in advance are vulnerable to losing sales to competitors willing to offer more attractive payment terms. Nonetheless, payment in advance may be the preferred form if the importer is a poor credit risk.

Open Account. From the importer's perspective, the safest form of payment is the **open account**, whereby goods are shipped by the exporter and received by the importer prior to payment. The exporter then bills the importer for the goods, stipulating the amount, form, and time at which payment is expected. Open accounts also can be used as a marketing tool because they offer potential buyers short-term financing. Use of an open account enables the importer to avoid the fees charged by banks for alternative means of payment such as letters of credit or documentary collection, which will be discussed shortly. An open account has the further advantage of requiring less paperwork than do these other forms of payment.

From the exporter's perspective, an open account may be undesirable for several reasons. First, the exporter must rely primarily on the importer's reputation for paying promptly. Second, since the transaction does not involve a financial intermediary like a bank, the exporter cannot fall back on such an intermediary's expertise if a dispute arises with the importer. Third, the exporter may pay a price for the advantage of doing less paperwork: if the importer refuses to pay, the lack of documentation can hamper the exporter's pursuit of a claim in the courts of the importer's home country. Finally, the exporter must tie up working capital to finance foreign accounts receivable. Borrowing working capital collateralized by foreign receivables is often expensive, because it may be difficult for domestically oriented lenders to evaluate the riskiness of a firm's portfolio of foreign receivables. Such borrowing is not impossible, however. Numerous firms engage in a specialized international lending activity called **factoring**, in which they buy foreign accounts receivable at a discount from face value. The size of the fees these firms charge (in the form of the discount from face value of the receivables) reflect both the time value of money and the factor's assessment of the portfolio's riskiness.

As a result, an open account is best suited for dealing with well-established, long-term customers or larger firms with impeccable credit ratings and reputations for timely payment of their bills. For example, U.S. video film distributors that deal with Blockbuster Video in the United States on an open account basis might offer the same arrangement to Citivision PLC, Blockbuster's subsidiary in the United Kingdom, particularly if Blockbuster pledged to honor Citivision's trade obligations. Similarly, foreign subsidiaries owned by a common parent corporation often deal with each other on an open account basis, since the risk of default in such circumstances is minimal. About 40 percent of U.S. international trade involves transactions between subsidiaries of a parent firm.[6]

Payment in advance and an open account share a basic similarity. Both shift the cash flow burden and risk of default to one party in the transaction: to the buyer in the case of payment in advance and to the seller in the case of an open account.

Documentary Collection. To get around the cash flow and risk problems caused by the use of payment in advance and open accounts, international businesses and banks have developed several other methods to finance transactions. One is **documentary collection**, whereby commercial banks serve as agents to facilitate the payment process. To initiate this method of payment, the exporter draws up a document called a **draft** (often called a *bill of exchange* outside the United States), in which payment is demanded from the buyer at a specified time. After the exporter ships its goods, it submits to its local banker the draft and appropriate shipping documents, such as the packing list and the bill of lading.[7] The **bill of lading** plays two important roles in documentary collection: it serves as both a contract for transportation between the exporter and the carrier and as title to the goods in question. Acting on the exporter's instructions, the exporter's bank then contacts its correspondent bank in the importer's country (or one of its own branches there, if it has any). The latter bank is authorized to release the bill of lading, thereby transferring title of the goods, when the importer honors the terms of the exporter's draft.[8] This process is shown in Fig. 18.1.

There are two major forms of drafts:

I A **sight draft** requires payment upon the transfer of title to the goods from the exporter to the importer. When the bank in the importer's country receives the bill of lading and the sight draft from the exporter's bank, it notifies the importer, which then pays the draft. Upon payment, the bank gives the bill of lading to the importer, which can then take title to the goods.

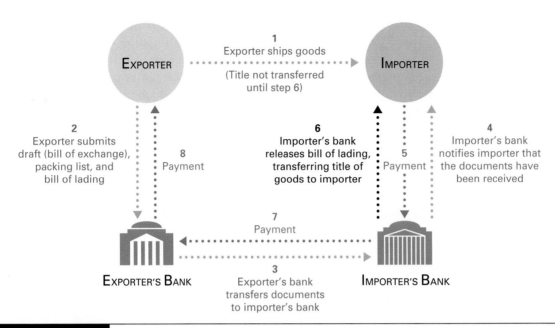

1
Exporter ships goods

EXPORTER .... ▷ IMPORTER

(Title not transferred
until step 6)

2
Exporter submits
draft (bill of exchange),
packing list, and
bill of lading

8
Payment

6
Importer's bank
releases bill of lading,
transferring title of
goods to importer

5
Payment

4
Importer's bank
notifies importer that
the documents have
been received

7
Payment

EXPORTER'S BANK

3
Exporter's bank
transfers documents
to importer's bank

IMPORTER'S BANK

FIGURE 18.1

Using a Sight Draft

Note: In the case of a time draft, the importer makes a promise to pay, not the actual payment, in step 5. Source: Based on *Dynamics of Trade Finance*, Chase Manhattan Bank, 1989, p. 42.

2 A **time draft** extends credit to the importer by requiring payment at some specified time, such as 30 or 60 days, after the importer receives the goods. (A variant of the time draft, the **date draft**, specifies a particular date on which payment will be made.)

To obtain title to the goods when a time draft is used, the importer must write "accepted" on the draft, thereby incurring a legal obligation to pay the draft when it comes due. An accepted time draft is called a **trade acceptance**, which under the laws of most countries is a legally enforceable and negotiable debt instrument. For a fee, the importer's bank may also accept a time draft, thereby adding its own obligation to pay the draft to the importer's. In this case, the time draft becomes a **banker's acceptance**.

The exporter may hold either a trade acceptance or a banker's acceptance until it comes due. But banks and other commercial lenders are often willing to buy acceptances at a discount, thereby allowing the exporter to receive immediate cash. Some acceptances are sold **without recourse**, meaning that the buyer of the acceptance is stuck with the loss if the importer does not pay. Others are sold **with recourse**, meaning that the exporter will have to reimburse the buyer of the acceptance in the case of nonpayment by the importer. Exporters planning to sell their accepted time drafts must balance the prices they will receive for them against the additional banking fees they must pay (in the case of banker's acceptances) and the degree of risk they are willing to bear (in the case of acceptances sold with recourse). Because of their greater riskiness, acceptances sold without recourse are sold at bigger discounts from face value than acceptances sold with recourse. Similarly, since banker's acceptances are guaranteed by the bank as well as by the importer, they are less risky and are usually discounted less than trade acceptances are.

For an exporter, payment through documentary collection has several advantages over the use of open accounts. First, the bank fees for documentary collection are quite reasonable because the banks act as agents rather than risk-takers (unless a banker's acceptance is involved). Second, a trade acceptance or a banker's acceptance is an enforceable debt instrument under the laws of most countries, thereby solidifying the exporter's legal position if the importer defaults on its promise to pay. Third, using banks simplifies the collection process for the exporter and substitutes the banks' superior expertise in effecting international payments for the exporter's presumably inferior knowledge. Further, because the collection agent is a local bank, and the importer does not want to jeopardize its business reputation with a local lender, the importer is more likely to pay a time draft promptly than an invoice sent under an open account. Finally, because of the enforceability of acceptances in courts of law, arranging financing for foreign accounts receivable is easier and less expensive when documentary collection is used than when open accounts are used.

With documentary collection, the exporter still bears some risks, however. Suppose local business conditions change or the importer finds a cheaper supply source. In such a case, an importer may simply refuse the shipment and decline to accept the draft, perhaps under a false pretext that the shipment was late or the goods improperly packed. The importer's default on the sales contract places the exporter in the unenviable position of having its goods piled up on a foreign loading dock (and running up storage fees known as *demurrage*) while receiving no payment for them. Alternatively, the importer may default on the time draft when it comes due. The exporter may have legal remedies in either case. But pursuing them is often costly in terms of time, energy, and money.

Letters of Credit. To avoid such difficulties, exporters often request payment using a **letter of credit**, a document that is issued by a bank and contains its promise to pay the exporter upon receiving proof that the exporter has fulfilled all requirements specified in the document. Because of the bank's pledge, the exporter bears less risk by using a letter of credit than by relying on documentary collection. However, cautious bankers are unlikely to issue a letter of credit unless they fully expect the importer to reimburse them. Thus, using a letter of credit has additional benefits in that the exporter benefits from the bank's knowledge of the importer's creditworthiness, the requirements of the importer's home country customs service, and any restrictions the importer's home country government imposes on currency movements.

Usually, an importer applies to its local bank—in most cases, one with which it has an ongoing relationship—for a letter of credit. The bank then assesses the importer's creditworthiness, examines the proposed transaction, determines whether it wants collateral, and, assuming everything is in order, issues the letter of credit. The bank typically charges the importer a small commission for this service. The letter of credit details the conditions under which the importer's bank will pay the exporter for the goods. The conditions imposed by the issuing bank reflect normal sound business practices. Most letters of credit require the exporter to supply an invoice, appropriate customs documents, a bill of lading, a packing list, and proof of insurance. Depending on the product involved, the importer's bank may demand additional documentation before funding the letter, such as the following:

♦ *Export licenses* are issued by an agency of the exporter's home country. They may be required for politically sensitive goods, such as nuclear fuels, or for high-technology goods that may have military uses.

♦ *Certificates of product origin* confirm that the goods being shipped were produced in the exporting country. They may be required by the importing country so that it can assess tariffs and enforce quotas.

♦ *Inspection certificates* may be needed to provide assurance that the products have been inspected and that they conform to relevant standards. For example, imported foodstuffs often must meet rigorous standards regarding pesticide residues, cleanliness, sanitation, and storage.

After issuing the letter of credit, the importer's bank sends it and the accompanying documents to the exporter's bank, which advises the exporter of the terms of the instrument, thereby creating an **advised letter of credit**. "Going Global" provides more information about the process of issuing an advised letter of credit. The exporter can also request its bank to add its own guarantee of payment to the letter of credit, thereby creating a **confirmed letter of credit**. This type of instrument is particularly appropriate when the exporter is concerned about political risk. If the importer's home country government later imposes currency controls or otherwise blocks payment by the importer's bank, the exporter can look to the confirming bank for payment.

Another type of letter of credit is the **irrevocable letter of credit**, which cannot be altered without the written consent of both the importer and the exporter. A bank may also issue a **revocable letter of credit**, which it may alter at any time and for any reason. An irrevocable letter of credit offers the exporter more protection than a revocable letter of credit does. However, amending such an instrument can be cumbersome, expensive, and time-consuming.

Banks that issue, advise on, and/or confirm letters of credit charge for their services. Therefore, international firms must determine which of these services they really need in order to avoid paying unnecessary fees.

When goods are sold under a letter of credit, payment does not depend on meeting the terms of the sales contract between the buyer and seller. Rather the bank issuing the letter of credit will make payment only when the terms of that letter have been fulfilled. Thus the exporter must carefully analyze the letter's terms before agreeing to them, to be sure that they are compatible with the sales contract.

Surprisingly, it is this feature of letters of credit—that they are paid when their terms are met, not when the sales contract is fulfilled—that makes them so useful in international trade. Once the exporter meets the letter's terms, the importer's bank is obligated to pay the exporter even if the importer refuses the shipment or fails to pay for the goods. Such difficulties become the problem of the importer's bank, not the exporter. But the likelihood of such difficulties arising are reduced because the importer is unlikely to jeopardize its business reputation or credit lines with its bank. Figure 18.2 shows how a letter of credit is used in a typical international transaction.

Although the issuing bank will not pay the exporter until all the terms of the letter of credit have been met, the exporter often can sell the letter prior to the expected payment date to its bank or another commercial lender at a discount from the face value. The discount will reflect the time value of money, the risk the buyer of the instrument bears if the issuing bank defaults on the transaction, and the buyer's administrative costs. Because confirmed and irrevocable letters of credit reduce the risk of secondary buyers, they sell for higher prices (or lower dis-

GOING GLOBAL

As an exporter, you may wonder now and again what your advising fee pays for. In addition to the obvious fax and courier expenses, there are a variety of services the advising bank performs before a letter of credit (L/C) is fully advised to you.

Advising banks have a responsibility to use reasonable care to check that any credit or amendment they advise to a beneficiary is authentic. Because of the large amounts of money involved, the letter of credit system has become a target for organized crime. To protect beneficiaries from fraud, advising banks check the validity of each credit and amendment through various private verification procedures. No credit is advised without some form of electronic test or authentication of signatures.

Banks are also required to review letters of credit and amendments for "boycott status." Commonly, L/Cs issued by Middle East banks carry stipulations relating to trade or commerce with Israel. Sometimes, under the Export Administration Act, these provisions are illegal and/or reportable to the government. Under the regulations, it is the responsibility of the advising bank to report boycott provisions in a letter of credit to the U.S. Department of Commerce or Treasury. This pertains not only to Mideast credits but credits worldwide.

The government also maintains a "Specially Designated Nationals" (SDN) list. This list contains names of businesses and individuals around the world who have forfeited their rights to export from or import to the United States. Companies or individuals on the SDN list are there because of their failure to comply with U.S. law. Each beneficiary and applicant on every credit is checked to make sure none is on the SDN list. This, too, is the advising bank's responsibility.

Another important function of the advising bank is to review credits for their workability. Surprisingly, many letters of credit are issued with conflicting stipulations, incorrect terms, and even expired availability dates. While the advising bank reviews the L/C for its "workability," it is important to remember that such review is from a banker's perspective and a bank's perspective on an L/C's "workability" may differ from that of an exporter. Exporters should also review the L/C for its "workability" from their perspective.

Finally, your advising fee pays for good, old-fashioned service. Often, exporters need clarification concerning the documentary requirements of the L/C, payment terms, or stipulations. A good advising bank will be ready, willing, and able to assist you with these and other questions.

What Your Advising Fees Buy

Source: Casey Ochs, "Export Letters of Credit," *Norwest Worldview*, August 1996, Vol. 3, No. 2. Copyright © 1996 Norwest Corporation. All rights reserved.

counts from face value) than do letters of credit without these features. Thus an exporter planning to sell a letter of credit prior to delivery must trade off the inconvenience or higher fees paid for these less risky types against the higher prices it will receive from secondary buyers of them.

Credit Cards. For small international transactions, particularly those between international merchants and foreign retail customers, credit cards such as American Express, VISA, and MasterCard may be used. A firm may tap into the well-established credit card network to facilitate international transactions, subject to the normal limitations of these cards. The credit card company collects transaction fees (usually 2 to 4 percent) from the merchant and in return assumes the costs of collecting the funds from the customer and any risks of nonpayment. Because credit card companies buy foreign currency in large quantities at whole-

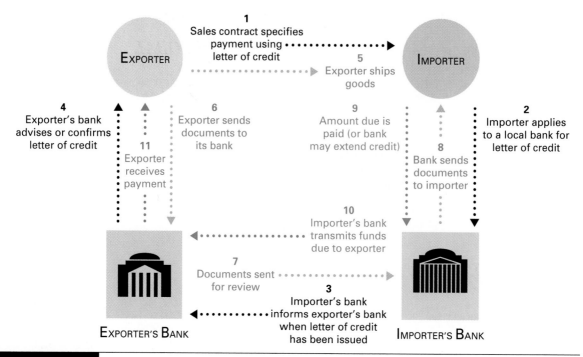

1
Sales contract specifies
payment using
letter of credit

EXPORTER

5
Exporter ships
goods

IMPORTER

4
Exporter's bank
advises or confirms
letter of credit

11
Exporter
receives
payment

6
Exporter sends
documents to
its bank

9
Amount due is
paid (or bank
may extend credit)

8
Bank sends
documents
to importer

2
Importer applies
to a local bank for
letter of credit

10
Importer's bank
transmits funds
due to exporter

7
Documents sent
for review

EXPORTER'S BANK

3
Importer's bank
informs exporter's bank
when letter of credit
has been issued

IMPORTER'S BANK

FIGURE 18.2

**Using a Letter
of Credit**

Source: Based on *Dynamics
of Trade Finance,* Chase
Manhattan Bank, 1989,
pp. 62–63.

sale rates, they typically charge only a 1 percent fee for converting currencies. However, they offer exporters and importers none of the help banks do in dealing with the paperwork and documentation requirements of international trade.

Countertrade. An additional method used for payment in international transactions is countertrade. **Countertrade** occurs when a firm accepts something other than money as payment for its goods or services. Forms of countertrade include barter, counterpurchase, buy-back, and offset purchase.

The simplest form of countertrade is **barter,** in which each party simultaneously swaps its products for the products of the other. For example, in 1996 the State Trading Corporation of India agreed to exchange wheat and other grains to Turkmenistan in return for cotton. Similarly, Azerbaijan agreed to import 100,000 tons of wheat from Romania, following a poor harvest in Azerbaijan and a bumper crop in Romania. Payment by Azerbaijan was in the form of crude oil.

A more sophisticated form of countertrade is **counterpurchase,** whereby one firm sells its products to another at one point in time and is compensated in the form of the other's products at some future time. Counterpurchase is the most common form of countertrade. It is sometimes called *parallel barter* as it disconnects the timing of contract performance by the participating parties. In this way, one part of the transaction can go ahead even if the second requires more time. Boeing, for example, has used counterpurchase to sell aircraft to Saudi Arabia in return for oil, and to India in return for coffee, rice, castor oil, and other goods.[9]

Another variant of countertrade involves **buy-back,** or compensation arrangements whereby one firm sells capital goods to a second firm and is compensated in the form of output generated as a result of their use. For example, Japan's Fukusuke Corporation sold ten knitting machines and raw materials to Chinatex, a Shanghai-based clothing manufacturer, in exchange for 1 million pairs of underwear to be produced on the knitting machines.[10] Similarly, Internationale Vine of Latvia agreed to buy equipment for producing apple juice concentrate from PKL of Switzerland, and paid for the equipment with output from the machinery. Because it links payment with output from the purchased goods, a buy-back is particularly useful when the buyer of the goods needs to ensure the exporter will provide necessary after-sale services such as equipment repairs or instructions on how to use the equipment.[11]

Another important type of countertrade involves **offset purchases,** whereby part of an exported good is produced in the importing country. Offset arrangements are particularly important in sales to foreign governments of expensive military equipment such as fighter jets or tanks. General Dynamics, for example, sold several hundred F-16 military jets to Belgium, Denmark, Norway, and the Netherlands by agreeing to allow those countries to offset the cost of the jets through coproduction agreements. As part of the deal, the countries were allowed to produce 40 percent of the value of the aircraft they purchased from General Dynamics. The firm sweetened the deal by authorizing the European countries to coproduce 10 percent of all F-16s sold to the U.S. military and 15 percent of any F-16s sold to other countries.[12]

Balancing export sales and counterpurchase obligations on a deal-by-deal basis is often cumbersome. To facilitate countertrade, firms may agree to establish **clearinghouse accounts.** Using this approach, as a firm exports goods and services to another, it incurs a counterpurchase obligation of an equivalent value, which is recorded in its clearinghouse account. When the firm buys goods from its partner, its clearinghouse obligation is reduced. Thus a firm does not need to balance any single countertrade transaction, although it must honor its cumulative set of obligations by the time its clearinghouse account expires.

Sometimes firms enter into countertrade agreements in order to expand their international sales, without having experience in or desire to engage in countertrade. In this case, countertrade agreements often permit the use of **switching arrangements,** whereby countertrade obligations are transferred from one firm to another. A variety of consulting firms, many headquartered in either London (because of access to capital markets) or Vienna (because of access to the former communist countries), are available to provide financing, marketing, and legal services needed by international businesses engaging in switching arrangements.[13] Japan's soga sosha are particularly skillful in the use of switching arrangements and clearinghouse accounts because of their extensive worldwide operations. A soga sosha might assist in the sale of Mitsubishi trucks in Ghana, taking payment in cocoa, which then can be sold to keiretsu-linked food processors back in Japan or to independent candymakers anywhere in the world.[14]

Some firms specialize in exploiting countertrade opportunities by constructing complicated multiple-market trades as part of their normal business. Consider, for example, Marc Rich & Co., which does over $3 billion in business annually in the former Soviet Union. In 1993 the firm engineered a complicated deal that began with its buying 70,000 tons of Brazilian raw sugar on the open market (see Map 18.1). It then hired a Ukrainian firm to refine the sugar and paid the refinery with part of the sugar. Next, it swapped the rest of the refined sugar to oil refineries in Siberia, which needed the sugar for their workers, in return for gasoline. It then swapped 130,000 tons of gasoline to Mongolia in return for 35,000 tons of copper concentrate. The copper concentrate was shipped to copper refineries in Kazakhstan, which received payment in kind. The

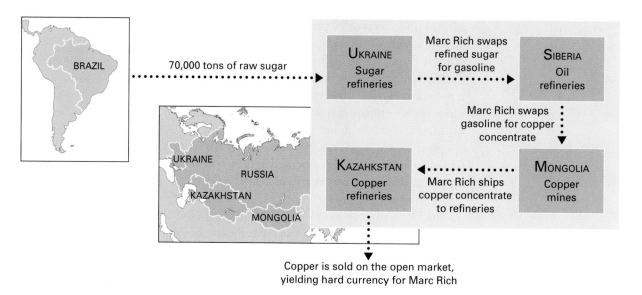

MAP 18.1

Countertrade by Marc Rich

refined copper was then sold on the world market. At that point, Marc Rich—after several months of efforts—was able to extract its profits on these countertrades in the form of hard currency.[15]

Countertrade is important to international businesses because of its widespread use. Informed estimates suggest that countertrade accounts for 15–20 percent of world trade, although some published reports claim that the proportion approaches 40 percent.[16] Countertrade is of particular importance to countries that lack a convertible currency and is often used as a means of reducing the drain on scarce holdings of convertible foreign currencies. The former Soviet Union, for example, was a major countertrade user. Often goods were traded between the Soviet Union and its former allies using clearinghouse accounts. The former communist countries also engaged in countertrade with capitalist countries.

Table 18.1 summarizes the benefits and costs of the various methods of payment. Techniques that reduce risk for the exporter generally are more expensive. Thus the exporter must decide how much risk it is willing to bear. In dealing with a new and unknown customer, an exporter may choose a safer but more expensive means of securing payment. In dealing with well-established clients, less expensive but riskier payment methods may be acceptable.

Financing Trade

Financing terms are often important in closing an international sale. In most industries, standard financing arrangements exist, and an international firm must be ready to offer those terms to its foreign customers. Depending on the product, industry practice may be to offer the buyer 30 to 180 days to pay after receipt of an invoice. For the sale of complex products such as commercial aircraft, which will be delivered several years in the future, the payment terms may be much more complicated. They may include down payments, penalty payments for cancellation or late delivery, inflation clauses, and concessionary interest rates for long-term financing. Outside of the Quad countries, capital markets are often not well developed, and local lenders may charge extremely high interest rates,

TABLE 18.1

Payment Methods for International Trade

METHOD	TIMING OF PAYMENT	TIMING OF DELIVERY OF GOODS	RISK(S) FOR EXPORTER	RISK(S) FOR IMPORTER	AVAILABILITY OF FINANCING FOR EXPORTER	CONDITION(S) FAVORING USE
Payment in advance	Prior to delivery of goods	After payment, when goods arrive in importer's country	None	Exporter may fail to deliver goods	N/A	Exporter has strong bargaining power; importer unknown to exporter
Open account	According to credit terms offered by exporter	When goods arrive in importer's country	Importer may fail to pay account balance	None	Yes, by factoring of accounts receivable	Exporter has complete trust in importer; exporter and importer are part of the same corporate family
Documentary collection	At delivery if sight draft is used; at specified later time if time draft is used	Upon payment if sight draft is used; upon acceptance if time draft is used	Importer may default or fail to accept draft	None	Yes, by discounting draft from its face value	Exporter trusts importer to pay as specified; when risk of default is low
Letter of Credit	After terms of letter are fulfilled	According to terms of sales contract and letter of credit	Issuing bank may default; documents may not be prepared correctly	Exporter may honor terms of letter of credit but not terms of sales contract	Yes, by discounting letter from its face value	Exporter lacks knowledge of importer; importer has good credit with local bank
Credit card	According to normal credit card company procedures	When goods arrive in importer's country	None	Exporter fails to deliver goods	N/A	Transaction size is small
Countertrade	When exporter sells countertraded goods	When goods arrive in importer's country	Exporter may not be able to sell countertraded goods	None	No	Importer lacks convertible currency; importer or exporter wants access to foreign distribution network

especially to smaller borrowers. Thus exporters with access to low-cost capital can gain a competitive advantage by offering financing to foreign customers that lack access to cheaper financing. Of course, by acting as a lender, the exporter increases the risk of not being paid for its goods. Before deciding to extend credit, the exporter must examine the trade-off between the benefits of increased sales and the higher risks of default.

As noted earlier in this chapter, banks and other commercial lenders are often willing to finance accounts receivable of exporters by purchasing letters of credit or time drafts or factoring open accounts at a discount from face value. Many developed countries supplement the services of these commercial lenders with government-supported financing programs to promote exports. For example, the Export-Import Bank of the United States (Eximbank) offers a working capital guarantee loan program to encourage U.S. exports. Under this program, commercial loans made to finance exportable inventory and foreign accounts receivable will be reimbursed 90 percent if the importer defaults on its obligations. Eximbank has made a special effort to serve the needs of small businesses; it approves over $2 billion of support annually for exports by U.S. small businesses. For example, in the

The ability of U.S. firms to secure contracts to supply the Three Gorges Dam has been hurt by the lack of Eximbank financing. The Eximbank believes this policy protects the environment; critics argue it protects European jobs and hurts the U.S. economy.

early 1990s, Ormat, Inc., a small Nevada producer of geothermal power generation equipment, beat out Japanese and Italian competitors for a $33.5 million contract with the National Power Corporation of the Philippines, thanks to Eximbank financing.[17] Eximbank also offers medium-term loan guarantees (up to seven years'

duration) and long-term guarantees (over ten years' duration) for telecommunications, electrical generation, and transportation infrastructure projects. However, as "Going Global" indicates, Export-Import Bank financing is often subject to political considerations and sometimes is unavailable to U.S. exporters.

Managing Foreign-Exchange Risk

By using contracts denominated in a foreign currency, KLM and other firms that conduct international trade are exposed to the risk that exchange-rate fluctuations may affect them adversely. Experts have identified three types of foreign-exchange exposure confronting international firms:[18]

1 Transaction

2 Translation

3 Economic

GOING GLOBAL

One of the largest and most expensive construction projects in the history of the world is under way in central China. Chinese engineers are busily directing the construction of the 607-foot-high, 1.3 mile-long Three Gorges Dam on the Yangtze River near the village of Sandouping, 3,000 miles from where the river starts at an altitude of 21,700 feet in the Tibetan Plateau and almost 1,000 miles from where it empties into the East China Sea at Shanghai. When the construction work is finished—estimated completion time is the year 2009—the $17 billion Three Gorges Dam will become the world's largest source of hydroelectric power and reduce the likelihood of devastating floods that have claimed 300,000 lives in the past hundred years. Its 18,200 megawatt capacity—the equivalent of eighteen nuclear power plants—will dwarf the 12,600 megawatt production of the second largest dam, the Itaipu Dam (on the Parana River between Brazil and Paraguay). Chinese planners believe the dam is critical to providing the electricity needed to power China's economic growth in the new millennium.

Foreign environmentalists, however, are appalled by the project. They argue that the 370 mile long lake created by the Three Gorges Dam will flood thousands of sites of archaeological value, including thirty Stone Age sites dating back 50,000 years, force 2 million people from their homes, clog the river with sediment, and threaten endangered species such as the Chinese river dolphin. They have successfully pressured the World Bank to refuse to provide financing for the dam because of its environmental cost.

U.S. environmentalists have waged a similar lobbying campaign and have convinced the U.S. Export-Import Bank (Eximbank) not to provide export guarantees or working capital loans for U.S. firms seeking Three Gorges contracts. But as Kermit the Frog once noted, it's not easy being green. While the U.S. government has chosen not to provide such loans, other countries continue to provide export financing for the massive project. For example, in August 1997 a consortium of three European manufacturers (Siemens, GEC Alsthom, and Asea Brown Boveri Ltd.) won a $740 million contract to supply the dam's power generators, while U.S. companies dropped out of the bidding because the Eximbank's decision left them uncompetitive against the European consortium. Because European governments continue to supply export financing for the project, U.S. critics of the Eximbank's policy argue that it does more to promote the profitability of European companies and hurt jobs in the United States than it does to protect the environment.

The Three Gorges Dam: It's Not a Feast For U.S. Firms

PER PERSON CONSUMPTION
OF ELECTRICITY, 1994

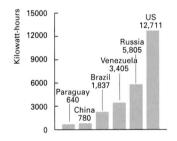

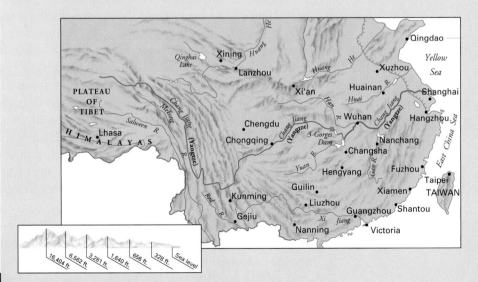

Map 18.2

Three Gorges Dam

Sources: "Europe Inc. Muscles Aside the U.S. and Japan in Asia," *Wall Street Journal,* October 2, 1997, p. A15; "China's Three Gorges," *National Geographic,* Vol. 192, No. 3, September 1997, pp. 2–33.

Transaction Exposure

A firm faces **transaction exposure** when the financial benefits and costs of an international transaction can be affected by exchange-rate movements that occur after the firm is legally obligated to complete the transaction. Many typical international business transactions denominated in a foreign currency can lead to transaction exposure, including the following:

- Purchase of goods, services, or assets
- Sales of goods, services, or assets
- Extension of credit
- Borrowing of money

For example, suppose that, in order to meet its Christmas needs, Saks Fifth Avenue agrees on April 10, 1999, to buy 5 million Swiss francs' worth of Rolex watches from Rolex's Swiss manufacturer, payable on delivery on October 10. Saks now faces the risk that exchange-rate fluctuations will raise the cost of the watches denominated in its home currency—in this case, U.S. dollars—by the time the transaction is completed on October 10. (Of course, exchange-rate movements could *lower* its costs.) Saks could avoid this risk by contracting in dollars, but then Rolex would face transaction exposure. In an international transaction, one of the parties has to bear transaction exposure.

Saks has several options for responding to this transaction exposure. In particular, it can

- Go naked
- Buy Swiss francs forward
- Buy Swiss franc currency options
- Acquire an offsetting asset

Go Naked. Saks can ignore the transaction exposure and deliberately assume the foreign-exchange risk by choosing to buy the necessary Swiss francs on October 10 when it needs to pay for the watches. By doing so, Saks is betting that the U.S. dollar will rise in value relative to the franc between April and October. This approach has several advantages. First, Saks does not have to tie up any capital in April for the transaction, since its only obligation is to pay 5 million Swiss francs October 10. Second, Saks can benefit from any appreciation of the U.S. dollar versus the Swiss franc. If this happens, it can pay its bill on October 10 using fewer dollars than it otherwise would have. This advantage, of course, can turn sour if the dollar falls relative to the franc. In this unfortunate circumstance, Saks would be forced to pay more U.S. dollars for the watches than it had anticipated. But by going naked, Saks avoids paying fees to any intermediaries, an expense that it would incur if it adopted any of the three other strategies, discussed next.

Buy Swiss Francs Forward. Saks has several ways of avoiding the transaction exposure if it wants. For example, it could buy Swiss francs forward in the foreign exchange market for delivery on October 10, thereby locking in the price in April that it will pay for the 5 million francs in October. This strategy has two advantages. First, Saks guarantees the dollar price it will pay for the imported watches and protects itself from declines in the value of the dollar. Second, it ties up none of its capital until it receives the goods, since its only agreement is to buy the currency on October 10 and pay Rolex the 5 million francs on delivery of the watches. On the other hand, with this strategy, Saks will miss the opportunity to benefit from any appreciation of the U.S. dollar relative to the Swiss franc. It also will bear some transaction costs in the form of fees and markups charged by the bank through which it buys the forward Swiss francs.

A variant of this approach is for Saks to purchase Swiss franc currency futures, as discussed in Chapter 5. Whether the firm chooses to buy currency futures or use the forward market depends on the price of francs in these two markets as well as the relative transaction costs of using the two markets.

Buy Swiss Franc Currency Options. Alternatively, Saks could acquire a currency options contract allowing it to buy 5 million Swiss francs in October. As discussed in Chapter 5, the purchase of an options contract gives the buyer the opportunity, but not the obligation, to buy a certain currency at a given price in the future. By buying an option, Saks can guarantee that it will pay no more for its francs than the price stated in its options contract. When payment for the watches is due in October, Saks can exercise the option if the U.S. dollar has declined in value relative to the franc or let the option expire if the U.S. dollar has increased in value—hence the advantage of an options contract over a forward contract or a futures contract. Saks is equally protected against depreciation of the dollar by all three types of foreign-exchange transactions; however, it can benefit from an appreciation of the U.S. dollar with an options contract (by letting it expire unused), but not with a forward or a futures contract. The options contract's disadvantage is that it is more expensive than other hedging techniques. Options typically cost from 3.0 to 5.5 percent of the transaction's total value. Accordingly, some MNCs prefer currency options to currency futures or forward contracts when hedging their transactions risk, because of the "heads I win, tails I don't lose" feature of options. Others find them too expensive relative to their expected benefit.[19]

Acquire an Offsetting Asset. Another option for Saks is for it to neutralize its liability of 5 million Swiss francs pending on October 10 by acquiring an offsetting asset of equivalent size denominated in Swiss francs. For example, suppose the interest rate in April on a six-month certificate of deposit (CD) in Switzerland is 8 percent annually (4 percent for six months). By purchasing a six-month CD in April from a Swiss bank such as Credit Suisse for 4,807,692 francs, Saks will receive 5 million francs ($4,807,692 \times 1.04$) in October when its payment obligation to Rolex comes due. By matching its assets denominated in francs with its liabilities denominated in francs, Saks will suffer no *net* transaction exposure. The disadvantage of this approach is that Saks has to tie up some of its capital in a Swiss bank until October. It will earn interest on the Swiss CD, but it may have been able to earn a higher rate of return if it utilized its capital elsewhere.

Of course, if Saks (or a member of its corporate family) already had an existing franc-denominated CD or receivable due in October, Saks could have used that asset to offset its pending franc-denominated liability to Rolex. Suppose, for example, Saks had licensed a Swiss T-shirt manufacturer to use the Saks logo on its shirts. If Saks expected to receive 5 million Swiss francs in royalties in October from the licensing deal, it could have offset those funds against its October liability to Rolex in order to neutralize its transaction exposure, rather than buying the Swiss CD. If the licensing deal were to yield only 2 million Swiss francs instead of 5 million, Saks could still pair up the two transactions. To eliminate its exposure totally, Saks would then need to cover its *net* transaction exposure of 3 million francs using one of the means just discussed.

Table 18.2 summarizes the benefits and costs of these different techniques available to manage transaction exposure (see also the following "Going Global"). Unfortunately, in many developing markets, these techniques are unavailable or very expensive to utilize. As a result, many companies operating in such economies choose to go naked. A recent survey conducted by Goldman Sachs of large Indonesian companies with large foreign debts suggested that half of them went naked (i.e., did not hedge these debts), and most of the rest hedged only a small portion of their foreign debts. No doubt the cost of hedging played an important role in their behavior. Consider the case of one Indonesian company that did hedge, Indo-Rama Synthetics. In 1997, just before the Asian currency crisis struck, it borrowed $175 million from a consortium of foreign lenders, payable over a five-year period, to finance an expansion of its operations. Indo-Rama paid a premium of about 10 percent of the face value of the loan to lock in an exchange rate of 2,650 rupiah per dollar for its loan repayments. In hindsight, this turned out to be a very fortunate move, for within a year the rupiah had fallen in value by over 80 percent against the dollar. But many of its compatriots were not so farsighted—or perhaps were unwilling at the time to pay the 10 percent premium to lock in a forward rate for repayment of their debts. There is little doubt

---

TABLE 18.2

Strategies for Managing Transaction Exposure

STRATEGY	BENEFIT(S)	COST(S)
Go naked	No capital outlay; potential for capital gain if home currency rises in value	Potential for capital loss if home currency falls in value
Buy forward currency	Elimination of transaction exposure; flexibility in size and timing of contract	Fees to banks; lost opportunity for capital gain if home currency rises in value
Buy currency future	Elimination of transaction exposure; ease and relative inexpensiveness of futures contract	Small brokerage fee; inflexibility in size and timing of contract; lost opportunity for capital gain if home currency rises in value
Buy currency option	Elimination of transaction exposure; potential for capital gain if home currency rises in value	Premium paid up front for option because of its "heads I win, tails I don't lose" nature; inflexibility in size and timing of option
Acquire offsetting asset	Elimination of transaction exposure	Effort or expense of arranging offsetting transaction; lost opportunity for capital gain if home currency rises in value

that the 1997–1998 Asian currency crisis was worsened by the failure of many Asian firms to manage their transaction exposure effectively.[20]

Translation Exposure

As part of reporting its operating results to its shareholders, a firm must integrate the financial statements of its subsidiaries into a set of consolidated financial statements. Problems can arise, however, when the financial statements of a foreign subsidiary are denominated in a foreign currency rather than the firm's home currency. **Translation exposure** is the impact on the firm's consolidated financial statements of fluctuations in exchange rates that change the value of foreign subsidiaries as measured in the parent's currency. If exchange rates were fixed, translation exposure would not exist. (Because translation exposure develops from the need to consolidate financial statements into a common currency, it is often called *accounting exposure*.)

The intricacies of international accounting are covered in Chapter 19, so here we present only a simple example of translation exposure. Suppose GM transfers $10 million to Deutsche Bank to open an account for its new German distribution subsidiary, General Motors Import & Distribution Company GmbH, so that the subsidiary can begin operations.[21] Further assume that the exchange rate on the day of the transfer is DM1.5/$1. Thus the subsidiary's sole asset is a bank account containing DM15 million. If the value of the dollar were to rise to 1.51 deutsche marks per dollar, the subsidiary would still have DM15 million. However, when GM's accountants prepared the firm's consolidated financial statements, its investment in the German subsidiary would be worth only $9,933,775 (15 million marks divided by 1.51 marks per dollar). GM thus would suffer a translation loss of $66,225 ($10,000,000 minus $9,933,775).

Financial officers can reduce their firm's translation exposure through the use of a balance sheet hedge. A **balance sheet hedge** is created when an international firm matches its assets denominated in a given currency with its liabilities denominated in that same currency. This balancing occurs on a currency-by-currency basis, not on a subsidiary-by-subsidiary basis. For example, Georgia-based AFLAC Inc. is the largest foreign provider of life insurance in Japan. To protect its $1.7 billion investment in Japan from translation exposure, the company utilizes a two-pronged balance sheet hedge. Its Japanese insurance subsidiary owns $1.4 billion of U.S. dollar-denominated securities, reducing the subsidiary's net exposure to changes in the yen-dollar exchange rate to $300 million. To finance its other operations, the parent company borrowed $300 million worth of yen from Japanese banks. Through these transactions, AFLAC effectively eliminated its translation exposure to changes in the yen.[22] Procter & Gamble and Owens-Corning follow a similar strategy to reduce their translation exposure.[23]

A controversy exists among financial experts over whether or not firms should protect themselves from translation exposure. Some experts believe that managers should ignore translation exposure and instead focus on reducing transaction exposure, arguing that transaction exposure can produce true cash losses to the firm, while translation exposure produces only paper, or accounting, losses. This, for example, is the approach used by General Motors.[24] Other experts disagree, stating translation exposure should not be ignored. For example, firms forced to take writedowns of the value of their foreign subsidiaries may trigger default clauses in their loan contracts if their debt-to-equity ratios fall too low. And in AFLAC's

GOING GLOBAL

Financial Derivatives: Blessing or Curse?

The most important change in financial markets in the past decade has been the growth of so-called financial derivatives. A financial derivative is a financial instrument whose price derives from some other bond, stock, or other asset. International financial derivatives such as currency forwards, futures, options, swaps, and swaptions (the option to enter into a swap at some later date) have helped international firms reduce their financial exposure to exchange-rate fluctuations.

Often firms use these contracts to hedge exchange-rate risks, as most MNCs do. Some firms use these instruments to speculate, hoping to make a financial killing by guessing correctly which way exchange rates will move in the future. However, sometimes these contracts seem to have been signed by financial managers who just didn't know what they were doing or who were violating company policy. Consider the following examples.

Kashima Oil lost $1.5 billion over several years by purchasing a huge number of forward contracts to buy dollars—far more than it needed for its actual operations. In effect, Kashima's major business became currency speculation, not petroleum refining. When the value of the dollar fell, Kashima was stuck with horrendous losses. The firm then used loopholes in the Japanese accounting system to hide the true extent of its losses, thereby compounding the damage to its reputation when those losses were ultimately revealed.

Daiwa Bank Ltd. lost $1.1 billion over a period of twelve years after rogue trader Toshihidi Igushi hid bond trading losses from management. In addition, Daiwa was fined $340 million after it pleaded guilty to a criminal cover-up. In early 1996 this led to the bank's forced closure in the United States and Igushi being sentenced to four years in prison. Not to be outdone, Yasuo Hamanaka traded in copper futures and successfully lost $2.6 billion for Sumitomo Corporation of Japan. And in Singapore, in 1995, Nick Leeson brought about the downfall of Britain's oldest bank—Baring's Bank. Baring's was one of the principal bankers for the Queen's accounts but collapsed after Leeson lost $1.4 billion in derivative speculations while trading on the Singapore futures market. He bet heavily on a recovery of the Japanese Nikkei 225 stock index. Unfortunately, Leeson did not count on "acts of God." In January 1995, the Japanese city of Kobe was hit by an earthquake that tragically killed 6000 people. The earthquake also depressed the stock market and left Leeson with an exposure that outweighed Baring's assets. Leeson compounded the problem when he invented a fictitious options trade to balance Baring's books. He also wrote false entries into Baring's accounts in an attempt to deceive the Singapore International Monetary Exchange (SIMEX). Leeson is currently serving a six and a half year sentence for fraud and forgery in Singapore's Changi Gaol.

case, its Japanese operations are so large relative to the rest of the company—over 80 percent of its premium income is generated there—that the company feels compelled to manage its translation exposure.

Economic Exposure

The third type of foreign-exchange exposure is economic exposure. **Economic exposure** is the impact on the value of a firm's operations of unanticipated exchange-rate changes. Toyota's financial executives estimate, for example, that each 1 percent increase in the value of the yen against the dollar, sustained over the course of the year, decreases Toyota's profitability by $100 million.[25] A similar rise in the value of the yen lowers Nissan's profits by $80 million.[26] From a strategic perspective, the threat of economic exposure deserves close attention from the

The saga is more extensive. Showa Shell Seikiyu KK, a Japanese oil refiner half-owned by Royal Dutch Shell, lost $1.05 billion in 1993 by speculating in foreign exchange futures, an action that violated Shell's company policy. Allied-Lyons, a U.K. food and beverage manufacturer, lost £150 million in 1991, by speculating on changes in the value of the dollar. Procter & Gamble (P&G) entered into a series of complex contracts involving interest rate differentials between German and treasury bonds in 1993 and 1994. If interest rates had continued to fall, P&G would have won handsomely. Unfortunately, those interest rates rose. P&G lost $157 million on the contracts, and its corporate treasurer lost his job. Nippon Steel & Chemical Co. lost $135 million in the early 1990s through ill-advised trades in the foreign exchange market. The loss was discovered only when an audit was conducted after the head of the firm's accounting department died in a railway accident.

Obviously, shareholders in these firms, and many other firms suffering similar losses, were not pleased. However, from the public's perspective, of even greater concern is the fact that trading in such instruments exposes the banking community to similarly large losses. In 1993, for example, Chemical Bank held derivative contracts totaling $2.4 *trillion*, while Bankers Trust and Citicorp each had contractual obligations of $1.9 *trillion*. Many other international banks in Europe and Japan have similarly large obligations. However, bankers calmly explain that while their gross exposure is quite large, their net exposure is much smaller. For example, a bank may buy British pounds forward in order to accommodate one client and sell an equivalent amount of British pounds forward to meet the needs of another client. As the two transactions effectively cancel each other out, the bank's net exposure is zero. Further, many transactions in this market are made between banks, so the banking system's net exposure is much smaller than the numbers suggest.

Banking regulators in Europe, Japan, and the United States are less sanguine. They fear that mismanagement by just one major bank of its derivative portfolio could lead to chaos in the international financial market. In their doomsday scenario, a failure by one bank to honor its obligations could trigger a series of defaults by other banks, whose ability to honor their obligations depends on the collapsed bank's honoring its own.

Source: "Beleaguered giant: As derivative losses rise, the huge industry fights to avert regulation," *Wall Street Journal*, August 25, 1994, p. A6; "Through a market, darkly," *Financial Times*, May 27, 1994, p. 15; "The beauty and the beast," *The Economist*, May 14, 1994, p. 21; "Just what firms do with 'derivatives' is suddenly a hot issue," *Wall Street Journal*, April 14, 1994, p. A1; Carol Loomis, "The risk that won't go away," *Fortune*, March 7, 1994, pp. 40ff; "Many Americans run hidden financial risk from 'derivatives,'" *Wall Street Journal*, August 10, 1993, p. A1; "Japan toughens financial disclosure law," *Wall Street Journal*, August 10, 1993, p. C1; "Loss focuses attention on detecting unauthorized trades," *Financial Times,* May 24, 1993; L. Hunt, "In search of Nick Leeson," *The Sunday Age*, March 24, 1996, Agenda, p. 2; *Sunday Weekend Argus* (South Africa), "Leeson is jailed for 6 1/2 years," December 2/3 1995, pp. 1, 31; "Behind the Sumitomo scandal: A drive to be the copper king," *The Australian Financial Review*, July 9, 1996, p. 13; "Daiwa trader sent to jail," *The Age,* December 18, 1996, p. C3; "Daiwa fined US $450m on cover-up count," *The Age,* March 1, 1996, p. B4; "Year of the great sale," *Herald Sun,* December 28, 1995, p. 13.

firm's highest policy makers, for it affects virtually every area of operations, including global production, marketing, and financial planning.

Unanticipated exchange-rate fluctuations may affect a firm's overall sales and profitability in numerous markets. In 1997, for example, the value of the U.S. dollar rose in world currency markets. U.S. exporters faced the unhappy choice of either raising their local currency prices in their export markets and seeing their market shares erode *or* holding the line on the prices they charge their foreign customers and seeing their profit margins cut.

Long-term investments in property, plant, and equipment are particularly vulnerable to economic exposure, even if they are located in a firm's home country. For example, the U.S. market is very important to German luxury automobile manufacturers such as Daimler-Benz, Porsche, and BMW. The decline in the U.S. dollar relative to the deutsche mark in the 1980s made upscale German cars increasingly expensive to U.S. motorists. German automakers thus lost market share in the luxury car segment of the U.S. market. To address this problem, both BMW and Daimler-Benz built assembly plants in the United States. By diversifying their production to better match the location of their customers, they reduced their economic exposure to fluctuations in the dollar/mark exchange rate. Sony has similarly tried to cut its economic exposure to exchange rate fluctuations by localizing its manufacturing, R&D, and parts procurement to better match its revenue flows and cost flows by country.[27]

Other innovative techniques exist for reducing economic exposure to exchange-rate changes. For example, in 1988 the Walt Disney Company developed a creative financial plan to reduce uncertainty regarding its proceeds from Tokyo Disneyland. Concerned about fluctuations in the value of the U.S. dollar relative to the yen, in 1988 the firm sold twenty years of projected royalties from Tokyo Disneyland to a group of Japanese investors at a time when the value of the yen was high relative to the dollar. The value of the payments was discounted back to 1988 terms at the prevailing 6 percent interest rate on long-term Japanese bonds and then converted from yen to dollars. Disney placed the proceeds ($750 million) in U.S. government bonds, which were yielding 10 percent at the time. By doing so, the firm locked in a favorable exchange rate for its yen earnings, thereby hedging against a drop in the yen's value.[28]

As this Disney example suggests, an important element of managing economic exposure is analyzing likely changes in exchange rates. (Map 18.3 shows exchange-rate changes versus the dollar in the mid-1990s.) A wide variety of exchange-rate experts are available to assist international businesses in this task. These range from private consultants to the staffs of international banks to the published forecasts of international organizations such as the World Bank and the International Monetary Fund. These experts scrutinize many of the factors discussed in Chapter 5. The theory of purchasing power parity, for example, provides guidance regarding long-term trends in exchange rates between countries. In the short term, forward exchange rates have been found to be unbiased predictors of future spot rates. Because of the importance of interest arbitrage in establishing equilibrium exchange rates, experts may also forecast countries' monetary policies in order to predict future currency values. BOP performance is also useful because it provides insights into whether a country's industries are remaining competitive in world markets and whether foreigners' short-term claims on a country are increasing. Prospects for inflation are also carefully assessed, since inflation can affect a county's export prospects, demand for imports, and future interest rates.

Management of Working Capital

Managing foreign-exchange exposure is related to another task that financial officers of international businesses perform—managing working capital, or cash, balances. This task is more complicated for MNCs than for purely domestic firms. An MNC's financial officers must consider the firm's working capital position for each of its foreign subsidiaries and in each currency in

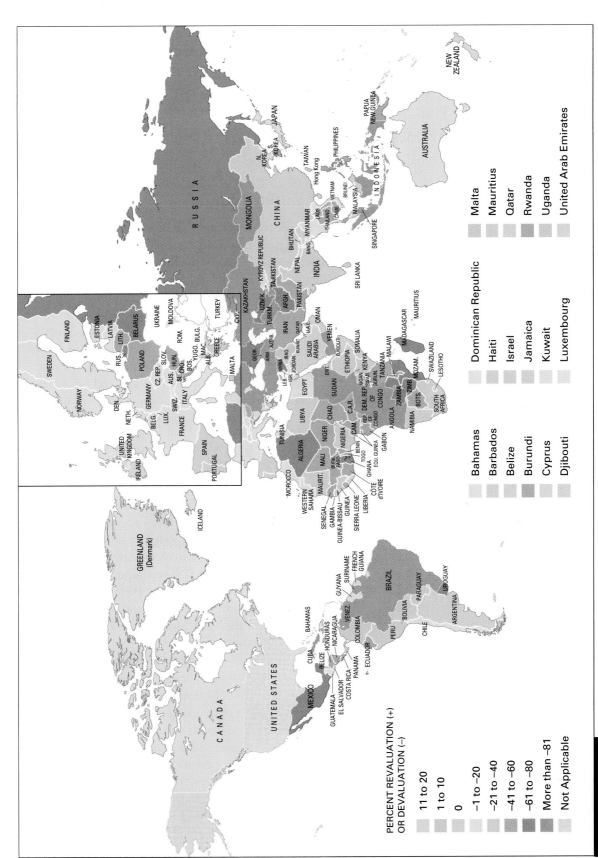

**PERCENT REVALUATION (+)
OR DEVALUATION (−)**

11 to 20

1 to 10

0

−1 to −20

−21 to −40

−41 to −60

−61 to −80

More than −81

Not Applicable

Bahamas

Barbados

Belize

Burundi

Cyprus

Djibouti

Dominican Republic

Haiti

Israel

Jamaica

Kuwait

Luxembourg

Malta

Mauritius

Qatar

Rwanda

Uganda

United Arab Emirates

MAP 18.3 **Changes in Currency Values Relative to the U.S. Dollar, February 1998 versus February 1993**

which the subsidiaries do business, as well as for the firm as a whole. KLM, for example, normally uses eighty currencies in its operations, and its financial officers must monitor its holdings of each of these currencies. In the process, they must balance three corporate financial goals:

1 Minimizing working capital balances

2 Minimizing currency conversion costs

3 Minimizing foreign-exchange risk

Minimizing Working Capital Balances

Financial officers seek to minimize the firm's working capital balances. Both domestic and international firms must hold working capital for two reasons: to facilitate day-to-day transactions and to cover the firm against unexpected demands for cash. (Note that the term cash refers here to actual cash, checking account balances, and highly liquid marketable securities that normally carry low yields.) Obviously, a firm does not want to run out of cash on hand. Failure to have sufficient cash to pay workers or suppliers can lead, at a minimum, to expensive emergency borrowings or, in the worst case, to an embarrassing loss of reputation that may cause suppliers and lenders to cut off future lines of credit. However, the rate of return on working capital is extremely low, and financial officers prefer to capture higher rates of return, if possible, by investing surplus funds in some other form than cash. Thus they need to balance the firm's needs for cash against the opportunity cost of holding the firm's financial assets in such low-yielding forms.

One technique MNCs can use to minimize their company-wide cash holdings is **centralized cash management.** A centralized cash manager, typically a member of the MNC's corporate treasury staff, coordinates the MNC's world-wide cash flows. Each of the MNC's subsidiaries sends to the centralized cash manager a daily cash report and an analysis of its expected cash balances and needs over the short run, which may range from a week to a month depending on the parent corporation's operating requirements. These reports are then assembled by the centralized cash manager's staff, who use them to reduce the precautionary balances held by the corporation as a whole and to plan short-term investment and borrowing strategies for the MNC. Instead of each subsidiary holding precautionary, "just in case" cash balances, the staff may direct each sub-sidiary to send cash in excess of its operational needs to a central corporate bank account. The centralized cash manager will pool these funds, funneling them to subsidiaries when and if emergencies arise. The unexpected need for additional cash by one subsidiary will often be offset by an unexpected excess of cash gener-ated by a second. Thus the central cash manager is able to reduce the precautio-nary cash balances held by the firm as a whole, and thereby reduce the amount of the firm's assets tied up in such a low-yielding form. Further, the expertise of the centralized cash manager's staff can be used to seek out the best short-term investment opportunities available for the firm's excess cash holdings and to monitor expected changes in the values of foreign currencies. By transferring these tasks from the subsidiaries to the parent corporation, this approach also reduces the number of highly trained, high-salaried financial specialists the cor-porate family needs. It is more efficient and cost-effective to concentrate such

GOING GLOBAL

Colefax and Fowler's Cash Flow Solution

Smaller businesses are also faced with the task of managing working capital and currency conversion costs. For example, U.K.-based Colefax and Fowler sells its high-priced, trendy wallpaper and fabric to upscale customers and distributors throughout Europe. However, its average invoice is only £96, and the bank charges its French and German customers pay for converting their local currencies into pounds typically total £15 per transaction. In the past, these customers often would seek to reduce their currency conversion costs by accumulating their invoices until their total reached some minimum amount. The typical customer paid an average of 86 days after receiving an invoice. This behavior played havoc with Colefax and Fowler's cash flow and increased the size of the working capital loans it needed.

Wanting to improve its cash flow but afraid of losing customers, the firm sought advice from a British financial services consulting firm. That firm recommended that Colefax and Fowler establish bank accounts in each country in which it did significant business. Its customers then could save conversion costs by writing checks denominated in their local currency for deposit in Colefax and Fowler's local accounts.

But Colefax and Fowler ultimately wants pounds, not French francs or deutsche marks. So it hired a Dutch firm, EDM, which specializes in handling large numbers of small payments for firms such as the publishers of *Newsweek* and *National Geographic*. EDM contracts with European banks to provide it with daily information about payments made to its clients' accounts. EDM then faxes this account information to its clients so that they can credit their customers' accounts. In the case of Colefax and Fowler, once local bank balances reach an agreed-upon level, EDM instructs the local banks to transfer funds to Colefax and Fowler's British bank account. Although the British firm now bears the currency conversion costs, the new system encourages its customers to buy more goods more often. And by speeding up the payment process, Colefax and Fowler has saved an estimated £45,000 annually in interest charges on its working capital loans. This savings more than pays for EDM's services.

Source: "Small cheques, big problems," *Financial Times*, June 21, 1994, p. 12.

financial information gathering and decision making in one unit of the corporation, rather than compelling each subsidiary to develop such expertise in-house. (For an innovative solution to working capital problems facing smaller businesses, see "Going Global.")

Minimizing Currency Conversion Costs

International businesses face another complication. Their foreign subsidiaries may continually buy and sell parts and finished goods among themselves. For example, Samsung, Korea's largest *chaebol,* has major assembly plants as well as company-owned parts suppliers and distribution companies throughout the world. The constant transfer of parts and finished goods among Samsung subsidiaries generates a blizzard of invoices and a constant need to transfer funds among the subsidiaries' bank accounts. Cumulative bank charges for transferring these funds and converting the currencies involved can be high. For large transactions involving two major currencies, currency conversion fees and expenses may average 0.3 percent of the value of the transaction. For smaller-sized transactions or for transactions involving minor currencies with narrow markets, such fees and expenses can easily be three or four times higher.[29]

FIGURE 18.3

**Payment Flows
without Netting**

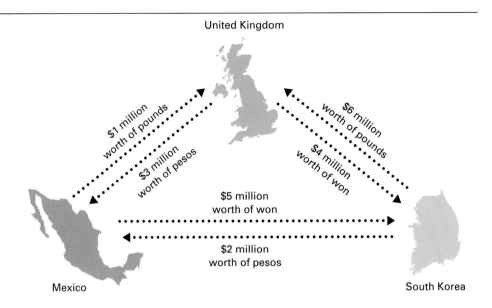

Let's consider Samsung's operations in just three countries: Mexico, the United Kingdom, and South Korea. As depicted in Fig. 18.3, the gross trade among the firm's subsidiaries in the three countries is $21 million (=1+3+6+4+5+2). (We have denominated their trade in a common currency (U.S. dollars) for simplicity.) If the costs of converting currencies total 0.5 percent of the transactions' value, Samsung would pay 0.5 percent times $21 million, or $105,000, to convert the currencies necessary to settle these transactions among its subsidiaries.

This cost can be cut considerably, however, if the subsidiaries engage in **bilateral netting,** in which two subsidiaries net out their mutual invoices. Consider Samsung's Mexican and British subsidiaries. Rather than have the Mexican subsidiary convert $1 million worth of pesos into pounds and the British subsidiary convert $3 million worth of pounds into pesos, it makes more sense for them to net out the difference. In this case, the British subsidiary should simply pay the Mexican subsidiary $2 million in pesos, making them even. In similar fashion, the South Korean subsidiary can pay the British subsidiary $2 million worth of pounds ($6 million − $4 million = $2 million), and the Mexican subsidiary can pay the Korean subsidiary $3 million worth of Korean won ($5 million − $2 million = $3 million). By engaging in bilateral netting, Samsung reduces its currency conversion costs to $35,000 (0.5 percent × $7 million).

Currency conversion costs can be reduced further if Samsung engages in **multilateral netting,** which is done among three or more business units. As shown in Table 18.3, the British subsidiary owes the equivalent of $7 million to the other two subsidiaries but is also owed $7 million by them. The South Korean subsidiary is owed $9 million but owes $8 million, for a net receipt of $1 million. The Mexican subsidiary is owed $5 million but owes $6 million, for a net debt of $1 million. When accompanied by the appropriate bookkeeping entries, all transactions among the three subsidiaries can be settled by the Mexican subsidiary transferring $1 million worth of won to the South Korean subsidiary. Because only $1 million is physically being converted in the foreign-exchange market and

TABLE 18.3

Multilateral Netting in Action (all quantities in millions of U.S. dollar equivalents)

		PAYMENTS OWED BY				
		South Korean subsidiary	Mexican subsidiary	British subsidiary	TOTAL RECEIPTS	NET TRANSFER
RECEIPTS DUE TO	South Korean subsidiary	—	5	4	9	+1
	Mexican subsidiary	2	—	3	5	−1
	British subsidiary	6	1	—	7	0
	TOTAL PAYMENTS	8	6	7	21	

transferred through the banking system, Samsung's conversion costs shrink to $5000 (0.5 percent × $1 million) as a result of the multilateral netting operation.

In concept, multilateral netting differs little from what children do on the playground all the time: "David owes Karen a quarter, but Karen owes LaTisha twenty cents, so David owes LaTisha twenty cents and Karen five cents, and Karen owes nobody anything." To complicate matters, however, some countries impose restrictions on netting operations in order to support their local banking industries, which benefit from the fees charged for currency exchange.[30] MNCs wanting to engage in netting operations often have to work around such government-imposed barriers.

Minimizing Foreign-Exchange Risk

Financial officers also typically adjust the mix of currencies that comprise the firm's working capital in order to minimize foreign-exchange risk. Often firms use a **leads and lags strategy** to try to increase their net holdings of currencies that are expected to rise in value and to decrease their net holdings of currencies that are expected to fall in value. For example, if the Thai baht were expected to decline in value, the financial officers would try to minimize the MNC's baht-denominated liquid assets, perhaps by demanding quicker (or *leading*) payment on baht-denominated accounts receivable or by reducing baht-denominated bank balances. The officers also would try to increase the firm's baht-denominated short-term liabilities, perhaps by slowing (or *lagging*) payment on baht-denominated accounts payable or by increasing short-term borrowing from Thai banks. Conversely, if the Mexican peso were expected to rise in value, the financial officers would try to maximize the firm's net holdings of pesos through reverse techniques.

Avon adopted these tactics as the Asian currency crisis worsened in late 1997. It bought most of the raw materials needed by its Asian factories locally; the working capital needs of these factories were supplied by local banks with the loans repayable in the local currency. By so doing, it increased its liabilities denominated in weakened currencies like the Indonesian rupiah, the Malaysian ringgit, and the Philippine peso. Its Asian subsidiaries were required to repatriate their earnings to headquarters on a weekly basis rather than on the monthly basis they had used previously. In this way, Avon minimized its holdings of these vulnerable currencies.[31]

In summary, an MNC's financial officers face a complex task. They must ensure each subsidiary maintains sufficient cash balances to meet expected ordinary day-to-day cash outflows, as well as an appropriate level of precautionary balances in order to respond quickly to sudden, unexpected increases in cash outflow. They also must balance each subsidiary's expected and unexpected demands for cash against the opportunity cost of holding the firm's financial assets in such low-yielding forms, while simultaneously controlling working capital-related currency conversion costs and foreign-exchange risk. Typically, such tasks are performed by a single unit of the firm, such as the treasury department of the parent corporation. For example, Tate & Lyle, a large British food processor, has followed this approach. Its centralized treasury provides cash management, in-house banking, currency conversion, and foreign-exchange risk-management services for all of the company's far-flung subsidiaries. Its centralized treasury handles over $6 billion of intracorporate cash flows a year.[32]

International Capital Budgeting

Another task financial officers of any business face is capital budgeting. Firms have limited funds for investment and often a seemingly endless set of projects from which to choose. They must establish mechanisms for developing, screening, and selecting projects in which the firm will make significant new investments. Numerous approaches for evaluating investment projects are available, but the most commonly used methods include net present value, internal rate of return, and payback period.

Net Present Value

The net present value approach is based on a basic precept of finance theory that a dollar today is worth more than a dollar in the future. To calculate the net present value of a project, a firm's financial officers estimate the cash flows the project will generate in each time period and then discount them back to the present. For many projects, the cash flow in the early years will be negative, since the firm must outlay cash for the initial investment and be prepared to suffer start-up operating losses in the first year or two. In later years, of course, the firm expects cash flows to be positive. Financial officers must decide which interest rate, called the *rate of discount*, to use in the calculation, based on the firm's cost of capital. For example, if the firm's cost of capital is 10 percent, then financial officers will use an annual interest rate of 10 percent to discount the cash flows generated by the project through time in order to calculate the present value. The firm will undertake only projects that generate a positive net present value.

The net present value approach can be used for both domestic and international projects. However, several additional factors must be considered when determining whether to undertake an international project.[33] These factors are risk adjustment, currency selection, and choice of perspective for the calculations.

Risk Adjustment. Because a foreign project may be riskier than a domestic project, international businesses may adjust either the discount rate upward or the expected cash flows downward to account for a higher level of risk. The amount of risk adjustment should reflect the degree of riskiness of operating in the country in question. For example, little if any risk adjustment is needed for Germany because of its political stability, well-respected court system, and superb infrastructure. In contrast, religious conflict in Algeria and civil war in Afghanistan warrant the use of much larger risk adjustments for potential investments in those countries.

Choice of Currency. The determination of the currency in which the project should be evaluated depends on the nature of the investment. If the project is an integral part of the business of an overseas subsidiary, use of the foreign currency is appropriate. For example, GM's German subsidiary Adam Opel AG invested millions of deutsche marks to build a new factory in Eisenach, Germany in the early 1990s. Constructing the plant was central to Opel's overall business plan, and the subsidiary's financial officers thus made the net present value calculation in deutsche marks. For foreign projects that are more properly viewed as integrated parts of a firm's global procurement strategy, translation into the home country currency may make sense. For example, Houston-based Compaq Computer allocates production between its U.S. and foreign factories as part of an overall strategy of global reduction of production costs. If Compaq invests £10 million to expand the output of its Scottish production facilities, it should calculate the project's net present value in U.S. dollars instead of pounds. To do this, it must estimate revenues and costs for the project and then convert them into dollars. It also must account for any expected changes in the exchange rate between the dollar and the pound over the life of the project.

Whose Perspective: Parent's or Project's? Another factor is determining whether the cash flows that contribute to the net present value of the capital investment should be evaluated from the perspective of the parent or that of the individual project. In practice, some international businesses analyze the cash flows of the individual project, others focus on the project's impact on the parent, and others do both.[34]

The cash flows to the parent can differ from those to the project for several reasons. MNCs often impose arbitrary accounting charges on the revenues of their operating units for the units' use of corporate trademarks or to cover general corporate overhead. These arbitrary charges may reduce the *perceived* cash flows generated by the project, but not the *real* cash flows returned to the parent. For example, suppose that when the corporate parent's accountants are calculating a subsidiary's profitability, they routinely assess a 5 percent fee against revenues for general corporate and administrative expenses. This technique may be a reasonable mechanism for allocating general corporate expenses across all the firm's operations. But the 5 percent charge does not represent a true drain on the cash flow generated by the subsidiary. Thus it should be ignored in the calculation of the net present value to the parent of a project the subsidiary proposes. Similarly, fees assessed against the subsidiary for the use of corporate trademarks, brand names, or patents should not be considered in the net present value calculation because the parent firm incurs no additional costs regardless of whether the subsidiary undertakes the project.[35]

Financial officers also must consider any governmental restrictions on currency movements that would affect the firm's ability to repatriate profits when it wants. A project proposed by a foreign subsidiary may be enormously profitable, but if the profits can never be repatriated to the parent, the project may not be desirable from the perspective of the parent and its shareholders. The importance of currency controls in determining the attractiveness of a project may also be a function of the parent's overall strategy. For example, PepsiCo has made a long-term commitment to the Ukrainian soft drink market. Any current Ukrainian restrictions on profit repatriation are of little concern to PepsiCo and its shareholders, since the firm expects to increase its investments in the country in the short and medium term. However, PepsiCo's shareholders would be concerned if the firm were never allowed to repatriate profits from its Ukrainian operations.

Internal Rate of Return

A second approach commonly used for evaluating investment projects is to calculate the internal rate of return. With this approach financial officers first estimate the cash flows generated by each project under consideration in each time period, as in the net present value analysis. They then calculate the interest rate—called the *internal rate of return*—that makes the net present value of the project just equal to zero. As with the net present value approach, the financial officers must adjust their calculations for any accounting charges that have no cash flow implications (intracorporate licensing fees, overhead charges for general corporate and administrative expenses, and so on). They then compare the project's internal rate of return with the **hurdle rate**—the minimum rate of return the firm finds acceptable for its capital investments. The hurdle rate may vary by country to account for differences in risk. The firm will undertake only projects for which the internal rate of return is higher than the hurdle rate.

Payback Period

A third approach for assessing and selecting projects is to calculate a project's **payback period**—the number of years it will take the firm to recover, or pay back, from the project's earnings the original cash investment. Vancouver's Placer Dome, Inc., often uses a payback approach to evaluate mining investments, such as a proposed $500 million investment in a Chilean copper mine as part of a joint venture with Finland's Outokumpu OY. After determining that this project's payback period would be less than five years, Placer decided to proceed with the deal.[36]

The payback period technique has the virtue of simplicity: all one needs is simple arithmetic to calculate the payback period. This approach ignores, however, the profits generated by the investment in the longer run. A project that earns large early profits but whose later profits diminish steadily over time may be

Before investing $500 million in this Chilean copper mine, the financial officers of Vancouver's Placer Dome Inc. carefully analyzed the risks and rewards of the project.

selected over a project that suffers initial start-up losses but makes large continuous profits after that.

Because of its simplicity, many firms use the payback period technique for a quick-and-dirty screening of projects and then follow with a more sophisticated method for further analysis of those that pass the preliminary screening.[37] A firm may choose different payback criteria for international projects than for domestic ones. Here, too, adjustments must be made to eliminate intracorporate charges that have no real effect on corporate cash flows.

Sources of International Investment Capital

Firms use capital budgeting techniques to allocate their financial resources toward those domestic and international projects that promise the highest rates of return. Having identified such profitable opportunities, firms must secure sufficient capital to fund them, from either internal or external sources. In doing so, an international business wants to minimize the worldwide cost of its capital, while also minimizing its foreign-exchange risk, political risk, and global tax burden.[38]

Internal Sources of Investment Capital

One source of investment capital for international businesses is the cash flows generated internally (for example, profits from operations and noncash expenses such as depreciation and amortization) by the parent firm and its various subsidiaries. The amount from such sources is significant: in 1996, foreign subsidiaries of U.S.-owned firms earned $98.9 billion, while U.S. subsidiaries of foreign-owned parents earned $32.1 billion.[39] Internal cash flows thus represent an important source of capital for funding subsidiaries' investment projects.

FIGURE 18.4

Internal Sources of Capital for International Businesses

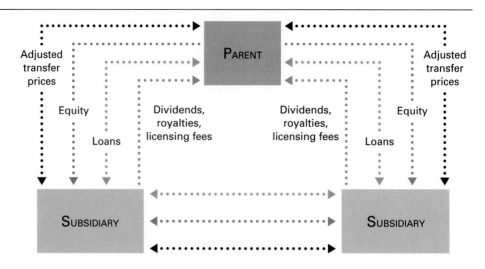

Subject to legal constraints, the parent firm may use the cash flow generated by any subsidiary to fund the investment projects of any member of the corporate family. The corporate parent may access the cash flow directly via the subsidiary's dividend payments to the parent. The parent then can channel those funds to another subsidiary through either a loan or additional equity investments in that subsidiary. Alternatively, one subsidiary can directly lend funds to a second subsidiary. Figure 18.4 summarizes the various internal sources of capital available to the parent and its subsidiaries.

Two legal constraints may affect the parent's ability to shift funds among its subsidiaries. First, if the subsidiary is not wholly owned by the parent, the parent must respect the rights of the subsidiary's other shareholders. Any intracorporate transfers of funds must be done on a fair market basis. This ensures the parent does not siphon off the subsidiary's profits through self-dealing, thereby harming the other shareholders' interests. If the subsidiary is wholly owned, transfers of funds are not a problem. Second, some countries impose restrictions on the repatriation of profits, thus blocking intracorporate transfers of funds. However, a parent may find that while it cannot shift funds in the form of dividends to itself, it can shift funds in the form of loans to other subsidiaries. Or, the parent may be able to recapture funds from the subsidiary by charging licensing fees for the use of the parent's brand names, trademarks, copyrights, or patents or by imposing fees for general corporate or administrative services. Such payments are not trivial. In 1996, foreign subsidiaries paid their U.S.-owned parents $30 billion in royalties and licensing fees, while U.S. subsidiaries paid their foreign-owned parents $7.3 billion for the same purpose.[40] (Please note that we do not mean to imply that any of these fees were paid to evade host country restrictions on currency movements.)

A parent corporation also may shift funds between its operating units by adjusting the transfer prices paid for goods and services in intracorporate transactions between a subsidiary and other branches of the corporate family. Suppose subsidiary B operates in a country that restricts profit repatriation, while subsidiary A does not. By raising the price charged by subsidiary A for a good purchased by subsidiary B, the MNC can transfer funds from B to A.

(Chapter 19 discusses the income tax implications of these pricing policies and the pitfalls awaiting firms that aggressively manipulate transfer prices.) Firms must be aware that transfer-pricing policies are least controversial when used between two wholly owned subsidiaries. Otherwise, the parent may be placing itself in the position of either defrauding the outside investors (in the case of subsidiary B) or enriching them (in the case of subsidiary A) at the expense of its own shareholders.

While such intracorporate transfers of funds may theoretically benefit the entire firm, they can create serious problems at the subsidiary and managerial level. From the parent's perspective, shifting cash flows from subsidiary to parent may be beneficial. However, it may cause operational problems and increased expenses for the subsidiary. The parent may consider it wise policy to siphon off the subsidiary's working capital and reduce its reported profitability by inflating royalty fees, administrative charges, or other transfer prices. Yet such approaches may result in a misleading picture of the subsidiary's performance in the marketplace. If the parent rewards managerial performance without making adjustments for these financial manipulations, morale among the subsidiary's managers may plummet, to the detriment of the parent.

External Sources of Investment Capital

When raising external financing for their investment projects, international businesses may choose from a rich source of debt and equity alternatives. Investment bankers, such as Goldman Sachs, and securities firms, such as Merrill Lynch and Nomura, can help firms acquire capital from external sources. For example, if a firm wants to increase its equity base, such an intermediary can place the firm's stock with investors in the home country, in the host country, or in other countries. To facilitate the raising of equity internationally, many MNCs list their common stock on stock markets in several different countries. For example, KLM shares are listed on the New York, Amsterdam, Brussels, and Frankfurt stock exchanges. Or consider Sony: its stock is listed on the New York, Pacific, Chicago, Toronto, London, Paris, Frankfurt, Dusseldorf, Brussels, Antwerp, Vienna, and Swiss stock exchanges, as well as on five Japanese stock exchanges.[41] Through multiple foreign listings, international businesses assure foreign investors that they can easily dispose of their shares should the need arise.

International firms also have many opportunities to borrow funds internationally on either a short-term or a long-term basis. They may shop for the best credit terms in their home country market, in the host country market, or in other markets. For example, consider New Jersey's Baltek Corporation, which annually produces $30 million in balsa wood products at its factory in Ecuador. In the early 1990s, Baltek relied on local Ecuadorian banks to finance its expansion into shrimp farming in the Gulf of Guayaquil. The firm found those banks more eager for its business than U.S. banks were—an example of the advantages of being a big fish in a small pond.[42] Larger MNCs may rely on syndicated short- and medium-term loans in which a consortium of international banks and pension fund managers join together to provide the capital. Often these syndicated loans use Eurocurrencies, since the absence of expensive central bank regulations reduces the cost of Eurocurrency-based loans. MNCs also may secure longer-term loans in the form of home country bonds, foreign bonds, and Eurobonds, as discussed in Chapter 5.

Securities firms and investment banks are continually developing innovative financing techniques to reduce the costs of borrowing for their MNC clients or to exploit gaps in national financial regulations.[43] For example, an MNC may issue dual-currency bonds, whereby it borrows money and pays interest in one currency but repays the principal in a second currency. Or bonds may be denominated as a basket of several currencies or be redeemable in gold. Some firms get very creative. For example, in October 1992, the Walt Disney Company issued $400 million in Eurobonds that had a different twist: their interest rate depended on the success of 13 Disney movies. Investors were guaranteed at least a 3 percent rate, with a possible return of 13.5 percent. Comparable quality bonds were yielding only 7–8 percent. Eager investors snapped up the bonds, betting that *The Muppet Christmas Carol* and other Disney movies would be box office hits.[44] Pleased with its ability to shift some movie-making risks to the bondholders through low minimum interest rates, in 1994 Disney offered a similar note linked to a new set of motion pictures.[45]

A particularly important facet of the international capital market is the **swap market**, in which two firms can exchange their financial obligations. Swaps are undertaken to change the cost and nature of a firm's interest obligations or to change the currency in which its debt is denominated. For example, suppose firm A has a fixed-rate obligation but prefers a floating-rate one, while firm B has a floating-rate obligation and wants a fixed-rate one. The two firms can swap their obligations. As noted by John Grout, a financial officer at Cadbury Schweppes, "The advantage of the swap market is that it allows you to adjust exposure profiles without having to undo the underlying transactions."[46] Often an international bank will facilitate such swaps by acting as a broker or by undertaking half of a swap for its own account.

MNCs also often engage in currency swaps, in order to shift their interest and payment obligations from a less preferred currency to a more preferred one. An MNC may consider its net obligations in one currency to be too large or may expect exchange-rate fluctuations to adversely affect its loan repayment costs. A swap may be arranged between two firms that have differing currency preferences. International banks play a key role in the currency swap market. Since they continually monitor foreign-exchange markets as well as their net currency exposures, they usually can accommodate any MNC's currency swap needs. Most international banks engage in currency swaps with corporate clients on an ongoing basis.

Through swaps, international businesses can manage both their interest costs and their exposure to exchange-rate fluctuations. For example, in the early 1990s Toronto-based Inco, the world's leading miner and refiner of nickel, swapped SFr200 million in 5.75 percent bonds and ECU70 million in 9.5 percent notes for debt obligations denominated in U.S. dollars bearing interest rates of 10.2 percent and 10.5 percent, respectively. Why would Inco agree to pay higher interest rates on the new bonds than it was paying on the old ones? One reason is that the firm receives much of its revenues in U.S. dollars and wants to match those dollar receipts with offsetting dollar obligations. Inco may also have believed that the U.S. dollar would depreciate in value and relished the prospect of paying off the bonds in the future with depreciated dollars.[47]

CHAPTER REVIEW

Summary

International firms face financial management challenges that are far more complex than those confronting purely domestic firms. Conflicts may arise between exporters and importers over the currency to use in invoicing international transactions. Exporting firms often find it difficult to check the creditworthiness of their foreign customers. Also, obtaining payment for goods from foreign customers may be more difficult because of greater geographical distances, differing legal systems, and unfamiliar business customs. Fortunately, many methods of payment have been developed over the centuries, including letters of credit, documentary collection, credit cards, and countertrade.

International firms must strive to minimize the impact of exchange-rate fluctuations on their operations. Three main types of exchange-rate exposure exist. Transaction exposure refers to the impact of exchange-rate fluctuations on the profitability of a business transaction denominated in a foreign currency. Translation exposure reflects the impact of exchange-rate fluctuations on the value of foreign operations in a firm's accounting records. Economic exposure is the impact unanticipated exchange-rate movements have on the value of the firm's operations.

Management of working capital balances presents international businesses with unique challenges. A firm and each of its operating subsidiaries must have sufficient cash to facilitate day-to-day operations and to meet unexpected demands for cash. Also, the firm must monitor its holdings of each currency in which it and its subsidiaries do business. MNCs often use centralized cash management and currency netting operations to control their working capital balances, reduce currency conversion costs, and minimize their exposure to adverse changes in exchange rates.

Financial officers of international firms must adjust capital budgeting techniques to meet the unique requirements of international business. Standard investment evaluation techniques, such as net present value, internal rate of return, and payback period analysis, must be changed to account for differences in risk, government restrictions on currency movements, and various payments between the parent firm and its foreign subsidiaries that do not affect net cash flows generated by an investment project.

Finally, financial officers must look worldwide for low-cost sources of capital. Ongoing operations of the parent firm and its foreign subsidiaries are often an important internal source of investment capital. Well-developed international debt and equity markets can provide external sources of such capital. Also, international businesses often use the swap market to reduce their exposure to adverse changes in currency values or interest rates.

Review Questions

1. What special problems arise in financing and arranging payment for international transactions?

2. What are the major methods of payment used for international transactions?

3. What are the different types of letters of credit?

4. How do a time draft and a sight draft differ? A trade acceptance and a banker's acceptance?

5. How do the various types of countertrade arrangements differ from each other?

6. What techniques are available to reduce transaction exposure? Discuss each.

7. What is translation exposure? What effect does a balance sheet hedge have on translation exposure?

8. Why do MNCs engage in currency netting operations?

9. What capital budgeting techniques are available to international businesses?

10. What is the difference between an interest rate swap and a currency swap?

Questions for Discussion

1. What are the advantages and disadvantages of each method of payment for international transactions from the exporter's perspective?

2. Which type of letter of credit is most preferable from the exporter's point of view?

3. Why do firms use countertrade? What problems do they face when they do?

4. How does capital budgeting for international projects differ from that for domestic projects?

5. The "Going Global" on page 667 noted that some U.S. companies are losing contracts to supply the Three Gorges Dam to European competitors because of the lack of support from the U.S. Export-Import Bank. Should the Eximbank change its policy to aid U.S. exporters? Or should the Eximbank maintain its pro-environment stance?

6. The government of Colefax and Fowler's home country, the United Kingdom, has chosen not to be a charter participant in the EU's single currency scheme. Will this put Colefax and Fowler at a disadvantage in competing for business in other EU countries? If so, is there anything it can do to reduce its disadvantage?

BUILDING GLOBAL SKILLS

Consider Belgian Lace Products (BLP), a hypothetical table linens manufacturer. BLP consists of a parent corporation, a wholly owned manufacturing subsidiary in Belgium, and four wholly owned distribution subsidiaries in Belgium, Germany, Japan, and the United States. Its manufacturing subsidiary buys inputs from various suppliers, manufactures high-quality lace napkins and tablecloths, and sells the output to the four BLP-owned distribution subsidiaries. The four distribution subsidiaries in turn sell the products to retail customers in their marketing areas. The distribution subsidiaries buy certain inputs, such as labor, warehouse space, electricity, and computers, from outside suppliers as well.

The following summarizes typical monthly transactions for each of the BLP operating units (BF = Belgian francs):

Manufacturing Subsidiary
Sales to Belgian distribution subsidiary: BF600,000
Sales to German distribution subsidiary: BF500,000
Sales to Japanese distribution subsidiary: BF700,000
Sales to U.S. distribution subsidiary: BF450,000
Cost of inputs purchased from Belgian suppliers: BF300,000

Costs of inputs purchased from German suppliers: DM50,000
Costs of inputs purchased from Japanese suppliers: ¥3,000,000
Costs of inputs purchased from U.S. suppliers: $5,000

Belgian Distribution Subsidiary
Sales to retail customers: BF2,000,000
Payments to BLP manufacturing subsidiary: BF600,000
Payments to external suppliers: BF30,000 and DM20,000

German Distribution Subsidiary
Sales to retail customers: DM150,000
Payments to BLP manufacturing subsidiary: BF500,000
Payments to external suppliers: DM10,000, BF40,000, and $9,000

Japanese Distribution Subsidiary
Sales to retail customers: ¥5,000,000
Payments to BLP manufacturing subsidiary: BF700,000
Payments to external suppliers: ¥3,000,000 and $8,000

U.S. Distribution Subsidiary

Sales to retail customers: $40,000

Payments to BLP manufacturing subsidiary:
BF450,000

Payments to external suppliers: $10,000 and
¥300,000

Exchange rates

BF20 = DM1
BF30 = $1.00
BF1 = ¥3

Use the above information to answer the following questions:

1. Calculate the profitability of each of BLP's five subsidiaries. (Because BLP is Belgian, perform the calculations in terms of Belgian francs.) Are

any of the subsidiaries unprofitable? On the basis of the information provided, would you recommend shutting down an unprofitable subsidiary? Why or why not?

2. Suppose it costs each subsidiary 1 percent of the transaction amount each time it converts its home currency into another currency in order to pay its suppliers. Develop a strategy by which BLP as a corporation can reduce its total currency conversion costs. Suppose your strategy costs BLP BF15,000 per month to implement. Should the firm still adopt your approach?

3. What effect would the creation of a single European currency have on BLP? On the benefits and costs of the strategy you developed to reduce its currency conversion costs?

WORKING WITH THE WEB: Building Global Internet Skills

Export Financing and the Internet

The promotion of exports is important to the economic health of most countries. However, many small businesses ignore export opportunities because they don't understand how they will be paid for their goods: letters of credit, time drafts, bills of lading, and the like all seem very confusing. If bankers can allay these fears and encourage small businesses to export, they stand to gain substantial revenues from providing trade financing to these new exporters.

Suppose you are on the marketing staff of a regional bank that has decided to target the small business trade financing market. One component of the bank's strategy is to develop a web site explaining to small businesses how the bank can help them export their goods

and get paid for their exports. You have been assigned to the team that will develop the bank's web site, and have been given two specific tasks. First, you have been asked to assess what information inexperienced exporters need about trade financing. Second, you have been asked to surf other banks' web sites and report back to the team which ones do an effective job of providing useful and understandable information to new exporters. After you have concluded these tasks, write a brief memo reporting your findings to the members of your team. Feel free to attach examples of effective web sites to your memo.

The textbook's web site provides linkages to several web sites that may be of help for this assignment.

CLOSING CASE

Janssen Pharmaceutica Cures Its Currency Ills[48]

Janssen Pharmaceutica, started by Dr. Paul Janssen in 1953, is one of the most innovative and success-

ful firms in the pharmaceutical industry. A subsidiary of Johnson & Johnson (J&J) since 1961, Janssen Pharmaceutica today employs 12,000 people worldwide. About 3,300 work in or near Beerse, the Belgian city where the firm was born and is headquartered.

Janssen's competitive strength lies in new drug development. Since 1970 only one firm in the world ranked higher than Janssen in the number of new drugs developed to cure humankind's ills. The Janssen-developed drugs Risperdal, Propulsid, and Itrizole, for example, combat such diverse medical problems as schizophrenia, nighttime heartburn, and fungal infections.

Janssen is also an important innovator in an area very different from pharmaceuticals: management of corporate treasury operations. Like many European firms, Janssen has production facilities and sales operations throughout Western Europe, the Americas, and Asia. It also purchases inputs and services from a wide variety of suppliers outside Belgium. Before 1984, handling the numerous incoming and outgoing cross-border invoices generated by its operations was very expensive. Much working capital was tied up as each of the firm's 32 far-flung subsidiaries maintained balances in their checking accounts sufficient to handle day-to-day operating needs and to protect against unexpected demands for cash. Further, every time a Janssen subsidiary paid an invoice denominated in a foreign currency, it paid currency conversion charges that averaged 0.5 percent of the amount in question.

In 1983 Belgium sought to improve the international competitiveness of its firms by authorizing the creation of so-called *coordination centers* to reduce the costs of corporate treasury activities. To qualify to establish a coordination center, a company had to have affiliates in at least four countries, to have sales of at least $300 million, and to employ a minimum of ten employees in its Belgian coordination center. Concomitant changes in Belgian tax laws reduced the corporate income tax burdens on coordination centers to near zero. By 1995 over 280 coordination centers had been established in Belgium, employing more than 8,000 highly trained professionals. The coordination centers have increased demand in Belgium for such corporate support services as accounting, auditing, legal research, and investment banking. Users resemble a who's who of international commerce, including such firms as IBM, British Petroleum, Monsanto, ABB Asea Brown Boveri, and Cable & Wireless PLC. About 30 percent of the coordination centers are owned by U.S. MNCs, 15 percent by Belgian MNCs, and 46 percent by

European MNCs headquartered outside of Belgium.

Janssen Pharmaceutica moved quickly to take advantage of the Belgian law by establishing a coordination center in June 1984. This center, a separately incorporated and wholly owned subsidiary of Janssen, provides a variety of financial services for the firm and its subsidiaries. Initially the coordination center focused on **treasury management**—the management of financial flows and of the currency and interest-rate risks associated with these flows. This mission involved three objectives:

1. Identify short- and medium-term financial risks on a worldwide basis.

2. Quantify such risks and recommend appropriate responses to Janssen's executives.

3. Manage and control these financial exposures on a worldwide basis subject to J&J's corporate rules and procedures (which encourage hedging but discourage speculation).

The center's treasury management activities include acting as a centralized cash manager and performing currency netting operations for the Janssen group of companies, thereby lowering the levels of cash balances held by the group and reducing the group's aggregate currency conversion costs. As Janssen has learned to use the center more efficiently, the center's duties have expanded. It now performs all currency and interest-rate exposure management and hedging activities for the Janssen group.

The coordination center has also taken over the bank management function. To benefit the whole group, it established checking accounts in the various countries in which Janssen does business. Suppose Janssen's German subsidiary buys paper and writing instruments from a French office supply wholesaler. The invoice (denominated in French francs) received by the German subsidiary will be sent to the coordination center, which will pay the invoice from its account at a French bank. By dealing with the banking system of only one country, Janssen can predict more reliably when checks will be debited or credited to its accounts. More important, however, this technique reduces currency conversion costs for the group as a whole. The German subsidiary, by shifting the responsibility for obtaining francs to the coordination center, avoids the cost of converting deutsche marks into francs. The coordination center can often obtain the necessary francs to pay French suppliers without converting any currencies. It does this by depositing franc-denominated revenues received by other Janssen subsidiaries into the coordination center's French bank account. This netting of payments and receipts on a corporate basis substantially reduces the need to convert currencies. The cumulative savings of currency conversion fees on hundreds of thousands of incoming and outgoing invoices amount to millions of dollars each year.

The managers of each Janssen subsidiary of course want credit for the revenues their subsidiary generates. Thus, at the end of the monthly accounting period, the coordination center nets out payments and receipts in all the currencies in which the subsidiary does business. It then sends each subsidiary either a *single* check or a *single* invoice, denominated in its local currency, that reflects the subsidiary's net position. And only 35 employees perform this monthly miracle for the Janssen group, although, as you can imagine, they work with an extremely sophisticated computer and telecommunications network.

In addition, the coordination center acts as an internal bank for the Janssen group. Its specialists interact continuously with the banking community worldwide, seeking the highest short-term interest rates for the group's excess cash balances. The center often can locate sources of low-cost loans for the Janssen subsidiaries. If a subsidiary needs to borrow money, the coordination center offers to match the best local terms available to that subsidiary. It uses a standardized loan document and so can offer 24-hour turnaround time on loan approvals. It also allocates to the borrowing subsidiary any tax benefits generated by the transaction.

As Janssen's coordination center honed its treasury management, bank management, and lending skills, J&J's corporate managers recognized that Janssen's expertise could be used to benefit the rest of the corporate family. Today, Janssen's coordination center provides financial services for the entire J&J family, with one significant change. When it served only the Janssen group, the center focused on managing exchange-rate risk in terms of the Belgian franc. However, because J&J is a U.S. firm, the center now manages exchange-rate risk in terms of the U.S. dollar.

Case Questions

1. In essence, to qualify for the tax breaks offered to a Belgian coordination center, a firm must be an MNC. Why would Belgium limit these tax breaks to multinationals? Are Belgian authorities happy that Janssen's coordination center is benefiting all of J&J's worldwide operations?

2. What are the advantages of having the Janssen coordination center act for J&J worldwide? Are there any disadvantages?

3. Can you think of any other strategies for reducing currency conversion costs that could be used by firms operating in Europe?

CHAPTER NOTES

1. *KLM Annual Report 1996/97 and 1993/94*; U.S. Department of Transportation, *U.S. International Air Passenger and Freight Statistics Calendar Year 1995*; *Fortune*, August 22, 1994, p. 190.

2. "Exporters get no help from slide in baht," *Financial Times*, September 10, 1997, p. 10; George Alogoskoufis and Richard Portes, "International costs and benefits from EMU," *European Economy*, Special Edition No. 1 (1991), p. 237.

3. S. Black, "International money and international monetary arrangements," in P. B. Kenen and R. W. Jones (eds.), *Handbook of International Economics*, Vol. 2 (Amsterdam: North-Holland, 1985).

4. "Small Firms Hit Foreign Obstacles in Billing Overseas," *Wall Street Journal*, December 8, 1992, p. B2.

5. An overview of methods of paying for international transactions may be found in *A Basic Guide to Exporting*, published by the U.S. Department of Commerce.

6. *Survey of Current Business*, February 1997, p. 24.

7. Richard Schaffer, Beverley Earle, and Filiberto Agusti, *International Business Law and Its Environment* (St. Paul, Minn.: West Publishing, 1990), pp. 154–155.

8. Chase Manhattan Bank, *Dynamics of Trade Finance* (New York: Chase Manhattan, 1984), pp. 41–58; Steve Murphy, *Complete Export Guide Manual* (Manhattan Beach, Calif.: Tran Publishing House, 1980).

9. "Saudis Agree to Trade Oil for Aircraft and Missiles," *Aviation Week and Space Technology*, September 20, 1985, p. 19.

10. Pompiliu Verzariu, *Countertrade Practices in East Europe, the Soviet Union and China: An Introductory Guide to Business* (Washington, D.C.: Department of Commerce, International Trade Administration, November 1984), pp. 98, 101.

11. Rolf Mirus and Bernard Yeung, "Economic Incentives for Countertrade," *The Journal of International Business Studies* (Fall 1986), pp. 27–39.

12. Ingemar Dorfer, *Arms Deal: The Selling of the F-16* (New York: Praeger, 1983).

13. Grant T. Hammond, *Countertrade, Offsets and Barter in International Political Economy* (New York: St. Martin's, 1990), p. 75.

14. Max Eli, *Japan Inc.* (Chicago: Probus Publishing, 1991), pp. 101–104.

15. "Marc Rich & Co. Does Big Deals at Big Risk in Former U.S.S.R.," *Wall Street Journal*, May 15, 1993, p. A1.

16. Hammond, op. cit., p. 11.

17. Export-Import Bank of the United States, *1991 Annual Report*, p. 7.

18. Boris Antl, "Measuring foreign exchange risk," in *The Management of Foreign Exchange Risk*, 2nd ed. (London: Euromoney Publications, 1982), p. 7.

19. "Foreign Currency Trades Slow at Merc as Firms Back Away," *Wall Street Journal*, October 20, 1992, p. C1.

20. "What Made the Indonesian Currency Plummet," *Wall Street Journal*, December 30, 1997, p. A4.

21. "German Unit Is Established for Importing, Distribution," *Wall Street Journal*, October 8, 1992, p. C15.

22. AFLAC Incorporated, *1996 Annual Report*, p. 44.

23. The Procter & Gamble Company, *1996 Annual Report*, p. 37; Owens Corning, *1996 Annual Report*, p. 42.

24. General Motors, *1996 Annual Report*, p. 70.

25. "Hard drive ahead to deal with a currency in turmoil," *Financial Times*, May 11, 1995, p. 15.

26. "Japan's Finance Chiefs Consider Risk of Hedging Their Bets Against Dollar," *Wall Street Journal*, February 8, 1996, p. A11.

27. *Sony Annual Report Year Ended March 31, 1996*, p. 31.

28. Christopher Knowlton, "How Disney Keeps the Magic Going," *Fortune*, December 4, 1989, pp. 111–132.

29. *European Economy*, No. 44 (October 1990), p. 66.

30. David K. Eiteman, Arthur I. Stonehill, and Michael H. Moffett, *Multinational Business Finance, 6th ed.* (Reading, Mass.: Addison-Wesley, 1992), p. 574.

31. "How U.S. Firm Copes with Asia Crisis," *Wall Street Journal*, December 26, 1997, p. A2.

32. "Centralisation lessens the risk," *Financial Times*, April 18, 1997, p. III.

33. Alan C. Shapiro, "Financial structure and cost of capital in the multinational corporation," *Journal of Financial and Quantitative Analysis* (June 1978), pp. 211–216.

34. Marjorie Stanley and Stanley Block, "An Empirical Study of Management and Financial Variables Influencing Capital Budgeting Decisions for Multinational Corporations in the 1980s," *Management International Review*, Vol. 23, No. 3 (1983), pp. 61–71.

35. Alan C. Shapiro, "Capital budgeting for the multinational corporation," *Financial Management* (Spring 1978), pp. 7–16.

36. "Placer Dome's Revamped Management Strikes Gold," *Wall Street Journal*, October 26, 1992, p. B4.

37. U. Rao Cherukuri, "Capital Budgeting in India," in S. Kerry Cooper, ed., *Southwest Review of International Business Research* (1992), pp. 194–204.

38. Eiteman, Stonehill, and Moffett, op. cit., p. 416.

39. *Survey of Current Business*, July 1997, p. 65.

40. Ibid.

41. *Sony Annual Report Year Ended March 31, 1996*, p. 61.

42. "When It's Smart to Use Foreign Banks," *International Business* (January 1992), pp. 17–18.

43. Gunter Dufey and Ian H. Giddy, "Innovation in the International Financial Market," *The Journal of International Business Studies* (Fall 1981), pp. 33–51.

44. "A Eurobond Issue Tied to Film Results," *Wall Street Journal*, October 12, 1992, p. C17.

45. "Walt Disney to Sell Notes Tied to Films' Results, With Initial Yield Linked to U.S. 7-Year Issue," *Wall Street Journal*, February 17, 1994, p. C20.

46. "Vital tool in minimizing costs," *Financial Times*, November 11, 1992, p. III.

47. Inco Ltd., *Annual Report 1990*, p. 38.

48. Johnson & Johnson, *1996 Annual Report*; lectures and personal interviews, staff of Janssen International N.V., May 25, 1994; "Visa plans small payments cross-border service," *Financial Times*, July 12, 1993, p. 1; "One Euro Currency Saves on Accounting But Not on Worries," *Wall Street Journal*, December 9, 1991, p. A9; "Belgium Steps Up Its Efforts to Keep Attracting Multinational Companies," *Wall Street Journal*, January 19, 1996, p. A9.

International Accounting and Taxation

Chapter Outline

National differences in accounting
The roots of differences
Differences in accounting practices
Impact on capital markets
Impact on corporate financial controls
Accounting in centrally planned economies

Efforts at harmonization

Accounting for international business activities
Accounting for transactions in foreign currencies
Foreign-currency translation

International taxation issues
Transfer pricing
Tax havens

Taxation of foreign income by the United States
Taxation of exports
Taxation of foreign branch income
Taxation of foreign subsidiary income

Resolving international tax conflicts
Tax credits
Tax treaties
"Bashing" of foreign firms

After studying this chapter you should be able to:

Discuss the various factors that influence the accounting systems countries adopt.

Describe the impact these national accounting differences have on international firms.

Analyze the benefits to international firms of harmonizing differences in national accounting systems.

Describe the accounting procedures used by U.S. firms engaged in international business.

Identify the major international taxation issues affecting international businesses.

Discuss the taxation of foreign income by the U.S. government.

Assess the techniques available to resolve tax conflicts among countries.

FAMOUS *MONTY PYTHON* SKETCH INVOLVES THE CAREER DILEMMA of a Mr. Anchovy, a London-based chartered accountant who finds his chosen profession, "Dull. Dull. My God it's dull, it's so desperately dull and tedious and stuffy and boring and des-per-ate-ly dull." He decides he wants to become a lion tamer but, unfortunately, because of the sheltered life he had led he had confused anteaters with lions. Upon learning the difference, he decides not to rush into a new career as a lion tamer. ▮▮ That may or may not be an accurate description of the life of an average English accountant in 1969, when this comedy sketch was first shown on British television. It is certainly not an accurate description of the market for international accounting services

Mr. Anchovy Was Wrong

today, which is anything but dull. If you're doubtful, just ask Iain Gerrard, a 33-year-old Arthur Andersen partner in Perth, Australia. As a result of a World Bank contract won by his firm, for the past three years he has been helping Erdenet, the biggest company in Mongolia, to modernize its accounting system. This task is critical to the Mongolian economy, for Erdenet accounts for 65 percent of the country's exports. And what do you do for fun in Ulan Bator, where the company is headquartered? In winter, Gerrard likes to go hunting wolves on the frozen Mongolian steppe—an activity he never dreamed of as a boy growing up in sunny Western Australia. ▮▮ For most of the 1990s, the accounting industry has been dominated by six firms prowling the global marketplace, devouring local competitors, and fighting for the lion's share of one of the fastest growing international service markets. These firms, collectively referred to as the Big Six, together provide accounting, auditing, and consulting services for the vast majority of the world's largest MNCs. All of the Big Six have enjoyed double-digit growth rates in recent years. ▮▮ The biggest of the Big Six is currently Andersen Worldwide, whose 2,760 partners and 92,000 employees generated $9.5 billion in accounting, auditing, and consulting revenues in 1996. In second place is KPMG Peat Marwick, with $8.1 billion in revenues in 1996. However, in September 1997, two members of the Big Six, Coopers & Lybrand and Price Waterhouse, announced that they would merge their operations. This merger would create the world's largest accounting firm, with 8,500 partners, 135,000 employees, and annual revenues of $11.8 billion. One month later, two other members of the Big Six—Ernst & Young and KPMG Peat Marwick—reported that they, too, would combine their operations. Although partners of the four firms approved the mergers, Ernst & Young and KPMG Peat Marwick later terminated their planned consolidation. The Coopers & Lybrand/Price Waterhouse proposal awaits the approvals of regulatory officials in Europe and North America before the merger can officially take place. ▮▮ Megamergers are nothing new in this industry. KPMG, for example, was formed by the 1987 merger of U.S.-based Peat Marwick Mitchell and

European-based Klynveld Main Goerdeler (KMG). Deloitte Touche Tohmatsu was created by the 1989 merger of Deloitte Haskins & Sells with Touche Ross & Company and its Japanese affiliate, Tohmatsu & Co. Similarly, Ernst & Young resulted from the 1989 merger of Ernst & Whinney and Arthur Young. Ernst & Whinney itself was the result of a merger between a U.S. and a U.K. accounting firm shortly after the end of World War II. ▌▌ This trend toward international expansion can be explained in part by the growth of international business. As their clients have globalized, accounting firms have felt compelled to expand their operations in order to meet their clients' needs—as well as to retain their business. To navigate among the various accounting regulations and tax laws of the nations in which its MNC clients do business, an accounting firm needs to be able to offer advice to its clients based on the operating needs of each of their foreign subsidiaries and of the parents themselves. The most effective way of providing this service is to have an office in each country in which the clients do business. Coopers & Lybrand, for example, employs 300 people in China to serve the needs of its multinational clients there. By merging with existing accounting firms, the Big Six have gained quick access to many domestic markets as well as to the existing client bases of the acquired firms. ▌▌ The Big Six are well positioned to continue to benefit from the increase in international business activity. Their clients' international activities are booming, and so their international accounting needs are also skyrocketing. That doesn't mean, however, that managers of the Big Six can afford to relax. They face the daunting challenge of managing their explosive growth, maintaining the quality of services they offer their clients, and nurturing and keeping their employees happy. For example, attitudes toward compensation vary considerably among business cultures. As a result of their rapid globalization, the Big Six firms must develop performance appraisal systems, compensation programs, and fringe benefit packages that meet the needs of employees in each country of the world yet preserve some semblance of equity within the organization. ▌▌ The Big Six must keep group-oriented Japanese partners happy while simultaneously satisfying "what's in it for me" U.S. partners. This problem is exacerbated because the Big Six have all developed extensive management consulting businesses in addition to their traditional auditing and accounting services. Because the consulting businesses have enjoyed more rapid growth than the accounting businesses in the past decade, many partners on the consulting side have argued that they deserve a bigger slice of the compensation pie, a suggestion not well received by the accounting partners. With the boom in international trade and investment, and the resultant need of MNCs to understand the complexities and differences in the accounting standards among countries, these accounting giants face a rosy future in spite of these challenges. ▌▌▌▌▌

The goal of an accounting system is to identify, measure, and communicate "economic information to permit informed judgments and decisions by users of the information."[1] These users are numerous. The accounting system provides operational information to line managers and financial performance data to top executives to help them make marketing, financial, and strategic decisions. Investors use information about a firm's performance to determine whether to purchase its stock and debt instruments. And the government uses this information to assess the firm's tax burdens and to regulate the issuance of its securities.

Accounting has been called the "language of business." Unfortunately for international firms, it is far from being a lingua franca. The accounting tasks of international businesses are much more complex than those of domestic firms. The accounting system of a purely domestic firm must meet the professional and regulatory standards of its home country. An MNC and its subsidiaries, however, must meet the sometimes contradictory standards of all the countries in which they operate. To effectively manage and control their operations, local managers need accounting information prepared according to local accounting concepts and denominated in the local currency. However, for corporate officers to assess a foreign subsidiary's performance and value, the subsidiary's accounting records must be translated into the parent's home currency using accounting concepts and procedures detailed by the parent. Investors around the world, seeking the highest possible returns on their capital, need to be able to interpret the firm's track record, even though it may be using a currency and an accounting system different from their own. The firm will also have to pay taxes to the countries in which it does business based on the accounting statements it develops in these countries. And when a parent corporation attempts to integrate the accounting records of its subsidiaries to create consolidated financial statements, additional complexities arise because of changes in the value of the host and home currencies over time.

This chapter discusses how international businesses deal with national differences in accounting and taxation systems. It first examines the causes of these differences and describes countries' attempts to reduce them. It goes on to describe how accountants of international businesses treat international business transactions in the firms' income statements and balance sheets. Finally, it discusses the impact of national taxation policies on international business and the strategies international firms adopt to reduce their global tax burdens.

National Differences in Accounting

An international business must develop an accounting system that provides both the internal information required by its managers to run the firm and the external information needed by shareholders, lenders, and government officials in the countries in which the firm operates. Yet, as you will see, differences in national accounting philosophies and practices make such a task easier said than done.

The Roots of Differences

A country's accounting standards and practices reflect the influence of legal, cultural, political, and economic factors, as Fig. 19.1 indicates.[2] Because these factors vary by country, the underlying goals and philosophy of national accounting systems also vary dramatically.

FIGURE 19.1

Influences on
a Country's
Accounting
System

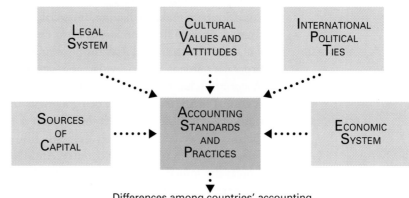

Differences among countries' accounting
practices affect a firm's decisions on:

- Reported income and profits
- Valuations of assets and inventories
- Tax reporting
- Desire to operate in a given country
- Use of accounting reserves

Consider first the difference between common law and code law countries. In common law countries such as the United Kingdom and the United States, accounting procedures normally evolve via decisions of independent standards-setting boards, such as the U.K.'s Accounting Standards Board or the U.S. Financial Accounting Standards Board (FASB). Each board works in consultation with professional accounting groups, such as the U.K.'s various Institutes of Chartered Accountants or the American Institute of Certified Public Accountants. Accountants in common law countries typically follow so-called generally accepted accounting principles (GAAP) that provide a "true and fair view" of a firm's performance based on the standards agreed on by these professional boards. Operating within the boundaries of these principles, accountants have leeway to exercise their professional discretion in reporting a "true and fair" depiction of a firm's performance.

Conversely, countries relying on code law are likely to codify their national accounting procedures and standards.[3] In these countries, accounting practices are determined by the law, not by the collective wisdom of professional accounting groups like the FASB.[4] For example, France's code law system and long tradition of strong central government control over the economy are reflected in its imposition on French firms of a national uniform chart of accounts—the *Plan Comptable Général*. This accounting system, which dates to 1673, creates accounting records designed to serve as proof in legal procedures. To facilitate this legal role, all corporate accounting records must be officially registered with the government. Similarly, German accounting practices adhere strictly to requirements laid down by law or court decisions.

A country's legal system also influences enforcement of accounting practices. Most developed countries rely on both private and public enforcement of business behavior, although the public/private mixture varies by country. Because French and German accounting procedures are laid down by law, the government plays a major role in monitoring accounting practices in those countries. In contrast, the U.S. system relies to a greater extent on private litigation to enforce the accuracy and honesty of firms' accounting practices. Any attempt to mislead private investors or creditors in the United States is likely to prompt a lawsuit; U.S. firms and their accountants have shelled out hundreds of millions of dollars settling such claims.[5] Thus, U.S. firms (and their accountants) are motivated to provide accurate information in their public accounting statements because of this threat of private litigation; French and German firms, in contrast, are more concerned about meeting governmental standards.

A country's accounting system also may reflect its national culture. The detailed accounting procedures laid down by the French government mirror France's statist tradition. Larger French firms also must publish a "social balance sheet" detailing their treatment and compensation of their work forces.[6] Australia's accounting requirements for public firms are generally permissive, reflecting the distrust of government power embedded in that country's culture. Strong anti-inflation biases are embedded in German accounting procedures, a reaction to the tragic hyperinflation of the early 1920s that wiped out much of the wealth of the German middle class and helped Adolf Hitler rise to the chancellorship in 1932.

International political ties are also important determinants of a country's accounting procedures. Most members of the British Commonwealth have adopted the accounting principles and procedures of the United Kingdom, while former colonies of France and the Netherlands have adopted those of their colonial rulers. Similarly, the accounting procedures of the Philippines follow those of the United States, which controlled that country from 1898 to 1946.

A country's economic system also influences its accounting practices. In a centrally planned economy (CPE) the accounting system is driven by the need to provide output-oriented information to the state planners. Such accounting systems focus on documenting how state funds are used and whether state-mandated production quotas are being met.[7] In market-oriented systems, on the other hand, managers and investors require profit- and cost-oriented information.

Capital markets may also affect national accounting standards. U.S. firms have historically raised capital by relying on public investors. U.S. accounting standards therefore emphasize the provision of accurate and useful information to help outsiders—private shareholders and bondholders—make appropriate investment decisions. As part of this goal, publicly owned firms must satisfy all the disclosure regulations of the Securities and Exchange Commission (SEC). In Germany, the dominant role of a few large banks in providing capital results in accounting practices that focus on the needs of creditors, for example, by tending to undervalue assets and overvalue liabilities. This conservative approach is favored by the lending banks. The public capital market has been much less important in Germany than in the United States, and German accounting practices provide less information to public investors than do U.S. ones.[8] For example, a German corporation does not need to consolidate the accounts of its subsidiaries if the subsidiaries' activities differ substantially from the parent's or if consolidation would be too expensive for the parent. This lack of consolidation makes it difficult for private investors to assess such a firm's overall performance. This is no problem for its bankers, however, who often sit on its board of directors and who in their role as lenders have access to all its financial information.

The situation is similar in Japan. Most publicly traded Japanese firms are members of a keiretsu. They have relatively few public shareholders because of the pervasive cross-ownership of shares among keiretsu members and the extensive share ownership by banks and other financial institutions. Most Japanese firms also have large debt-to-equity ratios by Western standards. Thus Japanese accounting standards are geared toward meeting the needs of the firm's lenders and keiretsu partners, both of which already have privileged access to the firm's financial records, rather than those of outside investors.

Differences in Accounting Practices

Political, cultural, legal, and economic forces affect each country's philosophy and attitude toward its accounting system. They also affect how the country's accountants treat different accounting issues. These differing treatments in turn impact a firm's reported profits, the value of its assets, its tax bill, and its decision to begin or continue to operate in the country. International businesses that rely on foreign accounting records but fail to recognize these differences may make expensive, perhaps fatal, strategic errors and operating mistakes. Let's look at some of the more important national accounting differences that affect international business.

Valuation and Revaluation of Assets. Most countries' accounting systems begin with the assumption that a firm's assets should be valued on an historical cost basis. That is, the asset is carried on the firm's books according to its original cost, less depreciation. Because of inflation, however, the market value of an asset is often higher than its historical cost. The resolution of this problem differs among national accounting systems. For example, Dutch firms are permitted to raise the value of such assets on their balance sheets to reflect their true replacement value. British accountants may exercise their professional discretion and value assets on an historical cost basis, a current cost basis, or a mixture of the two. Australia, an inheritor of British accounting philosophy, similarly grants a firm's accountants a great degree of professional discretion. Australian firms may alter the value of long-term assets on their balance sheets to take into account inflation or improved economic conditions. In the United States and Japan, however, such upward revaluations are illegal. These differences in asset revaluation procedures suggest the need for caution when comparing the strength of balance sheets of firms from different countries.

Valuation of Inventories. Every introductory accounting course discusses the two principle methods for valuing inventories: LIFO (last in, first out) and FIFO (first in, first out). In times of inflation, LIFO tends to raise the firm's reported costs of goods sold, lower the book value of its inventories, and reduce its reported profits (and, presumably, its taxes) more than FIFO does, while FIFO produces a clearer estimate of the value of the firm's existing inventories than does LIFO. Thus, in comparing the performance of two firms, one needs to know which technique they use to value their inventories. There are significant international differences in the use of the two methods: U.S., Japanese, and Canadian firms may use either approach. In Australia, LIFO cannot be used, while in New Zealand LIFO is allowed yet FIFO is generally used. Firms in Brazil and the United Kingdom normally use only FIFO.[9]

Dealing with the Tax Authorities. A firm's accounting records form the basis for assessing its income tax burden. In Germany, accounting procedures are explicitly detailed in the German Commercial Code and follow the requirements of German tax laws. A German firm's taxable income is measured by the contents of its financial records. Normally no distinction is made between financial statements reported to shareholders and financial statements reported to German tax authorities. The United States follows a very different approach. U.S. firms commonly report two different sets of financial statements—one to the Internal

Revenue Service (IRS) and one to shareholders. Such conduct is authorized by U.S. law and allows firms to take advantage of special tax code provisions to reduce their taxable income. For example, U.S. firms often use accelerated depreciation for tax purposes but not for financial reporting purposes. A German firm normally does not have this option. If it wants to use accelerated depreciation for tax-reporting purposes (to reduce its current-year taxes), it must also use accelerated depreciation in reporting to its shareholders (which reduces its reported income).

Forced to choose between higher taxes and lower reported income, most German firms opt for the latter. Managers and investors need to recognize that the reported profits of German firms are thus biased downward. The inflexibility of Germany's accounting system seems to put German firms at a disadvantage in raising capital. However, German firms typically obtain most of their capital from large financial intermediaries like banks and insurance firms. These inside investors have access to more detailed information about the firm's performance than is available in its public financial statements published in its annual report.

Tax laws also play a major role in French accounting practices, which follow well-defined procedures detailed by the French government in the national uniform chart of accounts. As in the German system, no deductions for tax purposes may be taken unless they have been entered into the firm's annual accounting records. Because of the dominance of tax law in accounting judgments, French firms are likely to bias their reported earnings and net assets downward in order to reduce their tax burdens.

Use of Accounting Reserves. Another important difference in national accounting systems is in the use of accounting reserves. Firms often use **accounting reserves** to adjust for foreseeable future expenses that affect their operations. An office supplies wholesaler, for example, might establish a reserve account for bad debts and for returned merchandise, knowing that when it ships merchandise, some retailers will ship the goods back and some will fail to pay their bills. The use of accounting reserves by U.S. firms is carefully monitored and limited by the IRS and the SEC. The IRS dislikes them because charges to accounting reserves reduce the firm's taxable income. The SEC fears that firms might manipulate their accounting reserves to provide misleading pictures of their financial performance.

In contrast to the restrictive U.S. system, the German Commercial Code liberally permits German firms to establish accounting reserves for various potential future expenses, such as deferred maintenance, future repairs, or exposure to international risks. Because these reserves reduce reported income on which taxes are based, most German firms use them aggressively. In 1996, for example, Deutsche Bank admitted that its hidden reserves amounted to over $14 billion.[10]

The use of such reserves hampers outside investors' ability to assess a German firm's performance. Often these firms use reserve accounts to smooth out fluctuations in their earning flows by adding large sums to their reserves in good years and dipping into their reserves in poor years. For example, Lufthansa, the German airline, reported in its 1993 annual report that in fiscal year 1992 it withdrew DM20.9 million from its reserves, and a year later it added DM9.9 million. No explanation was offered in the report for either of these transactions.[11] Because of their use of accounting reserves, the reported earnings of German firms often fluctuate less than those of U.S. firms, giving the misleading appearance that the former are less risky than the latter. These accounting differences complicate investors' decision making regarding how to diversify their portfolios internationally to reduce overall investments risk.[12]

Other Differences. Many other differences exist in how countries treat accounting issues, for example:

- *Capitalization of financial leases:* U.S., British, and Canadian firms must capitalize financial leases, while French and Swiss firms may do so but are not required to.

- *Preparation of consolidated financial statements:* Consolidation of financial statements is mandatory for U.S. and British firms, while German firms may exclude consolidating subsidiaries if their activities differ substantially from the parent's or if consolidation would be too expensive for the parent.

- *Capitalization of R&D expenses:* Most countries permit firms to capitalize R&D expenses, but this practice is forbidden in the United States except in limited circumstances.

- *Treatment of goodwill:* A firm that acquires a second firm often pays more than the book value of the acquired firm's stock. The excess payment is called **goodwill**. In the Netherlands, firms typically amortize goodwill over a five-year period, although they may write it off instantaneously or over a period of up to ten years. U.K. firms also are allowed to choose between immediately writing off goodwill or capitalizing it on their balance sheets and amortizing it over a period of time. French firms may amortize goodwill over five to twenty years. Japan, however, severely limits firms' ability to write off goodwill.

Table 19.1 summarizes important accounting differences among selected countries.

Impact on Capital Markets

The various national differences in accounting practices would be little more than a curiosity were it not for international businesspeople's need for information in order to make decisions. These differences can distort the measured performance of firms incorporated in different countries. As already noted, the earnings of German and French firms are often understated because of the congruency between financial reporting and tax reporting. And the price-to-earnings ratios of Japanese firms are often higher than those of U.S. firms, primarily because Japanese accounting practices often substantially reduce reported profits. For example, Japanese firms report depreciation expenses on an accelerated basis to their shareholders and are allowed to create generous reserve funds for future pension liabilities. Australia's accounting practices used to allow firms to appear more profitable than identically

Australian entrepreneurs took advantage of Australia's flexible accounting standards in building their corporate empires. Rupert Murdoch, head of Australia-based News Corporation, is well on his way to establishing a truly global media company, centered on the Fox Network in North America, STAR-TV in Asia, and Sky Broadcasting in Europe.

TABLE 19.1

Summary of International Accounting Differences

	UNITED STATES	JAPAN	UNITED KINGDOM	FRANCE	GERMANY	NETHERLANDS	SWITZERLAND	CANADA	ITALY	BRAZIL
Capitalization of research and development costs	Not allowed	Allowed in certain circumstances	Allowed in certain circumstances	Allowed in certain circumstances	Not allowed	Allowed in certain circumstances	Allowed in certain circumstances	Allowed in certain circumstances	Allowed in certain circumstances	Allowed
Fixed asset revaluations stated at amount in excess of cost	Not allowed	Not allowed	Allowed	Allowed	Not allowed	Allowed in certain circumstances	Allowed in certain circumstances	Not allowed	Required in certain circumstances	Allowed
Inventory valuation using LIFO	Allowed	Allowed	Allowed but rarely done	Allowed	Allowed in certain circumstances	Allowed	Allowed	Allowed	Allowed	Allowed but rarely done
Finance leases capitalized	Required	Allowed in certain circumstances	Required	Allowed	Allowed in certain circumstances	Required	Allowed	Required	Not allowed	Allowed in certain circumstances
Pension expense accrued during period of service	Required	Allowed	Required	Allowed	Required	Required	Allowed	Required	Allowed	Allowed
Book and tax timing differences presented on the balance sheet as deferred tax	Required	Allowed in certain circumstances	Required in certain circumstances	Required	Allowed in certain circumstances	Required	Allowed	Required	Generally required	Required
Current rate method used for foreign-currency translation	Required for foreign operations whose functional currency is other than the reporting currency	Generally required	Required	Required for self-sustaining foreign operations	Allowed	Required for self-sustaining foreign operations	Allowed	Required for self-sustaining foreign operations	Required	Required
Pooling method used for mergers	Required in certain circumstances	Allowed	Required in certain circumstances	Not allowed	Allowed in certain circumstances	Allowed but rarely done	Allowed but rarely done	Allowed in rare circumstances	Allowed in rare circumstances	Allowed but rarely done
Equity method used for 20–50 percent ownership	Required	Required	Required	Required	Required	Required	Allowed in certain circumstances	Required	Allowed	Required

Source: From Fredrick D.S. Choi, *International Accounting and Finance Handbook*, 2nd ed. Copyright © 1997 John Wiley & Sons, Inc. Reprinted by permission of John Wiley & Sons, Inc.

performing U.S. firms, an advantage that helped such Aussie entrepreneurs as Rupert Murdoch and Alan Bond to gain favorable access to additional capital and play the takeover game in the United States in the 1980s and 1990s, although subsequent changes in Australian accounting procedures have reduced this advantage.[13] The overall impact of these accounting differences is clear: comparing the financial reports of firms from different countries is exceedingly complex. Thus international investors find it more difficult to assess the performance of the world's businesses.

These differences can affect the global capital market in other ways. The New York Stock Exchange (NYSE), for example, is concerned about SEC-mandated accounting rules that must be followed by publicly traded corporations. Those rules emphasize full and comprehensive disclosure of a firm's financial performance information, and the NYSE fears that they discourage foreign firms from listing on the exchange, thereby threatening the exchange's global competitiveness.[14] Consider the Netherlands-based firm Philips NV. Under Dutch accounting standards, Philips assesses its assets on a current-value basis. To list its stock on the NYSE, Philips must undergo the expense of revaluing its assets on an historical cost basis to meet SEC requirements.[15]

The information-laden accounting practices used by U.S. firms do offer them certain advantages, however. A senior officer of the Long-Term Credit Bank of Japan believes that the United States is the easiest foreign locale in which his firm can lend because of U.S. public disclosure policies. Those policies result in reliable numbers for assessing the riskiness of potential loans.[16] In contrast, the German accounting system, which allows firms to lump together various cost categories and establish a variety of reserves, is much less helpful for a potential foreign lender. As one investment manager has noted, "The poor quality of financial information available from many German companies makes it difficult for investors to buy a stock with confidence, since valuations cannot be clearly established."[17] Similarly, some experts believe the economic problems of Southeast Asian companies triggered by the region's 1997–1998 currency crisis have been worsened by the lack of transparency in their accounting statements. When times were good in the region, investors seemingly overlooked the lack of information contained in financial reports and assumed the best about the companies' prospects; when the region's economy plunged into trouble after Thailand devalued the baht, investors assumed the worst, driving stock prices down even more. Despite the NYSE's concerns, investors' need for usable information apparently increasingly outweighs the regulatory burden imposed by the SEC's strict reporting requirements. In the past three years alone, the number of foreign companies listed on the NYSE has doubled, reaching a total of 326 by late 1997.[18]

Impact on Corporate Financial Controls

National differences in accounting procedures also complicate an MNC's ability to manage its foreign operations. An MNC's subsidiaries must provide the parent's senior executive officers with timely and uniform financial information prepared on a comparable basis in order to facilitate assessment of the subsidiaries' performances. So the parent typically dictates to the subsidiaries the form and procedures to be used for financial reports submitted to it. Coca-Cola, for example, has carefully developed for its subsidiaries an easy-to-use, standardized accounting manual that incorporates U.S. GAAP.[19]

Senior executives of an MNC must also determine whether to use the parent's or the subsidiary's currency in assessing the performances of foreign subsidiaries and their managers. The choice may seem obvious: translate each subsidiary's financial reports into the parent's currency, thereby allowing easy comparisons by the parent. However, the use of financial reports denominated in the parent's currency may induce the subsidiary's managers to focus their energies on beating the foreign-exchange market rather than on managing the local operations. In practice, there is no uniform answer to the question of which currency to use for performance evaluation: some MNCs choose the host currency and others the home currency, but most appear to use both.[20]

Accounting in Centrally Planned Economies

The accounting systems of CPEs offer special challenges to international businesses operating in those countries. The goals of these systems differ quite a bit from those in market economies. Their accounting systems are designed to provide information about an enterprise's aggregate production. This information is then passed from the enterprise to the central planners so that they can monitor the enterprise's success in fulfilling its performance goals in the economy's central plan and can make mid-plan adjustments as needed.

International businesses must approach financial statements developed in CPEs with great caution. General Electric (GE), for example, ran into several accounting problems in its 1990 purchase of the Hungarian lighting firm Tungsram. Tungsram was not required by Hungarian law to consolidate its transactions with those of its seventeen foreign sales subsidiaries. Because the bonuses of Tungsram's managers were tied to its sales revenues, the firm routinely shipped goods to the subsidiaries even though the subsidiaries might not be able to sell them. By so doing, Tungsram was able to claim increased sales and profits on its accounting statement, and managers were allowed to claim their bonuses. Had Tungsram been forced to consolidate its accounts, these sales to subsidiaries would have been recorded as increased inventory levels instead. In one case, GE discovered that Tungsram's French and German subsidiaries were warehousing $3 million worth of an obsolete automobile headlight that had not been marketed for over a decade.[21] Had GE recognized these accounting differences upfront, it might have either paid substantially less for Tungsram or walked away from the deal.

CPEs' accounting systems are of little use to international businesses trying to meet their own internal managerial and reporting requirements. These systems focus on recording production information needed by central planners but ignore "trivialities" such as revenues, costs, and profits that may be incompatible with Marxist ideology. China's old accounting system, for example, ignored bad debts and obsolete inventory but required foreign-currency transactions to be recorded at the official exchange rate, which often deviated substantially from market rates.[22] Fortunately, because these and other troublesome accounting procedures were perceived to be impediments to China's economic modernization, China's Ministry of Finance has undertaken significant reforms of the country's accounting procedures since 1993 to make them more compatible with the needs of external users.[23]

Efforts at Harmonization

Differences in accounting systems are confusing and costly to international businesses. Incompatibilities in these systems make it more difficult for firms to monitor their foreign operations and for investors to comprehend the relative performance of firms based in different countries.[24]

To help solve such problems, many accounting professionals and national regulatory bodies are attempting to harmonize the various national accounting practices. One of the most important of these efforts was the creation of the **International Accounting Standards Committee (IASC)** in 1973. IASC founding members were drawn from the professional accounting societies of the leading trading nations, including the United States, Germany, Japan, the United Kingdom, the Netherlands, Canada, Australia, Mexico, and Ireland. Today, the IASC membership consists of 116 professional societies from 85 countries. The IASC has issued a series of standards designed to harmonize national treatment of various accounting issues within its member countries. Among its most important goals is the promotion of comparability of financial statements across countries by establishing standards for inventory valuation, depreciation, deferred income taxes, and other matters. However, the IASC lacks enforcement powers. National governments often ignore its accounting standards if they disagree with them.[25]

The EU has undertaken a separate initiative to harmonize the accounting systems of its member states as part of its drive to complete the formation of its internal market. By so doing, the EU hopes to reduce the total accounting costs of European MNCs. In addition, as national accounting standards of the EU member states become more similar, investors will find it easier to assess the performance of those countries' firms. For example, the EU's Fourth Directive, issued in 1978, mandates that each member require its firms to adopt certain accounting practices and to ensure that financial statements provide a "true and fair view" of operations. The Seventh Directive, issued in 1983, requires firms to publish consolidated financial statements. Each directive, however, allows members a fair amount of discretion in establishing their national accounting standards. For example, inventories may be valued using LIFO, FIFO, actual cost, or weighted cost approaches. Similarly, consolidation is not required if a subsidiary's operations are immaterial to the parent, if the subsidiary's operations are substantially dissimilar from the parent's, or if consolidation would be expensive to perform. Other groups, such as the World Trade Organization and IOSCO (an international organization of national securities commissions), have also lobbied for the adoption of international accounting standards.

These harmonization efforts have their critics, however. The costs of harmonization are significant. Accountants, firms, and government officials must incur retooling costs if they abandon existing national accounting standards.[26] National pride has also affected the process. One EU official has proclaimed, "It would not be acceptable for Europe to delegate the setting of accounting standards to the U.S."[27] For its part, the U.S. Securities and Exchange Commission has shown little willingness to relax its accounting standards. Some analysts believe that harmonization may affect international competition among accountants. For example, the IASC standards have a strong bias toward British and U.S. accounting procedures. To the extent that the IASC's standards are adopted worldwide, these countries' accounting firms are favored in the international market for accounting services. As a result, other countries are resisting the universal adoption of IASC-endorsed procedures. France, for example, is aggressively promoting the rules developed by its own standards board, the Conseil National de la Comptabilité. So far this board's standards have been adopted by Bulgaria and Romania, thereby giving French accounting firms the inside track in selling accounting services in those countries.[28]

Nonetheless, there seems to be continual, albeit slow, progress toward harmonization. Much of this progress seems to be driven by the need of MNCs to access the global capital market: as globalization of the world's economies increases, the capital requirements of international firms also grow. To compete successfully with their foreign rivals, they must seek to acquire inputs—including capital—at the lowest possible cost. Change has been particularly noticeable among German firms. Major German MNCs like Daimler-Benz, Veba, Schering, Hoechst, Deutsche Bank, and Bayer have adopted the more transparent accounting procedures of IASC and/or the U.S. GAAP in order to improve their access to the global capital market and lower their cost of acquiring new capital.[29]

Accounting for International Business Activities

Besides the challenges posed by differences in national accounting systems, most international firms must also deal with two types of specific accounting problems that routinely develop when business is conducted internationally:

1 Accounting for transactions denominated in foreign currencies

2 Reporting the operating results of foreign subsidiaries in the firm's consolidated financial statements

Because of the collapse of the Bretton Woods system in 1971, both problems have become increasingly important to international businesses. Under the Bretton Woods fixed exchange-rate system, the accounting problems raised by international business activities denominated in foreign currencies tended to be minor. In the post–Bretton Woods era, however, currency values can change dramatically. Since 1971, accounting for the impact of exchange-rate changes on the value of international transactions and on the firm's consolidated financial statements has become a significant issue for international businesses.

Accounting for Transactions in Foreign Currencies

Chapter 18 introduced the concept of transaction exposure, which is the effect of exchange-rate fluctuations on the economic benefits and costs of an international transaction. Firms confront the problem of accounting for transactions in foreign currency whenever they agree to pay or receive payment in a foreign currency in settlement of a purchase or sale of goods, services, or assets. Under the existing flexible exchange-rate system, it is very likely that the exchange rate will change between the time a firm enters into an international transaction and the time it receives payment or pays for the goods, services, or assets in question. In accordance with FASB Statement 52, issued in 1981, U.S. firms must account for such international transactions by using the two-transaction approach in their financial statements.[30]

For example, Microsoft Corporation, the Seattle-based computer software giant, faces this problem when it ships copies of Windows 95, Office 97, or Microsoft Excel to a British computer store chain and agrees to accept £30,000 in payment in 90 days. If £1 is worth $1.60 when the contract is signed, making the transaction worth $48,000 (£30,000 × $1.60), Microsoft, by following FASB Statement 52, will account for the transaction as follows:

	DEBIT	CREDIT
Accounts Receivable	$48,000	
Sales Revenues		$48,000

Suppose that in 90 days, when Microsoft receives a check for £30,000, the value of the British pound has dropped to $1.50. In terms of its home currency, Microsoft has received only $45,000 rather than the $48,000 it expected. The actual receipt of the monies is accounted for as follows:

	DEBIT	CREDIT
Cash	$45,000	
Foreign-Exchange Loss	3,000	
Accounts Receivable		$48,000

This accounting procedure highlights any foreign-exchange loss or gain resulting from the sale or purchase. Ultimately, the firm's net income is affected by both the primary transaction and any foreign-exchange gains or losses. But the two-transaction approach has the benefit of separating out information about the success of the firm's core activities—selling its products—from its success in managing its exposure to fluctuations in foreign-currency values. In the example, Microsoft's managers would realize that they need to improve management of their transaction exposure to such fluctuations, perhaps by engaging in hedging operations through the use of the forward market or currency futures (discussed in Chapter 18).

Because the two-transaction approach distinguishes between the firm's core activities and its management of transaction exposure, it is of particular value to stock market analysts, who are often wary of firms that expose themselves to excessive foreign-exchange risk. Dell Computer, for example, lost 10 percent of its market value when it reported $38 million in currency-exchange losses in 1992, an amount equal to roughly one quarter of its annual profits at that time. Stock market analysts believed that the size of the losses meant that Dell was engaging in foreign-currency speculation, rather than merely hedging foreign-currency earnings from its export sales. Dell denied the allegations.[31]

Foreign-Currency Translation

A second type of international accounting problem confronts an MNC when it reports the results of its foreign subsidiaries' operations to its home country shareholders and tax officials. Because its foreign subsidiaries will normally conduct their business using their local currency, the firm must convert its subsidiaries' financial reports into its home currency (an accounting task discussed briefly in Chapter 18).

The process of transforming a subsidiary's reported operations denominated in a foreign currency into the parent's home currency is called **translation**. For most MNCs, the translation process is intertwined with the need to create consolidated financial statements. **Consolidated financial statements** report the combined operations of a parent and its subsidiaries in a single set of accounting statements denominated in a single currency.

Translating financial reports from one currency into another requires the use of an appropriate exchange rate to convert from the first currency to the second. Because the business activities captured in accounting records occur at different times, a question arises as to which exchange rate to use. Should the firm use the exchange rate on the date the transaction occurred (the historical rate), the rate on the date the financial statement is prepared (the current rate), a weighted average over time, or some other rate? For U.S. firms, FASB Statement 52 details the exchange rates and accounting procedures firms are to use in translating and then consolidating subsidiaries' financial statements denominated in a foreign currency.

The treatment of foreign investments under FASB Statement 52 depends upon the size of the parent's ownership stake in the foreign firm, as summarized in Table 19.2. A U.S. firm that has a portfolio investment in a foreign firm (less than 10 percent ownership) must use the **cost method**. With this method, the investment is recorded in the U.S. firm's accounting records at cost using the historical exchange rate—the exchange rate at the time the foreign shares were acquired. Any dividends the U.S. firm receives from its portfolio investment are to be reported in its income statement using the exchange rate in effect on the day it received the dividend. This is the approach Ford uses to account for its 9.4 percent ownership of Korea's Kia Motors.

A U.S. firm that owns between 10 and 50 percent of a foreign firm's stock must use the **equity method** to value its ownership stake. For example, Ford's 33 percent ownership stake in Mazda is entered into Ford's consolidated financial statements using this approach. The equity method calls for the U.S. firm to record its initial investment in the foreign firm at cost using the historical exchange rate. However, when the foreign firm earns profits or suffers losses, the value of the investment carried on the U.S. firm's consolidated financial statements is adjusted to reflect those profits or losses using the exchange rate prevailing when they were reported. Any dividends issued by the foreign firm reduce the value of the U.S. firm's investment in the foreign firm. This adjustment also is made using the exchange rate in effect on the day when the dividends were paid.

The most complicated accounting issues arise when a U.S. firm purchases more than 50 percent ownership of a foreign firm, such as Ford's purchase of all of the stock of the Jaguar Motor Company in 1990. In such cases, the U.S. firm must use the **consolidation method**. This method calls for the accounting records of the two firms to be consolidated when the U.S. firm reports its operating results to its shareholders and the SEC. Because the foreign subsidiary uses the accounting

---

TABLE 19.2

Parent's Ownership Stake and Accounting Treatment of Its Foreign Investments

OWNERSHIP STAKE	METHOD USED
Less than 10 percent	Cost method
Between 10 and 50 percent	Equity method
More than 50 percent	Consolidation method

rules prescribed by its national government or national professional association, the subsidiary's financial statements must first be restated using U.S. GAAP. The next step is to determine the **functional currency** of the subsidiary, defined as the currency of the principal economic environment in which the subsidiary operates. For example, the functional currency of GM's German subsidiary, Adam Opel AG, is the deutsche mark because Opel produces most of its parts in Germany, assembles its vehicles in Germany, and sells most of its output in Germany. In contrast, Compaq Computer's production facilities in Scotland and Singapore are integrated into the firm's worldwide sourcing program. Thus the functional currency of those two subsidiaries is their parent's currency, the U.S. dollar.

The U.S. firm will use one of two methods for translating a subsidiary's financial statements into the U.S. dollar (the parent's home currency), depending on the subsidiary's functional currency:

1 The **current rate method** is used if the subsidiary's functional currency is the host country's currency. This method assumes that the foreign subsidiary is a stand-alone operation. Any gains or losses arising from translation thus reflect the impact of exchange-rate changes, not the subsidiary's operational performance.

2 The **temporal method** is used if the subsidiary's functional currency is the U.S. dollar. This method assumes that the foreign subsidiary's operations are integrated into the parent's. Thus its profitability should be evaluated in terms of the parent's currency.

These two approaches differ mainly in how they treat translation losses and gains. Under the temporal method, translation losses and gains appear on the firm's income statement; under the current rate method, they appear as an adjustment to shareholders' equity. In some cases, a firm may use both approaches because of differences in the functional currencies of various subsidiaries. For example, Federal-Mogul, a $2 billion Detroit-based producer of motor vehicle parts, uses the temporal method to translate the results of its Brazilian and Argentinean subsidiaries, whose functional currency is the U.S. dollar. It uses the current rate method to translate the results of its British and German subsidiaries, whose functional currencies are the pound and the deutsche mark, respectively. The temporal method is less commonly used and more complicated than is needed for an introduction to international accounting, so we focus on the current rate method for illustrative purposes.

Applying the Current Rate Method to Income Statements. According to FASB Statement 52, a firm adopting the current rate method to translate a subsidiary's income statement uses either the exchange rate on the day a transaction occurred or a weighted average of exchange rates during the period the income statement covers. For simplicity's sake, firms often use the latter approach. Dividends, however, are translated using the exchange rate in effect on the day they are paid. Table 19.3 presents a simple example of the translation of an income statement of a Belgian subsidiary of a U.S. parent. The subsidiary's functional currency is the Belgian franc, and the average exchange rate between the Belgian franc and the U.S. dollar during the three months the statement covers is assumed to be BF35 = $1.

Applying the Current Rate Method to Balance Sheets. The foreign subsidiary's balance sheet also must be translated. Under the current rate method,

TABLE 19.3

Translation of Income Statement of Belgian Subsidiary of U.S. Firm Using the Current Rate Method for the Quarter Ending March 31, 1999

	IN FUNCTIONAL CURRENCY (BELGIAN FRANCS)	IN HOME CURRENCY (U.S. DOLLARS)
Revenues	350,000,000	10,000,000
Expenses		
Cost of goods sold	210,000,000	6,000,000
General and administrative	45,500,000	1,300,000
Depreciation	42,000,000	1,200,000
Income before Taxes	52,500,000	1,500,000
Income Taxes	24,500,000	700,000
Net Income after Taxes	28,000,000	800,000

the assets and liabilities shown on the subsidiary's balance sheet are translated using the exchange rate in effect on the date for which the balance sheet was prepared (March 31, 1999 for the example in Table 19.4). Equity accounts (common stock and retained earnings) are generally treated on an historical basis. Because two or more different exchange rates are being used, the subsidiary's assets are not likely to equal the sum of its liabilities and shareholders' equity when they are translated. To reconcile this discrepancy, the firm makes an accounting entry known as the **cumulative translation adjustment** (see Table 19.4), which

TABLE 19.4

Translation of Balance Sheet of Belgian Subsidiary of a U.S. Firm Using the Current Rate Method for the Quarter Ending March 31, 1999

	IN BELGIAN FRANCS	EXCHANGE RATE (BF/U.S. DOLLAR)	IN U.S. DOLLARS
ASSETS			
Cash	105,000,000	35	3,000,000
Accounts Receivable	70,000,000	35	2,000,000
Inventories	70,000,000	35	2,000,000
Plant and Equipment	140,000,000	35	4,000,000
Total	385,000,000		11,000,000
LIABILITIES AND SHAREHOLDERS' EQUITY			
Current Liabilities	87,500,000	35	2,500,000
Notes Payable	122,500,000	35	3,500,000
Common Stock	50,000,000	50	1,000,000
Retained Earnings	125,000,000	40	3,125,000
Cumulative Translation Adjustment*			875,000
Total	385,000,000		11,000,000

* Needed to make assets = liabilities + shareholders' equity when denominated in U.S. dollars.

TABLE 19.5

Consolidated Balance Sheet of Johnson & Johnson for 1996 (millions of U.S. dollars)

ASSETS

Current Assets	$9,370
Marketable securities, noncurrent, at cost	351
Property, plant, and equipment, net	5,651
Intangible assets, net	3,107
Other assets	1,531
Total Assets	$20,010

LIABILITIES AND STOCKHOLDERS' EQUITY

Current Liabilities	$5,184
Long-term debt	1,410
Deferred tax liability	170
Other liabilities	2,410
Total Liabilities	$9,174
Stockholders' Equity	
Common stock—par value $1.00 per share (authorized 1,080,000,000 shares; issued 767,372,000 shares)	1,535
Note receivable from employee stock ownership plan	(57)
Cumulative currency translation adjustments	(122)
Retained earnings	11,012
	12,368
Less common stock held in treasury, at cost (124,391,000 shares)	1,532
Total Stockholders' Equity	10,836
Total Liabilities and Stockholders' Equity	$20,010

Source: Johnson & Johnson 1996 Annual Report.

---

makes the firm's assets equal the sum of its liabilities and shareholders' equity, an equality necessary to make the balance sheet balance. FASB Statement 52 requires that when a parent consolidates the subsidiary's balance sheet into its own, it must enter the cumulative translation adjustment as an adjustment to the parent's shareholders' equity. Table 19.5 shows how Johnson & Johnson used the cumulative translation adjustment in its 1996 annual report to its shareholders.

Using the cumulative translation adjustment significantly benefits both the firm and investors. Under the current rate method, the cumulative translation adjustment is made directly to shareholders' equity rather than first flowing through the firm's income statement. Thus, translation gains and losses do not affect the firm's reported net income. Companies are able to avoid the temptation of engaging in expensive efforts to dampen fluctuations in reported earnings resulting from translation gains or losses, a temptation to which many firms suc-

TABLE 19.6

Cumulative Translation Adjustment (CTA) and Shareholders' Equity (SE) for Selected U.S. MNCs, 1996 (in millions of U.S. dollars)

FIRM	CTA	SE	CTA AS PERCENTAGE OF SE	FOREIGN ASSETS AS PERCENTAGE OF TOTAL ASSETS
Exxon	1,126	$43,542	2.6%	73.4%
Ford	(28)	26,762	0.1	35.1
GM	(113)	23,418	0.5	24.9
Gillette	(522)	4,491	11.6	66.3
Johnson & Johnson	(122)	10,836	1.1	41.0
Lucent Technologies	(191)	3,387	5.6	23.5
McDonald's	(175)	8,718	2.0	56.6
Procter & Gamble	(418)	11,722	3.6	40.5

Source: 1996 annual reports of firms listed.

cumbed under the FASB accounting requirement that preceded Statement 52.[32] Instead, the current rate method more properly focuses investors' attention on the impact of exchange-rate changes on the home currency value of the firm's equity in its foreign subsidiaries.

The cumulative translation adjustments of U.S. MNCs are often large in absolute terms, as Table 19.6 shows. As a percentage of total shareholders' equity, however, this adjustment varies widely from company to company. Not surprisingly, firms with more extensive foreign investments tend to have higher cumulative translation adjustments relative to their shareholders' equity. Of the firms listed in Table 19.6, the relative importance of the cumulative translation adjustment is greatest for Gillette. But 66.3 percent of Gillette's assets are located outside the United States, more than for any other firm listed in the table other than Exxon.

International Taxation Issues

A close relationship often exists between national accounting procedures and national taxation policies. A country's tax code affects a variety of business behaviors as firms seek to maximize their after-tax profitability. A country may use its tax code not only to raise revenue but also to stimulate certain activities, such as the hiring of persons with physical disabilities or an increase in firms' R&D expenditures. Location, production, and hiring decisions may all be influenced by the structure and level of taxes.

Like domestic firms, international firms seek to maximize their after-tax income. However, they also are challenged to meet the tax requirements (which unfortunately often are in conflict) of all the countries in which they operate. International businesses typically must navigate a careful path between taking advantage of tax incentives and sidestepping punitive taxes.

Transfer Pricing

Two common means international businesses adopt to reduce their overall tax burden are transfer pricing and tax havens. **Transfer pricing** refers to the prices one branch or subsidiary of a parent charges a second branch or subsidiary for goods or services. Transfer pricing is important to international business for several reasons. Intracorporate transfers of goods, technology, and other resources are common between subsidiaries located in different countries. By one estimate, intracorporate shipments account for 40 percent of U.S. international trade in goods.[33] Transfer prices also affect an MNC's ability to monitor the performance of individual corporate units and to reward (or punish) managers responsible for a unit's performance. Further, the transfer prices affect the taxes an MNC pays both to its home country and to the various host countries in which it operates.

In practice, transfer prices are calculated in one of two ways:

1 Market-based method

2 Nonmarket-based methods

Market-Based Transfer Prices. The market-based method utilizes prices determined in the open market to transfer goods between units of the same corporate parent. Suppose Hyundai wants to export memory chips from South Korea for use in assembling personal computers at one of its U.S. subsidiaries. It can establish the transfer price for the memory chips between its U.S. and Korean subsidiaries by using the open market price for such chips.

This market-based approach has two main benefits. First, it reduces conflict between the two units over the appropriate price. The higher the price charged in the intracorporate transfer, the better the selling subsidiary's performance appears and the poorer the buying subsidiary's performance appears. To the extent that the parent allocates managerial bonuses or investment capital to its subsidiaries on the basis of profitability, the unit managers have incentives to squabble over the transfer price, because they care about how the MNC's accounting system reports their unit's performance. From the parent's perspective, however, such arguments waste firm resources. Once the firm's accounting records are consolidated, its overall before-tax profits will remain the same regardless of whether the transfer price overstates unit A's profitability and understates unit B's, or vice versa. Assuming both subsidiaries recognize the basic equity of the market-based price, such intracorporate conflict will be reduced.

Second, the market-based approach promotes the MNC's overall profitability by encouraging the efficiency of the selling unit. If the price the unit can charge for intracorporate sales is limited to the market price, its managers know that the unit's profitability depends on their ability to control its costs. Moreover, they recognize that if they successfully produce the product in question more cheaply than their international competitors can, the parent's market-based transfer pricing will acknowledge their efforts in full. Motivated by the prospects of bonuses and lucrative promotions, unit managers have every incentive to improve the efficiency and profitability of their operations.

Nonmarket-Based Transfer Prices. Transfer prices may also be established using nonmarket-based methods. Prices may be set by negotiations between the buying and selling units or on the basis of cost-based rules of thumb, such as production costs plus a fixed markup. Some services of the corporate parent may be assessed as a percentage of the subsidiary's sales, such as charges for general corporate overhead or for the right to use technology or intellectual property owned by the parent.

MNCs commonly use nonmarket-based prices partly because, for some goods and services, no real market exists outside the firm. For example, the sole market for an engine produced in a Ford factory in Spain may consist of Ford automobile assembly plants in Belgium, Germany, and the United Kingdom. Because no external market exists for this engine, Ford may establish a transfer price for the engine based on production costs plus an allowance for overhead and profit. Similarly, Toyota's ability to design and develop new automobile models is not a service that is bought and sold in the open market. Yet Toyota may want to charge its North American, British, and Australian subsidiaries an appropriate fee for the use of its research, design, and development services.

The use of nonmarket-based prices has both disadvantages and advantages. One disadvantage is that managers of the buying and selling units may waste time and energy arguing over the appropriate transfer price, since it will affect their reported profits (even though it will have no overall impact on the parent's consolidated before-tax income). Nonmarket-based transfer prices may also reduce the selling unit's efficiency. A transfer price based on the seller's costs plus some markup may reduce the seller's incentive to keep its costs low because it can pass along any cost increases to other members of the corporate family through the nonmarket-based price.

However, strategic use of nonmarket-based transfer prices may benefit an international business, as Table 19.7 shows. Creative rearranging of intracorporate prices may allow the parent to lower its overall tax bill.[34] For example, an MNC can lessen the burden of an ad valorem import tariff by reducing the price the selling unit charges the buying unit, thereby lowering the basis on which the tariff is calculated. Further, such pricing may enable a firm to slash its total income taxes. Suppose an MNC operates in two countries, one with high corporate income tax rates and the second with low rates. The firm can raise the transfer prices charged to the subsidiary in the high-tax country and lower those charged to the subsidiary in the low-tax country. Doing this will reduce the profitability of the first subsidiary, as measured by its accounting records, while increasing the profitability of the second. The net effect is to shift the location of the MNC's profits from the high-tax country (which would tax them more) to the low-tax country (which taxes them less), thereby reducing the firm's overall tax burden. Ireland, for example, has effectively exempted exports of manufactured goods from Irish corporate taxation in order to give MNCs an incentive to locate factories in that country. But this tax break also encourages MNCs to manipulate the transfer prices charged by their Irish factories so as to increase the profits reported by those factories and lower the profits reported by their non-Irish subsidiaries.[35]

Clever structuring of transfer prices can even allow a firm to evade host country restrictions on repatriation of profits. Suppose, for example, that a host country blocks repatriation by forbidding dividend payments from the subsidiary to the parent. The parent can evade this restriction by raising the transfer prices it charges the subsidiary for goods and services produced by other units of the corporate family or by charging fees for general corporate services. By means of this technique, cash will flow from the subsidiary to other parts of the firm in the form of payments for goods or services, rather than through the forbidden dividend payments. The net effect is the same, however, funds (in some form) are repatriated from the host country.[36]

A firm's transfer prices often reflect a trade-off between tax consequences and legal constraints imposed by countries in which the firm operates.[37] Numerous studies conducted by researchers indicate that MNCs routinely engage in tax-shifting behavior through transfer pricing and other devices.[38]

TABLE 19.7

Strategic Use of Nonmarket-Based Transfer Prices

GOAL	TECHNIQUE	EFFECT
Decrease tariff paid on components imported from a subsidiary	Lower transfer price charged by the subsidiary	Lowering the price on which an ad valorem tariff is based decreases total amount of import tariff
Decrease overall corporate income tax	Raise transfer prices paid by subsidiaries in high-tax countries and/or lower transfer prices charged by those subsidiaries; lower transfer prices paid by subsidiaries in low-tax countries and/or raise transfer prices charged by those subsidiaries	Reported profits of subsidiaries in high-tax countries decrease, and reported profits of subsidiaries in low-tax countries increase; total corporate tax burden decreases
Repatriate profits from a subsidiary located in a host country that blocks repatriation	Raise transfer prices paid by the subsidiary; lower transfer prices charged by the subsidiary	Cash flows from the subsidiary to other units, circumventing restriction on repatriation

Government agencies, such as the IRS, are well aware of these opportunities to play accounting games. As a result, both home and host countries scrutinize the transfer-pricing policies of MNCs operating within their borders to ensure that the firms do not evade their tax obligations and that the governments receive their "fair share" of taxes from the firms. A common approach is to use an **arm's length test** whereby government officials attempt to determine the price that two unrelated firms operating at arm's length would have agreed on. But in many cases, an appropriate arm's length price is difficult to establish, leading to conflict between international businesses and tax authorities. For example, in 1994 Japan's National Tax Administration billed Coca-Cola $140 million for back taxes, claiming that the royalty rates the firm charged its Japanese subsidiary for the right to use its trademarks were too high. The firm immediately appealed the decision, asserting its royalty rates were reasonable. Of course, determining the appropriate arm's length price for a unique asset like Coca-Cola's trademark is not simple. Thus this kind of conflict will not be resolved easily or quickly.[39]

Tax Havens

A second device international businesses use to reduce their tax burdens is to locate their activities in **tax havens**, countries that impose little or no corporate income taxes. For a relatively small fee, an MNC may set up a wholly owned subsidiary in a tax haven. By manipulating payments such as dividends, interest, royalties, and capital gains between its various subsidiaries, an MNC may divert income from subsidiaries in high-tax countries to the subsidiary operating in the tax haven. By booking its profits in the tax haven subsidiary, the MNC escapes the clutches of revenue agents in other countries. For example, an MNC may give ownership of its trademarks to a subsidiary located in the Cayman Islands. That subsidiary can then charge each of the corporation's operating subsidiaries a fee for the use of the trademarks. The fees paid by the operating subsidiaries reduce their profitability and thus the corporate income taxes they must pay to their host governments. The government of the Cayman Islands, however,

Many MNCs and international banks establish subsidiaries in tax havens to benefit from those countries' low tax rates, friendly business climates, and excellent communications linkages to world financial centers. U.S. financial services firms have invested over $42 billion in tax havens in the Caribbean Islands in order to better serve their corporate clients.

imposes no income tax on the trademark licensing fees earned by the subsidiary located there—or on income, profits, capital gains, or dividends. Thus the MNC reduces its overall income tax burden. The following "Going Global" explores some of the ethical issues surrounding the use of tax havens and transfer prices to reduce corporate tax burdens.

Several other smaller countries, including Liechtenstein, Luxembourg, and the Netherlands Antilles, also have gone into the business of being tax havens. To attract MNCs, a tax haven must not only refrain from imposing income taxes but also provide a stable political and business climate, an efficient court system, and sophisticated banking and communications industries. In return, the tax haven is able to capture franchising and incorporation fees and generate numerous lucrative professional jobs far beyond what an economy of its size normally could.

Being a tax haven can create a thriving economy. For example, foreign-owned firms outnumber the 32,000 residents of the Cayman Islands. The Cayman Islands' success as a tax haven reflects the high-quality services it provides to international businesses; for example, an MNC can create and incorporate a Cayman Islands subsidiary within 24 hours if needed.[40] The firms create demand for highly paid professionals such as accountants, bankers, and lawyers. As a result, the Cayman Islands is a major world banking and finance center. Its banks have attracted $300 billion in deposits from foreign investors, or about $9.4 million per resident.[41] From the Cayman Islands' perspective, the tax-haven sector of the local economy represents the ultimate "clean" industry so beloved by economic development officials. But the existence of tax havens creates numerous headaches for the taxing authorities of other countries, as explained in the next section.

Taxation of Foreign Income by the United States

The tax treatment of foreign income varies by country, although some basic similarities exist among many developed countries. As an example, let's review U.S. tax treatment of foreign income from three common sources: exports, foreign branches, and foreign subsidiaries.

GOING GLOBAL

The Ethics of Tax Havens and Transfer Pricing

Multinational corporations can save millions of dollars in income and other taxes through the use of tax havens and transfer prices. For example, by manipulating transfer prices, an MNC can shift profits from high-tax countries to low-tax countries. But is such behavior ethical?

Skillful utilization of tax havens and transfer prices obviously benefits the MNC and its shareholders. However, such techniques reduce the revenues available to the home or host country government to solve important social problems such as poverty, homelessness, and drug addiction. An MNC's failure to pay its "fair share" of taxes in the countries in which it operates means that either the resources needed to solve these problems will be unavailable or other taxpayers will be forced to pick up the tab. Because an MNC benefits from various services the local governments provide, such as transportation infrastructure, educational facilities, and police protection, many people claim it is unethical for the MNC to shirk paying for its share of these services.

Others argue that so long as an MNC is engaging in tax avoidance, its use of transfer prices and tax havens to reduce its tax burden is ethical. (Experts distinguish between *tax avoidance*, whereby a firm uses legal tax code loopholes to minimize its tax burden, and *tax evasion*, whereby a firm engages in illegal activities to lessen its tax payments.) Many accountants argue that an MNC's officers are bound by their fiduciary duties to their shareholders to take advantage of tax avoidance opportunities provided by various national tax codes. Indeed, from this perspective a manager's failure to do so could be viewed as unethical.

Taxation of Exports

Ordinarily the U.S. tax code treats the profits associated with the export of goods and services the same as domestically generated income. Such exports are not trivial: In 1996, U.S. firms exported $612 billion of goods and $237 billion of services. However, to encourage firms to increase their export activities, the U.S. tax code allows firms to establish **foreign sales corporations (FSC)**. The tax code requires that an FSC engage in significant overseas activities, such as marketing, order processing, distribution, invoicing, and financing export sales. If a firm fully complies with all the provisions for establishing an FSC, it can significantly reduce its U.S. federal income taxes on its exporting activities.[42] Caterpillar, for example, reduced its 1996 tax burden by $49 million through the use of an FSC.[43]

Taxation of Foreign Branch Income

A foreign branch is an unincorporated unit of a corporation. It operates in a foreign country, but because legally it is identical to the parent, its income is treated as if it were the parent's. Thus any earnings of a foreign branch of a U.S. corporation create taxable income for the parent, regardless of whether or not the earnings are repatriated to the parent.

Taxation of Foreign Subsidiary Income

Subsidiaries incorporated in a foreign country are legally distinct from the home country parent corporation. In general, for U.S. tax purposes, a U.S. parent corporation does not need to include the earnings of its foreign subsidiaries in reporting its profits to the IRS. The **deferral rule** in the U.S. tax code allows such earnings to be taxed only when they are remitted to the parent in the form of dividends, thus allowing the parent to defer paying U.S. taxes on those earnings. For example, the deferral rule saved Caterpillar $10 million in 1996 U.S. federal corporate income taxes.

The deferral rule is intended to stimulate international business activity by U.S. firms. In Caterpillar's case, 51 percent of its sales are outside the United States, and the deferral rule has helped it penetrate key markets in Europe and Asia. However, one important exception to the deferral rule ensures that U.S. firms do not establish shell corporations in tax havens that do little but provide the parent with the ability to defer U.S. taxes. U.S. tax law requires a parent corporation to determine whether each of its foreign subsidiaries is a controlled foreign corporation. A **controlled foreign corporation (CFC)** is a foreign corporation in which U.S. shareholders—each of which holds at least 10 percent of the firm's shares—together own a majority of its stock. This definition may seem strange, but it is designed to focus on foreign firms that are controlled by a single U.S. firm or a group of U.S. firms acting in concert, rather than those owned by many small U.S. investors. For example, Ford's wholly owned Jaguar subsidiary is a CFC, but its 33 percent share of Mazda, which is primarily owned by Japanese investors, is not.

According to the U.S. tax code, the income of CFCs is divided into two types: active income and passive income (also called Subpart F income). **Active income** is income generated by traditional business operations such as production, marketing, and distribution. **Subpart F income**, or **passive income**, is generated by passive activities such as the collection of dividends, interest, royalties, and licensing fees—the type of activities typically performed by subsidiaries incorporated in tax havens. U.S. firms may defer active income earned by CFCs they control. In calculating their U.S. taxes, however, they generally may not defer Subpart F income. In the absence of this restriction, U.S. firms could escape federal corporate income taxes on earnings generated by their intellectual property and investment portfolios. They could do this by establishing subsidiaries in tax havens and transferring to those subsidiaries legal title to their trademarks, patents, brand names, and investment portfolios. The U.S. government, by treating active and passive earnings of foreign subsidiaries differently, is walking a fine line between stimulating U.S. firms' international business activities and limiting their ability to evade U.S. taxes through the creation of subsidiaries in tax havens.

Resolving International Tax Conflicts

Across countries, differences exist in tax rates as well as in the definition of what is to be taxed. International businesses must answer to the tax authorities of each country in which they operate. Often, national tax authorities may be in conflict or may cumulatively impose extremely burdensome levels of taxation on international firms. As a result, resolving international tax conflicts is very important to international businesspeople.

Tax Credits

The earnings of foreign subsidiaries are often taxed by the host country government. If the same earnings are also taxed by the home country government, this dual taxation may become too burdensome for the firm and discourage it from participating in the international marketplace. The home country may reduce the burden of this dual taxation of foreign subsidiary income by the home country and the host country by granting a tax credit to the parent corporation for income taxes paid to the host country. This tax credit reduces the level of home country taxes that the MNC must pay.

The U.S. tax code, for example, allows U.S. firms to reduce their federal corporate income taxes by the amount of foreign income taxes paid by their foreign branches or subsidiaries, subject to certain limitations. The foreign income tax credit cannot be larger than the foreign operation's U.S. tax burden. However, under certain circumstances firms may carry excess tax credits backward or forward for a limited number of years. But many common destinations for U.S. FDI impose higher corporate taxes than the United States does, so the foreign income tax credit offers U.S. MNCs only partial relief from high foreign taxes. Further, the tax credit may be taken only for income taxes, not for other forms of taxes such as value-added taxes or sales taxes. While these concepts are simple in principle, many provisions of the U.S. tax code dealing with foreign tax credits are far more complicated in practice. International firms generally hire professionals knowledgeable about the intricacies of the tax code's treatment of foreign tax credits.

Tax Treaties

To promote international commerce, many countries sign treaties that address taxation issues affecting international business. For example, the United States has signed over fifty-five tax treaties with foreign nations. While the details vary, many of these treaties contain provisions for reducing withholding taxes imposed on firms' foreign branches and subsidiaries. Sometimes these treaties reduce the overall tax burden imposed on foreign income earned by home country firms or completely exempt interest and royalty payments from taxation. Typically, such preferences are granted on a reciprocal basis: country A provides country B's firms with favorable treatment only if country B treats country A's firms the same way.[44]

"Bashing" of Foreign Firms

Another source of international tax conflict involves the "bashing" of foreign firms by domestic politicians who believe that such firms manipulate transfer prices or otherwise structure relationships between the parent corporation and the local subsidiary to avoid paying their "fair share" of taxes (see "Going Global"). For example, since 1993 Japan's National Tax Administration (NTA) has tripled its staff auditing the transfer-pricing policies of foreign firms. In 1996 it filed claims against fifty foreign firms, alleging underpayment of $492 million in Japanese taxes due to improperly calculated transfer prices. MNCs such as Roche, Goodyear, and Coca-Cola have been hit with such claims; most of these cases are as yet unresolved. However, the NTA's actions have created a boom in business for accounting firms: Arthur Andersen alone has quadrupled the number of transfer-pricing specialists employed in its Tokyo office since 1993.[45]

GOING GLOBAL

Pity the Poor Tax Collector

The United States has also attempted to boost its tax take from foreign firms by eliminating a tax loophole called "earnings stripping." In the U.S. tax code, firms are normally allowed to deduct interest payments in calculating their tax bills, but must pay taxes on any dividends that they earn. To take advantage of these provisions, many foreign MNCs provided capital to their U.S. subsidiaries in the form of loans from the parent corporation to the subsidiary rather than in the form of equity investment. Earnings generated by the subsidiary could then be repatriated back to the parent in the form of interest payments untaxed by the U.S. government. By repatriating profits in the form of nontaxed interest payments, earnings were thereby "stripped" from the income taxes that would otherwise have been paid to the U.S. government.

To eliminate this practice, in 1989 the U.S. tax code was revised to limit the deductability of interest payments made by a U.S. subsidiary to its foreign-owned parent to 50 percent of its taxable income. Foreign MNCs promptly changed their strategy. Instead of the parent corporation providing loans directly to the U.S. subsidiary, the parent corporation arranged and guaranteed bank loans for its U.S. subsidiary. Although this approach was more expensive than the parent lending the funds directly, many foreign MNCs found it a better alternative than paying taxes to the U.S. government.

To counteract this approach, the U.S. tax code was changed in 1994 so that bank loans to the U.S. subsidiary guaranteed by the parent corporation would be treated as loans from the parent. With this new law, the Internal Revenue Service thought it had at last outsmarted the foreign companies. However, the primary result to date is that they have developed even more creative means of avoiding U.S. taxes. Some U.S. subsidiaries have sold their assets and leased them back, thereby replacing bank loans with lease payments. Others have issued bonds convertible into the common stock of the foreign parent corporation, which has the effect of the parent guaranteeing the loan in substance but not in law.

Source: "Foreign Firms Fume, Seek Loopholes As U.S. Attempts to Collect More Taxes," *Wall Street Journal*, June 14, 1994, p. A10.

The U.S. Internal Revenue Service has similarly targeted foreign firms subsequent to a 1989 study that indicated that only 28 percent of foreign-owned firms operating in the United States paid any U.S. income tax. Yet it is unclear to what extent foreign firms are engaging in illegal tax evasion, as opposed to the legal use of tax code loopholes to avoid taxes. For example, in the late 1980s and early 1990s the IRS stepped up its enforcement of U.S. transfer-pricing rules. However, because of exemptions in the tax code, it obtained only 26.5 percent of the amount it originally sought. In two significant cases the IRS filed against Merck & Co. and Nestlé during this period, U.S. courts held that the firms were properly following the requirements of the U.S. tax code. To avoid costly and lengthy litigation, many MNCs, such as Matsushita Electric Industrial Co., have chosen to enter into advance pricing agreements with the IRS, in which both sides agree in advance to the transfer prices the company will charge for intracorporate transactions.[46] Nonetheless, some U.S. politicians have proposed requiring foreign firms to pay some minimum level of income taxes based on the profitability of their U.S. competitors. So far, Treasury Department officials have opposed such proposals, arguing that such taxes would violate existing tax treaties. U.S.-based MNCs have also fought such proposals, believing that unfair treatment of foreign firms by the United States would invite retaliation by foreign governments against foreign subsidiaries of U.S. firms.[47]

CHAPTER REVIEW

Summary

The accounting tasks international businesses confront are more complex than those purely domestic firms face. An international firm must meet the accounting requirements of both its home country and all the countries in which it operates. Unfortunately, significant philosophical and operational differences exist in the accounting standards and procedures of the world's countries.

To reduce the costs that differing national accounting systems impose on international businesses and international investors, several efforts are underway to harmonize the accounting systems of the major trading nations. The International Accounting Standards Committee (FASB) has played an important role in such efforts, as has the European Union.

Firms engaged in international business typically face two specific accounting challenges: accounting for transactions in foreign currencies and translating the reported operations of foreign subsidiaries into the currency of the parent firm for purposes of consolidation. FASB Statement 52 details the procedures U.S. corporations use to account for such international transactions.

International businesses are also challenged in dealing with various countries' taxation policies. MNCs try to maximize their after-tax profitability by taking advantage of tax breaks and avoiding punitive taxes. They may manipulate transfer prices to shift reported profits from high-tax countries to low-tax countries. A few smaller countries have built strong local economies by providing tax havens to attract MNCs through the elimination of corporate income taxes and the creation of favorable business climates.

Like many countries, the United States offers favorable tax incentives to encourage its firms to participate in international business. The U.S. tax code allows firms to establish foreign sales corporations to reduce the taxes they pay on exports. Under certain conditions, U.S. firms also may defer paying U.S. income taxes on income generated by their foreign subsidiaries. However, foreign branches of U.S. firms enjoy no such tax benefits.

Because of the revenue needs of governments, international businesses often find themselves in conflict with foreign governments. To reduce firms' tax burdens, many home governments offer their firms credits for taxes paid to foreign governments. They also negotiate tax treaties to both reduce firms' tax burdens and promote international commerce. But foreign firms are often the target of "bashing" by domestic politicians who rightly or wrongly believe those firms are not paying their fair share of domestic taxes.

Review Questions

1. What factors influence the accounting procedures a country adopts?

2. How do German firms use accounting reserves?

3. What problems do Western firms and investors face in analyzing the performance of firms in CPEs?

4. What is the impact of differing accounting standards on the international capital market?

5. Which organizations are promoting the harmonization of national accounting standards?

6. What is the two-transaction approach?

7. How do firms establish prices for goods sold by one subsidiary to another?

8. How do U.S. MNCs benefit from the deferral rule?

9. Why are the IRS rules regarding CFCs so complicated? What kind of behavior is the IRS trying to prevent?

10. What mechanisms have national governments adopted to lessen the burden of foreign governments' taxes on home country MNCs?

Questions for Discussion

1. The Big Six have globalized primarily through mergers. What advantages does this growth strategy offer these firms? What are the disadvantages of using mergers to globalize?

2. What impact would harmonization of national accounting standards have on international businesses?

3. What are the benefits of the two-transaction approach to international businesses and international investors?

4. How can an international firm use transfer pricing to increase its after-tax income?

5. The U.S. tax code distinguishes between active and passive income in permitting the deferral of foreign subsidiaries' income. Why has it made this distinction? Why is the distinction important? If tax havens were eliminated, would the tax code need to continue to distinguish between active and passive income?

6. Is the use of transfer pricing in order to reduce a firm's taxes ethical? Why or why not?

7. Are U.S. firms at a competitive disadvantage because they can't use accounting reserves as German firms do?

BUILDING GLOBAL SKILLS

International accounting is complex. As this chapter has shown, a firm's international activities affect its financial statements in many ways. To gain a better appreciation of this impact, obtain the most recent annual report of a publicly traded corporation that engages in international business. Most major firms listed on the NYSE, the American Stock Exchange, or NASDAQ are happy to provide you with their most recent annual report if you write or phone their investor relations department. Your local library or members of your family may also be able to provide you with a report. Some firms also provide access to their annual reports at their corporate web sites.

Next, answer the following questions regarding the firm you selected. (You may not be able to answer all of them. Some firms provide highly detailed information about their foreign operations, others very little.)

1. How large is the firm's cumulative translation adjustment in absolute terms? How large is the adjustment relative to shareholders' equity?

2. Did the firm use an FSC to save on its taxes? If so, how much did it save?

3. Did the firm benefit from the deferral rule on foreign subsidiary income? If so, by how much?

4. What percentage of the firm's assets are located in foreign countries? What percentage of its profits come from its foreign operations?

5. How much taxes did the firm pay to foreign countries?

6. How important is exporting to the firm?

7. Did the firm enjoy or suffer any foreign-currency transactions gains or losses? Did it engage in any hedging activities to protect itself from exchange-rate changes?

WORKING WITH THE WEB: Building Global Internet Skills

Hunting for Low Taxes

Mountain Sports, Inc. is a small U.S. manufacturer of snowboards. It markets its line of high-priced, high-tech snowboards to ski shops throughout the Rocky Mountains and New England. Recently, it has decided to expand into the European market, which it believes holds far greater opportunities than the increasingly crowded U.S. market. Its business plan predicts that it will sell $4 million in snowboards annually in Europe. To implement this initiative, Mountain Sports plans to establish a small, ten-person sales office somewhere in the Alps. The company estimates that it will pay each of its ten salespersons approximately $40,000. After deducting salaries, rent, travel expenses, and the cost of the snowboards themselves, Mountain Sports expects to gross $1 million in profits in Europe before paying taxes of any kind.

Mountain Sports has decided to locate its European sales office in Austria, Switzerland, or Italy, depending upon which country's tax laws are most favorable. To help Mountain Sports make this decision, you are assigned the task of obtaining information about each country's tax laws. In particular,

Mountain Sports is concerned about the payroll taxes and income taxes that it will have to pay for its European sales office. It is also unsure whether it should operate the office as a branch or as a subsidiary (i.e., should it incorporate the European sales office, thereby making it a subsidiary?). Accordingly, you need to collect information on the various taxes levied on payrolls and on corporate income in these three countries. You also need to determine if there are any advantages to operating as a subsidiary rather than a branch. After obtaining this information, write up a brief memo detailing what you have discovered and provide a recommendation to the CEO of Mountain Sports regarding which country the sales office should be located in and whether it should be incorporated or not. Make sure you justify your recommendation.

Fortunately, some accounting firms and other organizations provide summary information of the tax codes of the world's nations on their web sites. The textbook's web site provides linkages to these and other web sites that may be of help for this assignment.

CLOSING CASE

The Aramco Advantage[48]

Between the years 1979 and 1981, Saudi Arabia had a major disagreement with the other members of the Organization of Petroleum Exporting Countries (OPEC) about the appropriate price to charge for a barrel of crude oil. So-called OPEC "hawks" wanted to keep the price of oil high. Saudi Arabia, fearful that high prices would encourage other countries to explore for new, low-cost oil fields and stimulate consumers to conserve on energy usage, believed that the most profitable long-run strategy was to keep prices low. The Saudis' actions resulted in the creation of the "Aramco advantage" and the world's largest tax refund involving transfer pricing.

Aramco is a consortium of four U.S. oil companies—Chevron, Exxon, Mobil, and Texaco—that

originally controlled the Saudi oil fields. After their oil reserves were expropriated by the Saudi government in the 1970s, Aramco continued to play a major role in marketing Saudi oil. The Aramco advantage began in January 1979 when Ahmed Zaki Yamani, the Saudi oil minister, wrote a letter to Aramco forbidding it to sell Saudi oil for more than the price set by Yamani's ministry. This price was well below the world market price for crude oil. The Aramco partners, not wishing to displease the Saudi government, dutifully complied with Yamani's request. They sold the crude oil to their foreign refineries at Yamani's price and then refined it into gasoline, diesel fuel, and other petroleum products. But Yamani's directive involved only the price of crude oil. Each company was free to sell the refined products at their market prices, which they did.

Because they were buying the crude oil at less than the market price, the refining operations of the Aramco partners were soon making money hand over fist. (In case you are wondering, Yamani was not ignorant of the impact of his letter. He had numerous political reasons for his actions.)

The impact of the Aramco advantage was enormous. Exxon's refineries earned an additional $4.5 billion from 1979 to 1981, while Texaco's refineries netted an estimated $1.8 billion. And since these profits were earned by their foreign refinery subsidiaries, the profits could be sheltered from U.S. taxation because of the deferral rule—or so the companies thought. The Internal Revenue Service had a different view. It argued that it was the marketing activities of the two companies that were responsible for these profits, not the refining operations. Accordingly, the IRS claimed that $4.5 billion in income should be transferred to Exxon (the parent corporation) from its foreign refineries, while Texaco should make a similar shift of $1.8 billion. Having done so, the companies then should be required to pay U.S. corporate income taxes on these earnings.

Not surprisingly, the companies resisted the IRS's interpretation. They said that they were following the explicit instructions of the minister of a sovereign, friendly nation. Because of Yamani's directive, Texaco and Exxon asserted that the parent companies were unable to directly benefit from lower crude oil prices because they were forbidden to resell it. Rather, they noted that the Aramco advantage could only be captured by someone operating further down in the production-distribution chain. As it turned out, it was the next link in the chain—the foreign refineries owned by the individual Aramco partners—that garnered the Aramco advantage. Exxon and Texaco also pointed out that the United States had been putting great diplomatic pressure on the Saudis to lower the price of crude oil, and that U.S. officials were well aware that the result of this policy would be increased refining profits.

Texaco's case is the first to have completed its long journey through the U.S. judicial system. The U.S. Tax Court agreed with Texaco's interpretation. It found that the $1.8 billion in additional profits generated by the Aramco advantage were earned by Texaco's foreign refining subsidiaries and not subject to U.S. corporate income taxes unless and until they were repatriated back to the parent corporation in the form of dividends. A federal appeals court upheld the verdict of the Tax Court, and in April 1997 the U.S. Supreme Court refused to hear the IRS's appeal of the appeals court decision. Texaco officials estimate that their tax refund check will reach $700 million.

Case Questions

1. Which unit of Texaco really "earned" the Aramco advantage? Aramco itself? Texaco's foreign refineries? Texaco's marketing operations? Or the parent corporation?

2. Had Aramco sold the crude oil to Texaco's U.S. refineries, would Texaco have been able to avoid U.S. taxation on the Aramco advantage?

3. Since Minister Yamani created the Aramco advantage in part in response to U.S. diplomatic pressure, should Exxon and Texaco have been required to sell their allotment of Saudi crude oil to their domestic refineries?

4. The IRS lawyers argued that the appeals court ruling amounted to a "blueprint for the evasion of U.S. taxes. [It] … creates substantial tax incentives for United States corporations to encourage or to endure the adoption of profitable foreign 'legal restrictions' that 'require' such corporations to avoid United States taxation." Do you agree with the IRS position? Or is it just being a crybaby because it lost?

CHAPTER NOTES

1. American Accounting Association, *A Statement of Basic Accounting Theory* (Evanston, Ill.: AAA, 1966), p. 1.

2. Much of the discussion in this section is taken from Frederick D. S. Choi and Gerhard Mueller, *International Accounting*, 2nd ed. (Englewood Cliffs: Prentice Hall, 1992), Chapters 2 and 3, and from reports of the Working Group on Accounting Standards, Organisation for Economic Cooperation and Development, published in 1987: "Accounting Standards Harmonization, No. 2:

Consolidation Policies in OECD Nations" and "Accounting Standards Harmonization, No. 3: The Relationship between Taxation and Financial Reporting;" Frederick D. S. Choi (ed.). *International Accounting and Finance Handbook*. (New York: John Wiley & Sons, 1997).

3. Stephen B. Salter and Timothy S. Doupnik, "The Relationship between Legal Systems and Accounting Practices," in Kenneth S. Most (ed.), *Advances in International Accounting*, Vol. 5 (Greenwich, Conn.: JAI Press, 1992).

4. Hanns-Martin W. Schoenfeld, "International Accounting: Development, Issues, and Future Directions," *The Journal of International Business Studies* (Fall 1981), pp. 83–100.

5. "Accountancy," *The Economist*, October 17, 1992, p. 23.

6. Choi and Mueller, op. cit., p. 95.

7. "Chinese practitioners ready for their great leap forward," *Financial Times*, August 13, 1993, p. 20.

8. Timothy S. Doupnik, "Recent Innovations in German Accounting Practice," in Kenneth S. Most (ed.), *Advances in International Accounting*, Vol. 5 (Greenwich, Conn.: JAI Press, 1992).

9. Robert Bloom, Jayne Fuglister, and Jeffrey Kantor, "Toward Internationalization of Upper-Level Financial Accounting Courses," in Kenneth S. Most (ed.), *Advances in International Accounting*, Vol. 5 (Greenwich, Conn.: JAI Press, 1992), pp. 239–253; Frederick D. S. Choi and Richard Levich, *The Capital Market Effects of International Accounting Diversity* (Homewood, Ill.: Dow Jones–Irwin, 1990), pp. 115–117.

10. "Deutsche Bank Says Net Jumped 24% in 1995, Discloses Big Hidden Reserves," *Wall Street Journal*, March 29, 1996, p. A8.

11. Lufthansa, *Annual Report 1993*, p. 30.

12. Donald Lessard, "Principles of International Portfolio Selection," *International Financial Management* (New York: John Wiley and Sons, 1985), pp. 16–30.

13. "Shares of Murdoch's News Corp. Are Clouded by Australian Accounting, Critics Contend," *Wall Street Journal*, August 16, 1988, p. 53.

14. "Big Board Chief Renews His Pitch on Foreign Stocks," *Wall Street Journal*, January 7, 1992, p. A2.

15. S. J. Gray, J. C. Shaw, and L. B. McSweeney, "Accounting Standards and Multinational Corporations," *The Journal of International Business Studies* (Spring/Summer 1981), pp. 121–136.

16. Presentation of Tetsuo Sakamoto, Senior Vice President, The Long-Term Credit Bank of Japan, Ltd., Texas A&M University, June 1, 1992.

17. "Daimler-Benz gears up for a drive on the freeway," *Financial Times*, April 30, 1993.

18. "Asia Feels Bite of Lack of Transparency," *Wall Street Journal*, December 15, 1997, p. A18; "NY exchange sees wider horizons," *Financial Times*, September 24, 1997, p. 4.

19. Andrew L. Nodar, "Coca-Cola Writes an Accounting Procedures Manual," *Management Accounting*, Vol. 68 (October 1986), pp. 52–53.

20. Istemi S. Demirag, "Assessing Foreign Subsidiary Performance: The Currency Choice of U.K. MNCs," *Journal of International Business Studies*, Vol. 19, No. 2 (Summer 1988), pp. 257–275.

21. Shawn Tully, "GE in Hungary: Let There Be Light," *Fortune*, October 22, 1990, p. 142.

22. "Chinese practitioners ready for their great leap forward," *Financial Times*, August 13, 1993, p. 20.

23. Lee H. Radebough and Sidney J. Gray, *International Accounting and Multinational Enterprises* (New York: John Wiley & Sons, Inc., 1997), pp. 111–112.

24. John N. Turner, "International Harmonization: A Professional Goal," *Journal of Accountancy* (January 1983), pp. 58–59.

25. Choi and Mueller, op. cit., pp. 262ff.

26. Stephen B. Salter, *Classification of Financial Reporting Systems and a Test of Their Environmental Determinants*, unpublished Ph.D. dissertation, University of South Carolina (1991), p. 5.

27. "Language lessons for accountants," *Financial Times*, July 11, 1995, p. 4.

28. "France girds itself for an international market," *Financial Times*, June 28, 1991, p. 13.

29. "German conglomerate adopts U.S. system of filing accounts," *Financial Times*, March 28, 1996, p. 11; "Bonn signals softer line on accounting," *Financial Times*, May 22, 1995, p. 2; "German Firms Shift to More-Open Accounting," *Wall Street Journal*, March 15, 1995, p. C1.

30. Financial Accounting Standards Board, *Statement of Financial Accounting Standards No. 52: Foreign Currency Translation* (Stamford, Conn.: FASB, December 1981).

31. "Dell Computer at War with Analyst Critical of Its Currency Trades," *Wall Street Journal*, November 30, 1992,

p. A1; "Dell Computer Shares Drop by 9.8% on Analyst's Currency-Trading Report," *Wall Street Journal*, November 11, 1992, p. A5.

32. Robert G. Ruland and Timothy S. Doupnik, "Foreign Currency Translation and the Behavior of Exchange Rates," *Journal of International Business Studies*, Vol. 19, No. 3 (Fall 1988), p. 462.

33. F. Steb Hipple, "Multinational Companies and International Trade: The Impact of Intrafirm Shipments on U.S. Foreign Trade 1977–1982, *Journal of International Business Studies*, Vol. 21, No. 3 (Third Quarter, 1990), pp. 495–504.

34. J. Shulman, "When the Transfer Price Is Wrong—By Design," *Columbia Journal of World Business* (May–June 1967), pp. 69–76.

35. J. C. Stewart, "Transfer Pricing: Some Empirical Evidence from Ireland," *Journal of Economic Studies*, Vol. 16, No. 3, pp. 40–56.

36. D. J. Lecraw, "Some evidence on transfer pricing by multinational corporations," in A. M. Rugman and L. Eden (eds.), *Multinationals and transfer pricing* (New York: St. Martin's Press, 1985).

37. Mohammad F. Al-Eryani, Pervaiz Alam, and Syed H. Akhter, "Transfer Pricing Determinants of U.S. Multinationals," *Journal of International Business Studies*, Vol. 21, No. 3 (Third Quarter, 1990), pp. 409–425.

38. David Harris, Randall Morck, Joel Slemrod, and Bernard Yeung, "Income Shifting in U.S. Multinational Corporations," University of Michigan, mimeo, 1991; James R. Hines and Eric Rice, "Fiscal Paradise: Foreign Tax Havens and American Business," N.B.E.R. Working Paper #3477 (Cambridge, Mass., 1990); James Wheeler, "An Academic Look at Transfer Pricing in a Global Economy," *Tax Notes*, July 4, 1988.

39. "Japan Orders 60 Firms to Pay Back-Taxes," *Wall Street Journal*, October 12, 1994, p. A13.

40. "Cleaning Up by Cleaning Up," *Euromoney*, April 1991, pp. 73–77.

41. Howard W. French, "Offshore Banking Gets New Scrutiny with B.C.C.I. Scandal," *New York Times*, September 29, 1991, p. 7.

42. Bruce W. Reynolds and Alan R. Levenson, "Setting Up a Foreign Sales Corporation Can Cut Your Tax Bill," *Journal of European Business* (July/August 1992), pp. 59–64; Mark A. Goldstein and Arthur I. Aronoff, "Foreign Sales Corporations: Tax Incentives for U.S. Exporters," *Business Credit* (April 1991), pp. 20–23.

43. These and subsequent data are taken from Caterpillar's 1996 annual report.

44. Choi and Mueller, op. cit., p. 554.

45. "Japan's Tax Man Leans on Foreign Firms," *Wall Street Journal*, November 25, 1996, p. A13.

46. "Clinton's Economic Proposal Faces Problem: Taxes of Foreign Companies Won't Meet Goal," *Wall Street Journal*, November 11, 1992, p. A16.

47. "Lawmakers say tax fraud by foreign firms costs U.S. billions," *Houston Chronicle*, April 10, 1992, p. 10F; "Treasury Opposes Legislation to Impose Minimum Tax on Foreign Firms in U.S.," *Wall Street Journal*, July 22, 1992, p. A2.

48. "Court Blocks Challenge of Big Tax Refund for Texaco," *New York Times*, April 22, 1997, p. C1; "Texaco wins billion-dollar tax battle," *Houston Chronicle*, April 22, 1997, p. 1C.

International Human Resource Management and Labor Relations

After studying this chapter you should be able to:

Characterize the nature of human resource management in international business.

Discuss how firms recruit and select managers for international assignments.

Describe how international businesses train and develop expatriate managers.

Discuss how international firms conduct performance appraisals and determine compensation for their expatriate managers.

Discuss retention and turnover issues in international business.

Describe basic human resource issues involving nonmanagerial employees.

Describe labor relations in international business.

HEN AN INTERNATIONAL BUSINESS OPENS A NEW OFFICE, MANU-facturing plant, or other facility in a foreign country, one of its most important tasks is staffing that new facility with managers and operating employees. To do this, the firm must decide how many employees it needs for the new facility, what skills they must have, where they will be hired, how much they will be paid, and many other issues. Most firms think they do a pretty good job in this area. However, when it comes to staffing a foreign operation, Japanese companies are among the most careful and thorough in the world. ▪▪ Consider, for example, how Toyota approached the staffing of its first automobile assembly plant in the United States. In Japan, automakers and other manufacturers have set up special training programs in high schools. Students who are not likely to go to college can enter training and apprenticeship programs financed by these businesses. In the United States, such programs are rare. ▪▪ Toyota managers believe it takes a special kind of employee to succeed in their firm. The firm wants to hire only people who will conform to the Japanese emphasis on teamwork, corporate loyalty, and versatility along the production line. In Japan, prospective employees have been trained and screened along these dimensions while in high school. But to find such people in the United States, Toyota goes to what some observers see as extraordinary lengths. ▪▪ When Toyota was opening its first wholly owned U.S. plant in Kentucky, it received over 100,000 applications for 2,700 production jobs and 300 office jobs. Over half of these applicants were rejected immediately because they lacked the minimum education or experience Toyota deemed necessary. Other applicants were eliminated early in the screening process because they lacked one or more other essential qualifications. ▪▪ The thousands of applicants still under consideration were invited to participate in an exhaustive battery of tests. Applicants for even the lowest-level jobs in the plant were tested for over fourteen hours. The initial tests covered such areas as manual dexterity, job skills, and technical knowledge. Worker attitudes toward unionization were also assessed during this phase of testing because Toyota did not want its plant to be unionized by the United Auto Workers, the collective bargaining agent for U.S. automakers. ▪▪ Those applicants who passed the first level of tests were invited back to participate in an organizational simulation exercise. Although many firms use organizational simulations when hiring managers, Toyota uses it for all prospective employees. Results from the simulation eliminated still other applicants from the pool, while those who remained were invited back for still more testing. This third wave of testing involved performing mock production line jobs on a simulated conveyor belt under the observation of trained supervisors. Only one of every twenty applicants made it through this test and was invited back

Training for the World[1]

yet again, this time for an interview. ▌▌ The interview was conducted by a panel of officials and representatives from each department in the plant. These interviewers were trained to determine how well the applicant would fit into both the overall Toyota culture and the interviewers' specific departments. Finally, applicants who were favorably evaluated by the interviewers were asked to take a physical exam and drug tests. If they passed both, then—and only then—were they deemed to have met Toyota's standards. ▌▌ By the time the selection process is completed and Toyota actually hires a person, it has spent over $13,000 on testing and evaluating that individual. And, of course, it has already spent thousands of dollars more eliminating others at earlier stages. Even though Toyota's original U.S. plant has been open for a decade, the firm is just as selective now as in earlier times. The firm allows twenty-four people a day to sign up for its assessment center evaluation (many more apply each day). About one in a hundred eventually gets a job, although the entire evaluation process and time spent on the waiting list can stretch to up to two years before the individual can actually start to work. And Toyota has extended and refined its thorough selection approach into its new U.S. plants as well. For example, applicants for jobs at the firm's Indiana truck plant and West Virginia engine plant undergo the same rigorous assessment as applicants at the Kentucky factory. ▌▌ Other foreign automobile companies setting up shop in the United States also recognize that employees are critical to their success. When Mercedes-Benz began hiring people for its new factory in Alabama, 45,000 applications were received for 1,500 jobs. Like Toyota, Mercedes established a grueling and comprehensive system to identify just the workers it wanted. Other Japanese auto manufacturers also invest heavily in selecting employees for their U.S. operations. Each puts a slightly different twist on the process, however. Mazda, for example, uses more tests relating to job skills, while Mitsubishi puts more emphasis on group exercises and simulations. Honda emphasizes tests much less but subjects each applicant to a minimum of three interviews. Nissan takes yet another approach. Applicants who meet its preliminary screening criteria must go through forty hours of nonpaid pre-employment training. After that training is complete, their ability to meet Nissan's performance standards is assessed on a simulated assembly line. Those who meet the minimum acceptable standards may then be eligible for employment with the firm. ▌▌▌▌

At its most basic level, any organization—from a small neighborhood convenience store to the largest MNC—is nothing more than a collection of jobs, clusters of jobs, and interconnections among those jobs. The people who fill the jobs are a vital ingredient in determining how effectively the organization will be able to meet its goals, remain competitive, and satisfy its constituents. Toyota's care in selecting its U.S. work force shows that it understands that its employees are among its most important assets.

The Nature of Human Resource Management

Human resource management **(HRM)** is the set of activities directed at attracting, developing, and maintaining the effective work force necessary to achieve a firm's objectives. HRM includes recruiting and selecting nonmanagers and managers, providing training and development, appraising performance, and providing compensation and benefits. HR managers, regardless of whether they work for a purely domestic firm or an international one, must develop procedures and policies for accomplishing these tasks.

International HR managers, however, face challenges beyond those confronting their counterparts in purely domestic companies.[2] Specifically, differences in cultures, levels of economic development, and legal systems among the countries in which a firm operates may force it to customize its hiring, firing, training, and compensation programs on a country-by-country basis. Particularly troublesome problems develop when conflicts arise between the culture and laws of the home country and those of the host country. For example, prohibitions against gender discrimination in U.S. equal employment opportunity laws conflict with Saudi Arabian custom and law regarding the role of women. Such conflicts cause problems for U.S. MNCs that want to ensure that their female executives receive overseas assignments equivalent to those given to their male colleagues.

The international firm must also determine where various employees should come from—the home country, the host country, or third countries. The optimal mix of employees may differ according to the location of the firm's operations. A firm is likely to hire more employees from its home country to work in production facilities there than to work in foreign facilities. Local laws must also be considered, because they may limit or constrain hiring practices. For example, immigration laws may limit the number of work visas granted to foreigners, or employment regulations may mandate the hiring of local citizens as a requirement for doing business in a country.

International businesses also face more complex training and development challenges. For example, HR managers must provide cross-cultural training for corporate executives chosen for overseas assignments. Similarly, training systems for production workers in host countries must be adjusted to reflect the education offered by local school systems. For example, because of the tradition of employment as a lifetime commitment, Toyota, like other large Japanese corporations, goes to great lengths to hire just the right people to work in its factories and offices. As the chapter opener revealed, it has nurtured partnerships with local public school systems in Japan to help train and select future employees. But Toyota cannot rely on this approach in each country in which it does business because local school systems often are not prepared to operate such training partnerships with individual firms. The German secondary school system provides extensive vocational training for its students, but that training is less firm-specific. The United States, on the other hand, emphasizes general education and provides only modest vocational training opportunities through its public schools. And many countries have labor pools that, when measured along any dimension, are uneducated and unskilled. Toyota thus has adjusted its selection, recruitment, and training practices to meet the requirements of the countries in which it does business.

And, finally, because working conditions and the cost of living may vary dramatically by country, international HR managers often must tailor compensation systems to meet the needs of the host country's labor market. They must take into account variations in local laws, which may require the payment of a minimum wage or may mandate certain benefits, such as annual bonuses or health care coverage. These managers must also determine how to compensate executives on overseas assignments, who potentially face higher costs of living, reductions in the quality of their lifestyle, and unhappiness or stress due to separation from friends and relatives.

Strategic Significance of HRM

As with marketing, operations, finance, and accounting, the firm's managers must design an HRM strategy that promotes the company's overall corporate and business strategies. The cultural nuances inherent in international business heighten the complexities of developing an effective human resource strategy. The basic elements of the international HRM process are shown in Fig. 20.1, which provides the framework around which this chapter is organized. The starting point

FIGURE 20.1

The International
Human Resource
Management Process

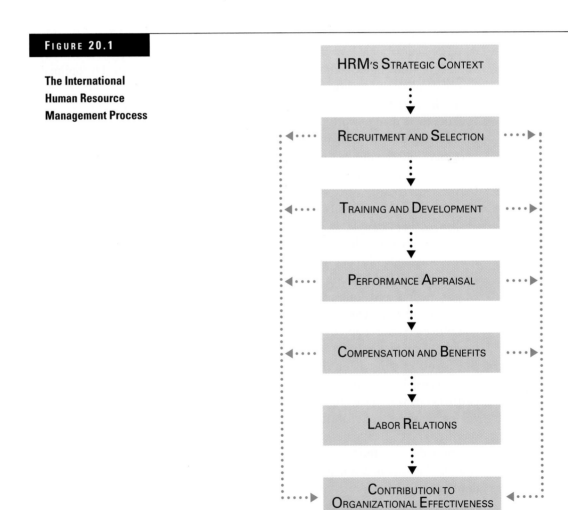

is recognizing and appreciating HRM's strategic position within the firm and the interconnection between overall firm strategy and HRM strategy.[3] For example, suppose that a firm decides to adopt a cost leadership strategy and subsequently identifies the opportunity to undercut competing firms by aggressively pricing its products in new international markets. In implementing this strategy, the firm could decide to purchase more inputs from outside suppliers, or it could shift production to a country with low-cost labor, such as Indonesia or Malaysia. This production location decision could result in less need for home country workers and more need for workers at the foreign facility. The firm's HR managers thus would have to develop severance packages and provide outplacement services for released workers in the home country as well as select, recruit, and train the new workers in the foreign country. Over time, the firm's HR managers would have to adjust their HR practices to meet the conditions in the host country, which are likely to differ from those in the home country.

The decision to shift production overseas has other HR consequences. HR managers have to select key managerial personnel to oversee the transfer of the firm's technology, operating policies, and proprietary skills to its new overseas factories.[4] Regardless of the skills or abilities of the selected international managers, few of them will be able to walk into a foreign operation and know exactly how to do things from the first day they arrive. Thus HR managers must provide them with training to help them function more effectively in a new culture.

HR managers must also be prepared to define performance effectiveness and assess how well each international manager is doing relative to that definition. And international managers must be compensated for their work. Further, firms invest a lot in their international managers, so HR managers must carefully assess the effectiveness of their management of retention and turnover.

International Managerial Staffing Needs

The staffing issues confronting international human resource managers can be divided into two broad categories. One of these is recruiting, training, and retaining managerial and executive employees. The other is recruiting, training, and retaining nonmanagerial employees, such as blue-collar production workers and white-collar office staff. For managerial employees, strategic and developmental issues are of primary importance. For nonmanagerial workers, differences in cultural, political, and legal conditions among countries may be of greater significance.

Scope of Internationalization

We begin by focusing on recruiting, training, and retaining managers. The size of this task depends on the scope of the firm's international involvement. Obviously, a firm's needs in the beginning stages of internationalization, such as in indirect exporting, are far less complex and comprehensive than those confronting an MNC with extensive investments in numerous countries. Consider the evolution of organizational structure discussed in Chapter 13.

1 *Export department.* A firm's initial foray into international business usually involves small-scale exporting using output from existing domestic production facilities. Its international activities are administered by an export department, whose manager reports to an existing company executive such as the vice president of marketing. The manager is likely to be a citizen of the home country and may or may not have special training in overseas marketing and financing. But as export sales increase, the firm quickly recognizes that it must increase its staff's expertise, so it hires specialists in export documentation, international trade financing, and overseas distribution and marketing. These specialists are often recruited from international banks, international freight forwarders, or export management companies.

2 *International division.* As its international operations grow in importance, a firm often creates a separate international division to administer all of its international activities. Typically, a firm's international division is housed at corporate headquarters in its home country and is headed by a home country citizen in order to facilitate communication and coordination between the domestic and international operations. The heads of the firm's foreign subsidiaries in turn report to the vice president of the international division. These foreign subsidiaries' managers (including their presidents as well as heads of functional departments such as finance, marketing, and production) may be either home country or host country citizens. Use of a home country manager facilitates communication and coordination with corporate headquarters because of shared cultural and educational backgrounds.[5] Use of a host country manager often improves the subsidiary's ability to adjust to changes in local economic and political conditions. As we discuss later in this chapter, cost considerations also play a major role in the choice between home country and host country managers.

3 *Global organization.* A firm further along in the internationalization process often adopts a global organization form. (Chapter 13 discussed the global product, global function, global area, and global customer forms.) Because of the complexity of its operations, a global organization must assemble a team of managers that have the expertise to produce, finance, and market its products worldwide while simultaneously coordinating its activities to achieve global production, financing, and marketing economies and synergies. To operate successfully, a global firm needs a team of managers that collectively possess expertise in and knowledge of the following:

♦ The firm's *product line.* Product managers must be aware of such factors as the latest manufacturing techniques, R&D opportunities, and competitors' strategies.

♦ The *functional skills* (accounting, logistics, marketing, manufacturing management, and so on) necessary to ensure global competitiveness. Functional specialists strive to capture global economies of scale and synergies in a firm's financial, marketing, and production activities.

♦ The *individual country markets* in which the firm does business. Country managers must understand such factors as local laws, culture, competitors, distribution systems, and advertising media. They play a key role in meeting the needs of local customers, ensuring compliance with host country rules and regulations, and enlarging the firm's market share and profitability in the host country.

- ◆ The firm's *global strategy*. High-level executives at corporate headquarters must formulate a global strategy for the firm and then control and coordinate the activities of the firm's product, functional, and country managers to ensure that its strategy is successfully implemented.[6]

Centralization versus Decentralization of Control

An international business's HRM needs are also affected by whether the firm wants decision making to be centralized at corporate headquarters or delegated (decentralized) to operating subsidiaries. Firms that use a centralized approach often favor employing home country managers; those that follow a decentralized decision-making philosophy are more likely to employ host country managers.

Certain organizational approaches and forms affect the choice of centralization or decentralization. Firms that view themselves as multi*domestic* rather than multi*national* are likely to favor decentralization of decision making. The global area form facilitates delegating responsibility to managers of the firm's foreign subsidiaries. Conversely, the international division form favors centralizing decision making at corporate headquarters.

Recall from Chapter 13 that most international businesses operate somewhere along the continuum from pure centralization to pure decentralization. In managing human resources, most adopt an overall HRM strategy at the corporate headquarters level, but delegate many day-to-day HR issues to local and regional offices. Doing this allows each foreign operation to meet its own needs and to more effectively deal with local conditions, cultures, and HR practices.

Staffing Philosophy

The extent of the firm's internationalization and its degree of centralization or decentralization affects (and is affected by) its philosophy regarding the nationality of its international managers. Firms can hire from three groups: parent-country nationals, host-country nationals, and third-country nationals.

Parent-country nationals (PCNs) are residents of the international business's home country. Use of PCNs in an MNC's foreign operations provides many advantages to the firm. Because PCNs typically share a common culture and educational background with corporate headquarters staff, they facilitate communication and coordination with corporate headquarters.[7] If the firm's global strategy involves exploiting new technologies or business techniques that were developed in the home market, PCNs are often best able to graft those innovations to a host country setting. For example, Toyota sent a team of executives from Japan to oversee the start-up of its U.S. operations. It wanted to ensure that its manufacturing techniques and corporate commitment to quality were successfully transplanted to Kentucky and the other U.S. plants it subsequently opened. Mercedes followed a similar staffing strategy when it started its Alabama plant.

However, using PCNs has several disadvantages. PCNs typically lack knowledge of the host country's laws, culture, economic conditions, social structure, and political processes. Although they can be trained to overcome these knowledge gaps, such training is expensive (particularly when the opportunity cost of the manager's time is considered) and is not a perfect substitute for having been born and raised in the host country. Further, PCNs are often expensive to relocate and maintain in the host country.[8] Finally, many host countries restrict the number of foreign employees who can be transferred in and/or mandate that a certain percentage of an international firm's payroll must be paid to domestic employees. Thus, an international business may not have total freedom to hire whomever it wants for international assignments. Because of these factors, PCNs are most likely to be used in upper-level and/or technical positions in host countries.

Host-country nationals (HCNs) are residents of the host country. HCNs are commonly used by international businesses to fill middle-level and lower-level jobs, but they also often appear in managerial and professional positions. Experienced MNCs such as Intel, Texas Instruments, IBM, DuPont, and Northern Telecom often hire HCNs instead of transferring home country employees to work in professional positions in their foreign operations.[9] Many smaller firms setting up operations abroad hire HCNs because they do not have enough managerial talent at home to send someone on a foreign assignment.[10]

Using HCNs offers two primary advantages. First, HCNs already understand the local laws, culture, and economic conditions. Second, the firm avoids the expenses associated with expatriate managers, such as relocation costs, supplemental wages paid for foreign service, and private schooling for children. However, using HCNs can have disadvantages. HCNs may be unfamiliar with the firm's business culture and practices, thus limiting their effectiveness. As noted earlier in this chapter, Toyota used Japanese executives to shepherd the development of its U.S. operations in order to ensure that its new employees understood the firm's emphasis on producing quality automobiles.

Andersen Consulting, the world's largest consulting firm, has developed an innovative approach to training HCNs in its corporate culture. All of Andersen's entry-level consultants, who staff 360 offices in 76 countries, must undergo an

International businesses increasingly recruit new employees from every market they serve. Andersen Consulting, for example, hires new consultants from around the world. Each recruit must complete an intensive training course at Andersen's Center for Professional Education in order to learn how the firm conducts business.

intensive three-week education program at its Center for Professional Education in St. Charles, Illinois. The newly recruited professionals learn about the Andersen way of doing business and solving clients' problems. By providing its multinational recruits with common training, the firm transmits its corporate culture throughout its international empire and promotes intracorporate networking of the new employees that transcends national boundaries.[11]

Finally, an international firm may hire **third-country nationals (TCNs),** who are not citizens of the firm's home country or of the host country. Like PCNs, TCNs are most likely to be used in upper-level and/or technical positions. TCNs and PCNs collectively are known as **expatriates,** or people working and residing in countries other than their native country. In the past, TCNs were likely to be used when they had special expertise that was not available to the firm through any other channel. Today, they are consciously being employed by some firms to promote a global outlook throughout their operations. For example, firms such as Nestlé and Philips NV rely heavily on TCNs because they believe those managers bring broader perspectives and experiences to the firm's host country operations. And some firms are recruiting more TCNs to serve on their boards of directors to help bring a more global orientation to the boards.[12]

Most international firms develop a systematic strategy for choosing among HCNs, PCNs, and TCNs for various positions. Some rely on the **ethnocentric staffing model,** whereby they use primarily PCNs to staff higher-level foreign positions. This approach is based on the assumption that home office perspectives should take precedence over local perspectives and that expatriate PCNs will be most effective in representing the views of the home office in the foreign operation. Other international firms follow a **polycentric staffing model;** that is, they emphasize the use of HCNs in the belief that HCNs know the local market best. Finally, the **geocentric staffing model** puts PCNs, HCNs, and TCNs on an equal footing. Firms that adopt this approach want to hire the best person available, regardless of where that individual comes from.[13]

National culture often affects the staffing model chosen by a firm. European MNCs are more likely than U.S. or Japanese ones to adopt the geocentric approach. This approach is encouraged by the EU in order to improve the mobility of workers and managers throughout its member countries. Japanese firms favor the ethnocentric staffing model, in part because their consensus-oriented approach to decision making is facilitated by employing Japanese managers in key roles in their foreign subsidiaries. But Japanese firms sometimes rely too heavily on this model, to their own disadvantage. While they usually hire HCNs for lower-level positions, they are reluctant to use non-Japanese managers in higher-level positions. When they do hire an HCN as a local manager, they have been accused of being too quick to send in a troubleshooter from the home office at the first sign of a problem.[14] Further, the non-Japanese managers often face a glass ceiling because the top positions in the firm are reserved for Japanese managers. Thus, the ethnocentric policy often results in the loss of the best HCN managers, who seek more challenge and responsibility by shifting to non-Japanese employers.

Recruitment and Selection

A firm's scope of internationalization, level of centralization, and staffing philosophy help determine the skills and abilities its international managers need. As shown in Fig. 20.2, these skills and abilities fall into two general categories: those needed to do the job and those needed to work in a foreign location.

The firm first must define the actual business skills necessary to do the job. For example, a firm that has an assembly plant in a foreign market needs a

FIGURE 20.2

Necessary Skills and Abilities for International Managers

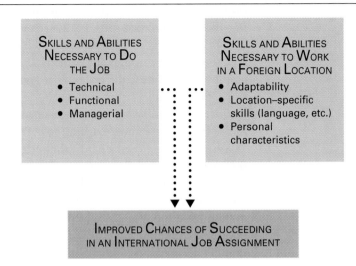

plant manager who understands the technical aspects of what is to be manufactured, what manufacturing processes will be utilized, and so on.[15] The firm's marketing managers must be knowledgeable about advertising media availability, distribution channels, market competition, and local consumers' demographic characteristics.

The firm next must determine the skills and abilities a manager must have to work and function effectively in the foreign location. These include the manager's ability to adapt to cultural change, ability to speak the local language, overall physical and emotional health, levels of independence and self-reliance, and appropriate levels of experience and education. Obviously, an HCN can meet these requirements far easier than a PCN or TCN can. Firms relying on the ethnocentric or geocentric staffing models thus must devote more resources to selecting and training PCNs and TCNs for foreign assignments than do firms that rely on the polycentric model.

Recruitment of Managers

Once the international business determines the skills and abilities an international manager must have, it next must develop a pool of qualified applicants for the job and then recruit and select the best candidate.

Recruitment of Experienced Managers. International businesses recruit experienced managers through a variety of channels. A common source of recruits is within the firm itself—among employees already working for the firm in the host country or those who, while currently employed in the home country, might be prepared for an international assignment in the host country. The latter group may include both managers who have never held an international assignment and managers who have already completed previous international assignments. For example, when Kal Kan's Canadian subsidiary entered the animal food market in Poland, the firm relied on a team of Polish-born Canadian executives to start up the new operation. Other companies are dipping into their pool of retired executives to fill short-term international assignments. Whirlpool rehired one of its retired senior engineers to help expand its Shanghai washing-machine factory, while Quaker Oats sent a team of five retired employees to oversee the start-up of a cereal plant in that same city. Retired employees are often eager to take on such tasks. For example, GTE has developed a pool of 725 former employees willing to tackle short-term foreign assignments.[16]

An international business may also attempt to identify prospective managers who work for other firms. These may be home country managers who are deemed to be qualified for an international assignment or managers already working in an international assignment for another firm.[17] For higher-level positions, firms often rely on so-called headhunters to help them locate prospective candidates. **Headhunters** are recruiting firms that actively seek qualified managers and other professionals for possible placement in positions in other organizations. In many parts of the world, including Japan, switching employers has long been frowned on. And until recently, headhunting in Europe was considered unethical. Both of these views are changing, however. More firms are finding that they can even entice highly qualified Japanese employees away from Japanese firms.[18]

A firm may sometimes even find it useful to relocate its facilities to be closer to a pool of qualified employees. For example, when Upjohn and Pharmacia (U.S. and Swedish pharmaceutical firms, respectively) merged in the mid-1990s, they initially selected London for their new corporate headquarters. But it quickly became apparent that there was not an adequate pool of managerial and technical talent available locally to staff the enterprise. And since London is among the world's most expensive cities, transferring in managers from other locations was not cost-effective. Thus, the firm recently announced that it was moving its headquarters to the east coast of the United States to be near several of its largest competitors. Managers reasoned that this would place them closer to a large talent pool of managers with pharmaceutical industry experience and therefore make recruiting a bit easier.[19]

One trend seems clear: as a result of the globalization of business, the market for executive talent is also becoming globalized. For example, fewer than half of the 150 highest-level executives at Imperial Chemical Industries PLC, Britain's largest chemical manufacturer, are British nationals. Firms increasingly value performance more than nationality. Nomura Securities, Japan's largest stock brokerage firm, typifies this trend. Concerned about losses in its global market share, in 1997 it turned to a seasoned U.S. securities executive, Max Chapman, to reinvigorate its global operations, which are headquartered in London. Similarly, when the directors of Compaq Computer became concerned about the company's direction several years ago, they promoted Eckhard Pfeiffer, a key executive in Compaq's European operations, to head the company. Pfeiffer used his knowledge of the worldwide computer market gained during his stint in Europe to set Compaq on an ambitious growth strategy with annual sales now approaching $20 billion.[20] Current estimates are that between 7 and 10 percent of all newly filled executive positions in U.S. firms go to foreigners.[21] And as described in "Going Global," many firms today are also seeking technical employees on a global scale.

Recruitment of Younger Managers. It is uncommon for large MNCs to hire new college graduates for immediate foreign assignments. Some firms, however, will hire new graduates they ultimately intend to send abroad and, in the short term, give them domestic assignments. Particularly attractive are graduates

GOING GLOBAL

The Global Talent Hunt

Finding the best employees is never an easy task. But in today's burgeoning high-technology age, finding good technical employees is a bit akin to looking for the proverbial needle in a haystack. One recent survey, for example, reported 190,000 unfilled programming and computer-related jobs in the United States alone. Little wonder, then, that the best firms in high-technology markets are casting a global net in their search for good help.

Electronic Data Systems, for example, a Dallas-based computer services company, currently recruits programmers on three continents for its Texas operations. Andersen Consulting, while not a high-technology firm per se, nevertheless needs to hire thousands of technical employees a year to support its management consulting operation. It recently added technical schools in Budapest and Manila to its growing list of recruiting sources. Texas Instruments looks to employees who have been cut loose from their employers in other countries.

Brazil, India, and Russia have become increasingly popular sources of computer talent. Skilled programmers in Brazil, for example, may be earning the equivalent of $30,000 a year. But by relocating to the United States, they can often more than double their salary. In addition, many U.S. firms cover relocation expenses and give foreign programmers a bonus after they work for three years. And even at this salary these programmers are often seen as bargains—a U.S. citizen with the same skills would probably command a salary of as much as $80,000.

There are also other countries where quality technical employees are available, and who may be interested in relocating. Some firms have had success, for example, in luring employees from Colombia, the Philippines, and South Africa. But even this approach can be difficult. For example, many of the best technical employees in South Africa learn their skills from trade schools that offer excellent training but no diplomas. This lack of a formal degree makes it more difficult for them to obtain immigration papers into countries like the United States.

Sources: "Forget the Huddled Masses: Send Nerds," *Business Week*, July 21, 1997, pp. 110–116; "A U.S. Recruiter Goes Far Afield to Bring in Techies," *Wall Street Journal*, January 8, 1998, pp. A1, A2.

with foreign language skills, international travel experience, and a major in international business or a related field.[22] A few firms have started taking a longer-term view of developing international managerial talent. Coca-Cola, for example, has developed an innovative strategy for recruiting managers for future international assignments. It actively seeks foreign students who are studying at U.S. colleges and universities and who intend to return to their home countries after receiving their degrees. The firm recruits and hires the best of these graduates and puts them through a one-year training program. The new managers then return home as Coca-Cola employees and take assignments in the firm's operations in their home countries.[23]

Colgate-Palmolive has mounted perhaps the most aggressive effort of this sort. This firm each year selects 15 new recruits (from an applicant pool of 15,000) to participate in its fast-track globalization program, which provides quick lessons in competing in the global marketplace. Colgate reaps several benefits from this program. It is able to hire excellent young talent because college graduates from around the world seek one of the coveted slots. By exposing management trainees and entry-level managers to a new culture, the firm can forcefully show its young talent the problems inherent in self-referencing one's culture in international markets. For example, a Dutch trainee brought to the United States was shocked by the huge assortment of goods in a typical U.S. supermarket. That visit created a vivid impression of the high level of competitiveness of the U.S. market and forced the trainee to recognize that marketing strategies that might work in the Netherlands could be dismal failures in the United States. A U.S. trainee sent by Colgate to a Romanian store had a similar experience. When the trainee asked Romanian shoppers which brands of soap they preferred—a perfectly logical question to market researchers in the United States—she was surprised by the response: the Romanian shoppers, accustomed to scarcity, bought whatever soap was available.[24]

Selection of Managers

After the pool of prospective managers has been identified, HR managers must decide which persons from that pool are the best qualified for the assignment. The most promising candidates share the following characteristics:

- Managerial competence (technical and leadership skills, knowledge of the corporate culture)
- Appropriate training (formal education, knowledge of the host market and its culture and language)
- Adaptability to new situations (ability to deal simultaneously with adjusting to a new work and job environment, adjusting to working with HCNs, and adjusting to a new national culture)[25]

The importance of the selection process cannot be overstated when dealing with expatriate managers. The costs to a firm of expatriate failure are extremely high. **Expatriate failure** is the early return of an expatriate manager to his or her home country because of an inability to perform in the overseas assignment.[26] Experts suggest that these costs are between $40,000 and $250,000 (these figures include the expatriate's original training, moving expenses, and lost managerial productivity, but do not include the decreased performance of the foreign subsidiary itself).[27]

Expatriate failure occurs far too often. Failure rates of 20–50 percent are common for many U.S. firms, and rates appear to be much higher for them than for European and Japanese firms. More than 76 percent of U.S. firms experience expatriate failure rates of over 10 percent (that is, at least one out of ten expatriate assignments were deemed failures), while only 14 percent of Japanese firms and only 3 percent of European firms experienced similar failure rates.[28]

The primary cause of expatriate failure is the inability of the manager and/or his or her spouse and family to adjust to the new locale. As a result, international HR managers increasingly are evaluating the nontechnical aspects of a candidate's suitability for a foreign assignment. Assessing certain skills and abilities is relatively easy. For example, measuring a prospect's language proficiency is a straightforward undertaking. But assessing a person's cultural adaptability is more difficult and must be accomplished through a variety of means. Most firms use a combination of tests (such as personality and aptitude tests) and interviews in their selection process. Assessment centers, which offer programs of exercises, tests, and interviews that last several days, are also useful because they provide an in-depth look at a set of prospective candidates under the same circumstances.

Another important consideration is the prospect's motivation for and interest in the foreign assignment. Some managers are attracted to foreign assignments, perhaps because they relish the thought of living abroad or because they see the experience as being useful in their future career plans. But others balk at the thought of uprooting their family and moving to a foreign environment, particularly one that is culturally distant from their own. As noted above, failure of the family to adjust to the new culture is a prominent cause of expatriate failure. Thus, most firms also consider the family's motivation for and interest in the foreign assignment. The manager's job performance will often deteriorate if he or she has to soothe an unhappy spouse cut off from friends and family and frustrated by dealing with a new culture. And clearly a foreign relocation is far more disruptive to the family than a domestic one. Dependent children may face problems integrating into a new school culture—particularly if they do not speak the local language—and may find that material covered in the courses at their new school is well ahead (or well behind) that at their home school. In addition, there's the dual career problem. The trailing spouse may find it difficult to take leave from his or her current position, thereby forcing a disruption in his or her career advancement. Still worse, labor laws in the new country may make it difficult or impossible for the spouse to obtain employment there legally.

Because of the risk of expatriate failure, firms often devote considerable resources to selection and training. AT&T, for example, prides itself on doing an especially thorough job of selecting managers for foreign assignments. The firm has long used personality tests and interviews as part of its selection process. It now also uses psychologists to help assess prospects and is investing more into learning about family considerations. In addition, the prospects complete a self-assessment checklist designed to help them probe their motivations for seeking a foreign transfer. Table 20.1 summarizes sample questions the firm uses to screen

---

TABLE 20.1

AT&T's Questionnaire for Screening Overseas Transferees

Would your spouse be interrupting a career to accompany you on an international assignment? If so, how do you think this will [affect] your spouse and your relationship with each other?

Do you enjoy the challenge of making your own way in new situations?

Securing a job upon reentry will be primarily your responsibility. How do you feel about networking and being your own advocate?

How able are you in initiating new social contacts?

Can you imagine living without television?

How important is it for you to spend significant amounts of time with people of your own ethnic, racial, religious, and national background?

As you look at your personal history, can you isolate any episodes that indicate a real interest in learning about other peoples and cultures?

Has it been your habit to vacation in foreign countries?

Do you enjoy sampling foreign cuisines?

What is your tolerance for waiting for repairs?

potential expatriates and their spouses. AT&T reports that this exercise increases managers' self-awareness. As a result, more managers now remove themselves from consideration for foreign assignments.[29]

General Motors spends almost $500,000 per year on cross-cultural training for 150 or so U.S. managers and their families heading to international assignments in order to reduce the risk of expatriate failure. The firm reports that fewer than 1 percent of its expatriates request an early return and attributes much of this success to its training efforts.[30]

Some international businesses are concerned with not only how well a prospective manager will adapt to the foreign culture but also how well he or she will fit into that culture. For example, for years some U.S. firms hesitated to send women managers on foreign assignments to some countries, such as Japan, because they assumed the women would not be accepted in a culture that frowned on women working outside the home. However, recent research indicates that this fear may be overstated. Host country citizens react primarily to these executives' foreignness, rather than their gender.[31]

Expatriation and Repatriation Issues

PCNs on long-term foreign assignments face great acculturation challenges. Working in and coping with a foreign culture can lead to **culture shock,** a psychological phenomenon that may lead to feelings of fear, helplessness, irritability, and disorientation. New expatriates experience a sense of loss regarding their old cultural environment as well as confusion, rejection, self-doubt, and decreased self-esteem from working in a new and unfamiliar cultural setting.[32] Acculturation, as shown in Fig. 20.3, typically proceeds through four phases.[33]

Culture shock reduces an expatriate's effectiveness and productivity, and so international businesses have developed various strategies to mitigate its effects. One simple solution is to provide expatriates (and their families) with pre-departure language and cultural training so that they can better understand and anticipate the cultural adjustments they must undergo. In addition to straightforward training, firms might also make initial foreign assignments relatively brief and make sure that the expatriate understands the role each particular international assignment plays in his or her overall career prospects.[34]

Interestingly, international businesses should pay almost as much attention to **repatriation**—bringing a manager back home after a foreign assignment has been completed—as they do to expatriation. If a manager and his or her family have been successfully expatriated, they become comfortable with living and working in the foreign culture. Returning home can be almost as traumatic to them as was the original move abroad.[35] One reason for the difficulty of repatriation is that people tend to assume that nothing has changed back home. They look forward to getting back to their friends, familiar surroundings, and daily routines. But their friends may have moved or developed new social circles and their coworkers may have been transferred to other jobs. Some expatriates who have returned to the United States have even been denied credit because they have no domestic financial history for several years![36] The repatriated manager also has to cope with change and uncertainty at work. The firm may not be sure what the manager's job is going to entail. Further, the manager may have been running the show at the foreign operation and enjoying considerable authority. Back home, however, he or she is likely to have much less authority and to be on a par with

FIGURE 20.3

**Phases in
Acculturation**

HONEYMOON
For the first few days or months, the new culture seems exotic and stimulating. Excitement of working in a new environment makes employee overestimate the ease of adjusting.

DISILLUSIONMENT
Differences between new and old environments are blown out of proportion. As employee and family face challenges of everyday living, differences become magnified. Many transplanted employees remain stuck in this phase.

ADAPTATION
With time, employee begins to understand patterns of new culture, gains language competence, and adjusts to everyday living.

BICULTURALISM
Anxiety has ended as transplanted employee gains confidence in ability to function productively in new culture.

many other managers reporting to more senior managers. Also, the manager and his or her family may have enjoyed a higher social status in the host country than they will after returning home. Thus, readjustment problems may be severe and need the attention of both manager and firm.

The repatriation problem can be expensive for a firm. By some estimates, one quarter of all repatriated employees leave their employer within a year after returning home. The average U.S. expatriate costs his or her employer about $300,000 per year and stays three to four years on an overseas assignment; thus, each repatriated executive who leaves the firm represents a million-dollar investment walking out the door.[37] One new strategy to help managers cope with repatriation has been successfully used by Nynex Corp (a unit of Bell Atlantic). Nynex brings home a manager who is to be repatriated about six weeks before the permanent move. The manager spends a couple of days getting reacquainted with the surroundings before coming back for good. This procedure helps reduce repatriation problems.[38]

The bottom line is that expatriation and repatriation problems can be reduced if international businesses systematically provide organizational career development programs for their expatriate managers. Recent research indicates that the likelihood of a manager being successful at an overseas assignment increases if the manager:

♦ Can freely choose whether to accept or reject the expatriate assignment

♦ Has been given a realistic preview of the new job and assignment

♦ Has been given a realistic expectation of what his or her repatriation assignment will be

♦ Has a mentor back home who will guard his or her interests and provide corporate and social support during the assignment

♦ Sees a clear link between the expatriate assignment and his or her long-term career path

Of these five elements, the last is the most critical in determining expatriate success.[39]

Training and Development

The international firm's HR managers must also provide training and development for its home and host country managers to help them perform more effectively. **Training** is instruction directed at enhancing specific job-related skills and abilities. For example, training programs might be designed to help employees learn to speak a foreign language, to use new equipment, or to implement new manufacturing procedures. Special acculturation training is important for employees who are given international assignments. **Development** is general education concerned with preparing managers for new assignments and/or higher-level positions. For example, a development program could be aimed at helping managers improve their ability to make decisions or to motivate subordinates to work harder.[40]

Assessing Training Needs

Before a firm can undertake a meaningful training or development program, it must assess its exact training and development needs. This assessment involves

New technology combined with global business opportunities dictates that international businesses continually train their employees in a variety of areas. Emerging computer-based communication networks are especially important. This Buddhist monk, for example, is conducting research on his computer at a monastery outside Bangkok.

determining the difference between what managers and employees can do and what the firm feels they need to be able to do. For example, suppose a firm that does business in Latin America wants its employees to be able to speak Spanish fluently. If most of its employees are fluent in Spanish, its language training needs may be minimal. But if relatively few employees are, extensive training may be called for. The assessment of training needs is an extremely important element of international HRM. Firms

FIGURE 20.4

Barriers to Entering Foreign Markets

Source: From "Cross-cultural training helps in leap abroad," *Houston Chronicle*, September 25, 1994, p. 1E. Reprinted with permission. Data: Ernst & Young survey.

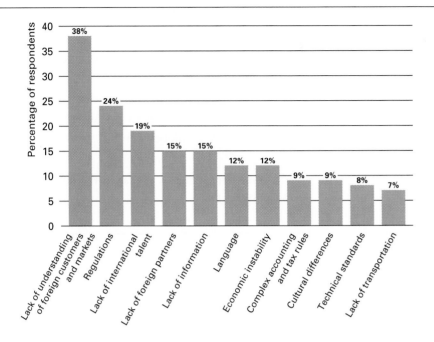

that underestimate training needs can encounter serious difficulties. Indeed, lack of knowledge about foreign customers and markets is a major barrier to successful entry into such markets, as Fig. 20.4 shows.

A firm just moving into international markets has different training and development needs from those of an established global firm. For example, the newly internationalizing firm is likely to have few, if any, experienced international managers. Thus, its training and development needs will be substantial.[41] In contrast, a global firm has a cadre of trained and experienced managers with international backgrounds, skills, and abilities.[42]

Basic Training Methods and Procedures

The first issue an international business must consider as it plans its training and development efforts is whether to rely on standardized programs or to develop its own customized programs. Certain kinds of training can be readily obtained in common retail outlets—for example, language-training programs and self-paced language training from cassette tapes. Prudential Insurance even offers packaged training programs for families of expatriates, a good idea in light of the importance of family problems in causing expatriate failure.[43] One advantage of standardized programs is that they tend to be less expensive than customized ones. On the other hand, a standardized program may not precisely fit the firm's needs.

As a result, most training and development programs are often customized to a firm's particular needs. Larger MNCs, for example, often have training and development departments that develop customized programs for the unique needs of individual managers and/or business units. Training and development activities may take place in regular classroom settings within the firm, on actual job sites, or off premises in a conference center or hotel. Customized programs are more costly than are standardized ones; however, they ensure that employees get the precise information deemed necessary. Regardless of whether training and development programs are standardized or customized, most use a variety of methods as instructional vehicles. Lectures and assigned readings are common, as are video-taped and software-based instruction. Role playing and other forms of experiential exercises are useful for helping people better understand other cultures. Case studies are also used, although not as frequently as other methods. Training materials must often be altered to fit different cultural contexts. For example, a consultant hired to make training videos for Bally of Switzerland initially assumed that he could use the same basic video for each of Bally's regional offices, with only minor script modifications. As the project progressed, however, he found that so many language and cultural differences affected the video that he essentially had to reshoot it for each office.[44]

The trainers themselves may also need to adapt how they do things. For example, one professional trainer reported difficulties in using her normal style when running a training program in Thailand. She prefers to be informal and to involve the participants through role playing and other forms of interaction. But she found that Thai managers were uncomfortable with her informality and resisted the role-playing approach. She eventually had to adopt a more formal style and use a straightforward lecture approach to get her points across.[45]

Developing Younger International Managers

The increasing globalization of business has prompted most MNCs to recognize the importance of internationalizing their managers earlier in their careers.[46] Until the late 1980s, most U.S. MNCs delayed giving their managers significant overseas assignments until they had spent seven to ten years with the firm. Today many of them are beginning to recognize that they need to develop the international awareness and competence of their managers earlier and to systematically integrate international assignments into individual career plans. For example, GE provides language and cross-cultural training to its professional staff even though they may not be scheduled for overseas postings. Such training is important because these employees, even if they never leave their home countries, are likely to work with GE employees from other countries and to deal with visiting executives from GE's foreign partners, suppliers, and customers. Such training also helps the employees gain a better understanding of the firm's international markets.

Other firms, such as American Express and Johnson & Johnson, have begun posting managers to overseas assignments after only eighteen to twenty months on the job. PepsiCo and Raychem are bringing young managers from their foreign operations to the United States to enrich their understanding of their firms' cultures and technologies.

U.S. firms aren't the only ones integrating international assignments into career development plans for younger managers. Honda's U.S. manufacturing subsidiary has been sending U.S. managers to Tokyo for multi-year assignments so that they can learn more about the firm's successful manufacturing and operating philosophies. Samsung regularly sends its executives abroad for various assignments. One of its more interesting strategies is to send younger managers to certain foreign locations for as long as a year with no specific job responsibilities. They are supposed to spend their time learning the local language and becoming familiar with the culture. The idea is that if they are transferred back to that same location in the future—when they are in a higher-level position—

they will be able to function more effectively. Even though the program costs Samsung about $80,000 per person per year, executives believe the firm will quickly recoup its investment.[47]

Performance Appraisal and Compensation

Another important part of international HRM consists of conducting performance appraisals and determining compensation and benefits. Whereas recruitment, selection, and training and development tend to focus on pre-assignment issues, performance appraisal and compensation involve ongoing issues that continue to have an effect well past the initial international assignment.

Assessing Performance in International Business

Performance appraisal is the process of assessing how effectively a person is performing his or her job. The purposes of performance appraisal are to provide feedback to individuals as to how well they are doing, to provide a basis for rewarding top performers, to identify areas in which additional training and development may be needed, and to identify problem areas that may call for a change in assignment.

Performance appraisals of an international business's top managers must be based on the firm's clear understanding of its goals for its foreign operations. A successful subsidiary in a mature and stable foreign market will have different goals than will a start-up operation in a growing but unstable market. Thus, a firm assigning two new managers to head up these different subsidiaries must understand that it cannot expect the same outcomes from each of them. Similarly, managers of foreign subsidiaries that serve as cost centers must be judged by different standards from those used for managers of profit centers.

In assessing a manager's actual performance, the firm may consider sales, profit margin, market share growth, or any other measures or indicators it deems important. And if a subsidiary has been having problems, performance may be more appropriately assessed in terms of how well the manager has helped to solve those problems. For example, reducing net losses or halting a decline in market share might be considered good performance, at least in the short term.

Expected and actual performance must be compared, and differences must be addressed. This step needs to have a strong diagnostic component: why and how has the manager's performance been acceptable or unacceptable? Are any problems attributable to the manager's lack of skills? Are some problems attributable to unforeseen circumstances? Is the home office accountable for some of the problems that may have arisen, perhaps because the manager was inadequately trained?

Circumstances will dictate how frequently performance appraisals occur. In a domestic firm, they may occur as often as every quarter. But geographical factors can limit the frequency with which international performance appraisals can occur. Generally, international managers are expected to submit reports on performance-based results to headquarters regularly. As long as these reports fall within acceptable parameters, the firm is likely to conduct a formal performance appraisal perhaps on an annual basis. But if standard reports reveal a problem, performance appraisals may be done more often in an effort to get things back on track.

Determining Compensation in International Business

Another important issue in international HRM is determining managerial compensation. To remain competitive, firms must provide prevailing compensation packages for their managers in a given market. These packages include salary and nonsalary items and are determined by labor market forces such as the supply and demand of managerial talent, occupational status, professional licensing requirements, standards of living, government regulations, tax codes, and similar factors.[48] For example, in Germany, employers customarily reimburse their executives for car expenses. In Japan, the executive may actually get a car plus expenses. Japanese executives also receive generous entertainment allowances and an allowance for business gifts. Similarly, British companies typically provide company cars to managers. In the United States, firms offer managers health care benefits because such benefits are free from income taxes.

Compensating Expatriate Managers. A more complex set of compensation issues apply to expatriate managers. Most international businesses find it necessary to provide these managers with differential compensation to make up for dramatic differences in currency valuation, standards of living, lifestyle norms, and so on.[49] When managers are on short-term assignments abroad, their home country salaries normally continue unchanged. (Of course, the managers are reimbursed for short-term living expenses such as for hotel rooms, meals, and transportation.) But if the foreign assignment is indefinite or longer-term, compensation is routinely adjusted to allow the manager to maintain his or her home country standard of living.[50] This adjustment is particularly important if the manager is transferred from a low-cost location to a high-cost location or from a country with a high standard of living to one with a lower standard of living. Table 20.2 summarizes cost-of-living differences for a number of international business centers.

The starting point in differential compensation is a **cost-of-living allowance.** This allowance is intended to offset differences in the cost of living in the home and host countries. The premise is that a manager who accepts a foreign assignment is entitled to the same standard of living he or she enjoyed at home. If the cost of living in the foreign country is higher than that at home, the manager's existing base pay will result in a lower standard of living and the firm will supplement the base pay to offset this difference. Of course, if the cost of living in the foreign location is lower than at home, no such allowance is needed.

Sometimes firms find they must supplement base pay in order to get a manager to accept an assignment in a relatively unattractive location. While it may not be difficult to find people willing to move to England or Japan, it may be much more difficult to entice people to move to Haiti, Somalia, or Afghanistan. Called either a **hardship premium** or a **foreign service premium,** this supplement is essentially an inducement to the individual to accept the international assignment.[51]

Finally, many international businesses also find they must set up a tax-equalization system. A **tax-equalization system** is a means of ensuring that the expatriate's after-tax income in the host country is similar to what the person's after-tax income would be in the home country. Each country has unique tax laws that apply to the earnings of its own citizens, to earnings within its borders by foreign citizens, and/or to earnings in another country by its own citizens. The most common tax-equalization system has the firm's own accounting department handling the taxes of its expatriates. A firm accountant determines what a manager's

TABLE 20.2

Annual Cost of Living in Selected Locations Worldwide, 1997

LOCATION	ANNUAL COST OF LIVING	INDEX
Tokyo, Japan	$160,157	285.1
Seoul, S. Korea	155,085	276.1
Moscow, Russia	124,246	221.2
Geneva, Switzerland	99,964	178.0
London, England	87,223	155.3
Rome, Italy	79,013	140.7
Helsinki, Finland	78,124	139.1
Munich, Germany	75,229	128.6
Sydney, Australia	70,484	125.5
Barcelona, Spain	65,775	117.1
Melbourne, Australia	65,253	116.2
Los Angeles, California	59,552	106.0
Mexico City, Mexico	59,020	105.1
Atlanta, Georgia	56,169	100.0
Montreal, Canada	51,014	90.8

The table above is based on a U.S. family of two with a base salary of $75,000. Total annual costs are based on a combination of housing, transportation, and goods & services. The total also includes a certain amount set aside for investments and savings. Taxes are not included because actual taxes will vary greatly depending upon the tax planning techniques used.

Housing costs are based on home or apartment rental and include utilities and renters insurance.

Transportation costs include both public commutation and private vehicle ownership and operating costs.

Goods & services include the total amounts paid (including sales tax) for food-at-home, food-away-from-home, tobacco & alcohol, household operations, clothing, domestic services, medical care, personal care, and recreation.

Source: Runzheimer International.

---

taxes will be where he or she is living and what they would be at home on the same income and then makes the appropriate adjustment to equalize the two.[52]

Figure 20.5 shows how Amoco creates compensation packages for its expatriate managers. The blocks in the center reflect an individual's U.S. base compensation prior to being posted to an international assignment. After an assignment has been made, the blocks above and below are then used to calculate appropriate adjustments to the employee's compensation. For example, suppose a U.S. executive being transferred abroad currently earns $100,000, of which $25,000 is paid in taxes, $10,000 is saved, and the remaining $65,000 consumed. Further suppose that the executive currently spends $2000 a month on housing (mortgage plus utilities). Amoco will adjust the executive's total compensation in order to make it as equal as possible to that currently earned in the United States. Assume that housing and utilities in the host country cost about 20 percent more than in the United States and other consumables cost about 10 percent more. Thus, Amoco will pay the executive a supplemental housing allowance that is equal to what the executive currently pays times 20 percent, or a total of $400 a month. The remaining part of the executive's consumption spending will be increased by 10 percent. Similar adjustments will be made to the other components of Fig. 20.5.

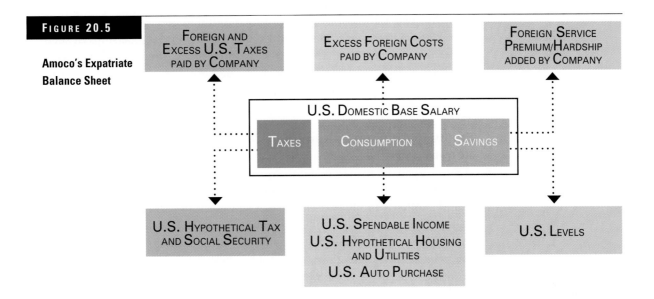

FIGURE 20.5

Amoco's Expatriate Balance Sheet

Benefits Packages for Expatriate Managers. International businesses must provide not only salary adjustments, but also special forms of benefits for their expatriate managers in addition to standard benefits such as health insurance and vacation allowances. Special benefits include housing, education, medical treatment, travel to the home country, and club memberships.

A common special benefit involves housing. Like other components of living costs, housing expenses vary in different areas. Duplicating the level of housing the executive enjoyed in his or her home country may be expensive, so housing is often treated as a separate benefit. If a manager is going on permanent or long-term assignment, the firm may buy the manager's existing home at fair market value. It may also help the manager buy a house in the host country if housing costs or interest rates are substantially different from those at home.

If the expatriate manager has a family, the firm may need to provide job location assistance for the spouse and help cover education costs for the children. For example, the children may need to attend private school, which the firm would pay for. Schooling represents a particularly important problem for Japanese expatriate managers, whose children may not do well in the national entrance exams for the most prestigious Japanese universities if their reading and writing skills atrophy as a result of living abroad. Thus, many Japanese firms pay for their expatriates' children to attend private schools that help students cram for those exams.[53]

Medical benefits may also need to be adjusted. For example, some people consider Malaysian health care facilities inadequate. Thus, managers on assignment there often request that their employer send them to Singapore whenever they need medical attention.

Most international businesses provide expatriates with a travel allowance for trips to the home country for personal reasons, such as to visit other family members or to celebrate holidays. The manager and his or her family may be allowed one or two trips home per year at company expense. If the manager's family remains at home during a short-term assignment, the manager may be given more frequent opportunities to travel home.

In some cultures, belonging to a certain club or participating in a particular activity is a necessary part of the business world. In Japan, for example, many business transactions occur during a round of golf. To be effective in Japan, a foreign manager may need to join a golf club. Memberships in such clubs, however, cost thousands of dollars and a single round of golf may cost ten times or more what it costs elsewhere. Because such activities are a normal part of doing business, firms often provide managers transferred to Japan with these benefits.[54]

Equity in Compensation. Thus far our discussion of compensating expatriate managers has not addressed the issue of equity between the compensation granted expatriate managers and that given to HCNs in similar positions. Often, the compensation package offered the expatriate manager is much more lucrative than that offered an HCN occupying an equivalent position of power and responsibility. The equity issue becomes even more complicated when dealing with TCNs. For example, if a U.S. international oil firm transfers a Venezuelan executive to its Peruvian operations, should the Venezuelan be paid according to Peruvian, Venezuelan, or U.S. standards?

Unfortunately there is no simple solution to this problem, and MNCs use a variety of approaches in grappling with it. For example, Hewlett-Packard pays expatriates on short-term assignments according to home country standards and those on long-term assignments according to host country standards. Minnesota Mining & Manufacturing (3M) compares the compensation package it offers in the expatriate's home country with what it normally pays HCNs and then gives the expatriate the higher pay package. Phillips Petroleum pegs a TCN's salary to that of the person's home country, but offers housing allowances, educational benefits, and home leaves based on costs in the host country.[55]

Retention and Turnover

Another important element of international HRM focuses on retention and turnover. **Retention** is the extent to which a firm is able to retain employees. **Turnover,** essentially the opposite, is the rate at which people leave a firm.

People choose to leave a firm for any number of reasons—for example, dissatisfaction with their current pay or promotion opportunities or receipt of a better offer to work elsewhere. Turnover is often a result of job transitions such as those associated with expatriation and repatriation: a worker contemplating changing work locations may also consider changing employers.[56] Turnover is a particular problem in international business because of the high cost of developing managers' international business skills.[57] Managers with strong reputations for having those skills are in high demand. As noted earlier, some firms even rely on headhunters to help them locate prospective managers currently working for other firms. For exactly the same reason—a scarcity of skilled, experienced managers—keeping successful managers should be a high priority for any international business.[58] One way to control managerial turnover is to develop strategies designed to reduce expatriate failure and repatriate failure. These may include providing career development counseling or cross-cultural training to ease the stress of relocation.

A firm may also have to provide special inducements or incentives to its most valuable international managers. For example, they may receive higher salaries or be given a greater say in choosing their assignments. The firm may also make stronger guarantees to them regarding the time frame of their assignments. For example, a firm may want to hire a particularly skillful TCN to run its operation in Italy. Because of the costs and other problems associated with relocation, the individual may consider the assignment only if the firm guarantees it will last for a minimum of, say, five years.[59]

Another important element of turnover management is the exit interview. An **exit interview** is an interview with an employee who is leaving a firm. Its purpose is to find out as much as possible about why the person decided to leave. Given the distances involved in international business, however, firms may be reluctant to do exit interviews. Yet the potential value of the information gleaned is high: managers can use it to reduce future employee losses. Thus, firms should give careful consideration to using such interviews as part of their strategy for reducing turnover.

Human Resource Issues for Nonmanagerial Employees

Next, we shift the focus of our discussion of HR issues to nonmanagerial employees in host countries. The standard HRM tasks associated with nonmanagerial employees—recruitment, selection, training, compensation, and so on—are strongly influenced by local laws, culture, and economic conditions. To prosper in the host country environment, HR managers must not fall prey to their own self-referencing criteria. They must be willing to do things the way the locals want, not the way things are done at home. In short, "When in Rome, do as the Romans do." Thus, many MNCs hire HCNs to staff their HR operations so as to incorporate their local knowledge into the policies and procedures of the HR department.

Recruitment and Selection

In international firms' foreign operations, nonmanagerial employees, such as blue-collar production workers and white-collar office workers, are typically HCNs. In most cases, there are economic reasons for this decision: HCNs are usually cheaper to employ than are PCNs or TCNs. HCNs are also used because local laws often promote the hiring of locals. Immigration and visa laws, for example, typically restrict jobs to citizens and legal residents of the country. A few exceptions to this rule exist. Construction firms in rich countries like Saudi Arabia or Kuwait often use Bangladeshi or Pakistani labor because local citizens dislike the working conditions. And oil firms and airlines often employ PCNs and TCNs for high-skilled jobs such as drilling supervisor and pilot.

Nonetheless, an international business must develop and implement a plan for recruiting and selecting its employees in a host country market. This plan should include assessments of the firm's human resources needs, sources of labor, labor force skills and talents, and training requirements and should also account for special circumstances that exist in the local labor market. The chapter opening, for example, detailed how Toyota goes about recruiting and selecting U.S. employees for its U.S. production facilities.

When firms are hiring PCNs for foreign assignments, they must adhere to their home country's hiring regulations, laws, and norms. But when hiring HCNs, they must be aware of those regulations, laws, and norms within the host country. For example, in the United States laws and regulations prohibit a firm from discriminating against someone on the basis of gender, race, age, religion, and assorted other characteristics. Toyota had to ensure that during its selection of its U.S. employees, it did not violate any of those laws and regulations. Because of these restrictions, the selection process in the United States emphasizes job relatedness. Job-related criteria such as skills, abilities, and education can be used to hire employees; non–job-related criteria such as gender or age cannot. In some other countries, however, characteristics such as gender, religion, and skin color are commonly used in hiring decisions. For example, firms in Israel and Northern Ireland often discriminate on the basis of religion, and those in Saudi Arabia discriminate on the basis of gender.

Training and Development

HR managers must also assess the training and development needs of the host country's work forces in order to help them perform their jobs more effectively.[60] The training and development needs of local work forces depend on several factors. An important one is the location of the foreign operation. In highly industrialized markets, firms usually find a nucleus of capable workers who may need only a bit of firm-specific training. But in an area that is relatively underdeveloped, training needs will be much greater. For example, when Hilton began operating hotels in Eastern Europe, it found that waiters, hotel clerks, and other customer service employees lacked the basic skills necessary to provide high-quality service to guests. These employees were so accustomed to working in a planned economy, where there was little or no need to worry about customer satisfaction, that they had difficulty recognizing why they needed to change their workplace behavior. Hilton had to invest much more in training new employees there than it had anticipated.[61]

Training also is a critical element if an international business wants to take full advantages of locating production abroad. For example, in recent years, MNCs have shown a marked tendency to move facilities to certain areas, such as Honduras, Malaysia, and Indonesia, in order to capitalize on inexpensive labor. But often the productivity of this labor is low, unless the firm is willing to invest in work force training. In Malaysia, for example, only one third of adults have more than a sixth-grade education; thus, training costs there can be quite high. And the owner of Quality Coils, Inc., a U.S. maker of electromagnetic coils, closed the firm's plant in Connecticut and opened one in Ciudad Juarez, Mexico, because hourly wage rates there were one third as much as in Connecticut. The owner soon discovered, however, that productivity was also only one third of what it had been. This, combined with higher absenteeism and the personal costs of running a facility in Mexico, prompted him to move the operation back to Connecticut.[62]

Japan is the world leader in training and development. On average, its workers receive more annual training on a regular basis than do workers in any other country.[63] Workers in Germany, South Korea, Singapore, and France also usually receive more annual training than do their U.S. counterparts. On the other hand, firms in Hong Kong are reputed to do a relatively poor job of training and development.[64] Firms in the United States have begun to recognize the importance of training and development and are closing the gap.

Compensation and Performance Appraisal

Compensation and performance appraisal practices for nonmanagerial employees also differ dramatically among countries, depending on local laws, customs, and cultures. Individualistic cultures such as that of the United States focus on assessing the individual's performance and then compensating the person accordingly. More group-oriented cultures such as Japan's emphasize training and motivating the group and place less emphasis on individual performance appraisal and compensation. The HR manager at each foreign operation must develop and implement a performance appraisal and reporting system most appropriate for that setting, given the nature of the work being performed and the cultural context.[65] For example, while U.S. workers often appreciate feedback from the appraisal system—thereby allowing them to do better in the future—German workers are often resentful of feedback, believing that it requires them to admit failures and shortcomings.[66]

Compensation practices also reflect local laws, culture, and economic conditions. Prevailing wage rates vary among countries, which has caused many labor-intensive industries to migrate to countries such as Malaysia, Indonesia, and Guatemala. To attract workers, HR managers must ensure that their firms' wage scales are consistent with local norms.

But compensation packages entail incentive payments and benefit programs in addition to wages. International business researchers have found that the mix among wages, benefits, and incentive payments varies as a function of national culture. For example, wages on average accounted for 85 percent of the total compensation package for workers in forty-one manufacturing industries in four Oriental countries. However, they amounted to only 56 percent of the total compensation package for workers in those same industries in five "Latin European" countries. By adjusting the composition of the compensation package to meet local norms, HR managers ensure that their workers (and the firm) get the maximum value from each compensation dollar spent.[67] Local laws also affect an international firm's compensation policies. For example, Mexican law requires employers to provide paid maternity leave, a Christmas bonus of fifteen days' pay, and at least three months' severance pay for dismissed workers.

Labor Relations

A final component of international HRM is labor relations. Because of their complexity and importance, labor relations are often handled as a separate organizational function, apart from human resource management.

Comparative Labor Relations

Labor relations in a host country often reflect its laws, culture, social structure, and economic conditions. For example, membership in U.S. labor unions has been steadily declining in recent years and today constitutes less than fifteen percent of the country's total work force. Labor relations in the United States are heavily regulated by various laws, and both the actions of management toward labor and those of labor toward management are heavily restricted. Further, the formal labor agreement negotiated between a firm and a union is a binding contract enforceable in a court of law. Because of the heavy regulation, most negotiations are relatively formal and mechanical, with both parties relying on the letter of law.

However, a different situation exists in most other countries. For example, in some countries union membership is very high and continues to grow. Over half the world's work force outside the United States belongs to labor unions.[68] In Europe, for example, labor unions are much more important than in the United States. Labor unions in many European countries are aligned with political parties, and their fortunes ebb and flow as a function of which party currently controls the government. Throughout most of Europe, temporary work stoppages are frequently used by unions in a bid for public backing for their demands. For example, the transport workers' union in Paris often calls for daily work stoppages that result in the city's buses, subways, and railroads being totally shut down. The union hopes that the inconvenienced public will call on elected officials to do whatever it takes to avoid such disruptions in the future. Foreign firms that try to alter prevailing host country labor relations may be buying trouble. For example, Toys 'R' Us's unwillingness to adopt the standard collective bargaining agreement used by most Swedish retailers led to a three-month strike against the firm in 1995 and denunciations by labor leaders who branded the firm "an anti-union interloper bent on breaking established traditions in Sweden," which was not the public image the firm was trying to create.[69]

In contrast, labor relations in Japan tend to be cordial. Labor unions are usually created and run by businesses themselves. Unions and management tend to work cooperatively toward their mutual best interests. The Japanese culture discourages confrontation and hostility, and these norms carry over into labor relations. Disputes are normally resolved cordially and through mutual agreement. In the rare event that a third-party mediator is necessary, there is seldom any hard feelings or hostility after a decision has been rendered. Thus, strikes are relatively rare in Japan. "Going Global" discusses labor relations issues in Chile, where a very different labor climate exists.

Collective Bargaining

Collective bargaining is the process used to make agreements between management and labor unions. As already noted, collective bargaining in the United States is highly regulated. But aside from passing the laws that regulate the process, government plays a relatively benign role in establishing labor agreements. Union and management representatives meet and negotiate a contract. That contract governs their collective working relationship until it expires, when a new contract is negotiated. Bargaining normally takes place on a firm-by-firm and union-by-union basis. For example, United Air Lines must bargain with a pilots' union, a flight attendants' union, a mechanics' union, and so on, one at a time. And each of these unions negotiates individually with each airline whose employees it represents.

In many other countries, the government is much more active in collective bargaining. For example, in some European countries collective bargaining is undertaken by representatives of several firms and unions, along with government officials. The outcome is an umbrella agreement that applies to entire industries and collections of related labor unions.[70] In Japan, collective bargaining also usually involves government officials, but is done on a firm-by-firm basis. A govern-

GOING GLOBAL

Labor laws and labor conditions vary dramatically from country to country. But in most industrialized nations there are at least clear rules and regulations that guide labor practices. As a result, managers, workers, and unions either know the rules that affect them or can track them down. But in Chile, the rules and regulations are sometimes so ambiguous as to defy understanding.

Unionization Patterns in Chile

Chile has one of the lowest levels of unionization in the Western hemisphere. One reason for this is that the country's laws specify that unions can only represent workers in individual companies, not across industries. Thus, the unions lack the clout that large worker organizations have elsewhere. In addition, there are few regulations or penalties for punishing a company that refuses to bargain collectively or that ignores existing contracts.

As a result, it is common for companies to pay workers extra wages in return for their refusal to join a union. Some firms also break down their operations into several small companies, thus segmenting the union into similar small groups. Overall, Chilean laws give employers the upper hand in wage negotiations, make it easy to terminate employees, and facilitate the widespread usage of temporary workers.

Chile's labor policies have become a rallying point for the AFL-CIO, which has lobbied against granting President Clinton fast-track authority to negotiate the extension of NAFTA to Chile. The AFL-CIO believes that Chile's labor laws limit workers' rights to organize and make it more difficult for U.S. workers to compete with their Chilean counterparts.

Source: "Chile's Labor Law Hobbles Its Workers and Troubles the U.S.," *Wall Street Journal*, October 15, 1997, pp. A1, A14.

ment official serves more as an observer, recording what transpires and answering any questions that arise during the negotiation.

Union Influence and Codetermination

Union influence can be manifested in various ways, including membership, strikes, and public relations. In Europe, much of the influence of labor unions arises from the premise of **industrial democracy**—the belief that workers should have a voice in how businesses are run. In some countries, most notably Germany, union influence extends far beyond traditional boundaries of labor-management relations. The approach taken in Germany is called **codetermination** and provides for cooperation between management and labor in running the business.

Codetermination is the result of a 1947 German law that required firms in the coal and steel industries to allow unions to have input into how the firms were run. The law has since been amended several times, and today it applies to all German firms with 2000 or more employees. The law requires all covered firms to establish a supervisory board. Half the seats on this board are elected by the firm's owners (much like the board of directors of a U.S. corporation); the other half are appointed or elected by labor. Of the labor seats, one third are union officials and two thirds are elected by the work force. One seat elected by labor must be occupied by a managerial employee, so management essentially controls a potential tie-breaking vote. The supervisory board oversees another board called the board of managers. This board, composed of the firm's top managers, actually runs the business on a day-to-day basis.

The German model represents the most extreme level of industrial democracy. However, other countries, including Sweden, the Netherlands, Norway, Luxembourg, Denmark, and France, take similar approaches in requiring some form of labor representation in running businesses. In contrast, Italy, Ireland, the United Kingdom, Spain, Greece, and Portugal have little or no mandated labor participation.[71] However, the EU has been attempting to standardize labor practices, employment regulations, and benefits packages throughout its member states.[72] The ongoing implementation of its **social charter** (sometimes called the **social policy**) focuses on such concerns as maternity leave, job training, and superannuation (pension) benefits. One motivation for the social charter is to reduce the potential loss of jobs from richer countries, such as Germany or Belgium, to countries with lower wages and poorer benefit programs, such as Portugal, Greece, and Spain. Worker participation reform is also spreading into Pacific Asia. For example, workers in Singapore have recently been given a considerably stronger voice in how businesses are operated.[73] And even though Japanese workers do not have a particularly strong voice in the management of their firms, they have traditionally enjoyed an abundance of personal power and control over how they perform their own jobs.

CHAPTER REVIEW

Summary

Human resource management is the set of activities directed at attracting, developing, and maintaining the effective work force necessary to achieve a firm's objectives. Because the human resource function is central to a firm's success, top managers should adopt a strategic perspective on it.

International human resource needs are partially dictated by a firm's degree of internationalization. The relative degree of centralization versus decentralization of control also plays an important role. A basic staffing philosophy should be developed and followed.

Recruitment and selection are important elements of international human resource management. Some firms choose to recruit experienced managers for foreign assignments, while others hire younger, and more likely inexperienced, managers. Various avenues may be used for either approach to recruiting. The selection of managers for foreign assignments usually involves consideration of both business and international skills. Managers and firms must address a variety of expatriation and repatriation issues.

Training and development are also important aspects of international human resource management. The two principal components of this activity are the assessment of training needs and the selection of basic training methods and procedures.

A firm also must assess the performance of its international managers and determine their compensation. Compensation for expatriate managers usually includes a cost-of-living adjustment as well as special benefits.

Given the high cost of training and development of expatriates, firms need to focus special attention on managing retention and turnover. Each part of international human resource management also must be addressed for the firm's nonmanagerial employees.

Labor relations pose an especially complex task for human resource managers and are often handled by a special department. One key aspect of labor relations is collective bargaining, or negotiating agreements with unions. Germany's practice of codetermination represents one interesting variation on labor relations.

Review Questions

1. What is human resource management?

2. Along what dimensions does domestic HRM differ from international HRM?

3. How does the degree of centralization or decentralization affect international staffing?

4. What are the basic issues involved in recruiting and selecting managers for foreign assignments?

5. What issues are at the core of expatriation and repatriation problems?

6. How does a firm go about assessing its training needs?

7. Why is performance appraisal important for international firms?

8. What special compensation and benefits issues arise in international HRM?

9. How does international HRM for nonmanagerial employees differ from that for managerial employees?

10. What is codetermination?

Questions for Discussion

1. How does HRM relate to other functional areas such as marketing, finance, and operations management?

2. Why and how does the scope of a firm's internationalization affect its HRM practices?

3. How are the different approaches to recruiting and selecting managers for foreign assignments similar and dissimilar?

4. Which are easier to assess, business skills or international skills? Why?

5. If you were being assigned to a foreign position, what specific training requests would you make of your employer?

6. Do you agree or disagree with the idea that some international assignments require special compensation?

7. How easy or difficult do you think it is to handle the equity issue in international compensation?

8. What does the high cost of replacing an international manager suggest regarding staffing philosophy?

9. Which do you think is easier, HRM for managerial employees or HRM for nonmanagerial employees? Why?

10. Do you think codetermination would work in the United States? Why or why not?

11. Given Korea's current financial difficulties, would you recommend that Samsung end its program of sending young managers on foreign assignments early in their careers?

BUILDING GLOBAL SKILLS

Assume that you are the top human resource manager for a large international firm. The head of your company's operation in Japan has just resigned unexpectedly to take a job with another firm. You must decide on a replacement as quickly as possible. You have developed the following list of potential candidates for the job:

♦ *Jack Henderson.* Henderson is a senior vice president based in your Chicago headquarters.

Jack has a long and distinguished career with your firm, is well regarded by everyone, and plans to retire in three years. He has never worked outside the United States but is strongly and visibly lobbying for the job in Japan. Because you and your spouse socialize with Jack and his wife outside of work, you know she does not want to move from Chicago.

♦ *Takeo Takahashi.* Takahashi is the number two manager in your Japanese operation now, although he has only served in that role for three months. He was born and raised in Japan. After attending college in the United States, he returned to Japan and went to work for your firm. Takeo is considered an emerging star in the company but is also relatively young and inexperienced. Your CEO prefers to appoint someone for the Japanese job with at least fifteen years of company experience, and Takeo has only eight years of experience. He was being groomed to eventually take over the operation, but the just-departed top executive had been expected to serve until he reached retirement age in another seven years.

♦ *Jane Yamaguichi.* Yamaguichi is a Hawaiian-born manager currently heading up a major division for your company in the United States. A dual economics and Asian studies major at the University of Hawaii, for the last several years she has been studying the Japanese market and become a true expert on that country. She enjoys traveling, and spends as much time in Asia as possible. You also know that she would be very interested in this job if it were offered, although you are concerned that her husband and two high-school-age children may not share her enthusiasm about living in Japan. In addition, you also worry that if she is not offered a new challenge soon, she might start looking for another position.

♦ *Jacques Moine.* Moine is your most experienced international manager. Originally from France, Jacques has held senior management positions in your firm's operations in Germany, Spain, Canada, Argentina, and Mexico. Moine appears to be quite satisfied with his current posting in Mexico. But because that operation is both stable and very efficient, it could likely be run by someone with less experience.

Working alone, carefully consider the strengths and weaknesses of each of the four leading candidates for the job. Select the individual that you think is the best candidate.

Then form small groups of four or five students. Share with each other your individual choices for the job in Japan, along with the reasons for making those choices.

WORKING WITH THE WEB: Building Global Internet Skills

Researching Expatriate Assignments

Assume you are a Boston-based manager for a growing international business. Your firm is among the leaders in its industry and has recently decided to emphasize its foreign operations even more. You have worked for the firm for ten years, and it is well known that you have been designated for fast-track consideration for top management. You have an MBA from a leading university program and currently earn $150,000 per year. You have two school-aged children—one loves to play soccer and one excels in swimming—and your spouse has a thriving medical practice. Neither you nor your spouse has ever lived outside the United States.

Your boss has just told you he would like you to get some international experience. An appropriate position for you has opened up in the company's London office, and your boss would like you to take it. He implies that a refusal to relocate would be a serious blow to your career with the firm. He also asks you to make a proposal regarding the compensation package you would require in order to accept this London assignment.

You have made the following list of issues and questions related to your move and your compensation package:

1. What are housing costs in London compared to those in Boston?

2. What are transportation options and costs in London relative to those in Boston?

3. What is the overall cost of living in London compared to that in Boston?

4. What career options exist in London for your spouse?

5. What schooling options exist in London for your children? How much will they cost?

6. What are average transportation costs between Boston and London? (You have a big family and anticipate many trips back and forth.)

7. What athletic options exist in London for your children?

8. What are the tax implications of this move for you?

Use the Internet to learn as much as you can about each of these questions.

CLOSING CASE

"You Americans Work Too Hard"[74]

Andreas Drauschke and Angie Clark work comparable jobs for comparable pay at department stores in Berlin and suburban Washington, D.C. But there is no comparison when it comes to the hours they put in.

Mr. Drauschke's job calls for a 37-hour week with six weeks' annual leave. His store closes for the weekend at 2 p.m. on Saturday afternoon and stays open one evening each week—a new service in Germany that Mr. Drauschke detests. "I can't understand that people go shopping at night in America," says the 29-year-old, who supervises the auto, motorcycle, and bicycle division at Karstadt, Germany's largest department-store chain. "Logically speaking, why should someone need to buy a bicycle at 8:30 p.m.?"

Mrs. Clark works at least 44 hours a week, including evening shifts and frequent Saturdays and Sundays. She often brings paperwork home with her, spends her days off scouting the competition, and never takes more than a week off at a time. "If I took any more, I'd feel like I was losing control," says the senior merchandising manager at J.C. Penney in Springfield, Va.

The 50-year-old Mrs. Clark was born in Germany but feels like an alien when she visits her native land. "Germans put leisure first and work second," she says. "In America it's the other way around."

While Americans often marvel at German industriousness, a comparison of actual workloads explodes such national stereotypes. In manufacturing, for instance, the weekly U.S. average is 37.7 hours and rising; in Germany it is 30 hours and has fallen steadily over recent decades. All German workers are guaranteed by law a minimum of five weeks' annual holiday.

A day spent at a German and an American department store also shows a wide gulf in the two countries' work ethic, at least as measured by attitudes toward time. The Germans fiercely resist any incursions on their leisure hours, while many J.C. Penney employees work second jobs and rack up 60 hours a week.

But long and irregular hours come at a price. Staff turnover at the German store is negligible; at J.C. Penney it is 40 percent a year. Germans serve apprenticeships of two to three years and know their wares inside out. Workers at J.C. Penney receive training of two to three days. And it is economic necessity, more than any devotion to work for its own sake, that appears to motivate most of the American employees.

"First it's need and then it's greed," says Sylvia Johnson, who sells full-time at J.C. Penney and works another 15 to 20 hours a week doing data entry at a computer firm. The two jobs helped her put one child through medical school and another through college. Now 51, Mrs. Johnson says she doesn't need to work so hard—but still does.

"My husband and I have a comfortable home and three cars," she says. "But I guess you always feel like you want something more as a reward for all the hard work you've done."

Mr. Drauschke, the German supervisor, has a much different view: Work hard when you're on the job and get out as fast as you can. A passionate gardener with a wife and young child, he comes in 20 minutes earlier than the rest of his staff but otherwise has no interest in working beyond the 37 hours his contract mandates, even if it means more money. "Free time can't be paid for," he says.

The desire to keep hours short is an obsession in Germany—and a constant mission of its powerful unions. When Germany introduced Thursday night shopping in 1989, retail workers went on strike. And Mr. Drauschke finds it hard to staff the extra two hours on Thursday evening, even though the late shift is rewarded with an hour less overall on the job. "My wife is opposed to my coming home late," one worker tells him when asked if he will work until 8:30 on a coming Thursday.

Mr. Drauschke, like other Germans, also finds the American habit of taking a second job inconceivable. "I already get home at 7. When should I work?" he asks. As for vacations, it is illegal—yes, illegal—for

Germans to work at other jobs during holidays, a time that "is strictly for recovering," Mr. Drauschke explains. He adds: "If we had conditions like in America, you would have to think hard if you wanted to go on in this line of work."

At J.C. Penney, the workday of the merchandising manager Mrs. Clark begins at 8 a.m. when she rides a service elevator to her windowless office off a stock room. Though the store doesn't open until 10 a.m., she feels she needs the extra time to check floor displays and schedules. Most of the sales staff clock in at about 9 a.m. to set up registers and restock shelves—a sharp contrast to Karstadt, where salespeople come in just moments before the shop opens.

Case Questions

1. How does HRM in the United States differ from HRM in Germany?

2. What do you see as the basic advantages and disadvantages of each system?

3. If you were the top HRM executive for an international department store chain with stores in both Germany and the United States, what basic issues would you need to address regarding corporate HR policies?

4. Are the issues more or less acute in the retailing industry versus other industries?

5. Under which system would you prefer to work?

CHAPTER NOTES

1. "Toyota Takes Pains, and Time, Filling Jobs at Its Kentucky Plant," *Wall Street Journal,* December 1, 1987, pp. 1, 29; "How Does Japan Inc. Pick Its American Workers?" *Business Week,* October 3, 1988, pp. 84–88; Louis Kraar, "Japan's Gung-Ho U.S. Car Plants," *Fortune,* January 30, 1989, pp. 98–108; Justin Martin, "Mercedes: Made in Alabama," *Fortune,* July 7, 1997, pp. 150–158; "Toyota Devises Grueling Workout for Job Seekers," *USA Today,* August 11, 1997, p. 3B.

2. Sakhawat Hossain and Herbert J. Davis, "Some Thoughts on International Personnel Management as an Emerging Field," in Albert Nedd (guest editor), Gerald R. Ferris and Kendrith M. Rowland (eds.), *Research in Personnel and Human Resources Management (Supplement 1: International Human Resources Management)* (Greenwich, Conn.: JAI Press, 1989), pp. 121–136.

3. John Milliman, Mary Ann Von Glinow, and Maria Nathan, "Organizational Life Cycles and Strategic

International Human Resource Management in Multinational Companies: Implications for Congruence Theory," *Academy of Management Review* (July 1991), pp. 318–339.

4. Ruth G. Shaeffer, "Matching International Business Growth and International Management Development," *Human Resource Planning*, Vol. 12, No. 1 (1992), pp. 29–35.

5. Nakiye Boyacigiller, "The Role of Expatriates in the Management of Interdependence, Complexity, and Risk in Multinational Corporations," *Journal of International Business Studies*, Vol. 21, No. 3 (Third Quarter 1990), pp. 357–382.

6. Christopher Lorenz, "Global executives walk a tightrope," *Financial Times*, October 12, 1992, p. 10.

7. Allan Bird and Roger Dunbar, "Getting the Job Done Over There: Improving Expatriate Productivity," *National Productivity Review* (Spring 1991), pp. 145–156.

8. "The High Cost of Expatriation," *Management Review* (July 1990), pp. 40–41.

9. "Like Factory Workers, Professionals Face Loss of Jobs to Foreigners," *Wall Street Journal*, March 17, 1993, pp. A1, A9.

10. Cynthia Fetterolf, "Hiring Local Managers and Employees Overseas," *The International Executive* (May–June 1990), pp. 22–26; Gretchen M. Spreitzer, Morgan W. McCall, Jr., and Joan D. Mahoney, "Early Identification of International Executive Potential," *Journal of Applied Psychology*, Vol. 82, No. 1 (1997), pp. 6–29.

11. Ronald Henkoff, "Inside Andersen's Army of Advice," *Fortune*, October 4, 1993, pp. 79ff.

12. "More U.S. Companies Venture Overseas for Directors Offering Fresh Perspectives," *Wall Street Journal*, January 22, 1992, pp. B1, B8.

13. Ellen Brandt, "Global HR," *Personnel Journal* (March 1991), pp. 38–44.

14. "Japan should give the locals a chance," *Financial Times*, November 15, 1991, p. 15.

15. Frank Heller, "Human Resource Utilization: A Model Based on East-West Research," *The International Executive* (January-February 1992), pp. 15–25.

16. "Companies Send Intrepid Retirees to Work Abroad," *Wall Street Journal*, March 2, 1998, p. B1.

17. Jennifer J. Laabs, "The Global Talent Search," *Personnel Journal* (August 1991), pp. 38–44.

18. "Long Frowned Upon, Switching Employers Is Climbing in Japan," *Wall Street Journal*, November 18, 1991, pp. B1, B4.

19. "Pharmacia to Move Headquarters to U.S. East Coast," *Wall Street Journal*, October 14, 1997, p. B14.

20. "U.S. Chief to Head Nomura's Global Operations," *Financial Times*, November 20, 1997, p. 19.

21. "Foreign Accents Proliferate in Top Ranks as U.S. Companies Find Talent Abroad," *Wall Street Journal*, May 21, 1992, pp. B1, B7.

22. Hugh Scullion, "Strategic Recruitment and Development of the Global Manager," in *Proceedings of the Third Conference on International Personnel and Human Resources Management*, Ashridge Management College, Berkhamsted, United Kingdom, 1992. See also "Glut of Graduates Lets Recruiters Pick Only the Best," *Wall Street Journal*, May 20, 1993, p. B1.

23. Richard M. Hodgetts and Fred Luthans, "U.S. Multinationals; Compensation Strategies," *Compensation & Benefits Review* (January-February 1993), pp. 57–62.

24. "Younger Managers Learn Global Skills," *Wall Street Journal*, March 31, 1992, p. B1.

25. J. Stewart Black and Gregory Stephens, "The Influence of the Spouse on American Expatriate Adjustment in Overseas Assignments," *Journal of Management*, Vol. 15 (1989), pp. 529–544.

26. M. G. Harvey, "The Multinational Corporation's Expatriate Problem: An Application of Murphy's Law," *Business Horizons*, Vol. 26 (1983), pp. 71–78.

27. Allan Bird and Roger Dunbar, "Getting the Job Done Over There: Improving Expatriate Productivity," *National Productivity Review* (Spring 1991), pp. 145–156.

28. Rosalie L. Tung, "Selection and training procedures of U.S., European, and Japanese multinationals," *California Management Review*, Vol. 25, No. 1 (1982), pp. 57–71.

29. "As Costs of Overseas Assignments Climb, Firms Select Expatriates More Carefully," *Wall Street Journal*, January 9, 1992, pp. B1, B6.

30. "Companies Use Cross-Cultural Training to Help Their Employees Adjust Abroad," *Wall Street Journal*, August 9, 1992, pp. B1, B6.

31. Nancy J. Adler and Dafna N. Izraeli, *Women in Management* (New York: M.E. Sharp, 1988).

32. Joel D. Nicholson, Lee P. Stepina, and Wayne Hochwarter, "Psychological Aspects of Expatriate Effectiveness," in Ben B. Shaw and John E. Beck (guest editors), Gerald R. Ferris and Kendrith M. Rowland (eds.), *Research in Personnel and Human Resources Management (Supplement 2: International Human Resources Management)* (Greenwich, Conn.: JAI Press, 1990), pp. 127–145.

33. Gary P. Ferraro, *The Cultural Dimension of International Business* (Englewood Cliffs, N.J.: Prentice Hall, 1990), pp. 143–144.

34. L. V. Newman, "A Process Perspective on Expatriate Adjustment," in *Proceedings of the Third Conference on International Personnel and Human Resources Management*, Ashridge Management College, Berkhamsted, United Kingdom, 1992.

35. J. Stewart Black and Hal B. Gregersen, "When Yankee Comes Home: Factors Related to Expatriate and Spouse Repatriation Adjustment," *Journal of International Business Studies* (Fourth Quarter 1991), pp. 671–694.

36. "Expatriates Find Long Stints Abroad Can Close Doors to Credit at Home," *Wall Street Journal*, May 17, 1993, pp. B1, B6.

37. Black and Gregersen, op. cit.

38. "As Costs of Overseas Assignments Climb," *Wall Street Journal*, op. cit., pp. B1, B4.

39. Daniel C. Feldman and David C. Thomas, "Career Management Issues Facing Expatriates," *Journal of International Business Studies*, Vol. 23, No. 2 (Second Quarter 1992), pp. 271–293; J. Stewart Black and Hal B. Gregersen, "The Other Half of the Picture: Antecedents of Spouse Cross-Cultural Adjustment," *Journal of International Business Studies*, Vol. 22, No. 3 (Third Quarter 1991), pp. 461–477.

40. Paul Vanderbroeck, "Long-Term Human Resource Development in Multinational Organizations," *Sloan Management Review* (Fall 1992), pp. 95–99.

41. Stephen H. Rhinesmith, "Going Global from the Inside Out," *Training & Development* (November 1991), pp. 42–47.

42. Joseph A. Petrick and Lisa Russell-Robles, "Challenges in the Education of the Contemporary U.S. International Manager," *The International Executive* (May-June 1992), pp. 251–261.

43. R. D. Albert, "Cultural Diversity and Cross-Cultural Training Approaches in Multinational Organizations: Major Issues and Approaches," in *Proceedings of the Third Conference on International Personnel and Human Resources Management*, Ashridge Management College, Berkhamsted, United Kingdom, 1992. See also "Employers Ignore Expatriate Wives at Their Own Peril," *Wall Street Journal*, March 2, 1992, p. A12.

44. Peter R. Schleger, "Making International Videos: An Odyssey," *Training & Development* (February 1992), pp. 25–32.

45. Michael J. Marquardt and Dean W. Engel, "HRD Competencies for a Shrinking World," *Training & Development* (May 1993), pp. 59–60.

46. Cynthia Lee and Miriam Erez, "Context-Oriented Strategies in Planning Career Promotion: A Cross-Cultural Comparison," in *Proceedings of the Third Conference on International Personnel and Human Resources Management*, Ashridge Management College, Berkhamsted, United Kingdom, 1992.

47. "Korea's Biggest Firm Teaches Junior Execs Strange Foreign Ways," *Wall Street Journal*, December 30, 1992, pp. A1, A4.

48. Wouter van Ginneken and Rolph van der Hoeven, "Industrialisation, Employment, and Earnings (1950–1987): An International Survey," *International Labour Review*, Vol. 128, No. 5 (1989), pp. 571–599.

49. K. S. Law, "A New Perspective on Determining an Organization-Wide Pay Structure," in *Proceedings of the Third Conference on International Personnel and Human Resources Management*, Ashridge Management College, Berkhamsted, United Kingdom, 1992.

50. "What's an Expatriate?" *Wall Street Journal*, April 21, 1993, pp. R1, R5.

51. Michael J. Bishko, "Compensating Your Overseas Executives, Part 1: Strategies for the 1990s," *Compensation & Benefits Review* (May-June 1990), pp. 33–43.

52. Richard M. Hodgetts and Fred Luthans, "U.S. Multinationals' Expatriate Compensation Strategies," *Compensation & Benefits Review* (January-February 1993), pp. 57–62.

53. "Cultural divide," *The Economist*, February 8, 1992, p. 33.

54. "For Executives Around the Globe, Pay Packages Aren't Worlds Apart," *Wall Street Journal*, October 12, 1992, pp. B1, B5.

55. "What's an Expatriate?" *Wall Street Journal*, op. cit., pp. R4–R5.

56. Yoram Zeira and Moshe Banai, "Selecting Managers for Foreign Assignments," *Management Decision*, Vol. 25 (1987), pp. 38–40.

57. Beverly Geber, "The Care and Breeding of Global Managers," *Training* (July 1992), pp. 32–37.

58. Richard A. Guzzo, Katherine A. Noonan, and Efrat Elron, "A Model of Organizational HR Practices and Expatriate Retention," in *Proceedings of the Third Conference on International Personnel and Human Resources Management*, Ashridge Management College, Berkhamsted, United Kingdom, 1992.

59. Larry Crump, "Developing Effective Personnel for International Business," *Management Japan* (Autumn 1990), pp. 31–36.

60. Mike Regan, "Developing the Middle Manager for Globalisation," in *Proceedings of the Third Conference on International Personnel and Human Resources Management*, Ashridge Management College, Berkhamsted, United Kingdom, 1992.

61. Robert O'Connor, "Retraining Eastern Europe," *Training* (November 1992), pp. 41–45.

62. "Some U.S. Companies Find Mexican Workers Not So Cheap After All," *Wall Street Journal*, September 15, 1993, pp. A1, A16.

63. Mitsuru Wakabayashi and George Graen, "Human Resource Development of Japanese Managers," in Albert Nedd (guest editor), Gerald R. Ferris and Kendrith M. Rowland (eds.), *Research in Personnel and Human Resources Management (Supplement 1: International Human Resources Management)* (Greenwich, Conn.: JAI Press, 1989), pp. 235–256.

64. Paul S. Kirkbride and Sara F. Y. Tang, "Training in Hong Kong," in Ben B. Shaw and John E. Beck (guest editors), Gerald R. Ferris and Kendrith M. Rowland (eds.), *Research in Personnel and Human Resources Management (Supplement 2: International Human Resources Management)* (Greenwich, Conn.: JAI Press, 1990), pp. 293–312.

65. Uco J. Wiersam, Peter T. van den Berg, and Gary P. Latham, "The Practicality of Performance Appraisal Instruments: A Replication and Extension," in *Proceedings of the Third Conference on International Personnel and Human Resources Management*, Ashridge Management College, Berkhamsted, United Kingdom, 1992.

66. Christopher Lorenz, "Learning to live with a cultural mix," *Financial Times*, April 23, 1993, p. 18.

67. Anthony M. Townsend, K. Dow Scott, and Steven E. Markham, "An Examination of Country and Culture-Based Differences in Compensation Practices," *Journal of International Business Studies*, Vol. 21, No. 4 (Fourth Quarter 1990), pp. 667–678.

68. David G. Blanchflower and Richard B. Freeman, "Unionism in the United States and Other Advanced OECD Countries," *Industrial Relations* (Winter 1992), pp. 56–79.

69. "Bitter Swedish Dispute Set to End," *Financial Times,* May 30, 1995, p. 3.

70. David A. MacPherson and James B. Stewart, "The Effect of International Competition on Union and Nonunion Wages," *Industrial and Labor Relations Review* (April 1990), pp. 434–446.

71. Dennis R. Briscoe, "Coping with the Human Resource Implications of the EC 1992," in *Proceedings of the Third Conference on International Personnel and Human Resources Management*, Ashridge Management College, Berkhamsted, United Kingdom, 1992.

72. Georges Spyropoulos, "Labour Law and Labour Relations in Tomorrow's Social Europe," *International Labor Review*, Vol. 129, No. 6 (1990), pp. 733–750.

73. Cheng Soo May, "Worker Participation in Private Companies in Singapore," in Albert Nedd (guest editor), Gerald R. Ferris and Kendrith M. Rowland (eds.), *Research in Personnel and Human Resources Management (Supplement 1: International Human Resources Management* (Greenwich, Conn.: JAI Press, 1989), pp. 97–120.

74. Daniel Benjamin and Tony Horwitz, "German View: 'You Americans Work Too Hard—and for What?," *Wall Street Journal*, July 14, 1994, pp. B5–B6. Reprinted by permission of the *Wall Street Journal*, © 1994 Dow Jones & Company, Inc. All Rights Reserved Worldwide.

Comprehensive Cases

Nomura is Number One No More

Technological innovation in telecommunications and computer systems has played a major role in the development and growth of the international capital market. Telecommunications make it easier to monitor changes in individual domestic capital markets and to obtain information about stock market prices, trends in interest rates, and the performance of individual firms anywhere in the world. Computers ease the task of acting on this information and utilizing the sophisticated investment and risk-reduction strategies developed from modern finance theory.

Commercial banks, investment banks, securities brokers, and large institutional investors such as pension funds and insurance companies are well aware of these innovations. They shop for the best advice, the best deals, and the best execution of their orders in a worldwide market. As a result, the financial services industry is becoming globalized. Although firms located in other cities participate in the industry, the major players are concentrated in three cities: London, New York, and Tokyo. London's preeminence stems from the pound's role in the nineteenth-century international monetary system. The "City of London," as London's financial district is known, developed expertise in international banking from managing and financing Britain's far-flung colonial empire. Despite its relatively small economy, the United Kingdom is still the world's leading center of international bank lending activities. Over 300,000 people are directly employed in the financial services industry in the Greater London area.

The second great center for financial services is New York City. U.S. financial service firms, benefiting from their location in the world's largest economy, are aggressive underwriters of equity and debt offerings by firms worldwide. U.S. firms are well-known for their innovative approaches to providing financial services, developing such products as money-market funds, automatic teller machines, and computer-executed program trading of complex bundles of stocks.

However, the dominance of British and U.S. financial services firms has been increasingly challenged by their Japanese counterparts, who benefited from Japan's growth into the world's second largest economy. As Table 5.1 showed, 11 of the world's 30 largest banks are in Japan. Their share of the international bank lending market is second only to the British. Tokyo is also the third-largest center for foreign exchange trading, after London and New York.

A similar pattern emerged in the global securities business. Tokyo's Nomura Securities Company, Ltd. claimed the number one position in the world's securities industry by the end of the 1980s. Like other securities firms, it buys and sells stocks and bonds on organized stock exchanges and in over-the-counter trading. It also engages in highly profitable underwriting activities in which it helps firms raise capital through public and private placements of debt and equity offerings. Its 134 domestic retail branches span Japan and serve 5 million clients. Nomura's retail salesforce is notoriously aggressive in pushing to those clients stocks and bonds favored by the firm's upper management, particularly ones underwritten or sponsored by Nomura's investment banking operations. Insulated from competition by a fixed commission system and governmental restrictions on domestic and foreign competitors, Nomura benefited substantially from the excellent performance of the Japanese economy in the 1980s. The firm's revenues grew at a compounded rate of 16.3 percent annually, while its income soared at an annual compounded rate of 20.9 percent.

During the 1980s, Nomura used its strong domestic base to expand its operations internationally. Currently it operates in 28 foreign countries; in 1996, 46 percent of its revenues were generated outside of Japan. It purchased a seat on the New York Stock Exchange in 1981 and one on the London Stock Exchange in 1986. During this boom decade for Japan, Nomura became a leading underwriter of Eurobonds (particularly dollar-denominated bonds sold by Japanese companies) and samurai bonds (foreign bonds denominated in yen). In 1988, attracted to the enormous profits earned by investment advisors in the 1980s takeover craze, it purchased a 20 percent share of the Wasserstein Perella Group, one of the world's leading merger and acquisitions specialists. By luring high-priced, talented investment bankers from other Wall Street firms, Nomura's North American operations have been profitable, although its activities have been limited to niche markets such as those for mortgage-based securities and junk bonds, and it has not yet succeeded in becoming a dominant player in the North American market like Goldman Sachs or Merrill Lynch.

Nomura's situation in Europe was not as comfortable. Its European operations were plagued by high costs, and its profits were disappointing. In the 1980s, Nomura primarily used its 16 European offices to peddle Japanese financial products to European investors. But Japanese stocks and bonds fell out of favor with foreign investors after Japan's "bubble" economy burst, starting in 1989. Suddenly Nomura's glaring weaknesses in Europe were exposed: it lacked both an extensive salesforce and knowledge of the local market. Moreover, U.S. and European securities brokers and investment bankers were well ahead of Nomura in developing the complex financial products, such as derivatives, warrants, and hybrid securities, that appealed to European money managers.

To address these problems, Nomura began in April 1994 to reorganize its European operations. Previously, the heads of its European offices reported directly to an executive in Tokyo. Now they report to the director of European operations headquartered in London. Their power was further weakened when their sales staffs were made members of teams directed by executives in London. For example, a bond salesperson in Zurich who previously reported to Nomura's Swiss country manager now reports to the division head in London who is in charge of fixed-income products. Through this restructuring, Nomura hopes to make its European operations less Japanese and more European in spirit and practice. Moreover, the restructuring improves the promotion opportunities available to its European staff (particularly in London); previously the highest position in Nomura's European operations was that of country manager, and such slots were reserved for Japanese executives. This reorganization seems to be bearing fruit. Nomura's European group has become the leading debt underwriter in the emerging markets of Central Europe, for example.

Yet organizational problems remain. Industry experts believe communication and coordination among Nomura's senior executives in Japan, Europe, and North America could be much improved. Lack of high-level communication is one reason Nomura has been unable to capture one of the important benefits of globalization, worldwide learning. While its U.S. operation has developed a much deserved reputation as an innovator in issuing mortgage-backed securities, and its European group in underwriting emerging market securities, little of this expertise has been absorbed by Nomura's Japanese staff. As one industry expert noted, most of Nomura's financial skills are centered in its 3,000 non-Japanese employees, not in its 12,000-strong Japanese staff.

Unfortunately, before Nomura had time to confront this problem, the performance of its domestic operations began to deteriorate. The crash of the Tokyo Stock Market in the early 1990s reduced trading volumes, which cut into Nomura's lucrative flow of commission income. And as the domestic recession in the early 1990s reduced corporate Japan's needs for new capital, Nomura's profits from underwriting new debt and equity issues plummeted. More threatening to the firm's long-run prospects has been the average Japanese household's growing distrust of investing in stocks. This reaction resembles that of U.S. investors, who shied away from the New York Stock Exchange after the 1929 crash. Confidence in the Japanese market was also disrupted by the news that Nomura, along with other leading Japanese securities firms (including the second-largest firm, Daiwa Securities), reimbursed large Japanese companies over $471 million for their stock market losses, but did not extend the same courtesy to little investors.

To make a difficult situation more difficult, as a result of trade conflicts between Japan and its major trading partners—the United States and the EU—the Japanese Ministry of Finance has increasingly allowed foreign competitors access to the domestic Japanese securities market. Moreover, it announced that it would deregulate the Japanese securities industry by the end of the century, thereby increasing competition within the industry.

Nomura has had difficulties responding quickly to innovations introduced by these foreign competitors, in part because of Japanese business culture. As we discussed in Chapter 9, this culture is very consensus-oriented, and pay scales tend to reward the achievements of the group rather than those of individuals. U.S. securities firms, on the other hand, seek to hire high-achieving superstars and are happy to reward their individual achievements. While Nomura was willing to adopt Western pay practices in its North American and European operations, it has been hesitant to do the same in Japan, thereby leaving itself vulnerable to raids on its personnel by Western securities firms operating in Japan.

As a result, despite the lackluster performance of the Japanese stock market in the past several years, foreign brokers have expanded their share of the Japanese market from 3 percent in 1988 to 20 percent in 1994, and to 33 percent in 1997. Three American firms—Salomon Brothers, Goldman Sachs, and Morgan Stanley—have been reaping record profits in Japan. They have done this by transferring to the Japanese stock market their U.S.-developed expertise in computerized arbitrage trading between the stock market and stock market index futures. Nomura and its fellow Japanese securities firms have been unable to match this success. What annoys the Japanese brokers most is their inability to harness their competitive advantages—their extensive retail branch networks and their understanding of the Japanese customer—to beat back the foreign invasion. As stated by one observer, the Americans' use of computerized arbitrage trading means there is "no need for customers. Nor for Japanese-speaking staff. Nor, indeed, for anyone who knows anything about Japanese companies."

By 1997, Nomura's financial condition had deteriorated further. In the fiscal year ending March 31, 1997, Nomura lost $722 million due to huge losses on nonperforming loans written by its real estate lending unit. After these losses were announced, the company was then badly hurt by news that Nomura had paid bribes to *sokaiya*, Japanese gangsters who blackmail companies by threatening to disrupt their annual shareholders' meetings. Japanese securities regulators later charged Nomura with illegally reimbursing a favored client linked to the *sokaiya* for his investment losses. Japan's Ministry of Finance indefinitely suspended Nomura from underwriting bonds issued by the Japanese government, taking away a profitable business in which it had enjoyed a 10 percent market share. Fifteen members of its board of directors resigned to atone for the scandal. Still worse, many of the company's important clients, such as the huge California Public Employers' Retirement System, Yasuda Trust Bank, and Shikoku Electric Power Company, announced they would refuse to

place orders with the company or hire it to underwrite securities. As a result, the company's share of the domestic stock brokerage industry quickly fell from first to fourth place, and it fell to fourth place within the global securities industry. No more was Nomura number one.

To address these problems, Nomura promoted Junichi Ujiie in April 1997 to be Nomura's president and CEO. The former head of Nomura's U.S. operations and a Ph.D. in Economics from the University of Chicago, Ujiie acted swiftly to reduce bureaucracy by flattening Nomura's organizational structure. He now plans to abandon the company's global area design and adopt a global product approach, so that Nomura can more profitably exploit product niches developed by its subsidiaries, such as the U.S. operation's expertise in developing mortgage-backed securities and derivatives trading—markets its Japanese unit has not yet mastered. He also has to win back the numerous former Nomura clients that severed their relationships with the firm after the *sokaiya* scandal broke.

Given the latent strengths of the Japanese economy, no doubt the Japanese stock market will eventually rise again. Japanese investors will return to the stock market, thereby allowing Nomura to benefit from its strong network of retail branches in Japan. And Nomura has a huge war chest to reclaim its lost turf: its equity capital totals some $12.3 billion. But Nomura will face tougher competition from domestic and foreign securities firms in its domestic market in the new century than it did in the 1970s, 1980s, and 1990s. The firm must also respond more quickly to the innovations of its foreign competitors and harness the expertise of its foreign subsidiaries if it wants to regain its position as the world's number one securities firm.

Discussion Questions

1. What can Nomura do to regain its former position as the world's largest securities firm?

2. Should Nomura temporarily place its international expansion efforts on hold, and concentrate on rebuilding its position in the Japanese market?

3. Nomura's North American operations have been profitable, but the firm's presence in the

market has been limited to specific niches. Should Nomura attempt to broaden its participation in the North American market even if it means sacrificing profits in the short run?

4. What effect will adopting a global product design have on Nomura's operations? On its profits?

5. Can Nomura survive if it doesn't have a presence in all areas of the Triad?

Sources

Nomura corporate web site (www.nomura.com/corporate/global); "Once there Were Four: Japanese Securities Firms," *The Economist*, September 27, 1997, p. 80; "Nomura begins global realignment around product reporting lines," *Investment Dealers' Digest*, August 18, 1997, p. 3; "Nomura changes its strategy," *Financial Times*, August 4, 1997, p. 17; "Japan Punishes Nomura, Dai-Ichi Over Rackets Cases," *Wall Street Journal*, July 31, 1997, p. A14; "Can This Man Save Nomura?," *Business Week*, May 12, 1997, p. 94; "New Broom at Nomura, *Financial Times*, April 25, 1997, p. 20; "Nomura directors step down," *Financial Times*, April 23, 1997, p.1; "Calpers Is Halting Trading with Nomura," *Wall Street Journal*, March 19, 1997, p. A20; "Financial Centres: Rise and Fall," *The Economist*, June 27, 1992, p. 4 of survey; "Unchain Japan's Financial Markets," *Wall Street Journal*, June 26, 1991, p. A10; "Chapman Says 'No' To Nomura Units Based in Europe," *Wall Street Journal*, May 18, 1994, p. B4; "Regulatory grip that has cost Tokyo dear," *Financial Times*, June 29, 1994, p. 9; Hoover et al., *Hoover's Handbook of World Business 1997* (Austin, Tex.: Reference Press, 1997), p. 249; Stefan Wagstyl, "Japan's scandal-hit traders may lose fixed commissions," *Financial Times*, August 10/11, 1991, p. 3; "Unfair Advantage," *Wall Street Journal*, June 25, 1991, p. A1; "Nomura Securities Fights to Regain the Confidence of Japanese Investors," *Wall Street Journal*, July 6, 1992, p. 3; Emiko Terazono, "Tokyo offers riches to foreign brokers," *Financial Times*, June 23, 1992, p. 19; "Gaijin, Gaijin, gone," *The Economist*, December 22, 1990, p. 96.

The Germans Come Roaring Back

The luxury car market holds a special place in the hearts of automobile manufacturers. Most cars sold today are mass-market products like those manufactured by Ford, Toyota, and Volkswagen. But the moderate prices that they can charge for products like the Taurus, Camry, and Jetta limit the profit margins they can earn on these bread-and-butter vehicles. Because luxury cars are sold at much higher prices, astute manufacturers can often achieve higher profit margins on these products. Consequently, while they may sell fewer luxury cars than other products, automobile manufacturers nevertheless still place a premium on luxury car sales and strive to maintain as large a market share and as strong a market position as possible in this product niche.

Because of the higher prices they must pay to get the exclusive products they want, luxury car buyers are more concentrated in developed nations; relatively fewer customers come from developing markets. Thus, while the Quad countries are important to every automobile manufacturer, they are especially vital to makers of luxury cars. Not surprisingly then, firms that make luxury cars pay close attention to their respective market shares in the Quad countries and work aggressively to hold onto their customers.

The U.S. market in particular is an important battlefield for luxury car manufacturers because of the large number of wealthy individuals who live there. For years, the dominant U.S. luxury car models were made by Ford's Lincoln division and General Motors' Cadillac division. The Chrysler Imperial was once a popular model as well, but was discontinued several years ago due to weak sales. German autos, however, have long enjoyed a special cachet among U.S. consumers. Much like wine connoisseurs associate imported French wines with high quality vintages, so too did U.S. car buyers see BMW and Mercedes as being special. Indeed, for most of the postwar period these German automobile companies were the only serious competitors for Ford's Lincoln products and General Motors' Cadillac products. As a result, if someone in the United States was in the market for an upscale car, they could buy a domestic product from one of these two manufacturers, or else buy an import from Germany. And many buyers did choose a BMW or Mercedes, along with some who might opt for an Audi or a Porsche (also German). And since Japanese automobile manufacturers had no products in this market, the competitive dynamics among Lincoln, Cadillac, BMW, and Mercedes were relatively straightforward and easy to understand.

The Germans, meanwhile, were well aware of the special niche they occupied in the U.S. automobile market. As a result, however, they began to treat U.S. consumers with a bit of a cavalier attitude. For example, because European consumers do not view their vehicles as dining rooms on wheels, German auto executives believed that it was safe to ignore complaints from U.S. consumers about the lack of cup holders in German-designed cars. They also saw little need to tailor other features of their products to the U.S. market. After all, they reasoned, their products were so superior that consumers would buy them even if they didn't precisely meet their needs. Their emphasis was on finely engineered, high-performance products with relatively little concern for customer tastes or preference. And it seemed to work: in 1986, BMW and Mercedes each achieved all-time record sales in the United States.

But everything changed just a few years later. Because they recognized their own manufacturing advantages and reputation for building quality products and observed the Germans' inattention to the needs of the U.S. market, Japanese auto manufacturers Honda, Toyota, and Nissan each decided to develop their own luxury car products and export them to the United States. Honda was first, in 1988, with the Acura. The following year Toyota and Nissan launched their products, the Lexus and the Infiniti, respectively. To ensure that consumers did not associate these new models with the less glamourous Camrys, Accords, and Altimas, sold by the hundreds of thousands, Toyota, Honda, and Nissan set up separate distribution and dealership networks to market their new upscale vehicles. This strategy succeeded: their new luxury cars were perceived to be as good—or better—than the German products. Just as important, they also were engineered and designed to better meet the tastes and preferences of U.S. consumers. These factors, along with the exciting new designs of the Japanese cars, helped attract customers to showroom floors in droves.

To compound the problems for the Germans, labor costs and exchange rates made it easy for the Japanese to undercut Mercedes' and BMW's pricing. For example, in 1989 Toyota was able to sell its top-of-the-line Lexus LS400 for about $35,000, whereas the comparable BMW car was selling for $52,000. Consumers who wanted an import luxury car, therefore, saw two clear choices: buy a Japanese product or a German product, with the Japanese option being generally seen as a better product at a lower price.

Not surprisingly, the Japanese cars were a big hit. While Lincoln and Cadillac were clearly affected, the Germans were initially hit the hardest. Sales of BMW and Mercedes plummeted, as did sales for other German companies such as Audi, Porsche, and Volkswagen. In 1991, sales bottomed out at 53,343 vehicles for BMW and 58,869 for Mercedes, down 45 percent and 41 percent, respectively, from their 1986 levels. And indeed, some of these German firms actually contemplated abandoning the U.S. market altogether.

Instead, however, the Germans decided to fight back against the Japanese in the United States and launched a number of important initiatives to regain their lost market share. First BMW and then Mercedes announced plans to begin assembling vehicles in the United States. Moreover, some of these products were ones specifically designed for the U.S. market. For example, the Alabama-built Mercedes M-Class sports utility vehicle was built primarily with the U.S. market in mind—and it has five cup holders! Clever advertising and promotional campaigns also boosted the allure of their vehicles. BMW tied the launch of its new Z-3 roadster and the latest redesign of its 7-Series auto to the two most recent James Bond movies (which featured the vehicles), reaping millions of dollars of free publicity and product exposure in the process.

Building in the United States also had several side benefits for BMW and Mercedes. For one thing, this approach reduces risks associated with fluctuating exchange rates. For another, labor costs in the U.S. are substantially lower than in Germany. And finally, even though consumers knew they were buying German products, the fact that BMW and Mercedes were making cars in the United States caused some buyers to appreciate the fact the jobs were being created for U.S. workers and shifted their interests away from Lexus and Infiniti. Both companies chose to ramp up U.S. production slowly to ensure that they could maintain the quality and the image of their U.S.-made vehicles.

As though to make things even easier for the Germans, the Japanese also hurt themselves with a bit of bumbling. Just as the Germans were making plans to fight back in the U.S. market, both Lexus and Infiniti boosted their prices to enhance profits. Exchange rate fluctuations then resulted in even higher prices for the Japanese imports. In addition, they were also uncharacteristically slow to launch new models and lost momentum just as the Germans came roaring back.

By 1998, German auto makers like BMW and Mercedes were back in the driver's seat. Sales of some BMW products in the United States have tripled since 1991, and Mercedes has even had to contend with long waiting lists for some of its products. Indeed, across the board all the Germany automobile manufacturers have experienced strong U.S. sales increases over the past few years. While Lexus managed to retain its share of the U.S. luxury car market, Infiniti and Acura both experienced sales drops, as did Lincoln and Cadillac. The table to the right shows U.S. market shares for these and other companies in the luxury market for 1991 and 1997.

Discussion Questions

1. Which strategy should firms adopt to compete in the luxury car market: international, multidomestic, global, or transnational?

2. If you ran Lincoln or Cadillac, what would you do to increase their share of the U.S. luxury car market?

3. Why do you think that Lexus has maintained its share of the U.S. luxury car market while Infiniti and Acura have not?

U.S. Market Shares in 1991 and 1997 for Luxury Cars

	1991	1997
Cadillac	19%	15%
Lincoln	16%	11%
BMW	5%	10%
Mercedes	5%	9%
Acura	12%	9%
Lexus	6%	7%
Volvo	6%	7%
Buick	12%	6%
Oldsmobile	6%	2%
Other	13%	24%

4. If you ran BMW or Mercedes, what would you do now?

Sources

"German Car Horns Are Tooting Again," *Wall Street Journal,* January 7, 1998, p. A18; "Germans in the Fast Lane," *Business Week,* April 13, 1998, pp. 78-82.

Lloyd's of London

Picture a smoky, seventeenth-century, English coffee house echoing with the mingled voices of merchants, farmers, and sea captains. Now picture a gleaming, modern skyscraper housing thousands of executives clustered around humming computers and fax machines. What do these two scenes have in common? Both are snapshots of the same organization, Lloyd's of London.

Today, Lloyd's of London is the world's best-known insurance organization. Athletes' legs and arms, rock singers' voices, and governments' satellites and military hardware are among the more unusual properties insured with Lloyd's. Lloyd's lost over $1 million when Luciano Pavarotti had to cancel a concert in Italy because of a sore throat. But Lloyd's loves to pay out on such claims, for they invariably yield a goldmine of free publicity that the organization's less known competitors envy. Even though Lloyd's is still headquartered in London, the organization does about 60 percent of its business outside the United Kingdom, with a third coming from the United States.

Lloyd's was started in 1688. At that time, coffee houses were a common forum for informal business transactions. Edward Lloyd's coffee house attracted a clientele of merchants, ship's captains, and others interested in foreign trade. These merchants and sea captains began to offer a share of the profits from their voyages in return for investors' sharing the risk of a loss at sea. An individual investor would agree to reimburse, or insure, the captain in the event of a loss (due to a shipwreck or to pirates, for example), and the captain would agree to pay the investor a share of the profits if there were no loss. The primary investor, in turn, would then line up other investors to help him cover his own losses, if any, in return for a share of his profits.

Today, Lloyd's is one of the world's largest insurance organizations, and it still conducts business much as it did 300 years ago. Individual insurance underwriters, called "working Names," accept risk on behalf of a group of outside investors, "external Names." Each collection of Names is called a syndicate. Some syndicates have thousands of members; others have only a few dozen.

Until the mid-1970s, Lloyd's was viewed as one of Britain's most exclusive clubs. One could not simply invest in Lloyd's by buying stock. Rather, one was elected to membership on the basis of one's wealth, and Lloyd's Names represented the cream of British society. A sound reason existed for this method of selection. Unlike many corporations, which limit the personal liability of their shareholders to the actual amount invested, each of the individual Names personally accepted unlimited liability for paying off his or her share of claims on insurance that his or her syndicate has underwritten. After 1975, however, Lloyd's became a less exclusive club. To expand its underwriting activities, it needed more capital and thus more Names, so it hired recruiters to attract new blood into its syndicates. These recruiters were quite successful: between 1975 and 1978, the number of Names nearly doubled, from 3,917 to 7,710; by 1989, it reached 34,218.

For most of its 300-year existence, the unlimited liability of Lloyd's Names was more a theoretical threat than a real possibility. For example, from 1967 to 1987, Lloyd's enjoyed profitable operations. But for several dark years after 1987, the threat turned into a nightmarish reality for many Names. Policies written from 1988 to 1991 to date have lost over $10 billion, and this figure is likely to rise because claims against those policies continue to pour into Lloyd's offices. An estimated $7.5 to $13 billion will be needed to settle all claims not yet filed against these policies.

Some of these losses are attributable to what might be considered "normal" events in the insurance industry—hurricanes, earthquakes, floods, destruction of North Sea oil rigs, even the grounding of the *Exxon Valdez*. But the real problem lies in so-called long-tailed risks, where claims are submitted many years after an insurance policy is written. Because of the hidden nature of such risks, they are often underestimated and the premiums therefore underpriced. Lloyd's long-tailed risk problem was centered in the United States, in particular on asbestosis and pollution insurance claims. Asbestosis may develop from exposure to asbestos that occurred decades ago; thus, assessing which firm was actually at fault is difficult. U.S. manufacturers and users of asbestos products settled most asbestosis litigation through a multibillion-dollar class action suit and then presented their insurance firms, including Lloyd's, with the bill.

But the impact of asbestosis on insurers pales in comparison to that of pollution claims. Legal liabilities under U.S. environmental laws are far reaching. The Superfund, created in 1980, has been particularly troublesome. The Superfund authorizes the U.S. Environmental Protection Agency to file suit against persons responsible for contaminating active or abandoned hazardous waste disposal sites. Usually these persons are the operators of the sites. However, landowners, former landowners, lenders, transporters of the wastes, and even customers of the hazardous waste sites have also been drawn into Superfund litigation because often the original defendant countersues them in order to spread the cost of cleaning up the disposal site. At one disposal site in Ohio, for example, 289 generators and transporters of hazardous wastes were found to be jointly and severally responsible for cleaning up the site. Inevitably, in such cases, the insurance providers of each party get drawn into the litigation as well.

Much of this legal liability was unanticipated by insurance firms. For example, an insurer of a motor carrier specializing in transportation of hazardous wastes would normally price its policy based on the carrier's past safety record, the quality of its employee training programs, and other factors controllable by its managers. Ignorant of its Superfund exposure, the insurer would not consider the likelihood that the carrier (and its insurer) would end up paying for the cleanup of the disposal site. Thus, it would, inadvertently, underprice its policies.

Long-tailed insurance risks like asbestosis and pollution liability account for much of the existing and expected losses suffered by Lloyd's Names. Legally, because of their unlimited liability, the Names who participated in insurance syndicates in the late 1980s will have to cough up billions of additional dollars to pay these claims. However, many of the Names have been financially devastated and so had little ability to honor their pledges to pay these claims. Lloyd's problems created a new sector of Britain's upper and upper-middle classes: *deficit millionaires,* persons who owe Lloyd's at least £1 million to cover past insurance losses. Titled gentlemen, society matrons, members of parliament, and former World War II RAF officers who valiantly defended their country in its darkest hour faced bills for millions of pounds they didn't have and so were forced to appear before Lloyd's Hardship Committee. This committee read them their financial last rights and stripped them of all their assets except "a modest and only home," which reverts to Lloyd's after their deaths. So far, over 1400 desperate Names have been forced to place their fate in the hands of the Hardship Committee. Others have filed for bankruptcy, and, sadly, at least seven have ended their own lives as a result of their financial troubles.

The most popular approach, however, was one familiar in the United States: many Names sued Lloyd's for negligence, fraud, and favoritism. By one estimate, 60 percent of the external Names filed lawsuits against Lloyd's. Newer Names claim they were duped into investing in the riskier syndicates, while more profitable insurance opportunities were reserved for the working Names and external Names of longer standing. Some external Names claimed that Lloyd's failed to warn them about the riskiness of its U.S. underwriting activities. They cite a 1981 letter from a Chicago law firm and a 1982 audit report from a London accounting firm warning about the potential liability of asbestosis claims. They say this information was not disseminated to them. Several groups of Names were successful in British courts, winning settlements totalling £3.2 billion. U.S. courts are still deciding whether they should hear claims that Lloyd's violated U.S. securities and racketeering laws.

Lloyd's 300-year reign as a major force in international insurance was perilously close to ending in the mid-1990s as a result of these catastrophic losses. Many Names withdrew from writing new insurance, fearing increased financial exposure. The number of Names dropped from its peak of 34,218 in 1989 to fewer than 20,000 in 1995; by 1998, individual Names plummeted to less than 7,000. To attract new capital and stave off further defections, Lloyd's was forced to change two of its long-standing traditions. Unlimited liability was effectively ended in 1992 with the creation of a mandatory stop-loss insurance policy, which placed a ceiling on individual losses at $3.6 million over a four-year period. Lloyd's also abandoned its reliance on individual investors by changing its rules in 1993 to allow corporate and institutional investors to participate in its underwriting business.

So far, these changes seem to be successful, and Lloyd's insurance underwriting has returned to profitability. In 1998, for example, Lloyd's announced that its investors earned $1.5 billion in profits for the 1995 year of account, which was a slight decrease from its $1.6 billion in earnings for 1994 and 1993. (Lloyd's accounting system operates three years in arrears in order to match claims, which may be filed long after the insurance is written, with premium income.) And the organization is expanding into new markets—more than 60 countries all told. For example, Lloyd's was able to begin directly underwriting insurance in Japan in 1997 as part of that country's evolving deregulation of its financial services industry.

Problems still remain, of course. Lloyd's lost market share in the global insurance market as the financial traumas facing its Names made front-page news in the worldwide financial press. Lloyd's suffered additional blows to its public image as a result of Parliamentary inquiries that condemned the organization for careless scrutiny of underwriting standards and of the financial wherewithal of newly recruited Names. New unexpected risk exposures have developed as well. For example, Lloyd's syndicates, like other insurance companies, are vulnerable to Year 2000 damage claims. (This refers to problems caused by older computer software that automatically translates "00" to mean the year 1900, potentially playing havoc with interest calculations, inventory control, etc.) U.K. insurance regulators are increasing their scrutiny of Lloyd's operations as a result of its past financial difficulties. And the influx of corporate capital—corporate investors now account for 60 percent of the organization's underwriting capacity—suggests that Lloyd's will have to restructure its rules and procedures to better serve the needs of these corporate investors. For example, Lloyd's will probably need to abandon its tradition of raising monies on a year-to-year basis, an approach which limits its ability to make long-term commitments to insurance clients.

As a result of these problems, many experts believe that Lloyd's increasingly will be dominated by insurance companies. Some insiders welcome such a change, arguing that "Names are tiresome and expensive to service." If true, Lloyd's 300 years of relying on individual Names will soon fade away like the smoke in Edward Lloyd's coffee house; but in the process, it may lose some of the entrepreneurship and individuality that have set it apart from other insurance providers over the past three centuries.

Discussion Questions

1. U.S. courts have yet to allow U.S. investors to pursue their legal claims against the organization in U.S. courts. Do you agree with this? Should U.S. citizens always have the right to have their claims against foreigners heard in U.S. courts? Why or why not? As a result of this decision, what precautions should potential U.S. Names take before deciding to invest in Lloyd's?

2. Should Lloyd's have gone further in assessing its exposure to asbestosis and pollution claims in the United States? More generally, what precautions should firms undertake when doing business in foreign markets?

3. How does ending the unlimited liability of Names affect Lloyd's operations?

4. What other changes will Lloyd's have to make if corporate investors continue to displace individual Names?

5. If you were in charge of Lloyd's, what would you do to restore the organization's faded luster?

Sources

"Composite syndicates gaining at Lloyd's," *National Underwriter Property & Casualty-Risk & Benefits Management,* February 9, 1998, p. 37; "Lloyd's still looking to diversify its business," *National Underwriter Property & Casualty-Risk & Benefits Management,* February 9, 1998, p. 2; "Lloyd's 1995 profit expected to fall 10 percent from 1994 to 917 million pounds sterling," *National Underwriter Property & Casualty-Risk & Benefits Management,* January 26, 1998, p. 46; "Names and numbers," *Financial Times,* June 6, 1997, p. 17; "After the storm," *The Economist,* May 10, 1997, p. 77; "Lloyd's of London—A Sketch History" (London: Lloyd's publications, no date); *United States v. Chem-Dyne Corp.,* 572 F. Supp. 802 (S.D. Ohio 1983); "Why Lloyd's Is Looking for Its Own Safety Net," *Business Week,* September 23, 1991, pp. 84–85; "Lloyd's of London, an Insurance Bulwark, Is a Firm Under Siege," *Wall Street Journal,* October 24, 1989, pp. A1, A18; "The New Broom at Lloyd's at London," *Business Week,* January 14, 1991, p. 54; "Lloyd's Plans to Put Cap on Exposure, Now Open-Ended, of Members to Losses," *Wall Street Journal,* January 16, 1992, p. A8; "Toughing it out," *The Economist,* February 22, 1992, p. 70; "Lloyd's wins one US judgment in dispute over jurisdiction," *Financial Times,* March 3, 1992, p. 22; "Lloyd's to Cap Loss Exposure, Rejects Bailout," *Wall Street Journal,* June 19, 1992, p. A8; Julian Barnes, "The Deficit Millionaires," *The New Yorker,* September 20, 1993, pp. 74ff; "Lloyd's 'Names' Vote to Admit New Investors," *Wall Street Journal,* October 21, 1993, p. A19; "Spurning the lifebelt," *The Economist,* January 22, 1994, p. 86; "Mess at Lloyd's May Have a Darker Side," *Wall Street Journal,* March 17, 1994, p. A10.

The Ethics of Global Tobacco Marketing

Cigarette smoking was once considered to be an elegant and glamorous pastime in the United States. Movie stars, athletes, politicians, and other public figures were often photographed holding or smoking a cigarette, and tobacco companies aggressively pushed their products as a basic commodity in the same way that firms today market soft drinks and fast foods. Driven in part by the allure of fashion and in part by this aggressive marketing, the annual consumption of cigarettes by U.S. smokers increased steadily from 54 per person in 1900 to a high of 4,345 in 1963.

In 1964, however, things began to change. The U.S. Surgeon General released a report that demonstrated a clear link between cigarettes and lung cancer. During the subsequent several years, numerous reforms were put in place that affected the ability of tobacco firms to market their products in the United States. Among the most stringent were bans on television and radio advertising, mandatory warning labels on cigarette packages, high sales taxes, and age restrictions for the legal purchase of cigarettes. These measures, combined with increased public awareness, caused the annual consumption of cigarettes by U.S. smokers to drop to 2,493 per person in 1994.

There are four major international cigarette makers today. Philip Morris, the world's largest, is a U.S. firm that manufactures such brands as Marlboro, Benson & Hedges, Parliament, and Virginia Slims. RJR Nabisco, also a U.S. firm, markets Camel, Doral, Salem, Winston, and other brands. B.A.T.

Industries, a British firm, sells such brands as Kool, Raleigh, and Viceroy (B.A.T.'s U.S. operation is called Brown & Williamson). Rothmans International, also a British firm, sells its Rothmans brand cigarette primarily outside the U.S. market.

As pressures to curb cigarette smoking in the United States increased during the 1970s and 1980s, U.S. cigarette makers began to adopt two diversification strategies in an effort to boost their profits. First, they branched into nontobacco markets, using cash flows generated by their tobacco profits to acquire leading firms outside their industry. Their experience in marketing premium-priced, brand-name consumer goods led them to focus on markets where this expertise would be useful. For example, Philip Morris purchased Kraft, General Foods, and Miller Brewing Company. Within the U.S. market, Philip Morris currently derives less than forty percent of its revenues from tobacco. RJR, previously known as R.J. Reynolds, acquired Nabisco in 1985 and became RJR Nabisco. It now sells a number of food and food-related products that came with that acquisition, including candy, gum, nuts, cookies, crackers, and cereals. And B.A.T. has insurance and financial services operations.

Second, these major tobacco marketers sought to diversify their tobacco sales geographically by focusing their efforts on markets other than the United States. These markets have two major advantages over the U.S. market. First, many of them place fewer restrictions on tobacco sales than is the case in the United States. Second, growth prospects in these markets are higher. Rising incomes and reduction of trade restrictions make such markets as Russia, the Czech Republic, Japan, and South Korea particularly appealing to U.S. tobacco companies. Thus, in one market after another, the four international giants, other international tobacco suppliers, and local tobacco brands are waging aggressive marketing wars in their efforts to increase sales of their products, especially to younger people.

Central and Eastern Europe is one battlefield. Communist government officials actively promoted the use of cigarettes and vodka. These commodities were cheap to make, and their addictive character helped maintain order and discipline in society. Indeed, after the collapse of communism and the move toward an open market in Russia, cigarette shortages caused riots in Moscow. Not surprisingly, then, cigarette makers rushed to enter the former

Soviet bloc countries, where total annual cigarette consumption is estimated to be as high as 700 billion, compared to 500 billion in the United States.

Philip Morris, RJR Nabisco, B.A.T., and Rothmans have discovered that consumers in this region crave affordable, high-quality, Western-style products. Cigarettes seem to fill at least part of the bill. Those firms have plastered cities throughout Central and Eastern Europe with billboards featuring the Marlboro Man—an icon of America, the West, and freedom—or symbols of other Western brands. Not surprisingly, the number of smokers in Central and Eastern Europe continues to escalate. Philip Morris is perhaps the most successful firm in this region so far, in part because it was able to buy the Czech cigarette monopoly, Tabak, in 1992 during that country's privatization program. It has also purchased majority interests in formerly state-owned cigarette factories in Hungary, Kazakhstan, Russia, and Ukraine. The other three major producers have also staked out positions in the region. R.J. Reynolds operates two joint ventures in Ukraine with local companies. B.A.T. bought a controlling interest in Uzbekistan's leading cigarette producer, while Rothmans has contracted with local producers to manufacture and sell its products in the Czech Republic and Poland.

Asia is another major battlefield. The Japanese, for example, have long been heavy smokers. The Japanese market was essentially closed to foreign firms until the Bush administration pressured the Japanese to reduce their high tariffs on imported cigarettes and end Japan Tobacco's monopoly over the domestic market. Because Japanese consumers have long been interested in products that they strongly associate with the United States (such as Levi Strauss jeans, McDonald's restaurants, and Disney films), U.S. cigarette makers are now finding Japan a fertile market for their brands.

The story is similar in the Philippines, Taiwan, Korea, Vietnam, Malaysia, Hong Kong, and Indonesia. Aggressive advertising, often targeted at young consumers and women, is inducing more and more people to become smokers. For example, a 1985 survey of high school students in Taiwan found that only 26 percent of males and 1 percent of females had ever smoked a cigarette. Six years later, a similar survey found 48 percent of males and 20 percent of females had smoked.

But perhaps China holds the greatest opportunity for cigarette makers. There are currently over 300 million smokers in China, most of whom currently smoke local brands. The four tobacco giants eagerly await any openings in this market, believing it to be the world's most lucrative one for their products. Rothmans, for example, has built a new factory in Shandong Province in a joint venture with the China National Tobacco Corporation.

But these efforts and strategies have been very controversial, raising ethical concerns about the behavior of the firms and the U.S. government. Critics argue, for example, that the tobacco giants are being socially irresponsible by taking advantage of uninformed, impressionable consumers who don't fully understand the health risks of smoking. One expert has predicted that lung-cancer deaths among Chinese men will increase from 30,000 in 1975 to 900,000 by 2025. Another observer notes that if U.S. tobacco firms are allowed full and free access to the Chinese market and can use the aggressive marketing techniques they have perfected elsewhere and if they increase the number of smokers by only 2 percent, three times as many Chinese will be killed by lung cancer than the number of Americans killed in wars this century.

The tobacco companies respond that they are doing nothing wrong. For example, they point out that local governments, especially in Central and Eastern Europe, have encouraged their investments. They also point out that they are simply taking advantage of legal market opportunities that already exist. Indeed, failing to do just what they are doing might seem to be a disservice to their stockholders and employees.

Among the most controversial issues are the marketing practices international tobacco companies employ. China again provides a good case in point. That country has a law that prohibits the advertising of cigarettes. But the law bans only the display of and actual mention of a cigarette. Philip Morris actively promotes its Marlboro brand without ever showing a picture of or mentioning cigarettes. One of its radio commercials, for example, proclaims, "This is the world of Marlboro. Ride through the rivers and mountains with courage. Be called a hero throughout the thousand miles. This is the world of Marlboro." And Philip Morris's efforts appear to be paying off: its brand recognition is high among Chinese consumers. One Canton factory manager, when asked by an interviewer why he smokes Marlboros, replied, "Marlboro shows my superior position to others. I'm more privileged."

More controversial has been the role of the U.S. government. Although it discourages cigarette usage at home, it has played an active role in opening foreign markets to U.S. tobacco firms. In the 1980s, the U.S. Trade Representative (USTR) (the government agency in charge of international trade negotiations) successfully hammered out agreements with Japan, South Korea, Taiwan, and Thailand to end their restrictions on the sale of foreign cigarettes. The USTR attacked foreign countries for utilizing public policies that the U.S. government itself had adopted. Taiwan, for example, previously disallowed all cigarette advertising as a means of discouraging cigarette consumption. As a result, most cigarettes were consumed by adult males. In 1986, however, the U.S. government exerted pressure on the Taiwanese government to allow greater access to its market by U.S. firms. Bowing to this pressure, Taiwan not only opened its market to Philip Morris and RJR Nabisco, but also relaxed its regulations on cigarette advertising. These Western firms have focused their marketing efforts on teenagers and females, believing that older males will continue to smoke domestic brands. U.S. brands now sell well among those targeted audiences. When Taiwanese health officials tried to strengthen the warning labels on cigarette packages, ban smoking by those under 18, and prohibit vending machine cigarettes sales, the USTR counterattacked, claiming that these efforts would hurt U.S. tobacco companies. The USTR took similar stances in trade negotiations with Japan, South Korea, and Thailand, threatening these countries with Super 301 retaliation if they did not open their markets to U.S. cigarettes.

All in all, the international marketing efforts of U.S. cigarette makers seem to be working. Exports to Asia alone account for 12 percent of U.S. cigarette production. These firms' primary target markets—teenagers, females, and the affluent—are purchasing U.S. cigarettes in record numbers. But the controversy rages on, however, as more and more critics line up in an effort to curtail the U.S. tobacco companies' efforts to indoctrinate people in other regions toward cigarette smoking.

Discussion Questions

1. Summarize the basic ethical and social responsibility issues that this case illustrates.

2. If you managed an international tobacco firm, what actions would you take today to protect your market opportunities abroad?

3. Do you think other foreign cigarette makers, such as those in Japan, will ever be able to crack the U.S. market? Why or why not?

4. In most Asian cultures, cigarette smoking is restricted to males. Should U.S. cigarette makers respect the cultural values of these countries and restrict their marketing efforts to males? Should females be targeted for marketing as well?

5. In February 1998, the U.S. State Department changed its tobacco policy, instructing all U.S. embassies to stop promoting sales of U.S. tobacco products. U.S. embassy personnel are also directed "to support, rather than challenge, local antismoking laws and regulations that may reduce U.S. tobacco company sales, as long as they are applied in a nondiscriminatory manner to both imported and domestic tobacco products." Do you agree with this policy change?

6. In formulating its international trade policies, should the U.S. government focus on protecting the interests of U.S. tobacco growers, workers, and manufacturers, or should it concentrate on protecting the lungs of Asians? More generally, what is the appropriate role of the U.S. government in foreign tobacco marketing?

Sources

"U.S. Embassies Stop Assisting Tobacco Firms," *Wall Street Journal*," May 14, 1998, p. B1; "Getting Acquainted," *Business Eastern Europe,* October 20, 1997, p. 4; "Rothmans Goes its Own Way in E. Europe," *World Tobacco,* July 1997, p. 21; "Smoke Signals," *Business Eastern Europe,* April 22, 1996, p. 17; "Stan Sesser, "Opium War Redux," *The New Yorker,* September 13, 1993, pp. 78–89; "Smoking Level Lowest in 50 Years," *USA Today,* November 17, 1994, p. D1; "Cigarettes May Find New Foe in Trade Rep," *Wall Street Journal,* August 1, 1994, p. B1; "Tobacco Companies Race for Advantage in Eastern Europe While Critics Fume," *Wall Street Journal,* December 28, 1992, pp. B1, B4; "U.S. Cigarette Firms Are Battling Taiwan's Bid to Stiffen Ad Curbs Like Other Asian Nations," *Wall Street Journal,* May 5, 1992, p. C25; "Opiate of the Masses," *Forbes,* April 11, 1994, pp. 74–75.

Glossary

The number in parentheses following each definition gives the page on which the term is introduced.

absolute advantage, theory of: theory stating that trade between nations occurs when one nation is absolutely more productive than other nations in the production of a good; according to Adam Smith, nations should export those goods for which they possess an absolute advantage and import goods for which other nations possess an absolute advantage (88)

accounting reserves: reserves created by firms for foreseeable future expenses (701)

acculturation: process of understanding and learning how to operate in a new culture (358)

acquisition strategy: form of foreign direct investment involving the purchase of existing assets in a foreign country (437)

active income: income generated by active business operations such as production, marketing, and distribution (719)

ad valorem tariff: tax assessed as a percentage of the market value of an imported good (214)

adjustable peg: feature of the Bretton Woods system by which a country had a limited right to adjust the value of its currency in terms of gold (132)

advised letter of credit: letter of credit in which the seller's bank advises the seller about the creditworthiness of the bank issuing the letter of credit (704)

affiliated bank: partly owned, separately incorporated overseas banking operation of a home country bank (188)

aggressive goal behavior: behavior based on the cultural belief that material possessions, money, and assertiveness underlie motivation and reflect the goals that a person should pursue (354)

agreeableness: a "big five" personality trait referring to a person's ability to get along with others (513)

Andean Pact: customs union composed of Bolivia, Colombia, Ecuador, Peru, and Venezuela (275)

antidumping duty: tax on imported goods designed to protect domestic firms from sales of imported goods at less than their cost of production or at prices less than they sell for in their home markets (203)

arbitrage: riskless purchase of a product in one market for immediate resale in a second market in order to profit from price differences between the markets (179)

arbitration: dispute resolution technique in which both parties agree to submit their cases to a private individual or body for resolution (308)

arm's length test: test imposed by the Internal Revenue Service to determine the appropriateness of transfer prices; reflects the price that one independent company would charge a second for a good or service (716)

Asia-Pacific Economic Cooperation (APEC): a group of countries on both sides of the Pacific working to promote trade among themselves through the reduction or elimination of trade barriers (277)

assigned arrangement: management arrangement in which one partner in a strategic alliance assumes primary responsibility for the operations of the alliance (468)

Australia-New Zealand Closer Economic Relations Trade Agreement (ANZCERTA or CER): an agreement between Australia and New Zealand intended to eliminate trade barriers between the two countries (276)

authoritarianism: personality trait determining the extent to which an individual believes that power and status differences are appropriate within hierarchical social systems like organizations (515)

backtranslation: technique used to check for translation errors; after one person translates a document from language A to language B, a second person translates the document from B back to A to check if the intended message is actually being sent (335)

Baker Plan: plan developed in 1985 by U.S. Treasury Secretary James Baker to solve the international debt crisis; stressed debt rescheduling, tight controls over domestic monetary and fiscal policies, and continued loans to debtor nations (141)

balance of payments (BOP) accounting system: accounting system that records commercial transactions between the residents of one country and residents of other countries (122)

balance on merchandise trade: difference between a country's merchandise exports and imports (144)

balance on services trade: difference between a country's service exports and imports (144)

balance sheet hedge: technique for eliminating translation exposure in which a firm matches its assets and liabilities denominated in a given currency on a consolidated basis (671)

banker's acceptance: time draft that has been endorsed by a bank, signifying the bank's promise to guarantee payment at the designated time (658)

barter: form of countertrade involving simultaneous exchange of goods or services between two parties (662)

beggar-thy-neighbor policies: domestic economic policies that ignore the economic damage done to other countries (125)

benchmarking: process of legally and ethically studying how other firms do something in a high-quality way and then either imitating or improving on their methods (570)

"big five" personality traits: popular personality model based on five dominant traits—agreeableness, conscientiousness, emotional stability, extroversion, and openness (513)

bilateral netting: netting of transactions between two business units (678)

bill of lading: international trade document that serves (1) as a contract between the exporter and the transporter and (2) as a title to the exported goods (657)

B-O-T project: variant of a turnkey project for market entry in which a firm builds a facility, operates it, and then later transfers ownership of the project to some other party (435)

Brady Plan: plan developed in 1989 by U.S. Treasury Secretary Nicholas Brady to solve the international debt crisis; involves writing off a portion of the debtor nations' debts or repurchase of their debts at less than face value (141)

branch bank: overseas banking operation of a home country bank that is not separately incorporated (188)

bureaucratic design: model of organization design based on rational rules, regulations, and standard operation procedures (481)

bureaucratic law: legal system based on interpretations, actions, and decisions of government employees (293)

buy-back: form of countertrade in which a firm is compensated in the form of goods produced by equipment or technology that it has sold to another firm (662)

BV: abbreviation used in the Netherlands to refer to a privately held, limited liability firm (11)

Cairns Group: group of major agricultural exporting nations, led by Argentina, Australia, and Canada, that lobbies for reductions in agricultural subsidies (247)

call option: publicly traded contract granting the owner the right, but not the obligation, to buy a specific amount of foreign currency at a specified price at a stated future date (177)

capacity planning: deciding how many customers a firm will be able to serve at a given time (641)

capital account: BOP account that records capital transactions between residents of one country and those of other countries (145)

Caribbean Basin Initiative (CBI): program developed by the United States to spur the economic development of countries in the Caribbean Basin; allows duty-free importation of selected goods into the United States from these countries (273)

centralized cash management: system controlled by a parent corporation that coordinates worldwide cash flows of its subsidiaries and pools their cash reserves (676)

centrally planned economy (CPE): economy in which government planners determine price and production levels for individual firms (313)

chaebol: any of the large business conglomerates that dominate the Korean economy (62)

channel length: number of stages in a distribution channel (610)

civil law: law based upon detailed codification of permissible and nonpermissible activities; world's most common form of legal system (293)

clearinghouse accounts: accounting system used to facilitate international countertrade; a firm must balance its overall countertrade transactions but need not balance any single countertrade transaction (663)

co-decision procedure: procedure that shares decision-making power between the European Parliament and the Council of the European Union (266)

codetermination: German system that provides for cooperation between management and labor in running a business (757)

cohesion fund: means of funneling economic development aid to countries whose per capita GDP is less than 90 percent of the EU average (263)

collective bargaining: process used to make agreements between management and labor unions (756)

collectivism: cultural belief that the group comes first (347)

comity, principle of: principle of international law that one country will honor and enforce within its own territory the judgments and decisions of foreign courts (308)

commodity agreement: agreement created by major producers and consumers of a good to control production and prices of that good (279)

commodity cartel: cartel created by producers of a good to control production and prices of that good (278)

common law: law that forms the foundation of the legal system in Anglo-American countries; based on cumulative findings of judges in individual cases (291)

common market: form of regional economic integration that combines features of a customs union with elimination of barriers inhibiting the movement of factors of production among members (255)

Commonwealth of Independent States: organization formed by twelve former Soviet republics to promote free trade and discuss issues of common concern (54)

comparative advantage, theory of: theory stating that trade between countries occurs when one country is relatively more productive than others in the production of a good (89)

compound tariff: tax that combines elements of an ad valorem tariff and a specific tariff (215)

comprehensive alliance: strategic alliance in which participants agree to perform together multiple stages of the process by which goods or services are brought to market (458)

confirmed letter of credit: letter of credit in which the seller's bank adds its promise to pay should the issuing bank fail to pay the seller (660)

confiscation: involuntary transfer of property, with little or no compensation, from a privately owned firm to the host government (303)

conglomerate: firm that uses a strategy of unrelated diversification (393)

conscientiousness: a "big five" personality trait referring to the order and precision a person imposes on activities (513)

consolidated financial statement: a financial statement combining the accounting records of a parent corporation and all its subsidiaries into a single set of statements denominated in a single currency (708)

consolidation method: technique used to consolidate accounting records of subsidiaries in which the parent company's ownership stake is more than 50 percent (709)

contingency fee: type of payment for legal services in which the fee paid is based on the size of monetary payments awarded to the client (308)

contract manufacturing: process of outsourcing manufacturing to other firms in order to reduce the amount of a firm's financial and human resources devoted to the physical production of its products (434)

control: process of monitoring and regulating activities in a firm so that targeted measures of performance are achieved or maintained (544)

control framework: managerial and organizational processes used to keep a firm on target toward its strategic goals (389)

control standard: desired level of a performance component a firm is attempting to control (554)

controlled foreign corporation (CFC): foreign corporation in which certain U.S. shareholders (each of which must own at least 10 percent of the foreign corporation's stock) cumulatively own at least 50 percent of the foreign corporation's stock (719)

controller: managerial position in an organization given specific responsibility for financial control (546)

convergence criteria: conditions that must be met in order to participate in the EU's single currency program, including numerical limits on members' inflation, interest rates, currency values, budget deficits, and outstanding national debts; designed to force convergence of participants' monetary and fiscal policies (264)

convertible currencies: currencies that are freely traded and accepted in international commerce; also called hard currencies (176)

Coordinating Committee for Multilateral Export Controls (COCOM): organization created by the Western allies to control the export of goods and technology with military value to the countries of the Soviet bloc (296)

coordination: process of linking and integrating functions and activities of different groups, units, or divisions (497)

corollary approach: approach whereby a firm delegates responsibility for processing international sales orders to individuals within an existing department, such as finance or marketing (482)

corporate culture: set of shared values that defines for its members what the organization stands for (499)

correspondent relationship: agency relationship whereby a bank in country A acts as an agent for a bank from country B, providing banking services in country A for both the B bank and its clients; typically done on a reciprocal basis (187)

cost-of-living allowance: compensation for managers on international assignment designed to offset differences in living costs (749)

cost method: technique used to consolidate accounting records of subsidiaries in which the parent company's ownership stake is less than 10 percent (709)

Council of the European Union: main decision-making body of the EU; composed of 15 members, who represent the interests of their home governments in Council deliberations (265)

counterpurchase: form of countertrade in which one firm sells its products to another at one point in time and is compensated in the form of the other's products at some future time (662)

countertrade: form of payment in which a seller accepts something other than money in compensation (662)

countervailing duty (CVD): ad valorem tariff placed on imported goods to offset subsidies granted by foreign governments (229)

country fund: mutual fund that specializes in investing in stocks and bonds issued by firms in a specific country (191)

country similarity theory: theory stating that international trade in manufactured goods will occur between countries with similar income levels and at similar stages of economic development (95)

covered-interest arbitrage: arbitrage that exploits geographic differences in interest rates and differences in exchange rates over time (185)

cross-cultural literacy: ability to understand and operate in more than one culture (358)

cross rate: exchange rate between two currencies, A and B, derived by using currency A to buy currency C and then using currency C to buy currency B (184)

cultural cluster: group of countries that share many cultural similarities (356)

cultural convergence: convergence of two or more cultures (358)

culture: collection of values, beliefs, behaviors, customs, and attitudes that distinguish and define a society (326)

culture shock: psychological phenomenon arising from being in a different culture; may lead to feelings of fear, helplessness, irritability, and disorientation (743)

cumulative translation adjustment: account created to balance any difference between a subsidiary's assets and its liabilities and stockholder's equity when the current rate method is used to value its balance sheet (711)

currency future: publicly traded contract involving the sale or purchase of a specific amount of foreign currency at a specified price with delivery at a stated future date (177)

currency option: publicly traded contract giving the owner the right, but not the obligation, to sell or buy a specific amount of foreign currency at a specified price at a stated future date (*see also* call option; put option) (177)

current account: BOP account that records exports and imports of goods, exports and imports of services, investment income, and gifts (143)

current account balance: net balance resulting from merchandise exports and imports, service exports and imports, investment income, and unilateral transfers (145)

current rate method: approach used to consolidate the financial statements of a foreign subsidiary when the subsidiary's functional currency is the subsidiary's home currency (710)

customs union: form of regional economic integration that combines features of a free trade area with common trade policies toward nonmember countries (254)

date draft: draft that requires payment at some specified date (658)

decision making: process of choosing one alternative from among a set of alternatives in order to promote the decision maker's objectives (529)

deferral rule: rule permitting U.S. companies to defer paying U.S. income taxes on profits earned by their foreign subsidiaries (719)

delegated arrangement: management arrangement in which partners in a strategic alliance play little or no management role, delegating responsibility to the executives of the alliance itself (468)

development: general education aimed at preparing managers for new assignments and/or higher-level positions (745)

differentiation strategy: business-level strategy that emphasizes the distinctiveness of products or services (394)

direct exchange rate: price of a foreign currency in terms of the home currency; also called a direct quote (166)

direct exporting: product sales to customers, either distributors or end-users, located outside the firm's home country (420)

direct quote: *see* direct exchange rate

direct sales: selling products to final consumers (610)

dirty float: *see* managed float

distinctive competence: component of strategy that answers the question "What do we do exceptionally well, especially as compared to our competitors?" (380)

distribution: process of getting a firm's products and services to its customers (608)

documentary collection: form of payment in which goods are released to the buyer only after the buyer pays for them or signs a document binding the buyer to pay for them (657)

draft: document demanding payment from the buyer (657)

dual use: products that may be used for both civilian and military purposes (296)

dumping: sale of imported goods either (1) at prices below what a company charges in its home market or (2) at prices below cost (203)

EC '92: common name given to the process of completing the internal market mandated by the Single European Act, which was to be finalized by December 31, 1992 (260)

eclectic theory: theory that foreign direct investment occurs because of location advantages, ownership advantages, and internalization advantages (107)

economic and monetary union (EMU): goal established by the Maastricht Treaty to create a single currency for the EU, thereby eliminating exchange-rate risks and the costs of converting currencies for intra-EU trade (263)

Economic Community of Central African States (CEEAC): organization promoting regional economic cooperation created by Central African countries (278)

Economic Community of West African States (ECOWAS): organization promoting regional economic cooperation created by 16 West African countries (278)

economic exposure: impact on the value of a firm's operations of unanticipated exchange-rate changes (672)

economic union: form of regional economic integration that combines features of a common market with coordination of economic policies among its members (255)

economies of scale: condition that occurs when average costs of production decline as the number of units produced increases (100)

economies of scope: condition that occurs when a firm's average costs decline as the number of different products it sells increases (100)

Edge Act corporation: bank that is domiciled outside the parent bank's home state and provides international banking services (182)

embargo: ban on the exporting and/or importing of goods to a particular country (211, 296)

emotional stability: a "big five" personality trait defining a person's poise, calmness, and resilience (513)

environmental scanning: the systematic collection of data about all elements of a firm's external and internal environments (386)

equity method: technique used to consolidate accounting records of subsidiaries in which the parent's ownership stake is between 10 and 50 percent (709)

errors and omissions: BOP account that results from measurement errors; equals the negative of the sum of the current account, the capital account, and the official reserves account (148)

ethnocentric approach: managerial approach in which a firm operates internationally the same way it does domestically (484, 588)

ethnocentric staffing model: approach that primarily uses PCNs to staff upper-level foreign positions (737)

Eurobond: bonds denominated in one country's currency but sold to residents of other countries (191)

Eurocurrencies: currency on deposit in banks outside its country of issue (190)

Eurodollars: U.S. dollars deposited in banks outside the borders of the United States (190)

European Commission: twenty-person group that acts as the EU's administrative branch of government and proposes all EU legislation (265)

European Court of Justice: fifteen-member court charged with interpreting EU law; also interprets whether the national laws of the 15 EU members are consistent with EU laws and regulations (266)

European Currency Unit (ECU): weighted "basket" of EU currencies used for accounting purposes within the EU (136)

European Economic Area: common market created by the EU and Iceland, Liechtenstein, and Norway (270)

European Free Trade Association (EFTA): trading bloc in Europe that works closely with the EU to promote intra-European trade; current members are Iceland, Liechtenstein, Norway, and Switzerland (270)

European Monetary Institute (EMI): organization created by the Maastricht Treaty as a first step in establishing a European Central Bank; plays a critical role in promoting economic and monetary union among EU members (263)

European Monetary System (EMS): system based on 1979 agreement among members of the European Union to manage currency relationships among themselves (136)

European Parliament: legislature with 626 members elected from districts in member countries that has a consultative role in EU decision making (266)

exchange rate: price of one currency in terms of a second currency (123)

Exchange-Rate Mechanism (ERM): agreement among European Union members to maintain fixed exchange rates among themselves within a narrow band (136)

exit interview: interview with an employee who is leaving the organization (753)

expatriate failure: early return of an expatriate manager to his or her home country because of an inability to perform in the overseas assignment (741)

expatriates: collective name for parent-country nationals (PCNs) and third-country nationals (TCNs) (737)

export and import brokers: agents who bring together international buyers and sellers of standardized commodities such as coffee, cocoa, and grains (427)

Export-Import Bank of the United States (Eximbank): U.S. government agency that promotes U.S. exports by offering direct loans and loan guarantees (228)

export management company (EMC): firm that acts as its clients' export department (424)

export of the services of capital: income that a country's residents earn from their foreign investments (144)

export promotion: economic development strategy based on building a vibrant manufacturing sector by stimulating exports, often by harnessing some advantage the country possesses, such as low labor costs (71, 210)

export-promotion strategy: *see* export promotion

export tariff: tax levied on goods as they leave the country (214)

export trading company (ETC): firm that may engage in various cooperative exporting practices without fear of violating U.S. antitrust laws (425)

exporting: selling products made in one's own country for use or resale in other countries (10)

expropriation: involuntary transfer of property, with compensation, from a privately owned firm to a host country government (303)

extraterritoriality: application of a country's laws to activities occurring outside its borders (298)

extroversion: a "big five" personality trait defining a person's comfort level with relationships, resulting in some people being sociable, talkative, and assertive, and others to be less sociable and more introverted (513)

factoring: specialized international lending activity in which firms buy foreign

accounts receivable at a discount from face value (657)

fair trade: trade between nations that takes place under active government intervention to ensure that the companies of each nation receive their fair share of the economic benefits of trade; also called managed trade (205)

fast-track authority: authority delegated by the U.S. Congress to the President allowing him/her to negotiate trade treaties with other countries; after treaty is negotiated, Congress may accept or reject it, but cannot amend or change it (273)

financial alliance: strategic alliance in which two or more firms work together to reduce the financial risks associated with a project (460)

financial derivative: financial instrument whose return derives from some bond, stock, or other asset (716)

first-mover advantage: competitive advantage gained by the first firm to enter a market, develop a product, introduce a technology, etc. (100)

fixed exchange-rate system: international monetary system in which each government promises to maintain the price of its currency in terms of other currencies (123)

flexible (or floating) exchange-rate system: system in which exchange rates are determined by supply and demand (135)

flight capital: money sent out of politically or economically unstable countries by investors seeking a safe haven for their assets (43, 148)

float: to allow a currency's value to be determined by forces of supply and demand (125)

focus strategy: business-level strategy targeting specific types of products for certain customer groups or regions (394)

foreign bonds: bonds issued by residents of one country to residents of a second country and denominated in the second country's currency (191)

Foreign Corrupt Practices Act (FCPA): U.S. law enacted in 1977 prohibiting U.S. firms, their employees, and agents acting on their behalf from paying or offering to pay foreign government officials in order

to influence official actions or policies or to gain or retain business (300)

foreign direct investment (FDI): acquisition of foreign assets for the purpose of controlling them; under U.S. regulations, FDI occurs when an investor owns at least 10 percent of the voting stock of a foreign company (11, 99)

foreign exchange: currencies issued by countries other than one's own (163)

foreign sales corporation (FSC): subsidiary of a U.S. MNC that enjoys substantial income tax savings from profits earned from exporting activities (718)

foreign service premium: *see* hardship premium

Foreign Sovereign Immunities Act of 1976: U.S. law that limits the ability of U.S. citizens to sue foreign governments in U.S. courts (308)

foreign trade zone (FTZ): geographical area in which imported or exported goods receive preferential tariff treatment (226)

forum shopping: attempt to seek a court system or judge that will be most sympathetic to an attorney's client (307)

forward discount: difference between the forward and the spot price of a currency expressed as an annualized percentage (assumes the forward price is *less* than the spot price) (*see also* forward premium) (178)

forward market: market for foreign exchange involving delivery of currency at some point in the future (176)

forward premium: difference between the forward and the spot price of a currency expressed as an annualized percentage (assumes the forward price is *more* than the spot price) (*see also* forward discount) (178)

franchisee: independent entrepreneur or organization that operates a business under the name of another (431)

franchising: special form of licensing allowing the licensor more control over the licensee while also providing more support from the licensor to the licensee (12, 431)

franchisor: firm that allows an independent entrepreneur or organization to operate a business under its name (431)

free trade: trade between nations that is unrestricted by governmental actions (205)

free trade area: regional trading bloc that encourages trade by eliminating trade barriers among its members (254)

freight forwarders: agents who specialize in the physical transportation of goods, arranging customs documentation and obtaining transportation services for their clients (427)

functional currency: currency of the principal economic environment in which a subsidiary operates (710)

General Agreement on Tariffs and Trade (GATT): international agreement that sponsors negotiations to promote world trade (244)

Generalized System of Preferences (GSP): system of reduced tariff rates offered on goods exported from developing countries (245)

generic organizational control: form of organizational control based on centralized generic controls across the entire organization (549)

geocentric approach: management approach in which a firm analyzes the needs of its customers worldwide and then adopts standardized operating practices for all markets it serves (588)

geocentric staffing model: approach using a mix of PCNs, HCNs, and TCNs to staff upper-level foreign positions (737)

geographic arbitrage: *see* two-point arbitrage (182)

global area design: form of organization design that centers a firm's activities around specific areas or regions of the world (487)

global bonds: large, liquid bond issues designed to be traded in numerous capital markets (191)

global corporation: organization that views the world as a single marketplace and strives to create standardized goods and services to meet the needs of customers worldwide (15)

global customer design: form of organization design centered around different customers or customer groups, each requiring special expertise or attention (491)

global functional design: form of organization design based on departments or divisions having worldwide responsibility for a single organizational function such as finance, operations, or marketing; also called U-form organization (488)

global matrix design: complex form of international organization design created by superimposing one form of design on top of an existing different form (492)

global product design: form of organization design that assigns worldwide responsibility for specific products or product groups to separate operating divisions within a firm (485)

goal orientation: cultural beliefs about motivation and the different goals toward which people work (354)

gold standard: international monetary system based on the willingness of countries to buy or sell their paper currencies for gold at a fixed rate (123)

goodwill: payment in excess of the book value of a firm's stock (702)

gray market: market created when products are imported into a country legally but outside the normal channels of distribution authorized by the manufacturer (597)

greenfield investment: form of investment in which the firm designs and builds a new factory from scratch, starting with nothing but a "green field" (358)

greenfield strategy: form of foreign direct investment that involves building new facilities (437)

gross domestic product (GDP): measure of market value of goods and services produced in a country (44)

gross national product (GNP): measure of market value of goods and services produced by resources owned by a country's residents (44)

hard currencies: currencies that are freely tradable; also called convertible currencies (176)

hard loan policy: World Bank lending policy requiring that loans be made only if they are likely to be repaid (127)

hardship premium: supplemental compensation to induce managers to accept relatively unattractive international assignments; also called foreign service premium (749)

harmonization: voluntary adoption of common regulations, policies, and procedures by members of a regional trading bloc to promote internal trade (259)

harmonized tariff schedule (HTS): classification scheme used by many nations to determine tariffs on imported goods (215)

headhunters: recruiting firms that actively seek qualified managers and other professionals for possible placement in positions in other organizations (739)

Heckscher-Ohlin theory: *see* relative factor endowments, theory of

H-form design: form of organization design in which products are unrelated to each other (485)

high-context culture: culture in which the context in which a discussion is held is equally as important as the actual words that are spoken in conveying the speaker's message to the listener (337)

home country: country in which a firm's headquarters is located (11)

host country: country other than a firm's home country in which it operates (11)

host-country nationals (HCNs): employees who are citizens of the host country where an international business operates (736)

human resource management (HRM): set of activities directed at attracting, developing, and maintaining the effective work force necessary to achieve a firm's objectives (731)

hurdle rate: minimum rate of return a firm finds acceptable for its capital investments (682)

IMF conditionality: restrictions placed on economic policies of countries receiving IMF loans (131)

import of the services of capital: payments that a country's residents make on capital supplied by foreigners (144)

import-substitution policy: economic development strategy that relies on the stimulation of domestic manufacturing firms by erecting barriers to imported goods (71, 210)

import tariff: tax levied on goods as they enter a country (214)

importing: buying products made in other countries for use or resale in one's own country (10)

Inc.: abbreviation for *incorporated*, meaning that the liability of the company's owners is limited to the extent of their investments if the company fails or encounters financial or legal difficulties (11)

income distribution: relative numbers of rich, middle-class, and poor residents in a country (45)

inconvertible currencies: currencies that are not freely traded because of legal restrictions imposed by the issuing country or that are not generally accepted by foreigners in settlement of international transactions; also called soft currencies (176)

indirect exchange rate: price of the home currency in terms of the foreign currency; also called indirect quote (166)

indirect exporting: sales of a firm's products to a domestic customer, which in turn exports the product, in either its original form or a modified form (419)

indirect quote: *see* indirect exchange rate

individualism: cultural belief that the person comes first (347)

industrial democracy: system based on the belief that workers should have a voice in how businesses are run (757)

industrial policy: economic development strategy in which a national government identifies key domestic industries critical to the country's economic future and then formulates policies that promote the international competitiveness of these industries (210)

infant industry argument: argument in favor of governmental intervention in trade: a nation should protect fledgling industries for which the nation will ultimately possess a comparative advantage (206)

informal management network: group of managers from different parts of the world who are connected to one another in some way (498)

information: data in a form that is of value to a manager (571)

information system: methodology created by a firm to gather, assemble, and provide data in a form or forms useful to managers (572)

intellectual property rights: intangible property rights that include patents, copyrights, trademarks, brand names, and trade secrets (250)

interindustry trade: international trade involving the exchange of goods produced in one industry in one country for goods produced in another industry in a different country (94)

intermediaries: third parties that specialize in facilitating imports and exports (423)

internalization advantages: factors that affect the desirability of a firm's producing a good or service itself rather than relying on other firms to control production (414)

internalization theory: theory stating that foreign direct investment occurs because of the high costs of entering into production or procurement contracts with foreign firms (107)

International Accounting Standards Committee (IASC): international organization whose mission is to harmonize the national accounting standards used by various nations (706)

International Bank for Reconstruction and Development (IBRD): official name of the World Bank, which was established by the Bretton Woods agreement to reconstruct the war-torn economies of Western Europe and whose mission changed in the 1950s to aid the development of less developed countries (126)

international banking facility (IBF): entity of a U.S. bank that is exempted from domestic banking regulations as long as it provides only international banking services (190)

international business: business that engages in cross-border commercial transactions with individuals, private firms, and/or public sector organizations; term is also used to refer to cross-border transactions (13)

International Development Association (IDA): World Bank affiliate that specializes in loans to less developed countries (128)

International Finance Corporation: World Bank affiliate whose mission is the development of the private sector in developing countries (128)

international Fisher effect: observation that differences in nominal interest rates among countries are due to differences in their expected inflation rates (186)

international investments: capital supplied by residents of one country to residents of another (11)

international logistics: management functions associated with the international flow of materials, parts, supplies, and finished products from suppliers to the firm, between units of the firm itself, and from the firm to customers (637)

international marketing: extension of marketing activities across national boundaries; *see also* marketing (584)

International Monetary Fund (IMF): agency created by the Bretton Woods Agreement to promote international monetary cooperation after World War II (130)

international monetary system: system by which countries value and exchange their currencies (122)

international operations management: transformation-related activities of an international firm (623)

international order cycle time: time between placement of an order and its receipt by the customer (609)

international service business: firm that transforms resources into an intangible output that creates utility for its customers (640)

international strategic management: comprehensive and ongoing management planning process aimed at formulating and implementing strategies that enable a firm to compete effectively internationally (348)

international strategies: comprehensive frameworks for achieving a firm's fundamental goals (372)

international trade: voluntary exchange of goods, services, or assets between a person or organization located in one country and a person or organization located in another country (85)

international trading company: firm directly engaged in importing and exporting a wide variety of goods for its own account (424)

intracorporate transfer: selling of goods by a firm in one country to an affiliated firm in another country (420)

intraindustry trade: trade between two countries involving the exchange of goods produced by the same industry (94)

invoicing currency: currency in which an international transaction is invoiced (43)

irrevocable letter of credit: letter of credit that cannot be changed without the consent of the buyer, the seller, and the issuing bank (704)

Jamaica Agreement: agreement among central bankers made in 1976, allowing each country to adopt whatever exchange-rate system it wished (135)

job satisfaction/dissatisfaction: an attitude that reflects the extent to which an individual is gratified by or fulfilled in his or her work (516)

joint venture: special form of strategic alliance created when two or more firms agree to work together and jointly own a separate firm to promote their mutual interests (439)

just-in-time (JIT) systems: systems in which suppliers are expected to deliver necessary inputs just as they are needed (10)

kabuskiki kaisha (KK): in Japan, term used to represent all limited-liability companies (11)

keiretsu: family of Japanese companies, often centered around a large bank or trading company, having extensive cross-ownership of shares and interacting with one another as suppliers or customers (58)

labor productivity: measure determined by dividing output by direct labor hours or costs; used to assess how efficiently an organization is using its work force (563)

leadership: use of noncoercive influence to shape the goals of a group or organization, to motivate behavior toward reaching those goals, and to help determine the group or organizational culture (525)

leads and lags strategy: money management technique in which an MNC attempts to increase its holding of currencies and assets denominated in currencies that are expected to rise in value and to decrease its holdings of currencies and assets denominated in currencies that are expected to fall in value (679)

Leontief paradox: empirical finding that U.S. exports are more labor-intensive than U.S. imports, which is contrary to the predictions of the theory of relative factor endowments (93)

letter of credit: document issued by a bank promising to pay the seller if all conditions specified in the letter of credit are met (659)

licensee: firm that buys the rights to use the intellectual property of another firm (427)

licensing: transaction in which a firm (called the licensor) sells the rights to use its intellectual property to another firm (called a licensee) in return for a fee (12, 427)

licensor: firm that sells the rights to use its intellectual property to another firm (427)

lingua franca: common language (334)

location advantages: factors that affect the desirability of host country production relative to home country production (413)

locus of authority: where the power to make various decisions resides within the organization (549)

locus of control: personality trait determining the extent to which people believe that their behavior has a real affect on what happens to them (514)

London Interbank Offer Rate (LIBOR): interest rate that London banks charge each other for short-term Eurocurrency loans (190)

long-term portfolio investments: portfolio investments with maturities of more than one year (145)

Louvre Accord: agreement made in 1987 among central bankers to stabilize the value of the U.S. dollar (137)

low-context culture: culture in which the words being spoken explicitly convey the speaker's message to the listener (337)

Ltd.: abbreviation used in the United Kingdom to indicate a privately held, limited-liability company (11)

Maastricht Treaty: common name given to the Treaty on European Union (262)

macropolitical risk: political risk that affects all firms operating within a country (310)

make-or-buy decision: decision for an organization to either make its own inputs or buy them from outside suppliers (629)

managed float: flexible exchange system in which government intervention plays a major role in determining exchange rates; also called a dirty float (135)

managed trade: *see* fair trade

management by objectives (MBO): a motivational technique whereby subordinates and managers agree on the subordinate's goals over some period of evaluation (523)

management contract: agreement whereby one firm provides managerial assistance, technical expertise, or specialized services to a second firm for some agreed-upon time in return for a fee (12, 434)

manufacturers' agents: agents who solicit domestic orders for foreign manufacturers, usually on a commission basis (425)

manufacturers' export agents: agents who act as an export department for domestic manufacturers, selling those firms' goods in foreign markets (425)

maquiladoras: Mexican factories, mostly located along the U.S.-Mexico border, that receive preferential tariff treatment (227)

marketing: process of planning and executing the conception, pricing, promotion, and distribution of ideas, goods, and services to create exchanges that satisfy individual and organizational objectives (584)

marketing alliance: strategic alliance in which two or more firms share marketing services or expertise (594)

marketing mix: how a firm chooses to address product development, pricing, promotion, and distribution (587)

market pricing: customization of prices on a market-to-market basis to maximize profits (596)

market pricing policy: pricing policy under which prices are set on a market-by-market basis (596)

market socialism: form of socialism that allows significant private ownership of resources (57)

Marshall Plan: massive U.S. aid program following World War II designed to help European nations rebuild themselves (21)

materials management: part of logistics management concerned with the flow of materials into the firm from suppliers and between units of the firm itself (637)

medium: communication channel used by an advertiser to convey a message (600)

mercantilism: economic philosophy based on the belief that a nation's wealth is measured by its holdings of gold and silver (82)

merchandise export: sale of a good to a resident of a foreign country (143)

merchandise exports and imports: trade involving tangible products (10)

merchandise import: purchase of a good from a resident of a foreign country (143)

Mercosur Accord: customs union composed of Argentina, Brazil, Paraguay, and Uruguay; Bolivia and Chile are associate members (273)

M-form design: form of organization design in which products are related in some way (485)

micropolitical risk: political risk that affects only specific firms or a specific industry operating within a country (310)

mission statement: definition of a firm's values, purpose, and directions (386)

most favored nation (MFN) principle: principle that any preferential treatment granted to one country must be extended to all countries (245)

motivation: overall set of forces that cause people to choose certain behaviors from a set of available behaviors (520)

multidomestic corporation: firm composed of relatively independent operating subsidiaries, each of which is focused on a specific domestic market (15)

Multifibre Agreement (MFA): commodity agreement among exporting and importing countries of textiles and apparel to control trade in those goods (247)

Multilateral Investment Guarantee Agency (MIGA): World Bank affiliate that offers political risk insurance to investors in developing countries (128, 313)

multilateral netting: netting of transactions between three or more business units (678)

multinational corporation (MNC): incorporated firm that has extensive involvement in international business, engages in foreign direct investment, and owns or controls value-adding activities in more than one country (13)

multinational enterprise (MNE): business that may or may not be incorporated and has extensive involvement in international business (14)

multinational organization (MNO): any organization—business or not-for-

profit—with extensive international involvement (14)

national competitive advantage, theory of: theory stating that success in international trade is based on the interaction of four elements: factor conditions, demand conditions, related and supporting industries, and firm strategy, structure, and rivalry (101)

national defense argument: argument in favor of governmental intervention in trade holding that a nation should be self-sufficient in critical raw materials, machinery, and technology (206)

national treatment: imposing the same standards, regulations, and so forth on foreign firms that are imposed on domestic firms (250)

nationalization: transfer of property from a privately owned firm to the government (303)

needs: the things an individual must have or wants to have (522)

neo-mercantilists: modern supporters of mercantilism, who hold that a country should erect barriers to trade to protect its industries from foreign competition; also called protectionists (87)

Newly Independent States (NIS): term used to refer collectively to the fifteen independent countries created as a result of the break-up of the Soviet Union (52)

nontariff barrier (NTB): any governmental regulation, policy, or procedure other than a tariff that has the effect of impeding international trade (218)

NV: in the Netherlands, abbreviation used to refer to a publicly held, limited-liability firm (11)

official reserves account: BOP account that records changes in official reserves owned by a central bank (147)

official settlements balance: BOP balance that measures changes in a country's official reserves (152)

offset purchases: form of countertrade in which a portion of the exported good is produced in the importing country (663)

open account: type of payment in which the seller ships goods to the buyer prior to payment; seller relies on the promise of the buyer that payment will be forthcoming (656)

openness: a "big five" personality trait referring to a person's rigidity of beliefs and range of interests (513)

operations control: level of control that focuses on operating processes and systems within both the organization and its subsidiaries and operating units (552)

operations management: set of activities used by an organization to transform different kinds of resource inputs into final goods and services (623)

opportunity cost: value of what is given up in order to get the good or service in question (89)

organizational commitment: an attitude reflecting an individual's identification with and loyalty to the organization

organizational control: level of control that focuses on the design of the organization itself (548)

organization change: any significant modification or alteration in a firm's strategy, organization design, technology, and/or employees (502)

organization design: overall pattern of structural components and configurations used to manage the total organization; also called organization structure (480)

Organization for Economic Cooperation and Development (OECD): organization whose 29 members are among the world's richest countries and consist of Canada, Mexico, the United States, Japan, Australia, New Zealand, South Korea, and 22 Western European countries (45)

Organization of Petroleum Exporting Countries (OPEC): commodity cartel created to control production and prices of crude oil (280)

organization structure: *see* organization design

overall cost leadership strategy: business-level strategy that emphasizes low costs (394)

overall productivity: productivity measure determined by dividing total outputs by total inputs; also called total factor productivity (563)

Overseas Private Investment Corporation (OPIC): U.S. government agency that promotes U.S. international business activities by providing political risk insurance (228, 313)

ownership advantages: resources owned by a firm that grant it a competitive advantage over its industry rivals (412)

ownership advantage theory: theory stating that foreign direct investment occurs because of ownership of valuable assets that confer monopolistic advantages in foreign markets (106)

paper gold: *see* special drawing rights

par value: official price of a currency in terms of gold (123)

parallel importing: market that results from products being imported into a country legally but outside the normal channels of distribution authorized by a manufacturer (synonymous with *grey market*) (597)

parent-country nationals (PCNs): employees who are citizens of an international business's home country and are transferred to one of its foreign operations (735)

passive goal behavior: behavior based on the cultural belief that social relationships, quality of life, and concern for others are the basis of motivation and reflect the goals that a person should pursue (354)

passive income: *see* Subpart F income (719)

payback period: number of years it takes a project to repay a firm's initial investment in that project (682)

pegged: tied to, as in "The gold standard created a fixed exchange-rate system because each country pegged the value of its currency to gold" (123)

per capita income: average income per person in a country (44)

perception: the set of processes by which an individual becomes aware of and interprets information about the environment (518)

performance appraisal: process of assessing how effectively a person is performing his or her job (748)

performance ratio: control technique based on a numerical index of performance that the firm wants to maintain (559)

personal selling: making sales on the basis of personal contacts (605)

personality: the relatively stable set of psychological attributes that distinguish one person from another (513)

planning process control: form of organizational control that focuses on the actual mechanics and processes a firm uses to develop strategic plans (551)

Plaza Accord: agreement made in 1985 among central bankers to allow the U.S. dollar to fall in value (137)

PLC: abbreviation used in the United Kingdom to indicate a publicly held, limited-liability company (11)

political risk: change in the political environment that may adversely affect the value of a firm (309)

political risk assessment: systematic analysis of the political risks that a firm faces when operating in a foreign country (309)

political union: complete political as well as economic integration of two or more countries (255)

polycentric approach: management approach in which a firm customizes its operations for each foreign market it serves (588)

polycentric staffing model: approach primarily using HCNs to staff upper-level foreign positions (737)

portfolio investments: passive holdings of stock, bonds, or other financial assets that do not entail active management or control of the securities' issuer by the investor (12, 104)

power orientation: cultural beliefs about the appropriateness of power and authority in hierarchies such as business organizations (350)

power respect: cultural belief that the use of power and authority is acceptable simply on the basis of position in a hierarchy (350)

power tolerance: cultural belief that the use of power and authority is not acceptable simply on the basis of position in a hierarchy (350)

principle of comity: *see* comity, principle of (308)

privatization: sale of publicly owned property to private investors (54, 286)

product: international marketing mix component that comprises both tangible factors that the consumer can see or touch and numerous intangible factors (591)

product-support services: assistance a firm provides for customers regarding the operation, maintenance, and/or repair of its products (641)

production alliance: strategic alliance in which two or more firms each manufacture products or provide services in a shared or common facility (459)

production management: international operations management decisions and processes involving the creation of tangible goods (627)

productivity: economic measure of efficiency that summarizes the value of outputs relative to the value of inputs used to create them (562)

promotion: set of all efforts by an international firm to enhance the desirability of its products among potential buyers (598)

promotion mix: mix of advertising, personal selling, sales promotion, and public relations used by a firm to market its products (599)

protectionists: *see* neo-mercantilists

Protestant ethic: belief that hard work, frugality, and achievement are means of glorifying God (341)

public choice analysis: branch of economics that analyzes public decision making (211)

public-private venture: joint venture involving a partnership between a privately owned foreign firm and a government (465)

public relations: efforts aimed at enhancing a firm's reputation and image (607)

purchasing power parity (PPP): theory stating that the prices of tradable goods, when expressed in a common currency, will tend to equalize across countries as a result of exchange-rate changes (180)

put option: publicly traded contract granting the owner the right, but not the obligation, to sell a specific amount of foreign currency at a specified price at a stated future date (177)

Quad: economic grouping of countries, consisting of Canada, the European Union, Japan, and the United States (41)

quality: totality of features and characteristics of a product or service that bear on its ability to satisfy stated or implied needs (565)

quota: deposit paid by a member nation when joining the International Monetary Fund (130)

quota: numerical limit on the quantity of a good that may be imported into a country (218)

R&D alliance: strategic alliance in which two or more firms agree to undertake joint research to develop new products or services (461)

R&D consortium: confederation of organizations that band together to research and develop new products and processes for world markets (461)

re-exporting: process of importation of a good into a country for immediate exportation, with little or no transformation of the good (63)

regional development banks: banks whose mission is to promote economic development of poorer nations within the region they serve (129)

related diversification: corporate-level strategy in which the firm operates in several different but related businesses, industries, or markets at the same time (390)

relative factor endowments, theory of: theory stating that a country will have a comparative advantage in producing goods that intensively use factors of production it has in abundance; also called Heckscher-Ohlin theory (92)

religious law: law based on officially established rules governing the faith and practice of a particular religion (293)

repatriate: to return to a home country (304)

repatriation: moving a manager back home after a foreign assignment has been completed (743)

resource deployment: component of strategy that answers the question "Given that we are going to compete in these markets, how will we allocate our resources to them?" (382)

responsibility center control: form of organizational control based on decentralized responsibility centers (549)

retention: extent to which a firm is able to retain its employees (752)

revocable letter of credit: letter of credit that can be changed by the bank without the consent of the buyer and the seller (704)

ringi system: Japanese approach to ensuring that decisions are made collectively, rather than by an individual (531)

royalty: compensation paid by a licensee to a licensor (429)

rules of origin: rules to determine which goods will benefit from reduced trade barriers in regional trading blocs (254)

sales promotion: specialized marketing efforts using such techniques as coupons and sampling (607)

sanctions: government-imposed restraints against commerce with a foreign country (295)

Schengen Agreement: accord among certain EU members abolishing passport controls at their common borders (260)

scope of operations: component of strategy that answers the question "Where are we going to conduct business?" (381)

screwdriver plant: domestic factory that assembles imported parts in which little value is added to the parts (271)

self-efficacy: personality trait determining a person's beliefs about his or her capabilities to perform a task (515)

self-esteem: personality trait determining the extent to which a person believes that she is a worthwhile and deserving individual (515)

self-reference criterion: unconscious use of one's own culture to assess and understand a new culture (358)

service export: sale of a service to a resident of a foreign country (144)

service exports and imports: trade involving intangible products (10)

service import: purchase of a service from a resident of a foreign country (144)

service operations management: international operations management decisions and processes involving the creation of intangible services (627)

shared management agreement: management arrangement in which each partner in a strategic alliance fully and actively participates in managing the alliance (467)

short-term portfolio investments: portfolio investments with maturities of one year or less (145)

sight draft: draft that requires payment upon transfer of the goods to the buyer (657)

single-business strategy: corporate-level strategy that calls for a firm to rely on a single business, product, or service for all its revenue (390)

Smithsonian Conference: meeting held in Washington, D.C. in December 1971, during which central bank representatives from the Group of Ten agreed to restore the fixed exchange-rate system but with restructured rates of exchange between the major trading currencies (134)

social charter: EU policy promoting common job-related benefits and working conditions throughout the EU; also called social policy (758)

social mobility: ability of individuals to move from one stratum of society to another (330)

social orientation: cultural beliefs about the relative importance of the individual and the groups to which an individual belongs (347)

social policy: *see* social charter

social stratification: organization of society into hierarchies based on birth, occupation, wealth, educational achievements, and/or other characteristics (329)

soft currencies: *see* inconvertible currencies (176)

soft loans: loans made by the World Bank Group that bear significant risk of not being repaid (128)

sogo sosha: large Japanese trading company (58)

sourcing: set of processes and steps a firm uses to acquire the various resources it needs to create its own products (627)

Southern African Development Community (SADC): free trade area created by twelve Southern African countries (278)

special drawing rights (SDRs): credits granted by the IMF that can be used to settle transactions among central banks; also called paper gold (134)

specific tariff: tax assessed as a specific dollar amount per unit of weight or other standard measure (215)

spot market: market for foreign exchange involving immediate delivery of the currency in question (176)

standard price policy: pricing policy under which a firm charges the same price for its products and services regardless of where they are sold (595)

statistical process control: family of mathematically based tools for monitoring and controlling quality (570)

statutory laws: laws enacted by legislative action (292)

sterling-based gold standard: gold standard in which the British pound is commonly used as an alternative means of settlement of transactions (123)

strategic alliance: business arrangement in which two or more firms choose to cooperate for their mutual benefit (448)

strategic business units (SBUs): "bundles" of businesses created by a firm using a corporate strategy of either related or unrelated diversification (393)

strategic control: process of monitoring how well an international business formulates and implements its strategies (545)

strategic goals: major objectives a firm wants to accomplish through the pursuit of a particular course of action (388)

strategic planning: process of developing a particular international strategy (372)

strategic trade theory: theory addressing the optimal policies through which a government may benefit its country by aiding domestic firms in monopolistic or highly oligopolistic industries (207)

stress: an individual's response to a strong stimulus (520)

stressor: a stimulus that results in stress (520)

Subpart F income: income earned from financial transactions, such as dividends, interest, and royalties; also called passive income (719)

subsidiary bank: separately incorporated overseas banking operation (188)

Super 301: section of U.S. trade law that requires the U.S. trade representative to publicly identify countries that flagrantly engage in unfair trade practices (231)

swap market: facet of international capital market in which two firms can exchange financial obligations (686)

swap transaction: transaction involving the simultaneous purchase and sale of a foreign currency with delivery at two different points in time (176)

switching arrangements: agreement under which firms may transfer their countertrade obligations to a third party (663)

SWOT analysis: analysis of a firm and its environment to determine its strengths, weaknesses, opportunities, and threats (386)

synergy: component of strategy that answers the question "How can different elements of our business benefit each other?" (383)

tactics: methods used by middle managers to implement strategic plans (388)

tariff: tax placed on a good involved in international trade (214)

tariff-rate quota: a type of quota that imposes a low tariff rate on a limited amount of imports of a specific good into the country, but then subjects all imports above that threshold to a prohibitively high tariff (218)

tax havens: countries that charge low, often zero, taxes on corporate incomes and that offer an attractive business climate (716)

tax-equalization system: system for ensuring that an expatriate's after-tax income in the host country is comparable to what the person's after-tax income would be in the home country (749)

temporal method: approach used to consolidate the financial statements of a foreign subsidiary whose functional currency is the U.S. dollar (710)

theocracy: country whose legal system is based on religious law (293)

theory of absolute advantage: *see* absolute advantage, theory of

theory of comparative advantage: *see* comparative advantage, theory of

theory of national competitive advantage: *see* national competitive advantage, theory of

theory of purchasing power parity: *see* purchasing power parity (PPP)

theory of relative factor endowments: *see* relative factor endowments, theory of

third-country nationals (TCNs): employees of an international business who are not citizens of the firm's home or host country (736)

three-point arbitrage: arbitrage based upon exploiting differences between the direct rate of exchange between two currencies and their cross rate of exchange using a third currency (184)

time draft: draft that requires payment at some specified time after the transfer of goods to the buyer (658)

time orientation: cultural beliefs regarding long-term versus short-term outlooks on work, life, and other aspects of society (356)

tort laws: laws covering wrongful acts, damages, and injuries (297)

total factor productivity: *see* overall productivity

total quality management (TQM): integrated effort to systematically and continuously improve the quality of an organization's products and/or services (569)

trade: voluntary exchange of goods, services, or assets between one person or organization and another (85)

trade acceptance: time draft that has been signed by the buyer signifying a promise to honor the payment terms (658)

trade creation: shifting of production from high-cost producers to low-cost producers within a regional trading bloc (257)

trade deflection: rerouting of exported goods to the member of a free trade area with the lowest barriers to imports from nonmember countries (254)

trade diversion: shifting of production to higher-cost producers located within a regional trading bloc from lower-cost producers located outside the trading bloc (257)

trade in invisibles: British term denoting trade in services (144)

trade in visibles: British term referring to merchandise trade (144)

training: instruction directed at enhancing job-related skills and abilities (745)

transaction costs: costs of negotiating, monitoring, and enforcing a contract (107)

transaction currency: currency in which an international transaction is denominated (173)

transaction exposure: financial risks that occur because the financial benefits and costs of an international transaction may be affected by exchange-rate movements occurring after the firm is legally obligated to the transaction (668)

transfer pricing: prices that one branch or subsidiary of a parent firm charges for goods, services, or property sold to a second branch or subsidiary of the same parent firm (298, 714)

transit tariff: tax levied on goods as they pass through one country bound for another (214)

translation: process of transforming the accounting statements of a foreign subsidiary into the home country's currency using the home country's accounting procedures (708)

translation exposure: impact on a firm's consolidated financial statements of fluctuations in foreign exchange rates that change the value of foreign subsidiaries as measured in the parent's currency (671)

transnational corporation: organization that seeks to combine the benefits of global scale efficiencies with the benefits of local responsiveness (15)

treasury management: management of financial flows and their associated currency and interest-rate risks (690)

Treaty of Amsterdam: 1997 treaty furthering integration among EU members (264)

Treaty of Rome: treaty signed in 1957 that established the European Economic Community; its original six signatories have expanded to 15 over time (257)

Treaty on European Union: treaty signed in 1992 that came into force on November 1, 1993, furthering economic and political integration of the EC's members; important provisions include the creation of an economic and monetary union, a cohesion fund, a pledge to cooperate on foreign and defense policies, and the renaming of the EC as the European Union; commonly known as the Maastricht Treaty (262)

Triad: grouping of countries that dominate the world economy, consisting of the European Union, Japan, and the United States (41)

Triffin paradox: paradox that resulted from reliance on the U.S. dollar as the primary source of liquidity in the Bretton Woods system; for trade to grow, foreigners needed to hold more dollars; the more dollars they held, however, the less faith they had in the U.S. dollar, thereby

undermining the Bretton Woods system (133)

turnkey project: contract under which a firm agrees to fully design, construct, and equip a facility and then turn the project over to the purchaser when it is ready for operation (435)

turnover: rate at which people leave an organization (752)

two-point arbitrage: riskless purchase of a product in one geographic market for immediate resale in a second geographic market in order to profit from price differences between the markets; also called geographic arbitrage (182)

two-tiered pricing policy: pricing policy under which a firm sets one price for all its domestic sales and a second price for all its international sales (595)

two-transaction approach: approach used by U.S. firms to account on their income statements for transactions denominated in foreign currencies (707)

U-form organization: form of organization design based on global functional design (488)

uncertainty acceptance: cultural belief that uncertainty and ambiguity are stimulating and present new opportunities (352)

uncertainty avoidance: cultural belief that uncertainty and ambiguity are unpleasant and should be avoided (353)

uncertainty orientation: cultural beliefs about uncertainty and ambiguity (352)

unilateral transfers: gifts made by residents of one country to residents of another country (144)

unrelated diversification: corporate-level strategy that calls for a firm to operate in several unrelated businesses, industries, or markets (391)

Uruguay Round: GATT negotiations (1986–1994) that created the World Trade Organization, slashed tariff rates, and strengthened enforcement of intellectual property rights (246)

value chain: technique for assessing a firm's strengths and weaknesses by identifying its most important activities (387)

values: the things that people believe to be important (522)

vertical integration: extent to which a firm either provides its own resources or obtains them from other sources (628)

voluntary export restraint (VER): promise by a country to limit its exports of a good to another country (220)

Webb-Pomerene association: group of U.S. firms that operate within the same industry and that are allowed by law to coordinate their export activities without fear of violating U.S. antitrust laws (424)

"wider vs. deeper": debate among EU members, with those arguing for "wider" wanting to expand membership as a first priority and those arguing for "deeper" wanting to more thoroughly integrate existing members as a first priority (270)

with recourse: term signifying that should a trade acceptance or banker's acceptance sold by an exporter to an investor fail to be paid, the exporter will reimburse the investor; the exporter retains the risk of default by the signer of the acceptance (658)

without recourse: term signifying that should a trade acceptance or banker's acceptance sold by an exporter to an investor fail to be paid, the exporter is not obligated to reimburse the investor; the investor retains the risk of default by the signer of the acceptance (658)

World Bank: *see* International Bank for Reconstruction and Development

World Bank Group: organization consisting of the World Bank and its affiliated organizations, the International Development Agency, the International Finance Corporation, and the Multilateral Investment Guarantee Agency (127)

world company: currently hypothetical firm that transcends national boundaries and has no national identity (16)

World Trade Organization (WTO): successor organization to the GATT founded in 1995; created by the Uruguay Round negotiations (246)

Photo Credits

About the Authors
Page vii (top and bottom): Mike Pustay.

Chapter 1
Page 13, Courtesy Boeing Aircraft; Page16, Courtesy Asea Brown Boveri Archive; Page 29, © Brian McInnis.

Chapter 2
Page 62 left, Jasmin/Liaison International; Page 62 right, Steve Proehl/The Image Bank.

Point/Counterpoint
Page 78, Reuters/Corbis-Bettmann; Page 79, Lincoln/Potter/Liaison International.

Chapter 3
Page 87, The Granger Collection; Page 92, James Pozarik/Liaison International; Page 98, AP/Wide World Photos.

Chapter 4
Page 127, UPI/Corbis-Bettmann; Page 129, MIGA Annual Report, 1996; Page 131, AP/Wide World Photos; Page 134, Copyright © *The New York Times* Company. Reprinted by permission. Photo by Susan Van Etten.

Chapter 5
Page 177, Hashimoto/Sygma.

Point/Counterpoint
Page 198, AP/Wide World Photos; Page 199, AP/Wide World Photos.

Chapter 6
Page 215, All STAR TREK® elements © 1995 by Paramount Pictures. All rights reserved. Photo by Susan Van Etten; Page 220, Courtesy of Collin Street Bakery.

Point/Counterpoint
Page 238, © Susan Van Etten; Page 239, © Susan Van Etten.

Chapter 7
Page 251, AP/Wide World Photos; Page 261, Mark Deville/The Gamma Liaison Network.

Chapter 8
Page 294, © Terry O'Neill; Page 304, Art Zamur/The Gamma Liaison Network.

Chapter 9
Page 343, © Robin Moyer/Time Magazine; Page 354 left and right, Mike Pustay.

Chapter 10
Page 370, UPI/Corbis-Bettmann; Page 381, Courtesy of Glasbau Hahn GmbH & Co. KG; Page 382, KiHo Park/Kistone.

Chapter 11
Page 410, © 1992 Malcolm Linton/Black Star; Page 421, Courtesy of Baskin-Robbins; Page 433, Peter Menzel/Stock, Boston.

Point/Counterpoint
Page 446, Courtesy The Seattle Mariners; Page 446, © Susan Van Etten.

Chapter 12
Page 451, Bachman/Stock Boston; Page 461, LGI/Corbis-Bettmann.

Chapter 13
Page 501, Peter Turnley/Black Star.

Chapter 14
Page 520, SuperStock, Inc. Page 533, Richard Wood/The Picture Cube;

Chapter 15
Page 551, Courtesy of Starbucks Coffee Company; Page 558, Wendy Stone/The Gamma Liaison Network; Page 560, Eric Vandeville/The Gamma Liaison Network; Page 570, Courtesy of Ford Motor Company/Photomedia.

Chapter 16
Page 600 right, Nicholas DeVore/Tony Stone Images; Page 600 left, Mike Yamashita/Woodfin Camp & Associates; Page 601, Courtesy of Colgate-Palmolive Company.

Chapter 17
Page 628, © Susan Van Etten; Page 639, © Susan Van Etten.

Point/Counterpoint
Page 650, Paulo Fridman/Liaison International; Page 651, John Chiasson/Liaison International.

Chapter 18
Page 666, Photograph by Bob Sacha, © 1997; Page 683, Courtesy of Placer Dome, Inc.

Chapter 19
Page 702, Porter Gifford/The Gamma Liaison Network; Page 717, The Gamma Liaison Network

Chapter 20
Page 736, Courtesy Arthur Anderson & Co.; Page 745, Jean-Lou Bersuder/Sipa Press.

Company Index

Subject Index